CTIA

Consolidated Treaties & International Agreements

Current Document Service: United States

2006

Volume 5

Containing

Department of State Documents 06-251 through 06-313
Issued between January 1, 2007 and February 28, 2007

Senate Treaty Documents 109-20 through 109-22

Oceana®
NEW YORK

OXFORD
UNIVERSITY PRESS

Oxford University Press, Inc., publishes works that further Oxford University's objective of excellence in research, scholarship, and education.

Published by Oxford University Press, Inc.
198 Madison Avenue, New York, New York 10016

This volume should be cited as **2006-5 CTIA.**

ISSN 1053-9905
ISBN: 978-0-19-536785-0

Note to Readers:

This publication is designed to provide accurate and authoritative information in regard to the subject matter covered. It is based upon sources believed to be accurate and reliable and is intended to be current as of the time it was written. It is sold with the understanding that the publisher is not engaged in rendering legal, accounting, or other professional services. If legal advice or other expert assistance is required, the services of a competent professional person should be sought. Also, to confirm that the information has not been affected or changed by recent developments, traditional legal research techniques should be used, including checking primary sources where appropriate.

(Based on the Declaration of Principles jointly adopted by a Committee of the American Bar Association and a Committee of Publishers and Associations.)

How to Use Consolidated Treaties & International Agreements

The **Consolidated Treaties & International Agreements** set is published semi-annually and contains all treaties and agreements in a given year to which the United States is a party. The agreements and treaties are made available by the Department of State and the Senate, as explained below.

The Department of State, under 1 U.S.C. §§ 112a and 112b, is obligated to report to Congress all international agreements and treaties to which the United States is a party within 60 days after the agreement or treaty has entered into force. The Department of State is also required to make available on their website within 180 days after the treaty or agreement has entered into force all reported agreements and treaties meeting the requirements for publication status in the U.S. government publication, *United States Treaties and Other International Agreements.* The Department of State numbers each agreement or treaty with a prefix based on the year reported and a suffix based on the order the agreement or treaty arrived to the Legal Affairs Office. For example, for the year 2005, the agreements would be numbered 05-01, 05-02, etc., and for 2006, the agreements would be numbered 06-01, 06-02, and so on.

The Senate, on the other hand, has a different procedure for formalizing and numbering treaties. All treaties requiring the Senate's consent to ratification are first submitted to the Senate Foreign Relations Committee for its review and recommendation. Thereafter, the treaty is introduced to the full Senate for its consent to ratification by a two-thirds vote of all members present. Once the Senate consents to its ratification, the treaty is presented to the President for formal ratification. However, the treaty is made available to the public upon the completed review and recommendation of the Foreign Relations Committee, although parts of the treaty text may remain concealed for security reasons. Senate treaty documents may remain in committee for many congressional sessions; thus, a treaty may be negotiated and signed in one year but not ratified until many years later. However, the treaty document is numbered based on the session the treaty was introduced to the Senate. For example, the Treaty between the United States of America and Japan on Mutual Legal Assistance in Criminal Matters is assigned as Senate Document No. 108-12, meaning it was introduced to the Senate during the 108th session of Congress and it was the 12th treaty submitted to the Foreign Relations Committee.

The editorial staff of the Law Division of Oxford University Press, Inc. (*fka* Ocean Publications) monitors the Department of State and the Senate throughout the year and gathers the agreements and treaties as they become available. Each agreement and treaty document is assigned an internal CTIA number and a subject. The CTIA number is used to track the agreement or treaty and its associated amendments, extensions and protocols. Each agreement or treaty document is assigned a CTIA prefix number with a suffix of ".000"; amendments, protocols and/or extensions of the agreement or treaty are assigned the same CTIA prefix, but a sequential CTIA suffix (*i.e.*, 2525.000 (main agreement), 2525.001 (amendment)).

The **Consolidated Treaties & International Agreements** set is organized by document number, beginning with the Department of State agreements and treaties, followed by the Senate treaty documents, and may also include any agreements for the year between the American Institute of Taiwan and the Taipei Economic and Cultural Representative Office. The Table of Contents for each volume provides all the key elements of the treaties published in the volume—agreement or treaty short title, date and place of signature and country.

The **Consolidated Treaties & International Agreements** set also contains three indices to help the reader locate documents. The last volume for any given year will include cumulative indices covering all agreement and treaty documents published in the volumes for that year.

The first index, Appendix I, organizes the treaties published in the volume by country and then by subject. Each treaty title includes the Department of State or Senate document number and the Oceana print citation.

The second index, Appendix II, is a complete listing of all multilateral agreements published in the volume. Each treaty title includes the Department of State or Senate document number and the Oceana print citation.

The third index, Appendix III, is the topical index, organizing each treaty published in the volume under its assigned subject in alphabetical order by country name and with the appropriate Department of State or Senate document number and Oceana print citation.

Table of Contents

* Due to a State Department numbering error, there is no document associated with 06-297

STATE DEPARTMENT DOCUMENT NUMBER: 06-251

STRATEGIC OBJECTIVE GRANT AGREEMENT AMENDMENT NUMBER FIVE BETWEEN THE UNITED STATES OF AMERICA AND THE ISLAMIC REPUBLIC OF AFGHANISTAN FOR THE STRATEGIC OBJECTIVE OF A THRIVING ECONOMY LED BY THE PRIVATE SECTOR

SIGNED AT KABUL,
SEPTEMBER 18, 2006
ENTERED INTO FORCE SEPTEMBER 18, 2006

CTIA DOCUMENT NUMBER: 12756.005

Dated as of: September *18*, 2006

AMENDMENT NO. FIVE
TO
STRATEGIC OBJECTIVE GRANT AGREEMENT

AMENDMENT NUMBER FIVE TO THE STRATEGIC OBJECTIVE GRANT AGREEMENT between the Government of the United States of America, acting through the United States Agency for International Development (USAID), and the Government of the Islamic Republic of Afghanistan (hereinafter referred to as the "Grantee" or the "GOA"), acting through the Ministry of Finance, dated as of September *18*, 2006

WHEREAS, the Grantee and USAID entered into a Strategic Objective Grant Agreement ("SOAG") for the strategic objective of "A Thriving Economy Led by the Private Sector" (USAID Grant Agreement No. SOAG–306–05–00) dated September 19, 2005 and subsequently amended the SOAG as of:

—September 30, 2005 (Amendment No. 1);

—April 6, 2006 (Amendment No. 2);

—May 11, 2006 (Amendment No. 3); and,

—June 28, 2006 (Amendment No. 4).

The SOAG as so amended is referred to hereinafter as the "Agreement."

WHEREAS, USAID and the Grantee wish to amend the Agreement further to: (a) increase the USAID contribution by **Sixty Nine Million Six Hundred Ten Thousand Seven Hundred Forty Eight** United States (U.S.) Dollars **(U.S.$ 69,610,748.00)**; (b) increase the Grantee Contribution by the U.S. Dollar equivalent of **Twenty Six Million One Hundred Thousand**

U.S. Dollars **(U.S.$ 26,100,000)**; (c) provide a mechanism for certain revisions to the illustrative financial plan; and (d) update the illustrative financial plan;

NOW, THEREFORE, the Parties hereto hereby agree that the Agreement shall be amended as follows:

1. The first sentence in Section 3.1(a), The Grant, of the Agreement is deleted in its entirety and the following is substituted therefor: "To help achieve the Objective set forth in this Agreement, USAID, pursuant to the *Foreign Assistance Act of 1961*, as amended, hereby grants to the Grantee under the terms of this Agreement not to exceed **Eight Hundred Sixty Five Million One Hundred Forty-Four Thousand Forty Four And Eighty-Two Hundredths** United States (U.S.) Dollars **(U.S.$ 865,144,044.82)** (the 'Grant')."

2. The first sentence of Section 3.2(b) of the Agreement is deleted in its entirety and the following is substituted therefor: "The Grantee's contribution, based on USAID's contribution in section 3.1(a), will not be less than the equivalent of **Fifty Million** U.S. Dollars **(U.S.$ 50,000,000)**, including in-kind contributions."

3. Article III, Funding, of Annex 1 to the Agreement is amended by adding, at the end thereof, the following sentence:

> "In addition, after such financial plan has been approved by the Parties or a revised financial plan has been approved by the Parties through an amendment to this Agreement or an Implementation Letter, changes between line items of such approved financial plan currently in effect may be made by USAID without prior consultation with the Grantee, provided that such changes do not, in the aggregate, affect more than fifteen percent (15%) of USAID's contribution under this Agreement, as specified in Section 3.1(a) of the Agreement."

4. The illustrative financial plan set forth in Attachment 1 to Annex 1 to the Agreement is deleted and the updated illustrative financial plan included as Attachment A to this Amendment is substituted therefor.

All other terms and conditions of the Agreement remain unchanged and in full force and effect. This Amendment is prepared in both English and Dari (capitalized terms not defined in this Amendment shall have the meanings ascribed thereto in the Agreement). In the event of ambiguity or conflict between the two versions, the English language version will control.

IN WITNESS WHEREOF, the United States of America and the Government of the Islamic Republic of Afghanistan, each acting through its duly authorized representatives, have caused this Amendment Number Five to be signed in their names and delivered as of the day, month and year first written above.

THE UNITED STATES OF AMERICA

By: [*Signature*]
Name: Leon S. Waskin
Title: Director, USAID Mission to Afghanistan

THE ISLAMIC REPUBLIC OF AFGHANISTAN

By: [*Signature*]
Name: Anwar-ul-Haq Ahady
Title: Minister of Finance

Attachment A

ILLUSTRATIVE FINANCIAL PLAN FOR FY 2005 TO FY 2010
In Thousands of U.S. Dollars

Objective and Activities	Amount Obligated prior to Amendment No. 5		Amount Obligated in Amendment No. 5		Cumulative Obligations in FY 2005–FY 2006 *		Amount Remaining to be Obligated in FY 2007–FY 2010 **		Total Estimated Contribution	
	USAID	Grantee	USAID	Grantee	USAID	Grantee	USAID	Grantee	USAID	Grantee
A THRIVING ECONOMY LED BY THE PRIVATE SECTOR USAID Grant Agreement No. SOAG–306–05–00										
Rehabilitate the rural economy	**226,686**		**13,114**		**239,800**		**794,701**		**1,034,501**	
Accelerate market-led growth in agricu1ture ***	52,471		7,948		60,420		228,980		284,400	
Accelerate rural development to generate alternative livelihoods—	174,215		5,166		179,381		570,720		750,101	
Increase Incomes through Economic Growth * **	**76,161**		**17,118**		**93,269**		**358,520**		**451,789**	
Expand Improved Access to Economic Infrastructure	**468,315**		**39,379**		**507,694**		**761,246**		**1,258,940**	
Stabilize Energy Services and Make them Affordable and More Accessible ***	187,622		27,000		214,622		389,826		604,448	
Expand and Improve Access to Transportation	267,265		12,379		279,644		150,848		430,292	

Continued

Objective and Activities	Amount Obligated prior to Amendment No. 5		Amount Obligated in Amendment No. 5		Cumulative Obligations in FY 2005–FY 2006 *		Amount Remaining to be Obligated in FY 2007–FY 2010 **		Total Estimated Contribution	
	USAID	Grantee	USAID	Grantee	USAID	Grantee	USAID	Grantee	USAID	Grantee
Expand and Improve Access to Water Supplies and Sanitation	13,428				13,428		210,772		224,200	
USAID Program Support	**24,350**				**24,380**		**18,540**		**42,920**	
TOTAL OBJECTIVE 5:	**795,533**	**23,900**	**89,611**	**26,100**	**865,144**	**50,000**	**1,923,006**	**212,900**	**2,788,150**	**262,900**

*NOTE *—References to "FY" refer to the USG fiscal year for the USAID contribution and the GOA contributions beginning in the second half of Afghan year 1384*

*NOTE **—These funds are subject to the availability of funds to USAID and the Grantee and the other conditions set forth respectively in Section 3.1(b) and Section 3.2(b) of the Agreement*

*NOTE ***—The illustrative financial plan previously included a line item for "Pre-existing Mortgages"; however, the funds in that line item are now included in the relevant programmatic line items indicated above*

STATE DEPARTMENT DOCUMENT NUMBER: 06-252

STRATEGIC OBJECTIVE GRANT AGREEMENT AMENDMENT NUMBER FIVE BETWEEN THE UNITED STATES OF AMERICA AND THE ISLAMIC REPUBLIC OF AFGHANISTAN FOR THE STRATEGIC OBJECTIVE OF A BETTER EDUCATED AND HEALTHIER POPULATION

SIGNED AT KABUL,
SEPTEMBER 18, 2006
ENTERED INTO FORCE SEPTEMBER 18, 2006

CTIA DOCUMENT NUMBER: 12755.005

Dated as of: September *18*, 2006

AMENDMENT NUMBER FIVE TO THE STRATEGIC OBJECTIVE GRANT AGREEMENT between the Government of the United States of America, acting through the United States Agency for International Development (USAID), and the Government of the Islamic Republic of Afghanistan (hereinafter referred to as the "Grantee" or the "GOA"), acting through the Ministry of Finance, dated as of September *18*, 2006.

WHEREAS, the Grantee and USAID entered into a Strategic Objective Grant Agreement ("SOAG") for the strategic objective of "A Better Educated and Healthier Population" (USAID Grant Agreement No. 306–07–00) dated September 19, 2005 and subsequently amended the SOAG as of:

—September 30, 2005 (Amendment No. 1);

—April 6, 2006 (Amendment No. 2);

—May 11, 2006 (Amendment No. 3); and,

—June 28, 2006 (Amendment No. 4).

The SOAG as so amended is referred to hereinafter as the "Agreement."

WHEREAS, USAID and the Grantee wish to amend the Agreement further to: (a) increase the USAID contribution by **Fifty Million Eight Hundred Eighty Four Thousand Eight Hundred Forty Three** United States (U.S.) Dollars (U.S.$ **50,884,843.00**); (b) provide a mechanism for certain revisions to the illustrative financial plan; and (c) update the illustrative financial plan;

NOW, THEREFORE, the Parties hereto hereby agree that the Agreement shall be amended as follows:

1. The first sentence in Section 3.1(a), The Grant, of the Agreement is deleted in its entirety and the following is substituted therefor: "To help achieve the Objective set forth in this Agreement,

USAID, pursuant to the *Foreign Assistance Act of 1961*, as amended, hereby grants to the Grantee under the terms of this Agreement not to exceed **Two Hundred Six Million Four Hundred Seventy Nine Thousand Eight Hundred Thirty and Seventy Hundreths** United States (U.S.) Dollars (U.S.$ **206,479,830.70**) (the 'Grant')."

2. Article III, Funding, of Annex 1 to the Agreement is amended by adding, at the end thereof, the following sentence:

> "In addition, after such financial plan has been approved by the Parties or a revised financial plan has been approved by the Parties through an amendment to this Agreement or an Implementation Letter, changes between line items of such approved financial plan currently in effect may be made by USAID without prior consultation with the Grantee, provided that such changes do not, in the aggregate, affect more than fifteen percent (15%) of USAID's contribution under this Agreement, as specified in Section 3.1(a) of the Agreement."

3. The illustrative financial plan set forth in Attachment 1 to Annex 1 to the Agreement is deleted and the updated illustrative financial plan included as Attachment A to this Amendment is substituted therefor.

All other terms and conditions of the Agreement remain unchanged and in full force and effect. This Amendment is prepared in both English and Dari (capitalized terms not defined in this Amendment shall have the meanings ascribed thereto in the Agreement). In the event of ambiguity or conflict between the two versions, the English language version will control.

IN WITNESS WHEREOF, the United States of America and the Government of the Islamic Republic of Afghanistan, each acting through its duly authorized representatives, have caused this Amendment Number Five to be signed in their names and delivered as of the day, month and year first written above.

THE UNITED STATES OF AMERICA

By: [*Signature*]
Name: Leon S. Waskin
Title: Director, USAID Mission to Afghanistan

THE ISLAMIC REPUBLIC OF AFGHANISTAN

By: [*Signature*]
Name: Anwar-ul-Haq Ahady
Title: Minister of Finance

Attachment A

ILLUSTRATIVE FINANCIAL PLAN FOR FY 2005 TO FY 2010
In Thousands of U.S. Dollars

Objective and Activities	Amount Obligated prior to Amendment No. 5		Amount Obligated in Amendment No. 5		Cumulative Obligations in FY 2005–FY 2006 *		Amount Remaining to be Obligated in FY 2007–FY 2010 **		Total Estimated Contribution	
	USAID	Grantee	USAID	Grantee	USAID	Grantee	USAID	Grantee	USAID	Grantee
A BETTER EDUCATED AND HEALTHIER POPULATION USAID Grant Agreement No. SOAG–306–07–00										
Increase Access of Women and Children Under 5 to Quality Basis Health Services, especially in rural and Underserved Areas	88,883		20,724		107,607		332,648		440,250	
Increase Access of Children, Youth, and Adults to Quality Teaching and Suitable Learning Environments ***	66,722		30,160		98,883		376,967		473,850	
USAID Program Support	**1,990**				**1,990**		**23,110**		**25,100**	
TOTAL OBJECTIVE 7:	**165,595**	**79,100**	**50,885**		**206,480**	**79,100**	**732,720**	**791,000**	**939,200**	**870,100**

*NOTE *—References to "FY" refer to the USG fiscal year for the USAID contribution and the GOA contributions beginning in the second half of Afghan year 1384*

*NOTE **—These funds are subject to the availability of funds to USAID and the Grantee and the other conditions set forth respectively in Section 3.1(b) and Section 3.2(b) of the Agreement*

*NOTE ***—The illustrative financial plan previously included a line item for "Pre-existing Mortgages"; however, the funds in that line item are now included in the relevant programmatic line items indicated above*

State Department Document Number: 06-253

Agreement Between the United States of America and the Kingdom of Swaziland Regarding the Surrender of Persons to the International Criminal Court

Signed at Mbabane,
May 10, 2006
Entered into force September 20, 2006

CTIA DOCUMENT NUMBER: 13081.000

Reaffirming the importance of bringing to justice those who commit genocide, crimes against humanity and war crimes,

Recalling that the Rome Statute of the International Criminal Court done at Rome on July 17, 1998 by the United Nations Diplomatic Conference of Plenipotentiaries on the Establishment of an International Criminal Court is intended to complement and not supplant national criminal jurisdiction,

Considering that the Government of the United States of America has expressed its intention to investigate and to prosecute where appropriate acts within the jurisdiction of the International Criminal Court alleged to have been committed by its officials, employees, military personnel or other nationals,

Bearing in mind Article 98 of the Rome Statute,

The Parties hereby agree as follows:

1. For purposes of this Agreement, "persons" are current or former Government officials, employees (including contractors), or military personnel or nationals of the United States of America.

2. Persons of the United States of America present in the territory of the Kingdom of Swaziland shall not, absent the express consent of the Government of the United States of America,

(A) Be surrendered or transferred by any means to the International Criminal Court for any purpose, or

(B) Be surrendered or transferred by any means to any other entity or third country, or expelled to a third country, for the purpose of surrender to or transfer to the International Criminal Court.

3. When the Government of the Kingdom of Swaziland extradites, surrenders, or otherwise transfers a person of the United States of America to a third country, the Government of the Kingdom

of Swaziland will not agree to the surrender or transfer of that person to the International Criminal Court by the third country, absent the express consent of the Government of the United States of America.

4. (1) This Agreement shall enter into force upon an exchange of Notes confirming that each Party has completed the necessary domestic legal requirements to bring the Agreement into force.

(2) This Agreement will remain in force until one year after the date on which one Party notifies the other of its intent to terminate this Agreement.

(3) The provisions of this Agreement shall continue to apply with respect to any act occurring, or any allegation arising, before the effective date of termination.

Done in the English language at MBABANE, Swaziland, this 10th day of May, 2006.

FOR THE GOVERNMENT OF
THE UNITED STATES OF AMERICA:

[Signature]
Lewis W. Lucke
Ambassador
United States of America

FOR THE GOVERNMENT OF
THE KINGDOM OF SWAZILAND:

[Signature]
Mathendele Dlamini
Foreign Minister
Kingdom of Swaziland

STATE DEPARTMENT DOCUMENT NUMBER: 06-254

AMENDMENT TO THE AIR TRANSPORT AGREEMENT OF MAY 8, 1997 BETWEEN THE UNITED STATES OF AMERICA AND THE REPUBLIC OF PANAMA

EFFECTED BY EXCHANGE OF NOTES AT PANAMA,
AUGUST 7 AND SEPTEMBER 27, 2006
ENTERED INTO FORCE SEPTEMBER 27, 2006

CTIA DOCUMENT NUMBER: 9642.001

DIPLOMATIC NOTE

No. 1221

The Embassy of the United States of America presents its compliments to the Ministry of Foreign Relations of the Republic of Panama and has the honor to refer to the Air Transport Agreement between the Government of the United States of America and the Government of Panama, signed at Panama City, Panama, May 8, 1997.

In light of recent discussions between the two governments concerning removal from the Agreement of provisions relating to regulation of computer reservation systems, the Embassy proposes that Annex III to the Agreement be deleted. If the Ministry concurs with this proposal, the Embassy further proposes that this note and the Ministry's affirmative note in reply shall constitute an agreement on this subject which shall enter into force on the date of the Ministry's note in reply.

The Embassy of the United States of America avails itself of this opportunity to reiterate to the Ministry of Foreign Relations of the Republic of Panama, the assurances of its highest consideration.

[Signature]

Embassy of the United States of America,
Panama, August 7, 2006.

UNOFFICIAL TRANSLATION

Republic of Panama
Ministry of Foreign Relations

Panama, 4, Panama

DT/421

To the Honorable Embassy of
The United States of America
City

The Ministry of Foreign Relations attentively greets the Honorable Embassy of the United States of America and has the honor of advising it of the receipt of its note No. 1221, dated August 7, 2006, through which the elimination of Annex 3 of the Air Transport Agreement between the Government of the Republic of Panama and the Government of the United States of America, signed in Panama on May 8, 1997, is proposed.

Regarding this matter, the Ministry of Foreign Relations is happy to inform the Honorable Embassy of the United States of America that the Government of the Republic of Panama accepts the elimination of the above-referenced Annex, through which the note of the Honorable Embassy and this letter constitute an agreement, which will enter into force as of the date of this letter.

The Ministry of Foreign Relations takes this opportunity to reiterate to the Honorable Embassy of the United States of America its assurance of its highest and distinguished considerations.

Panama, September 27, 2006

STATE DEPARTMENT DOCUMENT NUMBER: 06-255

AMENDMENT TO THE GRANT AGREEMENT OF NOVEMBER 21, 1997, AS AMENDED, BETWEEN THE UNITED STATES OF AMERICA AGENCY FOR INTERNATIONAL DEVELOPMENT (USAID) AND THE EUROPEAN BANK FOR RECONSTRUCTION AND DEVELOPMENT (EBRD) FOR THE CHERNOBYL UNIT 4 SHELTER IMPLEMENTATION PLAN

EFFECTED BY EXCHANGE OF LETTERS AT WASHINGTON D.C.
AND LONDON,
SEPTEMBER 21 AND 29, 2006
ENTERED INTO FORCE SEPTEMBER 29, 2006;
EFFECTIVE SEPTEMBER 21, 2006

CTIA DOCUMENT NUMBER: 13082.001

LETTERHEAD OF THE USAID
FROM THE AMERICAN PEOPLE

SEP 21 2006

Mr. Vincent Novak
Director, Nuclear Safety Department
European Bank for Reconstruction
and Development
London, U.K.

Subject: Amendment No. 8 to Grant No. ENI–G–00–98–00001–00

Dear Mr. Novak:

The United States Agency for International Development (USAID) hereby grants to the European Bank for Reconstruction and Development (hereinafter "the Grantee" or the "EBRD") additional incremental funding for the subject Grant in the amount of Thirty-Four Million One Hundred Forty-Seven Thousand United States Dollars ($34,147,000) to support the second pledge of the United States for the Chernobyl Unit 4 Shelter Implementation Plan in support of EBRD's Chernobyl Shelter Fund Program.

With this Amendment No. 8 to the Grant Agreement, the total amount obligated by USAID to date for the Chernobyl Shelter Fund Program is $142,282,000.

This Amendment No. 8 to the Grant is effective and obligation of the $34,147,000 is made as of the date of this letter and shall apply to expenditures made by the Grantee in furtherance of program objectives.

As the largest single country donor to the Chernobyl Shelter Fund Program, the U.S. continues to support selection of a contractor for the shelter construction though a fair and transparent process in accordance to EBRD rules. In this same spirit of openness, the U.S. would encourage the EBRD to make available to the Assembly of Contributors the supporting documents of the contract award.

Except as specifically amended hereby, including pursuant to the Schedule to this Amendment No. 8 (Tab 1 hereto), all other terms and conditions of the Grant, as subsequently amended, remain in full force and effect.

Please sign the four originals of this letter to acknowledge your acceptance of this Grant Amendment, retain one original for your records, and return the other three originals to the undersigned.

Sincerely,

[Signature]
Drew W. Luten
Acting Assistant Administrator
Bureau for Europe and Eurasia

ACKNOWLEDGED AND AGREED:

[*Signature*] Date: *29.9.06*
Vincent Novak
Director, Nuclear Safety Department
European Bank for Reconstruction and Development

Tab 1: Schedule to Amendment No. 8

U.S. Agency for International Development
1300 Pennsylvania Avenue, NW
Washington, DC 20523
www.usaid.gov

SCHEDULE to Amendment No. 8 to Grant No. ENI–G–00–98–00001–00

The referenced grant (Grant) is amended as follows:

1. Subsection 1. of Paragraph C. (*Amount of Grant and Payment*) of Attachment 1 (Schedule) is deleted in its entirety and the following is substituted therefor:

1. In addition to the initial obligation of $25,000,000, made as of November 21, 1997 under the Grant, and the subsequent obligations of $27,000,000, made as of April 10, 1998 under Amendment No. 1 to the Grant; $9,300,000, made as of May 17, 2000 under Amendment No. 2 to the Grant; $4,900,000, made as of September 26, 2001 under Amendment No. 3 to the Grant; $24,000,000, made as of September 24, 2002 under Amendment No. 4 to the Grant; $9,935,000, made as of November 10, 2003 under Amendment No. 5 to the Grant; and $8,000,000, made as of September 19, 2005 under Amendment No. 6 to the Grant, USAID hereby obligates an additional $34,147,000 (Thirty-Four Million One Hundred Forty-Seven Thousand United States Dollars) as of the effective date of Amendment No. 8, making for a total obligation by USAID of $142,282,000 (One Hundred Forty-Two Million Two Hundred Eighty-Two Thousand United States Dollars) for the purposes of this Grant. Funds obligated under this Grant will be in the form of a cash contribution to the Chernobyl Shelter Fund. The purpose of this Grant is met upon disbursement. The contribution under Amendment No. 8 covers the fourth tranche of the second pledge (Phase II). The total estimated funding of this Grant by USAID is $150,000,000 (One Hundred Fifty Million United States Dollars), subject to the availability of funds and the agreement of the Grantee and USAID to proceed.

Letterhead of the European Bank for Reconstruction and Development

Mr. Andres Doernberg
Energy Analyst, Energy & Infrastructure Division
Bureau for Europe and Eurasia
US Agency for International Development
Ronald Reagan Building
1300 Pennsylvania Avenue, N.W.
Room 5.8–124RRB
Washington, D.C. 20523
United States of America

29 September 2006

Dear Mr. Doernberg,

Re: Amendment No. 8 to Grant No. ENI–G–00–98–00001–00

Further to our email exchange and Mr. Luten's letter of 21 September 2006 I enclose three original letters of the Amendment No. 8 to the Grant Agreement between the Bank and USAID duly signed on 29 September 2006 by Mr. Novak, Director Nuclear Safety Department as requested.

I have retained an original letter for our files.

Yours sincerely,

[Signature]

Penelope J. Goldspink
Senior Administrative Officer, Nuclear Safety Department

cc: David Bleakney

STATE DEPARTMENT DOCUMENT NUMBER: 06-256

MILLENNIUM CHALLENGE COMPACT BETWEEN THE UNITED STATES OF AMERICA AND THE REPUBLIC OF ARMENIA, WITH ANNEXES

SIGNED AT WASHINGTON D.C.,
MARCH 27, 2006
ENTERED INTO FORCE SEPTEMBER 29, 2006

CTIA DOCUMENT NUMBER: 13083.000

This MILLENNIUM CHALLENGE COMPACT (the "***Compact***") is made between the United States of America, acting through the Millennium Challenge Corporation, a United States Government corporation ("***MCC***"), and the Government of the Republic of Armenia (the "***Government***") (referred to herein individually as a "***Party***" and collectively, the "***Parties***"). A compendium of capitalized terms defined herein is included in *Exhibit A* attached hereto.

RECITALS

WHEREAS, MCC, acting through its Board of Directors, has selected the Republic of Armenia as eligible to present to MCC a proposal for the use of Millennium Challenge Account ("***MCA***") assistance to help facilitate poverty reduction through economic growth in Armenia;

WHEREAS, the Government has carried out a consultative process with the country's private sector and civil society to outline the country's priorities for the use of MCA assistance and developed a proposal, which was submitted to MCC on March 28, 2005 (the "***Proposal***");

WHEREAS, the Proposal focused on increasing agricultural production in poor, rural areas of the country through investments in irrigation and rural roads;

WHEREAS, MCC has evaluated the Proposal and related documents to determine whether the Proposal is consistent with core MCA principles and includes proposed activities and projects that will advance the progress of Armenia towards achieving economic growth and poverty reduction;

WHEREAS, based on MCC's evaluation of the Proposal and related documents and subsequent discussions and negotiations between the Parties, the Government and MCC determined to enter into this Compact to implement a program using MCC Funding to advance Armenia's progress towards economic growth and poverty reduction (the "***Program***"); and

WHEREAS, the Government intends to establish a legal entity, in a form mutually agreeable to the Parties, which shall be responsible for the oversight and management of the implementation of this Compact on behalf of the Government ("***MCA-Armenia***").

NOW, THEREFORE, in consideration of the foregoing and the mutual covenants and agreements set forth herein, the Parties hereby agree as follows:

ARTICLE I
PURPOSE AND TERM

Section 1.1
Objectives

The overall objective of this Compact is to reduce rural poverty through a sustainable increase in the economic performance of the agricultural sector in Armenia (the "***Compact Goal***"). The Parties have identified the following project-level objectives (the "***Objectives***") to advance the Compact Goal, each of which is described in more detail in the Annexes attached hereto:

(a) Expand the access of rural communities to agricultural markets, non-farm income opportunities and social infrastructure by improving the condition of rural roads (the "***Rural Road Rehabilitation Objective***"); and

(b) Increase the productivity of the agricultural sector by extending and improving the quality of the irrigation system, strengthening the entities that manage the system and enabling farmers to commercialize their products (the "***Irrigated Agriculture Objective***").

The Government expects to achieve, and shall use its best efforts to ensure the achievement of, these Objectives during the Compact Term.

Section 1.2
Projects

The Annexes attached hereto describe the specific projects and the policy reforms and other activities related thereto (each, a "***Project***") that the Government will carry out, or cause to be carried out, in furtherance of this Compact to achieve the Objectives.

Section 1.3
Entry into Force; Compact Term

This Compact shall enter into force on the date of the last letter in an exchange of letters between the Principal Representatives of each Party confirming that each Party has completed its domestic requirements for entry into force of this Compact and that all conditions set forth in Section 4.1 have been satisfied by the Government and MCC (such date, the "***Entry into Force***"). This Compact shall remain in force for five (5) years from the Entry into Force of this Compact, unless earlier terminated in accordance with Section 5.4 (the "***Compact Term***").

ARTICLE II
FUNDING AND RESOURCES

Section 2.1
MCC Funding

(a) *MCC's Contribution*. MCC hereby grants to the Government, subject to the terms and conditions of this Compact, an amount not to exceed Two Hundred Thirty-Five Million Six Hundred Fifty Thousand United States Dollars (USD $235,650,000) ("***MCC Funding***") during the Compact Term to enable the Government to implement the Program and achieve the Objectives.

(i) Subject to Sections 2.1(a)(ii), 2.2(b) and 5.4, the allocation of MCC Funding within the Program and among and within the Projects shall be as generally described in *Annex II* or as otherwise agreed upon by the Parties from time to time.

(ii) If at any time MCC determines that a condition precedent to an MCC Disbursement has not been satisfied, MCC may, upon written notice to the Government, reduce the total amount of MCC Funding by an amount equal to the amount estimated in the applicable Detailed Financial Plan for the Program, Project or Project Activity for which such condition precedent has not been met. Upon the expiration or termination of this Compact, (1) any amounts of MCC Funding not disbursed by MCC to the Government shall be automatically released from any obligation in connection with this Compact and (2) any amounts of MCC Funding disbursed by MCC to the Government as provided in Section 2.1(b)(i), but not re-disbursed as provided in Section 2.1(b)(ii) or otherwise incurred as permitted pursuant to Section 5.4(e) prior to the expiration or termination of this Compact, shall be returned to MCC in accordance with Section 2.5(a)(ii).

(iii) Notwithstanding any other provision of this Compact and pursuant to the authority of Section 609(g) of the Millennium Challenge Act of 2003, as amended (the "***Act***"), upon the conclusion of this Compact (and without regard to the satisfaction of all of the conditions for Entry into Force required under Section 1.3), MCC shall make available Five Hundred Thousand United States Dollars (USD $500,000) ("***Compact Implementation Funding***") to facilitate certain aspects of Compact implementation as described in Schedule 2.1(a)(iii) attached hereto; *provided*, such Compact Implementation Funding shall be subject to (1) the limitations on the use or treatment of MCC Funding set forth in Section 2.3, as if such provision were in full force and effect, and (2) any other requirements for, and limitations on the use of, such Compact Implementation Funding as may be required by MCC in writing; *provided, further*, that any Compact Implementation Funding granted in accordance with this Section 2.1(a)(iii) shall be included in, and not additional to, the total amount of MCC Funding; and *provided, further*, any obligation to provide such Compact Implementation Funding shall expire upon the expiration or termination of this Compact or five (5) years from the conclusion of this Compact, whichever occurs sooner. Notwithstanding anything to the contrary in this Compact, this Section 2.1(a)(iii) shall provisionally apply prior to Entry into Force.

(b) *Disbursements*.

(i) *Disbursements of MCC Funding*. MCC shall from time to time make disbursements of MCC Funding (each such disbursement, an "***MCC Disbursement***") to a Permitted Account or through such other mechanism agreed by the Parties under and in accordance with the procedures and requirements set forth in *Annex I*, the Disbursement Agreement or as otherwise provided in any other relevant Supplemental Agreement.

(ii) *Re-Disbursements of MCC Funding*. The release of MCC Funding from a Permitted Account (each such release, a "***Re-Disbursement***"), shall be made in accordance with the procedures and requirements set forth in *Annex I*, the Disbursement Agreement or as otherwise provided in any other relevant Supplemental Agreement.

(c) *Interest*. Unless the Parties agree otherwise in writing, any interest or other earnings on MCC Funding that accrue (collectively, "***Accrued Interest***") shall be held in a Permitted Account and accrue in accordance with the requirements for the accrual and treatment of Accrued Interest as specified in *Annex I* or any relevant Supplemental Agreement. On a quarterly basis and upon the termination or expiration of this Compact, the Government shall return, or ensure the return of, all Accrued Interest to any United States Government account designated by MCC.

(d) *Conversion; Exchange Rate*. The Government shall ensure that all MCC Funding that is held in the Permitted Account(s) shall be denominated in the currency of the United States of America ("***United States Dollars***") prior to Re-Disbursement; *provided*, that a certain portion of MCC Funding may be transferred to a Local Account and may be held in such Local Account in the currency of the Republic of Armenia prior to Re-Disbursement in accordance with the requirements of

Annex I and any relevant Supplemental Agreement. To the extent that any amount of MCC Funding held in United States Dollars must be converted into the currency of the Republic of Armenia for any purpose, including for any Re-Disbursement or any transfer of MCC Funding into a Local Account, the Government shall ensure that such amount is converted consistent with *Annex I*, including the rate and manner set forth in *Annex I*, and the requirements of the Disbursement Agreement or any other Supplemental Agreement between the Parties.

(e) *Guidance*. From time to time, MCC may provide guidance to the Government through Implementation Letters on the frequency, form and content of requests for MCC Disbursements and Re-Disbursements or any other matter relating to MCC Funding. The Government shall apply such guidance in implementing this Compact.

Section 2.2
Government Resources

(a) The Government shall provide or cause to be provided such Government funds and other resources, and shall take or cause to be taken such actions, including obtaining all necessary approvals and consents, as are specified in this Compact or in any Supplemental Agreement to which the Government is a party or as are otherwise necessary and appropriate to effectively carry out the Government Responsibilities or other responsibilities or obligations of the Government under or in furtherance of this Compact during the Compact Term and through the completion of any post-Compact Term activities, audits or other responsibilities.

(b) If at any time during the Compact Term, the Government materially reallocates or reduces the allocation in its national budget or any other Armenian governmental authority at a departmental, municipal, regional or other jurisdictional level materially reallocates or reduces the allocation of its respective budget, of the normal and expected resources that the Government or such other governmental authority, as applicable, would have otherwise received or budgeted, from external or domestic sources, for the activities contemplated herein, the Government shall notify MCC in writing within fifteen (15) days of such reallocation or reduction, such notification to contain information regarding the amount of the reallocation or reduction, the affected activities, and an explanation for the reduction. In the event that MCC independently determines upon review of the executed national annual budget that such a material reallocation or reduction of resources has occurred, MCC shall notify the Government and, following such notification, the Government shall provide a written explanation for such reallocation or reduction and MCC may (i) reduce, in its sole discretion, the total amount of MCC Funding or any MCC Disbursement by an amount equal to the amount estimated in the applicable Detailed Financial Plan for the activity for which funds were reduced or reallocated or (ii) otherwise suspend or terminate MCC Funding in accordance with Section 5.4(b).

(c) The Government shall use its best efforts to ensure that all MCC Funding is fully reflected and accounted for in the annual budget of the Republic of Armenia on a multi-year basis.

Section 2.3
Limitations on the Use or Treatment of MCC Funding

(a) *Abortions and Involuntary Sterilizations*. The Government shall ensure that MCC Funding shall not be used to undertake, fund or otherwise support any activity that is subject to prohibitions on use of funds contained in (i) paragraphs (1) through (3) of section 104(f) of the Foreign Assistance Act of 1961 (22 U.S.C. 2151b(f)(1)–(3)), a United States statute, which prohibitions shall apply to the same extent and in the same manner as such prohibitions apply to funds made available to carry out Part I of such Act; or (ii) any provision of law comparable to the eleventh and fourteenth provisos under the heading "Child Survival and Health Programs Fund" of division E of Public Law 108–7 (117 Stat. 162), a United States statute.

(b) *United States Job Loss or Displacement of Production*. The Government shall ensure that MCC Funding shall not be used to undertake, fund or otherwise support any activity that is likely to cause a substantial loss of United States jobs or a substantial displacement of United States production, including:

(i) Providing financial incentives to relocate a substantial number of United States jobs or cause a substantial displacement of production outside the United States;

(ii) Supporting investment promotion missions or other travel to the United States with the intention of inducing United States firms to relocate a substantial number of United States jobs or a substantial amount of production outside the United States;

(iii) Conducting feasibility studies, research services, studies, travel to or from the United States, or providing insurance or technical and management assistance, with the intention of inducing United States firms to relocate a substantial number of United States jobs or cause a substantial displacement of production outside the United States;

(iv) Advertising in the United States to encourage United States firms to relocate a substantial number of United States jobs or cause a substantial displacement of production outside the United States;

(v) Training workers for firms that intend to relocate a substantial number of United States jobs or cause a substantial displacement of production outside the United States;

(vi) Supporting a United States office of an organization that offers incentives for United States firms to relocate a substantial number of United States jobs or cause a substantial displacement of production outside the United States; or

(vii) Providing general budget support for an organization that engages in any activity prohibited above.

(c) *Military Assistance and Training*. The Government shall ensure that MCC Funding shall not be used to undertake, fund or otherwise support the purchase or use of goods or services for military purposes, including military training, or to provide any assistance to the military, police, militia, national guard or other quasi-military organization or unit.

(d) *Prohibition of Assistance Relating to Environmental, Health or Safety Hazards*. The Government shall ensure that MCC Funding shall not be used to undertake, fund or otherwise support any activity that is likely to cause a significant environmental, health, or safety hazard. Unless MCC and the Government agree otherwise in writing, the Government shall ensure that activities undertaken, funded or otherwise supported in whole or in part (directly or indirectly) by MCC Funding comply with environmental guidelines delivered by MCC to the Government or posted by MCC on its website or otherwise publicly made available, as such guidelines may be amended from time to time (the "***Environmental Guidelines***"), including any definition of "likely to cause a significant environmental, health, or safety hazard" as may be set forth in such Environmental Guidelines.

(e) *Taxation*.

(i) *Taxes*. The Government shall ensure that the Program, all Program Assets, MCC Funding and Accrued Interest shall be free from any taxes imposed under laws currently or hereafter in effect in the Republic of Armenia during the Compact Term. This exemption shall apply to any use of any Program Asset, MCC Funding and Accrued Interest, including any Exempt Uses, and to any work performed under or activities undertaken in furtherance of this Compact by any person or entity (including contractors and grantees) funded by MCC Funding, and shall apply to all taxes, tariffs, duties, and other levies (each a "***Tax***" and collectively, "***Taxes***"), including:

(1) To the extent attributable to MCC Funding, income taxes and other taxes on profit or businesses imposed on organizations or entities, other than nationals of the Republic of Armenia, receiving MCC Funding, including taxes on the acquisition, ownership, rental, disposition or other use of real or personal property, taxes on investment or deposit requirements and currency controls in the Republic of Armenia, or any other tax, duty, charge or fee of whatever nature, except fees for specific services rendered; for purposes of this Section 2.3(e), the term "national" refers to organizations established under the laws of the Republic of Armenia, other than MCA-Armenia or any other entity established solely for purposes of managing or overseeing the implementation of the Program or any wholly-owned subsidiaries, divisions, or Affiliates of entities not registered or established under the laws of the Republic of Armenia;

(2) Customs duties, tariffs, import and export taxes, or other levies on the importation, use and re-exportation of goods, services, or the personal belongings and effects, including personally-owned automobiles, for Program use or the personal use of individuals who are neither citizens nor permanent residents of the Republic of Armenia and who are present in the Republic of Armenia for purposes of carrying out the Program or their family members, including all charges based on the value of such imported goods;

(3) Taxes on the income or personal property of all individuals who are neither citizens nor permanent residents of the Republic of Armenia, including income and social security taxes of all types and all taxes on the personal property owned by such individuals, to the extent such income or property are attributable to MCC Funding; and

(4) Taxes or duties levied on the purchase of goods or services funded by MCC Funding, including sales taxes, tourism taxes, value-added taxes ("***VAT***"), or other similar charges.

(ii) This Section 2.3(e) shall apply, but is not limited to (1) any transaction, service, activity, contract, grant or other implementing agreement funded in whole or in part by MCC Funding; (2) any supplies, equipment, materials, property or other goods (referred to herein collectively as "goods") or funds introduced into, acquired in, used or disposed of in, or imported into or exported from, the Republic of Armenia by MCC, or by any person or entity (including contractors and grantees) as part of, or in conjunction with, MCC Funding or the Program; (3) any contractor, grantee, or other organization carrying out activities funded in whole or in part by MCC Funding; and (4) any employee of such organizations (the uses set forth in clauses (1) through (4) are collectively referred to herein as "***Exempt Uses***").

(iii) If a Tax has been levied and paid contrary to the requirements of this Section 2.3(e), whether inadvertently, due to the impracticality of implementation of this provision with respect to certain types or amounts of taxes, or otherwise, the Government shall refund promptly to MCC to an account designated by MCC the amount of such Tax in the currency of the Republic of Armenia, within thirty (30) days (or such other period as may be agreed in writing by the Parties) after the Government is notified in writing according to procedures agreed by the Parties, whether by MCC or otherwise, of such levy and tax payment; *provided, however*, the Government shall apply national funds to satisfy its obligations under this Section 2.3(e)(iii) and no MCC Funding, Accrued Interest, or any assets, goods, or property (real, tangible, or intangible) purchased or financed in whole or in part (directly or indirectly) by MCC Funding ("***Program Assets***") may be applied by the Government in satisfaction of its obligations under this paragraph.

(iv) The Parties shall memorialize in a mutually acceptable Supplemental Agreement or Implementation Letter or other suitable document the mechanisms for implementing this Section

2.3(e), including (1) a formula for determining refunds for Taxes paid, the amount of which is not susceptible to precise determination, (2) a mechanism for ensuring the tax-free importation, use, and re-exportation of goods, services, or the personal belongings of individuals (including all Providers) described in paragraph (i)(2) of this Section 2.3(e), and (3) any other appropriate Government action to facilitate the administration of this Section 2.3(e).

(v) The Parties agree that this Section 2.3(e) shall supplement, without limiting in any manner, the provisions relating to tariffs, dues, customs duties, import taxes and other similar taxes or charges contained in the bilateral agreement entered into on December 12, 1992 between the Government of the United States of America and the Government of the Republic of Armenia Regarding Cooperation to Facilitate the Provision of Humanitarian and Technical Economic Assistance (the "***Bilateral Agreement***"), which agreement continues in full force and effect. In case of any inconsistency between the provisions of this Section 2.3(e) and the provisions relating to tariffs, dues, customs duties, import taxes and other similar taxes or charges contained in the Bilateral Agreement, the provisions of this Section 2.3(e) shall prevail.

(f) *Alteration*. The Government shall ensure that no MCC Funding, Accrued Interest or Program Assets shall be subject to any impoundment, rescission, sequestration or any provision of law now or hereafter in effect in the Republic of Armenia that would have the effect or requiring or allowing any impoundment, rescission or sequestration of any MCC Funding, Accrued Interest or Program Asset.

(g) *Liens or Encumbrances*. The Government shall ensure that no MCC Funding, Accrued Interest or Program Assets shall be subject to any lien, attachment, enforcement of judgment, pledge, or encumbrance of any kind (each a "***Lien***"), except with the prior approval of MCC in accordance with Section 3(c) of *Annex I*, and in the event of the imposition of any Lien not so approved, the Government shall promptly seek the release of such Lien; *provided, however*, the Government shall satisfy its obligations under this Section 2.3(g) at its own expense and no MCC Funding, Accrued Interest or Program Assets may be applied by the Government in satisfaction of its obligations under this Section 2.3(g).

(h) *Other Limitations*. The Government shall ensure that the use or treatment of MCC Funding, Accrued Interest and Program Assets shall be subject to such other limitations (i) as required by the applicable law of the United States of America now or hereafter in effect during the Compact Term, (ii) as advisable under or required by applicable United States Government policies now or hereafter in effect during the Compact Term, or (iii) to which the Parties may otherwise agree in writing.

(i) *Utilization of Goods, Services and Works*. The Government shall ensure that any Program Assets, services, facilities or works funded in whole or in part (directly or indirectly) by MCC Funding, unless otherwise agreed by the Parties in writing, shall be used solely in furtherance of this Compact.

(j) *Notification of Applicable Laws and Policies*. MCC shall notify the Government of any applicable United States law or policy affecting the use or treatment of MCC Funding, whether or not specifically identified in this Section 2.3, and shall provide to the Government a copy of the text of any such applicable law and a written explanation of any such applicable policy.

Section 2.4
Incorporation; Notice; Clarification

(a) The Government shall include, or ensure the inclusion of, all of the requirements set forth in Section 2.3 in all Supplemental Agreements to which MCC is not a party and shall use its best efforts to ensure that no such Supplemental Agreement is implemented in violation of the prohibitions set forth in Section 2.3.

(b) The Government shall ensure notification of all of the requirements set forth in Section 2.3 to any Provider and all relevant officers, directors, employees, agents, representatives, Affiliates, contractors, sub-contractors, grantees and sub-grantees of any Provider. The term "***Provider***" shall mean (i) MCA-Armenia and any Government Affiliate or Permitted Designee involved in any activities in furtherance of this Compact or (ii) any third party who receives at least USD $50,000 in the aggregate of MCC Funding (other than employees of MCA-Armenia) during the Compact Term or such other amount as the Parties may agree in writing, whether directly from MCC, indirectly through Re-Disbursements, or otherwise.

(c) In the event the Government or any Provider requires clarification from MCC as to whether an activity contemplated to be undertaken in furtherance of this Compact violates or may violate any provision of Section 2.3, the Government shall notify, or ensure that such Provider notifies, MCC in writing and provide in such notification a detailed description of the activity in question. In such event, the Government shall not proceed, and shall use its best efforts to ensure that no relevant Provider proceeds, with such activity, and the Government shall ensure that no Re-Disbursements shall be made for such activity, until MCC advises the Government or such Provider in writing that the activity is permissible.

Section 2.5
Refunds; Violation

(a) Notwithstanding the availability to MCC, or exercise by MCC of, any other remedies, including under international law, this Compact, or any Supplemental Agreement:

(i) If any amount of MCC Funding or Accrued Interest, or any Program Asset, is used for any purpose prohibited under this Article II or otherwise in violation of any of the terms and conditions of this Compact, any guidance in any Implementation Letter, or any Supplemental Agreement between the Parties, MCC may require the Government to repay promptly to MCC to an account designated by MCC or to others as MCC may direct the amount of such misused MCC Funding or Accrued Interest, or the cash equivalent of the value of any misused Program Asset, in United States Dollars, plus any interest that accrued or would have accrued thereon, within thirty (30) days (or such other period as may be agreed in writing by the Parties) after the Government is notified, whether by MCC or otherwise, of such prohibited use; *provided, however*, the Government shall apply national funds to satisfy its obligations under this Section 2.5(a)(i) and no MCC Funding, Accrued Interest or Program Assets may be applied by the Government in satisfaction of its obligations under this Section 2.5(a)(i); and

(ii) If all or any portion of this Compact is terminated or suspended and upon the expiration of this Compact, the Government shall, subject to the requirements of Sections 5.4(e) and 5.4(f), refund, or ensure the refund, to MCC to such account(s) designated by MCC the amount of any MCC Funding, plus any Accrued Interest, promptly, but in no event later than thirty (30) days after the Government receives MCC's request for such refund; *provided*, that if this Compact is terminated or suspended in part, MCC may request a refund for only the amount of MCC Funding, plus any Accrued Interest, then allocated to the terminated or suspended portion; *provided, further*, that any refund of MCC Funding or Accrued Interest shall be to such account(s) as designated by MCC.

(b) Notwithstanding any other provision in this Compact or any other agreement to the contrary, MCC's right under this Section 2.5 for a refund shall continue during the Compact Term and for a period of (i) five (5) years thereafter or (ii) one (1) year after MCC receives actual knowledge of such violation, whichever is later.

(c) If MCC determines that any activity or failure to act violates, or may violate, any Section in this Article II, MCC may refuse any further MCC Disbursements for or conditioned upon such activity, and may take any action to prevent any Re-Disbursement related to such activity.

ARTICLE III
IMPLEMENTATION

Section 3.1
Implementation Framework

This Compact shall be implemented by the Parties in accordance with this Article III and as further specified in the Annexes and in relevant Supplemental Agreements.

Section 3.2
Government Responsibilities

(a) The Government shall have principal responsibility for oversight and management of the implementation of the Program (i) in accordance with the terms and conditions specified in this Compact and relevant Supplemental Agreements, (ii) in accordance with all applicable laws then in effect in the Republic of Armenia, and (iii) in a timely and cost-effective manner and in conformity with sound technical, financial and management practices (collectively, the "***Government Responsibilities***"). Unless otherwise expressly provided, any reference to the Government Responsibilities or any other responsibilities or obligations of the Government herein shall be deemed to apply to any Government Affiliate and any of their respective directors, officers, employees, contractors, sub-contractors, grantees, sub-grantees, agents or representatives.

(b) The Government shall ensure that no person or entity shall participate in the selection, award, administration or oversight of a contract, grant or other benefit or transaction funded in whole or in part (directly or indirectly) by MCC Funding, in which (i) the entity, the person, members of the person's immediate family or household or his or her business partners, or organizations controlled by or substantially involving such person or entity, has or have a financial or other interest or (ii) the person or entity is negotiating or has any arrangement concerning prospective employment, unless such person or entity has first disclosed in writing to the Government the conflict of interest and, following such disclosure, the Parties agree in writing to proceed notwithstanding such conflict. The Government shall ensure that no person or entity involved in the selection, award, administration, oversight or implementation of any contract, grant or other benefit or transaction funded in whole or in part (directly or indirectly) by MCC Funding shall solicit or accept from or offer to a third party or seek or be promised (directly or indirectly) for itself or for another person or entity any gift, gratuity, favor or benefit, other than items of de minimis value and otherwise consistent with such guidance as MCC may provide from time to time.

(c) The Government shall not designate any person or entity, including any Government Affiliate, to implement, in whole or in part, this Compact or any Supplemental Agreement between the Parties (including any Government Responsibilities or any other responsibilities or obligations of the Government under this Compact or any Supplemental Agreement between the Parties) or to exercise any rights of the Government under this Compact or any Supplemental Agreement between the Parties, except as expressly provided herein or with the prior written consent of MCC; *provided, however*, the Government may designate MCA-Armenia or, with the prior written consent of MCC, such other mutually acceptable persons or entities, to implement some or all of the Government Responsibilities or any other responsibilities or obligations of the Government or to exercise any rights of the Government under this Compact or any Supplemental Agreement between the Parties (referred to herein collectively as "***Designated Rights and Responsibilities***"), in accordance with the terms and conditions set forth in this Compact or such Supplemental Agreement (each, a

"***Permitted Designee***"). Notwithstanding any provision herein or any other agreement to the contrary, no such designation shall relieve the Government of such Designated Rights and Responsibilities, for which the Government shall retain ultimate responsibility. In the event that the Government designates any person or entity, including any Government Affiliate, to implement any portion of the Government Responsibilities or other responsibilities or obligations of the Government, or to exercise any rights of the Government under this Compact or any Supplemental Agreement between the Parties, in accordance with this Section 3.2(c), then the Government shall (i) cause such person or entity to perform such Designated Rights and Responsibilities in the same manner and to the full extent to which the Government is obligated to perform such Designated Rights and Responsibilities, (ii) ensure that such person or entity does not assign, delegate, or contract (or otherwise transfer) any of such Designated Rights and Responsibilities to any other person or entity and (iii) cause such person or entity to certify to MCC in writing that it will so perform such Designated Rights and Responsibilities and will not assign, delegate, or contract (or otherwise transfer) any of such Designated Rights and Responsibilities to any person or entity without the prior written consent of MCC.

(d) The Government shall, upon a request from MCC, execute, or ensure the execution of, an assignment to MCC of any cause of action which may accrue to the benefit of the Government, a Government Affiliate or any Permitted Designee, including MCA-Armenia, in connection with or arising out of any activities funded in whole or in part (directly or indirectly) by MCC Funding.

(e) The Government shall ensure that (i) no decision of MCA-Armenia is modified, supplemented, unduly influenced or rescinded by any governmental authority, except by a non-appealable judicial decision or any judicial decision which MCA-Armenia, with the agreement of MCC, decides not to appeal, and (ii) the authority of MCA-Armenia shall not be expanded, restricted, or otherwise modified, except in accordance with this Compact, the Governance Agreement or any other Supplemental Agreement between the Parties.

(f) The Government shall ensure that all persons and individuals that enter into agreements to provide goods, services or works under the Program or in furtherance of this Compact shall do so in accordance with the Procurement Guidelines and shall obtain all necessary immigration, business and other permits, licenses, consents and approvals to enable them and their personnel to fully perform under such agreements.

Section 3.3
Government Deliveries

The Government shall proceed, and cause others to proceed, in a timely manner to deliver to MCC all Government deliveries required to be delivered by the Government under this Compact or any Supplemental Agreement between the Parties, in form and substance as set forth in this Compact or in any such Supplemental Agreement.

Section 3.4
Government Assurances

The Government hereby provides the following assurances to MCC that as of the date this Compact is signed:

(a) The information contained in the Proposal and any agreement, report, statement, communication, document or otherwise delivered or otherwise communicated to MCC by or on behalf of the Government on or after the date of the submission of the Proposal (i) are true, correct and complete in all material respects and (ii) do not omit any fact known to the Government that if disclosed would (1) alter in any material respect the information delivered, (2) likely have a material adverse effect on the Government's ability to effectively implement, or ensure the effective implementation of, the Program or any Project or to otherwise carry out its responsibilities or obligations under or in furtherance of this Compact, or (3) have likely adversely affected MCC's determination to enter into this Compact or any Supplemental Agreement between the Parties;

(b) Unless otherwise disclosed in writing to MCC, the MCC Funding made available hereunder is in addition to the normal and expected resources that the Government usually receives or budgets for the activities contemplated herein from external or domestic sources;

(c) This Compact does not conflict and will not conflict with any international agreement or obligation to which the Government is a party or by which it is bound; and

(d) No payments have been (i) received by any official of the Government or any other government body in connection with the procurement of goods, services or works to be undertaken or funded in whole or in part (directly or indirectly) by MCC Funding, except fees, taxes, or similar payments legally established in the Republic of Armenia or (ii) made to any third party, in connection with or in furtherance of this Compact, in violation of the United States Foreign Corrupt Practices Act of 1977, as amended (15 U.S.C. 78a *et seq.*).

Section 3.5
Implementation Letters; Supplemental Agreements

(a) MCC may, from time to time, issue one or more letters to furnish additional information or guidance to assist the Government in the implementation of this Compact (each, an "***Implementation Letter***"). The Government shall apply such guidance in implementing this Compact.

(b) The details of any funding, implementing and other arrangements in furtherance of this Compact may be memorialized in one or more agreements between (i) the Government (or any Government Affiliate or Permitted Designee) and MCC, (ii) MCC and/or the Government (or any Government Affiliate or Permitted Designee) and any third party, including any of the Providers or Permitted Designee or (iii) any third parties where neither MCC nor the Government is a party, before, on or after the Entry into Force (each, a "***Supplemental Agreement***"). The Government shall deliver, or cause to be delivered, to MCC within five (5) days of its execution a copy of any Supplemental Agreement to which MCC is not a party.

Section 3.6
Procurement; Awards of Assistance

(a) The Government shall ensure that the procurement of all goods, services and works by the Government or any Provider in furtherance of this Compact shall be consistent with the procurement guidelines (the "***Procurement Guidelines***") reflected in a Supplemental Agreement between the Government (and/or a mutually acceptable Government Affiliate such as MCA-Armenia) and MCC (the "***Procurement Agreement***"), which Procurement Guidelines shall include the following requirements:

(i) Internationally accepted procurement rules with open, fair and competitive procedures are used in a transparent manner to solicit, award and administer contracts, grants, and other agreements and to procure goods, services and works;

(ii) Solicitations for goods, services, and works shall be based upon a clear and accurate description of the goods, services or works to be acquired;

(iii) Contracts shall be awarded only to qualified and capable contractors that have the capability and willingness to perform the contracts in accordance with the terms and conditions of the applicable contracts and on a cost effective and timely basis; and

(iv) No more than a commercially reasonable price, as determined, for example, by a comparison of price quotations and market prices, shall be paid to procure goods, services, and works.

(b) The Government shall maintain, and shall use its best efforts to ensure that all Providers maintain, records regarding the receipt and use of goods, services and works acquired in furtherance of this Compact, the nature and extent of solicitations of prospective suppliers of goods, services and works acquired in furtherance of this Compact, and the basis of award of contracts, grants and other agreements in furtherance of this Compact.

(c) The Government shall use its best efforts to ensure that information, including solicitations, regarding procurement, grant and other agreement actions funded (or to be funded) in whole or in part (directly or indirectly) by MCC Funding shall be made publicly available in the manner outlined in the Procurement Guidelines or in any other manner agreed upon by the Parties in writing.

(d) The Government shall ensure that no goods, services or works funded in whole or in part (directly or indirectly) by MCC Funding are procured pursuant to orders or contracts firmly placed or entered into prior to the Entry into Force, except as the Parties may otherwise agree in writing.

(e) The Government shall ensure that MCA-Armenia and any other Permitted Designee follows, and uses its best efforts to ensure that all Providers follow, the Procurement Guidelines in procuring (including soliciting) goods, services and works and in awarding and administering contracts, grants and other agreements in furtherance of this Compact, and shall furnish MCC evidence of the adoption of the Procurement Guidelines by MCA-Armenia no later than the time specified in the Disbursement Agreement.

(f) The Government shall include, or ensure the inclusion of, the requirements of this Section 3.6 into all Supplemental Agreements between the Government or any Government Affiliate or Permitted Designee or any of their respective directors, officers, employees, Affiliates, contractors, subcontractors, grantees, sub-grantees, representatives or agents, on the one hand, and a Provider, on the other hand.

(g) The Government shall ensure that approvals of the procurement of goods, works and services in furtherance of this Compact by the Governing Council pursuant to the terms of the Procurement Agreement shall not be subject to any additional approval by the Government.

Section 3.7
Policy Performance; Policy Reforms

In addition to the specific policy and legal reform commitments identified in *Annex I* and the Schedules thereto, the Government shall seek to maintain and improve its level of performance under the policy criteria identified in Section 607 of the Act, and the MCA selection criteria and methodology published by MCC pursuant to Section 607 of the Act from time to time ("***MCA Eligibility Criteria***").

Section 3.8
Records and Information; Access; Audits; Reviews

(a) *Reports and Information*. The Government shall furnish to MCC, and shall use its best efforts to ensure that all Providers and any other third party receiving MCC Funding, as appropriate, furnish to the Government (and the Government shall provide to MCC), any records and other information required to be maintained under this Section 3.8 and such other information, documents and reports as may be necessary or appropriate for the Government to effectively carry out its obligations under this Compact, including under Section 3.12.

(b) *Government Books and Records*. The Government shall maintain, and shall use its best efforts to ensure that all Providers maintain, accounting books, records, documents and other evidence relating to this Compact adequate to show, to the satisfaction of MCC, without limitation, the use of all MCC Funding, including all costs incurred by the Government and the Providers in furtherance of this Compact, the receipt, acceptance and use of goods, services and works acquired in furtherance of this Compact by the Government and the Providers, agreed-upon cost sharing requirements, the nature and extent of solicitations of prospective suppliers of goods, services and works acquired by the Government and the Providers in furtherance of this Compact, the basis of award of Government and other contracts and orders in furtherance of this Compact, the overall progress of the of the implementation of the Program, and any documents required by this Compact or any Supplemental Agreement between the Parties or reasonably requested by MCC upon reasonable notice ("***Compact Records***"). The Government shall maintain, and shall use its best efforts to ensure that all Covered Providers maintain, Compact Records in accordance with generally accepted accounting principles prevailing in the United States, or at the Government's option and with the prior written approval by MCC, other accounting principles, such as those (i) prescribed by the International Accounting Standards Committee (an affiliate of the International Federation of Accountants) or (ii) then prevailing in the Republic of Armenia. Compact Records shall be maintained for at least five (5) years after the end of the Compact Term or for such longer period, if any, required to resolve any litigation, claims or audit findings or any statutory requirements.

(c) *Access*. Upon the request of MCC, the Government, at all reasonable times, shall permit, or cause to be permitted, authorized representatives of MCC, the Inspector General, the United States Government Accountability Office, any auditor responsible for an audit contemplated herein or otherwise conducted in furtherance of this Compact, and any agents or representatives engaged by MCC or a Permitted Designee to conduct any assessment, review or evaluation of the Program, at all reasonable times the opportunity to audit, review, evaluate or inspect activities funded in whole or in part (directly or indirectly) by MCC Funding or undertaken in connection with the Program, the utilization of goods and services purchased or funded in whole or in part (directly or indirectly) by MCC Funding, and Compact Records, including of the Government or any Provider, relating to activities funded or undertaken in furtherance of, or otherwise relating to, this Compact, and shall use its best efforts to ensure access by MCC, the Inspector General, the United States Government Accountability Office or relevant auditor, reviewer or evaluator or their respective representatives or agents to all relevant directors, officers, employees, Affiliates, contractors, representatives and agents of the Government or any Provider.

(d) *Audits*.

(i) *Government Audits*. The Government shall, on at least an annual basis and as the Parties may otherwise agree in writing, conduct, or cause to be conducted, financial audits of all MCC Disbursements and Re-Disbursements during the year since the Entry into Force or since the prior anniversary of the Entry into Force in accordance with the following terms, except as the Parties may otherwise agree in writing. As requested by MCC in writing, the Government shall use, or cause to be used, or select, or cause to be selected, an auditor named on the approved list of auditors in accordance with the *Guidelines for Financial Audits Contracted by Foreign Recipients* (the "***Audit Guidelines***") issued by the Inspector General (the "***Inspector General***") of the United States Agency for International Development ("***USAID***") and as approved by MCC, to conduct such annual audits. Such audits shall be performed in accordance with such Audit Guidelines and be subject to quality assurance oversight by the Inspector General in accordance with such Audit Guidelines. An audit shall be completed no later than 90 days after the first anniversary of the Entry into Force of this Compact and no later than 90 days after each anniversary of the Entry into Force thereafter, or such other period as the Parties may otherwise agree in writing.

(ii) *Audits of U.S. Entities*. The Government shall ensure that Supplemental Agreements between the Government or any Provider, on the one hand, and a United States nonprofit organization, on the other hand, state that the United States organization is subject to the applicable audit requirements contained in OMB Circular A–133, notwithstanding any other provision of this Compact to the contrary. The Government shall ensure that Supplemental Agreements between the Government or any Provider, on the one hand, and a United States for-profit Covered Provider, on the other hand, state that the United States organization is subject to audit by the cognizant United States Government agency, unless the Government and MCC agree otherwise in writing.

(iii) *Audit Plan*. The Government shall submit, or cause to be submitted, to MCC, no later than twenty (20) days prior to the date of its adoption, in form and substance satisfactory to MCC, a plan, in accordance with the Audit Guidelines, for the audit of the expenditures of any Covered Providers, which audit plan, in the form and substance as approved by MCA-Armenia, the Government shall adopt, or cause to be adopted, no later than sixty (60) days prior to the end of the first anniversary of the Entry into Force of this Compact or prior to the end of the first period to be audited.

(iv) *Covered Provider*. A "***Covered Provider***" is (1) a non-United States Provider that receives (other than pursuant to a direct contract or agreement with MCC) USD $300,000 or more of MCC Funding in any MCA-Armenia fiscal year or any other non-United States person or entity that receives (directly or indirectly) USD $300,000 or more of MCC Funding from any Provider in such fiscal year or (2) any United States Provider that receives (other than pursuant to a direct contract or agreement with MCC) USD $500,000 or more of MCC Funding in any MCA-Armenia fiscal year or any other United States person or entity that receives (directly or indirectly) USD $500,000 or more of MCC Funding from any Provider in such fiscal year.

(v) *Corrective Actions*. The Government shall use its best efforts to ensure that Covered Providers take, where necessary, appropriate and timely corrective actions in response to audits, consider whether a Covered Provider's audit necessitates adjustment of its own records, and require each such Covered Provider to permit independent auditors to have access to its records and financial statements as necessary.

(vi) *Audit Reports*. The Government shall furnish, or use its best efforts to cause to be furnished, to MCC an audit report in a form satisfactory to MCC for each audit required by this Section 3.8, other than audits arranged for by MCC, no later than 90 days after the end of the period under audit, or such other time as may be agreed by the Parties from time to time.

(vii) *Other Providers*. For Providers who receive MCC Funding under this Compact pursuant to direct contracts or agreements with MCC, MCC shall include appropriate audit requirements in such contracts or agreements and shall, on behalf of the Government, unless otherwise agreed by the Parties, conduct the follow-up activities with regard to the audit reports furnished pursuant to such requirements.

(viii) *Audit by MCC*. MCC retains the right to perform, or cause to be performed, the audits required under this Section 3.8 by utilizing MCC Funding or other resources available to MCC for this purpose, and to audit, conduct a financial review, or otherwise ensure accountability of any Provider or any other third party receiving MCC Funding, regardless of the requirements of this Section 3.8.

(e) *Application to Providers*. The Government shall include, or ensure the inclusion of, at a minimum, the requirements of:

(i) Paragraphs (a), (b), (c), (d)(ii), (d)(iii), (d)(v), (d)(vi), and (d)(viii) of this Section 3.8 into all Supplemental Agreements between the Government, any Government Affiliate, any Permitted Designee or any of their respective directors, officers, employees, Affiliates, contractors, sub-contractors, grantees, sub-grantees, representatives or agents (each, a "***Government Party***"), on the one hand, and a Covered Provider that is not a non-profit organization domiciled in the United States, on the other hand;

(ii) Paragraphs (a), (b), (c), (d)(ii), and (d)(viii) of this Section 3.8 into all Supplemental Agreements between a Government Party and a Provider that does not meet the definition of a Covered Provider; and

(iii) Paragraphs (a), (b), (c), (d)(ii), (d)(v) and (d)(viii) of this Section 3.8 into all Supplemental Agreements between a Government Party and a Covered Provider that is a non-profit organization domiciled in the United States.

(f) *Reviews or Evaluations*. The Government shall conduct, or cause to be conducted, such performance reviews, data quality reviews, environmental and social audits, or program evaluations during the Compact Term or otherwise and in accordance with the M&E Plan or as otherwise agreed in writing by the Parties.

(g) *Cost of Audits, Reviews or Evaluations*. MCC Funding may be used to fund the costs of any Audits, reviews or evaluations required under this Compact, including as reflected on *Exhibit A* to *Annex II*, and in no event shall the Government be responsible for the costs of any such Audits, reviews or evaluations from financial sources other than MCC Funding.

Section 3.9
Insurance

The Government shall, to MCC's satisfaction, insure or cause to be insured all Program Assets and shall obtain or cause to be obtained such other appropriate insurance and other protections to cover against risks or liabilities associated with the operations of the Program, including by requiring Providers to obtain adequate insurance and post adequate performance bonds or other guarantees. MCA-Armenia or the Implementing Entity, as applicable, shall be named as the payee on any such insurance and the beneficiary of any such guarantee, including performance bonds. MCC and, to the extent it is not named as the payee, MCA-Armenia shall be named as additional insureds on any such insurance or other guarantee, to the extent permissible under applicable laws. The Government shall ensure that any proceeds from claims paid under such insurance or any other form of guarantee shall be used to replace or repair any loss of Program Assets or to pursue the procurement of the covered goods, services or works; *provided, however*, at MCC's election, such proceeds shall be deposited in a Permitted Account as designated by MCA-Armenia and acceptable to MCC or otherwise as directed by MCC. To the extent MCA-Armenia is held liable under any indemnification or other similar provision of any agreement between MCA-Armenia, on the one hand, and any other Provider or other third party, on the other hand, the Government shall pay in full on behalf of MCA-Armenia any such obligation; *provided, further*, the Government shall apply national funds to satisfy its obligations under this Section 3.9 and no MCC Funding, Accrued Interest, or Program Asset may be applied by the Government in satisfaction of its obligations under this Section 3.9.

Section 3.10
Domestic Requirements

The Government shall proceed in a timely manner to seek any required ratification of this Compact or similar domestic requirement, which process the Government shall initiate promptly after the conclusion of this Compact. Notwithstanding anything to the contrary in this Compact, this Section 3.10 shall provisionally apply prior to the Entry into Force.

Section 3.11
No Conflict

The Government shall undertake not to enter into any agreement in conflict with this Compact or any Supplemental Agreement during the Compact Term.

Section 3.12
Reports

The Government shall provide, or cause to be provided, to MCC at least on each anniversary of the Entry into Force and otherwise within thirty (30) days of any written request by MCC, or as otherwise agreed in writing by the Parties, the following information:

(a) The name of each entity to which MCC Funding has been provided;

(b) The amount of MCC Funding provided to such entity;

(c) A description of the Program and each Project funded in furtherance of this Compact, including:

(i) A statement of whether the Program or any Project was solicited or unsolicited; and

(ii) A detailed description of the objectives and measures for results of the Program or Project;

(d) The progress made by the Republic of Armenia toward achieving the Compact Goal and Objectives;

(e) A description of the extent to which MCC Funding has been effective in helping the Republic of Armenia to achieve the Compact Goal and Objectives;

(f) A description of the coordination of MCC Funding with other United States foreign assistance and other related trade policies;

(g) A description of the coordination of MCC Funding with assistance provided by other donor countries;

(h) Any report, document or filing that the Government, any Government Affiliate or any Permitted Designee submits to any government body in connection with this Compact;

(i) Any report or document required to be delivered to MCC under the Environmental Guidelines, any Audit Plan, or any component of the Implementation Plan; and

(j) Any other report, document or information requested by MCC or required by this Compact or any Supplemental Agreement between the Parties.

ARTICLE IV
CONDITIONS PRECEDENT; DELIVERIES

Section 4.1
Conditions Prior to the Entry into Force and Deliveries

As conditions precedent to the Entry into Force, the Parties shall satisfy the conditions set forth in this Section 4.1.

(a) The Government (acting through a mutually acceptable Government Affiliate and/or MCA-Armenia) and MCC shall execute a Disbursement Agreement, which agreement shall be in full force and effect and, if required, ratified in Armenia as of the Entry into Force.

(b) (i) The Government (acting through a mutually acceptable Government Affiliate and/or MCA-Armenia) shall deliver one or more of the Supplemental Agreements identified in *Exhibit B* attached hereto, which agreements shall be duly executed by the parties thereto and in full force and effect and, if required, ratified in Armenia as of the Entry into Force, or (ii) the Government (acting through a mutually acceptable Government Affiliate and/or MCA-Armenia) and MCC execute one or more term sheets that set forth the material and principal terms and conditions that will be included in any such Supplemental Agreement that has not been entered into as of the Entry into Force (the "***Supplemental Agreement Term Sheets***").

(c) The Government (acting through a mutually acceptable Government Affiliate and/or MCA-Armenia) and MCC shall execute a Procurement Agreement, which agreement shall be in full force and effect and, if required, ratified in Armenia as of the Entry into Force.

(d) The Government shall deliver a written statement as to the incumbency and specimen signature of the Principal Representative and each Additional Representative executing any document under this Compact, such written statement to be signed by the Prime Minister or a duly authorized official of the Government other than the Principal Representative or any such Additional Representative.

(e) The Government shall deliver a letter signed and dated by the Minister of Justice of the Government certifying:

(i) That the Government has completed all of its domestic requirements for this Compact to be fully enforceable under Armenian law; and

(ii) That attached thereto are true, correct and complete copies of any decree, legislation, regulation or other governmental document relating to its domestic requirements for this Compact to enter into force, which MCC may post on its website or otherwise make publicly available.

(f) MCC shall deliver a letter signed and dated by the Principal Representative of MCC certifying that MCC has completed its domestic requirements for this Compact to enter into force.

(g) MCC shall deliver a written statement as to the incumbency and specimen signature of the Principal Representative and each Additional Representative executing any document under this Compact, such written statement to be signed by a duly authorized officer of MCC other than the Principal Representative or any such Additional Representative.

Section 4.2
Conditions Precedent to MCC Disbursements or Re-Disbursements

Prior to, and as condition precedent to, any MCC Disbursement or Re-Disbursement, the Government shall satisfy, or ensure the satisfaction of, all applicable conditions precedent in the Disbursement Agreement.

ARTICLE V
FINAL CLAUSES

Section 5.1
Communications

Unless otherwise expressly stated in this Compact or otherwise agreed in writing by the Parties, any notice, certificate, request, report, document or other communication required, permitted, or submitted by either Party to the other under this Compact shall be: (a) in writing; (b) in English; and

(c) deemed duly given: (i) upon personal delivery to the Party to be notified; (ii) when sent by confirmed facsimile or electronic mail, if sent during normal business hours of the recipient Party, if not, then on the next business day; or (iii) two (2) business days after deposit with an internationally recognized overnight courier, specifying next day delivery, with written verification of receipt to the Party to be notified at the address indicated below, or at such other address as such Party may designate:

To MCC:

Millennium Challenge Corporation
Attention: Vice President of Operations (with a copy to the Vice President and General Counsel)
875 Fifteenth Street, N.W.
Washington, DC 20005
United States of America
Facsimile: (202) 521–3700
Phone: (202) 521–3600
Email: VPOperations@mcc.gov (Vice President of Operations); VPGeneralCounsel@mcc.gov (Vice President and General Counsel)

To the Government:

Ministry of Finance and Economy
Attention: Minister of Finance and Economy
1, Melik-Adamyan Str.
Yerevan 375010
Republic of Armenia
Facsimile: +374 (10) 59–53–28
Phone: +374 (10) 59–52–22 or 23
Email: minister@mfe.am

Notwithstanding the foregoing, any audit report delivered pursuant to Section 3.8, if delivered by facsimile or electronic mail, shall be followed by an original in overnight express mail. This Section 5.1 shall not apply to the exchange of letters contemplated in Section 1.3 or any amendments under Section 5.3.

Section 5.2
Representatives

Unless otherwise agreed in writing by the Parties, for all purposes relevant to this Compact, the Government shall be represented by the individual holding the position of, or acting as, Minister of Finance and Economy, and MCC shall be represented by the individual holding the position of, or acting as, Vice President of Operations (each, a "***Principal Representative***"), each of whom, by written notice, may designate one or more additional representatives (each, an "***Additional Representative***") for all purposes other than signing amendments to this Compact. The names of the Principal Representative and any Additional Representative of each of the Parties shall be provided, with specimen signatures, to the other Party, and the Parties may accept as duly authorized any instrument signed by such representatives relating to the implementation of this Compact, until receipt of written notice of revocation of their authority. A Party may change its Principal Representative to a new representative of equivalent or higher rank upon written notice to the other Party, which notice shall include the specimen signature of the new Principal Representative.

Section 5.3
Amendments

The Parties may amend this Compact only by a written agreement signed by the Principal Representatives of the Parties and subject to the respective domestic approval requirements to which this Compact was subject.

Section 5.4
Termination; Suspension

(a) Subject to Section 2.5 and paragraphs (e) through (h) of this Section 5.4, either Party may terminate this Compact in its entirety by giving the other Party thirty (30) days' written notice.

(b) Notwithstanding any other provision of this Compact, including Section 2.1, or any Supplemental Agreement between the Parties, MCC may suspend or terminate this Compact or MCC Funding, in whole or in part, and any obligation or sub-obligation related thereto, upon giving the Government written notice, if MCC determines, in its sole discretion that:

(i) Any use or proposed use of MCC Funding or Program Assets or continued implementation of the Compact would be in violation of applicable law or United States Government policy, whether now or hereafter in effect;

(ii) The Government, any Provider, or any other third party receiving MCC Funding or using Program Assets is engaged in activities that are contrary to the national security interests of the United States;

(iii) The Government or any Permitted Designee has committed an act or omission or an event has occurred that would render Armenia ineligible to receive United States economic assistance under Part I of the Foreign Assistance Act of 1961, as amended (22 U.S.C. 2151 *et seq.*), by reason of the application of any provision of the Foreign Assistance Act of 1961 or any other provision of law;

(iv) The Government or any Permitted Designee has engaged in a pattern of actions or omissions inconsistent with the MCA Eligibility Criteria, or there has occurred a significant decline in the performance of the Republic of Armenia on one or more of the eligibility indicators contained therein;

(v) The Government or any Provider has materially breached one or more of its assurances or any covenants, obligations or responsibilities under this Compact or any Supplemental Agreement;

(vi) An audit, review, report or any other document or other evidence reveals that actual expenditures for the Program or any Project or any Project Activity were greater than the projected expenditure for such activities identified in the applicable Detailed Financial Plan or are projected to be greater than projected expenditures for such activities;

(vii) If the Government (1) materially reduces the allocation in its national budget or any other Government budget of the normal and expected resources that the Government would have otherwise received or budgeted, from external or domestic sources, for the activities contemplated herein; (2) fails to contribute or provide the amount, level, type and quality of resources required to effectively carry out the Government Responsibilities or any other responsibilities or obligations of the Government under or in furtherance of this Compact; or (3) fails to pay any of its obligations as required under this Compact or any Supplemental Agreement, including such obligations which shall be paid solely out of national funds;

(viii) If the Government, any Provider, or any other third party receiving MCC Funding or using Program Assets, or any of their respective directors, officers, employees, Affiliates, contractors, sub-contractors, grantees, sub-grantees, representatives or agents, is found to have been convicted of a narcotics offense or to have been engaged in drug trafficking;

(ix) Any MCC Funding or Program Assets are applied (directly or indirectly) to the provision of resources and support to, individuals and organizations associated with terrorism, sex trafficking or prostitution;

(x) An event or condition of any character has occurred that: (1) materially and adversely affects, or is likely to materially and adversely affect, the ability of the Government or any other party to effectively implement, or ensure the effective implementation of, the Program or any Project or to otherwise carry out its responsibilities or obligations under or in furtherance of this Compact or any Supplemental Agreement or to perform its obligations under or in furtherance of this Compact or any Supplemental Agreement or to exercise its rights thereunder; (2) makes it improbable that the Objectives will be achieved during the Compact Term; (3) materially and adversely affects the Program Assets or any Permitted Account; or (4) constitutes misconduct injurious to MCC, or constitutes a fraud or a felony, by the Government, any Government Affiliate, Permitted Designee or Provider, or any officer, director, employee, agent, representative, Affiliate, contractor, grantee, subcontractor or sub-grantee thereof;

(xi) The Government or any Permitted Designee or Provider has taken any action or omission or engaged in any activity in violation of, or inconsistent with, the requirements of this Compact or any Supplemental Agreement to which the Government or any Permitted Designee or Provider is a party;

(xii) There has occurred a failure to meet a condition precedent or series of conditions precedent or any other requirements or conditions in connection with MCC Disbursement as set out in and in accordance with any Supplemental Agreement between the Parties; or

(xiii) Any MCC Funding, Accrued Interest or Program Asset becomes subject to a Lien without the prior approval of MCC, and the Government fails to obtain the release of such Lien (at its own expense and not with MCC Funding, Accrued Interest or Program Assets) within 30 days after the imposition of such Lien.

(c) MCC may reinstate any suspended or terminated MCC Funding under this Compact or any Supplemental Agreement if MCC determines, in its sole discretion, that the Government or other relevant party has demonstrated a commitment to correcting each condition for which MCC Funding was suspended or terminated.

(d) The authority to suspend or terminate this Compact or any MCC Funding under this Section 5.4 includes the authority to suspend or terminate any obligations or sub-obligations relating to MCC Funding under any Supplemental Agreement without any liability to MCC whatsoever.

(e) All MCC Disbursements and Re-Disbursements shall cease upon expiration, suspension, or termination of this Compact; *provided, however*, (i) reasonable expenditures for goods, services and works that are properly incurred under or in furtherance of this Compact before expiration, suspension or termination of this Compact and (ii) reasonable expenditures for goods and services (including certain administrative expenses) properly incurred within one hundred and twenty (120) days after the expiration, suspension or termination of the Compact in connection with the winding up of the Program may be paid from MCC Funding, provided that in the case of clauses (i) and (ii) the request for such payment is (1) properly submitted within ninety (90) days after the expiration, suspension or termination of the Compact and (2) subject to the prior written consent of MCC.

(f) Other than payments permitted pursuant to Section 5.4(e), in the event of the suspension or termination of this Compact or any Supplemental Agreement, in whole or in part, each Party, shall suspend, for the period of the suspension, or terminate, or ensure the suspension or termination of, as applicable, any obligation or sub-obligation of the Parties to provide financial or other resources under this Compact or any Supplemental Agreement, or to the suspended or terminated portion of this Compact or such Supplemental Agreement, as applicable. In the event of such suspension or termination, the Government shall use its best efforts to suspend or terminate, or ensure the suspension or termination of, as applicable, all such noncancelable commitments related to the suspended or terminated MCC Funding. Any portion of this Compact or any such Supplemental Agreement that is not suspended or terminated shall remain in full force and effect.

(g) Upon the full or partial suspension or termination of this Compact or any MCC Funding, MCC may, at its expense, direct that title to Program Assets be transferred to MCC if such Program Assets are in a deliverable state; *provided*, for any Program Asset(s) partially purchased or funded (directly or indirectly) by MCC Funding, the Government shall reimburse to a United States Government account designated by MCC the cash equivalent of the portion of the value of such Program Asset(s).

(h) Prior to the expiration of this Compact or upon the termination of this Compact, the Parties shall consult in good faith with a view to reaching an agreement in writing on (i) the post-Compact Term treatment of MCA-Armenia, (ii) the process for ensuring the refunds of MCC Disbursements that have not yet been released from a Permitted Account through a valid Re-Disbursement nor otherwise committed in accordance with Section 5.4(e), or (iii) any other matter related to the winding up of the Program and this Compact.

Section 5.5
Privileges and Immunities

MCC is an agency of the Government of the United States of America and its personnel assigned to the Republic of Armenia will be notified pursuant to the Vienna Convention on Diplomatic Relations as members of the mission of the Embassy of the United States of America. The Government shall ensure that any personnel of MCC, including individuals detailed to or contracted by MCC, and the members of the families of such personnel, while such personnel are performing duties in the Republic of Armenia, shall enjoy the privileges and immunities that are enjoyed by a member of the United States Foreign Service, or the family of a member of the United States Foreign Service, as appropriate, of comparable rank and salary of such personnel, if such personnel or the members of the families of such personnel are not a national of, or permanently resident in the Republic of Armenia.

Section 5.6
Attachments

Any annex, schedule, exhibit, table, appendix or other attachment expressly attached hereto (collectively, the "***Attachments***") is incorporated herein by reference and shall constitute an integral part of this Compact.

Section 5.7
Inconsistencies

(a) Conflicts or inconsistencies between any parts of this Compact shall be resolved by applying the following descending order of precedence:

(i) Articles I through V; and

(ii) Any Attachments.

(b) In the event of any conflict or inconsistency between this Compact and any Supplemental Agreement between the Parties, the terms of this Compact shall prevail. In the event of any conflict or inconsistency between any Supplemental Agreement between the Parties and any other Supplemental Agreement, the terms of the Supplemental Agreement between the Parties shall prevail. In the event of any conflict or inconsistency between Supplemental Agreements between any parties, the terms of a more recently executed Supplemental Agreement between such parties shall take precedence over a previously executed Supplemental Agreement between such parties. In the event of any inconsistency between a Supplemental Agreement between the Parties and any component of the Implementation Plan, the terms of the relevant Supplemental Agreement shall prevail.

Section 5.8
Indemnification

The Government shall indemnify and hold MCC and any MCC officer, director, employee, Affiliate, contractor, agent or representative (each of MCC and any such persons, an "***MCC Indemnified Party***") harmless from and against, and shall compensate, reimburse and pay such MCC Indemnified Party for, any liability or other damages which (i) are (directly or indirectly) suffered or incurred by such MCC Indemnified Party, or to which any MCC Indemnified Party may otherwise become subject, regardless of whether or not such damages relate to any third-party claim, and (ii) arise from or as a result of the negligence or willful misconduct of the Government, any Government Affiliate, MCA-Armenia or any Permitted Designee, (directly or indirectly) connected with, any activities (including acts or omissions) undertaken in furtherance of this Compact; *provided, however*, the Government shall apply national funds to satisfy its obligations under this Section 5.8 and no MCC Funding, Accrued Interest, or Program Asset may be applied by the Government in satisfaction of its obligations under this Section 5.8.

Section 5.9
Headings

The Section and Subsection headings used in this Compact are included for convenience only and are not to be considered in construing or interpreting this Compact.

Section 5.10
Interpretation; Definitions

(a) Any reference to the term "including" in this Compact shall be deemed to mean "including without limitation" except as expressly provided otherwise.

(b) Any reference to activities undertaken "in furtherance of this Compact" or similar language shall include activities undertaken by the Government, any Government Affiliate, MCA-Armenia, any Permitted Designee, any Provider or any other third party receiving MCC Funding involved in carrying out the purposes of this Compact or any Supplemental Agreement, including their respective directors, officers, employees, Affiliates, contractors, sub-contractors, grantees, sub-grantees, representatives or agents, whether pursuant to the terms of this Compact, any Supplemental Agreement or otherwise.

(c) References to "day" or "days" shall be calendar days unless provided otherwise.

(d) The term "***United States Government***" shall, for the purposes of this Compact, mean any branch, agency, bureau, government corporation, government chartered entity or other body of the Federal government of the United States.

(e) The term "***Affiliate***" of a party is a person or entity that controls, is controlled by, or is under the same control as the party in question, whether by ownership or by voting, financial or other power or means of influence.

(f) The term "***Government Affiliate***" is an Affiliate, ministry, bureau, department, agency, government corporation or any other entity chartered or established by the Government.

(g) References to any Affiliate or Government Affiliate herein shall include any of their respective directors, officers, employees, affiliates, contractors, sub-contractors, grantees, sub-grantees, representatives, and agents.

(h) Any references to "***Supplemental Agreement between the Parties***" shall mean any agreement between MCC on the one hand, and the Government or any Government Affiliate or Permitted Designee on the other hand.

Section 5.11
Signatures

Other than a signature to this Compact or an amendment to this Compact pursuant to Section 5.3, a signature delivered by facsimile or electronic mail in accordance with Section 5.1 shall be deemed an original signature, and the Parties hereby waive any objection to such signature or to the validity of the underlying document, certificate, notice, instrument or agreement on the basis of the signature's legal effect, validity or enforceability solely because it is in facsimile or electronic form. Such signature shall be accepted by the receiving Party as an original signature and shall be binding on the Party delivering such signature.

Section 5.12
Designation

MCC may designate any Affiliate, agent, or representative to implement, in whole or in part, its obligations, and exercise any of its rights, under this Compact or any Supplemental Agreement between the Parties.

Section 5.13
Survival

Any Government Responsibilities, covenants, or obligations or other responsibilities to be performed by the Government after the Compact Term shall survive the termination or expiration of this Compact and expire in accordance with their respective terms. Notwithstanding the termination or expiration of this Compact, the following provisions shall remain in force: Sections 2.2, 2.3, 2.5, 3.2, 3.3, 3.4, 3.5, 3.8, 3.9 (for one year), 3.12, 5.1, 5.2, 5.4(d), 5.4(e) (for 120 days), 5.4(f), 5.4(g), 5.4(h), 5.5, 5.6, 5.7, 5.8, 5.9, 5.10, 5.11, 5.12, this Section 5.13, 5.14, and 5.15.

Section 5.14
Consultation

Either Party may, at any time, request consultations relating to the interpretation or implementation of this Compact or any Supplemental Agreement between the Parties. Such consultations shall begin at the earliest possible date. The request for consultations shall designate a representative for the requesting Party with the authority to enter consultations and the other Party shall endeavor to designate a representative of equal or comparable rank. If such representatives are unable to resolve the matter within 20 days from the commencement of the consultations then each Party shall forward the consultation to the Principal Representative or such other representative of comparable or higher rank. The consultations shall last no longer than 45 days from date of commencement. If the matter is not resolved within such time period, either Party may terminate this Compact pursuant to

Section 5.4(a). The Parties shall enter any such consultations guided by the principle of achieving the Compact Goal in a timely and cost-effective manner.

Section 5.15
MCC Status

MCC is a United States government corporation acting on behalf of the United States Government in the implementation of this Compact. As such, MCC has no liability under this Compact, is immune from any action or proceeding arising under or relating to this Compact and the Government hereby waives and releases all claims related to any such liability. In matters arising under or relating to this Compact, MCC is not subject to the jurisdiction of the courts or other body of the Republic of Armenia or any other jurisdiction.

Section 5.16
Language

This Compact is prepared in English and in the event of any ambiguity or conflict between this official English version and any other version translated into any language for the convenience of the Parties, this official English version shall prevail.

Section 5.17
Publicity; Information and Marking

The Government shall give appropriate publicity to this Compact as a program to which the United States, through MCC, has contributed, including by posting this Compact, and any amendments thereto, on the MCA-Armenia Website, identifying Program activity sites, and marking Program Assets; *provided*, any announcement, press release or statement regarding MCC or the fact that MCC is funding the Program or any other publicity materials referencing MCC, including the publicity described in this Section 5.17, shall be subject to prior approval by MCC and shall be consistent with any instructions provided by MCC from time to time in relevant Implementation Letters. Upon the termination or expiration of this Compact, MCC may request the removal of, and the Government shall, upon such request, remove, or cause the removal of, any such markings and any references to MCC in any publicity materials or on the MCA-Armenia Website.

IN WITNESS WHEREOF, the undersigned, duly authorized by their respective governments, have signed this Compact this 27th day of March, 2006 and this Compact shall enter into force in accordance with Section 1.3.

Done at Washington, D.C. in the English language.

FOR MILLENNIUM CHALLENGE CORPORATION, ON BEHALF OF THE UNITED STATES OF AMERICA
[Signature]

Name: John J. Danilovich
Title: Chief Executive Officer

FOR THE GOVERNMENT OF THE REPUBLIC OF ARMENIA

[Signature]

Name: Vardan Khachatryan
Title: Minister of Finance and Economy

EXHIBIT A
DEFINITIONS

The following compendium of capitalized terms that are used in this Compact is provided for the convenience of the reader. To the extent that there is a conflict or inconsistency between the definitions in this *Exhibit A* and the definitions elsewhere in the text of this Compact, the definition elsewhere in this Compact shall prevail over the definition in this *Exhibit A*. Defined terms importing the singular also include the plural and vice versa.

Accrued Interest *is any interest or other earnings on MCC Funding that accrues as specified in Section 2.1(c).*

Act *means the Millennium Challenge Act of 2003, as amended.*

Ad Hoc Evaluation *shall have the meaning set forth in Section 3(b) of Annex III.*

Additional Representative *is a representative as may be designated by a Principal Representative, by written notice, for all purposes other than signing amendments to this Compact.*

Affiliate *means the affiliate of a party, which is a person or entity that controls, is controlled by, or is under the same control as the party in question, whether by ownership or by voting, financial or other power or means of influence. References to Affiliate herein shall include any of their respective directors, officers, employees, affiliates, contractors, sub-contractors, grantees, sub-grantees, representatives, and agents.*

AMD *means Armenian Drams, the currency of the Republic of Armenia.*

Annex *means any annex to this Compact.*

ARD *means the Armenian Road Directorate that manages the main and republican roads.*

Attachments *means any annex, schedule, exhibit, table, appendix or other attachment to this Compact.*

Audit Guidelines *means the "Guidelines for Financial Audits Contracted by Foreign Recipients" issued by the Inspector General of the United States Agency for International Development.*

Auditor *means an auditor as defined in, and engaged pursuant to, Section 3(h) of Annex I and as required by Section 3.8(d) of the Compact.*

Auditor/Reviewer Agreement *is an agreement between MCA-Armenia and each Auditor or Reviewer, in form and substance satisfactory to MCC, that sets forth the roles and responsibilities of the Auditor or Reviewer with respect to the audit, review or evaluation, including access rights, required form and content of the applicable audit, review or evaluation and other appropriate terms and conditions such as payment of the Auditor or Reviewer.*

Bank(s) *means any bank holding a Permitted Account referenced in Section 4(d) of Annex I.*

Bank Agreement *means an agreement between MCA-Armenia and a Bank, satisfactory to MCC, that sets forth the signatory authority, access rights, anti-money laundering and anti-terrorist financing provisions, and other terms related to a Permitted Account.*

Beneficiaries *means the intended beneficiaries identified in accordance with Annex I.*

Bilateral Agreement *means the bilateral agreement entered into on December 12, 1992 between the Government of the United States of America and the Government of the Republic of Armenia Regarding Cooperation to Facilitate the Provision of Humanitarian and Technical Economic Assistance.*

Chair *means the Chair of the Governing Council.*

Chief Executive Officer *means the Chief Executive Officer of MCA-Armenia.*

Civil Society Members *are the five members of civil society appointed by the Stakeholders' Committee as described in Section 3(d)(ii)(2)(A)(vii) of Annex I, to serve as voting members on the Governing Council.*

Compact *means the Millennium Challenge Compact made between the United States of America, acting through the Millennium Challenge Corporation, and the Government of the Republic of Armenia.*

Compact Goal *means reducing rural poverty through a sustainable increase in the economic performance of the agricultural sector in Armenia.*

Compact Goal Indicator(s) *means the Indicators in the M&E Plan that will measure the results for the overall Program. A table of Compact Goal Indicators with their definitions is set forth at Section 2(a)(i) of Annex III.*

Compact Implementation Funding *shall have the meaning set forth in Section 2.1(a)(iii).*

Compact Records *shall have the meaning set forth in Section 3.8(b).*

Compact Reports *means any documents or reports delivered to MCC in satisfaction of the Government's reporting requirements under this Compact or any Supplemental Agreement between the Parties.*

Compact Term *means the term for which this Compact shall remain in force, which shall be the five (5) year period from the Entry into Force, unless earlier terminated in accordance with Section 5.4.*

Covered Provider *shall have the meaning set forth in Section 3.8(d)(iv).*

Designated Rights and Responsibilities *shall have the meaning set forth in Section 3.2(c).*

Detailed Financial Plan *means the financial plans that detail the annual and quarterly budget and projected cash requirements for the Program (including administrative costs) and each Project, projected both on a commitment and cash requirement basis.*

Disbursement Agreement *is a Supplemental Agreement that MCC, the Government (or a mutually acceptable Government Affiliate) and MCA-Armenia shall enter into that (i) further specifies the terms and conditions of any MCC Disbursements and Re-Disbursements, (ii) is in a form and substance mutually satisfactory to the Parties, and (iii) is signed by the Principal Representative of each Party (or in the case of the Government, the principal representative of the applicable Government Affiliate) and of MCA-Armenia.*

EMPs *means environmental management plans.*

Entry into Force *means the entry into force of this Compact, which shall be on the date of the last letter in an exchange of letters between the Principal Representatives of each Party confirming that all conditions set forth in Section 4.1 have been satisfied by the Government and MCC.*

Environmental Guidelines *means the environmental guidelines delivered by MCC to the Government or posted by MCC on its website or otherwise publicly made available, as such guidelines may be amended from time to time.*

Environmental Observer *is a representative of an environmentally focused NGO appointed by the Stakeholders' Committee to serve as an Observer on the Governing Council.*

ESI Officer *means the Environmental and Social Impact Officer within the Management Unit of MCA-Armenia who will ensure that environmental and social mitigation measures are followed for all Project Activities in accordance with the provisions set forth in this Compact and in relevant Supplemental Agreements.*

ESIAs *means environmental and social impact assessments.*

Evaluation Component *means the component of the M&E Plan that specifies a methodology, process and timeline for the evaluation of planned, ongoing, or completed Projects and Project Activities to determine their efficiency, effectiveness, impact and sustainability.*

Exempt Uses *shall have the meaning set forth in Section 2.3(e)(ii).*

Final Evaluation *shall have the meaning set forth in Section 3(a) of Annex III.*

Financial Plan *means collectively, the Multi-Year Financial Plan, each Detailed Financial Plan and each amendment, supplement or other change thereto.*

Financial Plan Annex *means Annex II of this Compact, which summarizes the Multi-Year Financial Plan for the Program.*

Fiscal Accountability Plan *shall have the meaning set forth in Section 4(c) of Annex I.*

Fiscal Agent *shall have the meaning set forth in Section 3(g) of Annex I.*

Fiscal Agent Agreement *is an agreement between MCA-Armenia and each Fiscal Agent, in form and substance satisfactory to MCC, that sets forth the roles and responsibilities of the Fiscal Agent and other appropriate terms and conditions, such as payment of the Fiscal Agent.*

GDP *means gross domestic product.*

Governance Agreement *is an agency agreement to be entered into by the Government, MCC and MCA-Armenia, that, in addition to the Governing Documents, sets forth the terms and conditions that govern MCA-Armenia and as is further described in Section 3(d)(i) of Annex I.*

Governing Council *means an independent governing council of MCA-Armenia to oversee MCA-Armenia's responsibilities and obligations under this Compact.*

Governing Documents *shall have the meaning set forth in Section 3(c)(i)(10) of Annex I.*

Government *means the Government of the Republic of Armenia.*

Government Affiliate *is an Affiliate, ministry, bureau, department, agency, government corporation or any other entity chartered or established by the Government. References to Government Affiliate shall include any of their respective directors, officers, employees, affiliates, contractors, sub-contractors, grantees, sub-grantees, representatives, and agents.*

Government Members *are the government members identified in Section 3(d)(ii)(2)(A)(i–vi) of Annex I serving as voting members on the Governing Council, and any replacements thereof in accordance with Section 3(d)(ii)(2)(A) of Annex I.*

Government Party *means the Government, any Government Affiliate, any Permitted Designee or any of their respective directors, officers, employees, Affiliates, contractors, sub-contractors, grantees, sub-grantees, representatives or agents.*

Government Responsibilities *shall have the meaning set forth in Section 3.2(a).*

HVA *means high value added.*

***IDP** means the Irrigation Development Project of the World Bank.*

***IFAD** means the International Fund for Agricultural Development.*

***Implementation Letter** is a letter that may be issued by MCC from time to time to furnish additional information or guidance to assist the Government in the implementation of this Compact.*

***Implementation Plan** is a detailed plan for the implementation of the Program and each Project, which will be memorialized in one or more documents and shall consist of: (i) a Financial Plan; (ii) a Fiscal Accountability Plan; (iii) Procurement Plans; (iv) Program and Project Work Plans; and (v) an M&E Plan.*

***Implementing Entity** means a Government Affiliate, nongovernmental organization or other public- or private-sector entity or persons to which MCA-Armenia may provide MCC Funding to implement and carry out the Projects or any other activities to be carried out in furtherance of this Compact.*

***Implementing Entity Agreement** is an agreement between MCA-Armenia and an Implementing Entity, in form and substance satisfactory to MCC, that sets forth the roles and responsibilities of such Implementing Entity and other appropriate terms and conditions, such as payment of the Implementing Entity.*

***Indicators** means the quantitative, objective and reliable data that the M&E Plan will use to measure the results of the Program.*

***Infrastructure Activity** is the Project Activity described in Section 2(a) of Schedule 2 of Annex I under the Irrigated Agriculture Project.*

***Inspector General** means the Inspector General of the United States Agency for International Development.*

***Irrigated Agriculture Objective** is an Objective of this Compact to increase the productivity of the agricultural sector by extending and improving the quality of the irrigation system, strengthening the entities that manage the system and enabling farmers to commercialize their products.*

***Irrigated Agriculture Project** means the Project described and summarized in Schedule 2 of Annex I that the Parties intend to implement in furtherance of the Irrigated Agriculture Objective.*

***Irrigation PIU** means the Water Sector Development and Institutional Project Implementation Unit under the authority of the State Water Committee that will implement the Infrastructure Activity of the Irrigated Agriculture Project.*

***Lien** means any lien, attachment, enforcement of judgment, pledge, or encumbrance of any kind.*

***LLN** means a lifeline network of roads from among the republican and local roads in Armenia, the objective of which is to ensure that all communities, towns and villages are linked to the main road network, either directly or through other communities.*

***Local Account** is an interest-bearing local currency of Armenia account at either the Central Bank of Armenia or at a commercial bank that is procured through a competitive process to which the Fiscal Agent may authorize transfers from any U.S. Dollar Permitted Account for the purpose of making Re-Disbursements payable in local currency.*

***M&E Annex** means Annex III of this Compact, which generally describes the components of the M&E Plan for the Program.*

***M&E Plan** means the plan to measure and evaluate progress toward achievement of the Compact Goal and Objectives of this Compact.*

Management Unit *means the management unit of MCA-Armenia that will have overall management responsibility for the implementation of this Compact.*

Material Agreement *shall have the meaning set forth in Section 3(c)(i)(3) of Annex I.*

Material Re-Disbursement *means any Re-Disbursement that requires MCC approval under applicable law, the Governing Documents, the Procurement Agreement, Procurement Guidelines, or any Supplemental Agreement.*

Material Terms of Reference *means any terms of reference for the procurement of goods, services or works that require MCC approval under applicable law, the Governing Documents, the Procurement Agreement, Procurement Guidelines, or any Supplemental Agreement.*

MCA *means the Millennium Challenge Account.*

MCA-Armenia *shall have the meaning set forth in the Recitals.*

MCA-Armenia Website *means the website operated by MCA-Armenia.*

MCA Eligibility Criteria *means the MCA selection criteria and methodology published by MCC pursuant to Section 607 of the Act from time to time.*

MCC *means the Millennium Challenge Corporation.*

MCC Disbursement *means the disbursement of MCC Funding by MCC from time to time to a Permitted Account or through such other mechanism agreed by the Parties as defined in and in accordance with Section 2.1(b)(i) of this Compact.*

MCC Disbursement Request *means the applicable request that the Government and MCA-Armenia will jointly submit for an MCC Disbursement as may be specified in the Disbursement Agreement.*

MCC Funding *shall have the meaning set forth in Section 2.1(a).*

MCC Indemnified Party *means MCC and any officer, director, employee, Affiliate, contractor, agent or representative of MCC.*

MCC Representative *is a representative appointed by MCC to serve as an Observer on the Governing Council.*

Monitoring Component *means the component of the M&E Plan that specifies how progress toward the Objectives and intermediate results of each Project and Project Activity set forth in the M&E Annex will be monitored.*

MoTC *means the Ministry of Transport and Communications.*

Multi-Year Financial Plan *means the multi-year financial plan for the Program and for each Project, which is summarized in Annex II.*

Multi-Year Financial Plan Summary *means a multi-year Financial plan summary attached to this Compact as Exhibit A of Annex II.*

NGOs *means non-governmental organizations.*

Objective(s) *are the following project-level objectives of this Compact that have been identified by the Parties, each of which is (i) key to advancing the Compact Goal and (ii) described in more detail in the Annexes attached hereto: (a) the Rural Road Rehabilitation Objective and (b) the Irrigated Agriculture Objective.*

***Objective Indicator** means the Indicator for each Objective in the M&E Plan that will measure the final results of the Projects to monitor their success in meeting each of the Objectives. A table of Objective Indicator definitions is set forth at Section 2(a)(ii) of Annex III.*

***Observers** means the non-voting observers of the Governing Council described in Section 3(d)(ii)(2) of Annex I.*

***Outcome Indicator** means the Indicator in the M&E Plan that will measure the intermediate results achieved under each of the Project Activities to provide an early measure of the likely impact of the Project Activities. A table of Outcome Indicator definitions is set forth at Section 2(a)(ii) of Annex III.*

***Outcomes** is the progress made toward the Objectives and the intermediate results of each Project and Project Activity.*

***Output Indicator** means the Indicator in the M&E Plan to measure the direct outputs of the Project Activities.*

***Outside Project Manager** means the qualified persons or entities engaged by MCA-Armenia, to serve as outside project managers in accordance with Section 3(f) of Annex I.*

***Parties** means the United States, acting through MCC, and the Government.*

***Party** means (i) the United States, acting through MCC or (ii) the Government.*

***Permitted Account(s)** shall have the meaning set forth in Section 4(d) of Annex I.*

***Permitted Designee** shall have the meaning set forth in Section 3.2(c).*

***Pledge** means any pledge of any MCC Funding or any Program Assets, or any guarantee (directly or indirectly) of any indebtedness.*

***Principal Representative** means (i) for the Government, the individual holding the position of, or acting as, the Minister of Finance and Economy, and (ii) for MCC, the individual holding the position of, or acting as, the Vice President of Operations.*

***Procurement Agent(s)** are the procurement agents that MCA-Armenia will engage to carry out and/or certify specified procurement activities in furtherance of this Compact on behalf of the Government, MCA-Armenia, any Outside Project Manager or Implementing Entity.*

***Procurement Agent Agreement** is an agreement between MCA-Armenia and each Procurement Agent, in form and substance satisfactory to MCC, that sets forth the roles and responsibilities of the Procurement Agent with respect to the conduct, monitoring and review of procurements and other appropriate terms and conditions, such as payment of the Procurement Agent.*

***Procurement Agreement** is a Supplemental Agreement between the Government (and/or a mutually acceptable Government Affiliate such as MCA-Armenia) and MCC, which includes the Procurement Guidelines, and governs the procurement of all goods, services and works by the Government or any Provider in furtherance of this Compact.*

***Procurement Guidelines** shall have the meaning set forth in Section 3.6(a).*

***Procurement Plan** means a procurement plan adopted by MCA-Armenia, which forecasts the upcoming six month procurement activities and be updated every six months.*

***Program** means the program to be implemented under this Compact using MCC Funding to advance Armenia's progress towards economic growth and poverty reduction.*

Program Annex *means Annex I to this Compact, which generally describes the Program that MCC Funding will support in Armenia during the Compact Term and the results to be achieved from the investment of MCC Funding.*

Program Assets *means (i) MCC Funding, (ii) Accrued Interest, or (iii) any assets, goods, or property (real, tangible, or intangible) purchased or financed in whole or in part by MCC Funding.*

Project(s) *are the specific projects and the policy reforms and other activities related thereto that the Government will carry out, or cause to be carried out in furtherance of this Compact to achieve the Objectives and the Compact Goal, specifically the Rural Road Rehabilitation Project and the Irrigated Agriculture Project.*

Project Activity *means the activities that will be undertaken in furtherance of each Project.*

Proposal *is the proposal for use of MCA assistance submitted to MCC by the Government on March 28, 2005.*

Provider *shall have the meaning set forth in Section 2.4(b).*

Re-Disbursement *is the release of MCC Funding from a Permitted Account.*

Reviewer *shall have the meaning set forth in Section 3(h) of Annex I.*

Rural Road Rehabilitation Objective *is an Objective of this Compact to expand the access of rural communities to agricultural markets, non-farm income opportunities and social infrastructure by improving the condition of rural roads.*

Rural Road Rehabilitation Project *means the Project described and summarized in Schedule 1 of Annex I that the Parties intend to implement in furtherance of the Rural Road Rehabilitation Objective.*

Stakeholders' Committee *is a committee that shall be representative of the various beneficiaries of the Program and as is further described in Section 3(d)(iv)(1) of Annex I.*

Supplemental Agreement *shall have the meaning set forth in Section 3.5(b).*

Supplemental Agreement between the Parties *means any agreement between MCC on the one hand, and the Government or any Government Affiliate or Permitted Designee on the other hand.*

Supplemental Agreement Term Sheets *shall have the meaning set forth in Section 4.1(b).*

Target *means each Indicator will have one or more expected results that specify the expected value and the expected time by which that result will be achieved.*

Tax(es) *shall have the meaning set forth in Section 2.3(e)(i).*

USAID *means the United States Agency for International Development.*

USDA *means the United States Department of Agriculture.*

United States Dollars or U.S. Dollars *(USD) means the currency of the United States of America.*

United States Government *means any branch, agency, bureau, government corporation, government chartered entity or other body of the Federal government of the United States.*

VAT *means value-added taxes.*

Voting Members *are the voting members on the Governing Council as described in Section 3(d)(ii)(2) of Annex I.*

Water-to-Market Activity *is the Project Activity described in Section 2(b) of Schedule 2 of Annex I under the Irrigated Agriculture Project.*

Work Plans *means work plans for the overall administration of the Program and for each Project.*

WSA *means the national Water Supply Agency.*

WUAs *means Water User Associations.*

EXHIBIT B
LIST OF CERTAIN SUPPLEMENTAL AGREEMENTS

1. Governance Agreement
2. Fiscal Agent Agreement
3. Implementing Entity Agreements
4. Bank Agreement

SCHEDULE 2.1(a)(iii)
DESCRIPTION OF COMPACT IMPLEMENTATION FUNDING

Compact Implementation Funding

The Compact Implementation Funding provided pursuant to Section 2.1(a)(iii) shall support the following activities and expenditures in an amount not to exceed the amounts specified below:

(a) Payments for reasonable and normal staff salaries and administrative expenses of MCA-Armenia (or mutually acceptable Government Affiliate) such as rent, computers, and other information technology equipment, in an amount not to exceed USD $500,000;[1] and

(b) Conduct fiscal and procurement administration activities, in an amount not to exceed USD $500,000.[2]

ANNEX I
PROGRAM DESCRIPTION

This *Annex I* to the Compact (the "***Program Annex***") generally describes the Program that MCC Funding will support in Armenia during the Compact Term and the results to be achieved from the investment of MCC Funding. Prior to any MCC Disbursement or Re-Disbursement, including for the Projects described herein, MCC, the Government (or a mutually acceptable Government Affiliate) and MCA-Armenia shall enter into a Supplemental Agreement that (i) further specifies the terms and conditions of such MCC Disbursements and Re-Disbursements, (ii) is in a form and substance mutually satisfactory to the Parties, and (iii) is signed by the Principal Representative of each Party (or in the case of the Government, the principal representative of the applicable Government Affiliate) and of MCA-Armenia (the "***Disbursement Agreement***").

Except as specifically provided herein, the Parties may amend this Program Annex only by written agreement signed by the Principal Representative of each Party. Except as defined in this Program Annex, each capitalized term in this Program Annex shall have the same meaning given such term elsewhere in this Compact. Unless otherwise expressly stated, each Section reference herein is to the relevant Section of the main body of the Compact.

---

[1] Notwithstanding the amount specified for this activity or payment, the total amount of funds disbursed in accordance with Section 2.1(a)(iii) shall not exceed the amount set forth in Section 2.1(a)(iii).

[2] Notwithstanding the amount specified for this activity or payment, the total amount of funds disbursed in accordance with Section 2.1(a)(iii) shall not exceed the amount set forth in Section 2.1(a)(iii).

1. Background; Consultative Process.

(a) *Background.* Economic development in Armenia suffered a severe setback in the early 1990s following the collapse of the Soviet Union. In 1994, Armenia adopted a comprehensive stabilization and reform program that transformed it into a liberal market economy and launched a period of uninterrupted growth with an average increase of eight percent of gross domestic product ("***GDP***") per year. In recent years, the Government has continued to focus on improving the business investment climate by pursuing macroeconomic stability, low inflation, strong fiscal discipline, and the privatization of state-owned enterprises.

Armenia's economic growth, however, has mainly benefited inhabitants of the capital Yerevan and a few other cities, and poverty remains widespread among the rural population. In 2004, per capita GDP was estimated at USD $1,100, with 35 percent of the population classified as poor. Data from household surveys show that the impact of agricultural sector growth on reducing rural poverty in Armenia has been much stronger than that of GDP growth. Consequently, specific policies and investments aimed at promoting sustainable growth in the agricultural sector are central to bringing about a reduction in rural poverty.

There are two important preconditions for growth in the Armenian agricultural sector: (i) investment in the rural road network, which is essential for improving access to markets and communities and (ii) investment in irrigated agriculture to increasing productivity. Only 10 percent of Armenia's rural road network is in good condition and there has been minimal investment in, or maintenance of, the network over the past decade. Currently, less than ten percent of total agricultural land is irrigated, while nearly 85 percent of total crop production is produced with irrigation.

(b) *Consultative Process.* In connection with the Program, Armenia engaged in a comprehensive consultative process based on the Poverty Reduction Strategy Paper initiated in 2003. In the initial priority-setting stage, the Government engaged a broad cross-section of the public, specifically civil society and rural communities, in a consultative process focused on MCA compact development. Issues were addressed through a continuous process that incorporated a feedback mechanism reaching out to stakeholders, particularly those involved in irrigation, rural road, policy development and advocacy, and groups that specialize in monitoring and evaluation.

The Government engaged in rounds of regional, municipal, and local village level meetings to seek input and feedback on potential Proposal components. Meetings were held outside of city centers with announcements published beforehand. In addition to face-to-face meetings, the Government utilized various forms of mass media to reach more remote areas of Armenia, including radio and television announcements and programs, electronic mailing lists that are managed by non-governmental organizations ("***NGOs***") throughout Armenia, and the printing of information brochures.

The selection of the irrigation and rural roads components of the Program also introduced new challenges that focused on issues ranging from communal land rights and responsibilities, sustainability of the investments and involvement of civil society in compact development and implementation. To address concerns of the NGO community, the Government offered to have the NGOs elect their own representatives to participate in the meetings of the MCA-Armenia Board of Trustees—an inter-governmental body, chaired by the Prime Minister that was established to oversee the MCC Proposal and Compact development process. Using existing NGO electronic mailing lists and a self-regulated selection process, NGOs voted to select three representatives to participate in the meetings.

The Government has created and maintains an interactive website (www.mca.am) (the "***MCA-Armenia Website***") that provides access to up-to-date information and a forum page on which to post and debate issues related to the Proposal process. The MCA-Armenia Website also makes publicly available the Board of Trustees meeting minutes and the minutes of all meetings convened to discuss the Proposal.

2. Overview.

(a) *Program*. The Program involves a series of specific and complementary interventions that the Parties expect will achieve the Irrigated Agriculture Objective and the Rural Road Rehabilitation Objective and advance the progress of Armenia toward the Compact Goal.

(b) *Projects*. To achieve the Objectives, the Parties have identified Projects that the Government will implement, or cause to be implemented, using MCC Funding, each of which is described in the Schedules to this Program Annex. The Schedules to this Program Annex identify the activities that will be undertaken in furtherance of each Project (each, a "***Project Activity***"). Notwithstanding anything to the contrary in this Compact, the Parties may agree to amend, terminate or suspend these Projects or Project Activities or create a new project by written agreement signed by the Principal Representative of each Party without amending this Compact; *provided, however*, any such amendment of a Project or Project Activity or creation of a new project is (i) consistent with the Objectives; (ii) does not cause the amount of MCC Funding to exceed the aggregate amount specified in Section 2.1(a) of this Compact; (iii) does not cause the Government's responsibilities or contribution of resources to be less than specified in Section 2.2 of this Compact or elsewhere in this Compact; and (iv) does not extend the Compact Term.

(c) *Beneficiaries*. The intended beneficiaries of each Project are described in the respective Schedule to this Program Annex and *Annex III* to the extent identified as of the date hereof. The intended beneficiaries shall be identified more precisely during the initial phases of the implementation of the Program. The Parties shall agree upon the description of the intended beneficiaries of the Program, including publishing such description on the MCA-Armenia Website.

(d) *Civil Society*. Civil society will participate in overseeing the implementation of the Program through its representation on the Stakeholders' Committee as further described in Section 3(d)(iv) of this Program Annex. In addition, the Work Plans for each Project shall note the extent to which civil society will have a role in the implementation of a particular Project Activity. Finally, members of civil society may be recipients of training or other public awareness programs that are related to the Project Activities.

(e) *Monitoring and Evaluation*. *Annex III* of this Compact generally describes the plan to measure and evaluate progress toward achievement of the Compact Goal and Objectives of this Compact (the "***M&E Plan***"). As outlined in the Disbursement Agreement and other Supplemental Agreements, continued payment of MCC Funding under this Compact will be contingent on successful achievement of targets set forth in the M&E Plan.

3. Implementation Framework.

The implementation framework and the plan for ensuring adequate governance, oversight, management, monitoring, evaluation and fiscal accountability for the use of MCC Funding is summarized below and in the Schedules attached to this Program Annex, or as may otherwise be agreed in writing by the Parties.

(a) *General*. The elements of the implementation framework will be further described in relevant Supplemental Agreements and in a detailed plan for the implementation of the Program and each Project (the "***Implementation Plan***"), which will be memorialized in one or more documents and shall consist of a Financial Plan, a Fiscal Accountability Plan, Procurement Plans, Program and Project Work Plans, and an M&E Plan. MCA-Armenia shall adopt each component of the Implementation Plan in accordance with the requirements and timeframe as may be specified in this Program Annex, the Disbursement Agreement or as may otherwise be agreed by the Parties from time to time. MCA-Armenia may amend the Implementation Plan or any component thereof without amending this Compact, *provided*, any material amendment of the Implementation Plan or any component thereof has been approved by MCC and is otherwise consistent with the requirements of this Compact and any relevant Supplemental Agreement between the Parties. By such time as may be specified in the Disbursement Agreement or as may otherwise be agreed by the Parties from time to time, MCA-Armenia shall adopt one or more work plans for the overall administration of the Program and for each Project (collectively, the "***Work Plans***"). The Work Plan(s) shall set forth the details of each activity to be undertaken or funded by MCC Funding as well as the allocation of roles and responsibilities for specific Project activities, or other programmatic guidelines, performance requirements, targets, or other expectations for a Project.

(b) *Government.*

(i) The Government shall promptly take all necessary and appropriate actions to carry out the Government Responsibilities under and in furtherance of this Compact, including undertaking or pursuing such legal, legislative or regulatory actions, procedural changes and contractual arrangements as may be necessary or appropriate to achieve the Objectives, to successfully implement the Program, and to establish MCA-Armenia. The Government shall promptly deliver to MCC certified copies of any documents, orders, decrees, laws or regulations evidencing such legal, legislative, regulatory, procedural, contractual or other actions.

(ii) During the Compact Term, the Government shall ensure that MCA-Armenia is duly authorized and organized and sufficiently staffed and empowered to fully carry out the Designated Rights and Responsibilities. Without limiting the generality of the preceding sentence, MCA-Armenia shall be organized, and have such roles and responsibilities, as described in Section 3(d) of this Program Annex and as provided in the Governance Agreement and any Governing Documents, which shall be in a form and substance satisfactory to MCC; *provided, however*, the Government may, subject to MCC approval, carry out any of the roles and responsibilities designated to be carried out by MCA-Armenia and described in Section 3(d) of this Program Annex or elsewhere in this Program Annex, applicable law, the Governing Documents, or any Supplemental Agreement prior to and during the initial period of the establishment and staffing of MCA-Armenia, but in no event longer than the earlier of (i) the formation of the Management Unit and the engagement of each of the officers and (ii) six months from the Entry into Force, unless otherwise agreed by the Parties in writing.

(c) *MCC.*

(i) Notwithstanding Section 3.1 of this Compact or any provision in this Program Annex to the contrary, and except as may be otherwise agreed upon by the Parties from time to time, MCC must approve in writing each of the following transactions, activities, agreements and documents prior to the execution or carrying out of such transaction, activity, agreement or document and prior to MCC Disbursements or Re-Disbursements in connection therewith:

(1) MCC Disbursements;

(2) The Financial Plan and any amendments and supplements thereto;

(3) Agreements (i) between the Government and MCA-Armenia, (ii) between the Government, MCA-Armenia or other Government Affiliate, on the one hand, and any Provider or Affiliate of a Provider, on the other hand, which require such MCC approval under applicable law, the Governing Documents, the Procurement Agreement or any other Supplemental Agreement,

or (iii) in which the Government, MCA-Armenia or other Government Affiliate appoints, hires or engages any of the following in furtherance of this Compact:

(A) Auditor or Reviewer;

(B) Fiscal Agent;

(C) Bank;

(D) Procurement Agent;

(E) Outside Project Manager;

(F) Implementing Entity; and

(G) Director, Observer, officer and/or other key employee or contractor of MCA-Armenia, including any compensation for such person.

(Any agreement described in clause (i) through (iii) of this Section 3(c)(i)(3) and any amendments and supplements thereto, each, a "***Material Agreement***");

(4) Any modification, termination or suspension of a Material Agreement, or any action that would have the effect of such a modification, termination or suspension of a Material Agreement;

(5) Any agreement that is (i) not at arm's length or (ii) with a party related to the Government, including MCA-Armenia, or any of their respective Affiliates;

(6) Any Re-Disbursement (each, a "***Material Re-Disbursement***") that requires such MCC approval under applicable law, the Governing Documents, the Procurement Agreement, Procurement Guidelines or any Supplemental Agreement;

(7) Terms of reference for the procurement of goods, services or works that require such MCC approval under applicable law, the Governing Documents, the Procurement Agreement, Procurement Guidelines or any Supplemental Agreement (each, a "***Material Terms of Reference***");

(8) The Implementation Plan, including each component plan thereto, and any material amendments and supplements to the Implementation Plan or any component thereto;

(9) Any pledge of any MCC Funding or any Program Assets or any guarantee (directly or indirectly) of any indebtedness (each, a "***Pledge***");

(10) Any decree, legislation, contractual arrangement or other document establishing or governing MCA-Armenia, including the Governance Agreement and the charter of MCA-Armenia (the "***Governing Documents***"), and any disposition (in whole or in part), liquidation, dissolution, winding up, reorganization or other change of (A) MCA-Armenia, including any revocation or modification of, or supplement to, any Governing Document, or (B) any subsidiary or Affiliate of MCA-Armenia;

(11) Any change in character or location of any Permitted Account;

(12) Formation or acquisition of any subsidiary (direct or indirect) or other Affiliate of MCA-Armenia;

(13) Any (A) change of a Director, Observer, officer or other key employee or contractor of MCA-Armenia, or in the composition of the Governing Council, including approval of the nominee for Chair, or (B) filling of any vacant seat of the Chair, a Director or an Observer or vacant position of an officer or other key employee or contractor of MCA-Armenia;

(14) The management information system to be developed and maintained by the Management Unit of MCA-Armenia, and any material modifications to such system;

(15) Any decision to amend, supplement, replace, terminate or otherwise change any of the foregoing; and

(16) Any other activity, agreement, document or transaction requiring the approval of MCC in this Compact, applicable law, the Governing Documents, the Procurement Agreement, Procurement Guidelines, the Disbursement Agreement, or any other Supplemental Agreement between the Parties.

The Chair of the Governing Council (the "***Chair***") and/or the Chief Executive Officer of MCA-Armenia (the "***Chief Executive Officer***") or other designated officer, as provided in applicable law and the Governing Documents, shall certify any documents or reports delivered to MCC in satisfaction of the Government's reporting requirements under this Compact or any Supplemental Agreement between the Parties (the "***Compact Reports***").

(ii) MCC shall have the authority to exercise its approval rights set forth in this Section 3(c) in its sole discretion and independent of any participation or position taken by the MCC Representative at a meeting of the Governing Council. MCC retains the right to revoke its approval of a matter if MCC concludes that its approval was issued on the basis of incomplete, inaccurate or misleading information furnished by the Government or MCA-Armenia.

(d) *MCA-Armenia*.

(i) *General*. Unless otherwise agreed by the Parties in writing, MCA-Armenia shall be responsible for the oversight and management of the implementation of this Compact. MCA-Armenia shall be governed by the Governing Documents, including the terms and conditions set forth in an agency agreement to be entered into by the Government, MCC and MCA-Armenia (the "***Governance Agreement***") on or before the Entry into Force, and based on the following principles:

(1) The Government shall ensure that MCA-Armenia shall not assign, delegate or contract any of the Designated Rights and Responsibilities without the prior written consent of the Government and MCC. MCA-Armenia shall not establish any Affiliates or subsidiaries (direct or indirect) without the prior written consent of the Government and MCC; and

(2) Unless otherwise agreed by the Parties in writing, MCA-Armenia shall consist of (a) an independent governing council (the "***Governing Council***") to oversee MCA-Armenia's responsibilities and obligations under this Compact (including any Designated Rights and Responsibilities) and (b) a management unit (the "***Management Unit***") to have overall management responsibility for the implementation of this Compact.

(ii) *Governing Council*.

(1) *Formation*. The Government shall ensure that the Governing Council shall be formed, constituted, governed, maintained and operated in accordance with applicable law and the terms and conditions set forth in this Section 3(d), the Governing Documents and relevant Supplemental Agreements.

(2) *Composition*. Unless otherwise agreed by the Parties in writing, the Governing Council shall consist of eleven (11) voting members (the "***Voting Members***") and two non-voting observers (the "***Observers***"), each of whom must be acceptable to MCC, taking into consideration appropriate gender and ethnic representation.

(A) The Voting Members shall be as follows, *provided*, that the members identified in subsections (i)–(vi) below (the "***Government Members***") may be replaced by another government official of comparable rank from a ministry or other government body relevant to the Program activities, subject to approval by the Government and MCC (such replacement to be referred to thereafter as a Government Member):

(i) Prime Minister;

(ii) Chief Economic Advisor to the President;

(iii) Minister of Finance and Economy;

(iv) Minister of Transport and Communication;

(v) Minister of Agriculture;

(vi) Minister of Territorial Administration; and

(vii) Five (5) members of civil society appointed by the Stakeholders' Committee (the "***Civil Society Members***").

The following provisions apply to the Voting Members:

a. Each Government Member may be replaced by another government official, subject to approval by the Government and MCC;

b. Subject to the Governing Documents, the Parties contemplate that the Prime Minister shall initially fill the seat of Chair;

c. Each Government Member position shall be filled by the individual then holding the office identified and such individuals shall serve in their capacity as the applicable Government official and not in their personal capacity. In the event that a Government Member is unable to participate in a meeting of the Governing Council such member's principal deputy or equivalent may participate in the member's stead; and

d. Each Civil Society Member may appoint an alternate, approved by majority vote of the other Civil Society Members, to serve when he or she is unable to participate in a meeting of the Governing Council.

(B) The Observers shall be:

(i) A representative appointed by MCC (the "MCC Representative"); and

(ii) A representative of an environmentally focused NGO appointed by the Stakeholders' Committee (the "Environmental Observer"); provided, that if one of the Civil Society Members on the Governing Council already represents an environmentally focused NGO, then such Civil Society Member shall also act as the Environmental Observer. The initial Environmental Observer shall serve for a period of one year from the date of the first Governing Council meeting after the Entry into Force, and on each anniversary thereof, the Stakeholders' Committee shall appoint another representative to serve as the Environmental Observer for the subsequent year. The Stakeholders' Committee may nominate an alternate to attend one or more meetings of the Governing Council in the event that the Environmental Observer is unable to attend.

The Observers shall have the right to attend all meetings of the Governing Council, participate in discussions of the Governing Council, and receive all information and documents provided to the Governing Council, together with any other rights of access to records, employees or facilities as would be granted to a member of the Governing Council under the Governance Agreement and any Governing Document.

(3) *Voting*. Unless otherwise agreed by the Parties, the Governing Documents of MCA-Armenia shall include voting and quorum provisions so as to require participation by the Civil Society Members in all decisions of the Governing Council.

(4) *Roles and Responsibilities*.

(A) The Governing Council shall oversee the overall implementation of the Program and the performance of the Designated Rights and Responsibilities.

(B) Certain actions may be taken, and certain agreements and other documents may be executed and delivered, by MCA-Armenia only upon the approval and authorization of the Governing Council as provided under applicable law and in the Governing Documents, including each MCC Disbursement Request, selection or termination of certain Providers, any component of the Implementation Plan, certain Re-Disbursements and certain terms of reference.

(C) The Chair shall certify the approval by the Governing Council of all Compact Reports or any other documents or reports from time to time delivered to MCC by MCA-Armenia (whether or not such documents or reports are required to be delivered to MCC), and that such documents or reports are true, accurate and complete.

(D) Without limiting the generality of the Designated Rights and Responsibilities, and subject to MCC's contractual rights of approval as set forth in Section 3(c) of this Program Annex or elsewhere in this Compact or any relevant Supplemental Agreement, the Governing Council shall have the exclusive authority for all actions defined for the Governing Council under applicable law and in the Governing Documents and which are expressly designated therein as responsibilities that cannot be delegated further.

(5) *Meetings*. The Governing Council shall hold at least quarterly meetings as well as such other periodic meetings or subcommittee meetings as may be necessary from time to time.

(6) *Indemnification of Civil Society Members; MCC Representative*. The Government shall ensure, at the Government's sole cost and expense, that appropriate insurance is obtained and appropriate indemnifications and protections are provided, acceptable to MCC, to ensure that Civil Society Members shall not be held personally liable for the actions or omissions of the Governing Council. Pursuant to Section 5.5 and Section 5.8 of this Compact, the Government and MCA-Armenia shall hold harmless the MCC Representative and the Environmental Observer for any liability or action arising out of their roles as non-voting Observers on the Governing Council. The Government hereby waives and releases all claims related to any such liability. In matters arising under or relating to the Compact, the MCC Representative is not subject to the jurisdiction of the courts or other body of Armenia.

(iii) *Management Unit*. Unless otherwise agreed in writing by the Parties, the Management Unit shall report, through the Chief Executive Officer or other officer as designated in the Governing Documents, directly to the Governing Council, and shall have the composition, roles and responsibilities described below and set forth more particularly in the Governing Documents.

(1) *Composition*. The Government shall ensure that the Management Unit shall be composed of qualified experts from the public or private sectors, including such officers and staff as may be necessary to carry out effectively its responsibilities, each with such powers and responsibilities as set forth in the Governance Agreement, any Governing Document, and from time to time in any Supplemental Agreement between the Parties, including without limitation the following: (i) a Chief Executive Officer, (ii) a chief financial officer, (iii) a monitoring and evaluation officer, (iv) an environment and social impact officer, (v) a rural roads project officer, (vi) an irrigation project officer,

(vii) a water-to-market project officer and (viii) a procurement officer. The Management Unit will be supported by an office manager and appropriate administrative and support personnel.

(2) *Appointment of Management Unit.* Unless otherwise specified in the Governance Agreement or any Governing Documents, the Governing Council shall appoint the Chief Executive Officer after an open and competitive recruitment and selection process, which appointment shall be subject to the approval of MCC. The remaining officers of the Management Unit shall be appointed by the Chief Executive Officer after an open and competitive recruitment and selection process, which appointments shall be subject to the approval of the Governing Council and MCC.

(3) *Roles and Responsibilities.*

(A) The Management Unit shall assist the Governing Council in overseeing the implementation of the Program and shall have principal responsibility (subject to the direction and oversight of the Governing Council and subject to MCC's rights of approval as set forth in Section 3(c) of this Program Annex or elsewhere in this Compact or any relevant Supplemental Agreement) for the overall management of the implementation of the Program.

(B) The Management Unit shall report to and meet with, on a quarterly basis, the Stakeholders' Committee, and shall include a report on the feedback provided by the Stakeholders' Committee and the ways in which that feedback has informed the activities of MCA-Armenia in the next following quarterly report to the Governing Council.

(C) Without limiting the foregoing general responsibilities or the generality of Designated Rights and Responsibilities that the Government may designate to MCA-Armenia, the Management Unit shall develop the components of the Implementation Plan, oversee the implementation of the Projects, manage and coordinate monitoring and evaluation, maintain internal accounting records, conduct and oversee certain procurements, and such other responsibilities as set out in the Governing Documents or delegated to the Management Unit by the Governing Council from time to time.

(D) Subject to the provisions of this Compact, the Procurement Agreement and the Governing Documents, appropriate officers of the Management Unit shall have the authority to contract on behalf of MCA-Armenia.

(E) The Management Unit shall have the obligation and right to approve certain actions and documents or agreements, including certain Re-Disbursements, certain human resources decisions, and certain procurement actions, as provided in the Governing Documents. The Management Unit shall also prepare MCC Disbursement Requests and Compact Reports for approval by the Governing Council.

(iv) *Stakeholders' Committee.*

(1) *Formation.* The Government shall ensure the establishment of a stakeholders' committee (the "***Stakeholders' Committee***") that shall be representative of the various beneficiaries of the Program. Unless otherwise agreed by the Parties, the Government shall invite members of the NGO community, representatives of the WUAs and farmer groups to participate in national and regional forums to elect the Stakeholders' Committee. The Government will provide adequate notice of such forums to ensure widespread participation. Initially, the Stakeholders' Committee will consist of eleven (11) members, taking into consideration appropriate gender and ethnic representation. The number of members of the Stakeholders' Committee may be increased, but in no event to more than fifteen (15) members, upon the majority vote of the then existing members and the vacancies created by such increase shall be filled by the majority vote of the then existing members, subject to the approval of MCA-Armenia and MCC. Each Stakeholders' Committee member may appoint an alternate,

approved by majority vote of the other members, to serve when he or she is unable to participate in a meeting of the Stakeholders' Committee.

(2) *Roles and Responsibilities*.

(A) The Stakeholders' Committee shall be a mechanism to provide representatives of the private sector, civil society and local and regional communities the opportunity to provide advice and input to MCA-Armenia regarding the implementation of the Compact.

(B) During quarterly meetings of the Stakeholders' Committee, the Management Unit shall present an update on the implementation of this Compact and progress towards achievement of the Objectives. The Management Unit shall provide copies of the M&E Plan, the Implementation Plan, and reports on the Projects and Project Activities. The Stakeholders' Committee will have an opportunity to regularly provide to the Chief Executive Officer and to the Governing Council its views and recommendations. The Governing Council may, in response to the Stakeholders' Committee, require the Management Unit to provide such other information and documents as the Governing Council deems advisable.

(C) The Management Unit shall include in its quarterly reports to the Governing Council, a report on the Stakeholders' Committee meetings that occurred during the period covered by such report.

(D) The Stakeholders' Committee shall appoint one of their members to be the secretary to, among other things, take official minutes of the meetings of the Stakeholders' Committee.

(3) *Meetings*. The Stakeholders' Committee shall hold quarterly meetings of the full Stakeholders' Committee as well as such other periodic meetings of the Stakeholders' Committee or subcommittees thereof designated along sectoral, regional, or other lines, as may be necessary or appropriate from time to time.

(4) *Accessibility; Transparency*. Stakeholders' Committee members will be accessible to the beneficiaries they represent to receive the beneficiaries' comments or suggestions regarding the Program. The minutes of all meetings of the Stakeholders' Committee and any subcommittees shall be made public on the MCA-Armenia Website in a timely manner.

(e) *Implementing Entities*. Subject to the terms and conditions of this Compact and any other Supplemental Agreement between the Parties, MCA-Armenia may provide MCC Funding, to one or more Government Affiliates or to one or more nongovernmental or other public- or private-sector entities or persons to implement and carry out the Projects or any other activities to be carried out in furtherance of this Compact (each, an "***Implementing Entity***"). The Government shall ensure that MCA-Armenia enters into an agreement with each Implementing Entity, in form and substance satisfactory to MCC, that sets forth the roles and responsibilities of such Implementing Entity and other appropriate terms and conditions, such as payment of the Implementing Entity (the "***Implementing Entity Agreement***"). An Implementing Entity shall report directly to MCA-Armenia as designated in the applicable Implementing Entity Agreement or as otherwise agreed by the Parties.

(f) *Outside Project Manager*. MCA-Armenia shall have the authority to engage qualified persons or entities to serve as outside project managers (each, an "***Outside Project Manager***") in the event that it is advisable to do so for the proper and efficient day-to-day management of a Project; *provided, however*, that the appointment or engagement of any Outside Project Manager after a competitive selection process shall be subject to approval by the Governing Council and MCC prior to such appointment or engagement. Upon Governing Council approval, MCA-Armenia may delegate, assign, or contract to the Outside Project Managers such duties and responsibilities as it deems appropriate with respect to the management of the Implementing Entities and the implementation of the specific Projects; and *provided, further*, that the Management Unit shall remain accountable for those duties and responsibilities and all reports delivered by the Outside Project Manager notwithstanding any such delegation, assignment or contract and the Outside Project Manager shall be subject to the oversight of the Fiscal Agent and Procurement Agent. The Governing Council may determine that it is advisable to engage one or more Outside Project Managers and instruct MCA-Armenia and, where appropriate, a Procurement Agent to commence and conduct the competitive selection process for such Outside Project Manager.

(g) *Fiscal Agent*. The Government shall ensure that MCA-Armenia engages one or more fiscal agents (each, a "***Fiscal Agent***"), who shall be responsible for, among other things, (i) ensuring and certifying that Re-Disbursements are properly authorized and documented in accordance with established control procedures set forth in the Disbursement Agreement, the Fiscal Agent Agreement and other relevant Supplemental Agreements, (ii) instructing a Bank to make Re-Disbursements from a Permitted Account, following applicable certification by the Fiscal Agent, (iii) providing applicable certifications for MCC Disbursement Requests, (iv) maintaining proper accounting of all MCC Funding financial transactions, and (v) producing reports on MCC Disbursements and Re-Disbursements (including any requests therefore) in accordance with established procedures set forth in the Disbursement Agreement, the Fiscal Agent Agreement or any other relevant Supplemental Agreements. Upon the written request of MCC, the Government shall ensure that MCA-Armenia terminates a Fiscal Agent, without any liability to MCC, and the Government shall ensure that MCA-Armenia engages a new Fiscal Agent, subject to the approval by the Governing Council and MCC. The Government shall ensure that MCA-Armenia enters into an agreement with each Fiscal Agent, in form and substance satisfactory to MCC, that sets forth the roles and responsibilities of the Fiscal Agent and other appropriate terms and conditions, such as payment of the Fiscal Agent ("***Fiscal Agent Agreement***").

(h) *Auditors and Reviewers*. The Government shall ensure that MCA-Armenia carries out the Government's audit responsibilities as provided in Sections 3.8(d), (e) and (f), including engaging one or more auditors (each, an "***Auditor***") required by Section 3.8(d). As requested by MCC in writing from time to time, the Government shall ensure that MCA-Armenia shall also engage an independent (i) reviewer to conduct reviews of performance and compliance under this Compact pursuant to Section 3.8(f), which reviewer shall have the capacity to (1) conduct general reviews of performance or compliance, (2) conduct environmental and social audits, and (3) conduct data quality assessments in accordance with the M&E Plan, as described more fully in *Annex III*, and/or (ii) evaluator to assess performance as required under the M&E Plan (each, a "***Reviewer***"). MCA-Armenia shall select the Auditor(s) or Reviewers in accordance with the Governing Documents or relevant Supplemental Agreement. The Government shall ensure that MCA-Armenia enters into an agreement with each Auditor or Reviewer, in form and substance satisfactory to MCC, that sets forth the roles and responsibilities of the Auditor or Reviewer with respect to the audit, review or evaluation, including access rights, required form and content of the applicable audit, review or evaluation and other appropriate terms and conditions such as payment of the Auditor or Reviewer (the "***Auditor / Reviewer Agreement***"). In the case of a financial audit required by Section 3.8(f), such Auditor / Reviewer Agreement shall be effective no later than 120 days prior to the end of the relevant fiscal year or other period to be audited; *provided, however*, if MCC requires concurrent audits of financial information or reviews of performance and compliance under this Compact, then such Auditor / Reviewer Agreement shall be effective no later than a date agreed by the Parties in writing.

(i) *Procurement Agent*. If requested by MCC, the Government shall ensure that MCA-Armenia engages one or more procurement agents (each, a "***Procurement Agent***") to carry out and/or certify specified procurement activities in furtherance of this Compact on behalf of the Government, MCA-Armenia, any Outside Project Manager or Implementing Entity. The roles and responsibilities of such Procurement Agent and the criteria for selection of a Procurement Agent shall be as set forth in the applicable Implementation Letter or Supplemental Agreement. The Government shall ensure that MCA-Armenia enters into an agreement with the Procurement Agent, in form and substance satisfactory to MCC, that sets forth the roles and responsibilities of the Procurement Agent with respect to the conduct, monitoring and review of procurements and other appropriate terms and conditions, such as payment of the Procurement Agent (the "***Procurement Agent Agreement***"). Any Procurement Agent shall adhere to the procurement standards set forth in the Procurement Agreement and Procurement Guidelines and ensure procurements are consistent with the procurement plan (the "***Procurement Plan***") adopted by MCA-Armenia, which plan shall forecast the upcoming six month procurement activities and be updated every six months.

4. Finances and Fiscal Accountability.

(a) *Financial Plan.*

(i) *Financial Plan.* The multi-year financial plan for the Program and for each Project (the "***Multi-Year Financial Plan***") is summarized in *Annex II* to this Compact.

(ii) *Detailed Financial Plan.* During the Compact Term, the Government shall ensure that MCA-Armenia delivers to MCC for approval timely financial plans that detail the annual and quarterly budget and projected cash requirements for the Program (including administrative costs) and each Project, projected both on a commitment and cash requirement basis (each a "***Detailed Financial Plan***"). Each Detailed Financial Plan shall be delivered by such time as specified in the Disbursement Agreement or as may otherwise be agreed by the Parties. The Multi-Year Financial Plan, each Detailed Financial Plan and each amendment, supplement or other change thereto are collectively, the "***Financial Plan***."

(iii) *Expenditures.* No financial commitment involving MCC Funding shall be made, no obligation of MCC Funding shall be incurred, and no Re-Disbursement shall be made or MCC Disbursement Request submitted for any activity or expenditure, unless the expense is provided for in the Detailed Financial Plan and unless uncommitted funds exist in the balance of the Detailed Financial Plan for the relevant period or unless the Parties otherwise agree in writing.

(iv) *Modifications to Financial Plan.* Notwithstanding anything to the contrary in this Compact, MCA-Armenia may amend or supplement the Financial Plan or any component thereof without amending this Compact, *provided*, any material amendment or supplement has been approved by MCC and is otherwise consistent with the requirements of this Compact and any relevant Supplemental Agreement between the Parties.

(b) *Disbursement and Re-Disbursement.* The Disbursement Agreement (and disbursement schedules thereto), as amended from time to time, shall specify the terms, conditions and procedures on which MCC Disbursements and Re-Disbursements shall be made. The obligation of MCC to make MCC Disbursements or approve Re-Disbursements is subject to the fulfillment or waiver of any such terms and conditions. The Government and MCA-Armenia shall jointly submit the applicable request for an MCC Disbursement (the "***MCC Disbursement Request***") as may be specified in the Disbursement Agreement. MCC will make MCC Disbursements in tranches to a Permitted Account from time to time as provided in the Disbursement Agreement or as may otherwise be agreed by the Parties, subject to Program requirements and performance by the Government, MCA-Armenia and other relevant parties in furtherance of this Compact. Re-Disbursements will be made from time to time based on requests by an authorized representative of the appropriate party designated for the size and type of Re-Disbursement in accordance with the Governing Documents and Disbursement Agreement; *provided, however*, unless otherwise agreed by the Parties in writing, no Re-Disbursement shall be made unless and until the written approvals specified herein or in the Governing Documents and Disbursement Agreement for such Re-Disbursement have been obtained and delivered to the Fiscal Agent.

(c) *Fiscal Accountability Plan*. By such time as specified in the Disbursement Agreement or as otherwise agreed by the Parties, MCA-Armenia shall adopt as part of the Implementation Plan a fiscal accountability plan that identifies the principles and mechanisms to ensure appropriate fiscal accountability for the use of MCC Funding provided under this Compact, including the process to ensure that open, fair, and competitive procedures will be used in a transparent manner in the administration of grants or cooperative agreements and the procurement of goods and services for the accomplishment of the Objectives (the "***Fiscal Accountability Plan***"). The Fiscal Accountability Plan shall set forth, among other things, requirements with respect to the following matters: (i) funds control and documentation; (ii) separation of duties and internal controls; (iii) accounting standards and systems; (iv) content and timing of reports; (v) policies concerning public availability of all financial information; (vi) cash management practices; (vii) procurement and contracting practices, including timely payment to vendors; (viii) the role of independent auditors; and (ix) the roles of fiscal agents and procurement agents.

(d) *Permitted Accounts*. The Government shall establish, or cause to be established, such accounts (each, a "***Permitted Account***," and collectively "***Permitted Accounts***") as may be agreed by the Parties in writing from time to time, including:

(i) A single, completely separate U.S. Dollar interest-bearing account at either the Central Bank of Armenia or at a commercial bank to receive MCC Disbursements;

(ii) If necessary, an interest-bearing local currency of Armenia account (the "***Local Account***") at either the Central Bank of Armenia or at a commercial bank that is procured through a competitive process to which the Fiscal Agent may authorize transfer from any U.S. Dollar Permitted Account for the purpose of making Re-Disbursements payable in local currency; and

(iii) Such other interest-bearing accounts to receive MCC Disbursements in such banks as the Parties mutually agree upon in writing.

No other funds shall be commingled in a Permitted Account other than MCC Funding and Accrued Interest thereon. All MCC Funding held in an interest-bearing Permitted Account shall earn interest at a rate of no less than such amount as the Parties may agree in the respective Bank Agreement or otherwise. MCC shall have the right, among other things, to view any Permitted Account statements and activity directly on-line or at such other frequency as the Parties may otherwise agree. By such time as shall be specified in the Disbursement Agreement or as otherwise agreed by the Parties, the Government shall ensure that MCA-Armenia enters into an agreement with each Bank, respectively, satisfactory to MCC, that sets forth the signatory authority, access rights, anti-money laundering and anti-terrorist financing provisions, and other terms related to the Permitted Account, respectively (each a "***Bank Agreement***"). For purposes of this Compact, any bank holding a Permitted Account referenced in Section 4(d) of this Program Annex are each a "***Bank***" and, are collectively referred to as the "***Banks***."

(e) *Currency Exchange*. The Bank shall convert MCC Funding to the currency of the Republic of Armenia at a rate to which the Parties mutually agree with the Bank in the Bank Agreement.

5. Transparency; Accountability.

Transparency and accountability to MCC and to the beneficiaries are important aspects of the Program and Projects. Without limiting the generality of the foregoing, in an effort to achieve the goals of transparency and accountability, the Government shall ensure that MCA-Armenia:

(a) Establishes an e-mail suggestion box as well as a means for other written comments that interested persons may use to communicate ideas, suggestions or feedback to MCA-Armenia;

(b) Considers as a factor in its decision-making the recommendations of the Stakeholders' Committee;

(c) Develops and maintains the MCA-Armenia Website in a timely, accurate and appropriately comprehensive manner, such MCA-Armenia Website to include postings of information and documents in English and Armenian and other languages where relevant; and

(d) Posts on the MCA-Armenia Website and otherwise makes publicly available from time to time the following documents or information:

(i) The Compact and all Compact Reports;

(ii) All minutes of the meetings of the Governing Council and Stakeholders' Committee;

(iii) The M&E Plan, as amended from time to time, along with periodic reports on Program performance;

(iv) All Project environmental and social impact assessments ("***ESIAs***") and supporting documents;

(v) All audit reports by an Auditor and any periodic reports or evaluations by a Reviewer;

(vi) Disbursement Agreement, as amended from time to time;

(vii) All procurement policies and procedures (including standard documents and procurement plans) and any other documents required to be made publicly available pursuant to the Procurement Agreement; and

(viii) A copy of any legislation and other documents related to the formation, organization and governance of MCA-Armenia, including the Governing Documents, and any amendments thereto.

SCHEDULE 1 to ANNEX I
RURAL ROAD REHABILITATION PROJECT

This *Schedule 1* describes and summarizes the key elements of the rural road rehabilitation project ("***Rural Road Rehabilitation Project***") that the Parties intend to implement in furtherance of the Rural Road Rehabilitation Objective. Additional details regarding the implementation of the Rural Road Rehabilitation Project will be included in the Implementation Plan and in relevant Supplemental Agreements.

1. Background.

Armenia's public road network consists of 7,703 km of roads, including 1,561 km of main roads, 1,800 km of secondary roads (referred to in Armenia as "republican" roads) and 4,342 km of local roads. Main and republican roads are managed by the Armenian Road Directorate ("***ARD***") and local roads are managed at the regional (*Marz*) level.

In 2002, the World Bank financed a rural infrastructure study which identified a lifeline network (the "***LLN***") from among the republican and local roads. The objective was to ensure all communities, towns and villages are linked to the main road network, either directly or through other communities. The resulting network comprises 2703 km, of which 759 km (28 percent) are republican roads, and 1943 km (72 percent) are local roads.

The Government is committed to bringing the entire LLN up to a maintainable standard and ensuring sustainable maintenance of this network. Moreover, the Government has committed to re-classifying the entire LLN as republican roads so that they will come under the management and maintenance responsibility of the ARD.

2. Summary of the Project.

(a) *Project Description*. MCC Funding will be used to rehabilitate up to 943 km of high priority LLN roads (45 percent of the LLN), consisting of 85 road segments throughout the country and amounting to 321 km of republican roads and 622 km of local roads. All rehabilitation works will be on existing alignments and will include pavement rehabilitation, improvements to up to 19 bridges, drainage facilities, and road safety features.

MCA-Armenia will select roads from among the LLN roads described above. MCC Funding will be provided to rehabilitate selected roads subject to the condition that each road must:

- Have an economic rate of return at least equal to 12.5 percent, calculated in a manner acceptable to MCC and based on a feasibility study and final design;
- Conform to Government requirements and MCC's Environmental Guidelines; and
- Conform to the World Bank policy on Involuntary Resettlement, where relevant.

MCC Funding will also be provided to ARD to conduct a technical audit of its existing performance based maintenance contracts and for technical assistance to create a long-term road maintenance strategic plan.

The M&E Plan (described in *Annex III*) will set forth anticipated results and, where appropriate, regular benchmarks that may be used to monitor implementation progress of the Rural Road Rehabilitation Project. Performance against these benchmarks and the overall impact of the Rural Road Rehabilitation Project will be assessed and reported at regular intervals to be specified in the M&E Plan or otherwise agreed by the Parties from time to time. The Parties expect that additional benchmarks may be identified during implementation of the Project. Estimated amounts of MCC Funding for the Rural Road Rehabilitation Project are identified in *Annex II* of this Compact. Conditions precedent and sequencing of the Project shall be set forth in the Disbursement Agreement or other relevant Supplemental Agreements.

(b) *Project Implementation*. The Rural Road Rehabilitation Project will be implemented through the ARD, under the authority of the Ministry of Transport and Communications ("***MoTC***"). ARD is responsible for planning, design and construction of all state owned roads in Armenia and is responsible for the maintenance of all main and republican roads. It has departments for design and tender, planning (road survey and economic evaluation), construction and rehabilitation and routine maintenance, as well as a road safety group and an on-site laboratory. ARD was the project implementation unit for two World Bank projects in the last 10 years and has a trained staff and the basic technical capacity to implement the Project. The Government will establish a rural roads coordination unit within the ARD, staffed with members of the former project implementation unit established by the World Bank for its completed transportation project. MCA-Armenia will enter into an Implementing Entity Agreement with the ARD that will set out the terms and conditions for the use of MCC Funding in implementing the Rural Road Rehabilitation Project.

3. Beneficiaries.

The principal beneficiaries of the Rural Road Rehabilitation Project are expected to be approximately 360,000 Armenians living in 265 rural communities connected by the rehabilitated LLN. Particular beneficiaries include: farmers who use the improved roads to get products to market and to get inputs to production; users of public transport; and other travelers.

4. Donor Coordination.

The Rural Road Rehabilitation Project will complement the rehabilitation and construction of larger roads and other rural roads recently undertaken by other donors. In addition, MCC support to the redefinition and management of the LLN will require collaboration and coordination with other donors active in the road sector. Although the World Bank's two transportation projects in Armenia, the Highway Project and the Transport Project, are closed, the World Bank takes an active interest in the sustainable maintenance arrangements of the roads. Coordination will also continue with the Lincy Foundation, which has completed several main road rehabilitation projects and is considering additional ones. Other donors include: the Japan International Cooperation Agency which is currently funding a landslide survey; the Kuwait Fund, which is currently considering a request to fund the rehabilitation of rural roads leading to places of historical and tourist significance; and the Asian Development Bank, which is establishing a country office in Armenia and has also expressed interest in road sector investments.

5. Sustainability.

(a) *Institutional Sustainability.*

The Government will ensure continued institutional support of the Project through the passage of appropriate legislation establishing the LLN as republican roads, placing them under the operations and maintenance jurisdiction of the ARD. The portion of the LLN to be rehabilitated with MCC Funding represents the initial phase of the establishment of this network and creates a commitment by the Government to build out the rest of the LLN, as well as establish a sustainable maintenance program for the LLN and main road network. The Rural Road Rehabilitation Project will further help to institutionalize performance based contracts, which were instituted by ARD in 2005 and provide a mechanism to promote local contractors by establishing a competitive and reliable contracting environment.

(b) *Financial Sustainability.*

Financial sustainability is a function of the Government's commitment to finance necessary annual road maintenance programs for the rehabilitated roads. Currently, the Government finances approximately USD $9 million annually of routine maintenance on the entire road network. As rehabilitation on the LLN proceeds, additional resources will be committed by the Government to cover routine maintenance on the additional roads. Moreover, the Government will establish a plan for financing periodic maintenance so as to ensure the long term sustainability of the entire road network. In addition, the Government agrees to fund any environmental mitigation costs associated with the Rural Road Rehabilitation Project in excess of MCC Funding allocated to cover such costs.

(c) *Environmental and Social Sustainability.*

The key to ensuring environmental and social sustainability of the Project is ongoing public consultation. The Environment and Social Impact Officer ("***ESI Officer***") within the Management Unit will ensure that environmental and social mitigation measures are followed for all Project Activities in accordance with the provisions set forth in this Compact and in relevant Supplemental Agreements. The ESI Officer will serve as the point of contact for comments and concerns of parties affected by the implementation of all Project Activities under the Compact and will lead the effort to find feasible resolutions to those problems. The ESI Officer will convene periodic public meetings to provide implementation updates and to identify and address public concerns. The Stakeholders' Committee will also appoint representatives of civil society to the Governing Council and provide a link between local NGOs and program managers.

Environmental and social analyses of the roads will be conducted as part of the technical survey and design to determine the environmental impacts and existence of economic and physical displacement. In addition to the analyses, environmental management plans ("***EMPs***") satisfactory to MCC will be developed, implemented and monitored during project implementation. Disbursement of MCC Funding will be contingent upon issuance of environmental licenses, as needed, or any other required permits.

6. Policy, Legal and Regulatory Reforms.

The Parties have identified the following policy, legal and regulatory reforms and actions that the Government will pursue in support of the Rural Road Rehabilitation Project to reach its full benefits. Satisfactory implementation of these reforms may be conditions precedent to certain MCC Disbursements as provided in the Disbursement Agreement:

(a) The Government will define and adopt into legislation the concept of a LLN of no less than 2,703 km of roads. LLN roads are to be defined as those which ensure road access from each community to the main road network. LLN roads should be classified as republican roads so that the maintenance of the LLN falls under the jurisdiction of the ARD.

(b) The Government will present an annual plan for the repair and routine maintenance of the entire LLN, acceptable to MCC, including the roads to be rehabilitated with MCC Funding.

(c) The Government will allocate sufficient funds in the budget for continued rehabilitation of a minimum of 532 km of the LLN over the Compact Term, with the following minimum annual km and threshold expenditure amounts:

(i) fiscal year 2006: 32 km; 1.01 billion AMD;[3]

(ii) fiscal year 2007: 100 km; 3.15 billion AMD;

(iii) fiscal year 2008: 100 km; 3.31 billion AMD;

(iv) fiscal year 2009: 120km; 3.97 billion AMD; and

(v) fiscal year 2010: 180 km; 5.95 billion AMD.

(d) The Government will allocate funds in the budget for routine maintenance of the entire Armenian road network in amounts at least equal to the amounts set out below for the following fiscal years, will expend such amounts for their intended purpose, and will make up any budget shortfall from the prior year's road maintenance budget:

(i) fiscal year 2006: 5.02 billion AMD;[4]

(ii) fiscal year 2007: 5.99 billion AMD;

(iii) fiscal year 2008: 6.29 billion AMD;

(iv) fiscal year 2009: 6.90 billion AMD; and

(v) fiscal year 2010: 7.36 billion AMD.

(e) The Government will submit a long-term routine and periodic maintenance plan for the entire road network by the end of the third year of the Compact Term.

SCHEDULE 2 to ANNEX I
IRRIGATED AGRICULTURE PROJECT

This *Schedule 2* describes and summarizes the key elements of the irrigated agriculture project that the Parties intend to implement in furtherance of the Irrigated Agriculture Objective (the "***Irrigated***

[3] Actual budgeted in Armenian Drams ("***AMD***").
[4] Actual budgeted in Armenian Drams ("***AMD***").

Agriculture Project"). Additional details regarding the implementation of the Irrigated Agriculture Project will be included in the Implementation Plan and in relevant Supplemental Agreements.

1. Background.

Armenian agricultural productivity and profitability are constrained by dilapidated irrigated infrastructure and an outdated system characterized by water losses, inefficient operations and high costs of electric pumping. Farmers operate on small plots of land and are limited by an underdeveloped market economy. In addition, agriculture lending in Armenia is at a very low level. Despite this, a reformed institutional environment for modern irrigation management and agribusiness development is emerging at a critical juncture in the post-Soviet era. The Irrigated Agriculture Project will address the conditions necessary to achieve higher rural incomes based on irrigated agriculture. It includes infrastructure improvements on targeted irrigation schemes, as well as technical support and training for key actors in the irrigation sector, namely: the national Water Supply Agency (the "***WSA***"), the Water User Associations (the "***WUAs***"), federations of WUAs and their member farmers. In addition, the Project will provide medium and long-term lending to farmers and enterprises participating in the Project through registered credit organizations.

2. Summary of the Project and Project Activities.

The Irrigated Agriculture Project addresses the physical, managerial and financial investments needed to generate sustainable increases in rural incomes through irrigated agriculture. These investments will be implemented through two critical activities:

- Improving dilapidated infrastructure to expand the land area under irrigated production and improvements to the overall efficiency of sourcing and delivering water to member farmers (the "***Infrastructure Activity***"); and

- Building the management capacities of the WSA and WUAs and providing training and access to credit for member farmers to transition to more profitable, market-oriented agriculture (the "***Water-to-Market Activity***").

The M&E Plan (described in *Annex III*) will set forth anticipated results and, where appropriate, regular benchmarks that may be used to monitor implementation progress. Performance against these benchmarks and the overall impact of the Irrigated Agriculture Project will be assessed and reported at the intervals to be specified in the M&E Plan or as otherwise agreed by the Parties from time to time. The Parties expect that additional benchmarks may be identified during the implementation of each Project Activity. Estimated amounts of MCC Funding for each Project Activity for this Irrigated Agriculture Project are identified in *Annex II* of this Compact. Conditions precedent to each Irrigated Agriculture Project Activity and sequencing of these Project Activities shall be set forth in the Disbursement Agreement or other relevant Supplemental Agreements.

(a) *Infrastructure Activity.*

(i) MCC Funding will be used to increase the land area under irrigated production and improve the overall efficiency of sourcing and water delivery to member farmers. This will be done by selectively:

(1) Rehabilitating infrastructure and equipment for up to 21 regional irrigation schemes, including:

(A) Conversion of part or all of 15 schemes from pump to gravity systems;

(B) Construction or rehabilitation of 7 reservoirs;

(C) Rehabilitation of 200 km of main canals;

(D) Renovation and resizing of 68 pumping stations; and

(E) Rehabilitation of tertiary canals utilizing a 15 percent beneficiary co-investment;

(2) Rehabilitating additional tertiary canal systems in up to nine WUAs utilizing a 15 percent beneficiary co-investment and not included in clause (i)(1)(E) above; and

(3) Renovating the drainage system serving the Ararat Valley production systems, including renovating open and closed drains, tube wells and artesian wells within 3 sub-regions.

MCA-Armenia will select individual components or groups of components from among the foregoing irrigation schemes for rehabilitation. MCC Funding will be provided to rehabilitate such components, subject to the condition that each individual component or group of components must:

- Have an economic rate of return at least equal to 12.5 percent, calculated in a manner acceptable to MCC and based on a feasibility study and final design;
- Conform to Government regulations and MCC's Environmental Guidelines; and
- Conform to the World Bank policy on Involuntary Resettlement, where relevant.

(ii) The Infrastructure Activity will be implemented through the Water Sector Development and Institutional Project Implementation Unit under the authority of the State Water Committee (the "***Irrigation PIU***"). Originally established for the World Bank's irrigation projects, the Irrigation PIU has a trained staff and the basic technical capacity to implement the Infrastructure Activity. MCC Funding will be used to recruit an outside project management advisor to assist the Irrigation PIU. MCA-Armenia will enter into an Implementing Entity Agreement with the Irrigation PIU that will set out the terms and conditions for the use of MCC Funding in implementing the Infrastructure Activity.

(b) *Water-to-Market Activity*.

(i) The Water-to-Market Activity will ensure that MCC Funding of the Infrastructure Activity is sustained through a combination of training, technical assistance, access to credit and essential equipment. Under the Water-to-Market Activity, MCC Funding will be used to build management capacities within the WSA and 53 WUAs and improve the ability of member farmers to convert the improved water supply to profitable production and pay for water charges through two sub-activities:

(1) *Strengthening Irrigation System Entities*. MCC Funding will be used to:

(A) Support organizational reforms and institutional strengthening of the WSA;

(B) Build administrative and operational capacity of the WUAs and the developing federations of WUAs; and

(C) Support the establishment of a professional irrigation association.

(2) *Improving the Profitability of WUA Member Farmers*. MCC Funding will be used to:

(A) Provide member farmers with access to technology and training in on-farm water management and higher value agricultural production;

(B) Provide training and consulting to individual member farmers, farmer groups and small and medium enterprises on post-harvest, processing and marketing investments; and

(C) Build capacity within credit organizations and provide funding to such credit organizations which will on-lend to member farmers and related enterprises.

(ii) The sub-activity to strengthen irrigation system entities will be managed in the Irrigation PIU. The sub-activity to improve profitability of WUA member farmers will be managed by an Outside Project Manager to be selected through a competitive international tender process.

3. Beneficiaries.

The beneficiaries of the Irrigated Agriculture Project will be the 53 WUAs and their approximately 250,000 member farmers who will benefit from more efficient and reliable irrigation water and intensive institutional strengthening. Among these member farmers, an estimated 60,000 will be reached with on-farm water management techniques. At least 30,000 member farmers will be reached with transition to higher value agriculture technology. A further subset of an estimated 15,000 member farmers will be reached with modern post-harvest, processing and marketing techniques. Some 300 enterprises involved with post-harvest, processing and marketing are expected to benefit leading to significant additional job creation.

4. Donor Coordination.

The Irrigated Agriculture Project builds upon and complements an extensive body of work by several donors in irrigation and agriculture.

(a) *World Bank and IFAD*. The World Bank has contributed to the irrigation sector through three operations: the Irrigation Dam Safety Projects I and II; the Irrigation Development Project (the "***IDP***"); and the Irrigation Rehabilitation Project. The International Fund for Agricultural Development ("***IFAD***") has also contributed to the sector under the latter two World Bank projects, as well as its own Agriculture Research Project. Regarding improvements in WUA members' capacity to pay for water services, the World Bank is initiating a loan package to support the agricultural sector called the Rural Enterprise and Small-Scale Commercial Agriculture Development Project. IFAD is also extending a loan focusing on providing credit, grants and training to rural enterprises in communities of mountainous regions. Coordination with the World Bank and IFAD programs is advantageous in the following areas: (i) the phase out of the Government's subsidy polices and establishment of effective cost recovery mechanisms; (ii) the co-financing contributions by the WUAs to capital investments in the tertiary canal system; (iii) institutional strengthening; and (iv) technical and marketing support programs for member farmers.

(b) *USAID and USDA*. USAID is currently funding a Water Management Program that focuses on national water policy (including drinking water) and the institutional framework for that policy. The Government and MCA-Armenia will align policy reform and support to the WSA and WUAs through this program's progress and insights. The USAID-supported Armenia SME Market Development Project will continue to support agribusiness, textiles and stone-work enterprises until September, 2006, and the Micro Enterprise Development Initiative provides management consulting services to financial institutions and business service providers also until September, 2006. United States Department of Agriculture ("***USDA***") funding supports the Center for Agribusiness and Rural Development to develop value-adding enterprises producing high quality product to meet market demand. The USAID and USDA programs represent economic development approaches that will be complemented by MCA-Armenia's support to WUA member farmers and related enterprises.

5. Sustainability.

(a) *Institutional Sustainability*.

The Government has taken substantial steps to strengthen the institutional framework for rural development. The management of Armenia's irrigation system has recently been decentralized to 53 regional WUAs. The Government has enhanced water management efficiency by merging responsibilities for irrigation and drainage. The Irrigated Agriculture Project will benefit from an extensive Water-to-Market Activity which will provide organizational support for the WSA reforms, management capacity building of the WUAs and developing regional federations of WUAs, and guidance for the formation of a professional irrigation association. Technical assistance will be targeted to ensure that the WSA, WUAs and federations of WUAs have systems to effectively manage and finance their operations. In addition, credit organizations will receive training and capital to expand financial services targeted at WUA member farmers.

(b) *Financial Sustainability.*

Armenia's irrigation system has suffered from a lack of resources for maintenance. The Irrigated Agriculture Project aims to address this problem, which has lead to the degradation of the system over time.

First, the Irrigated Agriculture Project is designed to rely less on pumping systems and more on gravity-based irrigation, which should decrease energy costs. However, to the extent pumping systems will be rehabilitated, the Government will present an adequate plan for coverage of operations and maintenance costs, including depreciation, before MCC Funding will be disbursed for civil works on these systems.

Second, the institutional strengthening of the WUAs under the Water-to-Market Activity will also increase the capacity of WUAs to finance themselves through member contributions and water charges. Investing in human capacities (farmers' technical and management skills and approach toward the market) to transform their enterprises to be profitable by competing in commercial markets significantly contributes to the financial sustainability of the irrigation system. Improved capacity of credit organizations to on-lend to rural borrowers will be sustained and expanded as new profit opportunities in the value chain emerge.

Third, the Government will continue its policy of WUA co-financing of tertiary canals consistent with the World Bank IDP and will implement such co-financing in a manner satisfactory to MCC. In addition, the Government agrees to fund any environmental mitigation costs associated with the Irrigated Agriculture Project in excess of MCC Funding allocated to cover such costs.

(c) *Environmental and Social Sustainability.*

The key to ensuring environmental and social sustainability of the Project is ongoing public consultation. The ESI Officer within the Management Unit will ensure that environmental and social mitigation measures are followed for all Project Activities in accordance with the provisions set forth in this Compact and in relevant Supplemental Agreements. The ESI Officer will serve as the point of contact for comments and concerns of parties affected by the implementation of all Project Activities and will lead the effort to find feasible resolutions to those problems. The ESI Officer will convene periodic public meetings to provide implementation updates and to identify and address public concerns. The Stakeholders' Committee will also appoint representatives of civil society to the Governing Council and provide a link between local NGOs and program managers.

ESIAs of the Irrigated Agriculture Project will be conducted as part of the technical survey and design. EMPs satisfactory to MCC will be developed, implemented and monitored during project implementation. Should the issue of involuntary resettlement arise, the Irrigated Agriculture Project will be conducted in compliance with the World Bank Policy on Involuntary Resettlement. To maximize the positive social impacts of the Project, the Implementing Entities for the Water-to-Market Activity will ensure that women are adequately represented in the groups targeted for assistance.

6. Policy Actions; Legislative and Regulatory Reform.

The Parties have identified the following policy actions and legislative and regulatory reforms that the Government will pursue in support of the Irrigated Agriculture Project to reach its full benefits. Satisfactory implementation of these reforms may be conditions precedent to certain MCC Disbursements as provided in the Disbursement Agreement:

(a) The Government will arrange for 15 percent WUA co-financing of investments in tertiary canal systems consistent with the World Bank IDP and will implement such co-financing in a manner satisfactory to MCC.

(b) Before the end of the second quarter of the second year of the Compact Term, the Government will adopt and implement a plan acceptable to MCC for the restructuring of the WSA.

(c) Before the end of the second year of the Compact Term, the Government will adopt appropriate legislation and/or regulations required by the Water Code of 2002 to establish a national policy on irrigation that will govern the relationships among the State Committee of Water Economy, the WSA, WUAs and the federations of WUAs.

(d) The Government will use its best efforts to ensure that water charges collected from WUAs continue towards the goal of full recovery of operations and maintenance costs. During the Compact Term, at least the following percentages of annual operations and maintenance costs will be covered:

(i) 2006: 46 percent;

(ii) 2007: 55 percent;

(iii) 2008: 60 percent;

(iv) 2009: 66 percent; and

(v) 2010: 70 percent.

These percentages will be calculated in a manner acceptable to MCC according to the following formula: WC/SC.

WC = Actual water charges collected during the most recently completed fiscal year as reported by the Board of WUAs and federations of WUAs pursuant to the Law on Water User Associations and Federations of Water User Associations.

SC = Operations and maintenance costs for the most recently completed fiscal year of the WSA and the WUAs as reported by the Board of WUAs and federations of WUAs pursuant to the Law on Water User Associations and Federations of Water User Associations.

(e) The Government will allocate funds to cover rehabilitation of the irrigation system in at least the amounts specified in the recommendation of the Technical Commission on Water System Operation and Maintenance, excluding any amounts provided for rehabilitation by MCC Funding.

(f) The Technical Commission on Water System Operation and Maintenance will make a recommendation with respect to the overall costs to cover depreciation of the irrigation system. The Government will ensure that such depreciation costs are reflected in its annual budgets throughout the life of the Program Assets.

(g) Before the end of the 18th month of the Compact Term, the Government will develop and adopt legislation and/or regulations, or amend existing legislation and regulations, to facilitate the establishment of agricultural cooperatives.

(h) By the end of the first year of the Compact Term, the Government will develop and adopt legislation and/or regulations to improve statistics on agriculture, including an accounting of the sector and data collection procedures.

(i) The Central Banking Authority will modify the regulatory framework for the licensing of MFIs as credit organizations.

(j) In an effort to ensure that the councils of the Water User Associations are more representative of their constituencies, the Government will adopt the amendment of Article 16 of the Law on Water User Associations and Federations of Water User Associations proposed by the Government on September 13, 2005.

(k) The Government will allocate in its budget and expend amounts satisfactory to MCC to fund the activities of the National Statistical Service, including conducting the Integrated Survey of Living Standards and the Community Survey. These surveys will be used by MCC as a key monitoring indicator and for impact evaluations. Funding by the Government should increase year-to-year to ensure sustainability post-Compact.

ANNEX II
FINANCIAL PLAN SUMMARY

This *Annex II* to the Compact (the "***Financial Plan Annex***") summarizes the Multi-Year Financial Plan for the Program. Except as defined in this Financial Plan Annex, each capitalized term in this Financial Plan Annex shall have the same meaning given such term elsewhere in this Compact.

1. General.

A multi-year financial plan summary ("***Multi-Year Financial Plan Summary***") is attached hereto as *Exhibit A*. By such time as specified in the Disbursement Agreement, MCA-Armenia will adopt, subject to MCC approval, a Multi-Year Financial Plan that includes, in addition to the multi-year summary of anticipated estimated MCC Funding and the Government's contribution of funds and resources, an estimated draw-down rate for the first year of the Compact based on the achievement of performance milestones, as appropriate, and the satisfaction or waiver of conditions precedent. Each year, at least 30 days prior to the anniversary of the Entry into Force, the Parties shall mutually agree in writing to a Detailed Financial Plan for the upcoming year of the Program, which shall include a more detailed plan for such year, taking into account the status of the Program at such time and making any necessary adjustments to the Multi-Year Financial Plan.

2. Implementation and Oversight.

The Multi-Year Financial Plan and each Detailed Financial Plan shall be implemented by MCA-Armenia, consistent with the approval and oversight rights of MCC and the Government as provided in this Compact, the Governance Agreement and the Disbursement Agreement.

3. Estimated Contributions of the Parties.

The Multi-Year Financial Plan Summary identifies the estimated annual contribution of MCC Funding for Program administration, monitoring and evaluation, and each Project. The Government's contribution of resources to Program administration, monitoring and evaluation, and each Project shall consist of (i) "in-kind" contributions in the form of Government Responsibilities and any other obligations and responsibilities of the Government identified in this Compact, including contributions identified in the notes to the Multi-Year Financial Plan Summary and (ii) such other contributions or amounts as may be identified in relevant Supplemental Agreements between the Parties or as may otherwise be agreed by the Parties; *provided*, in no event shall the Government's contribution of resources be less than the amount, level, type and quality of resources required to effectively carry out the Government Responsibilities or any other responsibilities or obligations of the Government under or in furtherance of this Compact.

4. Modifications.

The Parties recognize that the anticipated distribution of MCC Funding between and among the various Program activities and Project and Project Activities will likely require adjustment from time to time during the Compact Term. In order to preserve flexibility in the administration of the Program, the Parties may, upon agreement of the Parties in writing and without amending the Compact, change the designations and allocations of funds between Program administration and a Project, between one Project and another Project, between different activities within a Project, or between a Project identified as of the Entry into Force of this Compact and a new Project, without amending the Compact; *provided, however*, that such reallocation (i) is consistent with the Objectives, (ii) does not cause the amount of MCC Funding to exceed the aggregate amount specified in Section 2.1(a) of this Compact, and (iii) does not cause the Government's obligations or responsibilities or overall contribution of resources to be less than specified in Section 2.2(a) of this Compact, this *Annex II* or elsewhere in the Compact.

5. Conditions Precedent; Sequencing.

MCC Funding will be disbursed in tranches. The obligation of MCC to approve MCC Disbursements and Material Re-Disbursements for the Program and each Project is subject to satisfactory progress in achieving the Objectives and on the fulfillment or waiver of any conditions precedent specified in the Disbursement Agreement for the relevant Program activity or Project or Project Activity. The sequencing of Projects or Project Activities and other aspects of how the Parties intend the Projects to be implemented will be set forth in the Implementation Plan, including Work Plans for the applicable Project, and MCC Disbursements and Re-Disbursements will be disbursed consistent with that sequencing.

EXHIBIT A
Multi-Year Financial Plan Summary

Component	Year 1	Year 2	Year 3	Year 4	Year 5	Total
1. Rural Road Rehabilitation Project						
A. Infrastructure Improvements	$0.49	$17.92	$22.62	$13.46	$10.00	$64.50
B. Technical Audit of Performance Based Maintenance Contracts			$0.30			$0.30
C. Road Maintenance Strategic Plan				$0.30		$0.30
D. Project Administration	$0.40	$0.40	$0.40	$0.40	$0.40	$2.00
Sub-Total	**$0.89**	**$18.32**	**$23.32**	**$14.16**	**$10.40**	**$67.10**

Component	Year 1	Year 2	Year 3	Year 4	Year 5	Total
2. Irrigated Agriculture Project						
A. *Infrastructure Activity*						
Infrastructure*	$5.31	$30.16	$32.07	$25.17	$15.87	$108.59
Project Administration	$0.93	$0.93	$0.93	$0.93	$0.93	$4.67
B. *Water-to-Market Activity*						
Institutional Strengthening	$0.53	$0.98	$1.45	$0.69	$0.51	$4.16
Improved Profitability of WUA Members	$0.74	$4.55	$6.14	$6.99	$7.07	$25.50
Project Administration	$0.72	$0.61	$0.64	$0.41	$0.39	$2.76
Sub-Total	**$8.24**	**$37.24**	**$41.23**	**$34.20**	**$24.77**	**$145.67**
3. Monitoring and Evaluation	**$1.44**	**$0.92**	**$0.95**	**$0.97**	**$0.81**	**$5.08**
4. Program Administration and Control						
A. Program Administration	$1.41	$0.99	$1.06	$1.06	$1.09	$5.60
B. Audit	$0.17	$0.80	$0.93	$0.71	$0.52	$3.13
C. Fiscal Management	$0.49	$2.33	$2.70	$2.04	$1.50	$9.06
Sub-Total	**$2.06**	**$4.12**	**$4.69**	**$3.81**	**$3.11**	**$17.79**
MCC CONTRIBUTION	**$12.63**	**$60.61**	**$70.20**	**$53.13**	**$39.09**	**$235.65**

*Tertiary canals will be subject to a 15% farmer co-financing requirement.

ANNEX III
DESCRIPTION OF THE M&E PLAN

This *Annex III* to the Compact (the "***M&E Annex***") generally describes the components of the M&E Plan for the Program. Except as defined in this M&E Annex, each capitalized term in this M&E Annex shall have the same meaning given such term elsewhere in this Compact.

1. Overview.

MCC and the Government (or a mutually acceptable Government Affiliate or Permitted Designee) shall formulate, agree to and the Government shall implement, or cause to be implemented, an M&E Plan that specifies (1) how progress toward the Objectives and the intermediate results of each Project and Project Activity set forth in this M&E Annex (the "***Outcomes***") will be monitored (the "***Monitoring Component***"), (2) a methodology, process and timeline for the evaluation of planned, ongoing, or completed Projects and Project Activities to determine their efficiency, effectiveness, impact and sustainability (the "***Evaluation Component***"), and (3) other components of the M&E Plan described below. Information regarding the Program's performance, including the M&E Plan, and any amendments or modifications thereto, as well as periodically generated reports, will be made publicly available on the MCA-Armenia Website and elsewhere. The Objectives and Outcomes of the MCA-Armenia Program can be summarized as follows:

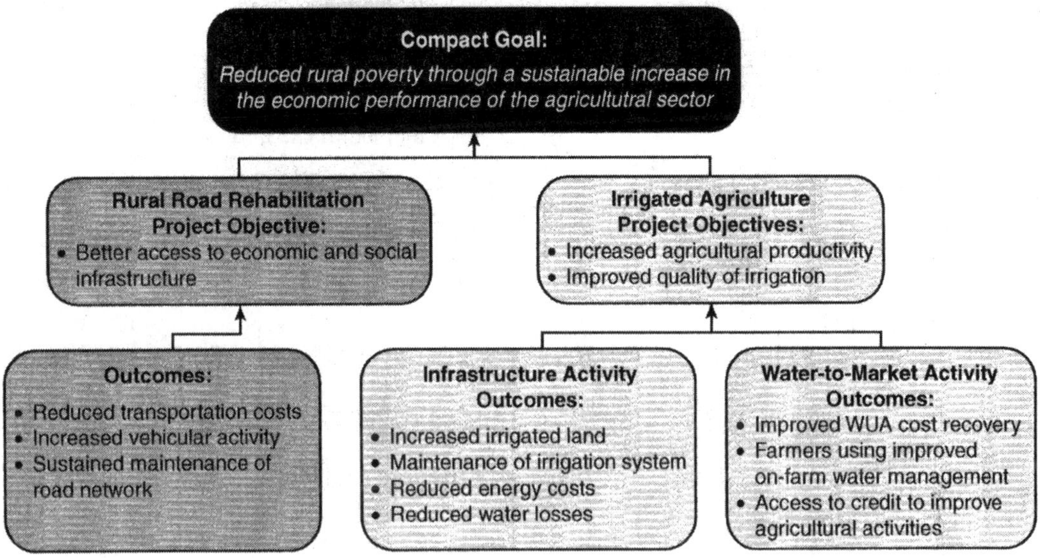

2. Monitoring Component.

To monitor progress toward the achievement of the Objectives and Outcomes, the Monitoring Component of the M&E Plan shall identify (a) the Indicators, (b) the party or parties responsible, the timeline, and the instrument for collecting data and reporting on each Indicator to MCA-Armenia, and (c) the method by which the reported data will be validated.

(a) *Indicators*. The M&E Plan shall measure the results of the Program using quantitative, objective and reliable data ("***Indicators***"). Each Indicator will have one or more expected results that specify the expected value and the expected time by which that result will be achieved (each, a "***Target***"). The M&E Plan will measure and report on Indicators at four levels. First, the Indicators for the Compact Goal (each, a "***Compact Goal Indicator***") will measure the results for the overall Program. Second, the Indicators for each Objective (each, an "***Objective Indicator***") will measure the final results of the Projects to monitor their success in meeting each of the Objectives, including results for the intended beneficiaries identified in accordance with *Annex I* (collectively, the "***Beneficiaries***"). Third, intermediate Indicators (each, an "***Outcome Indicator***") will measure the intermediate results achieved under each of the Project Activities to provide an early measure of the likely impact of the Project Activities. A fourth level of Indicators (each, an "***Output Indicator***") will be included in the M&E Plan to measure the direct outputs of the Project Activities. All Indicators will be disaggregated by gender, income level and age, to the extent practicable. Subject to prior written approval from MCC, MCA-Armenia may add Indicators or refine the Targets of existing Indicators.

(i) *Compact Goal Indicators*. The M&E Plan shall contain the Compact Goal Indicators listed in the table below with their definitions. The corresponding Targets to be achieved are in the following tables.

Compact Goal Indicators		
Purpose	**Indicator**	**Definition of Indicator**
Reduced rural poverty	Poverty rate in rural areas	Poverty rate in rural areas as measured by the National Statistical Service of Armenia
Increased economic performance of the agricultural sector	Change in real income from agriculture in rural areas	Change in real income from sale of agricultural produce per household member measured as an index

Compact Goal Targets						
Indicators	**Baseline**	**Year 4 2009**	**Year 5 2010**	**Year 6 2011**	**Year 7 2012**	**Year 8 2013**
Poverty rate in rural areas (percentage) Baseline: 2004	32%	31%	30%	29%	28%	26%
Change in real income from agriculture in rural areas (Index) Baseline: 2005 = 100	100	102	105	109	115	123

(ii) *Objective and Outcome Indicators*. The M&E Plan shall contain the Objective and Outcome Indicators listed in the tables below, with their definitions. The corresponding Targets to be achieved are in the tables following the definitions.

Rural Road Rehabilitation Project Indicators		
Purpose	**Indicator**	**Definition of Indicator**
Objective		
Better access to economic and social infrastructure	Satisfaction with public transportation in rural areas	Percentage satisfied
Outcomes		
Reduced transportation costs	International Roughness Index (IRI) for roads in Project area	Weighted index to measure road roughness (correlated with transportation costs)
Increased vehicular activity	Average daily traffic in Project area	Average daily number of vehicles on road sections in Project area weighted by length of corresponding road sections
Sustained maintenance of road network	Government budgetary allocations for rehabilitation of road sections in the road lifeline network	State budget expenditure on rehabilitation of road sections in the road lifeline network (AMD in millions)
	Government budgetary allocations for routine maintenance of the entire road network	State budget expenditures on routine maintenance of the entire road network (AMD in millions)

Rural Road Rehabilitation Project Targets						
Objective Level Indicators (Metric of Project success observable by end of Compact)	**Baseline**	**Year 1**	**Year 2**	**Year 3**	**Year 4**	**Year 5**
Satisfaction with public transportation in rural areas (percentage)[5]	TBD	TBD	TBD	TBD	TBD	TBD
Outcome Level Indicators (early Indicators of Project Activities impact on Objectives)						
International Roughness Index (IRI) for roads in Project area (m/km)	9.3	9.9	10.2	7.7	5.7	5.0
Average daily traffic in Project area (vehicles)	380	390	400	410	440	460
Government budgetary allocations for rehabilitation of road sections in the road lifeline network (AMD in millions)	n/a	1,010	3,150	3,310	3,970	5,950
Government budgetary allocations for routine maintenance of the entire road network (AMD in millions)	n/a	5,020	5,990	6,290	6,900	7,360

Irrigated Agriculture Project Indicators		
Purpose	**Indicator**	**Definition of Indicators**
Objectives		
Increased agricultural productivity	Increase in area covered by high value added ("***HVA***") crops	Increase in hectares covered by HVA crops (i.e., vegetables, potato, fruits, grapes)
Improved quality of irrigation	Share of respondents satisfied with irrigation services	Percentage of respondents satisfied with irrigation services

Infrastructure Activity Indicators		
Purpose	**Indicator**	**Definition of Indicators**
Outcomes		
Increased irrigated land	Additional land irrigated under Project	Annual increase in irrigated land in Project area (hectares)
Maintenance of irrigation system	Government budgetary allocations for maintenance of irrigation system	State budget expenditures on maintenance of irrigation system (AMD in millions)

[5] The Targets for this Indicator will be calculated using baseline information from the 2007 Integrated Survey of Living Standards (ISLS) to be conducted by the National Statistical Service of the Republic of Armenia.

Purpose	Indicator	Definition of Indicators
Reduced energy costs	Annual energy savings under Project	Reduction in Kilowatt hours used (thousand KWh)
Reduced water losses	Water losses in primary canals under Project	Share of water losses compared to total water intake (percentage)
	Water losses in tertiary canals under Project	Share of water losses compared to total water intake (percentage)
	Water-to-Market Activity Indicators	
Purpose	**Indicator**	**Definition of Indicators**
Outcomes		
Improved WUA cost recovery	Recovery of WUA operations and maintenance cost by water charges	Share of WUA water charges compared WUA annual operations and maintenance cost (percentage)
Farmers using improved on-farm water management	Number of farmers using better on-farm water management	Number of farmers using better on-farm water management: drip irrigation; ET Gage, and soil moisture monitoring
Access to credit to improve agricultural activities	Loans provided	Loans provided under the Project (USD in thousands)

Irrigated Agriculture Project Targets						
Objective Level Indicators (Metric of Project success observable by end of Compact)	**Baseline**	**Year 1**	**Year 2**	**Year 3**	**Year 4**	**Year 5**
Increase in area covered by high value added (HVA) crops (hectares)	0	0	110	1,100	4,020	2,540
Share of respondents satisfied with irrigation services (percentage)[6]	TBD	TBD	TBD	TBD	TBD	TBD
Infrastructure Activity: Outcome Level Indicators (Early Indicators of Project Activities impact on Objectives)	**Baseline**	**Year 1**	**Year 2**	**Year 3**	**Year 4**	**Year 5**
Additional land irrigated under Project (hectares)	0	0	0	2,400	10,900	20,340
Government budgetary allocations for maintenance of irrigation system (AMD in millions)[7]	TBD	TBD	TBD	TBD	TBD	TBD

[6] The Targets for this Indicator will be calculated using baseline information from the 2007 Integrated Survey of Living Standards (ISLS) to be conducted by the National Statistical Service of the Republic of Armenia.
[7] The Targets for this Indicator will be available at the end of the second quarter of 2006, when the recommendations of the Technical Commission on Water System Operation and Maintenance are due for Government confirmation.

Infrastructure Activity: Outcome Level Indicators	**Baseline**	**Year 1**	**Year 2**	**Year 3**	**Year 4**	**Year 5**
Annual energy savings under Project (thousand KWh)	0	0	0	0	2,800	25,520
Water losses in primary canals under Project (percentage)	28%	30%	31%	28%	23%	17%
Water losses in tertiary canals under Project (percentage)[8]	TBD	TBD	TBD	TBD	TBD	TBD
Water-to-Market Activity: Outcome Level Indicators (Early Indicators of Project Activities impact on objectives)	**Baseline**	**Year 1**	**Year 2**	**Year 3**	**Year 4**	**Year 5**
Recovery of WUA operations and maintenance cost by water charges (percentage)	n/a	46%	55%	60%	66%	70%
Number of farmers using improved on-farm water management (number; cumulative)	0	0	5,390	14,300	24,900	35,420
Loans provided (USD in thousands)	0	0	1,600	2,400	2,500	2,000

(b) *Data Collection and Reporting*. The M&E Plan shall establish guidelines for data collection and a reporting framework, including a schedule of Program reporting and responsible parties. The Management Unit shall conduct regular assessments of program performance to inform MCA-Armenia and MCC of progress under the Program and to alert these parties to any problems. These assessments will report the actual results compared to the Targets on the Indicators referenced in the Monitoring Component, explain deviations between these actual results and Targets, and in general, serve as a management tool for implementation of the Program. With respect to any data or reports received by MCA-Armenia, MCA-Armenia shall promptly deliver such reports to MCC along with any other related documents, as specified in the M&E Plan or as may be requested from time to time by MCC.

(c) *Data Quality Reviews*. From time to time, as determined in the M&E Plan or as otherwise requested by MCC, the quality of the data gathered through the M&E Plan shall be reviewed to ensure that data reported are as valid, reliable, and timely as resources will allow. The objective of any data quality review will be to verify the quality and the consistency of performance data, across different implementation units and reporting institutions. Such data quality reviews also will serve to identify where those levels of quality are not possible, given the realities of data collection. The data quality reviewer shall enter into an Auditor / Reviewer Agreement with MCA-Armenia in accordance with *Annex I*.

[8] The Targets for this Indicator will be incorporated once individual WUAs agree to the 15% co-financing required to proceed with the investments in tertiary canals.

3. Evaluation Component.

The Program shall be evaluated on the extent to which the interventions contribute to the Compact Goal. The Evaluation Component shall contain a methodology, process and timeline for analyzing data in order to assess planned, ongoing, or completed Project Activities to determine their efficiency, effectiveness, impact and sustainability. This component should use state-of-the-art methods for addressing selection bias and should make provisions for collecting data from both treatment and control groups, where practicable. The Evaluation Component shall contain two types of reports: Final Evaluations and Ad Hoc Evaluations, and shall be finalized before any MCC Disbursement or Re-Disbursement for specific Program activities or Project Activities.

(a) *Final Evaluation*. MCA-Armenia, with the prior written approval of MCC, may engage an independent evaluator to conduct an evaluation at the expiration or termination of the Compact Term ("***Final Evaluation***") or at MCC's election, MCC may engage such independent evaluator. The Final Evaluation must at a minimum (i) evaluate the efficiency and effectiveness of the Program; (ii) estimate, quantitatively and in a statistically valid way, the causal relationship between the Compact Goal (to the extent possible), the Objectives and Outcomes; (iii) determine if, and analyze the reasons why, the Compact Goal, Objectives and Outcomes were or were not achieved; (iv) identify positive and negative unintended results of the Program; (v) provide lessons learned that may be applied to similar projects; (vi) assess the likelihood that results will be sustained over time; and (vii) any other guidance and direction that will be provided in the M&E Plan. To the extent engaged by MCA-Armenia, such independent evaluator shall enter into an Auditor / Reviewer Agreement with MCA-Armenia in accordance with *Annex I*.

(b) *Ad Hoc Evaluations*. Either MCC or MCA-Armenia may request ad hoc or interim evaluations or special studies of Projects, Project Activities, or the Program as a whole prior to the expiration of the Compact Term ("***Ad Hoc Evaluations***"). If MCA-Armenia engages an evaluator, the evaluator will be an externally contracted independent source selected by MCA-Armenia, subject to the prior written approval of MCC, following a tender in accordance with the Procurement Guidelines, and otherwise in accordance with any relevant Implementation Letter or Supplemental Agreement. The cost of an independent evaluation or special study may be paid from MCC Funding. If MCA-Armenia requires an ad hoc independent evaluation or special study at the request of the Government for any reason, including for the purpose of contesting an MCC determination with respect to a Project or Project Activity or to seek funding from other donors, no MCC Funding or MCA-Armenia resources may be applied to such evaluation or special study without MCC's prior written approval.

4. Other Components of the M&E Plan.

In addition to the Monitoring and Evaluation Components, the M&E Plan shall include the following components for the Program, Projects and Project Activities, including, where appropriate, roles and responsibilities of the relevant parties and Providers:

(a) *Costs*. A detailed cost estimate for all components of the M&E Plan.

(b) *Assumptions and Risks*. Any assumptions and risks external to the Program that underlie the accomplishment of the Objectives and Outcomes; *provided*, such assumptions and risks shall not excuse performance of the Parties, unless otherwise expressly agreed to in writing by the Parties.

5. Implementation of the M&E Plan.

(a) *Approval and Implementation*. The approval and implementation of the M&E Plan, as amended from time to time, shall be in accordance with the Program Annex, this M&E Annex, the Governance Agreement, and any other relevant Supplemental Agreement.

(b) *Stakeholders' Committee*. The completed portions of the M&E Plan will be presented to the Stakeholders' Committee at the Stakeholders' Committee's initial meetings, and any amendments or modifications thereto or any additional components of the M&E Plan will be presented to the Stakeholders' Committee at appropriate subsequent meetings of the Stakeholders' Committee. The Stakeholders' Committee will have opportunity to present its suggestions to the M&E Plan, which the Governing Council will take into consideration in its review of any amendments to the M&E Plan during the Compact Term.

(c) *MCC Disbursement and Re-Disbursement for a Project Activity*. As a condition to each MCC Disbursement or Re-Disbursement there shall be satisfactory progress on the M&E Plan for the relevant Project or Project Activity, and substantial compliance with the M&E Plan, including any reporting requirements.

(d) *Modifications*. Notwithstanding anything to the contrary in the Compact, including the requirements of this M&E Annex, MCC and the Government (or a mutually acceptable Government Affiliate or Permitted Designee) may modify or amend the M&E Plan or any component thereof, including those elements described herein, without amending the Compact; *provided*, any such modification or amendment of the M&E Plan has been approved by MCC in writing and is otherwise consistent with the requirements of this Compact and any relevant Supplemental Agreement between the Parties.

STATE DEPARTMENT DOCUMENT NUMBER: 06-257

MILLENNIUM CHALLENGE COMPACT BETWEEN THE UNITED STATES OF AMERICA AND THE REPUBLIC OF BENIN, WITH ANNEXES

SIGNED AT WASHINGTON D.C.,
FEBRUARY 22, 2006
ENTERED INTO FORCE OCTOBER 6, 2006

CTIA DOCUMENT NUMBER: 13084.000

This MILLENNIUM CHALLENGE COMPACT (the "***Compact***") is made between the United States of America, acting through the Millennium Challenge Corporation, a United States Government corporation ("***MCC***"), and the Government of the Republic of Benin (the "***Government***") (referred to herein individually as a "***Party***" and collectively, the "***Parties***"). A compendium of capitalized terms defined herein is included, for convenience only, in *Exhibit A* attached hereto.

RECITALS

WHEREAS, MCC, acting through its Board of Directors, has selected the Republic of Benin as eligible to present to MCC a proposal for the use of Millennium Challenge Account ("***MCA***") assistance to help facilitate the advance of economic growth and poverty reduction in Benin;

WHEREAS, the Government has carried out a consultative process with the country's private sector and civil society to outline the country's priorities for the use of MCA assistance and developed a proposal, which final proposal was submitted to MCC on September 5, 2005 (the "***Proposal***");

WHEREAS, the Proposal focused on, among other things, improving core physical and institutional infrastructure to increase investment and private sector activity;

WHEREAS, MCC has evaluated the Proposal and related documents to determine whether the Proposal is consistent with core MCA principles and includes proposed activities and projects that will advance the progress of Benin towards achieving economic growth and poverty reduction; and

WHEREAS, based on MCC's evaluation of the Proposal and related documents and subsequent discussions and negotiations between the Parties, the Government and MCC determined to enter into this Compact to implement a program using MCC Funding to advance Benin's progress towards economic growth and poverty reduction (the "***Program***");

NOW, THEREFORE, in consideration of the foregoing and the mutual covenants and agreements set forth herein, the Parties hereby agree as follows:

ARTICLE I
PURPOSE AND TERM

Section 1.1
Objectives

The overall objective of this Compact is to increase investment and private sector activity in Benin ("***Program Objective***"), which is key to advancing the goal of economic growth and poverty reduction in Benin (the "***Compact Goal***"). The Parties have identified the following project-level objectives (each, an "***Project Objective***" and together, the "***Project Objectives***") of this Compact to advance the Program Objective and Compact Goal, each of which is described in more detail in the Annexes attached hereto:

(a) Strengthen property rights and investment (the "***Land Objective***");

(b) Expand access to financial services (the "***Financial Services Objective***");

(c) Improve ability of the justice system to enforce contracts and reconcile claims (the "***Justice Objective***"); and

(d) Improve access to markets through improvements to the Port of Cotonou ("***Markets Objective***").

The Government expects to achieve, and shall use its best efforts to ensure the achievement of, the Compact Goal, Program Objective and Project Objectives during the Compact Term. The Program Objective and the individual Project Objectives collectively referred to herein as "***Objectives***" and each individually as an "***Objective***."

Section 1.2
Projects

The Annexes attached hereto describe the specific projects and the policy reforms and other activities related thereto (each, a "***Project***") that the Government will carry out, or cause to be carried out, in furtherance of this Compact to achieve the Objectives and the Compact Goal.

Section 1.3
Entry into Force; Compact Term

This Compact shall enter into force on the date of the last letter in an exchange of letters between the Principal Representatives of each Party confirming that each Party has completed its domestic requirements for entry into force of this Compact (including as set forth in Section 3.10) and that all conditions set forth in Section 4.1 have been satisfied by the Government and MCC (the "***Entry into Force***"). This Compact shall remain in force for five (5) years from the Entry into Force, unless earlier terminated in accordance with Section 5.4 (the "***Compact Term***").

ARTICLE II
FUNDING AND RESOURCES

Section 2.1
MCC Funding

(a) *MCC's Contribution*. MCC hereby grants to the Government, subject to the terms and conditions of this Compact, an amount not to exceed Three Hundred Seven Million Two Hundred and Ninety

Eight Thousand and Forty United States Dollars (USD $307,298,040) ("***MCC Funding***") during the Compact Term to enable the Government to implement the Program and achieve the Objectives.

(i) Subject to Sections 2.1(a)(ii), 2.2(b) and 5.4(b), the allocation of the MCC Funding within the Program and among and within the Projects shall be as generally described in *Annex II* or as otherwise agreed upon by the Parties from time to time.

(ii) If at any time MCC determines that a condition precedent to an MCC Disbursement has not been satisfied, MCC may, upon written notice to the Government, reduce the total amount of MCC Funding by an amount equal to the amount estimated in the applicable Detailed Financial Plan for the Program, Project or Project Activity or sub-activity for which such condition precedent has not been met. Upon the expiration or termination of this Compact, (A) any amounts of MCC Funding not disbursed by MCC to the Government shall be automatically released from any obligation in connection with this Compact and (B) any amounts of MCC Funding disbursed by MCC to the Government as provided in Section 2.1(b)(i), but not re-disbursed as provided in Section 2.1(b)(ii) or otherwise incurred as permitted pursuant to Section 5.4(e) prior to the expiration or termination of this Compact, shall be returned to MCC in accordance with Section 2.5(a)(ii).

(iii) Notwithstanding any other provision of this Compact and pursuant to the authority of Section 609(g) of the Millennium Challenge Act of 2003, as amended (the "***Act***"), upon the conclusion of this Compact (and without regard to the satisfaction of all of the conditions for Entry into Force required under Section 1.3), MCC shall make available One Million Five Hundred Thirty Six Thousand Four Hundred and Ninety United States Dollars (USD $1,536,490) ("***Compact Implementation Funding***") to facilitate certain aspects of Compact implementation as described in *Schedule 2.1(a)(iii)* attached hereto; *provided*, such Compact Implementation Funding shall be subject to (A) the limitations on the use or treatment of MCC Funding set forth in Section 2.3, as if such provision were in full force and effect, and (B) any other requirements for, and limitations on the use of, such Compact Implementation Funding as may be required by MCC in writing; *provided, further*, that any Compact Implementation Funding granted in accordance with this Section 2.1(a)(iii) shall be included in, and not additional to, the total amount of MCC Funding; and *provided further*, any obligation to provide such Compact Implementation Funding shall expire upon the expiration or termination of this Compact or five (5) years from the conclusion of this Compact, whichever occurs sooner. Notwithstanding anything to the contrary in this Compact, this Section 2.1(a)(iii) shall provisionally apply prior to Entry into Force.

(b) *Disbursements*.

(i) Disbursements of MCC Funding. MCC shall from time to time make disbursements of MCC Funding (each such disbursement, an "***MCC Disbursement***") to a Permitted Account or through such other mechanism agreed by the Parties under and in accordance with the procedures and requirements set forth in *Annex I*, the Disbursement Agreement or as otherwise provided in any other relevant Supplemental Agreement.

(ii) Re-Disbursements of MCC Funding. The release of MCC Funding from a Permitted Account (each such release, a "***Re-Disbursement***"), shall be made in accordance with the procedures and requirements set forth in *Annex I*, the Disbursement Agreement or as otherwise provided in any other relevant Supplemental Agreement.

(c) *Interest*. Unless the Parties agree otherwise in writing, any interest or other earnings on MCC Funding that accrue (collectively, "***Accrued Interest***") shall be held in a Permitted Account and accrue in accordance with the requirements for the accrual and treatment of Accrued Interest as specified in *Annex I* or any relevant Supplemental Agreement. On a quarterly basis and upon the termination or expiration of this Compact, the Government shall return, or ensure the return of, all Accrued Interest to any United States Government account designated by MCC.

(d) *Conversion; Exchange Rate*. The Government shall ensure that all MCC Funding that is held in the Permitted Account(s) shall be denominated in the currency of the United States of America ("***United States Dollars***") prior to Re-Disbursement; *provided*, that a certain portion of MCC Funding may be transferred to a Local Account and may be held in such Local Account in the currency of the Republic of Benin prior to Re-Disbursement in accordance with the requirements of *Annex I* and any relevant Supplemental Agreement. To the extent that any amount of MCC Funding held in United States Dollars must be converted into the currency of the Republic of Benin for any purpose, including for any Re-Disbursement or any transfer of MCC Funding into a Local Account, the Government shall ensure that such amount is converted consistent with *Annex I*, including the rate and manner set forth in *Annex I*, and the requirements of the Disbursement Agreement or any other Supplemental Agreement between the Parties.

(e) *Guidance*. From time to time, MCC may provide guidance to the Government through Implementation Letters on the frequency, form and content of requests for MCC Disbursements and Re-Disbursements or any other matter relating to MCC Funding. The Government shall apply such guidance in implementing this Compact.

Section 2.2
Government Resources

(a) The Government shall provide or cause to be provided such Government funds and other resources, including any Government contributions set out forth on *Annex II* attached hereto, and shall take or cause to be taken such actions, including obtaining all necessary approvals and consents, as are specified in this Compact or in any Supplemental Agreement to which the Government is a party or as are otherwise necessary and appropriate to effectively carry out the Government Responsibilities or other responsibilities or obligations of the Government under or in furtherance of this Compact during the Compact Term and through the completion of any post-Compact Term activities, audits or other responsibilities. The Government shall submit to the Parliament on an annual basis the amount of the upcoming year's Government contribution for inclusion in the applicable finance law of Benin and such amount shall be committed in the national budget for that year for purposes of the Program, such contribution to be allocated within and in furtherance of the Program as agreed by the Parties. The Government shall disburse funds on a quarterly basis from this committed amount into an account, held at a bank acceptable to MCC, designated solely for this purpose.

(b) If at any time during the Compact Term, the Government materially reallocates or reduces the allocation in its national budget or any other Beninese governmental authority at a departmental, municipal, regional or other jurisdictional level materially reallocates or reduces the allocation of its respective budget of the normal and expected resources that the Government or such other governmental authority, as applicable, would have otherwise received or budgeted, from external or domestic sources, for the activities contemplated herein, the Government shall notify MCC in writing within fifteen (15) days of such reallocation or reduction, such notification to contain information regarding the amount of the reallocation or reduction, the affected activities, and an explanation for the reallocation or reduction. In the event that MCC independently determines, upon review of the executed national annual budget that such a material reallocation or reduction of resources has occurred, MCC shall notify the Government and, following such notification, the Government shall provide a written explanation for such reallocation or reduction and MCC may (i) reduce, in its sole discretion, the total amount of MCC Funding or any MCC Disbursement by an amount equal to the amount estimated in the applicable Detailed Financial Plan for the activity for which funds were reduced or reallocated or (ii) otherwise suspend or terminate MCC Funding in accordance with Section 5.4(b).

(c) The Government shall use its best efforts to ensure that all MCC Funding is fully reflected and accounted for in the annual budget of the Republic of Benin on a multi-year basis.

Section 2.3
Limitations on the Use or Treatment of MCC Funding

(a) *Abortions and Involuntary Sterilizations.* The Government shall ensure that MCC Funding shall not be used to undertake, fund or otherwise support any activity that is subject to prohibitions on use of funds contained in (i) paragraphs (1) through (3) of section 104(f) of the Foreign Assistance Act of 1961 (22 U.S.C. 2151b(f)(1)–(3), a United States statute, which prohibitions shall apply to the same extent and in the same manner as such prohibitions apply to funds made available to carry out Part I of such Act; or (ii) any provision of law comparable to the eleventh and fourteenth provisos under the heading "Child Survival and Health Programs Fund" of division E of Public Law 108–7 (117 Stat. 162), a United States statute.

(b) *United States Job Loss or Displacement of Production.* The Government shall ensure that MCC Funding shall not be used to undertake, fund or otherwise support any activity that is likely to cause a substantial loss of United States jobs or a substantial displacement of United States production, including:

(i) Providing financial incentives to relocate a substantial number of United States jobs or cause a substantial displacement of production outside the United States;

(ii) Supporting investment promotion missions or other travel to the United States with the intention of inducing United States firms to relocate a substantial number of United States jobs or a substantial amount of production outside the United States;

(iii) Conducting feasibility studies, research services, studies, travel to or from the United States, or providing insurance or technical and management assistance, with the intention of inducing United States firms to relocate a substantial number of United States jobs or cause a substantial displacement of production outside the United States;

(iv) Advertising in the United States to encourage United States firms to relocate a substantial number of United States jobs or cause a substantial displacement of production outside the United States;

(v) Training workers for firms that intend to relocate a substantial number of United States jobs or cause a substantial displacement of production outside the United States;

(vi) Supporting a United States office of an organization that offers incentives for United States firms to relocate a substantial number of United States jobs or cause a substantial displacement of production outside the United States; or

(vii) Providing general budget support for an organization that engages in any activity prohibited above.

(c) *Military Assistance and Training.* The Government shall ensure that MCC Funding shall not be used to undertake, fund or otherwise support the purchase or use of goods or services for military purposes, including military training, or to provide any assistance to the military, police, militia, national guard or other quasi-military organization or unit.

(d) *Prohibition of Assistance Relating to Environmental, Health or Safety Hazards.* The Government shall ensure that MCC Funding shall not be used to undertake, fund or otherwise support any activity that is likely to cause a significant environmental, health, or safety hazard. Unless MCC and the

Government agree otherwise in writing, the Government shall ensure that activities undertaken, funded or otherwise supported in whole or in part (directly or indirectly) by MCC Funding comply with environmental guidelines delivered by MCC to the Government or posted by MCC on its website or otherwise publicly made available, as such guidelines may be amended from time to time (the "***Environmental Guidelines***"), including any definition of "likely to cause a significant environmental, health, or safety hazard" as may be set forth in such Environmental Guidelines.

(e) *Taxation.*

(i) Taxes. The Government shall ensure that the Program, any Program Assets, MCC Funding and Accrued Interest shall be free from any taxes imposed under the laws currently or hereafter in effect in the Republic of Benin during the Compact Term. This exemption shall apply to any use of any Program Asset, MCC Funding and Accrued Interest, including any Exempt Uses, and to any work performed under or activities undertaken in furtherance of this Compact by any person or entity (including contractors and grantees) funded by MCC Funding, and shall apply to all taxes, tariffs, duties, and other levies (each a "***Tax***" and collectively, "***Taxes***"), including:

(1) To the extent attributable to MCC Funding, income taxes and other taxes on profit or businesses imposed on organizations or entities, other than nationals of the Republic of Benin, receiving MCC Funding, including taxes on the acquisition, ownership, rental, disposition or other use of real or personal property, taxes on investment or deposit requirements and currency controls in the Republic of Benin, or any other tax, duty, charge or fee of whatever nature, except fees for specific services rendered; for purposes of this Section 2.3(e), the term "*national*" refers to organizations established under the laws currently or hereafter in effect in the Republic of Benin, other than MCA-Benin or any other entity established solely for purposes of managing or overseeing the implementation of the Program or any wholly-owned subsidiaries, divisions, or Affiliates of entities not registered or established under the laws currently or hereafter in effect in the Republic of Benin;

(2) Customs duties, tariffs, import and export taxes, or other levies on the importation, use and re-exportation of goods, services, or the personal belongings and effects, including personally-owned automobiles, for Program use or the personal use of individuals who are neither citizens nor permanent residents of the Republic of Benin and who are present in the Republic of Benin for purposes of carrying out the Program or their family members, including all charges based on the value of such imported goods;

(3) Taxes on the income or personal property of all individuals who are neither citizens nor permanent residents of the Republic of Benin, including income and social security taxes of all types and all taxes on the personal property owned by such individuals, to the extent such income or property are attributable to MCC Funding; and

(4) Taxes or duties levied on the last transaction for the purchase of goods or services funded by MCC Funding, including sales taxes, tourism taxes, value-added taxes (VAT), or other similar charges. The term "last transaction" refers to the last transaction by which the goods or services were purchased for use in the activities funded by MCC Funding.

(ii) This Section 2.3(e) shall apply, but is not limited to (A) any transaction, service, activity, contract, grant or other implementing agreement funded in whole or in part by MCC Funding; (B) any supplies, equipment, materials, property or other goods (referred to herein collectively as "*goods*") or funds introduced into, acquired in, used or disposed of in, or imported into or exported from, the Republic of Benin by MCC, or by any person or entity (including contractors and grantees) as part of, or in conjunction with, MCC Funding or the Program; (C) any contractor, grantee, or other organization carrying out activities funded in whole or in part by MCC Funding; and (D) any employee of such organizations (the uses set forth in clauses (A) through (D) are collectively referred to herein as "***Exempt Uses***").

(iii) If a Tax has been levied and paid contrary to the requirements of this Section 2.3(e), whether inadvertently, due to the impracticality of implementation of this provision with respect to certain types or amounts of taxes, or otherwise, the Government shall refund promptly to MCC to an account designated by MCC the amount of such Tax in the currency of the Republic of Benin, within thirty (30) days (or such other period as may be agreed in writing by the Parties) after the Government is notified in writing of such levy and tax payment, in accordance with procedures agreed by the Parties, whether by MCC or otherwise; *provided, however*, the Government shall apply national funds to satisfy its obligations under this paragraph and no MCC Funding, Accrued Interest, or any assets, goods, or property (real, tangible, or intangible) purchased or financed in whole or in part (directly or indirectly) by MCC Funding ("***Program Assets***") may be applied by the Government in satisfaction of its obligations under this paragraph.

(iv) The Parties shall memorialize in a mutually acceptable Supplemental Agreement or Implementation Letter or other suitable document the mechanisms for implementing this Section 2.3(e), including (A) a formula for determining refunds for Taxes paid, the amount of which is not susceptible to precise determination, (B) a mechanism for ensuring the tax-free importation, use, and re-exportation of goods, services, or the personal belongings of individuals (including all Providers) described in paragraph (i)(2) of this Section 2.3(e), (C) a requirement for the provision by the Government of a tax-exemption certificate which expressly includes, *inter alia*, the thirty (30) day refund requirement of Section 2.3(e)(iii), and (D) any other appropriate Government action to facilitate the administration of this Section 2.3(e).

(f) *Alteration*. The Government shall ensure that no MCC Funding, Accrued Interest nor Program Assets shall be subject to any impoundment, rescission, sequestration or any provision of law now or hereafter in effect in the Republic of Benin that would have the effect of requiring or allowing any impoundment, rescission or sequestration of any MCC Funding, Accrued Interest or Program Asset.

(g) *Liens or Encumbrances*. The Government shall ensure that no MCC Funding, Accrued Interest, or Program Assets shall be subject to any lien, attachment, enforcement of judgment, pledge, or encumbrance of any kind (each a "***Lien***"), except with the prior approval of MCC in accordance with Section 3(c) of *Annex I*, and in the event of the imposition of any Lien not so approved, the Government shall promptly seek the release of such Lien and if required by final non-appealable order, shall pay any amounts owed to obtain such release; *provided, however*, the Government shall apply national funds to satisfy its obligations under this Section 2.3(g) and no MCC Funding, Accrued Interest, or Program Assets may be applied by the Government in satisfaction of its obligations under this Section 2.3(g).

(h) *Other Limitations*. The Government shall ensure that the use or treatment of MCC Funding, Accrued Interest, and Program Assets shall be subject to and in conformity with such other limitations (i) as required by the applicable law of the United States of America now or hereafter in effect during the Compact Term, (ii) as advisable under or required by applicable United States Government policies now or hereafter in effect during the Compact Term, or (iii) to which the Parties may otherwise agree in writing.

(i) *Utilization of Goods, Services and Works*. The Government shall ensure that any Program Assets, services, facilities or works funded in whole or in part (directly or indirectly) by MCC Funding, unless otherwise agreed by the Parties in writing, shall be used solely in furtherance of this Compact.

(j) *Notification of Applicable Laws and Policies*. MCC shall notify the Government of any applicable United States law or policy affecting the use or treatment of MCC Funding, whether or not specifically identified in this Section 2.3, and shall provide to the Government a copy of the text of any such applicable law and a written explanation of any such applicable policy.

Section 2.4
Incorporation; Notice; Clarification

(a) The Government shall include, or ensure the inclusion of, all of the requirements set forth in Section 2.3 in all Supplemental Agreements to which MCC is not a party and shall use its best efforts to ensure that no such Supplemental Agreement is implemented in violation of the prohibitions set forth in Section 2.3.

(b) The Government shall ensure notification of all of the requirements set forth in Section 2.3 to any Provider and all relevant officers, directors, employees, agents, representatives, Affiliates, contractors, sub-contractors, grantees and sub-grantees of any Provider. The term "***Provider***" shall mean (i) MCA-Benin and any Government Affiliate or Permitted Designee involved in any activities in furtherance of this Compact or (ii) any third party who receives at least USD $50,000 in the aggregate of MCC Funding (other than employees of MCA-Benin) during the Compact Term or such other amount as the Parties may agree in writing, whether directly from MCC, indirectly through Re-Disbursements, or otherwise.

(c) In the event the Government or any Provider requires clarification from MCC as to whether an activity contemplated to be undertaken in furtherance of this Compact violates or may violate any provision of Section 2.3, the Government shall notify, or ensure that such Provider notifies, MCC in writing and provide in such notification a detailed description of the activity in question. In such event, the Government shall not proceed, and shall use its best efforts to ensure that no relevant Provider proceeds, with such activity, and the Government shall ensure that no Re-Disbursements shall be made for such activity, until MCC advises the Government or such Provider in writing that the activity is permissible.

Section 2.5
Refunds; Violation

(a) Notwithstanding the availability to MCC, or exercise by MCC of, any other remedies, including under international law, this Compact, or any Supplemental Agreement:

(i) If any amount of MCC Funding or Accrued Interest, or any Program Asset, is used for any purpose prohibited under this Article II or otherwise in violation of any of the terms and conditions of this Compact, any guidance in any Implementation Letter, or any Supplemental Agreement between the Parties, MCC may, upon written notice, require the Government to repay promptly to MCC to an account designated by MCC or to others as MCC may direct the amount of such misused MCC Funding or Accrued Interest, or the cash equivalent of the value of any misused Program Asset, in United States Dollars, plus any interest that accrued or would have accrued thereon, within thirty (30) days after the Government is notified, whether by MCC or other duly authorized representative of the United States Government, of such prohibited use; *provided, however*, the Government shall apply national funds to satisfy its obligations under this Section 2.5(a)(i) and no MCC Funding, Accrued Interest, nor Program Assets may be applied by the Government in satisfaction of its obligations under this Section 2.5(a)(i); and

(ii) If all or any portion of this Compact is terminated or suspended and upon the expiration of this Compact, the Government shall, subject to the requirements of Sections 5.4(e) and 5.4(f), refund, or ensure the refund, to MCC to such account(s) designated by MCC the amount of any MCC Funding, plus any Accrued Interest, promptly, but in no event later than thirty (30) days after the Government receives MCC's request for such refund; *provided*, that if this Compact is terminated or suspended in part, MCC may request a refund for only the amount of MCC Funding, plus any Accrued Interest, then allocated to the terminated or suspended portion; *provided, further*, that any refund of MCC Funding or Accrued Interest shall be to such account(s) as designated by MCC.

(b) Notwithstanding any other provision in this Compact or any other agreement to the contrary, MCC's right under this Section 2.5 for a refund shall continue during the Compact Term and for a period of (i) five (5) years thereafter or (ii) one (1) year after MCC receives actual knowledge of such violation, whichever is later.

(c) If MCC determines that any activity or failure to act violates, or may violate, any Section in this Article II, MCC may refuse any further MCC Disbursements for or conditioned upon such activity, and may take any action to prevent any Re-Disbursement related to such activity.

Section 2.6
Bilateral Agreement

All MCC Funding shall be considered United States assistance under the Economic, Technical and Related Assistance Agreement by and between the Government of the United States of America and the Government of the Republic of Benin, dated May 27, 1961, as amended from time to time (the "***Bilateral Agreement***"). If there are conflicts or inconsistencies between any parts of this Compact and the Bilateral Agreement, as either may be amended from time to time, the provisions of this Compact shall prevail over those of the Bilateral Agreement.

ARTICLE III
IMPLEMENTATION

Section 3.1
Implementation Framework

This Compact shall be implemented by the Parties in accordance with this Article III and as further specified in the Annexes and in relevant Supplemental Agreements.

Section 3.2
Government Responsibilities

(a) The Government shall have principal responsibility for oversight and management of the implementation of the Program (i) in accordance with the terms and conditions specified in this Compact and relevant Supplemental Agreements, (ii) in accordance with all applicable laws then in effect in Benin, and (iii) in a timely and cost-effective manner and in conformity with sound technical, financial and management practices (collectively, the "***Government Responsibilities***"). Unless otherwise expressly provided, any reference to the Government Responsibilities or any other responsibilities or obligations of the Government herein shall be deemed to apply to any Government Affiliate and any of their respective directors, officers, employees, contractors, sub-contractors, grantees, sub-grantees, agents or representatives.

(b) The Government shall ensure that no person or entity shall participate in the selection, award, administration, or oversight of a contract, grant or other benefit or transaction funded in whole or in part (directly or indirectly) by MCC Funding, in which (i) the entity, the person, members of the person's immediate family or household or his or her business partners, or organizations controlled by or substantially involving such person or entity, has or have a direct or indirect financial or other interest or (ii) the person or entity is negotiating or has any arrangement concerning prospective employment, unless such person or entity has first disclosed in writing to the Government the conflict of interest and, following such disclosure, the Parties agree in writing to proceed notwithstanding such conflict. The Government shall ensure that no person or entity involved in the selection, award, administration, oversight or implementation of any contract, grant or other benefit or transaction funded in whole or in part (directly or indirectly) by MCC Funding shall solicit or accept from or offer to a third party or seek or be promised directly or indirectly for itself or for another person or entity any gift, gratuity, favor or benefit, other than items of *de minimis* value and otherwise consistent with such guidance as MCC may provide from time to time.

(c) The Government shall not designate any person or entity, including any Government Affiliate, to implement, in whole or in part, this Compact or any Supplemental Agreement between the Parties (including any Government Responsibilities or any other responsibilities or obligations of the Government under this Compact or any Supplemental Agreement between the Parties) or to exercise any rights of the Government under this Compact or any Supplemental Agreement between the Parties, except as expressly provided herein or with the prior written consent of MCC; *provided, however*, the Government may designate MCA-Benin or, with the prior written consent of MCC, such other mutually acceptable persons or entities, (each, a "***Permitted Designee***") to implement some or all of the Government Responsibilities or any other responsibilities or obligations of the Government or to exercise any rights of the Government under this Compact or any Supplemental Agreement between the Parties each in accordance with the terms and conditions set forth in this Compact or such Supplemental Agreement (referred to herein collectively as "***Designated Rights and Responsibilities***"). Notwithstanding any provision herein or any other agreement to the contrary, no such designation shall relieve the Government of such Designated Rights and Responsibilities, for which the Government shall retain ultimate responsibility. In the event that the Government designates any person or entity, including any Government Affiliate, to implement any portion of the Government Responsibilities or other responsibilities or obligations of the Government, or to exercise any rights of the Government under this Compact or any Supplemental Agreement between the Parties, in accordance with this Section 3.2(c), then the Government shall (i) cause such person or entity to perform such Designated Rights and Responsibilities in the same manner and to the full extent to which the Government is obligated to perform such Designated Rights and Responsibilities, (ii) ensure that such person or entity does not assign, delegate or contract (or otherwise transfer) any of such Designated Rights and Responsibilities to any person or entity and (iii) cause such person or entity to certify to MCC in writing that it will so perform such Designated Rights and Responsibilities and will not assign, delegate, or contract (or otherwise transfer) any of such Designated Rights and Responsibilities to any person or entity without the prior written consent of MCC.

(d) The Government shall, upon a request from MCC, execute, or ensure the execution of, an assignment to MCC of any cause of action which may accrue to the benefit of the Government, a Government Affiliate or any Permitted Designee, including MCA-Benin, in connection with or arising out of any activities funded in whole or in part (directly or indirectly) by MCC Funding.

(e) The Government shall ensure that (i) no decision of MCA-Benin is modified, supplemented, unduly influenced or rescinded by any governmental authority, except by a non-appealable judicial decision, and (ii) the authority of MCA-Benin shall not be expanded, restricted, or otherwise modified, except in accordance with this Compact, the Governance Agreement, the Governing Documents or any other Supplemental Agreement between the Parties.

(f) The Government shall ensure that all persons and individuals that enter into agreements to provide goods, services or works under the Program or in furtherance of this Compact shall do so in accordance with the Procurement Guidelines and shall obtain all necessary immigration, business and other permits, licenses, consents and approvals to enable them and their personnel to fully perform under such agreements.

Section 3.3
Government Deliveries

The Government shall proceed, and cause others to proceed, in a timely manner to deliver to MCC all reports, notices, certificates, documents or other deliveries required to be delivered by the Government under this Compact or any Supplemental Agreement between the Parties, in form and substance as set forth in this Compact or in any such Supplemental Agreement.

Section 3.4
Government Assurances

The Government hereby provides the following assurances to MCC that as of the date this Compact is signed:

(a) The information contained in the Proposal and any agreement, report, statement, communication, document or otherwise delivered or otherwise communicated to MCC by or on behalf of the Government on or after the date of the submission of the Proposal (i) are true, correct and complete in all material respects and (ii) do not omit any fact known to the Government that if disclosed would (A) alter in any material respect the information delivered, (B) likely have a material adverse effect on the Government's ability to effectively implement, or ensure the effective implementation of, the Program or any Project or to otherwise carry out its responsibilities or obligations under or in furtherance of this Compact, or (C) have likely adversely affected MCC's determination to enter into this Compact or any Supplemental Agreement between the Parties.

(b) Unless otherwise disclosed in writing to MCC, the MCC Funding made available hereunder is in addition to the normal and expected resources that the Government usually receives or budgets for the activities contemplated herein from external or domestic sources.

(c) This Compact does not conflict and will not conflict with any international agreement or obligation to which the Government is a party or by which it is bound.

(d) No payments have been (i) received by any official of the Government or any other government body in connection with the procurement of goods, services or works to be undertaken or funded in whole or in part (directly or indirectly) by MCC Funding, except fees, taxes, or similar payments legally established in the Republic of Benin (subject to Section 2.3(e)) and consistent with the applicable requirement of Beninese law or (ii) made to any third party, in connection with or in furtherance of this Compact, in violation of the United States Foreign Corrupt Practices Act of 1977, as amended (15 U.S.C. 78a *et seq.*).

Section 3.5
Implementation Letters; Supplemental Agreements

(a) MCC may, from time to time, issue one or more letters to furnish additional information or guidance to assist the Government in the implementation of this Compact (each, an "***Implementation Letter***"). The Government shall apply such guidance in implementing this Compact.

(b) The details of any funding, implementing and other arrangements in furtherance of this Compact may be memorialized in one or more agreements between (A) the Government (or any Government Affiliate or Permitted Designee) and MCC, (B) MCC and/or the Government (or any Government Affiliate or Permitted Designee) and any third party, including any of the Providers or Permitted Designee or (C) any third parties where neither MCC nor the Government is a party, before, on or after the Entry into Force (each, a "***Supplemental Agreement***"). The Government shall deliver, or cause to be delivered, to MCC within five (5) days of its execution a copy of any Supplemental Agreement to which MCC is not a party.

Section 3.6
Procurement; Awards of Assistance

(a) The Government shall ensure that the procurement of all goods, services and works by the Government or any Provider in furtherance of this Compact shall be consistent with the procurement guidelines (the "***Procurement Guidelines***") reflected in a Supplemental Agreement between the Government (and/or a mutually acceptable Government Affiliate or MCA-Benin) and MCC (the "***Procurement Agreement***"), which Procurement Guidelines shall include the following requirements:

(i) Internationally accepted procurement rules with open, fair and competitive procedures are used in a transparent manner to solicit, award and administer contracts, grants, and other agreements and to procure goods, services and works;

(ii) Solicitations for goods, services, and works shall be based upon a clear and accurate description of the goods, services or works to be acquired;

(iii) Contracts shall be awarded only to qualified and capable contractors that have the capability and willingness to perform the contracts in accordance with the terms and conditions of the applicable contracts and on a cost effective and timely basis; and

(iv) No more than a commercially reasonable price, as determined, for example, by a comparison of price quotations and market prices, shall be paid to procure goods, services, and works.

(b) The Government shall maintain, and shall use its best efforts to ensure that all Providers maintain, records regarding the receipt and use of goods, services and works acquired in furtherance of this Compact, the nature and extent of solicitations of prospective suppliers of goods, services and works acquired in furtherance of this Compact, and the basis of award of contracts, grants and other agreements in furtherance of this Compact.

(c) The Government shall use its best efforts to ensure that information, including solicitations, regarding procurement, grant and other agreement actions funded (or to be funded) in whole or in part (directly or indirectly) by MCC Funding shall be made publicly available in the manner outlined in the Procurement Guidelines or in any other manner agreed upon by the Parties in writing.

(d) The Government shall ensure that no goods, services or works may be funded in whole or in part (directly or indirectly) by MCC Funding which are procured pursuant to orders or contracts firmly placed or entered into prior to the Entry into Force, except as the Parties may otherwise agree in writing.

(e) The Government shall ensure that MCA-Benin and any other Permitted Designee follows, and uses its best efforts to ensure that all Providers follow, the Procurement Guidelines in procuring (including soliciting) goods, services and works and in awarding and administering contracts, grants and other agreements in furtherance of this Compact, and shall furnish MCC evidence of the adoption of the Procurement Guidelines by MCA-Benin no later than the time specified in the Disbursement Agreement.

(f) The Government shall include, or ensure the inclusion of, the requirements of this Section 3.6 into all Supplemental Agreements between the Government, any Government Affiliate or Permitted Designee or any of their respective directors, officers, employees, Affiliates, contractors, subcontractors, grantees, sub-grantees, representatives or agents, on the one hand, and a Provider, on the other hand.

Section 3.7
Policy Performance; Policy Reforms

In addition to the specific policy and legal reform commitments identified in *Annex I* and the Schedules thereto, the Government shall seek to maintain and to improve, its level of performance under the policy criteria identified in Section 607 of the Act, and the MCA selection criteria and methodology published by MCC pursuant to Section 607 of the Act from time to time ("***MCA Eligibility Criteria***").

Section 3.8
Records and Information; Access; Audits; Reviews

(a) *Reports and Information*. The Government shall furnish to MCC, and shall use its best efforts to ensure that all Providers and any other third party receiving MCC Funding, as appropriate, furnish to the Government (and the Government shall provide to MCC), any records and other information required to be maintained under this Section 3.8 and such other information, documents and reports as may be necessary or appropriate for the Government to effectively carry out its obligations under this Compact, including under Section 3.12.

(b) *Government Books and Records*. The Government shall maintain, and shall use its best efforts to ensure that all Providers maintain, accounting books, records, documents and other evidence relating to this Compact adequate to show, to the satisfaction of MCC, without limitation, the use of all MCC Funding, including all costs incurred by the Government and the Providers in furtherance of this Compact, the receipt, acceptance and use of goods, services and works acquired in furtherance of this Compact by the Government and the Providers, agreed-upon cost sharing requirements, the nature and extent of solicitations of prospective suppliers of goods, services and works acquired by the Government and the Providers in furtherance of this Compact, the basis of award of Government and other contracts and orders in furtherance of this Compact, the overall progress of the implementation of the Program, and any documents required by this Compact or any Supplemental Agreement between the Parties or reasonably requested by MCC upon reasonable notice ("***Compact Records***"). The Government shall maintain, and shall use its best efforts to ensure that all Covered Providers maintain, Compact Records in accordance with generally accepted accounting principles prevailing in the United States, or at the Government's option and with the prior written approval by MCC, other accounting principles, such as those (1) prescribed by the International Accounting Standards Committee (an affiliate of the International Federation of Accountants) or (2) then prevailing in Benin. Compact Records shall be maintained for at least five (5) years after the end of the Compact Term or for such longer period, if any, required to resolve any litigation, claims or audit findings or any statutory requirements.

(c) *Access*. Upon the request of MCC, the Government, at all reasonable times, shall permit, or cause to be permitted, authorized representatives of MCC, the Inspector General, the United States Government Accountability Office, any auditor responsible for an audit contemplated herein or otherwise conducted in furtherance of this Compact, and any agents or representatives engaged by MCC or a Permitted Designee to conduct any assessment, review or evaluation of the Program, at all reasonable times the opportunity to audit, review, evaluate or inspect activities funded in whole or in part (directly or indirectly) by MCC Funding or undertaken in connection with the Program, the utilization of goods and services purchased or funded in whole or in part (directly or indirectly) by MCC Funding, and Compact Records, including of the Government or any Provider, relating to activities funded or undertaken in furtherance of, or otherwise relating to, this Compact, and shall use its best efforts to ensure access by MCC, the Inspector General, the United States Government Accountability Office or relevant auditor, reviewer or evaluator or their respective representatives or agents to all relevant directors, officers, employees, Affiliates, contractors, representatives and agents of the Government or any Provider.

(d) *Audits*.

(i) Government Audits. The Government shall, on at least an annual basis and as the Parties may otherwise agree in writing, conduct, or cause to be conducted, financial audits of all MCC

Disbursements and Re-Disbursements during the year since the Entry into Force or since the prior anniversary of the Entry into Force in accordance with the following terms, except as the Parties may otherwise agree in writing. As requested by MCC in writing, the Government shall use, or cause to be used, or select or cause to be selected, an auditor named on the approved list of auditors in accordance with the "Guidelines for Financial Audits Contracted by Foreign Recipients" (the "***Audit Guidelines***") issued by the Inspector General of the United States Agency for International Development (the "***Inspector General***"), and as approved by MCC, to conduct such annual audits. Such audits shall be performed in accordance with such Audit Guidelines and be subject to quality assurance oversight by the Inspector General in accordance with such Audit Guidelines. An audit shall be completed and delivered to MCC no later than 90 days after the first period to be audited and no later than 90 days after each anniversary of the Entry into Force thereafter, or such other period as the Parties may otherwise agree in writing.

(ii) Audits of U.S. Entities. The Government shall ensure that Supplemental Agreements between the Government or any Provider, on the one hand, and a United States non-profit organization, on the other hand, state that the United States organization is subject to the applicable audit requirements contained in OMB Circular A–133, notwithstanding any other provision of this Compact to the contrary. The Government shall ensure that Supplemental Agreements between the Government or any Provider, on the one hand, and a United States for-profit Covered Provider, on the other hand, state that the United States organization is subject to audit by the cognizant United States Government agency, unless the Government and MCC agree otherwise in writing.

(iii) Audit Plan. The Government shall submit, or cause to be submitted, to MCC no later than 20 days prior to the date of its adoption a plan, in accordance with the Audit Guidelines, for the audit of the expenditures of any Covered Providers, which audit plan, in the form and substance as approved by MCC, the Government shall adopt, or cause to be adopted, no later than sixty (60) days prior to the end of the first period to be audited (such plan, the "***Audit Plan***").

(iv) Covered Provider. A "***Covered Provider***" is (A) a non-United States Provider that receives (other than pursuant to a direct contract or agreement with MCC) USD $300,000 or more of MCC Funding in any MCA-Benin fiscal year or any other non-United States person or entity that receives, directly or indirectly, USD $300,000 or more of MCC Funding from any Provider in such fiscal year or (B) any United States Provider that receives (other than pursuant to a direct contract or agreement with MCC) USD $500,000 or more of MCC Funding in any MCA-Benin fiscal year or any other United States person or entity that receives, directly or indirectly, USD $500,000 or more of MCC Funding from any Provider in such fiscal year.

(v) Corrective Actions. The Government shall use its best efforts to ensure that Covered Providers take, where necessary, appropriate and timely corrective actions in response to audits, consider whether a Covered Provider's audit necessitates adjustment of its own records, and require each such Covered Provider to permit independent auditors to have access to its records and financial statements as necessary.

(vi) Audit Reports. The Government shall furnish, or use its best efforts to cause to be furnished, to MCC an audit report in a form satisfactory to MCC for each audit required by this Section 3.8, other than audits arranged for by MCC, no later than 90 days after the end of the period under audit, or such other time as may be agreed by the Parties from time to time.

(vii) Other Providers. For Providers who receive MCC Funding under this Compact pursuant to direct contracts or agreements with MCC, MCC shall include appropriate audit requirements in such contracts or agreements and shall, on behalf of the Government, unless otherwise agreed by the Parties, conduct the follow-up activities with regard to the audit reports furnished pursuant to such requirements.

(viii) Audit by MCC. MCC retains the right to perform, or cause to be performed, the audits required under this Section 3.8 by utilizing MCC Funding or other resources available to MCC for this purpose, and to audit, conduct a financial review, or otherwise ensure accountability of any Provider or any other third party receiving MCC Funding, regardless of the requirements of this Section 3.8.

(e) *Application to Providers.* The Government shall include, or ensure the inclusion of, at a minimum, the requirements of:

(i) Paragraphs (a), (b), (c), (d)(ii), (d)(iii), (d)(v), (d)(vi), and (d)(viii) of this Section 3.8 into all Supplemental Agreements between the Government, any Government Affiliate, any Permitted Designee or any of their respective directors, officers, employees, Affiliates, contractors, sub-contractors, grantees, sub-grantees, representatives or agents (each, a "***Government Party***"), on the one hand, and a Covered Provider that is not a non-profit organization domiciled in the United States, on the other hand;

(ii) Paragraphs (a), (b), (c), (d)(ii), and (d)(viii) of this Section 3.8 into all Supplemental Agreements between a Government Party and a Provider that does not meet the definition of a Covered Provider; and

(iii) Paragraphs (a), (b), (c), (d)(ii), (d)(v) and (d)(viii) of this Section 3.8 into all Supplemental Agreements between a Government Party and a Covered Provider that is a non-profit organization domiciled in the United States.

(f) *Reviews or Evaluations.* The Government shall conduct, or cause to be conducted, such performance reviews, data quality reviews, environmental and social audits, or program evaluations during the Compact Term or otherwise and in accordance with the M&E Plan or as otherwise agreed in writing by the Parties.

(g) *Cost of Audits, Reviews or Evaluations.* MCC Funding may be used to fund the costs of any Audits, reviews or evaluations required under this Compact, including as reflected on *Exhibit A* to *Annex II*, and in no event shall the Government be responsible for the costs of any such Audits, reviews or evaluations from financial sources other than MCC Funding.

Section 3.9
Insurance; Performance Guarantees

The Government shall, to MCC's satisfaction, insure or cause to be insured all Program Assets and shall obtain or cause to be obtained such other appropriate insurance and other protections to cover against risks or liabilities associated with the operations of the Program, including by requiring Providers to obtain adequate insurance and post adequate performance bonds or other guarantees. MCA-Benin or the Implementing Entity, as applicable, shall be named as the payee on any such insurance and the beneficiary of any such guarantee, including performance bonds. MCC, and to the extent it is not named as the insured party, MCA-Benin shall be named as additional insureds on any such insurance or other guarantee, to the extent permissible under applicable laws. The Government shall ensure that any proceeds from claims paid under such insurance or any other form of guarantee shall be used to replace or repair any loss of Program Assets or to pursue the procurement of the covered goods, services, works, or otherwise; *provided, however*, at MCC's election, such proceeds shall be deposited in a Permitted Account as designated by MCA-Benin and acceptable to MCC or as otherwise directed by MCC. To the extent MCA-Benin is held liable under any indemnification or other similar provision of any agreement between MCA-Benin, on the one hand, and any other Provider or other third party, on the other hand, the Government shall pay in full on behalf of MCA-Benin any such obligation; *provided, further*, the Government shall apply national funds to satisfy its obligations under this Section 3.9 and no MCC Funding, Accrued Interest, or Program Asset may be applied by the Government in satisfaction of its obligations under this Section 3.9.

Section 3.10
Domestic Requirements

The Government shall proceed in a timely manner to seek ratification of this Compact, as necessary or required by the laws of the Republic of Benin, or similar domestic requirement, in order that (i) this Compact shall be given the status of an international agreement, (ii) this Compact shall take precedence and prevail over the domestic laws of Benin now or hereafter in effect and (iii) each of the provisions of this Compact is valid, binding and in full force and effect under Beninese law. The Government shall initiate such process promptly after the conclusion of this Compact. Notwithstanding anything to the contrary in this Compact, this Section 3.10 shall provisionally apply prior to Entry into Force.

Section 3.11
No Conflict

The Government shall undertake not to enter into any agreement in conflict with this Compact or any Supplemental Agreement during the Compact Term.

Section 3.12
Reports

The Government shall provide, or cause to be provided, to MCC at least on each anniversary of the Entry into Force (or such other anniversary agreed by the Parties in writing) and otherwise within thirty (30) days of any written request by MCC, or as otherwise agreed in writing by the Parties, the following information:

(a) The name of each entity to which MCC Funding has been provided;

(b) The amount of MCC Funding provided to such entity;

(c) A description of the Program and each Project funded in furtherance of this Compact, including:

(i) A statement of whether the Program or any Project was solicited or unsolicited; and

(ii) A detailed description of the objectives and measures for results of the Program or Project;

(d) The progress made by Benin toward achieving the Compact Goal and Objectives;

(e) A description of the extent to which MCC Funding has been effective in helping Benin to achieve the Compact Goal and Objectives;

(f) A description of the coordination of MCC Funding with other United States foreign assistance and other related trade policies;

(g) A description of the coordination of MCC Funding with assistance provided by other donor countries;

(h) Any report, document or filing that the Government, any Government Affiliate or any Permitted Designee submits to any government body in connection with this Compact;

(i) Any report or document required to be delivered to MCC under the Environmental Guidelines, any Audit Plan, or any component of the Implementation Plan; and

(j) Any other report, document or information requested by MCC or required by this Compact or any Supplemental Agreement between the Parties.

ARTICLE IV
CONDITIONS PRECEDENT; DELIVERIES

Section 4.1
Conditions Prior to the Entry into Force and Deliveries

As conditions precedent to the Entry into Force, the Parties shall satisfy the conditions set forth in this Section 4.1.

(a) The Government (or a mutually acceptable Government Affiliate) and MCC shall execute a Disbursement Agreement, which agreement shall be in full force and effect as of the Entry into Force.

(b) (i) The Government shall deliver one or more of the Supplemental Agreements or other document identified on *Exhibit B* attached hereto, which agreements or other documents shall be fully executed by the parties thereto and in full force and effect, or (ii) the Government (or a mutually acceptable Government Affiliate) and MCC execute one or more term sheets that set forth the material and principal terms and conditions that will be included in any such Supplemental Agreement or document that has not been entered into or effective as of the Entry into Force (the "***Supplemental Agreement Term Sheets***").

(c) The Government (or a mutually acceptable Government Affiliate) and MCC shall execute a Procurement Agreement, which agreement shall be in full force and effect as of the Entry into Force.

(d) The Government shall deliver a written statement as to the incumbency and specimen signature of the Principal Representative and each Additional Representative of the Government executing any document under this Compact, such written statement to be signed by a duly authorized official of the Government other than the Principal Representative or any such Additional Representative.

(e) The Government shall deliver a certificate signed and dated by the Principal Representative of the Government, or such other duly authorized representative of the Government acceptable to MCC, that:

(i) Certifies the Government has completed all of its domestic requirements for (1) this Compact to be given the status of an international agreement, (2) this Compact to take precedence and prevail over the domestic laws of Benin now or hereafter in effect and (3) each of the provisions of this Compact to be valid, binding and in full force and effect under Beninese law; and

(ii) Attaches thereto, and certifies that such attachments are, true, correct and complete copies of all decrees, legislation, regulations or other governmental documents relating to its domestic requirements for this Compact to enter into force and the satisfaction of Section 3.10, which MCC may post on its website or otherwise make publicly available.

(f) MCC shall deliver a written statement as to the incumbency and specimen signature of the Principal Representative and each Additional Representative of MCC executing any document under this Compact such written statement to be signed by a duly authorized official of MCC other than the Principal Representative or any such Additional Representative.

(g) The Government has not engaged subsequent to the conclusion of this Compact in any action or omission inconsistent with the MCA Eligibility Criteria, as determined by MCC in its sole discretion.

Section 4.2
Conditions Precedent to MCC Disbursements or Re-Disbursements

Prior to, and as condition precedent to, any MCC Disbursement or Re-Disbursement, the Government shall satisfy, or ensure the satisfaction of, all applicable conditions precedent in the Disbursement Agreement.

ARTICLE V
FINAL CLAUSES

Section 5.1
Communications

Unless otherwise expressly stated in this Compact or otherwise agreed in writing by the Parties, any notice, certificate, request, report, document or other communication required, permitted, or submitted by either Party to the other under this Compact shall be (a) in writing, (b) in English and (c) deemed duly given: (i) upon personal delivery to the Party to be notified; (ii) when sent by confirmed facsimile or electronic mail, if sent during normal business hours of the recipient Party, if not, then on the next business day; or (iii) three (3) business days after deposit with an internationally recognized overnight courier, specifying next day delivery, with written verification of receipt to the Party to be notified at the address indicated below, or at such other address as such Party may designate:

To MCC:

Millennium Challenge Corporation
Attention: Vice President of Operations (with a copy to the Vice President and General Counsel)
875 Fifteenth Street, N.W.
Washington, D.C. 20005
United States of America
Facsimile: (202) 521-3700
Phone: (202) 521-3600
Email: VPOperations@mcc.gov (Vice President of Operations); VPGeneralCounsel@mcc.gov (Vice President and General Counsel)

To the Government:

Ministry of Finance and Economy
Attention: Minister of Finance and Economy
Route de l'Aéroport
P.O. Box 302
Cotonou, Republic of Benin
Facsimile: 229 21 30 18 51
Phone: 229 21 30 69 38

With a copy to:

Office of the Head of State
Attention: Chief of Staff
Presidence de la République
Avenue de la Marina
Cotonou, Republic of Benin
Facsimile: 229 21 30 00 90
Phone: 229 21 30 06 36

MCA-Benin (to be formed)
Attention: National Coordinator
Immeuble Espace Dina, 6th Floor
Boulevard Saint Michel
Cotonou, Republic of Benin
Facsimile: 229 21 32 83 22
Phone: 229 21 32 83 19
E-mail: mcabenin@yahoo.com

Notwithstanding the foregoing, any audit report delivered pursuant to Section 3.8, if delivered by facsimile or electronic mail, shall be followed by an original in overnight express mail. This Section 5.1 shall not apply to the exchange of letters contemplated in Section 1.3 or any amendments under Section 5.3.

Section 5.2
Representatives

Unless otherwise agreed in writing by the Parties, for all purposes relevant to this Compact, the Government shall be represented by the individual holding the position of, or acting as, Minister of Finance and Economy of the Republic of Benin, and MCC shall be represented by the individual holding the position of, or acting as, Vice President for Operations (each, a "***Principal Representative***"), each of whom, by written notice to the other Party, may designate one or more additional representatives (each, an "***Additional Representative***") for all purposes other than signing amendments to this Compact. The names of the Principal Representative and any Additional Representative of each of the Parties shall be provided, with specimen signatures, to the other Party, and the Parties may accept as duly authorized any instrument signed by such representatives relating to the implementation of this Compact, until receipt of written notice of revocation of their authority. A Party may change its Principal Representative to a new representative of equivalent or higher rank upon written notice to the other Party, which notice shall include the specimen signature of the new Principal Representative.

Section 5.3
Amendments

The Parties may amend this Compact only by a written agreement signed by the Principal Representatives of the Parties and subject to the respective domestic approval requirements to which this Compact was subject.

Section 5.4
Termination; Suspension

(a) Subject to Section 2.5, either Party may terminate this Compact in its entirety by giving the other Party thirty (30) days' written notice.

(b) Notwithstanding any other provision of this Compact, including Section 2.1, or any Supplemental Agreement between the Parties, subject to Section 2.5, MCC may suspend or terminate this Compact or MCC Funding, in whole or in part, and any obligation or sub-obligation related thereto, upon giving the Government written notice, if MCC determines, in its sole discretion, that:

(i) Any use or proposed use of MCC Funding or Program Assets or continued implementation of the Compact would be in violation of applicable law or United States Government policy, whether now or hereafter in effect;

(ii) The Government, any Provider, or any other third party receiving MCC Funding or using Program Assets is engaged in activities that are contrary to the national security interests of the United States;

(iii) The Government or any Permitted Designee has committed an act or omission or an event has occurred that would render the Republic of Benin ineligible to receive United States economic assistance under Part I of the Foreign Assistance Act of 1961, as amended (22 U.S.C 2151 *et seq.*), by reason of the application of any provision of the Foreign Assistance Act of 1961 or any other provision of law;

(iv) The Government or any Permitted Designee has engaged in a pattern of actions or omissions inconsistent with the MCA Eligibility Criteria, or there has occurred a significant decline in the performance of the Republic of Benin on one or more of the eligibility indicators contained therein;

(v) The Government or any Provider has materially breached one or more of its assurances or any covenants, obligations or responsibilities under this Compact or any Supplemental Agreement;

(vi) An audit, review, report or any other document delivered in furtherance of the Compact or any Supplemental Agreement or any other evidence reveals that actual expenditures for the Program or any Project or Project Activity were greater than the projected expenditure for such activities identified in the applicable Detailed Financial Plan or are projected to be greater than projected expenditures for such activities;

(vii) If the Government (A) materially reallocates or reduces the allocation in its national budget or any other Government budget of the normal and expected resources that the Government would have otherwise received or budgeted, from external or domestic sources, for the activities contemplated herein, (B) fails to contribute or provide the amount, level, type and quality of resources required to effectively carry out the Government Responsibilities or any other responsibilities or obligations of the Government under or in furtherance of this Compact, or (C) fails to pay any of its obligations as required under this Compact or any Supplemental Agreement, including such obligations which shall be paid solely out of national funds;

(viii) If the Government, any Provider, or any other third party receiving MCC Funding or using Program Assets, or any of their respective directors, officers, employees, Affiliates, contractors, sub-contractors, grantee, sub-grantee, representatives or agents, is found to have been convicted of a narcotics offense or to have been engaged in drug trafficking;

(ix) Any MCC Funding or Program Assets are applied, directly or indirectly, to the provision of resources and support to, individuals and organizations associated with terrorism, sex trafficking or prostitution;

(x) An event or condition of any character has occurred that: (A) materially and adversely affects, or is likely to materially and adversely affect, the ability of the Government or any other party to effectively implement, or ensure the effective implementation of, the Program or any Project or to otherwise carry out its responsibilities or obligations under or in furtherance of this Compact or any Supplemental Agreement or to perform its obligations under or in furtherance of this Compact or any Supplemental Agreement or to exercise its rights thereunder; (B) makes it improbable that the Objectives will be achieved during the Compact Term; (C) materially and adversely affects the Program Assets or any Permitted Account or (D) constitutes misconduct injurious to MCC, or constitutes a fraud or a felony, by the Government, any Government Affiliate, Permitted Designee or Provider, or any officer, director, employee, agent, representative, Affiliate, contractor, grantee, subcontractor or sub-grantee of any of the foregoing;

(xi) The Government or any Permitted Designee or Provider has taken any action or omission or engaged in any activity in violation of, or inconsistent with, the requirements of this Compact or any Supplemental Agreement to which the Government or any Permitted Designee or Provider is a party;

(xii) There has occurred a failure to meet a condition precedent or series of conditions precedent or any other requirements or conditions in connection with MCC Disbursement as set out in and in accordance with any Supplemental Agreement between the Parties; or

(xiii) Any MCC Funding, Accrued Interest or Program Asset becomes subject to a Lien without the prior approval of MCC, and the Government fails to obtain the release of such Lien (at its own expense and not with MCC Funding, Accrued Interest, or Program Assets) within thirty (30) days after the imposition of such Lien.

(c) MCC may reinstate any suspended or terminated MCC Funding under this Compact or any Supplemental Agreement if MCC determines, in its sole discretion, that the Government or other relevant party has demonstrated a commitment to correcting each condition for which MCC Funding was suspended or terminated.

(d) The authority to suspend or terminate this Compact or any MCC Funding under this Section 5.4 includes the authority to suspend or terminate any obligations or sub-obligations relating to MCC Funding under any Supplemental Agreement without any liability to MCC whatsoever.

(e) All MCC Disbursements and Re-Disbursements shall cease upon expiration, suspension, or termination of this Compact; *provided, however*, (i) reasonable expenditures for goods, services and works that are properly incurred under or in furtherance of this Compact before expiration, suspension or termination of this Compact and (ii) reasonable expenditures for goods and services (including certain administrative expenses) properly incurred within one hundred and twenty (120) days after the expiration, suspension or termination of the Compact in connection with the winding up of the Program may be paid from MCC Funding, provided that in the case of clauses (i) and (ii) the request for such payment is (A) properly submitted within ninety (90) days after the expiration, suspension or termination of the Compact and (B) subject to the prior written consent of MCC.

(f) Other than payments permitted pursuant to Section 5.4(e), in the event of the suspension or termination of this Compact or any Supplemental Agreement, in whole or in part, the Party, at MCC's sole discretion, shall suspend, for the period of the suspension, or terminate, or ensure the suspension or termination of, as applicable, any obligation or sub-obligation of the Parties to provide financial or other resources under this Compact or any Supplemental Agreement, or to the suspended or terminated portion of this Compact or such Supplemental Agreement, as applicable. In the event of such suspension or termination, the Government shall use its best efforts to suspend or terminate, or ensure the suspension or termination of, as applicable, all such noncancelable commitments related to the suspended or terminated MCC Funding. Any portion of this Compact or any such Supplemental Agreement that is not suspended or terminated shall remain in full force and effect.

(g) Upon the full or partial suspension or termination of this Compact or any MCC Funding, MCC may, at its expense, direct that title to Program Assets be transferred to MCC if such Program Assets are in a deliverable state; *provided*, for any Program Asset(s) partially purchased or funded (directly or indirectly) by MCC Funding, the Government shall reimburse to a United States Government account designated by MCC the cash equivalent of the portion of the value of such Program Asset(s), such value as determined by MCC.

(h) Prior to the expiration of this Compact or upon termination of this Compact, the Parties shall consult in good faith with a view to reaching an agreement in writing on (i) the post-Compact Term treatment of MCA-Benin, (ii) the process for ensuring the refunds of MCC Disbursements that have not yet been released from a Permitted Account through a valid Re-Disbursement or otherwise committed in accordance with Section 5.4(e), or (iii) any other matter related to the winding up of the Program and this Compact.

Section 5.5
Privileges and Immunities

MCC is an agency of the Government of the United States of America and its personnel assigned to the Republic of Benin will be notified pursuant to the Vienna Convention on Diplomatic Relations as members of the mission of the Embassy of the United States of America. The Government shall ensure that any personnel of MCC so notified, including individuals detailed to or contracted by MCC, and the members of the families of such personnel, while such personnel are performing duties in the Republic of Benin, shall enjoy the privileges and immunities that are enjoyed by a member of the United States Foreign Service, or the family of a member of the United States Foreign Service so notified, as appropriate, of comparable rank and salary of such personnel, if such personnel or the members of the families of such personnel are not a national of, or permanently resident in, the Republic of Benin.

Section 5.6
Attachments

Any annex, schedule, exhibit, table, appendix or other attachment expressly attached hereto (collectively, the "***Attachments***") is incorporated herein by reference and shall constitute an integral part of this Compact.

Section 5.7
Inconsistencies

(a) Conflicts or inconsistencies between any parts of this Compact shall be resolved by applying the following descending order of precedence:

(i) Articles I through V and

(ii) Any Attachments.

(b) In the event of any conflict or inconsistency between this Compact and any Supplemental Agreement between the Parties, the terms of this Compact shall prevail. In the event of any conflict or inconsistency between any Supplemental Agreement between the Parties and any other Supplemental Agreement, the terms of the Supplemental Agreement between the Parties shall prevail. In the event of any conflict or inconsistency between Supplemental Agreements between any parties, the terms of a more recently executed Supplemental Agreement between such parties shall take precedence over a previously executed Supplemental Agreement between such parties. In the event of any inconsistency between a Supplemental Agreement between the Parties and any component of the Implementation Plan, the terms of the relevant Supplemental Agreement shall prevail.

Section 5.8
Indemnification

The Government shall indemnify and hold MCC and any MCC officer, director, employee, Affiliate, contractor, agent or representative (each of MCC and any such persons, an "***MCC Indemnified Party***") harmless from and against, and shall compensate, reimburse and pay such MCC Indemnified Party for, any liability or other damages which (i) are directly or indirectly suffered or incurred by such MCC Indemnified Party, or to which any MCC Indemnified Party may otherwise become subject, regardless of whether or not such damages relate to any third-party claim, and (ii) arise from or as a result of the negligence or willful misconduct of the Government, any Government Affiliate, MCA-Benin or any Permitted Designee, directly or indirectly connected with, any activities (including acts or omissions) undertaken in furtherance of this Compact; *provided, however*, the Government shall apply national funds to satisfy its obligations under this Section 5.8 and no MCC Funding, Accrued Interest, or Program Asset may be applied by the Government in satisfaction of its obligations under this Section 5.8.

Section 5.9
Headings

The Section and Subsection headings used in this Compact are included for convenience only and are not to be considered in construing or interpreting this Compact.

Section 5.10
Interpretation; Definitions

(a) Any reference to the term "including" in this Compact shall be deemed to mean "including without limitation" except as expressly provided otherwise.

(b) Any reference to activities undertaken "in furtherance of this Compact" or similar language shall include activities undertaken by the Government, any Government Affiliate, any Permitted Designee, any Provider or any other third party receiving MCC Funding involved in carrying out the purposes of this Compact or any Supplemental Agreement, including their respective directors, officers, employees, Affiliates, contractors, sub-contractors, grantees, sub-grantees, representatives or agents, whether pursuant to the terms of this Compact, any Supplemental Agreement or otherwise.

(c) References to "day" or "days" shall be calendar days unless provided otherwise.

(d) The term "***United States Government***" shall, for the purposes of this Compact, mean any branch, agency, bureau, government corporation, government chartered entity or other body of the Federal government of the United States.

(e) The term "***Affiliate***" of a party is a person or entity that controls, is controlled by, or is under the same control as the party in question, whether by ownership or by voting, financial or other power or means of influence.

(f) The term "***Government Affiliate***" is an Affiliate, ministry, bureau, department, agency, government corporation or any other entity chartered or established by the Government.

(g) References to any Affiliate or Government Affiliate herein shall include any of their respective directors, officers, employees, affiliates, contractors, sub-contractors, grantees, sub-grantees, representatives, and agents.

(h) Any references to "***Supplemental Agreement between the Parties***" shall mean any agreement between MCC on the one hand, and the Government or any Government Affiliate or Permitted Designee on the other hand.

(i) A compendium of capitalized terms defined herein is included, for convenience only, in *Exhibit A* attached hereto.

Section 5.11
Signatures

A signature to this Compact or an amendment to this Compact pursuant to Section 5.3 shall be delivered only as an original signature. With respect to all other signatures, a signature delivered by facsimile or electronic mail in accordance with Section 5.1 shall be deemed an original signature, and the Parties hereby waive any objection to such signature or to the validity of the underlying document, certificate, notice, instrument or agreement on the basis of the signature's legal effect, validity or enforceability solely because it is in facsimile or electronic form; without limiting the foregoing, a signature on an audit report or a signature evidencing any modification identified in Sections 2(b) and (4)(a)(iv) of *Annex I*, Section 4 of *Annex II* or Section 5(c) *Annex III* shall be followed by an original in overnight express mail. Such signature shall be accepted by the receiving Party as an original signature and shall be binding on the Party delivering such signature.

Section 5.12
Designation

MCC may designate any Affiliate, agent, or representative to implement, in whole or in part, its obligations, and exercise any of its rights, under this Compact or any Supplemental Agreement between the Parties. MCC shall inform the Government of any such designation.

Section 5.13
Survival

Any Government Responsibilities, covenants, or obligations or other responsibilities to be performed by the Government after the Compact Term shall survive the termination or expiration of this Compact and expire in accordance with their respective terms. Notwithstanding the termination or expiration of this Compact, the following provisions shall remain in force: Sections 2.2, 2.3, 2.5, 3.2, 3.3, 3.4, 3.5, 3.8, 3.9 (for one year), 3.12, 5.1, 5.2, 5.4(d), 5.4(e) (for one hundred and twenty days), 5.4(f), 5.4(g), 5.4(h), 5.5, 5.6, 5.7, 5.8, 5.9, 5.10, 5.11, 5.12, this Section 5.13, 5.14, and 5.15.

Section 5.14
Consultation

Either Party may, at any time, request consultations relating to the interpretation or implementation of this Compact or any Supplemental Agreement between the Parties. Such consultations shall begin at the earliest possible date. The request for consultations shall designate a representative for the requesting Party with the authority to enter consultations and the other Party shall endeavor to designate a representative of equal or comparable rank. If such representatives are unable to resolve the matter within 20 days from the commencement of the consultations then each Party shall forward the consultation to the Principal Representative or such other representative of comparable or higher rank. The consultations shall last no longer than 45 days from date of commencement. If the matter is not resolved within such time period, either Party may terminate this Compact pursuant to Section 5.4(a). The Parties shall enter any such consultations guided by the principle of achieving the Compact Goal in a timely and cost-effective manner and by the principles of international law. Any dispute arising under or related to this Compact shall be determined exclusively through the consultation mechanism set forth in this Section 5.14.

Section 5.15
MCC Status

MCC is a United States government corporation acting on behalf of the United States Government in the implementation of this Compact. As such, MCC has no liability under this Compact, is immune from any action or proceeding arising under or relating to this Compact and the Government hereby waives and releases all claims related to any such liability. In matters arising under or relating to this Compact, MCC is not subject to the jurisdiction of the courts or other body of Benin or any other jurisdiction and all disputes arising under or relating to this Compact shall be determined in accordance with Section 5.14.

Section 5.16
Language

This Compact is prepared in English and in the event of any ambiguity or conflict between this official English version and any other version translated into any language for the convenience of the Parties, this official English version shall prevail.

Section 5.17
Publicity; Information and Marking

The Government shall give appropriate publicity to this Compact as a program to which the United States, through MCC, has contributed, including by posting this Compact, and any amendments thereto, on the website operated by MCA-Benin ("***MCA-Benin Website***"), identifying Program activity sites, and marking Program Assets; *provided*, any announcement, press release or statement regarding MCC or the fact that MCC is funding the Program or any other publicity materials referencing MCC, including the publicity described in this Section 5.17, shall be subject to prior approval by MCC and shall be consistent with any instructions provided by MCC from time to time in relevant Implementation Letters. Upon the termination or expiration of this Compact, MCC may request the removal of, and the Government shall, upon such request, remove, or cause the removal of, any such markings and any references to MCC in any publicity materials or on the MCA-Benin Website. MCC may post this Compact, and any amendments thereto, on the website of MCC. MCC shall have the right to use any information or data provided in any report or document provided to MCC for the purpose of satisfying MCC reporting requirements or in any other manner.

IN WITNESS WHEREOF, the undersigned, duly authorized by their respective governments, have signed this Compact this 22nd day of February, 2006 and this Compact shall enter into force in accordance with Section 1.3.

Done at Washington, D.C. in English.

FOR MILLENNIUM CHALLENGE CORPORATION, ON BEHALF OF THE UNITED STATES OF AMERICA

[Signature]

Name: John J. Danilovich
Title: Chief Executive Officer

FOR THE GOVERNMENT OF THE REPUBLIC OF BENIN

[Signature]

Name: Cosme Sehlin
Title: Minister of Finance and Economy

EXHIBIT A
DEFINITIONS

The following compendium of capitalized terms that are used herein is provided for the convenience of the reader. To the extent that there is a conflict or inconsistency between the definitions in this *Exhibit A* and the definitions elsewhere in the text of this Compact, the definition elsewhere in this Compact shall prevail over the definition in this *Exhibit A*.

2006 Baseline Data Survey *shall have the meaning set forth in Section 2(a)(i) of Annex III.*

Accrued Interest *is any interest or other earnings on MCC Funding that accrues as specified in Section 2.1(c).*

Act *means the Millennium Challenge Act of 2003, as amended.*

Additional Representative *is a representative as may be designated by a Principal Representative, by written notice, for all purposes other than signing amendments to this Compact.*

ADR *means alternative dispute resolution.*

AFD *means the Agence Française de Développement.*

Advisory Council *shall have the meaning set forth in Section 3(e)(i) of Annex I.*

Affiliate *means the affiliate of a party, which is a person or entity that controls, is controlled by, or is under the same control as the party in question, whether by ownership or by voting, financial or other power or means of influence. References to Affiliate herein shall include any of their respective directors, officers, employees, affiliates, contractors, sub-contractors, grantees, sub-grantees, representatives, and agents.*

Arbitration Center Activity *is the Project Activity related to expansion of the arbitration center under the Justice Project described in Section 2(a) of Schedule 3 to Annex I.*

Attachments *are any annex, schedule, exhibit, table, appendix or other attachment expressly attached to this Compact.*

Audit Guidelines *means the "Guidelines for Financial Audits Contracted by Foreign Recipients" issued by the Inspector General of the United States Agency for International Development.*

Audit Plan *means a plan, in accordance with the Audit Guidelines, for the audit of the expenditures of any Covered Providers, which audit plan, in the form and substance as approved by MCC, the Government shall adopt, or cause to be adopted, no later than sixty (60) days prior to the end of the first period to be audited.*

Auditor *means the auditor(s) as defined in, and engaged pursuant to, Section 3(h) of Annex I and as required by Section 3.8(d) of the Compact.*

Auditor/Reviewer Agreement *is an agreement between MCA-Benin and each Auditor or Reviewer, in form and substance satisfactory to MCC, that sets forth the roles and responsibilities of the Auditor or Reviewer with respect to the audit, review or evaluation, including access rights, required form and content of the applicable audit, review or evaluation and other terms and conditions such as payment of the Auditor or Reviewer.*

Bank(s) *means each individually and collectively, any bank holding an account referenced in Section 4(d) of Annex I.*

***Bank Agreement** means an agreement between MCA-Benin and a Bank, satisfactory to MCC, that sets forth the signatory authority, access rights, anti-money laundering and anti-terrorist financing provisions, and other terms related to the Permitted Account.*

***BDS** means business development services.*

***Beneficiaries** means the intended beneficiaries identified in accordance with Annex I.*

***Bilateral Agreement** means the Economic, Technical and Related Assistance Agreement by and between the Government of the United States of America and the Government of the Republic of Benin, dated May 27, 1961, as amended from time to time.*

***BNC** means Benin National Committee.*

***Board** means the independent board of directors of MCA-Benin to oversee MCA-Benin's responsibilities and obligations under this Compact.*

***BOC** means the fish/seafood inspection handling facility at the Port.*

***Business Registration Activity** is the Project Activity related to the business registration center under the Justice Project described in Section 2(b) of Schedule 3 to Annex I.*

***CAMeC** means the Centre d'Arbitrage, Mediation et Conciliation.*

***Capacity Building Activity** is the Project Activity related to financial institution and borrower capacity building under the Financial Services Project described in Section 2(a) of Schedule 2 of Annex I.*

***Cellule** means the Cellule de Microfinance.*

***Chair** means the Chair of the Board of Directors.*

***Challenge Facility** means a financial innovation and expansion challenge facility or FINECF described in Section 2(a) of Schedule 2 to Annex I.*

***Chamber** means the Chamber of Commerce.*

***Civil Member(s)** means the representatives for the positions identified in Sections 3(d)(ii)(2)(A)(vii)–(xi) of Annex I designated to serve as voting members on the Board for a one-year period.*

***Compact** means the Millennium Challenge Compact made between the United States of America, acting through the Millennium Challenge Corporation, and the Government of the Republic of Benin.*

***Compact Goal** means advancing economic growth and poverty reduction in Benin.*

***Compact Goal Indicator(s)** means the Indicators that will measure the results for the overall Program on the intended Beneficiaries, as set out in the table at Section 2(a)(i) of Annex III.*

***Compact Implementation Funding** shall have the meaning set forth in Section 2.1(a)(iii).*

***Compact Records** shall have the meaning set forth in Section 3.8(b).*

***Compact Reports** are any documents or reports delivered to MCC in satisfaction of the Government's reporting requirements under this Compact or any Supplemental Agreement between the Parties.*

***Compact Term** means the term for which this Compact shall remain in force, which shall be the five (5) year period from the Entry into Force, unless earlier terminated in accordance with Section 5.4.*

Component *shall have the meaning set forth in Section 2(a)(ii)(7) in Schedule 2 of Annex I.*

Courts Activity *is the Project Activity related to improved services of courts under the Justice Project described in Section 2(c) of Schedule 1 to Annex I.*

Covered Provider *shall have the meaning set forth in Section 3.8(d)(iv).*

Designated Rights and Responsibilities *shall have the meaning set forth in Section 3.2(c).*

Detailed Financial Plan *means the financial plans that specify respectively the annual and quarterly detailed budget and projected cash requirements for the Program (including monitoring and evaluation and administrative costs) and each Project, projected both on a commitment and cash requirement basis.*

Disbursement Agreement *is a Supplemental Agreement that MCC, the Government (or a mutually acceptable Government Affiliate and MCA-Benin shall enter into that (i) further specifies the terms and conditions of any MCC Disbursements and Re-Disbursements, (ii) is in a form and substance mutually satisfactory to the Parties, and (iii) is signed by the Principal Representative of each Party (or in the case of the Government, the principal representative of the applicable Government Affiliate) and of MCA-Benin.*

EMICoV *means Benin's national household living standards measurement survey (L'Enquête Modulaire Integrée sur les Conditions de Vie).*

EMPs *means Environmental Management Plans.*

Entry into Force *shall have the meaning set forth in Section 1.3.*

Environmental Guidelines *means the environmental guidelines delivered by MCC to the Government or posted by MCC on its website or otherwise publicly made available, as such guidelines may be amended from time to time.*

ESI Officer *means the Environmental and Social Assessment Director, an Officer of MCA-Benin.*

ESIAs *means environmental and social impact assessments.*

EU *means the European Union.*

Evaluation Component *means the component of the M&E Plan that specifies a methodology, process and timeline for the evaluation of planned, ongoing, or completed Project Activities to determine their impact and likely sustainability.*

Exempt Uses *shall have the meaning set forth in Section 2.3(e)(ii).*

Facility Manager *means the qualified independent management entity or entities that shall manage and implement the Challenge Facility.*

Final Evaluation *shall have the meaning set forth in Section 3(a) of Annex III.*

Financial Advisory Committee *is a stakeholders group that will provide feedback and input to the Financial Services Project Division.*

Financial Enabling Environment Activity *is the Project Activity related to financial enabling environment under the Financial Services Project described in Section 2(b) of Schedule 2 to Annex I.*

Financial Plan *means collectively, the Multi-Year Financial Plan, each Detailed Financial Plan, and each amendment, supplement or other change thereto.*

Financial Plan Annex *means Annex II of this Compact, which summarizes the Multi-Year Financial Plan for the Program.*

Financial Services Objective *is a Project Objective of this Compact and means to expand access to financial services.*

Financial Services Project *is the Access to Financial Services Project, and the Project described in Schedule 2 to Annex I, that the Parties intend to implement in furtherance of the Financial Services Objective.*

FINECF *means a financial innovation and expansion challenge facility or the Challenge Facility described in Section 2(a) of Schedule 2 of Annex I.*

Fiscal Accountability Plan *shall have the meaning set forth in Section 4(c) of Annex I.*

Fiscal Agent *shall have the mean set forth in Section 3(g) of Annex I.*

Fiscal Agent Agreement *is an agreement between MCA-Benin and each Fiscal Agent, in form and substance satisfactory to MCC, that sets forth the roles and responsibilities of the Fiscal Agent and other appropriate terms and conditions, such as payment of the Fiscal Agent.*

"goods" refers to any supplies, equipment, materials, property or other goods.

Governing Document *means any decree, legislation, regulation, contractual arrangement (including a governance agreement by and among the Government (or a mutually acceptable Government Affiliate), MCA-Benin and MCC), or other charter document establishing or governing MCA-Benin.*

Government *means the Government of the Republic of Benin.*

Government Affiliate *is an Affiliate, ministry, bureau, department, agency, government, corporation or any other entity chartered or established by the Government. References to Government Affiliate shall include any of their respective directors, officers, employees, affiliates, contractors, sub-contractors, grantees, sub-grantees, representatives, and agents.*

Government Members *are the government members identified in Section 3(d)(ii)(2)(A)(i)–(vi) of Annex I serving as voting members on the Board, and any replacements thereof in accordance with Section 3(d)(ii)(2)(A) of Annex I.*

Government Party *means the Government, any Government Affiliate, any Permitted Designee or any of their respective directors, officers, employees, Affiliates, contractors, sub-contractors, grantees, sub-grantees, representatives or agents.*

Government Responsibilities *shall have the meaning set forth in Section 3.2(a).*

GTZ *means Deutsche Gessellschaft Für Technische Zusammenarbeit, GmbH.*

IEC *means information, education and communication campaign.*

IEC Activity *is the Project Activity related to information, education, and communication Project Activity under the Land Project described in Section 2(d) of Schedule 1 of Annex I.*

IFC *means the International Finance Corporation.*

Implementation Letter *is a letter that may be issued by MCC from time to time to furnish additional information or guidance to assist the Government in the implementation of this Compact.*

Implementation Plan *is a detailed plan for the implementation of the Program and each Project, which will be memorialized in one or more documents and shall consist of: (i) a Multi-Year Financial*

Plan; (ii) Detailed Financial Plans; (iii) Fiscal Accountability Plan; (iv) Procurement Plan; (v) Program and Project Work Plans; and (vi) M&E Plan.

Implementing Entity *means a Government Affiliate, nongovernmental organization or other public- or private-sector entity or persons to which MCA-Benin may provide MCC funding, directly or indirectly, through an Outside Project Manager, to implement and carry out the Projects or any other activities to be carried out in furtherance of this Compact.*

Implementing Entity Agreement *is an agreement between MCA-Benin (or the appropriate Outside Project Manager) and an Implementing Entity, in form and substance satisfactory to MCC, that sets forth the roles and responsibilities of such Implementing Entity and other appropriate terms and conditions, such as payment of the Implementing Entity.*

Indicators *shall mean the quantitative, objective and reliable data that the M&E Plan will use to measure the results of the Program.*

Initial Technical Studies *means the initial technical studies (engineering pre-feasibility, environmental and economic) related to the Markets Project described in Section 2(a) of Schedule 4 of Annex I.*

Inspector General *means the Inspector General of the United States Agency for International Development.*

ISPS *means the International Ship and Port Security Code.*

Justice Advisory Committee *is a stakeholders group that will provide feedback and input to the Justice Project Division.*

Justice Objective *is a Project Objective of this Compact and means to improve the ability of the judicial system to enforce contracts and resolve claims.*

Justice Project *is the Access to Justice Project, and the Project described in Schedule 3 of Annex I, that the Parties intend to implement in furtherance of the Justice Objective.*

Land Objective *is a Project Objective of this Compact and means to strengthen property rights and investment.*

Land Project *is the Access to Land Project, and the Project described in Schedule 1 to Annex I, that the Parties intend to implement in furtherance of the Land Project Objective.*

Land Project Steering Group *is a stakeholders group that will provide feedback and input to the Land Project Division.*

Lien *means any lien, attachment, enforcement of judgment, pledge, or encumbrance of any kind.*

Local Account *is an interest-bearing local currency of Benin bank account at a commercial bank, subject to MCC approval, to which the Fiscal Agent may authorize transfer from any U.S. Dollar Permitted Account for the purpose of making Re-Disbursements payable in local currency.*

M&E Annex *means Annex III of this Compact, which generally describes the components of the M&E Plan for the Program.*

M&E Plan *means the plan to measure and evaluate progress toward achievement of the Compact Goal and Objectives of this Compact.*

Management *means the management team or national program coordination team of MCA-Benin to have overall management responsibility for the implementation of this Compact.*

Markets Objective *is a Project Objective of this Compact and means to improve the Port of Cotonou.*

Markets Project *is the Access to Markets Project, and the Project described in Schedule 4 of Annex I, that the Parties intend to implement in furtherance of the Markets Objective.*

Material Agreement *shall have the meaning set forth in Section 3(c)(i)(5) of Annex I.*

Material Re-Disbursement *means any Re-Disbursement that requires MCC approval under applicable law, the Procurement Agreement, any Governing Document, or any Supplemental Agreement.*

Material Terms of Reference *means any terms of reference for the procurement of goods, services or works that requires MCC approval under applicable law, the Procurement Agreement, any Governing Document, or any Supplemental Agreement.*

MCA *means the Millennium Challenge Account.*

MCA-Benin *shall have the meaning set forth in Section 3(b) of Annex I and as is further described in Section 3(d) of Annex I.*

MCA-Benin Website *means the website operated by MCA-Benin.*

MCA Eligibility Criteria *means the MCA selection criteria and methodology published by MCC pursuant to Section 607 of the Act from time to time.*

MCA National Coordinator *means the National Coordinator of the Millennium Challenge Account under the Benin National Committee, as described in Section 1(b) of Annex I.*

MCC *means the Millennium Challenge Corporation.*

MCC Disbursement *means the disbursement of MCC Funding by MCC from time to time to a Permitted Account or through such other mechanism agreed by the Parties as defined in and in accordance with Section 2.1(b)(i).*

MCC Disbursement Request *means the applicable request that the Government and MCA-Benin will jointly submit for an MCC Disbursement as may be specified in the Disbursement Agreement.*

MCC Funding *shall have the meaning set forth in Section 2.1(a).*

MCC Indemnified Party *means MCC and any MCC officer, director, employee, Affiliate, contractor, agent or representative.*

MCC Representative *is a representative designated by MCC to serve as an Observer on the Board.*

MFIs *means micro-finance institutions.*

Monitoring Component *means the component of the M&E Plan that specifies how the implementation of the Program and progress toward the Compact Goal and Objectives will be monitored.*

MSMEs *means micro and small- and medium-scale enterprises.*

Multi-Year Financial Plan *means the multi-year financial plan for the Program and for each Project, which is summarized in Annex II to this Compact.*

Multi-Year Financial Plan Summary *means a multi-year Financial plan summary attached to this Compact as Exhibit A of Annex II.*

"national" means, for purposes of Section 2.3(e), organizations established under the laws currently or hereafter in effect in the Republic of Benin, other than MCA-Benin or any other entity

established solely for purposes of managing or overseeing the implementation of the Program or any wholly-owned subsidiaries, divisions, or Affiliates of entities not registered or established under the laws currently or hereafter in effect in the Republic of Benin.

National Coordinator *means the National Coordinator of MCA-Benin as defined in Section 3(c)(i) of Annex I.*

NGOs *means non-governmental organizations.*

Objective(s) *are the Program Objective together with the following project-level objectives of this Compact that have been identified by the Parties, each of which is (i) key to advancing the Compact Goal and (ii) described in more detail in the Annexes attached hereto: (a) the Land Objective, (b) the Financial Services Objective (c) the Justice Objective and (d) the Markets Objective.*

Objective Indicator *means the Indicator for each Objective that will measure the ultimate result for each of the individual Projects. A table of Objective Indicator definitions is set forth at Section 2(a)(ii) of Annex III.*

Observer(s) *means the non-voting members of the Board as identified in Section 3(d)(ii)(2)(B) of Annex I.*

Officers *shall have the meaning set forth in 3(d)(iii)(3) of Annex I.*

OHADA *means Organization for the Harmonization of Business Law in Africa.*

Outcome Indicator *means the Indicator in the M&E Plan that will measure the intermediate results achieved under each of the Project Activities in order to provide early measures of progress towards the accomplishment of the Project Objective. A table of Outcome Indicator definitions is set forth at Section 2(a)(ii) of Annex III.*

Output Indicator *means the Indicator in the M&E Plan to measure the direct outputs of the Project Activities.*

Outside Project Manager *means the qualified persons or entities engaged by Management, on behalf of MCA-Benin, to serve as outside project managers in accordance with Section 3(d)(iii)(5) of Annex I.*

PAC *means the Port Autonome de Cotonou.*

Panel *shall have the meaning set forth in Section 2(a)(ii)(3) of Schedule 2 to Annex I.*

Parties *means the United States of America, acting through MCC, and the Government.*

Party *means (i) the United States of America, acting through MCC or (ii) the Government.*

Permitted Account(s) *shall have the meaning set forth in Section 4(d) of Annex I.*

Permitted Designee *shall have the meaning set forth in Section 3.2(c).*

PFR *means Plan Foncier Rural.*

Pledge *means any pledge of any MCC Funding or any Program Assets, or any guarantee directly or indirectly of any indebtedness.*

Policy Activity *is the Project Activity related to policy and legal reform under the Land Project described in Section 2(a) of Schedule 1 of Annex I.*

Port *means the Port of Cotonou.*

Port Advisory Committee *is a stakeholders group representing the Markets Project beneficiaries that will provide feedback and input to the Markets Project Division.*

Port Institutional Activity *means the port institutional and systems improvements Project Activity of the Markets Project as described in Section 2(b) of Schedule 4 to Annex I.*

Port Security and Landside Improvements Activity *means the port security and landside improvements Project Activity of the Markets Project as described in Section 2(c) of Schedule 4 to Annex I.*

Principal Representative *means (i) for the Government, the individual holding the position of, or acting as the Minister of State in Charge of Planning and Development of the Republic of Benin, and (ii) for MCC, the individual holding the position of, or acting as, the Vice President for Operations.*

Procedural Code *shall have the meaning set forth in Section 2(c)(v)(1) of Schedule 3 to Annex I.*

Procurement Agent *shall have the meaning set forth in Section 3(i) of Annex I.*

Procurement Agent Agreement *is an agreement between MCA-Benin and each Procurement Agent, in form and substance satisfactory to MCC, that sets forth the roles and responsibilities of the Procurement Agent with respect to the conduct, monitoring, and review of procurements and other appropriate terms and conditions, such as payment of the Procurement Agent.*

Procurement Agreement *is a Supplemental Agreement between the Government (and/or a mutually accepted Government Affiliate or MCA-Benin) and MCC, which includes the Procurement Guidelines, and governs the procurement of all goods, services and works by the Government or any Provider in furtherance of this Compact.*

Procurement Guidelines *shall have the meaning set forth in Section 3.6(a).*

Procurement Plan *means a procurement plan adopted by MCA-Benin as set forth in Section 3(i) of Annex I.*

Program *means a program, to be implemented under this Compact, using MCC Funding to advance Benin's progress towards economic growth and poverty reduction.*

Program Annex *means Annex I to this Compact, which generally describes the Program that MCC Funding will support in Benin during the Compact Term and the results to be achieved from the investment of MCC Funding.*

Program Assets *means (i) MCC Funding, (ii) Accrued Interest, or (iii) any assets, goods, or property (real, tangible, or intangible) purchased or financed in whole or in part by MCC Funding.*

Program Objective *means the overall objective of the Program to which the Project Objectives contribute and means to increase investment and private sector activity in Benin, which is key to advancing the Compact Goal.*

Project(s) *are the specific projects and the policy reforms, and other activities related thereto that the Government will carry out, or cause to be carried out in furtherance of this Compact to achieve the Objectives and the Compact Goal, specifically the Land Project, the Financial Services Project, the Justice Project and the Markets Project.*

Project Activity *means the activities that will be undertaken in furtherance of each Project.*

Project Director *shall have the meaning set forth in Section 3(d)(iii)(3) of Annex I.*

Project Division *means the divisions that manage the implementation of each Project.*

Project Objective(s) *means the project-level objectives that will advance the Program Objective and Compact Goal, each of which is described in more detail in the Annexes of this Compact.*

Proposal *is the proposal for use of MCA assistance submitted to MCC, as revised, by the Government on September 5, 2005.*

Provider *shall have the meaning set forth in Section 2.4(b).*

PRSP *means the Poverty Reduction Strategy Paper.*

RAPs *means Resettlement Action Plans.*

Re-Disbursement *is the release of MCC Funding from a Permitted Account.*

Registration Activity *is the Project Activity related to achieving formal property rights under the Land Project described in Section 2(b) of Schedule 1 of Annex I.*

Reviewer *shall have the meaning set forth in Section 3(h) of Annex I.*

Services and Information Activity *is the Project Activity related to improving land registration services and land information management under the Land Project described in Section 2(c) of Schedule 1 of Annex I.*

Special Account *means a single, completely separate U.S. Dollar interest-bearing account at a commercial bank, acceptable to MCC, to receive MCC Disbursements.*

Studies Activity *means the feasibility studies and assessments Project Activity of the Markets Project described in Section 2(a) of Schedule 4 to Annex I.*

Supplemental Agreement *shall have the meaning set forth in Section 3.5(b).*

Supplemental Agreement between the Parties *means any agreement between MCC on the one hand, and the Government or any Government Affiliate or Permitted Designee on the other hand.*

Supplemental Agreement Term Sheets *means one or more term sheets that the Government (or mutually acceptable Government Affiliate) and MCC shall execute that set forth the material and principal terms and conditions of each of the Supplemental Agreements identified in Exhibit B attached hereto.*

Support Strategy Activity *is the Project Activity related to strategy and programmatic coordination under the Land Project described in Section 2(e) of Schedule 1 of Annex I.*

Target *means each Indicator will have one or more targets that quantifies the result and the expected time by which that result will be achieved.*

Tax(es) *shall have the meaning set forth in Section 2.3(e)(i).*

TEU *means twenty-foot equivalent unit, in Euro.*

TPI *shall have the meaning set forth in Section 2(c)(v) of Schedule 3 to Annex I.*

United States Dollars *(USD) means the currency of the United States of America.*

United States Government *shall mean any branch, agency, bureau, government corporation, government chartered entity or other body of the Federal government of the United States.*

WAEMU *means the West African Economic and Monetary Union.*

Waterside Improvements Activity *means the waterside improvements Project Activity described in Section 2(d) of Schedule 4 to Annex I.*

Work Plans *means work plans for the overall administration of the Program and for each Project.*

EXHIBIT B
LIST OF CERTAIN SUPPLEMENTAL AGREEMENTS

1. Governing Document Principles
2. Fiscal Agent Agreement
3. Procurement Agent Agreement
4. Form of Implementing Entity Agreement
5. Form of Bank Agreement

SCHEDULE 2.1(a)(iii)
DESCRIPTION OF COMPACT IMPLEMENTATION FUNDING

Compact Implementation Funding.

The Compact Implementation Funding provided pursuant to Section 2.1(a)(iii) shall support the following activities and expenditures in an amount not to exceed the amounts specified below:

(a) Conduct some or all Initial Technical Studies as described in Section 2(a)(i) of *Schedule 4* of *Annex I*, in an amount not to exceed USD $800,000.[1]

(b) Conduct the activities related to the 2006 Baseline Data Survey as described in Section 2(a)(i) of *Annex III*, including: communication and transportation of survey staff, supervision and quality assurance, and data management, in an amount not to exceed USD $600,000.[2]

(c) Conduct fiscal and procurement administration activities, in an amount not to exceed USD $500.000.[3]

(d) Payments for reasonable and normal staff salaries and administrative expenses of MCA-Benin (or mutually acceptable Government Affiliate) such as rent, computers, and other information technology equipment, in an amount not to exceed USD $500,000.[4]

[1] Notwithstanding the amount specified for this activity or payment, the total amount of funds disbursed in accordance with Section 2.1(a)(iii) shall not exceed the amount set forth in Section 2.1(a)(iii).

[2] Notwithstanding the amount specified for this activity or payment, the total amount of funds disbursed in accordance with Section 2.1(a)(iii) shall not exceed the amount set forth in Section 2.1(a)(iii).

[3] Notwithstanding the amount specified for this activity or payment, the total amount of funds disbursed in accordance with Section 2.1(a)(iii) shall not exceed the amount set forth in Section 2.1(a)(iii).

[4] Notwithstanding the amount specified for this activity or payment, the total amount of funds disbursed in accordance with Section 2.1(a)(iii) shall not exceed the amount set forth in Section 2.1(a)(iii).

ANNEX I
PROGRAM DESCRIPTION

This *Annex I* to the Compact (the "***Program Annex***") generally describes the Program that MCC Funding will support in Benin during the Compact Term and the results to be achieved from the investment of MCC Funding. Prior to any MCC Disbursement or Re-Disbursement, including for the Projects described herein, MCC, the Government (or a mutually acceptable Government Affiliate) and MCA-Benin shall enter into a Supplemental Agreement that (i) further specifies the terms and conditions of such MCC Disbursements and Re-Disbursements, (ii) is in a form and substance mutually satisfactory to the Parties, and (iii) is signed by the Principal Representative of each Party (or in the case of the Government, the principal representative of the applicable Government Affiliate) and of MCA-Benin (the "***Disbursement Agreement***").

Except as specifically provided herein, the Parties may amend this Program Annex only by written agreement signed by the Principal Representative of each Party. Each capitalized term in this Program Annex shall have the same meaning given such term elsewhere in this Compact. Unless otherwise expressly stated, each Section reference herein is to the relevant Section of the main body of the Compact.

1. Background and Benin Development Strategy; Consultative Process.

(a) *Background and Benin Development Strategy.*

Situated in West Africa, between Nigeria and Togo in the Gulf of Guinea, Benin is a small and very poor country with a population of nearly seven million, a third of which live in poverty. Progress in development is largely a result of reforms initiated in the early 1990s as Benin transitioned from a Marxist-Leninist state towards a pluralistic democracy and market economy.

Despite growth rates averaging 5% per year in the past decade, per capita income in Benin remains below the sub-Sahara African average and rural poverty has increased in recent years. Private sector activity and broad-based investment that would lead to sustainable growth and poverty reduction are hindered by land insecurity, lack of access to capital, an inefficient judicial system, and an uncompetitive Port of Cotonou.

The Program is a series of strategic investments designed to increase investment and private sector activity by improving core physical and institutional infrastructure. The objectives of the Compact are fully consistent with, and directly support, the priority areas identified by the Government in the Poverty Reduction Strategy Paper ("***PRSP***"). Benin's PRSP was developed in 2002 with broad participation from Beninese society. Its development plan is based on four pillars: (i) strengthening the macroeconomic framework over the medium-term; (ii) developing human capital and environmental management; (iii) strengthening good governance and institutional capacity; and (iv) promoting employment and strengthening the ability of the poor to participate in decision-making and production processes. The Program is focused primarily on supporting the fourth pillar of the PRSP.

(b) *Consultative Process.*

The Proposal was the product of a genuine, meaningful and participatory consultative process. By decree, the Government designated the National Coordinator of the Millennium Challenge Account ("***MCA National Coordinator***"), empowered the Benin National Committee ("***BNC***") to oversee the Proposal development and charged a Technical Team with shaping the Proposal.

The MCA National Coordinator sought the participation of various stakeholders through workshops, meetings, and radio and television events. Initially a vision for the Program was presented to representatives from the government (both central and municipal), the private sector, civil society, labor unions, artisans, and the agricultural sector. Among these groups, members were elected or delegated by their respective constituencies to form the BNC. This MCA working group consists of six government Ministers, three Chamber of Commerce representatives, three civil society representatives (elected), three labor union representatives, two representatives of the Agricultural Chamber (elected), and one representative of the artisan community. Included in the working group are two women, the Vice President of the Chamber of Commerce and another who was elected by NGOs promoting women's rights.

Working sessions were held based on the PRSP to discuss the major constraints to growth. Several iterations of the Proposal's projects were vetted by a broad audience through nationally broadcast radio programs to garner feedback from the targeted beneficiaries. In September the MCA National Coordinator convened a stakeholder meeting in which mayors from all 77 communes, and representatives of microfinance institutions, the donor community and the central government gathered to discuss the land tenure, and financial services components of the Proposal. Continuing consultation throughout the proposal development process has resulted in widespread endorsement by potential beneficiaries. On-going consultations with stakeholders and beneficiaries are planned during the Compact Term, including at the Project-level.

Following MCC's review of the Proposal and discussions and negotiations of the Parties, the Parties have identified certain mutually acceptable components of the Proposal and other components developed through the discussions of the Parties that together shall constitute the Program. The Program is fully consistent with, and directly supports PRSP, in particular the promoting employment and strengthening the ability of the poor to participate in decision-making and production processes as noted above.

2. Overview.

(a) *Program Objectives*. The Program Goal and Objectives of the Compact are expected to have a substantial impact on increasing economic growth and reducing poverty in Benin. The Program will accelerate economic growth and reduce poverty by removing constraints to investment in key sectors of the Beninese economy. The Program aims to increase investment and private sector activity by improving key institutional and physical infrastructures through four Projects: *Access to Land, Access to Financial Services, Access to Justice*, and *Access to Markets*. Respectively, the Projects will address: insecure land tenure rights; insufficient access to financial services for micro, small and medium-enterprises (MSMEs); an inefficient and under-equipped judicial system; and the degrading competitiveness of the Port. The Projects are complementary and support each other. The Land Project and Financial Services Project will enhance the use of land titles as collateral for loans or refinancing. The Justice Project will support this relationship by increasing the confidence in the judicial system to enforce contracts and collateral interests. The Markets Project will increase the flow of goods through the Port of Cotonou. In turn, improvements to the physical infrastructure will enhance the success of Projects focusing on the institutional environment. The sequencing and geographic selection criteria for activities undertaken in Projects will be influenced by each of the other Projects.

(b) *Projects*. The Parties have identified, for each Objective, Projects that the Government will implement, or cause to be implemented, using MCC Funding. Each Project is described in the Schedules to this Program Annex. The Schedules to this Program Annex identify the activities that will be undertaken in furtherance of each Project (each, a "***Project Activity***") as well as the various activities within a Project Activity. Notwithstanding anything to the contrary in this Compact, the Parties may agree to modify, amend, terminate or suspend these Projects or to create a new project by written agreement signed by the Principal Representative of each Party without amending this Compact; *provided, however*, any such modification or amendment of a Project or creation of a new project is (i) consistent with the Objectives; (ii) does not cause the amount of MCC Funding to exceed the aggregate amount specified in Section 2.1(a) of this Compact; (iii) does not cause the Government's responsibilities or contribution of resources to be less than specified in Section 2.2 of this Compact or elsewhere in this Compact; and (iv) does not extend the Compact Term. Certain Project Activities of the Program such as the policy reforms, the extension of financial services and court services, and improvements to the Port, will have an impact at the national level. The Land Project will be undertaken in targeted geographic areas of Benin, which are yet to be determined, but will be selected based on the criteria set forth in the applicable Schedule.

(c) *Beneficiaries*. The intended beneficiaries of each Project are described in the respective Schedule to this Program Annex and *Annex III* to the extent identified as of the date hereof. The intended beneficiaries shall be identified more precisely during the initial phases of implementation of the Program. The Government shall provide to MCC information on the population of the areas in which the Projects will be active, disaggregated by gender, income level and age. The Parties shall agree upon the description of the intended beneficiaries and the Parties will make publicly available a more detailed description of the intended beneficiaries of the Program, including publishing such description on the MCA-Benin Website. For each Project, the Government shall ensure that MCA-Benin presents to the Advisory Council (i) a detailed description of the intended beneficiaries and (ii) the methodology used to determine the intended beneficiaries within sixty (60) days after the commencement of the Project implementation and completion of the analysis of the intended beneficiaries therein, disaggregated, to the maximum extent practicable, by income level, gender, and age.

The Land Project is expected to assist an estimated 115,000 rural and urban households with more secure and useful tenure, contribute to a 50% reduction in court cases related to land disputes, and result in a 10% increase in investment in rural land and a 20% increase in investment in urban property. The Financial Services Project is expected to increase MSME value added and incomes of the poor that own, are employed by, or do business with those enterprises. The expected result is that by the end of the Compact Term, financial services to MSMEs will have expanded by nearly $60 million, which represents a multiple of three times the Project's funding. A more efficient Port will contribute to importer and exporter value-added through reducing transportation costs. Moreover, because Benin's road transport industry is relatively competitive, it is likely that the anticipated reduction in shipping costs will be passed on to wholesalers and traders, and ultimately be reflected in consumer prices. The Justice Project is expected to benefit land occupants, title holders, businesses and legal professionals in the jurisdictions where the Project will be active.

Overall, the Program is expected to impact an estimated five million beneficiaries and raise one quarter of a million Beninese out of poverty by 2015.

(d) *Civil Society*. Civil Society shall participate in overseeing the implementation of the program through its representation on the Board of Directors and the Advisory Council (which will include representatives from non-governmental organizations and private sector entities), as provided in Section 3(d) and Section 3(e), respectively, of this Program Annex. Stakeholders will be able to weigh in by a Land Project steering group and discussion groups for studies, the White Paper, and related legislative drafting. The Financial Services Project and the Markets Project will also incorporate the input of Stakeholders in advisory committees comprising non-governmental organizations and private sector entities. Finally, members of civil society may be recipients of training, technical assistance, or other public awareness programs that are integral to the Projects.

In addition, the Work Plans or Procurement Plans for each Project shall note the extent to which civil society will have a role in the implementation of or participation in a particular Project or Project Activity.

(e) *Monitoring and Evaluation ("M&E"). Annex III* of this Compact generally describes the plan to measure and evaluate progress toward achievement of the Compact Goal and Objectives of this Compact (the "***M&E Plan***"). As outlined in the Disbursement Agreement and other Supplemental Agreements, continued disbursement of MCC Funding under this Compact (whether as MCC Disbursements and Re-Disbursements) shall be contingent, among other things, on successful achievement of targets set forth in the M&E Plan.

3. Implementation Framework.

The implementation framework and the plan for ensuring adequate governance, oversight, management, monitoring, evaluation and fiscal accountability for the use of MCC Funding is summarized below and in the Schedules attached to this Program Annex, or as may otherwise be agreed in writing by the Parties.

(a) *General.* The elements of the implementation framework will be further described in relevant Supplemental Agreements and in a detailed plan for the implementation of the Program and each Project, which will be memorialized in one or more documents and shall consist of a Multi-Year Financial Plan, Detailed Financial Plans, a Fiscal Accountability Plan, a Procurement Plan, Program and Project Work Plans, and an M&E Plan (the "***Implementation Plan***"). MCA-Benin shall adopt each component of the Implementation Plan in accordance with the requirements and timeframe as may be specified in this Program Annex, the Disbursement Agreement or as may otherwise be agreed by the Parties from time to time. MCA-Benin may amend the Implementation Plan or any component thereof without amending this Compact, provided any material amendment of the Implementation Plan or any component thereof has been approved by MCC and is otherwise consistent with the requirements of this Compact and any relevant Supplemental Agreement between the Parties. By such time as may be specified in the Disbursement Agreement or as may otherwise be agreed by the Parties from time to time, MCA-Benin shall adopt one or more work plans for the overall administration of the Program and for each Project (collectively, the "***Work Plans***"). The Work Plan(s) shall set forth the details of each activity to be undertaken or funded by MCC Funding as well as the allocation of roles and responsibilities for specific Project activities, or other programmatic guidelines, performance requirements, targets, or other expectations for a Project.

(b) *Government.*

(i) The Government shall promptly take all necessary and appropriate actions to carry out the Government Responsibilities and other obligations or responsibilities of the Government under and in furtherance of this Compact, including undertaking or pursuing such legal, legislative or regulatory actions or procedural changes and contractual arrangements as may be necessary or appropriate to achieve the Objectives, to successfully implement the Program, to designate any rights or responsibilities to any Permitted Designee, and to establish a legal entity, in a form mutually agreeable to the Parties, the form, structure and other features of such legal entity to be determined and agreed upon by the Parties on or before the time specified in the Disbursement Agreement ("***MCA-Benin***"), which shall be a Permitted Designee and shall be responsible for the oversight and management of the implementation of this Compact on behalf of the Government. The Government shall promptly deliver to MCC certified copies of any documents, orders, decrees, laws or regulations evidencing such legal, legislative, regulatory, procedural, contractual or other actions.

(ii) The Government shall ensure that MCA-Benin is duly authorized and organized, sufficiently staffed and empowered to fully carry out the Designated Rights and Responsibilities. Without limiting the generality of the preceding sentence, MCA-Benin shall be organized, and have such roles and responsibilities, as described in Section 3(d) of this Program Annex and as provided in any Governing Documents; *provided, however*, the Government or another Permitted Designee may, subject to MCC approval, carry out any of the roles and responsibilities designated to be carried out by MCA-Benin and described in Section 3(d) of this Program Annex or elsewhere in this Program Annex, any Governing Document, or any other Supplemental Agreement prior to and during the initial period of the establishment and staffing and operational formation of MCA-Benin, but in no event longer than the earlier of (1) the formation and convening of organizational meetings of the Steering Committee, formation and operational establishment of MCA-Benin (including the selection and engagement of Officers and key employees), and engagement of the Officers and (2) six months from the Entry into Force, unless otherwise agreed by the Parties in writing.

(iii) Various ministries, bureaus and agencies of the Government may serve as Implementing Entities.

(c) *MCC.*

(i) Notwithstanding Section 3.1 of this Compact or any provision in this Program Annex to the contrary, and except as may be otherwise agreed upon by the Parties from time to time, MCC must approve in writing each of the following transactions, activities, agreements and documents prior to the execution or carrying out of such transaction, activity, agreement or document and prior to MCC Disbursements or Re-Disbursements in connection therewith:

(1) MCC Disbursements;

(2) Each Detailed Financial Plan, and any amendments thereto;

(3) The Multi-Year Financial Plan and any amendments and annual supplements thereto;

(4) Any Audit Plan;

(5) Agreements (i) between the Government and MCA-Benin, (ii) between the Government, a Government Affiliate, MCA-Benin or any other Permitted Designee on the one hand, and any Provider or Affiliate of a Provider, on the other hand, which require such MCC approval under applicable law, the Procurement Agreement, any Governing Document, or any other Supplemental Agreement or (iii) in which the Government, a Government Affiliate, MCA-Benin or any other Permitted Designee appoints, hires, or engages any of the following in furtherance of this Compact:

(A) Auditor;

(B) Reviewer;

(C) Fiscal Agent;

(D) Procurement Agent;

(E) Each Bank;

(F) Outside Project Manager;

(G) Implementing Entity; and

(H) Board of Directors member, Observer, Officer, and other key employee of MCA-Benin (including any compensation for such person).

(Any agreement described in clause (i) through (iii) of this Section 3(c)(i)(5) and any amendments and supplements thereto, each, a "***Material Agreement***");

(6) Any modification, termination or suspension of a Material Agreement, or any action that would have the effect of such a modification, termination or suspension of a Material Agreement;

(7) Any agreement that is (A) not at arm's length or (B) with a party related to the Government or MCA-Benin or any of their respective Affiliates;

(8) Any Re-Disbursement (each, a "***Material Re-Disbursement***") that requires such MCC approval under applicable law, the Procurement Agreement, any Governing Document, or any Supplemental Agreement;

(9) Any terms of reference (each, a "***Material Terms of Reference***") for the procurement of goods, services or works that requires such MCC approval under applicable law, the Procurement Agreement, any Governing Document, or any Supplemental Agreement;

(10) The Implementation Plan, including each component plan thereto, and any material amendments and supplements to the Implementation Plan or any component thereto;

(11) Any pledge of any MCC Funding or any Program Assets or any guarantee directly or indirectly of any indebtedness (each, a "***Pledge***");

(12) Any decree, legislation, regulation, contractual arrangement (including a governance agreement by and among the Government (or a mutually acceptable Government Affiliate), MCA-Benin and MCC), or other charter document establishing or governing MCA-Benin ("***Governing Document***");

(13) Any disposition (in whole or in part), liquidation, dissolution, winding up, reorganization or other change of (A) MCA-Benin, including any revocation or modification of or supplement to any Governing Document related thereto, or (B) any subsidiary or Affiliate of MCA-Benin;

(14) Any change in character or location of any Permitted Account;

(15) Formation or acquisition of any subsidiary (direct or indirect) or other Affiliate of MCA-Benin;

(16) Any (A) change of a Board of Directors member, Observer, Officer or other key employee or contractor of MCA-Benin, or change in the composition of the Board of Directors of MCA-Benin, including approval of the nominee for Chair, (B) filling of any vacant seat of the Chair, Board of Directors member, or an Observer or vacant position of an Officer, key employee or contractor of MCA-Benin, (C) filling of the seats designated as representatives nominated by the Advisory Council, if any, to the Board of Directors, and (D) filling any vacant seat on the Advisory Council;

(17) The management information system to be developed and maintained by the Management of MCA-Benin, and any material modifications to such system;

(18) Any decision to amend, supplement, replace, terminate, or otherwise change any of the foregoing; and

(19) Any other activity, agreement, document or transaction requiring the approval of MCC in this Compact, applicable law, any Governing Document, the Procurement Agreement, the Disbursement Agreement, or any other Supplemental Agreement between the Parties.

The Chair of the Board of Directors (the "***Chair***") and/or the National Coordinator of MCA-Benin (the "***National Coordinator***") or other designated Officer, as provided in applicable Governing Document, shall certify any documents or reports delivered to MCC in satisfaction of the Government's reporting requirements under this Compact or any Supplemental Agreement between the Parties (the "***Compact Reports***").

(ii) MCC shall have the authority to exercise its approval rights set forth in this Section 3(c) in its sole discretion and independent of any participation or position taken by the MCC Representative at a meeting of the Board of Directors. MCC retains the right to revoke its approval of any matter, agreement, or action if MCC concludes, in its sole discretion, that its approval was issued on the basis of incomplete, inaccurate or misleading information furnished by the Government, MCA-Benin, or any Government Affiliate or Permitted Designee. Notwithstanding any provision in this Compact or any Supplemental Agreement to the contrary, the exercise by MCC of its approval rights under this Compact or any Supplemental Agreement shall not (1) diminish or otherwise affect the Government Responsibilities or any other obligations or responsibilities of the Government under this Compact or any Supplemental Agreement, (2) transfer any such obligations or responsibilities of the Government, or (3) otherwise subject MCC to any liability.

(d) *MCA-Benin.*

(i) General. Unless otherwise agreed by the Parties in writing, MCA-Benin shall, as a Permitted Designee, be responsible for the oversight and management of the implementation of this Compact. MCA-Benin shall be governed by applicable law and any Governing Documents, each such Governing Document to be in a form and substance satisfactory to MCC and effective on or before the time specified in the Disbursement Agreement, and based on the following principles:

(1) The Government shall ensure that MCA-Benin shall not assign, delegate or contract any of the Designated Rights and Responsibilities without the prior written consent of the Government and MCC. MCA-Benin shall not establish any Affiliates or subsidiaries (direct or indirect) without the prior written consent of the Government and MCC.

(2) Unless otherwise agreed by the Parties in writing, MCA-Benin shall consist of (a) an independent board of directors (the "***Board***") to oversee MCA-Benin's responsibilities and obligations under this Compact (including any Designated Rights and Responsibilities) and (b) a management team or national program coordination team ("***Management***") to have overall management responsibility for the implementation of this Compact.

(ii) Board.

(1) Formation. The Government shall ensure that the Board shall be formed, constituted, governed and operated in accordance with the terms and conditions set forth in the applicable Governing Document and any other relevant Supplemental Agreement.

(2) Composition. Unless otherwise agreed by the Parties in writing, the Board shall consist of at least nine (9) and no more than eleven (11) voting members, one of whom shall be appointed as the Chair as provided in applicable law, any Governing Document and subject to MCC approval, and the non-voting observers identified below.

(A) The Board shall initially be composed of eleven voting members as follows, provided that the Government members identified in subsections (i)–(vi) below (the "***Government Members***") may be replaced by another government official of comparable rank from a ministry or other government body relevant to the Program activities, subject to approval by the Government and MCC (such replacement to be referred to thereafter as a Government Member):

(i) Chief of Staff of the Office of the Presidency of the Republic of Benin;

(ii) Chief of Staff of the Ministry of Economy and Finance;

(iii) Chief of Staff of the Ministry of Planning and Development;

(iv) Chief of Staff of the Ministry of Agriculture;

(v) Chief of Staff of the Ministry of Public Works and Transportation;

(vi) Chief of Staff of the Ministry of the Environment, Housing and Urban Planning;

(vii) Representative from civil society (selected following a national assembly of the non-governmental organizations and civil society and based upon selection criteria to be agreed by the Parties, including the capacity and expertise of the individual to hold such position);

(viii) President of the Chamber of Commerce and Industry;

(ix) The Chairman of the Chamber of Agriculture;

(x) Representative from the Mayors' Council (which shall be the public official holding the relevant office as such office is selected following a national assembly of the mayors throughout Benin); and

(xi) A member of the Board of the National Assembly as designated by the National Assembly.

(B) The non-voting observers (each, an "***Observer***") shall be:

(i) A representative designated by MCC (the "MCC Representative");

(ii) A representative from the Advisory Council; and

(iii) Representatives-elect for Civil Members (defined below), who will be non-voting observers for a one-year period.

(C) Each Government Member position shall be filled by the individual, during the Compact Term, holding the office identified and such individuals shall serve in their capacity as the applicable Government official and not in their personal capacity; in the event that such member is unable to participate in a meeting of the Board such member's principal deputy may participate in the member's stead.

(D) The positions identified in Section 3(d)(ii)(2)(A)(vii)–(xi) of this Program Annex shall be each individually referred to as a "***Civil Member***" and collectively as "***Civil Members***." Each Civil Member position shall be filled by the individual, during the Compact Term, holding the office or position identified in, or selected pursuant to, Section 3(d)(ii)(2)(A)(viii)–(xi) and such individuals shall serve in their capacity as the incumbent in such office or position and not in their personal capacity; in the event that such member is unable to participate in a meeting of the Board such member's principal deputy may participate in the member's stead, *provided, however*, any action shall be taken only by a proxy signed by the Civil Member. The Civil Member identified in Section 3(d)(ii)(2)(A)(vii) shall serve in their personal capacity and if such member is unable to participate in a meeting of the Board, such member may only send a substitute as permitted in the applicable Governing Document, *provided*, any action shall be taken only by a proxy signed by the Civil Member. The term of each Civil Member's appointment to the Board shall be thirty (30) months; other than the Civil Member identified in Section 3(d)(2)(ii)(A)(viii) and (ix) which position shall be filled by the individual holding such position during the Compact Term; *provided, further* if the Civil Member designated pursuant to Section 3(d)(ii)(2)(A)(xi) resigns or is removed from the Board of the National Assembly, the National Assembly shall designate another member of the Board of the National Assembly to fill this seat on the Board.

(E) The voting members identified in Section 3(d)(ii)(2)(A) by majority vote may alter the size of the Board in accordance with the applicable Governing Document, so long as the total does not exceed eleven members; in the event that such action is taken, any change in the composition of the voting seats shall be subject to the approval of the Government and MCC.

(F) Subject to the Governing Documents, the Parties contemplate that the Chief of Staff of the Office of the Presidency shall initially fill the seat of Chair.

(G) Each Observer shall have rights to attend all meetings of the Board, participate in the discussions of the Board, and receive all information and documents provided to the Board, together with any other rights of access to records, employees or facilities as would be granted to a member of the Board under any Governing Document.

(H) The voting members identified in Section 3(d)(ii)(2)(A) shall exercise their duties solely in accordance with the best interests of MCA-Benin and the Program and its Objectives and may not undertake any action that is contrary to those interests or would result in personal gain or a conflict of interest.

(3) Roles and Responsibilities.

(A) The Board shall oversee the Management, the overall implementation of the Program, and the performance of the Designated Rights and Responsibilities.

(B) Certain actions may be taken and certain agreements, documents or instruments executed and delivered, as the case may be, by MCA-Benin only upon the approval and authorization of the Board provided under applicable law or as set forth in any Governing Document, including each MCC Disbursement Request, selection or termination of certain Providers, any component of the Implementation Plan, certain Re-Disbursements and certain terms of reference.

(C) The Chair shall certify the approval by the Board of all Compact Reports or any other documents or reports from time to time delivered to MCC by MCA-Benin (whether or not such documents or reports are required to be delivered to MCC), and that such documents or reports are true, correct and complete.

(D) Without limiting the generality of the Designated Rights and Responsibilities that the Government may designate to MCA-Benin, and subject to MCC's contractual rights of approval as set forth in Section 3(c) of this Program Annex or elsewhere in this Compact or any relevant Supplemental Agreement, the Board shall have the exclusive authority as between the Board and the Management for all actions defined for the Board in any Governing Document and which are expressly designated therein as responsibilities that cannot be delegated further.

(4) Indemnification of Civil Members; Observers; and Officers. The Government shall ensure, at the Government's sole cost and expense, that appropriate insurance is obtained and appropriate indemnifications and other protections are provided, acceptable to MCC and to the fullest extent permitted under the laws of the Republic of Benin, to ensure that (A) as Civil Members and Observers shall not be held personally liable for the actions or omissions of the Board or MCA-Benin and (B) as Officers shall not be held personally liable for the actions or omissions of the Board, MCA-Benin or

actions or omissions of the Officer so long as properly within the scope of Officer's authority. Pursuant to Section 5.5 and Section 5.8 of this Compact, the Government and MCA-Benin shall hold harmless the MCC Representative for any liability or action arising out of the MCC Representative's role as a non-voting observer on the Board. The Government hereby waives and releases all claims related to any such liability and acknowledges that the MCC Representative has no fiduciary duty to MCA-Benin. In matters arising under or relating to the Compact, the MCC Representative is not subject to the jurisdiction of the courts or any other body of Benin. MCA-Benin shall provide a written waiver and acknowledgement that no fiduciary duty to MCA-Benin is owed by the MCC Representative.

(iii) Management. Unless otherwise agreed in writing by the Parties, the Management shall report, through the National Coordinator or other Officer as designated in any Governing Document, directly to the Board and shall have the composition, roles and responsibilities described below and set forth more particularly in any Governing Document.

(1) Appointment of the National Coordinator. The National Coordinator of MCA-Benin shall be selected by the Board and hired after an open and competitive recruitment and selection process, which appointment shall be subject to MCC approval. Such appointment shall be further evidenced by such document as the Parties may agree.

(2) Appointment of Other Officers. Unless otherwise specified in any Governing Document, the other Officers of MCA-Benin shall be selected and hired by the National Coordinator after an open and competitive recruitment and selection process, which appointment shall be subject to the approval of the Board and MCC.

(3) Composition. The Government shall ensure that the Management shall be composed of qualified experts from the public or private sectors, including such offices and staff as may be necessary to carry out effectively its responsibilities, each with such powers and responsibilities as set forth in any Governing Document, and from time to time in any Supplemental Agreement between the Parties, including without limitation the following: (i) National Coordinator; (ii) Administration and Finance Director; (iii) Monitoring and Evaluation Director; (iv) Land Project Director, Financial Services Project Director, Justice Project Director and Markets Project Director (each a, "***Project Director***"); (v) Environmental and Social Assessment Director; (vi) Legal Counsel and (vii) Procurement Director (the persons holding the positions in sub-clauses (i) through (vii) and such other offices as may be created and designated in accordance with any Governing Document and any other Supplemental Agreement between the Parties, shall be collectively referred to as "***Officers***"). In addition, MCA-Benin will have an implementation staff in each of the Project divisions as described below and administrative or other assistants and staff in other divisions as appropriate and budgeted in the Detailed Financial Plan and provided for in the applicable Work Plan or other Implementation Plan component, and as otherwise agreed by MCC. The Administration and Finance Division and the Procurement Division shall have separate authorizations, duties and responsibilities and each shall report directly only to the National Coordinator and the Board. The Parties contemplate that for purposes of the initial period of operations, and in no event longer than six months, MCA-Benin may appoint an acting National Coordinator, subject to the approval of MCC; *provided*, following such period, the Board shall ratify the actions of such acting National Coordinator and the Board shall select a permanent National Coordinator through a competitive selection process and subject to MCC approval in accordance with this *Annex I*. The divisions that manage the implementation of each Project ("***Project Division***") shall have the following general organizational structure, or such other structure as may be agreed by the Parties in writing and specified in the applicable Governing Document:

(A) Land Project Division. In addition to the Project Director, there shall be (i) a Senior Land Administration Advisor for period to be specified in the Work Plan, (ii) a National Land Policy

Reform Coordinator, and (iii) up to two Activity Implementation Managers. The Land Project Division will also receive feedback and input from a stakeholders group (the "***Land Project Steering Group***"), the composition and formation of which shall be specified in the applicable Governing Document or Implementation Plan.

(B) Financial Services Project Division. In addition to the Project Director, there shall be (i) an Enabling Environment Activity Coordinator and (ii) a Capacity Building Activity Coordinator. The Financial Services Project Division will also receive feedback and input from a stakeholders group (the "***Financial Advisory Committee***"), the composition and formation of which shall be specified in the applicable Governing Document or Implementation Plan.

(C) Justice Project Division. In addition to the Project Director, there shall be a Justice Project Coordinator. The Justice Project Division will also receive feedback and input from a stakeholders group (the "***Justice Advisory Committee***"), the composition and formation of which shall be specified in the applicable Governing Document or Implementation Plan component.

(D) Markets Project Division. The Markets Project Division will also receive feedback and input from a stakeholders group representing the Markets Project beneficiaries (the "***Port Advisory Committee***"), the composition and formation of which shall be specified in the applicable Governing Document or Implementation Plan.

(4) Roles and Responsibilities.

(A) Management shall assist the Board in overseeing the implementation of the Program and shall have principal responsibility (subject to the direction and oversight of the Board and subject to MCC's contractual rights of approval as set forth in Section 3(c) of this Program Annex or elsewhere in this Compact or any relevant Supplemental Agreement) for the overall management of the implementation of the Program.

(B) Without limiting the foregoing general responsibilities or the generality of Designated Rights and Responsibilities that the Government may designate MCA-Benin, Management shall develop the components of the Implementation Plan, oversee the implementation of the Projects, manage and coordinate monitoring and evaluation, maintain internal accounting records, conduct and oversee certain procurements, and such other responsibilities as set out in the applicable Governing Document or delegated to Management by the Board from time to time.

(C) Appropriate Officers as designated in the Governing Documents shall have the authority to contract on behalf of MCA-Benin under any procurement under the Program undertaken in accordance with the Procurement Agreement and Procurement Guidelines.

(D) Management shall have the obligation and right to approve certain actions and documents or agreements, including certain Re-Disbursements, MCC Disbursement Requests, Compact Reports, certain human resources decisions and other certain actions, as provided in the applicable Governing Document.

(5) Additional Resources. Management, on behalf of MCA-Benin, shall have the authority to engage qualified persons or entities to serve as outside project managers (each, an "***Outside Project Manager***") in the event that it is advisable to do so for the proper and efficient day-to-day management of a Project; *provided, however*, that the appointment or engagement of any Outside Project Manager, after a competitive selection process, shall be subject to approval by the Board and MCC prior to such appointment or engagement. Upon Board approval, Management, on behalf of MCA-Benin, may delegate, assign, or contract to the Outside Project Managers such duties and responsibilities as it deems appropriate with respect to the management of the Implementing Entities and the implementation of the specific Projects or Project Activities, subject to Section 3.2(c) of the Compact; *provided, however*, that the Management and the relevant Project Manager shall remain accountable for those duties and responsibilities and all reports delivered by the Outside Project

Manager. Independent of any request from Management, the Board may determine that it is advisable for MCA-Benin to engage one or more Outside Project Managers and the Board may direct Management to commence and conduct the competitive selection process for such Outside Project Manager. Upon a finding by the Board that Management has not responded to such a Board directive, the Board may direct the Procurement Agent to commence and conduct the competitive selection process for one or more Outside Project Managers.

(e) *Advisory Council.*

(i) Formation and Composition. The Government shall ensure the establishment of an advisory council with both governmental, private sector and non-governmental representatives (the "***Advisory Council***") consisting of at least eight (8) and no more than eleven (11) members, unless otherwise agreed by the Parties, and comprised of the following members: (A) Chief of Staff of the Ministry of Foreign Affairs and African Integration; (B) Chief of Staff of the Ministry of Industry and Commerce; (C) Chief of Staff of the Ministry of the Interior, Security, and Decentralization; (D) Chief of Staff of the Ministry of Justice; (E) a representative from the Private Sector (selected following a national assembly of the private sector); (F) a representative from the labor unions (selected following a national assembly of the labor unions); (G) a representative from the regional organizations (selected following a national assembly of the regional organizations); and (H) a representative from the National Artisan Federation (selected following a national assembly of the National Artisan Federation). Representatives described in (E) through (H) shall be selected and vacancies filled in accordance with the manner and criteria set forth in the applicable Governing Document, subject to MCC approval. Following the selection of the representatives described in (E) through (H), the results of the selection shall be posted on the MCA-Benin Website and published in the local newspaper. The Government shall take all action necessary and appropriate actions to ensure the Advisory is established consistent with this Section 3(e) and as otherwise specified in the Governing Document or otherwise agreed in writing by the Parties. The composition of the Advisory Council may be adjusted by agreement of the Parties from time to time to ensure, among other things, a cross-section representative of the intended beneficiaries. The number of members of the Advisory Council may be increased, but in no event more than eleven (11), upon the majority vote of the then existing members and the vacancies created by such increase shall be filled by the majority vote of the then existing members, subject to the approval of the Government and MCC.

(1) Each member position identified in Sections 3(e)(i) of this Program Annex shall be filled by the individual, during the Compact Term, holding the office identified and such individuals shall serve in their capacity as the applicable Government official and not in their personal capacity. In the event that such member is unable to participate in a meeting of the Advisory Council such member's principal deputy may participate in the member's stead.

(2) In the event of a vacancy in positions identified in Sections 3(e)(i)(E) through (H) such vacancy to be filled by nomination of the organization or group for whom such seat is designated and in the same manner as described in Section 3(e)(i) for the initial designation and as otherwise set forth in the applicable Governing Document.

(ii) Role. The Advisory Council shall be a mechanism to provide representatives of the private sector, civil society and local and regional governments the opportunity to provide advice and input to MCA-Benin regarding the implementation of the Compact. During quarterly meetings of the Advisory Council, Management shall present an update on the implementation of this Compact and progress towards achievement of the Objectives. The Advisory Council will have an opportunity to regularly provide to the Board, via the Chair, its views or recommendations on the performance and progress on the Projects and Project Activities, components of the Implementation Plan, procurement, financial management or such other issues as may be presented from time to time to the Advisory Council or as otherwise raised by the Advisory Council. Management shall provide copies of the M&E Plan and related reports to the Advisory Council simultaneously with the transmittal to the Advisory Council of such documents and reports. The Board may, in response to the Advisory Council, require Management to provide such other information and documents as the Board deems advisable and subject to appropriate treatment of the information by the Advisory Council and its members.

(iii) Meetings. The Advisory Council shall hold quarterly meetings of the full Advisory Council as well as such other periodic meetings of the Advisory Council or subcommittees thereof designated along sectoral, regional, or other lines, as may be necessary or appropriate from time to time.

(iv) Board Observer. The Advisory Council shall nominate, by majority decision, one individual, either from the Advisory Council or otherwise, to serve as an Observer to the Board for a one-year term. The Advisory Council shall rotate its representative each year. Any vacancy of the Observer seat designated for the Advisory Council shall be filled by the Advisory Council in same manner as it would the annual nomination.

(v) Accessibility; Transparency. Advisory Council members will be accessible to the beneficiaries they represent to receive the beneficiaries' comments or suggestions regarding the Program. The minutes of all meetings of the Advisory Council meetings and any subcommittees shall be made public on the MCA-Benin Website in a timely manner.

(f) *Implementing Entities*. Subject to the terms and conditions of this Compact and any other Supplemental Agreement between the Parties, MCA-Benin may provide MCC Funding, directly or indirectly through an Outside Project Manager, to one or more Government Affiliates or to one or more nongovernmental organizations or other public- or private-sector entities or persons to implement and carry out the Projects or any other activities to be carried out in furtherance of this Compact (each, an "***Implementing Entity***"). The Government shall ensure that MCA-Benin (or the appropriate Outside Project Manager) enters into an agreement with each Implementing Entity, in form and substance satisfactory to MCC, that sets forth the roles and responsibilities of such Implementing Entity and other appropriate terms and conditions, such as payment of the Implementing Entity (the "***Implementing Entity Agreement***"). An Implementing Entity shall report directly to the relevant Project Manager or Outside Project Manager, as designated in the applicable Implementing Entity Agreement or as otherwise agreed by the Parties. The Implementing Entities shall be either (i) predetermined ministries, bureaus or agencies of the Government based on their sector expertise with respect to certain activities or (ii) government bodies, businesses, micro-finance institutions ("***MFIs***") and/or non-governmental organizations, vendors and contractors selected according to a the Procurement Guidelines.

(g) *Fiscal Agent*. The Government shall ensure that MCA-Benin engages one fiscal agent following an international competitive process (a "***Fiscal Agent***") who shall be responsible for, among other things: (i) assisting MCA-Benin in preparing the Fiscal Accountability Plan, (ii) ensuring and certifying that Re-Disbursements are properly authorized and documented in accordance with established control procedures set forth in the Disbursement Agreement, the Fiscal Agent Agreement and other relevant Supplemental Agreements; (iii) Re-Disbursing from, cash management and account reconciliation of a Bank Account established and maintained by the Fiscal Agent for the purpose of instructing Bank to make Re-Disbursements from a Permitted Account (to which Fiscal Agent has sole signature authority), following applicable certification by the Fiscal Agent; (iv) providing applicable certifications for MCC Disbursement Requests; (v) maintaining and retaining proper accounting, records and document disaster recovery system of all MCC Funded financial transactions and certain other accounting functions; (vi) producing reports on MCC Disbursements and Re-Disbursements (including any requests therefore) in accordance with established procedures set forth in the Disbursement Agreement, the Fiscal Agent Agreement, the Fiscal Accountability Plan, or any other relevant Supplemental Agreements, (vii) preparing budget development procedures and the Compact implementation budget, (viii) managing funds control, (ix) inventory control, and (x) internal management of the Fiscal Agent operations. Upon the written request of MCC, the Government shall ensure that MCA-Benin terminates the Fiscal Agent, without any liability to MCC, and the Government shall ensure that MCA-Benin engages a new Fiscal Agent, subject to the approval by the Board and MCC. The Government shall ensure that MCA-Benin enters into an agreement with each Fiscal Agent, in form and substance satisfactory to MCC, that sets forth the roles and responsibilities of the Fiscal Agent and other appropriate terms and conditions, such as payment of the Fiscal Agent (each, a "***Fiscal Agent Agreement***"), such Fiscal Agent Agreement shall not be terminated until MCA-Benin has engaged a successor Fiscal Agent or as otherwise agreed by MCC in writing.

(h) *Auditors and Reviewers*. The Government shall ensure that MCA-Benin carries out the Government's audit responsibilities as provided in Sections 3.8(d), (e) and (f) of this Compact, including engaging one or more auditors (each, an "***Auditor***") required by Section 3.8(d) of this Compact. As requested by MCC in writing from time to time, the Government shall ensure that MCA-Benin also engages (i) an independent reviewer to conduct reviews of performance and compliance under this Compact pursuant to Section 3.8(f) of this Compact, which reviewer shall have the capacity to (A) conduct general reviews of performance or compliance, (B) conduct environmental audits, (C) conduct data quality assessments in accordance with the M&E Plan, as described more fully in *Annex III*, and/or (ii) an independent evaluator to assess performance as required under the M&E Plan (each, a "***Reviewer***"). MCA-Benin shall select the Auditor(s) or Reviewers in accordance with any Governing Document or other relevant Supplemental Agreement. The Government shall ensure that MCA-Benin enters into an agreement with each Auditor or Reviewer, in form and substance satisfactory to MCC, that sets forth the roles and responsibilities of the Auditor or Reviewer with respect to the audit, review or evaluation, including access rights, required form and content of the applicable audit, review or evaluation and other appropriate terms and conditions such as payment of the Auditor or Reviewer (the "***Auditor/Reviewer Agreement***"). In the case of a financial audit required by Section 3.8(f) of the Compact, such Auditor/Reviewer Agreement shall be effective no later than 120 days prior to the end of the relevant fiscal year or other period to be audited; *provided, however*, if MCC requires concurrent audits of financial information or reviews of performance and compliance under this Compact, then such Auditor/Reviewer Agreement shall be effective no later than the date agreed by the Parties in writing.

(i) *Procurement Agent*. The Government shall ensure that MCA-Benin engages one or more procurement agents through international competitive process (each, a "***Procurement Agent***") to carryout and/or certify specified procurement activities in furtherance of this Compact on behalf of the Government, MCA-Benin, the Project Manager or Implementing Entity. The roles and responsibilities of such Procurement Agent and the criteria for selection of a Procurement Agent shall be as set forth in the applicable Implementation Letter or Supplemental Agreement. The Government shall ensure that MCA-Benin enters into an agreement with the Procurement Agent, in form and substance satisfactory to MCC, that sets forth the roles and responsibilities of the Procurement Agent with respect to the conduct, monitoring and review of procurements and other appropriate terms and conditions, such as payment of the Procurement Agent (the "***Procurement Agent Agreement***"). Any Procurement Agent shall adhere to the procurement standards set forth in the Procurement Agreement and Procurement Guidelines and ensure procurements are consistent with the procurement plan adopted by MCA-Benin pursuant to the Procurement Agreement (the "***Procurement Plan***").

4. Finances and Fiscal Accountability.

(a) *Financial Plans.*

(i) Multi-Year Financial Plan. The multi-year financial plan for the Program and for each Project (the "***Multi-Year Financial Plan***") is summarized in *Annex II* to this Compact.

(ii) Detailed Financial Plan. During the Compact Term, the Government shall ensure that MCA-Benin timely delivers to MCC financial plans that specify respectively the annual and quarterly detailed budget and projected cash requirements for the Program (including monitoring and evaluation and administrative costs) and each Project, projected both on a commitment and cash requirement basis (each a "***Detailed Financial Plan***"). Each Detailed Financial Plan shall be delivered by such time as specified in the Disbursement Agreement or as may otherwise be agreed by the Parties. The Multi-Year Financial Plan and each Detailed Financial Plan and each amendment, supplement or other change thereto are collectively, the "***Financial Plan***."

(iii) Expenditures. No financial commitment involving MCC Funding shall be made, no obligation of MCC Funding shall be incurred, and no Re-Disbursement shall be made or MCC Disbursement Request submitted for any activity or expenditure, unless the expense is provided for in the Detailed Financial Plan and unless uncommitted funds exist in the balance of the Detailed Financial Plan for the relevant period or unless the Parties otherwise agree in writing.

(iv) Modifications to Multi-Year Financial Plan or Detailed Financial Plan. Notwithstanding anything to the contrary in this Compact, MCA-Benin may amend or supplement the Multi-Year Financial Plan, or any component thereof or any Detailed Financial Plan without amending this Compact, provided any material amendment or supplement has been approved by MCC and is otherwise consistent with the requirements of this Compact including Section 4 of *Annex II* and any relevant Supplemental Agreement between the Parties; *provided, however*, MCA-Benin may modify the Detailed Financial Plan to reallocate MCC Funding without MCC prior approval to the extent that in the aggregate during the Compact Term the:

(1) Reallocation of funds within a Project would not reduce or increase any line item in the Detailed Financial Plan for a Project Activity more than the lesser of 10% of such relevant line item in the Detailed Financial Plan or USD $2,000,000, taking into account any modifications made pursuant to paragraph (B) such that any modifications made pursuant to (A) and (B) in the aggregate shall not exceed USD $2,000,000;

(2) Re-allocation of funds within a Project Activity would not reduce or increase any line item in the Detailed Financial Plan for a sub-activity more than the lesser of 10% of the relevant line item in the Detailed Financial Plan or USD $2,000,000 taking into account any modifications made pursuant to paragraph (A) such that any modifications made pursuant to (A) and (B) in the aggregate shall not exceed USD $2,000,000;

(3) Re-allocation of funds between Projects would not reduce or increase any line item in the Detailed Financial Plan for a Project Activity more than the lesser of 10% of the relevant line item in the Detailed Financial Plan or USD $500,000;

(4) Re-allocation of funds within Monitoring and Evaluation category of the Detailed Financial Plan would not reduce or increase more than the lesser of 10% of the relevant line item in the Detailed Financial Plan for the M&E activity or USD $500,000; or

(5) Re-allocation of funds within Program Administration category of the Detailed Financial Plan would not reduce or increase more than the lesser of 10% of the relevant line item in the Detailed Financial Plan for the Program Administration expense category or USD $500,000.

With respect to any modification pursuant to subparagraphs (1)–(5) above, such modification (A) shall be consistent with the Objectives and the Implementation Plan; (B) shall not materially adversely impact the applicable Project, Project Activity, sub-activity, M&E activity or Program administration activity; (C) shall not cause the amount of MCC Funding to exceed the aggregate amount specified in Section 2.1(a) of this Compact; and (D) shall not cause the Government's obligations or responsibilities or overall contribution of resources to be less than as specified in Section 2.2(a) of this Compact, this *Annex I* or elsewhere in this Compact; *provided, further*, that MCA-Benin shall promptly deliver to MCC any such modified Detailed Financial Plan, together with a modified Multi-Year Financial Plan to reflect the corresponding modifications, and further reflected in the Detailed Financial Plan submitted with the MCC Disbursement Request at the next Disbursement Period.

(b) *Disbursement and Re-Disbursement.* The Disbursement Agreement (and disbursement schedules thereto), as amended from time to time, shall specify the terms, conditions and procedures on which MCC Disbursements and Re-Disbursements shall be made. The obligation of MCC to make MCC Disbursements or approve Re-Disbursements is subject to the fulfillment, waiver or deferral of any such terms and conditions. The Government and MCA-Benin shall jointly submit the applicable request for an MCC Disbursement (the "***MCC Disbursement Request***") as may be specified in the Disbursement Agreement. MCC will make MCC Disbursements in tranches to a Permitted Account from time to time as provided in the Disbursement Agreement or as may otherwise be agreed by the Parties, subject to Program requirements and performance by the Government, MCA-Benin and other relevant parties in furtherance of this Compact. Re-Disbursements will be made from time to time based on requests by an authorized representative of the appropriate party designated for the size and type of Re-Disbursement in accordance with any Governing Document and Disbursement Agreement; *provided, however*, unless otherwise agreed by the Parties in writing, no Re-Disbursement shall be made unless and until the written approvals specified herein or in any Governing Document and Disbursement Agreement for such Re-Disbursement have been obtained and delivered to the Fiscal Agent.

(c) *Fiscal Accountability Plan.* By such time as specified in the Disbursement Agreement or as otherwise agreed by the Parties, MCA-Benin shall adopt as part of the Implementation Plan a fiscal accountability plan that identifies the principles, mechanisms and procedures to ensure appropriate fiscal accountability for the use of MCC Funding provided under this Compact, including the process to ensure that open, fair, and competitive procedures will be used in a transparent manner in the administration of grants or cooperative agreements and the procurement of goods and services for the accomplishment of the Objectives (the "***Fiscal Accountability Plan***"). The Fiscal Accountability Plan shall set forth, among other things, requirements with respect to the following matters: (i) Re-Disbursement, cash management and account reconciliation; (ii) funds control and documentation; (iii) accounting standards and systems; (iv) content and timing of reports; (v) preparing budget development procedures and the Compact implementation budget; (vi) policies concerning records, document disaster recovery and public availability of all financial information; (vii) procurement and contracting practices, including timely payment to vendors; (viii) inventory control; (ix) the role of independent auditors; (x) the roles of fiscal agents and procurement agents; (xi) separation of duties and internal controls; and (xii) certifications, powers, authorities and delegations.

(d) *Permitted Accounts.* The Government shall establish, or cause to be established, such accounts (each, a "***Permitted Account***," and collectively "***Permitted Accounts***") as may be agreed by the Parties in writing from time to time, including:

(i) A single, completely separate U.S. Dollar interest-bearing account (the "***Special Account***") at a commercial bank, subject to MCC approval, that is procured through a competitive process;

(ii) If necessary, an interest-bearing local currency of Benin account (the "***Local Account***") at a commercial bank, subject to MCC approval, that is procured through a competitive process to which the Fiscal Agent may authorize transfer from any U.S. Dollar Permitted Account for the purpose of making Re-Disbursements payable in local currency; and

(iii) Such other interest-bearing accounts to receive MCC Disbursements in such banks as the Parties mutually agree upon in writing.

No other funds shall be commingled in a Permitted Account other than MCC Funding and Accrued Interest thereon. All MCC Funding held in an interest-bearing Permitted Account shall earn interest at a rate of no less than such amount as the Parties may agree in the respective Bank Agreement or otherwise. MCC shall have the right, among other things, to view any Permitted Account statements and activity directly on-line, where feasible, or at such other frequency as the Parties may otherwise agree. By such time as shall be specified in the Disbursement Agreement or as otherwise agreed by the Parties, the Government shall ensure that MCA-Benin enters into an agreement with each Bank, respectively, satisfactory to MCC, that sets forth the signatory authority, access rights, anti-money laundering and anti-terrorist financing provisions, and other terms related to the Permitted Account, respectively (each, a "***Bank Agreement***"). For purposes of this Compact, the banks holding an account referenced in Sections 4(d) of this Program Annex are each a "***Bank***" and are collectively referred to as the "***Banks***."

(e) *Currency Exchange*. The Bank shall convert MCC Funding to the currency of Benin at a rate to which the parties to the Bank Agreement mutually agree with the Bank in the Bank Agreement, subject to MCC approval.

5. Transparency; Accountability.

Transparency and accountability to MCC and to the beneficiaries are important aspects of the Program and Projects. Without limiting the generality of the foregoing, in an effort to achieve the goals of transparency and accountability, the Government shall ensure that MCA-Benin:

(a) Establishes an e-mail suggestion box as well as a means for other written comments that interested persons may use to communicate ideas, suggestions or feedback to MCA-Benin.

(b) Considers as a factor in its decision-making the recommendations of the Board, particularly in MCA-Benin's deliberations over pending key Management decisions and key Board decisions as shall be specified in the relevant Governing Document.

(c) Develops and maintains the MCA-Benin Website in a timely, accurate and appropriately comprehensive manner, such MCA-Benin Website to include postings of information and documents in English and French.

(d) Posts on the MCA-Benin Website and otherwise makes publicly available via appropriate mediums (including radio and print) in the appropriate language the following documents or information from time to time:

(i) All minutes of the meetings of the Advisory Council and the meetings of the Board; *provided, however*, in certain instances of sensitivity and solely as specified and in accordance with the Governing Documents meeting minutes may be maintained solely in the corporate records of MCA-Benin without public release;

(ii) The M&E Plan, as amended from time to time, along with periodic reports on Program performance;

(iii) Such financial information as may be required by this Compact or as may otherwise be agreed from time to time by the Parties;

(iv) All Compact Reports;

(v) All audit reports by an Auditor and any periodic reports or evaluations by a Reviewer;

(vi) All relevant Environmental Impact Assessments and supporting documents, and such other environmental documentation as MCC may request;

(vii) A copy of the Disbursement Agreement, as amended from time to time;

(viii) A copy of any documents related to the formation, organization and governance of MCA-Benin including any Governing Documents, together with any amendments thereto;

(ix) A copy of the Procurement Agreement (including Procurement Guidelines), as amended from time to time and any procurement policies or procedures and standard documents; and

(x) A copy of information derived from each Procurement Plan, as specified in the Procurement Agreement, and all bid requests and awarded contracts.

SCHEDULE 1 to ANNEX I
ACCESS TO LAND PROJECT

This *Schedule 1* generally describes and summarizes the key elements of an Access to Land Project (the "***Land Project***") that the Parties intend to implement in furtherance of the Land Project Objective. Additional details regarding the implementation of the Land Project will be included in the Implementation Plan and in relevant Supplemental Agreements.

1. Background.

Insecure access to land is a determinant of poverty and a major barrier to income growth in Benin as reflected in the Government's Action Plan and the Poverty Reduction Strategy Document. Investment climate studies list land access among the top constraints to business development in Benin. Therefore, the Government's Access to Land proposal was met with strong civil society support. Inclusion of the Land Project in the Program reflects an understanding of the importance of sound property rights to overall economic growth and to the owners and users of land across Benin.

Currently, the title registration system is expensive, slow, and complex. For a small urban land parcel, titling and registration costs approximately $1,400 and can take up to two years to complete. As a result, only 1% of households hold a formal title to their land and a majority of the rural population relies on oral customary land rights. In urban areas, individuals occupy land under a weak administrative permit while enterprises occupy state land by concession. Land disputes are prevalent and are estimated to comprise more than 70% of all civil court cases in Benin. Women are often disadvantaged under current practices while investors are unable to acquire sites with confidence. Public investment in infrastructure is hindered by the lack of land use planning and adequate property tax administration. The lack of registered land rights also limits access to credit, particularly since Benin adheres to agreements under the Organization for Harmonization of Business Law in Africa ("***OHADA***") requiring land titles as a basis for pledging real property as collateral.

The Government is committed to changing this scenario. The Government has demonstrated a commitment to adopting improved laws, regulations, administrative processes and techniques to meet its ambitious land policy vision. It has already undertaken important legal reforms and experimented with new approaches to formalizing property rights. The Government's view of the importance of converting to titles, albeit in a progressive, voluntary approach, will be promoted and ways to make the process easier will be identified through this Project. With MCA support, a new land policy framework will be developed and over 100,000 households will attain registered land rights. The Land Project will serve both rural and urban areas and will lead to: significantly reduced time and costs to obtain titles and record transfers; fewer land disputes; and increased sense of land security. These improvements should, in turn, motivate investment and contribute, along with other Projects, to income growth.

2. Summary of Projects and Activities in Project and Expected Results.

The Land Project is designed to establish secure access to land and efficient land administration services. MCC Funding will support the following Project Activities:

- *Policy and Legal Reform:* To enable sustainable, efficient land registration services, gender equity, land dispute resolution and expanded use of land as collateral, MCC Funding will support legal, regulatory, administrative and informational reforms within a national land policy framework encompassing both rural and urban land.
- *Achieving Formal Property Rights to Land:* To provide citizens with more secure and useful records of their land rights, MCC Funding will support conversion of 30,000 occupancy permits to land titles in urban areas and formally document land rights to 300 rural villages directly benefiting around 85,000 households with certificates or titles.
- *Improve Land Registration Services and Land Information Management:* To reduce time and costs to register land and expand access to land information for public and private uses, MCC Funding will be used to upgrade and decentralize title registration services in twenty four communes and introduce map-based land information systems in twelve of these communes.
- *Information, Education and Communication:* To create broad awareness of land policy reform, especially among more vulnerable groups, in order to help citizens understand, protect and use their land rights.
- *Support Land Program Coordination:* To strengthen the capacity to manage the reform process and to encourage active participation of key stakeholder representatives, support policy and program coordination advisors, convene a Project steering group, and establish working groups for particular studies.

The M&E Plan (described in *Annex III*) will set forth anticipated results and, where appropriate, regular benchmarks that may be used to monitor implementation progress. Performance against these benchmarks and the overall impact of the Land Project will be assessed and reported at the intervals to be specified in the M&E Plan or as otherwise agreed by the Parties from time to time. The Parties expect that additional indicators will be identified during the implementation of the Land Project. The *expected results* from, and the *key benchmarks* to measure progress on the Project, Project Activities and sub-activities undertaken or funded under the Land Project are set forth in *Annex III.*

Estimated amounts of MCC Funding for each Project Activity for the Land Project are identified in *Annex II* of this Compact. Conditions precedent to each Land Project Activity and sequencing of these Project Activities shall be set forth in the Disbursement Agreement or other relevant Supplemental Agreements or component of the Implementation Plan.

The following summarizes the Land Project Activities:

(a) ***Project Activity: Policy and Legal Reform (the "Policy Activity")***

Building from the Government's commitment to land reform, under this Policy Activity, MCC funds will support three-stages to establish a more cohesive, functional land policy. The three stages are analysis, policy formulation and legal reform. This Policy Activity is national in scope and will address both urban and rural issues. MCA-Benin shall take account of the relevant outputs of the Policy Activity, as described below, in the full Implementation Plan (to be adopted following the completion of the relevant assessments in this Policy Activity). It is also anticipated that the Policy Activity will affect the implementation strategy to be used for certain other Land Project activities or sub-activities.

Detailed assessments of a series of topics will be produced by commissioned experts working in consultation with key stakeholder representatives. As a result, decision-makers will be better informed of best options for detailing the legal, administrative and technical solutions needed to achieve secure land rights and efficient land access. Based on the assessment process, a Land Policy White Paper will be prepared to guide public and private actors regarding the reform process. Endorsement from senior Government of Benin officials, including all relevant Ministers will be sought by MCA-Benin. The Policy Activity will also support drafting of a National Land Policy Decree, drafting of any needed legislation and/or amendments, and, finally, the compilation of land laws into a new Land Code to reinforce cohesiveness.

MCC Funding will support the following activities:

(i) Conduct of assessments that will inform policy decisions and Land Project implementation strategies. The assessments will further clarify issues and provide recommendations for refining the reform strategy. Efficiency, affordability, sustainability, gender equity, and the ability to manage the reform process with minimum risk will be considered. The assessments listed below will be conducted by experts and MCA-Benin will convene working groups of stakeholder representatives that will consult on the terms of reference for and the preparation of the assessments described below. MCA-Benin shall ensure that the results of these assessments are incorporated as relevant in the complete and final Work Plans for the activities described in Sections 2(b)–(d) of this *Schedule 1*. The assessments shall include the following topics, unless otherwise agreed by the Parties:

(1) A review of current practice and proposed reforms related to the administrative structure and functions of national, regional and local agencies involved in implementation of land policy; clarify roles and responsibilities and propose an approach to achieve greater operational efficiency and coherence;

(2) A review of the processes for titling (conversion) and registration to identify specific bottlenecks to an accelerated, quality implementation pace, including a review of technical norms, administrative procedures, evidences accepted and proofs required to participate; taxes, fees and budget parameters; and the technical specifications of the certification processes (particularly of the Plan Foncier Rural "***PFR***"); make recommendations for changes to make the process more affordable and/or efficient and its results more sustainable;

(3) An assessment of the number and types of land conflicts encountered in the past under rural and urban pilot activities and how/if these conflicts have been resolved; recommend a strategy for strengthening the capacity to resolve land conflicts under formal and informal means;

(4) An analysis of how to effectively improve women's access to land and the security of their tenure; propose a gender strategy on policy, legal, administrative, and/or project implementation measures and provide guidelines for its implementation;

(5) Following the completion of the assessment described in paragraph (1) above, compare technology options to meet information management needs at national, regional and local levels including mapping data, registration data, land market information and land use planning; compare initial investment costs as well as implied operational and maintenance costs and capacity to sustain the systems; and

(6) An analysis of the operational modalities for the communes in implementing the proposed new rural land law and related financing needs; make recommendations for the content for the regulations to this law.

(ii) Development, formalization and dissemination of a new land policy framework for Benin, that draws on the assessments conducted under the sub-activity described in Section 2(a)(i) above:

(1) Draft and promote a Land Policy White Paper covering rural and urban land and addressing the findings of the assessments conducted under sub-activity described in Section 2(a)(i); seek its immediate endorsement by relevant senior Government of Benin officials for use in implementation of Projects and also a legislative mandate for compliance with its key provisions;

(2) Upon completion of sub-activity described in Section 2(a)(i) above, prepare a new procedural manual for the transformation of urban and rural certificates into land titles;

(3) Review of relevant current law and proposed legislation compared to the requirements of the Land Policy White Paper;

(4) Based on the conclusions reached in paragraph 3 of this Section 2(a)(ii), support the drafting of new or amended laws and regulations as called for such that the resulting body of land legislation removes disincentives to register land rights and transactions, facilitates compliance with relevant agreements under OHADA; and safeguards vulnerable populations to the extent feasible from risks and undue tax burdens;

(5) Following completion of the sub-activity described in paragraph (4) of this Section 2(a)(ii), support the preparation of a draft unified Land Code for submission to Parliament; and

(6) Conduct public consultation on and dissemination of the new legislation and procedures.

(b) ***Project Activity: Achieving Formal Property Rights (the "Registration Activity")***

By providing roughly 115,000 citizens with more secure and useful property rights, this Registration Activity will demonstrate the effectiveness of Benin's new policy and approaches. Support will be provided for the conversion of urban housing land use permits into land titles in selected neighborhoods primarily in Cotonou, Parakou and Porto Novo. In roughly 300 selected rural villages, the recording of rural land rights through written land plans and certificates of customary ownership will be undertaken using an existing methodology. Additionally, converting rural land certificates to land titles will also be facilitated for beneficiaries that choose to participate. To facilitate progress in the Government's title conversion approach, the Registration Activity will support mapping and related technology improvements and will help communities to identify and resolve any case-specific issues that could arise during tenure formalization.

Specifically, MCC Funding will support the following:

(i) Expansion of formal registration of land rights in urban areas. Based on lessons learned in a pilot project recently conducted by the Government, improve and continue the process of transforming urban housing land permits to titles in selected neighborhoods in Cotonou, Parakou, Porto Novo and possibly other cities. For each neighborhood selected:

(1) Investigation of the current status of land tenure and records and take measures to organize data and prepare the areas for the conversion process;

(2) Organization and engagement of the community as active and informed participants in the conversion process; and

(3) Measurement and mapping individual parcels, conduct public review of parcel maps to gain agreement among community members on the boundaries indicated on the maps, and issuance of registered land titles (incorporating recommendations of the relevant assessments conducted under sub-activity described in Section 2(a)(i)).

(ii) Expansion of formal land rights in rural areas. Consistent with existing standards and guidelines, expand the creation of rural land plans, land tenure certificates and local land management capacity:

(1) For each rural commune meeting the site selection criteria and chosen by MCA-Benin for participation, (A) conduct of information campaigns, (B) assessment of the socio-economic and land tenure conditions of villages in the area and (C) prepare village profiles including documentation of any location-specific land tenure terms and norms;

(2) Based on the conclusions reached in paragraph (1) above and the application of the more general site selection criteria to the villages within each commune, final selection of villages for implementing the PFR process;

(3) For selected villages, production of land use and tenure maps (the PFR) using a participatory method and submission of the plan for public review and comment; and

(4) Based on the PFR, issuance of rural land use certificates and facilitation of formal, written records of subordinate land rights such as tenancies using improved approaches (e.g., standard lease template).

(iii) Facilitation of voluntary, "on-demand" conversion of rural land certificates into land titles. Conversion of rural land certificates to land titles through an efficient, affordable process. Priority will be given to villages that already have a PFR in place.

(iv) Improvements in capacity for mapping and surveying. To facilitate more rapid registration of land rights and to establish databases that support land information services e.g., for planning and fiscal purposes and for land market research, support the following actions, incorporating as relevant recommendations from sub-activity described in Section 2(a)(i):

(1) Creation of up-to-date digital imagery of Benin's land resources;

(2) Creation of regional scale maps for selected areas of the country indicating major topographic features and infrastructure systems, such regional scale maps will be an important tool to the production of an integrated set of parcel maps generated through the process of property rights formalization; and

(3) Following the completion of the design strategy described in Section 2(d)(iii), training for public and private professionals in use of digital imagery and in improved surveying and mapping techniques.

(v) Improvement of local capacity to adapt to changing land tenure and use patterns and to resolve case-specific issues that might arise during the implementation of land tenure reforms by:

(1) Supporting communes in rural areas to develop improved social programs and planning for the specific needs of landless peasants and migrants;

(2) Supporting the provision of paralegal, informational and other advisory services related to land access and tenure security to citizens who otherwise would not have access to such services;

(3) Improvement of the capacity of citizens, local authorities and tribunals to resolve disputes related to land tenure;

(4) Establishment of transitional measures, in urban areas, to protect the rights of land occupants with certificates who delay or opt-out of the conversion process; and

(5) In a few pilot sites, introduction of the use of parcel layout plans in irregularly developed neighborhoods as a step prior to the permit-title conversion process (any site in which such plans would call for resettlement of persons to sites outside the neighborhood prior to the conversion of permits to titles may not be selected for participation).

The activities contemplated under this Registration Activity may begin with preparatory activities such as those described in Sections 2(b)(i)(1) and (2), 2(b)(ii)(1) and (2), and 2(b)(v) above under a provisional work plan; *provided, however*, full implementation will require a complete and final work plan which adopts, to MCC's satisfaction, the recommendations and findings of the relevant reports produced under the Project Activity described in Section 2(a)(i).

(c) ***Project Activity: Improve Land Registration Services and Land Information Management (the "Services and Information Activity")***

To launch the process of moving Benin's land registration system services to the local level, new offices of the national property registry will be established (i.e., deconcentration), and, select communes will be supported as authority is transferred to them to manage their land (i.e., decentralization). This Activity will help design, equip and adequately staff new local registry offices. Communes should be chosen from among those in which implementation of the Registration Activity will occur, unless otherwise agreed in writing with MCC. Some communes will also experiment with a cadastre or parcel-based registration system that may include additional land information used for planning and fiscal purposes. Finally, the Services and Information Activity will help make reliable land market information (e.g., recent sales and prices) available for use by households, investors and public offices.

Pending completion of the relevant studies in Policy Activity and incorporation of the recommendations into implementation plans, MCC Funding will support the design and implementation of more accessible, efficient, reliable land registration and information services. The implementation strategy for each sub-activity described below in paragraphs (i), (ii) and (iii) shall promote, to the extent practicable, the harmonization of national, regional, and communal land data and uses including the mapping and certificate lists generated during the PFR process.

Specifically, MCC Funding will support:

(i) Deconcentration of the National Land Registration Services.

(1) The establishment of regional offices in Benin's 12 prefectures and communal service offices in 24 selected communes; and

(2) In the offices established pursuant to paragraph (1) of this Section 2(c)(i), replacement of the manual system of document administration with an automated, digital records

management system and training of land registry office staff in the operation of these systems.

(ii) Decentralization of Land Administration.

(1) Assist in development of capacity of approximately 50 communes for land administration, such assistance to include training, acquisition of equipment and transitional operational support; and

(2) Design and implementation of a pilot parcel-based or cadastre-registration system in 12 of the communes where MCC Funding will support decentralization; this sub-activity will support a more comprehensive, systematic approach to the establishment of a cadastre may be demonstrated in three of these twelve communes (one rural, one urban and one peri-urban).

(iii) Design and establishment of an electronic national land market data system.

(iv) Provision of technical assistance, training (consistent with the design strategy completed pursuant to Section 2(d)(iii)) and in relation to the capacity to manage and to quality control the land information systems established in (i) and (ii) of this Section 2(c).

(d) ***Project Activity: Information, Education and Communication ("IEC") (the "IEC Activity")***

MCA-Benin has an opportunity to promote good governance through appropriate transparency and consultation on the Project throughout the Compact Term. Moreover, informed and widespread participation in planning, dispute resolution and decision-making are necessary for an effective system of land registration. The IEC Activity will ensure citizens have a clear understanding of their rights and responsibilities, and are able to participate fully in the new processes of planning, land securitization and dispute resolution.

Specifically, MCC Funding will support IEC campaigns throughout the Compact Term to include but not limited to the following topics (other topics for these campaigns may be implemented, subject to MCC approval):

(i) Creation of broad awareness and understanding of the changing land policy regime and how it affects the rights of citizens; new processes and services; gender considerations, and, land markets and access to credit.

(ii) Conduct of specific public notice and awareness of each activity and sub-activity and of the results relevant to particular groups or communities.

(iii) Design of a training strategy precedent to implementation of any training in the Registration Activity or Services and Information Activity.

(e) ***Project Activity: Support Strategy and Programmatic Coordination (the "Support Strategy Activity")***

This Project Activity will ensure coordination across the various Project Activities and sub-Activities of the Land Project, across agencies involved in the land policy reform process, and facilitate ongoing consultation with stakeholder groups. In the near term, this is critical to the Project effectiveness in undertaking a comprehensive and diverse set of reform actions. By the end of the Compact Term, the MCA-Benin Access to Land Project division could be transformed into a national coordination unit to lead the completion of the reform implementation process over a longer time period.

Specifically, in addition to an overall Land Project Director and the ordinary Project-related operating expenses, MCC Funding will support:

(i) Complement MCA-Benin management staff with a group of professionals dedicated to "change management and coordination," namely a National Land Policy Reform Coordinator and a long term policy advisor familiar with international best practice in land administration. Among their roles are, potentially, to (A) lead the process of incorporation of the results of the Policy Activity into practice by both project implementing partners and more generally, in Benin; (B) provide guidance on policy and implementation oversight issues to senior Government officials and MCA-Benin management; (C) facilitate linkages with the Financial Services Project activities as relevant; (D) engage other donors in Project specific coordination; and, (E) respond to beneficiary requests and queries.

(ii) Establishment (including rules regarding selection, composition, roles and frequency of meetings) and convening of a Steering Group for periodic consultations on the implementation of the Land Project e.g., the development of annual work plans, key terms of reference, draft reports and otherwise as appropriate; including key stakeholder representatives, at least one person from each of the MCA-Benin Finance Services Project and the Justice Project divisions, and a gender expert.

(iii) Convening of discussion groups for each of the assessments in Section (2)(a)(i) and for the White Paper and corresponding legal reform work.

(iv) Selection of sites for activities undertaken under this Project. Sites shall be chosen by applying selection criteria developed by MCA-Benin, subject to MCC approval, in a fair and transparent manner. MCA-Benin will publicize, including posting on the MCA-Benin Website, both the criteria for selection and the actual sites chosen, giving a brief justification for each site. These criteria will ensure that sites have the following characteristics, among others: representation of the North, South and Central regions of Benin; sites that exhibit both poverty and near-term economic opportunity e.g., urbanizing areas, high-value crop production sites, and places where market participation is expanding; willingness to comply with Benin's Family Code; site of activity under the Financial Services Project and the Justice Project; and location within the scope of the decentralized registry and land information systems to be established under Services and Information Activity set forth in Section 2(c) of this *Schedule 1*. These characteristics will be strategic to choosing sites that will more readily experience near-term, economically meaningful results including for the poor and women. The completion of this site selection shall be a condition precedent to certain activities under this Project.

(v) Strengthening of the National Land Commission for the transformation of urban land permits to titles by providing the resources and guidance to enhance the quality and quantity of work it can perform.

3. Beneficiaries.

The Land Project will encourage investment in urban and rural land. A new policy framework will enable a progressive transition between customary and administrative land management to markets and a title registration system. With lower transactions costs and fewer disputes, the climate for investment, productivity and finance will be improved. The Land Project will strengthen women's land rights under the law and, more importantly, work to ensure the new family code is practiced widely. In Cotonou, Porto-Novo and Parakou, the three main cities in Benin, up to 30,000 properties currently under administrative certificates will have titles. In twenty four selected rural communes, as many as 83,000 families in 300 villages will receive a certificate, which can be subsequently turned into a land title. Other rural land users, without full ownership rights, will also have recorded agreements. Accurate land rights information will benefit potential local and international investors, including Benin's diaspora. For example, reliable and cost-effective inquiries of local records will be possible before entering leases or purchasing land. Finally, there will be better capacity for local planning and tax administration which will benefit local municipalities and civil society.

Roughly 115,000 rural and urban households will have more secure and useful tenure, affordable access to reliable land related information and services; a 50% reduction in court cases related to land disputes is targeted, and a modest 10% to 20% investment response is expected to boost income earning opportunities.

4. Donor Coordination; Private Sector; Role of Civil Society.

In rural Benin, both Deutsche Gesellschaft für Technische Zusammenarbeit ("***GTZ***") GmbH (German) and Agence Française de Développement ("***AFD***") (French) have supported successful land use pilot projects under the Program for Natural Resources Conservation and Management. A first phase of these pilot projects has recently ended and both donors have expressed interested in continuing this work. The approach has been standardized and guidelines established which will be used in implementation of this Project.

In urban areas the Government recently completed a pilot titling project that had positive but limited results. The limited results were due to substantial titling fees, a reluctance to being the initial participant ("first adopter"), insufficient public outreach, and administrative problems relating to certificates previously pledged as collateral. These limitations were identified in the Proposal and will be further addressed in the Implementation Plan for the Registration Activity.

The "Transformation of Assets into Usable Capital in the Least Developed Countries" project initiated by the International Land Coalition has chosen Benin as a pilot country. Under this International Land Coalition initiative, the UNDP will support a stakeholder analysis that could be used to refine the relevant components of the Project Activity Implementation Plans. The Foreign Investors Advisory Service of the International Finance Corporation ("***IFC***") will soon complete a study of land access and investment. Their preliminary recommendations are generally consistent with this Project, with some sub-activities herein having been derived from it.

Private professionals, e.g., surveyors, are currently called on by the government to implement tasks within the formalization process. To the extent feasible, the Land Project will promote outsourcing and development of private sector services related to land registration and land markets. Among the key stakeholders that will guide the project implementation planning and participate in the studies undertaken pursuant to the Policy Activity, are bankers and businessmen and civil society organizations, e.g., women's groups. These are the end-users of the improved formal property registration system and their perspectives will provide much-needed insight into final definition of land policy and of the most practical approaches to implementation.

5. U.S. Agency for International Development.

No USAID projects focus specifically on land access and security in Benin. However, MCA-Benin will continue to dialogue with USAID to identify areas in which it can complement or coordinate with e.g., women's legal aid.

6. Sustainability.

One of the prime concerns that will underlie the series of evaluations conducted in the Policy Activity is the need to ensure that investments can be sustained and that near-term results translate into long-term sustainable change. The Government has set ambitious targets for decreasing costs of land titling and registration and will be considering further rationalizing fee structures. The final choice of technical solutions for information management and for supporting the process of formalizing land tenure will be chosen on a best-value for cost in the specific context of Benin. The extensive consultation, information dissemination and training embedded across all the Project Activities will reinforce consensus and make it more likely that people can take advantage of the new land policy framework. The review of the law will identify and address disincentives to keep land records formal over time. All together, these features lend themselves to sustainability.

7. Policy; Legal Reform; and Procedural Changes.

The Parties have identified the following policy, legal and regulatory reforms and actions that the Government shall pursue in support, and to reach the full benefits, of the Land Project, the satisfactory implementation of which will be conditions precedent to certain MCC Disbursements as provided in the Disbursement Agreement:

(a) Undertake policy, legal and/or procedural changes as called for in the final approved assessment reports produced under the Policy Activity: to simplify, streamline and make affordable all processes related to formal registration of land rights;

(b) Endorse a Land Policy White Paper produced in conjunction with this Project; issue a National Land Policy Decree endorsing its vision, adopt a law requiring compliance with it and pass a unified Land Code to consolidate the body of law that affects land rights;

(c) Reform laws, regulations and administrative processes as needed to remove constraints to the use of land as collateral;

(d) Undertake measures to improve the enforcement of Benin's Family Code, Rural Code, and other legislation, as identified in the gender strategy undertaken pursuant to the Policy Activity, which give and protect women's rights to land; and

(e) Undertake measures to ensure the property taxes do not discourage registration of land transactions and that safeguard against undue tax burdens.

8. Proposals.

Under the Land Project, public solicitations for proposals are anticipated to procure goods and services, as needed, to implement all Land Project Activities. MCA-Benin will develop, subject to MCC approval, a process for consideration of both such proposals. While competitive procurement will be the norm for this Land Project, MCA-Benin may also consider, using a process developed subject to MCC approval, any unsolicited proposals it might receive.

Under Strategy Support Activity of this Land Project, a Land Project Steering Group and several working groups will be comprised to guide implementation planning and implementation of the assessments to be conducted under the Policy Activity. MCA-Benin will determine the number and types of participants in these groups. A public call for expressions of interest to participate will be made and candidates will be selected by a panel comprised of MCA-Benin's Land Project Director, Finance Project Director and one other person to be determined by MCA-Benin with MCC approval. The composition of this panel shall be made publicly available as will be their final selection for any particular group.

This Land Project also involves selection of particular communes, villages or urban neighborhoods to participate in Project Activities described in Sections 2(b) and (c) of this *Schedule 1*. As described in Sections 2(b) and (c), selection criteria for identifying communes, villages or urban neighborhoods to participate and a method to apply these will be developed by MCA-Benin, subject to MCC approval. The criteria, method and final selections (including justifications) will be made known to the public. In addition, MCA-Benin will incorporate into the method for applying the selection criteria a process for consideration of unsolicited offers of participation by particular communes, villages or urban neighborhoods.

SCHEDULE 2 to ANNEX I
ACCESS TO FINANCIAL SERVICES PROJECT

This *Schedule 2* generally describes and summarizes the key elements of the Access to Financial Services Project (the "***Financial Services Project***") that the Parties intend to implement in furtherance of the Financial Services Objective. Additional details regarding the implementation of the Financial Services Project will be included in the Implementation Plan and in relevant Supplemental Agreements.

1. Background.

Benin has a shallow financial sector that provides limited services to micro and small- and medium-scale enterprises (one or more of such categories of enterprises, "***MSMEs***"), particularly those that are involved directly or indirectly in the production of goods in Benin. For example, the banking sector, while possessing significant liquidity, has focused much of its credit services on short-term financings and on larger companies, such as multinationals with branches in Benin. Savings services in Benin have had limited penetration, with only a small fraction of the population owning a bank account. Although the microfinance sector is relatively vibrant in Benin, it faces significant challenges, including the weak institutional capacity of many MFIs and the need for additional monitoring and supervision. Moreover, much of the financial sector has focused on urban areas and on short-term commerce rather than long-term production.

The following factors contribute to the limited scope of financial services to MSMEs:

- High transaction costs, especially in rural areas;
- Lack of reliable information on clients;
- Lack of creditworthiness of many borrowers;
- Limited resources and capacity of some of the financial intermediaries; and
- Perceived risk of clients, in part due to lack of sufficient collateral (such as title) and the inability of lenders to effectively enforce debts or sell collateral upon default, and price and yield risks inherent in agriculture.

These factors constrain the growth of MSMEs in Benin. The high cost or unavailability of credit and other financial services, including savings, limits the capacity of small businesses in Benin to expand production and employment, to respond to business opportunities and to manage risk. Accordingly, alleviating these constraints, and creating a broader and deeper financial sector, should increase incomes of the poor that own, are employed by, or do business with MSMEs.

2. Summary of Projects and Activities in Project and Expected Results.

The Financial Services Project is designed to improve the ability of MSMEs, particularly those directly or indirectly involved in production in Benin, to access financial services that will help them improve the sustainability of their businesses.

The Financial Services Project includes the following two Project Activities:

- *Financial Institution and Borrower Capacity Building Activity*: This Project Activity aims to (a) improve the capacity of financial institutions to expand existing or establish new services for MSMEs and (b) improve the capacity of MSMEs to access and use expanded financial services productively by improving their creditworthiness; and
- *Financial Enabling Environment Activity*: This Project Activity will undertake to identify and support legal and policy changes that are needed to facilitate the expansion of the financial sector in Benin.

The M&E Plan (described in *Annex III*) will set forth anticipated results and, where appropriate, regular benchmarks that may be used to monitor implementation progress. Performance against these benchmarks and the overall impact of Financial Services Project will be assessed and reported at the intervals to be specified in the M&E Plan or as otherwise agreed by the Parties from time to time. The Parties expect that additional indicators will be identified during the implementation of the Financial Services Project. The *expected results* from, and the *key benchmarks* to measure progress on, the Project, Project Activities and sub-activities undertaken or funded under the Financial Services Project are set forth in *Annex III*.

Estimated amounts of MCC Funding for each Project Activity for the Financial Services Project are identified in *Annex II* of this Compact. Conditions precedent to each Financial Services Project Activity and sequencing of these Project Activities shall be set forth in the Disbursement Agreement or other relevant Supplemental Agreements or applicable component of the Implementation Plan.

The following summarizes the Financial Services Project Activities:

(a) ***Project Activity: Financial Institution and Borrower Capacity Building (the "Capacity Building Activity")***

The overall goal of this Project Activity is to broaden and deepen the financial sector in Benin by improving both the supply of and demand for financial services. It is intended to build the capacity of financial institutions, as well as to improve MSMEs' creditworthiness and ability to use financial services productively.

This Project Activity involves two sub-activities:

- Demand and feasibility assessments; and
- A financial innovation and expansion challenge facility ("***FINECF***" or the "***Challenge Facility***")

(i) Demand and Feasibility Assessments. This sub-activity is intended to help shape the criteria and guidelines for the Challenge Facility described in Section 2(a)(ii), and to build on existing studies and improve the quality of information available to potential applicants. Satisfactory completion of these studies, and dissemination of the key findings, shall therefore be conditions precedent to the Challenge Facility. The below studies shall be conducted by an expert or experts retained after an international competitive procurement; terms of reference and procurement for these studies shall be subject to MCC approval. The results of the studies may be further divided or combined into one or more reports, so long as they cover the topics mentioned below or such other topics as the Parties may agree in writing. MCC and MCA-Benin shall consider cost structures where public and private costs for the studies are shared, with the private portion to expand over time.

MCC Funding, together with potential parallel or co-financing from other sources, shall support the following:

(1) Conduct of demand study for services to MSMEs. This will study the demand for innovative and expanded financial services (especially credit and savings) that may be provided to MSMEs by MFIs, banks and other financial institutions. To the extent practical, the study will assess demand particularly among MSMEs involved in production in Benin and in areas where Land Project is likely to be active.

(2) Conduct of economic feasibility and cost assessment. An economic feasibility and cost assessment will determine the effectiveness of certain MFI investments in technologies that have the potential to reduce operating costs, increase the scale of operations and expand services to MSMEs in previously underserved regions and sectors. The

technologies that may be explored and identified include, without limitation, smart cards, e-payment systems, management information systems, and biometric technology. To the extent practical, these studies will focus on MFIs operating in areas where the Land Project is likely to be active.

(3) Conduct of demand study for business development services. This will study the demand for, and capacity within Benin to supply, business development services ("***BDS***") to MSMEs involved in agricultural and non-agricultural sectors. In order to determine capacity to supply such services, the study will investigate specialized BDS providers, MFIs and agricultural and rural organizations. To the extent practical, these studies will focus on BDS in areas where the Land Project is likely to be active.

(4) Conduct of follow-up research and studies or assessments, as needed during the Compact Term, in the areas covered by the studies and assessments, set forth in paragraphs (1)–(3) of this sub-activity or other similar types of studies.

(ii) Financial Innovation and Expansion Challenge Facility. MCC Funding shall support a demand-driven and competitive mechanism that will co-fund with participants technical assistance and capacity building for both financial institutions and MSMEs. This mechanism requires potential beneficiaries to compete for support based on transparent criteria and to contribute a significant portion of the project costs. These elements help ensure that resources are directed to the most motivated institutions and to the most promising projects. MCC Funding shall finance up to 66% of the cost of selected projects with the share funded by MCC Funding decreasing over time (this is a cap, and in some cases the program criteria may set a lower percentage of support by MCC Funding). Operating costs shall not be eligible for support and the remainder of a project's costs must be provided by private enterprises (which may include NGOs). The Challenge Facility shall emphasize and encourage support for local service providers.

A qualified independent management entity or entities shall manage and implement the Challenge Facility (the "***Facility Manager***"), acceptable to MCC and MCA-Benin, selected after a competitive tender. Funding for the Challenge Facility shall be conditioned upon: (a) feasibility and demand studies having been satisfactorily concluded; (b) terms of reference and procurement of Facility Manager being satisfactory to MCC and (c) operating guidelines and criteria for each Component of Challenge Facility having been developed in form and substance satisfactory to MCC. The Challenge Facility itself will not be making debt or equity investments or issuing guarantees to recipients of support; however, its support, it is expected, will enable institutions to better mobilize that capital from others.

MCC Funding will support the following activities, to be undertaken in the manner described:

(1) Identification of viable applicants. The Facility Manger shall filter expressions of interest and identify viable applicants for the three facility components described below in paragraph (7).

(2) Provision of guidance to applicants and development of operating manual. The Facility Manager will provide guidance to applicants throughout the application procedure; including guiding viable applicants through the process of preparing a brief concept note for review, and ultimately providing assistance with development of the full application. Challenge Facility funds shall assist (where appropriate, based on need) in the development of applications that submit a concept note with significant potential. The Facility Manager shall develop a policy as part of the operating manual that will identify criteria for this assistance.

(3) Review of applications and selection of funding awards. Following submission of applications, an independent panel (the "***Panel***") shall review applications and make

awards based on selection criteria described below and subject to MCC approval. MCA-Benin shall post on the MCA-Benin Website the names and descriptions of applications that receive awards, including amounts of awards.

(4) Development of award criteria. The Facility Manager shall develop (A) award criteria consistent with paragraph (6) below and (B) an operating procedures manual, each subject to MCC and MCA-Benin approval. In developing the award criteria, efforts shall be made to support activities that extend financial services to places outside Cotonou where the Land Project is (or is likely to be) active. Awards, if practical, will be awarded in kind rather than in cash, where technical assistance or equipment or services are required. Unless otherwise agreed by the Parties, the Facility Manager shall be responsible for selecting the provider through a competitive tender, in accordance with the procurement guidelines that govern the Compact.

(5) Support of donor coordination related to the Project Activity. The Facility Manager, to the extent practical, shall support capacity building activities that leverage other donor support or enable the beneficiary to attract financing from other sources (for example, enabling an MFI to attract long-term financing from a bank or enabling an MSME to obtain a loan). MCA-Benin and the Facility Manager shall seek to coordinate with other donors to ensure that the MCA assistance is as effective as possible.

(6) Development of criteria for support by the Challenge Facility. The selection criteria for funding under the Components shall be determined by the Facility Manager, subject to approval by MCC and MCA-Benin. The Parties anticipate that the criteria will include (without limitation) the following categories:

(A) *Market demand* (there must be a demonstrated need for the project);

(B) *Impact* (the project must be expected to contribute, directly or indirectly, to improved incomes and opportunities for a substantial number of poor people; the applicant's commitment to gender issues will be a positive factor);

(C) *Effectiveness* (the project's impact must be expected to exceed its costs);

(D) *Implementation Capacity* (applicants must have the capacity to implement the project successfully);

(E) *Demonstration effect* (the project must be unlikely to be undertaken without the requested financial support. In particular, projects suggested by for-profit entities, while permitted, shall be scrutinized. In addition, pilot projects shall be preferred over projects that involve larger, untested ideas);

(F) *Commitment* (applicants must show their commitment through the share of project funding they are willing to contribute);

(G) *Sustainability* (the project must be expected to lead to the improved financial sustainability of funding recipients, and the impact of the project must be expected to extend beyond the termination of funding);

(H) *Timing* (the financial support of the project must be completed prior to the termination of the proposed Program);

(I) *Limitations on Use of Funding* (the proposed project must comply with the limitations on use and treatment of MCC Funding as set forth in Section 2.3 of this Compact); and

(J) *Other* (the Facility Manager shall develop such other selection criteria for Components, including any criteria unique to particular Component).

MCA-Benin shall post on the MCA-Benin Website the selection criteria developed by the Facility Manager, as approved by MCC and MCA-Benin.

(7) Implementation of Challenge Facility Projects. Unless otherwise agreed by the Parties, there shall be the following three sub-facilities (each a "***Component***" and each described more fully below) and to be funded equally; *provided, however*, there may be changes in allocations between the Components, subject to MCC approval:

- The Innovation Component;
- The Institutional Strengthening Component; and
- The MSME Business Development Component.

Support under each Component is expected to range from $25,000 to $250,000 per institution. Applications can come from individual institutions or groups of up to ten institutions with one institution taking the lead. Where the total project cost exceeds $500,000, the application shall be subject to heightened review and additional selection criteria. A call for applications shall be made up to twice per year, and the guidelines and criteria will be clearly communicated. Applications must be supported by a sound business plan by one of the eligible parties. In the event MCA-Benin receives any unsolicited written applications or proposals and such proposals have not been otherwise submitted to the Facility Manager through the call for applications, MCA-Benin shall forward such applications to the Facility Manager. The Facility Manager will evaluate such unsolicited applications in the same manner as those received through the call and identify viable applications in accordance with paragraph (1) above.

(A) The *Innovation Component* shall support financial institutions (non-banks and banks) that expand their product offering to MSMEs in previously underserved regions and sectors or introduce innovative technologies that lead to economies of scale and reduced operating costs and risks. For example, funding may be used to support investments in technology, management information or communications services, or to provide technical assistance and staff training to assist with the design, implementation and marketing of new financial products or services.

(B) The *Institutional Strengthening Component* shall seek to strengthen the capacity of selected microfinance institutions in Benin by improving internal controls, transparency, management, and ability to access additional stable financial resources from commercial banks and investors at reduced costs. As a result, MFIs shall be able to provide better quality and cheaper products and services to MSMEs. This Component shall fund technical assistance and grants for equipment or supplies to build capacity within MFIs that significantly serve MSMEs. Unless otherwise agreed by the Parties, 10% of grants under this Component shall go to each of the following:

(i) Promotion of transparency and good governance at MFIs, such as external audits and ratings and internal controls.

(ii) Improvement of management/analysis of long-term credit extended by MFIs with national or regional scope.

(iii) Training or other mechanisms to improve the ability of MFI management to access long-term financing and other stable resources.

(iv) Assistance with compliance with regulatory requirements.

(v) Evaluations of, and technical assistance to improve, operating capacity and efficiency of MFIs.

(C) The *MSME Business Development Component* shall support business development services for agricultural and non-agricultural MSMEs. The objective is to improve access to finance by improving the MSMEs' creditworthiness and ability to use financial services productively. This Component may include the following types of funding:

(i) Funding to financial institutions, such as MFIs: Assistance designed to improve financial literacy and business management (including through improved marketing, internal controls and accounting), as well as to improve the ability of borrowers to complete credit applications and access credit.

(ii) Funding to rural networks and organizations (such as co-ops and associations): Training and technology to agricultural and rural networks and organizations that present plans to build the creditworthiness and productivity of their MSME members.

(iii) Funding to specialized BDS providers: Training and technology to assist local specialized business development service providers in improving their capacity to provide sustainable services.

(8) Monitoring of progress of the Challenge Facility projects. Funding agreements with entities receiving benefits shall include annual performance benchmarks to indicate progress in meeting objectives, with the form of such agreements subject to the approval of MCA-Benin and MCC and will be specified as conditions to certain Re-Disbursements for the selected Challenge Facility project. In the case of the Institutional Strengthening Component, this might include items such as capitalization and other financial reporting requirements. In the case of the Innovation Component, this might include items such as increased amount of services, number of new clients for all services and number of new credit clients. Failure to meet these benchmarks may lead to termination of project support and in some cases a requirement that the entity repay a portion of the assistance received. Repaid funds shall be used as grant funding to finance other activities under the Challenge Facility.

(9) Conduct of information, education, and communications campaign. To improve the quality and responsiveness of proposals, a portion of the MCC Funding for FINECF shall be used to support market information campaigns. The campaigns shall inform potential applicants about FINECF's objectives and guidelines for targeted technical assistance and grants. Where appropriate, certain trainings, technical assistance, and services will be provided through FINECF to incorporate information on strategies for avoiding environmental and social risks, using environmental and social review criteria and enhancing the sustainability of loans.

(b) ***Project Activity: Financial Enabling Environment Activity (the "Financial Enabling Environment Activity")***

The objective of the Financial Enabling Environment Activity is to identify and support legal and policy changes that are needed to facilitate the deepening and expansion of the financial sector in Benin.

The Financial Enabling Environment Activity consists of the following sub-activities:

- *Strengthening of Microfinance Supervision*: Support for Cellule de Microfinance ("***Cellule***"), microfinance supervisory authority in the Ministry of Finance, and for audits of microfinance institutions.
- *Multi-stakeholder forums*: Conduct of electronic and/or physical forums to discuss potential improvements to laws and policies relating to an expanded financial sector and use of land titles as collateral.
- *Improvement of regulatory environment*: Support for financial sector regulatory changes by funding the analysis of and advocacy for such changes.
- *Credit Bureau capacity building*: Building the capacity of the MFI credit information bureau so that it can track the payment history of borrowers more accurately.
- *Land titles as collateral*: Provision of support to assist ability of financial institutions to use land titles as collateral in loans or refinancings.

MCC Funding will support the following activities:

(i) Strengthening of Microfinance Supervision.

(1) Build capacity of the Ministry of Finance and Economy's Cellule de Microfinance, which currently serves as the supervisory authority for microfinance in Benin, by providing support in areas such as technical assistance, training, and acquisition of software and equipment. The goal of this support is to improve the supervision, transparency and governance of MFIs in Benin. MCC Funding will not be used for salaries of Cellule staff. This sub-activity will improve the capacity of the Cellule to increase its monitoring and licensing activities and use resources more effectively;

(2) Improvement of rules and procedures for microfinance. An outside advisor shall be engaged to work with the Cellule to improve rules and procedures in Benin regarding microfinance, and improve the efficiency and effectiveness of the Cellule. It is intended that the advisor shall come for approximately two weeks a quarter, at least for the first year, with limited follow-up visits thereafter; and

(3) Conduct of audits of microfinance institutions, with the goal of further strengthening the supervision of MFIs in Benin. Institutions to be audited will be recommended by the Cellule, with the criteria for selection submitted to MCC for approval. Funding for audits will be conditioned on the development by the Ministry of Finance and Economy of a plan, approved by MCC, for the sustainability of the conduct of audits beyond the Compact Term.

(ii) Multi-stakeholder forums.

(1) Design workshops and electronic forums to promote the discussion and exchange of ideas on policies and strategies for expanding access to financial services. Where relevant, implementers of other Projects in this Program (especially Land Project and Justice Project) will also have representatives involved in the design and implementation of these forums; and

(2) Conduct of workshops and electronic forums designed under paragraph (1) above. Topics for these forums shall be approved by MCC and MCA-Benin and are expected to include, for example (1) actions and initiatives needed to ensure successful use of land titles as collateral for loans (with the participation of the implementers of the Land Project, including the MCA-Benin Land Project division); and (2) legal and regulatory hurdles, at the national and regional level, to development and implementation of

expanded financial services and new products. The Government, including the Ministry of Finance, shall participate in these forums and respond to reasonable issues raised therein. The presentations to and results or feedback generated from these forums shall be posted on the MCA-Benin Website.

(iii) Improvement of regulatory environment. Following completion of initial multi-stakeholder forums convened pursuant to paragraph (ii) above, MCC Funding shall support analysis of, and advocacy for, changes in West African regional and Benin national regulations of the financial sector that are intended to expand access to financial services prudently. On an annual basis, areas of focus for these regulatory changes shall be agreed upon between MCC and MCA-Benin, and are expected to include the priority reforms identified in the multi-stakeholder forums described above. Other stakeholders may, at this stage, present to MCA-Benin unsolicited proposals for interventions or activities that were not identified in the multi-stakeholder forums. In implementing these activities, MCA-Benin shall coordinate with other development organizations and government agencies involved in the financial sector in Benin and in West Africa.

MCC Funding will support the following:

(1) Technical assistance in identifying areas of regulatory reform; and

(2) Drafting of regulations and/or policy papers, and other acceptable advocacy and consensus building mechanisms in areas of regulatory focus approved by MCC and MCA-Benin of the areas of focus.

(iv) Credit bureau capacity building. To build the capacity of the Consortium Alafia (a microfinance trade association) credit information bureau, MCC Funding will support the following:

(1) Conduct of studies to assess demand, feasibility and cost-effectiveness of the recommended improvements; and

(2) Improvements to Consortium Alafia (a microfinance trade association) credit information bureau, following completion of the studies conducted pursuant to paragraph (1) above and subject to agreement between MCC and MCA-Benin that: there is sufficient demand, that the feasibility has been demonstrated, and that the proposed costs are acceptable. This activity will build capacity of the credit information bureau to track information and more precisely identify customers in a credit information database, including not just negative (i.e., missed payment) information, but also positive (i.e., satisfied payment) information of clients. The activity may also link the credit bureau database with databases that include bank customer data.

(v) Land titles as collateral for loans. This sub-activity will provide technical assistance and other capacity building for financial institutions, particularly MFIs, to support their ability to make title-based-loans or refinance portfolios of loans secured by land titles. The financial institutions to receive this assistance shall be selected based on criteria developed by MCA-Benin, subject to MCC approval. It is expected that these financial institutions shall be located or serve areas covered by the Land Project. MCA-Benin shall post on the MCA-Benin Website the selection criteria.

The activities MCC Funding will support under this sub-activity are expected to include, without limitation:

(1) Technical assistance to MFIs to improve credit management and assessment for secured loans and to assist them in using portfolios of secured loans as collateral for MFI financing obtained from banks;

(2) Development of standardized forms; and

(3) Installation of mechanisms of collaboration between financial institutions and land authorities to facilitate and accelerate the treatment of the files of application for credit.

3. Beneficiaries.

The principal beneficiaries of the Financial Services Project are expected to be people who own, are employed by, or do business with MSMEs in Benin. Particular efforts shall be made to reach MSMEs in traditionally underserved areas of the country, as well as in areas where the Land Project is likely to be active.

The urban and rural poor will benefit directly, due to their (or the MSME with whom they do business or are employed) gaining access to a broader and more effective menu of financial products and services. They will also benefit indirectly, because financial sector deepening has been shown to lead to economic growth and disproportionately benefit the poor. The Financial Services Project, in particular, will benefit poor women. When managed effectively, microfinance has significant economic and social benefits for women, and by strengthening the microfinance sector in Benin, this Project will extend these benefits to a larger percent of the population. Showing commitment to gender issues will be weighted positively in the criteria for allocating funding in FINECF.

4. Donor Coordination; Private Sector; Role of Civil Society.

Donor Coordination: The Financial Services Project complements the activities of other donors. The World Bank, United Nations Development Program, African Development Bank, and several bilateral donors have been active in MFI and other financial sector activities. The demand-driven nature of the FINECF and the requirement for applicants to demonstrate the need for funding should enhance rather than duplicate donor efforts. In addition, policy and regulatory initiatives funded under this Project will be designed to complement and support the efforts of other donors that are leading similar initiatives at the regional level.

Private Sector: MSMEs are a particular focus of this project, and an assessment of their financial services needs will help drive the focus of the Challenge Facility and efforts to support policy and legal reforms.

Civil Society: The multi-stakeholder forums are designed to solicit suggestions from a wide range of voices in society to improve the regulatory and policy environment. In addition, a number of the recipients of FINECF funding are likely to be local NGOs.

5. U.S. Agency for International Development.

USAID was consulted during the design of the Project, and their input will be solicited throughout the implementation and monitoring of the Financial Services Project. This Project will benefit from the lessons learned from USAID's main microfinance project which is nearing the end of its term. To the extent applicable, this Project will be coordinated with ongoing and future agricultural and other programs focused on increasing the breadth and quality of demand for financial services.

6. Sustainability.

The Financial Services Project is not intended to create a new, sustainable institution or financial mechanism. Rather, it is intended to enhance the success of existing commercial actors that service MSMEs and make them more sustainable. Beneficiary institutions of the Challenge Facility, for example, can be expected to continue to implement improvements in financial technologies and institutional capacities after Program support ends, since participating institutions are required to present sustainable, economically viable, plans for assistance and demonstrate their financial commitment to the project. Moreover, by demonstrating best practices, the Project will also encourage other financial institutions or business development service providers to follow the innovations of participating institutions.

Support for portions of the Financial Enabling Environment Activity shall be conditioned on Benin having presented and developed a funding and sustainability plan for the microfinance supervisory authority in the Ministry of Finance that is satisfactory to MCC; such plan may include mechanism for funding via national funds and private funds and adjustments in staffing.

7. Policy; Legal Reform; and Procedural Changes.

The Parties have identified the following policy, legal and regulatory reforms and actions that the Government shall pursue in support, and to reach the full benefits, of the Financial Services Project, the satisfactory implementation of which will be conditions precedent to certain MCC Disbursements as provided in the Disbursement Agreement:

(a) The implementers of the Financial Services Project, including the MCA-Benin Financial Services Project division, shall participate in the development of the Land Policy White Paper through representation on the Land Project Steering Committee and in the relevant working group(s). The Government shall commit to adopt the reforms consistent with this Land Policy White Paper that are necessary to ensure effective use of land titles as collateral for loans and to enable financial institutions to effectively enforce their collateral interest in such title;

(b) The Government shall develop a funding and sustainability plan for the Cellule that shows appropriate use of MCC Funding and is satisfactory to MCC, including a commitment to finance significantly increased and adequate staffing for the Cellule as soon as practical through the budget, fees, or another sustainable mechanism. The amount funded by this sustainable funding mechanism must grow over time and eventually replace the MCC Funding. This commitment must be in form and substance acceptable to MCC. In addition, the Government shall commit to working with the outside advisor to the Cellule funded under the Compact and adopting reasonable reforms suggested by advisor;

(c) The Government shall develop and seek MCC approval of a funding and sustainability plan for the implementation of regular audits of microfinance institutions, as well as of a plan for selection of these institutions;

(d) Support for improvements to the credit bureau for microfinance shall be conditioned upon the results of a study (or studies) of feasibility and demand (with procurement approved by MCC). An implementation plan and detailed budget for improvements, based on the results of the feasibility and demand study (or studies), shall be submitted to MCC for approval;

(e) The National Policy for Microfinance shall be adopted in form and substance satisfactory to MCC; and

(f) The Government shall develop and advocate for, and use its best efforts to adopt and implement, those reasonable legal and regulatory reforms, if any, that are identified by the multi-stakeholder forums in the Financial Enabling Environment Activity as necessary to expand, significantly and sustainably, financial services offered to MSMEs. A yearly report, including a summary of the forums and a resulting work plan, shall be submitted to MCC for approval.

8. Proposals.

Mechanisms for consideration of solicited and unsolicited Challenge Facility applications shall be as described above in Section 2(a)(ii).

Mechanisms for consideration of solicited and unsolicited proposals for regulatory reforms shall be as described above in Section 2(b)(ii).

In addition, as appropriate, MCA-Benin will develop, subject to MCC approval, a process for consideration of solicited and unsolicited proposals. With respect to solicited proposals, the evaluation process will include, consistent as appropriate with the Procurement Guidelines, the issuance of a published request for proposals with specific identified evaluation criteria and peer reviewers.

SCHEDULE 3 to ANNEX I
ACCESS TO JUSTICE

This *Schedule 3* generally describes the key elements of an Access to Justice Project (the "***Justice Project***") that the Parties intend to implement. Additional details regarding the implementation of the Access to Justice Project will be included in the Implementation Plan and in relevant Supplemental Agreements.

1. Background.

A major obstacle to Benin's economic growth is the inadequate physical and institutional infrastructure of the judicial system. The judicial system and courthouses serving Benin at independence in 1960 are largely the same system and courthouses that serves Benin now. Archaic laws, few and insufficiently trained judges, insufficient administrative capacity, and poor access to legal information combine with few and old courthouses to deny access to justice to many Beninese. If individuals or businesses dare to proceed into the maze of the courts, expense, delays (it takes an average of 570 days to enforce a contract), and the risk of corruption mean that justice is a highly uncertain result. Business decisions are skewed, and business expansion is stifled by the reality of slow, costly and uncertain justice.

Throughout West Africa alternative dispute resolution ("***ADR***") is becoming an increasingly viable means to resolve commercial disputes. As part of Benin's obligations under OHADA, the Centre d'Arbitrage, Mediation et Conciliation ("***CAMeC***") has been formed within the Chamber of Commerce and Industry in Cotonou. It has not yet begun to conduct arbitrations or other ADR activities.

The Chamber of Commerce (the "***Chamber***") has initiated and is managing a successful program in business registration that this Justice Project will build upon. Rather than a lengthy corporate registration proceeding through many offices in many agencies, the Chamber has developed a service that has already reduced the average time for the registration of companies from over three months to ten days by centrally managing the process of corporate registrations. The Business Registration Center is based in Cotonou with small satellite offices in Porto-Novo, Abomey, and Parakou.

The Government has already begun an extensive process of legal reform: hiring additional new judges and court personnel, improving court administration, and building new courthouses. In addition, other donors have already made commitments to the improvement of Benin's judicial infrastructure. The Inspection General service provides supervision for the courts. It assures that courts are all performing with uniform quality, provides guidance to new judges, and initiates investigations when improper behavior by court personnel is reported. MCC's contribution will fit with Benin's ongoing legal reform plans and complement the work of other donors.

A notable failure of the current judicial system is the lack of access to legal information and the absence of a central location for legal information—whether it is the decisions of courts, the laws of Benin, or legal texts, either in paper or electronic form. Greater knowledge of the laws and courts of Benin for large numbers of people will lead to greater certainty in commercial transactions, reduced demand for courts in minor disputes, and less fear of the judicial system for more serious disputes. Informed public awareness of legal and judicial issues is critical to public confidence in the judicial system. For this reason, the Government proposed the creation of a Legal Information Center.

This Project also aims at assisting litigants in Benin currently suffering from case backlogs and litigants or potential litigants who live great distances from current courts. New courts will be built, to an established modern design, beginning late in the year two of the Justice Project. Training of current judges and other court personnel will begin in year one of the Justice Project. A financing facility to support legal aid to assist poorer litigants will also be established. The construction of the courts will be linked to growth and training of new judges; as noted Section 6 below, the Government of Benin will hire new judges and other personnel on an appropriate schedule to staff the new courts and to allow for training prior to their assignment to the courts.

Finally, the Justice Project will increase the likelihood of success of both the Land Project and Financial Services Project by increasing speed and likelihood of contract enforcement.

2. Summary of Project Activities.

The overall objective of the Justice Project is to improve the investment climate by increasing the confidence in the judicial system to enforce contracts. In response to the conditions noted above, this Project has three main components:

- Support the expansion of the Center of Arbitration, Mediation and Conciliation at the Chamber of Commerce;
- Improvement of the Registration Center (*Guichet Unique*); and
- Improved services of courts including capacity building and training for judges, court personnel, legal aid, and Inspection General service; creation of a legal information center; development of a public awareness campaign; and the construction of new courthouses.

The following summarizes the contemplated Justice Project Activities. The M&E Plan (described in *Annex III*) will set forth anticipated results and, where appropriate, regular benchmarks that may be used to monitor implementation progress. Performance against the benchmarks and the overall impact of the Justice Project will be assessed and reported at the intervals to be specified in the M&E Plan or as otherwise agreed by the Parties from time to time. The Parties expect that additional benchmarks will be identified during the implementation of the Justice Project. Estimated amounts of MCC Funding for each Project Activity for the Justice Project are identified in *Annex II* of this Compact. Conditions precedent to each Project Activity and sequencing of the Project Activities shall be set forth in the Disbursement Agreement, other relevant Supplemental Agreements, or component of the Implementation Plan.

(a) ***Project Activity: Expansion of the Arbitration Center ("Arbitration Center Activity")***

Increased access to ADR will reduce the burden on courts, reduce the cost of dispute resolution, and allow for faster resolution of commercial disputes. Companies and individuals engaging in commercial activities are the expected beneficiaries for this Project Activity. Increased economic activity and a growing number of entrants to commercial activity are expected results, supporting the Program Objective. This Project Activity will facilitate a plan to fully launch operations of CAMeC involves capacity building, public outreach, and budgetary support (e.g., staff costs).

MCC Funding will support the following activities:

(i) Training for arbitrators and CAMeC staff in arbitration procedures and ADR and arbitration management.

(ii) Development of institutional management and operational procedures.

(iii) Promotion of public outreach, including production of training and publicity materials and maintaining of website with relevant documents and information.

(iv) Support for staff salaries at the CAMeC; *provided, however*, MCC Funding will gradually phase out over the Compact Term as an incentive for CAMeC to promote a commercially viable pricing structure for provision of and access to services of the Arbitration Center and to ensure sustainability of the activity after the Compact Term.

(v) Acquisition of new equipment and some additional rented space for CAMeC as increased caseload warrants.

(b) ***Project Activity: Business Registration Center (Guichet Unique) ("Business Registration Activity")***

The Business Registration Project Activity is intended to greatly reduce the steps required to register a company. This Project Activity will track the reduction of registration time year by year, from the current average of twenty days. MCC support will strengthen current operations in Cotonou, Porto-Novo, Abomey and Parakou and support opening new satellite offices in Natitingou and Lokossa. Investment in existing and new offices will further speed, simplify and reduce the cost of corporate registration, and make this service available to more enterprises. It is expected that these improvements will encourage the formation of companies, boost employment in the formal sector and increase incomes.

MCC Funding will support the following activities:

(i) Evaluation of the performance of existing offices to identify necessary improvements and assist with design of new offices and services of the Business Registration Center.

(ii) Introduction of new services such as a system for registration under the Investment Code.

(iii) Training of new staff in regulations, rules and procedures related to formation of companies.

(iv) Development and maintenance of an electronic database of companies in Benin.

(v) Provision of computers and other office equipment for new offices of the Business Registration Center.

(vi) Conduct of public outreach to business community including seminars and publicity or informational materials.

(c) ***Project Activity: Improved Services of Courts ("Courts Activity")***

The Courts Activity will allow Benin to move forward its ten year plan for improvement of the judiciary by providing basic training, court management, guidance, and physical and institutional infrastructure.

MCC Funding will support the following activities:

(i) Training of judges and court personnel.

(1) Prior to commencing of activities described in paragraphs (2) through (5) below, design of a comprehensive capacity building strategy for judges and court personnel;

(2) Training of both new and current judges in substantive and procedural matters, particularly in commercial issues as the laws of Benin are modernized and harmonized, under the OHADA process, with the rest of francophone West Africa;

(3) Training of court personnel, including clerks and court officials, in modern case management procedures, use of technology, and other substantive and procedural matters as the courts modernize;

(4) Continuing training of current judges and court staff as well training of new hires, particularly on commercial issues. This activity will build on training programs already underway supported by various European aid agencies; and

(5) Development of comprehensive training materials and judicial bench-books and other documents to support improved functioning of the courts and further development of local training capacity, to support efforts to institutionalize the capacity building process.

(ii) Inspection General Service. To improve the efficiency of the Inspection General Service and its ability to serve the increased number of courts contemplated by Benin's legal reform plan, the work of other donors and this Project:

(1) Training of new and existing personnel of the Inspection General Service to improve their ability to supervise the courts, advise court staff, and identify unethical behavior; and

(2) Development of training materials to build Inspection General Service capacity.

(iii) Legal Information Center. The proposed Legal Information Center to be located in Cotonou will serve not just as law library, but as a center for the disseminating of court decisions, laws, and other legal information. The Legal Information Center will be open to the public, both physically and electronically. The Legal Information Center will: serve as a central location for case records; convert case records and other legal documents to electronic media; provide public access to laws and other legal documents; serve as a resource and training center for judges, court personnel, and government officials.

MCC Funding will support the following activities:

(1) Following the completion of the Category B environmental and social assessment framework specified in Section 2(c)(v)(3) and an individual EMP or environmental assessment (including an EMP) as determined according to the framework and subject to adoption of the Procedural Code and other Codes specified in Section 2(c)(v)(1), construction and equipment of a new Legal Information Center. Hazardous and toxic materials will not be permitted to be used or result as by-products from construction and operation of the buildings;

(2) Development of an electronic database of legal information and documents; and

(3) Conduct of a public awareness campaign to demystify law and legal proceedings to the broader public. This will involve "open days" at the courts and the Legal Information Center, publication of legal information for non-lawyers, information dissemination via the media, and other outreach efforts such as coordination with the outreach activities of the CAMeC and Business Registration Center to introduce consumers and the broader public to the workings of each institution. Media outreach will also be an important aspect to the public awareness campaign, along with publication of informational and legal materials in French and major local languages, and the development of a web-based information system based at the Legal Information Center.

(iv) Legal Aid.

(1) Support of poorer litigants gaining access to legal services by law professionals (lawyers and others) and to information materials such as on processes and rights by establishing a fund for this purpose. Initial funding will be USD$1,000,000. An additional matching amount of up to USD$1,500,000 will be provided from MCC Funding on a dollar for dollar basis to

match funds provided by non-MCC sources, such as other bi-lateral or multilateral donors, foundations or corporations; and

(2) Funding shall be provided to, and services provided by, existing non-governmental organizations ("***NGOs***") active in Benin, or by a not-for-profit entity established in the future to provide these services. MCA-Benin shall conduct a competitive selection process to determine the best value providers of legal aid services eligible for funding. The selection process shall include an evaluation by, among others, the Justice Project Manager of proposals by candidate NGO for use of funds. Final selection of NGOs and awards shall be subject to MCC approval. Funding shall support selected NGOs implement the proposed legal aid services.

(v) New Courthouses.

This sub-activity, the capstone to the Justice Project, will support the creation of new courthouses—one appellate court in Abomey, a region that is currently lacking in appellate court capacity, and eight courts of first instance (*Tribunaux de Premier Instance*) ("***TPI***") distributed throughout the country. Another key requirement for this activity will be that a system for case management is developed as described in Section 2(c)(vi) and that support of legal aid services is undertaken as described in Section 2(c)(iv), likewise in keeping with modern best practices, and implemented prior to construction of the courthouses.

MCC Funding will support the following:

(1) Evaluation of Codes to be adopted. As condition to MCC Disbursements and prior to commencement of construction, a new Code of Civil Commercial, Administrative and Social Procedure of Benin ("***Procedural Code***") and such other codes as may be identified by the time specified in the Disbursement Agreement and agreed by the Parties, must be passed by the legislature and adopted by the Government. The Procedural Code, as passed by the legislature must be in keeping with regional best practices, as determined by independent experts;

(2) Select sites for courthouses. MCA-Benin shall select sites based on its identification of viable sites. MCA-Benin shall consider input from civil society and other stakeholders, including any unsolicited proposals for sites from communities or others. The criteria for selection of courthouse locations shall be as follows: (i) population density in surrounding area; (ii) commercial activity in the surrounding area; (iii) proximity of proposed court site to underserved populations and other courts; (iv) links to other Projects, in particular the Land Project and Financial Services Project and (v) restrictions on selection of sites that are (A) contaminated with toxic or hazardous waste, (B) require major service infrastructure improvements (such as new roads, water supply or treatment, transmission lines or sewage treatment), or (C) in sensitive locations as defined in Appendix C of the Environmental Guidelines;

(3) Preparation of a Category B environmental and social assessment, pursuant to the Environmental Guidelines, for the courthouses and the Legal Information Center will be required to provide pertinent guidance in the form of a framework document. This will allow more rapid and efficient environmental and social assessment of the courthouses and the Legal Information Center. This document will be used to screen sites, according to MCC Environmental Guidelines, focus the content of Environmental Management Plans ("***EMPs***") or any Resettlement Action Plans ("***RAPs***"), and provide standard contract/bid clauses for impact mitigation during construction and operation. The framework document will provide criteria for determining when individual environmental and social assessments or solely EMPs of the buildings are needed and will incorporate procedures to address economic or

physical displacement consistent with the World Bank policy on Involuntary Resettlement in effect as of the date hereof;

(4) Subject to completion and satisfactory results of the environmental and social assessment framework conducted under paragraph (1) above and an individual EMP or environmental and social assessment (including an EMP) for each construction, as determined according to the framework, construction of courthouses. Construction of four TPI and one appellate court can commence as early as the end of year two of compact, assuming code modernization, case management, and training goals and other conditions precedent have been achieved. Process of construction of final four courthouses may commence one year after construction starts for first set of TPI, assuming continued satisfaction of conditions precedent and other criteria such as case management and training. Hazardous and toxic materials will not be permitted to be used or result as by-products from construction and operation of the buildings; and

(5) Following the construction undertaken in accordance with paragraph (2) above, equip newly constructed courthouses. This includes computers, furniture, and other necessary items and systems.

(vi) Case Management. To the facilitate increasing the speed and efficiency of the processing cases through judicial system, MCC Funding will support the following:

(1) Conduct of a survey of current case management system and develop recommendations for improvement in case management and will include recommendations regarding administrative risks including time limits to process cases, procedures for assignment of judges to cases, and technology to manage case flow though court system; and

(2) Development by the courts of improved regulations and more effective administrative processes to manage cases and implementation of those regulations and processes. Implementation will include incorporation of recommendations developed in paragraph (1) above which MCA-Benin and MCC deem advisable.

3. Beneficiaries.

The intended beneficiaries of the Justice Project will be ordinary citizens as well as MSMEs and other commercial actors. Currently only 8% of commercial cases received in a given year are treated by the system. This case backlog diminishes confidence in the system and increases the potential for corruption. Benin was recently rated by the World Bank's "Doing Business in 2006" as among the most difficult countries in the world to do business. By improving the capacity of the court system to resolve claims, the Project will benefit all users hindered by delays and backlogs. It will also support the benefits of the Land Project and Financial Services Project by increasing the likelihood of timely and appropriate enforcement of contracts and resolution of other disputes. The Legal Information Center is expected to reach a large class of beneficiaries including judges, government officials, business representatives, and the general public. Poorer litigants will benefit from the legal aid services.

4. Donor Coordination; Role of Private Sector and Civil Society.

(a) *Donors*. The Justice Project will benefit significantly from lessons learned by the European Union ("***EU***") regarding the construction and equipping of new courthouses. A current EU project is underway to refurbish several existing courthouses and build four new TPIs and appellate court. Assuming the Beninese and others are satisfied with the design of the courts being built by the EU, the Justice Project would follow the same design. Several donors have been engaged with projects related to Access to Justice. Bi-lateral assistance from France and Belgium has supported re-drafting of codes for which MCC will require enactment as conditions precedent to court construction. MCC will coordinate with in particular AFD in connection with the adoption and development of the Procedural Code as the AFD has supported the code redrafting efforts. Their involvement provides some comfort that the codes are modern and harmonized, where appropriate, with codes of neighboring countries. Neither the World Bank nor the African Development Bank have justice sector projects in Benin but both are interested in promoting passage of modernized codes as it will increase the likelihood and degree of success of other World Bank programs. It is anticipated that some of the NGOs supported by the legal aid services activity described in Section 2(c)(iv) may funded as well by other donors and it is also possible that some of the matching funds contemplated with respect to that activity could be provided by other bilateral or multilateral donors (as well as private sector or other sources).

(b) *Private Sector*. It is anticipated that members of the private bar and business sector will actively participate in the public outreach and other activities of the Business Registration Center, Legal Information Center, and the CAMeC.

(c) *Civil Society*. Civil society and other stakeholders, including communities or municipalities, will have the opportunity to participate in courthouse selection process or submit proposals for sites as described in Section 2(c)(v)(2).

5. U.S. Agency for International Development.

USAID supports a Women's Legal Rights Initiative in Benin that has offered valuable assistance in the development of this Project.

6. Sustainability.

To sustain the Justice Project there will need to be sufficient demand for Alternative Dispute Resolution in Benin and satisfaction by the Government of key conditions precedent related to of court construction, and court design and maintenance. To mitigate the risk of insufficient ADR-related demand, market pricing mechanisms will be built into the CAMeC support. This will promote development of a fee-supported ADR system. Initiation of court construction process will be set at the end of year two of the Compact Term, which will give the Government time to make necessary required Project-related legal reforms. Construction and maintenance will also benefit, respectively, from EU experience in court construction, and be sustained by the increased annual budget of the Ministry of Justice. The Government will ensure the sustainability of the Legal Information Center by ensuring support for adequate staffing of Legal Information Center during and following the Compact Term.

The key to ensuring environmental and social sustainability of the Project is ongoing public consultation. By the time specified in the Disbursement Agreement, MCA-Benin shall engage the Environment and Social Assessment Director, subject to MCC approval, as described in Section 3(d)(iii)(3) of *Annex I*.

Environmental and social analyses of the courthouses and the Legal Information Center will be conducted as part of the technical survey and design to determine the environmental impacts and existence of economic and physical displacement. In addition to the analyses, EMPs satisfactory to MCC will be developed, implemented and monitored during project implementation. Disbursement of MCC Funding will be contingent upon issuance of environmental licenses, as needed, or any other required permits and subject to the environmental and social assessment review described as requirements under Sections 2(c)(v)(3) and (4).

7. Policy; Legal Reform; and Procedural Changes.

The Parties have identified the following policy, legal and regulatory reforms and actions that the Government shall pursue in support, and to reach the full benefits, of the Justice Project, the satisfactory implementation of which will be conditions precedent to certain MCC Disbursements as provided in the Disbursement Agreement:

(a) Passage of the new Procedural Code and other codes as identified in accordance with Section 2(c)(v)(1). The new Procedural Code should include adequate provisions pertaining to the speed with which court cases are heard, and the means by which cases proceed through the courts;

(b) Development and implementation of enhanced case management techniques and implementation of the case management system developed based on recommendations formed pursuant to Section 2(c)(vi), including modernized methods of case assignment and case tracking, even though not required as part of the Procedural Code;

(c) Development of CAMeC activities by measures, acceptable to MCC, to facilitate the removal of old cases from the TPI to CACeM;

(d) Undertake, as necessary, steps to support the enforceability of arbitral awards;

(e) As necessary and if evaluation of Business Registration Center indicates warranted, undertake improvements in regulations, policies or procedures related to business registration and company formation;

(f) Hire and train new judges and court personnel sufficient to staff new courts; and

(g) Commitment by the Government of budgetary resources to support salaries for judges and other court personnel and for the maintenance of those courts constructed under this Project.

8. Proposals.

Objective selection criteria for the selection of NGOs to be supported by the legal aid sub-activity of the Courts Activity shall be as specified in Section 2(c)(iv)(2).

Objective selection criteria and procedures for determining the locations (towns) of the courthouses to be constructed under the Courts Activity shall be as specified in Section 2(c)(v)(2).

SCHEDULE 4 to ANNEX I
ACCESS TO MARKETS PROJECT

This *Schedule 4* generally describes and summarizes the key elements of an Access to Markets Project that the Parties intend to implement in furtherance of the Markets Objective (the "***Markets Project***"). Additional details regarding the implementation of the Access to Markets Project will be included in the Implementation Plan and in relevant Supplemental Agreements.

1. Background.

Benin's economy is dependent on cotton production, subsistence agriculture and an increasingly uncompetitive Port of Cotonou (the "***Port***"). Key impediments to sustainable economic growth are its poor investment climate and lack of dynamic private sector activity. Benin has long been a strategic trading center and a keystone in the trade corridor that links the landlocked countries of the West African Economic and Monetary Union ("***WAEMU***") with Nigeria, Europe, and the Americas. Trade and transport have traditionally made up a large part of the nation's economy, and limitations in Benin's transportation network have increased costs for raw materials to the country and the region. The bottleneck at the Port has impeded access to external markets by agricultural and fish/shrimp producers and processors. Improved Port facilities will lower production and marketing costs and encourage greater agricultural production as well as increased trade between Benin and other countries.

This Project is designed to promote access to markets by improvements to the Port of Cotonou, including a fish inspection facility. This Project aims to improve Port performance and security, expand capacity, and reduce costs. A more efficient Port will contribute to importer and exporter value-added through reducing transportation costs and improving product quality. Moreover, because Benin's road transport industry is relatively competitive, it is likely that the anticipated reduction in shipping costs will be passed on to wholesalers and traders, and ultimately be reflected in consumer prices. Finally, both the Project Activities and the policy or other actions the Government will undertake as set forth in Section 6 of this *Schedule 4* are designed to reduce the potential for corruption at the Port.

Expanding the Port to meet Benin's long-term developmental needs will require a significant number of large investments. Due to the complexity and scope of the Port expansion plan, not only will it take several years to design, build and construct the facilities to meet a growing future demand but it will also be necessary to accommodate current demands by upgrading existing Port facilities.

2. Summary of Projects and Activities in Project and Expected Results.

The objective of the Markets Project is to improve the Port of Cotonou through increasing the efficiency at the Port and volume of goods flowing through the Port and reducing vehicle operating costs.

The Markets Project includes the following Project Activities:

- *Studies and Port Institutional Activity*: This Project Activity will include key feasibility studies, environmental assessments and revision of master plan for the Port, as well as the computerization and streamlining of customs clearance procedures for merchandise, technical assistance and training in information systems and Port management, and improvements to legal, fiscal and institutional frameworks that govern the sub-activities.
- *Port Security and Landside Improvements*: This Project Activity will address the safety and security aspects of the Port for compliance with international safety requirements (conforming to International Ship and Port Security Code ("***ISPS***") standards). The expansion and reconfiguration plan for the Port under this Project Activity includes: major improvements to the physical infrastructure including the access gates, access road, vehicle access facilities, storage areas, and the construction of a compulsory inspection facility for fish and seafood products with associated training and technical assistance.
- *Waterside Improvements*: This Project Activity will support the construction of a new South wharf to accommodate additional containerized merchant marine vessels and a dry bulk conveyor system; environmental management improvements; and, an environmentally appropriate solution to address sedimentation of the Port's entrance.

The M&E Plan (described in *Annex III*) will set forth anticipated results and, where appropriate, regular benchmarks that may be used to monitor implementation progress. Performance against these benchmarks and the overall impact of the Markets Project will be assessed and reported at the intervals to be specified in the M&E Plan or as otherwise agreed by the Parties from time to time. The Parties expect that additional indicators will be identified during the implementation of the Markets Project. The *expected results* from, and the *key benchmarks* to measure progress on the Project, Project Activities and sub-activities undertaken or funded under the Markets Project are set forth in *Annex III*.

Estimated amount of MCC Funding for the Project Activity for this Markets Project is identified in *Annex II* of this Compact. Conditions precedent to the Project Activities and sequencing of the Project Activities shall be set forth in the Disbursement Agreement or other relevant Supplemental Agreements or component of the Implementation Plan.

The following summarizes the Markets Project:

The Project will address institutional, landside and waterside improvements necessary to meet the unmet demand and address resulting inefficiencies. Because of the complexity and timing of the sub-activities, the environmental and social assessment requirements will be implemented in a phased manner.

To support the expansion and improvement of the Port, MCC Funding will be used for the following activities:

(a) ***Project Activity: Feasibility Studies and Assessments ("Studies Activity")***

(i) Conduct of initial technical studies (engineering pre-feasibility, environmental and economic) ("***Initial Technical Studies***") to evaluate in further detail the costs, engineering and environmental aspects of the key waterside components of the Markets Project. These Initial Technical Studies will:

(1) Objectively evaluate alternative schemes that address sedimentation of the harbor access, including but not limited, to the use of other studies and proposals related to erosion control and environmental impacts;

(2) Evaluate the dredging for the new South wharf;

(3) Perform any additional sampling and testing of sediments related to the wharf or other areas to be dredged as part of the harbor access;

(4) Determine needs as well as options for disposal of dredged material;

(5) Evaluate the engineering to the pre-feasibility level; and

(6) Provide expanded information on costs and benefits.

Based on the recommendations of the Initial Technical Studies, the Government shall select, subject to MCC approval, its preferred option that will both reduce sedimentation of the Port access channel and not adversely impact coastal erosion and also select, subject to MCC approval, disposal of dredged material and other key waterside component options.

(ii) Following the satisfactory completion of the Initial Technical Studies, conduct of detailed engineering and economic feasibility studies of the entire Markets Project, including studies to ensure appropriate scheduling and budgeting have been established. These feasibility studies shall include, but not be limited to, studies regarding:

(1) Port container scanning system; and

(2) A dry port facility at Tori.

(iii) Following the satisfactory completion of the Initial Technical Studies, conduct of Environmental and Social Impact Assessments ("***ESIAs***") for landside improvements described in Section 2(c)(ii), fish/seafood inspection and handling facility services described in Section 2(c)(iii), and waterside improvements described in Section 2(d). The ESIAs will address landside and waterside in the following manner:

(1) The ESIA for Port landside rehabilitation/restructuring shall incorporate an Environmental Management Plan/System (based on an audit of existing operations as

well as the assessment of the proposed activities), an overall Environmental Management Plan, language for bid solicitations and construction contracts to implement the EMP, and, if needed, a Resettlement Action Plan (consistent with World Bank Policy on Involuntary Resettlement), all of which shall be subject to MCC approval. Port Autonome de Cotonou ("***PAC***") shall adopt the EMP/EMS, implement the HIV/AIDS awareness program and implement any RAP, prior to initiation of construction under the landside improvements activity described in Section 2(c)(ii).

(2) The ESIA for waterside improvements will include an EMP as well as language for bid solicitations and construction contracts to implement the EMP, all of which shall be subject to MCC approval. Such language must cover capital and maintenance dredging and dredged material disposal as well as construction work. PAC shall adopt the EMP prior to initiation of any construction. The ESIA for the waterside may be combined with the ESIA for the landside, if timing of construction activity permits.

(iv) Following the satisfactory completion of the Initial Technical Studies and feasibility studies work to be conducted under Section 2(a)(ii), development of a revised master plan for the Port that consolidates the expected improvements, operational environment and land use for long term planning purposes which master plan shall be completed in conjunction with the feasibility studies work to be conducted under Section 2(a)(ii) and which master plan may be updated periodically thereafter.

(b) ***Project Activity: Port Institutional and Systems Improvements ("Port Institutional Activity")***

(i) Computerization and streamlining of customs clearance procedures for merchandise including information technology systems, warehouse computer management system, and transit cargo system;

(ii) Improvements in the legal, fiscal and institutional frameworks that govern Port activities including restructuring concession agreements with stevedoring companies, conducting independent financial audits and project reviews, and implementing with additional consultants the existing and new Port rules and regulations based upon consultant recommendations for port best practices. PAC and the Government will cooperate with the MCA-Benin consultant(s) including providing unlimited access to the PAC Director General, Customs Department and other PAC related entities for development, recommendation and evaluation of potential improvements in PAC and Customs Department policies, procedures, rules and regulation; and

(iii) Training for tug boat and ship pilots for night docking of petroleum cargo ships.

(c) ***Project Activity: Port Security and Landside Improvements (the "Port Security and Landside Improvements Activity")***

Subject to the satisfactory results of the Studies Activity assessments and studies described in Section 2(a), a plan for renegotiation of PAC concessions and reallocation of berths and land usage satisfactory to MCC, implementation of any RAP, adoption of the EMP and implementation of the HIV/AIDS awareness plan, MCC Funding will support the following capital improvements and other goods and services at the Port:

(i) Port security. Acquisition and installation of, and training associated with, an integrated security system for compliance with ISPS standards, including oceanographic monitoring systems, video surveillance systems, and radio communications systems.

(ii) Landside Improvements.

(1) Front-end engineering and design for major civil and mechanical facilities and works, which shall be completed prior to any sub-activities set forth in this Section 2(c)(ii);

(2) Port road construction and rehabilitation including upgrading and expanding existing Port roads, illumination, and gate system. Other works include constructing an east-side gate, rezoning by berth usage, land and warehousing to achieve efficient operations;

(3) Construction of a dry bulk conveyor system leading to storage/truck loading bins provided by private sector operators;

(4) North wharf structural improvements including reinforcements to wharf substructure (as needed) to accommodate rail mounted gantries and mobile cranes;

(5) Acquisition and implementation of pollution control equipment necessary to respond to significant discharges of hazardous materials in the Port and other equipment and activities related to the EMP/EMS;

(6) Installation of fire control and prevention equipment;

(7) Construction of a compulsory inspection base for fish and seafood products and facilities for efficiently off-loading and handling product before transport to processing centers, market, or ships for export; and

(8) Technical assistance and training of appropriate regulatory agency staff in seafood/fish inspection and safety administration.

(iii) Fish/seafood inspection and handling facility ("***BOC***") services.

(1) Development and adoption of a management plan for the BOC including required training and technical assistance program targeted at inspectors, other employees, and user associations;

(2) Adoption of improved design and procedures for BOC including mechanized off-loading based on required demand study; and

(3) Development and implementation of a user fee system to defray some operation and maintenance costs of the BOC.

(d) ***Project Activity: Waterside Improvements (the "Waterside Improvements Activity")***

Upon completion, satisfactory to MCC, of the Studies Activity described in Section 2(a) and the execution of PAC concessions and reallocation of berths and land usage, each with results satisfactory to MCC and subject to adoption of the EMP and implementation of the HIV/AIDS awareness plan, MCC Funding will support the following waterside improvements:

(i) Front-end engineering and design for major civil and mechanical facilities, works and dredging and dredged material disposal, which shall be completed prior to any sub-activities set forth in this Section 2(d).

(ii) New South wharf construction of approximately 595 meters of berth space for new terminal operations, and mitigating measures associated with dredging and dredged material disposal, in accordance with the results of the Initial Technical Studies.

(iii) Sedimentation control scheme that permits reduction of the sedimentation at the Port entrance and does not adversely impact coastal erosion, in accordance with the results of the Initial Technical Studies.

(iv) Acquisition of additional tug boat with necessary pilot training.

3. Beneficiaries.

The principal beneficiaries of the Markets Project are expected to be Beninese importers, exporters and consumers, including individuals and businesses, through improved quality of transportation services and fish processing facilities following the upgrades to and expansion of the Port. The intended beneficiaries will be identified more precisely, and where possible disaggregated by gender, age, location and income level during the initial phases of the implementation of the Markets Project.

The principal intended beneficiaries of this Project are potentially quite broad. As the economy of Benin is driven by foreign trade and that foreign trade is dependent the Port, both consumers of imported products and exporters of Beninese products will benefit directly or indirectly from efficiency gains in Port operations that translate into lower transportation costs of goods or increased operating margins for Beninese operators and businesses.

4. Donor Coordination; Private Sector.

(a) *Donor Coordination*. The World Bank has been working with the Government to expand private management at the Port. The Markets Project Activities will be coordinated with the study of privatization options and competitiveness at the Port that the World Bank expects to complete by December 2006. The Danish and Dutch governments have been active in supporting analyses of improvements at the Port. The Danish and other studies were used to assess the sedimentation and erosion control problems. MCC will coordinate with DANIDA (the Danish aid agency), the Dutch embassy, the Japanese International Cooperation Agency, the World Bank, Islamic Development Bank, African Development Bank, Arab Bank for Economic Development in Africa, OPEC Funds, Saudi Funds, and the Government to (i) assess and address the erosion and port sedimentation problems and (ii) ensure all sub-activities support Port improvements to maximize the benefits available of donor activities.

(b) *Private Sector*. In order to achieve the expected benefits from MCC Funding, several improvements at the Port are dependent on private sector complementary investments and expanded private sector management services associated with the operations of the Port. MCA-Benin will work with PAC to coordinate with existing private sector operators at the Port, and MCA-Benin and PAC will establish the appropriate private sector participation at each stage of the sub-activities including renegotiation of existing concession agreements to provide for the appropriate investments by the private operators in the Port.

5. U.S. Agency for International Development; U.S. Government Agencies.

MCC will seek to coordinate with USAID during the Compact Term, as appropriate, though there is not currently any USAID activity in this area. In addition MCC will seek to coordinate with the U.S. Department of Homeland Security and U.S. Coast Guard on the Markets Project.

6. Sustainability.

(a) Improvements to the cargo handling operations and the physical layout of the Port will improve the financial performance of the Port. The introduction of private sector participation in operations is also critical to the sustainability of the Markets Project. Part of the restructuring of the Port needs to include revenue from the concessions, which are now paid to a different Government agency as a conduit to the state owned stevedoring company, in order to support port services and to increase transparency and Port efficiency.

(b) Investments by private sector tenants and other users of the Port will provide complementary improvements that will contribute to the long-term sustainability of the Port's ability to meet market demand.

(c) The Port's financial condition has suffered from declining revenues and from increasing labor costs. In addition, its revenues have been declining recently due to restrictions on Nigerian import policies.

(d) A rationalized user fee schedule for the BOC will be developed as part of a required demand study to help defray some of the inspection costs associated with its operation and maintenance.

(e) Essential to the environmental sustainability of the Markets Project is the conduct of the Initial Technical Studies, as well as the landside ESIA, the waterside ESIA and the associated EMPs, each as described in Section 2(a).

(f) The key to ensuring environmental and social sustainability of the Project is ongoing public consultation. By the time specified in the Disbursement Agreement, MCA-Benin shall engage the Environment and Social Assessment Director ("***ESI Officer***"), subject to MCC approval, as described in Section 3(d)(iii)(3) *Annex I*.

7. Policy; Legal Reform; and Procedural Changes.

The Parties have identified the following policy, legal and regulatory reforms and actions that the Government shall pursue in support, and to reach the full benefits, of the Access to Markets, the satisfactory implementation of which will be conditions precedent to certain MCC Disbursements as provided in the Disbursement Agreement:

(a) Renegotiation of existing lease and concession agreements and port leases on terms acceptable to MCC that provide for capital investment based upon the market demand for Port services; in all cases, for any concession within the port right-of-way the PAC shall be the grantor and the beneficiary of the income resulting from the concession or lease. To the extent not covered in the renegotiation of the existing concession agreements, completion of new concession agreements for terminal operations of the new South wharf berths shall include private capital investments acceptable to MCC based upon the demand for Port services;

(b) The Government and PAC shall agree to enforce maritime-related international and regional conventions and agreements to which they are signatory, including the MARPOL International Convention for the Prevention of Pollution from Ships and the UN Convention on the Law of the Sea, and shall also agree to internationally accepted practices, such as the London Dumping Convention and Protocol (to which Benin is not signatory) for the disposal of dredged material, including contaminated material, and the control of pollution in the harbor, its entrance and the landside Port operations;

(c) By the time specified in the Disbursement Agreement, PAC shall create and fill the permanent staff position of PAC Environmental Manager, whose qualifications, selection and replacement shall be acceptable to MCC. The PAC Environmental Manager shall serve as the PAC representative concerning the environmental aspects of the Project Activities and other environmental management activities of PAC. The Government shall ensure that the PAC provides appropriate resources to the PAC Environmental Manager as identified by PAC and as recommended by MCA-Benin port advisor consultant as provided for in Section 2(b)(ii) above and the ESI Officer.

(d) The Government and PAC shall provide a permanent office for the MCA-Benin port advisor adjacent to the office of the Director General of the PAC. The Government and PAC Board of Directors shall facilitate and endorse the assistance by the MCA-Benin port advisor to the Director General of the PAC in the implementation of private management activities and operational improvements associated with the Markets Project;

(e) Execution of private management or concession agreements satisfactory to MCC for the dry bulk conveyor, and the BOC, and other new facilities to be constructed at the Port;

(f) Satisfactory progress on meeting ISPS certification, in particular implementing recommendations as specified by MCC in the Disbursement Agreement or otherwise;

(g) Development and ongoing satisfactory implementation of a program to accomplish financial control and other recommendations as may be specified by the independent financial auditor contemplated by the Markets Project;

(h) Commitment shall be made by the Government to fund, or commitments shall be made by another funding source satisfactory to MCC, for amounts in excess of budgeted amount in the financial plan including amounts that may be necessary for environmental mitigation and remediation. All Beninese environmental and other permits (including any necessary or advisable environmental certificates under Benin law) shall be issued, valid and in full effect;

(i) Support the redesign of the BOC to ensure that specifications address likely traffic and activity requirements, including equipment for mechanical unloading of seafood cargo, and that a demand study is completed as specified by MCC;

(j) Support the design, approval and implementation of a rationalized user fee system for the BOC;

(k) Support the design, approval, and implementation of a capacity building training and technical assistance plan for cold chain, product quality assurance;

(l) Satisfactory results from customs and warehouse systems implementation reflected in reduced in Port cargo processing time;

(m) The Government agrees not to institute a container scanning system at the Port (1) until after a study of the effectiveness of such a scanning system has been completed pursuant to Section 2(a)(i) or (2) in the event that MCC determines that the Government proposed scanning system would be detrimental to the effectiveness of MCC investments at the Port;

(n) The Government agrees not to institute or continue a tax, levy, duty, or other charge or any delivery procedure or requirement at the Port or elsewhere since commencement of MCC review on August 1, 2005 of the port proposal which may affect the competitiveness of the Port without the prior consent of MCC; and

(o) Completion of the World Bank privatization and competitiveness study by the time specified in the Disbursement Agreement, with commitments by the PAC and other Government Affiliates to implement recommendations as requested by MCC and satisfactory implementation of such recommendations.

ANNEX II
SUMMARY OF MULTI-YEAR FINANCIAL PLAN

This Annex II to this Compact (the "***Financial Plan Annex***") summarizes the Multi-Year Financial Plan for the Program. Each capitalized term in this Financial Plan Annex shall have the same meaning given such term elsewhere in this Compact.

1. General.

A multi-year financial plan summary ("***Multi-Year Financial Plan Summary***") is attached hereto as *Exhibit A*. By such time as specified in the Disbursement Agreement, MCA-Benin will adopt, subject to MCC approval, a Multi-Year Financial Plan that includes, in addition to the multi-year summary of anticipated estimated MCC Funding and the Government's contribution of funds and resources, an estimated draw-down rate for the first year of the Compact Term based on the achievement of performance milestones, as appropriate, and the satisfaction or waiver of conditions precedent. Each year, at least 30 days prior to the anniversary of Entry into Force, the Parties shall mutually agree in writing to a Detailed Financial Plan for the upcoming year of the Program, which shall include a more detailed plan for such year, taking into account the status of the Program at such time and making any necessary adjustments to the Multi-Year Financial Plan.

2. Implementation and Oversight.

The Multi-Year Financial Plan and each Detailed Financial Plan shall be implemented by MCA-Benin, consistent with the approval and oversight rights of MCC and the Government as provided in this Compact, the Governing Documents and the Disbursement Agreement.[5]

3. Estimated Contributions of the Parties.

The Multi-Year Financial Plan Summary identifies the estimated annual contribution of MCC Funding for Program administration, monitoring and evaluation, and each Project. The Government's contribution of resources to Program administration, monitoring and evaluation, and each Project shall consist of (a) "in-kind" contributions in the form of Government Responsibilities and any other obligations and responsibilities of the Government identified in this Compact, including contributions identified in the notes to the Multi-Year Financial Plan Summary, (b) such other contributions or amounts as identified in notes to the Multi-Year Financial Plan Summary, and (c) such other contributions or amounts as may be identified in relevant Supplemental Agreements between the Parties or as may otherwise be agreed by the Parties; *provided*, in no event shall the Government's contribution of resources be less than the amount, level, type and quality of resources required to effectively carry out the Government Responsibilities or any other responsibilities or obligations of the Government under or in furtherance of this Compact.

4. Modifications.

The Parties recognize that the anticipated distribution of MCC Funding between and among the various Program activities and Project and Project Activities will likely require adjustment from time to time during the Compact Term. In order to preserve flexibility in the administration of the Program, in addition to Section 4(a)(iv) of *Annex I*, the Parties may, upon agreement of the Parties in writing and without amending this Compact, change the designations and allocations of funds between Program administration and a Project, between one Project and another Project, between different activities within a Project, or between a Project identified as of the Entry into Force and a new Project, without amending this Compact; *provided, however*, that such reallocation (a) is consistent with the Objectives, (b) does not cause the amount of MCC Funding to exceed the aggregate amount specified in Section 2.1(a) of this Compact, and (c) does not cause the Government's obligations or responsibilities or overall contribution of resources to be less than specified in Section 2.2(a) of this Compact, this *Annex II* or elsewhere in this Compact.

5. Conditions Precedent; Sequencing.

MCC Funding will be disbursed in tranches. The obligation of MCC to approve MCC Disbursements and Material Re-Disbursements for the Program and each Project is subject to satisfactory progress in achieving the Objectives and on the fulfillment or waiver of any conditions precedent specified in the Disbursement Agreement for the relevant Program activity or Project or Project Activity. The sequencing of Project Activities or sub-activities and other aspects of how the Parties intend the Projects to be implemented will

[5] The role of civil society in the implementation of this Compact (including through participation on the Stakeholders' Committee and Steering Committee), the responsibilities of the Government and MCC in achieving the Compact Goal and Objectives, and the process for the identification of beneficiaries are addressed elsewhere in this Compact and therefore are not repeated here.

be set forth in the Implementation Plan, including Work Plans for the applicable Project, and MCC Disbursements and Re-Disbursements will be disbursed consistent with that sequencing.

EXHIBIT A
MULTI-YEAR FINANCIAL PLAN SUMMARY

Project	Year 1	Year 2	Year 3	Year 4	Year 5	Total
1. Access to Land						
(a) Policy Activity	520,000	260,000	520,000	0	0	1,300,000
(b) Registration Activity	3,310,000	6,550,000	4,605,000	4,375,000	4,320,000	23,160,000
(c) Services and Information Activity[1]	510,000	3,350,000	3,205,000	2,775,000	620,000	10,460,000
(d) IEC Activity	100,000	150,000	100,000	100,000	50,000	500,000
(e) Support Strategy Activity	120,000	120,000	120,000	120,000	120,000	600,000
Sub-Total	4,560,000	10,430,000	8,550,000	7,370,000	5,110,000	36,020,000
2. Access to Financial Services						
(a) Capacity Building Activity	1,770,000	3,570,000	3,870,000	3,570,000	270,000	13,050,000
(b) Financial Enabling Environment Activity	1,380,000	1,850,000	1,540,000	1,140,000	690,000	6,600,000
Sub-Total	3,150,000	5,420,000	5,410,000	4,710,000	960,000	19,650,000
Project	Year 1	Year 2	Year 3	Year 4	Year 5	Total
3. Access to Justice						
(a) Arbitration Center (CAMeC) Activity	400,000	160,000	140,000	180,000	0	880,000
(b) Business Registration Activity	470,000	830,000	330,000	200,000	0	1,830,000
(c) Courts Activity[2, 3]	2,960,000	6,860,000	8,590,000	6,590,000	6,560,000	31,560,000
Sub-Total	3,830,000	7,850,000	9,060,000	6,970,000	6,560,000	34,270,000

4. Access to Markets						
(a) Studies Activity	5,993,000	2,101,000	0	0	0	8,094,000
(b) Port Institutional Activity	3,251,000	4,876,000	1,196,000	980,000	1,016,000	11,319,000
(c) Port Security and Landside Improvements Activity[4]	200,000	23,154,000	42,158,000	8,151,000	200,000	73,863,000
(d) Waterside Improvements Activity[5]	0	0	22,939,000	53,232,000	0	76,171,000
Sub-Total	9,444,000	30,131,000	66,293,000	62,363,000	1,216,000	169,447,000
Monitoring and Evaluation	3,190,000	1,690,000	1,240,000	1,240,000	1,420,000	8,780,000
Sub-Total	3,190,000	1,690,000	1,240,000	1,240,000	1,420,000	8,780,000
Program Administration and Control						
(a) Program Administration[6]	3,395,000	2,795,000	2,933,000	2,919,000	3,015,000	15,057,000
Project	Year 1	Year 1	Year 1	Year 1	Year 1	Total
(b) Fiscal and Procurement Agent	3,398,688	3,398,688	3,398,688	3,398,688	3,398,688	16,993,440
(c) Audits	1,416,120	1,416,120	1,416,120	1,416,120	1,416,120	7,080,600
Sub-Total[7]	8,209,808	7,609,808	7,747,808	7,733,808	7,829,808	39,131,040
Total Estimated MCC Contribution[8]	32,383,808	63,130,808	98,300,808	90,386,808	23,095,808	307,298,040

[1] MCC Disbursements in connection with this Activity shall be conditioned upon, among others, the completion, satisfactory to MCC, of the relevant studies in Policy Activity and incorporation of the recommendations into implementation plans as appropriate.

[2] After the first $1 million for the legal aid services sub-activity described in Section 2(c)(iv) of *Schedule 3* to *Annex I*, any additional MCC Disbursement for this sub-activity shall be conditioned upon the Government obtaining matching funds to support the legal aid services program described in Section 2(c)(iv) of *Schedule 3* of *Annex I*.

[3] MCC Disbursements in connection with the new courthouses sub-activity described in Section 2(c)(v) of *Schedule 3* to *Annex I*, shall be conditioned upon, among others, passage of the Procedural Code and certain other codes, which codes should contain adequate provisions in areas as may be specified by MCC in the relevant Supplemental Agreement (including with respect to the Procedural Code, provisions pertaining to the speed with which court cases are heard, and the means by which cases proceed through the courts).

[4] MCC Disbursements in connection within the landside improvements sub-activity described in Section 2(c)(ii) of *Schedule 4* of *Annex I* shall be conditioned upon, among others, the following: (i) renegotiation of existing concession and lease agreements on terms acceptable to MCC that provide for capital investment based upon the demand for Port services, (ii) a contract management program of the dry bulk conveyor system acceptable to MCC, (iii) the completion of Initial Technical Studies, (iv) a Government commitment of funding, or commitments obtained from another funding source (satisfactory to MCC) for amounts in excess of budgeted amount in the Detailed Financial Plan, including amounts that may be necessary for environmental and mitigation, and (v) subject to results, satisfactory to MCC, of feasibility studies and ESIA that includes an environmental audit and EMP, (vi) redesign of the fish inspection facility, (vii) completion of a World Bank privatization and competitiveness study, and (viii) selection of a construction management agent.

[5] MCC Disbursement in connection with the waterside improvements sub-activity described in Section 2(d) of *Schedule 4* of *Annex I* shall be conditioned upon, among others, the following: (i) satisfactory results of the Initial Technical Studies, (ii) demonstration, satisfactory to MCC, of improvements in customs and warehouse systems operations, (iii) implementation of recommendations of the independent financial auditor, (iv) obtaining environmental permits, (v) a Government commitment of funding, or commitments obtained from another funding source (satisfactory to MCC) for amounts in excess of budgeted amount in the Detailed Financial Plan, including amounts that may be necessary for environmental and mitigation, (vi) results, satisfactory to MCC, of feasibility studies and ESIA that includes an environmental audit and EMP and (vii) the completion of a long-term management services agreement for the operation of a Port sedimentation facility (or other harbor dredging program, as appropriate) on terms satisfactory to MCC.

[6] The total administration budget as a percentage of the Program cost is equal to 5.61%.

[7] The total implementation budget as a percentage of the Program cost is equal to 14.59%.

[8] Total Government contribution of 5 billion CFA to be included in the annual national budget (1.25 billion CFA per year during the first four years of Compact) and to be allocated in a manner agreed upon by the Parties in writing.

ANNEX III
DESCRIPTION OF THE M&E PLAN

This *Annex III* to the Compact (the "***M&E Annex***") generally describes the components of the Monitoring and Evaluation (M&E) Plan for the Benin Program, and how progress toward the Compact Goal will be measured. Each capitalized term in this *Annex III* shall have the same meaning given such term elsewhere in this Compact. This Annex represents the agreement between the Government of Benin and the MCC on the Goals and Objectives of the MCA program and the timeline for achieving them.

1. Overview.

Prior to disbursement for any Project (other than administrative expenses), the parties shall formulate an M&E Plan that specifies (a) how the implementation of the Program and progress toward the Compact Goal and Objectives will be monitored (the "***Monitoring Component***"), (b) a methodology, process and timeline for the evaluation of planned, ongoing, or completed Project Activities to determine their impact and likely sustainability (the "***Evaluation Component***"), and (c) other components of the M&E Plan described below. Information regarding the Program's performance, including the M&E Plan, and any amendments or modifications thereto, as well as periodically-generated reports, will be made publicly available on the MCA-Benin Website and elsewhere. The Compact Goal, Objectives and Outcomes of the MCA-Benin Program are summarized in the following diagram:

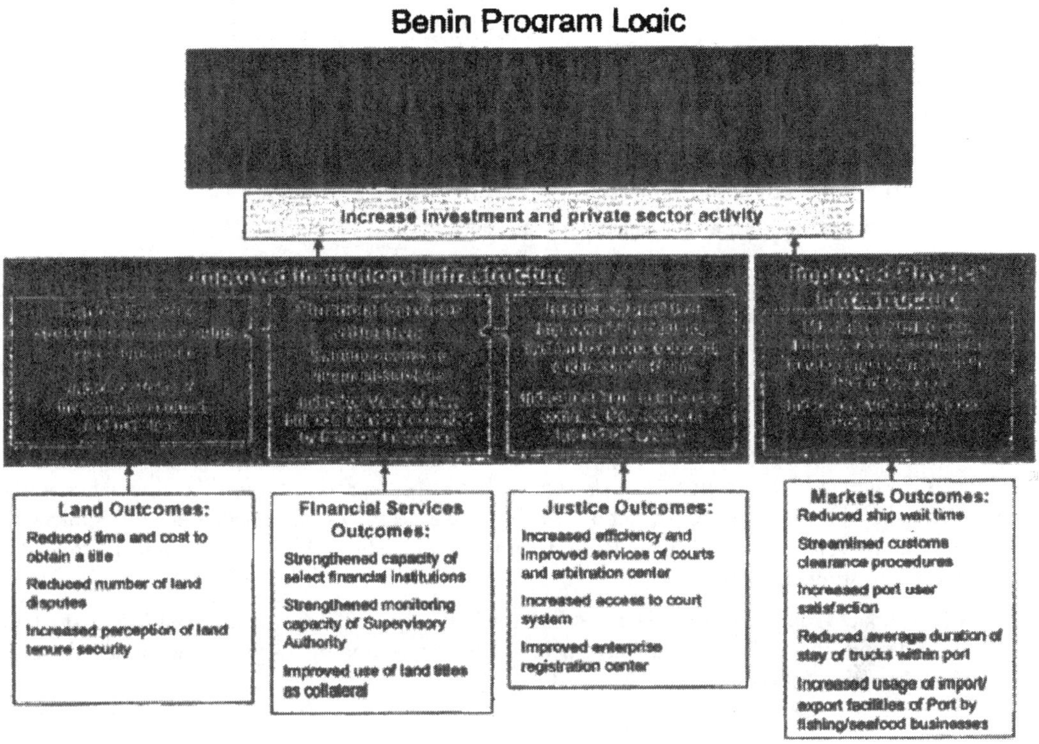

2. Monitoring Component.

To monitor progress toward the achievement of the Compact Goal, Objectives and Outcomes, the Monitoring Component of the M&E Plan shall contain the following elements:

(a) *Indicators*.

The M&E Plan shall measure the results of the Program using quantitative, objective and reliable data ("***Indicators***"). Each Indicator will have one or more targets that quantifies the result and the expected time by which that result will be achieved ("***Target***"). The M&E Plan will detail the process for measuring and reporting on Indicators at several levels. First, the indicators for the Compact Goal (each, a "***Compact Goal Indicator***") will measure the results for the overall Program on the intended beneficiaries (collectively, the "***Beneficiaries***").

Second, the indicators for each Objective (each, an "***Objective Indicator***") will measure the ultimate result for each of the individual Projects. Third, intermediate indicators (each, an "***Outcome Indicator***") will measure the intermediate results achieved under each of the Project Activities in order to provide early measures of progress towards the accomplishment of the Project Objective. Further, other indicators will be included in the M&E Plan to measure the direct outputs of the Project Activities (each, an "***Output Indicator***").

Benin's national household living standards measurement survey (*L'Enquête Modulaire Integrée sur les Conditions de Vie* ("***EMICoV***") will provide baseline data where identified. MCC Funding will support the 2006 baseline survey as well as regular follow-up surveys as described in the M&E Plan ("***2006 Baseline Data Survey***"). The Government will also fund a portion of the 2006 baseline survey. All EMICoV data will be disaggregated by gender, income and age group where appropriate. MCC Funding in connection with the 2006 Baseline Data Survey shall support activities such as the following:

- Training of field and data entry staff;
- Conducting pilot test of survey questionnaire;
- Communication and transportation for survey staff;
- Supervision and Quality Assurance; and
- Data Management.

For all indicators, data collection will be disaggregated by gender, income level and age, where appropriate and to the extent practicable. For some indicators baseline data was not available as of the date of conclusion on the Compact. For such indicators identified in the tables that follow, the M&E Plan and Disbursement Agreement will specify requirements for baseline data collection that shall be met prior to disbursing funds for each Project or Project Activity. Subject to prior written approval from MCC, MCA-Benin may modify and add Indicators or refine the Targets of existing Indicators.

(i) Compact Goal Indicators. The M&E Plan shall contain the Compact Goal Indicators and their definitions, as listed in the table below. The corresponding Targets to be achieved are in the tables that follow.

Compact Goal Indicators		
Purpose	**Indicator**	**Definition of Indicator**
Increase household income in land and finance-targeted areas	Average annual household income in the land and finance areas	Average revenue and consumption level per household in land/finance areas measured through the national living standards measurement survey (EMICoV)
Increase value added to MSMEs	Profits and wages of MSMEs benefiting from Access to Finance capacity building activity	Additional profits and wages of MSMEs that are clients of institutions that are beneficiaries of the Challenge Facility
Increase value added due to port infrastructure improvements	Profits and wages of Port users	Additional profits and wages of Port users

Compact Goal Targets						
Indicators	**Baseline**	**Year 1**	**Year 2**	**Year 3**	**Year 4**	**Year 5**
Average household income in the land and finance areas	TBD[1]					Estimated at 7% increase in treated areas compared to untreated areas
Profits and wages of MSMEs benefiting from the Capacity Building Activity	Zero[2]					USD$5 million
Additional annual profits and wages of Port users	Zero					USD$36 million[3]

[1]EMICoV will provide baseline data to be available starting in August 2006. 2004 GNP per capita is estimated at USD$538.

[2]Benin will estimate current wages and profits of client enterprises of MFIs in the Demand Study at the end of the third quarter, Year 1 of the Compact Term.

[3]Port users include: ship-owners, firms operating within the port and trucks transporting cargo to and from the Port.

(ii) Objective and Outcome Indicators. The M&E Plan shall contain the Objective and Outcome Indicators and their definitions, as listed in the tables below. The corresponding Targets to be achieved are in the tables following the definitions.

Access to Land Project Indicators		
Purpose	**Indicator**	**Definition of Indicator**
Objective		
Strengthen property rights and increase investment in rural and urban land	Total value of additional investment in targeted rural land parcels	Value of investments made to rural land parcels per year; land investment data will come from self-reported data through EMICoV
	Total value of additional investment in targeted urban land parcels	Value of investments made to urban land parcels per year; land investment data will come from self-reported data through EMICoV
Outcomes		
Reduced time to obtain new land title	Average time required to obtain a new land title	Average time associated with obtaining land title, disaggregated by rural and urban areas[1]
Reduced costs to obtain new land title	Average cost required to obtain a new land title	Average cost associated with obtaining land title, disaggregated by rural and urban areas[1]

Purpose	Indicator	Definition of Indicator
Perception of land tenure security increased	Percent of respondents perceiving greater land security	Share of respondents perceiving land tenure security; as measured through EMICoV. Data should be disaggregated by inhabitants of communities benefiting from the Registration Activity and those that are not.
Reduction in number of land disputes	Number of land disputes brought to court	Total number of land disputes registered at TPIs, per year.
	Number of land disputes reported by commune heads	Total number of land disputes (not brought to formal court) as reported by commune heads as measured through EMICoV

[1]Disaggregated time and costs to obtain a land title was not available as of the date of conclusion of the Compact. Going forward, data will be collected and reported for the rural and urban areas separately.

Access to Land Project Targets						
Objective Level Indicators (Metric of Project success observable by end of Compact Term)	**Baseline**	**Year 1**	**Year 2**	**Year 3**	**Year 4**	**Year 5**
Total value of additional investment in targeted rural land parcels	Zero[1]			5% increase from baseline		10% increase from baseline
Total value of additional investment in targeted urban land parcels	Zero (Current level for Cotonou only is USD $310 million)			8% increase from baseline	15% increase from baseline	20% increase from baseline
Outcome Level Indicators (Early indicators of Project Activities impact on Objectives)	**Baseline**	**Year 1**	**Year 2**	**Year 3**	**Year 4**	**Year 5**
Average time required to obtain a new land title	12 months			10 months		6 months

Outcome Level Indicators	Baseline	Year 1	Year 2	Year 3	Year 4	Year 5
Average cost required to obtain a new land title	USD$ 1,300					USD$180
Percent of respondents perceiving greater land security	TBD[1]			30% increase from baseline for benefi-ciary communes		50% increase from baseline for benefi-ciary communi-ties
Number of land disputes brought to court	8000[2]					50% reduction in MCA-targeted zones
Number of land disputes reported by commune heads	TBD[1]					

[1]EMICoV will provide baseline data to be available starting in August 2006.

[2]This baseline figure is an estimate. Data will be verified by quarter 3 of Year 1 of the Compact Term.

Access to Finance Project Indicators		
Purpose	**Indicator**	**Definition of Indicator**
Objective		
Expand access to financial services	Value of new financial services offered by financial institutions	Total incremental increase in value of new credit extended and savings received by financial institutions participating in the project[1]
Outcomes		
Strengthened capacity of select financial institutions	Average portfolio-at-risk > 30 days of participating MFIs	Share of value of all loans outstand-ing that have one or more install-ments of principal past due over 30 days. Participating institutions will be compared to a national average
	Operational self-sufficiency of participating MFIs (%)	Operating revenue/(financial expense + loan loss provision + operating expense). Measures extent of cost coverage from operating revenues. Participating institutions will be compared to national average. Indicator values are illustrative of each class/cohort's performance

Continued

Purpose	Indicator	Definition of Indicator
Strengthened monitoring capacity of Supervisory Authority	Number of MFIs supervised by the Microfinance Cellule	Total number of micro finance institutions that are supervised and have received recommendations from the Ministry of Finance Supervisory Authority
Improved use of land titles as collateral	Number of new bank credits guaranteed with land titles	Total number of loans guaranteed by land titles, per year

[1]Indicator and target will be amended if services other than credit and savings are offered.

Access to Finance Project Targets						
Objective Level Indicators (Metric of Project success observable by end of Compact Term)	**Baseline**	**Year 1**	**Year 2**	**Year 3**	**Year 4**	**Year 5**
Value of new financial services offered by financial institutions	USD$155 Million in Credit and USD$73 Million in savings[1]			USD$24 Million		USD$59 Million
Access to Finance Project Targets						
Outcome Level Indicators (Early indicators of Project Activities impact on Objectives)	**Baseline**	**Year 1**	**Year 2**	**Year 3**	**Year 4**	**Year 5**
Average portfolio-at-risk > 30 days of participating financial institutions	10%[2]		8%	7%	6%	5%
Operational self-sufficiency of participating financial institutions	103%[2]		106%	109%		112%
Number of MFIs supervised by the Microfinance Cellule	27		35	40	50	75
Number of new bank credits guaranteed with land titles	60			100	150	200

[1]Current aggregate value of savings and credit offered in system as cited in National Policy for Micro finance.

[2]These baseline values represent the national average. Once financial institutions are selected, baselines will be recalculated. Targets values are average values for cohort/class entering the Program after 2, 3, 4, and 5 years.

Access to Justice Project Indicators		
Purpose	**Indicator**	**Definition of Indicator**
Objective		
Improved ability of justice system to enforce contracts and reconcile claims	Average time required to enforce a contract	Number of days associated with filing payment dispute in court until moment of actual payment
	Percent of firms reporting confidence in the judicial system	Percent of manufacturing firms who agree with statement "I have confidence in the judicial system"
Outcomes		
Increased efficiency and improved services of courts and the arbitration center	Number of cases processed at Arbitration Center	Number of cases processed at Chamber of Commerce Arbitration Center, per year
	Percent of all cases resolved in TPI courts per year	Share of number of cases resolved of total cases filed at all TPIs, per year
	Percent of all cases resolved in court of appeals per year	Share of number of cases resolved of total cases filed at court of appeals, per year
Purpose	**Indicator**	**Definition of Indicator**
Increased access to court system	Average distance required to reach TPI (km)	Distance between village and jurisdictional TPI in kilometers
Improved enterprise registration center	Number of enterprises registered through the registration center	Annual number of enterprises registered with Chamber of Commerce *Guichet Unique* central or satellite offices
	Average time required to register an enterprise (days)	Number of days associated with registering enterprise with Chamber of Commerce *Guichet Unique* central or satellite offices, per year

Access to Justice Project Targets						
Objective Level Indicators (Metric of Project success observable by end of Compact Term)	**Baseline**	**Year 1**	**Year 2**	**Year 3**	**Year 4**	**Year 5**
Average time required to enforce a contract (days)	570			470		370
Percent of firms reporting confidence in the judicial system	35%			47%		60%

Continued

Outcome Level Indicators (Early indicators of Project Activities impact on Objectives)	**Baseline**	**Year 1**	**Year 2**	**Year 3**	**Year 4**	**Year 5**
Number of cases processed at Arbitration Center	0		25	150	200	250
Percent of all cases resolved in TPIs per year	40%			45%		50%
Percent of all cases resolved in court of appeals per year	8%	12%	15%	18%	21%	24%
Average Distance required to reach TPI (km)	50					34
Number of enterprises registered through the business registration center	9,600 (total to 2004)			1,400	1,000	500
Average time required to register an enterprise (days)	20			10		3

Access to Markets Project Indicators		
Purpose	**Indicator**	**Definition of Indicator**
Objective		
Improve access to markets through improvements to the Port of Cotonou	Volume of merchandise traffic through the PAC (million metric tons)	Total volume of exports and imports passing through Port of Cotonou, per year in million metric tons
	Port surcharges due to delay	Surcharge associated with congestion per twenty-foot equivalent unit ("*TEU*"), in Euro
Outcomes		
Reduced ship wait time	Bulk ship carriers waiting times at the Port (days)	Number of days bulk carrier must wait at anchor (before proceeding to berth) and at berth
Streamlined customs clearance procedures	Average customs clearance times at Port	Time associated with moving merchandise through customs procedures
Increased satisfaction with Port operations among users	Port user satisfaction	Share of port users satisfied with Port operations, estimated through Port user survey
Reduced average duration of stay of trucks at Port	Average duration of stay of trucks at Port	Average duration of stay of trucks at Port

Purpose	Indicator	Definition of Indicator
Increased usage of import/ export facilities of Port among fishing/seafood businesses	Volume of seafood exports processed through BOC (tons)	Total volume of seafood exports processed through the BOC (tons)

Access to Markets Project Targets						
Objective Level Indicators (Metric of Project success observable by end of Compact Term)	**Baseline**	**Year 1**	**Year 2**	**Year 3**	**Year 4**	**Year 5**
Volume of merchandise traffic through the PAC (million metric tons)	4.1	4.9	5.2	5.6	5.9	6.3
Port surcharges due to delay (Euros)	125				50	25
Outcomes	**Baseline**	**Year 1**	**Year 2**	**Year 3**	**Year 4**	**Year 5**
Bulk ship carriers waiting times at the Port (days)	7				5	3
Average customs clearance times at the Port (days)	5			3		1
Outcomes	**Baseline**	**Year 1**	**Year 2**	**Year 3**	**Year 4**	**Year 5**
Port user satisfaction	50%			65%	70%	75%
Average duration of stay of trucks at Port (hours)	24			18	12	7
Volume of seafood exports processed through BOC (tons)	0				250	500

Note: Attainment of most targets in the Markets Project tables in the years specified depends on the successful completion of early sub-activities.

(iii) The final M&E Plan will also include a number of activity-level (Output) measures that will track progress toward realizing the direct outputs of the Projects and Activities. Examples of the indicators likely to be included are:

(1) Number of villages with *plan foncier rural* (PFRs);

(2) Number of urban land titles transformed from *permis d'habiter* or living permits in Cotonou, Parakou and Porto Novo;

(3) Number of clients of financial service providers trained;

(4) Average cost of registering an enterprise with Chamber of Commerce *Guichet Unique*;

(5) Number of judicial employees receiving pre-service training; and

(6) Port meeting ISPS standards.

(b) *Beneficiaries*. The M&E plan shall describe the beneficiaries of the Program in detail, including the expected number of beneficiaries, their income, gender and other general demographic characteristics.

(c) *Data Collection and Reporting*. The M&E Plan shall establish guidelines for data collection and a reporting framework, including a schedule of Program reporting and responsible parties. In addition, MCA-Benin shall conduct regular assessments of program performance to measure progress on the Goals and Objectives and to alert all parties to any problems in implementation. These assessments will report actual results compared to the Targets on the Indicators referenced in the Monitoring Component, explain deviations between these actual results and Targets, and describe any planned actions to address performance problems. With respect to any data or reports received by MCA-Benin, MCA-Benin shall promptly deliver such reports to MCC along with any other related documents, as specified in the M&E Plan or as may be requested from time to time by MCC, and will make these assessments available to the public on their website.

(d) *Data Quality Reviews*. As determined in the M&E Plan or as otherwise requested by MCC, the quality of the data gathered through the M&E Plan shall be reviewed to ensure that data reported are as reliable, timely and valid as resources will allow. The objective of any data quality review will be to verify the quality and the consistency of performance data, across different implementation units and reporting institutions. Such data quality reviews also will serve to identify where consistent levels of quality are not possible, given in-country capacity or other constraints.

3. Evaluation Component.

The Program shall be evaluated on the extent to which the interventions contribute to the Compact Goal and Objectives. The Evaluation Component shall contain the methodology for conducting the most rigorous impact evaluations feasible and cost-effective, as well as the process and timeline for analyzing data. The Evaluation Component shall contain two types of reports: a Final Program Evaluation and Project, Project Activity, or Interim Evaluations.

(a) *Final Evaluation*. MCC will engage an independent evaluator to conduct a program evaluation at the expiration or termination of the Program ("***Final Evaluation***"). The evaluation methodology, timeline, data collection, and analysis requirements will be finalized and detailed in the M&E Plan. The Final Evaluations must at a minimum (i) estimate quantitatively and in a statistically valid way, the causal relationship between the Compact Goals (to the extent possible), the Objectives and

Outcomes; (ii) determine if and analyze the reasons why the Compact Goals, Objectives and Outcomes were or were not achieved; and (iii) assess the overlapping benefits of the Projects.

(b) *Project or Interim Evaluations*. The Evaluation Component in the M&E Plan will also describe other individual Project, Project Activity, or Interim Evaluations. The evaluation methodology, timeline, data collection, and analysis requirements will be finalized and detailed in the M&E Plan. Determination of the evaluation methodologies will be condition precedent for specified MCC Disbursements.

(c) *Ad Hoc Evaluations or Special Studies*. In addition to the evaluations described in the M&E Plan, MCC may require ad hoc evaluations or special studies prior to the expiration of the Compact Term. If MCA-Benin engages an evaluator, the evaluator will be an externally contracted independent source subject to the prior written approval of MCC for terms of reference and final selection, following a tender in accordance with the Procurement Guidelines, and otherwise in accordance with any relevant Implementation Letter or Supplemental Agreement. The cost of an independent evaluation or special study may be paid from MCC Funding. If MCA-Benin requires an ad hoc independent evaluation or special study at the request of the Government for any reason, including for the purpose of contesting an MCC determination with respect to a Project or Project Activity or to seek funding from other donors, no MCC Funding or MCA-Benin resources may be applied to such evaluation or special study without MCC's prior written approval.

4. Other Components of the M&E Plan.

In addition to the Monitoring and Evaluation Components, the M&E Plan shall include the following components for the Program, Projects and Project Activities, including, where appropriate, roles and responsibilities of the relevant parties and Providers:

(a) *Costs*. A detailed annual budget estimate for all components of the M&E Plan.

(b) *Assumptions and Risks*. Any assumptions and risks external to the Program that underlie the accomplishment of the Objectives and Outcomes; provided such assumptions and risks shall not excuse performance of the Parties, unless otherwise expressly agreed to in writing by the Parties.

5. Implementation of the M&E Plan.

(a) *Approval and Implementation*. The approval and implementation of the M&E Plan, as amended from time to time, shall be in accordance with this M&E Annex, and any other relevant Supplemental Agreement. Stakeholders' Committee's review of the completed portions of the M&E Plan shall be required prior to the expiration of the first year of the Program. Review and approval of the M&E Plan shall be completed by time specified in the Disbursement Agreement.

(b) *MCC Disbursement and Re-Disbursement for a Project Activity*. As a condition to each MCC Disbursement or Re-Disbursement there shall be satisfactory progress on the M&E Plan for the relevant Project or Project Activity, and substantial compliance with the M&E Plan, including any reporting requirements. In addition, for certain activities, collection of baseline data will be condition precedent for specified MCC Disbursements.

(c) *Modifications*. Notwithstanding anything to the contrary in the Compact, including the requirements of this M&E Annex, the Parties may modify or amend the M&E Plan or any component thereof, including those elements described herein, without amending the Compact; provided, any such modification or amendment of the M&E Plan is reviewed by the Stakeholders' Committee and has been approved by MCC in writing and is otherwise consistent with the requirements of this Compact and its Objectives, and any relevant Supplemental Agreement between the Parties.

State Department Document Number: 06-258

Memorandum of Understanding Among the National Aeronautics and Space Administration (NASA) and the National Oceanic and Atmospheric Administration (NOAA) Jointly and the Centre National D'Etudes Spatiales (CNES) and the European Organisation for the Exploitation of Meteorological Satellites (EUMETSAT) for Cooperation In the Ocean Surface Topography Mission

Signed at Washington D.C., Darmstadt and Paris, March 21, 24, and 30, and April 7, 2006
Entered into force April 7, 2006

CTIA Document Number: 13085.000

Preamble

The National Aeronautics and Space Administration (hereinafter referred to as "NASA") and the National Oceanic and Atmospheric Administration (hereinafter referred to as "NOAA"), both agencies of the United States Government, acting jointly as one Party to this Memorandum of Understanding (MOU), and as represented by their Administrators;

The Centre National d'Etudes Spatiales (hereinafter referred to as "CNES"), established under the provisions of the French Law 61-1382, dated December 19,1961, setting up a national center for space research and, as represented by its President; and

The European Organisation for the Exploitation of Meteorological Satellites (hereinafter referred to as "EUMETSAT"), established by the Convention which entered into force on June 19,1986, as amended by the Amending Protocol which entered into force on November 19,2000, and as represented by its Director-General,

hereinafter referred to as the "Parties" to this Memorandum of Understanding,

RECALLING the cooperative effort of NASA and CNES mat led to the launch of the TOPEX/Poseidon mission by an Ariane launch vehicle from the Kourou launch site in French Guiana, on August 10, 1992,

RECALLING the cooperative effort of NASA and CNES that led to the launch of the Jason mission by a Boeing Delta II launch vehicle from Vandenberg Air Force Base in California, on December 7,2001,

RECOGNIZING that both the TOPEX/Poseidon mission and the Jason mission have demonstrated clearly that global sea surface topography measurements of unparalleled accuracy can be obtained from space; and further, that such measurements can create new opportunities for monitoring ocean phenomena and developing models to predict global climatic change,

RECOGNIZING the important contribution that the Jason mission has brought to operational activities that led EUMETSAT and NOAA to express a strong interest in participating in the program,

RECALLING the success of NASA in research and development on a variety of environmental programs and the extensive experience of NOAA in operating civilian satellites for the benefit of users of environmental data and the World Meteorological Organization (WMO),

RECALLING NOAA's performance of various domestic and international missions including observation and reporting of the state of the oceans and preparation and issuance of warnings and forecasts of atmospheric, flood, and ocean conditions to ensure protection of life and property; operation of environmental satellites and data archives for the United States; and provision of products and services to users and managers of oceanic, atmospheric, and coastal zone programs,

RECALLING that the primary objective of EUMETSAT is to establish, maintain, and exploit European systems of operational meteorological satellites, taking into account as far as possible the recommendations of the WMO, and that a further objective of EUMETSAT is to contribute to the operational monitoring of the climate and the detection of global climatic changes,

TAKING INTO ACCOUNT the Enabling Resolution EUM/C/0 I/Res. VII on the Optional EUMETSAT Jason-2 Altimetry Programme, adopted at the 49th meeting of the EUMETSAT Council, in which the Council approved the execution, within the framework of the EUMETSAT Convention, of an Optional Jason-2 Altimetry Programme, and which tasked the Director-General with the preparation of the necessary cooperation agreements with international partners contributing to the overall Ocean Surface Topography Mission (OSTM),

TAKING INTO ACCOUNT that Declaration EUM/C/01/Decl. I on the Optional EUMETSAT Jason-2 Altimetry Programme adopted by EUMETSAT Potential Participating States on December 4-5, 2001, entered into force on June 27, 2003,

RECALLING that EUMETSAT and NOAA have enjoyed long-standing and fruitful cooperation in the field of operational Earth observation from space for meteorological purposes,

RECALLING that the CNES Board of Governors approved the program proposal (Phase B/C/D) for Jason-2/OSTM implementation on April 29, 2004,

TAKING INTO ACCOUNT the requirement for satellite ocean altimetry observations expressed by the WMO, the Global Ocean Data Assimilation Experiment (GODAE), the Global Ocean Observing System (GOOS), the Ocean Observations Program Committee (OOPC), and the Integrated Global Observing Strategy Partnership (IGOS-P),

TAKING NOTE OF the common interest of the Parties to continue using radar altimetry to study the oceans from space,

RECOGNIZING the imperative need that this measurement set be continued on an operational basis, and

HAVING IDENTIFIED a mutual interest in the conduct of OSTM, HAVE AGREED as follows:

Article I
Purpose

The Parties each set forth in this MOU their respective responsibilities and the terms and conditions under which they have agreed to cooperate on OSTM. The Parties will use reasonable efforts to carry out their respective responsibilities in accordance with this MOU and to avoid changes that will have a negative effect on another Party with regard to scientific return, implementation approach, cost, and/or schedule, and where they cannot be avoided, to minimize these negative effects.

Article II
Definitions

As used in this MOU, the following terms will have the specified meanings:

1. "Damage" means:

 a. harm to, impairment of the health of, or death of any person;

 b. harm to, destruction or loss of, or loss of use of any property;

 c. other direct, indirect, or consequential damage.

2. "Data Products" are those resulting from processing of the Payload Instrument Data and any necessary supporting Housekeeping Data and/or ancillary data. These fall into two general categories:

 a. Near Real Time (NRT) Products, available within a few hours of acquisition by the satellite; and

 b. Offline Products, available with a delay of several days or weeks after additional processing.

3. "OSTM Ground Segment[5]" means all elements and facilities required to operate the satellite, acquire its Telemetry, process, distribute, and archive Telemetry and Data Products.

4. "Partner" refers to NASA and to NOAA, when they are acting individually, and to CNES and to EUMETSAT.

5. "Proprietary Information" means information embodying trade secrets or comprising commercial or financial information that is privileged or confidential, excluding such information that:

 a. is in the public domain at the time of disclosure or thereafter enters the public domain without breach of the receiving Partner (or a Related Entity of the receiving Partner);

 b. is known to the receiving Partner at the time of disclosure;

 c. has been disclosed to the receiving Partner without restriction from the disclosing Partner;

 d. has been independently developed by the receiving Partner, or

 e. has become known to the receiving Partner without similar restrictions from a source other than the disclosing Partner, that source having the right to disclose.

6. "PROTEUS" is the name of the satellite platform.

7. "Related Entity" means:

 a. a contractor, subcontractor, or grant recipient of a Partner at any tier;

 b. a user or customer having a contractual link with a Partner at any tier;

c. a contractor or subcontractor of a user or customer or grant recipient of a Partner at any tier; or

d. a scientific investigator. The terms "contractors" and "subcontractors" include suppliers of any kind.

8. "Satellite," sometimes referred to as "Jason-2" is the satellite composing the space component of OSTM. It consists of a PROTEUS platform, a payload module, and payload instruments.

9. "Telemetry" is downlinked data comprising of:

a. "Housekeeping Data" (measurements of spacecraft performance and health and welfare of the satellite); and

b. "Payload Instrument Data" (raw instrument data).

10. "Validated Data" are Data Products based upon Telemetry after successful completion of the relevant product assessment and verification.

Article III
Mission Description and Participation

The objective of OSTM is to bring high-precision altimetry to a full operational status through the continuation of the TOPEX/Poseidon and Jason missions and their collection of measurements of sea surface height (SSH), significant wave height (SWH), wind speed at the ocean surface, and other parameters.

OSTM will provide Data Products to the operational and research user communities in support of:

- Marine meteorology and sea state forecasting;
- Operational oceanography;
- Seasonal forecasting;
- Climate monitoring;
- Ocean, Earth system and climate research.

CNES will provide the PROTEUS platform and payload module; NASA and CNES will jointly provide the payload instruments. CNES will provide a Poseidon-3, dual-frequency radar altimeter with its antenna and the Doppler Orbitography and Radiopositioning Integrated by Satellite (DORIS) receiver package.

NASA will provide an Advanced Microwave Radiometer (AMR) with its antenna, a laser retroreflector array (LRA), and a Global Positioning System Payload (GPSP) receiver package.

NASA will provide launch services for the satellite.

CNES will provide a command and control center for the satellite, a European Earth Terminal and data processing, and archiving and distribution infrastructure for the mission.

NOAA will provide a control center for the satellite, command and data acquisition (CDA) stations, and data processing and archiving and distribution infrastructure for the mission.

EUMETSAT will provide a site and infrastructure for accommodation of the European Earth terminal to be integrated into the EUMETSAT Ground Segment infrastructure and data processing, rolling archiving and distribution infrastructure for the mission.

The Partners are to jointly establish and operate an OSTM Ground Segment Telemetry is to be made available to the Partners and Data Products to the broader international user community through data centers and services under the responsibility of the Partners consistent with Article XII (Data Policy).

Data Products will be, at a minimum, consistent with TOPEX/Poseidon and Jason data products and will be defined in the Operational Service Specification (OSS) together with the associated services to the users.

OSTM operations are planned for 5 years. The mission operation is divided into six phases, the objectives of each being as follows:

1. Launch and Early Orbit Phase (LEOP). The satellite is launched and maneuvered into injection orbit. Satellite and instrument systems are activated and checked out.

2. Orbit Acquisition Phase. The satellite is maneuvered into its operational orbit. This phase is concurrent with the Assessment Phase.

3. Assessment Phase. This phase begins at the end of LEOP and ends when:

   a. the satellite and instrument systems are functionally certified;

   b. the satellite is in its operational orbit; and

   c. the ground system is ready to operate routinely.

4. Verification Phase. This phase overlaps the Assessment Phase and continues until the data and processing algorithms are satisfactorily calibrated and validated.

5. Initial Routine Operation Phase. This phase begins after completion of the Assessment Phase and is consistent with the 3-year mission design life.

6. Extended Routine Operation Phase. Assuming useful data are still being collected, this phase extends the mission an additional 2 years or any additional period feat may be agreed by the Parties. This phase will include end-of-life activities.

In this MOU, the term “Routine Operation Phases” is used for both “Initial Routine Operation Phase” and “Extended Routine Operation Phase.”

Article IV
CNES Responsibilities

To implement this MOU, CNES will use reasonable efforts to:

1. Establish, with the support of all Partners, the overall systems engineering function for OSTM;

2. Establish and maintain, with the support of the other Partners, and make available to the Partners the OSTM Project Plan, OSS, System Requirements, Operational Concept, Project Schedule, and other Project Documents, to be approved by the Partners as defined in the Project Plan, including relevant interface control documents and in-orbit assessment and verification plans;

3. Support NASA with information as required for the preparation and maintenance of the OSTM Safety Plan; provide NASA with information to verify compliance with the OSTM Safety Plan;

4. Establish a Mission Assurance Plan (MAP) for its own contribution, make it available to the other Partners, and review the MAPs of the other Partners;

5. Conduct or support, together with the other Partners as necessary, OSTM project reviews, as defined in the OSTM Project Plan;

6. Provide interface, design, fabrication, and test information and support as necessary for the other Partners to fulfill their respective responsibilities under this MOU;

7. Design, fabricate, test, calibrate, and prepare to integrate the PROTEUS platform and the payload module;

8. Design, fabricate, assemble, test, and calibrate the CNES instruments (the Poseidon-3 altimeter and the DORIS receiver package) and provide fully tested instruments to be integrated with the satellite;

9. Provide a site and infrastructure for instrument integration and testing of the fully integrated satellite;

10. Conduct, with NASA support, integration of the fully tested instruments onto the platform; perform functional tests of the satellite; transport the flight-ready satellite to the NASA designated launch site and support launch site processing and testing;

11. Provide ground support equipment and qualified personnel at appropriate sites to support payload and system integration, testing, and launch operations;

12. Upgrade the CNES Command and Control Center (CCC) and the data processing, archival, and distribution center (SSALTO);

13. Test the CNES elements of the OSTM Ground Segment, as defined in the OSTM Project Plan;

14. Provide to NASA all satellite information necessary for NASA to ensure satellite and launch vehicle compatibility, as defined in the OSTM Project Plan;

15. Conduct, with the support of other Partners, satellite, ground system, and overall system-level testing, evaluation of test results, and preparation for operations, as defined in the OSTM Project Plan;

16. Perform quality control of all products generated by CNES;

17. Operate and control the satellite from launch until handover of this responsibility to NOAA, including operations of the European Earth terminal, and support routine operations at NOAA and EUMETSAT, as defined in the OSTM Project Plan;

18. Lead and conduct, with the support of other Partners, the OSTM Assessment and Verification Phases, as defined in the OSTM Project Plan, and perform evaluation and calibration activities to verify the OSTM performance achieved on-orbit;

19. Coordinate operations from a system perspective, in all phases, throughout the OSTM lifetime;

20. Archive all Telemetry, as defined in the OSTM Project Plan consistent with Article XH (Data Policy), and perform offline monitoring of Housekeeping Data during all OSTM Phases;

21. Process and archive Offline Products and distribute them to users, as defined in the OSTM OSS consistent with Article XII (Data Policy), and archive NRT Products generated by NOAA and EUMETSAT;

22. Provide, test, and deliver to EUMETSAT a European Earth terminal, including a set of spare parts, and requirements for its accommodation and operations at a EUMETSAT-designated site;

23. Provide, test, and deliver to EUMETSAT Headquarters a fully tested NRT processing system; support integration and testing of the system at the EUMETSAT-specified location;

24. Provide, test, and deliver to NOAA a fully tested NRT processing system; support integration and testing of the system at the NOAA-specified location;

25. Provide to NOAA a satellite performance and analysis function and engineering and operation support for anomaly resolution for CNES instruments and satellite for the total life of the satellite;

26. Conduct, together with NASA, the preparation and release of relevant Research Announcements and, in coordination with EUMETSAT, the selection of European Investigators as specified in Article XI (OSTM Science Investigations and Application Demonstrations) of this MOU; and

27. Inform the Partners promptly of any technical or programmatic problems that may affect overall OSTM schedules, cost, or performance.

Article V
NASA Responsibilities

To implement this MOU, NASA will use reasonable efforts to:

1. Support CNES for the overall systems engineering function for OSTM;

2. Support, along with the other Partners, the preparation and maintenance of the OSTM Project Plan, OSS, System Requirements, Operational Concept, Project Schedule, and other Project Documents, to be approved by the Partners as defined in the Project Plan, including relevant interface control documents and in-orbit assessment and verification plans;

3. With support from CNES, establish and maintain the OSTM Safety Plan in response to NASA requirements; verify compliance with controls, procedures, testing, and policies, as defined in the OSTM Safety Plan;

4. Establish a MAP for its own contribution, make it available to the other Partners, and review the MAPs of the other Partners;

5. Conduct or support, together with the other Partners as necessary, OSTM project reviews, as defined in the OSTM Project Plan;

6. Provide interface, design, fabrication, and test information and support as necessary for the other Partners to fulfill their respective responsibilities under this MOU;

7. Design, fabricate, assemble, test, and calibrate the NASA instruments (an AMR with its antenna, an LRA, and the GPSP receiver package), and provide fully tested instruments to be integrated with the satellite;

8. Support CNES in the integration of the NASA instruments onto the Payload module and functional testing of the satellite;

9. Provide launch services compatible with the Jason-2 satellite and OSTM mission requirements; conduct, with support of other Partners, launch site processing and testing activities;

10. Provide ground support equipment and qualified personnel at appropriate sites to support payload and system integration, testing, and launch operations;

11. Provide to CNES all necessary launch vehicle information, and support CNES in the verification of the compatibility of satellite interfaces with the launch vehicle;

12. Support CNES, along with the other Partners, in ground system and overall system-level testing, evaluation of test results, and preparation for operations;

13. Support CNES checkout and operation of the satellite during LEOP, including additional Earth terminals such as the Transportable Orbital Tracking System (TOTS), to provide data tracking, and Flight Dynamic Facility Center involvement to provide CNES with improved satellite position;

14. Support, along with the other Partners, the OSTM Assessment and Verification Phases, as defined in the OSTM Project Plan, and perform evaluation and calibration activities to verify the OSTM performance achieved on-orbit;

15. Provide to NOAA and CNES engineering support for anomaly resolution for NASA instruments throughout the OSTM lifetime;

16. Conduct, together with CNES, the preparation and release of relevant Research Announcements and, in coordination with NOAA, the selection of U.S. Investigators as specified in Article XI (OSTM Science Investigations and Application Demonstrations) of this MOU; and

17. Inform the Partners promptly of any technical or programmatic problems, which may affect overall OSTM schedules, cost, or performance.

Article VI
EUMETSAT Responsibilities

To implement this MOU, EUMETSAT will use reasonable efforts to:

1. Support CNES for the overall systems engineering function for OSTM;

2. Support, along with the other Partners, the preparation and maintenance of the OSTM Project Plan, OSS, System Requirements, Operational Concept, Project Schedule, and other Project Documents, to be approved by the Partners as defined in the Project Plan, including relevant interface control documents and in-orbit assessment and verification plans;

3. Establish a MAP for its own contribution, make it available to the other Partners, and review the MAPs of the other Partners;

4. Conduct or support, together with the other Partners as necessary, OSTM project reviews, as defined in the OSTM Project Plan;

5. Provide interface, design, fabrication, and test information and support, as necessary, for the other Partners to fulfill their respective responsibilities under this MOU;

6. Provide a mission-compliant site and infrastructure for accommodation of the European Earth terminal, support its installation, testing, arid on-site acceptance, and perform its integration with CNES support into EUMETSAT Ground Segment infrastructure, and maintain it throughout OSTM operations;

7. Support the installation, testing, and acceptance of a near real-time processing system at EUMETSAT Headquarters, and perform its integration into the EUMETSAT Ground Segment infrastructure with CNES support;

8. Establish and test the EUMETSAT elements of the OSTM Ground Segment with support of CNES, as defined in the OSTM Project Plan;

9. Support ground system and overall system-level integration, testing, and preparation of operations and assessment of readiness for launch and operations, as defined in the OSTM Project Plan, including training of key personnel;

10. Perform quality control of all products generated by EUMETSAT;

11. During all OSTM Phases, retrieve all Telemetry acquired at the European Earth terminal and make it available to the other Partners, as defined in the OSTM Project Plan;

12. During OSTM Assessment, Verification, and Routine Operations Phases, produce NRT Products from Telemetry acquired at the European Earth terminal and make them available to the other Partners, as defined in the OSTM Project Plan;

13. During OSTM Assessment, Verification, and Routine Operations Phases, make available the NRT Products produced at EUMETSAT and those generated and made available by NOAA, to users, as defined in the OSTM OSS and consistent with the Article XII (Data Policy);

14. Maintain an online storage of Telemetry acquired by EUMETSAT until such Telemetry is safely archived at the long term archives of CNES and NOAA; archive NRT Products generated by EUMETSAT and NOAA;

15. Support, along with the other Partners, the OSTM Assessment and Verification Phases, as defined in the OSTM Project Plan, and support evaluation and calibration activities to verify the OSTM performance achieved on orbit;

16. Provide a support service to users of NRT Products and a European focal point for offline users of wind-wave products, as defined in the OSTM OSS;

17. During all OSTM Phases, support NOAA and CNES in conducting mission operations;

18. Support the relevant Research Announcement process, and assess the relevance of investigation results to future operational services as specified in Article XI (OSTM Science Investigations and Application Demonstrations) of this MOU; and

19. Inform the Partners promptly of any technical or programmatic problems which may affect overall OSTM schedules, cost, or performance.

Article VII
NOAA Responsibilities

To implement this MOU, NOAA will use reasonable efforts to:

1. Support CNES for the overall systems engineering function for OSTM;

2. Support, along with the other Partners, the preparation and maintenance of the OSTM Project Plan, OSS, System Requirements, Operational Concept, Project Schedule, and other Project Documents, to be approved by the Partners, as defined in the Project Plan, including relevant interface control documents and in-orbit assessment and verification plans;

3. Provide NASA with required information necessary for NASA to establish and maintain the OSTM Safety Plan;

4. Establish a MAP for its own contribution, make it available to the other Partners, and review the MAPs of the other Partners;

5. Conduct or support, together with the other Partners as necessary, OSTM project reviews, as defined in the OSTM Project Plan;

6. Provide interface, design, fabrication, and test information and support as necessary to the other Partners to fulfill their respective responsibilities under this MOU;

7. Upgrade the NOAA Satellite Operations Control Center, CDA stations, and the data processing, archival, and distribution centers; integrate the OSTM-specific equipment, hardware, and real-time processing system into the NOAA infrastructure and communication system;

8. Test, with the support of NASA and CNES, the NOAA elements of the OSTM Ground Segment, as defined in the OSTM Project Plan;

9. Support the installation, testing, and acceptance of a near real time processing system at the NOAA-specified location, and perform its integration into the NOAA Ground Segment infrastructure with CNES support; procure and/or install the associated hardware as specified by CNES;

10. Archive all Telemetry, as defined in the OSTM Project Plan and consistent with Article XII (Data Policy), and perform offline monitoring of Housekeeping Data during all OSTM Phases;

11. Perform quality control of all products generated by NOAA;

12. Support ground system and overall system-level integration, testing, and preparation of operations and assessment of readiness for launch and operations, as defined in the OSTM Project Plan, including training of key personnel;

13. Support, along with the other Partners, the OSTM Assessment and Verification Phases, as defined in the OSTM Project Plan, and support evaluation and calibration activities to verify the OSTM performance achieved on orbit;

14. Support real-time mission operations before handover, and prepare for Routine Operations Phases with CNES support;

15. Operate and control the satellite after handover of this responsibility from CNES, including operation of the European Earth terminal;

16. During all OSTM Phases, acquire all Telemetry from the NOAA CDA Stations and make it available to the other Partners, as defined in the OSTM Project Plan;

17. During OSTM Assessment, Verification, and Routine Operations Phases, produce NRT Products from Telemetry acquired at the NOAA CDA Stations and make them available to the other Partners, as defined in the OSTM Project Plan;

18. During OSTM Assessment, Verification, and Routine Operations Phases, make available the NRT Products produced at NOAA and those generated and made available by EUMETSAT to users, as defined in the OSTM OSS and consistent with the Article XII (Data Policy);

19. Provide for long-term archival of OSTM Data Products and provide for access thereto, and make available the Offline Products generated by CNES to users, as defined in the OSTM OSS and consistent with the Article XII (Data Policy);

20. Support the relevant Research Announcement process, and assess the relevance of investigation results to future operational services, as specified in Article XI (OSTM Science Investigations and Application Demonstrations) of this MOU; and

21. Inform the Partners promptly of any technical or programmatic problems which may affect overall OSTM schedules, cost, or performance.

Article VIII
Program and Project Management

1. Each Partner will designate an OSTM Program and/or Project Manager responsible for fulfilling its respective responsibilities as defined in this MOU and based on mechanisms defined in the OSTM Project Plan.

2. The Partners will establish an OSTM Joint Steering Group (JSG) to provide oversight for the mission. The JSG will be comprised of up to two senior representatives from each Partner, as designated by the Partners in writing.

3. The JSG will meet at least once a year and, additionally, upon agreement of the Partners. The Partners' Program/Project Managers, Program or Mission Scientists, Project Scientists and others of their Project or Program staff, as agreed, will support these meetings,

4. The JSG will review project status, resolve conflicts as foreseen in Article XXJJI (Settlement of Disputes), and provide institutional resources to ensure timely delivery of mission elements. The JSG will be co-chaired by NASA and CNES during mission development, until handover of satellite operations, and by NOAA and EUMETSAT following handover of the satellite operations and control functions. Decision-making by the JSG will be made by consensus.

5. Changes that may impact other Partners in terms of OSTM cost, mission performance, schedule, and end of life of mission will require the approval of the JSG.

Article IX
Mission Reviews, Integration, and Flight Readiness

1. To implement OSTM, there will be a series of mission-level reviews, as defined in the OSTM Project Plan to evaluate the readiness of the Space and Ground Segments to proceed to implementation, integration, test, and final launch preparation. The JSG, which serves as the steering committee for these reviews, will ensure that representatives from all Partners, or each Partner's designees, are invited to serve on the boards of these reviews. All Partners will furnish relevant engineering and programmatic data and will participate in these reviews. The review process will be further described in the OSTM Project Plan.

2. Taking into account the results of the relevant reviews and key milestones, the Partners will jointly:

a. make a final determination on the system's readiness for operations;

b. make a final determination on the readiness of the satellite for integration with the launch vehicle; and

c. make a final determination on the overall readiness of the system for launch.

Article X
Project Plan and Operational Service Specification

1. CNDES will prepare, in close coordination with the other Partners, the OSTM Project Plan. This plan will contain detailed statements as to how this cooperative project is to be carried out, including mission planning, provision of the satellite, instruments, and ground systems, description of interfaces, conduct of mission operations, and data delivery, overall delivery schedule, plan for formal and informal reviews, process and configuration control, data delivery timeline, and other such

information as the Partners' Program/Project Managers deem necessary to control the project. The OSTM Project Plan will be approved by the JSG and maintained by the CNES Project Manager.

2. The Partners will establish and publish an OSTM OSS defining the OSTM standard Data Products and services that the Partners agree to make available jointly to the operational and Science user community. The OSTM OSS will be consistent with the Data Policy, approved by the JSG, and maintained by the CNES Project Manager.

3. In case of conflict between the OSTM Project Plan, OSS, or any other project document and this MOU, this MOU will prevail.

Article XI
OSTM Science Investigations and Application Demonstrations

1. Program or Mission Scientists: Each Partner will designate a Program or Mission Scientist responsible for its contribution to the joint OST Research Announcement (RA) process and related interactions with the operational user community. The designated Program or Mission Scientists will, in particular:

a. oversee the selection of an Ocean Surface Topography Science Team (OSTST) supporting TOPEX/Poseidon, Jason, and OSTM;

b. stimulate relevant interactions between selected OST investigators and the operational user community, including the establishment of agreed mechanisms for assessing the relevance of investigation results to future operational services; and

c. ensure relevant scientific input and feedback from the operational community to the JSG.

2. The OSTST: The suite of activities within the OSTST will be selected through competitions (the RA process) every 4 years or at a time as mutually agreed by the Partners. The activities will include scientific investigations and innovative application demonstration projects for OSTM. NASA, in coordination with NOAA, will select proposals to be funded by the United States, and CNES, in coordination with EUMETSAT, will select proposals expected to be funded by European funding agencies. The Partners will jointly select investigators from outside the United States and Europe. The OSTST will be a major contributor to geophysical calibration of OSTM, geophysical correction models update, and validation of data prior to release.

3. Project Scientists: NASA and CNES will designate Project Scientists to oversee the work of the OSTST and its interaction with the OSTM Project. They will be jointly responsible for the development of the scientific aspects of OSTM and for assuring that all data are effectively used across the OSTST and that the investigation results are expeditiously produced and made available. They will also be jointly responsible for coordinating science requirements, calibration and validation plans, and associated field experiments with other organizations.

Article XII
Data Policy

1. The Partners will make available to each other all Telemetry and Data Products in a timely manner and without any conditions as to the Partners' use of Telemetry and Data Products.

2. As a joint contribution to the worldwide exchange of meteorological and related data and products under the auspices of the WMO, the Partners will treat all Data Products listed in the OSTM OSS as "essential data and products," as defined in WMO Resolution 40 (Cg-XII), and will make them available as such to other users on a free and unrestricted basis.

3. The Partners will make available Payload Instrument Data and Data Products to Investigators selected through the joint RA process and ensure that OSTM Investigators provide a report to the Partners on the results of their investigations.

4. Subject to Article XIX (Exchange of Technology and Goods), algorithms developed for the purposes of processing payload instrument data into higher level data and science data products will be made available to the OSTST and, upon request, to other interested members of the scientific community for purposes of scientific calibration and validation.

5. All Telemetry and Data Products obtained from the OSTM system will be archived in appropriate data centers of the Partners, as defined in the OSTM Project Plan, and Data Products will be made available to all users. Additionally, pertinent ground-based and correlative observations made in support of Payload Instrument Data and Data Product validation will be archived and made available. Notwithstanding termination of this MOU, all Telemetry and Data Products will be archived by the Partners for at least 10 years after the termination of OSTM, unless otherwise agreed by the Partners.

6. There will be no period of exclusive use of Validated Data. The goal should be the release of Validated Data in some preliminary form at the start of the Initial Routine Operation Phase.

Article XIII
Publication of Public Information and Results

1. The Partners retain the right to release public information regarding their own activities under this MOU. The Partners will coordinate with each other in advance concerning public information activities which relate to the other Partner's responsibilities or performance under this MOU.

2. The Partners will ensure that the analyzed results obtained from the OSTM will be made available to the general scientific community through publication in appropriate journals or presentations at scientific conferences as soon as possible and consistent with good scientific practices. In the event that such reports or publications are copyrighted, the Partners will have a royalty free right under the copyright to reproduce, distribute, and use such copyrighted work for their own purposes.

Article XIV
Intellectual Property Rights

1. Nothing in this MOU will be construed as granting or implying any rights to, or interest in, patents owned or inventions which are independently developed by a Partner or a Related Entity.

2. All intellectual property conceived or developed solely by a Partner or Related Entity, in the performance of the activities of this MOU, will be owned by such Partner or a Related Entity.

3. In the event that an invention is jointly made by employees of more than one Partner and/or a Related Entity of more than one Partner during the implementation of this MOU, the Partners concerned will consult and agree as to the responsibilities and costs of actions to be taken to establish and maintain patent protection (in any country) for such invention and on the terms and conditions of any license or other rights to be exchanged or granted by or between the Partners.

Article XV
Customs/Taxes/Immigration

1. In accordance with applicable laws and regulations, each Partner will endeavor to facilitate free customs clearance and waiver of all applicable customs duties and taxes for equipment and related

goods necessary for the implementation of this MOU. In the event that any customs, duties, or taxes of any kind are nonetheless levied on such equipment and related goods, such customs duties or taxes will be borne by the Partner having its headquarters in the country levying such customs, duties, or taxes. Such arrangements will be fully reciprocal.

2. Subject to applicable laws and regulations, each Partner will endeavor to facilitate provision of the appropriate entry and residence documentation for personnel of the other Partners in order to carry out the activities under this MOU.

Article XVI
Exchange of Personnel

To facilitate coordination related to the OSTM, the Partners will support the exchange of a limited number of personnel from each Partner, at a time and under conditions as mutually agreed between the Partners' Project Managers, pursuant to necessary administrative authorizations. In the event of such an exchange, the Partners will provide necessary office space and administrative support at the host location, including such additional support' services as may be agreed between the Partners' Project Managers. Salary and all other expenses will be borne by the employing Partner of the personnel throughout the duration of their assignment.

Article XVII
Financial Arrangements

Each Partner will bear the costs of discharging its respective responsibilities, including travel and subsistence of personnel and transportation of all equipment and other items for which it is responsible. Further, it is understood that each Partner's obligations are subject to the availability of appropriated funds. Should any Partner encounter budgetary problems that may affect the activities to be carried out under this MOU, the Partner encountering the problems will notify and consult with the other Partners as soon as possible.

Article XVIII
Ownership of Elements and Equipment

For the purposes of this MOU, each Partner will retain ownership of elements and equipment it furnishes to another Partner, except as otherwise agreed. Any equipment not launched into space will be returned to the furnishing Partner at such time as mutually agreed, unless otherwise agreed. Each Partner will transport its equipment to the delivery points, as specified in the OSTM Project Plan, and, where appropriate, from such delivery points, when the equipment is to be returned to the furnishing Partner.

Article XIX
Exchange of Technology and Goods

The Parties will transfer only that technology (including algorithms, software, and source code) and those goods necessary to fulfill their respective responsibilities under this MOU, in accordance with the following provisions:

1. All activities of the Parties will be carried out in accordance with applicable laws and regulations, including their export control laws and regulations and those pertaining to the control of classified information.

2. The transfer of technology for the purpose of discharging the Parties' responsibilities with regard to interface, integration, and safety will normally be made without restriction, except as provided in paragraph 1 above.

3. All transfers of goods and proprietary or export-controlled technology are subject to the following provisions: In the event a Partner or its Related Entity finds it necessary to transfer goods or to transfer proprietary or export-controlled technology, for which protection is to be maintained, such goods will be specifically identified and such proprietary or export-controlled technology will be marked. The identification for goods and the marking on proprietary or export-controlled technology will indicate that the goods and proprietary or export-controlled technology will be used by the receiving Partner or its Related Entity only for the purposes of fulfilling the receiving Partner's or its Related Entity's responsibilities under this MOU, and that the identified goods and marked proprietary technology or marked export-controlled technology will not be disclosed or retransferred to any other entity without the prior written permission of the furnishing Partner or its Related Entity. The receiving Partner or its Related Entity will abide by the terms of the notice and protect any such identified goods and marked proprietary technology or marked export-controlled technology from unauthorized use and disclosure. The Partners to this MOU will cause their Related Entities to be bound by the provisions of this Article related to use, disclosure, and retransfer of goods and marked technology through contractual mechanisms or equivalent measures.

4. All goods exchanged in the performance of this MOU will be used by the receiving Partner or its Related Entity exclusively for the purposes of the MOU. Upon completion of the activities under the MOU, the receiving Partner or its Related Entity will return or, at the request of the furnishing Partner or its Related Entity, destroy, or otherwise dispose of, as mutually agreed, all goods and marked proprietary technology or marked export-controlled technology provided under this MOU.

Article XX
Liability

1. The Parties agree that a comprehensive cross-waiver of liability will enhance participation in space exploration, use, and investment. The cross-waiver of liability will be broadly construed to achieve this objective. The terms of the waiver are set out below.

2. As used in this Article:

   a. "Launch Vehicle" means an object or any part thereof intended for launch, launched from Earth, or returning to Earth which carries payloads;

   b. "Payload" means all property to be flown or used on or in a launch vehicle; and

   c. "Protected Space Operations" means all activities pursuant to this MOU, including launch vehicle activities and payload activities on Earth, in outer space, or in transit between Earth and outer space. Protected Space Operations begin at the entry into force of this MOU and end when all activities done in implementation of this MOU are completed. It includes, but is not limited to:

      (i) research, design, development, test, manufacture, assembly, integration, operation, disposal or use of launch or transfer vehicles, payloads, or instruments, as well as related support equipment and facilities and services; and

      (ii) all activities related to ground support, test, training, simulation, or guidance and control equipment and related facilities or services.

   Protected Space Operations excludes activities on Earth that are conducted on return from space to develop further a payload's product or process for use other than for the joint activity in question.

3.

a. Each Party agrees to a cross-waiver of liability pursuant to which each Party waives all claims against any of the entities or persons listed in subparagraphs (i) through (iii) below based on Damage arising out of Protected Space Operations. This cross-waiver of liability will apply only if the person, entity, or property causing the Damage is involved in Protected Space Operations and the person, entity, or property damaged is damaged by virtue of its involvement in Protected Space Operations. The cross-waiver of liability will apply to any claims for Damage, whatever the legal basis for such claims, including but not limited to delict and tort (including negligence of every degree and kind) and contract, against:

(i) another Party;

(ii) a Partner or a Related Entity of a Partner; and

(iii) the employees of any of the entities identified in subparagraphs (i) and (ii) immediately above.

b. In addition, each Partner will extend the cross-waiver of liability, as set forth in subparagraph 3.a above, to its Related Entities by requiring them, by contract or otherwise, to agree to waive all claims against the entities or persons identified in subparagraphs 3.a (i) through 3.a (iii) above.

c. Notwithstanding the other provisions of this Article, this cross-waiver of liability will not be applicable to:

(i) claims between a Partner and its own Related Entity or between its own Related Entities;

(ii) claims made by a natural person, his/her estate, survivors, or subrogees for bodily injury, other impairment of health or death of such natural person, except where the subrogee is a Partner;

(iii) claims for Damage caused by willful misconduct;

(iv) intellectual property claims;

(v) claims for Damage resulting from a failure of a Partner to extend the cross-waiver of liability, as set forth in subparagraph 3.b, or from a failure of a Partner to ensure that its Related Entities extend the cross-waiver of liability as set forth in subparagraph 3.b; or

(vi) contract claims between the Partners based on the explicit contractual provisions.

d. Nothing in this Article will be construed to create the basis for a claim or suit where none would otherwise exist.

e. For avoidance of doubt, this cross-waiver of liability includes a cross-waiver of liability arising from the Convention on International Liability for Damage Caused by Space Objects of March 29, 1972, where the person, entity, or property causing the Damage is involved in Protected Space Operations and the person, entity, or property is damaged by virtue of its involvement in Protected Space Operations.

4. In the event of third-party claims for which any of the Partners may be liable, the Partners will consult promptly to determine an appropriate and equitable apportionment of any potential liability and on the defense of any such claims.

5. NASA and NOAA, jointly, and CNES, have requested their respective governments to conclude an agreement that includes a cross-waiver of liability between their respective governments. All rights and obligations under this MOU related to the responsibility to launch as provided by paragraph 9 of Article V (NASA Responsibilities), will be contingent upon the conclusion between France and the United States of such an agreement.

Article XXI
Registration of Satellite and Frequencies

1. CNES will perform all the procedures enabling the Government of France to register the Jason-2 satellite as a space object in accordance with the Convention on Registration of Space Objects Launched into Outer Space of January 14, 1975. Registration pursuant to this Article will not affect the rights or obligations of the Parties under the 1972 Convention on International Liability for Damage Caused by Space Objects.

2. CNES will also take the necessary steps to ensure registration of the Jason-2 satellite frequencies by the International Telecommunication Union (ITU), with the support of the other Parties as required.

Article XXII
Provision for Future Cooperation

The Partners will consider working together, as appropriate, on a long-term basis to help define the research and operational requirements for implementation of future ocean surface topography missions involving Europe and the United States, with the objective of ensuring fitness for purposes of research and continuity of data and services for all applications.

In the event a mission failure unexpectedly terminates the OSTM prior to its planned end of lifetime, the Partners agree to consult regarding the resulting gaps in data collection.

Article XXIII
Settlement of Disputes

Disputes relating to this MOU will be resolved exclusively by the Parties.

Any dispute in the interpretation or implementation of the terms of this MOU that is not resolved by the Project and Program Managers will be referred to the JSG for settlement. Should the JSG be unable to resolve the dispute, it will be submitted to the representatives of each Partner as mentioned in the Preamble of this MOU, or their designees, for an amicable resolution.

Article XXIV
Entry into Force, Duration, Amendment, and Termination

1. This MOU will enter into force upon signature by all Parties. It will remain in force until completion of the Extended Routine Operation Phase. This MOU may be amended and extended by written agreement of the Parties. Any Party may terminate its participation in this MOU at any time upon at least 12 months written notice to the other Parties. In that event, the terminating Party will consult with the other Parties and will endeavor to minimize negative impacts of such termination on the other Parties and the mission.

2. Termination or expiration of this MOU will not affect the Parties' continuing obligations under Articles XII (Data Policy), XIII (Publication of Public Information and Results), XIV (Intellectual Property Rights), XIX (Exchange of Technology and Goods), and XX (Liability) of this MOU.

Done, in four originals, in the English and French languages, both language versions being equally authentic.

Signed at: Washington, DC
Date: March 21, 2006

[Signature]
FOR THE NATIONAL AERONAUTICS AND SPACE ADMINISTRATION

Signed at: Wash. DC
Date: 3/24/06

[Signature]
FOR THE NATIONAL OCEANIC AND ATMOSPHERIC ADMINISTRATION

Signed at: Paris
Date: April 7th, 2006

[Signature]
FOR THE CENTRE NATIONAL D'ETUDES SPATIALES

Signed at: Darmstadt
Date: 30/3/06

[Signature]
FOR THE EUROPEAN ORGANISATION FOR THE EXPLOITATION OF METEOROLOGICAL SATELLITES

I hereby certify that this is a true copy of the signed original.

[Signature] 10-4-06
Devon Fleming

State Department Document Number: 06-259

Amendment to the Memorandum of Understanding Between the United States of America National Aeronautics and Space Administration (NASA) and the European Space Agency Concerning Cooperation with Respect to the Hubble Space Telescope Program

Signed at Washington D.C.,
April 20 and 24, 2006
Entered into force April 24, 2006

CTIA DOCUMENT NUMBER: 13086.001

The United States National Aeronautics and Space Administration (NASA) and the European Space Agency (ESA),

Desiring to continue their cooperation with respect to the Hubble Space Telescope Program under their Memorandum of Understanding of October 7, 1977 (the "MOU"), as amended and extended on October 23, 2001,

Desiring to continue this successful cooperation until the end of operations of the HST, Deciding to amend the MOU in accordance with its ARTICLE 21,

Hereby agree as follows:

Replace the existing ARTICLE 22 of the MOU as follows:

> This Memorandum of Understanding shall remain in force until December 31, 2010. At least 1 year before the expiration of this Memorandum of Understanding, the Parties agree to consult as to continuation of this Memorandum of Understanding. This Memorandum of Understanding may be terminated by either Party after 6 months notice of its intention to terminate.

This amendment shall enter into force on the date of the last signature below.

FOR THE UNITED STATES NATIONAL AERONAUTICS AND SPACE ADMINISTRATION

[Signature]
Michael D. Griffin

20 Apr 2006
Date:

FOR THE EUROPEAN SPACE AGENCY

[Signature]
Jean-Jacques Dordain

24 April 2006
Date:

STATE DEPARTMENT DOCUMENT NUMBER: 06-260

EXTENSION AGREEMENT BETWEEN THE UNITED STATES OF AMERICA NATIONAL AERONAUTICS AND SPACE ADMINISTRATION (NASA) AND FEDERAL SPACE AGENCY, THE RUSSIAN FEDERATION, ON THE FLIGHT OF THE RUSSIAN HIGH ENERGY NEUTRON DETECTOR (HEND) INSTRUMENT ON THE UNITED STATES 2001 MARS ODYSSEY ORBITER MISSION

SIGNED AT WASHINGTON D.C.,
SEPTEMBER 12 AND 18, 2006
ENTERED INTO FORCE SEPTEMBER 18, 2006

CTIA DOCUMENT NUMBER: 13087.001

The United States National Aeronautics and Space Administration (hereinafter referred to as "NASA"), and the Federal Space Agency, the Russian Federation (hereinafter referred to as "Roscosmos"), both NASA and Roscosmos may be hereinafter referred to as a "Party" or collectively as "the Parties,"

Desiring to continue their cooperation with respect to the Russian HEND on the U.S. 2001 Mars Odyssey orbiter mission under the terms and conditions of the *Implementing Agreement Between the United States National Aeronautics, and Space Administration and the Russian Aviation and Space Agency on the Flight of the Russian High Energy Neutron Detector (HEND) on the United States 2001 Mars Odyssey Orbiter Mission* of April 6, 2001 (hereinafter referred to as "the Implementing Agreement"), during the extended operations and data analysis phase of the U.S. 2001 Mars Odyssey orbiter mission,

Recognizing that although the Implementing Agreement, expired on April 30, 2006, the Parties desire to continue to be bound by the terms and conditions of the Implementing Agreement,

Hereby agree as follows:

1. The Parties agree to continue to be bound by the same terms and conditions of the Implementing Agreement with the exception of the termination date in Paragraph 1 of ARTICLE XV.

2. All references to the "Russian Aviation and Space Agency" and "Rosaviakosmos" throughout the Implementing Agreement shall be replaced with "the Federal Space Agency, the Russian Federation" and "Roscosmos," respectively.

3. This Agreement shall enter into force on the date of the last signature below and shall remain in force until April 30, 2009, or the end of the U.S. 2001 Mars Odyssey orbiter mission operations and data analysis period, whichever is later.

FOR THE UNITED STATES NATIONAL AERONAUTICS AND SPACE ADMINISTRATION

[Signature]
Date: *9/18* 2006

FOR THE FEDERAL SPACE AGENCY, THE RUSSIAN FEDERATION

[Signature]
Date: *9/12* 2006

I hereby certify that this is a true copy of the original.

[Signature] 10/5/06
Timothy Tawney

State Department Document Number: 06-261

Arrangement Between the Nuclear Regulatory Commission of the United States of America (USNRC) and the Nuclear Power Inspectorate of Sweden (SKI) for the Exchange of Technical Information and Cooperation in the Regulation of Nuclear Safety, with Addenda

Signed at Vienna,
September 19, 2006
Entered into force September 19, 2006

CTIA Document Number: 13088.000

The Nuclear Regulatory Commission of the United States of America (hereinafter called the USNRC) and the Nuclear Power Inspectorate of Sweden, hereinafter called the SKI), the two together hereinafter referred to as the Parties;

Having a mutual interest in a continuing exchange of information pertaining to regulatory matters and of standards required or recommended by their organizations for the regulation of safety and environmental impact of nuclear facilities and activities, including management and final storage of spent fuel and nuclear waste;

Having similarly cooperated under the terms of a five-year Arrangement for the exchange of technical information cooperation in the regulation of nuclear safety, originally signed on December 6, 1974, between the United States Atomic Energy Commission (USAEC) and the SKI, and having already extended such Arrangement for five-year periods beginning October 30, 1979, January 24, 1985, October 4, 1989, December 12, 1994, and December 13, 2001; having indicated their mutual desire to continue the established cooperation for another five years;

Have agreed as follows:

I. SCOPE OF THE ARRANGEMENT

A. *Technical Information Exchange*

To the extent that the USNRC and SKI are permitted to do so under the laws, regulations, and policy directives of their respective authorities, the Parties will continue to exchange technical and regulatory information relating to the safety, safeguards, physical protection, transport safety, and environmental impact of nuclear facilities, materials, and activities, as designated by mutual consent.

1. Legislation, regulations, guides, and standards;
2. Major safety reviews, safety initiatives, and licensing decisions;

3. Reports on incidents and other operational experience of substantial significance;

4. Safety-related research, including the development of methods for safety regulation and supervision (See Addenda A and B. This area may require a separate agreement which would be subject at least to the terms of the present agreement, as determined to be necessary by one or both of the Parties.); and

5. Activities of immediate public interest.

II. ADMINISTRATION

A. The exchange of information under this Arrangement may be accomplished by post or appropriate means of electronic communication, including telephone, and by visits and meetings arranged in advance on a case-by-case basis.

B. An administrator will be designated by each Party to supervise and coordinate its participation in the overall exchange. The administrators will be the recipients of all documents transmitted under the exchange, unless the Parties decide otherwise. One or more technical coordinators may be appointed as direct contacts for specific disciplinary areas.

C. Meetings of persons implementing this Arrangement on behalf of the two Parties will be arranged only when the Parties mutually deem it to be appropriate. Any visit made under this Arrangement will take place only after consultation between administrators.

D. The transmitting Party does not warrant the suitability of any information for any particular use or application, and the application or use of such information exchanged or transferred between the Parties under this Arrangement will be the responsibility of the Receiving Party.

E. Nothing contained in this Arrangement will require either Party to take any action which would be inconsistent with its existing laws, regulations, and policy directives. No nuclear information related to proliferation-sensitive technologies will be exchanged under this Arrangement. Should any conflict arise between the terms of this Arrangement and those laws, regulations, and policy directives, the Parties agree to consult before any action is taken.

F. Unless otherwise agreed, all costs resulting from cooperation pursuant to this Arrangement will be the responsibility of the Party that incurs them. The ability of the Parties to carry out their obligations is subject to the appropriation of funds by the appropriate governmental authority and to the laws and regulations applicable to the Parties.

III. EXCHANGE AND USE OF INFORMATION

A. *General*

The Parties support the widest possible dissemination of information provided or exchanged under this Arrangement, subject both to the need to protect proprietary or other confidential or privileged information as may be exchanged hereunder, and to the provisions of Addendum C and the Intellectual Property Addendum, which are integral parts of this Arrangement.

B. *Confidentiality*

1. The Parties will inform each other about any information that is to be treated as confidential pursuant to this Arrangement.

2. The Parties are committed to protect any information that has been identified as confidential information. Such information will not be published or transmitted to any third party without prior written agreement from the Transmitting Party.

C. *Intellectual Property*

Without prejudice to the provisions of the Intellectual Property Addendum of this Arrangement, the Parties will jointly and effectively protect intellectual property in Accordance with the Parties' laws and concluded international agreements, which the Parties have undertaken to comply with.

D. *Consultation*

If one of the Parties becomes aware that it will be, or may reasonably be expected to become, unable to meet the provisions of this Article in order to comply with applicable laws or regulations or any other reason, it will immediately inform the other Party. The Parties will thereafter consult to define an appropriate course of action.

E. *Other*

Nothing contained in this Arrangement will preclude a Party from using or disseminating information received without restriction by a Party from sources outside of this Arrangement.

F. *Dispute Resolution*

The laws and regulations of the respective countries will govern cooperation under this Arrangement. Any dispute or questions among the Parties concerning the interpretation or application of this Arrangement arising during its term will be settled by mutual agreement of the parties.

IV. FINAL PROVISIONS

A. This Arrangement will enter into force upon signature and, subject to paragraph B. of this Article, will remain in force for a period of five years unless extended for a further period of time by written agreement of the Parties.

B. Either Party may withdraw from this Arrangement after providing the other Party with 180 days prior written notice of its intent to withdraw.

C. All information protected by proprietary or other confidential or privileged information will remain so protected for the duration of this Arrangement and after this Arrangement has expired or been terminated, unless otherwise specifically agreed by the Parties in writing.

DONE at Vienna, Austria on this 19th day of September 2006.

FOR THE NUCLEAR REGULATORY COMMISSION OF THE UNITED STATES OF AMERICA:

[Signature]

Dale E. Klein, Chairman

FOR THE NUCLEAR POWER INSPECTORATE OF SWEDEN:

[Signature]

Judith A. Melin, Director General

Addendum "A"
USNRC–SKI Safety Research Exchange
Areas In Which the USNRC Is Performing or Sponsoring Safety Research

1. Reactor Vessel and Piping Integrity
2. Aging of Reactor Components
3. Reactor Equipment Qualification
4. Thermal Hydraulic Code Applications and Maintenance
5. Plant Performance
6. Human Performance
7. Core Melt and Reactor Coolant System Failure
8. Reactor Containment Safety
9. Containment Structural Integrity
10. Seismic Safety
11. Probabilistic Risk Assessment
12. Severe Accident Analysis
13. Radiation Protection and Health Effects
14. Radionuclide Transport and Waste Management
15. Nuclear Fuel Analysis
16. Dry Cask Storage and Transport
17. Decommissioning
18. Advanced Reactor Designs
19. Fire Protection

ADDENDUM "B"
USNRC–SKI Nuclear Safety Research Exchange Areas
in Which the SKI is Performing or Sponsoring Safety Research

1. Integrated Safety Assessment
2. Safety Analysis
3. Man-Technology-Organization (MTO)
4. Material and Chemistry
5. Solid Mechanics
6. Control and Material Testing
7. Thermal Hydraulics
8. Fuel Safety
9. Severe Accidents

10. Safety and Process Instrumentation and Control

11. Nuclear Waste

12. Nuclear Non-Proliferation

13. Regulatory Management

14. Emergency Preparedness

15. Support to Universities and Nordic Research

16. Miscellaneous

ADDENDUM "C"
Information Exchange and Use

A. *Definitions*

For the purposes of this Arrangement:

1. The term "information" means nuclear energy-related regulatory, safety, safeguards, waste management, scientific, or technical data, including information on results or methods of confirmatory assessment, research, and any other knowledge intended to be provided or exchanged under this Arrangement.

2. The term "proprietary information" means information made available under this Arrangement which contains trade secrets or other privileged or confidential information (such that the person having the information may derive an economic benefit from it or may have a competitive advantage over those who do not have it), and may only include information which:

(a) has been held in confidence by its owner;

(b) is of a type which is customarily held in confidence by its owner;

(c) has not been transmitted by the owner to other entities (including the Receiving Party) except on the basis that it be held in confidence;

(d) is not otherwise available to the Receiving Party from another source without restrictions on its further dissemination; and

(e) is not already in the possession of the Receiving Party.

3. The term "other confidential or privileged information" means information, other than "proprietary information," which is protected from public disclosure under the laws and regulations of the country providing the information and which has been transmitted and received in confidence.

B. *Marking Procedures for Documentary Proprietary Information*

A Party receiving documentary proprietary information pursuant to this Arrangement will respect the privileged nature thereof, *provided* such proprietary information is clearly marked with the following (or substantially similar) restrictive legend:

> This document contains proprietary information furnished in confidence under an Arrangement dated September 19, 2006 between the Nuclear Regulatory Commission of the United States of America and the Nuclear Power Inspectorate of Sweden and will not be disseminated outside these organizations, their consultants, contractors, and licensees, and concerned departments and agencies of the Government of the United States and the Government of Sweden without the prior approval of (*name of the Transmitting Party*). This notice will be marked on any reproduction hereof, in whole or in part.

These limitations will automatically terminate when this information is disclosed by the owner without restrictions.

[Missing in original.]

D. *Marking Procedures for Other Confidential or Privileged Information of a Documentary Nature*

A Party receiving under this Arrangement other confidential or privileged information will respect its confidential nature, *provided* such information is clearly marked so as to indicate its confidential or privileged nature and is accompanied by a statement indicating:

1. that the information is protected from public disclosure by the Government of the Transmitting Party, and
2. that the information is transmitted under the condition that it be maintained in confidence.

E. *Dissemination of Other Confidential or Privileged Information of a Documentary Nature*

Other confidential or privileged information may be disseminated in the same manner as that set forth in paragraph D., *Dissemination of Documentary Proprietary Information.*

F. *Non-Documentary Proprietary or Other Confidential or Privileged Information*

Non-documentary proprietary or other confidential or privileged information provided in seminars and other meetings arranged under this Arrangement, or information arising from attachments of staff, use of facilities, or joint projects, will be treated by the Parties according to the principles specified for documentary information in this Arrangement; *provided*, however, that the Party communicating such proprietary or other confidential or privileged information has placed the recipient on notice as to the character of the information communicated.

INTELLECTUAL PROPERTY ADDENDUM

Pursuant to Article III. of this Arrangement:

The Parties shall ensure adequate and effective protection of intellectual property created or furnished under this Arrangement and relevant implementing arrangements. The Parties agree to notify one another in a timely fashion of any inventions or copyrighted works arising under this Arrangement and to seek protection for such intellectual property in a timely fashion. Rights to such intellectual property shall be allocated as provided in this Addendum.

I. SCOPE

1. This Addendum is applicable to all cooperative activities undertaken pursuant to this Arrangement, except as otherwise specifically agreed by the Parties or their designees.

2. For purposes of this Arrangement, "intellectual property" shall have the meaning found in Article 2 of the Convention Establishing the World Intellectual Property Organization, done at Stockholm, July 14, 1967; *viz.*, 'intellectual property' shall include the rights relating to:

—literary, artistic and scientific works,

—performances of artists, phonograms, and broadcasts,

—inventions in all fields of human endeavor,

—scientific discoveries,

—industrial designs,

—trademarks, service marks, and commercial names and designations,

—protection against unfair competition,

and all other rights resulting from intellectual activity in the industrial, scientific, literary, or artistic fields."

3. This Addendum addresses the allocation of rights, interests, and royalties between the Parties. Each Party shall ensure that the other Party can obtain rights to intellectual property allocated in accordance with the Addendum by obtaining those rights from its own participants through contracts or other legal means, if necessary. This Addendum does not otherwise alter or prejudice the allocation between a Party and its nationals, which shall be determined by that Party's laws and practices.

4. Disputes concerning intellectual property arising under this Arrangement should be resolved through discussions between the concerned participating institutions or, if necessary, the Parties or their designees. Upon mutual agreement of the Parties, a dispute shall be submitted to an arbitral tribunal for binding arbitration in accordance with the applicable rules of international law. Unless the Parties or their designees agree otherwise in writing, the arbitration rules of the United Nations Commission on International Trade Law (UNCITRAL) shall govern.

5. Termination or expiration of this Arrangement shall not affect rights or obligations under this Addendum.

II. *ALLOCATION OF RIGHTS*

1. Each party shall be entitled to a non-exclusive, irrevocable, royalty-free license in all countries to translate, reproduce, and publicly distribute scientific and technical journal articles, reports, and books directly arising from cooperation under this Arrangement. All publicly distributed copies of copyrighted work prepared under this provision shall indicate the names of the authors of the work unless an author explicitly declines to be named.

2. Rights to all forms of intellectual property, other than those rights described in Section II.1., above, shall be allocated as follows:

a. Visiting researchers, for example, scientists visiting primarily in furtherance of their education, shall receive intellectual property rights under the policies of the host institution. In addition, each visiting researcher named as an inventor shall be entitled to share in a portion of any royalties earned by the host institution from the licensing of such intellectual property.

b. (1) For intellectual property created during joint research, for example, when the Parties, participating institutions, or participating personnel have agreed in advance on the scope of work, each Party shall be entitled to obtain all rights and interests in its own country. The Party in whose country the invention was made shall have first option to acquire all rights and interests in third countries. If research is not designated as "joint research," rights to intellectual property arising from the research will be allocated in accordance with paragraph II.2.a., above. In addition, each person named as an inventor shall be entitled to share in a portion of any royalties earned by either institution from the licensing of the property.

(2) Notwithstanding paragraph II.2.b.(1), above, if a type of intellectual property is available under the laws of one Party but not of the other Party, the Party whose laws provide for this type of protection shall be entitled to all rights and interests worldwide. Persons named as inventors of the property shall nonetheless be entitled to royalties as provided in paragraph II.2.b.(1), above.

STATE DEPARTMENT DOCUMENT NUMBER: 06-262

ACQUISITION AND CROSS-SERVICING AGREEMENT BETWEEN THE UNITED STATES OF AMERICA AND THE REPUBLIC OF MALI, WITH ANNEXES

SIGNED AT BAMAKO,
SEPTEMBER 20, 2006
ENTERED INTO FORCE SEPTEMBER 20, 2006

CTIA DOCUMENT NUMBER: 13089.000

Effective Date: *20 Sep 06*

PREAMBLE

The Government of the United States of America and the Government of the Republic of Mali, represented respectively by the Department of Defense of the United States of America and the Ministry of Defense and Veterans of the Republic of Mali, hereinafter referred to as the Parties, desiring to further the interoperability, readiness, and effectiveness of their respective military forces through increased logistic cooperation, have resolved to conclude this Acquisition and Cross-Servicing Agreement (USA–MLI–01).

ARTICLE I
DEFINITIONS

As used in this Agreement and in any Implementing Arrangements which provide specific procedures, the following definitions apply:

a. *Equal Value Exchange.* Payment for a transfer conducted under this Agreement in which it is agreed that the Receiving Party shall replace Logistic Support, Supplies, and Services that it receives with Logistic Support, Supplies, and Services of an equal monetary value.

b. *Implementing Arrangement.* A written supplementary arrangement for Logistic Support, Supplies, and Services that specifies details, terms, and conditions to implement this cross-servicing agreement effectively.

c. *Invoice.* A document from the Supplying Party which requests reimbursement or payment for specific Logistic Support, Supplies, and Services rendered pursuant to this Agreement and any applicable Implementing Arrangements.

d. *Logistic Support, Supplies, and Services.* Food, water, billeting, transportation (including airlift), petroleum, oils, lubricants, clothing, communication services, medical services, ammunition, base operations support (and construction incident to base operations support), storage services, use of facilities, training services, spare parts and components, repair and maintenance services, calibration services, and port services. This term also includes the temporary use of general purpose vehicles and other nonlethal items of military equipment, where such lease or loan is permitted under the national laws and regulations of the Parties.

e. *Order*. A written request, in an agreed upon format and signed by an authorized individual, for the provision of specific Logistic Support, Supplies, and Services pursuant to this Agreement and any applicable Implementing Arrangement.

f. *Point of Contact*. An entity (usually an office or agency) which is authorized by a Party to bind that Party by signing an Order requesting or agreeing to supply Logistic Support, Supplies, and Services under this Agreement, or by collecting or making payments for Logistic Support, Supplies, and Services supplied or received under this Agreement.

g. *Receiving Party*. The Party ordering and receiving support.

h. *Replacement-In-Kind*. Payment for a transfer conducted under this Agreement in which it is agreed that the Receiving Party shall replace Logistic Support, Supplies, and Services that it receives with Logistic Support, Supplies, and Services of an identical, or substantially identical, nature under agreed conditions.

i. *Supplying Party*. The Party providing support.

j. *Transfer*. Selling (whether for payment in currency, Replacement-In-Kind, or exchange of supplies or services of equal value), leasing, loaning, or otherwise temporarily providing Logistic Support, Supplies, and Services under the terms of this Agreement.

ARTICLE II
PURPOSE

This Agreement is entered into for the purpose of establishing basic terms, conditions, and procedures to facilitate the reciprocal provision of Logistic Support, Supplies, and Services as that term is defined in Article I of this Agreement.

ARTICLE III
APPLICABILITY

1. This Agreement is designed to facilitate reciprocal logistic support between the Parties to be used primarily during combined exercises, training, deployments, operations, or other cooperative efforts, and for unforeseen circumstances or exigencies in which one of the Parties may have a need for Logistic Support, Supplies, and Services.

2. This Agreement applies to the provision of Logistic Support, Supplies, and Services from the military forces of one Party to the military forces of the other Party in return for either cash payment or the reciprocal provision of Logistic Support, Supplies, and Services to the military forces of the Supplying Party.

3. All activities of the Parties under this Agreement and any Implementing Arrangements shall be carried out in accordance with their respective national laws and regulations. All obligations of the Parties under this Agreement and any Implementing Arrangements shall be subject to the availability of funds for such purposes. Unless otherwise agreed in advance, a Party shall not place an Order and receive support under this Agreement and any Implementing Arrangement unless it has funds (or agreed-upon in-kind support) available to pay for such support. If a Party discovers that it does not have the funds to perform its obligations, it shall promptly notify the other Party who

shall have the right to discontinue its provision of any support that was to be paid with such funds. This shall not affect the obligation of a Party to pay for support already received.

4. The following items are not eligible for transfer under this Agreement and are specifically excluded from its coverage:

a. weapon systems;

b. major end items of equipment (except for the lease or loan of general purpose vehicles and other nonlethal items of military equipment where such lease or loan is permitted under the national laws and regulations of the Parties); and

c. initial quantities of replacement and spare parts associated with the initial order of major items of organizational equipment; however, individual replacement and spare parts needed for immediate repair and maintenance services may be transferred.

5. Also excluded from transfer by either Party under this Agreement are any items the transfer of which are prohibited by its national laws or regulations. In accordance with U.S. law and regulation, the United States may not currently transfer the following items under this Agreement:

a. guided missiles;

b. naval mines and torpedoes;

c. nuclear ammunition (including such items such as warheads, warhead sections, projectiles, demolition munitions, and training ammunition);

d. cartridge and propellant-actuated devices;

e. chaff and chaff dispensers;

f. guidance kits for bombs or other ammunition;

g. chemical munitions or ammunition (other than riot-control agents);

h. source, byproduct, or special nuclear materials, or any other material, article, data, or thing of value the transfer of which is subject to the *Atomic Energy Act of 1954* (Title 42, United States Code, Section 2011, et. seq.);

i. items of military equipment designated as Significant Military Equipment on the United States Munitions List (Part 121 of Title 22 of the U.S. Code of Federal Regulations) for temporary use (e.g. lease or loan).

ARTICLE IV
TERMS AND CONDITIONS

1. Each Party shall make its best efforts, consistent with national priorities, to satisfy requests from the other Party under this Agreement for Logistic Support, Supplies, and Services. However, when an Implementing Arrangement contains a stricter standard for satisfying such requests, the standard in the Implementing Arrangement shall apply.

2. Orders may be placed or accepted only by the points of contact, or designees, identified by the Parties in Annexes B through I of this Agreement. When military forces of United States European Command (USEUCOM) require Logistic Support, Supplies, or Services outside the USEUCOM Area of Responsibility (AOR), they may place orders directly with the cognizant point of contact or may seek the assistance of USEUCOM, or a USEUCOM Component Command, to place an order with a non-USEUCOM point of contact.

3. An Implementing Arrangement under this Agreement may be negotiated on behalf of the U.S. Department of Defense by Headquarters, USEUCOM, the Headquarters of other United States

combatant commands, or their designees. Implementing Arrangements may be negotiated on behalf of the Republic of Mali Ministry of Defense and Veterans by the Ministry of Defense and Veterans. Implementing Arrangements must identify points of contact and their specific authorizations or limitations.

4. Prior to submitting a written Order, the ordering Party should initially contact the Supplying Party's point of contact by telephone, fax, or e-mail to ascertain availability, price, and desired method of repayment for required materiel or services. Orders must include all the data elements in Annex A, as well as any other terms and details necessary to carry out the transfer. Minimum Essential Data Elements, a Standard ACSA Order Form with completion instructions are attached at Annex A. The number of this Agreement, USA–MLI–01, should be annotated on all Orders and related correspondence.

5. Both Parties shall maintain records of all transactions.

6. The Receiving Party is responsible for:

a. arranging pickup and transportation of supplies acquired under this Agreement. This does not preclude the Supplying Party from assisting with loading supplies acquired under this Agreement onto the transportation conveyance.

b. obtaining any applicable customs clearance and arranging other official actions required by national customs regulations.

7. The individual designated by the Receiving Party to receive the Logistic Support, Supplies, and Services on behalf of the Receiving Party shall sign the Standard ACSA Order Form (Annex A / Tab B) in the appropriate block as evidence of receipt. If the standard order form is not available at the Supplying Party's point of issue, the individual receiving the support, supplies, and services shall sign the receipt document provided by the Supplying Party as a substitute. The number of this Agreement, USA–MLI–01, shall be entered on the receipt document.

8. The Supplying Party shall be responsible for:

a. notifying the Receiving Party when and where Logistic Support, Supplies, and Services are available to be picked up; and

b. forwarding the signed receipt document to the point of contact authorized to accept Orders under this Agreement. The signed receipt document shall be attached to the original Order Form.

9. Logistic Support, Supplies, and Services received through this Agreement shall not be retransferred, either temporarily or permanently, to any entity other than the Receiving Party without the prior written consent of the Supplying Party.

ARTICLE V
REIMBURSEMENT

1. For transfers of Logistic Support, Supplies, and Services under this Agreement, the Parties shall agree for payment either by cash ("reimbursable transaction"), or by Replacement-In-Kind or an Equal Value Exchange (both of which are exchange transactions). The Receiving Party shall pay the Supplying Party as provided in either paragraph 1a. or paragraph 1b. of this Article.

a. *Reimbursable Transaction*. The Supplying Party shall submit Invoices to the Receiving Party after delivery or performance of the Logistic Support, Supplies, and Services. Both Parties shall provide for the payment of all transactions and each Party shall invoice the other Party at least once every three months for all transactions not previously invoiced. Invoices shall be accompanied by necessary support documentation and shall be paid within 30 days of the date prepared. Payment shall be made in the currency of the Supplying Party or as otherwise agreed in the Order. In pricing a reimbursable transaction, the Parties agree to the following reciprocal pricing principles:

(1) In the case of specific acquisition by the Supplying Party from its contractors on behalf of a Receiving Party, the price shall be no less favorable than the price charged the military forces by the contractor of the Supplying Party for identical items or services, less any amounts excluded by Article VI of this Agreement. The price charged may take into account differentials due to delivery schedules, points of delivery, and other similar considerations.

(2) In the case of transfer from the Supplying Party's own resources, the Supplying Party shall charge the same price charged its own military forces for identical Logistic Support, Supplies, and Services, as of the date delivery or performance occurs, less amounts excluded by Article VI of this Agreement. In any case where a price has not been established or charges are not made for one's own military forces, the Parties shall agree on a price in advance, reflecting reciprocal pricing principles, excluding charges that are precluded under these same reciprocal pricing principles.

b. *Exchange Transaction.* Exchange transactions may be by Replacement-In-Kind or Equal-Value-Exchange. The Receiving Party shall pay by transferring to the Supplying Party Logistic Support, Supplies, and Services that are agreed between the Parties to be identical (or substantially identical) or to be of equal monetary value to the Logistic Support, Supplies, and Services delivered or performed by the Supplying Party. When Equal Value Exchange is the agreed method of payment, prior to the provision of the requested support both Parties will agree, to the extent possible, on the goods and services that will be accepted for payment. The Receiving Party is responsible for arranging return transportation and delivery of the replacement logistic support, supplies and services to the location mutually agreed between the Parties at the time the order is signed. If the Receiving Party does not complete the exchange within the terms of a replacement schedule agreed to or in effect at the time of the original transaction, which may not exceed one year from the date of the original transaction, the transaction shall be deemed reimbursable and governed by paragraph 1a above, except that the price shall be established using actual or estimated prices in effect on the date payment would otherwise have been due.

c. *Establishment of Price or Value.* The following pricing mechanisms are provided to clarify application of the reciprocal pricing principles. The price established for inventory stock materiel shall be the Supplying Party's stock list price. The price for new procurement shall be the same price paid to the contractor or vendor by the Supplying Party. The price for services rendered will be the Supplying Party's standard price, or, if not applicable, the costs directly associated with providing the services. Prices charged shall exclude all taxes and duties which the Receiving Party is exempted from paying under other agreements which the Governments of the Parties have concluded. Upon request, the Parties agree to provide information sufficient to verify that these reciprocal pricing principles have been followed and that prices do not include waived or excluded costs.

2. When a definitive price for the Order is not agreed to in advance, the Order, pending agreement on final price, shall set forth a maximum liability for the Receiving Party. The Parties shall then promptly enter into negotiation to establish the final price.

3. Points of contact for payments and collections for each Party are identified in annexes to this Agreement.

4. The price for Logistic Support, Supplies, and Services under this Agreement shall not be higher than the price for the same Logistic Support, Supplies, and Services available under any other agreement between the Parties or their Governments.

ARTICLE VI
WAIVED OR EXCLUDED COSTS

Insofar as national laws and regulations permit, the Parties shall ensure that any readily identifiable duties, taxes, and similar charges are not imposed on activities conducted under this Agreement. The Parties shall cooperate to provide proper documentation to maximize tax and customs relief. The provisions of any applicable tax and customs relief agreements shall also apply under this Agreement. The Parties shall inform each other whether the price charged for Logistic Support, Supplies, or Services includes taxes or duties. In determining whether duties, taxes and similar charges should be levied, the pricing principles in Article V, and in particular Article V, paragraph 1, subparagraph c, will govern the value of the support, supplies, or services provided by the Supplying Party.

ARTICLE VII
SECURITY OF INFORMATION

It is the intent of the Parties that activities under this Agreement and any Implementing Arrangements be carried out at the unclassified level. Unless specifically authorized by separate written agreement or arrangement, no classified information or material shall be provided or generated under this Agreement or any Implementing Arrangements.

ARTICLE VIII
DISPUTE RESOLUTION, AMENDMENT OF THE AGREEMENT, AND REVISION OF INFORMATION

1. Any disagreements regarding the interpretation or application of this Agreement, any Implementing Arrangements, or transactions executed hereunder shall be resolved through consultation between the Parties and shall not be referred to any international tribunal or third party for settlement.

2. Either Party may, at any time, request amendment of this Agreement by giving the other Party written notice. In the event such a request is made, the Parties shall promptly enter into negotiations. This Agreement may be amended only by written agreement between the Parties. Replacement of Annexes B through I, which list points of contact, may be done by a Party transmitting the replacement annex to the other Party through military channels, without formal amendment of this Agreement.

ARTICLE IX
ENTRY INTO FORCE AND TERMINATION

This Agreement, USA–MLI–01, which consists of a Preamble, Articles I–IX, and Annexes A through I, shall enter into force upon the date of the last signature. This Agreement shall remain in force unless terminated by the mutual consent of the Parties or by either Party giving not less than 180 days notice in writing to the other Party of its intent to terminate. Notwithstanding termination of this Agreement, all reimbursement obligations incurred pursuant to its terms shall remain binding on the responsible Party until satisfied.

IN WITNESS WHEREOF, the undersigned, being duly authorized by their respective governments, have signed this Agreement, USA–MLI–01.

DONE, in duplicate in the English and French languages, each being equally authentic.

FOR THE GOVERNMENT OF THE UNITED STATES OF AMERICA REPRESENTED BY THE DEPARTMENT OF DEFENSE

[Signature]

MICHAEL J. LYDEN
Rear Admiral, SC, USN
Director, Logistics and
Security Assistance
HQ, European Command
at: *Bamako, Mali*
on: *20 Sep 06*

FOR THE GOVERNMENT OF THE REPUBLIC OF MALI REPRESENTED BY THE MINISTRY OF DEFENSE AND VETERANS

[Signature]

ABDOU KARIM DIOP
Brigadier General, Malian Army
Secretary General
Ministry of Defense and Veterans

at: *Bamako, Mali*
on: *20 Sep 06*

LIST OF ANNEXES

ANNEX G—USSOUTHCOM Points of Contact

ANNEX H—USNORTHCOM Points of Contact

ANNEX I—USTRANSCOM Points of Contact

ANNEX A
ACSA ORDERING INFORMATION

TAB A—Minimum Essential Data Elements

TAB B—Standard ACSA Order Form—2006

TAB C—Instructions for manual completion of Standard ACSA Order Form—2006

ANNEX A / TAB A
MINIMUM ESSENTIAL DATA ELEMENTS

1) Implementing Arrangements or support Agreement

2) Date of Order

3) Designation and address of office to be billed

4) Numerical listing of stock numbers of items, if any

5) Quantity and description of material/services requested

6) Quantity furnished

7) Unit of Measurement

8) Unit price in currency of billing country or as otherwise agreed to

9) Quantity furnished (6) multiplied by unit price (8)

10) Currency of billing country or other billing currency as agreed to

11) Total Order amount expressed in currency of billing country or as otherwise agreed to

12) Name (typed or printed), signature, and title of authorized Ordering or requisitioning representative

13) Payee to be designated on remittance

14) Designation and address of office to receive remittance

15) Recipient's signature acknowledging service or supplies received on the Order or requisition or a separate supplementary document

16) Document number of Order or requisition

17) Receiving organization

18) Issuing organization

19) Transaction type

20) Fund citation or certification of availability of funds when applicable under Parties' procedures

21) Date and place of original transfer; in the case of an exchange transaction, a replacement schedule including time and place of replacement transfer

22) Name, signature and title of authorized acceptance official

23) Additional special requirement, if any, such as transportation, packaging, etc.

24) Limitation of government liability

25) Name, signature, date and title of Supplying Party official who actually issues supplies or services.

ANNEX A / TAB B
Standard ACSA Order Form—2006

ACQUISITION AND CROSS-SERVICING AGREEMENT (ACSA)/MUTUAL LOGISTICS SUPPORT (MLS) ORDER FORM

1. Requisition No.	2. Support Agreement	3. Operation/Theater	4. Order Date
5. Requesting Unit	6. Requesting Nation	7. Providing Unit	8. Providing Nation
9. Deliver to Unit	10. Deliver to Country	11. Deliver Place	12. Deliver Time

13. REQUESTED LINE ITEM SUMMARY (SEE ATTACHED LINE ITEM DETAIL SHEET)

No	Sub	Attch	Stock No & Description	Unit of Mea	Quantity Request (less Previously Received)	Quantity Received	Unit Price	Total

14. Method of Payment	15. Currency	16. Not to Exceed Amount	17. Line Item Cost
[ ] Cash [ ] Replacement-in-Kind (RIK) [ ] Equal-Value-Exchange (EVE)			

<table>
<tr><th colspan="6">ACQUISITION AND CROSS-SERVICING AGREEMENT (ACSA)/MUTUAL LOGISTICS SUPPORT (MLS) ORDER FORM</th></tr>
<tr><td colspan="3">22. Authorized Requestor</td><td colspan="2">23. Authorized Supplier</td><td>18. Trans Costs</td></tr>
<tr><td colspan="3">Signature</td><td colspan="2">Signature</td><td>19. Other Costs</td></tr>
<tr><td colspan="2">Name (Last, First MI, Rank/Title)</td><td>Date</td><td>Name (Last, First MI, Rank/Title)</td><td>Date</td><td>20. Total Claimed</td></tr>
<tr><td>Unit/Office</td><td colspan="2">Nation/Organization</td><td>Unit/Office</td><td>Nation/Organization</td><td>21. Agreed Return Date</td></tr>
<tr><td>24. Purchase Order No</td><td>25. Fund Citation</td><td>26. Bill To</td><td colspan="3" rowspan="2">30. Remarks</td></tr>
<tr><td>27. Invoice No.</td><td>28. Account No./Finance Tracking No.</td><td>29. Pay To</td></tr>
<tr><td colspan="3">31. Receipt</td><td colspan="3">32. Invoice

I Certify that the amount invoiced is exclusive of all taxes fro which exemption has been granted under provisions of existing agreements and that the invoice is correct.</td></tr>
<tr><td colspan="3">Signature</td><td colspan="3">Signature</td></tr>
<tr><td colspan="2">Name (Last, First MI, Rank/Title)</td><td>Date</td><td colspan="2">Name (Last, First MI, Rank/Title)</td><td>Date</td></tr>
<tr><td>Unit/Office</td><td colspan="2">Nation/Organization</td><td>Unit/Office</td><td colspan="2">Nation/Organization</td></tr>
</table>

ANNEX A / TAB C
INSTRUCTIONS FOR MANUAL COMPLETION OF STANDARD ACSA ORDER FORM—2006

For manual Order, if the ACSA Global Automated Tracking and Recording Systems (AGATRS) is not available

1. REQUEST NUMBER: Enter an order identification number, with a unit / organization (Ex . . . USA, USAFE, etc. . . . .) Specific prefix, Julian calendar date, and sequence number (001, 002, 003. . . . .).

2. SUPPORT AGREEMENT: Enter the ACSA agreement number (such as USA–XXX–01), and the number of any associated Implementing Arrangement that the order will be done under.

3. OPERATION / THEATER: Enter the Operations / Theater where support is being provided (such as Bosnia, Kosovo, etc. . . . .).

4. ORDER DATE: Self explanatory.

5. REQUESTING UNIT / DEMANDER: Enter the unit / organization actually receiving the LSSS.

6. REQUESTING NATION / ORGANIZATION: Enter the nation or organization (such as SHAPE, etc. . . . .) of the Requesting Party.

7. PROVIDING UNIT / SUPPLIER: Enter the unit / organization actually providing the LSSS.

8. PROVIDING NATION / ORGANIZATION: Enter the nation or organization (such as US, SHAPE, etc. . . . .).

9. DELIVER TO UNIT / DESTINATION: Enter Location of Unit to receive delivery.

10. DELIVERY TO COUNTRY: Enter the name of nation receiving delivery.

11. DELIVER PLACE: Enter Bldg Number / Location of delivery.

12. DELIVER TIME: Enter Date-Time (ZULU) Group (DDTTTTZ MMM YY) of desired delivery date and time (example: 061400Z AUG 04).

13. REQUESTED LINE ITEM SUMMARY:

a. Enter National Stock Number if applicable.

b. Enter a general description of each item requested.

c. Enter the appropriate or the agreed to unit of measure for specified type of LSSS.

d. Enter quantity of the specified item based on entered Unit of Measure.

e. Enter Unit Price of the specified item.

f. Enter Total Amount on the specified item(s) based on the entered Unit of Measure and Unit Price.

14. METHOD OF PAYMENT: Mark the appropriate block for “Cash”, Replacement-In-Kind”, or “Equal Value Exchange”.

15. CURRENCY: Enter currency to be paid in.

16. NOT TO EXCEED AMOUNT: Maximum liability if applicable.

17. LINE ITEM COST: Enter the total amount of the order.

18. TRANSPORTATION COST: Enter the costs of transportation if any.

19. OTHER COSTS: Enter all additional costs (for example: customs, packing fees, etc. . . . .).

20. TOTAL CLAIMED: Enter the total amount of the order.

21. AGREED RETURN DATE: Enter return date for Replacement-In-Kind (RIK), or Equal Value Exchange (EVE) transactions, or for Temporary Transfers (Loans or Leases). Note: Dates RIK and EVE may not exceed one year from date of initial delivery.

22. AUTHORIZED REQUESTOR: Information for authorized (must hold office of listed POC organization in the POC Annex of applicable ACSA or IA) approving official for the requesting party. Enter Name, Title and Unit/Office of Requesting Official.

23. AUTHORIZED SUPPLIER/APPROVING OFFICIAL FOR SUPPLYING PARTY: Approving official (must hold office of listed POC organization in POC Annex of applicable ACSA or IA) for Supplying Party. Enter Name, Title and Unit/Office of Approving Official.

24–29: TO BE FILLED IN BY INVOICING AUTHORITY

30. REMARKS: Enter date range for support or services that are continuous in nature (Example: Billeting Services that are scheduled from 1 January to 31 March).

31–32: TO BE FILLED IN BY INVOICING AUTHORITY

ANNEX B
REPUBLIC OF MALI, MINISTRY OF DEFENSE AND VETERANS
POINTS OF CONTACT

ACSA ORDERING AND APPROVING POINTS OF CONTACT

1. The Republic of Mali, Ministry of Defense and Veterans agency responsible for **approving, placing, and accepting orders** is:

a. Unit: **MINISTRY OF DEFENSE AND VETERANS**

b. Commercial Telephone: **(223) 16 41**

c. 24 hour/after duty hours contact telephone: **(222) 50 21**

d. Commercial Fax: **(223) 16 41**

e. Mailing Address: **BP 2083 Bamako, Mali**

ACSA FINANCIAL POINTS OF CONTACT

2. Republic of Mali, Ministry of Defense and Veterans agency responsible for **collecting and making payments** for support, supplies, and services is:

a. Unit: **ADMINISTRATIVE DIRECTORATE OF FINANCE**

b. Commercial Telephone: **(222) 00 66**

c. Commercial Fax: **(222) 00 66**

d. Mailing Address: **BP 2083 Bamako, Mali**

ANNEX C
USCENTCOM
POINTS OF CONTACT, ORDERING AND FINANCIAL RESPONSIBILITIES

TAB A—HQ USCENTCOM

TAB B—USARCENT (Army)

TAB C—USNAVCENT (Navy)

TAB D—USCENTAF (Air Force)

TAB E—USMARCENT (Marine Corps)

TAB F—SOCCENT (Special Operations)

ANNEX C / TAB A
U.S. CENTRAL COMMAND (USCENTCOM)

1. The USCENTCOM POC for coordinated **placement and acceptance of orders** under this agreement is the USCENTCOM J4-Operations Directorate, Multinational Logistics and Contracting Branch (CCJ4–O/MLC).

a. Unit:	CCJ4–O/MLC
b. Telephone:	Com'l: 813–827–6420/5822 DSN: 651–6420/5822
c. Fax:	Com'l: 813–827–5828 DSN: 651–5828
d. Message Address:	USCENTCOM//J4/O/MLC//
e. Mailing Address:	USCENTCOM ATTN: CCJ4–O/MLC 7115 South Boundary Boulevard MacDill AFB, FL 33621–5101

2. The USCENTCOM agency responsible for **payments and collections** in support of this agreement is the USCENTCOM COMPTROLLER OFFICE.

a. Unit:	CCCO
b. Telephone:	Com'l: 813–827–5884 DSN: 651–5884
c. Fax:	Com'l: 813–827–4218/4648 DSN: 651–4218/4648
d. Message Address:	USCENTCOM//CCCO//
e. Mailing Address:	USCENTCOM ATTN: CCCO 7115 South Boundary Boulevard MacDill AFB, FL 33621–5101

ANNEX C / TAB B
THIRD U.S. ARMY / U.S. ARMY FORCES CENTRAL COMMAND (USARCENT)

1. The USARCENT POC responsible for **approving, placing, and accepting orders** is the G–4, Logistics Sustainment Division.

a. Unit:	Third U.S. Army, G–4
b. Telephone:	Com'l: 404–464–2927 DSN: 367–2927
c. Fax:	Com'l: 404–464–4030 DSN: 367–4030 Com'l: 404–464–4579 (Classified) DSN: 367–4579 (Classified)
d. Message Address:	COMUSARCENT FT MCPHERSON GA//G4//
e. Mailing Address:	Third U.S. Army, ATTN: G–4, AFRD–GD–LS 18881 Hardee Ave SW Ft McPherson, GA 30330

2. The USARCENT agency responsible for **payments and collections** in support of this agreement is the USARCENT Comptroller.

a. Unit:	Third U.S. Army, Comptroller
b. Telephone:	Com'l: 404–464–4885/4049 DSN: 367–4885/4049
c. Fax:	Com'l: 404–464–4823 DSN: 367–4823
d. Message Address:	COMUSARCENT FT MCPHERSON GA//COMPTROLLER//
e. Mailing Address:	Third U.S. Army, ATTN: Comptroller, AFRD–CM 18881 Hardee Ave SW Ft McPherson, GA 30330

ANNEX C / TAB C
U.S. NAVAL FORCES CENTRAL COMMAND (USNAVCENT)

1. The USNAVCENT POC for coordinated **placement and acceptance of orders** under agreement is the USNAVCENT N4.

a. Unit:	COMUSNAVCENT-BAHRAIN Code: N4/Coalition Logistics Officer
b. Telephone:	Com'l: (CC) 973–1785–3721/3722 DSN: 318–439–3721/3722
c. Fax:	Com'l: 973–1785–9936 DSN: 318–439–9936 Com'l: 973–1785–4579 (Classified) DSN: 318–439–4579 (Classified)
d. Message Address:	COMUSNAVCENT//N4//COALITION LOGISTICS OFFICER//
e. Mailing Address:	COMUSNAVCENT Code: N4/LRC/Coalition Logistics Officer/ FPO AE 09501–6008

2. The USNAVCENT agency responsible for **payments and collections** in support of this agreement is the COMUSNAVCENT COMPTROLLER.

a. Unit:	COMUSNAVCENT Comptroller, CODE NOOCF
b. Telephone:	Com'l: 973–1785–3029/4254 DSN: 318–439–3029/4254
c. Fax:	Com'l: 973–1785–9936 DSN: 318–439–9936
d. Message Address:	COMUSNAVCENT//N00CF//
e. Mailing Address:	COMUSNAVCENT Code: NOOCF FPO AE 09501–6503

ANNEX C / TAB D
U.S. AIR FORCES CENTRAL COMMAND (USCENTAF)

1. The USCENTAF POC for coordinated **placement and acceptance of orders** under this agreement is the A4, Logistics Plans Office.

a. Unit:	US CENTAF/ A4–LGXP
b. Telephone:	Com'l: 803–895–4460/4455 DSN: 965–4460
c. Fax:	Com'l: 803–895–2947 DSN: 965–2947
d. Message Address:	COMUSCENTAF SHAW AFB SC//A4//
e. Mailing Address:	US CENTAF/ A4–LGXP 524 Shaw Drive, Suite 135 Shaw AFB, SC 29152

2. The USCENTAF agency responsible for **payments and collections** in support of this agreement is the 9th Air Force Financial Management Analysis Branch.

a. Unit:	9 AF/FMA
b. Telephone:	Com'l: 803–895–2806 DSN: 965–2806
c. UNCLASSIFIED Fax:	Com'l: 803–895–2809 DSN: 965–2809
d. Message Address:	USCENTAF SHAW AFB SC//FMA//
e. Mailing Address:	US CENTAF/9th AF–FMA 524 Shaw Drive, Suite 237 Shaw AFB, SC 29152

ANNEX C / TAB E
U.S. MARINE FORCES CENTRAL COMMAND (USMARCENT)

1. The USMARCENT POC for coordinated **placement and acceptance of orders** under this agreement is the MARFORPAC G–4–CENTCOM BRANCH.

a. Unit:	MARFORPAC, G4-RESOURCE BRANCH
b. Telephone:	Com'l: 808–477–8341 DSN: 477–8341
c. Fax:	Com'l: 808–477–8709 DSN: 477–8709 Com'l: 808–477–0077 (Classified) DSN: 477–0077 (Classified)
d. Message Address:	COMUSMARCENT//G4//
e. Mailing Address:	USMARCENT, G–4 ATTN: Resource Branch (Multinational Logistics) Box 64118 Camp H. M. Smith, HI 96861–4118

2. The USMARCENT agency responsible for **payments and collections** in support of this agreement is the USMARCENT G–8.

a. Unit:	USMARCENT G–8
b. Telephone:	Com'l: 808–477–8557 DSN: 477–8557
c. Fax:	Com'l: 808–477–8702 DSN: 477–8702 Com'l: 808–477–0077 (Classified) DSN: 477–0077 (Classified)
d. Message Address:	COMUSMARCENT//G8//
e. Mailing Address:	USMARCENT, G–8 Box 64112 Camp H. M. Smith, HI 96861–4112

ANNEX C / TAB F
SPECIAL OPERATIONS COMMAND CENTRAL (SOCCENT)

1. The Special Operations Command Central (SOCCENT) POC for **coordinated placement and acceptance of orders** under this agreement is the SOCCENT, J4.

a. Unit:	SOCCCENT, J4
b. Telephone:	Com'l: 813–828–0297 DSN: 968–0297
c. Fax:	Com'l: 813–828–4826 DSN: 968–4826 Com'l: 813–828–8372 (Classified) DSN: 968–8372 (Classified)
d. Message Address:	COMSOCCENT MACDILL AFB FL//J4//
e. Mailing Address:	HQ, SOCCENT ATTN: SOCCENT, J4 7115 South Boundary Boulevard MacDill AFB, FL 33621–5101

2. The Special Operations Command Central (SOCCENT) agency responsible for **payments and collections** in support of this agreement is the SOCCENT Comptroller.

a. Unit:	SOCCENT, Comptroller
b. Telephone:	Com'l: (813) 828–4614//DSN: 968–4614
c. Fax:	Com'l: 813–828–8747 DSN: 968–8747 Com'l: 813–828–1894 (Classified) DSN: 968–1894 (Classified)
d. Message Address:	COMSOCCENT MACDILL AFB FL//SOCCO//
e. Mailing Address:	HQ SOCCENT ATTN: SOCCO 7115 South Boundary Boulevard MacDill AFB, FL 33621–5101

ANNEX D
USPACOM/USFJ/USFK
POINTS OF CONTACT, ORDERING AND FINANCIAL RESPONSIBILITIES

TAB A—USPACOM

TAB B—PACFLT (Navy)

TAB C—USARPAC (Army)

TAB D—MARFORPAC (Marines)

TAB E—PACAF (Air Force)

TAB F—SOCPAC (Special Operations Command)

TAB G—USFJ (Japan)

TAB H—USARJ (Army)

TAB I—MARFORJ (Marines)

TAB J—USAFJ (Air Force)

TAB K—USFK (Korea)

ANNEX D / TAB A
COMMANDER, U.S. PACIFIC COMMAND (CDRUSPACOM)

1. The USPACOM POC for coordinated **placement and acceptance of orders** under this agreement is the J45, Security Assistance and International Logistics Division:

a. Unit:	CDRUSPACOM J4
b. Telephone:	Com'l (808) 477–0387
c. Fax:	Com'l (808) 477–6669 Com'l (808) 477–0844 (Classified)
d. Message Address:	CDRUSPACOM HONOLULU HI//J4//
e. Mailing Address:	HQ CDRUSPACOM J4 Bldg 400, Box 64020 Camp H. M. Smith, HI 96861–4020

2. The USPACOM POC responsible for **payments and collections** in support of this agreement is the Comptroller:

a. Unit:	CDRUSPACOM J05
b. Telephone:	Com'l (808) 477–6680
c. Fax:	Com'l (808) 477–0535
d. Message Address:	CDRUSPACOM HONOLULU HI//J05//
e. Mailing Address:	HQ CDRUSPACOM J05 Box 64037 Camp H. M. Smith, HI 96861–4037

ANNEX D / TAB B
COMMANDER, U.S. PACIFIC FLEET (PACFLT)

1. The CDRPACFLT POC responsible for **approving, placing, and accepting orders** is:

a. Unit:	COMPACFLT (N401)
b. Telephone:	Com'l (808) 474–6445
c. Fax:	Com'l (808) 474–6448
d. Message Address:	COMPACFLT PEARL HARBOR HI//N401H//
e. Mailing Address:	Commander, U.S. Pacific Fleet Code N401 251 Makalapa Drive Pearl Harbor, HI 96860–3131

2. The CDRPACFLT POC for **collecting and making payments** for support, supplies, and services is:

a. Unit:	COMPACFLT (N00F)
b. Telephone:	Com'l (808) 474–6950
c. Fax:	Com'l (808) 474–6937
d. Message Address:	COMPACFLT PEARLHARBOR HI//N00F//
e. Mailing Address:	Commander, U.S. Pacific Fleet Code N00F 250 Makalapa Drive Pearl Harbor, HI 96860–3131

ANNEX D / TAB C
U.S. ARMY PACIFIC (USARPAC)

1. The USARPAC POC responsible for **approving, placing, and accepting orders** under this agreement is Headquarters USARPAC Logistics Plans and International Programs:

a. Unit:	USARPAC/APLG–PIL
b. Telephone:	Com'l (808) 438–8615
c. Fax:	Com'l (808) 438–3460
d. Message Address:	CDRUSARPAC FT SHAFTER HP//APLG–PIL//
e. Mailing Address:	Commander, U.S. Army, Pacific Attn: APLG–PIL, Logistics Plans and International Programs Ft. Shafter, HI 96858

2. The USARPAC POC responsible for **payments and collections** for this agreement is the Defense Finance and Accounting Service, Honolulu Operating Location:

a. Unit:	DFAS
b. Telephone:	Com'l (808) 472–3760
c. Fax:	Com'l (808) 472–8250
d. Message Address:	DFAS HONOLULU HI//
e. Mailing Address:	DFAS Box 77, Building 1392 Pearl Harbor, HI 96860–7552

ANNEX D / TAB D
MARINE FORCES PACIFIC (MARFORPAC)

1. The MARFORPAC POC responsible for **approving, placing, and accepting orders** under this agreement is:

a. Unit:	HQ MARFORPAC/G4
b. Telephone:	Com'l (808) 477–2066/2067
c. Fax:	Com'l (808) 477–0260
d. Message Address:	COMMARFORPAC//G4//
e. Mailing Address:	Commander MARFORPAC (GA Ops) Box 64118 Camp H. M. Smith, HI 96861–4118

2. The MARFORPAC POC responsible for **payments and collections** in support of this agreement is:

a. Unit:	MARFORPAC/G8
b. Telephone:	Com'l (808) 477–5051
c. Fax:	Com'l (808) 477–7100
d. Message Address:	COMMARFORPAC//G8//
e. Mailing Address:	Commander USMARFORPAC (G–8) Box 64112 Camp H. M. Smith, HI 96861–4112

ANNEX D / TAB E
PACIFIC AIR FORCES (PACAF)

1. The PACAF POC responsible for **approving, placing, and accepting orders** under this agreement is Headquarters PACAF Logistics Plans and Programs, Plans Branch:

a. Unit:	PACAF/LGR
b. Telephone:	Com'l (808) 449–3778
c. Fax:	Com'l (808) 449–3690
d. Message Address:	HQ PACAF HICKAM AFB HI//LGR//
e. Mailing Address:	HQ PACAF/LGR 25 E. Street, Suite H–302 Hickam AFB, HI 96853–5427

2. The PACAF POC responsible for **payments and collections** for this agreement is Headquarters PACAF Logistics Plans and Programs, Plans Branch:

a. Unit:	DFAS Pacific-AIF
b. Telephone:	Com'l (808) 472–7908
c. Fax:	Com'l (808) 472–5816
d. Message Address:	DFAS Honolulu// HI//LGXW//
e. Mailing Address:	DFAS Pacific-AIF 477 Essex Street Pearl Harbor, HI 96860–5806

ANNEX D / TAB F
SPECIAL OPERATIONS COMMAND PACIFIC (SOCPAC)

1. The SOCPAC POC responsible for **approving, placing, and accepting orders** under this agreement is:

a. Unit:	SOCPAC/SOJ4
b. Telephone:	Com'l (808) 477–0615
c. Fax:	Com'l (808) 477–2908
d. Message Address:	COMSOCPAC HONOLULU HI//SOJ4//
e. Mailing Address:	HQ SOCPAC/SOJ4 Box 64046 Camp H. M. Smith, HI 96861–4046

2. The SOCPAC POC responsible for **payments and collections** in support of this agreement is:

a. Unit:	SOCPAC/SOJ08
b. Telephone:	Com'l (808) 477–2603
c. Fax:	Com'l (808) 477–3880
d. Message Address:	COMSOCPAC HONOLULU HI//SOJO8//
e. Mailing Address:	HQ SOCPAC/SOJO8 Box 64046 Camp H. M. Smith, HI 96861–4046

ANNEX D / TAB G
US FORCES JAPAN (HQ USFJ)

1. The USFJ POC responsible for **approving, placing, and accepting orders** under this agreement is:

a. Unit:	USFJ/J43
b. Telephone:	Com'l: 0425–52–2511 ext. 5–2445 DSN: 225–2445
c. Fax:	Com'l: 0425–52–2511 ext. 5–4709 DSN: 225–4709
d. Message Address:	COMUSJAPAN YOKOTA AB JA//J4//
e. Mailing Address:	Headquarters, United States Forces, Japan Logistics Directorate/J4, Yokota Air Base Fussa-Shi, Tokyo 197

2. The USFJ agency responsible for **payments and collections** under this agreement is:

a. Unit:	DFAS–J
b. Telephone:	Com'l: 0425–52–2511, ext. 5–9838 DSN: 225–9838
c. Fax:	Com'l 0425–52–2511, ext. 5–9841 DSN: 225–3213
d. Message Address:	DFAS JAPAN YOKOTA JA//
e. Mailing Address:	DFAS–J, Unit 5220, Bldg 206 Yokota Air Base Fussa-Shi, Tokyo 197

ANNEX D / TAB H
US ARMY JAPAN (USARJ)

1. The USARJ POC responsible for **approving, placing, and accepting orders** under this agreement is:

a. Unit:	USARJ, DCS, G4
b. Telephone:	Com'l: 0462–51–1788 ext. 263–7204 DSN: 263–5471
c. Fax:	Com'l: 0462–51–1788 ext. 263–8372 DSN: 263–8372
d. Message Address:	CDRUSARJ 9th TSC CP ZAMA JA//DSCLOG//
e. Mailing Address:	HQ, USARJ/DCS, G4 ATTN: APAJ–GD–LOG, (ACSA POC) Camp Zama, Zama-Shi Kanagawa-Ken, 288–0000

2. The USARJ POC responsible for **approving, placing, and accepting orders** for the 836th U.S. Army Transportation Battalion under this agreement is:

a. Unit:	836th U.S. Army Transportation Bn
b. Telephone:	Com'l: 0454–53–4840 ext. 269–6630 DSN: 269–6330
c. Fax:	Com'l: 0454–53–4840 ext. 269–6246 DSN: 269–6739
d. Message Address:	CDR 836TH TRANS BN YOKOHAMA JA//SDPC–YO–XO//
e. Mailing Address:	836th U.S. Army Transportation Bn ATTN: SDPC–YO–XO Mizuho Sanbashi Kanagawa-Ku Yokohama-Shi, 221–0034

3. The USARJ POC responsible for approving, placing, and accepting orders for the 835th U.S. Army Transportation Bn under this agreement is:

a. Unit:	835th U.S. Army Transportation Bn
b. Telephone	Com'l: 098–857–3844 DSN: 648–7729
c. Fax:	Com'l: 098–892–5111 ext. 648–7731 DSN: 648–7731
d. Message Address:	CDR 835TH TRANS BN OKINAWA JA//MTPC–OK–XO//
e. Mailing Address:	835th U.S. Army Transportation Bn ATTN: MTPC–OK–XO Shisetsu, Bldg, 305 Nahagunko-Nai, Kakinohana-Cho Naha-Shi, Okinawa 900

4. The USARJ agency responsible for **payments and collections** under this agreement is:

a. Unit:	DFAS–J (Army Accounting)
b. Telephone:	Com'l: 042–552–2511 ext. 5–5340 DSN: 225–5340
c. Fax:	Com'l: 042–552–2511 ext. 5–3523 DSN: 225–3523
d. Message Address:	DFAS JAPAN YOKOTA JA//
e. Mailing Address:	DFAS–J (Army Accounting) Unit 5220 ATTN: AAOA Yokota Air Base Fussa-Shi, Tokyo 197

ANNEX D / TAB I
MARINE FORCES JAPAN (MARFORJ)

1. The MARFORJ POC responsible for **approving, placing, and accepting orders** for the III MEF under this agreement is:

a. Unit:	III Marine Expeditionary Force (G–4/Supply)
b. Telephone:	Com'l: 0988–92–5111 ext. 622–7137 DSN: 622–7137
c. Fax:	Com'l: 0988–92–5111 ext. 622–9019 DSN: 622–9019
d. Message Address:	CG III MEF//G4//
e. Mailing Address:	Commanding General ATTN: AC/S G4/MRB/SUP Unit 35601 FPO AP 96606–5061

2. The MARFORJ POC responsible for **approving, placing, and accepting orders** for Marine Forces Japan, Camp Butler under this agreement is:

a. Unit:	Marine Corps Base, Camp S.D. Butler (G–4/)
b. Telephone:	Com'l: 0988–92–5111 ext. 645–7223 DSN: 645–7223
c. Fax:	Com'l: 098–892–5111 ext. 645–7231 DSN: 6457231
d. Message Address:	CG MCB CP BUTLER JA//G4//SUPPLY//
e. Mailing Address:	Commanding General, Marine Corps Base, Camp S.D. Butler (G4) ATTN: ACSA POC Unit 35001 FPO AP 96373–5001, Central Post Office, Naha-shi, Okinawa-ken 900

3. The MARFORJ agency responsible for **payments and collections** under this agreement is:

a. Unit:	Marine Forces Japan, Camp Butler (Comptroller)
b. Telephone:	Com'l: 098–892–5111 ext. 645–7310 DSN: 645–7310
c. Fax:	Com'l: 098–892–5111 ext. 645–7351 DSN: 645–7759
d. Message Address:	DMS CG MCBUTLER COMPT JA//COMPT//
e. Mailing Address:	Commanding General Marine Forces Japan (Comptroller) Unit 35001 ATTN: ACSA POC FPO AP 96373–5001 Central Post Office, Naha-shi, Okinawa-ken 900

ANNEX D / TAB J
US AIR FORCES JAPAN (USAFJ)

1. The USAFJ POC responsible for **approving, placing, and accepting orders** under this agreement is:

a. Unit:	HQ 5AF 605 ASUS/LGX (Logistics Plans and Programs)
b. Telephone:	Com'l: 0425–52–2511, ext. 5–4173 DSN: 225–4173
c. Fax:	Com'l: 0425–52–2511, ext. 5–8831 DSN: 225–8831
d. Message Address:	5AF YOKOTA AB JA/LGX//
e. Mailing Address:	HQ 5AF 605 Air Support Squadron/LGX Logistics Division, Plans and Programs Branch ATTN: ACSA POC, Yokota Air Base, Fussa-Shi, Tokyo 197

2. The USAFJ agency responsible for **payments and collections** under this agreement is:

a. Unit:	DFAS–J
b. Telephone:	Com'l: 0425–52–2511, ext. 5–9838 DSN: 225–9838
c. Fax:	Com'l: 0425–52–2511, ext. 5–9841 DSN: 225–3213
d. Message Address:	DFAS JAPAN YOKOTA JA//
e. Mailing Address:	DFAS–J, Unit 5220, Bldg 206 Yokota Air Base, Fussa-Shi, Tokyo 197

ANNEX D / TAB K
US FORCES KOREA (HQ USFK)

1. The HQ USFK POC for coordinated **placement and acceptance of orders** under this agreement is the J45, Security Assistance and International Logistics Division:

a. Unit:	CDRUSPACOM J4
b. Telephone:	Com'l (808) 477–0387
c. Fax:	Com'l (808) 477–6669 Com'l (808) 477–0844 (Classified)
d. Message Address:	CDRUSPACOM HONOLULU HI//J4//
e. Mailing Address:	HQ CDRUSPACOM J4 Bldg 400, Box 64020 Camp H. M. Smith, HI 96861–4020

2. The HQ USFK POC responsible for **payments and collections** in support of this agreement is the Comptroller:

a. Unit:	CDRUSPACOM J05
b. Telephone:	Com'l (808) 477–6680
c. Fax:	Com'l (808) 477–0535
d. Message Address:	CDRUSPACOM HONOLULU HI//J05//
e. Mailing Address:	HQ CDRUSPACOM J05 Box 64037 Camp H. M. Smith, HI 96861–4037

ANNEX E
UNITED STATES EUROPEAN COMMAND (USEUCOM) POINTS OF CONTACT, ORDERING AND FINANCIAL RESPONSIBILITIES

TAB A—USEUCOM

TAB B—USAFE (Air Force)

TAB C—USAREUR (Army)

TAB D—USNAVEUR (Navy)

TAB E—USMARFOREUR (Marine Corps)

TAB F—SOCEUR (Special Operations)

TAB G—USAREUR SFOR (Bosnia and Herzegovina)

TAB H—USAREUR KFOR (Kosovo)

ANNEX E / TAB A
HQ U.S. EUROPEAN COMMAND (USEUCOM) POINTS OF CONTACT POINTS OF CONTACT, POLICY, LEGAL, ORDERING, AND FINANCIAL RESPONSIBILITIES

1. The USEUCOM POC for **policy issues** under this agreement is the ECJ4 Logistics Sustainment Division, Multinational Logistics Branch, ACSA Program:

a. Unit:	HQ USEUCOM ECJ4–LS–ML–ACSA
b. Telephone:	Commercial 49–711–680–7474 / 1490 DSN 430–7474 / 1490
c. Fax:	Commercial 49–711–680–7476 DSN 430–7476
CLASSIFIED Fax:	Commercial 49–711–680–7402 DSN 430–7402
d. Message Address:	CDRUSEUCOM VAIHINGEN GE//ECJ4–LS//
e. Mailing Address:	HQ USEUCOM, ECJ4–LS ATTN: ML–ACSA Unit 30400, Box 1000 APO AE 09131

2. The EUCOM agency responsible for policy issues regarding **international law and legal matters** in support of this agreement is the Staff Judge Advocate:

a. Unit:	HQ USEUCOM–ECJA
b. Telephone:	Commercial 49–711–680–8001 DSN 430–8001
c. Fax:	Commercial 49–711–680–5370 DSN 430–5370
d. Message Address:	CDRUSEUCOM VAIHINGEN GE//ECJA//
e. Mailing Address:	HQ USEUCOM–ECJA Unit 30400 APO AE 09131

3. The USEUCOM POC's for coordination and authorized for **approving, placing, and acceptance of orders** under this agreement is:

3.1. The ECJ4 Logistics Sustainment Division, Multinational Logistics Branch, ACSA Program:

a. Unit:	HQ USEUCOM ECJ4–LS–ML–ACSA
b. Telephone:	Commercial 49–711–680–7474 / 1490 DSN 430–7474 / 1490
c. Fax:	Commercial 49–711–680–7476 DSN 430–7476
CLASSIFIED Fax:	Commercial 49–711–680–7402 DSN 430–7402
d. Message Address:	CDRUSEUCOM VAIHINGEN GE//ECJ4–LS//
e. E-mail Address:	acsa@eucom.mil
f. Mailing Address:	HQ USEUCOM, ECJ4–LS ATTN: ML–ACSA Unit 30400, Box 1000 APO AE 09131

3.2. The ECJ4 EUCOM Deployment and Distribution Operation Center (EDDOC), to include the Logistics Readiness Center (LRC):

a. Unit:	HQ USEUCOM ECJ4–EDDOC
b. Telephone:	Commercial 49–711–680–8766 (24 hour) DSN 430–8766 (24 hour)
c. Fax:	Commercial 49–711–680–6104 (24 hour) DSN 430–7476 (24 hour)
CLASSIFIED Fax:	Commercial 49–711–680–7402 (24 hour) DSN 430–7402 (24 hour)
d. Message Address:	CDRUSEUCOM VAIHINGEN GE// ECJ4–EDDOC//
e. Mailing Address:	HQ USEUCOM, ECJ4–EDDOC Unit 30400, Box 1000 APO AE 09131

4. The EUCOM agency responsible for policy issues regarding **payments and collections** in support of this agreement is the Comptroller:

a. Unit:	HQ USEUCOM–ECCM
b. Telephone:	Commercial 49–711–680–5119 or 7105 DSN 430–5119 or 7105
c. Fax:	Commercial 49–711–680–5370 DSN 430–5370
d. Message Address:	CDRUSEUCOM VAIHINGEN GE//ECCM//
e. Mailing Address:	HQ USEUCOM–ECCM Unit 30400 APO AE 09131

ANNEX E / TAB B
HQ U.S. AIR FORCES EUROPE (HQ USAFE) POINTS OF CONTACT
ORDERING AND FINANCIAL RESPONSIBILITIES

1. The HQ USAFE agency responsible for approving, placing and accepting orders under this agreement is Headquarters USAFE Logistics Readiness Division, International Logistics Branch:

a. Unit:	HQ USAFE/A4RI
b. Telephone:	Commercial 49–6371–47–6788 DSN 480–6788
c. Fax:	Commercial 49–6371–47–9255 DSN 480–9255
d. Message	HQ USAFE RAMSTEIN AB GE//A4RI//
e. Mailing Address:	
(Military) HQ USAFE/A4RI Unit 3050, Box 105 APO AE 09094–0105	(Commercial) HQ USAFE/A4RI Gebäude 528, Zim. 102; Flugplatz 66877 Ramstein-Miesenbach, GE

2. The HQ USAFE agency responsible for payments and collections for this agreement is the Defense Finance and Accounting Service, Ramstein AB:

a. Unit:	DFAS–ADCJ
b. Telephone:	Com'l 49–6371–47–2068 DSN 480–2068
c. Fax:	Com'l 49–6371–47–7582 DSN 480–7582
d. Message Address:	USAFE DFAS–CCE/MSA Office
e. Mailing Address:	
(Military) HQ USAFE/DFAS CCE/MSA Unit 3050, Box 5 APO AE 09094–0505	(Commercial) HQ USAFE/DFAS CCE/MSA Gebäude 413, Zim. 210, Flugplatz 66877 Ramstein-Miesenbach, GE

ANNEX E / TAB C
U.S. ARMY EUROPE (USAREUR)

The HQ USAREUR agencies responsible for **approving, placing, and accepting orders** under this agreement are:

1. For logistics support, supplies, and services **in connection with training**:

a. Unit/Address:	Commander 7th Army Training Command ATTN: AETT–RM–MGT Unit 28130, APO AE 09114–8130 Grafenwoehr Lager D–92655 Grafenwoehr, Germany
b. Telephone:	Commercial 49–9641–83–7159 DSN 475–7159
c. Fax:	Commercial 49–9641–83–8416 DSN 475–8416
d. Message Address:	CDR7ATC GRAFENWOEHR GE// AETT–RM–MGT//

2. For **all other logistics support, supplies, and services**:

a. Unit/Address:	HQ USAREUR/7A ATTN: AEAGF–PB–TCS Unit 29351, APO AE 09014–9351 Roemerstr. 168 69128 Heidelberg, Germany
b. Telephone:	Commercial 49–6221–57–6375 DSN 370–6375
c. Fax:	Commercial 49–6221–57–6194 DSN 370–6194
d. Message Address:	CGUSAREUR HEIDELBERG GE// AEAGF–PM–TCS//

3. **Paying Office** for HQ USAREUR/7A:

a. Unit/Address:	DFAS Europe Army Vendor Pay Unit 23122 APO AE 09227 Mannheimer Strasse 218/219 D–67657 Kaiserslautern, Germany
b. Telephone:	Commercial 49–631–413–4278/4183/4109/4111 DSN 484–4278/4183/4109/4111
c. Fax:	Commercial 49–631–413–4290/4293 DSN 484–4290/4293

4. Paying Office for Balkans Area of Operations:

a. Unit/Address:	Commercial Vendor Service (CVS) Finance Detachment, Bldg 1330–C Camp Bondsteel Kosovo APO AE 09340
b. Telephone:	Commerical 49–621–730–781–5467 DSN 781–5467
c. Fax:	Commercial 49–621–730–781–5465 DSN 781–5465

ANNEX E / TAB D
U.S. NAVY EUROPE (USNAVEUR)

1. The USNAVEUR agency responsible for **approving, placing, and accepting orders** is:

a. Unit:	COMUSNAVEUR (NEPO LOG PLANS)
b. Telephone:	Com'l 39–081–568–5083 DSN 626–5083
c. Fax:	Com'l 39–081–568–8202 DSN 626–8202
d. Message Address:	COMSNAVEUR NAPLES IT//NEPO LOG PLANS//
e. Mailing Address:	
(Military) COMUSNAVEUR (NEPO LOG PLANS) PSC 817, Box 111 FPO AE 09622	(Commercial) COMUSNAVEUR (NEPO LOG PLANS) Marina Militarie Americana Viale Fulco Ruffo Di Calabria Aereoporto Capodichino Napoli Italie 80144

2. The USNAVEUR agency for **collecting and making payments** for support, supplies, and services is:

a. Unit:	COMUSNAVEUR (COMPTROLLER)
b. Telephone:	Com'l 39–081–568–5295 DSN 626–5295
d. Message Address:	COMUSNAVEUR NAPLES IT//COMPT//
e. Mailing Address:	
(Military) COMUSNAVEUR (COMPTROLLER) PSC 817, Box 111 FPO AE 09622	(Commercial) COMUSNAVEUR (COMPTROLLER) Marina Militare Americana Viale Fulco Ruffo Di Calabria Aereoporto Capodichino Napoli Italie 80144

ANNEX E / TAB E
MARINE FORCES EUROPE (MARFOREUR)

1. The HQ MARFOREUR agency responsible for **approving, placing, and accepting orders** under this agreement is:

a. Unit:	HQ MARFOREUR/G4
b. Telephone:	Commercial 49–7031–15–438 DSN 431–2438
c. Fax:	Commercial 49–7031–15–519 DSN 431–2519
d. Message Address:	HQ MARFOREUR BOEBLINGEN GE//G4//
e. Mailing Address:	Commanding Officer Headquarters Marine Forces Europe Panzer Kaserne APO AE 09046

2. The HQ MARFOREUR agency responsible for **payments and collections** in support of this agreement is:

a. Unit:	HQ MARFOREUR/G4
b. Telephone:	Commercial 49–7031–15–438 DSN 431–5438
c. Fax:	Commercial 49–7031–15–519 DSN 431–5519
d. Message Address:	HQ MARFOREUR BOEBLNGEN GE//G4//
e. Mailing Address:	Commanding Officer Headquarters Marine Forces Europe Panzer Kaserne APO AE 09046

ANNEX E / TAB F
SPECIAL OPERATIONS COMMAND EUROPE (SOCEUR)

1. The HQ SOCEUR agency responsible for **approving, placing, and accepting orders** under this agreement is:

a. Unit:	SOCEUR/J4
b. Telephone:	Commercial 49–711–680–5250 DSN 430–5250
c. Fax:	Commercial 49–711–680–577 DSN 430–0577
d. Message Address:	COMSOCEUR VAIHINGEN GE//J4//
e. Mailing Address:	HQ USEUCOM SOCEUR/SOJ4 Unit 30400 APO AE 09131

2. The SOCEUR agency responsible for **payments and collections** in support of this agreement is:

a. Unit:	SOCEUR/J8
b. Telephone:	Commercial 49–711–680–7249 DSN 430–7249
c. Fax:	Commercial 49–711–5771 DSN 430–5771
d. Message Address:	COMSOCEUR VAIHINGEN GE//SOJ1//
e. Mailing Address:	HQ USEUCOM SOCEUR/SOJ8 Unit 30400 APO AE 09131

ANNEX E / TAB G
U.S. ARMY EUROPE (USAREUR) Stabilization Forces (SFOR)

1. The USAREUR SFOR agency responsible for **approving, placing, and accepting orders** for logistics support, supplies, and services under this agreement are:

A. Unit/Address:	Multinational Support Cell ATTN: G4, MNSC EAGLE BASE, TUZLA APO AE 09789
B. Telephone: Commercial	DSN 762–8856
C. Fax: Commercial	DSN 762–2287
D. Message Address:	EAGLE CAMP//S–4//

2. **Paying Office** for SFOR (Bosnia):

a. Unit/Address:	Finance Office Eagle Base, Tuzla Operation Joint Forge APO AE 09789
b. Telephone:	DSN 762–2116
c. Fax:	Commercial 49–631–413–4300 DSN 370–4300

ANNEX E / TAB H
U.S. ARMY EUROPE (USAREUR) Kosovo Forces (KFOR)

1. The USAREUR KFOR agency responsible for **approving, placing, and accepting orders** for logistics support, supplies, and services under this agreement are:

a. Unit/Address:	Multinational Support Cell ATTN: G4, MNSC Camp Bondsteel, Kosovo APO AE 09340
b. Telephone: Commercial	DSN 781–4272
c. Fax: Commercial	DSN 781–3891
d. Message Address:	CAMP BONDSTEEL//S–4//

2. The USAREUR KFOR **Paying Office**:

a. Unit/Address: Finance Office	Camp Bondsteel, Kosovo Task Force Falcon/ OJG APO AE 09340
b. Telephone:	DSN 781–3720
c. Fax:	Commercial 49–631–413–4300 DSN 370–4300

ANNEX F
USJFCOM
POINTS OF CONTACT, ORDERING AND FINANCIAL RESPONSIBILITIES

TAB A—USJFCOM

TAB B—ACC (Air Force)

TAB C—CINCLANTFLT (Navy)

TAB D—MARFORLANT (Marine Corps)

TAB E—FORSCOM (Army)

ANNEX F / TAB A
U.S. JOINT FORCES COMMAND (USJFCOM)

1. The USJFCOM POC for coordinated **placement and acceptance of orders** under this agreement is the J4 Plans, Programs, and Policy Division:

a. Unit:	USJFCOM J45
b. Telephone:	Com'l: (757) 836–8344 or 5924 DSN: 836–8344 or 5924
c. Fax:	Com'l: (757) 836–5937 DSN: 836–5937
d. Message Address:	COMUSJFCOM NORFOLK VA//J45//
e. Mailing Address:	Commander HQ, U.S. Joint Forces Command (J45) 1562 Mitscher Avenue, Suite 200 Norfolk, VA 23551–2488

2. The USJFCOM agency responsible for **payments and collections** in support of this agreement is the Comptroller:

a. Unit:	USJFCOM J02F3
b. Telephone:	Com'l: (757) 836–5901 DSN: 836–5901
c. Fax:	Com'l: (757) 836–5901 DSN: 836–6648
d. Message Address:	COMUSJFCOM NORFOLK VA//J02F//
e. Mailing Address:	Commander HQ, U.S. Joint Forces Command (J02) 1562 Mitscher Avenue, Suite 200 Norfolk, VA 23551–2488

3. The USJFCOM agency for **legal matters** is J02L:

a. Unit:	USJFCOM J02L
b. Telephone:	Com'l: (757) 836–6416 or 6414 DSN: 836–6416 or 6414
c. Fax:	Com'l: (757) 836–5959 DSN: 836–5959
d. Message Address:	COMUSJFCOM NORFOLK VA//J02L//
e. Mailing Address:	Commander, U.S. Joint Forces Command (J02L) 1562 Mitscher Avenue Suite 200 Norfolk, VA 23551–2488

ANNEX F / TAB B
AIR COMBAT COMMAND (ACC)

1. The ACC POC for coordinated **placement and acceptance of orders** and for **payment and collections** under this agreement is:

a. Unit:	Command Staff
b. Telephone:	Com'l: (757) 764–5462 DSN: 574–5462
c. Fax:	Com'l: (757) 764–3909 DSN: 574–3909
d. Message Address:	HQ ACC LANGLEY AFB VA//CS//
e. Mailing Address:	Headquarters Air Combat Command Langley AFB, VA 23665–5000

ANNEX F / TAB C
COMMANDER, ATLANTIC FLEET (CDRLANTFLT)

1. The CDRLANTFLT POC for coordinated **payment and collections** under this agreement is:

a. Unit:	N413
b. Telephone:	Com'l: (757) 836–3789 DSN: 836–3789
c. Fax:	Com'l: (757) 836–3772 DSN: 836–3772
d. Message Address:	CDRLANTFLT NORFOLK VA//N413
e. Mailing Address:	Commander, U.S Atlantic Fleet Code N413 1562 Mitscher Avenue, Suite 250 Norfolk, VA 23551–2487

2. The CDRLANTFLT POC for coordinated **placement and acceptance of orders** under this agreement is:

a. Unit:	N02F
b. Telephone:	Com'l: (757) 836–6929 DSN: 836–6929
c. Fax:	Com'l: (757) 836–6987 DSN: 836–6987
d. Message Address:	CDRLANTFLT NORFOLK VA//N02F
e. Mailing Address:	Commander, U.S Atlantic Fleet Code N02F 1562 Mitscher Avenue, Suite 250 Norfolk, VA 23551–2487

ANNEX F / TAB D
MARINE FORCES ATLANTIC (MARFORLANT)

1. The MARFORLANT POC for coordinated **payment and collections** under this agreement is:

a. Unit:	G4A
b. Telephone:	Com'l: (757) 836–1647 DSN: 836–1647
c. Fax:	Com'l: (757) 836–1678 DSN: 836–1678
d. Message Address:	COMMARFORLANT//G4
e. Mailing Address:	U.S. Marine Corps Forces Atlantic Code G4A 1468 Ingram Street Norfolk, VA 13551

2. The MARFORLANT POC for coordinated **placement and acceptance of orders** under this agreement is:

a. Unit:	G8
b. Telephone:	Com'l: (757) 836–1582 or 1583 DSN: 836–1582 or 1583
c. Fax:	Com'l: (757) 836–1753 DSN: 836–1753
d. Message Address:	COMMARFORLANT//G8
e. Mailing Address:	U.S. Marine Corps Forces Atlantic Code G8 1468 Ingram Street Norfolk, VA 13551

ANNEX F / TAB E
ARMY FORCES COMMAND (FORSCOM)

1. The FORSCOM POC for coordinated **payment and collections** under this agreement is:

a. Unit:	AFLG–POFP
b. Telephone:	Com'l: (404) 464–5636 DSN: 367–5636
c. Fax:	Com'l: (404) 464–5685 DSN: 367–5685
d. Message Address:	CDRFORSCOM FT MCPHERSONGA// AFLG–POT
e. Mailing Address:	Headquarters Forces Command Code AFLG–POT 1777 Hardee Avenue Ft. McPherson, GA 30330–1062

2. The FORSCOM POC for coordinated **placement and acceptance of orders** under this agreement is:

a. Unit:	AFRM–RI–O
b. Telephone:	Com'l: (404) 464–5460 or 6213 DSN: 367–5460 or 6213
c. Fax:	Com'l: (404) 464–6564 DSN: 367–6564
d. Message Address:	CDRFORSCOM FT MCPHERSONGA// AFRM–RI–O//
e. Mailing Address:	Headquarters Forces Command Code AFRM–RI–O 1777 Hardee Avenue Ft. McPherson, GA 30330–1062

ANNEX G
USSOUTHCOM
POINTS OF CONTACT, ORDERING AND FINANCIAL RESPONSIBILITIES
U.S. SOUTHERN COMMAND (USSOUTHCOM)

1. The USSOUTHCOM POC for coordinated **placement and acceptance of orders** under this agreement is the SCJ4 Joint Logistics Operations Center:

a. Unit:	SOUTHCOM–SCJ4
b. Telephone:	Com'l: (305) 437–1412 or 1400 DSN: 567–1412 or 1400
c. Fax:	Com'l: (305) 437–1443 DSN: 567–1443 Com'l: (305) 437–1444 (Classified) DSN: 567–1444 (Classified)
d. Message Address:	CDR USSOUTHCOM MIAMI FL//SCJ4//(CM)
e. Mailing Address:	COMMANDER HQ USOUTHCOM–SCJ4 3511 NW 91st Ave Miami, FL 33172–1217

2. The USSOUTHCOM agency responsible for coordinating **payments and collections** in support of this agreement is the Comptroller:

a. Unit:	USSOUTHCOM–SCJ8
b. Telephone:	Com'l: (305) 437–1814 or 1811 DSN: 567–1814 or 1811
c. Fax:	Com'l: (305) 437–1840 DSN: 567–1840
d. Message Address:	CDR USSOUTHCOM MIAMI FL//SCJ8//(CM)
e. Mailing Address:	COMMANDER HQ USSOUTHCOM (Attn: SCJ8) 3511 NW 91st Ave Miami, FL 33172–1217

ANNEX H
USNORTHCOM
POINTS OF CONTACT, ORDERING AND FINANCIAL RESPONSIBILITIES
U.S. NORTHERN COMMAND (USNORTHCOM)

1. The USNORTHCOM POC for coordinated **placement and acceptance of orders** under this agreement is:

a. Unit:	NORAD–USNORTHCOM/J4P
b. Telephone:	Com'l: (719) 554–2651 or 3205 DSN: 692–2651 or 3205
c. Fax:	Com'l: (719) 554–3062 or 0813 DSN: 692–3062 or 0813
d. Message Address:	NORAD–NORTHCOM PETERSON AFB CO//J4//
e. Mailing Address:	250 Vandenberg St. Ste. B016 Peterson AFB CO 80914–3816

2. The USNORTHCOM agency responsible for **payments and collections** in support of this agreement is:

a. Unit:	NORAD–USNORTHCOM/J8
b. Telephone:	Com'l: (719) 554–6327 DSN: 692–6327
c. Fax:	Com'l: (719) 556–0335 DSN: 834–0335
d. Message Address:	NORAD–NORTHCOM PETERSON AFB CO//J8//
e. Mailing Address:	250 Vandenberg St. Rm 1031 Peterson AFB CO 80914–3816

ANNEX I
USTRANSCOM
POINTS OF CONTACT, ORDERING AND FINANCIAL RESPONSIBILITIES
U.S. TRANSPORTATION COMMAND (USTRANSCOM)

1. The USTRANSCOM POC for coordinated **placement and acceptance of orders** under this agreement is the TCJ3 Deployment and Distribution Operations Center (DDOC):

a. Unit:	USTRANSCOM–TCJ3–R
b. Telephone:	Com'l: (618) 229–4172 or 1045 DSN: 779–4172 or 1045
c. Fax:	Com'l: (618) 256–1363 DSN: 576–1363 Com'l: (618) 256–6859 (Classified) DSN: 576–6859 (Classified)
d. Message Address:	USTRANSCOM SCOTT AFB IL//TCJ3–R//
e. Mailing Address:	HQ USTRANSCOM TCJ3–R (DDOC) 508 Scott Drive Bldg. 1900 Scott AFB IL, 62225–5357

2. The USTRANSCOM agency responsible for **payments and collections** in support of this agreement is the TCJ8 Program Analysis and Financial Management Directorate:

a. Unit:	USTRANSCOM–TCJ8
b. Telephone:	Com'l: (618) 229–1099 DSN: 779–1099
c. Fax:	Com'l: (618) 256–8097 DSN: 576–8097
d. Message Address:	USTRANSCOM SCOTT AFB IL//TCJ8//
e. Mailing Address:	HQ USTRANSCOM–TCJ8 508 Scott Drive Bldg. 1900 Scott AFB

STATE DEPARTMENT DOCUMENT NUMBER: 06-263

MEMORANDUM OF ARRANGEMENT BETWEEN THE UNITED STATES OF AMERICA JOINT FORCES COMMAND AND THE MINISTER OF NATIONAL DEFENCE OF THE REPUBLIC OF POLAND REGARDING ASSIGNMENT OF LIAISON OFFICERS, WITH ANNEX

SIGNED ON SEPTEMBER 22, 2006
ENTERED INTO FORCE SEPTEMBER 22, 2006

CTIA DOCUMENT NUMBER: 13090.000

City/County of *Norfolk*
Commonwealth of Virginia
I certify this to be a complete, exact and true copy of the original document. Certified this *27th* day of *September*, 2006

[*Signature*] Notary Public
My commission expires *31 August 2008*

INTRODUCTION

The United States Joint Forces Command and the Minister of National Defence of the Republic of Poland (each referred to herein individually as a "Participant" and together as the "Participants"), recognizing the Protocol to the North Atlantic Treaty on the Accession of Poland, signed in Brussels and entered into force December 16, 1997; the Agreement between the Parties to the North Atlantic Treaty regarding the Status of their Forces, signed at London on June 19, 1951, entered into force August 23, 1953; the agreement concerning exchange of research and development information, with appendix (Master Information Exchange Agreement), signed at Warsaw June 9, 1995, entered into force June 9, 1995, and any other arrangement between the participants concerning research and development and information sharing apply to this Memorandum of Arrangement and, desiring to establish formal liaison between the Participants to coordinate theater security cooperation events and to provide a consistent and established affiliation between the U.S. Joint Forces Command and the Minister of National Defence of the Republic of Poland, undertake abide by the following terms and conditions regarding the assignment of individuals to serve as Liaison Officers to the other Participant.

SECTION I
DEFINITIONS

In addition to any terms defined in other provisions of this Arrangement, the following terms will have the following meanings when used herein:

1.1. "*Classified Information*" will mean official information of a Participant that requires protection in the interests of national security of such Participant and is so designated by the application of security classification markings. This information may be in oral, visual, electronic, or documentary form, or in the form of material, including equipment, or technology.

1.2. "*Contact Officer*" will mean a U.S. Department of Defense (DoD) official designated in writing to oversee and control all contacts, requests for information, consultations, access, and other activities of Foreign Liaison Officers who are assigned to, or are visiting, a DoD component or subordinate organization.

1.3. "*Controlled Unclassified Information*" will mean unclassified information of a Participant to which access or distribution limitations have been applied in accordance with national laws, policies, and regulations of such Participant. It includes U.S. information that is exempt from public disclosure or subject to export controls.

1.4. "*Foreign Liaison Officer*" will mean a military member or civilian employee of the Parent Participant who, upon approval of or certification by the Host Participant or Government, is authorized by the Parent Participant to act as its official representative in connection with programs, projects, or arrangements of interest to the Participants' Governments.

1.5. "*Host Government*" will mean the national government of the Host Participant.

1.6. "*Host Participant*" will mean the Participant to which the Foreign Liaison Officer acts as a liaison pursuant to an assignment by a Parent Participant under SECTION III.

1.7. "*International Visits Program (IVP)*" will mean the program established to process visits by, and assignments of, foreign representatives to United States Department of Defense Components and Department of Defense contractor facilities. It is designed to ensure that classified and controlled unclassified information to be disclosed to foreign nationals has been properly authorized for disclosure to their governments; that the requesting foreign government provides a security assurance on such foreign nationals and their sponsoring organization or firm, when Classified Information is involved in the visit or assignment, and that administrative arrangements (e.g., date, time and place) for the visit or assignment are provided.

1.8. "*Parent Government*" will mean the national government of the Parent Participant.

1.9. "*Parent Participant*" will mean the Participant that assigns a Foreign Liaison Officer pursuant to SECTION III.

SECTION II
SCOPE

2.1. During the term of this Arrangement, subject to the mutual concurrence of the Participants, the Minister of National Defence of the Republic of Poland may assign a military member of the Polish Armed Forces to serve as a Foreign Liaison Officer to the Headquarters, U.S. Joint Forces Command, in accordance with the terms of this Arrangement. The Parent Participant will ensure that the person assigned is a senior officer whose rank is at least equivalent to a U.S. O–6. The Polish military member assigned will represent the Minister of National Defence of the Republic of Poland to the U.S. Joint Forces Command.

2.2. The establishment of each Foreign Liaison Officer position under this Arrangement will be based upon the demonstrated need for, and the mutual benefit of, this position to the Participants.

Once established, each Foreign Liaison Officer position will be subject to periodic review by either Participant to ensure that the position continues to be required by, and is of mutual benefit to, the Participants. A Foreign Liaison Officer position no longer required by, or of mutual benefit to, either Participant will be subject to elimination.

2.3. Commencement of such a tour of duty by a Foreign Liaison Officer will be subject to any requirements that may be imposed by the Host Participant or its Government regarding formal certification by or approval of Foreign Liaison Officers. Foreign Liaison Officers to be assigned by their Parent Participant to locations in the United States will be requested pursuant to the IVP, as defined in Paragraph 1.7. of this Arrangement.

2.4. Unless otherwise mutually determined, the normal tour of duty for a Foreign Liaison Officer will be three (3) years.

2.5. An individual may serve as a Foreign Liaison Officer to only one major military command of the Host Participant at any point in time.

SECTION III
DUTIES AND ACTIVITIES

3.1. The Foreign Liaison Officer will represent the Parent Participant to the Host Participant. The Foreign Liaison Officer will not perform duties reserved by the laws or regulations of the Host Government to officers or employees of the Host Government, nor will the Foreign Liaison Officer provide any labor or services to the Host Government or any of its agencies, including the Host Participant.

3.2. The Foreign Liaison Officer shall comply with all applicable Host Government policies, procedures, laws and regulations. The Host Participant will assign a Contact Officer to provide guidance to the Foreign Liaison Officer concerning policies, procedures, laws and regulations of the Host Participant, and to arrange for activities consistent with such requirements and the purposes of this Arrangement.

3.3. The Foreign Liaison Officer may request access to Host Participant facilities by submitting a request to the Contact Officer. Access to Host Participant facilities may be granted if such access promotes the purposes of this Arrangement, is consistent with the terms of any applicable certification or approval issued by the Host Government, and is permitted under the applicable policies, procedures, laws and regulations of the Host Government. Approval of such requests will be at the discretion of the Host Participant. Any request for access that exceeds the terms of an applicable certification or approval will be submitted through the IVP.

3.4. The Foreign Liaison Officer will not be granted access to technical data or other information of the Host Participant, whether or not classified, except as authorized by the Host Participant, and only to the extent necessary to fulfill the Foreign Liaison Officer's functions hereunder and consistent with the Agreement concerning security measures for the protection of classified military information, signed at Washington February 17, 1995 and entered into force February 17, 1995.

3.5. All information to which the Foreign Liaison Officer is granted access while serving as a liaison to the Host Participant will be treated as information provided in confidence to the Parent Government and will not be further released or disclosed by the Foreign Liaison Officer to any other person, firm, organization, or government without the prior written authorization of the Host Government. Disclosure of information to the Foreign Liaison Officer will not be deemed to be a license or authorization to use such information for any purpose other than the purposes described in SECTION II.

3.6. The Foreign Liaison Officer will not be permitted to participate in exercises, deployments, or civil-military actions, unless expressly authorized in writing to do so by both the Host and Parent Participants.

3.7. The Parent Participant will not place or keep a Foreign Liaison Officer in duty assignments in which direct hostilities with forces of third states are likely to occur or have commenced, unless approved in writing by the Parent Participant and Host Participant.

3.8. The Foreign Liaison Officer will be required to comply with the dress regulations of the Parent Participant but, if requested by the Host Participant, will also wear such identification necessary to identify the Foreign Liaison Officer's nationality, rank and status as a Foreign Liaison Officer. The order of dress for any occasion will be that which most closely conforms to the order of dress for the particular organization of the Host Participant where the Foreign Liaison Officer is located. The Foreign Liaison Officer will be required to comply with the customs of the Host Participant with respect to the wearing of civilian clothing.

3.9. Prior to the commencement of a Foreign Liaison Officer's tour, the Parent Participant will notify the Host Participant of the specific Parent Participant organization that will exercise operational control over the Foreign Liaison Officer and, if different, the Parent Participant organization that will provide administrative support to the Foreign Liaison Officer and the Foreign Liaison Officer's dependents.

3.10. At the end of a Foreign Liaison Officer's tour, or as otherwise mutually determined by the Participants, the Parent Participant may, subject to the provisions of SECTION II, replace the Foreign Liaison Officer with another individual who meets the requirements of this Arrangement.

SECTION IV
FINANCIAL ARRANGEMENTS

4.1. The Parent Participant will bear all costs and expenses of the Foreign Liaison Officer, including, but not limited to:

4.1.1. All pay and allowances of the Foreign Liaison Officer;

4.1.2. All travel by the Foreign Liaison Officer and the Foreign Liaison Officer's dependents, including, but not limited to, travel to and from the duty location;

4.1.3. All costs and expenses associated with the assignment or placement of the Foreign Liaison Officer and the Foreign Liaison Officer's dependents at the duty location, including travel, office space, clerical support, housing, messing, medical and dental services, unless specifically stated otherwise in an applicable international agreement;

4.1.4. Compensation for loss of, or damage to, the personal property of the Foreign Liaison Officer, or the personal property of the Foreign Liaison Officer's dependents;

4.1.5. The movement of the household effects of the Foreign Liaison Officer and the Foreign Liaison Officer's dependents;

4.1.6. Preparation and shipment of remains and funeral expenses associated with the death of the Foreign Liaison Officer or the Foreign Liaison Officer's dependents;

4.1.7. Formal and informal training of the Foreign Liaison Officer, other than briefings on Host Participant requirements provided by the Contact Officer; and

4.1.8. All expenses in connection with the return of a Foreign Liaison Officer whose assignment has ended or been terminated, along with the Foreign Liaison Officer's dependents.

4.2. The Host Participant may provide such office facilities, equipment, supplies and services as may be necessary for the Foreign Liaison Officer to fulfill the purposes of this Arrangement, subject to reimbursement by the Parent Participant for the cost of the Foreign Liaison Officer's use of such facilities at rates determined by the Host Participant. Where the United States is the Host Participant, reimbursement for such facilities, equipment, supplies, and services will be made through Foreign Military Sales (FMS). The Host Participant will provide the Parent Participant advanced notice of rates for use of facilities, equipment, supplies and services, if any, and procedures for billing and reimbursement through Foreign Military Sales.

4.3. The assignment of a Foreign Liaison Officer pursuant to this Arrangement will be subject to the Parent Participant's authorization and availability of Parent Participant's funds for such purposes.

SECTION V
SECURITY

5.1. The Host Participant will establish the maximum substantive scope and classification levels within which the disclosure of any classified information or controlled unclassified information (CUI) to the Foreign Liaison Officer will be permitted. The Host Participant will inform the Parent Participant of the level of security clearance required to permit the Foreign Liaison Officer access to such information. The Foreign Liaison Officer's access to such information and facilities will be consistent with, and limited by the terms of the Foreign Liaison Officer's assignment, the provisions of this SECTION and subject to all provisions and safeguards provided for under the U.S.-Poland Agreement concerning Security measures for the Protection of Classified Military Information, signed at Washington February 17, 1995, and any other arrangement between the Participants or their governments concerning access to such information and facilities. Further, access will at all times be limited to the minimum required to accomplish the purposes of this Arrangement, and, at its discretion, the Host Participant may prohibit the Foreign Liaison Officer's right of access to any Host Participant facility or require that such access be supervised by Host Participant personnel. Nothing in this MOA shall be construed by the Participants to authorize unfettered access to classified information or CUI residing in the Host Participant's facilities or computers.

5.2. Each Participant will cause security assurances to be filed, through the Polish Embassy in Washington, DC, in the case of Polish personnel, and through the U.S. Embassy in Warsaw in the case of U.S. personnel, stating the security clearances for the Foreign Liaison Officer being assigned by such Participant. The security assurances will be prepared and forwarded through prescribed channels in compliance with established Host Participant procedures. For the United States, the prescribed channels will be the IVP, as defined in Paragraph 1.7. of this Arrangement.

5.3. The Parent Participant will ensure that each assigned Foreign Liaison Officer is fully cognizant of, and complies with, applicable laws and regulations concerning the protection of proprietary information (such as patents, copyrights, know-how, and trade secrets), classified information and CUI disclosed to the Foreign Liaison Officer. This obligation will apply both during and after termination of an assignment as a Foreign Liaison Officer. Prior to taking up duties as a Foreign Liaison Officer, the Foreign Liaison Officer from Poland will be required to sign the certification at Annex A. Only individuals who execute the certification will be permitted to serve as Foreign Liaison Officers with the U.S. Joint Forces Command.

5.4. The Parent Participant will ensure that the Foreign Liaison Officer, at all times, complies with the security laws, regulations and procedures of the Host Government. Any violation of security procedures by a Foreign Liaison Officer during Foreign Liaison Officer's assignment will be reported to the Parent Participant for appropriate action. Upon request by the Host Participant, the Parent Participant will remove any Foreign Liaison Officer who violates security laws, regulations, or procedures during his/her assignment.

5.5. All Classified Information made available to the Foreign Liaison Officer will be considered to be Classified Information furnished to the Government of Poland. Classified Information made available under the Arrangement shall not be shared outside the Government of Poland without the express written consent of U.S. Joint Forces Command.

5.6. The Foreign Liaison Officer will not take custody of classified information or CUI in tangible form (for example, documents or electronic files), except as expressly permitted by the terms of the Host Participant certification of the Foreign Liaison Officer (and requested in writing by the Parent Government) for the following situations:

5.6.1. Couriers. The Foreign Liaison Officer may take custody of classified information to perform courier functions when authorized by the Host Participant certification for the Foreign Liaison Officer. The classified information will be packaged and receipted for in compliance with Host Participant requirements.

5.6.2. On-Site Storage. The Foreign Liaison Officer may be furnished a secure container for the temporary storage of classified information, consistent with the terms of the certification, provided the security responsibility and control of the container and its contents remains with the Host Participant.

SECTION VI
TECHNICAL AND ADMINISTRATIVE MATTERS

6.1. The Host Participant's certification or approval of an individual as a Foreign Liaison Officer will not bestow diplomatic or other special privileges on that individual.

6.2. To the extent authorized by the laws and regulations of the Host Government, and in accordance with SECTION IV of this Arrangement, the Host Participant may provide such administrative support as is necessary for the Foreign Liaison Officer to fulfill the purposes of this Arrangement, subject to reimbursement by the Parent Participant.

6.3. Exemption from taxes, customs or import duties, or similar charges for the Foreign Liaison Officer or the Foreign Liaison Officer's dependents will be governed by applicable laws and regulations or international agreements between the Host and Parent Governments.

6.4. If office space is provided to the Foreign Liaison Officer by the Host Participant, the Host Participant will determine the normal working hours for the Foreign Liaison Officer.

6.5. The Parent Participant will ensure that the Host Participant is informed as far in advance as possible of any absences of the Foreign Liaison Officer.

6.6. The Foreign Liaison Officer and the Foreign Liaison Officer's dependents will be provided care in military medical and dental facilities to the extent permitted by applicable national law and policy, and/or applicable international agreement. Where a reciprocal agreement for health care exists between the Participants, the access entitlement of the Foreign Liaison Officer and the Foreign Liaison Officer's dependents is specified. For those personnel covered by such an agreement, care is generally provided free of charge. All Foreign Liaison Officers and their dependents not covered by a reciprocal agreement may be offered health care, on a reimbursable basis, in military facilities. Where military facilities are not available, the Foreign Liaison Officer will be responsible for all medical and dental costs incurred by himself/herself and the Foreign Liaison Officer's dependents. The Parent Participant will ensure that the Foreign Liaison Officer and the Foreign Liaison Officer's dependents are physically fit prior to the Foreign Liaison Officer's tour of duty. The Parent Participant will be responsible for familiarizing itself with the medical and dental services available to the Foreign Liaison Officer and Foreign Liaison Officer's dependents, and the costs of, and the procedures for, use of such services.

6.7. The Foreign Liaison Officer and the Foreign Liaison Officer's dependents will be accorded the use of military commissaries, exchanges, theaters and similar morale and welfare activities, in accordance with the laws, regulations, and policies of the Host Participant and international agreements to which the Host and Parent Participants are parties.

6.8. To the extent permitted by the laws and regulations of the Host Government, and subject to reimbursement by the Parent Participant, the Host Participant will provide, if available, housing and messing facilities for the Foreign Liaison Officer and the Foreign Liaison Officer's dependents on the same basis and priority as for its own personnel of comparable rank and assignment. At locations where housing and messing facilities are not provided by the Host Participant, the Host Participant will use reasonable efforts to assist the Parent Participant to locate such facilities for the Foreign Liaison Officer and the Foreign Liaison Officer's dependents.

6.9. The Parent Participant will ensure that the Foreign Liaison Officer and the Foreign Liaison Officer's dependents have all documentation required by the Host Government for entry into and exit from the country of the Host Government at the time of such entry or exit. Unless exempted under an applicable international agreement between the Participants, Foreign Liaison Officers and their dependents entering the United States will be required to comply with United States Customs Regulations.

6.10. The Parent Participant will ensure that the Foreign Liaison Officer and those dependents accompanying the Foreign Liaison Officer will obtain motor vehicle comprehensive insurance coverage for their private motor vehicles, in accordance with applicable laws, regulations and policies of the Host Participant.

SECTION VII
DISCIPLINE AND REMOVAL

7.1. Except as provided in Paragraph 7.2., neither the Host Participant nor the armed forces of the Host Government may take disciplinary action against a Foreign Liaison Officer who commits an offense under the military laws or regulations of the Host Participant, nor will the Host Participant exercise disciplinary powers over the Foreign Liaison Officer's dependents. The Parent Participant, however, will take such administrative or disciplinary action against the Foreign Liaison Officer as may be appropriate under the circumstances, to ensure compliance with this Arrangement, and the Participants will cooperate in the investigation of any offenses under the laws or regulations of either Participant.

7.2. The certification or approval of a Foreign Liaison Officer may be withdrawn, modified or curtailed at any time by the Host Participant for any reason, including, but not limited to, the violation of the regulations or laws of the Host Participant or the Host Government. In addition, at the request of the Host Participant, the Parent Government will remove the Foreign Liaison Officer or a dependent of the Foreign Liaison Officer from the territory of the Host Government. The Host Participant will provide an explanation for its removal request, but a dispute between the Participants concerning the sufficiency of the Host Participant's reasons will not be grounds to delay the removal of the Foreign Liaison Officer or a Foreign Liaison Officer's dependents.

7.3. A Foreign Liaison Officer will not exercise any supervisory or disciplinary authority over military or civilian personnel of the Host Participant.

SECTION VIII
SETTLEMENT OF DISPUTES

8.1. Disputes arising under or relating to this Arrangement will be resolved only through consultations between the Participants and will not be referred to an individual, national or international tribunal, or to any other forum for settlement.

SECTION IX
ENTRY INTO EFFECT, AMENDMENT, DURATION, AND TERMINATION

9.1. All obligations of the Participants under this Arrangement will be subject to national laws and the availability of appropriated funds for such purposes.

9.2. The Parent Participant will ensure that the Foreign Liaison Officer complies with all obligations and restrictions applicable to the Foreign Liaison Officer under this Arrangement.

9.3. This Arrangement may be amended by the mutual written concurrence of the Participants.

9.4. This Arrangement may be terminated at any time with the written concurrence of both Participants. In the event both Participants determine to terminate this Arrangement, the Participants will consult prior to the date of termination.

9.5. Either Participant may terminate this Arrangement upon 180 days written notification to the other Participant.

9.6. In the event of conflict between the terms of this Arrangement and the terms of an applicable Letter of Offer and Acceptance (LOA), the terms of the LOA will control. Any LOAs associated with or related to this Arrangement will terminate in accordance with their terms.

9.7. The respective rights and responsibilities of the Participants under SECTION V (Security) will continue, notwithstanding the termination or expiration of this Arrangement.

9.8. No later than the effective date of expiration or termination of this Arrangement, each Participant will remove its Foreign Liaison Officer and such Foreign Liaison Officer's dependents from the territory of the other Participant and pay any money owed to the other Participant under this Arrangement. Any costs or expenses for which a Participant is responsible pursuant to SECTION IV of this Arrangement, but were not billed in sufficient time to permit payment prior to termination or expiration of this Arrangement will be paid promptly after such billing.

9.9. This Arrangement will supersede any and all prior arrangements regarding Foreign Liaison Officers entered into by the Participants or their organizations, units, or agencies.

9.10. This Arrangement will enter into effect upon signature by both Participants. This Arrangement will remain in effect for five (5) years, and may be extended with the written concurrence of the Participants.

9.11. This Arrangement consists of nine (9) SECTIONs. Annex A is a sample of the Foreign Liaison Officer's certification detailed in Section 5.3 of this Arrangement.

IN WITNESS WHEREOF, the undersigned, being duly authorized, have signed this Arrangement.

ON BEHALF OF
U.S. JOINT FORCES COMMAND

[Signature]

LANCE SMITH
General, U.S. Air Force
Commander

22 Sep 06

Date

ON BEHALF OF
Minister of National Defence of
the Republic of Poland
[Signature]

FRANCISZEK GAGOR
General, Chief of General
Staff of the Polish Armed
Forces
22/Sept/2006

Date

ANNEX A
SAMPLE CERTIFICATION

[Date]

SECTION I
FOREIGN LIAISON OFFICER
LEGAL STATUS OF CERTIFICATION

As a representative of the Minister of National Defence of the Republic of Poland under the auspices of a Foreign Liaison Officer Assignment to the U.S. Joint Forces Command, I am subject to the jurisdiction of United States federal, state, and local laws, except as provided by treaty, other specific legal authority, or the terms of any diplomatic immunity that I may have been granted. I understand that my acceptance of the Foreign Liaison Officer position does not bestow upon me diplomatic or other special privileges.

SECTION II
FOREIGN LIAISON OFFICER
CONDITIONS OF CERTIFICATION

(1) **Responsibilities**: I understand that my activities shall be limited to the representational responsibilities of my Government and that I am expected to present the views of my Government with regard to the issues that my Government and the U.S. Government have a mutual interest. I shall not perform duties that are reserved by law or regulation to an officer or employee of the U.S. Government.

(2) **Costs**: I understand that all costs associated with my duties as a Foreign Liaison Officer will be the responsibility of my government, including, but not limited to, travel, office space, clerical services, housing, messing, and medical and dental services.

(3) **Extensions and Revalidation**: I understand that if my Government desires to request an extension or revalidation of my position beyond the original dates for which I am certified, a new visit request will be submitted not later than thirty (30) days prior to the expiration date of the current Foreign Liaison Officer Assignment Authorization.

(4) **Contact Officer**: I understand that when the certification process is completed, a Contact Officer will be assigned to sponsor me during my visit to the U.S. Joint Forces Command. I further understand that I will coordinate, through my Contact Officer, all requests for information, visits, and other business that fall under the terms of my certification. I also understand that requests for information that are beyond the terms of my certification will be made through the Office of the Defense Attaché.

(5) **Other Visits**: I understand that visits to facilities for which the purpose does not directly relate to the terms of my certification will be made through the Office of the Defense Attaché.

(6) **Uniform**: I understand that I will wear my national uniform when conducting business at the U.S. Joint Forces Command or other Department of Defense facilities, unless otherwise directed. I will comply with my Parent Government's service uniform regulations.

(7) **Duty Hours**: I understand that my duty hours are Monday through Friday, from 0800 to 1700. Should I require access to my work area during non-duty hours, I am required to request permission from the Command Security Officer through my Contact Officer.

(8) **Security**:

a. I understand that access to U.S. Government information shall be limited to that information determined by my Contact Officer to be necessary to fulfill the functions of a Foreign Liaison Officer. I also understand that I may not have access to U.S. Government computer systems, unless all information accessible by the computer is releasable to my government in accordance with applicable U.S. law, regulations and policy.

b. All information to which I may have access during my certification shall be treated as information provided in confidence to my Government and will not be further released or disclosed by me to any other person, firm, organization, or government without the prior written authorization of the U.S. Government.

c. I shall immediately report to my Contact Officer should I obtain or become knowledgeable of U.S. Government information for which I am not authorized to have access. I further agree that I will report to my Contact Officer any incidents of my being offered or provided information that I am not authorized to have.

d. If required, I will display a security badge on my outer clothing so that it is clearly visible. The U.S. Government will supply this badge.

(9) **Compliance**: I have been briefed on, fully understand, and will comply with the terms and conditions of my certification. Failure to comply may result in termination of my certification. I further understand that the termination of my certification does not preclude further disciplinary action in accordance with any applicable Status of Forces Agreement or other government-to-government arrangements or agreements.

(10) **Definitions of Terms**: Terms not defined herein will have the definitions ascribed to them in the applicable Arrangement governing my assignment as a Foreign Liaison Officer.

SECTION III
FOREIGN LIAISON OFFICER
TERMS OF CERTIFICATION

(1) **Contact Officer**: ______________________________ has been assigned as my Contact Officer.

(2) **Certification**: I am certified to the U.S. Joint Forces Command and will represent the Minister of National Defence of the Republic of Poland to the U.S. Joint Forces Command, as mutually determined by both Participants.

(3) **Travel**: I may visit the following locations under the terms of my certification, with the permission of my Contact Officer:

—U.S. Joint Forces Command facilities;

—U.S. Joint Forces Command subordinate activities; and

—Designated areas within the Pentagon.

SECTION IV
FOREIGN LIAISON OFFICER CERTIFICATION OF IN-BRIEFING

I, ______________________________, understand and acknowledge that I have been certified as a Foreign Liaison Officer to the U.S. Joint Forces Command, as determined between the Minister of National Defence of the Republic of Poland and U.S. Joint Forces Command. I further acknowledge that I fully understand and have been briefed on: (1) the legal status of my certification; (2) the conditions of my certification; and (3) the terms of my certification. I further acknowledge that I shall comply with the conditions and responsibilities of my certification.

____
(SIGNATURE OF LIAISON OFFICER)
(TYPED NAME OF LIAISON OFFICER)

____
(RANK AND/OR TITLE)

____
(DATE)

____
(SIGNATURE OF BRIEFER)

____
(TYPED NAME)

____
(LOCATION)

State Department Document Number: 06-264

Memorandum of Agreement Between the Department of Defense of the United States of America and the Ministry of Defense of the Italian Republic for Research, Development, Test and Evaluation Projects, with Annex and Appendix

Signed at Washington D.C. and Rome,
September 15 and 26, 2006
Entered into force September 26, 2006

CTIA Document Number: 13091.000

Certified to be a true copy:

[Signature]

F. R. BEER
Director, International Agreements Division
Navy International Programs Office

PREAMBLE

The Department of Defense of the United States of America (U.S. DoD) and the Ministry of Defense of the Italian Republic (IT MoD), hereinafter referred to as the "Parties":

Having a common interest in defense;

Recognizing the benefits to be obtained from rationalization, standardization, and interoperability of military equipment;

Considering the Memorandum of Understanding between the Government of Italy and the Government of the United States of America Concerning the Principles Governing Mutual Cooperation in the Research, Development, Production and Procurement of Defense Equipment, dated September 11, 1978, and its Annexes;

Seeking to make the best use of their respective research, development, test and evaluation capacities, eliminate unnecessary duplication of work, and obtain the most efficient and cost-effective results through cooperation in Research, Development, Test, and Evaluation (RDT&E) Projects; and

Recognizing the need to develop collectively emerging technologies to field technologically superior weapons;

Have agreed as follows:

ARTICLE I
DEFINITIONS AND ABBREVIATIONS

The Parties have agreed upon the following definitions and abbreviations for terms used in this RDT&E MOA and PAs under this MOA:

1.1. Definitions:

Classified Information	Official information that requires protection in the interests of national security and is so designated by the application of a security classification marking. It may be in oral, visual, magnetic, or documentary form, or in the form of equipment or technology.
Contract	Any mutually binding legal relationship that obligates a Contractor to furnish supplies or services, and obligates one or both of the Parties to pay for them.
Contracting	The obtaining of supplies or services by Contract from sources outside the government organizations of the Parties. Contracting includes description of supplies and services required, solicitation and selection of sources, preparation, and award of Contracts, and all phases of Contract administration.
Contracting Agency	The entity within the government organization of a Party that has authority to enter into, administer, or terminate Contracts.
Contracting Officer	A person representing a Contracting Agency of a Party who has the authority to enter into, administer, or terminate Contracts.
Contractor	Any entity awarded a Contract by a Party's Contracting Agency.
Contractor Support Personnel	Persons specifically identified as providing administrative, managerial, scientific, or technical support services to a Party under a support Contract.
Controlled Unclassified Information	Unclassified information to which access or distribution limitations have been applied in accordance with applicable national laws or regulations. It includes information that has been declassified but remains controlled.
Cooperative Project Personnel (CPP)	Military members or civilian employees of a Parent Party assigned to a Joint Project Office who perform managerial, engineering, technical, administrative, Contracting, logistics, financial, planning or other functions in furtherance of a Project.
Defense Purposes	Manufacture or other use in any part of the world by or for the armed forces of either Party.
Designated Security Authority (DSA)	The security office approved by national authorities to be responsible for the security aspects of this MOA and its PAs.
Financial Costs	Project costs met with monetary contributions.

Host Party	The Party whose nation serves as the location of the Joint Project Office established under a Project Agreement.
National Security Authority (NSA)	The government entity responsible for national security policy guidance. It may include DSA's responsibilities.
Non-financial Costs	Project costs met with non-monetary contributions.
Parent Party	The Party that sends its CPP to the Joint Project Office located in the nation of the other Party.
Party	A signatory to this MOA represented by its military and civilian personnel. Contractors and Contractor Support Personnel shall not be representatives of a Party under this MOA or its PAs.
Patent	Grant by a government of the right to exclude others from making, using, or selling an invention. The term refers to any and all patents including, but not limited to, patents of implementation, improvement, or addition, petty patents, utility models, appearance design patents, registered designs, and inventor certificates or like statutory protection as well as divisions, reissues, continuations, renewals, and extensions of any of these.
Project	Specific collaborative activity described in a PA concluded pursuant to this RDT&E MOA.
Project Agreement	An implementing agreement, added after the RDT&E MOA has come into effect, which specifically details the provisions of collaboration on a specific Research, Development, Test, and Evaluation Project.
Project Background Information	Information not generated in the performance of a PA.
Project Equipment	Any materials, equipment, end item, subsystem, component, special tooling, or test equipment jointly acquired or provided for use in a PA.
Project Foreground Information	Information generated in the performance of a specific PA.
Project Information	Any information provided to, generated in, or used in a PA regardless of form or type, including, but not limited to, that of a scientific, technical, business, or financial nature, and also including photographs, reports, manuals, threat data, experimental data, test data, designs, specifications, processes, techniques, inventions, drawings, technical writings, software and associated documentation, sound recordings, pictorial representations, and other graphical presentations, whether in magnetic tape, computer memory, or any other form and whether or not subject to copyright, Patent, or other legal protection.

Project Invention	Any invention or discovery formulated or made (conceived or first actually reduced to practice) in the course of work performed under a PA. The term "first actually reduced to practice" means the first demonstration, sufficient to establish to one skilled in the art to which the invention pertains, of the operability of an invention for its intended purpose and in its intended environment.
Prospective Contractor	Any entity that seeks to enter into a Contract to be awarded by a Party's Contracting Agency and that, in the case of a solicitation involving the release of export-controlled information, is eligible to receive such information.
Third Party	A government other than the government of a Party and any person or other entity whose government is not the government of a Party.

1.2. Abbreviation List:

AP	Agreement Principal
CPP	Cooperative Project Personnel
DSA	Designated Security Authority
EA	Executive Agent
JPO	Joint Project Office
NAD	National Armament Director
NSA	National Security Authority
PA	Project Agreement
PO	Project Officer
SC	Steering Committee
RDT&E	Research, Development, Test, and Evaluation

ARTICLE II
OBJECTIVE

2.1. The objective of this MOA is to promote collaboration on research of technologies and systems by defining and establishing the general provisions that apply to the initiation, conduct, and management of RDT&E Projects established by separate Project Agreements (PAs) entered into by representatives of the Parties authorized in accordance with this MOA. Areas of cooperation shall be identified and reviewed by RDT&E MOA Principals for potential PAs.

2.2. PAs shall be entered into pursuant to this MOA and shall incorporate by reference the provisions of this MOA. Detailed provisions of each individual PA shall include, as a minimum, provisions concerning the objective, scope of work, management structure, financial arrangements, contractual arrangements (if required), security classification, responsibilities of the Parties, and other provisions as required, in accordance with the format attached as Annex A (to be used as a guideline).

ARTICLE III
SCOPE OF WORK

3.1. The scope of work for this MOA shall encompass collaboration, within the respective institutional authorities of the Parties, in research, development, testing, and evaluation potentially leading to new or improved military capability. PAs may encompass one or more of the following activities: basic research, applied research, advanced technology development, concept of operation studies and analysis, advanced concept technology demonstrations, system prototypes, system development and demonstration (engineering and manufacturing development), developmental test and evaluation of system/subsystem efforts, and evolutionary acquisition/spiral development efforts associated with low rate initial production or production programs.

3.2. Information exchange for the purposes of harmonizing the Parties' respective RDT&E capabilities and requirements, and for formulating, developing, and negotiating PAs is permitted under this MOA.

3.3. No technical information relating to production may be transferred under this MOA or its implementing PAs.

3.4. This MOA does not preclude the Parties from entering into any other agreement in the area of research, development, test, and evaluation.

ARTICLE IV
MANAGEMENT (ORGANIZATION AND RESPONSIBILITY)

4.1. The Director, International Cooperation in the Office of the Under Secretary of Defense (Acquisition, Technology and Logistics) is designated as the U.S. RDT&E MOA Principal (AP). The Deputy of the Secretary General (NAD) is designated as the Italian RDT&E AP. The RDT&E APs shall be responsible for:

4.1.1. monitoring implementation of this MOA and exercising executive-level oversight;

4.1.2. monitoring overall use and effectiveness of the MOA;

4.1.3. recommending amendments to the MOA to the Parties; and

4.1.4. resolving issues brought forth by the Executive Agents.

4.2. The appropriate U.S. Military Department Acquisition Executive or Defense Agency Director, or designee, is designated as the U.S. RDT&E Executive Agent (U.S. RDT&E/EA) for those Projects within the respective Military Department or Defense Agency. The Chief of 5th Department for Research and Technology of the Secretariat General/NAD, or designated representative, is designated as the Italian RDT&E Executive Agent (Italian RDT&E/EA). The RDT&E/EAs shall be responsible for:

4.2.1. concluding appropriate PAs in accordance with this MOA and national policies and procedures;

4.2.2. establishing an appropriate management structure for overseeing their PAs and, for each PA, considering the PA's scope and the requirement for a Steering Committee (SC);

4.2.3. appointing SC members when deemed necessary, and Project Officers (PO), as appropriate;

4.2.4. providing administrative direction to appropriate SCs, if established, or POs appointed to their Projects;

4.2.5. approving plans for disposal of jointly acquired Project Equipment if an SC is not established;

4.2.6. ensuring security is administered during all phases of PAs;

4.2.7. designating a point of contact for exchange of information to harmonize requirements for the development and negotiation of potential PAs, in accordance with paragraph 3.2. of Article III (Scope of Work); and

4.2.8. resolving issues brought forth by the SC, or, if no SC is established, by the POs. If the issue cannot be resolved by the EAs, then the EAs are responsible for bringing the issue to the attention of the APs.

4.3. If an SC is established under a particular PA, it shall be responsible for:

4.3.1. providing policy and management direction to the POs during PA execution;

4.3.2. monitoring overall PA implementation, including technical, cost, and schedule performance against requirements;

4.3.3. approving plans for transfers of Project Equipment or disposal of jointly acquired Project Equipment, in accordance with Article VIII (Project Equipment);

4.3.4. resolving issues brought forth by the POs, or raising the issues to the EAs;

4.3.5. maintaining oversight of the security aspects of a PA and appointing a Project security officer;

4.3.6. approving assignment of personnel working on a Project at the other Party's facilities in accordance with the provisions set forth in Appendix (1) to Annex A;

4.3.7. approving the detailed financial procedures of a PA established by the POs in the event that one Party contracts on behalf of the other Party or on behalf of both Parties;

4.3.8. employing its best efforts to resolve, in consultation with the export control authorities of the Parties, any export control issues raised by the POs in accordance with paragraph 4.4. or raised by a Party's SC representative in accordance with paragraph 4.6.; and

4.3.9. reporting status of activity of assigned PAs at least every six months to the RDT&E/EAs and RDT&E/APs.

4.4. In accordance with the provisions of the PA, the POs shall have primary responsibilities for effective implementation, efficient management and direction of their assigned PA including technical, cost, and schedule performance against requirements. The POs shall monitor export control arrangements required to implement any PA and, if applicable, shall immediately refer to the SC any export control issues that could adversely affect the implementation of the PA. Additionally, if no SC is established for the PA, the POs shall have the obligations under paragraph 4.3., except that the EAs shall be responsible for resolving issues brought forth by the POs and for approving plans for the disposal of jointly acquired Project Equipment. The POs shall also maintain a list of all Project Equipment transferred by either of the Parties.

4.5. As provided in a PA and in accordance with the provisions set forth in Appendix (1) to Annex A of this MOA, a Party may assign Cooperative Project Personnel (CPP) to the Joint Project Office (JPO) established under the PA to assist in the implementation of the PA.

4.6. If a Party finds it necessary to exercise a restriction on the retransfer of export-controlled information as set out in paragraph 9.1.3. of Article IX (Disclosure and Use of Project Information), it will promptly inform the other Party. If a restriction is then exercised and the affected Party objects, that Party's SC representative or PO shall promptly notify the other Party's SC representative or PO, and they shall immediately consult in order to discuss ways to resolve such issues or mitigate any adverse effects.

4.7. The RDT&E/EAs, SCs, and POs shall meet as required on a regular basis, alternatively in the United States and Italy. The Chairman for each meeting shall be the senior official of the Host Party. During such meetings, all decisions shall be made unanimously with each Party having one vote. In the event the Parties are unable to reach a timely decision on an issue, each Party shall refer the issue to its higher authority for resolution. In the meantime, the approved PA shall continue to be implemented without interruption under the direction of the POs while the issue is being resolved by higher authority.

ARTICLE V
FINANCIAL PROVISIONS

5.1. Each Party shall contribute its equitable share of the full Financial Costs and Non-financial Costs incurred in performing, managing, and administering its responsibilities and activities under each PA, including overhead costs, administrative costs, and costs of claims, and each Party shall receive an equitable share of the results of the PA. The tasks to be performed by each Party shall be established in each PA. The assignment of tasks shall represent an equitable sharing of the costs and work to be performed under each PA.

5.2. This MOA creates no Financial or Non-financial Costs regarding individual PAs. Detailed descriptions of the financial and non-financial arrangements for a specific Project, including, at a minimum, each Party's share of the total Project cost, shall be contained in that PA.

5.3. The following costs shall be borne entirely by the Party incurring the costs or on whose behalf the costs are incurred:

5.3.1. costs associated with any unique national requirements identified by a Party; and

5.3.2. any other costs not expressly stated as shared costs or any costs that are outside the scope of this MOA and its PAs.

5.4. A Party shall promptly notify the other Party if available funds are not adequate to fulfill its obligations under a PA. If a Party notifies the other Party that it is terminating or reducing its funding for a PA, both Parties shall immediately consult with a view toward continuation on a changed or modified basis.

5.5. For a Project where one Party contracts on behalf of the other Party or on behalf of both Parties, the POs shall be responsible for establishing the detailed financial management procedures under which the Project shall operate. These procedures, which must accord with the national laws and accounting and audit requirements of the Parties, shall be detailed in a Financial Management Procedures Document (FMPD) prepared by the POs and subject to the approval of the SC, as appropriate.

5.6. For a Project where one Party contracts on behalf of the other Party or both Parties, each Party shall provide funds for the Project in accordance with the estimated schedule of financial contributions contained in the FMPD, which shall be consistent with paragraph 5.10.

5.7. For PAs with shared costs that involve the establishment of a JPO with Cooperative Project Personnel (CPP) assignments, the PA shall address the financial and non-financial contributions required for JPO administration and associated support services including, but not limited to, JPO costs of travel incurred in support of Project efforts, JPO training costs, Contract award, Contract administration, office space, security services, information technology services, communications services, and supplies.

5.8. In addition to the shared costs of JPO administration and associated support services costs described in paragraph 5.7., the cost of personnel in the JPO shall be borne as follows:

5.8.1. The Host Party shall bear the costs of all pay and allowances of Host Party personnel in the JPO.

5.8.2. The Parent Party shall bear the following CPP-related costs:

5.8.2.1. all pay and allowances of CPP assigned to the JPO;

5.8.2.2. transportation of CPP, CPP dependents, and their personal property to the JPO location prior to commencement of the CPP assignment in the JPO, and return transportation of the foregoing from the JPO location upon completion or termination of the CPP assignment;

5.8.2.3. compensation for loss of, or damage to, the personal property of CPP or CPP dependents, subject to the laws and regulations of the Parent party's government; and

5.8.2.4. preparation and shipment of remains and funeral expenses in the event of the death of CPP or CPP dependents.

5.9. For PAs without shared costs that involve the establishment of one or more multinational offices with CPP assignments, the Parties shall bear costs related to multilateral offices established under such PAs as follows.

5.9.1. The Host Party shall bear the following costs:

5.9.1.1. all pay and allowances of Host Party personnel assigned to the multinational office; and

5.9.1.2. multinational office costs including, but not limited to, CPP assignment-related administrative and support services costs such as CPP costs of travel incurred in support of Project efforts, CPP-related training costs, Contract award, Contract administration, office space, security services, information technology services, communications services, and supplies.

5.9.2. The Parent Party shall bear the following costs:

5.9.2.1. all pay and allowances of CPP assigned to the multinational office;

5.9.2.2. transportation of CPP, CPP dependents, and their personal property to the JPO location prior to commencement of the CPP assignment at a location specified by the Host Party, and return transportation of the foregoing from this location upon completion or termination of the CPP assignment;

5.9.2.3. compensation for loss of, or damage to, the personal property of CPP or CPP dependents, subject to the laws and regulations of the Parent Party's government; and

5.9.2.4. preparation and shipment of remains and funeral expenses in the event of the death of CPP or CPP dependents.

5.10. The Parties recognize that in performing Contracting responsibilities under a PA, it may become necessary for one Party to incur contractual or other obligations for the benefit of the other Party or both Parties prior to the receipt of the other Party's funds. In the event one Party incurs such obligations, the other Party shall make such funds available in such amounts and at such times as may be required by the Contract or other obligation, and shall pay any damages and costs that may accrue from the performance of or cancellation of the Contract or other obligation in advance of the time such payments, damages, or costs are due.

ARTICLE VI
CONTRACTING PROVISIONS

6.1. Prior to the signature of a PA, each Party, in consultation with the other Party, shall determine if Contracting is necessary to fulfill its responsibilities under that PA and so indicate in the PA. In such event, that Party shall contract in accordance with its respective national laws, regulations, and procedures.

6.2. When one Party individually contracts to undertake a task under a PA, it will be solely responsible for its own Contracting, and the other Party shall not be subject to any liability arising from such Contracts.

6.3. If the Parties determine that it is necessary under a PA that one Party contract on behalf of the other Party or both Parties for tasks under the PA, the Party shall contract in accordance with its respective national laws, regulations, and procedures. The Contracting Officer shall be the exclusive source for providing contractual direction and instructions to Contractors. The POs shall be responsible for the coordination of activities relating to this MOA and its PAs, and shall cooperate with the Contracting Officer in the areas of Contract procedures, Contract negotiation, evaluation of offers, and Contract award. The Contracting Officer shall also keep the POs advised of all financial arrangements with Contractors.

6.4. For all Contracting activities performed by either Party, the PO shall, upon request, provide a copy of all statements of work for information prior to the issuance of solicitations.

6.5. Each Party's Contracting Agency shall negotiate to obtain the rights to use and disclose Project Information required by Article IX (Disclosure and Use of Project Information). During the Contracting process, each Party's Contracting Officer shall advise Prospective Contractors of their obligation to notify the Contracting Agency immediately if they are subject to any license or agreement that shall restrict that Party's freedom to disclose information or permit its use. The Contracting Officer shall also advise Prospective Contractors to employ their best efforts not to enter into any new agreement or arrangement that shall result in restrictions.

6.6. In the event a Party's Contracting Agency is unable to secure adequate rights to use and disclose Project Information as required by Article IX (Disclosure and Use of Project Information), or is notified by Contractors or Prospective Contractors of any restrictions on the disclosure and use of information, that Party's PO shall notify the other Party's PO of the restriction(s).

6.7. Each Party's Contracting Agency shall insert into its prospective Contracts (and require its Contractors to insert in subcontracts) provisions that satisfy the requirements of this MOA, including Article IX (Disclosure and Use of Project Information), Article X (Controlled Unclassified Information), Article XII (Security), Article XIII (Third Party Sales and Transfers), and Article XVI (General Provisions), including the export control provisions in accordance with this MOA, in particular paragraphs 6.8. and 6.9.

6.8. Each Party shall legally bind its Contractors to a requirement that the Contractor shall not retransfer or otherwise use export-controlled information furnished by the other Party for any purpose other than the purposes authorized under this MOA or a PA under this MOA. The Contractor shall also be legally bound not to retransfer the export-controlled information to another Contractor or subcontractor unless that Contractor or subcontractor has been legally bound to limit use of the information to the purposes authorized under this MOA or a PA under this MOA. Export-controlled information furnished by one Party under this MOA or a PA under this MOA may only be retransferred by the other Party to its Contractors if the legal arrangements required by this paragraph have been established.

6.9. Each Party shall legally bind its Prospective Contractors to a requirement that the Prospective Contractor shall not retransfer or otherwise use export-controlled information furnished by the other Party for any purpose other than responding to a solicitation issued in furtherance of the purposes authorized under this MOA or a PA under this MOA. Prospective Contractors shall not be authorized use for any other purpose if they are not awarded a Contract. The Prospective Contractors shall also be legally bound not to retransfer the export-controlled information to a prospective subcontractor unless that prospective subcontractor has been legally bound to limit use of the export-controlled information for the purpose of responding to the solicitation. Export-controlled information furnished by one Party under this MOA or a PA under this MOA may only be retransferred by the other Party to its Prospective Contractors if the legal arrangements required by this paragraph have been established. Upon request by the furnishing Party, the receiving Party shall identify its Prospective Contractors and prospective subcontractors receiving such export-controlled information.

6.10. Each Party's PO shall promptly advise the other Party's PO of any cost growth, schedule delay, or performance problems of any Contractor for which its Contracting Agency is responsible.

ARTICLE VII
WORK SHARING

7.1. After the scope of a Project has been fully defined with regard to both the technical and the financial contents, each Party shall work toward the goal that the work to be performed under a PA to this MOA shall be equitably shared, taking into account the technical merit, and the need to achieve the timely, economical, and efficient execution of the Project. This work shall encompass those requirements contained in the Scope of Work of the PA that are common to the Parties and are funded under the Project.

7.2. Each Party shall encourage its Contractors to provide competitive opportunities to sources from the other Party to participate in the work of a Project, provided that such participation does not adversely affect the Project.

7.3. No requirement shall be imposed by either Party for work sharing or other industrial or commercial compensation in connection with this MOA and any PA that is not in accordance with this MOA.

ARTICLE VIII
PROJECT EQUIPMENT

8.1. For the purpose of carrying out a PA, each Party may provide to the other Party such Project Equipment identified as being necessary for the corresponding Project. A list of all Project Equipment provided by one Party to another Party shall be developed, maintained, and amended by the POs. If an SC is formed, the SC will approve the list of Project Equipment.

8.2. Project Equipment is provided only for the purposes set forth in Article II (Objectives) of the applicable PA, unless otherwise consented in writing by the providing Party. The providing Party shall furnish the receiving Party all the relevant technical information needed to use, inspect, maintain, and repair the Project Equipment. Project Equipment shall remain the property of the providing Party. In addition, the receiving Party shall maintain Project Equipment in good order, repair, and operable condition and shall return it in as good condition as received, normal wear and tear excepted, unless the providing Party has approved in the PA the expenditure or consumption of Project Equipment as necessary for the purposes of the PA. Such expenditure or consumption shall be without reimbursement to the providing Party. However, the receiving Party shall bear the cost of any damage to (other than normal wear and tear) or loss of Project Equipment provided to it that is not approved for expenditure or consumption. If the Project Equipment is damaged beyond economical repair, the receiving Party shall return the Project Equipment to the providing Party (unless otherwise specified in writing by the providing Party) and pay its replacement value as computed pursuant to the providing Party's national laws and regulations. If Project Equipment is lost while in the custody of the receiving Party, the receiving Party shall issue a certificate of loss to the providing Party and pay the replacement value as computed pursuant to the providing Party's national laws and regulations. The replacement value of the Project Equipment shall be specified in the list of Project Equipment referenced in paragraph 8.1. of this Article.

8.3. The providing Party shall furnish the Project Equipment in a serviceable and usable condition for the purposes of the PA. However, the providing Party makes no warranty or guarantee of fitness of the Project Equipment for a particular purpose or use, and makes no commitment to alter, improve, or adapt the Project Equipment or any part thereof.

8.4. The providing Party shall deliver the Project Equipment to the receiving Party at a mutually agreed location. Custody of the Project equipment shall pass from the providing Party to the receiving Party at time of receipt. Any further transportation is the responsibility of the receiving Party.

8.5. The receiving Party shall inspect and inventory the Project Equipment upon receipt. The receiving Party shall also inspect and inventory the Project Equipment prior to its return (unless the Project Equipment is to be expended or consumed).

8.6. Prior to expiration or termination of the PA, the receiving Party shall return Project Equipment to the providing Party at a mutually agreed location. Any further transportation is the responsibility of the providing Party. The receiving Party shall provide written notice of consumption or expenditure of Project Equipment not intended for return. In the event the intended consumption or expenditure does not occur, the receiving Party shall return the Project Equipment to the providing Party at a mutually agreed location. Any further transportation is the responsibility of the providing Party.

8.7. The Parties shall ensure, by all reasonable means, the protection of any intellectual property rights in the Project Equipment.

8.8. Any Project Equipment that is jointly acquired on behalf of the Parties for use under this MOA and a PA shall be disposed of during the applicable Project or when the Project ends as agreed by RDT&E EA or SC, as appropriate.

8.9. Disposal of jointly acquired Project Equipment may include a transfer of the interest of one Party in such Project equipment to the other Party, or the sale of such Project Equipment to a Third Party in accordance with Article XIII (Third Party Sales and Transfers). The Parties shall share the consideration from jointly acquired Project Equipment transferred or sold to a Third Party in the same ratio as costs are shared under the PA.

ARTICLE IX
DISCLOSURE AND USE OF PROJECT INFORMATION

9.1. General

9.1.1. Both Parties recognize that successful collaboration depends on full and prompt exchange of information necessary for carrying out each PA and the use of the results. The nature and amount of Project Information to be acquired shall be in accordance with Article II (Objective), Article VI (Contractual Provisions) and the PAs to this MOA. Subject to the rights both Parties are accorded under this MOA, title to Project Foreground Information generated by a Party or its Contractor shall reside in that Party or its Contractors, in accordance with that Party's national laws, regulations, and policies.

9.1.2. As set forth in paragraph 3.2. of Article III (Scope of Work), the Parties may exchange information under this MOA for the purpose of harmonizing the Parties' requirements for formulating, developing, and negotiating PAs. The Party furnishing such information shall clearly indicate to the receiving Party that it is furnishing such information for this purpose. Until a PA is signed, or if no PA is signed, a Party may use information received under paragraph 3.2. only for information and evaluation purposes and shall not disclose or transfer such information to a Third Party.

9.1.3. Transfer of Project Information will be consistent with the furnishing Party's applicable export control laws and regulations. Unless otherwise restricted by duly authorized officials of the furnishing Party at the time of transfer to the other Party, all export-controlled information furnished by that Party to the other Party may be retransferred to the other Party's Contractors, subcontractors, Prospective Contractors, and prospective subcontractors, subject to the requirements of paragraphs 6.8. and 6.9. of Article VI (Contracting Provisions). Export-controlled information may be furnished by Contractors, subcontractors, Prospective Contractors, and prospective subcontractors of one Party's nation to the Contractors, subcontractors, Prospective Contractors, and prospective subcontractors of the other Party's nation pursuant to this MOA or PA under this MOA subject to the conditions established in licenses or other approvals issued by the Government of the former Party in accordance with its applicable export control laws and regulations.

9.2. Government Project Foreground Information

9.2.1. Disclosure: Project Foreground Information generated in the performance of the Project by a Party's military or civilian employees shall be disclosed without charge to both Parties.

9.2.2. Use: Each Party may use all government Project Foreground Information without charge for Defense Purposes. The Party generating government Project Foreground Information shall also retain its rights of use thereto. A sale or other transfer to a Third Party shall be subject to the provisions of Article XIII (Third Party Sales and Transfers) of this MOA.

9.3. Government Project Background Information

9.3.1. Disclosure: Each Party, upon request, shall disclose to the other Party any relevant government Project Background Information generated by its military or civilian employees outside the scope of this MOA, provided that:

9.3.1.1. such Project Background Information is necessary to or useful in the Project, with the Party in possession of the information determining whether it is "necessary to" or "useful in" the Project;

9.3.1.2. such Project Background Information may be made available without incurring liability to holders of proprietary rights; and

9.3.1.3. disclosure is consistent with national disclosure policies and national regulations of the furnishing Party.

9.3.2. Use: Government Project Background Information disclosed by one Party to the other may be used without charge by the other Party for the Project purposes of the particular PA. However, subject to proprietary rights held by other than the Parties and subject to the provisions of paragraph 13.4. of Article XIII (Third Party Sales and Transfers), such Project Background Information may be used for other Defense Purposes by the other Party without charge when the use of such information is necessary for the use of the Project Foreground Information. The furnishing Party, in consultation with the other Party, shall determine whether the use of such information is necessary. The furnishing Party shall retain all its rights with respect to such Project Background Information.

9.4. Contractor Project Foreground Information

9.4.1. Disclosure: Project Foreground Information generated and delivered by Contractors shall be disclosed without charge to both Parties.

9.4.2. Use: Each Party may use without charge for its Defense Purposes all Contractor Project Foreground Information generated and delivered by Contractors of the other Party. The Party whose Contractors generate and deliver Contractor Project Foreground Information shall also retain rights of use thereto in accordance with the applicable Contract(s). Any sale or other transfer to a Third Party of Contractor Project Foreground Information shall be subject to the provisions of Article XIII (Third Party Sales and Transfers) of this MOA.

9.5. Contractor Project Background Information

9.5.1. Disclosure: Any relevant Project Background Information, (including information subject to proprietary rights) generated and delivered by Contractors or other entities under Contracts awarded by a Party outside the scope of this MOA shall be made available to the other Party provided the following conditions are met:

9.5.1.1. such Project Background Information is necessary to or useful in the Project, with the Party in possession of the information determining whether it is "necessary to" or "useful in" the Project;

9.5.1.2. such Project Background Information may be made available without incurring liability to holders of proprietary rights; and

9.5.1.3. disclosure is consistent with national disclosure policies and national regulations of the furnishing Party.

9.5.2. Use: Project Background Information furnished by one Party's Contractors and disclosed to the other Party may be used without charge by the other Party for the Project purposes of the particular PA. However, subject to any further restrictions by holders of proprietary rights, and subject to the provisions of paragraph 13.4. of Article XIII (Third Party Sales and Transfers), such Project Background Information may be used for other Defense Purposes in accordance with such fair and reasonable terms as are arranged with the Contractor. However, the furnishing Party shall retain all its rights with respect to such Project Background Information.

9.6. Alternative Uses of Project Information

9.6.1. The prior written consent of each Party shall be required for the use of any Project Foreground Information for purposes other than those provided for in this MOA or any PA under it.

9.6.2. Any Project Background Information provided by one Party shall be used by the other Party only for the purposes set forth in this MOA or any PA under it, unless otherwise consented to in writing by the providing Party.

9.7. Proprietary Project Information

9.7.1. All unclassified Project Information subject to proprietary interests shall be identified and marked, and it shall be handled as Controlled Unclassified Information. All classified Project Information subject to proprietary rights shall be so identified and marked.

9.7.2. The provisions of the NATO Agreement on the Communication of Technical Information for Defence Purposes, done at Brussels on October 19, 1970, and the Implementing Procedures for the NATO Agreement on the Communication of Technical Information for Defence Purposes, approved by the North Atlantic Council on January 1, 1971, shall apply to proprietary Project Information related to this MOA.

9.8. Patents

9.8.1. Where a Party owns title to a Project Invention, or has the right to receive title to a Project Invention, that Party shall consult with the other Party regarding the filing of a Patent application for such Project Invention. The Party that has or receives title to such Project Invention shall, in other countries, file, cause to be filed, or provide the other Party with the opportunity to file on behalf of the Party holding title, or its Contractors, as appropriate, Patent applications covering that Project Invention. If a Party having filed or caused to be filed a Patent application decides to stop prosecution of the application, that Party shall notify the other Party of that decision and permit the other Party to continue the prosecution.

9.8.2. The other Party shall be furnished with copies of Patent applications filed and Patents granted with regard to Project Inventions.

9.8.3. The other Party shall acquire a non-exclusive, irrevocable, royalty-free license to practice or have practiced, by or on behalf of the Party, throughout the world for Defense Purposes, any Project Invention.

9.8.4. Patent applications which contain Classified Information, to be filed under this MOA, shall be protected and safeguarded in accordance with the requirements contained in the NATO Agreement for the Mutual Safeguarding of Secrecy of Inventions Relating to Defense and for Which Applications for Patents Have Been Made, done at Paris on September 21, 1960, and its Implementing Procedures.

9.8.5. Each Party shall notify the other Party of any Patent infringement claims made in its territory arising in the course of work performed under a PA. Insofar as possible, the other Party shall provide information available to it that may assist in defending the claim. Each Party shall be responsible for handling all Patent infringement claims made in its territory, and shall consult with the other Party during the handling, and prior to any settlement, of such claims. The Parties shall share the costs of resolving Patent infringement claims in the same percentage as costs are shared under a PA, unless otherwise specified in the PA. The Parties shall, in accordance with their national laws and practices, give their authorization and consent for all use and manufacture in the course of work performed under a PA of any invention covered by a Patent issued by their respective countries.

ARTICLE X
CONTROLLED UNCLASSIFIED INFORMATION

10.1. Except as otherwise provided in this MOA or as authorized in writing by the originating Party, Controlled Unclassified Information (CUI) provided or generated pursuant to this MOA or a PA to this MOA shall be controlled as follows:

10.1.1. Such information shall be used only for the purposes authorized for use of Project Information as specified in Article IX (Disclosure and Use of Project Information).

10.1.2. Access to such information shall be limited to personnel whose access is necessary for the permitted use under subparagraph 10.1.1., and shall be subject to the provisions of Article XIII (Third Party Sales and Transfers).

10.1.3. Each Party shall take all lawful steps, which may include national classification, available to it to keep such information free from further disclosure (including requests under any legislative provisions), except as provided in subparagraph 10.1.2., unless the originating Party consents to such disclosure. In the event of unauthorized disclosure, or if it becomes probable that the information may have to be further disclosed under any legislative provision, immediate notification shall be given to the originating Party.

10.2. To assist in providing the appropriate controls, the originating Party shall ensure that CUI is appropriately marked to ensure its "in confidence" nature. The Parties' export-controlled information shall be marked in accordance with the applicable Party's export control markings as documented in the Project Security Instruction (PSI), or in Article XII (Special Provisions) of the applicable PA, as appropriate. The Parties shall also decide, in advance and in writing, on the markings to be placed on any other types of CUI and describe such markings in the PSI or in Article XII (Special Provisions) of the applicable PA, as appropriate.

10.3. CUI provided or generated pursuant to a PA to this MOA shall be handled in a manner that ensures control as provided for in paragraph 10.1.

10.4. Prior to authorizing the release of CUI to Contractors, the Parties shall ensure the Contractors are legally bound to control such information in accordance with the provisions of this Article.

ARTICLE XI
VISITS TO ESTABLISHMENTS

11.1. Each Party shall permit visits to its government establishments, agencies, and laboratories, and Contractor industrial facilities by employees of the other Party or by employees of the other Party's Contractor(s), provided that the visit is authorized by both Parties and the employees have any necessary and appropriate security clearances and a need-to-know.

11.2. All visiting personnel shall be required to comply with security regulations of the Host Party. Any information disclosed or made available to visitors shall be treated as if supplied to the Party sponsoring the visiting personnel, and shall be subject to the provisions of this MOA.

11.3. Requests for visits by personnel of one Party to a facility of the other Party shall be coordinated through official channels, and shall conform with the established visit procedures of the host country. Requests for visits shall bear the name of this MOA and the appropriate PA.

11.4. Lists of personnel of each Party required to visit, on a continuing basis, facilities of the other Party shall be submitted through official channels in accordance with recurring international visit procedures.

ARTICLE XII
SECURITY

12.1. All Classified Information provided or generated pursuant to this MOA and any of its PAs shall be stored, handled, transmitted, and safeguarded in accordance with the General Security Agreement between the Republic of Italy and the United States of America, of August 4, 1964, amended September 2, 1982, and including the Industrial Security Annex thereto, of November 27, 1985, amended January 27, 1988.

12.2. Classified Information shall be transferred only through official government-to-government channels or through channels approved by the Designated Security Authorities (DSAs) or National Security Authorities (NSA), as appropriate, of the Parties. Such Classified Information and material shall bear the level of classification, denote the country of origin, the conditions of release, and the fact that the information relates to this MOA and the applicable PA.

12.3. Each Party shall take all lawful steps available to it to ensure that Classified Information provided or generated pursuant to this MOA and any of its PAs is protected from further disclosure, except as permitted by paragraph 12.8., unless the other Party consents to such disclosure. Accordingly, each Party shall ensure that:

12.3.1. The recipient shall not release the Classified Information to any government, national, organization, or other entity of a Third Party except as permitted under the procedures set forth in Article XIII (Third Party Sales and Transfers).

12.3.2. The recipient shall not use the Classified Information for other than the purposes provided for in this MOA and any of its PAs.

12.3.3. The recipient shall comply with any distribution and access restrictions on information that is provided under this MOA and any of its PAs.

12.4. The Parties shall investigate all cases in which it is known or where there are grounds for suspecting that Classified Information provided or generated pursuant to this MOA and any of its PAs has been lost or disclosed to unauthorized persons. Each Party also shall promptly and fully inform the other Party of the details of any such occurrences, and of the final results of the investigation and of the corrective action taken to preclude recurrence.

12.5. When a PA contains provisions for the exchange of Classified Information, the POs shall prepare a PSI and a Classification Guide (CG) for the PA. The PSI and the CG shall describe the methods by which Project Information and material shall be classified, marked, used, transmitted, and safeguarded, and shall require that markings for all export-controlled Classified Information also include the applicable export control markings identified in the PSI in accordance with paragraph 10.2. of Article X (Controlled Unclassified Information) of this MOA. The PSI and CG shall be developed by the PO within three months after the PA comes into effect. They shall be reviewed and forwarded to the appropriate DSA or NSA, and shall be applicable to all government and Contractor personnel participating in the PA. The CG shall be subject to regular review and revision with the aim of downgrading the classification whenever this is appropriate. The PSI and the CG shall be approved by the appropriate DSA or NSA prior to the transfer of any Classified Information or CUI.

12.6. The DSA or NSA, as appropriate, of a Party that awards a classified Contract under this MOA shall assume responsibility for administering within its territory security measures for the protection of the Classified Information, in accordance with its national laws and regulations. Prior to the release to a Contractor, Prospective Contractor or subcontractor of any Classified Information received under this MOA, the DSAs, or NSAs, as appropriate, shall:

12.6.1. ensure that such Contractor, Prospective Contractor, or subcontractors and their facility(ies) have the capability to protect the Classified Information adequately;

12.6.2. grant a security clearance to the facility(ies), if appropriate;

12.6.3. grant a security clearance for all personnel whose duties require access to Classified Information, if appropriate;

12.6.4. ensure that all persons having access to the Classified Information are informed of their responsibilities to protect the Classified Information in accordance with national security laws and regulations, and the provisions of this MOA and the applicable PA;

12.6.5. carry out periodic security inspections of cleared facilities to ensure that the Classified Information is properly protected; and

12.6.6. ensure that access to the Classified Information is limited to those persons who have a need-to-know for purposes of a Project.

12.7. Contractors, Prospective Contractors, or subcontractors which are determined by the DSA or NSA, as appropriate, to be under financial, administrative, policy, or management control of nationals or entities of a Third Party, may participate in a Contract or subcontract requiring access to Classified Information provided or generated pursuant to this MOA and any of its PAs only when enforceable measures are in effect to ensure that other entities of a Third Party shall not have access to Classified Information. If enforceable measures are not in effect to preclude access by other entities of a Third Party, the other Party shall be consulted for approval prior to permitting such access.

12.8. For any facility wherein Classified Information is to be used, the responsible Party or Contractor shall approve the appointment of a person or persons to exercise effectively the responsibilities for safeguarding at such facility the information pertaining to this MOA and any of its PAs. These officials shall be responsible for limiting access to Classified Information or material involved in the MOA and any PAs to those persons who have been properly approved for access and have a need-to-know.

12.9. Each Party shall ensure that access to the Classified Information is limited to those persons who possess requisite security clearances and have a specific need for access to the Classified Information in order to participate in this MOA and any of its PAs.

12.10. A Party may consider on a case-by-case basis a person who is a citizen of another NATO country or who is a citizen of Austria, Finland, Sweden, or Switzerland as eligible for access to Classified Information furnished or generated pursuant to this MOA and any of its PAs, provided that the following conditions are met:

12.10.1. Access to such Classified Information may not be granted or implemented until appropriate U.S. Government authorization is secured either as part of the original sale or export authorization, which may permit sharing of such Information with citizens of the aforementioned countries who are employees or agents of the Parties, or as a retransfer or re-export authorization. Italian Government authorization for transfers, export, or retransfer or re-export, may be required with respect to Classified Information of Italian origin.

12.10.2. Eligibility for access is necessary in support of activities undertaken pursuant to this MOA and any of its PAs.

12.10.3. The person is granted a personal security clearance based on a clearance procedure that is no less rigorous than that required for a citizen of the Party's country in accordance with the Party's security policy and procedures, and shall sign a non-disclosure agreement.

12.10.4. Eligibility for access shall be limited to Classified Information that is classified no higher than SECRET. Access shall not be provided to TOP SECRET Information, intelligence Information, special access program Information, communications security Information, ATOMAL Information, Information carrying out specific dissemination limitations, or other Information subject to other access controls.

12.10.5. The person shall be eligible to obtain access only to that Classified Information that is required for the person to perform the specific Project-related tasks that are assigned to him or her and only for the period of time necessary to perform such tasks. Subject to the requisite appropriate additional U.S. or Italian Government authorizations referred to above, the person may have access only during working hours (not including weekends) and shall not remove or transmit in any form Classified Information from the office. The person shall not be permitted to reproduce Classified Information. The person shall be required to certify in writing that he or she is aware of and shall comply with security procedures and restrictions on re-transfers and access by unauthorized persons. The control of access to Classified Information shall be the responsibility of the security officer of the facility or organization at which the access is provided. Such security officer shall be a citizen of the country of the Party that provides the access.

12.10.6. There shall be a security of information agreement or other legally binding security arrangement between the government of the Party wishing to provide access and the government of the country of citizenship of the person who is to be eligible for such access.

12.10.7. Before confirming eligibility for access to Classified Information, the government of the Party that is to extend eligibility for such access shall ensure that it has sufficient jurisdiction and control over the person to effectively prosecute the person and hold him or her accountable for the proper handling of the Classified Information.

12.10.8. The Party extending eligibility for access to Classified Information to a citizen from another NATO country or a citizen of Austria, Finland, Sweden, or Switzerland shall provide thirty (30) days prior notification to the other Party of the nationality and identity of the citizens of the aforementioned countries who shall be eligible for such access and shall ensure that records are maintained of any such access.

12.10.9. The government of the Party that is to extend eligibility for access to the Classified Information shall be willing to provide access to its own Classified Information of a similar type and classification level to the country of citizenship of the person who shall be eligible for access under the conditions stated herein.

12.10.10. Information or material provided or generated pursuant to this MOA and any of its PAs may be classified as high as SECRET. The existence of this MOA is UNCLASSIFIED and the contents are UNCLASSIFIED. The classification of a specific PA and its content shall be stated in that PA.

ARTICLE XIII
THIRD PARTY SALES AND TRANSFERS

13.1. Each Party shall retain the right to sell, transfer title to, disclose, or transfer possession of Project Foreground Information:

13.1.1. which is generated solely by either that Party or that Party's Contractors in the performance of that Party's work allocation under a PA; and

13.1.2. which does not include any Project Foreground Information or Project Background Information of the other Party and whose generation, test, or evaluation has not relied on the use of Project Equipment of the other Party.

13.2. In the event questions arise as to whether the Project Foreground Information (or any item produced either wholly or in part from Project Foreground Information) that a Party intends to sell, transfer title to, disclose, or transfer possession of to a Third Party is within the scope of paragraph 13.1., the matter shall be brought to the immediate attention of the other Party's PO. The Parties shall resolve the matter prior to any sale or other transfer of such Project Foreground Information (or items produced wholly or in part from such Project Foreground Information) to a Third Party.

13.3. Except to the extent permitted in paragraph 13.1., the Parties shall not sell, transfer title to, disclose, or transfer possession of Project Foreground Information (or any item produced either wholly or in part from Project Foreground Information) or jointly acquired Project Equipment to any Third Party without the prior written consent of the government of the other Party. Furthermore, neither Party shall permit any such sale, disclosure, or transfer, including by the owner, without the prior written consent of the government of the other Party. Such consent shall not be given unless the government of the intended recipient agrees in writing with the Parties that it shall:

13.3.1. not retransfer, or permit the further retransfer of, any equipment or information provided; and

13.3.2. use, or permit the use of, the equipment or information provided only for the purposes specified by the Parties.

13.4. A Party shall not sell, transfer title to, disclose, or transfer possession of Project Equipment or Project Background Information provided by the other Party to any Third Party without the prior written consent of the government of the Party that provided such equipment or information.

The providing Party's government shall be solely responsible for authorizing such transfers and, as applicable, specifying the method and conditions for implementing such transfers.

ARTICLE XIV
LIABILITY AND CLAIMS

14.1. Claims against either Party or its personnel shall be dealt with in accordance with the terms of Article VIII of the NATO Status of Forces Agreement (NATO SOFA) dated June 19, 1951. Civilian employees of the Parties assigned to duty within their government's Defense Department or Ministry shall be deemed for the purpose of Article VIII of NATO SOFA to be members of a civilian component within the meaning of Article I of the NATO SOFA while present in the territory of the other Party for the purpose of this MOA. However, claims for loss of or damage to Project Equipment provided under Article VIII (Project Equipment) shall be dealt with in accordance with paragraph 8.2.

14.2. Claims arising under or related to any Contract awarded pursuant to Article VI (Contracting Provisions) shall be resolved in accordance with the provisions of the Contract.

14.3. Employees and agents of Contractors shall not be considered to be civilian personnel employed by a Party for the purpose of paragraph 14.1.

14.4. In case of damage caused to or by jointly acquired Project Equipment, where the cost of making good such damage is not recoverable from other persons, such cost shall be borne by the Parties according to the same percentages as costs are shared under the PA.

ARTICLE XV
CUSTOMS DUTIES, TAXES, AND SIMILAR CHARGES

15.1. Customs duties, import and export taxes, and similar charges shall be administered in accordance with each Party's respective national laws and regulations. Insofar as existing national laws and regulations permit, the Parties shall endeavor to ensure that such readily identifiable duties, taxes and similar charges, as well as quantitative or other restrictions on imports and exports, are not imposed in connection with work carried out under each PA.

15.2. Each Party shall use its best efforts to ensure that customs duties, import and export taxes, and similar charges are administered in a manner favorable to the efficient and economical conduct of the work. If any such duties, taxes, or similar charges are levied, the Party in whose country they are levied shall bear such costs.

ARTICLE XVI
GENERAL PROVISIONS

16.1. Disputes between the Parties arising under or relating to this MOA shall be resolved only by consultation between the Parties and shall not be referred to a national court, an international tribunal, or to any other person or entity for settlement.

16.2. In the event of a conflict between the terms of this MOA and any PA, this MOA shall take precedence.

16.3. All activities of the Parties under this MOA shall be carried out in accordance with their respective national laws and regulations, including their respective export control laws and regulations.

16.4. The obligations of the Parties shall be subject to the availability of appropriated funds for such purposes.

ARTICLE XVII
LANGUAGE

17.1. The working language for this MOA and its PAs shall be the English language.

17.2. All data and information generated under this MOA, its PAs, and its implementing Contracts, and provided by one Party to the other Party shall be furnished in the English language.

ARTICLE XVIII
AMENDMENT, TERMINATION, COMING INTO EFFECT, AND DURATION

18.1. This MOA may be amended only by the mutual written agreement of the Parties. Any of the PAs under this RDT&E MOA may be amended only by the written agreement of authorized representatives of the Parties.

18.2. The Parties may, upon written consent, terminate at any time this MOA and any of its PAs. In the event both Parties agree to terminate this MOA or one of its PAs, the Parties shall consult prior to the date of termination to ensure termination on the most economical and equitable terms.

18.3. Either Party may terminate this MOA or any PA at any time and the termination will take effect 180 days after its written notification to the other Party. Such notice shall be the subject of immediate consultation to decide upon the appropriate course of action.

18.4. In the event of termination of this MOA or any of its PAs, the following rules apply:

18.4.1. The terminating Party shall continue participation, financial or otherwise, up to the effective date of termination.

18.4.2. Except as to Contracts awarded on behalf of both Parties, each Party shall be responsible for its own Project-related costs associated with termination of the Project. For Contracts awarded on behalf of both Parties, the terminating Party shall pay for all Contract modification and termination costs that would not otherwise have been incurred but for the decision to terminate. However, in no event shall a terminating Party's total financial contribution, including Contract termination costs, exceed that Party's total financial contribution for the PA being terminated.

18.4.3. All Project Information and rights therein received under the provisions of this MOA and any of its PAs prior to the termination shall be retained by the Parties, subject to the provisions of this MOA and its PAs.

18.4.4. If requested by the other Party, the terminating Party may continue to administer Project Contract(s) that it awarded on behalf of the other Party on a reimbursable basis.

18.4.5. Each Party shall make available to the other Party all Project Foreground Information generated and delivered prior to termination, and that has not been provided to the other Party prior to the termination.

18.5. The respective rights and responsibilities of the Parties regarding Article VIII (Project Equipment), Article IX (Disclosure and Use of Project Information), Article X (Controlled Unclassified Information), Article XII (Security), Article XIII (Third Party Sales and Transfers), Article XIV (Liability and Claims), and this Article XVIII (Amendment, Termination, Coming into Effect and Duration) shall continue notwithstanding termination or expiration of this MOA and any of its PAs.

18.6. This MOA, which consists of 18 Articles, one Annex, and one Appendix to the Annex, shall come into effect upon signature by both Parties and shall remain in effect for 25 years. It may be extended by written agreement of the Parties. All PAs shall automatically terminate upon the termination or expiration of this MOA.

IN WITNESS WHEREOF, the undersigned, duly authorized by their respective Parties, have signed this MOA.

DONE, in duplicate, in the English language.

FOR THE DEPARTMENT OF DEFENSE OF THE UNITED STATES OF AMERICA

[Signature]

Signature

Hon. Kenneth J. Krieg

Name

Under Secretary of Defense, Acquisition, Technology and Logistics

Title

1 September 2006

Date

WASHINGTON, DC

Location

FOR THE MINISTRY OF DEFENSE OF THE ITALIAN REPUBLIC

[Signature]

Signature

Gen. C.A. Gianni BOTONDI

Name

Seq.Gen. & NAD

Title

26 September 2006

Date

Rome-IT

Location

ANNEX A (SAMPLE PROJECT AGREEMENT)
TO THE
U.S. DoD-ITALIAN MoD RESEARCH, DEVELOPMENT, TEST, AND EVALUATION PROJECTS MEMORANDUM OF AGREEMENT
DATED
PROJECT AGREEMENT NO. _________[1]
BETWEEN
THE DEPARTMENT OF DEFENSE
OF THE UNITED STATES OF AMERICA
AND
THE MINISTRY OF DEFENSE
OF THE ITALIAN REPUBLIC
CONCERNING
(FULL DESIGNATION OF THE PROJECT)

INTRODUCTION

This Project Agreement (PA) hereby establishes the ____________________________ (**insert name of Project**) as a Project in accordance with the MOA between the Department of Defense of the United States of America (U.S. DoD) and the Ministry of Defense of the Italian Republic (IT MoD) for Research, Development, Test, and Evaluation (RDT&E) Projects, (***date***), the terms of which are hereby incorporated by reference.

ARTICLE I
DEFINITION OF TERMS AND ABBREVIATIONS

(Define only those terms used in this PA that have not been defined in the RDT&E MOA).

ARTICLE II
OBJECTIVES

The objectives of this ____________________________ Project are:

(**For example:**

a. the development of ____________________________
____

b. the improvement of ____________________________
____

c. the investigation of ____________________________
____________________________)

[1] The Project Agreement Numbers shall be structured as follows: RDT&E: IT XX–NN–nnnn where XX is a U.S. Military Department or Defense Agency designator such as N for Navy, A for Army, AF for Air Force, DA for DARPA, etc.; NN is the calendar year, and nnnn is a sequential number.

ARTICLE III
SCOPE OF WORK

The following tasks shall be undertaken under this PA.

(For example:

a. Research ______________________________
____

b. Develop ______________________________
____

c. Evaluate ______________________________
____

d. Design, fabricate and test ______________________________)

ARTICLE IV
SHARING OF TASKS

(Applicable when the work may be apportioned into discrete work packages that are assigned as an individual Party's primary responsibility)

The sharing of tasks shall be as follows:

(For example:

a. The U.S. DoD shall
____
____

b. The IT MoD shall ______________________________
____

c. U.S. DoD and IT MoD shall jointly
____
______________________________)

ARTICLE V
BREAKDOWN AND SCHEDULE OF TASKS

(OPTIONAL)

(When the tasks covered under Project may be performed using multiple phases, requiring milestones or decision points).

The Project shall proceed according to the following phases and schedule.

Phase 1	*Start*	*End*
Description of Phase 1	MM/YY	MM/YY

(Milestone 1) (e.g., Transmittal of Feasibility Report)

Phase 2	*Start*	*End*
Description of Phase 2	MM/YY	MM/YY

(Milestone 2) (e.g., Decision to proceed to phase 3)

Phase 3	*Start*	*End*
Description of Phase 3	MM/YY	MM/YY

(Milestone 3) (e.g., Evaluation, analysis of results)

(Add as many phases as necessary)

The final report must be transmitted to the Executive Agents (or Steering Committee) six months before the termination date for this PA.

ARTICLE VI
MANAGEMENT

1. Steering Committee:

(It is anticipated that most Projects shall not need the establishment of a Steering Committee (SC); however, for such instances where an SC is deemed to be required, the following provides for the designation of SC members).

U.S. Co-Chairman

Title/Position ______________________________

Organization ______________________________

Address ______________________________

____

____

Italian Co-Chairman

Title/Position ______________________________

Organization ______________________________

Address ______________________________

____

____

2. Project Officers:

U.S. PO

Title/Position ______________________________

Organization ______________________________

Address ______________________________

____

____

Italian PO

Title/Position ______________________________

Organization ______________________________

Address ______________________________

____

____

3. Particular Management Procedures:

(Mention only those additional management responsibilities not covered under Article IV of the RDT&E MOA. For instance, if a PA shall be administered by a Joint Program Office that includes CPPs, add the following paragraph):

4. A Joint Program Office (JPO) will be established in [location]. Provisions for Cooperative Project Personnel (CPP) in the JPO are provided in Appendix 1 of this PA.

ARTICLE VII
FINANCIAL ARRANGEMENTS

The Parties estimate that the cost of performance of the tasks under this PA shall not exceed *X* U.S. dollars plus *Y* Euro.

Cooperative efforts of the Parties over and above the jointly agreed tasks set forth in the SCOPE OF WORK, SHARING OF TASKS and FINANCIAL ARRANGEMENTS Articles shall be subject to amendment to this PA or signature of a new PA.

(If a PA will involve the assignment of CPP, the PA shall include a provision that refers to paragraphs 5.7.–5.9. of the RDT&E MOA, identifies which Party is sending or hosting CPP, and specifies the number of CPP to be assigned. In addition, the PA shall include the amount of financial and non-financial contributions related to CPP in one of the two alternatives below in this Article).

(If a PA will not involve one Party Contracting for the other or for both Parties, and no funds shall be exchanged between the Parties, use Alternative 1 below for the Financial Arrangements. Both financial and non-financial contributions should be included in the total DoD and MoD costs).

Alternative 1

The U.S. DoD tasks shall not cost more than *X* U.S. dollars. The IT MoD tasks shall not cost more than *Y* Euro.

Or:

If a PA shall involve one Party Contracting for the other Party or both Parties, or the Parties shall transfer or exchange funds between them, use the following format for the Financial Provisions).

Alternative 2

Cost of performance includes Financial and Non-financial Costs.

	Year 1	Year 2	Year 3	Year 4	Year 5	Total
Italy						
U.S.						

(Using the above table and whatever description is necessary, explain, and demonstrate how the PA shall be funded. Identify both financial (funds) and non-financial (e.g., range time, use of equipment, etc). contributions).

(For Alternative 2, the Financial Management Procedures Document (FMPD) should be developed by the POs and submitted to the SC (if appropriate) for approval. The FMPD should include as a minimum schedule, handling, funding levels by year, and auditing procedures for monetary contributions anticipated for this PA).

ARTICLE VIII
CONTRACTING PROVISIONS

(if applicable)

The ______________________________ (acting through the ______________________________) shall be responsible for Contracting under this PA in accordance with its national laws, regulations, and procedures and with Article VI (Contracting Provisions) of the RDT&E MOA.

ARTICLE IX
LEVEL OF CLASSIFICATION

Only one of the three following possibilities must be selected:

a. No Classified Information shall be exchanged under this PA; **or**

b. The highest level of Classified Information exchanged under this PA is Confidential; **or**

c. The highest level of Classified Information exchanged under this PA is Secret.

ARTICLE X
PRINCIPAL ORGANIZATIONS INVOLVED

(List government laboratories, research centers, and other organizations for both the United States and Italy)

ARTICLE XI
PROJECT EQUIPMENT

1. In the event that the collaborative efforts under this PA required the provision of Project Equipment to either Party, the POs shall prepare a list of such Project Equipment using the following table as a guideline:

Providing Party	Receiving Party	QTY	Description	Part/ Stock #	Consumables\ Non-Consumables	Approx. Value

ARTICLE XII
SPECIAL PROVISIONS

1. All activities of the Parties under this PA shall be carried out in accordance with the Parties' national laws and regulations, including their export control laws and regulations.

(In the event a PSI and CG shall not be created for the Project, the following paragraph shall be used).

2. All U.S. export-controlled Information to be provided to the Italian MoD under this PA shall be marked "International Traffic in Arms Regulations (ITAR)-Controlled" or "Export Administration Control Regulations (EAR) Controlled," as appropriate, or such other markings as is notified by the U.S. DoD to the Italian MoD. Italian MoD export-controlled Information shall be marked as (Italy to provide), or such other markings as is notified by the Italy MoD to the U.S. DoD.

(Identify any procedures, specifications, or other necessary attributes of the Project not delineated in other Articles).

ARTICLE XIII
COMING INTO EFFECT, DURATION, AND TERMINATION

This ______________________________ PA, a Project under the MOA between the Department of Defense of the United States of America and the Ministry of Defense of the Italian Republic for Research, Development, Test, and Evaluation (RDT&E) Projects, shall come into effect upon its signature, and shall remain in effect for _________ years unless terminated by either Party. It may be extended by mutual written agreement of the Parties.

FOR THE DEPARTMENT OF DEFENSE OF THE UNITED STATES OF AMERICA	FOR THE MINISTRY OF DEFENSE OF THE ITALIAN REPUBLIC
______________________	______________________
Signature	Signature
______________________	______________________
Name	Name
______________________	______________________
Title	Title
______________________	______________________
Date	Date
______________________	______________________
Location	Location

APPENDIX (1)
COOPERATIVE PROJECT PERSONNEL

1.0. Purpose and Scope

1.1. This appendix to the PA establishes the terms and conditions for Cooperative Project Personnel (CPP) assigned for work under this PA. CPP must be able to perform all responsibilities for the positions assigned to them under this PA. Commencement of assignments shall be subject to the requirements that may be imposed by the Host Party or its government regarding acceptance of CPP, such as, but not limited to, visas and visit request documentation. The Host Party and Parent Party shall determine the length of tour for the positions at the time of initial assignment.

1.2. CPP shall be assigned to perform work under this PA and shall report to a supervisor to be identified by the Host Party. CPP shall have a position description mutually determined by the Parent Party and Host Party. CPP shall not act as liaison officers for their Parent Party. However, such personnel may act from time to time on behalf of the Parent Party's SC representative if the latter so authorizes in writing.

1.3. CPP shall not be assigned to command or other positions that would require them to exercise responsibilities that are reserved by national law or regulation to an officer or employee of the Host Party's government.

2.0. Security

2.1. The Host Party shall establish the level of security clearance required, if any, to permit CPP to have access to Classified Information and facilities. Access to Classified Information and facilities in which Classified Information is used shall be limited by the scope of this PA.

2.2. The Parent Party shall file visit requests through prescribed channels in compliance with the Host Party's procedures. As part of the visit request procedures, each Party shall cause security assurances to be filed, through the Italian Embassy in Washington, DC, in the case of Italian personnel, and through the U.S. Embassy in Rome, Italy, in the case of United States personnel, specifying the security clearances for the CPP being assigned.

2.3. The Host and Parent Party shall use their best efforts to ensure that CPP assigned to a Host Party's facility to conduct work under the PA are aware of the requirements of the RDT&E MOA and this PA. On arrival, CPP and their dependents shall be informed by the Host Party's representative about applicable national laws, orders, regulations, and customs and the need to comply with them. Prior to commencing assigned duties, CPP shall sign a certification concerning the conditions and responsibilities of CPP.

2.4. CPP shall at all times be required to comply with the national security and export control laws, regulations, and procedures of the Host Party's government. Any violation of national security procedures by CPP during their assignment shall be reported to the Parent Party for appropriate action. CPP committing significant violations of national security laws, regulations, or procedures during their assignments shall be withdrawn from the Project with a view toward appropriate administrative or disciplinary action by their Parent Party.

2.5. All Classified Information made available to CPP shall be considered as Classified Information furnished to the Parent Party, and shall be subject to all provisions and safeguards provided for in Article XII (Security).

2.6. CPP shall not have personal custody of Classified Information or CUI unless approved by the Host Party and as authorized by their Parent Party. They shall be granted access to such Information in accordance with Article X (Controlled Unclassified Information), Article XII (Security), and the applicable PSI during normal duty hours and when access is necessary to perform work for the Project.

2.7. CPP assigned to a Host Party's facility to conduct Project work shall not serve as a conduit between the Host Party and Parent Party for requests and/or transmission of Classified Information or CUI outside the scope of their assignment, unless specifically authorized by the PSI.

3.0. Technical and Administrative Matters

3.1. Consistent with the Host Party's laws and regulations, and subject to applicable multilateral and bilateral treaties, agreements, and arrangements of the governments of the Host Party and Parent Party, CPP and their authorized dependents shall be accorded:

3.1.1. exemption from any Host Party's government tax upon income received from the Parent Party; and

3.1.2. exemption from any Host Party's government customs and import duties or similar charges levied on items entering the country for their official or personal use, including their baggage, household effects, and private motor vehicles.

3.2. On or shortly after arrival CPP and their dependents shall be provided briefings arranged by the Host Party's representative regarding (subject to applicable multilateral and bilateral agreements) entitlements, privileges, and obligations such as:

3.2.1. any medical and dental care that may be provided to CPP and their dependents at local medical facilities, subject to the requirements of applicable national laws and regulations, including reimbursement when required;

3.2.2. purchasing and patronage privileges at military commissaries, exchanges, theaters, and clubs for CPP and their dependents, subject to the requirements of applicable national laws and regulations; and

3.2.3. responsibility of CPP and their accompanying dependents to obtain motor vehicle liability insurance coverage in accordance with the national laws and regulations applicable in the area where they are residing. In case of claims involving the use of private motor vehicles by CPP, the recourse shall be against such insurance.

3.3. The Host Party shall, in consultation with the CPP, establish standard operating procedures for CPP in the following areas:

3.3.1. working hours, including holiday schedules;

3.3.2. leave authorization, consistent to the extent possible with the military and civilian personnel regulations and practices of the Host Party and Parent Party;

3.3.3. dress regulations, consistent to the extent possible with the military and civilian personnel regulations and practices of the Host Party and Parent Party; and

3.3.4. performance evaluations, recognizing that such evaluations shall be rendered in accordance with the Parent Party's military or civilian personnel regulations and practices.

3.4. CPP committing an offense under the national laws of the government of the Host Party or Parent Party may be withdrawn from this Project with a view toward further administrative or disciplinary action by the Parent Party. Disciplinary action, however, shall not be taken by the Host Party against CPP, nor shall CPP exercise disciplinary powers over the Host Party's personnel. In accordance with Host Party's government laws and regulations, the Host Party shall assist the Parent Party in carrying out investigations of offenses involving CPP.

STATE DEPARTMENT DOCUMENT NUMBER: 06-265

AGREEMENT BETWEEN THE UNITED STATES OF AMERICA AND THE REPUBLIC OF ICELAND REGARDING THE WITHDRAWAL OF UNITED STATES FORCES FROM AND THE RETURN TO ICELAND OF CERTAIN AGREED AREAS AND FACILITIES IN ICELAND, WITH ATTACHMENTS

SIGNED AT WASHINGTON D.C. AND REYKJAVIK,
SEPTEMBER 27 AND 29, 2006
ENTERED INTO FORCE SEPTEMBER 29, 2006

CTIA DOCUMENT NUMBER: 13092.000

Preamble

Recognizing and reaffirming the rights and obligations deriving from the "Defense Agreement Pursuant to the North Atlantic Treaty Between the United States of America and the Republic of Iceland," signed at Reykjavik on May 5, 1951 (hereafter, the 1951 Agreement), the Government of the United States of America (hereafter, the United States) and the Government of the Republic of Iceland (hereafter, Iceland) (hereafter, the Parties),

Noting that the Parties have cooperated earnestly and successfully for more than 55 years to ensure the security of the Icelandic people and of the North Atlantic Treaty Area;

Taking into account the evolving strategic environment;

Desiring to establish the conditions under which the United States will withdraw its forces from and return to Iceland certain agreed areas and facilities in Iceland following the notification by the United States to Iceland of March 15, 2006 that, given the current strategic environment and the intense demand for United States conventional military resources in other parts of the world, permanent United States military presence in Iceland would cease by the end of September 2006;

Noting that facilities in such agreed areas are comprised of both United States and NATO-funded facilities for which the United States has fulfilled host nation responsibilities with respect to NATO; and

As a result of discussions regarding the return to Iceland of these agreed areas and facilities, including the environmental conditions of and compensation for residual value of such agreed areas and facilities, the United States and Iceland have agreed as follows:

Article I

Iceland shall, in accordance with the 1951 Agreement, continue to provide access to United States and other North Atlantic Treaty Organization (hereinafter, NATO) forces within and through the territory of Iceland as is necessary to support the future defense needs of Iceland and of the North Atlantic Treaty Area and for other activities agreed to by the Parties.

Article II

The United States recognizes the importance to Iceland of the Keflavik International Airport and agrees to support and facilitate a smooth transfer of airport operations to Iceland in order to ensure uninterrupted air traffic operations.

Article III

1. By September 30, 2006, the United States shall withdraw from and return to Iceland the use of the following agreed areas, provided to the United States under the 1951 Agreement, as well as all United States-funded facilities thereon, as described more completely in the diagrams appended to this Agreement depicted in Annexes A through E, which shall be considered to be an integral part of this Agreement:

A. Main Agreed Area (Naval Air Station Keflavik, H–1/Rockville-Midnesheidi, Helguvik and Sandgerdi);

B. Whale Bay/Hvalfjordur;

C. H–2/Gunnolfsvikurfjall;

D. H–3/Stokksnes;

E. H–4/Bolafjall.

2. Iceland shall accept from the United States such agreed areas, as well as all United States-funded facilities thereon, in the condition existing at the time of their return without expectation that the United States will make improvements or remediation, including environmental remediation, of any kind following return of such agreed areas and facilities. Should an imminent and substantial endangerment to human health and safety due to environmental contamination of the agreed areas returned pursuant to this Agreement, and present but unknown prior to the date of this Agreement, become known at any time during a four (4) year period from said date, Iceland and the United States shall jointly consult to assess the character, source, time of creation, and extent of the contamination and to consider what further action by the Parties is necessary.

3. The United States shall provide to Iceland its plans, drawings, and records relating to the improvements it has made on or to such agreed areas, as well as information regarding the location and nature of its activities and operations thereon.

Article IV

Iceland and the United States shall jointly recommend to NATO that Iceland assume host nation responsibility for all NATO-funded facilities in Iceland as soon as possible after the return of agreed areas. To ensure continuity of airport operations, Iceland and the United States shall jointly recommend to NATO that Iceland assume user nation responsibility for those NATO-funded facilities that Iceland has identified as being necessary for airport operations. As the current user nation, the United States has committed in accord with NATO requirements to be responsible to NATO for the guarding and maintaining of all other NATO-funded facilities pending a decision by NATO on the final disposition of these facilities and for a period not to exceed twelve months following United States notification to NATO military authorities that the United States no longer requires the use of these facilities. With respect to the NATO facilities that Iceland intends to use for airport operations and upon return of the agreed areas, Iceland shall accept all responsibility relating to use, operation, preservation, and maintenance. Upon request the United States will support and assist Iceland in its consultations with NATO.

Article V

The United States shall retain the communications facility at Grindavik as an agreed area and be responsible for the continued maintenance and operation of the facility. Iceland shall cooperate as necessary to maintain the continuity of the required contracts and continued access to the facility.

Article VI

Iceland shall save, hold harmless, release, and discharge the United States and any agency, instrumentality, contractor, agent, or employee thereof from any and all claims, demands, or actions for damages, expenses or liability, whatsoever, arising from injury to person or property which may be advanced in connection with the use, possession, or operation of the aforementioned agreed areas and facilities in the past or in the future. Iceland shall assume responsibility for, and, at the request of the United States, provide defense of, any claims or legal proceedings brought against the United States, its agencies, instrumentalities, contractors, agents, or employees, in connection with its previous use, possession, or operation of the aforementioned agreed areas and facilities.

This Agreement shall enter into force upon the date of signature of the Parties.

DONE at *Washington*
This *27* day of *September*, 2006.
[Signature]

FOR THE GOVERNMENT OF THE UNITED STATES OF AMERICA:

DONE at *Reykjavik*
This *29* day of *September*, 2006.
[Signature]

FOR THE GOVERNMENT OF THE REPUBLIC OF ICELAND:

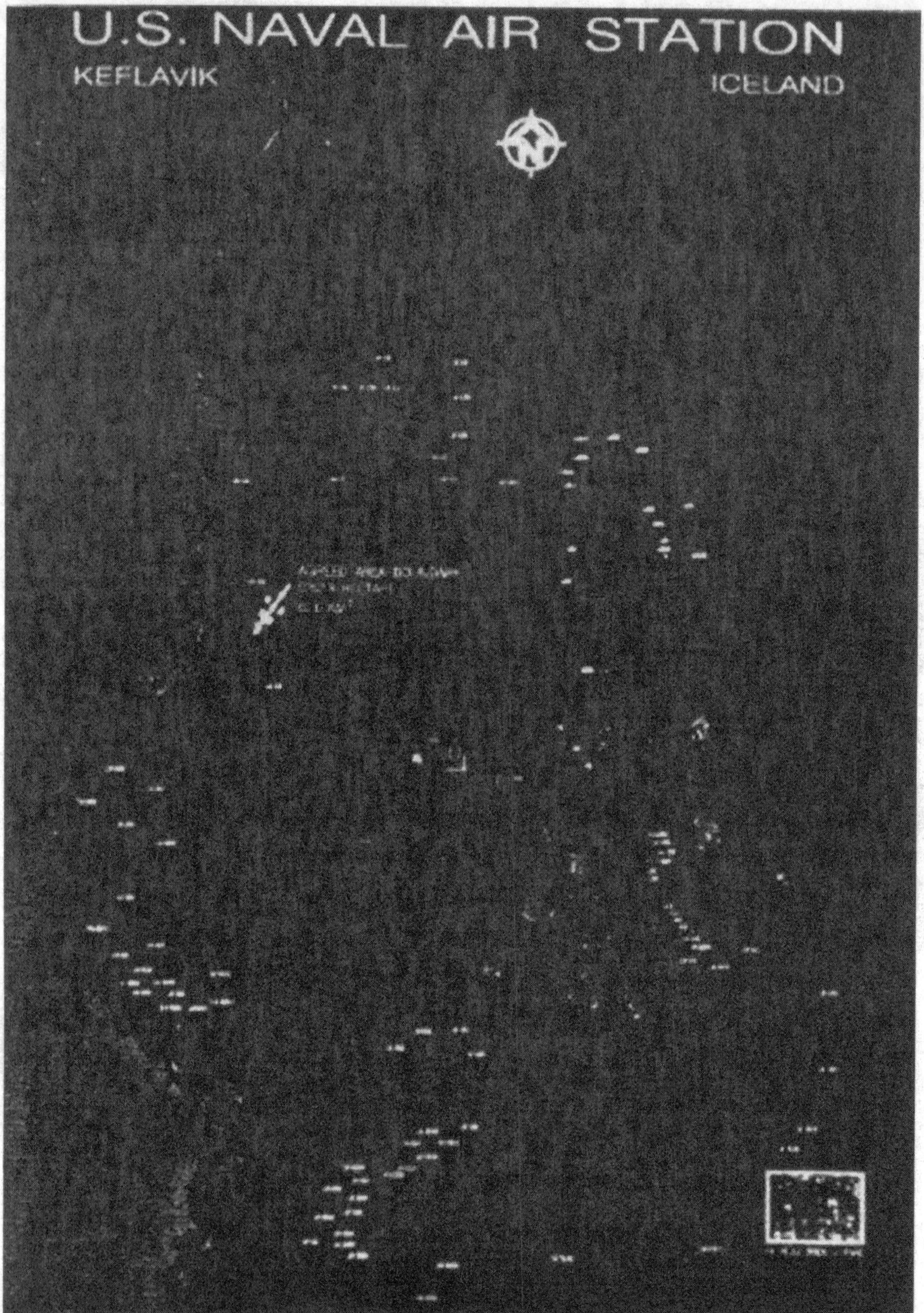
U.S. NAVAL AIR STATION
KEFLAVIK
ICELAND

POINT_ID	coord_x	coord_y	unit_d	Latitude	Longitude
1	330539.710	375577.290	M	63ø50′32.96248″N	22ø26′42.46254″W
2	330545.880	377608.240	M	63ø51′38.45643″N	22ø26′50.10931″W
3	328544.949	377614.190	M	63ø51′35.10602″N	22ø29′16.37761″W
4	328539.752	375913.452	M	63ø50′40.26247″N	22ø29′09.89607″W
5	328613.828	375582.936	M	63ø50′29.73796″N	22ø29′03.15308″W
6	328938.921	375582.169	M	63ø50′30.29100″N	22ø28′39.40560″W
7	328938.364	375431.758	M	63ø50′25.44049″N	22ø28′38.84137″W
8	329938.910	375429.080	M	63ø50′27.12527″N	22ø27′25.75383″W
9	329939.390	375579.110	M	63ø50′31.96342″N	22ø27′26.31865″W
102	324753.774	392759.419	M	63ø59′36.55440″N	22ø34′56.22127″W
106	324534.343	393096.563	M	63ø59′47.02218″N	22ø35′13.74069″W
110	324286.001	393417.220	M	63ø59′56.90482″N	22ø35′33.31831″W
401	330192.669	375578.342	M	63ø50′32.38538″N	22ø27′07.81559″W
402	330540.335	375782.723	M	63ø50′39.58726″N	22ø26′43.23553″W
410	325700.321	391230.235	M	63ø58′48.97977″N	22ø33′40.38088″W
411	325749.539	391153.117	M	63ø58′46.58295″N	22ø33′36.44926″W
412	326042.806	390630.395	M	63ø58′30.26281″N	22ø33′12.76547″W
413	326098.726	390550.702	M	63ø58′27.79492″N	22ø33′08.33280″W
414	326164.987	390479.374	M	63ø58′25.61543″N	22ø33′03.17600″W
415	326222.682	390431.211	M	63ø58′24.16721″N	22ø32′58.74358″W
802	330300.950	377608.990	M	63ø51′38.04923″N	22ø27′08.01433″W
803	330301.728	377853.591	M	63ø51′45.93713″N	22ø27′08.93483″W
804	330546.430	377852.953	M	63ø51′46.34757″N	22ø26′51.04546″W
400A	325922.491	391429.739	M	63ø58′55.81551″N	22ø33′24.89869″W
KF5133	323209.982	389250.866	M	63ø57′40.60771″N	22ø36′34.85499″W
LM–006	318139.679	389214.993	M	63ø57′29.97414″N	22ø42′46.54558″W
LM02	324121.207	390779.196	M	63ø58′31.55469″N	22ø35′34.39812″W
LM07	324390.815	396183.335	M	64ø01′26.27484″N	22ø35′37.18147″W
LM12	324295.474	395635.345	M	64ø01′08.43305″N	22ø35′41.89689″W
LM14	326221.414	396787.894	M	64ø01′49.10720″N	22ø33′25.10996″W
LM3409	325936.829	386229.963	M	63ø56′08.19969″N	22ø33′02.38597″W
LM601	325448.131	397637.011	M	64ø02′15.07540″N	22ø34′25.50262″W
LM602	325065.284	397761.946	M	64ø02′18.40400″N	22ø34′54.18162″W
LM603	324828.819	397736.540	M	64ø02′17.15225″N	22ø35′11.46758″W
LM604	324500.975	397540.342	M	64ø02′10.22606″N	22ø35′34.75924″W
LM605	324271.673	397309.596	M	64ø02′02.36608″N	22ø35′50.65625″W
LM607	324328.877	397098.075	M	64ø01′55.65183″N	22ø35′45.56384″W
LM61	326177.339	396220.435	M	64ø01′30.73201″N	22ø33′26.00044″W
LM610	323788.841	399091.245	M	64ø02′58.91678″N	22ø36′33.65091″W

POINT_ID	coord_x	coord_y	unit_d	Latitude	Longitude
LM62	326038.066	396617.260	M	64ø01′43.27277″N	22ø33′37.88425″W
LM63	325901.890	396682.374	M	64ø01′45.12443″N	22ø33′48.16691″W
LM660	324662.207	394284.637	M	64ø00′25.55921″N	22ø35′09.30497″W
LM880	324929.760	394901.509	M	64ø00′45.93641″N	22ø34′52.21856″W
LM97	323812.499	392325.486	M	63ø59′20.83879″N	22ø36′03.52254″W
LM–G01	317290.939	389836.016	M	63ø57′48.38032″N	22ø43′51.47341″W
LM–G01A	317316.003	390241.619	M	63ø58′01.50268″N	22ø43′51.39286″W
LM–G02	317325.952	390664.277	M	63ø58′15.14602″N	22ø43′52.49511″W
LM–G04	317553.919	391925.135	M	63ø58′56.22400″N	22ø43′41.23225″W
LM–G05	317108.611	392181.445	M	63ø59′03.63758″N	22ø44′15.02758″W
LM–G06	317364.922	392626.752	M	63ø59′18.48080″N	22ø43′58.14719″W
LM–G07	317810.230	392370.442	M	63ø59′11.06610″N	22ø43′24.34814″W
LM–G10	319635.297	393968.755	M	64ø00′06.04194″N	22ø41′17.23003″W
LM–G12	319358.123	395559.492	M	64ø00′56.79922″N	22ø41′44.42511″W
LM–G14	319503.947	397050.168	M	64ø01′45.12834″N	22ø41′40.11843″W
LM–G15	321001.275	397048.766	M	64ø01′47.89555″N	22ø39′50.02755″W
LM–G16	321053.972	398455.248	M	64ø02′33.33543″N	22ø39′52.15409″W
LM–G16A	321371.363	398443.226	M	64ø02′33.54112″N	22ø39′28.75659″W
LM–G17	321938.419	398421.985	M	64ø02′33.91364″N	22ø38′46.95501″W
LM–G18	321731.755	398930.829	M	64ø02′49.93274″N	22ø39′04.32096″W
LM–G19	322565.445	398890.804	M	64ø02′50.19278″N	22ø38′02.81634″W
LM–G19A	322552.892	398398.948	M	64ø02′34.31290″N	22ø38′01.65760″W
LM–G20	322533.885	397850.510	M	64ø02′16.59690″N	22ø38′00.73435″W
LM–G21	322241.370	397505.626	M	64ø02′04.93544″N	22ø38′20.78587″W
LM–G22	322389.693	397047.072	M	64ø01′50.42792″N	22ø38′07.93717″W
LM–G22A	323443.258	397046.095	M	64ø01′52.34608″N	22ø36′50.46639″W
LM–G35A	325733.259	391729.506	M	63ø59′05.13622″N	22ø33′40.02974″W
LM–G36	325755.601	391708.271	M	63ø59′04.49222″N	22ø33′38.30172″W
LM–G37	325895.880	391519.411	M	63ø58′58.65822″N	22ø33′27.22287″W
LM–G40	326282.039	390192.422	M	63ø58′16.57611″N	22ø32′53.40343″W
LM–G40A	326382.744	390087.593	M	63ø58′13.37872″N	22ø32′45.58226″W
LM–G41	326599.557	389942.856	M	63ø58′09.10458″N	22ø32′29.07839″W
LM–G41A	326912.283	389865.390	M	63ø58′07.17191″N	22ø32′05.81538″W
LM–G42	327395.135	389994.628	M	63ø58′12.20888″N	22ø31′30.91793″W
LM–G43	328971.723	389486.711	M	63ø57′58.65722″N	22ø29′33.17368″W
LM–G50A	321030.452	385229.909	M	63ø55′26.94194″N	22ø38′57.66337″W
LM–G50B	320808.408	385398.200	M	63ø55′31.95322″N	22ø39′14.64003″W
LM–G51	320776.899	385422.413	M	63ø55′32.67499″N	22ø39′17.05064″W
LM–G51A	320850.131	385560.925	M	63ø55′37.27681″N	22ø39′12.27353″W

POINT_ID	coord_x	coord_y	unit_d	Latitude	Longitude
LM–G51B	320981.584	385807.957	M	63ø55′45.48551″N	22ø39′03.69061″W
LM–G51C	321030.984	385901.092	M	63ø55′48.58002″N	22ø39′00.46601″W
LM–G51D	321085.406	386127.878	M	63ø55′55.99236″N	22ø38′57.43922″W
LM–G51E	321112.273	386240.699	M	63ø55′59.67945″N	22ø38′55.94843″W
LM–G52	321164.111	386462.853	M	63ø56′06.93764″N	22ø38′53.09072″W
LM–G52A	321410.928	386518.692	M	63ø56′09.19711″N	22ø38′35.24152″W
LM–G52B	321633.643	386568.944	M	63ø56′11.23108″N	22ø38′19.13402″W
LM–G53	321793.987	386605.918	M	63ø56′12.72075″N	22ø38′07.54040″W
LM–G53A	322127.454	386820.228	M	63ø56′20.24798″N	22ø37′44.00668″W
LM–G54	322308.118	386936.646	M	63ø56′24.33561″N	22ø37′31.25658″W
LM–G54A	322463.402	387036.538	M	63ø56′27.84321″N	22ø37′20.29605″W
LM–G54B	322591.992	387119.184	M	63ø56′30.74527″N	22ø37′11.21877″W
LM–G55	322816.301	387259.429	M	63ø56′35.68078″N	22ø36′55.36697″W
LM–G56	322878.344	388380.637	M	63ø57′11.94121″N	22ø36′55.52449″W
LM–G57	322601.145	388745.292	M	63ø57′23.18499″N	22ø37′17.38298″W
LM–G58	322486.356	388666.804	M	63ø57′20.44241″N	22ø37′25.47029″W
LM–G59	322043.876	388374.912	M	63ø57′10.21281″N	22ø37′56.68547″W
LM–HG44	328433.001	388244.647	M	63ø57′17.64890″N	22ø30′07.64380″W
LM–HG44A	328011.931	387296.501	M	63ø56′46.32560″N	22ø30′34.65860″W
LM–HG45	328631.687	387205.995	M	63ø56′44.51599″N	22ø29′48.85535″W
LM–HG46	327836.528	387078.416	M	63ø56′38.97979″N	22ø30′46.62825″W
LM–HG47	326610.628	385489.326	M	63ø55′45.54020″N	22ø32′09.96954″W
LM–HG48	324355.700	385353.044	M	63ø55′37.04939″N	22ø34′54.60463″W
LM–HG49	322466.373	385237.034	M	63ø55′29.83610″N	22ø37′12.51746″W
LM–HG50	322136.099	384672.737	M	63ø55′11.03342″N	22ø37′34.33579″W
LM–N001	317957.257	391570.227	M	63ø58′45.55018″N	22ø43′10.09578″W
LM–N002	318811.636	389554.505	M	63ø57′42.18996″N	22ø41′58.72903″W
LM–N003	318877.869	389125.232	M	63ø57′28.47701″N	22ø41′52.02781″W
LM–N004	318544.836	389087.528	M	63ø57′26.63230″N	22ø42′16.28680″W
LM–N005	318481.974	389094.357	M	63ø57′26.73354″N	22ø42′20.92568″W
LM–N007	318056.067	389283.151	M	63ø57′32.01273″N	22ø42′52.97087″W
LM–N008	317959.028	389411.500	M	63ø57′35.96603″N	22ø43′00.64085″W
LM–N010	317565.979	389590.641	M	63ø57′40.99407″N	22ø43′30.23956″W
LM–N011	317846.894	389999.431	M	63ø57′54.70538″N	22ø43′11.40404″W
LMN64	326169.887	396120.810	M	64ø01′27.50652″N	22ø33′26.13573″W
LMN65	326238.782	396054.271	M	64ø01′25.48638″N	22ø33′20.79544″W
ML–N009	317854.766	389444.856	M	63ø57′36.84340″N	22ø43′08.4309″W

ISN–93 GRID COORDINATES AND WGS–84 LAT/LONG

POINT_ID	coord_x	coord_y	unit_d	Latitude	Longitude
LM–G01A	317316.003	390241.619	M	63ø58′01.50268″N	22ø43′51.39286″W
LM–G02	317325.952	390664.277	M	63ø58′15.14602″N	22ø43′52.49511″W

HJORSEY DATUM 1955

POINT_ID				Latitude	Longitude
LM–G01A				63° 58′ 02.59″	22° 43′ 52.25″
LM–G02				63° 58′ 16.24″	22° 43′ 53.35″

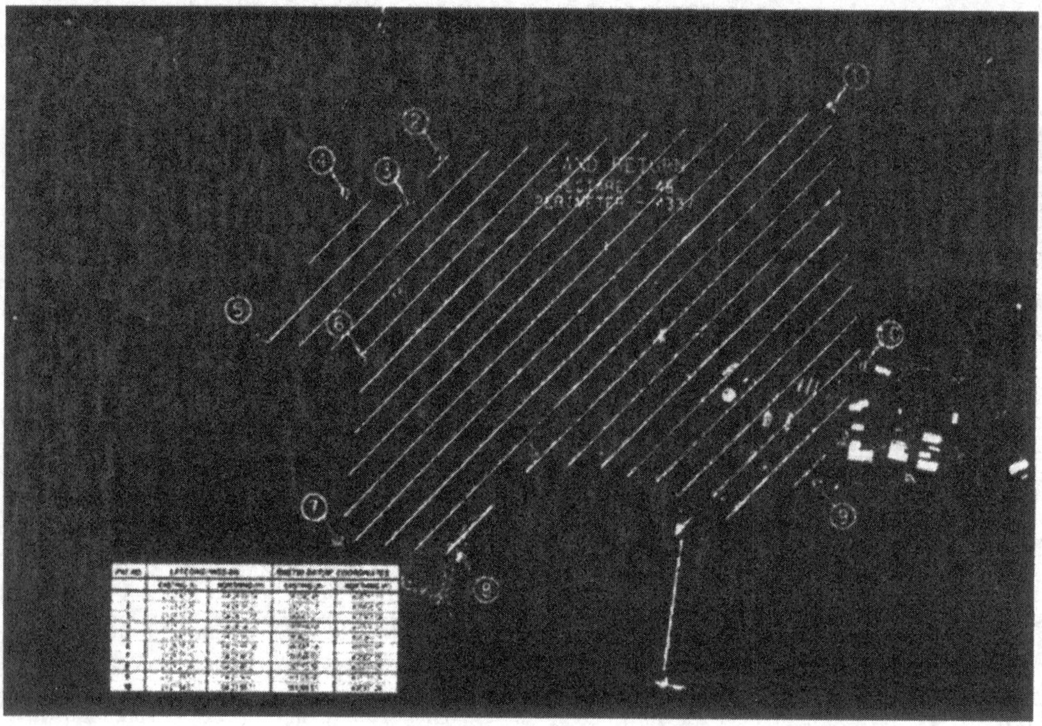

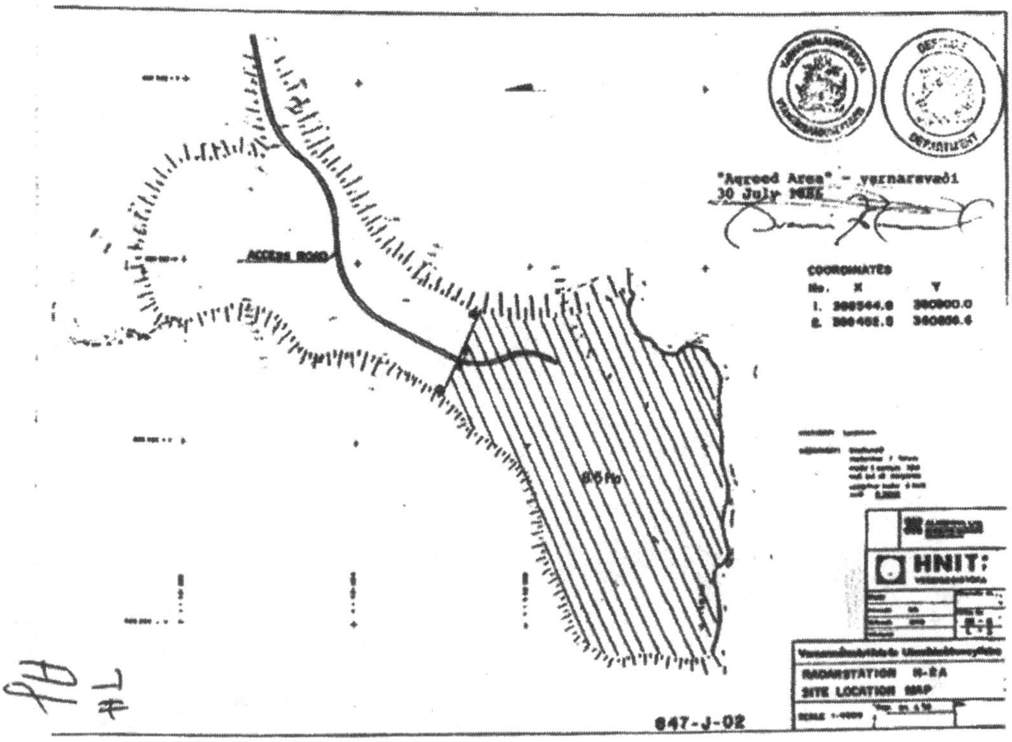
"Agreed Area" - varnarsvaði
ACCESS ROAD
COORDINATES
HNIT:
RADARSTATION
SITE LOCATION MAP
847-J-02

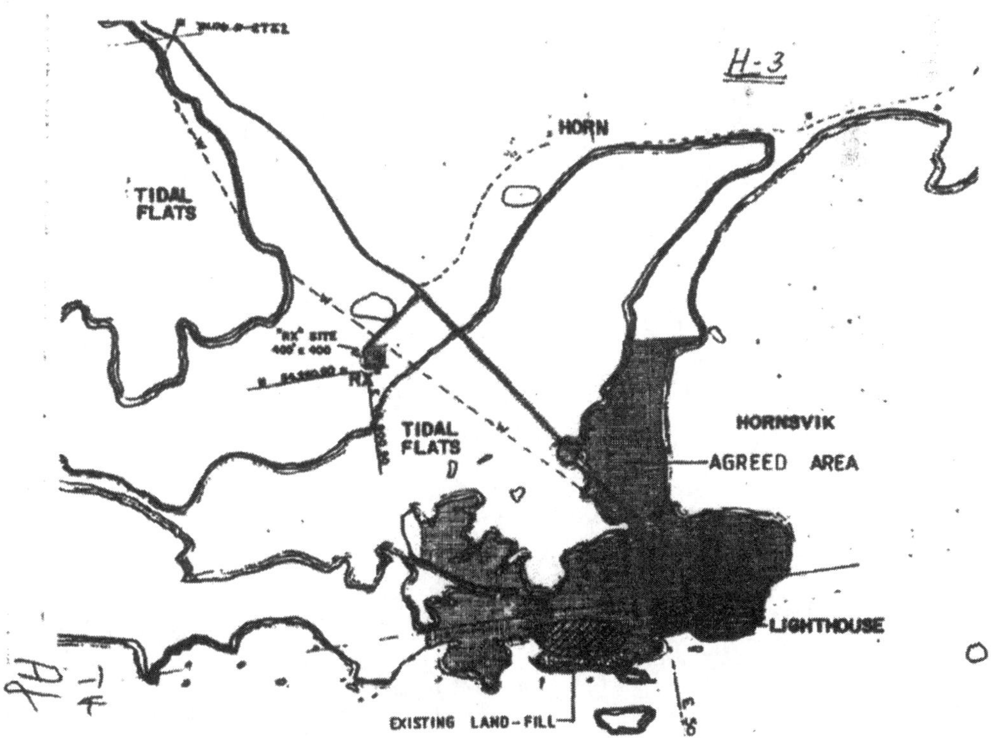
H-3
HORN
TIDAL FLATS
"RX" SITE
RX
TIDAL FLATS
HORNSVIK
AGREED AREA
LIGHTHOUSE
EXISTING LAND-FILL

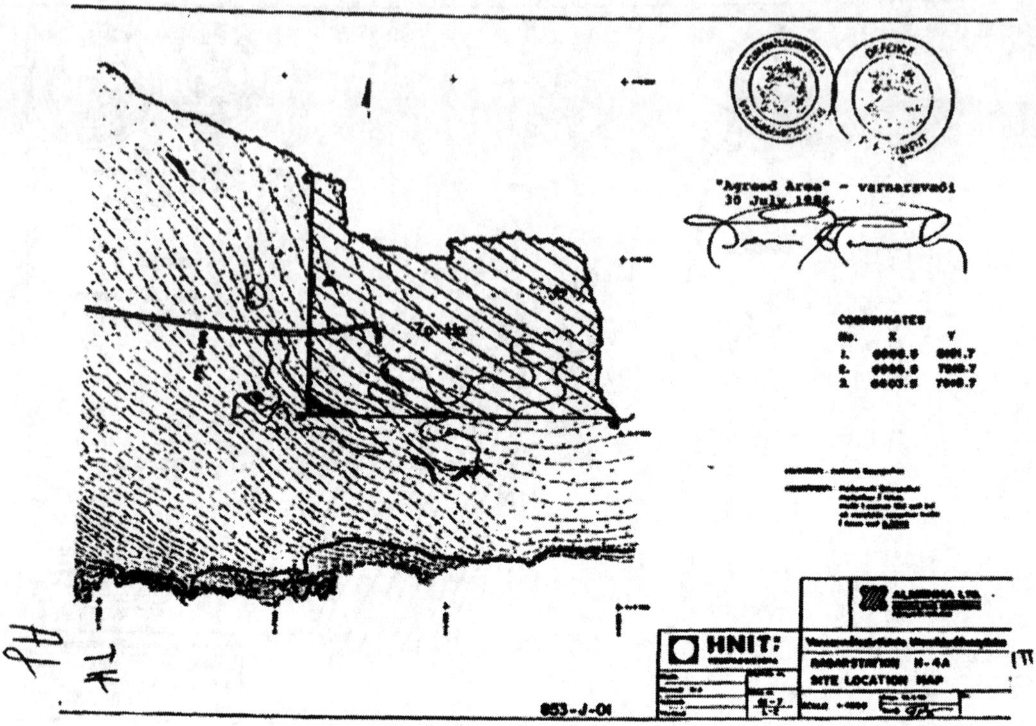
"Agreed Area" - varnarsvaði
COORDINATES
No. X Y
HNIT
SITE LOCATION MAP
853-J-01

STATE DEPARTMENT DOCUMENT NUMBER: 06-266

STRATEGIC OBJECTIVE GRANT AGREEMENT AMENDMENT NUMBER SIX BETWEEN THE UNITED STATES OF AMERICA AND THE ISLAMIC REPUBLIC OF AFGHANISTAN FOR THE THRIVING ECONOMY LED BY THE PRIVATE SECTOR, WITH ATTACHMENT

SIGNED AT KABUL,
SEPTEMBER 30, 2006
ENTERED INTO FORCE SEPTEMBER 30, 2006

CTIA DOCUMENT NUMBER: 12756.006

Dated as of: September *30*, 2006

AMENDMENT NO. SIX
TO
STRATEGIC OBJECTIVE GRANT AGREEMENT

AMENDMENT NUMBER SIX TO THE STRATEGIC OBJECTIVE GRANT AGREEMENT between the Government of the United States of America, acting through the United States Agency for International Development (USAID), and the Government of the Islamic Republic of Afghanistan (hereinafter referred to as the "Grantee" or the "GOA"), acting through the Ministry of Finance, dated as of September *30*, 2006.

WHEREAS, the Grantee and USAID entered into a Strategic Objective Grant Agreement ("SOAG") for the strategic objective of "A Thriving Economy Led by the Private Sector" (USAID Grant Agreement No. SOAG–306–05–00) dated September 19, 2005 and subsequently amended the SOAG as of:

—September 30, 2005 (Amendment No. 1);

—April 6, 2006 (Amendment No. 2);

—May 11, 2006 (Amendment No. 3);

—June 28, 2006 (Amendment No. 4); and,

—September 18, 2006 (Amendment No. 5).

The SOAG as so amended is referred to hereinafter as the "Agreement."

WHEREAS, USAID and the Grantee wish to amend the Agreement further to: (a) increase the USAID contribution by **Sixty Million Four Hundred Thirty Three Thousand Eight Hundred Sixty Eight** United States (U.S.) Dollars **(U.S.$ 60,433,868.00)**; and (b) update the illustrative financial plan;

NOW, THEREFORE, the Parties hereto hereby agree that the Agreement shall be amended as follows:

1. The first sentence in Section 3.1(a), The Grant, of the Agreement is deleted in its entirety and the following is substituted therefor: "To help achieve the Objective set forth in this Agreement, USAID, pursuant to the *Foreign Assistance Act of 1961*, as amended, hereby grants to the Grantee under the terms of this Agreement not to exceed **Nine Hundred Twenty-Five Million Five Hundred Seventy-Seven Thousand Nine Hundred Twelve And Eighty-Two Hundredths** United States (U.S.) Dollars **(U.S.$ 925,577,912.82)** (the 'Grant')."

2. The illustrative financial plan set forth in Attachment 1 to Annex 1 to the Agreement is deleted and the updated illustrative financial plan included as Attachment A to this Amendment is substituted therefor.

All other terms and conditions of the Agreement remain unchanged and in full force and effect. This Amendment is prepared in both English and Dari (capitalized terms not defined in this Amendment shall have the meanings ascribed thereto in the Agreement). In the event of ambiguity or conflict between the two versions, the English language version will control.

IN WITNESS WHEREOF, the United States of America and the Government of the Islamic Republic of Afghanistan, each acting through its duly authorized representatives, have caused this Amendment Number Six to be signed in their names and delivered as of the day, month and year first written above.

THE UNITED STATES OF AMERICA

By: [*Signature*]
Name: Leon S. Waskin
Title: Director, USAID Mission to Afghanistan

THE ISLAMIC REPUBLIC OF AFGHANISTAN

By: [*Signature*]
Name: Wahldullah Shahrani
Title: Deputy Minister of Finance, Signing in his capacity as Acting Finance Minister

Attachment

ILLUSTRATIVE FINANCIAL PLAN FOR FY 2005 TO FY 2010
Amendment No. 6
In Thousands of U.S. Dollars

Objective and Activities	Amount Obligated prior to Amendment No. 6		Amount Obligated in Amendment No. 6		Cumulative Obligations in FY 2005–FY2006 *		Amount Remaining to be Obligated in FY 2007–FY 2010 **		Total Estimated Contribution	
	USAID	Grantee	USAID	Grantee	USAID	Grantee	USAID	Grantee	USAID	Grantee
A THRIVING ECONOMY LED BY THE PRIVATE SECTOR USAID Grant Agreement No. SOAG–306–05–00										
Rehabilitate the rural economy	**239,800**		–		**239,800**		**794,701**		**1,034,501**	
Accelerate market-led growth in agriculture***	60,420		–		60,420		223,980		284,400	
Accelerate rural development to generate alternative livelihoods—	179,381		–		179,381		570,720		750,101	
Increase Incomes through Economic Growth* **	**93,269**		**1,500**		**94,769**		**357,020**		**451,789**	
Expand Improved Access to Economic Infrastructure	**507,694**		**58,934**		**566,628**		**692,312**		**1,258,940**	
Stabilize Energy Services and Make them Affordable and More Accessible***	214,622				214,622		389,826		604,448	

Continued

Objective and Activities	Amount Obligated prior to Amendment No. 6		Amount Obligated in Amendment No. 6		Cumulative Obligations in FY 2005–FY2006 *		Amount Remaining to be Obligated in FY 2007–FY 2010 **		Total Estimated Contribution	
	USAID	Grantee	USAID	Grantee	USAID	Grantee	USAID	Grantee	USAID	Grantee
Expand and Improve Access to Transportation	279,644		58,934		338,578		91,714		430,292	
Expand and Improve Access to Water Supplies and Sanitation	13,428		–		13,428		210,772		224,200	
USAID Program Support	**24,380**		–		**24,380**		**18,540**		**42,920**	
TOTAL OBJECTIVE 5:	**865,144**	**50,000**	**60,434**	–	**925,578**	**50,000**	**1,862,572**	**212,900**	**2,788,150**	**262,900**

*NOTE *—References to "FY" refer to the USG fiscal year for the USAID contribution and the GOA contributions beginning in the second half of Afghan year 1384*

*NOTE **—These funds are subject to the availability of funds to USAID and the Grantee and the other conditions set forth respectively in Section 3.1(b) and Section 3.2(b) of the Agreement*

*NOTE ***—The illustrative financial plan previously included a line item for "Pre-existing Mortgages"; however, the funds in that line item are now included in the relevant programmatic line items indicated above*

STATE DEPARTMENT DOCUMENT NUMBER: 06-267

ACQUISITION AND CROSS-SERVICING AGREEMENT BETWEEN THE DEPARTMENT OF DEFENSE OF THE UNITED STATES OF AMERICA AND THE MINISTRY OF DEFENSE OF LEBANON

SIGNED AT BEIRUT,
MAY 3 AND 20, 2006
ENTERED INTO FORCE SEPTEMBER 30, 2006

CTIA DOCUMENT NUMBER: 13093.000

Effective Date: __________

PREAMBLE

The Department of Defense of the United States of America and the Ministry of Defense of Lebanon, hereinafter referred to as the Parties, desiring to further the interoperability, readiness, and effectiveness of their respective military forces through increased logistic cooperation, have resolved to conclude this Acquisition and Cross-Servicing Agreement (the Agreement).

ARTICLE I
PURPOSE

This Agreement is entered into for the purpose of establishing basic terms, conditions, and procedures to facilitate the reciprocal provision of logistic support, supplies, and services as that term is defined in Article III of this Agreement.

ARTICLE II
APPLICABILITY

1. This Agreement is designed to facilitate reciprocal logistic support between the Parties to be used primarily during combined exercises, training, deployments, operations, or other cooperative efforts, and for unforeseen circumstances or exigencies in which one of the Parties may have a need for logistic support, supplies, and services.

2. This Agreement applies to the provision of logistic support, supplies, and services from the military forces of one Party to the military forces of the other Party in return for either cash payment or the reciprocal provision of logistic support, supplies, and services to the military forces of the Supplying Party.

3. All activities of the Parties under this Agreement and any Implementing Arrangements shall be carried out in accordance with their respective national laws and regulations. All obligations of the Parties under this Agreement and any Implementing Arrangements shall be subject to the availability of funds for such purposes. Unless otherwise agreed in advance, a Party shall not place an Order and receive support under this Agreement and any Implementing Arrangement unless it has funds (or agreed-upon in-kind support) available to pay for such support. If a Party discovers that it does not have the funds to perform its obligations, it shall promptly notify the other Party who shall have the right to discontinue its provision of any support that was to be paid with such funds. This shall not affect the obligation of a Party to pay for support already received.

4. The following items are not eligible for transfer under this Agreement and are specifically excluded from its coverage:

a. weapon systems;

b. major end items of equipment (except for the lease or loan of general purpose vehicles and other nonlethal items of military equipment where such lease or loan is permitted under the national laws and regulations of the Parties);

c. initial quantities of replacement and spare parts associated with the initial order of major items of organizational equipment; however, individual replacement and spare parts needed for immediate repair and maintenance services may be transferred.

5. Also excluded from transfer by either Party under this Agreement are any items the transfer of which are prohibited by its national laws or regulations. In accordance with U.S. law and regulation, the United States may not currently transfer the following items under this Agreement:

a. guided missiles;

b. naval mines and torpedoes;

c. nuclear ammunition (including such items such as warheads, warhead sections, projectiles, demolition munitions, and training ammunition);

d. cartridge and propellant-actuated devices;

e. chaff and chaff dispensers;

f. guidance kits for bombs or other ammunition;

g. chemical munitions or ammunition (other than riot-control agents);

h. source, byproduct, or special nuclear materials, or any other material, article, data, or thing of value the transfer of which is subject to the *Atomic Energy Act of 1954* (Title 42, United States Code, Section 2011, et. seq.);

i. items of military equipment designated as Significant Military Equipment on the United States Munitions List (Part 121 of Title 22 of the U.S. Code of Federal Regulations) not included in the definition of logistic support, supplies and services.

ARTICLE III
DEFINITIONS

1. As used in this Agreement and in any Implementing Arrangements which provide specific procedures, the following definitions apply:

a. *Equal value exchange*. Payment for a transfer conducted under this Agreement in which it is agreed that the Receiving Party shall replace logistic support, supplies, and services that it receives with logistic support, supplies, and services of an equal monetary value.

b. *Implementing Arrangement.* A written supplementary arrangement for logistic support, supplies, and services that specifies details, terms, and conditions to implement cross-servicing agreements effectively.

c. *Invoice.* A document from the Supplying Party which requests reimbursement or payment for specific logistic support, supplies, and services rendered pursuant to this Agreement and any applicable Implementing Arrangements.

d. *Logistic support, supplies, and services.* Food, water, billeting, transportation (including airlift), petroleum, oils, lubricants, clothing, communication services, medical services, ammunition, base operations support (and construction incident to base operations support), storage services, use of facilities, training services, spare parts and components, repair and maintenance services, calibration services, and port services. This term also includes the temporary use of general purpose vehicles and other nonlethal items of military equipment, where such lease or loan is permitted under the national laws and regulations of the Parties.

e. *Order.* A written request, in an agreed upon format and signed by an authorized individual, for the provision of specific logistic support, supplies, and services pursuant to this Agreement and any applicable Implementing Arrangement.

f. *Receiving Party.* The Party ordering and receiving support.

g. *Replacement-in-kind.* Payment for a transfer conducted under this Agreement in which it is agreed that the Receiving Party shall replace logistic support, supplies, and services that it receives with logistic support, supplies, and services of an identical, or substantially identical, nature under agreed conditions.

h. *Supplying Party.* The Party providing support.

i. *Transfer.* Selling (whether for payment in currency, replacement-in-kind, or exchange of supplies or services of equal value), leasing, loaning, or otherwise temporarily providing logistic support, supplies, and services under the terms of this Agreement.

ARTICLE IV
TERMS AND CONDITIONS

1. Each Party shall make its best efforts, consistent with national priorities, to satisfy requests from the other Party under this Agreement for logistic support, supplies, and services. However, when an Implementing Arrangement contains a stricter standard for satisfying such requests, the standard in the Implementing Arrangement shall apply.

2. Orders may be placed or accepted only by the points of contact (POCs), or designees, identified by the Parties in Annexes B through I of this Agreement. When military forces of Lebanon require logistics support, supplies, or services outside the U.S. Central Command (USCENTCOM) Area of Responsibility (AOR), they may place orders directly with the cognizant POC or may seek the assistance of USCENTCOM, or a USCENTCOM Component Command, to place an order with a non-USCENTCOM POC.

3. An Implementing Arrangement under this Agreement may be negotiated on behalf of the U.S. Department of Defense by Headquarters, CENTCOM, the Headquarters of other United States combatant commands, or their designees. Implementing Arrangements may be negotiated on behalf of the Lebanese Ministry of Defense by the Minister of National Defense or his designees. Implementing Arrangements must identify POCs and their specific authorizations or limitations.

4. Prior to submitting a written Order, the ordering Party should initially contact the Supplying Party's POC by telephone, fax, or e-mail to ascertain availability, price, and desired method of repayment for required materiel or services. Orders must include all the data elements in Annex A, as well as

any other terms and details necessary to carry out the transfer. Instructions and a standard order form are attached at Annex A. The number of this Agreement, US–LB–01, should be annotated on all Orders and related correspondence.

5. Both Parties shall maintain records of all transactions.

6. The Receiving Party is responsible for:

a. Arranging pickup and transportation of supplies acquired under this Agreement. This does not preclude the Supplying Party from assisting with loading supplies acquired under this Agreement onto the transportation conveyance.

b. Obtaining any applicable customs clearance and arranging other official actions required by national customs regulations.

7. The individual designated by the Receiving Party to receive the logistic support, supplies, and services on behalf of the Receiving Party shall sign the standard order form (Annex A) in the appropriate block as evidence of receipt. If the standard order form is not available at the Supplying Party's point of issue, the individual receiving the support, supplies, and services shall sign the receipt document provided by the Supplying Party as a substitute. The number of this Agreement, US–LB–01, shall be entered on the receipt document.

8. The Supplying Party shall be responsible for:

a. notifying the Receiving Party when and where logistic support, supplies, and services are available to be picked up; and

b. forwarding the signed receipt document to the POC authorized to accept Orders under this Agreement. The signed receipt document shall be attached to the original Order Form.

9. Logistic support, supplies, and services received through this Agreement shall not be retransferred, either temporarily or permanently, to any entity other than the Receiving Party without the prior written consent of the Supplying Party.

ARTICLE V
REIMBURSEMENT

1. For transfers of logistic support, supplies, and services under this Agreement, the Parties shall agree for payment either by cash ("reimbursable transaction"), or by replacement-in-kind or an equal-value exchange (both of which are exchange transactions). The Receiving Party shall pay the Supplying Party as provided in either paragraph 1a. or paragraph 1b. of this Article.

a. *Reimbursable Transaction*. The Supplying Party shall submit Invoices to the Receiving Party after delivery or performance of the logistic support, supplies, and services. Both Parties shall provide for the payment of all transactions and each Party shall invoice the other Party at least once every 3 months for all transactions not previously invoiced. Invoices shall be accompanied by necessary support documentation and shall be paid within 90 days of the date prepared. Payment shall be made in the currency of the Supplying Party or as otherwise agreed in the Order. In pricing a reimbursable transaction, the Parties agree to the following reciprocal pricing principles:

(1) In the case of specific acquisition by the Supplying Party from its contractors on behalf of a Receiving Party, the price shall be no less favorable than the price charged the military forces by the contractor of the Supplying Party for identical items or services, less any amounts excluded by Article VI of this Agreement. The price charged may take into account differentials due to delivery schedules, points of delivery, and other similar considerations.

(2) In the case of transfer from the Supplying Party's own resources, the Supplying Party shall charge the same price charged its own military forces for identical logistic support, supplies, and services, as of the date delivery or performance occurs, less amounts excluded by Article VI of this Agreement. In any case where a price has not been established or charges are not made for one's own military forces, the Parties shall agree on a price in advance, reflecting reciprocal pricing principles, excluding charges that are precluded under these same reciprocal pricing principles.

b. *Exchange Transaction.* Exchange transactions may be by replacement-in-kind or equal-value-exchange. The Receiving Party shall pay by transferring to the Supplying Party logistic support, supplies, and services that are agreed between the Parties to be identical (or substantially identical) or to be of equal monetary value to the logistic support, supplies, and services delivered or performed by the Supplying Party. When Equal Value Exchange is the agreed method of payment, prior to the provision of the requested support both Parties will agree, to the extent possible, on the goods and services that will be accepted for payment. The Receiving Party is responsible for arranging return transportation and delivery of the replacement logistic support, supplies and services to the location mutually agreed between the Parties at the time the order is signed. If the Receiving Party does not complete the exchange within the terms of a replacement schedule agreed to or in effect at the time of the original transaction, which may not exceed one year from the date of the original transaction, the transaction shall be deemed reimbursable and governed by paragraph 1a above, except that the price shall be established using actual or estimated prices in effect on the date payment would otherwise have been due.

c. *Establishment of Price or Value.* The following pricing mechanisms are provided to clarify application of the reciprocal pricing principles. The price established for inventory stock materiel shall be the Supplying Party's stock list price. The price for new procurement shall be the same price paid to the contractor or vendor by the Supplying Party. The price for services rendered will be the Supplying Party's standard price, or, if not applicable, the costs directly associated with providing the services. Prices charged shall exclude all taxes and duties which the Receiving Party is exempted from paying under other agreements which the Governments of the Parties have concluded. Upon request, the Parties agree to provide information sufficient to verify that these reciprocal pricing principles have been followed and that prices do not include waived or excluded costs.

2. When a definitive price for the Order is not agreed to in advance, the Order, pending agreement on final price, shall set forth a maximum liability for the Party ordering the logistic support, supplies, and services. The Parties shall then promptly enter into negotiation to establish the final price.

3. POCs for payments and collections for each Party are identified in annexes to this Agreement.

4. The price for logistic support, supplies, and services under this Agreement shall not be higher than the price for the same logistic support, supplies, and services available under any other agreement between the Parties or their Governments.

ARTICLE VI
WAIVED OR EXCLUDED COSTS

Insofar as national laws and regulations permit, the Parties shall ensure that any readily identifiable duties, taxes, and similar charges are not imposed on activities conducted under this Agreement. The Parties shall cooperate to provide proper documentation to maximize tax and customs relief. The provisions of any applicable tax and customs relief agreements shall also apply under this Agreement. The Parties shall inform each other whether the price charged for logistic support, supplies, or services includes taxes or duties. In determining whether duties, taxes and similar charges should be levied, the pricing principles in Article V, and in particular Article V, paragraph 1, subparagraph c, will govern the value of the support, supplies, or services provided by the Supplying Party.

ARTICLE VII
SECURITY OF INFORMATION

It is the intent of the Parties that activities under this Agreement and any Implementing Arrangements be carried out at the unclassified level. No classified information or material shall be provided or generated under this Agreement or any Implementing Arrangements.

ARTICLE VIII
INTERPRETATION, AMENDMENTS, AND REVISION OF INFORMATION

1. Any disagreements regarding the interpretation or application of this Agreement, any Implementing Arrangements, or transactions executed hereunder shall be resolved through consultation between the Parties and shall not be referred to any international tribunal or third party for settlement.

2. Either Party may, at any time, request amendment of this Agreement by giving the other Party written notice. In the event such a request is made, the Parties shall promptly enter into negotiations. This Agreement may be amended only by written agreement between the Parties. Replacement of Annexes B through I, which list POCs, may be done by a Party transmitting the replacement annex to the other Party through military channels, without formal amendment of this Agreement.

ARTICLE IX
ENTRY INTO FORCE AND TERMINATION

This Agreement, which consists of a Preamble, Articles I–IX, and Annexes A through I, shall be provisionally applied from the date of its signature and shall enter into force on the date that the Government of Lebanon provides written notification through diplomatic channels to the Government of the United States of America that it has completed its internal procedures for entry into force of this Agreement. This Agreement shall remain in force unless terminated by the mutual consent of the Parties or by either Party giving not less than 180 days notice in writing to the other Party of its intent to terminate. Notwithstanding termination of this Agreement, all reimbursement obligations incurred pursuant to its terms shall remain binding on the responsible Party until satisfied.

IN WITNESS WHEREOF, the undersigned, being duly authorized by their respective governments, have signed this Agreement.

DONE, in duplicate, in the English and Arabic languages, each being equally authentic.

FOR THE DEPARTMENT OF DEFENSE OF THE UNITED STATES OF AMERICA

[Signature]

BRIAN I. GEEHAN
MG, USA
DIRECTOR OF LOGISTICS
US CENTRAL COMMAND

at:

on: *3 MAY 06*

FOR THE MINISTRY OF NATIONAL DEFENSE OF LEBANON

[Signature]

MICHEL SLEIMAN
COMMANDING GENERAL
LEBANESE ARMED FORCES

at:

on: *20/5/2006*

LETTERHEAD OF THE REPUBLIQUE LIBANAISE
Ministère des Affaires Etrangères et des Émigrés

Centre des Etudes Juridiques,
des Recherches et de la Documentation

No. 857/15

The Ministry of Foreign Affairs and Emigrants presents its compliments to the Embassy of United States of America and has the honor to notify the Embassy that the "Acquisition and Cross-servicing Agreement between the Ministry of Defense of Lebanon and the Department of Defense of United States of America" has been ratified by decree no. 17 728 dated on 25th of September 2006.

According to its article 9, the Agreement shall enter into force on the date this Ministry provide written notification through diplomatic channel that Lebanon has fulfilled all of its internal procedures necessary for the Agreement to enter into force.

The Embassy is kindly requested to notify the Ministry on the date of entry into force of this Agreements.

The Ministry of Foreign Affairs and Emigrants avails itself of this opportunity to renew to the Embassy of United States of America the assurances of its consideration.

Beirut, 30 September 2006

[Seal]

Embassy of United States of America
Beirut

State Department Document Number: 06-268

Agreement Between the United States of America and the Democratic Republic of Congo Regarding Grants Under the Foreign Assistance Act of 1961, as Amended, or Successor Legislation, and the Furnishing of Defense Articles, Defense Services and Related Training, Including Pursuant to the United States International Military and Education Training Program (IMET) and the Peacekeeping Operation (PKO) Program

Effected By Exchange of Notes at Kinshasa,
June 5 and October 11, 2006
Entered into force October 11, 2006

CTIA Document Number: 13094.000

DIPLOMATIC NOTE

No. 06/120

The Embassy of the United States of America presents its compliments to the Ministry of Foreign Affairs of the Democratic Republic of Congo and has the honor to refer to earlier discussions between representatives of the two Governments regarding the provision of defense articles, related training, and other defense services on a grant basis pursuant to the *Foreign Assistance Act of 1961*, as amended, or successor legislation, and to the provision of articles and services, including training and training materials, pursuant to the International Military Education and Training (IMET) program and the Peacekeeping Operations (PKO) program. In this regard the Embassy refers to the Agreement concerning the provision of training related to defense articles under the United States International Military Education and Training (IMET) Program, effected by exchange of notes at Kinshasa on December 22, 1983 and June 16, 1984 (the 1984 Agreement).

In accordance with these discussions, it is proposed that the Government of the Democratic Republic of Congo agree:

A. That unless the consent of the Government of the United States of America has been first obtained the Government of the Democratic Republic of Congo shall not:

(I) Permit any use of such defense articles, related training, other defense services, other articles, and other services (hereinafter "articles and services") by anyone not an officer, employee or agent of the Government of the Democratic Republic of Congo;

(II) Transfer, or permit any officer, employee or agent of the Government of the Democratic Republic of Congo to transfer, such articles and services by gift, sale or otherwise; or

(III) Use, or permit the use of, such articles and services for purposes other than those for which provided;

B. That such articles and services shall be returned to the Government of the United States of America when no longer needed for the purposes for which they were furnished, unless the Government of the United States of America consents to another disposition;

C. That the net proceeds of sale received by the Government of the Democratic Republic of Congo in disposing of, with prior written consent of the Government of the United States of America, any such articles and services furnished by the Government of the United States of America on a grant basis, including scrap from any related equipment and training materials, shall be paid to the Government of the United States of America;

D. That the Government of the Democratic Republic of Congo shall maintain the security of such articles and services; that it shall provide substantially the same degree of security protection afforded to such articles and services by the Government of the United States of America; that it shall, as the United States of America may require, permit continuous observation and review by, and furnish necessary information to, representatives of the Government of the United Stats of America with regard to the use thereof by the Government of the Democratic Republic of Congo; and

E. That the Government of the United States of America may also, from time to time, make the provision of articles and services furnished under other authority (except the *United States Arms Export Control Act*) subject to the terms and conditions of the agreement proposed herein. (Transfers under the *United States arms Export Control Act* shall continue to be governed by the requirements of that Act and United States regulations applicable to such transfers.)

The Ministry's note stating that the foregoing is acceptable to the Government of the Democratic Republic of Congo shall, together with this note, constitute an agreement between the two Governments, which shall supersede the 1984 Agreement in its entirety and shall enter into force on the date of the Ministry's note.

The Embassy of the United States of America avails itself of this opportunity to renew to the Ministry of Foreign Affairs of the Democratic Republic of the Congo, the assurances of its highest consideration.

Embassy of the United States of America,
Kinshasa, June 5, 2006.

[Seal]

Letterhead of the U.S. Department of State
Office of Language Services
Translating Division

LS No. 10–2007–0272
French/English
ALK/HNC

Translation

Democratic Republic of Congo
Ministry of Foreign Affairs and International Cooperation

No. 130/01/ASS/NKL/4019/2006

Embassy of the United States of America,
Kinshasa.

The Ministry of Foreign Affairs and International Cooperation of the Democratic Republic of Congo presents its compliments to the Embassy of the United States of America at Kinshasa and has the honor to acknowledge receipt of Embassy note No. 06/120 dated June 5, 2005, which reads as follows:

[See U.S. Text]

The Ministry of Foreign Affairs and International Cooperation of the Democratic Republic of Congo has the honor to confirm that the proposals set forth in the Embassy's note are acceptable to the Government of the Democratic Republic of Congo and that the Embassy's note, together with this note in response, shall constitute an agreement between the two governments, which shall replace the Agreement on the provision of training related to defense articles under the United States International Military Education and Training (IMET) Program, effected by exchange of notes at Kinshasa on December 22, 1983, and June 16, 1984, and shall enter into force on this date.

[Complimentary clause]

Done at Kinshasa, October 11, 2006
[Initialed]
[Illegible stamp]

STATE DEPARTMENT DOCUMENT NUMBER: 06-269

AGREEMENT BETWEEN THE UNITED STATES OF AMERICA AND JAPAN CONCERNING A CASH CONTRIBUTION BY JAPAN FOR ADMINISTRATIVE AND RELATED EXPENSES ARISING FROM IMPLEMENTATION OF THE MUTUAL DEFENSE ASSISTANCE AGREEMENT OF MARCH 8, 1954

EFFECTED BY EXCHANGE OF NOTES AT TOKYO,
OCTOBER 13, 2006
ENTERED INTO FORCE OCTOBER 13, 2006

CTIA DOCUMENT NUMBER: 4058.003

LETTERHEAD OF THE EMBASSY OF THE UNITED STATES OF AMERICA

No. 721

Excellency,

I have the honor to acknowledge the receipt of Your Excellency's Note of today's date, which reads as follows:

> Excellency,
>
> I have the honor to refer to the Mutual Defense Assistance Agreement between Japan and the United States of America signed at Tokyo on March 8, 1954.
>
> Paragraph 2 of Article VII of the Agreement provides that the Government of Japan will make available, from time to time, to the Government of the United States of America funds in yen for the administrative and related expenses of the latter Government in connection with carrying out the Agreement.
>
> Paragraph 3 of Annex G of the Agreement provides that, in consideration of the contributions in kind to be made available by the Government of Japan, the amount of yen to be made available as a cash contribution by the Government of Japan for any Japanese fiscal year shall be as agreed upon between the two Governments.

> Accordingly, I have the honor to propose on behalf of the Government of Japan the following arrangements concerning the amount of the cash contribution referred to above for the Japanese fiscal year 2006:
>
> > In consideration of the contributions in kind to be made available by the Government of Japan during the Japanese fiscal year from April 1, 2006 to March 31, 2007, the amount of the cash contribution to be made available by the Government of Japan for the said fiscal year shall be one hundred and twenty six million three hundred and thirty eight thousand yen (¥126,338,000).
>
> I have further the honor to propose that the present Note and Your Excellency's Note in reply confirming on behalf of the Government of the United States of America the foregoing arrangements shall be regarded as constituting an agreement between the two Governments, which will enter into force on the date of Your Excellency's reply.
>
> I avail myself of this opportunity to renew to Your Excellency the assurance of my highest consideration.

I have further the honor to confirm on behalf of the Government of the United States of America the foregoing arrangements and to agree that Your Excellency's Note and this Note shall be regarded as constituting an agreement between the two Governments, which will enter into force on the date of this reply.

I avail myself of this opportunity to renew to Your Excellency the assurance of my highest consideration.

[Signature]

Embassy of the United States of America,
October 13, 2006

Translation

Tokyo, October 13, 2006

His Excellency
Mr. John Thomas Schieffer
Ambassador Extraordinary
and Plenipotentiary
of the United States of America

Excellency,

I have the honor to refer to the Mutual Defense Assistance Agreement between Japan and the United States of America signed at Tokyo on March 8, 1954.

Paragraph 2 of Article VII of the Agreement provides that the Government of Japan will make available, from time to time, to the Government of the United States of America funds in yen for the administrative and related expenses of the latter Government in connection with carrying out the Agreement.

Paragraph 3 of Annex G of the Agreement provides that, in consideration of the contributions in kind to be made available by the Government of Japan, the amount of yen to be made available as a cash contribution by the Government of Japan for any Japanese fiscal year shall be as agreed upon between the two Governments.

Accordingly, I have the honor to propose on behalf of the Government of Japan the following arrangements concerning the amount of the cash contribution referred to above for the Japanese fiscal year 2006:

> In consideration of the contributions in kind to be made available by the Government of Japan during the Japanese fiscal year from April 1, 2006 to March 31, 2007, the amount of the cash contribution to be made available by the Government of Japan for the said fiscal year shall be one hundred and twenty-six million three hundred and thirty eight thousand yen (¥126,338,000).

I have further the honor to propose that the present Note and Your Excellency's Note in reply confirming on behalf of the Government of the United States of America the foregoing arrangements shall be regarded as constituting an agreement between the two Governments, which will enter into force on the date of Your Excellency's reply.

I avail myself of this opportunity to renew to Your Excellency the assurance of my highest consideration.

Taro Aso
Minister for Foreign Affairs
of Japan

STATE DEPARTMENT DOCUMENT NUMBER: 06-270

EXTENSION OF THE AGREEMENT BETWEEN THE UNITED STATES OF AMERICA AND THE KINGDOM OF NORWAY FOR COOPERATION IN THE CIVIL USES OF OUTER SPACE

SIGNED AT WASHINGTON D.C.,
OCTOBER 23, 2006
ENTERED INTO FORCE OCTOBER 23, 2006;
EFFECTIVE NOVEMBER 14, 2006

CTIA DOCUMENT NUMBER: 11585.001

The United States of America and the Kingdom of Norway, pursuant to Article 11 of the *Agreement Between the United States of America and the Kingdom of Norway for Cooperation in the Civil Uses of Outer Space,* signed October 20, 2000 and November 14, 2001, agree to extend the duration of this Agreement for 10 years, thus extending the expiration date of the Agreement until November 14, 2016.

FOR THE UNITED STATES OF AMERICA:

October 23, 2006
Date

[Signature]
Mr. Michael O'Brien
Assistant Administrator
NASA Office of External Relations

FOR THE KINGDOM OF NORWAY:

October 23, 2006
Date

[Signature]
His Excellency Knut Vollebaek
Ambassador Extraordinary and
Plenipotentiary

I hereby certify that this is a true copy of the original.

[Signature]

STATE DEPARTMENT DOCUMENT NUMBER: 06-271

AMENDMENT TO THE AGREEMENT OF DECEMBER 30, 2002, BETWEEN THE DEPARTMENT OF DEFENSE OF THE UNITED STATES OF AMERICA AND THE MINISTRY OF DEFENSE OF GEORGIA CONCERNING COOPERATION IN THE AREA OF PREVENTION OF PROLIFERATION OF TECHNOLOGY, PATHOGENS AND EXPERTISE RELATED TO THE DEVELOPMENT OF BIOLOGICAL WEAPONS

SIGNED AT TBILISI AND WASHINGTON D.C.,
MARCH 19 AND 23, 2004
ENTERED INTO FORCE JULY 22, 2004

CTIA DOCUMENT NUMBER: 11506.003

Pursuant to Article VII of the Agreement between the Department of Defense of the United States of America and the Ministry of Defense of Georgia Concerning Cooperation in the Area of Prevention of Proliferation of Technology, Pathogens and Expertise Related to the Development of Biological Weapons, dated 30 December 2002, hereinafter referred to as "the Agreement", the Department of Defense of the United States of America and the Ministry of Defense of Georgia hereby agree:

1. To amend Article III, Paragraph 1 by replacing the words "five (5) million" with the words "fifteen (15) million."
2. To amend Article IV of the Agreement by adding new Paragraphs 4, 5, 6 and 7 as follows:

> "4. The MOD or its designated agent shall collect and facilitate the transfer of requested pathogen samples to DoD for prophylactic, protective or other peaceful purposes, and share data with DoD generated by the disease surveillance networks of MOD or its designated agents in order for the parties to better detect, diagnose and monitor disease outbreaks in Georgia.
>
> 5. The MOD or its designated agent shall consolidate and store all dangerous pathogens at the National Center for Disease Control, or at other secure centralized laboratories designated in writing by DoD (hereinafter centralized laboratories). DoD may provide molecular diagnostics capabilities, improved electronic communications, and equipment for the safe and timely transport of field pathogen samples to the centralized laboratories.
>
> 6. Dangerous pathogens placed in centralized laboratories shall remain in those laboratories for the duration of the Proliferation Prevention Agreement unless removal is agreed to in writing by DoD.
>
> 7. The MOD or its designated agent shall cooperate with DoD annually to develop a plan describing the underlying assumptions, requirements and responsibilities for each project being undertaken pursuant to the Agreement, and the MOD or its designated executive agent shall certify each such plan as accurate."

This Amendment shall enter into force upon the date on which the Parties exchange written notifications confirming the completion by each Party of all applicable procedures required for the entry into force of the Amendment, and shall remain in force for the duration of the Agreement. Notwithstanding termination of the Agreement, Paragraph 6 shall continue to apply as between the Parties for the duration of the Proliferation Prevention Agreement.

In witness whereof, the undersigned, being duly authorized by their respective governments, have signed this Amendment.

Done at Washington, this *23rd* day of *March*, 2004, and at Tbilisi, this *19th* day of *March*, 2004, in duplicate, each in the English and Georgian languages, both texts being equally authentic.

For the Department of
Defense of the United States of America:

[Signature]

For the Ministry of
Defense of Georgia:

[Signature]
Paata GAPRINDASHVILI
Deputy Defense Minister

STATE DEPARTMENT DOCUMENT NUMBER: 06-272

AGREEMENT BETWEEN THE NATIONAL PARK SERVICE OF THE UNITED STATES OF AMERICA AND THE SECRETARIAT OF ENVIRONMENT AND NATURAL RESOURCES OF THE UNITED MEXICAN STATES ON COOPERATION IN THE MANAGEMENT AND PROTECTION OF NATIONAL PARKS AND OTHER PROTECTED NATURAL AREAS

SIGNED AT WASHINGTON D.C.,
MARCH 23, 2006
ENTERED INTO FORCE MARCH 23, 2006

CTIA DOCUMENT NUMBER: 13102.000

The National Park Service of the Department of the Interior of the United States of America (NPS), and the Secretariat of Environment and Natural Resources (SEMARNAT) of the United Mexican States, hereinafter referred to as "the Parties",

RECOGNIZING the advanced cooperation that exists between NPS and National Commission of Natural Protected Areas (CONANP) of SEMARNAT, in the sustainable management of natural resources and the establishment and conservation of protected natural areas that are their natural heritage;

NOTING the mutual interest in national parks and other natural protected areas, for the purpose of conserving ecosystems and promoting ecotourism;

RECOGNIZING the mutual interest in strengthening cooperation between the Parties in the exchange of information and informal education activities for the management and operation of national parks and other natural protected areas;

RECOGNIZING that the national parks and natural protected areas of the Parties share numerous migratory wildlife species, similar ecosystems, and other resources that are best protected and enjoyed through communication, consultation and cooperation;

RECOGNIZING the advantages of facilitating, coordinating and amplifying efforts in conservation, management, development and research of natural resources in protected natural areas of interest to both Parties;

RECOGNIZING that the conservation policy in force in Mexico contemplates working in coordination and consultation with rural communities to conserve and use in a sustainable way the natural protected areas and their resources, in a fashion that guarantees the preservation of biological diversity and equilibrium of ecosystems, seeking sustainable development;

RECOGNIZING that the policy of NPS is to conserve the resources and values of units of the U.S. national park system and to provide for the enjoyment of the same in such manner and by such means as will leave them unimpaired for the enjoyment of future generations, and that such conservation is best achieved through communication, consultation and cooperation;

RECOGNIZING the need for the joint development of appropriate strategies that support the conservation and restoration of biodiversity in both countries, including strategies to restore shared native species in the national parks of the United States and the corresponding protected natural areas of Mexico;

Have agreed as follows:

ARTICLE 1

This Agreement has as its objective the creation of a framework for cooperation between the Parties concerning: the conservation of protected natural areas and their biodiversity and, to the extent possible, the enjoyment of these areas by visitors and recognition of sustainable development alternatives for rural Mexican communities located in those areas; and the exploration of strategies for related cooperation with rural communities, citizens groups and scientific and other organizations of both countries accepted within the legal framework of each country.

ARTICLE 2

1. The Parties will meet periodically as necessary, but at least annually, in a mutually agreed location, to review, formulate and update ongoing and proposed cooperative technical projects and activities to accomplish the objectives of this Agreement.

2. Each Party shall designate a Coordinator to direct, approve, and monitor the progress of cooperative technical projects and activities developed to accomplish the objectives outlined in this Agreement. The Coordinators will be: for the National Park Service, the Director of NPS or a designated representative; and for SEMARNAT, the President of CONANP or a designated representative.

3. The Coordinators will be responsible for receiving documentation, for reviewing and obtaining decisions on proposed cooperative projects and activities, and for all communications between the Parties regarding formal project proposals, schedules and responsibilities. The Coordinators shall decide by mutual consent whether to approve proposed projects and to continue ongoing projects undertaken through this Agreement.

4. Cooperative technical projects and activities carried out under the terms of this Agreement may be outlined in a work program to be jointly negotiated and mutually approved by the Coordinators. Documentation and information in support of proposed projects and activities may be submitted by either Party and shall contain a project description, project objectives, procedures, a calendar of events and target conclusion date, a statement of required equipment and personnel, and estimated costs for each Party.

5. The Parties shall be considered principal collaborators on all projects and activities approved under the terms of this Agreement. Each project will be under the joint supervision of an NPS and CONANP team leader, selected respectively by the Coordinators for each of the Parties. The team leaders will jointly develop and submit a final report on each project.

6. Any changes to the agreed projects shall require the concurrence of both Coordinators.

7. The Coordinators and Team Leaders from both parties may meet as often as necessary to develop or carry out cooperative projects and activities.

8. Those projects and activities that, in the opinion of the Coordinators, require special or urgent consideration may be reviewed and approved by them at any time by mutual consent.

9. The Coordinators will transmit an annual summary report on activities under this agreement to the Natural Resources Working Group of the U.S.-Mexico Binational Commission.

ARTICLE 3

1. The forms of cooperative activities under this Agreement may consist of exchanges of information for the management, enjoyment, and use of natural heritage; equal exchange of information regarding planning, management, and operations of national parks and other natural protected areas and planning and conduct of courses, conferences, and symposia pertaining to the same; research in protected areas; and personnel exchanges in fields of mutual interest within the scope of ongoing programs of both countries, related to the objectives of this Agreement. Specific areas of mutual interest for cooperative activities may include, but are not limited to:

a. Collaboration between specialists in the research and management of natural heritage and natural resources; and in the planning and design of visitor programs and facilities;

b. Specialized projects related to the management of protected natural areas, including, but not limited to, arid and semi-arid environments and marine coastal zones;

c. Exchange of information regarding the objectives of this Agreement;

d. Development of educational and public information focusing on the environment and in understanding protected natural areas;

e. Completion of studies that will support, among other things, the identification and formulation of strategies for the rational and sustainable use of natural resources;

f. Technical cooperation to protect, conserve, and maintain the flora and fauna protected by one or both countries.

2. For any actions or commitments requested by SEMARNAT that extend into subjects outside the scope of NPS, NPS may seek, in a manner compatible with existing laws, regulations and policies of the United States of America, to involve other organizations or agencies of the United States of America. For any actions or commitments requested by NPS that extend into subjects outside the scope of SEMARNAT, SEMARNAT may seek, in a manner compatible with existing laws, regulations and policies of the United Mexican States, to involve other organizations or agencies of the United Mexican States. The Parties shall consult regarding the identity and parameters for the involvement of any such other organizations or agencies.

ARTICLE 4

Cooperation under this agreement shall be subject to the availability of funds, personnel, and other resources of each Party; as well as to the policies, laws and regulations of each country. Funding for each project shall be determined in accordance with the terms and conditions jointly agreed by the Parties. Nothing in this agreement abrogates or in any way infringes upon the sovereign rights and authorities of each of the Parties to exclusively manage, acquire, dispose of, or otherwise administer lands within their respective borders.

ARTICLE 5

Information transmitted by one Party to the other Party under this Agreement shall be accurate to the best knowledge and belief of the transmitting Party. The transmitting Party does not warrant the suitability of the information transmitted for any particular use of or application by the receiving Party.

ARTICLE 6

Any differences in interpretation or application of this Agreement shall be resolved solely by consultation of the Parties. Nothing in this Agreement shall be construed to prejudice other existing or future agreements concluded between the United States and Mexico, or affect the rights and obligations of the United States and Mexico under international agreements to which they are a party.

ARTICLE 7

1. This Agreement shall enter into force upon signature and shall remain in force for five (5) years.

2. This Agreement may be extended or amended by written agreement of the Parties.

3. This Agreement may be terminated at any time by either Party upon written notification from one Party to the other ninety days in advance of such termination. The Parties shall consult in a timely manner to determine the disposition of cooperative activities planned or underway at the time of notice of termination.

DONE at Washington this 23rd of March, 2006, in duplicate in the English and Spanish languages, both texts being equally authentic.

FOR THE DEPARTMENT OF THE INTERIOR OF THE UNITED STATES OF AMERICA

[Signature]

FOR THE SECRETARIAT OF ENVIRONMENT AND NATURAL RESOURCES OF THE UNITED MEXICAN STATES

[Signature]

State Department Document Number: 06-273

Amendment to the Agreement of August 26, 1993, as Amended, Between the Department of Defense of the United States of America and the Federal Space Agency of the Russian Federation Concerning Cooperation in the Elimination of Strategic Offensive Arms

Signed at Washington D.C. and Moscow,
May 15 and 25, 2006
Entered into force May 25, 2006

CTIA Document Number: 7360.013

Pursuant to Article VIII of the Agreement Between the Department of Defense of the United States of America and the Federal Space Agency Concerning Cooperation in the Elimination of Strategic Offensive Arms, dated August 26, 1993, as amended April 3, 1995, June 19, 1995, May 27, 1996, April 11, 1997, February 11, 1998, June 9, 1998, August 16, 1999, August 8, 2000, June 9, 2003, September 25, 2003, and January 14, 2005, and as amended and extended August 30, 2002, hereinafter referred to as the Agreement,

The Department of Defense of the United States of America (DoD) and the Federal Space Agency (Roscosmos), which is an Executive Agent for the Russian Federation to implement the Agreement Between the United States of America and the Russian Federation Concerning the Safe and Secure Transportation, Storage and Destruction of Weapons and the Prevention of Weapons Proliferation (with respect to the elimination of strategic missile complexes and heavy bombers), hereinafter referred to as the Parties, have agreed as follows:

To amend Article III, Paragraph 1 of the Agreement by replacing the words "one billion, one hundred thirty-two million, nine hundred seventy thousand U.S. Dollars" with the words "one billion, one hundred ninety-three million U.S. Dollars".

This Amendment shall enter into force upon the date of its signature by both Parties and shall remain in force for the duration of the Agreement.

Done at Washington this *15th* day of *May*, 2006, and at Moscow, this *25* day of *MAY*, 2006, in duplicate, each in the English and Russian languages, both texts being equally authentic.

FOR THE DEPARTMENT OF DEFENSE OF THE UNITED STATES OF AMERICA	FOR THE FEDERAL SPACE AGENCY
[Signature]	[Signature]

STATE DEPARTMENT DOCUMENT NUMBER: 06-274

EXTENSION TO THE AGREEMENT OF JANUARY 29, 2001 BETWEEN THE UNITED STATES OF AMERICA AND THE ARAB REPUBLIC OF EGYPT ON SCIENCE AND TECHNOLOGY COOPERATION

EFFECTED BY EXCHANGE OF NOTES AT CAIRO,
MAY 11 AND AUGUST 27, 2006
ENTERED INTO FORCE AUGUST 27, 2006
EFFECTIVE SEPTEMBER 1, 2005

CTIA DOCUMENT NUMBER: 10146.001

LETTERHEAD OF THE EMBASSY OF THE UNITED STATES OF AMERICA

No. 477

The Embassy of the United States of America has the honor to refer the Ministry of Foreign Affairs of the Arab Republic of Egypt to the Agreement Between the Government of the United States of America and the Government of the Arab Republic of Egypt on Science and Technology Cooperation, signed at Cairo January 29, 2001 (the Agreement).

Considering science and technology cooperation to be an important field in which to strengthen the bilateral relationship between our two countries; and in regards to Article XIV of the Agreement, which provides that "it may be amended or extended for further five-year periods by written agreement of the Parties", the Embassy proposes, on behalf of the Government of the United States of America, that the Agreement be extended for a five-year period as from September 1, 2005.

In addition, the Embassy wishes to inform the Ministry of Foreign Affairs that the limitations concerning research under the Agreement set forth in the United States' side letter of December 11, 2000, are operative only with respect to cooperation which might produce pharmaceuticals.

If the Government of the Arab Republic of Egypt agrees with the proposal set forth above, the Embassy further proposes that this note and the Ministry's affirmative reply to it shall constitute an agreement between our two governments, which shall enter into force on the date of the Ministry's reply.

The Embassy of the United States of America avails itself of this opportunity to renew to the Ministry of Foreign Affairs of the Arab Republic of Egypt the assurances of its highest consideration.

[Signature]

Embassy of the United States of America,
Cairo, May 11, 2006.

The Foreign Ministry

The Office of the Assistant Foreign Minister
For International Cultural and Scientific Relations
And Technical Cooperation

Dated: August 27, 2006

Memorandum

The MFA extends its best regards to the U.S. Embassy in Cairo and refers to the Embassy's memorandum No. 447 dated May 11, 2006 regarding the Scientific and Technological Agreement between the Arab Republic of Egypt and the United States of America that was signed in Cairo on March 22, 1995 and extended on January 29, 2001 (to be in effect) as of September 1, 2005 for five years from that date.

Taking into account scientific and technological cooperation as a major field for strengthening bilateral relations between the two countries, and (taking into account) Article 14 of the aforementioned agreement on the possibility of amending or extending it for additional periods of five years each by mutual agreement of the two parties in writing, and (taking into account) the Embassy's suggestion on behalf of the USG to extend the agreement for five additional years as of September 1, 2005, in addition to the Embassy's desire to mention that the restrictions imposed on implementing the aforementioned agreement—with regard to researches by virtue of the side-letter sent by the United States of American dated January 11, 2001—should apply only to cooperation in the field of pharmaceutical industry.

We would like to notify you that the Embassy's memorandum is acceptable by the Arab Republic of Egypt and, therefore, your aforementioned memorandum and this reply of ours hereof are considered an agreement between our two governments that takes effect on the date of this memorandum.

The MFA seizes this opportunity to express its deepest appreciation and respect for the American Embassy in Cairo.

STATE DEPARTMENT DOCUMENT NUMBER: 06-275

ARRANGEMENT BETWEEN THE UNITED STATES OF AMERICA NUCLEAR REGULATORY COMMISSION (USNRC) AND THE FINNISH RADIATION AND NUCLEAR SAFETY AUTHORITY (SATEILYTURVAKESKUS) FOR THE EXCHANGE OF TECHNICAL INFORMATION AND COOPERATION IN NUCLEAR SAFETY MATTERS, WITH ADDENDA

SIGNED AT VIENNA,
SEPTEMBER 20, 2006
ENTERED INTO FORCE SEPTEMBER 20, 2006

CTIA DOCUMENT NUMBER: 13103.000

The Nuclear Regulatory Commission of the United States of America (hereinafter called the USNRC) and the Finnish Radiation and Nuclear Safety Authority (Sateilyturvakeskus, hereinafter called the STUK), the two together hereinafter referred to as the Parties;

Considering the desirability of a continuing exchange of information pertaining to regulatory matters and of standards required or recommended by their organizations for the regulation of safety and environmental impact of nuclear facilities;

Having similarly cooperated under the terms of a five-year Arrangement for the exchange of technical information cooperation in nuclear safety matters, signed on September 26, 1980, in Helsinki, Finland, and subsequent Arrangements for five-year periods beginning September 25, 1985, July 9, 1990, April 9, 1996, and December 31, 2001, and now having indicated their mutual desire to continue the established cooperation for another five years;

Have agreed as follows:

I. SCOPE OF THE ARRANGEMENT

A. *Technical Information Exchange*

To the extent that the USNRC and STUK are permitted to do so under the laws, regulations, and policy directives of their respective countries, the Parties agree to exchange of the following types of technical information relating to the regulation of

[Missing in original.]

4. Information in the field of confirmatory safety research which the Parties have the right to disclose, either in the possession of one of the Parties or available to it, including light water reactor safety information from the technical areas described in Addendum "A", attached hereto

and made a part hereof. Exchanges in the field of reactor safety research may require a separate agreement, as determined to be necessary by the research organizations of one or both of the Parties. Each Party will transmit immediately to the other information concerning research results that requires early attention in the interest of public safety, along with an indication of significant implications.

5. Reports on operating experience, such as reports on nuclear incidents, accidents and shutdowns, and compilations of historical reliability data on components and systems.

6. Regulatory procedures for the safety, safeguards (materials accountancy and control and physical protection), waste management, and environmental impact evaluation of nuclear facilities.

7. Early advice of important events, such as serious operating incidents and government-directed reactor shutdowns, that are of immediate interest to the Parties.

8. Copies of regulatory standards required to be used, or proposed for use, by the regulatory organizations of the Parties.

B. *Cooperation in Confirmatory Nuclear Safety Research*

The execution of joint programs and projects of safety research and development, or those programs and projects under which activities are divided between the two Parties, including the use of test facilities and/or computer programs owned by either Party, will be agreed upon on a case-by-case basis and may be the subject of a separate agreement, as determined to be necessary by one or both of the Parties. Other times, it may be accomplished by an exchange of letters between the Parties. Such separate agreements or exchange of letters will be subject at least to the terms and conditions of the present Arrangement. Technical areas specified by such exchanges of letters may be modified subsequently by mutual consent. Temporary assignments of personnel by one Party in the other Party's agency will also be considered on a case-by-case basis and subject to the terms and conditions of the present Arrangement.

C. *Training and Assignments*

Within the limits of available resources and subject to the availability of appropriated funds, the USNRC will try to assist the STUK by providing certain training and experience for STUK safety personnel. Unless otherwise agreed, costs of salary, allowances, and travel of STUK participants will be paid by the STUK. The following are typical of the kinds of training and experience that may be provided:

1. STUK inspector accompaniment of USNRC inspectors on operating reactor and reactor construction inspection visits in the U.S., including extended briefings at USNRC regional inspection offices.

2. Participation by STUK employees in USNRC staff training courses.

3. Assignment of STUK employees for 6–24 month periods within the USNRC staff to work on USNRC staff duties and gain on-the-job experience.

4. Possible training assignments within the radiation control programs of interested USNRC Agreement States.

D. *Additional Safety Advice*

To the extent that the documents and other information provided by the USNRC as described in the SCOPE OF THE ARRANGEMENT, above, are not adequate to meet STUK needs for technical advice, the parties will consult on the best means for fulfilling such needs.

II. ADMINISTRATION

A. The exchange of information under this Arrangement will be accomplished through letters, reports, and other documents, and by visits and meetings arranged in advance on a case-by-case basis. Meetings will be held at such times as mutually agreed to review the exchange of information, to recommend revisions to the provisions of the Arrangement, and to discuss topics within the scope of the exchange. The time, place, and agenda for such meetings will be agreed upon in advance. Visits which take place under the Arrangement, including their schedules, will have the prior approval of the Arrangement administrators referred to in paragraph II.B.

B. An administrator will be designated by each Party to coordinate its participation in the overall exchange. The administrators will be the recipients of all documents transmitted under the exchange, including copies of all letters unless otherwise agreed. Within the terms of the exchange, the administrators will be responsible for developing the scope of the exchange, including agreement on the designation of the nuclear energy facilities subject to the exchange, and on specific documents and standards to be exchanged. One or more technical coordinators may be appointed as direct contacts for specific disciplinary areas. These technical coordinators will assure that both administrators receive copies of all transmittals. These detailed arrangements are intended to assure, among other things, that a reasonably balanced exchange giving access to equivalent available information is achieved and maintained.

C. The administrators will determine the number of copies to be provided of the documents exchanged. Each document will be accompanied by an abstract in English, 250 words or less, describing its scope and content.

D. The application or use of any information exchanged or transferred between the Parties under this Arrangement will be the responsibility of the Receiving Party, and the Transmitting Party does not warrant the suitability of such information for any particular use or application.

E. Recognizing that some information of the type covered in this Arrangement is not available within the agencies which are Parties to this Arrangement, but is available from other agencies of the governments of the Parties, each Party will assist the other to the maximum extent possible by organizing visits and directing inquiries concerning such information to appropriate agencies of the government concerned. The foregoing will not constitute a commitment of other agencies to furnish such information or to receive such visitors.

F. Nothing contained in this Arrangement will require either Party to take any action which would be inconsistent with its national laws, regulations, and policy directives. No nuclear information related to proliferation-sensitive technologies will be exchanged under this Arrangement. Should any conflict arise between the terms of this Arrangement and those laws, regulations, and policy directives, the Parties agree to consult before any action is taken.

G. Unless otherwise agreed, all costs resulting from cooperation pursuant to this Arrangement will be the responsibility of the Party that incurs them. The ability of the each of the Parties to carry out their obligations is subject to the availability of appropriated funds and to the laws and regulations of such Party.

III. EXCHANGE AND USE OF INFORMATION

A. *General*

The Parties support the widest possible dissemination of information provided or exchanged under this Arrangement, subject both to the need to protect proprietary or other confidential or privileged information as may be exchanged hereunder, and to the provisions of the Intellectual Property Addendum, which is an integral part of this Arrangement.

B. *Definitions*

For the purposes of this Arrangement:

1. The term "information" means nuclear energy-related regulatory, safety, safeguards, waste management, scientific, or technical data, including information on results or methods of confirmatory assessment, research, and any other knowledge intended to be provided or exchanged under this Arrangement.

2. The term "proprietary information" means information made available under this Arrangement which contains trade secrets or other privileged or confidential information (such that the person having the information may derive an economic benefit from it or may have a competitive advantage over those who do not have it), and may only include information which:

(a) has been held in confidence by its owner;

(b) is of a type which is customarily held in confidence by its owner;

(c) has not been transmitted by the owner to other entities (including the Receiving Party) except on the basis that it be held in confidence;

(d) is not otherwise available to the Receiving Party from another source without restrictions on its further dissemination; and

(e) is not already in the possession of the Receiving Party.

3. The term "other confidential or privileged information" means information, other than "proprietary information," which is protected from public disclosure under the laws and regulations of the country providing the information and which has been transmitted and received in confidence.

C. *Marking Procedures for Documentary Proprietary Information*

A Party receiving documentary proprietary information pursuant to this Arrangement will respect the privileged nature thereof, *provided* such proprietary information is clearly marked with the following (or substantially similar) restrictive legend:

> This document contains proprietary information furnished in confidence under an Arrangement dated September 20, 2006 between the Nuclear Regulatory Commission of the United States of America and the Finnish Radiation and Nuclear Safety Authority and will not be disseminated outside these organizations, their consultants, contractors, and licensees, and concerned departments and agencies of the Government of the United States and the Government of Finland without the prior approval of (*name of the Transmitting Party*). This notice will be marked on any reproduction hereof, in whole or in part. These limitations will automatically terminate when this information is disclosed by the owner without restrictions.

This restrictive legend will be respected by the receiving Party and proprietary information bearing this legend will not be used for commercial purposes, made public, or disseminated in any manner unspecified by or contrary to the terms of this Arrangement without the consent of the transmitting Party whose consent will presumed to be authorized where the owner and the transmitting party differ.

D. *Dissemination of Documentary Proprietary Information*

1. In general proprietary information received under this Arrangement may be freely disseminated by the Receiving Party without prior consent to persons within or employed by the Receiving Party,

and to concerned Government departments and Government agencies in the country of the Receiving Party.

2. In addition, except where expressly prohibited by the originating party, proprietary information may be disseminated without prior consent

(a) to prime or subcontractors or consultants of the Receiving Party located within the geographical limits of that Party's nation, for use only within the scope of work of their contracts with the Receiving Party in work relating to the subject matter of the proprietary or other confidential or privileged information;

(b) to domestic organizations permitted or licensed by the Receiving Party to construct or operate nuclear production or utilization facilities, or to use nuclear materials and radiation sources, provided that such proprietary or other confidential or privileged information is used only within the terms of the permit or license; and

(c) to domestic contractors of organizations identified in D.2.(b), above, for use only in work within the scope of the permit or license granted to such organizations;

Provided that any dissemination of proprietary information under D.2.(a), (b), and (c), above, will be on an as-needed, case-by-case basis, will be pursuant to an agreement of confidentiality, and will be marked with a restrictive legend substantially similar to that appearing in C., above.

3. With the prior written consent of the Party furnishing proprietary information under this Arrangement, the Receiving Party may disseminate such proprietary information more widely than otherwise permitted in subsections 1. and 2. The Parties will cooperate in developing procedures for requesting and obtaining approval for such wider dissemination, and each Party will grant such approval to the extent permitted by its national policies, regulations, and laws.

E. *Marking Procedures for Other Confidential or Privileged Information of a Documentary Nature*

A Party receiving under this Arrangement other confidential or privileged information will respect its confidential nature, *provided* such information is clearly marked so as to indicate its confidential or privileged nature and is accompanied by a statement indicating

1. that the information is protected from public disclosure by the Government of the Transmitting Party, and

2. that the information is transmitted under the condition that it be maintained in confidence.

F. *Dissemination of Other Confidential or Privileged Information of a Documentary Nature*

Other confidential or privileged information may be disseminated in the same manner as that set forth in paragraph D., *Dissemination of Documentary Proprietary Information*.

G. *Non-Documentary Proprietary or Other Confidential or Privileged Information*

Non-documentary proprietary or other confidential or privileged information provided in seminars and other meetings arranged under this Arrangement, or information arising from attachments of staff, use of facilities, or joint projects, will be treated by the Parties according to the principles specified for documentary information in this Arrangement; *provided*, however, that the Party communicating such proprietary or other confidential or privileged information has placed the recipient on notice as to the character of the information communicated.

H. *Consultation*

If, for any reason, one of the Parties becomes aware that it will be, or may reasonably be expected to become, unable to meet the non-dissemination provisions of this Article, it will immediately inform the other Party. The Parties will thereafter consult to define an appropriate course of action.

I. *Other*

Nothing contained in this Arrangement will preclude a Party from using or disseminating information received without restriction by a Party from sources outside of this Arrangement.

J. *Dispute Resolution*

Cooperation under this Arrangement will be governed by the laws and regulations of the respective countries. Any dispute or question between the parties concerning the interpretation or application of this Arrangement arising during its term will be settled by mutual agreement of the parties.

IV. FINAL PROVISIONS

A. This Arrangement will enter into force upon signature and, subject to paragraph B. of this Article, will remain in force for a period of five years. It may be extended for a further period of time by written agreement of the Parties.

B. Either Party may withdraw from this Arrangement after providing the other Party written notice 180 days prior to its intended date of termination.

C. All information protected by provisions of this Arrangement as proprietary or other confidential or privileged information will remain so protected for the duration of this Arrangement and after this Arrangement has expired or been terminated, unless otherwise specifically agreed by the Parties in writing.

DONE at Vienna, Austria on this 20th day of September 2006.

FOR THE UNITED STATES NUCLEAR REGULATORY COMMISSION:

[Signature]

Dale E. Klein, Chairman

FOR THE FINNISH RADIATION AND NUCLEAR SAFETY AUTHORITY:

[Signature]

Jukka Laaksonen, Director General

CERTIFIED A TRUE COPY
BY [Signature]
Office of the Secretary

Addendum "A"

USNRC–STUK Safety Research Exchange
Areas In Which the USNRC Is Performing or Sponsoring Safety Research

1. Reactor Vessel and Piping Integrity

2. Aging of Reactor Components

3. Reactor Equipment Qualification

4. Thermal Hydraulic Code Applications and Maintenance

5. Plant Performance

6. Human Performance

7. Core Melt and Reactor Coolant System Failure

8. Reactor Containment Safety

9. Containment Structural Integrity

10. Seismic Safety

11. Probabilistic Risk Assessment

12. Severe Accident Analysis

13. Radiation Protection and Health Effects

14. Radionuclide Transport and Waste Management

15. Nuclear Fuel Analysis

16. Dry Cask Storage and Transport

17. Decommissioning

18. Advanced Reactor Designs

19. Fire Protection

INTELLECTUAL PROPERTY ADDENDUM

Pursuant to Article III. of this Arrangement:

The Parties shall ensure adequate and effective protection of intellectual property created or furnished under this Arrangement and relevant implementing arrangements. The Parties agree to notify one another in a timely fashion of any inventions or copyrighted works arising under this Arrangement and to seek protection for such intellectual property in a timely fashion. Rights to such intellectual property shall be allocated as provided in this Addendum.

I. SCOPE

1. This Addendum is applicable to all cooperative activities undertaken pursuant to this Arrangement, except as otherwise specifically agreed by the Parties or their designees.

2. For purposes of this Arrangement, "intellectual property" shall have the meaning found in Article 2 of the Convention Establishing the World Intellectual Property Organization, done at Stockholm, July 14, 1967; *viz.*, 'intellectual property' shall include the rights relating to:

—literary, artistic and scientific works,

—performances of artists, phonograms, and broadcasts,

—inventions in all fields of human endeavor,

—scientific discoveries,

—industrial designs,

—trademarks, service marks, and commercial names and designations,

—protection against unfair competition,

and all other rights resulting from intellectual activity in the industrial, scientific, literary, or artistic fields.

3. This Addendum addresses the allocation of rights, interests, and royalties between the Parties. Each Party shall ensure that the other Party can obtain rights to intellectual property allocated in accordance with the Addendum by obtaining those rights from its own participants through contracts or other legal means, if necessary. This Addendum does not otherwise alter or prejudice the allocation between a Party and its nationals, which shall be determined by that Party's laws and practices.

4. Disputes concerning intellectual property arising under this Arrangement should be resolved through discussions between the concerned participating institutions or, if necessary, the Parties or their designees. Upon mutual agreement of the Parties, a dispute shall be submitted to an arbitral tribunal for binding arbitration in accordance with the applicable rules of international law. Unless the Parties or their designees agree otherwise in writing, the arbitration rules of the *United Nations Commission on International Trade Law* (UNCITRAL) shall govern.

5. Termination or expiration of this Arrangement shall not affect rights or obligations under this Addendum.

II. *ALLOCATION OF RIGHTS*

1. Each party shall be entitled to a non-exclusive, irrevocable, royalty-free license in all countries to translate, reproduce, and publicly distribute scientific and technical journal articles, reports, and books directly arising from cooperation under this Arrangement. All publicly distributed copies of copyrighted work prepared under this provision shall indicate the names of the authors of the work unless an author explicitly declines to be named.

2. Rights to all forms of intellectual property, other than those rights described in Section II.1., above, shall be allocated as follows:

a. Visiting researchers, for example, scientists visiting primarily in furtherance of their education, shall receive intellectual property rights under the policies of the host institution. In addition, each visiting researcher named as an inventor shall be entitled to share in a portion of any royalties earned by the host institution from the licensing of such intellectual property.

b. (1) For intellectual property created during joint research, for example, when the Parties, participating institutions, or participating personnel have agreed in advance on the scope of work, each Party shall be entitled to obtain all rights and interests in its own country. The Party in whose country the invention was made shall have first option to acquire all rights and interests in third countries. If research is not designated as "joint research," rights to intellectual property arising from the research will be allocated in accordance with paragraph II.2.a., above. In addition, each person named as an inventor shall be entitled to share in a portion of any royalties earned by either institution from the licensing of the property.

(2) Notwithstanding paragraph II.2.b.(1), above, if a type of intellectual property is available under the laws of one Party but not of the other Party, the Party whose laws provide for this type of protection shall be entitled to all rights and interests worldwide. Persons named as inventors of the property shall nonetheless be entitled to royalties as provided in paragraph II.2.b.(1), above.

STATE DEPARTMENT DOCUMENT NUMBER: 06-276

AMENDMENT NO. 1 TO THE MEMORANDUM OF UNDERSTANDING OF SEPTEMBER 29, 2004 BETWEEN THE DEPARTMENT OF DEFENSE OF THE UNITED STATES OF AMERICA AS REPRESENTED BY THE DEFENSE ENERGY SUPPORT CENTER AND THE MINISTRY OF DEFENCE OF THE UNITED KINGDOM AND NORTHERN IRELAND AS REPRESENTED BY THE DEFENCE FUELS GROUP ACTING ON BEHALF OF THE ROYAL NAVY CONCERNING THE EXCHANGE AND REPLACEMENT OR REIMBURSEMENT OF MARINE AVIATION AND PROPULSION FUELS AT SEA AND AT MILITARY INSTALLATIONS WORLDWIDE

SIGNED AT FORT BELVOIR,
OCTOBER 6, 2006
ENTERED INTO FORCE OCTOBER 6, 2006

CTIA DOCUMENT NUMBER: 11473.001

Dated: October 12, 2006
I certify that this is a true and complete copy of the original Amendment One to the Memorandum of Understanding Between the United States Department of Defense as Represented by the Defense Energy Support Center and the Ministry of Defence of the United Kingdom of Great Britain and Northern Ireland as Represented by the Defence Fuels Group on Behalf of the Royal Navy Concerning the Exchange and Replacement or Reimbursement of Marine Aviation and Propulsion Fuels at Sea and at Military installations Worldwide.
[Signature]

Timothy A. Raezer, Assistant Counsel
Defense Energy Support Center

The "Memorandum of Understanding between the Department of Defense of the United States of America, as Represented by the Defense Energy Support Center and the Ministry of Defence of the United Kingdom of Great Britain and Northern Ireland, as Represented by the Defence Fuels Group, Acting on Behalf of the Royal Navy, Concerning the Exchange and Replacement or Reimbursement, of Marine Aviation and Propulsion Fuels at Sea and at Military Installations Worldwide," dated September 29, 2004 is amended as follows.

1. Amend SECTION I: PURPOSE AND SCOPE, by:

a. Adding Paragraph 1.3. with the following:

"1.3. Third-Party NATO Countries may participate in this Agreement when mutually agreed by the Participants. The balance of one Participant or third-party NATO Country may be reconciled against the account of another Participant or third-party NATO Country."

2. Amend SECTION III: RESPONSIBILITIES, by:

a. Deleting Paragraph 3.1.3. and replacing it with the following:

"3.1.3. Meet to reconcile accounts quarterly."

3. Amend SECTION IV: OPERATIONS, by:

a. Deleting Paragraph 4.2. and replacing it with the following:

"4.2. The Participants will exchange letters regarding minor technical and administrative changes to the annexes without formal amendment to the MOU. These changes include providing updated point-of-contact listings when necessary. When a jointly decided number of such changes have accumulated, an amendment to this MOU, or a new MOU, will be renegotiated as provided in Section V, paragraph 5.4."

b. Deleting Paragraph 4.3.

4. Amend ANNEX C, RECONCILIATION, by:

a. Deleting Paragraph C.2. and replacing it with the following:

"C.2. Quarterly Account Reconciliation."

b. Deleting Paragraph C.2.1. and replacing it with the following:

"C.2.1. The Participants intend to reconcile and settle account transactions on a quarterly basis. Reconciliation of accounts may be accomplished by meeting or exchange of correspondence as mutually agreed between the Participants. After reconciliation, the Participants will mutually agree how reimbursement of any balance will be settled."

c. Deleting Paragraph C.2.2. and replacing it with the following:

"C.2.2. Balances may be replaced in kind (Annex E) or reimbursed in monetary terms (Annex D). The Participants intend that balances of less than five (5) million U.S. gallons (18,927,063 litres) may be carried forward to the next reconciliation meeting, with the consent of the Participant owed. Balances of five (5) million U.S. gallons (18,927,063 litres) or greater will be repaid in kind or by monetary equivalent in accordance with this MOU."

d. Adding Paragraphs C.2.3.7. and C.2.3.8. as follows:

"C.2.3.7. For the purpose of reconciliation and settlement, the following conversion factors will be used at the same temperature:

C.2.3.7.1. One (1) litre equals 0.264172 U.S. gallons

C.2.3.7.2. One (1) cubic metre equals 1,000 litres

C.2.3.7.3. One (1) barrel equals 42 U.S. gallons"

"C.2.3.8. Equal Value Exchange. Equal Value Exchange (EVE) is the process of converting a quantity of one grade of product to an equivalent financial value of another grade of product. Price determination of products will be in accordance with Annex D. Equal value exchange of products will be mutually agreed by the Participants."

5. Amend ANNEX D, PAYMENT IN CASH, by deleting Paragraph D.1. and replacing it with the following:

"D.1. Price Determination.

D.1.1. DESC Repayment to DFG. For DESC repayment to DFG, DESC will repay based on the DFG's "weighted average monthly stock price" in effect at the time in which product was received by DESC.

D.1.2. DFG Repayment to DESC. For DFG repayment to DESC, DFG will repay based on DESC's "standard price" in effect for the year in which product was received by DFG."

This Amendment One to the "Memorandum of Understanding between the Department of Defense of the United States of America, as Represented by the Defense Energy Support Center and the Ministry of Defence of the United Kingdom of Great Britain and Northern Ireland, as Represented by the Defence Fuels Group, Acting on Behalf of the Royal Navy, Concerning the Exchange and Replacement or Reimbursement of Marine Aviation and Propulsion Fuels as Sea and at Military Installations Worldwide," will enter into effect upon the signature of both Participants.

In witness thereof, the undersigned, being duly authorized by their Governments, have signed this Amendment.

FOR THE
DEFENSE ENERGY SUPPORT CENTER

[Signature]

RICHARD J. CONNELLY
Director
Defense Energy Support Center

4 Oct 2006
DATE SIGNED

Fort Belvoir, VA
PLACE OF SIGNATURE

FOR THE
DEFENCE FUELS GROUP

[Signature]

A. C. SPINKS, Air Commodore, RAF
Director
Defence Fuels Group

6 Oct 06
DATE SIGNED

Fort Belvoir, VA
PLACE OF SIGNATURE

State Department Document Number: 06-277

Amendment to the Agreement of October 22, 2001, as Amended, Between the Department of Defense of the United States of America and the Ministry of Defense of the Republic of Uzbekistan Concerning Cooperation in the Area of Demilitarization of Biological Weapons Associated Facilities and the Prevention of Proliferation of Biological Weapons Technology

Signed at Tashkent and Washington D.C.,
September 29 and October 11, 2006
Entered into force October 11, 2006

CTIA Document Number: 10123.005

Pursuant to Article IX of the Agreement Between the Department of Defense of the United States of America and the Ministry of Defense of the Republic of Uzbekistan Concerning Cooperation in the Area of Demilitarization of Biological Weapons Associated Facilities and the Prevention of Proliferation of Biological Weapons Technology, dated October 22, 2001, as amended July 29, 2003, May 17, 2004, September 10, 2004, and December 19, 2005, hereinafter referred to as "the Agreement," the Department of Defense of the United States of America and the Ministry of Defense of the Republic of Uzbekistan hereby agree to amend Article III of the Agreement by replacing the words "seventy million" with the words "eighty-five million".

This Amendment shall enter into force upon signature and shall remain in force for the duration of the Agreement.

IN WITNESS WHEREOF, the undersigned, being duly authorized by their respective governments, have signed this Amendment.

DONE at Washington, this 11th of October, 2006, and at Tashkent, this 29 day of 09, 2006, in duplicate, in the English and Russian languages. In case of differences in interpretation, the English language text shall prevail.

**FOR THE
DEPARTMENT OF DEFENSE
OF THE UNITED STATES OF AMERICA:**

[Signature]

**FOR THE
MINISTRY OF DEFENSE OF
THE REPUBLIC OF UZBEKISTAN:**

[Signature]

STATE DEPARTMENT DOCUMENT NUMBER: 06-278

AGREEMENT BETWEEN THE REPUBLIC OF ARMENIA AND THE UNITED STATES OF AMERICA ON EMPLOYMENT OF DEPENDENTS OF MEMBERS OF DIPLOMATIC MISSIONS AND CONSULAR POSTS

EFFECTED BY EXCHANGE OF NOTES AT YEREVAN,
SEPTEMBER 20 AND DECEMBER 30, 2005
ENTERED INTO FORCE OCTOBER 16, 2006

CTIA DOCUMENT NUMBER: 13111.000

LETTERHEAD OF MINISTRY OF FOREIGN AFFAIRS OF THE REPUBLIC OF ARMENIA

The Ministry of Foreign Affairs of the Republic of Armenia presents its compliments to the State Department of the United States of America and with reference to recent discussions between the Government of the Republic of Armenia and the Government of the United States of America regarding the employment of dependents of employees assigned to official duty in the Receiving State, has the honour to inform, that guiding by desire of the Government of the Republic of Armenia and the Government of the United States of America sign the Agreement for the employment of the dependents of members of diplomatic missions, consular offices and missions to international organizations in respective countries, the Ministry of Foreign Affairs of the Republic of Armenia has the honour to propose the terms attached to this note.

If the terms attached to this note are acceptable for the Government of the United States of America, the Ministry of Foreign Affairs of the Republic of Armenia has the honour to propose that this note and the reply of the Government of the United States of America will constitute an Agreement between the Government of the Republic of Armenia and the Government of the United States of America, which will enter into force on the date of the last written notification of parties on completion of their legal procedures necessary for the entry into force of this Agreement.

The Ministry of Foreign Affairs of the Republic of Armenia avails itself of this opportunity to renew to the State Department of the United States of America the assurances of its highest consideration.

Yerevan, September 30 2005
[Seal]

The State Department of the
United States of America
Washington

Annex
on the employment of dependents of employees assigned to official duty in the Receiving State

The Government of the Republic of Armenia and the Government of United States of America, hereinafter referred to as the "Parties",

Wishing to set up conditions for the employment of the dependents of members of diplomatic missions, consular offices and missions to international organizations in respective countries,

Have agreed as follows:

Article 1
Definitions

For the purpose of this Agreement the following terms shall mean:

"Employees assigned to official duty" – diplomatic agents, consular officers and members of the support (administrative and technical) staff assigned to diplomatic missions, consular offices and missions to international organizations.

"Dependents" – a) in the case of Armenia dependents: spouses, unmarried dependent children under 18 years of age, and unmarried children who are physically or mentally disabled,

b) in the case of America dependents: spouses, unmarried dependent children under 21 years of age, unmarried dependent children under 23 years of age who are in full-time attendance as students at a postsecondary educational institution, and unmarried children who are physically or mentally disabled.

"Receiving State" – a State, where the diplomatic mission, consular offices and/or missions to international organizations of one of the Party are located.

Article 2
The right to employment of dependents in the Receiving State

Dependents of employees of one Party assigned to official duty in the State of the other Party have a right to employment in the Receiving State in accordance to the procedure described in the Article 3.

Article 3
Procedure for acceptance of the employment

In the case of dependents who seek employment in the Receiving State the diplomatic mission of one Party must make an official request to the Ministry of Foreign Affairs (the Department of State). Upon verification that the person is a dependent of an employee assigned to official duty and processing of the official request, the Ministry of Foreign Affairs (the Department of State) will inform the diplomatic mission that the dependent may accept employment.

Article 4
Duties and limits of Immunities of dependents who obtain employment under this Agreement

The dependents who obtain employment under this Agreement and who have immunity from the jurisdiction of the Receiving State in accordance with the Vienna Convention on diplomatic relations or any other applicable international agreement between the Contracting Parties:

a) enjoy no immunity from civil and administrative jurisdiction with respect to matters arising out of such employment.

b) are liable for payment of income and social security taxes on any remuneration received as a result of employment in the Receiving State.

DIPLOMATIC NOTE

No. 689/05

The Embassy of the United States of America presents its compliments to the Ministry of Foreign Affairs of the Republic of Armenia and has the honor to respond to the Ministry's note No. 16/10683, concerning the employment of dependents of members of diplomatic missions, consular offices, and missions to international organizations in respective countries. The Government of the United States of America has the honor to agree to the terms attached to this note and to notify the Republic of Armenia that all necessary legal formalities for its entry into force have been completed.

The Embassy of the United States of America avails itself of this opportunity to renew to the Ministry of Foreign Affairs of the Republic of Armenia the assurances of its highest consideration.

Embassy of the United States of America [Seal]
Yerevan, December 30, 2005

AGREEMENT

between the Government of the Republic of Armenia and the Government of the United States of America on the employment of dependents of employees assigned to official duty in the Receiving State

The Government of the Republic of Armenia and the Government of United States of America, hereinafter referred to as the "Parties",

Wishing to set up conditions for the employment of the dependents of members of diplomatic missions, consular offices and missions to international organizations in respective countries,

Have agreed as follows:

Article 1
Definitions

For the purpose of this Agreement the following terms shall mean:

"Employees assigned to official duty" – diplomatic agents, consular officers and members of the support (administrative and technical) staff assigned to diplomatic missions, consular offices and missions to international organizations.

"Dependents" – a) in the case of Armenian dependents: spouses; unmarried dependent children under 18 years of age and unmarried dependent children who are physically or mentally disabled.

b) in the case of American dependents: spouses, unmarried dependent children under 21 years of age, unmarried dependent children under 23 yeas of age who are in full-time attendance as students at a post-secondary educational institution; and unmarried children who are physically or mentally disabled.

"Receiving State" – a State, where the diplomatic mission, consular offices and/or missions to international organizations of one of the Party are located.

Article 2
The right to employment of dependents in the Receiving State

Dependents of employees of one Party assigned to official duty in the State of the other Party have a right to employment in the Receiving State in accordance to the procedure described in the Article 3.

Article 3
Procedure for acceptance of the employment

In the case of dependents who seek employment in the Receiving State the diplomatic mission of one Party must make an official request to the Ministry of Foreign Affairs (the Department of State). Upon verification that the person is a dependent of an employee assigned to official duty and processing of the official request, the Ministry of Foreign Affairs (the Department of State) will inform the diplomatic mission that the dependent may accept employment.

Article 4
Duties and limits of Immunities of dependents who obtain employment under this Agreement

The dependents who obtain employment under this Agreement and who have immunity from the jurisdiction of the Receiving State in accordance with the Vienna Convention on diplomatic relations or any other applicable international agreement between the Contracting Parties:

a) enjoy no immunity from civil and administrative jurisdiction with respect to matters arising out of such employment.

b) are liable for payment of income and social security taxes on any remuneration received as a result of employment in the Receiving State.

Article 5
Termination of Employment

The employment of the dependent is terminated 30 days after the date of termination of the service of the employee assigned to official duty.

Article 6
Dispute

Any dispute between the Parties arising from the application and interpretation of this Agreement shall be settled through diplomatic channels by mutual consent.

Article 7
Entry into Force

This Agreement shall enter into force on the date when the Parties have notified each other that all necessary legal formalities for its entry into force have been completed. It may be amended upon the mutual written agreement of the Parties.

This Agreement shall remain in force until terminated by either Party upon ninety (90) days written notice to the other Party.

STATE DEPARTMENT DOCUMENT NUMBER: 06-279

MEMORANDUM OF UNDERSTANDING BETWEEN THE MINISTRY OF DEFENCE OF THE REPUBLIC OF HUNGARY AND THE UNITED STATES OF AMERICA JOINT FORCES COMMAND REGARDING ASSIGNMENT OF LIAISON OFFICERS, WITH ANNEX

SIGNED AT BUDAPEST AND NORFOLK,
SEPTEMBER 22 AND OCTOBER 23, 2006
ENTERED INTO FORCE OCTOBER 23, 2006

CTIA DOCUMENT NUMBER: 13112.000

INTRODUCTION

The Ministry of Defence of the Republic of Hungary and the U.S. Joint Forces Command, (each referred to herein individually as a "Participant" and together as the "Participants"), desiring to establish formal liaison between them to coordinate theater security cooperation events and to provide a consistent and established affiliation between the Ministry of Defence of the Republic of Hungary and the U.S. Joint Forces Command undertake the following terms and conditions regarding the assignment of individuals to serve as Liaison Officers to the other Participant.

SECTION I
DEFINITIONS

In addition to any terms defined in other provisions of this Arrangement, the following terms will have the following meanings when used herein:

1.1 "*Classified Information*" will mean official information of a Participant that requires protection in the interests of national security of such Participant and is so designated by the application of security classification markings. This information may be in oral, visual, electronic, or documentary form, or in the form of material, including equipment, or technology.

1.2 "*Contact Officer*" will mean a U.S. Department of Defense (DoD) official designated in writing to oversee and control all contacts, requests for information, consultations, access, and other activities of Foreign Liaison Officers who are assigned to, or are visiting, a DoD component or subordinate organization.

1.3 "*Controlled Unclassified Information*" will mean unclassified information of a Participant to which access or distribution limitations have been applied in accordance with national laws, policies, and regulations of such Participant. It includes U. S. information that is exempt from public disclosure or subject to export controls.

1.4 "*Foreign Liaison Officer*" will mean a military member or civilian employee of the Parent Participant who, upon approval of or certification by the Host Participant, and under the direction and supervision of the Hungarian National Liaison Representative assigned to NATO's allied Command Transformation, Norfolk, Virginia, is authorized by the Parent Participant to act as its official representative in connection with programs, projects, or arrangements of interest to the Participants' Governments.

1.5 "*Host Government*" will mean the national government of the Host Participant.

1.6 "*Host Participant*" will mean the Participant to which the Foreign Liaison Officer acts as a liaison pursuant to an assignment by the Parent Participant under SECTION III.

1.7 "*International Visits Program (IVP)*" will mean the program established to process visits by, and assignments of, foreign representatives to United States Department of Defense Components and DoD contractor facilities. It is designed to ensure that classified and controlled unclassified information to be disclosed to foreign nationals has been properly authorized for disclosure to their governments; that the requesting foreign government provides a security assurance on such foreign nationals and their sponsoring organization or firm, when Classified Information is involved in the visit or assignment, and that administrative arrangements (e.g., date, time and place) for the visit or assignment are provided.

1.8 "*Parent Government*" will mean the national government of the Parent Participant.

1.9 "*Parent Participant*" will mean the Participant that assigns a Foreign Liaison Officer pursuant to SECTION III.

SECTION II
SCOPE

2.1 During the term of this Arrangement, subject to the mutual concurrence of the Participants, the Ministry of Defence of the Republic of Hungary may assign a Foreign Liaison Officer to the Headquarters, U.S. Joint Forces Command, in accordance with the terms of this Arrangement. The Parent Participant will ensure that the person assigned is a senior officer whose rank is at least equivalent to a U.S. 0–5. The Foreign Liaison Officer will represent the Ministry of Defence of the Republic of Hungary to the Host Participant.

2.2 The establishment of each Foreign Liaison Officer position under this Arrangement will be based upon the demonstrated need for, and the mutual benefit of, this position to the Participants. Once established, each Foreign Liaison Officer position will be subject to a periodic review of every six months by either Participant to ensure that the position continues to be required by, and is of mutual benefit to, the Participants. A Foreign Liaison Officer position no longer required by, or of mutual benefit to, either Participant will be subject to elimination.

2.3 Commencement of such a tour of duty by a Foreign Liaison Officer will be subject to any requirements that may be imposed by the Host Participant or by the Parent Government regarding formal certification by or approval of Foreign Liaison Officers.

Foreign Liaison Officers to be assigned by the Parent Participant to locations in the United States will be requested pursuant to the IVP, as defined in Paragraph 1.7 of this Arrangement.

2.4 Unless otherwise mutually determined, the normal tour of duty for a Foreign Liaison Officer will not exceed three (3) years.

2.5 An individual may serve as a Foreign Liaison Officer to only one major military command of the Host Participant at any point in time.

SECTION III
DUTIES AND ACTIVITIES

3.1 The Foreign Liaison Officer will represent the Parent Participant to the Host Participant. The Foreign Liaison Officer will not perform duties reserved by the laws or regulations of the Host Government to officers or employees of the Host Government, nor will the Foreign Liaison Officer provide any labor or services to the Host Government or any of its agencies, including the Host Participant.

3.2 The Foreign Liaison Officer shall comply with all applicable Host Government policies, procedures, laws and regulations. The Host Participant will assign a Contact Officer to provide guidance to the Foreign Liaison Officer concerning policies, procedures, laws and regulations of the Host Participant, and to arrange for activities consistent with such requirements and the purposes of this Arrangement.

3.3 The Foreign Liaison Officer may request access to Host Participant facilities by submitting a request to the Contact Officer. Access to Host Participant facilities may be granted if such access promotes the purposes of this Arrangement, is consistent with the terms of any applicable certification or approval issued by the Host Government, and is permitted under the applicable policies, procedures, laws and regulations of the Host Government. Approval of such requests will be at the discretion of the Host Participant. Any request for access that exceeds the terms of an applicable certification or approval will be submitted through the IVP.

3.4 The Foreign Liaison Officer will not be granted access to technical data or other information of the Host Participant, whether or not classified, except as authorized by the Host Participant, and only to the extent necessary to fulfill the Foreign Liaison Officer's functions hereunder.

3.5 All information to which the Foreign Liaison Officer is granted access while serving as a liaison to the Host Participant will be treated as information provided in confidence to the Parent Government and will not be further released or disclosed by the Foreign Liaison Officer to any other person, firm, organization, or government without the prior written authorization of the Host Government. Disclosure of information to the Foreign Liaison Officer will not be deemed to be a license or authorization to use such information for any purpose other than the purposes described in SECTION II.

3.6 The Foreign Liaison Officer will not be permitted to participate in exercises, deployments, or civil-military actions, unless expressly authorized in writing to do so by both the Host and Parent Participants.

3.7 The Parent Participant will not place or keep a Foreign Liaison Officer in duty assignments in which direct hostilities with forces of third states are likely to occur or have commenced, unless approved in writing by the Parent Participant and Host Participant.

3.8 The Foreign Liaison Officer will be required to comply with the dress regulations of the Parent Participant but, if requested by the Host Participant, will also wear such identification necessary to identify the Foreign Liaison Officer's nationality, rank and status as a Foreign Liaison Officer. The order of dress for any occasion will be that which most closely conforms to the order of dress for the particular organization of the Host Participant where the Foreign Liaison Officer is located. The Foreign Liaison Officer will be required to comply with the customs of the Host Participant with respect to the wearing of civilian clothing.

3.9 Prior to the commencement of a Foreign Liaison Officer's tour, the Parent Participant will notify the Host Participant of the specific Parent Participant organization that will exercise operational control over the Foreign Liaison Officer and, if different, the Parent Participant organization that will provide administrative support to the Foreign Liaison Officer and the Foreign Liaison Officer's dependents.

3.10 At the end of a Foreign Liaison Officer's tour, or as otherwise mutually determined by the Participants, the Parent Participant may, subject to the provisions of SECTION II, replace the Foreign Liaison Officer with another individual who meets the requirements of this Arrangement.

SECTION IV
FINANCIAL ARRANGEMENTS

4.1 The Parent Participant will bear all costs and expenses of the Foreign Liaison Officer, including, but not limited to:

4.1.1 All pay and allowances of the Foreign Liaison Officer;

4.1.2 All travel by the Foreign Liaison Officer and the Foreign Liaison Officer's dependents, including, but not limited to, travel to and from the duty location;

4.1.3 All costs and expenses associated with the assignment or placement of the Foreign Liaison Officer and the Foreign Liaison Officer's dependents at the duty location, including travel, office space, clerical support, housing, messing, medical and dental services, unless specifically stated otherwise in an applicable international agreement;

4.1.4 Compensation for loss of, or damage to, the personal property of the Foreign Liaison Officer or the personal property of the Foreign Liaison Officer's dependents;

4.1.5 The movement of the household effects of the Foreign Liaison Officer and the Foreign Liaison Officer's dependents;

4.1.6 Preparation and shipment of remains and funeral expenses associated with the death of the Foreign Liaison Officer or the Foreign Liaison Officer's dependents;

4.1.7 Formal and informal training of the Foreign Liaison Officer, other than briefings on Host Participant requirements provided by the Contact Officer; and

4.1.8 All expenses in connection with the return of a Foreign Liaison Officer whose assignment has ended or been terminated, along with the Foreign Liaison Officer's dependents.

4.2 The Host Participant may provide such office facilities, equipment, supplies and services as may be necessary for the Foreign Liaison Officer to fulfill the purposes of this Arrangement, subject to reimbursement by the Parent Participant for the cost of the Foreign Liaison Officer's use of such facilities at rates determined by the Host Participant through the Foreign Military Sales (FMS).

4.3 The assignment of a Foreign Liaison Officer pursuant to this Arrangement will be subject to the Parent Participants' authorization and availability of Parent Participants' funds for such purposes.

SECTION V
SECURITY

5.1 The Host Participant will establish the maximum substantive scope and classification levels within which the disclosure of any Classified Information or controlled unclassified information (CUI) to the Foreign Liaison Officer will be permitted. The Host Participant will inform the Parent Participant of the level of security clearance required to permit the Foreign Liaison Officer access to such information. The Foreign Liaison Officer's access to such information and facilities will be consistent with, and limited by the terms of the Foreign Liaison Officer's assignment, the provisions of this SECTION and the Agreement between the Government of the United States of America and the Government of the Republic of Hungary concerning Security Measures for the Protection of Classified Military Information, signed at Washington on May 16, 1995, and any other arrangement between the Participants or their governments concerning access to such information and facilities. Further, access will at all times be limited to the minimum required to accomplish the purposes of this Agreement, and, at its discretion, the Host Participant may prohibit the Foreign Liaison Officer's right of access to any Host Participant facility or require that such access be supervised by Host Participant personnel. Nothing in this Arrangement shall be considered by the Participants to authorize unfettered access to Classified Information or CUI residing in the Host Participant's facilities or computers.

5.2 Each Participant will cause security assurances to be filed, through the Hungarian Embassy in Washington, DC, in the case of Hungarian personnel, and through the U.S. Embassy in Budapest in the case of U.S. personnel, stating the security clearances for the Foreign Liaison Officer being assigned by such Participant. The security assurances will be prepared and forwarded through prescribed channels in compliance with established Host Participant procedures. For the United States, the prescribed channels will be the IVP, as defined in Paragraph 1.7 of this Arrangement.

5.3 The Parent Participant will ensure that each assigned Foreign Liaison Officer is fully cognizant of, and complies with, applicable laws and regulations concerning the protection of proprietary information (such as patents, copyrights, know–how, and trade secrets), Classified Information and CUI disclosed to the Foreign Liaison Officer. This obligation will apply both during and after termination of an assignment as a Foreign Liaison Officer. Prior to taking up duties as a Foreign Liaison Officer, the Foreign Liaison Officer will be required to sign the certification at Annex A. Only individuals who execute the certification will be permitted to serve as Foreign Liaison Officers with the U.S. Joint Forces Command.

5.4 The Parent Participant will ensure that the Foreign Liaison Officer, at all times, complies with the security laws, regulations and procedures of the Host Government. Any violation of security procedures by a Foreign Liaison Officer during the Foreign Liaison Officer's assignment will be reported to the Parent Participant for appropriate action. Upon request by the Host Participant, the Parent Participant will remove any Foreign Liaison Officer who violates security laws, regulations, or procedures during his/her assignment.

5.5 All Classified Information made available to the Foreign Liaison Officer will be considered to be Classified Information furnished to the Government of Hungary and subject to the provisions of the Agreement concerning Security Measures for the Protection of Classified Military Information, signed at Washington May 16, 1995 and entered into force June 4, 1996. Classified Information made available under the agreement shall not be shared outside the Republic of Hungary without the express written consent of U.S. Joint Forces Command.

5.6 The Foreign Liaison Officer will not take custody of Classified Information or CUI in tangible form (for example, documents or electronic files), except as expressly permitted by the terms of the Host Participant certification of the Foreign Liaison Officer (and requested in writing by the Parent Government) for the following situations:

5.6.1 Couriers. The Foreign Liaison Officer may take custody of Classified Information to perform courier functions when authorized by the Host Participant certification for the Foreign Liaison Officer. The Classified Information will be packaged and receipted for in compliance with Host Participant requirements.

5.6.2 On-Site Storage. The Foreign Liaison Officer may be furnished a secure container for the temporary storage of Classified Information, consistent with the terms of the certification, provided the security responsibility and control of the container and its contents remains with the Host Participant.

SECTION VI
TECHNICAL AND ADMINISTRATIVE MATTERS

6.1 The Host Participant's certification or approval of an individual as a Foreign Liaison Officer will not bestow diplomatic or other special privileges on that individual.

6.2 To the extent authorized by the laws and regulations of the Host Government, and in accordance with SECTION IV of this Arrangement, the Host Participant may provide such administrative support as is necessary for the Foreign Liaison Officer to fulfill the purposes of this Arrangement, subject to reimbursement by the Parent Participant.

6.3 Exemption from taxes, customs or import duties, or similar charges for the Foreign Liaison Officer or the Foreign Liaison Officer's dependents will be governed by applicable laws and regulations or international arrangements or agreements between the Host and Parent Governments.

6.4 If office space is provided to the Foreign Liaison Officer by the Host Participant, the Host Participant will determine the normal working hours for the Foreign Liaison Officer.

6.5 The Parent Participant will ensure that the Host Participant is informed as far in advance as possible of any absences of the Foreign Liaison Officer.

6.6 The Foreign Liaison Officer and the Foreign Liaison Officer's dependents will be provided care in military medical and dental facilities to the extent permitted by applicable national law and policy, and applicable international agreements. Where a reciprocal agreement for health care exists between the Participants, the access entitlement of the Foreign Liaison Officer and the Foreign Liaison Officer's dependents is specified. For those personnel covered by such an agreement, care is generally provided free of charge. All Foreign Liaison Officers and their dependents not covered by a reciprocal agreement may be offered health care, on a reimbursable basis, in military facilities. Where military facilities are not available, the Foreign Liaison Officer will be responsible for all medical and dental costs incurred by himself/herself and the Foreign Liaison Officer's dependents. The Parent Participant will ensure that the Foreign Liaison Officer and the Foreign Liaison Officer's dependents are physically fit prior to the Foreign Liaison Officer's tour of duty. The Parent Participant will be responsible for familiarizing itself with the medical and dental services available to the Foreign Liaison Officer and Foreign Liaison Officer's dependents, and the costs of, and the procedures for, use of such services.

6.7 The Foreign Liaison Officer and the Foreign Liaison Officer's dependents will be accorded the use of military commissaries, exchanges, theaters and similar morale and welfare activities, in accordance with the laws, regulations, and policies of the Host Participant and international agreements to which the Host and Parent Participants are party.

6.8 To the extent permitted by the laws and regulations of the Host Government, and subject to reimbursement by the Parent Participant, the Host Participant will provide, if available, housing and messing facilities for the Foreign Liaison Officer and the Foreign Liaison Officer's dependents on the same basis and priority as for its own personnel of comparable rank and assignment. At locations where housing and messing facilities are not provided by the Host Participant, the Host Participant will use reasonable efforts to assist the Parent Participant to locate such facilities for the Foreign Liaison Officer and the Foreign Liaison Officer's dependents.

6.9 The Parent Participant will ensure that the Foreign Liaison Officer and the Foreign Liaison Officer's dependents have all documentation required by the Host Government for entry into and exit from the country of the Host Government and at the time of such entry or exit. Unless exempted under an applicable international agreement between the Participants, Foreign Liaison Officers and their dependents entering the United States will be required to comply with United States Customs Regulations.

6.10 The Parent Participant will ensure that the Foreign Liaison Officer and those dependents accompanying the Foreign Liaison Officer will obtain motor vehicle liability insurance coverage for their private motor vehicles, in accordance with applicable laws, regulations and policies of the Host Participant, or the political subdivisions of the country of the Host Participant in which the Foreign Liaison Officer and the Foreign Liaison Officer's dependents are located.

SECTION VII
DISCIPLINE AND REMOVAL

7.1 Except as provided in Paragraph 7.2, neither the Host Participant nor the armed forces of the Host Government may take disciplinary action against a Foreign Liaison Officer who commits an offense under the military laws or regulations of the Host Participant, nor will the Host Participant exercise disciplinary powers over the Foreign Liaison Officer's dependents. The Parent Participant, however, will take such administrative or disciplinary action against the Foreign Liaison Officer as may be appropriate under the circumstances, to ensure compliance with this Arrangement, and the Participants will cooperate in the investigation of any offenses under the laws or regulations of either Participant.

7.2 The certification or approval of a Foreign Liaison Officer may be withdrawn, modified or curtailed at any time by the Host Participant for any reason, including, but not limited to, the violation of the regulations or laws of the Host Participant or the Host Government. In addition, at the request of the Host Participant, the Parent Government will remove the Foreign Liaison Officer or a dependent of the Foreign Liaison Officer from the territory of the Host Government. The Host Participant will provide an explanation for its removal request, but a dispute between the Participants concerning the sufficiency of the Host Participant's reasons, will not be grounds to delay the removal of the Foreign Liaison Officer or Foreign Liaison Officer's dependents.

7.3 A Foreign Liaison Officer will not exercise any supervisory or disciplinary authority over military or civilian personnel of the Host Participant.

SECTION VIII
SETTLEMENT OF DISPUTES

8.1 Disputes arising under or relating to this Arrangement will be resolved only through consultations between the Participants and will not be referred to an individual, national or international tribunal, or to any other forum for settlement.

SECTION IX
ENTRY INTO EFFECT, AMENDMENT, DURATION, AND TERMINATION

9.1 All obligations of the Participants under this Arrangement will be subject to national laws and the availability of appropriated funds for such purposes.

9.2 The Parent Participant will ensure that the Foreign Liaison Officer complies with all obligations and restrictions applicable to the Foreign Liaison Officer under this Arrangement.

9.3 This Arrangement may be amended by the mutual written concurrence of the Participants.

9.4 This Arrangement may be terminated at any time with the written concurrence of both Participants. In the event both Participants determine to terminate this Arrangement, the Participants will consult prior to the date of termination.

9.5 Either Participant may terminate this Arrangement upon 180 days written notification to the other Participant.

9.6 In the event of conflict between the terms of this Arrangement and the terms of an applicable Letter of Offer and Acceptance (LOA) , the terms of the LOA will control. Any LOAs associated with or related to this Arrangement will terminate in accordance with their terms.

9.7 The respective rights and responsibilities of the Participants under SECTION V (Security) will continue, notwithstanding the termination or expiration of this Arrangement.

9.8 No later than the effective date of expiration or termination of this Arrangement, each Participant will remove its Foreign Liaison Officer and such Foreign Liaison Officer's dependents from the territory of the other Participant and pay any money owed to the other Participant under this Arrangement. Any costs or expenses for which a Participant is responsible pursuant to SECTION IV of this Arrangement, but were not billed in sufficient time to permit payment prior to termination or expiration of this Arrangement, will be paid promptly after such billing.

9.9 This Arrangement will supercede any and all prior arrangements regarding Foreign Liaison Officers entered into by the Participants or their organizations, units, or agencies.

9.10 This Arrangement will enter into effect upon signature by both Participants. This Arrangement will remain in force for five (5) years, and may be extended with the written concurrence of the Participants.

9.11 This Arrangement consists of nine (9) SECTIONS and an Annex.

IN WITNESS WHEREOF, the undersigned, being duly authorized, have signed this Arrangement.

ON BEHALF OF
THE MINISTRY OF DEFENCE OF THE
REPUBLIC OF HUNGARY

[Signature]

JANOS MIKITA
Lieutenant General Eng.
Deputy Chief of Defence Staff,
Ministry of Defence
of the Republic of Hungary

22 September 2006
Date

ON BEHALF OF
UNITED STATES
U.S. JOINT FORCES COMMAND

[Signature]

JOHN R. WOOD
Lieutenant General, U.S. Army
Deputy Commander
U.S. Joint Forces Command

23 October 2006
Date

ANNEX A – CERTIFICATION

[Date]

SECTION I
FOREIGN LIAISON OFFICER
LEGAL STATUS OF CERTIFICATION

As a representative of the Ministry of Defence of the Republic of Hungary, under the auspices of a Foreign Liaison Officer Assignment to the U.S. Joint Forces Command, I am subject to the jurisdiction of United States federal, state, and local laws, except as provided by treaty, other specific legal authority, or the terms of any diplomatic immunity that I may have been granted. I understand that my acceptance of the Foreign Liaison Officer position does not bestow upon me diplomatic or other special privileges.

SECTION II
FOREIGN LIAISON OFFICER
CONDITIONS OF CERTIFICATION

(1) **Responsibilities**: I understand that my activities shall be limited to the representational responsibilities of my Government and that I am expected to present the views of my Government with regard to the issues that my government and the U.S. Government have a mutual interest. I shall not perform duties that are reserved by law or regulation to an officer or employee of the U.S. Government.

(2) **Costs**: I understand that all costs associated with my duties as a Foreign Liaison Officer will be the responsibility of my Government, including, but not limited to, travel, office space, clerical services, housing, messing, and medical and dental services.

(3) **Extensions and Revalidation**: I understand that if my Government desires to request an extension or revalidation of my position beyond the original dates for which I am certified, a new visit request will be submitted not later than thirty (30) days prior to the expiration date of the current Foreign Liaison Officer Assignment Authorization.

(4) **Contact Officer**: I understand that when the certification process is completed, a Contact Officer will be assigned to sponsor me during my visit to the U.S. Joint Forces Command. I further understand that I will coordinate, through my Contact Officer, all requests for information, visits, and other business that fall under the terms of my certification. I also understand that requests for information that are beyond the terms of my certification will be made through the Office of the Defence Attaché.

(5) **Other Visits**: I understand that visits to facilities for which the purpose does not directly relate to the terms of my certification will be made through the Office of the Defence Attaché.

(6) **Uniform**: I understand that I will wear my national uniform when conducting business at the U.S. Joint Forces Command or other Department of Defense facilities, unless otherwise directed. I will comply with my Parent Government's service uniform regulations.

(7) **Duty Hours**: I understand that my duty hours are Monday through Friday, from 0800 to 1700. Should I require access to my work area during non-duty hours, I am required to request permission from the Command Security Officer through my Contact Officer.

(8) **Security**:

a. I understand that access to U.S. Government information shall be limited to that information determined by my Contact Officer to be necessary to fulfill the functions of a Foreign Liaison Officer. I also understand that I may not have access to U.S. Government computer systems, unless all information accessible by the computer is releasable to my Government in accordance with applicable U.S. law, regulations and policy.

b. All information to which I may have access during my certification shall be treated as information provided in confidence to my Government and will not be further released or disclosed by me to any other person, firm, organization, or government without the prior written authorization of the U. S. Government.

c. I shall immediately report to my Contact Officer should I obtain or become knowledgeable of U.S. Government information for which I am not authorized to have access. I further agree that I will report to my Contact Officer any incidents of my being offered or provided information that I am not authorized to have.

d. If required, I will display a security badge on my outer clothing so that it is clearly visible. The U.S. Government will supply this badge.

(9) **Compliance**: I have been briefed on, fully understand, and will comply with the terms and conditions of my certification. Failure to comply may result in termination of my certification. I further understand that the termination of my certification does not preclude further disciplinary action in accordance with any applicable Status of Forces Agreement or other government–to–government arrangements or agreements.

(10) **Definitions of Terms**: Terms not defined herein will have the definitions ascribed to them in the applicable Arrangement governing my assignment as a Foreign Liaison Officer.

SECTION III
FOREIGN LIAISON OFFICER
TERMS OF CERTIFICATION

(1) **Contact Officer**: __________ has been assigned as my Contact Officer.

(2) **Certification**: I am certified to the U.S. Joint Forces Command and will represent the Ministry of Defence of the Republic of Hungary, to the U.S. Joint Forces Command, as mutually determined by both Participants.

(3) **Travel**: I may visit the following locations under the terms of my certification, with the permission of my Contact Officer:

–U.S. Joint Forces Command facilities;
–U.S. Joint Forces Command subordinate activities; and
–Designated areas within the Pentagon.

SECTION IV
FOREIGN LIAISON OFFICER CERTIFICATION OF IN-BRIEFING

I,__________________, understand and acknowledge that I have been certified as a Foreign Liaison Officer to the U.S. Joint Forces Command, as determined between the Ministry of Defence of the Republic of Hungary and the U.S. Joint Forces Command. I further acknowledge that I fully understand and have been briefed on: (1) the legal status of my certification; (2) the conditions of my certification; and (3) the terms of my certification. I further acknowledge that I shall comply with the conditions and responsibilities of my certification.

____
(SIGNATURE OF LIAISON OFFICER)

(TYPED NAME OF LIAISON OFFICER)

(RANK AND/OR TITLE)

____
(DATE)

____
(SIGNATURE OF BRIEFER)

____
(TYPED NAME)

____
(LOCATION)

STATE DEPARTMENT DOCUMENT NUMBER: 06-280

AMENDMENT TO THE AGREEMENT OF DECEMBER 30, 2002, AS AMENDED, BETWEEN THE DEPARTMENT OF DEFENSE OF THE UNITED STATES OF AMERICA AND THE MINISTRY OF DEFENSE OF GEORGIA CONCERNING COOPERATION IN THE AREA OF PREVENTION OF PROLIFERATION OF TECHNOLOGY, PATHOGENS, AND EXPERTISE RELATED TO THE DEVELOPMENT OF BIOLOGICAL WEAPONS

SIGNED AT TBILISI AND WASHINGTON D.C.,
JUNE 21 AND 23, 2006
ENTERED INTO FORCE OCTOBER 25, 2006

CTIA DOCUMENT NUMBER: 11506.004

Pursuant to Article VII of the Agreement between the Department of Defense of the United States of America and the Ministry of Defense of Georgia "*Concerning Cooperation In The Area Of Prevention Of Proliferation Of Technology, Pathogens And Expertise Related To The Development Of Biological Weapons*", dated December 30, 2002, as amended in March 23, 2004, August 30, 2004, and November 3, 2005 (hereinafter referred to as "the Agreement"), the Department of Defense of the United States of America and the Ministry of Defense of Georgia hereby agree to amend Article III, Paragraph 1 by replacing the words "sixty (60) million" with the words "ninety five (95) million".

This Amendment shall enter into force upon the date on which the parties exchange written notifications confirming the completion by each Party of all applicable procedures, and it shall remain in force for the duration of the Agreement.

IN WITNESS WHEREOF, the undersigned, being duly authorized by their respective governments, have signed this Amendment.

Done at Tbilisi, this *21st* day of *June*, 2006, and at Washington, this *23rd* day of *June*, 2006, in duplicate, each in the Georgian and English leanguages, both texts being equally authentic.

SIGNATURES:

on behalf of the Department of Defense of the United States of America:

[Signature]

on behalf of the Ministry of Defense of Georgia:

[Signature]

STATE DEPARTMENT DOCUMENT NUMBER: 06-281

AMENDMENT AND EXTENSION OF THE MEMORANDUM OF UNDERSTANDING BETWEEN THE UNITED STATES OF AMERICA NATIONAL AERONAUTICS AND SPACE ADMINISTRATION (NASA) AND THE EUROPEAN SPACE AGENCY CONCERNING ESA PARTICIPATION IN THE HUBBLE SPACE TELESCOPE PROGRAM

SIGNED ON OCTOBER 19 AND
OCTOBER 23, 2001
ENTERED INTO FORCE OCTOBER 23, 2001

CTIA DOCUMENT NUMBER: 13086.002

The United States National Aeronautics and Space Administration (NASA) and the European Space Agency (ESA),

Desiring to continue their cooperation with respect to the Hubble Space Telescope Program under their Memorandum of Understanding of October 7, 1977 (the "MOU"),

Desiring to. continue this successful cooperation until the end of operations of the HST,

Deciding to amend and extend the MOU as specified herein,

Hereby agree as follows:

1. All references to "Space Telescope" throughout the MOU shall be replaced with "Hubble Space Telescope," and all references to "ST" throughout the MOU shall be replaced by "HST."

2. Add a new paragraph (h) to ARTICLE 7 of the MOU, as follows:

> The science operations facility referred to in Article 7(g) as being established by NASA is the Space Telescope Science Institute (STScI) located in Baltimore, Maryland. The STScI is a NASA contractor-operated facility. NASA and ESA recognize that certain HST activities are supported by the STScI and the Space Telescope European Coordinating Facility (ST-ECF) in Garching, Germany. Both Parties acknowledge that ESA personnel resident at STScI as provided for in Article 4(c) are fully integrated members of the STScI team.

3. Replace the existing paragraph (b)(v) of ARTICLE 8 of the MOU with the following:

The parties are obligated to transfer only those technical data (including software) and goods necessary to fulfill their respective responsibilities under this Memorandum of Understanding, in accordance with the following provisions:

(1) Transfer of technical data necessary for interface, integration or safety purposes:

The transfer of technical data (excluding software) for the purpose of discharging the Parties' responsibilities with regard to interface, integration, and safety shall normally be made without restriction, except as required by national laws and regulations relating to export control or the control of classified data. If design, manufacturing, and processing data and associated software, which are proprietary but not export controlled, or are necessary for interface, integration, or safety purposes, the transfer shall be made and the data and associated software shall be appropriately marked.

(2) All other transfers of proprietary technical data, export-controlled goods and export-controlled technical data are subject to the following provisions:

In the event a Party finds it necessary to transfer goods which are subject to export control or technical data which are proprietary or subject to export controls, and for which protection is to be maintained, such goods shall be specifically identified and such technical data shall be marked with a notice to indicate that they shall be used and disclosed by the receiving Party and its related entities (e.g., contractors and subcontractors) only for the purposes of fulfilling the receiving Party's responsibilities under the programs implemented by this MOU, and that the identified goods and marked technical data shall not be disclosed or retransferred to any other entity without the prior written permission of the furnishing Party.

The receiving party shall abide by the terms of the notice, and shall protect any such identified goods and marked technical data from unauthorized use and disclosure, and shall also obtain these same obligations from its related entities prior to the transfer.

(3) All goods, marked proprietary data, and marked or unmarked technical data subject to export control, which are transferred under this MOU shall be used by the receiving Party exclusively for the purposes of the programs implemented by this MOU.

(4) The Parties are not required to transfer goods or technical data contrary to national laws and regulations relating to export control or control Of classified data.

4. Replace the existing ARTICLES 14 and 15 of the MOU, including their titles, with the following:

Rights in Resulting Data

1. Final results of the experiments shall be made available to the scientific community through publication in appropriate journals or other established channels as soon as practicable and consistent with good scientific practice. Reprints of scientific and technical reports and publications resulting from this project will be exchanged between ESA and NASA. In the event such reports or publications are copyrighted, NASA and ESA shall have a royalty-free right under the copyright to reproduce, distribute, and use such copyrighted work for their purposes. Final reports and publications will be placed in the Data Library of ESA and in the science operations facility at the STScL

2. Following the period of first publication, records or copies of processed data will be deposited in the HST data archive at STScI and in the Data Library of ES A. It is currently planned that at the end of the HST mission, the processed data would be deposited in the U.S. National Space Science Data Center (NSSDC).

5. Replace the existing ARTICLE 22 of the MOU as follows:

This Memorandum of Understanding shall remain in force until April 24, 2006. At least 1 year before the expiration of this Memorandum of Understanding, the Parties agree to consult as to continuation of this Memorandum of Understanding. This Memorandum of Understanding may be terminated by either Party after 6 months notice of its intention to terminate.

This amendment shall enter into force on the date of the last signature below:

FOR THE UNITED STATES
NATIONAL AERONAUTICS AND
SPACE ADMINISTRATION

[Signature]
Date: *10/19/01*

FOR THE EUROPEAN SPACE AGENCY:

[Signature]
Date: *23/10/01*

Letterhead of European Space Agency

Mr Daniel S. Goldin
Administrator
NASA Headquarters
Washington, D.C. 20546-0001
U.S.A.
Paris. 23 AVR. 2001

Dear Mr Goldin.

I refer to your letter of 20 April 2001 proposing that the Memorandum of Understanding (MoU) between the European Space Agency (ESA) and the National Aeronautical Space Administration (NASA) for cooperation on the Hubble Space Telescope of 7 October 1977 be amended, extending its current expiration date of 24 April 2001 for six months, that is, until 24 October 2001, and that in the intervening time period NASA and ESA will continue to negotiate additional amendments to the MoU permitting the cooperation to continue for an additional 4 ½ years from the date of expiration of this extension, that is, until 24 April 2006.

I am pleased to inform you that your proposal is acceptable to ESA and therefore consider that your above-referenced letter, together with this affirmative reply, constitute an extension of the MoU.

Yours sincerely,

[Signature]

ACTING DIRECTOR GENERAL
Antonio Rodota

Letterhead of National Aeronautics and
Space Administration
Office of the Administrator
Washington, DC 20546-0001

Mr. Antonio Rodota
Director General
European Space Agency
8-10, rue Mario Nikis
75738 Paris Cedex. 15
France

Dear Mr. Rodota:

Pursuant to Article 21 of the Memorandum of Understanding (MOU) between the European Space Agency (ESA) and the United States National Aeronautics and Space Administration (NASA) for cooperation on the Hubble Space Telescope (HST) signed on October 7, 1977, and in order to continue our beneficial collaboration on the HST, I propose that we amend the MOU extending its current expiration date of April 24, 2001, for 6 months, that is, until October 24, 2001. In the intervening time period, NASA and ESA will continue to negotiate additional amendments to the MOU permitting the cooperation to continue for an additional 4½ years from the date of expiration of this extension, that is, until April 24, 2006.

If this proposal is acceptable to ESA, I propose that this letter, together with your affirmative written reply, constitute an amendment of the MOU.

Sincerely,

[Signature]

Daniel S. Goldin
Administrator

MEMORANDUM OF UNDERSTANDING BETWEEN THE EUROPEAN SPACE AGENCY AND THE UNITED STATES NATIONAL AERONAUTICS AND SPACE ADMINISTRATION

ARTICLE 1
Purpose

The European Space Agency (ESA) and the United States National Aeronautics and Space Administration (NASA), desiring to extend the fruitful cooperation developed in previous space projects, agree that ESA will participate in the NASA 2-4 Meter Space Telescope (ST) Project, as described below.

ARTICLE 2
Mission

The mission of the ST Project is to provide a space observatory for use by the international astronomy community to extend the sensitivity, resolving power and spectral range of astronomical observations decisively beyond those achievable from earth observatories.

ARTICLE 3
Participation

1. To carry out this project, NASA plans to launch the ST by means of the Space Shuttle in 1983/1984 and to operate it for a period of 10 to 15 years. ESA agrees to assist in the provision of scientific instruments and subsystems for the ST, in the operation of the ST and related facilities, in the in-orbit maintenance, major refurbishments and reflights, at anticipated intervals of two or three years, and to arrange for participation of ESA-sponsored astronomers in the observation programs.

2. ESA will carry out its participation in accordance with the plans, specifications and schedules contained in the NASA/ESA ST Project Plan annexed to this Memorandum of Understanding. This plan may be subject to change as defined in Article 7 (d) below.

ARTICLE 4
ESA responsibilities

To implement the cooperation in this project ESA will:

(a) Provide the Faint Object Camera (FOC), a scientific instrument of high sensitivity for high resolution imagery in the ultraviolet, visual, and near infrared portions of the spectrum. The performance specification for this instrument is included in the NASA/ESA ST Project Plan annexed to this Memorandum of Understanding.

With respect to the provision of the FOC, ESA will:

(i) design, fabricate, test, calibrate and deliver for integration into the ST the FOC, comprising the camera optics and an Imaging Photon Counting System (IPCS). The FOC models and associated hardware together with the schedule for their delivery are defined in the NASA/ESA ST Project Plan;

(ii) provide personnel and equipment to support NASA activities relating to testing, integration of the FOC with the ST, and launch site operations, as defined in the NASA/ESA ST Project Plan;

(iii) set up an ESA Instrument Science Team (IST) to ensure the scientific integrity of the definition and design of the FOC, and its compatibility with the telescope, and to provide scientific advice for the ESA project management, which will manage FOC development. It is agreed that at least one NASA-appointed scientist will be a member of the IST;

(iv) provide participation in NASA reviews in accordance with Article 8 (b) (iii) below;

(v) develop the ground and flight software packages uniquely required for the FOC, as defined in the NASA/ESA ST Project Plan;

(vi) provide a team of two to four instrument and data scientists to support the operations of the FOC after launch, as mutually agreed; and,

(vii) refurbish the FOC for reflight, and provide necessary support for maintenance or modification of the FOC in-orbit, when mutually agreed. In the event NASA wishes to refurbish or modify the FOC and ESA does not desire to do either, ESA will provide the available documentation and other support as agreed between the Project Managers.

(b) Provide the ST Solar Array. In this respect, ESA will:

(i) design, fabricate, test and deliver to the NASA Support Systems Module (SSM) contractor for integration with the Space Telescope a complete solar array and associated hardware, the performance specification, interface requirements, number of models and hardware parts and their delivery schedule being defined in the NASA/ESA ST Project Plan;

(ii) provide personnel and equipment to support the handling and testing of the solar arrays while they are not attached to the ST spacecraft, as defined in the NASA/ESA Project Plan;

(iii) provide appropriate representation in NASA reviews in accordance with Article 8 (b) (iii) below;

(iv) maintain continuing engineering liaison with NASA ST project elements which interface with the ESA solar array;

(v) provide personnel and equipment to support NASA activities relating to testing, integration of the solar array with the ST, and launch site operations, as defined in the NASA/ESA ST Project Plan; and

(vi) refurbish, repair, and/or replace the solar array and provide support to NASA for its maintenance or modification in-orbit, as mutually agreed and reflected in the NASA/ESA ST Project Plan.

(c) Participate in the activities of the science operations facility as described in Article 7 (g) below. In this respect ESA will, in particular:

(i) provide a team of approximately six persons to support one shift of the

scientific planning and operation tasks of the science operations facility;

(ii) provide a team of approximately seven persons to support the ST scientific data reduction shift of the science operations facility;

(iii) provide membership to this facility, as mutually agreed, in order to participate in the definition and implementation of the ST science activities; and

(iv) provide a representative to NASA to serve as a focal point for NASA/ESA consultations regarding the establishment and operation of the science operations facility;

it being understood that the members of the ESA teams mentioned in (i) and (ii) above will be considered functionally as members of the science operations facility.

ARTICLE 5
NASA responsibilities

To carry out the cooperation in this project, NASA will:

(a) Design, fabricate, test, integrate and prepare for launching the complete ST assembly.

(b) Define jointly with ESA the solar array interfaces, design requirements, and test and handling specification, and provide this information to ESA in accordance with the schedule defined in the NASA/ESA ST Project Plan.

(c) Test the solar array when it is integrated on the ST and supply ESA with relevant engineering data. NASA is responsible for handling of the solar array after its acceptance at the integration site.

(d) Provide appropriate representation at ESA reviews in accordance with Article 8 (b) (iv) below.

(e) Provide and transport to the launch site all necessary ST ground support equipment, including items delivered by ESA to the test and integration sites to support the FOC and the solar array.

(f) Transport to the launch site the flight qualified ST and perform necessary tests and checkout prior to launch.

(g) Provide initial launching of the ST on a Space Shuttle, release the ST into the designated orbit, and conduct, with ESA participation, checkout of the ST as required for a period of approximately 30 days following launch.

(h) Provide all tracking and data acquisition services during the lifetime of the project.

(i) Exercise all in-orbit control functions. To accomplish this, NASA will organise, equip, staff, train and operate an operations center.

(j) Include the FOC in the payload of the first flight of the ST and operate it in accordance with the provisions of Article 6 below.

(k) Establish a science operations facility to conduct scientific operations, as outlined in Article 7 (g) below.

(l) Provide In-orbit maintenance, and retrieve and relaunch the ST when necessary according to operations plans, and conduct refurbishment and in-orbit modification operations assists! by ESA as provided in Articles 4 (a) (vii) and 4 (b) (vi) above.

ARTICLE 6
Flight and Operation of the ESA-supplied F0C

1. The following principles shall apply to the flights of the ESA-supplied FOC:

(a) Assuming normal functioning, it will be operated by NASA for a nominal initial period of thirty months.

(b) Following this period, it will be flown as long as it is decided to be a component of the scientifically optimum payload.

(c) Following the initial or subsequent operating periods, both parties may nevertheless agree that NASA will continue to fly it In modified form, in application of Article 4 (a) (vii), or replace it for a given period by another scientific instrument.

(d) If the FOC fails to meet the minimum scientific requirements laid down in the performance specification as defined In the NASA/ESA ST Project Plan, or if the delivery by ESA would substantially delay the first flight, NASA may decide, after consultation with ESA, to launch the ST without the FOC. In this event, provided that, at the relevant time, the FOC does meet the minimum scientific requirements referred to above, NASA will take its availability into account when funding the development of ST instruments for subsequent flights and accept it as a candidate instrument for those flights.

2. Decisions concerning the implementation of the provision of the foregoing paragraph shall be made by the NASA Associate Administrator for Space Science and the appropriate Director at ESA Headquarters, subject to the application of the provisions of Article 18 of this Memorandum of Understanding.

ARTICLE 7
Management and Organisation

Unless otherwise provided in this Memorandum of Understanding, the management arrangements are understood by NASA and ESA to be as follows:

(a) NASA will establish a ST Project Office to provide for project planning and management, with the following responsibilities:

(i) Overall responsibility for the design, fabrication, test, integration, launch, In-orbit verification, and operation of the ST;

(ii) flight performance evaluation, and planning for and carrying out in-orbit maintenance and modification; and

(iii) planning and carrying out ST refurbishments.

(b) The Project Office will be headed by a NASA Project Manager. To carry out the ST Project, the Project Manager will be supported by a full-time staff of managers and engineers. Full responsibility for management of the ST Project resides with the NASA Project Manager. The Project Office provides the principal means for carrying out these management responsibilities.

(c) ESA will:

(i) Designate an ESA Project Manager for overall coordination, planning and execution of the ESA tasks described in this Memorandum of Understanding, and will assign appropriate representation to the ST Project Office, as mutually agreed; and

(ii) appoint an ESA Project Scientist.

(d) Management and technical decisions which have a bearing on the execution of ESA tasks as described under this Memorandum of Understanding or affect the contents of the annexed NASA/ESA ST Project Plan, and items with respect to which mutual agreement is necessary in accordance with provisions of this Memorandum, shall be taken in common by the NASA and the ESA Project Managers. If they are unable to come to an agreement on a particular issue, it shall be referred to the NASA Associate Administrator for Space Science for resolution in consultation with the appropriate Director at ESA Headquarters, subject to the application of the provisions of Article 18 of this Memorandum of Understanding.

(e) NASA will establish a Space Telescope Science. Working Group (ST-SWG) which will be the principal mechanism for scientific input to the Project Office during the development of the ST. The ST-SWG will be chaired by the ST Project Scientist designated by NASA. The ESA membership on the ST-SWG will consist of the ESA Project Scientist referred to in paragraph (c) of this Article and of the Chairman of the ESA IST referred to in Article 4 (a) (iii), who will be assisted by such members of his team as he desires to be present for specific ST-SWG meetings.

(f) NASA will establish a mission operations center, as defined in the NASA/ESA Project Plan to:

(i) Carry out mission operations planning;

(ii) execute ST command and control;

(iii) acquire data on and evaluate ST engineering performance;

(iv) report ST anomalies;

(v) reduce ST engineering data; and

(vi) acquire and process ST scientific data.

(g) NASA will establish a science operations facility to carry out scientific management of the observatory in orbit. Operational support of the investigators by this facility will include, but is not limited to:

(i) Planning long-term scientific operations;

(ii) scheduling daily scientific observations;

(iii) conducting real time scientific observations; and

(iv) performing ST scientific data management, including making available ST scientific data to investigators in a form suitable for analysis.

ESA will be represented and participate in this facility in accordance with the provisions of Article 4 (c).

ESA participation in the daily activities of the science operations facility will include, but will not be limited to the provision of the support provided under Article 4 (a) (vi) and 4 (c) above.

ARTICLE 8
Technical Interfaces

The management of the technical interfaces on the ST will be carried out with a minimum of documentation and formal reviews. It is understood between ESA and NASA that the following principles and procedures will apply:

(a) General Responsibilities for Technical Interfaces:

(i) The NASA Project Manager, in accordance with Article 7 (b) above. Is responsible for the management of the interfaces, including documentation, general control of the use of such documentation, and the conduct of technical reviews on all systems for which NASA is responsible.

(ii) The ESA Project Manager is responsible to work to such requirements and interfaces as he and the NASA Project Manager have mutually agreed to, and for the conduct of technical reviews to insure that all systems and hardware for which ESA is responsible comply with ST interface requirements.

(b) Specific Responsibilities and Procedures:

(i) The NASA Project Manager will review and mutually agree with the ESA Project Manager, as to which standards and specifications will be considered to constitute the requirements for control purposes in the ST Project. The agreed standards and specifications, if any, will be referenced as part of the NASA/ESA ST Project Plan.

(ii) ESA will supply data to NASA for the generation of appropriate Interface Requirements Documentation (IRD's), Interface Control Drawings (ICD's) and Contract End Item (CEI) Specifications Part I for the Solar array and the FOC. The CEI Specifications Part II for the Solar array and the FOC will be generated by ESA. The Project Managers will mutually agree on these documents, and the NASA Project Manager will approve them in accordance with a schedule in the NASA/ESA ST Project Plan. Subsequent modifications to either the IRD's, the ICD's, or the CEI Specifications will be approved by appropriate change control procedures identified in the NASA/ESA ST Project Plan. Should such modifications seem unacceptable to either Project Manager for financial or schedule reasons, the provisions of Article 18 will apply.

(iii) NASA will make final determination of the overall readiness of the ST for launching. This determination will be based on periodic reviews chaired by NASA to address the concept, design, and readiness for flight of the ST. ESA will have appropriate representation at selected reviews and will furnish engineering data as agreed by the Project Managers.

(iv) Determination of the readiness for integration of the solar array and the FOC will be based on periodic reviews, chaired by ESA, of the concept, design and readiness for flight of the hardware. NASA will have appropriate representation at these reviews as agreed between the Project Managers and will furnish engineering data as agreed by the Project Managers. Final determination of the readiness for integration of the solar array and the FOC will be the responsibility of the NASA Project Manager, based on recommendations from the ESA Project Manager and review committees.

(v) NASA and ESA shall have full access to, and the right to use and disclose, non-proprietary data necessary to discharge their respective responsibilities under this Memorandum of Understanding. In principle, there will be no transfer of documents bearing proprietary or other restrictive markings. To achieve this, optimal use will be made of mathematical models, mock ups and simulators, as appropriate to assure hardware interface and operations compatibility. Should either party consider that the above limitation prevents it from carrying out a particular responsibility under this Memorandum of Understanding, the Project Managers will determine a mutually agreeable solution on a case-by-case basis. In the event that the solution must involve the transfer of proprietary data, the furnishing party, with the consent of the proprietor, shall furnish the data and shall mark them with a notice limiting the use and disclosure of the information for ST Project purposes only, and the receiving party will use its best efforts to comply with such limitations.

(vi) Detailed arrangements for working level technical interfaces, including NASA and ESA contractors, are defined in the NASA/ESA ST Project Plan.

ARTICLE 9
Apportionment of Observing Time

1. The term "observing time" as used in this Article is understood to mean that time during which the ST instruments are in operation, less idle time and time necessary for calibration, testing and maintenance.

2. NASA and ESA agree that ST observing time will be made available to investigators from the international community of astronomers on the basis of the scientific merit of proposals made.

3. Subject to the application of this principle, and in consideration of ESA's participation as defined in this Memorandum of Understanding, ESA will obtain, for use by ESA-sponsored astronomers, a portion of the observing time on the total complement of scientific instruments of the ST. It is

expected and intended that this portion will be not less than 15% of the observing time on the average over the lifetime of the ST Project.

ARTICLE 10
Selection of Observing Programs

1. All proposals for observing programs from astronomers in ESA member States will be submitted In accordance with ESA procedures to the ST Proposal Review Committee (STPRC). which will be the primary body for the review and evaluation of all proposals for observing programs to be carried out on the ST.

2. The STPRC will have an appropriate European membership (minimum of two) the number to be agreed between ESA and NASA Headquarters. It will make recommendations for observing programs to the NASA Associate Administrator for Space Science, who, after consultation with ESA as necessary, will make a final determination of the observing programs.

3. Should ESA consider that the observing programs so determined are inconsistent with the provisions of Article 9, or should there be a major alteration in the ESA participation in the ST Project, either party may request a joint review of the evaluation and selection process.

ARTICLE 11
Deposit Accounts

Should ESA desire that NASA procure goods and services on ESA's behalf to assist ESA in carrying out an ESA responsibility under this Memorandum of Understanding, NASA 1s prepared to consider such requests on a case-by-case basis under the provisions of a Deposit Account Agreement to be negotiated separately. Similar requests from NASA will be treated by ESA accordingly.

ARTICLE 12
Funding Arrangements

Each Agency will arrange to meet the cost of discharging its responsibilities, including travel and subsistence for its own authorised personnel and transportation charges on all equipment and flight hardware for which it is responsible. Other than deposit account transactions referred to in Article 11, there will be no exchange of funds between ESA and NASA.

ARTICLE 13
Customs and Visas

ESA and NASA will use their best efforts to arrange free customs clearance for equipment required in the ST project. NASA-will use its best efforts to facilitate the issuance of visas to European astronomers and ESA contractors collaborating in the ST Project.

ARTICLE 14
Data rights

Use of ST scientific data for scientific analysts will be reserved to investigators for a twelve month period, beginning with the receipt of data and any associated spacecraft data in a form suitable for analysis. Investigators may occasionally be requested to share data to enhance efficient utilisation of the observatory and of ground observing operations. Immediately after the period reserved to the investigator reduced data will be deposited with the National Space Science Data Center (NSSDC) and with the science operations facility. In addition, European investigators will deposit their data in the Data Library of the European Space Operations Center (ESOC). Such records will then be available to the international scientific community through the World Data Center for Rockets and Satellites. It is agreed that a listing of all observations will be published at least every six months in sources readily available to astronomers.

ARTICLE 15
Publication of Results

Subject to the provisions of Article 14 above, results of the experiments will be made available to the scientific community in general through publication in appropriate journals or other established channels as soon as possible and consistent with good scientific practice. Reprints of scientific and technical reports and publications resulting from this project will be exchanged between ESA and NASA. In the event that such reports or publications are copyrighted, ESA and NASA shall have a royalty free right under the copyright to reproduce and use such copyrighted work for their purposes. Final reports and publications will be placed in the Data Library of ESOC and 1n the science operations facility.

ARTICLE 16
Public Information

Each Agency may release information to the public regarding its own activities covered by this Memorandum of Understanding. Each Agency undertakes to coordinate with the other in advance those public information activities which relate to the other Agency's responsibilities or performance in the ST project. Implementing arrangements for these public information activities will be agreed separately.

ARTICLE 17
Limits of obligation

It is understood that the ability of ESA and NASA to carry out their obligations under this Memorandum of Understanding is subject to the availability of appropriate funds.

ARTICLE 18
Disputes

1. Any dispute as to the interpretation or implementation of the terms of this Memorandum of Understanding shall be referred to the NASA Administrator and the Director General of ESA for settlement.

2. Should the NASA Administrator and the Director General of ESA be unable to resolve such disputes, they will be submitted to such other form of resolution or arbitration as they may agree.

ARTICLE 19
Liability

1. NASA shall bear responsibility for damage to US nationals in the course of this cooperative project, unless such nationals are employees of ESA.

2. ESA shall bear full responsibility for such damage to ESA employees.

3. NASA shall be liable for damage to those items delivered to it by ESA in accordance with Article 4, after the accomplishment of the relevant receiving inspections defined 1n the NASA/ESA ST Project Plan, but shall not be liable for damage occuring to such items in connection with the Space Shuttle launch, flight or descent.

4. In the event of damage to other persons or property, for which damage there is liability under international law or the principles of the Convention on International Liability for Damage caused by Space Objects, NASA and ESA shall consult promptly on an equitable sharing of any payments that have been or may be agreed In settlement. If agreement is not reached within 180 days, the two Agencies will act promptly to arrange for early arbitration to settle the sharing of such claims following the 1958 model rules on arbitral procedure of the International Law Commission.

ARTICLE 20
Patent use – Authorization. Consent and Indemnification

1. In order to avoid any possible interruption to the conduct of this cooperative project which might arise from patent infringement litigation in U.S. Courts, NASA hereby gives authorization and consent (without prejudice to any rights of indemnification) for all use and manufacture by ESA of any invention described in and covered by a patent of the United States in the performance of any obligations under this Memorandum of Understanding, including the performance of any such obligations by any contractor or subcontractor, providing such use and manufacture is confined entirely to the discharge of the obligations of this Memorandum of Understanding.

2. In the event any liability is incurred by the US Government for the practice of inventions covered by privately owned U.S. patents, either as royalties owed under an existing patent license inuring to the benefit of NASA or as judgement and litigation costs resulting from a suit for patent infringement in the U.S. Court of Claims, and such liability is incurred as a result of ESA's and/or any of its contractors' or subcontractors' performance of obligations under this Memorandum of Understanding, or as a result of NASA's use under this Memorandum of Understanding of the items furnished by ESA under this Memorandum of Understanding, ESA agrees to indemnify NASA or any other j U.S. Agency against, and make reimbursement for, such royalties and/or costs. ESA shall provide such information and assistance as it has available in the defense of any such patent Infringement suit brought in the U.S. Court of Claims.

ARTICLE 21
Amendments

Each party may propose to the other amendments to this Memorandum of Understanding, in writing. Agreements on such amendments shall be established by the parties in the form of riders to this Memorandum of Understanding.

ARTICLE 22
Termination

This Memorandum of Understanding shall enter into force when both the NASA Administrator and Director General of ESA have signed it, and It shall remain in effect for a first period of eleven years from the first launching of the ST. It is anticipated that this period will include at least ten years of ST space operations. At least one year before the expiration of the eleven year period, the parties agree to consult as to continuation or termination of this Memorandum of Understanding. The Memorandum of Understanding will continue in its present form unless it is terminated or amended.

For the National Aeronautics and Space Administration	For the European Space Agency
[Signature] Date: *7 Oct 1977*	[Signature] Date: *7 Oct 1977*

STATE DEPARTMENT DOCUMENT NUMBER: 06-282

STRATEGIC OBJECTIVE GRANT AGREEMENT BETWEEN THE UNITED STATES OF AMERICA AND THE REPUBLIC OF INDONESIA TO SUPPORT IMPROVED QUALITY OF DECENTRALIZED BASIC EDUCATION IN INDONESIA, WITH ANNEXES

SIGNED AT JAKARTA,
AUGUST 30, 2004
ENTERED INTO FORCE AUGUST 30, 2004

CTIA DOCUMENT NUMBER: 13065.000

Dated: August 30, 2004

Between

The Government of the United States of America, acting through the United States Agency for International Development ("USAID")

and

The Government of the Republic of Indonesia, acting through the Coordinating Ministry of People's Welfare (hereinafter referred to as the "Grantee")

WHEREAS, the Grantee and USAID (the "Parties) hereby express their commitment to support the improved quality of decentralized basic education in Indonesia as described herein;

NOW, THEREFORE, the Parties hereby agree as follows:

Article 1: Purpose.

The purpose of this Strategic Objective Grant Agreement ("Agreement") is to set out the understanding of the Parties named above about the Strategic Objective described below.

Article 2: Strategic Objective and Results.

Section 2.1. Strategic Objective. The Strategic Objective ("Objective") is to support the improved quality of decentralized basic education in Indonesia.

Section 2.2. Results. In order to achieve this Objective, the Parties agree to work together to strengthen the decentralized management and governance of schools, improve the quality of teaching and learning, and increase the relevance of junior secondary and non-formal education to work and life skills for youth in Indonesia, (the "Results") as described in Annex 1. Within the limits of the definition of the Objective in Section 2.1, this Section 2.2 may only be changed by written agreement of the authorized representatives of the Parties with formal amendment to the Agreement.

Section 2.3. Annex 1, Amplified Program Description. Annex 1, attached, amplifies the above Objective and Results. Annex 1 may be changed by written agreement of the authorized representatives of the Parties without formal amendment of this Agreement.

Article 3: Contributions of the Parties.

Section 3.1. USAID Contribution.

(a) The Grant. To help achieve the Objective set forth in this Agreement, USAID, pursuant to the Foreign Assistance Act of 1961, as amended, and in accordance with the budget contained in Annex 1, hereby grants to the Grantee under the terms of the Agreement up to Nineteen Million United States ("U.S.") Dollars ($19,000,000) (the "Grant").

(b) Total Estimated USAID Contribution. USAID's total estimated contribution to achievement of the Objective will be One Hundred Thirty Three Million U.S. Dollars ($133,000,000), which will be provided in increments. Subsequent increments will be subject to the availability of funds to USAID for this purpose and the mutual agreement of the Parties, at the time of each subsequent increment, to proceed.

(c) If at any time USAID determines that its contribution under Section 3.1(a) exceeds the amount which reasonably can be committed for achieving the Objective or Results or activities during the current or next U.S. fiscal year, USAID may, upon written notice to the Grantee, withdraw the excess amount, thereby reducing the amount of the Grant as set forth in Section 3.1(a). Actions taken pursuant to this subsection will not revise USAID's total estimated contribution set forth in 3.1(b). USAID will report at least annually in a format to be agreed upon by the Parties on its contribution.

Section 3.2. Grantee Contribution.

(a) The Grantee agrees to provide or cause to be provided all funds, in addition to those provided by USAID and any other donor identified in Annex 1, and all other resources required to complete, on or before the Completion Date, all activities necessary to achieve the Results.

(b) The Grantee's Total Estimated Planned Contributions to the Objective will not be less than the equivalent of Twenty-Five (25%) of USAID's Total Estimated Contribution in section 3.1(b) that is determined by USAID to fund activities that involve substantial Government of Indonesia benefit or involvement. No Government of Indonesia budgetary contributions are required. The Government of Indonesia will meet this requirement through attributions derived from existing nationally-implemented sectoral programs and contributions on an in-kind basis only. Acceptable attributions may include: capital goods, counterpart personnel, services and studies that support attainment of the Objective, rental or purchase of materials for operations or construction, administrative costs, land contributed by the Government of Indonesia to attainment of the Objective, and costs related to the above items, subject to availability of funds to the Grantee for this purpose, the mutual agreement of the Parties, at the time of each subsequent increment, to proceed, and USAID providing the total estimated amount in Section 3.1 (b). The Grantee will report at least annually in a format to be agreed upon by the Parties on its cash and "in-kind" contributions.

Article 4: Completion Date.

(a) The Completion Date, which is September 30, 2009, or such other date as the two Parties may agree to in writing, is the date by which the two Parties estimate that all the activities necessary to achieve the Objective and Results will be completed.

(b) Except as USAID may otherwise agree to in writing, USAID will not issue or approve documentation which would authorize disbursement of the Grant for services performed or goods furnished after the Completion Date.

(c) Requests for disbursement, accompanied by necessary supporting documentation prescribed in Implementation Letters, are to be received by USAID no later than nine (9) months following the Completion Date, or such other period as USAID agrees to in writing before or after such period. After such period USAID, at any time or times, may give notice in writing to the Grantee and reduce the amount of the Grant by all or any part thereof for which requests for disbursement, accompanied by necessary supporting documentation prescribed in Implementation Letters, were not received before the expiration of such period.

Article 5: Conditions Precedent to Disbursement.

Section 5.1. First Disbursement. Prior to the first disbursement under the Grant, or to the issuance by USAID of documentation pursuant to which disbursement will be made, the Grantee will, except as the Parties may otherwise agree in writing, furnish to USAID in form and substance satisfactory to USAID, a statement in the name of the person holding or acting in the office of the Grantee specified in Section 7.2, and of any additional representatives, together with a specimen signature of each person specified in such statement.

Section 5.2. Notification. USAID will promptly notify the Grantee when USAID has determined that a condition precedent has been met.

Section 5.3. Terminal Dates for Conditions Precedent. The terminal date for meeting the conditions specified in Section 5.1 -is 30 days from the date of this Agreement or such later date as USAID may agree to in writing before or after the above terminal date. If the conditions precedent in Section 5.1, have not been met by the above terminal date, USAID, at any time, may terminate this Agreement by written notice to the Grantee.

Article 6: Special Covenants

Section 6.1. Standard Provisions, Section F.1, F.2, and F.3 of Annex 2. After a thorough review, the Parties have determined that the activities proposed for funding under this Agreement do not in any way relate to the terms of Standard Provisions F.1, F.2, and F.3 of Annex 2. Should potential issues arise in the future under this Agreement, the Parties agree to work together to resolve any concerns related to Standard Provisions F.1, F.2, and F.3 of Annex 2.

Section 6.2. Implementation. In support of the Objectives of this Agreement, the Parties may conclude implementation arrangements as fully described in Section E.4, Coordination, of Annex 1 and Section A.2, Implementation Letters, of Annex 2.

Section 6.3. Contractors, Grantees and Other Organizations. Funding under this Agreement may be provided directly by USAID in the form of contracts, grants, cooperative agreements and other mechanisms to international and national private voluntary organizations, commercial entities, universities, international and national non-governmental organizations and other U.S. Government agencies that work as USAID partners to implement the Objective through the Amplified Program Description in Annex 1.

Section 6.4. Visas and Assignment Approvals. The Grantee, in conjunction with appropriate Government of the Republic of Indonesia ministries and offices, will ensure the prompt and timely approval and issuance of visas and assignment approvals for the employees, consultants, and experts of any contractor, grantee or other organization carrying out activities financed by USAID under this Agreement through an established procedure agreed to in writing by the Grantee and USAID.

Section 6.5. Taxation Exemption. Any contractor, grantee or other organization and their employees, except citizens of Indonesia, carrying out activities financed by USAID under this Agreement shall be exempt from taxation, including but not limited to custom duties, tariffs, import taxes, income tax, and value added taxes on income, equipment and property financed, leased or imported with USAID funding under this Agreement, as fully described in Section B.4 of the Standard Provisions in Annex 1, through an established procedure agreed to in writing by the Grantee and USAID.

Commodities acquired by USAID and its implementing partners (including contractors, grantees, sub-contractors and sub-grantees) that are financed under this Agreement shall be exempt from taxation including value-added taxes (VAT) and custom duties imposed by Indonesia. The Government of Indonesia shall provide reimbursement in a timely fashion to USAID or its partners for all taxes including VAT and custom duties that are imposed or it may be subject to a U.S. Congressional mandated withholding penalty of future U.S. foreign assistance. Commodities include materials, articles, supplies, goods and equipment.

In the event of a conflict, Section B.4 of the Standard Provisions is the controlling provision of the Agreement.

Article 7: Miscellaneous.

Section 7.1. Communications. Any notice, request, document, or other communication submitted by either Party to the other under this Agreement will be in writing or by telegram, telefax or cable, and will be deemed duly given or sent when delivered to such Party at the following address:

To USAID:

Mail Address:

United States Agency for International Development
American Embassy
Jl. Medan Merdeka Selatan 3–5
Jakarta 10110, Indonesia
Attention: Mission Director

Telefax: (62-21) 380-6694
Tel: (62-21)3435-9000

To the Grantee:

Mail Address:

Coordinating Ministry for People's Welfare
Jl. Medan Merdeka Barat 3
Jakarta 10110, Indonesia
Attention: Deputy for Education and State Administration

Telefax: (62-21) 345-3675
Tel: (62-21) 345-3675

All such communications will be in English, unless the Parties otherwise agree in writing. Other addresses may be substituted for the above upon the giving of notice.

Section 7.2. Representatives. For all purposes relevant to this Agreement, the Grantee will be represented by the individual holding or acting in the Office of Deputy for Education and State Administration, and USAID will be represented by the individual holding or acting in the Office of the Mission Director, each of whom, by written notice, may designate additional representatives for all purposes and any conditions governing actions of additional representatives other than signing formal amendments to the Agreement or exercising the power under Sections 2.2 or 2.3 to revise the Results or Annex 1. The names of the representatives of the Grantee, with specimen signatures, will be provided to USAID, which may accept as duly authorized any instrument signed by such representatives in implementation of this Agreement, until receipt of written notice of revocation of their authority.

Section 7.3. Standard Provisions Annex. A "Standard Provisions Annex" (Annex 2) is attached to and forms part of this Agreement.

IN WITNESS WHEREOF, the United States of America and the Grantee, each acting through its duly authorized representatives, have caused this Agreement to be signed in their names and delivered as of the day and year first above written.

GOVERNMENT OF
THE UNITED STATES OF
AMERICA

BY:

[Signature]

Name: Jon D. Lindborg

&Title: Acting USAID Mission
Director to Indonesia

BY:

[Signature]

Name: Ralph L. Boyce

Title: U.S. Ambassador to
Indonesia

GOVERNMENT OF
THE REPUBLIC OF INDONESIA

BY:

[Signature]

Name: Dr. Jahja Umar

Title: Deputy for Education and
State Administration, Coordinating
Ministry for People's Welfare

WITNESSED

BY:

[Signature]

Name: A. Malik Fajar

Title: Coordinating Minister for
People's Welfare

SOAG Annex 1
Amplified Description

A. Purpose

This USAID program is designed to support government and non-governmental actions and priorities to strengthen the management and quality of basic education services in Indonesia. This Annex provides an amplified description of the program and contains an illustrative list of activities. Nothing in this Annex shall be construed as amending any of the definitions or terms of the Strategic Objective Grant Agreement between the Government of the Republic of Indonesia (GOI) and the Government of the United States of America to Support Improved Quality of Decentralized Basic Education in Indonesia (the Agreement).

B. Background

The new USAID strategy for 2004 to 2009 is organized around four major program areas: (1) improved quality of decentralized basic education, (2) higher quality basic human services utilized, (3) effective democratic and decentralized governance, and (4) effective systems of economic governance to increase trade and investment and drive new job creation.

The quality of basic education in public and private schools and madrasahs throughout Indonesia is often poor. As a result, many Indonesian children are being deprived of the skills and knowledge required to participate in a global economy. Decentralized education management is mandated but often inadequate. Many teachers do not yet have sufficient expertise in key subject areas. Approximately half the children who start primary school and madrasahs do not complete junior secondary level. With rising drop out rates, Indonesia is unable to meet the demand for nonformal education services.

The USAID/Indonesia program will focus on achieving three results:

- More Effective Decentralized Education Management and Governance
- Improved Quality of Teaching and Learning; and
- Increased Relevance of Junior Secondary school and madrasah and Non-formal Education to Work and Life Skills.

The program will work primarily at the local level, seek to leverage the assistance of other donors, and mobilize private sector support for basic education in Indonesia. The program will also support capacity building at the national, provincial, and district level to support the achievement of the Objective.

C. Program Description

In line with the GOI's priorities and based on long-standing cooperation in key sectors, USAID's program is designed to achieve the following priorities:

a) More Effective Decentralized Education Management and Governance;

b) Improved Quality of Teaching and Learning; and

c) Increased Relevance of Junior Secondary and Non-formal Education to Work and Life Skills.

C.1. Illustrative Results Framework

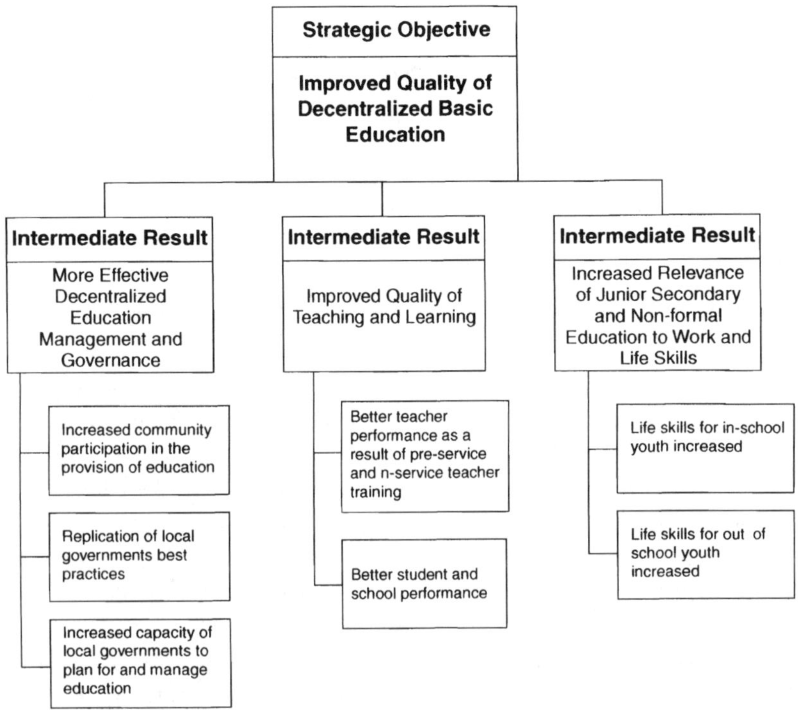

C.2. **IR 1: More Effective Decentralized Education Management and Governance**

Interventions will seek to increase the capacity of local governments to plan for and manage education services and increase community participation in the provision of education services, replicating best practices in other districts. During the period covered under this Agreement, illustrative activities may include but not be limited to:

- Technical assistance, training, fellowships and other support to responsible government units at district and sub-district levels to increase effectiveness and transparency in managing and monitoring the education system including: producing education development plans; managing education personnel, school maintenance, and supplies; monitoring and evaluation; and rational allocation of education funding.
- Technical assistance, training, fellowships and other support to communities, responsible government units, education councils, and school committees to increase community participation in and demand for quality education services.

C.3. **IR 2: Improved Quality of Teaching and Learning.**

The major question facing the GOI and all donors now is how to improve the quality of the education system. These interventions are intended to improve teaching performance in the classroom and elevate the quality of student learning that occurs. During the period covered under this Agreement, illustrative activities may include but not be limited to:

- Technical assistance and training to support in-service training for teachers focusing on Indonesian, Math, Science, and Civics and ensure that primary teachers across the public/private school and madrasah spectrum are prepared to teach the basic subjects using modern teaching and learning techniques.

- Technical assistance and training, and other support to kindergartens, schools and madrasah, and communities to improve student performance, particularly in Basic Literacy, Math, Science, English and Civics, through the provision of better instructional and learning materials, equipment, practices, and multi-media programming and including a focus on early childhood materials and supplies.
- Technical assistance, training, fellowships and other support to work with a targeted group of teacher training institutions to improve pre-service training and build better linkages with schools.

C.4. **IR 3: Increased Relevance of Junior Secondary and Non-formal Education to Work and Life Skills**

Interventions will enable in-school and out-of-school youth to better compete for jobs and develop the skills needed to contribute to Indonesia's development by ensuring that basic education in school directly relates to the life and work skills needed upon entering the workforce. During the period covered under this Agreement, illustrative activities may include but not be limited to:

- Technical assistance, training, and other support to increase life skills for junior high school level youth by supporting: the participatory development of local content curriculum, English language studies, and employment preparation and awareness programs that encourage positive attitudes about work and entrepreneurship.
- Technical assistance, training, and other support to increase life skills for out-of-school junior high school level youth by supporting community learning centers, local NGO efforts, and the development of equivalence materials and curricula, including collaborative work with the Government of Indonesia on Paket B.

D. Funding

D.1. Funds Supporting the Government of Indonesia Program

Subject to the availability of funds to USAID for this purpose, funding under this Agreement may be provided directly by USAID, in the form of contracts, grants, cooperative agreements and other types of agreements, to international private voluntary organizations, commercial entities, universities, non-governmental organizations, and other U.S. Government agencies that work as USAID partners for the following purposes, including but not limited to:

- Technical Assistance
- Training
- Fellowships
- Research
- Supplies and Commodities
- Assessments, performance monitoring and evaluations
- Audits
- Other purposes as deemed appropriate

D.2. Financial Plan

The financial plan for the Program is set forth in the attached table (Illustrative SOAG Budget). Changes may be made to the financial plan by representatives of the Parties without formal amendment to the Agreement, if such changes do not cause (1) USAID's contribution to exceed the amount specified in Section 3.1 of the Agreement, or (2) the Grantee's contribution to be less than the amount specified in Section 3.2 of the Agreement.

D.3. Other USAID Program Support Obligated Outside this Agreement

In addition to the amount that may be made available under this Agreement, USAID will also contribute additional technical and program support for activities that may be obligated outside of this Strategic Objective Agreement. All funding provided by USAID not obligated in this Agreement for assistance to achieve the Strategic Objective and Results shall be treated as assistance provided to Indonesia under the Economic and Technical Cooperation Agreement between the Government of the United States of America and the Government of the Republic of Indonesia on October 16, 1950 and its related annex. Funding may be provided by USAID/Washington or USAID/Indonesia through other financial mechanisms.

E. Roles and Responsibilities of the Parties

USAID, the Grantee, international private voluntary organizations, commercial entities, universities, non-governmental organizations, and other U.S. Government agencies will achieve the Strategic Objective together in partnership with the citizens of Indonesia.

E.1 The Grantee

The Grantee will be responsible for facilitating the necessary administrative support for the provision of technical assistance under the Strategic Objective program. The Coordinating Ministry for People's Welfare shall act as the executing agency of the GOI. The Coordinating Ministry for People's Welfare will liaise with other GOI ministries and agencies to ensure that the GOI fulfills its responsibility to facilitate visa and assignment approvals; fee, tariff and tax exemptions; and customs clearances in accordance with this Agreement.

E.2 USAID

USAID will solicit, manage, finance and take overall responsibility for goods and technical services to be procured which contribute to the Strategic Objective of this Agreement. USAID's Basic Education Strategic Objective Team will be responsible for the day-to-day, overall management of the Strategic Objective program and for monitoring progress toward achievement of the Strategic Objective. All recipients of assistance under this Agreement will be selected and funded by USAID in accordance with United States Government rules and regulations. USAID will approve the scopes of work and proposals from the implementing partners. USAID will monitor and supervise all financial and implementation actions of the program.

E.3 Implementing Partners

USAID may use various mechanisms, such as contracts, grants, cooperative agreements, with international private voluntary organization, commercial entities, international and national universities, international and national non-governmental organizations and other U.S. Government agencies in implementing activities under this Strategic Objective with funding provided by USAID. These implementing partners will prepare performance monitoring reports in accordance with the terms of their respective agreements.

E.4 Coordination

USAID will coordinate overall program implementation with the Coordinating Ministry of People's Welfare. Within this framework and given the cross-cutting and integrated nature of the assistance to be provided under this Agreement, the Parties will collaborate closely with the Ministry of Education, the Ministry of Religious Affairs, Bappenas, and other relevant GOI ministries and institutions on specific areas of assistance. The Parties agree to establish appropriate working-level implementation mechanisms to achieve the Objective.

USAID implementing partners may enter into working groups and memoranda of understanding with appropriate implementing GOI agencies to facilitate program implementation provided such actions do not contravene the terms and conditions of this Agreement nor any contract, grant, cooperative agreement or other type of agreement entered into by USAID and its partners to implement the Objective. USAID and the Grantee acknowledge that such arrangements do not constitute a legally binding commitment on the Governments of the Republic of Indonesia nor on the Government of the United States.

E.5 Monitoring and Evaluation

USAID and the Grantee agree to establish a program of reviewing, evaluating and reporting on progress made and results achieved as part of this Agreement. Except as both Parties may otherwise agree in writing, the program will include during the implementation of this Agreement the following: 1) submission of an annual performance report by USAID to the Grantee, in a mutually agreed upon format, on the activities which are addressing the achievement of the overall objective; 2) review of progress on a frequent and continual basis through site visits and other monitoring mechanisms by USAID and the implementing partners.

Annex 1
Attachment 1

Improved Quality of Decentralized Basic Education in Indonesia, SO-18
FY 2004 - FY 2008
Budget Summary (August 2004)

USAID			
Components	Obligation under this SOAG FY 2004 (A)	Future Obligation Under SOAG Amendments FY 2005- FY 2008* (B)	Life of Strategic Objective Activities Funding Under this SOAG (C) = (A) + (B)
1. Program Implementation	17,824,919	108,451,081	126,276,000
Activities: * Managing Basic Education * More Effective Decentralized Education Mgt. in Indonesia * Improved Quality of Teaching and Learning * Greater Education Relevance to Life & Employment Skills for Formal and Non-Formal Junior High School Programs.			
2. Administrative and Program Support	975,000	5,749,000	6,724,000
* Evaluation * Staffing & Logistics for Administrative Support			
Strategic Objective Agreement Total	18,799,919	114,200,081	133,000,000

NOTES

* Subject to the availability of funds

The GOI has agreed, pursuant to Section 3.2, to provide contribution on an in-kind basis and report on that contributions on an annual basis

USAID anticipates providing up to $24 million in additional support for this SOAG through the U.S. Embassy Public Affairs Section in FY 2004–2008.

Annex 2
Standard Provisions

Article A: Definitions and Implementation Letters.

Section A.1. Definitions. As used in this Annex, the "Agreement" refers to the Strategic Objective Grant Agreement to which this Annex is attached and of which this Annex forms a part. Terms used in this Annex have the same meaning or reference as in the Agreement.

Section A.2. Implementation Letters. To assist the Grantee in the implementation of the Agreement, USAID, from time to time, will issue Implementation Letters that will furnish additional information about matters stated in this Agreement. The Parties may also issue jointly agreed-upon Implementation Letters to confirm and record their mutual understanding on aspects of the implementation of this Agreement. Implementation Letters can also be issued to record revisions or exceptions which are permitted by the Agreement.

Article B: General Covenants.

Section B.1. Consultation. The Parties will cooperate to assure that the Objective and Results of this Agreement will be accomplished. To this end, the Parties, at the request of either, will exchange views on progress towards the Objective and Results, the performance of obligations under this Agreement, the performance of any consultants, contractors, or suppliers engaged under the Agreement, and other matters relating to the Agreement.

Section B.2. Execution of Agreement. The Grantee will:

(a) Carry out the Agreement or cause it to be carried out with due diligence and efficiency, in conformity with sound technical, financial, and management practices, and in conformity with those documents, plans, specifications, contracts, schedules, or other arrangements, and with any modifications therein, approved by USAID pursuant to this Agreement; and

(b) Provide qualified and experienced management for, and train such staff as may be appropriate for the maintenance and operation of activities financed under the Agreement, and, as applicable for continuing activities, cause those activities to be operated and maintained in such manner as to assure the continuing and successful achievement of the Objective and Results of the Agreement.

Section B.3. Utilization of Goods and Services.

(a) Any goods and services financed under this Agreement, unless otherwise agreed in writing by USAID, will be devoted to the Agreement until the completion or termination of the Agreement, and thereafter (as well as during any period of suspension of the Agreement) will be used to further the Objective of the Agreement and as USAID may direct in Implementation Letters.

(b) Goods or services financed under this Agreement, except as USAID may otherwise agree in writing, will not be used to promote or assist a foreign aid project or activity associated with or financed by a country not included in USAID Geographic Code 935 as in effect at the time of such use.

Section B.4. Taxation.

(a) General Exemption. The Agreement and the assistance there under are free from any taxes imposed under laws in effect in the territory of the Grantee.

(b) Except as provided otherwise in this provision, the General Exemption in subsection (a) applies to, but is not limited to (1) any activity, contract, grant or other implementing agreement financed by USAID under this Agreement; (2) any transaction or supplies, equipment, materials, property or other goods (hereinafter collectively "goods") under (1) above; (3) any contractor, grantee, or other organization carrying out activities financed by USAID under this Agreement; (4) any employee of such organizations; and (5) any individual contractor or grantee carrying out activities financed by USAID under this Agreement.

(c) Except as provided otherwise in this provision, the General Exemption in subsection (a) applies to, but is not limited to, the following taxes:

(1) Exemption 1. Customs duties, tariffs, import taxes, or other levies on the importation, use and re-exportation of goods or the personal belongings and effects (including personally-owned automobiles) for the personal use of non-national individuals or their family members. Exemption 1 includes, but is not limited to, all charges based on the value of such imported goods, but does not include service charges directly related to services performed to transfer goods or cargo.

(2) Exemption 2. Taxes on the income, profits or property of all (i) non-national organizations of any type, (ii) non-national employees of national and non-national organizations, or (iii) non-national individual contractors and grantees. Exemption 2 includes income and social security taxes of all types and all taxes on the property, personal or real, owned by such non-national organizations or persons. The term "national" refers to organizations established under the laws of the Grantee and citizens of the Grantee, other than permanent resident aliens in the United States.

(3) Exemption 3. Taxes levied on the last transaction for the purchase of goods or services financed by USAID under this Agreement, including sales taxes, value-added taxes (VAT), or taxes on purchases or rentals of real or personal property. The term "last transaction" refers to the last transaction by which the goods or services were purchased for use in the activities financed by USAID under this Agreement.

(d) If a tax has been levied and paid contrary to the provisions of an exemption, USAID may, in its discretion, (1) require the Grantee to refund to USAID or to others as USAID may direct the amount of such tax with funds other than those provided under the Agreement, or (2) offset the amount of such tax from amounts to be disbursed under this or any other agreement between the Parties.

(e) In the event of a disagreement about the application of an exemption, the Parties agree to promptly meet and resolve such matters, guided by the principle that the assistance furnished by USAID is free from direct taxation, so that all of the assistance furnished by USAID will contribute directly to the economic development of the country of the Grantee.

Section B.5. Reports and Information, Agreement Books and Records, Audits, and Inspections.

(a) Reports and Information. The Grantee shall furnish USAID accounting records and such other information and reports relating to the Agreement as USAID may reasonably request.

(b) Grantee Agreement Books and Records. If USAID funds are expended directly by the Grantee, it shall maintain accounting books, records, documents and other evidence relating to the Agreement, adequate to show, without limitation, all costs incurred by the Grantee under the Agreement, the receipt and use of goods and services acquired under the Agreement by the Grantee, agreed-upon cost sharing requirements, the nature and extent of solicitations of prospective suppliers of goods and services acquired by the Grantee, the basis of award of Grantee contracts and orders, and the overall progress of the Agreement toward completion ("Agreement books and records"). The Grantee shall maintain Agreement books and records in accordance with generally accepted accounting principles prevailing in the United States, or at the Grantee's option, with approval by USAID, other accounting principles, such as those (1) prescribed by the International Accounting Standards Committee (an affiliate of the International Federation of Accountants) or (2) prevailing in the country of the Grantee. Agreement books and records shall be maintained for at least three years after the date of last disbursement by USAID or for such longer period, if any, required to resolve any litigation, claims or audit findings.

(c) Grantee Audit. If $300,000 or more of USAID funds are expended directly by the Grantee in its fiscal year under the Agreement, the Grantee shall have financial audits made of the expenditures in accordance with the following terms, except as the Parties may otherwise agree in writing:

(1) With USAID approval, the Grantee shall use its Supreme Audit Institution or select an independent auditor in accordance with the "Guidelines for Financial Audits Contracted by Foreign Recipients" issued by the USAID Inspector General ("Guidelines"), and the audits shall be performed in accordance with the "Guidelines"; and

(2) The audit shall determine whether the receipt and expenditure of the funds provided under the Agreement are presented in accordance with generally accepted accounting principles agreed to in section (b) above and whether the Grantee has complied with the terms of the Agreement. Each audit shall be completed no later than nine months after the close of the Grantee's year under audit.

(d) Sub-recipient Audits. The Grantee, except as the Parties may otherwise agree in writing, shall submit to USAID, in form and substance satisfactory to USAID, a plan for the audit of the expenditures of "covered" sub-recipients, as defined below, that receive funds under this Agreement pursuant to a direct contract or agreement with the Grantee.

(1) A "covered" sub-recipient is one who expends $300,000 or more in its fiscal year in "USAID awards" (i.e., as recipients of USAID cost reimbursable contracts, grants or cooperative agreements and as sub-recipients under USAID strategic objective and other grant agreements with foreign governments).

(2) The plan shall describe the methodology to be used by the Grantee to satisfy its audit responsibilities for covered sub-recipients. The Grantee may satisfy such audit responsibilities by relying on independent audits of the sub-recipients; expanding the scope of the independent financial audit of the Grantee to encompass testing of sub-recipients' accounts; or a combination of these procedures.

(3) The plan shall identify the funds made available to covered sub-recipients that will be covered by audits conducted in accordance with other audit provisions that would satisfy the Grantee's audit responsibilities. (A nonprofit organization organized in the United States is required to arrange for its own audits. A for-profit contractor organized in the United States that has a direct contract with USAID is audited by the cognizant U.S. Government Agency. A private voluntary organization organized outside the United States with a direct grant from USAID is required to arrange for its own audits. A host-country contractor should be audited by the Grantee's auditing agency.)

(4) The Grantee shall ensure that covered sub-recipients under direct contracts or agreements with the Grantee take appropriate and timely corrective actions; consider whether sub-recipients' audits necessitate adjustment of its own records; and require each such sub-recipient to permit independent auditors to have access to records and financial statements as necessary.

(e) Audit Reports. The Grantee shall furnish or cause to be furnished to USAID an audit report for each audit arranged for by the Grantee in accordance with this Section within 30 days after completion of the audit and no later than nine months after the end of the period under audit.

(f) Other Covered Sub-recipients. For "covered" sub-recipients who receive funds under the Agreement pursuant to direct contracts or agreements with USAID, USAID will include appropriate audit requirements in such contracts or agreements and will, on behalf of the Grantee, conduct the follow-up activities with regard to the audit reports furnished pursuant to such requirements.

(g) Cost of Audits. Subject to USAID approval in writing, costs of audits performed in accordance with the terms of this Section may be charged to the Agreement.

(h) Audit by USAID. USAID retains the right to perform the audits required under this Agreement on behalf of the Grantee by utilizing funds under the Agreement or other resources available to USAID for this purpose, conduct a financial review, or otherwise ensure accountability of organizations expending USAID funds regardless of the audit requirement.

(i) Opportunity to Audit or Inspect. The Grantee shall afford authorized representatives of USAID the opportunity at all reasonable times to audit or inspect activities financed under the Agreement, the utilization of goods and services financed by USAID, and books, records and other documents relating to the Agreement.

(j) Sub-recipient Books and Records. The Grantee will incorporate paragraphs (a), (b), (d), (e), (g), (h) and (i) of this provision into all sub-agreements with non-U.S. organizations which meet the $300,000 threshold of paragraph (c) of this provision. Sub-agreements with non-U.S. organizations, which do not meet the $300,000 threshold, shall, at a minimum, incorporate paragraphs (h) and (i) of this provision. Sub-agreements with U.S. organizations shall state that the U.S. organization is subject to the audit requirements contained in OMB Circular A-133.

Section B.6. Completeness of Information. The Grantee confirms:

(a) that the facts and circumstances of which it has informed USAID, or caused USAID to be informed, in the course of reaching agreement with USAID on the Agreement, are accurate and complete, and include all facts and circumstances that might materially affect the Agreement and the discharge of responsibilities under this Agreement; and

(b) that it will inform USAID in timely fashion of any subsequent facts and circumstances that might materially affect, or that it is reasonable to believe might so affect, the Agreement or the discharge of responsibilities under this Agreement.

Section B.7. Other Payments. Grantee affirms that no payments have been or will be received by any official of the Grantee in connection with the procurement of goods or services financed under the Agreement, except fees, taxes, or similar payments legally established in the country of the Grantee. Section B.8. Information and Marking. The Grantee will give appropriate publicity to the Agreement as a program to which the United States has contributed, identify Agreement activity sites, and mark goods financed by USAID, as described in Implementation Letters.

Article C: Procurement Provisions.

Section C.1. Source and Origin.

C.1. Source and Origin.

(a) Foreign Exchange Costs. Disbursements for Foreign Exchange Costs will be used exclusively to finance the costs of goods and services required for the Agreement having, with respect to goods, their source and origin and, with respect to the suppliers of goods and services, their nationality, in the United States (USAID Geographic Code 000), except as USAID may otherwise agree in writing.

(b) Local Currency Costs. Disbursements for Local Currency Costs will be used exclusively to finance the costs of goods and services required for the Agreement which meet the requirements of USAID's local procurement policy which will be provided in an Implementation Letter.

(c) The source and origin of ocean and air shipping will be deemed to be the ocean vessel's or aircraft's country of registry at the time of shipment.

(d) Provisions concerning restricted and ineligible goods and services may be provided in an Implementation Letter.

(e) Transportation by air of property or persons financed under this agreement will be on carriers holding United States certification, to the extent service by such carriers is available under the Fly America Act. This requirement may be further described by USAID in Implementation Letters.

Section C.2. Eligibility Date. No goods or services may be financed under the Agreement which are procured pursuant to orders or contracts firmly placed or entered into prior to the date of this Agreement, except as the Parties may otherwise agree in writing.

Section C.3. Plans, Specifications and Contracts. In order for there to be mutual agreement on the following matters, and except as the Parties may otherwise agree in writing:

(a) The Grantee will furnish to USAID upon preparation:

(1) any plans, specifications, procurement or construction schedules, contracts, or other documentation between the Grantee and third parties, relating to goods or services to be financed under the Agreement, including documentation relating to the prequalification and selection of contractors and to the solicitation of bids and proposals. Material modifications in such documentation will likewise be furnished USAID on preparation; and

(2) such documentation will also be furnished to USAID, upon preparation, relating to any goods or services, which, though not financed under the Agreement, are deemed by USAID to be of major importance to the Agreement. Aspects of the Agreement involving matters under this subsection (a)(2) will be identified in Implementation Letters.

(b) Documents related to the prequalification of contractors, and to the solicitation of bids or proposals for goods and services financed under the Agreement will be approved by USAID in writing prior to their issuance, and their terms will include United States standards and measurements;

(c) Contracts and contractors financed under the Agreement for engineering and other professional services, for construction services, and for such other services, equipment, or materials as may be specified in Implementation Letters, will be approved by USAID in writing prior to execution of the contract. Material modifications in such contracts will also be approved in writing by USAID prior to execution; and

(d) Consulting firms used by the Grantee for the Agreement but not financed under the Agreement, the scope of their services and such of their personnel assigned to activities financed under the Agreement as USAID may specify, and construction contractors used by the Grantee for the Agreement but not financed under the Agreement, shall be acceptable to USAID.

Section C.4. Reasonable Price. No more than reasonable prices will be paid for any goods or services financed, in whole or in part, under the Agreement. Such items will be procured on a fair and, to the maximum extent practicable, competitive basis.

Section C.5. Notification to Potential Suppliers. To permit all United States firms to have the opportunity to participate in furnishing goods and services to be financed under the Agreement, the Grantee will furnish USAID such information with regard thereto, and at such times, as USAID may request in Implementation Letters.

Section C.6. Transportation

(a) In addition to the requirements in Section C.1(a), costs of ocean or air transportation and related delivery services may not be financed under the Grant, if the costs are for transportation under an ocean vessel or air charter which has not received prior USAID approval.

(b) Unless USAID determines that privately owned United States-flag commercial ocean vessels are not available at fair and reasonable rates for such vessels, or otherwise agrees in writing:

(1) at least fifty percent (50%) of the gross tonnage of all goods (computed separately for dry bulk carriers, dry cargo liners and tankers) financed by USAID which may be transported on ocean vessels will be transported on privately owned United States-flag commercial vessels; and

(2) at least fifty percent (50%) of the gross freight revenue generated by all shipments financed by USAID and transported to the territory of the Grantee on dry cargo liners shall be paid to or for the benefit of privately owned United States-flag commercial vessels. Compliance with the requirements of (1) and (2) of this subsection must be achieved with respect to both any cargo transported from U.S. ports and any cargo transported from non-U.S. ports, computed separately.

Section C.7. Insurance.

(a) Marine insurance on goods financed by USAID which are to be transported to the territory of the Grantee may be financed as a Foreign Exchange Cost under this Agreement provided

(1) such insurance is placed at the most advantageous competitive rate;

(2) such insurance is placed in a country which is authorized under Section C.1(a); and

(3) claims there under are payable in U.S. dollars or any freely convertible currency unless USAID agrees otherwise in writing.

If the Grantee (or government of the Grantee), by statute, decree, rule, regulation, or practice discriminates with respect to USAID-financed procurement against any marine insurance company authorized to do business in any State of the United States, then all goods shipped to the territory of the Grantee financed by USAID hereunder shall be insured against marine risks and such insurance shall be placed in the United States with a company or companies authorized to do marine insurance business in the United States.

(b) Except as USAID may otherwise agree in writing, the Grantee will insure, or cause to be insured, goods financed under the Agreement imported for the Agreement against risks incident to their transit to the point of their use under the Agreement; such insurance will be issued on terms and conditions consistent with sound commercial practice and will insure the full value of the goods. Any indemnification received by the Grantee under such insurance will be used to replace or repair any material damage or any loss of the goods insured or will be used to reimburse the Grantee for the replacement or repair of such goods. Any such replacement will be of source and origin of countries listed in USAID Geographic Code 935 as in effect at the time of replacement and, except as the Parties may agree in writing, will be otherwise subject to the provisions of the Agreement.

Section C.8. U.S. Government-Owned Excess Property. The Grantee agrees that wherever practicable United States Government-owned excess personal property, in lieu of new items financed under the Grant, should be utilized. Funds under the Agreement may be used to finance the costs of obtaining such property.

Article D: Disbursements.

Section D.1. Disbursement for Foreign Exchange Costs.

(a) After satisfaction of conditions precedent, if any, the Grantee may obtain disbursements of funds under the Agreement for the Foreign Exchange Costs of goods or services required for the Agreement in accordance with its terms, by such of the following methods as may be mutually agreed upon:

(1) by submitting to USAID, with necessary supporting documentation as prescribed in Implementation Letters, (A) requests for reimbursement for such goods or services, or, (B) requests for USAID to procure commodities or services in Grantee's behalf for the Agreement; or,

(2) by requesting USAID to issue Letters of Commitment for specified amounts directly to one or more contractors or suppliers, committing USAID to pay such contractors or suppliers for such goods or services.

(b) Banking charges incurred by the Grantee in connection with Letters of Commitment will be financed under the Agreement unless the Grantee instructs USAID to the contrary. Such other charges as the Parties may agree to may also be financed under the Agreement.

Section D.2. Disbursement for Local Currency Costs.

(a) After satisfaction of conditions precedent, if any, the Grantee may obtain disbursements of funds under the Agreement for Local Currency Costs required for the Agreement in accordance with terms of this Agreement, by submitting to USAID, with necessary supporting documentation as prescribed in Implementation Letters, requests to finance such costs.

(b) The local currency needed for such disbursements may be purchased by USAID with U.S. Dollars. The U.S. Dollar equivalent of the local currency made available hereunder will be the amount of U.S. Dollars required by USAID to obtain the local currency.

Section D.3. Other Forms of Disbursement. Disbursements may also be made through such other means as the Parties may agree to in writing.

Section D.4. Rate of Exchange. If funds provided under the Agreement are introduced into the Cooperating Country by USAID or any public or private agency for purposes of carrying out obligations of USAID hereunder, the Grantee will make such arrangements as may be necessary so that such funds may be converted into local currency at the highest rate of exchange which, at the time the conversion is made, is not unlawful in the country of the Grantee to any person for any purpose.

Article E: Termination; Remedies.

Section E.1. Suspension and Termination.

(a) Either Party may terminate this Agreement in its entirety by giving the other Party 30 days written notice. USAID also may terminate this Agreement in part by giving the Grantee 30 days written notice, and suspend this Agreement in whole or in part upon giving the Grantee written notice. In addition, USAID may terminate this Agreement in whole or in part, upon giving the

Grantee written notice, if (i) the Grantee fails to comply with any provision of this Agreement, (ii) an event occurs that USAID determines makes it improbable that the Objective or Results of the Agreement or the assistance program will be attained or that the Grantee will be able to perform its obligations under this Agreement, or (iii) any disbursement or use of funds in the manner herein contemplated would be in violation of the legislation governing USAID, whether now or hereafter in effect.

(b) Except for payment which the Parties are committed to make pursuant to non-cancellable commitments entered into with third parties prior to such suspension or termination, suspension or termination of this entire Agreement or part thereof will suspend (for the period of the suspension) or terminate, as applicable, any obligation of the Parties to provide financial or other resources to the Agreement, or to the suspended or terminated portion of the Agreement, as applicable. Any portion of this Agreement which is not suspended or terminated shall remain in full force and effect.

(c) In addition, upon such full or partial suspension or termination, USAID may, at USAID's expense, direct that title to goods financed under the Agreement, or under the applicable portion of the Agreement, be transferred to USAID if the goods are in a deliverable state.

Section E.2. Refunds.

(a) In the case of any disbursement which is not supported by valid documentation in accordance with this Agreement, or which is not made or used in accordance with this Agreement, or which was for goods or services not used in accordance with this Agreement, USAID, notwithstanding the availability or exercise of any other remedies under this Agreement, may require the Grantee to refund the amount of such disbursement in U.S. Dollars to USAID within sixty (60) days after receipt of a request therefor.

(b) If the failure of Grantee to comply with any of its obligations under this Agreement has the result that goods or services financed or supported under the Agreement are not used effectively in accordance with this Agreement, USAID may require the Grantee to refund all or any part of the amount of the disbursements under this Agreement for or in connection with such goods or services in U.S. Dollars to USAID within sixty (60) days after receipt of a request there for.

(c) The right under subsections (a) or (b) to require a refund of a disbursement will continue, notwithstanding any other provision of this Agreement, for three years from the date of the last disbursement under this Agreement.

(d) (1) Any refunds under subsections (a) or (b), or (2) any refund to USAID from a contractor, supplier, bank or other third party with respect to goods or services financed under the Agreement, which refund relates to an unreasonable price for or erroneous invoicing of goods or services, or to goods that did not conform to specifications, or to services that were inadequate, will (A) be made available first for the Agreement, to the extent justified, and (B) the remainder, if any, will be applied to reduce the amount of the Grant.

(e) Any interest or other earnings on funds disbursed by USAID to the Grantee under this Agreement prior to the authorized use of such funds for the Agreement will be returned to USAID in U.S. Dollars by the Grantee, unless USAID otherwise agrees in writing.

Section E.3. Non-waiver of Remedies. No delay in exercising any right or remedy accruing to a Party in connection with its financing under this Agreement will be construed as a waiver of such right or remedy.

Section E.4. Assignment. The Grantee agrees, upon request, to execute an assignment to USAID of any cause of action which may accrue to the Grantee in connection with or arising out of the contractual performance or breach of performance by a Party to a direct U.S. Dollar contract which USAID financed in whole or in part out of funds granted by USAID under this Agreement.

Article F: Miscellaneous.

Section F.1. Investment Promotion.

(a) Except as specifically set forth in the Grant or otherwise authorized by USAID in writing, no funds or other support provided hereunder may be used for any activity that involves investment promotion in a foreign country.

(b) In the event the Grantee is requested or wishes to provide assistance in the above area or requires clarification from USAID as to whether the activity would be consistent with the limitation set forth above, the Grantee must notify USAID and provide a detailed description of the proposed activity. The Grantee must not proceed with the activity until advised by USAID that it may do so.

(c) The Grantee must ensure that its employees and subcontractors and sub-recipients providing investment promotion services hereunder are made aware of the restrictions set forth in this clause and must include this clause in all subcontracts and other sub-agreements entered into hereunder.

Section F.2. Prohibition on Assistance to Drug Traffickers.

(a) USAID reserves the right to terminate this Agreement or take other appropriate measures if a key individual of the Grantee responsible for this program is found to have been convicted of a narcotics offense or to have been engaged in drug trafficking as defined in 22 CFR Part 140 and the Grantee does not take satisfactory legal proceedings against such individual.

(b) USAID reserves the right to terminate assistance to, or take other appropriate measures with respect to, any participant approved by USAID who is found to have been convicted of a narcotics offense or to have been engaged in drug trafficking as defined in 22 CFR Part 140.

(c) The Grantee agrees not to disburse, or sign documents committing the Grantee to disburse, funds to a sub-recipient designated by USAID ("Designated Sub-recipient") until advised by USAID that: (1) any United States Government review of the Designated Sub-recipient and its key individuals has been completed; (2) any related certifications have been obtained; and (3) the assistance to the Designated Sub-recipient has been approved.

(1) The Grantee shall insert the following clause, or its substance, in its agreement with the Designated Sub-recipient:

(2) The Grantee reserves the right to terminate this Agreement or take other appropriate measures if the [Sub-recipient] or a key individual of the [Sub-recipient] is found to have been convicted of a narcotic offense or to have been engaged in drug trafficking as defined in 22 CFR Part 140."

Section F.3. Workers' Rights.

(a) Except as specifically set forth in the Grant or otherwise authorized by USAID in writing, no funds or other support provided hereunder may be used for any activity that involves workers' rights in a foreign country.

(b) In the event the Grantee is requested or wishes to provide assistance in the above area or requires clarification from USAID as to whether the activity would be consistent with the limitation set forth above, the Grantee must notify the USAID and provide a detailed description of the proposed activity. The Grantee must not proceed with the activity until advised by USAID that it may do so.

(c) The Grantee must ensure that all employees and subcontractors and sub-recipients providing employment-related services hereunder are made aware of the restrictions set forth in this clause and must include this clause in all subcontracts and other sub-agreements entered into hereunder.

STATE DEPARTMENT DOCUMENT NUMBER: 06-283

AMENDMENT NO. 1 TO THE STRATEGIC OBJECTIVE GRANT AGREEMENT BETWEEN THE UNITED STATES OF AMERICA AND THE REPUBLIC OF INDONESIA TO SUPPORT IMPROVED QUALITY OF DECENTRALIZED BASIC EDUCATION IN INDONESIA, WITH ANNEX

SIGNED AT JAKARTA,
JULY 8, 2005
ENTERED INTO FORCE JULY 8, 2005

CTIA DOCUMENT NUMBER: 13065.002

Date: July 8, 2005

This AMENDMENT No 1 is entered into by and between the Government of the REPUBLIC OF INDONESIA, acting through the Coordinating Ministry of People's Welfare ("Grantee") and the UNITED STATES OF AMERICA, acting through the United States Agency for International Development ("USAID").

WHEREAS, the Grantee and USAID (the "Parties") entered into a Strategic Objective Grant Agreement for Improved Quality of Decentralized Basic Education in Indonesia on August 30, 2004, whereby USAID granted to the Grantee an amount not to exceed Eighteen Million Seven Hundred and Ninety Nine Thousand, Nine Hundred and Nineteen U.S. Dollars ($18,799,919).

WHEREAS, the Parties desire to amend the Grant Agreement to provide a new increment of USAID grant financing in the amount of **$22,476,839** and make related changes in the Budget Summary to the Grant Agreement.

NOW, THEREFORE, the Grantee and USAID hereby agree to amend the Grant Agreement as amended as follows:

1. In order to increase the amount of the current Grant of $18,799,919 by a new increment of **$22,476,839**, the first sentence of Section 3.1(a) (*The Grant: Current Increment*) is amended and restated in its entirety to read:

> "To help achieve the Objective set forth in this Agreement, USAID, pursuant to the Foreign Assistance act of 1961, as amended, hereby grants to the Grantee under the term of the Agreement an amount not to exceed – **Forty One Million Two Hundred Seventy Six Thousand Seven Hundred Fifty Eight United States Dollars ($41,276,758)**"

2. In order to reflect the increase in USAID grant funding made hereinabove, the financial plan is amended and restated its entirety to read in the form of the Revised Budget Summary (**May 2005**) attached hereto as Attachment 1.

3. Except as amended herein, the terms and conditions of the Grant Agreement shall remain in full force and effect.

IN WITNESS WHEREOF, the Grantee and US AID, each acting through its duly authorized representative, have caused this Amendment No. 1 to be signed in their names and delivered as of the day and year first above written.

FOR THE GOVERNMENT OF
THE UNITED STATES OF AMERICA

[Signature]

William M. Frej
Mission Director to Indonesia
United States Agency for
International Development

FOR THE GOVERNMENT OF THE
REPUBLIC OF INDONESIA

[Signature]

Prof. Fuad Abdul Hamied, Ph.D.
Deputy for Education and State
Administration, Coordinating Ministry
for People's Welfare

WITNESSED

[Signature]

B. Lynn Pascoe
United States Ambassador to Indonesia

[Signature]

Dr. Alwi Shihab
Coordinating Minister for
People's Welfare

Annex 1
Attachment 1

Improved Quality of Decentralized Basic Education in Indonesia, SO-18
FY 2004 - FY 2009
Revised Budget Summary (May 2005)

	USAID				
Components	Total Previously Obligated under this SOAG FY 2004 (A)	Obligation under this SOAG Amendment #1 FY 2005 (B)	Total Obligation to date under this SOAG, including Amendment #1 (C) = (A) + (B)	Future Obligation Under SOAG Amendments FY 2006 - 2009 ** (D)	Life of Strategic Objective Activities Funding under this SOAG (E) = (C) + (D)
1. **Program Implementation** Activities: * Managing Basic Education * More Effective Decentralized Education Mgt. in Indonesia * Improved Quality of Teaching and Learning * Greater Education Relevance to Life & Employment Skills for Formal and Non-Formal Junior High School Programs.	17,824,919	20,976,839	38,801,758	87,474,242	126,276,000
2. Administrative and Program Support * Evaluation and Audit * Staffing & Logistics for Administrative Support	975,000	1,500,000	2,475,000	4,249,000	6,724,000

Continued

Components	Total Previously Obligated under this SOAG FY 2004 (A)	Obligation under this SOAG Amendment #1 FY 2005 (B)	Total Obligation to date under this SOAG, including Amendment #1 (C) = (A) + (B)	Future Obligation Under SOAG Amendments FY 2006 - 2009 ** (D)	Life of Strategic Objective Activities Funding under this SOAG (E) = (C) + (D)
Strategic Objective Agreement Total	18,799,919	22,476,839	41,276,758	91,723,242	133,000,000

NOTES

1. ** Subject to the availability of funds.
2. The GOI has agreed, pursuant to Section 3.2, to provide contribution on an in-kind basis and report on that contributions on an annual basis.
3. USAID anticipates providing up to $24 million in additional support for this SOAG through the U.S. Embassy Public Affairs Section in FY-2004-2009.

STATE DEPARTMENT DOCUMENT NUMBER: 06-284

AGREEMENT BETWEEN THE UNITED STATES OF AMERICA AND THE GOVERNMENT OF THE HASHEMITE KINGDOM OF JORDAN CONCERNING THE TRAINING OF IRAQI POLICE IN JORDAN

SIGNED AT AMMAN AND WASHINGTON D.C.,
SEPTEMBER 24, 2004
ENTERED INTO FORCE SEPTEMBER 6, 2005

CTIA DOCUMENT NUMBER: 13113.000

PREAMBLE

The Government of the United States of America and the Government of the Hashemite Kingdom of Jordan, the Parties to this Letter of Agreement (hereinafter each individually a "Party" and collectively "the Parties"),

Desiring to cooperate towards working on the restoration of the conditions of security and stability in Iraq by means of rebuilding the capacity of the Iraqi civilian police force,

Recalling United Nations Security Council Resolutions 1483 and 1546,

Sharing a mutual interest in combating transnational crime and developing closer regional law enforcement cooperation,

Noting that the Jordan International Police Training Center was established pursuant to the "Contractual Agreement between the Coalition Provisional Authority in Iraq and the Government of the Hashemite Kingdom of Jordan Concerning Access to and Use of the Facilities in Jordan for Iraq Police Training" of October 13, 2003,

Noting further that the Coalition Provisional Authority in Iraq has ceased to function as an entity effective on the transfer of sovereignty to the Government of Iraq,

Desiring to continue the Training of Iraqi Police in Jordan to provide a secure training facility, a curriculum of instruction in police skills, a cadre of multinational instructors, and logistic support for Iraqi police cadets and trainers,

Have agreed as follows:

Article I
GENERAL

1. The Parties will continue to support a project designed to provide civilian police training for Iraqi police force trainees in Jordan. The purpose of this Letter of Agreement ("LOA") is to continue the project commenced under the Agreement entered into on October 13, 2003 by the Coalition Provision Authority ("CPA") in Iraq and the Hashemite Kingdom of Jordan entitled "Contractual Agreement between the Coalition Provision Authority in Iraq and the Government of the Hashemite Kingdom of Jordan Concerning Access to and Use of Facilities in Jordan for Iraq Police Training" (hereinafter "JIPTC Agreement"), and to identify the respective rights and obligations of the Parties necessary to carry out and complete the project goals, to include security and base operations support for the Jordan International Police Training Center at Muwaqqar, Jordan and the training staff housing facility at Jawa, Jordan.

2. The actions to be taken and the resources to be provided by the Government of the United States of America ("USG") and the Hashemite Kingdom of Jordan ("GOJ") in support of this LOA are set forth below and constitute the clear understanding of each Party. Funds to be granted by the USG under the terms of this LOA will be specified under separate cover. Future funding for these projects by the USG is contingent upon the availability of duly authorized and appropriated funds, satisfactory progress towards project goals, and approval by the U.S. Department of State.

Article II
DEFINITIONS

As used in this Letter of Agreement, the terms below shall have the following meanings:

"JIPTC Agreement" refers to the Agreement entered into on October 13, 2003 by the Coalition Provision Authority ("CPA") in Iraq and the Hashemite Kingdom of Jordan entitled "Contractual Agreement between the Coalition Provision Authority in Iraq and the Government of the Hashemite Kingdom of Jordan Concerning Access to and Use of Facilities in Jordan for Iraq Police Training."

"JIPTC personnel" includes the military and civilian personnel of the governmental entities who were participating in or were agents of the JIPTC for the purposes of the JIPTC Agreement, together with USG and governmental entity contractor employees, not nationals or permanent residents of the Hashemite Kingdom of Jordan, in connection with the JIPTC Agreement or this LOA or in connection with a contract or similar agreement entered into pursuant to or in furtherance of the JIPTC Agreement or this LOA.

"JIPTC contractors" includes companies and firms employed by the former or current JIPTC or its designated representatives or governmental agents in connection with the JIPTC Agreement, this LOA, or in connection with a contract or similar agreement entered into pursuant to or in furtherance of the JIPTC Agreement or this LOA.

"Governmental entities" means entities, including subdivisions, of states participating as members of the JIPTC, who are acting on behalf of or as agents for the JIPTC for purposes of this Letter of Agreement, or for purposes of a contract or similar agreement entered into pursuant to or in furtherance of the JIPTC Agreement or this LOA.

"IP trainees" means Iraqi residents receiving police training in Jordan in connection with the JIPTC Agreement or this LOA.

"Base Services" means those facility, grounds, and physical infrastructure-related services necessary to maintain and operate the buildings, grounds, and physical support infrastructure required to achieve the training mission.

"Facilities management" includes the planning, direction, and leadership required to effect actions related to all physical infrastructure, utility systems, facilities, and other major and minor equipment, whether for routine, scheduled or emergency services.

"Facilities maintenance" includes all physical infrastructure, utility systems, facilities, and other major and minor equipment, whether for routine, scheduled, or emergency services.

"Facilities operations and administration" includes provisioning, storing, assembling, and applying spare parts and components, as well as repair and maintenance services required by JIPTC.

Article III
PROJECT DESCRIPTION

The project is designed to train Iraqi police officers in Jordan. Under the terms of this LOA, the GOJ will provide facilities, security, and base operations and maintenance for the International Police Training Center at Muwaqqar, Jordan, hereafter referred to as "Jordan International Police Training Center" ("JIPTC"), and the training staff housing complex at Jawa, Jordan. The USG will be responsible for administering the training program and will compensate the GOJ through the Public Security Directorate ("PSD") for the costs of providing the required facilities, utilities, services, supplies, equipment and capabilities enumerated herein. Toward that goal, the USG and the GOJ shall take actions and commit resources on an annual basis as authorized by their respective legislative processes to support this LOA.

A. JIPTC ADMINISTRATION

1. The JIPTC will be directed by the USG, or its designated representatives, in close coordination with the PSD. The provisions of Article III, Program Development, Administration, Management and Costs, specifically subparagraphs a, c, d, e, and h of the JIPTC Agreement shall apply, *mutatis mutandis*, inclusive of changes herein. Accordingly,

a. the JIPTC, or its designated representative, in close coordination with the PSD, shall develop, manage, and administer the JIPTC training program at the Muwaqqar facility with a view toward providing support for as many as 3,000 Iraqi Police ("IP") trainees and 1,500 trainers and staff at any given time;

b. except as otherwise noted in this LOA or in the JIPTC Agreement, the USG shall bear, on a reimbursable basis, the costs specified in this LOA related to the programs offered by the JIPTC, and of the costs of improvements to the Muwaqqar and Jawa facilities and their operation and maintenance in connection with this LOA;

c. PSD will continue to provide Arabic/English translators and accredited Jordanian Police Officers/Instructors for the JIPTC for the duration of this LOA, the costs of which will be reimbursed by the USG;

d. the PSD will provide a security unit and a base command group as needed in the overall command structure, and in a manner that reflects the very high level of concern for the safety and security of all individuals concerned;

e. the Parties agree that the command and control relationships concerning the administration and provision of security for the facilities are accurately portrayed in the JIPTC Agreement, incorporated herein by reference.

2. The JIPTC and its duly authorized personnel, to include agents and contractors, shall have unrestricted use of and access to facilities in Muwaqqar and Jawa, as appropriate, so long as the USG determines that these sites, or any of them, are needed to achieve the training mission.

3. The Director, Jordan International Police Training Center, as the senior JIPTC representative, shall manage, direct, and administer the operations of the JIPTC, in close coordination with the PSD Base Commander. The Director shall be responsible for establishing and modifying training requirements and the instructional curriculum, and coordinating student scheduling and travel arrangements. The JIPTC internal security force, under the overall direction of the Director JIPTC, is responsible for internal security at the JIPTC and shall request assistance from the PSD security forces when necessary in emergency situations. In such cases, onsite JIPTC staff will inform both the JIPTC management and USG staff as soon as reasonably possible.

4. The Base Commander shall be responsible for base operations and services, under the direction of the Director, JIPTC.

5. The USG shall return, as the sole and unencumbered property of Jordan, all buildings, facilities, or areas at the Muwaqqar and Jawa facilities once they are no longer used by the JIPTC in connection with this LOA, including any construction or improvement carried out on the building, facilities, or areas by the JIPTC, less reasonable fair wear and tear. This provision does not apply to removable property of the JIPTC, the governmental entities or their contractors. Removable property of the GOJ remains the property of the GOJ.

6. The JIPTC, the governmental entities or their contractors shall keep original title to all their equipment, materials, supplies, relocatable structures, and other property they have imported into or acquired within Jordan in connection with this LOA that does not become a fixture or otherwise permanently attached to buildings or other real property in Jordan.

7. In accordance with applicable laws and regulations, the JIPTC and its designated representative(s) or agent(s) may award contracts or other similar agreements for construction, repairs, maintenance, and other goods/services as needed at the Muwaqqar and Jawa facilities identified in Article II of the JIPTC Agreement encouraging the employment of Jordanian nationals. The JIPTC, the government entities, and their contractors present in Jordan for the purposes set forth herein may also carry out related work regarding the facilities and locations identified in Article II of the JIPTC Agreement, under the general direction of JIPTC.

8. The Parties agree to coordinate with each other concerning the joint control of entry into and exit from the facilities.

9. The Parties shall issue instructions as needed to ensure that the obligations provided by this LOA are fully implemented.

10. The Parties may enter into contracts, implementing arrangements, or other similar agreements with third parties or implementing arrangements with each other to carry out the provisions of this LOA. In the event of conflict between a contract, implementing arrangement, or other similar agreement and this LOA, the terms of this LOA shall govern Settlement of Disputes.

11. The Parties may increase, amend, or terminate projects undertaken in conjunction with this LOA as agreed to by the Parties in writing. Such projects shall be subject to the terms and conditions of this LOA. The planned life of this project is until approximately 32,000 Iraqi students have been trained, or a number that is mutually agreeable to both Governments.

12. Settlement of Disputes: Any dispute or disagreement regarding interpretation or application of this LOA shall be resolved by consultation between the Parties and shall not be referred to any third party or international tribunal for settlement.

B. RESPONSIBILITIES OF THE GOJ

The GOJ agrees to provide the following according to the qualifications and standards to be outlined in the Statement of Work provided by the USG, at the price agreed to by the Parties. The GOJ may designate representatives to provide these services on its behalf.

a command group element to include a Head of Security to serve as the Base Commander and his supporting staff;

b. when needed, upon request of the JIPTC, sufficient senior level PSD officers to prepare for a potential transition from USG management;

c. exterior perimeter security using PSD security forces;

d. emergency assistance to the JIPTC with internal security matters, upon the request of the JIPTC security staff;

e. at the levels currently provided, training program personnel to be integrated into the JIPTC training program, including General Policing Instructors, Operational Policing Instructors, Cadet Brigade Command Drill Instructors, Language Assistants and other staff support required;

f. upon request of the JIPTC, followed by written confirmation, temporary or emergency staffing support from PSD personnel;

g. upon written request of the USG, if additional permanent staff are required beyond the levels currently provided, the GOJ will provide such personnel in accordance with the terms of this LOA;

h. transportation for Police Students/Cadets which will include transporting them to the JIPTC upon their arrival in Jordan and back to the point of departure from the JIPTC upon completion or termination of the training, and such other transportation as needed or as requested in writing by the JIPTC;

i. transportation for Language Assistants from designated pick up points to and from the JIPTC;

j. transportation for Instructors to and from the facilities at Jawa and Muwaqqar;

k. telephone service capability to the facilities, via microwave technology, for telephone and internet service network capability to the Jawa and Muwaqqar sites for JIPTC use supporting uninterrupted telecommunications operation to all facilities;

l. invoices for all utilities including electricity, water, and sewage services for all JIPTC facilities;

m. operational performance of all physical infrastructure, utility systems, HVAC (Heating, Ventilation, Air Conditioning), grounds, and facilities (to include integrity, usability, and availability) at the Jawa and Muwaqqar sites to support the mission, including but not limited to:

> i. major or minor equipment, routine, scheduled, and emergency maintenance services for all mechanical, electrical, and plumbing at the facility level, common building level, and individual quarters level;
>
> ii. major or minor, routine, scheduled, and emergency maintenance services for street and security lighting, for all fencing, walls, roads, walkways and curbs;
>
> iii. stock, assemble, and apply spare parts and components to provide and effect repairs and services requested by JIPTC personnel;

n. diesel fuel, petrol, oil and lubrications supplies and services at the Muwaqqar and Jawa sites;

o. housekeeping and janitorial services for classrooms, dining areas, sleeping quarters, canteens, warehouses, outside yards, outside sports areas, offices, sitting areas, bathrooms, and other JIPTC designated areas at the Muwaqqar and Jawa sites;

p. pest and vermin control and eradication services at the Muwaqqar and Jawa sites;

q. trash removal and disposal at the Muwaqqar and Jawa sites;

r. potable water sufficient to meet the continuous needs of a community of approximately 4,500 at the Muwaqqar and Jawa sites;

s. emergency response services and on site fire departments fully equipped to ensure fire protection for the facilities and the JIPTC community at the Muwaqqar and Jawa sites;

t. routine and emergency medical and dental support for the IP trainees and staff, consistent with services provided prior to the signing of this LOA, until superseded by a separate agreement specifically related to the provision of medical and dental care.

C. RESPONSIBILITIES OF THE USG

The USG will provide the following:

a. subject to the availability of appropriated funds authorized for the purpose, compensation to the GOJ for the direct and indirect costs associated with the provision of support required by this LOA;

b. management and oversight of the JIPTC in close coordination with GOJ;

c. statement of requirements and statements of work detailing services areas and minimum acceptable standards for all base facility operations, performance of maintenance, maintenance of security and all other requested services;

d. reimbursement to PSD for invoiced utilities covering JIPTC facilities;

e. reimbursement to PSD for invoiced diesel and petrol consumed;

f. as deemed necessary by the Parties, training for PSD officers to transition the JIPTC from USG management;

g. a director for the Jordan International Police Training Center.

Article IV
PERFORMANCE GOALS AND MEASUREMENTS OF EFFECTIVENESS

Bearing in mind the mutual goals set forth in the Preamble to this Agreement, the measurements of effective performance shall be set forth in detail in the Statement of Work, to be provided separately.

Article V
SERVICES

The USG will provide to the GOJ a list of all currently identified service areas in which the PSD may be interested in performing. All service areas (new and existing) will have a Statement of Work ("SOW") defined by the JIPTC. Each such SOW will contain standards, measurable and quantifiable performance metrics, performance measures, and the appropriate performance-reporting period(s). The JIPTC staff, with assistance as necessary from other USG staff, will work with the PSD to clarify any subject matter or procedural or process area required to plan, implement, and conclude PSD work in any of the desired service areas. At the conclusion of these discussions, an approved and operative SOW agreement will be signed by the JIPTC and PSD duly authorized representatives; such signatures shall mean that the parties understand the SOW and the operational procedures required by each service area, and that PSD agrees to provide the services under the terms and conditions stipulated, including but not limited to written requirements, standards, costs/pricing, invoicing and payment procedures, performance metrics, measures, and reporting requirements.

Article VI
JOINT REVIEW BOARD

Representatives of the USG and the GOJ will meet at least once per quarter to review performance, and evaluate program progress towards the overall training goals and objectives. This quarterly meeting will also provide the joint forum in which the Parties may raise other issues related to this LOA. Project progress will be evaluated jointly, in accordance with the performance measurements and other criteria developed in accordance with the service area SOWs and subsequent discussions. Information to be considered in conducting these evaluations will include both qualitative and quantitative indicators. To facilitate this process, the JIPTC will prepare an agenda in advance of each meeting. JIPTC will also prepare a summary report of each meeting, which will be presented each quarter to the appropriate senior representatives of the USG and GOJ. These evaluations are in addition to the ongoing monitoring of the programs and activities conducted by relevant personnel of both governments.

Article VII
STANDARD PROVISIONS

A. FUNDS

1. Disbursement of USG funds shall be for acquisition and or use of property, equipment, supplies, material (hereinafter collectively "property"), utilities, and services provided or to be prepared to provide.

It is the intent of the Parties that this LOA shall constitute an obligating document. It will be accompanied by a face sheet setting forth the amount and other documentation required.

2. Funds obligated by the USG that have not been spent within twelve months following the close of the USG fiscal year in which the LOA is signed may be de-obligated by the USG. An extension of this period may be granted by the USG, the Bureau of International Narcotics and Law Enforcement Affairs ("INL") acting on its behalf.

3. The GOJ shall support the project(s) in the LOA by ensuring adequate funding for normal administrative and related expenses for Jordanian personnel within its areas of responsibility. These expenses include the payment of rents, telephone costs, salaries and benefits (including medical and other insurance protections), per diem, and travel costs within Jordan, personal equipment and uniforms, and recruiting and retaining competent personnel. This provision does not apply to those Jordanian Police officers participating in the JIPTC whose compensation the USG has agreed to fund.

B. PROPERTY

1. Property furnished to the GOJ through funds provided by the USG shall be used to further the object and purpose of this LOA. The GOJ shall return to the USG, or reimburse the USG for the original purchase price of, any property that it obtains through funds provided by the USG that is not used in accordance with this provision.

2. The GOJ shall not authorize the export, re-export, transfer, loan, sale or other disposition of any property provided to it under this LOA without the prior written authorization of the USG. Funds derived from the export, re-export, transfer, loan, sale or other disposition of any property furnished or funded by the USG to GOJ under this LOA shall be used to further the objective of the LOA.

3. All property furnished or funded under this LOA shall be accounted for to the U.S. Embassy by the GOJ in no less rigorous manner than would be used if the property was acquired by the GOJ with GOJ funds.

4. Unless otherwise specified, the GOJ shall hold the title to all fixed property procured with funds provided by the USG under this LOA.

C. MONITORING AND EVALUATION

1. Each Party shall have the right:

a. to examine any property furnished or funded by that Party under this LOA to determine that such property is being used in accordance with the terms of the LOA, and;

b. to inspect and audit any records and accounts with respect to funds, property, or services furnished or funded by that Party under this LOA to determine that such funds, property, and services are being utilized in accordance with the terms of this LOA.

2. In addition to periodic evaluations, the Parties shall monitor the progress of implementation of this LOA, including the use of funds, property, and services furnished or funded under this LOA at least annually. Each Party shall assign qualified personnel to participate in the monitoring and evaluation process.

3. Each Party shall furnish the other with information necessary to evaluate the effectiveness of project operations under the terms of this LOA.

D. APPLICABLE LAWS

1. Each party shall expend funds and support project operations in accordance with its applicable laws and regulations.

2. Whenever feasible and reasonable, all property furnished or funded by the USG under this LOA shall be procured in and shipped from the United States unless otherwise provided for in this LOA, or in any project annex, or as otherwise authorized in writing by the USG.

E. IMPORTATION, EXPORTATION, TAXES, PRIVILEGES AND IMMUNITIES

1. The provisions of Article V of the JIPTC Agreement, "Contracting," paragraph a, c, and d only, shall apply, *mutatis mutandis*. Accordingly, in accordance with applicable laws and regulations, the JIPTC and its designated representative(s) or agent(s) may:

a. award contracts or other similar agreements for construction and major repair and maintenance at the Muwaqqar and Jawa facilities identified in Article II of the JIPTC Agreement. The JIPTC, and its contractors present in Jordan for the purposes set forth herein may also carry out construction work with JIPTC personnel regarding the facilities and locations identified in Article II of the JIPTC Agreement;

b. employ nationals of states who are participating members of the multi-national force in Iraq, permanent residents or citizens of Jordan, and nationals of other countries in connection with this LOA or in connection with a contract or similar agreement entered into pursuant to or in furtherance of this LOA. The JIPTC, its personnel and contractors shall be exempted from payment of all dues and customs, duties, taxes, personal or real, or similar charges by Jordan, its instrumentalities or any subdivision thereof for the acquisition of goods and services in Jordan on behalf of the JIPTC in connection with this LOA, or in connection with a contract or similar agreement entered into pursuant to or in furtherance of this LOA.

2. The provisions of Article VII of the JIPTC Agreement, "Importation, Exportation, and Taxes," shall apply, mutatis mutandis. Accordingly:

a. all materials, equipment, supplies, relocatable structures and other property (including funds) required by the JIPTC or its contractors in connection with this LOA, or in connection with a contract or similar agreement entered into pursuant to or in furtherance of this LOA, and such property required for the personal use of JIPTC personnel, and JIPTC trainees in Jordan in connection with this LOA or in connection with a contract or similar agreement entered into pursuant to or in furtherance of this LOA shall be permitted entry into, acquired, used within and exportation from, Jordan free of customs duties, taxes and related charges. Taxes include but are not limited to import tax, value added tax on zero base and excise tax.

b. JIPTC contractors (excluding Jordanian corporations, citizens and permanent residents) shall be exempt from payment of taxes on income, salaries and emoluments, or on any property in Jordan due to their presence there in connection with the LOA or in connection with a contract or similar agreement entered into pursuant to or in furtherance of this LOA.

3. The provisions of Article VTII of the JIPTC Agreement, "Privileges and Immunities," shall apply, *mutatis mutandis*. Accordingly:

a. JIPTC personnel and IP trainees shall be accorded a status equivalent to that provided to the administrative and technical staff of the U.S. Embassy in Amman under the Vienna Convention on Diplomatic Relations concluded April 18, 1961. This status includes the right of temporary entry of privately owned motor vehicles.

b. upon notification by the JIPTC, Jordan shall accord the Director, International Police Training Center, and all International Police Training Center Deputy Directors, who are not Jordanian citizens or permanent residents, privileges and immunities equivalent to those accorded to diplomatic agents under the Vienna Convention on Diplomatic Relations concluded April 18, 1961.

F. ENTRY AND EXIT

GOJ shall facilitate the entry into, movement to and from the MUWAQAR and JAWA facilities, and exit from Jordan of JIPTC personnel, its contractors and their employees, and JIPTC trainees entering and exiting Jordan in connection with this LOA or similar agreement entered into pursuant to or in furtherance of this LOA. Procedures for the expedited issue of visas and other required accommodations by Jordan shall be in accordance with procedures as mutually agreed. Jordan shall not charge for visas and residence permits issued in connection with this LOA, or in connection with a contract or similar agreement entered into pursuant to or in furtherance of this LOA.

G. HUMAN RIGHTS

The Parties recognize that the protection of human rights is an important element of this LOA. Towards this end, the Parties understand that:

1. USG funding provided to the GOJ in exchange for security, base support, material supplies and services in support of the Iraq police training program is conditioned on the GOJ actively protecting human rights in Jordan.

2. in accordance with United States law and policy, no USG assistance or funds shall be provided under this LOA to or for use by a unit of the security forces of the GOJ if the USG has credible evidence that such a unit has committed gross violations of human rights, unless the USG determines that the GOJ is taking effective measures to bring the responsible members of the security forces unit to justice. The Parties understand that "effective measures" means that the Hashemite Kingdom of Jordan is carrying out a credible investigation and that the individuals involved face appropriate disciplinary action or impartial prosecution in accordance with Jordanian law.

Article VIII
FINAL CLAUSES

1. After this LOA has been signed by duly authorized representatives of the Parties, this LOA shall enter into force upon ratification by the Jordanian Council of Ministers. The terms of the LOA may only be amended by mutual written agreement.

2. Upon the entry into force of this Agreement, contracts in place under the JIPTC Agreement may remain in effect during a period of transition of one hundred fifty (150) days to permit the Parties to solicit and compete such contracts for goods and services as may be required to implement this agreement. The USG also encourages the GOJ and/or its agents, if they so desire, to compete in accordance with Article III, A., 7 of this LOA. The USG will give due consideration to responses from Jordanian firms to any such full and open competition.

3. Either Party may terminate this LOA by giving the other Party ninety (90) days prior written notice of its intention to terminate. The USG may suspend its obligations under this LOA in whole or in part upon giving the GOJ written notice with immediate effect.

4. Notwithstanding the termination of this LOA, the obligations of GOJ under Article VII, Paragraph B of this LOA relating to the use of property shall continue to apply without respect to time unless otherwise agreed in writing by the Parties.

DONE at Amman and the City of Washington, in duplicate, in the English and Arabic languages, both texts being equally authentic.

For the Government of the
United States of America

[Signature]
William E. Todd
Principal Deputy Asst. Secretary
Bureau of International Narcotics
and Law Enforcement Affairs

Date: *9/24/2004*

For the Government of the
Hashemite Kingdom of Jordan

[Signature]
General Tahsin Shurdom
Director of Public Security

Date: *9/24/2004*

STATE DEPARTMENT DOCUMENT NUMBER: 06-285

AMENDMENT NO. 1 TO THE STRATEGIC OBJECTIVE GRANT AGREEMENT OF JULY 11, 2005 BETWEEN THE UNITED STATES OF AMERICA AND THE REPUBLIC OF INDONESIA TO SUPPORT EFFECTIVE DEMOCRATIC AND DECENTRALIZED GOVERNANCE IN INDONESIA

SIGNED AT JAKARTA,
NOVEMBER 16, 2005
ENTERED INTO FORCE NOVEMBER 16, 2005

CTIA DOCUMENT NUMBER: 12665.002

Dated: NOVEMBER 16, 2005

This AMENDMENT No. 1 is entered into by and between the Government of the United States of America, acting through the United States Agency for International Development ("USAID") and the Government of the REPUBLIC OF INDONESIA, acting through the National Development Planning Agency, BAPPENAS ("Grantee").

WHEREAS, the Grantee and USAID entered into a Strategic Objective Grant Agreement for Effective Democratic and Decentralized Governance in Indonesia ("Grant Agreement") on July 11, 2005, whereby USAID agreed, subject to the availability of funds, to grant to the Grantee up to Thirty One Million Eight Hundred and Four Thousand Six Hundred Eighty Four United States Dollars ($31,804,684).

WHEREAS, USAID and the Grantee desire to amend the Grant Agreement to provide an additional increment of USAID Grant financing in the amount of Nine Million United States Dollars ($9,000,000) and to make other changes in the Grant Agreement relating to the total USAID contribution.

NOW, THEREFORE, the Grantee and USAID hereby agree to amend the Grant Agreement ("Amendment No.1") as follows:

1. In order to increase the amount of the current Grant of $31,804,684 by a new increment of **$9,000,000** the first sentence of Section 3.1 (a) (*The Grant.*) is amended and restated in its entirety to read:

> Section 3.1. (a) The Grant. To help achieve the Objective set forth in this Agreement, USAID, pursuant to the Foreign Assistance Act of 1961, as amended, and in accordance with the budget contained in Annex 1, hereby grants to the Grantee under the terms of the Agreement up to **Forty Million Eight**

Hundred and Four Thousand Six Hundred Eighty Four United States ("U.S") Dollars ($40,804,684) (the "Grant")."

2. In order to increase that total estimated contribution to the achievement of the Objective by a new increment of **$9,000,000** the first sentence of Section 3.1. (b) (Total Estimated USAID Contribution) is amended and restated in its entirety to read:

> "Section 3.1 (b) Total Estimated USAID Contribution. USAID's total estimated contribution to the achievement of the Objective will be **One Hundred and Twenty-Nine Millions U.S. Dollars ($129,000,000),** which will be provided in increments. Subsequent increments will be subject to the availability of funds to USAID for this purpose, and the mutual agreement of the Parties, at the time of each subsequent increment, to proceed. The Estimated Contribution under this Strategic Objective Agreement supports the five-year (2004-2008) USAID Democratic and Decentralized Governance Strategy."

3. In order to reflect the increase in USAID grant funding, the Financial Plan of Annex 1, Attachment 1 of the Original Grant Agreement is amended and restated in its entirety to read in the form of the attached Revised Financial Plan (October 2005) Attachment 1 to this Amendment No. 1.

4. Section C.4 of the Amplified Description, Annex 1 is amended to add Section C.4 (f) and is restated in its entirety in the attached Amplified Description, Annex 1 to this Amendment No.1.

5. Except as amended herein, the terms and conditions of the Grant Agreement shall remain in full force and effect.

IN WITNESS WHEREOF, the Grantee and USAID each acting through its duly authorized representative, have caused the Amendment No. 1 to be signed in their names and delivered as of the day and year first above written.

FOR THE GOVERNMENT OF
THE REPUBLIC OF INDONESIA

[Signature]

Mr. I Dewa Putu Rai
Deputy Minister for Political, Law, Defense and Security Affairs
National Development Planning Agency (BAPPENAS)

FOR THE GOVERNMENT OF
THE UNITED STATES OF AMERICA

[Signature]

Mr. William M. Frej
USAID Mission Director to Indonesia

WITNESSED BY:

[Signature]

Dr. Sri Mulyani Indrawati
Minister of State for National Development Planning

WITNESSED BY:

[Signature]

Mr. James R. Kunder
Assistant Administrator for Asia and Near East (ANE) Bureau,
USAID/Washington, DC

State Department Document Number: 06-286

Amendment No. 1 to the Memorandum of Understanding of March 3, 2001 Between the NOAA National Weather Service of the United States of America and the Saudi Arabia Meteorology and Environmental Protection Administration for Technical Cooperation in a Meteorological and Environmental Program

Signed at Jeddah and Washington D.C.,
March 15 and April 27, 2006
Entered into force April 27, 2006

CTIA DOCUMENT NUMBER: 10119.001

Title: Technical Cooperation in a Meteorological and Environmental Program.

Period of performance of this Memorandum is hereby extended to September 1, 2006.

[Signature]

APPROVED BY:

[Signature] Presidency of Meteorology and Environment Kingdom of Saudi Arabia	*March 15 2006* Date
[Signature] National Oceanic and Atmospheric Administration United States of America	*4/27/06* Date

STATE DEPARTMENT DOCUMENT NUMBER: 06-287

MEMORANDUM OF UNDERSTANDING BETWEEN THE UNITED STATES OF AMERICA NATIONAL AERONAUTICS AND SPACE ADMINISTRATION (NASA) AND THE INDIAN SPACE RESEARCH ORGANISATION (ISRO) ON COOPERATION CONCERNING NASA'S MINIATURE SYNTHETIC APERTURE RADAR INSTRUMENT ON ISRO'S CHANDRAYAAN-1 MISSION

SIGNED AT BANGALORE,
MAY 9, 2006
ENTERED INTO FORCE MAY 9, 2006

CTIA DOCUMENT NUMBER: 13114.000

Preamble

The United States National Aeronautics and Space Administration (hereinafter referred to as NASA) and the Indian Space Research Organisation (hereinafter referred to as ISRO);

As the Parties to this Memorandum of Understanding (MOU) (hereinafter the Parties);

CONSIDERING that the United States and India have agreed upon a major initiative to enhance joint activities in space cooperation;

CONSIDERING ISRO's plan to fly a mission, Chandrayaan-1, designed to map the Moon from polar lunar orbit in 2007;

CONSIDERING the release of the Announcement of Opportunity by ISRO, calling for proposals from interested foreign investigators to fly instruments on Chandrayaan-1;

CONSIDERING the selection by ISRO of the "Mini-SAR: An Imaging Radar for the Chandrayaan-1 Mission" proposal to characterize and map the environment and deposits of the lunar polar regions;

RECOGNIZING the need for a mission to collect these data to understand better the nature and properties of the lunar polar regions, this information being critical to the future of humanity on the Moon; and

CONSIDERING that cooperation on such a mission would be beneficial to both nations and to future human activities on the Moon;

Have agreed as follows:

Article 1 – Purpose

This MOU sets forth the terms and conditions under which the Parties will cooperate on the Chandrayaan-1 Mission with regard to the Miniature Synthetic Aperture Radar (Mini-SAR) instrument.

Article 2 – Definitions

As used in this MOU, the following terms shall have the specified meanings:

2.1 "S-band radar data" is data as received from the Mini-SAR instrument, including sensor and housekeeping data.

2.2 "Payload resource evaluation data" is the portion of the S-band radar data composed of the instrument sensor data.

2.3 "Instrument housekeeping data" is engineering health and status data necessary for the daily operation of the Mini-SAR instrument in flight as well as for providing surface location knowledge necessary to produce validated flight data products.

Article 3 – Mission Description and Participation

3.1 The primary objective of the Chandrayaan-1 Mission is to map key properties of the Moon from polar orbit to better understand its history, evolution, and current state. These objectives include the mapping of Polar Regions and their deposits to address the scientific and resource questions regarding the volatile content of the lunar poles.

3.2 The NASA-sponsored Miniature Synthetic Aperture Radar (Mini-SAR) instrument, selected by ISRO for flight on Chandrayaan-1 after an international solicitation and competition, is a collaboration between NASA and ISRO on the acquisition and interpretation of data from the Mini-SAR developed for NASA and flown by ISRO. The Mini-SAR instrument is to be designed, developed, fabricated, integrated and tested by the Naval Air Warfare Center (NAWC), with support from the Johns Hopkins University Applied Physics Laboratory (JHU/APL), and is to be provided to ISRO for integration and flight on the Chandrayaan-1 spacecraft by JHU/APL.

3.3 The Chandrayaan-1 Mission is conceived, designed, built and flown by ISRO. This Indian mission is aimed at expanding the scientific knowledge about the Moon, and is to provide, through the independent initiative and effort of India, an exceptional international contribution to planetary research. The NASA Mini-SAR instrument on the Indian Chandrayaan-1 spacecraft has been accepted in exchange for the joint sharing of the collected scientific final data products. The Chandrayaan-1 spacecraft, integrated and tested under ISRO responsibility, is to carry the Mini-SAR instrument, which is to be operated by the plan and procedure that will be provided by a resource evaluation and engineering team at JHU/APL during the Chandrayaan-1 Mission. The Payload Operations Center (POC), which. is to prepare the plan and procedure to operate the instrument in flight, process and archive the data to the NASA international Planetary Data System (PDS), is to be located at JHU/APL. The POC is a ground system comprising two primary subsystems (a) a command/sequence generation subsystem for instrument operations, and (b) a data processing subsystem for calibrating and processing raw scientific flight data of the lunar surface (the Indian Space Science Data Center (ISSDC) is to also have a POC Data Processing Subsystem replica (delivered by JHU/APL) to mutually process collected raw scientific and resource-related flight data).

3.4 Mini-SAR is to map both poles from 80 degrees latitude poleward in both right-and left-circular polarizations at a resolution of 150 m (75 m/pixel). The poles are to be mapped in both left- and right-look directions to minimize ambiguities.

3.5 In order to develop and sequence Mini-SAR operating commands, Mini-SAR instrument engineering health and status raw flight data is required, as well as other ISRO supplied ancillary data, e.g., ephemeris data, metadata indicating where the instrument bore sight/alignment is relative to the spacecraft, and spacecraft clock correlation data (initial and as updated). These data streams are to be transmitted upon receipt electronically between the POC and the ISSDC.

3.6 The Chandrayaan-1 spacecraft is planned to operate for a nominal period of 2 years. The satellite is to be operated by ISRO throughout the life of the mission. The U.S. Mini-SAR Team is to plan and command the Mini-SAR instrument by providing commands to the ISRO satellite control center for uplink. Following Mini-SAR instrument raw flight data collection both the U.S. resource evaluation and ISRO science teams are to mutually oversee the production of fully calibrated and processed data products. Both teams are to have replicas of the fully integrated and tested POC ground system (hardware, software, and related documentation) for processing the raw flight data. Upon receipt of the Mini-SAR instrument raw flight data from the spacecraft, the ISSDC is to electronically transmit a complete set of Mini-SAR instrument raw flight data to the POC. Both teams are to process the Mini-SAR raw flight data mutually and simultaneously. Fully calibrated and processed Mini-SAR flight data are to then be shared and reconciled between the two teams. Any improvements of processing POC software, and processed data products are to be mutually transferred and shared between the two teams as this occurs. Fully processed final data products that have been mutually scientifically validated and mutually agreed upon by both teams, are to be distributed in a timely manner to the international scientific community via public domain Planetary Data Systems (PDSs). This data production process is to be continuous throughout the Chandrayaan-1 Mission. The focus of this effort is on those aspects related to topography, shadow, and ice and information necessary for future exploration of the lunar poles. Scientific/resource evaluation data repository/publication is to then occur in the public domain.

3.7 Payload resource evaluation data and data products are to be made available to the Chandrayaan-1 ISRO science team and the broader international user community according to the policies outlined in Article 16.

Article 4 – ISRO Responsibilities

To implement this collaborative effort, ISRO shall use reasonable efforts to:

4.1 Provide the overall systems engineering function for the Chandrayaan-1 Mission, including developing overall satellite system specifications, and developing, jointly with NASA and its related entity, JHU/APL, an Interface Control Document (ICD) which will define the Chandrayaan-1/Mini-SAR instrument hardware/software interfaces.

4.2 Provide spacecraft engineering, develop a spacecraft configuration document, establish requirements for overall spacecraft-level payload interface testing, plan and conduct spacecraft-level payload interface tests, evaluate test results to certify flight readiness, and provide a mutually agreed upon Chandrayaan-1/Mini-SAR instrument ICD.

4.3 Support integration of the Mini-SAR instrument onto the Chandrayaan-1 spacecraft, perform spacecraft-level functional and environmental testing, and launch the spacecraft from the Indian launch facility.

4.4 Support end-to-end, system-level testing by performing functional tests of the Chandrayaan-1 spacecraft, including interface testing to and from the POC with NASA-provided data archival centers.

4.5 Provide spacecraft-level ground support equipment and qualified personnel at appropriate sites to support payload and system integration, testing, launch, and operations.

4.6 Receive, process, archive and provide to JHU/APL raw and processed Mini-SAR instrument and related spacecraft data upon receipt, as specified in the Chandrayaan-1/Mini-SAR Implementation Plan; provide JHU/APL with instrument-generated telemetry and spacecraft telemetry, as needed, to assess the health and safety of the Mini-SAR instrument, in agreed-upon formats; retain this data to enable it to be rerequested by JHU/APL, if needed; provide JHU/APL with "geometry," e.g., Space, Planet, Instrument, Camera-matrix, and Events kernel data, as needed; and receive Mini-SAR instrument commands and integrate them into the overall command load to be sent to the Chandrayaan-1 spacecraft.

4.7 Perform system-level testing between the spacecraft and the ISRO ground system, including joint testing with the POC.

4.8 Provide the spacecraft support necessary for the Mini-SAR instrument to perform on-orbit calibration activities, as agreed, after launch and according to a schedule defined in the Chandrayaan-1/ Mini-SAR Implementation Plan, to verify the performance achieved in lunar orbit by the Mini-SAR instrument, and such that the POC can provide calibrated data products to NASA, ISRO and the international community.

4.9 Arrange with the appropriate Indian research organizations to support and prepare the Indian and other international members of the science teams and Indian and other international users to analyze and validate the Chandrayaan-1 non-Mini-SAR payload resource evaluation data and related data products and publish their findings in accordance with Articles 8, 16, and 17; in particular, in archiving and/or making available, as appropriate, Chandrayaan-1 science data products to the scientific community.

4.10 Inform NASA and JHU/APL promptly of any technical or programmatic problems which may affect overall Mini-SAR instrument and POC development and operations, schedule, cost, or technical performance.

4.11 Provide mutual access to the Mini-SAR instrument flight data products from Chandrayaan-1. If deemed of interest for scientific analysis of Mini-SAR instrument data, the Parties may agree to provide mutual access to correlative data products from other missions.

4.12 Agree with NASA to investigate the issues related to coordinated measurements between Chandrayaan-1 and NASA's Lunar Reconnaissance Orbiter Mission (LRO), specifically, the possibility of conducting a bistatic imaging and far-side gravity experiment using compatible equipment on both spacecraft, which would be studied scientifically and operationally, and if feasible, incorporated into a joint operational plan.

4.13 Place the science data of the other Chandrayaan-1 instruments into the public domain for use by the international science and space technology community.

4.14 ISRO shall provide appropriate transmit filtering of its X-band downlink signal to preclude any harmful interference into deep space earth station receiving operations in the 8400 – 8450 MHz band in compliance with the Space Frequency Coordination Group (SFCG) Recommendation REC 21-2R2 and Decision 25-1.

Article 5 – NASA Responsibilities

To implement this cooperative project, NASA shall use reasonable efforts to:

5.1 Provide Mini-SAR instrument and Chandrayaan-1/Mini-SAR instrument interface system engineering and develop overall Mini-SAR and POC system specifications and requirements documents which will define the Chandrayaan-1/Mini-SAR instrument interfaces, including those to the POC that demonstrate compliance with mission requirements.

5.2 Develop, in coordination with ISRO, an ICD which will define the Chandrayaan-1/Mini-SAR instrument hardware/software interfaces.

5.3 Provide requirements for overall payload-level testing, the planning and conduct of payload system-level tests, evaluation of test results and certification of payload flight readiness.

5.4 Design, fabricate, assemble, and test the Mini-SAR instrument.

5.5 Provide information on Mini-SAR instrument interfaces to the Chandrayaan-1 spacecraft.

5.6 Design, fabricate, and test the NASA-provided ground system.

5.7 Design, fabricate, and test the NASA POC and install a replica at ISSDC.

5.8 Perform end-to-end Mini-SAR instrument and POC system-level testing.

5.9 Transport the pay load to the ISRO-designated site, in preparation for satellite integration.

5.10 Provide pay load ground support equipment including a payload simulator and qualified personnel at appropriate sites to support satellite and system integration, testing, launch, and operations.

5.11 Provide the necessary plan and procedure to ISRO to carry out Mini-SAR instrument flight operations and instrument management

5.12 Perform Mini-SAR instrument evaluation and calibration activities, as agreed, after launch and according to a schedule defined in the Chandrayaan-1 Project Plan, to verify the performance achieved on-orbit by the Mini-SAR and provide results to ISRO.

5.13 Process and archive all Mini-SAR instrument data and make the payload resource data and related flight data products available to ISRO, in a timely manner and in accordance with Article 16.

5.14 Support the U.S. resource evaluation team members in analyzing and validating Mini-SAR flight data and related data products and in publishing their findings, in accordance with Articles 7, 16, and 17.

5.15 Inform ISRO promptly of any Mini-SAR technical or programmatic problems which may affect overall Chandrayaan-1 Mission schedule, cost, or technical performance.

5.16 Provide mutual access to the Mini-SAR instrument flight data products from Chandrayaan-1. If deemed of interest for scientific analysis of Mini-SAR instrument data, the Parties may agree to provide mutual access to correlative data products from other missions.

5.17 Provide support to JHU/APL to configure its 18 m ground station to allow its use by the Chandrayaan-1 Mission. Upon request by ISRO, this station may be used for tracking, commanding, receipt of housekeeping telemetry, and receipt of science data.

Article 6 – Project and Program Management

6.1 A Chandrayaan-1/Mini-SAR Joint Steering Group (JSG) shall be established to provide implementation oversight for the collaborative effort. The Chandrayaan-1/Mini-SAR JSG shall be composed of senior-level NASA and ISRO representatives involved in the development of the Chandrayaan-1/Mini -SAR collaborative effort. The JSG shall review the effort's implementation status, resolve implementation conflicts, and provide institutional resources to ensure timely delivery of collaborative effort elements.

6.2 The NASA Mini-SAR Principal Investigator (PI) function is a shared responsibility between NAWC and JHU/APL. The NASA Program Manager shall provide end-to-end Mini-SAR oversight in consultation with the Chandrayaan-1 Project Director and is the NASA official responsible for the success of the project.

6.3 The Mini-SAR Project Manager shall prepare, in close coordination with the ISRO Chandrayaan-1 Project Director, the Chandrayaan-1 Mini-SAR Implementation Plan, which shall then be subject to approval by the Parties. In case of conflict between this Chandrayaan-1 Mini-SAR Implementation Plan and the MOU, the MOU shall prevail. This plan shall detail how the Mini-SAR contribution to the Chandrayaan-1 Mission will be accomplished, including mission planning, instrument development and delivery, rough description of the interfaces (to be more specifically defined in an Interface Control Document), data flow and downlink options, conduct of mission operations, and data delivery. The delivery process and timeline for Mini-SAR data from ISRO shall be defined.

6.4 The Parties shall act in accordance with the schedules to be defined in the Chandrayaan-1 Mini-SAR Implementation Plan and to avoid changes that will have a negative effect on the other Party with regard to scientific return, implementation approach, cost, and/or schedule, and where they cannot be avoided, to minimize these negative effects. To the extent that changes made by NASA or ISRO to the Chandrayaan-1 Mini-SAR Implementation Plan cause schedule or other problems that go beyond either Party's program constraints, the Mini-SAR Project Manager and ISRO Chandrayaan-1 Project Director shall discuss potential options to address such problems and submit their proposal to NASA and ISRO Management.

Article 7 – U.S. Resource Evaluation Team

7.1 The U.S. Resource Evaluation Team, formed by the NASA Mini-SAR PI, shall be responsible for the resource evaluation management of the Mini-SAR experiment on the Chandrayaan-1 Mission. The Mini-SAR U.S. Resource Evaluation Team shall be the principal scientific and technical forum for instrument oversight, validation of resource data, and initial resource data evaluation studies.

7.2 Additionally, the Mini-SAR U.S. Resource Evaluation Team may select scientists or other specialists with an expertise in the area, to perform resource data evaluation. The Parties reserve the right to establish guest investigator programs for validation and resource data evaluation studies.

7.3 The Mini-SAR PI shall be responsible for the development of the scientific and technical aspects of the Mini-SAR experiment and for assuring that the resource data products are effectively used and that the results are expeditiously produced and made available, according to Article 16. The Mini-SAR PI shall also be responsible for coordinating Mini-SAR resource evaluation requirements with the other U.S. resource evaluation team organizations.

Article 8 – ISRO Chandrayaan-1 Science Working Team

8.1 The ISRO Chandrayaan-1 Science Working Team, formed by ISRO, shall be responsible for the science management of the Chandrayaan-1 Mission. The ISRO Science Team consists of scientists from ISRO and other Indian research institutions, as well as the PIs from each of the international guest payloads. The ISRO science team shall be the principal scientific forum for mission oversight, mission validation of science data, and initial mission-level science data evaluation studies.

8.2 Additionally, the ISRO Science Team may select scientists with relevant expertise to perform science data evaluation. The Parties reserve the right to establish guest investigator programs for validation and science data evaluation studies for their respective instruments.

8.3 The ISRO science team shall be responsible for the development of the scientific aspects of the Chandrayaan-1 Mission and for assuring that the mission-level science data products are effectively used and that the results are expeditiously produced and made available, according to Article 16. They shall also be responsible for coordinating mission-level science requirements with the other international science team organizations.

Article 9 – Mission Reviews, Integration, and Flight Readiness

9.1 To implement the Mini-SAR experiment, there will be a series of interface reviews to evaluate the readiness of the flight and ground segments to proceed to implementation, integration, test, and final launch preparation. Representatives from both Parties shall attend these reviews. Both Parties shall furnish engineering and programmatic data and shall participate in payload to spacecraft interface reviews, as mutually agreed. As required, as a result of these reviews, the Chandrayaan-1/ Mini-SAR instrument ICD shall be updated accordingly.

9.2 NASA and ISRO shall jointly make a final determination of the overall readiness to proceed with integration of the payload to the spacecraft and the readiness of the payload for flight.

Article 10 – Exchange of Personnel

Each of the Parties shall facilitate the movement of persons necessary to implement this MOU into and out of its country subject to its laws and regulations. To facilitate coordination related to the Chandrayaan-1 Mission, the Parties may exchange a limited number of liaison visits from each Party, at times and under conditions as mutually agreed by the NASA Mini-SAR Project Manager and ISRO Chandrayaan-1 Project Director, pursuant to necessary administrative authorizations. In the event of such an exchange, each Party shall provide necessary office space and administrative support at the host location, including such additional support services as may be agreed by the Parties. Salary and all other personnel expenses and living and travel expenses, shall be borne by the employing Party of the liaison(s) throughout the duration of their assignment.

Article 11 – Funding

Each Party shall bear the costs of discharging its respective responsibilities under this MOU, including travel and subsistence of each Party's personnel and transportation of its own equipment and associated documentation. The obligations of the Parties under this MOU are subject to their respective funding procedures and the availability of appropriated funds.

Article 12 – Customs and Taxes

Each Party shall facilitate the arrangement of free customs clearance and waiver of applicable duties and taxes for equipment and related goods necessary for the implementation of this MOU. Such facilitation of arrangements shall be fully reciprocal. In the event that any customs fees and/or taxes of any kind are still levied on the equipment and related goods for implementation of this MOU, after seeking to obtain the appropriate free customs clearance and waiver of applicable duties and taxes, such customs fees and/or taxes shall be borne by the Party of the country levying the fees and/or taxes.

Article 13 – Ownership of Elements and Equipment

For the purposes of this MOU, each Party shall retain ownership of elements and equipment it furnishes to the other Party. Any equipment not launched into space shall be returned to the furnishing Party expeditiously, as mutually agreed. Each Party shall transport its equipment to the designated delivery points, as specified in the Chandrayaan-1/Mini-SAR Implementation Plan, and, where appropriate, from such delivery points, when the equipment is to be returned to the furnishing Party.

Article 14 – Transfer of Goods and Technical Data

The Parties are obligated to transfer only those technical data (including software) and goods necessary to fulfill their respective responsibilities under this MOU, in accordance with the following provisions, notwithstanding any other provision of this MOU:

14.1 All activities of the Parties shall be carried out in accordance with their national laws and regulations, including those pertaining to export control and the control of classified information.

14.2 The transfer of technical data for the purpose of discharging the Parties' responsibilities with regard to interface, integration, and safety shall normally be made without restriction, except as provided in paragraph 14.1 above.

14.3 All transfers of goods and proprietary or export-controlled technical data are subject to the following provisions. In the event a Party or its related entity (e.g., contractor, subcontractor, grantee, cooperating entity) finds it necessary to transfer goods or to transfer proprietary or export-controlled technical data, for which protection is to be maintained, such goods shall be specifically identified and such proprietary or export-controlled technical data shall be marked. The identification for goods and the marking on proprietary or export-controlled technical data shall indicate that the goods and proprietary or export-controlled technical data shall be used by the receiving Party or related entities only for the purposes of fulfilling the receiving Party's or related entity's responsibilities under this MOU, and that the identified goods and marked proprietary technical data or marked export-controlled technical data shall not be disclosed or retransferred to any other entity without the prior written permission of the furnishing Party or its related entity. The receiving Party or related entity shall abide by the terms of the notice and protect any such identified goods and marked proprietary technical data or marked export-controlled technical data from unauthorized use and disclosure. The Parties to this MOU shall cause their related entities to be bound by the provisions of this Article related to use, disclosure, and retransfer of goods and marked technical data through contractual mechanisms or equivalent measures.

14.4 All goods exchanged in the performance of this MOU shall be used by the receiving Party or related entity exclusively for the purposes of the MOU. Upon completion of the activities under the MOU, the receiving Party or related entity shall return or, at the request of the furnishing Party or its related entity, otherwise dispose of all goods and marked proprietary technical data or marked export-controlled technical data provided under this MOU, as directed by the furnishing Party or related entity.

Article 15 – Intellectual Property

15.1 For the purposes of this Article, "Related Entity" includes, but is not limited to, contractors, subcontractors, grantees, or cooperating entities (or any lower tier contractor, subcontractor, grantee, or cooperating entities) of a Party.

15.2 PATENTS

15.2.1 Nothing in this Agreement shall be construed as granting, either expressly or by implication, to the other Party any rights to, or interest in, any inventions of a Party or its Related Entities made prior to the entry into force of, or outside the scope of, this Agreement, including any patents or other forms of protection (in any country) corresponding to such inventions.

15.2.2 Any rights to, or interest in, any invention made in the performance of this Agreement solely by one Party or any of its Related Entities, including any patents or other forms of protection (in any country) corresponding to such invention, shall be owned by such Party or, subject to paragraph 15.2.4 of this Article, such Related Entity.

15.2.3 It is not anticipated that there will be any joint inventions made in the performance of this Agreement. Nevertheless, in the event that an invention is jointly made by the Parties in the performance of this Agreement, the Parties shall, in good faith, consult and agree as to: a) the allocation of rights to, or interest in, such joint invention, including any patents or other forms of protection (in any country) corresponding to such joint invention; b) the responsibilities, costs, and actions to be taken to establish and maintain patents or other forms of protection (in any country) for each such joint invention; and c) the terms and conditions of any license or other rights to be exchanged between the Parties or granted by one Party to the other Party.

15.2.4 With respect to any invention created in the performance of this Agreement and involving a Related Entity, allocation of rights between a Party and its Related Entity to such invention, including any patents or other forms of protection (in any country) corresponding to such invention, shall be determined by such Party's laws, regulations, and applicable contractual obligations.

15.3 COPYRIGHTS

15.3.1 Nothing in this Agreement shall be construed as granting, either expressly or by implication, to the other Party any rights to, or interest in, any copyrights of a Party or its Related Entities created prior to the entry into force of, or outside the scope of, this Agreement.

15.3.2 Any copyrights in works created solely by one Party or any of its Related Entities, as a result of activities undertaken in performance of this Agreement, shall be owned by such Party or Related Entity. Allocation of rights between such Party and its Related Entities to such copyrights shall be determined by such Party's laws, regulations, and applicable contractual obligations.

15.3.3 For any jointly authored work, should the Parties decide to register the copyright in such work, they shall, in good faith, consult and agree as to the responsibilities, costs, and actions to be taken to register copyrights and maintain copyright protection (in any country).

15.3.4 Subject to the provisions of Articles 14 and 17, each Party shall have an irrevocable, royalty free right to reproduce, prepare derivative works, distribute copies to the public, and perform publicly and display publicly, and authorize others to do so on its behalf, any copyrighted work resulting from activities undertaken in the performance of this Agreement for its own purposes, regardless of whether the work was created solely by, or on behalf of, that Party or jointly with the other Party, and without consulting with or accounting to the other Party.

Article 16 – Instrument Flight Data Policy

Access to Chandrayaan-1 and Mini-SAR instrument flight data shall be as follows:

16.1 The Parties shall release scientific data from the Mini-SAR to the international scientific community after a period of no longer than 12 months. The 12-month data validation and verification period begins with the receipt of the data from the spacecraft.

16.2 Data produced by the Mini-SAR instrument shall be jointly reduced and analyzed by the Mini-SAR Resource Evaluation Team and scientists of ISRO.

16.3 In all cases, the Parties shall provide immediate access to all Mini-SAR instrument flight data and data products, free of charge, for members of the teams, as well as designated representatives of team members, including associates, staff and coworkers. The Parties shall also provide, free of charge, payload flight data and data products necessary to the scientists selected for validation. The Parties shall have the right to use the data (processed and unprocessed) at any time for support of their respective responsibilities but shall not prejudice the PIs and Co-Is' first publication rights, which are established in accordance with paragraph 16.1 above.

16.4 After the 12-month validation and verification period, the Parties shall make the data from the Mini-SAR, including required calibration and spacecraft data, available to the international scientific community in a form suitable for analysis.

16.5 NASA shall make flight data products available to the public and the international community in standard Planetary Data System (PDS) format after the appropriate flight data calibration and validation. In order to promote rapid access to flight data products, some preliminary data products shall be archived after initial verification, but prior to full validation, and made available to all users at no more than the cost of fulfilling the user request.

16.6 All S-band radar data, payload data and related flight data products, and applicable ancillary data obtained from the Mini-SAR instrument shall be archived in the PDS and at the JHU/APL POC and the ISSDC. Copies of the Mini-SAR instrument flight data products shall be exchanged between the Parties.

16.7 The Mini-SAR Resource Evaluation Team members (including designated representatives) shall provide a report to the Parties on the results of their analysis and validation investigations and the results of their investigations on validated Mini-SAR instrument flight data.

16.8 Notwithstanding the termination of this MOU, any S-band radar data and payload data products, related flight data products, and applicable ancillary data obtained from the Mini-SAR instrument (as defined in the Chandrayaan-1/Mini-SAR Implementation Plan) shall be archived by NASA for at least 10 years after completion of the Chandrayaan-1 Mission, unless otherwise agreed by the Parties.

16.9 To enhance scientific and technical analysis of Mini-SAR instrument data, Announcements of Opportunity may be issued by the Parties.

16.10 The Parties note that NASA intends to include a Mini-SAR technology demonstration on the forthcoming LRO Mission. The Parties shall provide mutual access to the Mini-SAR flight data products from Chandrayaan-1 and the LRO Mission. The Parties shall agree on the terms of data access. If deemed of interest for scientific analysis of Mini-SAR data, the Parties may agree to provide mutual access to correlative data products from other missions.

16.11 Complementary data from ISRO-provided instruments on the Chandrayaan-1 Mission shall be made available, free of charge, to NASA Mini-SAR PI, upon request for the purpose of collaboration with ISRO.

16.12 Scientific data obtained by Chandrayaan-1 Mission are to be released to the international scientific community in a form suitable for analysis after a period that shall not exceed 1 year. This 1 year period shall begin with the receipt by the PIs/Co-Is of usable scientific data from the spacecraft in a form suitable for analysis. The period for producing usable scientific data should not nominally exceed 6 months following receipt of data from the spacecraft.

Article 17 – Publication of Public Information and Results

17.1 The Parties retain the right to release public information regarding their own activities under this Agreement. The Parties shall coordinate with each other in advance concerning releasing to the public information that relates to the other Party's responsibilities or performance under this Agreement.

17.2

17.2.1 The Parties shall make the final results obtained from the Chandrayaan-1 Mission available to the general scientific community through publication in appropriate journals or by presentations at scientific conferences as soon as possible and in a manner consistent with good scientific practices.

17.2.2 Each Party shall have an irrevocable, royalty-free right to reproduce, prepare derivative works from, distribute to the public copies of, present publicly, and authorize others to do so on its behalf, the scientific information included in each such publication or presentation for its own purposes. The royalty-free right shall exist irrespective of any copyright protection applicable to each such publication or presentation.

17.2.3 Raw data, analyzed data and final results primarily obtained from the Chandrayaan-1 Mini-SAR science data, or other scientific information regarding results obtained from the implementation of this Agreement, shall be disclosed by the Party, or its investigators that collected the data, analyzed the data or generated the results, to the other Party prior to any publication or presentation. The first presentation/publication will be done jointly by designated scientists of the Parties.

17.3 The Parties acknowledge that the following data or information does not constitute public information and that such data or information shall not be included in any publication or presentation by a Party under this Article without the other Party's prior written permission: 1) data furnished by the other Party in accordance with Article 14 of this Agreement which is export-controlled, classified or proprietary; or 2) information about an invention of the other Party before a patent application has been filed covering the same, or a decision not to file has been made.

Article 18 – Liability

18.1 The purpose of this Article is to establish a cross-waiver of liability between the Parties and their related entities in the interest of encouraging participation in the exploration, exploitation, and use of outer space. This cross-waiver of liability shall be broadly construed to achieve this objective.

18.2 As used in this cross-waiver,

18.2.1 The term "Related Entity" means:

(i) a contractor or subcontractor of a Party at any tier;

(ii) a user or customer of a Party at any tier; or

(iii) a contractor or subcontractor of a user or customer of a Party at any tier. "Contractors" and "subcontractors" include suppliers of any kind.

18.2.2 The term "damage" means:

(i) bodily injury to, or other impairment of health of, or death of, any person;

(ii) damage to, loss of, or loss of use of any property;

(iii) loss of revenue or profits; or

(iv) other direct, indirect, or consequential damage.

18.2.3 The term "payload" means any property to be flown or used on or in the launch vehicle.

18.2.4 The term "launch vehicle" means an object or any part thereof intended for launch, launched from Earth, or returning to Earth which carries payloads or persons, or both.

18.2.5 The term "Protected Space Operations" means all launch vehicle and payload activities on Earth, in outer space, or in transit between Earth and outer space done in implementation of this MOU. Protected Space Operations begins upon entry into force of this MOU and ends when all activities done in implementation of this MOU are completed. It includes, but is not limited to:

(i) research, design, development, test, manufacture, assembly, integration, operation, disposal, or use of launch or transfer vehicles, payloads, or instruments, as well as related support equipment and facilities and services;

(ii) all activities related to ground support, test, training, simulation, or guidance and control equipment and related facilities or services. "Protected Space Operations" excludes activities on Earth which are conducted on return from space to develop further a payload's product or process for use other than for launch vehicle-related activities necessary to complete implementation of this MOU.

18.3

18.3.1 Each Party agrees to a cross-waiver of liability pursuant to which each Party waives all claims against any of the entities or persons listed in subparagraphs (i) through (iii) of this section based on damage arising out of Protected Space Operations. This cross-waiver shall apply only if the person, entity, or property causing the damage is involved in Protected Space Operations and the person, entity, or property damaged is damaged by virtue of its involvement in Protected Space Operations. The cross-waiver shall apply to any claims for damage, whatever the legal basis for such claims, against:

(i) the other Party;

(ii) a related entity of the other Party;

(iii) the employees of any of the entities identified in sub-paragraphs (i) and (ii) above.

18.3.2 In addition, each Party shall extend the cross-waiver of liability as set forth in paragraph 18.3.1 of this section to its own related entities by requiring them, by contract or otherwise, to agree to waive all claims against the entities or persons identified in sub-paragraphs 18.3.1 (i) through (iii).

18.3.3 For avoidance of doubt, this cross-waiver of liability includes a cross-waiver of liability arising from the Convention on International Liability for Damage Caused by Space Objects of March 29, 1972, where the person, entity, or property causing the damage is involved in Protected Space Operations and the person, entity, or property damaged is damaged by virtue of its involvement in Protected Space Operations.

18.3.4 Notwithstanding the other provisions of this Article, this cross-waiver of liability shall not be applicable to the following:

(i) claims between a Party and its own related entity or between its own related entities;

(ii) claims made by a natural person, his/her estate, survivors, or subrogees for bodily injury, other impairment of health or death of such natural person, except where the subrogee is a Party to this MOU or has otherwise agreed to be bound by the promises of this cross-waiver;

(iii) claims for damage caused by willful misconduct;

(iv) intellectual property claims;

(v) contract claims between the Parties based on the express contractual provisions of this MOU; or

(vi) claims for damage based on a failure of the Parties or their related entities to flow down the cross-waiver.

18.3.5 Nothing in this Article shall be construed to create the basis for a claim or suit where none would otherwise exist.

Article 19 – Registration of Space Objects

ISRO shall request that the Government of India register the Chandrayaan-1 spacecraft as a space object in accordance with the Convention on Registration of Space Objects Launched into Outer Space of January 14, 1975. Registration pursuant to this section shall not affect the rights or obligations of either Party or its Government under the 1972 Convention on International Liability for Damage Caused by Space Objects.

Article 20 – Settlement of Disputes

Any disputes not settled through the mechanisms provided in Article 6 (Project and Program Management), or any other issue concerning the interpretation or implementation of the terms of the MOU that cannot be resolved otherwise, shall be referred to the appropriate level of management of the Parties for consideration and joint amicable resolution.

Article 21 – Entry into Force, Duration, Amendment, and Termination

21.1 This MOU shall enter into force upon signature and remain in force until ten years after the Chandrayaan-1 spacecraft has been launched. This MOU may be amended and extended by written agreement of the Parties. Either Party may terminate this MOU at any time upon at least 12 months written notice to the other Party. In that event, the Parties shall endeavor to minimize negative impacts of such termination on other Parties.

21.2 Termination of the MOU shall not affect a Party's continuing obligations under Articles 6 (Project and Program Management), 13 (Ownership of Elements and Equipment), 14 (Transfer of Goods and Technical Data), 15 (Intellectual Property), 16 (Instrument Flight Data Policy), 17 (Publication of Public Information and Results), and 18 (Liability), unless otherwise agreed to by the Parties.

FOR THE UNITED STATES
NATIONAL AERONAUTICS
AND SPACE ADMINISTRATION:

[Signature]
Michael D. Griffin
Administrator

Date: 9 May 2006

Place: Bangalore, India

FOR THE INDIAN SPACE
RESEARCH ORGANISATION:

[Signature]
G. Madhavan Nair
Chairman

Date: 9 May 2006

Place: Bangalore, India

I certify this to be a true copy of the signed original.

[Signature]
Kent Bress

STATE DEPARTMENT DOCUMENT NUMBER: 06-288

MEMORANDUM OF UNDERSTANDING BETWEEN THE UNITED STATES OF AMERICA NATIONAL AERONAUTICS AND SPACE ADMINISTRATION (NASA) AND THE INDIAN SPACE RESEARCH ORGANISATION (ISRO) ON COOPERATION CONCERNING NASA'S MOON MINERALOGY MAPPER (M3) INSTRUMENT ON ISRO'S CHANDRAYAAN-1 MISSION

SIGNED AT BANGALORE,
MAY 9, 2006
ENTERED INTO FORCE MAY 9, 2006

CTIA DOCUMENT NUMBER: 13115.000

Preamble

The United States National Aeronautics and Space Administration (hereinafter referred to as NASA), and the Indian Space Research Organisation (hereinafter referred to as ISRO);

As the Parties to this Memorandum of Understanding (MOU) (hereinafter the Parties);

CONSIDERING that the United States and India have agreed upon a major initiative to enhance joint activities in space cooperation;

CONSIDERING ISRO's plan to fly a mission, Chandrayaan-1, designed to explore the Moon from polar lunar orbit in 2007;

CONSIDERING the release of the Announcement of Opportunity by ISRO, calling for proposals from interested foreign investigators to fly instruments on Chandrayaan-1;

CONSIDERING the selection by ISRO of the Moon Mineralogy Mapper (M3) proposal to use a visible-near infrared imaging spectrometer to map the mineralogy of the Moon;

RECOGNIZING the need for a mission to collect these data to characterize and map the lunar surface composition in the context of its geologic evolution and to assess Moon mineral resources at high spatial resolution; and

CONSIDERING that cooperation on such a mission would be beneficial to both nations and to future human activities on the Moon;

Have agreed as follows:

Article 1 - Purpose

This MOU sets forth the terms and conditions under which the Parties shall cooperate in the Chandrayaan-1 Mission with regard to the M3 instrument.

Article 2 - Definitions

As used in this MOU, the following terms shall have the specified meanings:

2.1 "ISRO Chandrayaan-1 Science Working Team" consists of scientists from ISRO and other Indian research institutions, as well as the Principal Investigators (PIs) responsible for the non-Indian instruments on the Chandrayaan-1 Mission.

2.2 "M3 Science Team" consists of only those scientists selected by the M3 PI to carry out specific tasks to meet M3 science objectives, and a Co-Investigator selected by ISRO.

2.3 "M3 Instrument Data" are data received from the payload, including sensor and housekeeping data.

2.4 "Science Data Products" are data products resulting from the processing of the M3 instrument data.

Article 3 - Mission Description and Participation

3.1 The primary objective of the Chandrayaan-1 Mission is to map key properties of the Moon from polar orbit to better understand its history, evolution, and current state. These objectives include mapping the mineral resources of the Moon. To accomplish these science objectives, the Chandrayaan-1 Mission is to carry several ISRO remote sensing instruments and an impact probe, as well as a number of contributed instruments from foreign countries including the M3 sponsored by NASA.

3.2 The M3, selected by ISRO for flight on Chandrayaan-1 after an international solicitation and competition and after a NASA peer-reviewed selection, is a collaboration between NASA, which developed and fabricated the M3 instrument, and ISRO, which included the M3 instrument on its flight. The M3 Project is to be led by a PI of Brown University who is to have overall responsibility for project resources and mission success. The M3 instrument will be designed and developed at the Jet Propulsion Laboratory (JPL).

3.3 The Chandrayaan-1 Mission is conceived, designed, built, and flown by ISRO. The Chandrayaan-1 spacecraft, integrated and tested under ISRO responsibility, is to carry the M3 instrument designed and provided by JPL.

3.4 The requirements for the M3 instrument were developed by the M3 Science Team and the instrument team at JPL. These requirements define the spatial coverage, spectral resolution, and signal-to-noise value of the observations necessary to map the minerals of the Moon.

3.5 The Chandrayaan-1 Mission is to collect science data and products for the entire lunar surface.

3.6 ISRO plans for the Chandrayaan-1 spacecraft to operate for a nominal period of two years. ISRO is to operate the spacecraft throughout the life of the mission. NASA is to provide ISRO with a plan and procedure for commanding the M3 instrument from the ISRO satellite control center. NASA is to process M3 instrument data and science products, as defined in Article 5 – NASA Responsibilities and Article 16 – Science Data Policy, below. The Indian Space Science Data Center (ISSDC) is also to have an M3 Data Processing Subsystem (a replica of the Payload Operating Center (POC) workstation, to be delivered by NASA) to process collected raw scientific and resource related flight data.

3.7 M3 instrument data and science data products are to be made available to the Chandrayaan-1 Science Team and the broader international user community according to Article 16 – Science Data Policy.

Article 4 - ISRO Responsibilities

To implement this cooperative project, ISRO shall use reasonable efforts to:

4.1 Provide overall systems engineering function for the Chandrayaan-1 Mission, including in developing overall system specifications and developing jointly with JPL an Interface Control Document (ICD) which shall define the NASA/ISRO interfaces.

4.2 Provide spacecraft engineering, develop a spacecraft specification document and establish requirements for overall spacecraft-level testing, plan and conduct spacecraft-level tests, evaluate test results, certify flight readiness and provide a Payload Design Interface Specification (PDIS) between the platform and the payload.

4.3 Integrate the M3 instrument onto the Chandrayaan-1 platform, perform functional and environmental testing, and launch the spacecraft from the Indian launch facility.

4.4 Carry out end-to-end, system-level testing by performing functional tests of the satellite, including providing assistance with testing of the M3 instrument data telemetry with NASA-provided ground control and data archival centers.

4.5 Provide ground support equipment and qualified personnel at appropriate sites to support instrument and system integration, testing, launch, and operations.

4.6 Perform checkout of the Chandrayaan-1 spacecraft during the launch campaign.

4.7 Operate the spacecraft throughout the life of the mission.

4.8 Design, fabricate, test, and operate the Chandrayaan-1 Mission Control Center (MCC).

4.9 Receive, process, archive, and provide to JPL raw and processed M3 instrument data and related spacecraft data upon receipt as specified in the Chandrayaan-1 /M3 Implementation Plan.

4.10 Perform system-level testing between the spacecraft and the MCC including joint testing with the NASA-provided M3 POC workstation located at JPL.

4.11 Perform evaluation and calibration activities, as agreed, after launch and according to a schedule defined in the Chandrayaan-1 M3 Implementation Plan, to verify the performance achieved in lunar orbit.

4.12 Perform analysis and validation of M3 telemetry data during the overall mission.

4.13 Arrange with the appropriate Indian research organizations to support and prepare the Indian members of the science teams, Indian scientists, and Indian users to analyze and validate the M3 instrument data and science data products and publish their findings in accordance with Article 7 – Science Team, Article 16 – Science Data Policy, and Article 17 - Publication of Public Information and Results; in particular, in archiving and/or making available, as appropriate, Chandrayaan-1 science data products to the scientific community.

4.14 Inform NASA promptly of any technical or programmatic problems which may affect overall Chandrayaan-1 Mission schedules or performance.

Article 5 - NASA Responsibilities

To implement this cooperative project, NASA shall use reasonable efforts to:

5.1 Provide system engineering and overall system specifications for M3 and develop, with the support of ISRO, the M3 instrument/platform ICD which shall define the NASA/ISRO interfaces that demonstrate compliance to mission requirements.

5.2 Provide requirements for overall M3 instrument-level testing, the planning and conduct of M3 instrument system-level tests, evaluation of test results, and certification of flight readiness.

5.3 Design, fabricate, assemble, and test the M3 instrument.

5.4 Provide information on interfaces of the M3 instrument to the Chandrayaan-1 spacecraft

5.5 Assemble, integrate, and test the M3 instrument on Chandrayaan-1 spacecraft.

5.6 Design, fabricate, and test the NASA POC and install a replica at the ISSDC.

5.7 Perform end-to-end, system-level testing, including system-level testing between the M3 instrument data telemetry system and the NASA-provided ground system.

5.8 Transport the M3 instrument to the ISRO-designated site, in preparation for satellite integration.

5.9 Provide ground support equipment, including an M3 instrument engineering model and qualified personnel at appropriate sites, to support satellite and system integration, testing, launch, and operations.

5.10 Provide the necessary plan and procedure to ISRO for carrying out M3 instrument operations management.

5.11 Perform M3 evaluation and calibration activities, as agreed, after launch and according to a schedule defined in the Chandrayaan-1 M3 Implementation Plan, to verify the performance achieved on-orbit by the M3 instrument and provide results to ISRO.

5.12 Process and archive M3 instrument data and make the instrument data and science data products available to ISRO via the POC, as required, in a timely manner and in accordance with Article 16 - Science Data Policy.

5.13 Support the U.S. science team members in analyzing and validating M3 science data and science data products and in publishing their findings, in accordance with Article 7 – Science Team, Article 16 – Science Data Policy and Article 17 -Publication of Public Information and Results.

5.14 Inform ISRO promptly of any technical or programmatic problems which may affect the overall Chandrayaan-1 schedules or performance.

Article 6 - Project and Program Management

6.1 A Chandrayaan-1/M3 Joint Steering Group (JSG) shall be established to provide implementation oversight for the M3 instrument. The Chandrayaan-1/M3 JSG shall be composed of the M3 Program Executive and the M3 Program Scientist at NASA Headquarters, the Discovery Program Director, and ISRO representatives involved in the development of the Chandrayaan-1 Mission. The JSG shall review M3 implementation status and resolve implementation conflicts to facilitate timely delivery of the M3 instrument.

6.2 The NASA M3 PI has assigned mission implementation responsibility to the M3 Mission Management Team (MMT). The M3 Project is part of the Discovery Program which has designated a Mission Manager to oversee the M3 Project. The M3 MMT shall provide end-to-end mission planning and day-to-day management. The MMT shall be located at JPL and shall be led by the NASA/JPL M3 Project Manager who shall serve as interface to the JSG and the Discovery Program.

Article 7 - Science Team

7.1 The M3 Science Team, formed by the NASA M3 PI, shall be responsible for the science management of the M3 experiment on the Chandrayaan-1 Mission. The M3 Science Team shall be the principal scientific forum for instrument oversight, algorithm development, validation of science data, and initial science data evaluation studies. ISRO will select a Co-Investigator on the M3 Science Team, as described in Article 2.2 above.

7.2 Additionally, the Science Team may invite scientists with an expertise in the area to perform science data evaluation. The Parties reserve the right to establish guest investigator programs for science activities related to their respective payloads.

7.3 The M3 PI shall be a member of the ISRO Chandrayaan-1 Science Working Team and shall be responsible for oversight of the M3 Science Team in Chandrayaan-1 science analyses and for coordinating science requirements and plans with other organizations.

7.4 The M3 PI, supported by the Science Team, shall be responsible for the development of the scientific aspects of the experiment and for assuring that the science data products are effectively used and that the results are expeditiously produced and made available, according to Article 16 – Science Data Policy, below.

Article 8 - Chandrayaan-1 M3 Implementation Plan

8.1 The NASA M3 Project Manager shall prepare, in close coordination with the ISRO Chandrayaan-1 Project Director, the Chandrayaan-1 M3 Implementation Plan, which shall then be subject to approval by the Parties. In case of conflict between this Chandrayaan-1 M3 Implementation Plan and the MOU, the MOU shall prevail. This plan shall detail how the M3 contribution to the Chandrayaan-1 Mission will be accomplished, including mission planning, instrument development and delivery, rough description of the interfaces (to be more specifically defined in an Interface Control Document), data flow and downlink options, conduct of mission operations, and data delivery. The delivery process and timeline for M3 data from ISRO shall be defined.

8.2 To ensure mission success, NASA and ISRO shall provide mutual insight into the elements under their respective responsibility, consistent with Article 14 – Transfer of Goods and Technical Data.

8.3 Meetings and reviews required to carry out the responsibilities set forth in this MOU shall also be included in the Chandrayaan-1 M3 Implementation Plan and shall be held periodically in the United States, India, or at other sites as mutually agreed. The Parties agree to invite each other to these meetings and reviews. The reviews shall be chaired by NASA or ISRO, as agreed.

8.4 The Parties shall act in accordance with the schedules to be defined in the M3 Chandrayaan-1 M3 Implementation Plan and to avoid changes that will have a negative effect on the other Party with regard to scientific return, implementation approach, cost, and/or schedule, and where they cannot be avoided, to minimize these negative effects. To the extent that changes made by NASA or ISRO to the Chandrayaan-1 M3 Implementation Plan cause schedule or other problems that go beyond either Party's program constraints, the NASA Instrument Project Manager and ISRO Chandrayaan-1 Project Director shall discuss potential options to address such problems and submit their proposal to NASA and ISRO Management.

Article 9 - Mission Reviews, Integration, and Flight Readiness

9.1 To implement the M3 experiment, there shall be a series of reviews to evaluate the readiness of the flight and ground segments to proceed to implementation, integration, test, and final launch preparation. Representatives from both Parties shall serve on the boards of these reviews, in particular, the Readiness and Pre-Ship Review boards. Both Parties shall furnish engineering and programmatic data and shall participate in these mission reviews, as mutually agreed.

9.2 NASA and ISRO shall jointly make a final determination of the overall readiness to proceed with integration of the pay load to the spacecraft.

Article 10 - Exchange of Personnel

Each of the Parties shall facilitate the movement of persons necessary to implement this MOU into and out of its country subject to its laws and regulations. To facilitate coordination related to the Chandrayaan-1 Mission, the Parties may exchange a limited number of liaison visits from each Party, at times and under conditions as mutually agreed by the NASA M3 Project Manager and ISRO Chandrayaan-1 Project Director pursuant to necessary administrative authorizations. In the event of such an exchange, the Parties each shall provide necessary office, space and administrative support at the host location, including such additional support services as may be agreed by the Parties. Salary and all other personnel expenses and living and travel expenses shall be borne by the employing Party of the liaison(s) throughout the duration of their assignment.

Article 11 - Funding

Each Party shall bear the costs of discharging its respective responsibilities under this MOU, including travel and subsistence of each Party's personnel and transportation of its own equipment and associated documentation. The obligations of the Parties under this MOU are subject to their respective funding procedures and the availability of appropriated funds.

Article 12 - Customs and Taxes

Each Party shall facilitate the arrangement of free customs clearance and waiver of applicable duties and taxes for equipment and related goods necessary for the implementation of this MOU. Such facilitation of arrangements shall be fully reciprocal. In the event that any customs fees and/or taxes of any kind are still levied on the equipment and related goods for implementation of this MOU, after seeking to develop the necessary free customs clearance and waiver of applicable duties and taxes, such customs fees and/or taxes shall be borne by the Party of the country levying the fees and/or taxes.

Article 13 - Ownership of Elements and Equipment

For the purposes of this MOU, each Party shall retain ownership of elements and equipment it furnishes to the other Party. Any equipment not launched into space shall be returned to the furnishing Party expeditiously, as mutually agreed. Each Party shall transport its equipment to the designated delivery points, as specified in the Chandrayaan-1 M3 Implementation Plan, and, where appropriate, from such delivery points, when the equipment is to be returned to the furnishing Party.

Article 14 - Transfer of Goods and Technical Data

The Parties are obligated to transfer only those technical data (including software) and goods necessary to fulfill their respective responsibilities under this MOU, in accordance with the following provisions, notwithstanding any other provision of this MOU:

14.1 All activities of the Parties shall be carried out in accordance with their national laws and regulations, including those pertaining to export control and the control of classified information.

14.2 The transfer of technical data for the purpose of discharging the Parties' responsibilities with regard to interface, integration, and safety shall normally be made without restriction, except as provided in paragraph 14.1 above.

14.3 All transfers of goods and proprietary or export-controlled technical data are subject to the following provisions. In the event a Party or its related entity (e.g., contractor, subcontractor, grantee, cooperating entity) finds it necessary to transfer goods or to transfer proprietary or export-controlled technical data, for which protection is to be maintained, such goods shall be specifically identified and such proprietary or export-controlled technical data shall be marked. The identification for goods and the marking on proprietary or export- controlled technical data shall indicate that the goods and proprietary or export-controlled technical data shall be used by the receiving Party or related entities only for the purposes of fulfilling the receiving Party's or related entity's responsibilities under this MOU, and that the identified goods and marked proprietary technical data or marked export-controlled technical data shall not be disclosed or retransferred to any other entity without the prior written permission of the furnishing Party or its related entity. The receiving Party or related entity shall abide by the terms of the notice and protect any such identified goods and marked proprietary technical data or marked export-controlled technical data from unauthorized use and disclosure. The Parties to this MOU shall cause their related entities to be bound by the provisions of this Article related to use, disclosure, and retransfer of goods and marked technical data through contractual mechanisms or equivalent measures.

14.4 All goods exchanged in the performance of this MOU shall be used by the receiving Party or related entity exclusively for the purposes of the MOU. Upon completion of the activities under the MOU, the receiving Party or related entity shall return or, at the request of the furnishing Party or its related entity, otherwise dispose of all goods and marked proprietary technical data or marked export-controlled technical data provided under this MOU, as directed by the furnishing Party or related entity.

Article 15 - Intellectual Property

15.1 For the purposes of this Article, "Related Entity" includes but is not limited to contractors, subcontractors, grantees, or cooperating entities (or any lower tier contractor, subcontractor, grantee, or cooperating entities) of a Party.

15.2 PATENTS

15.2.1 Nothing in this Agreement shall be construed as granting, either expressly or by implication, to the other Party any rights to, or interest in, any inventions of a Party or its related entities made prior to the entry into force of, or outside the scope of, this Agreement, including any patents or other forms of protection (in any country) corresponding to such inventions.

15.2.2 Any rights to, or interest in, any invention made in the performance of this Agreement solely by one Party or any of its related entities, including any patents or other forms of protection (in any country) corresponding to such invention, shall be owned by such Party or, subject to paragraph 15.2.4 of this Article, such related entity.

15.2.3 It is not anticipated that there will be any joint inventions made in the performance of this Agreement. Nevertheless, in the event that an invention is jointly made by the Parties in the performance of this Agreement, the Parties shall, in good faith, consult and agree as to: a) the allocation of rights to, or interest in, such joint invention, including any patents or other forms of protection (in any country) corresponding to such joint invention; b) the responsibilities, costs, and actions to be taken to establish and maintain patents or other forms of protection (in any country) for each such joint invention; and c) the terms and conditions of any license or other rights to be exchanged between the Parties or granted by one Party to the other Party.

15.2.4 With respect to any invention created in the performance of this Agreement and involving a related entity, allocation of rights between a Party and its related entity to such invention, including any patents or other forms of protection (in any country) corresponding to such invention, shall be determined by such Party's laws, regulations, and applicable contractual obligations.

15.3 COPYRIGHTS

15.3.1 Nothing in this Agreement shall be construed as granting, either expressly or by implication, to the other Party any rights to, or interest in, any copyrights of a Party or its related entities created prior to the entry into force of, or outside the scope of, this Agreement.

15.3.2 Any copyrights in works created solely by one Party or any of its related entities, as a result of activities undertaken in performance of this Agreement, shall be owned by such Party or related entity. Allocation of rights between such Party and its related entities to such copyrights shall be determined by such Party's laws, regulations, and applicable contractual obligations.

15.3.3 For any jointly authored work, should the Parties decide to register the copyright in such work, they shall, in good faith, consult and agree as to the responsibilities, costs, and actions to be taken to register copyrights and maintain copyright protection (in any country).

15.3.4 Subject to the provisions of Articles 14 and 17, each Party shall have an irrevocable, royalty free right to reproduce, prepare derivative works, distribute copies to the public, and perform publicly and display publicly, and authorize others to do so on its behalf, any copyrighted work resulting from activities undertaken in the performance of this Agreement for its own purposes, regardless of whether the work was created solely by, or on behalf of, that Party or jointly with the other Party, and without consulting with or accounting to the other Party.

Article 16 - Science Data Policy

Access to Chandrayaan-1 and M3 science data shall be as follows:

16.1 The Parties shall release scientific data from the M3 to the international scientific community after a period of no longer than 12 months. The 12-month data validation and verification period begins with the receipt, by either Party, of the data from the spacecraft.

16.2 In all cases, the Parties shall provide immediate access to all M3 instrument data and science data products, free of charge, for members of the M3 science team, as well as designated representatives of M3 science team members, including associates, staff, and coworkers. The Parties shall also provide, free of charge, M3 instrument data and science data products to NASA or ISRO-selected participating scientists. The Parties shall have the right to use the data (processed and unprocessed) at any time for support of their respective responsibilities but shall not prejudice the M3 PI and Co-I's first publication rights, which are established in accordance with paragraph 16.1 above.

16.3 After the 12 month validation and verification period, the Parties shall make the data from the M3 instrument, including required calibration and spacecraft data, available to the international scientific community in a form suitable for analysis.

16.4 NASA shall make science data products available to the public and the science community in standard Planetary Data System (PDS) format after the appropriate science calibration and validation. In order to promote rapid access to science data products, some preliminary science data products shall be archived after initial verification, but prior to full validation, and made available to all users at no more than the cost of fulfilling the user request.

16.5 All M3 instrument data and science data products shall be archived in appropriate NASA data centers and the ISSDC, as defined in the Chandrayaan-1 M3 Implementation Plan. Copies of the M3 science data products shall be exchanged between the Parties.

16.6 The M3 Science Team members (including designated representatives) must provide a report to the Parties on the results of their analysis and validation investigations and the results of their investigations on validated M3 science data.

16.7 Notwithstanding the termination of this MOU, any M3 instrument data and science data products obtained from the M3 experiment (as defined in the Chandrayaan-1 M3 Implementation Plan) shall be archived by NASA for at least 10 years after completion of the Chandrayaan-1 Mission, unless otherwise agreed by the Parties.

16.8 If deemed of interest for scientific analysis of M3 instrument data, the Parties may agree to provide mutual access to correlative data products from other instruments or missions.

16.9 To enhance scientific analysis of Chandrayaan-1 M3 instrument data, research announcements may be issued by the Parties.

16.10 Complementary data from ISRO-provided instruments on the Chandrayaan-1 Mission shall be made available, free of charge, to NASA M3 PI, upon request, for the purpose of collaboration with ISRO.

16.11 Scientific data obtained by Chandrayaan-1 Mission are to be released to the international scientific community in a form suitable for analysis after a period that shall not exceed 1 year. This one year period shall begin with the receipt by the Pis/Co-Is of usable scientific data from the spacecraft in a form suitable for analysis. The period for producing usable scientific data should not nominally exceed 6 months following receipt of data from the spacecraft

Article 17 - Publication of Public Information and Results

17.1 The Parties retain the right to release public information regarding their own activities under this Agreement The Parties shall coordinate with each other in advance concerning releasing to the public information that relates to the other Party's responsibilities or performance under this Agreement.

17.2

17.2.1 The Parties shall make the final results obtained from the Chandrayaan-1 Mission available to the general scientific community through publication in appropriate journals or by presentations at scientific conferences as soon as possible and in a manner consistent with good scientific practices.

17.2.2 Each Party shall have an irrevocable, royalty free right to reproduce, prepare derivative works from, distribute to the public copies of, present publicly, and authorize others to do so on its behalf, the scientific information included in each such publication or presentation for its own purposes. The royalty free right shall exist irrespective of any copyright protection applicable to each such publication or presentation.

17.2.3 Raw data, analyzed data and final results primarily obtained from the Chandrayaan-1 M3 science data, or other scientific information regarding results obtained from the implementation of this Agreement, shall be disclosed by the Party, or its investigators that collected the data, analyzed the data or generated the results, to the other Party prior to any publication or presentation. The first presentation/publication will be done jointly by designated scientists of the Parties.

17.3 The Parties acknowledge that the following data or information does not constitute public information and that such data or information shall not be included in any publication or presentation by a Party under this article without the other Party's prior written permission: 1) data furnished by the other Party in accordance with Article 14 of this Agreement which is export-controlled, classified or proprietary; or 2) information about an invention of the other Party before a patent application has been filed covering the same, or a decision not to file has been made.

Article 18 - Liability

18.1 The purpose of this Article is to establish a cross-waiver of liability between the Parties and their related entities in the interest of encouraging participation in the exploration, exploitation, and use of outer space. This cross-waiver of liability shall be broadly construed to achieve this objective.

18.2 As used in this cross-waiver,

18.2.1 the term "Related Entity" means:

(i) a contractor or subcontractor of a Party at any tier;

(ii) a user or customer of a Party at any tier; or

(iii) a contractor or subcontractor of a user or customer of a Party at any tier.

"Contractors" and "subcontractors" include suppliers of any kind.

18.2.2 the term "damage" means:

(i) bodily injury to, or other impairment of health of, or death of, any person;

(ii) damage to, loss of, or loss of use of any property;

(iii) loss of revenue or profits; or

(iv) other direct, indirect, or consequential damage.

18.2.3 The term "payload" means any property to be flown or used on or in the launch vehicle.

18.2.4 The term "launch vehicle" means an object or any part thereof intended for launch, launched from Earth, or returning to Earth which carries payloads or persons, or both.

18.2.5 The term "Protected Space Operations" means all launch vehicle and payload activities on Earth, in outer space, or in transit between Earth and outer space done in implementation of this MOU. Protected Space Operations begins upon entry into force of this MOU and ends when all activities done in implementation of this MOU are completed. It includes, but is not limited to:

(i) research, design, development, test, manufacture, assembly, integration, operation, disposal, or use of launch or transfer vehicles, payloads, or instruments, as well as related support equipment and facilities and services;

(ii) all activities related to ground support, test, training, simulation, or guidance and control equipment and related facilities or services. "Protected Space Operations" excludes activities on Earth which are conducted on return from space to develop further a payload's product or process for use other than for launch vehicle-related activities necessary to complete implementation of this MOU.

18.3

18.3.1 Each Party agrees to a cross-waiver of liability pursuant to which each Party waives all claims against any of the entities or persons listed in subparagraphs 18.3.1 (i) through 18.3.1 (iii) of this section based on damage arising out of Protected Space Operations. This cross-waiver shall apply only if the person, entity, or property causing the damage is involved in Protected Space Operations and the person, entity, or property damaged is damaged by virtue of its involvement in Protected Space Operations. The cross-waiver shall apply to any claims for damage, whatever the legal basis for such claims, against:

(i) the other Party;

(ii) a related entity of the other Party;

(iii) the employees of any of the entities identified in sub-paragraphs (i) and (ii) above.

18.3.2 In addition, each Party shall extend the cross-waiver of liability as set forth in paragraph 18.3.1 of this section to its own related entities by requiring them, by contract or otherwise, to agree to waive all claims against the entities or persons identified in sub-paragraphs 18.3.1 (i) through 18.3.1 (iii).

18.3.3 For avoidance of doubt, this cross-waiver of liability includes a cross-waiver of liability arising from the Convention on International Liability for Damage Caused by Space Objects of March 29, 1972, where the person, entity, or property causing the damage is involved in Protected Space Operations and the person, entity, or property damaged is damaged by virtue of its involvement in Protected Space Operations.

18.3.4 Notwithstanding the other provisions of this Article, this cross-waiver of liability shall not be applicable to the following:

(i) claims between a Party and its own related entity or between its own related entities;

(ii) claims made by a natural person, his/her estate, survivors, or subrogees for bodily injury, other impairment of health or death of such natural person, except where the subrogee is a Party to this MOU or has otherwise agreed to be bound by the promises of this cross-waiver;

(iii) claims for damage caused by willful misconduct;

(iv) intellectual property claims;

(v) contract claims between the Parties based on the express contractual provisions of this MOU; or

(vi) claims for damage based on a failure of the Parties or their related entities to flow down the cross-waiver.

18.3.5 Nothing in this Article shall be construed to create the basis for a claim or suit where none would otherwise exist.

Article 19 - Registration of Space Objects

ISRO shall request that the Government of India register the Chandrayaan-1 spacecraft as a space object in accordance with the Convention on Registration of Space Objects Launched into Outer Space of January 14, 1975. Registration pursuant to this section shall not affect the rights or obligations of either Party or its Government under the 1972 Convention on International Liability for Damage Caused by Space Objects.

Article 20 - Settlement of Disputes

Any disputes not settled through the mechanisms provided in Article 6 – Project and Program Management, or any other issue concerning the interpretation or implementation of the terms of the MOU that cannot be resolved otherwise, shall be referred to the appropriate level of management of the Parties for consideration and joint amicable resolution.

Article 21 - Entry into Force, Duration, Amendment, and Termination

21.1 This MOU shall enter into force upon signature and remain in force until ten years after the Chandrayaan-1 spacecraft has been launched. This MOU may be amended and extended by written agreement of the Parties. Either Party may terminate this MOU at any time upon at least twelve months written notice to the other Party. In that event, the Parties shall endeavor to minimize negative impacts of such termination on other Parties.

21.2 Termination of the MOU shall not affect a Party's continuing obligations under Articles 6 (Project and Program Management), 13 (Ownership of Elements and Equipment), 14 (Transfer of Goods and Technical Data), 15 (Intellectual Property), 16 (Science Data Policy), 17 (Publication of Public Information and Results), and 18 (Liability), unless otherwise agreed to by the Parties.

FOR THE UNITED STATES
NATIONAL AERONAUTICS
AND SPACE ADMINISTRATION:

[Signature]
Michael D. Grtffin
Administrator

Date: 9 May 2006

Place: Bangalore, India

FOR THE INDIAN SPACE RESEARCH
ORGANISATION

[Signature]
G. MadhavanNair
Chairman

Date: 9 May 2006

Place: Bangalore, India

I certify this to be a true copy of the signed original.

[Signature]
Kent Bress

STATE DEPARTMENT DOCUMENT NUMBER: 06-289

AGREEMENT ON SCIENCE AND TECHNOLOGY COOPERATION BETWEEN THE UNITED STATES OF AMERICA AND THE KINGDOM OF SWEDEN, WITH ANNEXES

SIGNED AT STOCKHOLM,
JUNE 29, 2006
ENTERED INTO FORCE JUNE 29, 2006

CTIA DOCUMENT NUMBER: 13116.000

THE GOVERNMENT OF THE UNITED STATES OF AMERICA
and
THE GOVERNMENT OF THE KINGDOM OF SWEDEN,

(hereinafter referred to as "the Parties"),

CONSIDERING the importance of science and technology for their economic and social development;

RECOGNIZING that the Parties are pursuing research and technological activities in a number of areas of common interest, and that participation in each other's research and development activities on a basis of reciprocity will provide mutual benefits;

DESIRING to establish a formal basis for cooperation in scientific and technological research which will extend and strengthen the conduct of cooperative activities in areas of common interest and encourage the application of the results of such cooperation to their economic and social benefit;

HAVE AGREED AS FOLLOWS:

ARTICLE 1
Purpose

The Parties shall encourage, develop and facilitate cooperative activities in fields of common interest where they are pursuing research and development activities in science and technology.

ARTICLE 2
Definitions

For the purposes of this Agreement:

(a) "Cooperative activity" means any activity which the Parties undertake or support pursuant to this Agreement;

(b) "Information" means scientific or technical data, results or methods of research and development stemming from cooperative activities, and any other data relating to cooperative activities;

(c) "Intellectual Property" means the subject matter listed in Article 2 of the Convention Establishing the World Intellectual Property Organization, done at Stockholm July 14, 1967, and may include other subject matter as agreed by the Parties;

(d) "Participants" means any individual or entity, including, inter alia, the Parties' scientific and technological organizations and agencies, private persons, undertakings, research centers, universities and colleges, subsidiaries of U.S. and Swedish entities, or any other legal entity involved in cooperative activities;

(e) "Science" shall include all fields of research.

ARTICLE 3
Principles

Cooperative activities shall be conducted on the basis of the following principles:

(a) Mutual benefit based on an overall balance of advantages;

(b) Reciprocal opportunities to engage in cooperative activities;

(c) Equitable and fair treatment for the participants; and

(d) Timely exchange of information which may affect cooperative activities.

ARTICLE 4
Areas of Cooperative Activities

(a) Priority will be given to collaboration that can advance common goals in science and technological research.

(b) The Parties may jointly pursue cooperative activities with third parties.

ARTICLE 5
Forms of Cooperative Activities

(a) Subject to applicable laws, regulations and policies, the Parties shall foster, to the fullest extent practicable, the involvement of participants in cooperative activities under this Agreement with a view to providing comparable opportunities for participation in their scientific and technological research and development activities.

(b) Cooperative activities may take the following forms:

1. coordinated research projects;
2. joint task forces;
3. joint studies;
4. joint organization of scientific seminars, conferences, symposia and workshops;
5. training of scientists and technical experts;
6. exchanges or sharing of equipment and materials;
7. visits and exchanges of scientists, engineers or other appropriate personnel;
8. exchanges of scientific and technological information as well as information on practices, laws, regulations and programs relevant to cooperation under this Agreement.

ARTICLE 6
Coordination, Facilitation and Implementation of Cooperative Activities

(a) The coordination and facilitation of cooperative activities under this Agreement shall be carried out on behalf of the Government of the United States of America by the Department of State, and on behalf of the Government of the Kingdom of Sweden by the Ministry of Education, Research and Culture or a Government appointed Executive Agent. The Parties or their duly authorized representatives shall meet regularly to decide which common goals should be given priority and periodically review cooperative activities under this agreement.

(b) Upon request of either Party, representatives of the Parties shall meet to consider matters related to the implementation of this Agreement. Groups of experts may be designated to discuss specific questions.

(c) Each Party shall designate a national contact person to maintain contacts between meetings.

(d) Moreover, each Party shall designate a national contact person for the notification and approval of requests for authorization for access to the waters under national jurisdiction for the purpose of scientific research, and will treat those requests with diligence, taking into account the significance of these activities to the advancement of scientific knowledge.

(e) Implementing arrangements setting forth the details and procedures of specific cooperative activities under this Agreement may be made between the two Parties or their participants. These arrangements may describe, as appropriate, the nature and the duration of cooperation for a specific area or purpose, treatment of intellectual property, funding, allocation of costs, and other relevant matters. The implementing arrangements should make a reference to this Agreement. Any arrangements deviating from any of the provisions in this Agreement, including the annexes, shall be concluded in writing.

ARTICLE 7
Funding and Legal Considerations

(a) Cooperative activities shall be subject to the availability of appropriated funds, resources, and personnel and to the applicable laws and regulations, policies and programs of the United States of America and Sweden.

(b) Unless otherwise provided for in an implementing arrangement, each Party, its agency or scientific organization or participant shall bear the costs of its participation and that of its personnel engaged in cooperative activities under this Agreement.

ARTICLE 8
Entry of Personnel and Equipment

(a) Each Party shall take all reasonable steps and use its best efforts, within applicable laws and regulations, to facilitate entry to and exit from its territory of persons, material, data and equipment involved in or used in cooperative activities under this Agreement.

(b) Each Party shall endeavor to ensure that all participants in agreed cooperative activities under this Agreement have access to facilities and personnel within its country as needed to carry out those activities.

ARTICLE 9
Treatment of Intellectual Property

The allocation and protection of intellectual property rights under this Agreement shall be in accordance with the provisions of Annex I unless the Parties or their designees agree otherwise in writing. Reciprocal security obligations related to sensitive information or equipment and unclassified export-controlled information or equipment transferred under the Agreement are contained in Annex II. Annexes I and II form integral parts of this Agreement.

ARTICLE 10
Other Agreements and Transitional Provisions

(a) The Parties shall endeavor, where appropriate, to bring under the terms of this Agreement new arrangements that facilitate scientific and technological cooperation between the Parties that fall under the scope of Article 4.

(b) This Agreement is without prejudice to rights and obligations under other agreements between the Parties and any agreement or arrangement between either of the Parties and any third parties. Cooperative activities concerning the exploration and peaceful use of outer space will be undertaken pursuant to the Framework Agreement Between the Government of the United States of America and the Government of Sweden for Cooperative Activities in the Exploration and Use of Outer Space for Peaceful Purposes, done on October 14, 2005.

ARTICLE 11
Entry into Force, Termination and Dispute Settlement

(a) This Agreement shall enter into force on the date of signature thereof.

(b) This Agreement may be terminated at any time by either Party upon six months' written notice to the other Party. The expiration or termination of this Agreement shall not affect the validity or duration of any arrangements made under it, or any specific rights and obligations that have accrued in compliance with Annexes I and II.

(c) This Agreement may be amended by written agreement of the Parties.

(d) All questions or disputes related to the interpretation or implementation of this Agreement shall be settled by mutual agreement of the Parties. This paragraph does not affect any implementing arrangement between non-governmental participants.

IN WITNESS WHEREOF the undersigned, being duly authorized by their respective Governments, have signed this Agreement.

DONE at Stockholm in duplicate, this 29th day of June 2006, in the English and Swedish languages, each text being equally authentic.

FOR THE GOVERNMENT OF THE UNITED STATES OF AMERICA:	FOR THE GOVERNMENT OF THE KINGDOM OF SWEDEN:
[Signature]	[Signature]

ANNEX I
Intellectual Property Rights

I. General Obligation

The Parties shall ensure adequate and effective protection of intellectual property created or furnished under this Agreement and relevant implementing arrangements. Rights to such intellectual property shall be allocated as provided in this Annex.

II. Scope

A. This Annex is applicable to all cooperative activities undertaken pursuant to this Agreement, except as otherwise specifically agreed by the Parties or their designees.

B. For purposes of this Agreement, "intellectual property" shall mean the subject matter listed in Article 2 of the Convention Establishing the World Intellectual Property Organization, done at Stockholm, July 14, 1967 and may include other subject matter as agreed by the Parties.

C. This Annex does not otherwise alter or prejudice the allocation between a Party and its nationals, which shall be determined by that Party's laws and practices.

D. Except as otherwise provided in this Agreement, disputes concerning intellectual property arising under this Agreement shall be resolved through discussions between the concerned participating institutions, or, if necessary, the Parties or their designees. Upon mutual agreement of the Parties, a dispute shall be submitted to an arbitral tribunal for binding arbitration in accordance with the applicable rules of international law. Unless the Parties or their designees agree otherwise in writing, the arbitration rules of UNCITRAL shall govern.

E. Termination or expiration of this Agreement shall not affect rights or obligations under this Annex.

III. Allocation of Rights

A. To the extent consistent with applicable law, each Party shall be entitled to a non-exclusive, irrevocable, royalty-free license in all countries to translate, reproduce, and publicly distribute scientific and technical journal articles, reports, and books directly arising from cooperation under this Agreement. All publicly distributed copies of a copyrighted work prepared under this provision shall indicate the names of the authors of the work unless an author explicitly declines to be named.

B. To the extent consistent with applicable law, rights to all forms of intellectual property, other than those rights described in paragraph IIIA. above, shall be allocated as follows:

(1) Visiting researchers shall receive rights, awards, bonuses and royalties in accordance with the policies of the host institution.

(2) (a) Any intellectual property created by persons employed or sponsored by one Party under cooperative activities other than those covered by paragraph III.B.(l) shall be owned by that Party. Intellectual property created by persons employed or sponsored by both Parties shall be jointly owned by the Parties. In addition, each creator shall be entitled to awards, bonuses and royalties in accordance with the policies of the institution employing or sponsoring that person.

(b) Unless otherwise agreed in an implementing or other arrangement, each Party shall have within its territory a right to exploit or license intellectual property created in the course of the cooperative activities.

(c) The rights of a Party outside its territory shall be determined by mutual agreement considering the relative contributions of the Parties and their participants to the cooperative activities, the degree of commitment in obtaining legal protection and licensing of the intellectual property and such other factors deemed appropriate.

(d) Notwithstanding paragraphs III.B(2)(a) and (b) above, if either Party believes that a particular project is likely to lead to or has led to the creation of intellectual property not protected by the laws of the other Party, the Parties shall immediately hold discussions to determine the allocation of rights to the intellectual property. If an agreement cannot be reached within three months of the date of the initiation of the discussions, cooperation on the project in question shall be terminated at the request of either Party. Creators of intellectual property shall nonetheless be entitled to awards, bonuses and royalties as provided in paragraph III.B(2)(a).

(e) For each invention made under any cooperative activity, the Party employing or sponsoring the inventor(s) shall disclose the invention promptly to the other Party together with any documentation and information necessary to enable the other Party to establish any rights to which it may be entitled. Either Party may ask the other Party in writing to delay publication or public disclosure of such documentation or information for the purpose of protecting its rights in the invention. Unless otherwise agreed in writing, the delay shall not exceed a period of six months from the date of disclosure by the inventing Party to the other Party.

IV. Business Confidential Information

In the event that information identified in a timely fashion as business-confidential is furnished or created under this Agreement, each Party and its participants shall protect such information in accordance with applicable laws, regulations, and administrative practices. Information may be identified as "business-confidential" if a person having the information may derive an economic benefit from it or may obtain a competitive advantage over those who do not have it, and the information is not generally known or publicly available from other sources, and the owner has not previously made the information available without imposing in a timely manner an obligation to keep it confidential.

ANNEX II

Security Obligations

I. Protection of Information

Unless otherwise agreed in relevant implementing arrangements, no information or equipment requiring protection in the interests of national defense or foreign relations of either Party and classified in accordance with the applicable national laws and regulations shall be provided under this Agreement. In the event that information or equipment which is known or believed to require such protection is identified in the course of cooperative activities undertaken pursuant to this Agreement, it will be brought immediately to the attention of the appropriate officials and the Parties shall consult concerning the need for and level of appropriate protection to be accorded such information or equipment.

II. Technology Transfer

The transfer of export-controlled information or equipment between the two countries shall be in accordance with the relevant laws and regulations of each Party to prevent the unauthorized transfer or retransfer of such information or equipment provided or produced under this Agreement. If either Party deems necessary, detailed provisions for the prevention of unauthorized transfer or retransfer of such information or equipment shall be incorporated into the contracts or implementing arrangements.

STATE DEPARTMENT DOCUMENT NUMBER: 06-290

MEMORANDUM OF UNDERSTANDING BETWEEN THE DEPARTMENT OF DEFENSE OF THE UNITED STATES OF AMERICA AND THE DEPARTMENT OF DEFENCE OF AUSTRALIA CONCERNING COOPERATION ON LAND FORCE CAPABILITY MODERNIZATION, WITH ANNEXES

SIGNED AT WASHINGTON D.C.,
JULY 26, 2006
ENTERED INTO FORCE JULY 26, 2006

CTIA DOCUMENT NUMBER: 13117.000

CERTIFICATION OF AUTHENTICITY
I hereby certify this to be a true copy of the Memorandum of Understanding Between the Department of Defense of the United States of America and the Department of Defence of Australia Concerning Cooperation on Land Force Capability Modernization (Short Title: Land Force Capability Modernization MOU).
The Office of the Deputy Assistant Secretary of the Army for Defense Exports and Cooperation, Armaments Cooperation Division, maintains custody of a signed copy of the amendment.

[Signature]
LAURA MCMAHON
DEPUTY, INTERNATIONAL AGREEMENTS

INTRODUCTION

The Department of Defense of the United States of America (U.S. DoD) and the Department of Defence of Australia (ADOD), hereinafter referred to as the "Participants":

Recognizing the Agreement between the Government of the United States of America and the Government of Australia Concerning Certain Mutual Defense Commitments, which entered into force on December 1, 1995 (Chapeau Agreement);

Recognizing the Agreement Concerning Security Measures for the Protection of Classified Information between the Governments of Australia and the United States of America, which entered into force November 7, 2002 (Security Agreement);

Having a common interest in defense;

Recognizing the benefits to be obtained from standardization, rationalization, and interoperability of military equipments;

Desiring to improve their mutual conventional defense capabilities through the application of emerging technology;

Having a mutual interest in the design, analysis, development, test and evaluation of the land force systems to satisfy national interoperability requirements;

Having independently conducted research and exploratory development related to land force capability modernization, recognize the benefits of cooperation in Land Force Capability Modernization (LFCM) programs of mutual interest; and

Desiring to carry out cooperative research, design, analysis, development, test and evaluation of LFCM efforts to address their respective needs;

Have reached the following understandings:

SECTION I
DEFINITIONS AND ABBREVIATIONS

The Participants have jointly decided upon the following definitions and acronyms for this MOU:

ACTD	Advanced Concept Technology Demonstration
Background Information	Information not generated in the performance of a Land Force Capability Modernization (LFCM) Activity.
C4ISR	Command, Control, Communication, Computing, Intelligence, Surveillance, and Reconnaissance
Classified Information	Official information that requires protection in the interests of national security and is so designated by the application of a security classification. This information may be in oral, visual, magnetic, electronic, or documentary form or in the form of material, equipment, or technology.
Contract	Any mutually binding legal relationship under national laws that obligates a Contractor to furnish supplies or services, and obligates one or both of the Participants to pay for them.
Contracting	The obtaining of supplies or services by Contract from sources outside the government organizations of the Participants. Contracting includes description (but not determination) of supplies and services required, solicitation and selection of sources, preparation and award of Contracts, and all phases of Contract administration.
Contracting Agency	The entity within the government organization of a Participant that has authority to enter into, administer, and/or terminate Contracts.
Contracting Officer	A person representing a Contracting Agency of a Participant who has the authority to enter into, administer, and/or terminate Contracts.
Contractor	Any entity awarded a Contract under a Project Arrangement (PA) by a Participant's Contracting Agency.
Contractor Support Personnel	Persons specifically identified for support Contracts who provide administrative, managerial, scientific, or technical support services to a Participant under a Contract with that Participant that prohibits using information received under the Contract for any purpose other than those authorized under this MOU.

Controlled Unclassified Information	Unclassified information to which access or distribution limitations have been applied in accordance with applicable national laws or regulations. It could include information that has been declassified but remains controlled. Whether the Information is provided or generated under this MOU or its PAs, the Information will be marked to identify its "in confidence" nature. U.S. export-controlled Information will be marked as "International Traffic in Arms Regulations (ITAR)-Controlled". AS export-controlled information will be marked as "Australian Export Controlled".
Cooperative Project Personnel (CPP)	Military members or civilian employees of a Participant assigned to a Joint Project Office (JPO) or a facility of the other Participant under a specific PA who perform managerial, engineering, technical, administrative, Contracting, logistics, financial, planning, or other functions in furtherance of a PA.
Defense Purposes	Manufacture or other use in any part of the world by or for the armed forces of either Participant.
Designated Security Authority (DSA)	The security office approved by national authorities to be responsible for the security aspects of this MOU.
Equipment and Material	Any material, equipment, end item, subsystem, component, Special Tooling or test equipment that is either owned by one Participant and provided for use pursuant to a PA or Equipment and Material Transfer Arrangement (E&MTA) by that Participant, or is jointly acquired by both Participants and provided for use in a PA or an E&MTA.
Financial Costs	Any costs that, due to their nature, will be paid using monetary contributions from the Participants.
Foreground Information	Information generated in the performance of an LFCM Activity.
Host Participant	The Participant whose nation serves as the location where CPP are assigned for duty pursuant to a PA under this MOU.
Information	Any information provided to, generated in, or used in a LFCM Activity regardless of form or type, including, but not limited to, that of a scientific, technical, business, or financial nature, and also including photographs, reports, manuals, threat data, experimental data, test data, designs, specifications, processes, techniques, inventions, drawings, technical writings, sound recordings, pictorial representations, and other graphical presentations, whether in magnetic tape, computer memory, or any other form and whether or not subject to Intellectual Property Rights or other legal protection.
Intellectual Property Rights	All copyright and neighboring rights and all rights in relation to inventions (including Patent rights), registered and unregistered trademarks (including service marks), registered and unregistered designs, undisclosed information (including trade secrets and know-how), mask works fixed in semiconductor chip products, layout designs of integrated circuits, geographical indicators, and any other rights resulting from creative activity in the industrial, scientific, literary and artistic fields.

Invention	Any product or process, in any field of technology, provided it is new, conceived or "first actually reduced to practice" or involves an inventive step and is capable of industrial application. The term "first actually reduced to practice" means the first demonstration, sufficient to establish to one skilled in the art to which the invention pertains, of the operability of an invention for its intended purpose and in its intended environment.
Land Force Capability Modernization (LFCM)	A cooperative program aimed at enhancing interoperability between U.S. DoD and ADOD systems that also permits cooperation on warfighting requirements and challenges, and complementary efforts/ development for mutually beneficial needs across the domains of doctrine, organization, training and materiel, leader development, personnel, and facilities. This may include, but is not limited to, battle command, C4ISR, system architectures, sustainment, unmanned systems, modeling, simulation/training, lethality, survivability, and mobility.
LFCM Activity	Any activity in support of Section III (SCOPE OF WORK) of this MOU.
Non-Financial Costs	Any costs that, due to their nature, will be met using non monetary contributions from the Participants.
Patent	Legal Protection of the right to exclude others from making, using or selling an invention. The term refers to any and all patents including, but not limited to, Patents of implementation, improvement, or addition; petty Patents; utility models; appearance design Patents; registered designs; and inventor certificates or like statutory protection as well as divisions, reissues, continuations, renewals, and extensions of any of these.
Participant	A signatory to this MOU represented by its military and civilian personnel. Contractors and Contractor Support Personnel will not be representatives of a Participant under this MOU.
Parent Participant	The Participant that sends its CPP to the nation of the other Participant pursuant to a PA under this MOU.
Project Arrangement (PA)	An implementing arrangement concluded after this MOU has entered into effect that specifies the provisions for cooperation for an LFCM Activity between the Participants.
Project Plan	The document that provides a description of a PA's major events, delivery requirements and milestones that is updated periodically by the Project Officers.

Project Purposes	Any use by or for a Participant in connection with the activities of a particular PA.
Special Tooling	Jigs, dies, fixtures, molds, patterns, tapes, gauges, other equipment and manufacturing aids, and all components of these items, which are of such a specialized nature that without substantial modification or alteration their use is limited to the development or production of particular supplies or parts thereof or to the performance of particular services and excluding material, special test equipment, facilities (except foundations and similar improvements necessary for installing Special Tooling), general or special machine tools, or similar capital items.
Third Party	A government other than the government of a Participant and any person or other entity whose government is not the government of a Participant.

SECTION II
OBJECTIVE

2.1 This MOU establishes a comprehensive framework for implementing a program of cooperation on mutually determined topics related to LFCM. This includes research, design, development, test and evaluation, and System Development and Demonstration (SDD). The specific level of cooperation will be determined through discussions conducted by the Participants under this MOU, consistent with their respective national interests.

2.2 The Participants intend to enhance interoperability by cooperating on warfighting concept and capability development, where mutually beneficial, in the areas of doctrine, organization, training and materiel, leader development, personnel and facilities. This may include, but is not limited to, battle command, C4ISR, system architectures, sustainment, unmanned systems, modeling, simulation/ training, lethality, survivability and mobility.

SECTION III
SCOPE OF WORK

3.1 The overall work to be carried out under this MOU includes, but is not limited to:

3.1.1 establishing a foundation to maximize land force interoperability;

3.1.2 facilitating and conducting cooperative conceptualization, research, experimentation, design, analysis, development, test and evaluation of land force systems;

3.1.3 promoting a common understanding of each other's capabilities, limitations and operating environments;

3.1.4 providing a mechanism for information exchange and cooperation on land warfare innovations, emerging concepts and technology;

3.1.5 providing guidance to enhance current, emerging and future forces; and

3.1.6 sharing networking strategies to develop interoperability across the spectrum of conflict through combined participation in experimentation and related activities.

3.2 The following mechanisms will be utilized to undertake the LFCM Activities described in paragraph 3.1:

3.2.1 *Information Exchange:*

3.2.1.1 Information exchange will take place on an equitable basis as mutually determined by the Participants in all areas concerning LFCM. This MOU permits the exchange of Information for any purpose under the scope of this MOU, including, but not limited to, harmonization and alignment of LFCM capability requirements of the Participants and the formulating, developing, and negotiating of any LFCM Activity. Information exchange need not necessarily coincide in time or technical field.

3.2.1.2 Computer databases, computer software or computer software documentation associated with LFCM Activities may be transferred under this MOU in accordance with national procedures, subject to the following limitations:

3.2.1.2.1 Such transfers must be necessary or useful to the conduct of the LFCM Activities as determined by the providing Participant; and

3.2.1.2.2 Such transfers may occur only when the providing Participant has obtained national authority for such release. Such release may be subject to restrictions on use imposed by the providing Participant.

3.2.2 *Working Groups (WGs):*

WGs may be established to explore, study, and report on specific LFCM issues. A WG will be limited in scope to a single, well defined area and will endeavor to assess the LFCM issue based on Information provided by both Participants in such a way as to arrive at a jointly determined position within a set time limit. Each WG will have its own written Terms of Reference (TOR).

3.2.3 *PAs:*

Each PA will be subject to the terms of this MOU concerning the objectives, scope of work, sharing of tasks, management, financial arrangements, security classification, E&MTA, entry into effect, duration and termination, and any other provisions as required. PAs will conform to the format in Annex A (MODEL PROJECT ARRANGEMENT).

3.2.4 *ACTDs:*

The Participants recognize that it may be to their mutual advantage to conduct technology demonstrations, such as ACTDs, to evaluate evolving technology and LFCM concepts. The plan for the demonstrations will be documented in a PA.

3.2.5 *E&MTAs:*

The Participants recognize that it may be necessary or desirable to transfer Equipment and Material for the purpose of implementing this MOU. When E&MTAs are performed outside of a PA, the Participants may execute an E&MTA in accordance with Annex C (MODEL EQUIPMENT AND MATERIAL TRANSFER ARRANGEMENT).

3.2.6 *Familiarization Visits:*

Familiarization visits may occur, in accordance with Section XI (VISITS TO ESTABLISHMENTS).

3.2.7 *CPP:*

CPP may be assigned pursuant to a PA under this MOU to either a JPO or a facility of the other Participant and will report to their designated supervisor regarding that work.

SECTION IV
MANAGEMENT (ORGANIZATION AND RESPONSIBILITY)

4.1 LFCM Activity will be directed and administered on behalf of the Participants by an organization consisting of a Steering Committee (SC), Project Managers (PMs) and Project Officers (POs) appointed by the Participants. The SC will have overall authority over the PMs. The PMs will have primary responsibility for effective implementation and efficient management of LFCM Activities, and direction of POs for subsequently developed PAs. The Participants may assign military or civilian employees to serve as CPPs in support of PAs.

4.2 The SC will consist of the U.S. Army's Program Manager Unit of Action (PM UA), and the ADOD Director General Land Development (DGLD). The SC will meet annually, with additional meetings held at the request of either Participant. The representative hosting the meeting will chair the meeting. The Participants will alternate hosting the SC meetings unless otherwise mutually determined. The host Participant will provide administrative support for the meeting at its own expense. Decisions of the SC will be made unanimously. In the event that the SC is unable to reach a timely decision on an issue, each SC representative will refer the issue to their higher authorities for resolution. Ongoing LFCM Activities will continue to be implemented without interruption under the direction of the PMs pending resolution of the issue. The SC's responsibilities include, but are not limited to:

4.2.1 Exercising executive-level oversight;

4.2.2 Reviewing the status reports submitted by the PMs;

4.2.3 Maintaining oversight of the security aspects of this MOU;

4.2.4 Resolving issues brought forth by the PMs;

4.2.5 Reviewing and forwarding to the Participants for approval recommended amendments to this MOU in accordance with Section XVIII (ENTRY INTO EFFECT, AMENDMENT, DURATION AND TERMINATION);

4.2.6 Reviewing and forwarding to the Participants recommendations for the establishment of PAs and E&MTAs;

4.2.7 Monitoring Third Party Sales and Transfers authorized in accordance with Section XIII (THIRD PARTY SALES AND TRANSFERS);

4.2.8 Approving PM plans for the transfer of Equipment and Material provided by a Participant in accordance with Section VIII (EQUIPMENT AND MATERIAL TRANSFERS);

4.2.9 Approving PM plans for the disposal of jointly acquired Equipment and Material under this MOU in accordance with Section VIII (EQUIPMENT AND MATERIAL TRANSFERS); and

4.2.10 Approving the assignment and duties of CPP.

4.3 Program offices will be established in the United States and Australia to manage LFCM Activities. The PM UA will appoint the U.S. PM, and the DGLD will appoint the AS PM, both of whom will be responsible for oversight of LFCM Activities under this MOU. The PMs will be responsible for:

4.3.1 Managing the day-to-day activities associated with this MOU;

4.3.2 Establishing WGs, approving their TOR, and keeping the SC informed;

4.3.3 Recommending LFCM Activities, as described in Section III (SCOPE OF WORK), to the SC for approval;

4.3.4 Referring issues to the SC that cannot be resolved by the PMs;

4.3.5 Developing and recommending amendments to this MOU and its Annexes to the SC;

4.3.6 Ensuring appointment of project security officers;

4.3.7 Ensuring development of and forwarding to the SC a Project Security Instruction (PSI) and a Classification Guide (CG) for the MOU within three months after signature of the MOU, and implementing them upon final approval by the respective DSAs;

4.3.8 Providing status reports to the SC; and

4.3.9 Implementing actions as directed by the SC.

4.4 For each PA, the Participants will each appoint one Project Officer (PO). The POs' duties will be specified in each PA. However, generally they will be responsible for:

4.4.1 Managing and executing the cost, schedule, performance requirements, and technical and financial aspects in accordance with Section V (FINANCIAL PROVISIONS) of the PA;

4.4.2 Maintaining a list of all equipment and/or material transferred by either Participant under a PA or E&MTA;

4.4.3 Appointing a PA security officer;

4.4.4 Ensuring development of and forwarding to the PMs the CG for the PA and any proposed updates to the MOU PSI within three months after signature of a PA, and implementing them upon final approval by the respective DSAs;

4.4.5 Developing, if required, the Financial Management Procedures Document (FMPD) for approval by the PMs and SC; and

4.4.6 Transmitting a final report through the PMs to the SC six months before the termination date for each PA.

4.5 WGs will be established by the PMs as necessary to examine areas of mutual interest and/or to perform work under specific PAs under this MOU. WGs will consist of representatives from the Participants. Each Participant will have one vote in WG matters, although a Participant may have as many representatives attend WG meetings as the Participant deems necessary. The location and chairmanship of the WG meetings will alternate between the Participants, unless otherwise mutually determined, with the hosting Participant providing, without charge, appropriate meeting facilities, including security and administrative support. WGs will be responsible for:

4.5.1 Developing and submitting a TOR and any required changes to the PMs;

4.5.2 Recommending potential LFCM Activities through the PMs for review and endorsement to the SC;

4.5.3 Interacting with and providing information to other WGs, as directed by the PMs; and

4.5.4 Referring issues to the PMs that cannot be resolved at the WG level.

SECTION V
FINANCIAL PROVISIONS

5.1 This MOU creates no financial commitments regarding individual PAs. Detailed descriptions of the financial provisions for a specific project, including the total cost of the project and each Participant's cost share, will be contained in that PA.

5.2 Each Participant will contribute its equitable share of the full Financial Costs and Non-Financial Costs of a PA, as mutually determined by the Participants and as set out in each PA, including overhead costs, administrative costs, and costs of claims, and each Participant will receive an equitable share of the results of each PA, as mutually determined by the Participants.

5.3 For each PA, the POs will be responsible for establishing the detailed financial management procedures under which the project will operate. These procedures may be specified in an FMPD proposed by the POs and subject to the approval of the PMs and SC.

5.4 Each Participant will perform, or have performed, its tasks and will use its best efforts to perform the tasks within the cost estimates specified in each PA. Each Participant will bear the full costs it incurs for performing, managing, and administering its own activities under this MOU and participation in each PA, including its share of the costs of any Contracts awarded pursuant to paragraph 5.10.

5.5 The following costs will be borne entirely by the Participant incurring the costs or on whose behalf the costs are incurred:

5.5.1 Costs associated with national representation at meetings;

5.5.2 Costs associated with any unique national requirements identified by a Participant; and

5.5.3 Any other costs not expressly stated as shared costs or any costs that are outside the scope of this MOU and its PAs.

5.6 For PAs with shared costs that involve the establishment of a JPO with CPP assignments, the PA will specify the Financial Costs and Non-Financial Costs required to be contributed by each Participant for JPO administration and associated support services including, but not limited to, JPO costs of travel incurred in support of PA efforts, JPO training costs, Contract award, Contract administration, office space, security services, information technology services, communications services, and supplies.

5.7. In addition to the shared costs of JPO administration and associated support services costs described in paragraph 5.6, the costs of CPP assigned to the JPO or a facility of the other Participant will be borne as follows:

5.7.1. The Host Participant will bear the costs of all pay and allowances of its CPP assigned to the JPO. Where CPP are assigned to a facility of the Host Participant, the Host Participant will bear the following costs including, but not limited to, CPP assignment-related administrative and support services costs such as CPP costs of travel incurred in support of PA efforts, CPP-related training costs, office space, security services, information technology services, communications services, and supplies.

5.7.2 The Parent Participant will bear the following CPP-related costs:

5.7.2.1 All pay and allowances of its CPP assigned to the JPO or a facility of the other Participant;

5.7.2.2 Transportation of its CPP, CPP dependents, and their personal property to the JPO location or a facility of the other Participant prior to commencement of the CPP assignment in the JPO or a facility of the other Participant, and return transportation of the foregoing from the JPO location or facility of the other Participant upon completion or termination of the CPP assignment;

5.7.2.3 Compensation for loss of, or damage to, the personal property of its CPP or CPP dependents, subject to the laws and regulations of the Parent Participant's Government; and

5.7.2.4 Preparation and shipment of remains and funeral expenses in the event of the death of its CPP or CPP dependents.

5.8 A Participant will promptly notify the other Participant if available funds will not be adequate to fulfill its obligations as mutually determined under any PA to this MOU, or if it appears that the cost estimates in a PA will be exceeded. The Participants will immediately consult with a view toward continuation on a modified basis.

5.9 For a PA where a Participant contracts on behalf of the other Participant or on behalf of both Participants, the PO will be responsible for establishing the detailed financial management procedures under which the PA will operate prior to the transfer of funds between the Participants. The procedures, which will accord with national accounting and audit requirements of the Participants, will be specified in an FMPD. Each Participant will provide funds in the amounts and at the times set out in the estimated schedule for monetary contributions, as specified in the FMPD.

5.10 For PAs, the Participants recognize that, in performing Contracting responsibilities on behalf of the other Participant, it may become necessary for the Contracting Participant to incur contractual or other responsibilities for the benefit of the other Participant prior to the receipt of the other Participant's funds. In such event the other Participant will make such funds available in such amounts and at such times as required by the Contract or other responsibility and will pay its equitable share, as mutually determined, of any damages and costs that may accrue from the performance or cancellation of the Contract or other responsibility, after consultation within the SC, in advance of the time such payments, damages, or costs are due.

5.11 Each Participant will be responsible for the audit of its activities or its Contractors' activities pursuant to a PA. A Participant's audits will be in accordance with its own national practices. For PAs where funds are transferred between the Participants, the receiving Participant will be responsible for the internal audit regarding administration of the other Participant's funds in accordance with the receiving Participant's national practices. Audit reports of such funds will be promptly made available by the receiving Participant to the other Participant.

SECTION VI
CONTRACTING PROVISIONS

6.1 If either Participant determines that Contracting is necessary to fulfill its obligations under the scope of work of any PA, that Participant will contract in accordance with its respective national laws, regulations, and procedures. Sources from both Participants' industries will be allowed to compete on an equal basis for such Contracts.

6.2 When one Participant contracts on its own behalf to perform a task under a PA, it will be solely responsible for its own Contracting, and the other Participant will not be subject to any liability arising from such Contracts.

6.3 If the Participants determine that it is necessary under a PA that one Participant contract on behalf of the other Participant or for both Participants for tasks under that PA, the Contracting Agency will contract in accordance with its national laws, regulations, and procedures. Such contractual arrangements will be detailed in the particular PA. Sources from both Participants' industries will be allowed to compete on an equal basis for such Contracts. The Contracting Officer will be the exclusive source for providing contractual direction and instructions to Contractors and prospective Contractors. The PMs will be responsible for the coordination of activities relating to this MOU and its PAs and will cooperate with the Contracting Officer in the areas of Contract procedures, Contract negotiation, evaluation of offers, and Contract award. The Contracting Officer will also keep the PMs advised of all financial arrangements with Contractors.

6.4 Upon mutual written consent, consistent with Section II (OBJECTIVES), a Participant may Contract for the unique national requirements of the other Participant.

6.5 For all Contracting activities performed by either Participant, the PMs will be provided a copy of all statements of work prior to the development of solicitations to ensure that they are consistent with the provisions of this MOU and the applicable PA.

6.6 For all Contracting activities performed by either Participant, each Participant's Contracting Agency will negotiate to obtain the rights to use and disclose Information required by Section IX (DISCLOSURE AND USE OF INFORMATION). Each Participant's Contracting Agency will insert into its prospective Contracts (and require its Contractors to insert in subcontracts) suitable provisions to satisfy the requirements of this MOU and the specific PA, including Section IX (DISCLOSURE AND USE OF INFORMATION), Section X (CONTROLLED UNCLASSIFIED INFORMATION), Section XII (SECURITY), Section XIII (THIRD PARTY SALES AND TRANSFERS) and Section XVIII (ENTRY INTO EFFECT, AMENDMENT, DURATION AND TERMINATION), including suitable provisions to require compliance with the Participants' respective export control laws and regulations. During the Contracting process, each Participant's Contracting Officer will advise prospective Contractors of their obligation to notify the Contracting Agency immediately if they are subject to any license or agreement that will restrict that Participant's freedom to disclose Information or permit its use. The Contracting Officer will also advise prospective Contractors to employ their best efforts not to enter into any new agreement or arrangement that will result in such restrictions.

6.7 The transfer of export-controlled Information furnished by one Participant will be authorized by the Government of the furnishing Participant only to those Contractors of the other Participant who will limit the end use of the Information received for the sole purpose of furthering the purposes authorized under this MOU or the applicable PA. The Participants will establish legal arrangements with their Contractors to require that their Contractors do not retransfer or otherwise use export-controlled Information for any purpose other than the purposes authorized under this MOU or the applicable PA. Such legal arrangements will also provide that the Contractor will not retransfer the export-controlled Information to another Contractor without the written consent of the Government of the furnishing Participant.

6.8 In the event a Participant's Contracting Agency is unable to secure adequate rights to use and disclose Information as required by Section IX (DISCLOSURE AND USE OF INFORMATION), or is notified by Contractors or prospective Contractors of any restrictions on the disclosure and use of Information, that Participant will notify the other Participant of the restrictions before the Contract or subcontract is signed. The Participants will immediately consult, at the appropriate level, to assess the consequences and determine the way ahead.

6.9 The Contracting Officer will ensure that the PMs are provided with sufficient information concerning the Contract and its execution to enable them to fulfill their relevant responsibilities.

6.10 Should a Participant's Contracting Agency determine that quality assurance services, pricing or cost investigation services are required, such services will be obtained through the responsible national authorities of the Participant within whose territories the performing Contractor or subcontractor is located, consistent with the Details of Agreement Between the Defense Authorities of the United States of America and the Commonwealth of Australia for Mutual Acceptance of Government Quality Assurance, dated November 29, 1994.

6.11 Each Participant will promptly advise the other Participant of any cost growth, schedule delay, or performance problems of any Contractor for which its Contracting Agency is responsible.

SECTION VII
WORK SHARING

7.1 The Participants will work toward the goal that the work to be performed under this MOU and each PA will be shared in proportion to the financial and non-financial contribution of the Participants to the maximum extent practicable, consistent with high technical merit, reasonable cost, and the need to achieve the timely, economical, and efficient execution of the PA. This work will encompass those requirements contained in Section III (SCOPE OF WORK) of this MOU that are common to the Participants and are funded under this MOU.

7.2 Sources from both nations will be permitted to bid on PA work. Each Participant will encourage its Contractors to provide competitive opportunities to sources from the other Participant to participate in the work of a PA, provided that such participation does not adversely impact the PA.

7.3 No requirement will be imposed by either Participant for work sharing or other industrial or commercial compensation in connection with this MOU that is not in accordance with this MOU or the applicable PA.

SECTION VIII
EQUIPMENT AND MATERIAL TRANSFERS

8.1 For the purpose of carrying out a PA, each Participant may transfer, without charge to the other Participant, such Equipment and Material identified as being necessary for implementing a PA. The PA will provide specific details of any transfer of Equipment and Material. Equipment and Material identified at the time of PA signature will be specified in the PA as set out in Annex A (MODEL PROJECT ARRANGEMENT). Equipment and Material that cannot be identified at the time of PA signature will be documented, when identified, in a list to be developed and maintained by the POs. Approval for all E&MTAs will be in accordance with national procedures.

8.2 For E&MTAs concluded pursuant to Annex C, each Participant may transfer, without charge to the other Participant, Equipment and Material, in accordance with the model at Annex C (EQUIPMENT AND MATERIAL TRANSFER ARRANGEMENT).

8.3 The receiving Participant of the E&MTA, in accordance with the provisions of this MOU and its national laws, regulations, and policies, will provide without charge the results of any testing or evaluation to the other Participant.

8.4 The providing Participant will make every effort to ensure that the Equipment and Material are furnished in a serviceable and usable condition according to the intended purpose. However, the providing Participant makes no warranty or guarantee of fitness of the Equipment and Material for a particular purpose or use, and makes no commitment to alter, improve, or adapt the Equipment and Material, or any part thereof.

8.5 The receiving Participant will maintain any such Equipment and Material in good order, repair, and operable condition. Unless the providing Participant has authorized the Equipment and Material to be expended or otherwise consumed without reimbursement to the providing Participant, the receiving Participant will return the Equipment and Material to the providing Participant in as good condition as received, normal wear and tear excepted, or return the Equipment and Material and pay the cost to restore it. If the Equipment and Material are damaged beyond economical repair, the receiving Participant will return the Equipment and Material to the providing Participant (unless otherwise specified in writing by the providing Participant) and pay the replacement value as computed pursuant to the providing Participant's national laws, regulations, and procedures. If the Equipment and Material are lost or stolen while in the custody of the receiving Participant, the receiving Participant will issue a certificate of loss to the providing Participant and pay the replacement value as computed pursuant to the providing Participant's national laws, regulations, and procedures.

8.6 The providing Participant, at its expense, will deliver the Equipment and Material to the receiving Participant at a mutually determined location. Possession and responsibility for the Equipment and Material will pass from the providing Participant to the receiving Participant at the time of receipt of the Equipment and Material. Any further transportation is the responsibility of the receiving Participant.

8.7 All Equipment and Material that is transferred will be used by the receiving Participant only for the purposes of carrying out this MOU and the applicable PA or E&MTA, unless otherwise consented to in writing by the providing Participant. In addition, in accordance with Section XIII (THIRD PARTY SALES AND TRANSFERS), Equipment and Material will not be retransferred to a Third Party without the prior written consent of the providing Participant.

8.8 The providing Participant will transfer the Equipment and Material for the mutually determined transfer period. The transfer period may be extended by written mutual consent of the Participants provided that the duration of the transfer period will not exceed the effective period of the PA or E&MTA.

8.9 The providing Participant will furnish the receiving Participant such Information as is necessary to enable the Equipment and Material to be used. If the Participants mutually determine that specific training is required for use of Equipment and Material, they will mutually determine the appropriate arrangements for the provision of such training.

8.10 The receiving Participant will inspect and inventory the Equipment and Material upon receipt. The receiving Participant will also inspect and inventory the Equipment and Material prior to its return (unless the Equipment and Material are to be expended or consumed).

8.11 Upon expiration or termination of the transfer period specified in the PA or the E&MTA (taking into account any extension), the receiving Participant will return the Equipment and Material, at its expense, to the providing Participant at a location mutually determined. Possession and responsibility for the Equipment and Material will pass from the receiving Participant to the providing Participant at the time of its receipt. Any further transportation is the responsibility of the providing Participant.

8.12 The receiving Participant will provide written notice of consumption or expenditure of Equipment and Material approved for such consumption or expenditure. In the event the intended consumption or expenditure does not occur, the receiving Participant will, unless otherwise determined by the providing Participant, return the Equipment and Material, at its expense, to the providing Participant to the location mutually determined in the PA or E&MTA. Any further transportation is the responsibility of the providing Participant.

8.13 The Participants will ensure, by all reasonable means, the protection of Intellectual Property Rights in Equipment and Material.

8.14 Equipment and Material transferred to one Participant under an E&MTA or under a PA will be returned to the providing Participant prior to the termination or expiration of this MOU.

8.15 Each Participant waives all claims against the other Participant for damage to or loss of jointly acquired Equipment and Material arising from the performance of official duties. However, if the Participants mutually decide to repair damaged jointly acquired Equipment and Material in order to complete a PA, the cost of such repair will be shared in a manner that results in sharing the total costs of the PA in the proportions established for the Participants' contributions under the PA. In any case, if the Participants mutually determine that damage or loss is caused by reckless acts, reckless omission, willful misconduct or gross negligence of one of the Participants, the costs of any liability, including the cost of repairs, will be borne by that Participant

8.16 Any Equipment and Material that is jointly acquired on behalf of both Participants for use in a PA will be disposed of during the PA, or when the PA expires or is terminated, as approved or directed by the SC. Jointly acquired Equipment and Material will remain the property of both Participants in the same ratio as Financial Costs and Non-Financial Costs are shared in the PA under which it is acquired. The Participant who has custody of the jointly acquired Equipment and Material will maintain such jointly acquired Equipment and Material in good order and operable condition, normal wear and tear excepted, unless the Participants have mutually determined in writing that it may be expended or otherwise consumed by that Participant in connection with this MOU and applicable PA. If jointly acquired Equipment and Material are damaged or lost while in custody of a Participant, the provisions of this Section will apply. Where a person or entity, other than the Participants (including their personnel), damages jointly acquired Equipment and Material, and the cost of making good such damage is not recoverable from such person or entity, the Participants will share such costs in the same ratios as the financial contributions to the PA.

8.17 Disposal of jointly acquired Equipment and Material may include a transfer of the interest of one of the Participants in such Equipment and Material to the other Participant; the sale or transfer to a U.S. or AS entity; or, the sale or transfer of such Equipment and Material to a Third Party, in accordance with Section XIII (THIRD PARTY SALES AND TRANSFERS) of this MOU. The Participants will share the consideration from jointly acquired Equipment and Material transferred or sold to a Third Party, or other U.S. or AS entity in the same ratio as Financial Costs and Non-Financial Costs are shared in the relevant PA.

SECTION IX
DISCLOSURE AND USE OF INFORMATION

9.1 Both Participants recognize that successful cooperation depends on full and prompt exchange of Information necessary for carrying out each LFCM Activity. The Participants intend to acquire sufficient Information and rights to use such Information to promote the objectives of this MOU. The nature and amount of Information to be acquired will be consistent with the objectives stated in Section II (OBJECTIVE) and Section III (SCOPE OF WORK) of this MOU and any applicable PA. Subject to the rights both Participants are accorded under this MOU, title to Foreground Information generated by a Participant or its Contractor will reside with that Participant and/or its Contractors, in accordance with that Participant's national laws, regulations, and policies. Nothing in this MOU will affect title to Background Information of the Participants or their Contractors. Transfer of such Information to Contractors will be in accordance with each Participant's applicable respective export control laws and regulations.

Information Exchange, WGs, and Familiarization Visits

9.2 The disclosure and use provisions that govern Information exchanges, WGs, and Familiarization Visits authorized in Section III (SCOPE OF WORK) are as follows:

9.2.1 Disclosure: Each Participant, upon request, will disclose to the other Participant any relevant Information, provided that:

9.2.1.1 Such Information is necessary to or useful in a LFCM Activity, with the furnishing Participant determining whether it is "necessary to" or "useful in" the LFCM Activity;

9.2.1.2 Information subject to Intellectual Property Rights may be disclosed only without incurring liability to holders of Intellectual Property Rights;

9.2.1.3 Disclosure is consistent with national disclosure policies and regulations of the furnishing Participant; and

9.2.1.4 Any disclosure or transfer of such Information to Contractors is in accordance with the furnishing Participant's export control laws and regulations.

9.2.2 Use: Use of Information will be for information and evaluation purposes only. Written permission from the furnishing Participant will be required for any other use.

Project Arrangements

9.3 Government Foreground Information.

9.3.1 Disclosure: Government Foreground Information generated by a Participant's military or civilian employees will be disclosed without charge to the other Participant.

9.3.2 Use: Each Participant may use all Government Foreground Information without charge for Defense Purposes only. The Participant generating Government Foreground Information will also retain its rights of use thereto. Any sale or other transfer to a Third Party will be subject to the provisions of Section XIII (THIRD PARTY SALES AND TRANSFERS) of this MOU.

9.4 Government Background Information.

9.4.1 Disclosure: Each Participant, upon request, will disclose to the other Participant any relevant Government Background Information generated by its military or civilian employees, provided that:

9.4.1.1 Such Government Background Information is necessary to or useful in the PA, with the furnishing Participant determining whether it is "necessary to" or "useful in" the PA;

9.4.1.2 Such Government Background Information subject to Intellectual Property Rights may be disclosed only without incurring liability to holders of Intellectual Property Rights;

9.4.1.3 Disclosure is consistent with national disclosure policies and regulations of the furnishing Participant; and

9.4.1.4 Any disclosure or transfer of such Government Background Information to Contractors is in accordance with the furnishing Participant's export control laws and regulations.

9.4.2 Use: Government Background Information disclosed by one Participant to the other may be used without charge by the other Participant for Project Purposes only. However, subject to any Intellectual Property Rights held by other than the Participant. Government Background Information may be used for Defense Purposes by the receiving Participant without charge when the use of such Government Background Information is necessary to enable the use of Foreground Information. The furnishing Participant (after consultation with the receiving Participant) will determine whether such use of Government Background Information is necessary. The furnishing Participant will retain all its rights with respect to such Government Background Information.

9.5 Contractor Foreground Information.

9.5.1 Disclosure: Contractor Foreground Information generated and delivered by Contractors will be disclosed without charge to the other Participant.

9.5.2 Use: Each Participant may use all Contractor Foreground Information generated and delivered by Contractors of the other Participant without charge for Defense Purposes only. The Participant whose Contractors generate and deliver Contractor Foreground Information will also retain rights of use thereto in accordance with the applicable Contract(s). Any sale or other transfer to a Third Party of Contractor Foreground Information will be subject to the provisions of Section XIII (THIRD PARTY SALES AND TRANSFERS) of the MOU.

9.6 Contractor Background Information.

9.6.1 Disclosure: Any Contractor Background Information (including information subject to Intellectual Property Rights), which is or has been generated outside of an LFCM Activity and delivered by Contractors, will be disclosed to the other Participant provided the following provisions are met:

9.6.1.1 Such Contractor Background Information is necessary to or useful in the PA, with the furnishing Participant determining whether it is "necessary to" or "useful in" the PA;

9.6.1.2 Such Contractor Background Information may be made available without incurring liability to holders of Intellectual Property Rights;

9.6.1.3 Disclosure is consistent with national disclosure policies and regulations of the furnishing Participant; and

9.6.1.4 Any disclosure or transfer of such Contractor Background Information to Contractors is consistent with the furnishing Participant's export control laws and regulations.

9.6.2 Use: Contractor Background Information furnished by one Participant's Contractors and disclosed to the other Participant may be used without charge by the other Participant for Project Purposes only, and may be subject to further restrictions by holders of Intellectual Property Rights. The furnishing Participant will retain all its rights with respect to such Contractor Background Information. Subject to any Intellectual Property Rights held by the furnishing Participant or its Contractors, where the use of Contractor Background Information is necessary to enable the use of Foreground Information, such Contractor Background Information may be used for Defense Purposes. The furnishing Participant (after consultation with the receiving Participant) will determine whether such use of Contractor Background Information is necessary.

9.7 Jointly Generated Foreground Information.

9.7.1 Disclosure: All jointly generated Foreground Information generated under an LFCM Activity will be disclosed to both Participants promptly and without charge.

9.7.2 Use: Each Participant generating or receiving jointly generated Foreground Information may use or have used such Information without charge only for its Defense Purposes, unless mutually determined otherwise in writing.

9.7.3 Information generated by PA WGs will be treated as jointly generated Foreground Information unless mutually determined otherwise in writing.

9.8 Alternative Uses of Information.

9.8.1 Any Background Information provided by one Participant will be used by the other Participant only for the purposes set out in this MOU, unless otherwise agreed to in writing by the furnishing Participant.

9.8.2 The prior written consent of each Participant will be required for the use of Foreground Information for any purposes other than those provided for in this MOU.

9.9 Intellectual Property Rights.

9.9.1 All unclassified Information subject to Intellectual Property Rights will be identified and marked, and it will be handled as Controlled Unclassified Information in accordance with Section X (CONTROLLED UNCLASSIFIED INFORMATION).

9.9.2 All Classified Information subject to Intellectual Property Rights will be identified, marked and handled in accordance with Section XII (SECURITY).

9.9.3 In addition to Section 10.4 of this MOU, prior to transferring Information subject to Intellectual Property Rights to Contractors, the Participants will ensure the Contractors are legally bound to adhere to such Intellectual Property Rights.

9.10 Inventions and Patents.

9.10.1 Reporting of Inventions. A Participant will disclose to the other Participant any Invention made by its respective employees or Contractors pursuant to work undertaken under this MOU or applicable PA as promptly as possible after the Invention is made. The disclosure will be in the form of a written report listing the inventor(s) and describing the manner and process of making and using the Invention in sufficient technical detail as to enable any person skilled in the art to which it pertains to make and use the Invention.

9.10.2 Title to Inventions. Each Participant will retain title to each Invention made by its respective employees under this MOU or applicable PA.

9.10.2.1 The Participant retaining title to such Inventions will grant to the other Participant at least a royalty-free, nonexclusive, irrevocable license to practice or have practiced worldwide for Defense Purposes by or on behalf of the other Participant such Inventions covered by any resulting Patents.

9.10.2.2 The Participant retaining title to such Inventions may, in its discretion, grant rights in such Inventions covered by any resulting Patents to the other Participant (in addition to the rights granted by 9.10.2.1), or any other person or entity, upon such terms and conditions as it deems appropriate.

9.10.3 Title to Joint Inventions. Title to Inventions made jointly by employees of both Participants will be held jointly by the Participants unless otherwise mutually determined.

9.10.3.1 The Participants may grant rights in such joint Inventions to any other person or entity, upon such terms and conditions, as the Participants mutually determine.

9.10.4 Contractor-Generated Inventions. Title to Inventions made by Contractors will be held in accordance with the terms of the respective Contract. Where any Contract fails to specify how title in any Patent will be held, title will be determined in accordance with the national laws governing Inventions by Contractors of the Participant who awarded the Contract.

9.10.4.1 Contractor-Generated Inventions in Unique National Variants. Where Inventions are made in connection with unique national variants, paid for fully by or on behalf of only one Participant, regardless of who is the Contracting Agency, the Contracting Agency must ensure that the Contract grants to the Participant funding the national variant any rights as directed by that Participant.

9.10.4.2 Contractor Generated Inventions of Participants. Where a Contract is awarded by a Participant on its own behalf or by a Contracting Agency on behalf of the other Participant or both Participants, the Contract so awarded must ensure that the owner of any Invention made by a Contractor, pursuant to that contract, will grant to the Participants at least a royalty-free. non-exclusive, irrevocable license to practice or have practiced worldwide for Defense Purposes by or on behalf of the Participants the Invention covered by any resulting Patents.

9.10.5 Patent Applications. A Participant having the right to hold title to an Invention may elect to file Patent applications or otherwise seek Patent protection thereon provided it so advises the other Participant of its intention to do so and the countries in which it intends to seek Patent protection within 60 days from the date it reports the Invention to the other Participant.

9.10.5.1 If a Participant initially elects to seek Patent protection, but later decides not to continue seeking Patent protection, or if a Participant decides not to share the costs of seeking Patent protection of a joint Invention, then the other Participant may elect (but is not required) to seek Patent protection on such Invention in those countries in which the Participant has not elected to seek Patent protection.

9.10.5.2 If the other Participant elects to seek Patent protection in those countries, the Participant initially having the right to seek Patent protection on the Invention is deemed to consent to such filing by the other Participant and the Participants will equitably share, as mutually determined by the Participants, any royalties from the licensing of any resulting Patents taking into consideration the expenses incurred by each Participant in securing Patent protection.

9.10.5.3 A Participant will not file or cause to be filed any Patent application outside the United States of America or Australia, or publish or cause to be published any such application or Patent thereon anywhere, without the other Participant's prior written consent where the application contains either:

9.10.5 3.1 the other Participant's Background Information; or

9.10.5.3.2 jointly generated Foreground Information.

9.10.5.4 Patent applications on Inventions which contain Classified Information to be filed under this MOU or any of its PAs, will be protected and safeguarded in accordance with the requirements contained in Section XII (SECURITY) of this MOU.

9.10.6 Patent Prosecution.

9.10.6.1 The expenses attendant to seeking Patent protection as specified above will be borne by the Participant seeking Patent protection. Where both Participants jointly seek Patent protection, the expenses attendant to seeking the Patent protection will be shared equally between the Participants, unless mutually determined otherwise.

9.10.6.2 Each Participant will provide the other Participant with copies of Patent applications it files in. Patent offices, along with a power to inspect and make copies of all documents retained in the files of the applicable Patent office that are available for inspection and copying by a Participant seeking Patent protection.

9.10.6.3 A Participant seeking Patent protection will have the right to control the Patent prosecution where it is solely funding the expenses attendant to seeking the Patent protection. Where both Participants are seeking Patent protection, they will jointly control the Patent prosecution if each is funding a portion of the expenses attendant to seeking the Patent protection. The Participants will cooperate with each other in seeking Patent protection.

9.10.7 Maintenance Fees. The fees payable to a Patent office in order to maintain the Patent on an Invention will be paid by the Participant having title to the Patent or will be shared equally if title is held jointly by both Participants. If one Participant decides not to pay the required maintenance fees, it will immediately notify the other Participant, who may pay the maintenance fees if it desires to maintain the enforcement of the Patent. In this case, the Participant who has decided not to pay the maintenance fees will assign its rights to the other Participant.

9.10.8 Infringement. Each Participant will notify the other Participant of any Patent infringement claims made in its territory arising in the course of work performed under any PA of this MOU.

Insofar as possible, the other Participant will provide information available to it that may assist in defending the claim. Each Participant will be responsible for handling all Patent infringement claims made in its territory, and will consult with the other Participant during the handling, and prior to any settlement, of such claims. Unless the Participants otherwise mutually determine in writing, the costs of resolving Patent infringement claims will be handled as follows. The Participants will share in the costs of resolving Patent infringement claims in the same percentage as they share the full Financial Costs and Non-Financial Costs of the applicable PA. If the infringement claim does not arise under a PA, then the Participants will share in the costs of resolving Patent infringement claims equally. The Participants will, in accordance with their national laws and practices, give their authorization and consent for all use and manufacture in the course of work performed under this MOU or a PA of any Invention covered by a Patent issued by their respective countries.

SECTION X
CONTROLLED UNCLASSIFIED INFORMATION

10.1 Except as otherwise provided in this MOU or as authorized in writing by the originating Participant, Controlled Unclassified Information provided or generated pursuant to this MOU will be controlled as follows:

10.1.1 Such Information will be used only for the purposes authorized according to Section IX (DISCLOSURE AND USE OF INFORMATION).

10.1.2 Access to such Information will be limited to personnel whose access is necessary for the permitted use under subparagraph 10.1.1 and will be subject to the provisions of Section XIII (THIRD PARTY SALES AND TRANSFERS).

10.1.3 Each Participant will take all applicable steps, which may include national classification, available to it to keep such information free from further disclosure (including requests under any legislative provisions), except as provided in subparagraph 10.1.2, unless the originating Participant consents in writing to such disclosure. In the event of unauthorized disclosure, or if it becomes probable that the Information may have to be further disclosed under any legislative provisions, immediate notification will be given to the originating Participant.

10.2 To assist in providing the appropriate controls, the originating Participant will ensure that Controlled Unclassified Information is appropriately marked. The Participants will decide, in advance and in writing, on the markings to be placed on the Controlled Unclassified Information. The appropriate markings will be specified in the PSI.

10.3 Controlled Unclassified Information provided or generated pursuant to this MOU will be handled in a manner that ensures control as provided for in paragraph 10.1.

10.4 Prior to authorizing the release of Controlled Unclassified Information to Contractors, the Participants will ensure the Contractors are legally bound to control such Information in accordance with the provisions of this Section.

SECTION XI
VISITS TO ESTABLISHMENTS

11.1 All visits will be in accordance with the Security Agreement.

11.2 Each Participant will permit visits to its Government establishments, agencies and laboratories, and Contractor industrial facilities by employees of the other Participant or by employees of the other Participant's Contractor(s), provided that the visit is authorized in writing by both Participants and the employees have all necessary and appropriate security clearances and a need to know.

11.3 All visiting personnel will be required to comply with the security regulations of the host Participant. Any Information disclosed or made available to visitors will be treated as if supplied to the Participant sponsoring the visiting personnel, and will be subject to the provisions of this MOU.

11.4 Requests for visits by personnel of one Participant to a facility of the other Participant will be coordinated through official channels, and will conform to the established visit procedures of the host Participant. Requests for visits will bear the name of this MOU and the applicable LFCM Activity.

11.5 Lists of personnel of each Participant required to visit, on a continuing basis, facilities of the other Participant will be submitted through official channels in accordance with recurring international visit procedures.

SECTION XII
SECURITY

12.1 All Classified Information provided or generated pursuant to this MOU will be stored, handled, transmitted, and safeguarded in accordance with the Security Agreement.

12.2 Classified Information will be transferred only through official government-to-government channels or through channels approved in writing by the Designated Security Authorities (DSAs) of the Participants. Such Classified Information will bear the level of classification, denote the country of origin, the conditions of release, and the fact that the information relates to this MOU and the applicable LFCM Activity.

12.3 Each Participant will take all applicable steps available to it to ensure that Classified Information provided or generated pursuant to this MOU is protected from further disclosure, except as permitted by paragraph 12.8, unless the other Participant consents in writing to such disclosure. Accordingly, each Participant will ensure that:

12.3.1 The receiving Participant will not release the Classified Information to any government, national, organization, or any other entity of a Third Party without the prior written consent of the originating Participant in accordance with the procedures detailed in Section XIII (THIRD PARTY SALES AND TRANSFERS);

12.3.2 The receiving Participant will not use the Classified Information for purposes other than those provided for in this MOU and applicable PA;

12.3.3 The receiving Participant will comply with any distribution and access restrictions on Classified Information that are required under this MOU; and

12.3.4 The recipient will not change the national security classification assigned by the furnishing Participant without the prior written consent of the furnishing Participant.

12.4 The Participants will investigate all cases in which it is known or where there are grounds for suspecting that Classified Information provided or generated pursuant to this MOU has been lost or disclosed to unauthorized persons. Each Participant also will promptly and fully inform the other Participant of the details of any such occurrences, of the final results of the investigation, and of the corrective action taken to preclude recurrences.

12.5 The PM will prepare a PS1 and a CG for the MOU. The PSI and the CG will describe the methods by which Information will be classified, marked, used, transmitted, and safeguarded. The PSI will be reviewed and a CG will be developed by the PO within three months after the PA enters into effect and in accordance with the Security Agreement. The CG will be subject to regular review and revision with the aim of downgrading the classification whenever this is appropriate. Prior to the transfer of any Classified Information or Controlled Unclassified Information, the PSI and the applicable CG will be approved by the respective DSAs and will be applicable to all Government and Contractor personnel of the Participants.

12.6 The DSA of the Participant that awards a classified Contract pursuant to this MOU will assume responsibility for administering within its territory security measures for the protection of the Classified Information, in accordance with its laws and regulations. Prior to the release to a Contractor, prospective Contractor, subcontractor, or prospective subcontractor of any Classified Information provided or generated under this MOU, the DSA will:

12.6.1 Ensure that such Contractor, prospective Contractor, subcontractor, or prospective subcontractor and their facility or facilities have the capability to protect the Classified Information adequately under each Participant's respective industrial security program;

12.6.2 Grant a security clearance to the facility or facilities;

12.6.3 Grant a security clearance for all personnel whose duties require access to Classified Information;

12.6.4 Ensure that all persons having access to the Classified Information are informed of their responsibilities to protect the Classified Information in accordance with national security laws and regulations, and provisions of this MOU; and

12.6.5 Ensure that access to the Classified Information is limited to those persons who have a need to know for the purposes of the MOU and any LFCM Activities.

12.7 The DSAs may carry out periodic security inspections of cleared facilities to ensure that the Classified Information is properly protected.

12.8 Contractors, prospective Contractors, subcontractors, or prospective subcontractors who are determined by DSAs to be under financial, administrative, policy, or management control of nationals or entities of a Third Party, may participate in a Contract or subcontract requiring access to Classified Information provided or generated pursuant to this MOU only when enforceable measures are in effect to ensure that nationals or other entities of a Third Party will not have access to Classified Information. If enforceable measures are not in effect to preclude access by nationals or other entities of a Third Party, the other Participant will be consulted for written approval prior to permitting such access.

12.9 For any facility wherein Classified Information is to be used, the responsible Participant or Contractor will approve the appointment of a person or persons to exercise effectively the responsibilities for safeguarding at such facility the Classified Information pertaining to this MOU. These officials will be responsible for limiting access to Classified Information involved in this MOU to those persons who have been properly approved for access and have a need to know.

12.10 Each Participant will ensure that access to the Classified Information is limited to those persons who possess requisite security clearances and have a specific need for access to the Classified Information in order to participate in this MOU.

12.11 Information provided or generated pursuant to this MOU may be classified up to and including SECRET. Information exchanged or generated pursuant to a PA may, on a case-by-case basis, be classified up to and including TOP SECRET. All Classified Information provided or generated under this MOU will be consistent with the national disclosure policies of the Participants. The existence of this MOU is UNCLASSIFIED and the contents are UNCLASSIFIED. The classification of the existence of any PA or E&MTA and its contents will be stated in that PA or E&MTA.

SECTION XIII
THIRD PARTY SALES AND TRANSFERS

13.1 Except to the extent permitted in paragraph 13.2, the Participants will not sell, transfer title to, disclose, or transfer possession of Foreground Information (or any item produced either wholly or in part from Foreground Information) or jointly acquired or produced Equipment and Material, to any Third Party without the prior written consent of the Government of the other Participant. Furthermore, neither Participant will permit any such sale, disclosure, or transfer, including by the owner of the item, without the prior written consent of the Government of the other Participant. Such consent will not be given unless the Government of the intended recipient consents in writing with the Participants that it will:

13.1.1 not retransfer, or permit the further retransfer of, any Equipment and Material or Information provided; and

13.1.2 use, or permit the use of, the Equipment and Material or Information provided only for the purposes specified by the Participants.

13.2 Each Participant will retain the right to sell, transfer title to, disclose, or transfer possession of Foreground Information that:

13.2.1 is generated solely by either that Participant or that Participant's Contractors in the performance of that Participant's work allocation under Section III (SCOPE OF WORK); and

13.2.2 does not include any Foreground Information or Background Information of the other Participant, and whose generation, test, or evaluation has not relied on the use of Equipment and Material of the other Participant.

13.3 In the event questions arise as to whether the Foreground Information (or any item produced either wholly or in part from the Foreground Information) that a Participant intends to sell, transfer title to, disclose, or transfer possession of to a Third Party is within the scope of paragraph 13.2, the matter will be brought to the immediate attention of the other Participant. The Participants will resolve the matter prior to any sale or other transfer of such Foreground Information (or any item produced either wholly or in part from the Foreground Information) to a Third Party.

13.4 The Participants will not sell, transfer title to, disclose, or transfer possession, grant, donate or transfer usage rights of Equipment and Material or Background Information provided by the other Participant to any Third Party without the prior written consent of the Government of the Participant that provided such Equipment and Material or Information. The providing Participant's Government will be solely responsible for authorizing such transfers and, as applicable, specifying the method and provisions for implementing such transfers. For Project Equipment or Background Information that has been provided by a furnishing PA Participant to a receiving PA Participant, the Participants recognize that any sale, transfer of title to, disclosure of, or transfer of possession of such Project Equipment or Background Information by the receiving PA Participant to any non-Third Party will be in accordance with the applicable provisions of this MOU, including Section VII (CONTRACTING PROVISIONS), Section VIII (PROJECT EQUIPMENT) and Section IX (DISCLOSURE AND USE OF INFORMATION).

13.5 Consent for Third Party sales and transfers of Foreground Information, jointly acquired or produced Equipment and Material, or any item produced either wholly or in part from Foreground Information will be subject to foreign policy, national security considerations, and national laws, regulations, and policies of the Governments of both Participants. A Participant's Government's written approval of the other Participant's Government's proposed sale or transfer to a Third Party will take into account their willingness to sell or transfer such Equipment and Material or Information to the same Third Party.

SECTION XIV
LIABILITY AND CLAIMS

14.1 Claims arising under this MOU and any PA will be dealt with in accordance with paragraph 1 of the Chapeau Agreement.

14.2 The Participants will share any costs required to be shared under subparagraph l(b)(ii) of the Chapeau Agreement in the same proportions as the Financial Costs and Non-Financial Costs are shared in the applicable PA.

14.3 The Participants will share any costs required to be shared under subparagraph l(b)(iv) of the Chapeau Agreement on the following basis:

14.3.1 For Contracts where one Participant contracts solely on its own behalf, the Participant awarding the Contract will pay the cost of claims arising under that Contract.

14.3.2 For Contracts where one Participant contracts on behalf of the other Participant, the Participant on whose behalf the Contract was awarded will pay the cost of claims arising under that Contract. The Contracting Participant will not indemnify Contractors against third party liability claims, unless otherwise mutually determined in the applicable PA.

14.3.3 For Contracts awarded on behalf of both Participants, the costs of claims arising under such Contracts will be shared in the same proportions as costs are shared in the applicable PA. The Contracting Participant will not indemnify Contractors against third party liability claims, unless otherwise mutually determined in the applicable PA.

SECTION XV
PARTICIPATION OF ADDITIONAL NATIONS

15.1 The Participants recognize that other nations may wish to join this MOU.

15.2 Mutual consent of the Participants will be required to conduct discussions with potential additional participants. The Participants will discuss the arrangements under which another participant might join, including the furnishing of releasable Information for evaluation prior to joining. If the disclosure of Information is necessary to conduct discussions, such disclosure will be in accordance with Section IX (DISCLOSURE AND USE OF PROJECT INFORMATION), Section X (CONTROLLED UNCLASSIFIED INFORMATION), Section XII (SECURITY) and Section XIII (THIRD PARTY SALES AND TRANSFERS).

15.3 The addition of new participants will require amendment to this MOU or the establishment of a new MOU.

SECTION XVI
CUSTOMS DUTIES, TAXES, AND SIMILAR CHARGES

16.1 Customs duties, import and export taxes, and similar charges will be administered in accordance with each Participant's respective laws and regulations. Insofar as existing national laws and regulations permit, the Participants will endeavor to ensure that such readily identifiable duties, taxes, and similar charges, as well as quantitative or other restrictions on imports and exports, are not imposed in connection with work carried out under this MOU.

16.2 Each Participant will use its best efforts to ensure that customs duties, import and export taxes, and similar charges are administered in a manner favorable to the efficient and economical conduct of the work. If any such duties, taxes, or similar charges are levied, the Participant in whose country they are levied will bear such costs as a cost to that Participant over and above that Participant's financial contribution under this MOU.

SECTION XVII
SETTLEMENT OF DISPUTES

Disputes between the Participants arising under or relating to this MOU will be resolved only by consultation between the Participants and will not be referred to a national court, to an international tribunal, or to any other person or entity for settlement.

SECTION XVIII
ENTRY INTO EFFECT, AMENDMENT, DURATION AND TERMINATION

18.1 All activities of the Participants under this MOU will be carried out in accordance with their respective national laws and regulations, including their respective export control laws and regulations. The obligations of the Participants will be subject to the availability of funds for such purposes.

18.2 In the event of a conflict between the terms of this MOU, any PA, or E&MTA under this MOU, this MOU will take precedence.

18.3 This MOU, or any arrangement under this MOU, may be amended by the mutual written consent of the Participants.

18.4 This MOU, or any arrangement under this MOU, may be terminated at any time upon the mutual written consent of the Participants. In the event both Participants consent to terminate this MOU or any arrangement under this MOU the Participants will consult prior to the date of termination to ensure termination on the most economical and equitable terms. Termination of this MOU will result in the termination of all arrangements under this MOU.

18.5 Either Participant may terminate this MOU, or any arrangement under this MOU, upon 180 days written notification of its intent to terminate to the other Participant. Such notice will be the subject of immediate consultation by the Participants to mutually determine the appropriate course of action to conclude the activities under this MOU or any arrangement. In the event of such termination, the following rules apply:

18.5.1 If this MOU is terminated, the Participants will continue participation, financial or otherwise, in all LFCM Activities, up to the effective date of termination. Each Participant will make available to the other Participant all Foreground Information generated prior to termination and which has not been provided to the other Participant prior to the termination.

18.5.2 Except as to Contracts awarded on behalf of both Participants, each Participant will be responsible for its own project-related costs associated with termination of a PA. For Contracts awarded on behalf of both Participants, the terminating Participant will pay all Contract modification or termination costs that would not otherwise have been incurred but for the decision to terminate; in no event, however, will a terminating Participant's total financial contribution, including Contract termination costs, exceed that Participant's total financial contribution for the PA being terminated.

18.5.3 All Information and rights therein received under the provisions of this MOU or any arrangement prior to the termination of the MOU will be retained by the Participants, subject to the provisions of this MOU.

18.5.4 Additional termination provisions consistent with this Section may be established in the arrangements.

18.6 The respective rights and obligations of the Participants regarding Section VIII (EQUIPMENT AND MATERIAL TRANSFERS). Section IX (DISCLOSURE AND USE OF INFORMATION), Section X (CONTROLLED UNCLASSIFIED INFORMATION), Section XII (SECURITY),

Section XIII (THIRD PARTY SALES AND TRANSFERS), Section XIV (LIABILITY AND CLAIMS), Section XVn (DISPUTES), and this Section XVIII (ENTRY INTO EFFECT, AMENDMENT, DURATION, AND TERMINATION) will continue to apply notwithstanding termination or expiration of this MOU or any arrangement under this MOU.

18.7 This MOU, which consists of eighteen (18) Sections and three (3) Annexes, will enter into effect on the date of last signature and will remain in effect for twenty (20) years unless terminated by either Participant. It may be extended by the written mutual determination of the Participants The foregoing represents the understandings reached between the Department of Defense of the United States of America and the Department of Defence of Australia upon the matters referred to herein.

The foregoing represents the understandings reached between the Department of Defense of the United States of America and the Department of Defence of Australia upon the matters referred to herein.

SIGNED, in duplicate, in the English language.

FOR THE DEPARTMENT OF DEFENSE OF THE UNITED STATES OF AMERICA:	FOR THE DEPARTMENT OF DEFENCE OF AUSTRALIA:
[Signature]	[Signature]
Major General Charles A. Cartwright Name	Brigadier Damian S.M. Roche CSC Name
Program Manager, Future Combat Systems (Brigade Combat Team) Title	Military Attaché and Assistant Defence Attaché Title
26 July 2006 Date	*26 July 2006* Date
Washington, DC, USA Location	Washington, DC, USA Location

ANNEX A
MODEL PROJECT ARRANGEMENT
PA NUMBER – (-XXXX*)
TO THE
MEMORANDUM OF UNDERSTANDING
BETWEEN
THE DEPARTMENT OF DEFENSE
OF THE UNITED STATES OF AMERICA
AND
THE DEPARTMENT OF DEFENCE
OF AUSTRALIA
CONCERNING
COOPERATION ON LAND FORCE CAPABILITY
MODERNIZATION

DATED
CONCERNING
(FULL DESIGNATION OF THE PROJECT)

INTRODUCTION

This Land Force Capability Modernization (LFCM) Project Arrangement (PA) is entered into pursuant to the Memorandum of Understanding (MOU) between the Department of Defense of the United States of America (U.S. DoD) and the Department of Defence of Australia (ADOD) concerning Cooperation on Land Force Capability Modernization, which entered into effect on *(date)*

SECTION I
DEFINITIONS AND ABBREVIATIONS

(Define only those terms used in this PA that have not been defined in the MOU.)

SECTION II
OBJECTIVES

The objectives of this__________ PA are:

a. The development of ____.

b. The improvement of ____.

SECTION III
SCOPE OF WORK

The following work will be undertaken under this PA.

a. Develop____.

b. Evaluate____.

c. Design, fabricate and test______________________________.

*The U.S. DoD will assign the Project Arrangement Number.

SECTION IV
SHARING OF TASKS

The sharing of tasks will be as follows:

a. The U. S. DoD will____________________________________.

b. The ADOD will____________________________________.

c. U.S. DoD and ADOD will jointly____________________________.

SECTION V
BREAKDOWN AND SCHEDULE OF TASKS
(OPTIONAL)

(Use this format when the tasks covered under this project may be performed using multiple phases, requiring milestones or decision points.)

The project will proceed according to the following phases and schedule. Note that national priorities may pre-empt mutually determined schedules in PAs.

Phase 1	*Start*	*End*
Description of Phase 1	Month X	Month Y

(Milestone 1) (e.g., Transmittal of Feasibility Report)

Phase 2	*Start*	*End*
Description of Phase 2	Month X	Month Y

(Milestone 2) (e.g., Decision to proceed to Phase 3)

Phase 3	*Start*	*End*
Description of Phase 3	Month X	Month Y

(Milestone 3) (e.g., Evaluation, analysis of results)

(Add as many phases as necessary.)

The final report will be transmitted to the Steering Committee (SC) six months before the termination date for this PA.

SECTION VI
MANAGEMENT

1. The POs are:

U.S. DoD PO Title/Position__________________________

Organization__________________________________

ADOD PO Title/Position___________________________

Organization__________________________________

2. Project Offices will be established in_________***(Name of U.S. location)*** and in__________ ***(Name of AS location)***. ***(The management structure and names, position, organization and address of key personnel.)***

3. Particular Management Procedures:

(Mention only those additional management responsibilities not covered under Section IV (MANAGEMENT (ORGANIZATION AND RESPONSIBILITIES) of the MOU.)

SECTION VII
FINANCIAL PROVISIONS

The Participants estimate that the cost of performance of the tasks under this PA will not exceed________U.S. Dollars or_________AS Dollars.

Cooperative efforts of the Participants over and above the mutually determined tasks set out in the SCOPE OF WORK, SHARING OF TASKS and FINANCIAL PROVISIONS Sections will be subject to amendment to this PA or signature of a new PA.

(If a PA will involve the assignment of CPP, the PA will include a provision that refers to paragraphs 5.6–5.7 of the MOU, identifies which Participant is sending or hosting CPP, and specifies the number of CPP to be assigned. In addition, the PA will include the amount of financial and non-financial contributions related to CPP in one of the two alternatives below in this section.)

(If a PA will not involve one Participant contracting for the other or both Participants, and no funds will be exchanged between the Participants, use the following format for the Financial Arrangements. Both financial and non-financial contributions should be included in the total U.S. DoD and ADOD costs.)

Alternative 1

The U.S. DOD tasks will not cost more than:___U.S. Dollars or AS Dollars.

The ADOD tasks will not cost more than:_________AS Dollars or_________U.S. Dollars.

Or

(If a PA will involve one Participant contracting for the other Participant or both Participants, or the Participants will transfer or exchange funds between them, use the following format for the Financial Arrangements.)

Alternative 2

(Cost of performance includes Financial Costs and Non-Financial Costs.)

	Year 1	Year 2	Year 3	Year 4	Year 5	Total
U.S. DoD						
ADOD						

(Using the above table and whatever description is necessary, explain and demonstrate how the PA will be funded. Identify both financial (funds) and non-financial (for example, use of equipment) contributions and identify the amount of funds to be transferred between the Participants, as well as the rate of currency exchange.)

(The Financial Management Procedures Document (FMPD) should be developed by the POs and submitted to the PMs and SC (if appropriate) for approval. The FMPD should include, as a minimum, schedule, handling, funding levels by year, and auditing procedures for monetary contributions anticipated for this PA.)

SECTION VIII

SPECIAL DISCLOSURE AND USE OF INFORMATION PROVISIONS (OPTIONAL)

(Insert any special disclosure and use of information provisions unique to the PA.)

SECTION IX
CLASSIFICATION

(Select only one of the four following possibilities:)

a. No Classified Information will be exchanged under this PA;

b. The highest level of Classified Information that may be exchanged under this PA is CONFIDENTIAL;

c. The highest level of Classified Information that may be exchanged under this PA is SECRET; or

d. The highest level of Classified Information that may be exchanged under this PA is TOP SECRET.

The existence of this PA is ***[Insert classification]*** and its contents are ***[Insert classification]***

SECTION X
PRINCIPAL ORGANIZATIONS INVOLVED

(List the organizations of the Participants.)

SECTION XI

EQUIPMENT AND MATERIAL TRANSFERS (OPTIONAL)

Providing Participant	Receiving Participant	Qty	Description	Part/ Stock#	Consumable/ Non-Consumable	Return Date	Estimated Replacement Value*	Security Classification

* Estimated Replacement Value is a good faith estimate of the replacement value at the time of the loan.

(NOTES:

1. In the event that the cooperative efforts under the PA requires the provision of Equipment and Material to either Participant, a list of such Equipment and Material must be developed in general accordance with the proceeding table. (Equipment and Material that cannot be identified at the time of PA signature will be documented, when identified, in a list to be developed and maintained by the PM in the format above.)

2. If jointly acquired Equipment and Material is an aspect of the cooperative effort under the PA, terms and conditions for the disposal of such jointly acquired Equipment and Material must be included in the PA.)

SECTION XII
SPECIAL PROVISIONS

(Identify any procedures, specifications, or other necessary attributes of the project not delineated in other Sections).

SECTION XIII

ENTRY INTO EFFECT. DURATION AND TERMINATION.

This______________________________Project Arrangement, a project under the Memorandum of Understanding between the Department of Defense of the United States of America and the Department of Defence of Australia concerning Cooperation on Land Force Capability Modernization, will enter into effect on the date of last signature by the Participants, and will remain in effect for____years unless terminated.

FOR THE DEPARTMENT OF DEFENSE OF THE UNITED STATES OF AMERICA:

____
[Signature]

____
Name

____
Title

____
Date

____
Location

FOR THE DEPARTMENT OF DEFENCE OF AUSTRALIA:

____
[Signature]

____
Name

____
Title

____
Date

____
Location

ANNEX B

COOPERATIVE PROJECT PERSONNEL (CPP)

ASSIGNMENT OF LAND FORCE CAPABILITY MODERNIZATION COOPERATIVE PROJECT PERSONNEL

1. Purpose and Scope:

1.1 This Annex establishes the provisions that will govern the conduct of Cooperative Project Personnel (CPP). The Parent Participant will assign military members or civilian employees to the Joint Project Office (JPO) or other office or facility in accordance with Section IV (MANAGEMENT) and this Annex. CPP will be able to perform all the responsibilities assigned to them under this MOD and the relevant PA. Commencement of assignments will be subject to any requirements that may be imposed by the Host Participant or its Government regarding acceptance of CPP, such as, but not limited to, visas and visit request documentation. The Participants will mutually determine the length of tour for the positions at the time of initial assignment.

1.2 CPP will be assigned to a JPO or other office or facility for PA work and will report to their designated supervisor regarding that work. The POs will be responsible for the creation of a document describing the duties of each CPP position, which will be subject to approval by the SC. CPP will not act as liaison officers on behalf of the Parent Participant. CPP may act from time to time on behalf of their respective SC member if the latter so authorizes in writing.

1.3 CPP will not be assigned to command or other positions that would require them to exercise responsibilities that are reserved by law or regulation to an officer or employee of the Host Participant's Government.

2.0 Security:

2.1 The Participants will ensure CPP have the minimum level of security clearance required, if any, to permit them to have access to Classified Information and facilities in which Classified Information is used in accordance with the Project Security Instruction (PSI) and Classification Guide (CG). Access to Classified Information and facilities in which Classified Information is used will be consistent with, and limited by, Section II (OBJECTIVES) and Section III (SCOPE OF WORK) of this MOU and will be kept to the minimum required to accomplish the work assignments.

2.2 The Parent Participant will file visit requests for the CPP through prescribed channels in compliance with the Host Participant's procedures. As part of the visit request procedures, the Parent Participant will cause security assurances to be filed, through the Parent Government's embassy located in the Host Participant's country, specifying the security clearances for the CPP being assigned.

2.3 The Host Participant and Parent Participant will use their best efforts to ensure that CPP assigned to a JPO or other office or facility are aware of, and comply with, applicable laws and regulations as well as the requirements of Section IX (DISCLOSURE AND USE OF INFORMATION), Section X (CONTROLLEDUNCLASSIFIEDINFORMATION),SectionXI(VISITSTOESTABLISHMENTS), Section XII (SECURITY), and Section XVIII (ENTRY INTO EFFECT, AMENDMENT, DURATION AND TERMINATION) of this MOU and the provisions of the applicable PSI and CG. Prior to commencing assigned duties, CPP will, if required by the Host Government's laws, regulations, policies, or procedures, sign a certification concerning the conditions and responsibilities of CPP.

2.4 CPP will at all times be required to comply with the security and export control laws, regulations, and procedures of the Host Government. Any violation of security procedures by CPP during their assignment will be reported to the Parent Participant for appropriate action. CPP committing violations of security and export control laws, regulations, or procedures during their assignments may be withdrawn from the project with a view toward appropriate administrative or disciplinary action by the Parent Participant.

2.5 All Classified Information made available to CPP will be considered as Classified Information furnished to the Parent Participant, and will be subject to all provisions and safeguards provided for in Section XII (SECURITY), the PSI, and CG.

2.6 CPP will not have personal custody of Classified Information or Controlled Unclassified Information unless approved by the Host Participant and as authorized by the Parent Participant. They will be granted access to such Information in accordance with Section X (CONTROLLED UNCLASSIFIED INFORMATION), Section XII (SECURITY), and the PSI during normal duty hours at the JPO or other office or facility and when access is necessary to perform PA work.

2.7 CPP assigned to a JPO or other office or facility will not serve as a conduit between the Host Participant and Parent Participant for requests and/or transmission of Classified Information or Controlled Unclassified Information unless specifically authorized by the PSI.

3.0 Technical and Administrative Matters:

3.1 Consistent with Host Government's laws and regulations, and subject to applicable multilateral or bilateral agreements or arrangements, CPP will be subject to the same restrictions, conditions, and privileges as Host Participant personnel of comparable rank and in comparable assignments. Further, to the extent authorized by Host Government's laws and regulations, and any applicable multilateral or bilateral agreements or arrangements, CPP and their authorized dependents will be accorded:

3.1.1 exemption from any Host Government' s tax upon income received from the Parent Participant; and

3.1.2 exemption from any Host Government's customs and import duties or similar charges levied on items entering the country for their official or personal use, including their baggage, household effects, and private motor vehicles.

3.2 On arrival, CPP will be provided briefings arranged by the JPO or other office or facility about applicable laws, orders, regulations, and customs and the need to comply with them. CPP will also be provided briefings arranged by the JPO or other office or facility regarding entitlements, privileges, and obligations such as:

3.2.1 Any medical and dental care that may be provided to CPP and their authorized dependents at Host Participant medical facilities, subject to the requirements of applicable laws, regulations, and any applicable multilateral or bilateral agreements or arrangements;

3.2.2 Purchasing and patronage privileges at military commissaries, exchanges, theaters, and clubs for CPP and their authorized dependents;

3.2.3 Subject to the requirements of applicable laws, regulations, and provision by any applicable multilateral or bilateral agreements or arrangements, the Host Participant will provide if available, housing and messing facilities for CPP and their authorized dependents on the same basis and priority as for its own personnel;

3.2.4 Paying messing and housing charges to the same extent as Host Participant personnel. At locations where facilities are not provided by the Host Participant for its own personnel or facilities are not available, the Parent Participant will make suitable arrangements for its CPP; and

3.2.5 Paying motor vehicle liability insurance coverage in accordance with the laws and regulations applicable in the area where they are residing. In case of claims involving the use of private motor vehicles by CPP, the recourse will be against such insurance.

3.3 The PO, through the JPO or other office or facility, will, in consultation with the CPP, establish standard operating procedures for CPP in the following areas:

3.3.1 Working hours, including holiday schedules;

3.3.2 Leave authorization, consistent to the extent possible with the military and civilian personnel regulations and practices of the Host Participant and Parent Participant;

3.3.3 Dress regulations, consistent to the extent possible with the military and civilian personnel regulations and practices of the Host Participant and Parent Participant;

3.3.4 Performance evaluations, recognizing that such evaluations will be rendered in accordance with the Parent Participant's military or civilian personnel regulations and practices; and

3.3.5 Wearing of a building or installation pass or badge. CPP will be required to wear in clear view, when required by security procedures, a U.S. DoD or similar building or installation pass or badge that clearly identifies CPP. CPP will not be provided nametags, codes or titles that could imply CPP are U.S. DoD persons.

3.4 CPP committing an offense under the laws of the Government of the Host Participant or Parent Participant may be withdrawn from the project with a view toward further administrative or disciplinary action by the Parent Participant. Disciplinary action, however, will not be taken by the Host Participant against CPP, nor will the CPP exercise disciplinary powers over the Host Participant's personnel. In accordance with Host Participant's Government laws and regulations, the Host Participant will assist the Parent Participant in carrying out investigations of offenses involving CPP.

3.5 During their assignment, CPP will not be placed in the following duty status or environments unless it is consented to in writing by the Parent Participant:

3.5.1 Areas of political sensitivity where their presence may jeopardize the interests of either the Host Participant or Parent Participant, or where, in the normal course of their duty, they may become involved in activities that may embarrass either Participant:

3.5.2 Deployments in non-direct hostility situations, such as UN peacekeeping or multi-national operations, or third countries; and

3.5.3 Duty assignments in which direct hostilities are likely. Should a JPO or other office or facility to which CPP are assigned become involved unexpectedly in hostilities, assigned CPP will not be involved in the hostilities. Any such CPP approved by the Parent Participant for involvement in hostilities will be given specific guidance as to the conditions under which the assignment will be carried out by the appropriate authorities of the Host Participant and Parent Participant.

APPENDIX 1

COOPERATIVE PROJECT PERSONNEL POSITION DESCRIPTION

1. Position:

a. Title: Cooperative Project Personnel

2. Position Location:

3. Security Clearance Level Required for the Position:

4. Qualifications/Skills Required for Position:***(Insert appropriate data, e.g., Accredited degree in a scientific or related subject, land staff and/or operational experience in land systems. Military specialty similar to U.S. FCS Product Manager and/or acquisition engineering experience.)*** The CPP will perform the following tasks and responsibilities as mutually determined by the Project Managers (PMs).

5. General Categories of Information to which access will be required:***(Insert appropriate categories, e.g., Provided oral and visual access to information required to perform the duties outlined in this position description.)***

6. Description of Specific Duties:

a.**CPP**.will be primarily responsible for***(Insert responsibilities, e.g., coordinating the administration of the LFCM MOU). CPP will require information access to (Insert specific information access requirements, e.g., research, development and engineering programs involving manned systems);***

b. Identify specific duties;

c. The CPP requires access to computer word processing systems for preparing reports;

d. Identify anticipated travel requirements and locations;

e. The CPP will attend technical meetings and symposiums as required in performance of assigned duties;

f. Identify reporting requirements***(e.g., Provide a monthly summary of the U.S. /AS LFCM programs that are undertaken as separate PA's under the MOU)***.and any detail requirement ***(e.g., This report is to cover upgrade plans and program execution, associated technology programs in the ADOD, U.S. DoD, industry, and in-service support and engineering issues. It should also include forecasts of forthcoming trials, tests and program reviews.);***

g. Attend AS and U.S. project reviews and provide a summary report of PA activities at that venue as required;

h. In support of the PA advise the PM on respective national procurement and fielding policy, support and logistics doctrine and organization; and

i. Provide administrative support and coordination for the SC and other project meetings. In particular, to:

(1) Request inputs from the PA WGs at least two weeks prior to each meeting;

(2) Provide written briefs to the PM at least one week prior to each meeting;

(3) Provide draft minutes for each meeting within 10 days;

(4) Provide written briefs on PA activities to the PM every six weeks;

(5) Coordinate with key players in all PAs so as to ensure timely progress;

(6) Facilitate routing requests for information from both sides regarding PAs; and

(7) Attend PA meetings and provide administrative support where necessary.

ANNEX C

MODEL EQUIPMENT AND MATERIAL TRANSFER ARRANGEMENT E&MTA NUMBER (EMT-XXXX*)

TO THE MEMORANDUM OF UNDERSTANDING BETWEEN THE DEPARTMENT OF DEFENSE OF THE UNITED STATES OF AMERICA AND THE DEPARTMENT OF DEFENCE OF AUSTRALIA CONCERNING COOPERATION ON LAND FORCE CAPABILITY MODERNIZATION

BETWEEN

(Insert titles of the Organizations participating in the transfer.)

* The U.S. DoD will assign the E&MTA number.

INTRODUCTION

This Equipment and Material Transfer Arrangement (E&MTA) is entered into pursuant to the Memorandum of Understanding between the Department of Defense of the United States of America and the Department of Defence of Australia concerning Cooperation on Land Force Capability Modernization (the "LFCM MOU"), which entered into effect on ***(Insert effective date of the LFCM MOU).***This E&MTA is executed by authorized representatives of the providing and receiving Participants pursuant to Section VIII (EQUIPMENT AND MATERIAL TRANSFERS) of the LFCM MOU.

SECTION I

DESCRIPTION AND QUANTITY.

1.1 The following Equipment and Material will be transferred by the providing Participant to the receiving Participant:

Providing Participant	Receiving Participant	Qty	Description	Part/ Stock#	Consumable/ Non-Consumable	Return Date	Estimated Replacement Value*	Security Classification

(Fill in as appropriate)

* Estimated replacement value is a good faith estimate of the replacement value at the time of the loan.

1.2 ***(Choose one of the following alternatives, or use both if both situations apply.)***

Alternative A –Use when return of Equipment and Material is planned.

None of the Equipment and Material identified in paragraph 1.1 is intended to be consumed or expended during the course of the LFCM Activities described in paragraph 2.1.1.

Alternative B –Use when return of Equipment and Material is not planned due to its consumption during the activity.

The Equipment and Material described in paragraph 1.1 is intended to be consumed or expended during the course of the LFCM Activities described in paragraph 2.1.1.

SECTION II
PURPOSE

2.1 The purpose of this E&MTA is to support the following LFCM Activities.

2.1.1 ***(Fill in as appropriate)***

SECTION III
MANAGEMENT AND RESPONSIBILITIES

3.1 Each Participant will establish a point of contact (POC) who will be responsible for implementing this E&MTA.

3.1.1 For the providing Participant the POC is *

3.1.2 For the receiving Participant the POC is *

- Insert the appropriate names, title/office symbols, addresses, and telephone numbers of the individuals assigned to implement the E&MTA.

3.2 Responsibilities of the Providing Participant

3.2.1 Transfer of the Equipment and Material The providing Participant will transfer the Equipment and Material listed above for the duration of the transfer period specified in paragraph 6.4 unless extended by mutual written consent.

3.2.2 Equipment and Material Delivery – The providing Participant will deliver the Equipment and Material **(specify arrangements)** Possession and responsibility for the Equipment and Material will pass from the providing Participant to the receiving Participant at the time of receipt of the Equipment and Material at the mutually determined location specified. Any further transportation is the responsibility of the receiving Participant unless otherwise specified in this paragraph.

3.2.3 Information ... The providing Participant will furnish the receiving Participant such information as is necessary to enable the Equipment and Material to be used in the activities described in paragraph 2.1.1 in accordance with Section IX (DISCLOSURE AND USE OF INFORMATION) of the MOU.

3.3 Responsibilities of the Receiving Participant

3.3.1 *Inspection and Inventory*– The receiving Participant will inspect and inventory the Equipment and Material upon receipt. The receiving Participant will also inspect and inventory the Equipment and Material prior to its return to the providing Participant, unless the Equipment and Material is consumed in accordance with paragraph 3.3.2.

3.3.2 **(Choose one of the following alternatives, or use both if both situations apply.)**

Alternative A – Use when return of Equipment and Material is planned.

Return of Equipment and Material– Upon expiration or termination of the transfer period specified in paragraph 6.4 (taking into account any approved extensions by the providing Participant), the receiving Participant will return the Equipment and Material to the providing Participant (specify arrangements). Possession and responsibility for the Equipment and Material will pass from the receiving Participant to the providing Participant at the time of receipt of the Equipment and Material at the mutually determined location specified. If the Equipment and Material is lost, unintentionally destroyed, or damaged beyond economical repair, while in the custody of the receiving Participant, the receiving Participant will issue a certificate of loss/destruction/irreparable damage to the providing Participant.

Alternative B – Use when return of Equipment and Material is not planned due to it consumption during the activity.

Consumption of Equipment and Material– It is intended that the receiving Participant will consume the Equipment and Material specified in paragraph 1.1 during the course of the activities described in paragraph 2.1.1. If this does occur, the receiving Participant will provide written notice of its consumption to the providing Participant. In the event consumption does not occur prior to the end of the transfer period specified in paragraph 6.4, the receiving Participant will return the Equipment and Material to the providing Participant (specify arrangements). Possession and responsibility for the Equipment and Material will pass from the receiving Participant to the providing Participant at the time of receipt of the Equipment and Material at the mutually determined location specified. If the Equipment and Material is lost, unintentionally destroyed, or damaged beyond repair prior to its intended consumption while in the custody of the receiving Participant, the receiving Participant will issue a certificate of loss/destruction/irreparable damage to the providing Participant.

3.4 This E&MTA provides only for transfer of Equipment and Material associated with the activities described in paragraph 2.1.1. Signature of this E&MTA does not imply any commitment by a Participant to participate in any activities beyond the E&MTA described herein.

SECTION IV

SPECIAL PROVISIONS (OPTIONAL)

4.1 (Insert any special provisions as required.)

SECTION V CLASSIFICATION

5.1(Insert only one of the two following paragraphs; note that one of these two options must be selected.)

a. No classified Equipment and Material will be transferred under this E&MTA.

b. The highest level of classified Equipment and Material transferred under this E&MTA is CONFIDENTIAL.

c. The highest level of classified Equipment and Material transferred under this E&MTA is SECRET.

SECTION VI MODIFICATION. TRANSFER PERIOD AND TERMINATION

6.1 The provisions of this E&MTA may be amended or extended in accordance with Section XVIII of the LFCM MOU.

6.2 The Equipment and Material Transfer described in this E&MTA may be terminated in accordance with Section XVIII of the LFCM MOU. Additionally, this E&MTA may be terminated unilaterally by the providing Participant at any time.

6.3 Responsibilities regarding security and protection against unauthorized use, disclosure, or transfer that accrued prior to termination or expiration of the transfer period will continue to apply without limit of time in accordance with Section XVIII (ENTRY INTO EFFECT, AMENDMENT. DURATION AND TERMINATION) of the LFCM MOU.

6.4 The transfer period for the Equipment and Material described herein begins on the date of the last signature below, and unless terminated or extended, will continue until ***(enter date or amount of time).***

FOR THE DEPARTMENT OF DEFENSE OF THE UNITED STATES OF AMERICA

[Signature]

Name

Title

Date

Location

FOR THE DEPARTMENT OF DEFENCE OF AUSTRALIA

[Signature]

Name

Title

Date

Location

STATE DEPARTMENT DOCUMENT NUMBER: 06-291

AGREEMENT REGARDING THE TECHNICAL EXCHANGE AND COOPERATION ARRANGEMENT BETWEEN THE NUCLEAR REGULATORY COMMISSION OF THE UNITED STATES OF AMERICA (USNRC) AND THE INSTITUT DE RADIOPROTECTION ET DE SÛRETÉ NUCLÉAIRE OF FRANCE (IRSN) IN THE FIELD OF NUCLEAR SAFETY RESEARCH

SIGNED AT ROCKVILLE AND PARIS,
JULY 26 AND AUGUST 4, 2006
ENTERED INTO FORCE AUGUST 4, 2006

CTIA DOCUMENT NUMBER: 13118.000

The Parties: the United States Nuclear Regulatory Commission, hereinafter referred to as the USNRC, and the Institut de Radioprotection et de Sûreté Nucléaire of France, hereafter referred to as IRSN;

Considering that:

1) They have a mutual interest in cooperation in the field of nuclear reactor safety research, with the objective of improving and thus ensuring the safety of nuclear facilities on an international basis;

(2) They have cooperated in the field of LWR safety under the terms of successive five-year technical exchange Arrangements, originally concluded September 23 and October 16, 1974, between the United States Atomic Energy Commission (USAEC) and the Commissariat à l'Energie Atomique (CEA), continued after January 19, 1975, as between the USNRC and the Institut de Protection et de Sûreté Nucléaire (IPSN), currently known as the Institut de Radioprotection et de Sûreté Nucléaire (IRSN);

(3) They have indicated their mutual wish to continue the cooperation established by the previous Arrangement and, accordingly, will continue their cooperation pending the execution of this Arrangement;

HEREBY AGREE AS FOLLOWS:

ARTICLE 1 - OBJECTIVE

The USNRC and the IRSN will continue their cooperation in the field of nuclear safety research in accordance with the provisions of this Arrangement and on the basis of a reasonably balanced exchange. Nothing contained in this Arrangement will require either Party to take any action which would be inconsistent with its laws, regulations and national policy. Should any conflict arise between the terms of this Arrangement and those laws, regulations and national policy, the Parties agree to consult before any action is taken.

ARTICLE 2 - FORMS OF COOPERATION

Cooperation between the Parties may take the following forms:

2.1 The exchange of information in the form of technical reports, experimental data, correspondence, newsletters, visits, joint experts meetings, and such other means as the Parties agree.

2.2 The temporary assignment of personnel of one Party or of its contractors to the laboratory or facilities owned by the other Party or in which it sponsors research. Each such assignment will be considered on a case-by-case basis and generally be the subject of a separate attachment-of-staff agreement between appropriate representatives of the recipient and assigning organizations.

2.3 The execution of joint programs and projects, including those involving a division of activities between the Parties. Each such joint program and project will be considered on a case-by-case basis and may be the subject of a separate agreement between the Parties, if determined to be necessary by the research organizations of one or both of the Parties. Otherwise, it will be accomplished by an exchange of letters between the research organizations of the Parties, subject at least to the terms and conditions of this Arrangement.

2.4 The use by one Party of facilities which are owned by the other Party or in which research is being sponsored by the other Party; such use of facilities will be the subject of separate agreements between the relevant entities and may be subject to commercial terms and conditions.

2.5 If either Party wishes to visit, assign personnel or use the facilities owned or operated by entities other than the Parties to this Arrangement, the Parties recognize that the prior approval of such entities will be required with respect to the terms upon which such visit, assignment or use shall be made.

2.6 Any other form agreed between the Parties.

ARTICLE 3 - SCOPE OF INFORMATION EXCHANGE

3.1 Each Party will make available to the other information in the field of nuclear safety research which it has the right to disclose, either in its possession or available to it, in the technical areas (listed in Appendices A and B) in which the Parties are sponsoring nuclear safety research. These Appendices may be modified by common agreement of the Administrators (see Article 4).

3.2 Each Party will promptly transmit and call to the other Party's attention any information on its research results appearing to have significant safety implications. If the transmitting Party denotes such information to be of a proprietary nature, the recipient Party will control the further dissemination of the information in accordance with the provisions of Article 5.

3.3 As agreed upon, the Parties may also exchange information on any other topic related to nuclear safety.

3.4 Information furnished by one Party to the other under this Arrangement will be accurate to the best knowledge and belief of the Party supplying the information. However, neither Party gives any warranty as to the accuracy of such information nor will have any responsibility for the consequences of any use to which such information may be put by the other Party or by any third Party.

ARTICLE 4 - ADMINISTRATION OF THE ARRANGEMENT

Each Party will designate, as Administrator, a senior representative to coordinate its participation in the overall exchange. The Administrators will establish agreed-upon procedures for implementing the Arrangement. Approximately annually, the Administrators will meet to review the status of exchange and cooperation established under this Arrangement, to recommend revisions for improving and developing the cooperation, and to discuss topics within the scope of the cooperation. The time, place, and agenda for such meetings will be agreed upon in advance.

ARTICLE 5 - EXCHANGE AND USE OF INFORMATION AND INTELLECTUAL PROPERTY

5.1 General

The Parties support the widest possible dissemination of information provided, created or exchanged under this Arrangement, subject to the requirements of each Party's national laws, regulations and policies and the need to protect proprietary and other sensitive or privileged information, and subject to the provisions of the Intellectual Property Annex, hereby incorporated into this Arrangement.

5.2 Definitions

5.2.1 The term "information" means unclassified nuclear energy-related regulatory, safety, safeguards, waste management, scientific, or technical data, including information on results or methods of assessment, research, and any other knowledge provided, created or exchanged under this Arrangement.

5.2.2 The term "proprietary information" means information created or exchanged under this Arrangement which contains trade secrets or other privileged or sensitive commercial information (such that the person having the information may derive a commercial benefit from it or may have a commercial advantage over those who do not have it), and may only include information which:

a. has been held in confidence by its owner;

b. is of a type which is customarily held in confidence by its owner;

c. has not been transmitted by the owner to other entities (including the receiving Party) except on the basis that it be held in confidence;

d. is not otherwise available to the receiving Party from another source without restriction on its further dissemination; and

e. is not already in the possession of the receiving Party.

5.2.3 The term "other confidential or privileged information" means non-classified information, other than "proprietary information," which has been transmitted and received in confidence under this Arrangement and is protected from public disclosure under the laws, regulations, or policies of the country of the Party providing the information, or is otherwise restricted by the provider.

5.3 *Marking Procedures for Documentary Proprietary Information*

A Party receiving documentary proprietary information pursuant to this Arrangement will respect the privileged nature of such information, provided that such proprietary information is clearly marked with the following (or substantially similar) restrictive legend:

> "This document contains proprietary information furnished in confidence under an Arrangement dated______between the United States Nuclear Regulatory Commission and the Institut De Radioprotection et De Sûreté Nucléaire of France and will not be disseminated outside these organizations, their consultants, contractors, and licensees, or concerned departments and agencies of the Government of the United States and the Government of France, without the prior written

approval of (*name of transmitting Party*). This notice will be marked on each page of any reproduction hereof, in whole or in part. These limitations will automatically terminate when the proprietary information is disclosed by the owner without restriction."

This restrictive legend shall be respected by the Parties to this Arrangement. Proprietary information bearing this restrictive legend shall not be made public or otherwise disseminated in any manner unspecified or contrary to the terms of this Arrangement without the prior written consent of the transmitting Party. Proprietary information bearing this restrictive legend shall not be used by the receiving Party or its contractors and consultants for any commercial purposes without the prior written consent of the transmitting Party.

5.4 *Dissemination of Documentary Proprietary Information*

5.4.1 In general, proprietary information received under this Arrangement may be disseminated by the receiving Party without prior consent to persons within or employed by the receiving Party, and to concerned Government departments and Government agencies in the country of the receiving Party, provided

a. such dissemination is made on a case-by-case basis to persons or departments and agencies having a legitimate need for the proprietary information; and

b. such proprietary information shall bear the restrictive legend appearing in section 5.3 of this Arrangement.

5.4.2 Proprietary information received under this Arrangement may be disseminated by the receiving Party without prior consent to contractors and consultants of the receiving Party located within the geographical limits of that Party's nation, provided

a. that the proprietary information is used by such contractors and consultants only for work within the scope of their contracts with the receiving Party relating to the subject matter of the proprietary information, and shall not be used by such contractors and consultants for any other private commercial purposes; and

b. that such dissemination is made on a case-by-case basis to contractors and consultants having a legitimate need for the proprietary information and who have executed a non-disclosure agreement; and

c. that such proprietary information shall bear the restrictive legend appearing in Article 5.3 of this Arrangement.

5.4.3 With the prior written consent of the Party furnishing proprietary information under this Arrangement, the receiving Party may disseminate such proprietary information more widely than otherwise permitted under the terms set forth in this Arrangement. The Parties will endeavor to grant such approval to the extent permitted by their respective national laws, regulations and policies, provided

a. that the entities receiving proprietary information under Article 5.4.3 of this Arrangement, including domestic organizations permitted or licensed by the receiving Party to construct or operate nuclear production or utilization facilities, or to use nuclear materials and radiation sources, have a legitimate need for the proprietary information and have executed a non-disclosure agreement; and

b. that the entities receiving proprietary information under Article 5.4.3 of this Arrangement, including domestic organizations permitted or licensed by the receiving Party to construct or operate nuclear production or utilization facilities, shall not use such proprietary information for any private commercial purposes; and

c. that those entities receiving proprietary information under Article 5.4.3 of this Arrangement that are domestic organizations permitted or licensed by the receiving Party, agree to use the proprietary information only for activities carried out under or within the terms of their specific permit or license.

5.5 *Marking Procedures for Other Confidential or Privileged Information of a Documentary Nature*

A Party receiving under this Arrangement other confidential or privileged information will respect its confidential nature, *provided* such information is clearly marked so as to indicate its confidential or privileged nature and is accompanied by a statement indicating:

5.5.1 that the information is protected from public disclosure by the Government of the transmitting Party; and

5.5.2 that the information is transmitted under the condition that it be maintained in confidence.

5.6 *Dissemination of Other Confidential or Privileged Information of a Documentary Nature*

Other confidential or privileged information may be disseminated in the same manner as that set forth in paragraph 5.4, *Dissemination of Documentary Proprietary Information*.

5.7 *Non-Documentary Proprietary or Other Confidential or Privileged Information*

Non-documentary proprietary or other confidential or privileged information provided in seminars and other meetings arranged under this Arrangement, or information arising from the attachments of staff, use of facilities, or joint projects, will be treated by the Parties according to the principles specified for documentary information in this Arrangement; *provided*, however, that the Party communicating such proprietary or other confidential or privileged information has placed the recipient on notice as to the character of the information communicated.

5.8 *Consultation*

If, for any reason, one of the Parties becomes aware that it will be, or may reasonably be expected to become, unable to meet the non-dissemination provisions of this Arrangement, it will immediately inform the other Party. The Parties will, thereafter, consult to define an appropriate course of action.

5.9 *Codes*

5.9.1 All USNRC and IRSN computer codes disseminated under this Arrangement are to be considered privileged information unless otherwise noted, are protected as such by the USNRC and IRSN respectively, and shall be treated likewise by the Parties. They are, in particular, subject to all the provisions of this Article including the requirements for an agreement of confidentiality (Article 5.4) prior to dissemination, with the exception that they need not be marked with the restrictive designation. The codes are subject to this protection in both object and source forms and as recorded in any media.

5.9.2 The USNRC and IRSN codes and other related analytical techniques covered under this Arrangement and any improvements, modifications or updates to such codes or techniques, are for the purpose of reactor and plant systems safety research and licensing and will not be used for commercial purposes, or for other benefits not related to the study of reactor safety without the prior consent of USNRC or IRSN as appropriate.

Among the code uses that will be permitted under this Arrangement are those related to research in the reactor safety area and analyses performed by the Parties or their contractors that can assist regulators and plant personnel in assessing the safety of the plant, analyzing operating events, and training of operators. Specific examples of permitted analyses include: design basis accidents (e.g., loss-of-coolant accidents), anticipated transients, accident management and emergency operating procedures, mid-loop operation, analyses to support PRA success criteria, power upgrades and reload.

Prohibited uses of the USNRC code include: (1) analyses to develop a new reactor design and (2) analyses to support power upgrades and reload in the U.S. unless performed by a U.S. subsidiary.

Prohibited uses of the IRSN code include: (1) analyses to develop a new reactor design and (2) analyses to support power upgrades and reload in France unless performed by a French subsidiary.

5.9.3 The USNRC and IRSN codes and other related analytical techniques will not be advertised directly or by implication to obtain contracts related to the construction or servicing of nuclear facilities, nor will advertising imply that the USNRC or IRSN has endorsed any particular analyses or techniques.

5.10 *Other*

Nothing contained in this Arrangement will preclude a Party from using or disseminating information received without restriction by a Party from sources outside of this Arrangement.

ARTICLE 6 - COSTS

Except when otherwise specifically agreed upon by the Parties, all costs arising in the implementation of this Arrangement will be borne by the Party that incurs them. It is understood that the ability of the Parties to carry out their obligations covered by Article 2 of the present Arrangement is subject to the appropriation of funds by the appropriate governmental authority and to the laws and regulations applicable to the Parties.

ARTICLE 7 - FINAL PROVISIONS

7.1 This Arrangement will enter into force upon the last date of signature, and, subject to paragraph 7.2, will remain in force for a period of five years, unless extended for a further period of time by agreement of the Parties.

7.2 Either Party may withdraw from the present Arrangement after providing the other Party written notice six months prior to its intended date of withdrawal.

7.3 All information protected by provisions of this Arrangement as proprietary, confidential, privileged, or otherwise subject to restriction on disclosure will remain so protected indefinitely, unless and until the removal of such restriction is agreed to by the Parties in writing.

7.4 Any dispute or questions, between the Parties concerning the interpretation or application of this Arrangement arising during its term will be settled by mutual agreement of the Parties.

FOR THE UNITED STATES NUCLEAR REGULATORY COMMISSION:

BY: [Signature]
Luis A Reyes

TITLE: Executive Director for Operations

DATE: *7/26/06*

PLACE: Rockville, Maryland

FOR THE INSTITUT DE RADIOPROTECTION ET DE SÛRETÉ NUCLÉAIRE OF FRANCE:

BY: [Signature]
Jacques Repussad

TITLE: Director General

DATE: *8/4/06*

PLACE: *Clamart*

CERTIFIED A TRUE COPY
BY [Signature]
Office of the Secretary

APPENDIX A

NUCLEAR SAFETY RESEARCH AREAS IN WHICH THE USNRC IS CURRENTLY PERFORMING OR SPONSORING RESEARCH

– Reactor Vessel and Piping Integrity

– Aging of Reactor Components

– Reactor Equipment Qualification

– Thermal Hydraulic Code Application and Maintenance

– Plant Performance

– Human Performance

– Core Melt and Reactor Coolant System Failure

– Reactor Containment Safety

– Containment Structural Integrity

– Seismic Safety

– Probabilistic Risk Assessment

– Severe Accident Analysis

– Radiation Protection and Health Effects

– Radionuclide Transport and Waste Management

– Nuclear Fuel Analysis

– Dry Cask Storage and Transport

– Decommissioning

– Advanced Reactor Designs

– Fire Protection

– PWR Containment Sump and Recirculation

– Knowledge Management

APPENDIX B

IRSN'S NUCLEAR SAFETY RESEARCH AREAS

1. Operating Reactors: Lessons Learned from Reactor Operations
2. Thermal Hydraulic Transients and Simulators for Analysis
3. Fuel Degradation and Fission Products Release in Accident Conditions
4. Equipment Qualification
5. Seismic and External Hazards
6. Probabilistic Risk Assessment
7. Accident Management and Mitigation
8. Safety of Nuclear Waste Repository
9. Radiation Protection and Health Effects
10. Containment Safety
11. Aging of Reactor Components
12. Reactor Vessel and Piping Integrity
13. Criticality
14. Nuclear Fuel Behavior Under Reactivity Insertion Accident, Loss of Coolant Accident and Storage Pool Accident conditions.
15. Fire Propagation and Protection
16. Safety and Severe Accident Analysis for Research Reactors and Operating Reactors
17. Knowledge Management
18. Containment Sump and Recirculation

INTELLECTUAL PROPERTY ANNEX

Pursuant to Article 5 of this Technical Exchange and Cooperation Arrangement:

The Parties shall ensure adequate and effective protection of intellectual property created or furnished under this Technical Exchange and Cooperation Arrangement and relevant implementing arrangements. The Parties agree to notify one another in a timely fashion of any inventions or copyrighted works arising under this Technical Exchange and Cooperation Arrangement and to seek protection for such intellectual property in a timely fashion. Rights to such intellectual property shall be allocated as provided in this Annex.

I. SCOPE

A. Annex is applicable to all cooperative activities undertaken by the Parties pursuant to this Technical Exchange and Cooperation Arrangement, except as otherwise specifically agreed by the Parties or their designees.

B. For purposes of this Arrangement, "intellectual property" shall have the meaning found in Article 2 of the Convention Establishing the World Intellectual Property Organization, done at Stockholm, July 14,1967; viz., 'intellectual property' shall include the rights relating to:

– literary, artistic and scientific works,

– performances of artists, phonograms, and broadcasts,

– inventions in all fields of human endeavor,

– scientific discoveries,

– industrial designs,

– trademarks, service marks, and commercial names and designations,

– protection against unfair competition, and all other rights resulting from intellectual activity in the industrial, scientific, literary or artistic fields."

C. This Annex addresses the allocation of rights, interests, and royalties between the Parties. Each Party shall ensure that the other Party can obtain rights to intellectual property allocated in accordance with the Annex. The allocation between a Party and participants on behalf of this Party in the cooperative activities, which shall be determined by the Party's laws and practices, shall not be altered or prejudiced by this Annex.

D. Disputes concerning intellectual property arising under this Technical Exchange and Cooperation Arrangement should be resolved through discussions between the concerned participating institutions or, if necessary, the Parties or their designees. Upon mutual agreement of the Parties, a dispute shall be submitted to an arbitral tribunal for binding arbitration in accordance with the applicable rules of international law. Unless the Parties or their designees agree otherwise in writing, the arbitration rules of the United Nations Commission on International Trade Law (UNCITRAL) shall govern.

E. Termination or expiration of this Technical Exchange and Cooperation Arrangement shall not affect rights or obligations under this Annex.

II. ALLOCATION OF RIGHTS

A. Each Party shall be entitled to a non-exclusive, irrevocable, royalty-free license in all countries to translate, reproduce, and publicly distribute scientific and technical journal articles, publicly available reports and books directly arising from cooperation under this Technical Exchange and Cooperation Arrangement. All publicly distributed copies of copyrighted work prepared under this provision shall indicate the names of the authors of the work unless an author explicitly declines to be named. Each Party shall have the right to review a translation prior to public distribution.

B. Rights to all forms of intellectual property, other than those rights described in Section II.A. above, shall be allocated as follows:

1. Visiting researchers, for example, scientists visiting primarily in furtherance of their education, shall receive intellectual property rights under the policies of the host institution, unless a specific agreement is or has been signed between the host and forwarding institution. In addition, each visiting researcher named as an inventor shall be entitled to treatment as a national of the host country with regard to awards, bonuses, benefits, or any other rewards, in accordance with the policies of the host institution.

2. (a) For intellectual property created during joint research, the Parties shall jointly develop a technology management plan either prior to the start of their cooperation, for example in research areas likely to lead rapidly to industrial applications, or within a reasonable time from the time a party becomes aware of the creation of the intellectual property. The technology management plan shall consider the relative contributions of the Parties, the benefits of exclusive or nonexclusive licensing by territory or for fields of use, requirements imposed by the Parties' domestic laws, and other factors deemed appropriate. If needed, the technology management plan shall be jointly modified or completed in a timely fashion subject to approval of both parties.

(b) If the Parties cannot reach agreement on a joint technology management plan within a reasonable time not to exceed six months from the time a Party becomes aware of the creation of the intellectual property in question, each party may designate one co-exclusive licensee to have world wide rights to said intellectual property. Each party should notify the other two months prior to making a designation under this paragraph. When both Parties (or their licensees) exploit the intellectual property in a country, they shall share equally the reasonable cost of intellectual property protection in that country. The Parties will designate licensees to commercially exploit and protect intellectual property resulting from this Arrangement.

(c) A specific program of research will be regarded as joint research for purposes of this Annex when it is designated as such in the relevant implementing arrangements. Otherwise the allocation of rights to intellectual property will be in accordance with paragraph II.B.1.

(d) In the event that either Party believes that a particular joint research project under this Arrangement will lead or has led to the creation or furnishing of intellectual property of a type not protected by the applicable laws of one of the Parties, the Parties shall immediately hold discussions to determine the allocation of the rights to the said intellectual property; the joint activities in question will be suspended during the discussions unless otherwise agreed by the parties thereto. If no agreement can be reached within a three month period from the date of the request for discussions, the Parties shall cease the cooperation in the project in question; notwithstanding paragraphs II.B.2(a) and 2(b), rights to any intellectual property which has been created will be resolved in accordance with provisions of paragraph I.D.

STATE DEPARTMENT DOCUMENT NUMBER: 06-292

AMENDMENT NO. 4 TO THE STRATEGIC OBJECTIVE GRANT AGREEMENT OF FEBRUARY 23, 2004, AS AMENDED, BETWEEN THE UNITED STATES OF AMERICA AND THE HASHEMITE KINGDOM OF JORDAN FOR THE IMPROVED ECONOMIC OPPORTUNITIES FOR JORDANIANS STRATEGIC OBJECTIVE, WITH ANNEX

SIGNED AT AMMAN,
AUGUST 10, 2006
ENTERED INTO FORCE AUGUST 10, 2006

CTIA DOCUMENT NUMBER: 12676.002

DATED: 10 AUG 2006

APPN:
BPC:
RCN:

Certified conformed copy of agreement
signed on August 10, 2006
[Signature]
Tracy Thoman
Acting Director
Office of Program Management

BETWEEN the Hashemite Kingdom of Jordan (Grantee or GOJ) acting through the Ministry of Planning and International Cooperation, and the United States of America, acting through the United States Agency for International Development (USAID).

WHEREAS, on February 23, 2004, the Grantee and USAID (Parties) entered into a Grant Agreement for the Improved Economic Opportunities for Jordanians Strategic Objective (Agreement) whereby USAID granted to the Grantee Eighteen Million Five Hundred Thousand United States (U.S.) Dollars (U.S. $18,500,000) to finance foreign exchange and local currency costs of achieving the Strategic Objective; and

WHEREAS, on June 22, 2004, the Parties amended the Agreement to, among other things, provide additional USAID grant funding of Nineteen Million Fifty Thousand U.S. Dollars (U.S. $19,0.50,000) to finance foreign exchange and local currency costs of achieving the Strategic Objective; and

WHEREAS, on April 18, 2005, the Parties amended the Agreement to, among other things, provide additional USAID grant funding of Twelve Million U.S. Dollars (U.S. $12,000,000) to finance foreign exchange and local currency costs of achieving the Strategic Objective; and

WHEREAS, on July 20, 2005, the Parties amended the Agreement to, among other things, provide additional USAID grant funding of Thirty Five Million Three Hundred Seventy Seven Thousand Four Hundred Fifty Six U.S. Dollars (U.S. $35,377,456) to finance foreign exchange and local currency costs of achieving the Strategic Objective; and

WHEREAS, the Parties now wish to amend the Agreement to, among other things, provide additional USAID grant funding of Thirty Seven Million Seven Hundred Twenty Two Thousand Three Hundred Ninety Five U.S. Dollars (U.S. $37,722,395) to finance foreign exchange and local currency costs of achieving the Strategic Objective;

NOW THEREFORE, the Parties hereby agree to further amend the Agreement as follows:

1. ***Article 3: Contributions of the Parties, Section 3.1. USAID Contribution, Subsection (a) The Grant***, is amended by deleting the amount of "Eighty Four Million Nine Hundred Twenty Seven Thousand Four Hundred Fifty Six United States Dollars (U.S. $84,927,456)" and replacing it with "One Hundred Twenty Two Million Six Hundred Forty Nine Thousand Eight Hundred Fifty One United States Dollars (U.S. $122,649,851)".

2. Attachment No. 1 to Annex 1 to the Agreement is deleted and hereby replaced in its entirety with the revised Attachment No. 1 to Annex 1 attached hereto.

3. Except as amended herein, the Agreement, as amended, remains in full force and effect.

IN WITNESS WHEREOF, the Parties, each acting through their duly authorized representative(s), have caused this Amendment to be signed in their names and delivered as of the day and year first above written.

THE HASHEMITE KINGDOM OF JORDAN

BY: [Signature]

H.E.Ms. Suhair Al-Ali
Minister of Planning and International Cooperation

THE UNITED STATES OF AMERICA

BY: [Signature]

David Hale
U.S. Ambassador

BY:[Signature]
Anne Aarnes
USAID/Jordan Director

ANNEX 1, ATTACHMENT 1

ILLUSTRATIVE STRATEGIC OBJECTIVE BUDGET (US$)

SO: Improved Economic Opportunities for Jordanians

INTERMEDIATE RESULT	PROGRAM FUNDING			
	PREVIOUS OBLIGATIONS	THIS AMENDMENT	TOTAL	LIFE OF SO
1. Transparent, Efficient and Responsive Public Sector	20,686,456	19,033,000	39,719,456	83,300,000
2. More Effective Policy and Regulatory Reform	21,100,000	5,883,000	26,983,000	83,300,000
3. Increased Depth of Private Sector Growth	43,141,000	12,806,395	55,947,395	83,400,000
TOTAL	84,927,456	37,722,395	122,649,851	250,000,000

STATE DEPARTMENT DOCUMENT NUMBER: 06-293

AMENDMENT NO. 2 TO THE STRATEGIC OBJECTIVE GRANT AGREEMENT OF JUNE 2, 2004, AS AMENDED, BETWEEN THE UNITED STATES OF AMERICA AND THE HASHEMITE KINGDOM OF JORDAN FOR THE IMPROVED SOCIAL SECTOR DEVELOPMENT AND GOVERNANCE STRATEGIC OBJECTIVE, WITH ANNEX

SIGNED AT AMMAN,
AUGUST 10, 2006
ENTERED INTO FORCE AUGUST 10, 2006

CTIA DOCUMENT NUMBER: 10797.002

DATED: 10 AUG 2006

APPN:
BPC:
RCN:

[Seal]

Certified conformed copy of agreement
signed on August 10, 2006

[Signature]

Tracy Thoman
Acting Director
Office of Program Management

BETWEEN the Hashemite Kingdom of Jordan (Grantee or GOJ) acting through the Ministry of Planning and International Cooperation, and the United States of America, acting through the United States Agency for International Development (USAID).

WHEREAS, on June 2, 2004, the Grantee and USAID (Parties) entered into a Grant Agreement for the Improved Social Sector Development and Governance Strategic Objective (Agreement) whereby USAID granted to the Grantee Thirty Million Three Hundred Fifty Thousand United States (U.S.) Dollars (U.S.$30,350,000) to finance foreign exchange and local currency costs of achieving the Strategic Objective; and

WHEREAS, on July 20, 2005, the Parties amended the Agreement to, among other things, provide additional USAID grant funding of Sixty Million Two Hundred Fifty Ninc Thousand Three Hundred Sixty Eight .U.S. Dollars (U.S.$60,259,368) to finance foreign exchange and local currency costs of achieving the Strategic Objective; and

WHEREAS, the Parties now wish to amend the Agreement to, among other things, provide additional USAID grant funding of Forty Five Million Five Hundred Fifty Five Thousand Eight Hundred

Thirty Two U.S. Dollars (U.S.$45,555,832) to finance foreign exchange and local currency costs of achieving the Strategic Objective;

NOW THEREFORE, the Parties hereby agree to further amend the Agreement as follows:

1. ***Article 3: Contributions of the Parties, Section 3.1. USAID Contribution, Subsection (a) The Grant***, is amended by deleting the amount of "Ninety Million Six Hundred Nine Thousand Three Hundred Sixty Eight United States Dollars (U.S:$90,609,368)" and replacing it with "One Hundred Thirty Six Million One Hundred Sixty Five Thousand Two Hundred United States Dollars (U.S.$136,165,200)".

2. Attachment No. 1 to Annex 1 to the Agreement is deleted and hereby replaced in its entirety with the revised Attachment No. 1 to Annex 1 attached hereto.

3. In Annex 1, Section III, the Subsection entitled "Other Health/Population Resources that Support Intermediate Result 9.1" is deleted and hereby replaced in its entirety with the following revised section:

Other Health/Population Resources that Support Intermediate Result 9.1:

Resources outside this Agreement (and therefore financed with funds neither obligated by this Agreement nor included in the Financial Plan set forth in Section VI of this Annex 1) are being made available, or may in the future be made available, from USAID to achieve Intermediate Result 9.1. Those resources are being provided or will in the future be provided through USAID/Washington's Bureau for Global Health (GH) in Washington, D.C. (USAID/W) under projects and programs administered by them, and are or will be additional to the funds obligated hereunder. These important projects directly support the other projects and activities in the Population and Health portfolio.

The following sets forth a description of the additional resources being provided for Intermediate Result 9.1. from GH in fiscal year 2006 (FY 2006). In FY 2006-support for the following projects/ activities includes:

i. Health Policy Initiative (replaces POLICY II), $600,000: The Futures Group International. This project will continue to provide technical assistance and other relevant support to the Higher Population Council (HPC) and the Ministry of Health (MOH) to reduce population growth through improving the policy environment for family planning and reproductive health. The project will also assist the HPC prepare for Phase II of the Reproductive Health Action Plan in support of the National Population Strategy to ensure achieving population goals of replacement fertility by 2020.

ii. DELIVER Project, $100,000: John Snow, Inc. This project will continue to provide selected technical assistance to the MOH in the design, development and implementation of improved systems for forecasting, procurement, storage, distribution, performance monitoring, and information collected. It will also continue to assist the MOH and the HPC finalize the contraceptive security strategic plan under the Reproductive Health Action Plan.

iii. Central Contraceptive Procurement, Global Health, USAID/W, $500,000: This project provides technical assistance and contraceptive supplies to the MOH, RMS, UNRWA and NGOs.

iv. Measure Phase II Demographic and Health Survey Project, $200,000: Macro International, Inc. This project provides technical assistance and training support to the Department of Statistics in implementing the Jordan Population and Family Health Survey scheduled for mid-2007.

While there can be no assurance, additional resources may be available from USAID/W in the future for the Intermediate Result.

The additional resources described above are only available in the form of goods and services (e.g., technical assistance, services, information, training, research, medical and computer equipment, contraceptives.). While the costs of those resources to USAID are indicated above, the resources are not available to USAID/Jordan or the GOJ in the form of money. Bureau for Global Health (GH) contractors and cooperating agencies have pre-existing contracts/agreements with GH which specify which resources they can and cannot provide, and to the extent that these resources are being or will be provided by USAID/W to the GOJ, the GOJ can utilize these resources to enhance its own programs.

The assistance represented by these resources will only be provided upon USAID/Jordan receiving a request for such assistance from the GOJ. By signing this Agreement, the GOJ hereby acknowledges that it has requested all of the assistance described above and already being provided by USAID. With respect to any assistance not described above which may be provided by USAID in the future for the Intermediate Result, the Minister of Health, or a certified representative of the MOH or GOJ, shall be authorized to make requests for such assistance.

All of the additional resources being made available by USAID to the GOJ, or which may be made available by USAID to the GOJ in the future, for the Intermediate Result, are being or will be made available by USAID to the GOJ on the understanding that all USAID assistance funded there from will be entitled to the privileges and immunities accorded under the agreements entered into in June of 1957 between the Government of the United States and the Government of Jordan governing USAID economic assistance to Jordan. By signing this Agreement, the GOJ acknowledges and agrees to the application of the 1957 agreements to the assistance provided by these resources and to the personnel carrying out that assistance.

4. Except as amended herein, the Agreement, as amended, remains in full force and effect.

IN WITNESS WHEREOF, the Parties, each acting through their duly authorized representative(s), have caused this Amendment to be signed in their names and delivered as of the day and year first above written.

THE HASHEMITE KINGDOM OF JORDAN

BY: [Signature]
H.E. Ms. Suhair Al-Ali
Minister of Planning and International Cooperation

THE HASHEMITE KINGDOM OF JORDAN

BY: [Signature]
David Hale
U.S. Ambassador

BY: [Signature]
Anne Aarnes
USAID/Jordan Director

ANNEX 1, ATTACHMENT 1

ILLUSTRATIVE STRATEGIC OBJECTIVE BUDGET (US$)

SO: Improved Social Sector Development and Governance

INTERMEDIATE RESULT	**PROGRAM FUNDING**			
	PREVIOUS OBLIGATIONS	THIS AMENDMENT	TOTAL	LIFE OF SO
1. Improved Health Status for All Jordanians	36,486,456	15,585,277	52,071,733	106,000,000
2. Improved Education and Life Skills	32,626,456	14,985,277	47,611,733	48,000,000
3. Improved Governance and Expanded Civic Participation	21,496,456	14,985,278	36,481,734	48,000,000
TOTAL	90,609,368	45,555,832	136,165,200	202,000,000

STATE DEPARTMENT DOCUMENT NUMBER: 06-294

AMENDMENT NO. 2 TO THE STRATEGIC OBJECTIVE GRANT AGREEMENT OF JUNE 2, 2004, AS AMENDED, BETWEEN THE UNITED STATES OF AMERICA AND THE HASHEMITE KINGDOM OF JORDAN FOR THE ENHANCED INTEGRATED WATER RESOURCES STRATEGIC OBJECTIVE, WITH ANNEX

SIGNED AT AMMAN,
AUGUST 10, 2006
ENTERED INTO FORCE AUGUST 10, 2006

CTIA DOCUMENT NUMBER: 10796.002

DATED: 10 AUG 2006	Certified conformed copy of agreement signed on August 10, 2006
APPN: BPC: RCN:	[Signature]
[Seal]	Tracy Thoman Acting Director Office of Program Management

BETWEEN the Hashemite Kingdom of Jordan (Grantee or GOJ) acting through the Ministry of Planning and International Cooperation, and the United States of America, acting through the United States Agency for International Development (USAID).

WHEREAS, on June 2, 2004, the Grantee and USAID (Parties) entered into a Grant Agreement for the Enhanced Integrated Water Resources Strategic Objective (Agreement) whereby USAID granted to the Grantee Thirty Nine Million Five Hundred Eighty Thousand Eight Hundred Sixteen United States (U.S.) Dollars (U.S. $39,580,816) to finance foreign exchange and local currency costs of achieving the Strategic Objective;

WHEREAS, on July 20, 2005, the Grantee and USAID amended the Agreement to, among other things, provide additional USAID grant funding of Forty Nine Million Nine Hundred Sixty Seven Thousand Five Hundred Ninety Eight U.S. Dollars (U.S. $49,967,598) to finance foreign exchange and local currency costs of achieving the Strategic Objective; and

WHEREAS, the Parties now wish to amend the Agreement to, among other things, provide additional USAID grant funding of Forty Five Million Ninety Five Thousand Four Hundred Seventy

Seven U.S. Dollars (U.S. $45,095,477) to finance foreign exchange and local currency costs of achieving the Strategic Objective;

NOW THEREFORE, the Parties hereby agree to further amend the Agreement as follows:

1. ***Article 3: Contributions of the Parties, Section 3.1. USAID Contribution, Subsection (a) The Grant***, is amended by deleting the amount of "Eighty Nine Million Five Hundred Forty Eight Thousand Four Hundred Fourteen United States Dollars (U.S. $89,548,414)" and replacing it with "One Hundred Thirty Four Million Six Hundred Forty Three Thousand Eight Hundred Ninety One United States Dollars (U.S. $134,643,891)".

2. Attachment 1 to Annex 1 to the Agreement is deleted and hereby replaced in its entirety with the revised Attachment 1 to Annex 1 attached hereto.

3. Except as amended herein, the Agreement, as amended, remains in full force and effect.

IN WITNESS WHEREOF, the Parties, each acting through their duly authorized representative(s), have caused this Amendment to be signed in their names and delivered as of the day and year first above written.

THE HASHEMITE KINGDOM OF JORDAN

[Signature]

H.E. Ms. SuhairAl-Ali
Minister of Planning and International Cooperation

THE UNITED STATES OF AMERICA

[Signature]

David Hale
U.S. Ambassador

[Signature]
Anne Aarnes
USAID/Jordan Director

ANNEX 1, ATTACHMENT 1

ILLUSTRATIVE STRATEGIC OBJECTIVE BUDGET (US$)

SO: Enhanced Integrated Water Resources

INTERMEDIATE RESULT	**PROGRAM FUNDING**							
	PREVIOUS OBLIGATIONS		THIS AMENDMENT		TOTAL	LIFE OF SO		
	USAID	GOJ	USAID	GOJ		USAID	GOJ	TOTAL
1. Improved Environmental Protection	6,532,598	0	6,566,874	0	13,099,472	18,600,000	0	18,600,000
2. Optimization of Water Resources	44,250,000	0	25,400,000	0	69,650,000	198,900,000	15,000,000	213,900,000
3. Strengthened Water Policies and Systems	12,515,000	0	5,628,603	0	18,143,603	50,000,000	0	50,000,000
4. Improved Resources Allocation	26,250,816	0	7,500,000	0	33,750,816	92,500,000	15,000,000	107,000,000
TOTAL	89,548,414	0	45,095,477	0	134,643,891	360,000,000	30,000,000	390,000,000

STATE DEPARTMENT DOCUMENT NUMBER: 06-295

AMENDMENT NO. 3 TO THE STRATEGIC OBJECTIVE GRANT AGREEMENT OF MARCH 23, 2004, AS AMENDED, BETWEEN THE UNITED STATES OF AMERICA AND THE HASHEMITE KINGDOM OF JORDAN FOR THE CASH TRANSFER SPECIAL OBJECTIVE, WITH ANNEX

SIGNED AT AMMAN,
AUGUST 10, 2006
ENTERED INTO FORCE AUGUST 10, 2006

CTIA DOCUMENT NUMBER: 10792.002

DATED: 10 AUG 2006

Certified conformed copy of agreement signed on August 10, 2006

APPN:
BPC:
RCN:

[Signature]

[Seal]

Tracy Thoman
Acting Director
Office of Program Management

BETWEEN the Hashemite Kingdom of Jordan (Grantee or GOJ), acting through the Ministry of Planning and International Cooperation, and the United States of America, acting through the United States Agency for International Development (USAID).

WHEREAS, on March 23, 2004, the Grantee and USAID (Parties) entered into a Grant Agreement for the Cash Transfer Special Objective (Agreement) whereby USAID granted to the Grantee one hundred and thirty eight million five hundred and twenty five thousand United States ("U.S.") Dollars ($138,525,000) to finance foreign exchange and local currency costs of achieving the Special Objective; and

WHEREAS, on June 22, 2004, the Parties amended the Agreement to, among other things, provide additional USAID grant funding of one hundred million U.S. Dollars (U.S.$100,000,000) to finance foreign exchange and local currency costs of achieving the Special Objective;

WHEREAS, on July 20, 2005, the Parties amended the Agreement to, among other things, provide additional USAID grant funding of one hundred eighty eight million U.S. Dollars (U.S.$188,000,000) to finance foreign exchange and local currency costs of achieving the Special Objective; and

WHEREAS, the Parties now wish to amend the Agreement to, among other things, provide additional USAID grant funding of one hundred seventeen million five hundred thousand U.S. Dollars (U.S.$117,500,000) to finance foreign exchange and local currency costs of achieving the Special Objective;

NOW THEREFORE, the Parties hereby agree to further amend the Agreement as follows:

1. Every reference in the Agreement to "Special Objective" is hereby deleted and replaced with "Strategic Objective. "

2. ***Article 3: Contributions of the Parties, Section 3.1. USAID Contribution, Subsection (a) The Grant***, is amended by deleting the amount of "four hundred and twenty six million five hundred and twenty five thousand United States ("U.S.") Dollars ($426,525,000)" and replacing it with "five hundred and forty four million twenty five thousand United States ("U.S.") Dollars ($544,025,000)."

3.***Article 5: Conditions Precedent to Disbursement*** is hereby deleted and replaced with a new Article 5 as follows:

"Article 5: Conditions Precedent to Disbursement

Section 5.2. FY 2004 Cash Transfer, General Conditions Precedent

Prior to disbursement of the cash transfer of one hundred seventeen million five hundred thousands United States Dollars envisaged under Amendment No. 3 of this Agreement (hereinafter referred to as "cash transfer"), or prior to the issuance by USAID of documentation pursuant to which such disbursement will be made, the Grantee will, except as the Parties may otherwise agree in writing, furnish to USAID, in form and substance satisfactory to USAID:

(a) Evidence that the Grantee has established the Separate Dollar Account described in Article 8 of this Agreement, together with the Grantee's certification that such bank account has been established and will be maintained as required by this Agreement and/or subsequent Implementation Letters ("ILs"); and

(b) Evidence that the Grantee has established the Local Currency Account described in Article 9 of this Agreement, together with the Grantee's certification that such account has been established and will be maintained as required by this Agreement and/or subsequent Implementation Letters.

Section 5.3. FY 2004 Cash Transfer, Policy Reform Conditions Precedent

Prior to the disbursement of the cash transfer, or prior to the issuance by USAID of documentation pursuant to which such disbursement will be made, the Grantee shall, except as the Parties may otherwise agree in writing, meet the following policy reform and related Conditions Precedent and furnish to USAID, in form and substance satisfactory to USAID, evidence of the following actions:

5.3.1 The Central Bank of Jordan drafts, issues and implements new instructions on Anti-Money Laundering in accordance with international standards.

5.3.2 The Government of Jordan produces a plan for a unified intellectual property rights (IPR) policy and regulatory framework, which will meet international commitments on IPR, and project a clear statement of the importance of IPR to the national economy, while dedicating adequate financial resources to fulfill the plan.

5.3.3 The Government of Jordan eliminates the minimum capital requirement and the paid-in capital requirement for Limited Liability Companies (except those providing financial services).

5.3.4 The Government of Jordan (through JISM) sends a letter to Bureau Veritas (BV), informing BV that the government will not continue with the DAMAN program pre-shipment inspection system and will not be renewing its four-year contract with BV which ends in August 2007. The Government of Jordan approves a plan for a sustainable internal system to monitor product standards through post-market surveillance and other means that do not pose technical barriers to trade.

5.3.5 The Government of Jordan defines ministerial and agency roles in export controls and licensing of controlled items, establishes a formal process to resolve inter-agency differences on license requests, and establishes a centralized national control list compatible with existing international control regimes.

5.3.6 The Government of Jordan issues instructions to outline the implementation of Article 9a of the Temporary Agriculture Law to facilitate the importation of agricultural produce into Jordan.

5.3.7 The Government of Jordan effectively combines the two customs administrations in Jordan: the Jordan Customs Department and the Aqaba Special Economic Zone Customs Office.

5.3.8 The Jordan Customs Department launches an English version of the Customs Integrated Tariff System (CITS) on the internet.

5.3.9 The Government of Jordan accedes to the revised Kyoto Convention.

5.3.10 The Government of Jordan adopts regulations for civilian procurement that are compliant with the WTO Government Procurement Agreement (GPA).

5.3.11 The Government of Jordan issues instructions to all government bodies requiring a public notice and a comment period to increase consultation in the formulation of proposed legislation and draft regulations.

5.3.12 The Government of Jordan enables the Jordan Authority for Enterprise Development (JAED) to function as an independent agency under the Ministry of Industry and Trade, consistent with the authorities described in the current temporary JAED Law.

5.3.13 The Government of Jordan lifts all restrictions that prohibit academic researchers from concurrently working for publicly funded research institutions and the private sector.

5.3.14 The Government of Jordan increases the allocations for the Ministry of Tourism and Antiquities and the allocations for the Department of Antiquities by 10% annually. The budget increase will be allocated towards improved tourism site management and other programs.

5.3.15 The Jordan Institute for Standards and Meteorology (JISM) amends Jordanian Standard 1005/2003 to require purple color coding on pipe used for all reclaimed water systems.

5.3.16 The Minister of Water and Irrigation improves monitoring and enforcement of the Groundwater Control Bylaw through the issuance of instructions to the Water Authority of Jordan (WAJ) for application and full implementation of the Bylaw.

5.3.17 The Minister of Water and Irrigation instructs each regional Groundwater Basin Office to prepare annual reports on the impact of implementing the Groundwater Bylaw on groundwater withdrawals.

5.3.18 The Government of Jordan issues amended standards for biosolids reused in irrigated agriculture or disposed in a landfill.

5.3.19 The Government of Jordan grants approval for the Water Authority of Jordan to hire five full-time Information Technology personnel and two senior financial professionals in order to bring online the financial accounting system.

5.3.20 The Government of Jordan adopts two revised policies relating to irrigation efficiency: 1- "Irrigation Water Efficiency/ Crop Water Requirements". 2- "Irrigation Water Efficiency/ Irrigation Equipment Standards and System Design Code".

5.3.21 The Government of Jordan, through the Ministry of Water and Irrigation (MWI), directs the Water Authority of Jordan (WAJ) to purchase 710 new water meters, over a three year period, to be installed on private non-WAJ wells.

5.3.22 The Ministry of Justice designs, approves and implements a new mechanism for the identification and appointment of judges based upon publicly defined acceptance criteria and selection protocols.

5.3.23 The Ministry of Justice allocates adequate resources for the construction of a new Judicial Institute building.

Section 5.4. Notification

USAID will promptly notify the Grantee when USAID has determined that all conditions precedent have been met.

Section 5.5. Terminal Date for Conditions Precedent

If all the conditions specified in Sections 5.2 and 5.3 of this Agreement have not been met within ninety days from the date of the execution of Amendment No. 3 to this Agreement, or such later date as USAID may agree to in writing, USAID, at its option, may terminate this Agreement by written notice to the Grantee."

4. ***Article 8: General Terms and Conditions Relating to Use of the Cash Transfer, Section 8.1, Use of the Cash Transfer***, is hereby amended as follows:

The opening clause of paragraph (a) is hereby deleted and replaced in its entirety with the following: "The cash transfer provided under Amendment No. 3 to this Agreement shall be utilized by the Grantee to cover payments and/or reimbursements for payments made during the period from October 1, 2005 or after (as the cash transfer provided under the original Agreement and Amendment No. 1 to the Agreement was utilized by the Grantee to cover payments and/or reimbursements for payments made during the period from October 1, 2003 or after and as the cash transfer provided under Amendment No. 2 to the Agreement was utilized by the Grantee to cover payments and/or reimbursements for payments made during the period from October 1, 2004 or after) in the following categories, in order of precedence:"

5. ***Article 9: General Terms and Conditions Relating to the Local Currency Account associated with the Cash Transfer, Section 9.2, Deposit into the Local Currency Account*** is hereby deleted and replaced with a new Section 9.2 as follows:

"For the cash transfer under Amendment No. 3, the Local Currency equivalent of the total value of the cash transfer will be deposited into the Local Currency Account in four installments as described below or as the Parties may otherwise agree in writing through an exchange of ILs. Four equal installments, each in the amount of the Jordanian Dinar equivalent of U.S. $29,375,000, will be made within 15 working days after the beginning of following months in calendar year 2006: August 1, 2006; September 1, 2006; October 1, 2006 and, November 1, 2006, calculated at the highest legally obtainable rate of exchange as determined by the Central Bank of Jordan, which, as of the date of deposit, is not unlawful in Jordan."

6. ***Article 10: Trust Fund Account*** shall be amended to read as follows:

Insert a new paragraph (d), Article 10 as follows:

> "(d) For the FY 2006 cash transfer, the Grantee shall transfer from the Local Currency Account the equivalent of two million five hundred thousand U.S. Dollars (U.S.$. 2,500,000) in Jordanian Dinars to the USAID Trust Fund Account established pursuant to the Commodity Import Program Agreement between the Parties dated September 23, 1993, as amended. The Jordanian Dinars shall be provided at the highest legally obtainable exchange rate as determined by the Central Bank of Jordan, as of the date of deposit, in two equal installments of the equivalent of one million two hundred fifty thousand United States Dollars each, with one installment due on May 1, 2007 and the other due on October 1, 2007. These funds will help meet a portion of USAID administrative expenses beginning October 1, 2007 through September 30, 2008."

7. Attachment No. 1 to Annex 1 to the Agreement is deleted and hereby replaced in its entirety with the revised Attachment No. 1 to Annex 1 attached hereto.

8. Except as amended herein, the Agreement, as amended, remains in full force and effect.

IN WITNESS WHEREOF, the Parties, each acting through their duly authorized representative(s), have caused this Amendment to be signed in their names and delivered as of the day and year first above written.

THE HASHEMITE KINGDOM OF JORDAN

By: [Signature]
H.E. Ms. SuhairAl-Ali
Minister of Planning and International Cooperation

THE UNITED STATES OF AMERICA

By: [Signature]
David Hale
U.S. Ambassador

By: [Signature]
Anne Aarnes
USAID/Jordan Director

ANNEX 1, ATTACHMENT 1

ILLUSTRATIVE STRATEGIC OBJECTIVE BUDGET (US$)

SO: Strategic Objective – Cash Transfer

INTERMEDIATE RESULT	PROGRAM FUNDING			
	PREVIOUS OBLIGATIONS	THIS AMENDMENT	TOTAL	LIFE OF SO TOTAL
1. Improved Environment for Sustained Policy Reform	425,500,000	116,500,000	542,500,000	663,975,000
2. Increased Technical Capacity to Implement Policy Reform	1,025,000	1,000,000	2,025,000	2,025,000
TOTAL	426,525,000	117,500,000	544,025,000	666,000,000

STATE DEPARTMENT DOCUMENT NUMBER: 06-296

MEMORANDUM OF UNDERSTANDING BETWEEN THE UNITED STATES OF AMERICA TRANSPORTATION COMMAND (USTRANSCOM) AND THE AUSTRALIAN DEFENCE FORCE REGARDING ASSIGNMENT OF AN OPERATIONAL LOGISTICS LIAISON OFFICER TO USTRANSCOM, WITH ANNEX

SIGNED AT CANBERRA AND BELLEVILLE,
JULY 27 AND AUGUST 25, 2006
ENTERED INTO FORCE AUGUST 25, 2006

CTIA DOCUMENT NUMBER: 13119.000

INTRODUCTION

The United States Transportation Command (USTRANSCOM) and the Australian Defence Force (ADF) (each referred to herein individually as a "Participant" and together as the "Participants"), recognising that the Exchange of Notes constituting an Agreement between the Government of the United States of America and the Government of Australia concerning Certain Mutual Defense Commitments done on 1 December 1995 (Chapeau Agreement) and the Agreement between the Government of Australia and the Government of the United States of America concerning Security Measures for the Protection of Classified Information (GSOIA), that entered into force on 7 November 2002 apply to this Memorandum of Understanding, desiring to establish formal liaison between the Participants in connection with combined logistics efforts, mutually determine the following terms and conditions regarding the assignment of individuals to serve as Australian Operational Logistics Foreign Liaison Officers to USTRANSCOM.

SECTION I
DEFINITIONS

In addition to any terms defined in other provisions of this Memorandum of Understanding (MOU) the following terms will have the following meanings when used herein:

1.1 "*Classified Information*" will mean official information of a Participant that requires protection in the interests of national security of such Participant and is so designated by the application of security classification markings. The information may be in oral, visual, electronic, or documentary form, or in the form of material, including equipment, or technology.

1.2 "*Contact Officer*" will mean a U.S. Department of Defense (DoD) official designated in writing to oversee and control all contacts, requests for information, consultations, access, and other activities of Foreign Liaison Officers who are assigned to, or are visiting, a DoD component or subordinate organization.

1.3 "*Controlled Unclassified Information*" will mean unclassified information of a Participant to which access or distribution limitations have been applied in accordance with national laws, policies, and regulations of such Participant. It includes United States information that is exempt from public disclosure or subject to export controls.

1.4 "*Foreign Liaison Officer*" will mean a military member of the ADF or civilian employee of the Australian DoD who, upon approval of or certification by the Host Participant or Government, is authorized by the Parent Participant to act as its official representative in connection with programs, projects, or arrangements of interest to the Participants' Governments.

1.5 "*Host Government*" will mean the national government of the Host Participant.

1.6 "*Host Participant*" will mean the Participant to which the Foreign Liaison Officer acts as a liaison pursuant to an assignment by a Parent Participant under Section III.

1.7 "*International Visits Program (IVP)*" will mean the program established to process visits by, and assignments of, foreign representatives to DoD and DoD contractor facilities. It is designed to ensure that Classified and Controlled Unclassified Information to be disclosed to foreign nationals has been properly authorized for disclosure to their governments; that the requesting foreign government provides a security assurance on such foreign nationals and their sponsoring organization or firm, when Classified Information is involved in the visit or assignment, and that administrative arrangements (e.g., date, time, and place) for the visit or assignment are provided.

1.8 "*Parent Government*" will mean the national government of the Parent Participant.

1.9 "*Parent Participant*" will mean the Participant that assigns a Liaison Officer pursuant to Section III.

SECTION II
SCOPE

2.1 During the term of this MOU, subject to the mutual concurrence of the Participants, the ADF may assign a military member of the ADF or civilian employee of the Australian DoD to serve as a Foreign Liaison Officer to USTRANSCOM in accordance with the terms of this MOU. The Australian military member or civilian employee assigned will act as the official representative to USTRANSCOM in connection with programs, projects or arrangements of interest to the Participants' Governments.

2.2 The establishment of each Foreign Liaison Officer position under this MOU will be based on the demonstrated need for, and the mutual benefit of, this position to the Participants. Once established, each Foreign Liaison Officer position will be subject to periodic review by either Participant to ensure that the position continues to be required by, and is of mutual benefit to, the Participants. A Foreign Liaison Officer position no longer required by, or of mutual benefit to, either Participant will be subject to elimination.

2.3 Commencement of such a tour of duty will be subject to any requirements that may be imposed by the Host Participant or its Government regarding formal certification by or approval of Foreign Liaison Officers. Foreign Liaison Officers to be assigned by their Parent Participant to locations in the United States will be requested pursuant to the IVP, as defined in Paragraph 1.7 of this MOU.

2.4 Unless otherwise mutually determined, the normal tour of duty for a Foreign Liaison Officer will be two (2) years.

2.5 At the discretion of the Parent Participant, and with the written concurrences of the Commander, USTRANSCOM, and the Chairman of the Joint Chiefs of Staff, the individual occupying the Foreign Liaison Officer position established pursuant to this MOU may concurrently occupy the existing ADF Foreign Liaison Officer position at the Directorate of Logistics, Joint Staff. In the event a conflict should arise between the demands of the Foreign Liaison Officer positions, the Parent Participant will decide which position has priority.

SECTION III
DUTIES AND ACTIVITIES

3.1 The Foreign Liaison Officer will not perform duties reserved by the laws or regulations of the Host Government to officers or employees of the Host Government, nor will the Foreign Liaison Officer provide any labour or services to the Host Government or any of its agencies, including the Host Participant.

3.2 The Foreign Liaison Officer shall comply with all applicable Host Government policies, procedures, laws and regulations. The Host Participant will assign a Contact Officer to provide guidance to the Foreign Liaison Officer concerning policies, procedures, laws and regulations of the Host Government, and to arrange for activities consistent with such requirements and the purposes of this MOU.

3.3 The Foreign Liaison Officer may request access to Host Participant facilities by submitting a request to the Contact Officer. Access to Host Participant facilities may be granted if such access promotes the purposes of this MOU, is consistent with the terms of any applicable certification or approval issued by the Host Government, and is permitted under the applicable policies, procedures, laws and regulations of the Host Government. Approval of such requests will be at the discretion of the Host Participant. Any request for access that exceeds the terms of an applicable certification or approval will be submitted through the IVP.

3.4 The Foreign Liaison Officer will not be granted access to technical data or other information of the Host Participant, whether or not classified, except as authorized by the Host Participant, and only to the extent necessary to fulfil the Foreign Liaison Officer's functions hereunder.

3.5 All information to which the Foreign Liaison Officer is granted access while serving as a liaison to the Host Participant will be treated as information provided in confidence to the Parent Government, and will not be further released or disclosed by the Foreign Liaison Officer to any other person, firm, organization, or government without the prior written authorization of the Host Government. Disclosure of information to the Foreign Liaison Officer will not be deemed to be a license or authorization to use such information for any purpose other than the purposes described in Section II.

3.6 The Foreign Liaison Officer will not be permitted to participate in exercises, deployments, or civil-military actions, unless expressly authorized in writing to do so by both the Host and Parent Participants.

3.7 The Host Participant will not place or keep a Foreign Liaison Officer in duty assignments in which direct hostilities with forces of third states are likely to occur or have commenced, unless approved by the Parent Participant and Host Participant, in writing.

3.8 The Foreign Liaison Officer will be required to comply with the dress regulations of the Parent Participant but, if requested by the Host Participant, will also wear such identification necessary to identify the Foreign Liaison Officer's nationality, rank and status as a Foreign Liaison Officer. The order of dress for any occasion will be that which most closely conforms to the order of dress for the particular organization of the Host Participant where the Foreign Liaison Officer is located. The

Foreign Liaison Officer will be required to comply with the customs of the Host Participant with respect to the wearing of civilian clothing.

3.9 Prior to the commencement of a Foreign Liaison Officer's tour, the Parent Participant will notify the Host Participant of the specific Parent Participant organization that will exercise operational control over the Foreign Liaison Officer and, if different, the Parent Participant organization that will provide administrative support to the Foreign Liaison Officer and the Foreign Liaison Officer's dependents.

3.10 At the end of the Foreign Liaison Officer's tour, or as otherwise mutually determined by the Participants, the Parent Participant may, subject to the provisions of Section II, replace the Foreign Liaison Officer with another individual who meets the requirements of this MOU.

SECTION IV
FINANCIAL ARRANGEMENTS

4.1 The Parent Participant will bear all costs and expenses of the Foreign Liaison Officer, including, but not limited to:

4.1.1 All pay and allowances of the Foreign Liaison Officer;

4.1.2 All travel by the Foreign Liaison Officer and the Foreign Liaison Officer's dependents, including, but not limited to, travel to and from the duty location;

4.1.3 All costs and expenses associated with the assignment or placement of the Foreign Liaison Officer and the Foreign Liaison Officer's dependents at the duty location, including travel, office space, clerical support, housing, messing, and medical and dental services, unless specifically stated otherwise in an applicable international agreement;

4.1.4 Compensation for loss of, or damage to, the personal property of the Foreign Liaison Officer or the Foreign Liaison Officer's dependent(s);

4.1.5 The movement of the household effects of the Foreign Liaison Officer and the Foreign Liaison Officer's dependents;

4.1.6 Preparation and shipment of remains and funeral expenses associated with the death of the Foreign Liaison Officer or the Foreign Liaison Officer's dependent(s);

4.1.7 Formal and informal training of the Foreign Liaison Officer, other than briefings on Host Participant requirements provided by the Contact Officer; and

4.1.8 All expenses in connection with the return of a Foreign Liaison Officer whose assignment has ended or been terminated, along with the Foreign Liaison Officer's dependent(s).

4.2 The Host Participant may provide such office facilities, equipment, supplies and services as may be necessary for the Foreign Liaison Officer to fulfil the purposes of this MOU.

4.3 The assignment of the Foreign Liaison Officer pursuant to this MOU will be subject to the Parent Participant's authorization and availability of Parent Participant's funds for such purposes.

SECTION V
SECURITY

5.1 The Host Participant will establish the maximum substantive scope and classification levels within which the disclosure of any Classified Information or Controlled Unclassified Information (CUI) to the Foreign Liaison Officer will be permitted. The Host Participant will inform the Parent Participant of the level of security clearance required to permit the Foreign Liaison Officer access to such information. The Foreign Liaison Officer's access to such information and facilities will be consistent with, and limited by the terms of his/her assignment, the provisions of this Section and any other agreement between the Participant's or their Governments concerning access to such information and facilities. Further, access will at all times be limited to the minimum required to accomplish the purposes of this MOU, and, at its discretion, the Host Participant may prohibit the Foreign Liaison Officer's right of access to any Host Participant facility or require that such access be supervised by Host Participant personnel. Nothing in this MOU shall be construed by the Participants to authorize unfettered access to Classified Information or CUI residing in the Host Participant's facilities or computers.

5.2 The ADF will cause security assurances to be filed, through the Australian Embassy in Washington, D.C stating the security clearances for the Foreign Liaison Officer being assigned. The security assurances will be prepared and forwarded through prescribed channels in compliance with established Host Participant procedures. For the United States, the prescribed channels will be the IVP, as defined in paragraph 1.7 of this MOU.

5.3 The Parent Participant will ensure that each assigned Foreign Liaison Officer is fully cognizant of, and complies with, applicable laws and regulations concerning the protection of proprietary information (such as patents, copyrights, know-how, and trade secrets), Classified Information and CUI disclosed to the Foreign Liaison Officer. This obligation will apply both during and after termination of an assignment as a Foreign Liaison Officer. Prior to taking up duties as a Foreign Liaison Officer, the Australian Foreign Liaison Officer will be required to sign the certification at Annex A. Only individuals who execute the certification will be permitted to serve as Foreign Liaison Officers with USTRANSCOM.

5.4 The Parent Participant will ensure that the Foreign Liaison Officer, at all times, complies with the security laws, regulations and procedures of the Host Government. Any violation of security procedures by a Foreign Liaison Officer during his or her assignment will be reported to the Parent Participant for appropriate action. Upon request by the Host Participant, the Parent Participant will remove any Foreign Liaison Officer who violates security laws, regulations, or procedures during his/her assignment.

5.5 Parent Participant. All Classified Information made available to the Foreign Liaison Officer will be considered to be Classified Information furnished to the Government of Australia, and shall be subject to all the provisions and safeguards provided for under the GSOIA.

5.6 The Foreign Liaison Officer will not take custody of Classified Information or CUI in tangible form (for example, documents or electronic files), except as expressly permitted by the terms of the Host Participant certification of the Foreign Liaison Officer (and requested in writing by the Parent Government) for the following situations:

5.6.1 Couriers. The Foreign Liaison Officer may take custody of Classified Information to perform courier functions-, when authorized by the Host Participant certification for the Foreign Liaison Officer. The Classified Information will be packaged and an acknowledgement for receipt provided for in compliance with Host Participant requirements.

5.6.2 On-Site Storage. The Foreign Liaison Officer may be furnished a secure container for the temporary storage of Classified Information, consistent with the terms of the certification, provided the security responsibility for the container and control of the container and its contents remains with the Host Participant.

SECTION VI
TECHNICAL AND ADMINISTRATIVE MATTERS

6.1 The Host Participant's certification or approval of an individual as a Foreign Liaison Officer will not bestow diplomatic or other special privileges on that individual.

6.2 To the extent authorized by the laws and regulations of the Host Government, and in accordance with Section IV of this MOU, the Host Participant may provide such administrative support as is necessary for the Foreign Liaison Officer to fulfil the purposes of this MOU, subject to reimbursement by the Parent Participant.

6.3 Exemption from taxes, customs or import duties, or similar charges for the Foreign Liaison Officer or the Foreign Liaison Officer's dependent(s) will be governed by applicable laws and regulations or any applicable international agreements between the Host and Parent Governments.

6.4 If office space is provided to the Foreign Liaison Officer by the Host Participant, the Host Participant will determine the normal working hours for the Foreign Liaison Officer.

6.5 The Parent Participant will ensure that the Host Participant is informed as far in advance as possible of any absences of the Foreign Liaison Officer.

6.6 The Foreign Liaison Officer and the Foreign Liaison Officer's dependent(s) will be provided care in military medical and dental facilities to the extent permitted by applicable Host Government law, policy, and/or applicable international agreement. Where a reciprocal agreement for health care exists between the Participants, the access entitlement of the Foreign Liaison Officer and the Foreign Liaison Officer's dependent(s) is specified. For those personnel covered by such an agreement, care in military medical and dental facilities is generally provided free of charge. All Foreign Liaison Officers and their dependent(s) not covered by a reciprocal agreement may be offered health care, on a reimbursable basis, in military facilities. Where military facilities are not available, the Foreign Liaison Officer will be responsible for all medical and dental costs incurred by himself/herself and his/her dependent(s). The Parent Participant will ensure that the Foreign Liaison Officer and his/her dependent(s) are physically fit prior to the Foreign Liaison Officer's tour of duty. The Parent Participant will be responsible for familiarizing itself with the medical and dental services available to the Foreign Liaison Officer and his/her dependent(s), and the costs of, and the procedures for, use of such services.

6.7 The Foreign Liaison Officer and the Foreign Liaison Officer's dependent(s) may be accorded the use of military commissaries, exchanges, theatres and similar morale and welfare activities, in accordance with the laws, regulations, and policies of the Host Participant and any applicable international agreements or arrangements between the Host and Parent Participants.

6.8 To the extent permitted by the laws and regulations of the Host Government, and subject to reimbursement by the Parent Participant, the Host Participant may provide, if available, housing and messing facilities for the Foreign Liaison Officer and the Foreign Liaison Officer's dependent(s) on the same basis and priority as for its own personnel of comparable rank and assignment. At locations where housing and messing facilities are not provided by the Host Participant, the Host Participant will use reasonable efforts to assist the Parent Participant to locate such facilities for the Foreign Liaison Officer and the Foreign Liaison Officer's dependent(s).

6.9 The Parent Participant will ensure that the Foreign Liaison Officer and the Foreign Liaison Officer's dependent(s) have all documentation required by the Host Government for entry into, and exit from, the country of the Host Government. Unless exempted under an applicable international agreement between the Participants, Foreign Liaison Officers and their dependents entering the

United States will be required to comply with United States Customs and Border Protection regulations.

6.10 The Parent Participant will ensure that the Foreign Liaison Officer and dependent(s) accompanying the Foreign Liaison Officer in the country of the Host Participant will obtain motor vehicle liability insurance coverage for their private motor vehicles, in accordance with applicable laws, regulations and policies of the Host Participant.

SECTION VII DISCIPLINE AND REMOVAL

7.1 Except as provided in Section 7.2, neither the Host Participant nor the armed forces of the Host Government may take disciplinary action against a Foreign Liaison Officer who commits an offence under the military laws or regulations of the Host Participant, nor will the Host Participant exercise disciplinary powers over the Foreign Liaison Officer's dependent(s). The Parent Participant, however, will take such administrative or disciplinary action against the Foreign Liaison Officer as may be appropriate under the circumstances, to ensure compliance with this MOU, and the Participants will cooperate in the investigation of any offences under the laws or regulations of either Participant.

7.2 The certification or approval of a Foreign Liaison Officer may be withdrawn, modified or curtailed at any time by the Host Participant for any reason, including, but not limited to, the violation of the regulations or laws of the Host Participant or the Host Government. In addition, at the request of the Host Participant, the Parent Government will remove the Foreign Liaison Officer or a dependent of the Foreign Liaison Officer from the territory of the Host Government. The Host Participant will provide an explanation for its removal request, but a disagreement between the Participants concerning the sufficiency of the Host Participant's reasons will not be grounds to delay the removal of the Foreign Liaison Officer or the dependent(s).

7.3 A Foreign Liaison Officer will not exercise any supervisory or disciplinary authority over military or civilian personnel of the Host Participant.

SECTION VIII CLAIMS

8.1 Claims arising under this MOU will be dealt with in accordance with paragraph 1 of the Chapeau Agreement. The Participants will share any costs required to be shared under subparagraph 1(b) (ii) of the Chapeau Agreement on the following basis:

8.1.1 Where the Participants mutually determine in respect of any claim that the damage, injury or death can be specifically attributed to one Participant, the cost of handling and settling the claim will be the sole responsibility of that Participant;

8.1.2 Where it is mutually determined that both Participants are responsible for the damage, injury or death, the Participants will enter into consultation to resolve the handling and settling of the claim, with each Participant paying an apportioned share according to their degree of responsibility for the damage, injury or death; and

8.1.3 Where it is mutually determined that it not possible to attribute responsibility for damage, injury or death, the costs of handling and settling the claim will be distributed equally between the Participants.

8.2 Claims arising under a contract will be resolved in accordance with the contract. Unless otherwise mutually determined by the Participants, the costs of claims arising as a consequence of a contract awarded pursuant to this MOU will be the sole responsibility of the Participant which is the party to the contract.

SECTION IX
SETTLEMENT OF DISPUTES

9.1 Disputes arising under or relating to this MOU will be resolved only though consultations between the Participants and will not be referred to a third party, national or international tribunal, or to any other forum for settlement.

SECTION X
ENTRY INTO EFFECT, AMENDMENT, DURATION AND TERMINATION

10.1 All obligations of the Participants under this MOU will be subject to national laws and the availability of appropriated funds for such purposes.

10.2 The Parent Participant will ensure that the Foreign Liaison Officer complies with all obligations and restrictions applicable to the Foreign Liaison Officer under this MOU.

10.3 This MOU may be amended by the mutual written concurrence of the Participants.

10.4 This MOU may be terminated at any time by written concurrence of both Participants. In the event both Participants determine to terminate this MOU, the Participants will consult prior to the date of termination.

10.5 Either Participant may terminate this MOU upon thirty (30) days' written notification to the other Participant.

10.6 The respective rights and responsibilities of the Participants under Section V (Security) and Section VIII (Claims) will continue, notwithstanding the termination or expiration of this MOU.

10.7 No later than the effective date of expiration or termination of this MOU, each Participant will remove its Foreign Liaison Officer(s) and such Foreign Liaison Officer's dependents from the territory of the Host Participant and pay any money owed to the other Participant under this MOU. Any costs or expenses for which the Parent Participant is responsible pursuant to Section IV (Financial Arrangements) of this MOU, but which were not billed in sufficient time to permit payment prior to termination or expiration of this MOU, will be paid promptly after such billing.

10.8 This MOU will enter into force upon signature by both Participants. This MOU Arrangement will remain in force for five (5) years and may be extended by written concurrence of the Participants.

10.9 This MOU consists often (10) Sections and an Annex.

IN WITNESS WHEREOF, the undersigned, being duly authorized, have signed this MOU.

ON BEHALF OF
UNITED STATES TRANSPORTATION COMMAND

[Signature]

NORTON A. SCHWARTZ
General, U.S. Air Force
Commander

Dated: 22 Aug 06

ON BEHALF OF
AUSTRALIAN DEFENCE FORCE

[Signature]

CHRISTOHPHER G. SPENCE
Air Vice-Marshal
Commander Joint Logistics

Dated: 27 July 2006

ANNEX A - CERTIFICATION

SECTION I
FOREIGN LIAISON OFFICER
LEGAL STATUS OF CERTIFICATION

As a representative of the Parent Participant under the auspices of a Foreign Liaison Officer assignment to the United States Transportation Command (USTRANSCOM), I am subject to the jurisdiction of United States Federal, state, and local laws, except as provided by treaty, other specific legal authority, or the terms of any diplomatic immunity that I may have been granted. I understand that my acceptance of the Foreign Liaison Officer position does not bestow upon me diplomatic or other special privileges.

SECTION II
LIAISON OFFICER
CONDITIONS OF CERTIFICATION

(1) **Responsibilities:** I understand that my activities as the Operational Logistics Foreign Liaison Officer shall be limited to the representational responsibilities of my Government and that I am expected to present the views of my Government with regard to the issues in which my government and the U.S. Government have a mutual interest. I shall not perform duties that are reserved by law or regulation to an officer or employee of the U.S. Government. I will work issues pertaining to the logistics systems of the Participants, particularly as they relate to combined operations between the United States and Australia, and, when requested by USTRANSCOM, provide national operational planning and coordination in support of contingency operations.

(2) **Costs:** I understand that all costs associated with my duties as a Foreign Liaison Officer will be the responsibility of my Government, including, but not limited to, travel, office space, clerical services, housing, messing, and medical and dental services.

(3) **Extensions and Revalidation:** I understand that if my Government desires to request an extension or revalidation of my position beyond the original dates for which I am certified, a new visit request will be submitted not later than 30 days prior to the expiration date of the current Foreign Liaison Officer assignment authorization.

(4) **Contact Officer:** I understand that when the certification process is completed, a Contact Officer will be assigned to sponsor me during my visit to USTRANSCOM. I further understand that I shall coordinate, through my Contact Officer, all requests for information, visits, and other business that fall under the terms of my certification. I also understand that requests for information which are beyond the terms of my certification will be made through the Office of the Defense Attaché in Washington D.C.

(5) **Other Visits:** I understand that visits to facilities for which the purpose does not directly relate to the terms of my certification will be made through the Office of the Defense Attaché in Washington D.C.

(6) **Uniform:** I understand that I will wear my national uniform when conducting business at USTRANSCOM or other Department of Defense facilities, unless otherwise directed. I will comply with my Australian service uniform regulations.

(7) **Security:**

a. I understand that access to U.S. Government information shall be limited to that information determined by my Contact Officer to be necessary to fulfil the functions of a Foreign Liaison Officer. I also understand that I may not have access to U.S. Government computer systems, unless the information accessible by the computer is releasable to my Government in accordance with applicable U.S. law, regulations and policy.

b. All information to which I may have access during my certification shall be treated as information provided in confidence to my government and will not be further released or disclosed by me to any other person, firm, organization, or government without the prior written authorization of the United States Government.

c. I may be allowed to take possession of classified material in the performance of my duties provided I safeguard this material in accordance with the Agreement between the Government of Australia and the Government of the United States of America concerning Security Measures for the Protection of Classified Information (GSOIA), that entered into force on 7 November 2002.

d. I shall immediately report to my Contact Officer should I obtain or become knowledgeable of United States Government information for which I am not authorized to have access. I further agree that I shall report to my Contact Officer any incidents of my being offered or provided information that I am not authorized to have.

e. If required, I shall display a security badge on my outer clothing so that it is clearly visible. The United States Government will supply this badge.

(8) **Compliance:** I have been briefed on, fully understand, and will comply with the terms and conditions of my certification. Failure to comply may result in termination of my certification. I further understand that the termination of my certification does not preclude further disciplinary action in accordance with any applicable government-to-government agreements or arrangements between the United States and Australia.

(9) **Definitions of Terms:** Terms not defined herein will have the definitions ascribed to them in the applicable MOU governing my assignment as a Foreign Liaison Officer.

SECTION III
LIAISON OFFICER – TERMS OF CERTIFICATION

(1) Contact Officer: ______________________________ has been assigned as my Contact Officer.

(2) Certification: I am certified to USTRANSCOM and will act as the official representative to USTRANSCOM in connection with programs, projects or arrangements of interest to the Participants' Governments . As such, I am allowed to visit sites, offices, and briefings that support the issues stemming from the logistic systems of the Australian Defence Force and USTRANSCOM, and other venues in support of Operational Logistics Foreign Liaison Officer duties with USTRANSCOM.

(3) Travel: I may visit the following locations under the terms of my certification, with the permission of my Contact Officer:

- USTRANSCOM facilities;
- USTRANSCOM subordinate activities;
- Defense Logistics Agency;
- Designated areas within the Pentagon;
- Other such locations as my Contact Officer may permit in the future.

SECTION IV
FOREIGN LIAISON OFFICER - CERTIFICATION OF IN-BRIEFING

I, *(NAME OF FOREIGN LIAISON OFFICER)*, understand and acknowledge that I have been certified as an Operational Logistics Foreign Liaison Officer to USTRANSCOM, as mutually determined upon between the Australian Defence Force and USTRANSCOM. I further acknowledge that I fully understand and have been briefed on: (1) the legal status of my certification; (2) the conditions of my certification; and (3) the terms of my certification. I further acknowledge that I shall comply with the conditions and responsibilities of my certification.

______________________________	______________________________
(Signature of Foreign Liaison Officer)	(Signature of Briefer)
______________________________	______________________________
(Name of Foreign Liaison Officer)	(Name of Briefer)
(Rank and/or Title):____________________	(Location):________________________
(Date):______________________________	

State Department Document Number: 06-298

Amendment No. 4 to the Agreement of September 11, 2003, as Amended, Between the Kingdom of Cambodia and the United States of America, the Strategic Objective Grant Agreement for Improved Health Services in HIV/AIDS and Infectious Diseases as well as in Maternal, Child and Reproductive Health, with Annex

Signed at Phnom Penh,
September 18, 2006
Entered into force September 18, 2006

CTIA DOCUMENT NUMBER: 13120.001

AMENDMENT NUMBER FOUR dated September 18, 2006 between The Kingdom of Cambodia ("Grantee"), represented by the Ministry of Foreign Affairs and International Cooperation of the Royal Government of Cambodia ("RGC"), and The United States of America, acting through the United States Agency for International Development ("USAID")

WHEREAS, the Grantee and USAID ("Parties") entered into a Grant Agreement on September 11, 2003 for Twenty Two Million Six Hundred Four Thousand Five Hundred Thirty-Two U.S. Dollars ($22,604,532) for the Strategic Objective of Improved Health Services in HIV/AIDS and Infectious Diseases as well as in Maternal, Child and Reproductive Health, and

WHEREAS, the Parties amended the Agreement on August 03, 2004 to obligate an additional Twenty-Nine Million Five Hundred Sixty Thousand U.S. Dollars ($29,560,000), on June 30, 2005 to obligate an additional Twenty-Eight Million Seven Hundred Thousand U.S. Dollars ($28,700,000), and on September 27, 2005 to obligate an additional One Million and Two Hundred Thousand U.S. Dollars ($1,200,000), and

WHEREAS, the Parties now wish to amend the Agreement to increase the amount of the USAID Grant by $30,509,000, to increase the amount of the total estimated USAID contribution, and to make corresponding changes in the Financial Plan.

NOW, THEREFORE, the Parties hereby agree as follows:

1. To reflect the additional Thirty Million Five Hundred and Nine Thousand United States Dollars ($30,509,000) obligated by this Amendment, Subsection (a) (The Grant) of Section 3.2 is hereby deleted in its entirety and replaced with, "To help achieve the objective set forth in this agreement, USAID, pursuant to the Foreign Assistance Act of 1961, as amended, hereby obligates to the Grantee under the terms of the Agreement not to exceed One Hundred Twelve Million Five

Hundred Seventy Three Thousand Five Hundred Thirty-Two "U.S." Dollars ($112,573,532) (the "Grant") for the purpose of direct funding by USAID of nongovernmental organizations as described in Article 6 hereof

2. To increase the total estimated USAID contribution for the Strategic Objective, Subsection (b) (Total Estimated USAID Contribution) of Section 3.2 of the Agreement (USAID Contribution) is hereby amended by deleting "$82,064,532 million" and substituting therefore "One Hundred Fifty Nine Million Six Hundred Eighty One Thousand Five Hundred Thirty-Two "U.S." Dollars ($159,681,532)"

3. To amend and restate the Financial Plan set forth in Attachment 1 to Annex 1 of the Agreement in its entirety in the form of attachment A to this Amendment Number Four

4. To increase the amount of the total estimated grantee contribution, Section 3.3 of the Agreement (Grantee Contribution) is hereby amended by deleting "Four Million and Four Hundred Thousand U.S. Dollars" ($4,400,000) and substituting therefore "Fifteen Million Eighty Four Thousand and Five Hundred U.S. Dollars ($15,084,500)."

5. To change the SO title, Section 2.1 of the Agreement is amended by deleting "Increased Use of High Impact HIV/AIDS and Family Health Services and Appropriate Health Seeking Behaviors" and substituting therefore "Improved Health Services in HIV/AIDS and Infectious Diseases as well as in Maternal, Child and Reproductive Health"

6. To extend the Completion Date of the Strategic Objective, Subsection (a) of Section 4.1 (The Completion Date) is amended by deleting "September 30, 2006 and substituting therefore "September 30, 2011"

7. Except as amended herein, the terms and conditions of the Agreement remain in full force and effect.

IN WITNESS WHEREOF, the Kingdom of Cambodia and the United States of America, each, acting through its duly authorized representative, have caused this Amendment Number Four to the Agreement to be signed in their names and delivered as of the day and year first above written.

For the Government of the
United States of America

[Signature]

M. Erin Soto
Mission Director
USAID Cambodia

For the Royal Government
of Cambodia

[Signature]

LONG Visalo
Acting Minister
Secretary of State
Ministry of Foreign Affairs and
International Cooperation

STRATEGIC OBJECTIVE GRANT AGREEMENT
Improved Health Services in HIV/AIDS and Infectious Diseases as well as in Maternal, Child and Reproductive Health
(SO 442-009)

Accounting Classification & Appropriation Data

Project No.	Project Element No.	Proj. Element Name	Appropriation	Fund Code	DOCNO	Amount
4420009.01	1	Child Survival, Maternal Health, TB & Malaria	726/71095	06/07-CD	SOAG 442009 AM#04	$9,175,353.00
4420009.01	2	Population	726/71095	06/07-CD-POP	SOAG 442009 AM#04	$2,970,000.00
4420009.01	3	HIV/AIDS	726/71095	06/07-CD-AIDS	SOAG 442009 AM#04	$14,313,353.00
		HIV/AIDS (GHAI)	7219X1030	06-GAI-X6	SOAG 442009 AM#04	$1,953,000.00
				Sub-total		$28,411,706.00
				Field Support		$2,058,647.00
				IT Cost Recovery		*$38,647.00*
				SOAG Obligation total		$30,509,000.00

Obligation Summary

From SOAG Inception through Amendment No. 04

Project Element No. / Name	Prior Cumulative Obligations	Increase (Decrease) This Amendment	Cumulative Obligations to date
Funds Allowed to the Mission:			
1 – Child Survival, Maternal Health, TB, Malaria	$24,930,225	$9,175,353	$34,105,578
2 – Population	8,282,612	2,970,000	11,252,612
3 – HIV/AIDS	26,895,225	16,266,353	43,161,578
4 – FY 02 Carryover Funds	504,532	0	504,532
Total Funds Allowed to the Mission	**$60,612,594**	**$28,411,706**	**$89,024,300**
Field Support Funds	**21,415,000**	**$2,058,647**	**23,473,647**
IT Cost Recovery	**36,938**	**38,647**	**75,585**
SOAG Total	**$82,064,532**	**$30,509,000**	**$112,573,532**

ATTACHMENT A TO AMENDMENT NUMBER FOUR TO THE GRANT AGREEMENT FOR Strategic Objective Grant Agreement *"Improved Health Services in HIV/AIDS and Infectious Diseases as well as in Maternal, Child and Reproductive Health." (in US$)*

Table 1 : Financial Plan

Budget Item	Year 1-3 (FY03-05)	Year 4 (FY06)	Year 5 (FY07)	Year 6 (FY08)	Total
USAID: **PC10:** Improve Child Survival, Health and Nutrition	7,663,000	3,215,000	3,132,000	3,593,000	17,603,000
PC17: Improve Maternal Health and Nutrition	4,697,000	1,933,000	2,022,000	2,297,000	10,949,000
PC21: Prevent and Control Infectious Diseases of Major Importance	17,127,258	5,786,000	4,837,000	3,840,000	31,590,258
PC32: Reduce Transmission and Impact of HIV/AIDS	43,877,273	16,605,000	14,652,000	7,000,000	82,134,273
PC33: Support Family Planning	8,700,001	2,970,000	2,735,000	3,000,000	17,405,001
Total USAID Contribution	**82,064,532**	**30,509,000**	**27,378,000**	**19,730,000**	**159,681,532**
RGC: In-kind Contributions (staff, offices, equipment, and utilities).	3,900,000	3,157,500	3,436,000	3,491,000	13,984,500
Tax and Customs Duty on vehicles and equipment *	500,000	200,000	200,000	200,000	1,100,000
Total RGC Contribution **	**4,400,000**	**3,357,500**	**3,636,000**	**3,691,000**	**15,084,500**
Total Program	**86,464,532**	**33,866,500**	**31,014,000**	**23,421,000**	**174,766,032**

* As necessary, the RGC will provide funds out of the RGC's own budget resources for direct payment to RGC tax authorities in the amount of the taxes being exempted for commodities, supplies, materials, equipment, vehicles and other goods financed by USAID and imported into Cambodia. (See SOAG, Section 7.1 (g)).

** Total and details subject to negotiations with RGC/MoH.

Annex 1
Amplified Description

List of Acronyms

ADB	Asian Development Bank
AIDS	Acquired Immune- Deficiency Syndrome
ARI	Acute Respiratory Infection
BSS	(Sexual) Behavioral Sentinel Survey
CARE	CARE International
CDC	Centers for Disease Control
CPA	Complementary Package of Activities
DFID	Department For International Development
DHF	Dengue Hemorrhagic Fever
DOTS	Directly Observed Treatment Short-Course
EmOC	Emergency Obstetric Care
EPI	Expanded Program of Immunization
EU	European Union
FHI/ IMPACT	Family Health International/Implementing AIDS Prevention and Care Project
HC	Health center
HIV/AIDS	Human Immuno-deficiency Virus/ Acquired Immunodeficiency Syndrome
HKI	Helen Keller International
HSSHIV/AIDS	Sentinel Surveillance
IEC	Information, Education, Communication
I/NGOs	International Non-Governmental Organizations
IMCI	Integrated Management of Childhood Illnesses
IRs	Intermediate Results
KHANA	Khmer HIV/AIDS National Alliance
MCH	Maternal and Child Health
MOH	Ministry Of Health
MPA+	Minimum Package of Activities plus
NTP	National Tuberculosis Plan
OD	Operational District
ORS	Oral Rehydration Salts
PFD	Partners for Development
PLWHA	Persons Living With HIV/AIDS
PMTCT	Prevention of Mother to Child Transmission
PSI	Population Services International
RACHA	Reproductive and Child Health Alliance
RCH	Reproductive and Child Health
RGC	Royal Government of Cambodia
RHAC	Reproductive Health Association of Cambodia
STD	Sexually Transmitted Disease
STI	Sexually Transmitted Infection
TB	Tuberculosis

URC	University Research Corporation
USAID	United States Agency for International Development
VCT	Voluntary Counseling and Testing
VCCT	Voluntary Confidential Counseling and Testing
VDC	Village Development Committee
VHSG	Village Health Support Group
WHO	World Health Organization

I. Introduction

This annex describes the activities to be undertaken and the results to be achieved with the funds obligated under this agreement. Nothing in Annex 1 shall be construed as amending any of the definitions or terms of the Agreement.

II. Background

After the end of civil war in October 1991, the United States is one among the principal donors to help reconstruct Cambodia. The USG national interest lies in assuring that its investment in that process is not lost. The United States' main foreign policy objectives in Cambodia are promotion of democracy, good governance, economic growth, protection of the environment and natural resources, and continued improvement of human rights. Addressing global problems of infectious diseases, especially HIV/AIDS and tuberculosis (TB), and serious concerns related to maternal and child health are also high priorities.

The programs of the USAID Office of Public Health are specifically directed at mitigating the devastating affects of HIV/AIDS and other infectious diseases such as TB, as well as reducing morbidity and mortality related to maternal and child health (MCH) and Reproductive Health (RH) in geographically-focused areas in Cambodia.

a) Health Sector in Cambodia

The Problem

The need for reproductive and child health (RCH), HIV/AIDS and infectious disease (ID) interventions is compelling. Cambodia's maternal, infant and child morbidity and mortality rates are the highest in the South-East Asia region as is Cambodia's HIV/AIDS prevalence rate. The burden of tuberculosis is amongst the top 22 countries in the world. Malaria is a leading cause of morbidity and mortality. Dengue hemorrhagic fever is a significant cause of death among children aged 1-5 years. And, poor health conditions are more than just a health sector problem: mounting evidence suggests that household expenditures for health care are a leading cause of landlessness and indebtedness.

The problems are formidable. The capacity of the health system to address these problems is, however, extremely limited. Numerous non-governmental organizations (NGOs) and other donors have been contributing to the strengthening of the health system and delivery of health information and services. These efforts are often quite limited in scope and scale, however. Most Cambodians rely on private service providers who have little or no medical knowledge.

Although progress is being made by the Ministry of Health in implementing a national health coverage plan, it will take time to achieve the goal of full access and availability of health services nationwide. The need to deliver RCH, HIV/AIDS and ID interventions is urgent and cannot wait for the full development of the health care system. At the same time, interventions cannot be delivered without such a system and will always be constrained by the level and pace of health systems development.

USAID/Cambodia will therefore proceed on two tracks simultaneously: strengthening the nascent service delivery system, and promoting the delivery of specific, well-targeted interventions addressing the HIV/AIDS, maternal and child health, and infectious disease challenges in Cambodia.

The health sector in Cambodia faces enormous and persistent challenges.

HIV/AIDS: The HIV/AIDS prevalence rate in Cambodia remains the highest in Southeast Asia. Prevention is hampered by low use of condoms with intimate partners, a lack of quality counseling and testing services, and a paucity of information and services geared to the needs of especially vulnerable groups such as youth and mobile populations. The need to provide care and support to people affected by HIV/AIDS is mounting. And the number of orphans and vulnerable children are increasing.

Safe Motherhood: Cambodia's maternal mortality rate is the highest in the region. This is directly associated with low antenatal attendance at health centers, low level of deliveries assisted by trained health providers, and harmful traditional practices during pregnancy, childbirth, and postpartum. Most maternal deaths are due to complications related to unsafe induced abortion or direct obstetric causes.

Family Planning/Birth Spacing: The problems that need to be addressed are low contraceptive prevalence, large unmet need and demand for family planning services, and a high prevalence of unsafe abortions.

Child Health: The problems of greatest concern are high infant, child and neonatal mortality rates, low use of oral rehydration salts, low Expanded Program of Immunization (EPI) coverage, poor nutrition, and indiscriminate use of antibiotics for childhood infections.

Infectious Diseases: Tuberculosis, malaria, and dengue hemorrhagic fever continue to be leading causes of morbidity and mortality. HIV/AIDS-TB co-infection is increasing rapidly. And Avian Influenza is a growing threat throughout the region.

Service Delivery: The still nascent public health system is not yet playing a major role in responding to these public health challenges. The system's existing workforce, is grossly inadequate in skills. Salaries are so low as to create little or no incentive to work. Supplies and equipment at health centers are not adequate or appropriate for many health care situations. The general population relies heavily on private service providers who most often have little or no medical knowledge.

Existing health services

The RGC launched its ongoing health sector reform program in 1995 with the presentation of the National Health Coverage Plan for 1996-2000. Key features of the plan included the creation of the Operational District (OD) (a population-based unit comprising anywhere from 100,000 to 300,000 people) as the functional focus of health reform efforts, designation of health centers (HC) as the first level of health care, and a stated intention to provide a Minimum Package of Activities (MPA) and Complementary Package of Activities (CPA) at the health centers and referral hospitals respectively. The plan called for the establishment of 940 health centers. As of 2006, over 900 of these health centers have been built throughout the country. Priority has been given to establishing the physical infrastructure and strengthening clinical services; outreach has not been a high priority. The range and quality of services offered at these public health facilities varies widely.

The bulk of Cambodia's public health staff were recruited and trained quickly during the Vietnamese occupation from 1979-89. Many of the skills learned by these individuals are not adequate to respond to the country's burden of disease. Moreover, the planning, management and supervisory systems and skills needed to support the health care delivery system are similarly weak. Local and international

NGOs are helping to fill this gap in many important ways but such heavy reliance on external assistance should not delay the strengthening of the public health system's own capacity to meet basic health care needs.

Most Cambodians look to non-government outlets (pharmacies, traditional healers, drug sellers) as their preferred sources of services for most health problems including delivery assistance, birth spacing methods, sexually transmitted disease (STD) drugs and abortion. An uncontrolled drug industry and widespread self-treatment have serious implications for the quality and appropriateness of treatment. A number of studies have suggested that very few of the personnel at unregulated private sector outlets are familiar with common symptoms of reproductive health problems, correct drug dosage or potential side effects, or correct management procedures for many of the health problems they treat. In consequence, most Cambodians are receiving very poor quality of care, and little value for their money, at either public or private sources of health services. Nevertheless, high household expenditures for health care are an enormous financial burden for many families, particularly in rural areas.

Opportunities for high-impact interventions

HIV/AIDS. While awareness of HIV/AIDS is high and concern is increasing, the social environment is still highly permissive with a very active sex trade and many people engaged in high-risk behavior. Behavior change has occurred in some target groups, but in general, high-risk sexual behavior remains unacceptably high.

The past three years' successes in reaching high-risk populations and changing behaviors demonstrate that Cambodians will act when provided with adequate information and services. Most Cambodians, however, lack access to appropriate health education, voluntary counseling and testing, condoms, and sexually transmitted infection (STI) diagnosis and treatment – resulting in considerable unmet demand for these critical services, especially among high-risk and mobile populations.

Good models of successful interventions with high-risk populations have been developed, although these are mostly limited in scope and coverage. These models need to be scaled up significantly and rapidly to reach a broader segment of high-risk populations, including police and military personnel, factory workers and commercial sex workers. Successful approaches need to be expanded to other high-risk populations such as indirect sex workers, injecting drug users/drug users, migrant workers, truck drivers and other mobile populations.

Major opportunities to improve the technical quality of services, availing full advantage of all available channels for HIV/AIDS prevention, and improving cost-effectiveness have been missed by channeling health services through various vertical structures. Service delivery needs to be integrated at the OD-level in order to ensure that links are made between HIV/AIDS and all other health interventions. This would entail defining and implementing the package of essential health services[1]. HIV/AIDS-related services that need to be strengthened at the OD-level include voluntary counseling and testing, STD diagnosis and treatment, and dissemination of more appropriate and effective information about HIV/AIDS prevention. Integrated programming should result in a higher impact and would contribute to the identification of more effective approaches that could be replicated in other geographic areas by the RGC and other donors. Advocacy and policy development and support are paramount to successful interventions.

[1] The MoH-sanctioned "Minimum Package of Activities-Plus" or MPA+, whereby the "plus" refers to HIV/AIDS and STD prevention activities.

As the epidemic evolves, issues related to pediatric AIDS, and care and support for those infected with and affected by HIV/AIDS have become more pronounced in recent times. OD-level interventions could contribute to the prevention of mother-to-child transmission of HIV through expansion of voluntary counseling and testing services and significant improvements in the provision of antenatal and other key reproductive health services. OD-level interventions would also foster synergies between HIV/AIDS and other core program approaches such as Reproductive Health and Family Planning, contributing to reducing overall maternal and child morbidity and mortality, consistent with USAID's global priorities and strategies in the health sector.

Given the extremely limited capacity of the public health system, continued emphasis needs to be placed on developing and expanding effective community-based approaches to care and support of those infected and affected by HIV/AIDS.

Cambodia's HIV sentinel surveillance and behavioral surveillance systems, developed largely with USAID funding, have contributed significantly to effective program planning and creating a policy environment conducive to AIDS prevention. These systems need to be refined and expanded to include new high-risk populations.

Maternal health. Cambodia's very high levels of maternal, infant and child mortality are clear indicators of the weaknesses in existing health service delivery systems. The vast majority of Cambodian women deliver at home assisted by untrained birth attendants, receive no antenatal care prior to delivery, and no tetanus toxoid immunization. A large proportion of pregnant women are anemic and suffer from Vitamin A and iodine deficiencies. Access to emergency obstetric care is extremely limited. Postpartum services are virtually non-existent, despite the fact that postpartum hemorrhage is a common killer. Delivery practices of traditional birth attendants are known to include harmful practices.

Within the context of an integrated health service delivery strategy at the provincial and OD-levels, there is clear need and opportunity to continue to upgrade the skills of midwives and foster linkages between nurses, midwives and Traditional Birth Attendants in order to ensure access to necessary and appropriate antenatal and postpartum services, and reduce harmful delivery practices. NGOs and the private sector have an important role to play in outreach activities.

Family planning/birth spacing. Despite a rapid increase in contraceptive knowledge and use over the last five years, the unmet need for family planning services is considerable – due mainly to the absence of extensive service delivery systems. Although the government policy environment toward birth spacing is favorable and permits distribution of a complete range of contraceptive methods, the only methods currently available to any significant extent are pills, injectables and condoms – and even these are not always available in rural areas. Anecdotal evidence suggests that this limited availability of birth spacing services is at least partially responsible for Cambodia's high incidence of unsafe abortions. Notably lacking is emergency contraception for which the need may be great given the reportedly high incidence of rape, which bears especially heavily on the adolescent population.

Contraceptive products need to be made routinely available at the community level by strengthening and expanding information and services through community-based approaches, thus moving beyond the current health center medical model. These approaches would extend and complement the outreach activities of the health center staff without undermining or competing with them. Increased availability could also be achieved through expanding partnerships with private providers of reproductive health services, expanding social marketing in rural areas, and improving the health system's capacity to provide post-abortion care.

Expanded voluntary family planning services at the OD-level would address the needs of married couples not yet using a contraceptive method, and who have said they want to limit or prevent future pregnancies. Information, Education and Communication (IEC) efforts are needed to promote the practice of three-year birth intervals. Expanded OD-level services would also respond to the needs of a large group of women who resort to abortion as a means of achieving their fertility preferences and provide post-abortion care. Adolescents at risk of unwanted pregnancies, especially in the burgeoning garment industry and the growing urban middle class, need specially designed youth-friendly information and services, including emergency contraception.

Child health. The chief causes of infant and child mortality are neonatal tetanus, acute respiratory infection, diarrhea, meningitis, septicemia, typhoid, malaria, and dengue. Child health service coverage is extremely low: the majority of children are not fully immunized , do not receive Vitamin A prophylaxis, oral rehydration therapy , or treatment for acute respiratory infections (ARI) by a trained provider. Half the children are malnourished. Child health interventions need to be strengthened within the context of the MPA+ package, with special emphasis on ARI, diarrhea and malnutrition (particularly optimal breastfeeding and infant feeding practices and use of micronutrients, especially Vitamin A). There are also opportunities to work with UNICEF and WHO to support the Royal Government of Cambodia (RGC) pilot testing of Integrated Management of Childhood Illness (IMCI), and to scale up that activity in selected ODs.

Infectious diseases. TB, malaria and dengue hemorrhagic fever (DHF) continue to be leading causes of morbidity and mortality. The emergence of drug-resistant malaria strains has been confounded by extensive national and cross-border mobility. There have been increasingly large DHF epidemics every two to three years. In recent years, transmission has spread from the urban centers of Phnom Penh and Battambang to smaller towns and villages.

There is a clear need for continued surveillance and increased capacity to deliver effective and appropriate clinic services, health education and control activities in high risk areas. Related to malaria, there is a continuing need for monitoring of drug-resistant malaria, drug-use practices and drug quality, and the development and implementation of interventions to improve the rational use of anti-malarial drugs. Efforts to control and manage DHF should be focused on geographic areas of highest risk, including Phnom Penh and Battambang.

A strategy for addressing tuberculosis, including HIV/AIDS-TB co-infection, was finalized in September 2003. This strategy calls for strengthening of planning and management skills at the national and provincial levels in communicable disease control; operational research on diagnostic issues and alternative service delivery mechanisms; expansion of the directly observed treatment short-course (DOTS) to the health center level and into communities; and, continued support for IEC and advocacy on TB.

Demand for quality health care. Individuals, families and communities need to be empowered to demand high quality care, change their health seeking behavior, and actively participate in and influence the systems responsible for delivery of health care services.

III. Funding

Financial Plan. The financial plan for the program is set forth in the attached tables below.

Strategic Objective Grant Agreement for "Improved Health Services in HIV/AIDS and Infectious Diseases as well as in Maternal, Child and Reproductive Health." (in US$)

Table 1: Financial Plan					
Budget Item	**Year 1-3 (FY03-05)**	**Year 4 (FY06)**	**Year5 (FY07)**	**Year 6 (FY08)**	**Total**
USAID: **PC10**: Improve Child Survival, Health and Nutrition	7,663,000	3,215,000	3,132,000	3,593,000	17,603,000
PC17: Improve Maternal Health and Nutrition	4,697,000	1,933,000	2,022,000	2,297,000	10,949,000
PC21 : Prevent and Control Infectious Diseases of Major Importance	17,127,258	5,786,000	4,837,000	3,840,000	31,590,258
PC32: Reduce Transmission and Impact of HIV/AIDS	43,877,273	16,605,000	14,652,000	7,000,000	82,134,273
PC33: Support Family Planning	8,700,001	2,970,000	2,735,000	3,000,000	17,405,001
Total USAID Contribution	**82,064,532**	**30,509,000**	**27,378,000**	**19,730,000**	**159,681,532**
RGC: In-kind Contributions (staff, offices, equipment, and utilities).	3,900,000	3,157,500	3,436,000	3,491,000	13,984,500
Tax and Customs Duty on vehicles and equipment *	500,000	200,000	200,000	200,000	1,100,000
Total RGC Contribution **	**4,400,000**	**3,357,500**	**3,636,000**	**3,691,000**	**15,084,500**
Total Program	**86,464,532**	**33,866,500**	**31,014,000**	**23,421,000**	**174,766,032**

* As necessary, the RGC will provide funds out of the RGC's own budget resources for direct payment to RGC tax authorities in the amount of the taxes being exempted for commodities, supplies, materials, equipment, vehicles and other goods financed by USAID and imported into Cambodia. (See SOAG, Section 7.1 (g)).

** Total and details subject to negotiations with RGC/MoH.

IV. Results To Be Achieved/Results Framework

A. Strategic Objective

USAID/Cambodia and the Ministry of Health together will collaborate with their implementing organizations to achieve the Strategic Objective of "Improved Health Services in HIV/AIDS and Infectious Diseases as well as in Maternal, Child and Reproductive Health. "

B. Program Components:

USAID/Cambodia activities have focused on five Program Components (PCs) to assist in achieving the overall Strategic Objectives. These are:

- child survival, health and nutrition is improved;
- maternal health and nutrition is improved;
- infectious diseases of major importance is prevented and controlled;
- transmission and impact of HIV/AIDS is reduced;
- knowledge of family planning is improved

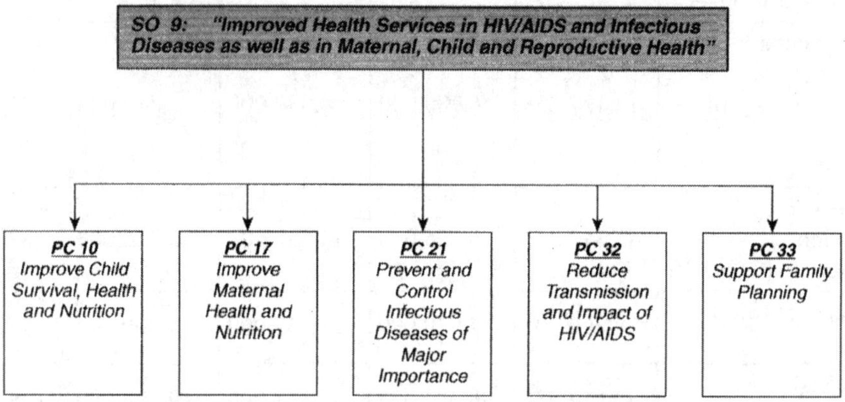

Working in collaboration with government (RGC), principally the Ministry of Health, international and local non-governmental organizations (I/NGOs), private commercial sector partners and other donors, USAID assistance will support critical elements of the primary health care information and service delivery system, community outreach and help strengthen the performance of the overall health system. USAID assistance will ensure that access to information and the utilization of essential services (including a comprehensive package of HIV/AIDS prevention and care, reproductive health, maternal and child health, prevention and treatment of sexually-transmitted infections) and the control of selected infectious diseases (i.e., TB, malaria, and dengue), including emerging infectious diseases, particularly avian influenza, will continue.

USAID assistance will also improve and strengthen the existing health system and its requisite systems (administrative, management, health information, quality assurance, supervision and monitoring, logistics/reporting, and service delivery systems). It will support the Government's decentralization efforts by strengthening the institutional, management, and technical capabilities of provincial and operational district health offices and facilities. Finally, USAID assistance will strengthen the management and technical capabilities of local non-governmental and community organizations in order to improve and expand NGO and community-based organizations involvement in the delivery of health information and services at the community level and in concert with the government's priorities.

Currently, USAID is supporting the provision of health care information and services and selected aspects of the health care delivery system through activities that are implemented by PVO/NGOs, indigenous NGOs, and community/international organizations. USAID is working to preserve, strengthen and appropriately expand the following health care services and information: a comprehensive package of HIV/AIDS prevention and care; reproductive health; maternal and child health; prevention and treatment of sexually-transmitted infections; and, the control of selected infectious diseases (TB, malaria, AI, and dengue), including appropriate monitoring and disease surveillance systems.

V. Activities/Activity Selection

PC10: *Improve Child Survival, Health and Nutrition*

As with maternal mortality, Cambodia's under-five mortality rate is the highest in Southeast Asia. Neonatal death accounts for one third of infant mortality. Aside from the epidemiological component of the RGC National Child Survival Program, the other National Child Survival Program components are not well organized and urgent action is needed to increase service utilization and quality of care. In particular, there has been little attention to newborn health, aside from breastfeeding, and newborn care needs particular attention as a major contributor to under-five mortality.

- Improved infant and young child feeding practices
  - Number of infants with breastfeeding initiated within one hour of birth
  - Number of infants under 6 months exclusively breastfed
  - Number of breastfed infants 6-9 months receiving semi-solid food
- Increased micronutrient supplementation
  - Coverage of population aged 6-59 months receiving vitamin A
- Expanded provision of immunizations to children
  - Coverage of infants receiving dose of measles vaccine
- Improved diagnosis and treatment of common childhood illnesses
  - Number of children with fast and difficult breathing in the last 2 weeks who received medical care
  - Number of children with diarrhea in the last 2 weeks who received ORT
- Improved motivation and capacity of health care providers, managers, volunteers and government workers
  - Number of people trained in child health, by category, by sex
  - Number of health providers trained in child health according to national curriculum, by sex
- Expanded linkages with referral level
  - Number of completed referrals (child illness)
- Demonstrated linkages with malaria
  - Number of children who slept under ITN previous night
  - Number of children living in malarious area with fever in the last 2 weeks who received anti-malarial prophylaxis

Illustrative Activities and Approaches

- Behavior change approaches including mass media and interpersonal counseling
- Partnerships between public and private sector for distribution/sale of commodities through public sector and private/NGO sector outlets
- School and public education programs
- Community-based savings and equity programs for fees and transport for emergencies
- Outreach programs for health education and service delivery
- Quality improvement approaches
- Formal and on-the-job training of service providers, volunteers, managers, educators
- Coordination with NGO, donor, UN, and government partners
- Information dissemination on results, successful innovations, and lessons learned

PC 17: *Improve Maternal Health and Nutrition*

The maternal mortality ratio is the highest in Southeast Asia. Ninety percent of births occur at home and less than a third of all births are attended by skilled birth attendants. The priorities are to prevent unwanted pregnancy that can end up in abortion, increase use and provision of proven preventive behaviors and care for reducing maternal deaths and obstetric complications, and improve referrals for emergency obstetric care

- Provision of services to the community expanded
  - Postpartum vitamin A coverage
  - Antepartum and postpartum iron folate coverage
  - Anemia prevalence among women of reproductive age
- Increased use of key maternal health services and interventions in the antenatal, delivery and postpartum periods
  - ANC + 4 coverage
  - Skilled birth attendant coverage (home and facility)
  - Number of health centers (HCs) implementing active management of the third stage of labor as maternal intervention
  - Number of post abortion complication cases receiving appropriate treatment and care
  - Coverage of pregnant women receiving tetanus toxoid 2 (TT2)
- Improved motivation and capacity of health care providers, managers, volunteers and government workers
  - Number of people trained in maternal health by category, by sex
  - Number of health providers trained in maternal health according to national curriculum, disaggregated by sex
- Improved and expanded quality of newborn care services provision
  - Number of HCs implementing comprehensive package of newborn care

- Number of HCs implementing basic newborn care package (without antibiotics)
- Number of villages implementing community newborn care

- Demonstrated linkages with malaria and HIV/AIDS programs
  - Number of pregnant women who received HIV counseling and testing for PMTCT and received their test results
  - Number of ANC clients provided with insecticide-treated nets (ITN)

Illustrative Activities and Approaches

- Behavior change approaches including mass media and interpersonal counseling
- Partnerships between public and private sector for distribution/sale of commodities through public sector and private/NGO sector outlets
- School and public education programs
- Community-based savings and equity programs for fees and transport for emergencies
- Outreach programs for health education and service delivery
- Quality improvement approaches
- Formal and on-the-job training of service providers, volunteers, managers, educators
- Coordination with NGO, donor, UN, and government partners
- Information dissemination on results, successful innovations, and lessons learned

PC 21: *Prevent and control infectious diseases of major importance*

Cambodia is one of the worlds' 22 **tuberculosis** (TB) high-burden countries. Despite good progress in expanding Directly-Observed Treatment Short Course (DOTS) to health center and community levels, TB remains a major killer and public health challenge in Cambodia – especially given the high HIV/AIDS prevalence rate. **Malaria** continues to be a major public health and economic burden in Cambodia. It is currently the second most common cause of hospital mortality. Although during the past few years there has been a steady reduction in the severe case fatality rate, as well as in the total number of clinically diagnosed and treated malaria cases in the country, morbidity and mortality in Cambodia remain unacceptably high. Malaria treatment and control have been hampered by the spread of resistance to common antimalarial drugs. Access to preventive educational messages and commodities remains a challenge for disease control efforts given the remoteness and mobility of target populations. Cambodia is a **dengue-endemic** country with increasingly large scale epidemics every two to three years. Epidemiological evidence suggests that dengue is spreading from urban to rural areas. Effective prevention and management of dengue and dengue hemorrhagic fever is key to reducing the case fatality rate among children. Quality and appropriateness of services in public and private facilities is still a challenge for public health efforts.

Program interventions focus on improvement of access to prevention and treatment services/ commodities related to three key infectious diseases: Tuberculosis (TB), Malaria, and Dengue among vulnerable populations in one or more of the 11 priority provinces.

Anticipated Results and Proposed Indicators:

- Improved knowledge and practices for disease prevention and health seeking behaviors for appropriate care.
  - Number of community volunteers, care providers, target population trained on disease prevention, danger signs and appropriate care seeking, by sex

  - Number of simple cases referred by volunteers and self-referred cases to health facilities according to health education guidance, disaggregated by disease and by sex
  - Number of severe cases referred to appropriate facilities for care, disaggregated by disease and by sex
- Increased Community DOTS (C-DOTS) coverage to health centers and community levels
  - Number of TB new cases detected
  - Number of registered TB patients receiving complete treatment course
  - Number of registered TB patients cured
  - Number of HCs in each OD implementing C-DOTS
  - Number of villages in each OD implementing C-DOTS
- Increased referral links between TB and HIV/AIDS services in coverage areas.
  - Number of ODs implementing TB/HIV program
  - Number of TB patients accessing HIV/AIDS VCCT services
  - Number of TB/HIV co-infected patients receiving AIDS treatment and care services according to national guidelines
- Increase coverage of impregnated bed-net distribution, re-treatment of bed-nets and increased access to long lasting nets.
  - Number of population living in endemic areas having sufficient insecticide-treated nets (ITN) as defined by National Program
  - Number of population at risk seeping under ITN in the previous night
- Increased referral links to quality care and treatment services for severe cases of malaria, malaria in pregnancy, and dengue during outbreak.
  - Number of severe malaria cases, under-five children, and pregnant women with confirmed malaria referred to appropriate health care facilities
  - Number of children with dengue receiving care and treatment at health facilities according to national guidelines
- Increased access to other commodities for disease prevention, diagnosis and treatment such as malaria rapid diagnosis test kits and drugs through both public and private sector.
  - Availability (coverage) of socially marketed products for malaria prevention and treatment
- Increased capacity of health care providers (where there is a gap) and communities for appropriate management of diseases.
  - Case fatality rate in the supported health facilities
  - Number of health center staff and private providers trained according to national guidelines, by sex
  - Number of community volunteers, leaders and caregivers trained in danger signs appropriate community based care, and referral guidelines, by sex

Illustrative Activities and approaches:

Activities should include health education on disease prevention, improving health seeking behaviors for early diagnosis and treatment, improving linkages/referrals from communities to appropriate public and private health services, improving treatment compliance by involvement of communities, and strengthening capacity of providers, community volunteers and care-takers. Applicants are welcome to suggest different activities to meet the results listed below.

- Effective behavior change approaches using mass media, interpersonal communication and other community initiatives consistent with national programs' strategies and guidelines
- Expand C-DOTS services to all health centers and scale up coverage at community level and promote active case finding in communities.
- Partnership among public health system, NGOs and national level partners to ensure support for quality TB diagnosis and treatment.
- Support the expansion of linkages between TB and HIV/AIDS services
- Expand coverage of preventative, diagnostic and treatment commodities to communities in partnership with public health system, social marketing and other private partners (such as insecticide treated nets, long lasting insecticide treated nets, pre-packaged combination malaria drugs etc.)
- Community mobilization to promote and sustain community based environmental hygiene and vector control measures.
- Strengthen the capacity of public and private health care providers, volunteers, managers, and communities
- Advocate for community saving system and/or equity funds or other "insurance" schemes to support referral for early diagnosis and treatment and emergency referral of severe cases.

PC32: *Reduce transmission and impact of HIV/AIDS*

Prevalence in Cambodia is among the highest of all countries in Asia, despite the successful reduction in prevalence levels in the general population, from 3% in 1997, to 1.9% in 2003. The challenge is to intensify prevention efforts and behavior change interventions for high risk groups, while addressing male behaviors in the general population that are contributing to increases in new infections among monogamous Cambodian women, and the associated threat of HIV transmission from mother-to-child. Maintenance and expansion of prevention activities with high risk groups and their sexual partners must be balanced with expansion of quality care, support, mitigation, and treatment services to children affected and persons living with AIDS throughout priority USG provinces.

Anticipated Results and Proposed Indicators:

- Increased numbers of pregnant HIV+ women receive counseling and prophylaxis to prevent mother to child transmission
    - Number of pregnant women who received HIV counseling and testing for PMTCT and received their test results
    - Number of pregnant women provided with a complete course of antiretroviral prophylaxis for PMTCT

- Reduced risk of HIV/AIDS infection and transmission contains and slows the epidemic
    - Number of individuals reached through community outreach that promotes HIV/AIDS prevention through abstinence and/or being faithful
    - Number of individuals reached through community outreach that promotes HIV/AIDS prevention through other behavior change beyond abstinence and/or being faithful
    - Number of high risk persons adopting consistent and correct condom use
    - Number of HIV+ individuals and sero-discordant couples reached with condom and other prevention and family planning services

Illustrative Activities and Approaches:

- Develop and promote community-based strategies to increase pregnant women's ANC attendance and demand for PMTCT services, including voluntary HIV counseling and testing
- Increase access of PLHA, sero-discordant couples, and persons engaged in high risk behaviors to HIV prevention approaches such as behavior change interventions and prevention commodities such as condoms and syndromic treatment for STIs
- Increase coverage of community-based prevention programs for the general population, with a special emphasis on risky male behaviors and addressing harmful community norms
- Link HIV prevention interventions to reproductive health activities and strengthen referral systems between prevention activities and HIV/AIDS/STI/TB diagnostic, treatment, and care and support services

Counseling and Testing

Expansion of Voluntary Confidential Counseling and Testing (VCCT) services, especially into rural and remote communities serves not only as a prevention activity but also as the entry point into care and treatment and support services for persons infected with HIV/AIDS and their partners and families.

Anticipated Results and Proposed Indicators:

- Increased numbers of persons know their sero-status and are able to protect themselves and their partners from HIV infection and transmission
    - Number of individuals who received counseling and testing for HIV and received their test results
    - Number of VCCT outlets providing counseling and testing according to national and international standards
- Increased proportion of PLHA screened for TB
    - Number of HIV+ persons tested for TB disease
- Increased referrals of TB patients to quality VCCT services
    - Number of TB patients receiving counseling and testing for HIV

Illustrative Activities and Approaches:

- Support quality improvement and expansion of VCCT services to ensure broader availability of counseling and testing services and ensure links to care and treatment
- Increase referrals of PLHA for TB screening and referrals of TB patients to quality VCCT services

Care, Support and Mitigation

Care activities will include home-based care and strengthened referrals for PLHA to clinical care and other services provided through the Continuum of Care (CoC) network. Support and mitigation activities for PLHA and orphans and vulnerable children will address psycho-social, economic and spiritual problems associated with life-threatening illness.

Anticipated Results and Proposed Indicators:

- Increased numbers of HIV + individuals receive clinical, community based, and/or home-based HIV-related palliative care
  - Number of individuals provided with facility-based, community based, and/or home-based HIV-related palliative care (including those HIV-infected individuals receiving clinical prophylaxis and/or treatment for TB)
- Lay health workers and community members are trained to provide community and Home-based HIV palliative care
  - Number of individuals trained to provide community and home-based HIV palliative care (including HIV/TB)
- Strong referral procedures link co-infected TB patients to HIV/AIDS testing, care and treatment services
  - Number of HIV-TB co-infected clients attending HIV care/treatment services that are receiving treatment for TB disease
- Strong referral procedures link HIV+ patients to TB preventative therapy
  - Number of HIV-infected clients given TB preventive therapy
- AIDS orphans and other vulnerable children receive quality comprehensive care and services supporting their needs for health, education and social well-being
  - Number of OVC served by an OVC program
  - Number of providers/caretakers trained in caring for OVC
- Quality of life of HIV infected and affected individuals improved through receipt of psychosocial, income-generation, and spiritual support services
  - Number of individuals infected or affected by HIV receiving support and mitigation services offered by the program

Illustrative Activities and Approaches:

- Strengthen skills of home based care teams to increase proficiency in care provision, in monitoring side effects, and promotion of treatment adherence
- Improve referrals and follow up between community-based HIV/AIDS care and clinical care and treatment services

- Respond to health, nutritional, psychosocial, economic, and educational needs of PLHA and OVC
- Link community-based HIV prevention activities to the protection of older OVCs, especially young girls who are at risk for infection from exposure to forced or unwanted sex

Treatment

Treatment activities at the non-clinical, community level could include improving linkages to PMTCT programs to ensure that treatment is available to HIV-positive mothers and effective follow-up is available for their children and partners. Similarly, barriers to access to ART by treatment-eligible PLHAs can be reduced by improving referral systems and by building lay health worker capacity to support success of ART, for example through adherence support, community outreach, and improved links between TB programs and ARV services.

Anticipated Results and Proposed Indicators:

- Increased numbers of medically-eligible HIV/AIDS clients receive quality ARV services according to Cambodian national and/or international treatment standards
    - Number of individuals receiving ARV therapy at the end of reporting period
    - Number of individuals who ever received ARV therapy by the end of reporting period
    - Number of HIV-infected clients attending HIV care /treatment services that are receiving treatment for TB disease
- Access to quality ART services for medically-eligible HIV/AIDS clients is improved in the intervention province(s)
    - Number of service outlets providing antiretroviral therapy (includes PMTCT sites)
- Increased numbers of health workers are providing quality ART services according to Cambodian national and/or international treatment standards
    - Number of health workers trained to deliver ART services according to national and/or international standards (includes PMTCT)

Illustrative Activities and Approaches:

- Increase access to treatment for children and integration of non-clinical support for pediatric AIDS patients into community based health services
- Support training of lay health workers and home based care teams to promote treatment readiness and counseling for adherence, management of side effects and provision of non-clinical drugs (in accordance with national and/or international guidelines for non-clinical ART care and support)
- Provide support for transport and improved access by ART patients of laboratory services, related clinical monitoring services, and commodities for pain management and dual protection from HIV/STI and pregnancy, such as condoms

PC33: *Support Family Planning*

Contraceptive prevalence has at least doubled since the 1990s, but remains low overall with the expected below-average results for less-educated and rural women, who are also less likely to receive needed care in pregnancy. Knowledge and receptivity to family planning are improving, although knowledge is constrained by low literacy and intention to use family planning is constrained by fears around side effects and cultural beliefs. Birth intervals need to be widened for their benefits to maternal and child health, and services and referrals for modern, long term and permanent contraceptive methods for both men and women need to be improved and expanded.

Reproductive health and family planning (RH/FP) activities should respond to:

- High unmet need for family planning services
- Quality RH/FP service provision through community-based approaches, especially in rural areas and for the urban poor
- Broad-based, innovative, state-of-the-art behavior change communication to increase knowledge, strengthen the enabling environment for informed RH/FP decision-making, and change behavior.

Anticipated Results and Proposed Indicators:

- Increased use of family planning (birth spacing and birth limiting services).
    - Contraceptive Prevalence Rate (CPR)
    - Total Fertility Rate (TFR)
- Increased use of family planning methods by: postpartum women; young low parity women; zero parity women; and engaged couples
    - Coverage of current family planning users by target group (postpartum women, young low parity women, zero parity women; and engaged couples)
    - Couple Years of Protection (CYP) by target group and method
- Increased knowledge by women, men, and health providers of importance of family planning and appropriate birth spacing in improving nutrition and health status of mother and newborn
    - Numbers of men/women/providers who know about health and nutrition benefits for mother, child and newborn associated with waiting 24 months after the last birth before attempting a pregnancy
    - Numbers of women/men/providers who can correctly identify the recommended number of months women should wait after a birth or an induced or spontaneous abortion before attempting a pregnancy
    - Numbers of women in the 15-19 age group delaying first birth until age 20
- Increased quality of contraceptive counseling—emphasis on side effects, and ensuring that clients receive the method they prefer
    - Increased numbers of clients reporting quality side effects counseling
    - Dropout rate among family planning users
- Increased referrals from community agents to health facility for birth spacing or limiting services
    - Numbers of referees receiving needed FP/RH services
- Increased access of RH/FP services
    - Number public/private providers trained in RH/FP, by sex

- Number Health Centers having sufficient RH/FP commodities
- Number of villages with at least one shop that sells oral contraceptives and condoms

- Increased coverage of reproductive health education
    - Numbers of women/men/adolescents who trained in RH/FP/STI
    - Numbers of women/men/adolescents who understand the meaning of "dual protection"
    - Numbers of married women who participate in training on negotiating condom use
    - Numbers of men/women/providers who participate in gender-based violence education
    - Number of schools implementing adolescent sexual and reproductive health (ASRH) programs
    - Number of Village and private sectors (such as garment factories) implemented ASRH program

Illustrative Activities and Approaches

- Behavior change approaches including mass media, interpersonal counseling, and group education on FP/RH
- Partnerships between public and private sector for distribution/sale of commodities through public and private outlets
- Increased linkages between RH/FP, school and public education programs
- Community-based savings programs for fees and transport for family planning and reproductive services
- Outreach programs for health education and service delivery
- Quality improvement approaches
- Coordination and improved information sharing among NGO, donor, UN and government partners
- Promote use of state-of-the-art, evidence-based tools, best practices and training materials
- Social mobilization to educate women, men and adolescents about birth spacing and birth limiting services as a maternal and child health intervention
- Life skills/RH/gender-based violence education workshops for male and female adolescents
- Workshops/training for women, men, and couples on communication skills and condom use negotiation
- Training to strengthen midwives' technical and business skills
- Identifying and addressing fears about side effects, myths, and traditional beliefs that inhibit care seeking behavior and use of reproductive health and family planning services
- Community postpartum care to include FP and exclusive breastfeeding counseling

VI. Roles and Responsibilities of the Parties

A. Ministry of Health

To achieve the strategic objective and intermediate results of this SOAG, the MOH will:

1) Serve as the implementing RGC partner for the SOAG;

2) Participate with USAID in determining program direction, including review of project proposal and work-plans, in providing input to project implementation plans in support of Cambodian national goals, and in monitoring and evaluating the program's activities;

3) Work with USAID and other donors to ensure RGC and donor support from all sources is mutually supportive and utilized to achieve the RGC's health sector objectives;

4) Facilitate official approval at all necessary levels within the RGC for implementing program activities, and assign appropriate RGC counterparts to the implementing organizations conducting activities under the program;

5) Collaborate and support the implementing organizations in carrying out the specific projects for which they are responsible at the national, provincial, and district levels, including communication to appropriate authorities at those levels that the activities of those implementing organizations should receive support;

6) Assist those implementing organizations that are counterparts with the MOH's institutions/ units in getting entry visas for their approved international employees, and their family members, and when requested, for expert consultants and visitors who are needed for successful execution of the program

7) Arrange, or assign, relevant import tax exemption and VAT tax exemption for all goods, supplies, equipment, vehicles and services provided for the implementation of the program and,

8) Carry out its other obligations under the SOAG.

B. USAID

To achieve the strategic objective and intermediate results of this SOAG, the USAID will:

1) Provide, through implementing organizations, appropriate technical assistance for implementing the program;

2) Contribute to the achievement of the national health strategic plan and the Cambodian Millennium Development Goals (MDGs);

3) Ensure that USAID supported implementing organizations provide reports on program activities to the MOH on a semi-annual basis and that other relevant documents and information produced by the program be provided to the MOH on a timely basis;

4) Consult with the MOH on regular, mutually agreed upon intervals, or at the request of the MOH, on progress towards the achievement of the: a) program's objective; b) performance of obligations under the SOAG; and c) performance of USAID supported implementing organizations, and other matters related to this SOAG; and

5) Carry out its other obligations as stipulated in this SOAG.

VII. Performance Monitoring

The health environment in Cambodia is a dynamic one where diffusion of innovations is rapid and where strategic planning expertise and a commitment to collaborative alliances among public and private partners have the potential to contribute significantly to improvements in the health infrastructure and health outcomes. Given the epidemiological, demographic, behavioral, geographic, organizational, and institutional profile of Cambodia, the developmental nature of the interventions currently being implemented, and the changing political and policy environment, the ability to efficiently modify and redirect programs based on quality program evaluation, surveillance, and research data will be a decided advantage.

In close consultation with the Ministry of Health, USAID will continue support for epidemiological, demographic and behavior research. USAID's support for the HSS and BSS and other applied field research has provided essential information on the HIV/AIDS epidemic, related behaviors and on effective interventions.

In order to manage its assistance and track progress in meeting the objective and the supporting intermediate results, USAID will carry out population-based health surveys in each of the targeted operational districts periodically. These will be designed to complement the national level data already collected through the 2000 and 2005 Demographic and Health Surveys and the 1998 National Health Survey. USAID with other donors will also consider supporting a national level demographic and health survey (including HIV/AIDS and infectious diseases modules) in line with the Ministry's five year Strategic Plan. Periodic facility-based health assessments of health centers in each of the target operational districts may be used to measure progress in improving health information, quality of care and management. These will be carefully coordinated with RGC and other donor-financed data collection and use efforts. Annual sales data will track progress in expanding access to social marketing products.

In consultation with the MOH and other development partners, USAID will continue support to strengthen and expand as necessary the HSS and BSS surveys to provide more complete, national-level information on HIV/AIDS. USAID will also work to improve provincial and OD-level capacities to use these data in the development and evaluation of province and district-specific strategies. USAID will help managers at all levels to use health service statistics, survey data and other information to better manage and monitor their programs.

USAID-funded Partners:

- CARE
- Family Health International (FHI)
- Population Services International (PSI)
- Reproductive Health Association of Cambodia (RHAC)
- Khmer HIV/AIDS NGO Alliance (KHANA)
- Reproductive and Child Health Alliance (RACHA)
- University Research Corp. (URC)
- Helen Keller International (HKI)
- Catholic Relief Service (CRS)
- BASICS
- ACCESS
- A2Z
- Academy for Educational Development (AED)

- US Pharmacopeia-Drug Quality and Information (USP-DQI)
- Management Sciences for Health (MSH)
- Tuberculosis Coalition for Technical Assistance (TBCTA)
- World Health Organization (WHO)
- UNICEF
- Food and Agricultural Organization (FAO)

USAID Donor and Development Partners:

- World Health Organization (WHO) - infectious diseases and child survivial
- Japan Embassy/JICA - USAID Partnership for Global Health, TB
- UNICEF - child survival including immunization and micronutrients
- UNAIDS - HIV/AIDS
- DFID - social marketing, BCC
- United States Centers for Disease Control and Prevention (US-CDC)

STATE DEPARTMENT DOCUMENT NUMBER: 06-299

AMENDMENT TO THE AGREEMENT OF JUNE 21, 1997 BETWEEN THE UNITED STATES OF AMERICA AND MALAYSIA REGARDING AIR TRANSPORT SERVICES

EFFECTED BY EXCHANGE OF NOTES AT KUALA LUMPUR,
AUGUST 7 AND OCTOBER 20, 2006
ENTERED INTO FORCE OCTOBER 20, 2006

CTIA DOCUMENT NUMBER: 9333.001

DIPLOMATIC NOTE

No. 854

The Embassy of the United States of America presents its compliments to the Ministry of Foreign Affairs of Malaysia and refers to the Air Transport Agreement between the Government of the United States of America and the Government of Malaysia, signed at San Francisco, California on June 21, 1997 (the "Agreement").

In light of October 2004 discussions between the two governments concerning removal from the Agreement of provisions relating to regulation of computer reservation systems, the Embassy proposes that Annex III to the Agreement be deleted. If the Ministry concurs with this proposal, the Embassy further proposes that this note and the Ministry's affirmative note in reply shall constitute an agreement on this subject which shall enter into force on the date of the Ministry's note in reply.

The Embassy of the United States of America avails itself of the opportunity to renew to the Ministry of Foreign Affairs of Malaysia the assurances of its highest consideration.

[Seal]

Embassy of the United States of America,
Kuala Lumpur, August 7, 2006.

[Signature]
Conze M. Rabb
Vice Council
United States of America

LETTERHEAD OF THE MINISTRY OF FOREIGN AFFAIRS OF MALAYSIA

CU 773/06 (AME)

The Ministry of Foreign Affairs of Malaysia presents its compliments to the Embassy of the United States of America and with reference to the latter's note (ref. no. 854) dated 7 August 2006 has the honour to inform that the Government of Malaysia is agreeable to the proposed amendments as stated in the above mentioned note.

The Ministry has further the honour to inform that this note in reply thereto shall constitute an agreement between the two Governments on this matter, which shall enter into force on the date of this note.

The Ministry of Foreign Affairs of Malaysia avails itself of the opportunity to renew to the Embassy of the United States of America the assurances of its highest consideration.

Embassy of the United States of America,
KUALA LUMPUR
20 October 2006

[SEAL]

State Department Document Number: 06-300

Agreement Between the United States of America and the Dominican Republic on Trade in Textile and Apparel Goods

Effected by Exchange of Letters at
Santo Domingo and Washington D.C.,
October 19 and 24, 2006
Entered into force October 24, 2006

CTIA Document Number: 13121.000

LETTERHEAD OF EXECUTIVE OFFICE OF THE PRESIDENT
OFFICE OF THE UNITED STATES TRADE REPRESENTATIVE
WASHINGTON, D.C. 20508

October 24, 2006

Vilma I. Arbaje
Directora de Comercio Exterior
Secretaría de Estado de Industria y Comercio
Santo Domingo, República Dominicana

Dear Ms. Arbaje:

I am pleased to acknowledge your letter of October 19, 2006, which reads as follows:

"I have the honor to confirm the following understandings reached between our Governments regarding the Dominican Republic–Central America–United States Free Trade Agreement signed on August 5, 2004 (the "Agreement"):

(1) The Governments of the Dominican Republic and the United States shall consult to determine additional measures to maintain the competitiveness of trouser and suit manfacturers in the Dominican Republic, while at the same time preserving and promoting the use of U.S. fabrics for such garments. Both parties will jointly consult with private sector interests in both countries, and shall conclude the consultation by March 31, 2007.

(2) Subject to the acceptance by the other Parties to the Agreement of any modifications proposed by the Dominican Republic or the United States as a result of the consultations described in paragraph (1), and after the proposed modifications are approved in accordance with the applicable legal procedures of each of the Parties, the Dominican Republic and the United States shall implement the proposed modifications on a date the Parties shall determine. The Governments of the Dominican Republic and the United States shall seek to implement the necessary modifications to the Agreement as expeditiously as possible.

(3) After the Agreement enters into force, the United States will propose a modification to the Agreement's rules of origin, pursuant to Article 3.25 of the Agreement. This modification will provide that, if an apparel good contains a pocket or pockets, the pocket bag fabric must be formed and finished in the territory of one or more of the Parties to the Agreement from yarn wholly formed in the territory of one or more of the Parties to the Agreement in order for that apparel good to qualify as an originating good under the Agreement ("pocket fabric rule of origin modification").

(4) The Dominican Republic is prepared to engage in Article 3.25 consultations immediately after the Agreement enters into force, and will agree to the pocket fabric rule of origin modification in those consultations without condition or delay.

(5) The application by the Dominican Republic of the pocket bag fabric rule of origin modification will provide a benefit to the United States that satisfies the requirements of Article 3.20.3 of the Agreement.

(6) In light of the Dominican Republic's unconditional commitment to agree to the pocket bag fabric rule of origin modification, the United States will provide duty refunds as provided for under Article 3.20.1 of the Agreement with respect to imports of textile or apparel goods of the Dominican Republic that were imported into the United States between January 1, 2004 and the date of entry into force of the Agreement for the Dominican Republic and that satisfy the other requirements of that article.

(7) After the Agreement enters into force, the Dominican Republic will propose a modification to the Agreement's rules of origin, pursuant to Article 3.25 of the Agreement. This modification will provide that apparel goods classifiable in tariff items 6202.91.2011 and 6203.39.9020 shall be considered originating goods under the Agreement regardless of the origin of the fibers, yarns, or fabrics used in the production of the component of the good that determines the tariff classification of the good, provided that the good satisfies all other applicable requirements of Chapter Four (Rules of Origin and Origin Procedures) of the Agreement.

(8) The United States is prepared to engage in Article 3.25 consultations regarding the proposed rule of origin modification described in paragraph (7) immediately after the Agreement enters into force, and will agree to the proposed modification in those consultations without condition or delay.

(9) After the Agreement enters into force, the Dominican Republic will propose a modification pursuant to Article 22.2 of the Agreement. This modification will provide that:

(a) for nonoriginating goods classifiable in tariff items 6202.11.00, 6203.31.90, 6203.33.10, 6203.41.18, 6203.42.40, 6203.43.30, and 6204.62.40, the duty rate to be applied by the United States shall be 0.5 percentage points lower than its MFN rate of duty (for example, if the MFN duty were 20.0 percent, the United States would apply a duty of 19.5 percent), and

(b) for nonoriginating goods classifiable in tariff items 6203.12.2020, 6203.43.40, and 6204.63.35, the duty rate to be applied by the United States shall be 2.0 percentage points lower than its MFN rate of duty (for example, if the MFN duty were 20.0 percent, the United States would apply a duty of 18.0 percent),

provided that the goods are cut or knit to shape, and sewn or otherwise assembled, in the territory of a Party and that the goods meet the conditions for originating goods in Chapter Rules 1 (subject to the limitation in the second sentence of Chapter Rule 2), 3, and 4 for Chapter 62 in Annex 4.1 of the Agreement and paragraph (3) above.

(10) The United States is prepared to engage in consultations regarding the proposed modification described in paragraph (9) immediately after the Agreement enters into force, and will agree to the proposed modification in those consultations without condition or delay.

(11) Subject to the acceptance of the proposed modifications described in paragraphs (3), (7), and (9) by the other Parties to the Agreement, and after the proposed modifications are approved in

accordance with the applicable legal procedures of each of the Parties, the Dominican Republic and the United States shall implement the proposed modifications on a date the Parties shall determine.

I have the honor to propose that this letter and your letter of confirmation in reply shall constitute an agreement between our two Governments."

I have the honor to confirm that the understandings referred to in your letter are shared by my Government, and that your letter and this reply shall constitute an agreement between our two Governments.

Sincerely,
[Signature]
Scott D. Quesenberry
Special Textile Negotiator

LETTERHEAD OF REPUBLICA DOMINICANA
Secretaría de Estado de Industria y Comercio
Santo Domingo, Distritio Nacional
"Afto de la Generación de Empleos"

Courtesy Translation

October 19, 2006

Mr. Scott D. Quesenberry
Special Textile Negotiator
Office of the United States Trade Representative
600 Seventeenth Street, N.W.
Washington, DC 20508

Dear Mr. Quesenberry:

I have the honor to confirm the following understandings reached between our Governments regarding the Dominican Republic–Central America–United States Free Trade Agreement signed on August 5, 2004 (the "Agreement"):

(1) The Governments of the Dominican Republic and the United States shall consult to determine additional measures to maintain the competitiveness of trouser and suit manfacturers in the Dominican Republic, while at the same time preserving and promoting the use of U.S. fabrics for such garments. Both parties will jointly consult with private sector interests in both countries, and shall conclude the consultation by March 31, 2007.

(2) Subject to the acceptance by the other Parties to the Agreement of any modifications proposed by the Dominican Republic or the United States as a result of the consultations described in paragraph (1), and after the proposed modifications are approved in accordance with the applicable legal procedures of each of the Parties, the Dominican Republic and the United States shall implement the imposed modifications on a date the Parties shall determine. The Governments of the Dominican Republic and the United States shall seek to implement the necessary modifications to the Agreement as expeditiously as possible.

(3) After the Agreement enters into force, the United States will propose a modification to the Agreement's rules of origin, pursuant to Article 3.25 of the Agreement. This modification will provide that, if an apparel good contains a pocket or pockets, the pocket bag fabric must be formed and finished in the territory of one or more of the Parties to the Agreement from yarn wholly formed in the territory of one or more of the Parties to the Agreement in order for that apparel good to qualify as an originating good under the Agreement ("pocket fabric rule of origin modification").

(4) The Dominican Republic is prepared to engage in Article 3.25 consultations immediately after the Agreement enters into force, and will agree to the pocket fabric rule of origin modification in those consultations without condition or delay.

(5) The application by the Dominican Republic of the pocket bag fabric rule of origin modification will provide a benefit to the United States that satisfies the requirements of Article 3.20.3 of the Agreement.

(6) In light of the Dominican Republic's unconditional commitment to agree to the pocket bag fabric rule of origin modification, the United States will provide duty refunds as provided for under Article 3.20.1 of the Agreement with respect to imports of textile or apparel goods of the Dominican Republic that were imported into the United States between January 1, 2004 and the date of entry into force of the Agreement for the Dominican Republic and that satisfy the other requirements of that article.

(7) After the Agreement enters into force the Dominican Republic will propose a modification to the Agreement's rules of origin; pursuant to Article 3.25 of the Agreement. This modification will provide that apparel goods classifiable in tariff items 6202.91.2011 and 6203.39.9020 shall be considered originating goods under the Agreement regardless of the origin of the fibers, yarns, or, fabrics used in the production of the component of the good that determines the tariff classification of the good, provided that the good satisfies all other applicable requirements of Chapter Four (Rules of Origin and Origin Procedures) of the Agreement.

(8) The United States is prepared to engage in Article 3.25 consultations regarding the proposed rule of origin modification described in paragraph (7) immediately after the Agreement enters into force, and will agree to the proposed modification in those consultations without condition or delay.

(9) After the Agreement enters into force, the Dominican Republic will propose a modification pursuant to Article 22.2 of the Agreement. This modification will provide that:

(a) for nonoriginating goods classifiable in tariff items 6202.11.00, 6203.31.90, 6203.33.10. 6203.41.18, 6203.42.40, 6203.43.30, and 6204.62.40, the duty rate to be applied by the United States shall be 0.5 percentage points lower than its MFN rate of duty (for example, if the MFN duty were 20.0 percent, the United States would apply a duty of 19.5 percent), and

(b) for nonoriginating goods classifiable in tariff items 6203.12.2020, 6203.43.40, and 8204.63.35, the duty rate to be applied by the United States shall be 2.0 percentage points lower than its MFN rate of duty (for example, if the MFN duty were 20.0. percent, the United States would apply a duty of 18.0 .percent),

provided that the goods are cut or knit to shape, and sewn or otherwise assembled in the territory of a Party and that the goods meet the conditions for originating goods in Chapter Rules 1 (Subject to the limitation in the second sentence of Chapter Rule 2). 3, and 4 for Chapter 62 in Annex 4.1 of the Agreement and paragraph (3) above.

(10) The United States is prepared to engage in consultations regarding the proposed modification descried in paragraph (9) immediately after the Agreement enters into force, and will agree to the proposed modification in those consultations without condition or delay.

(11) Subject to the acceptance of the proposed modifications described in paragraphs (3), (7), and (9) by the other Parties to the Agreement, and after the proposed modifications are approved in accordance with the applicable legal procedures of each of the Parties, the Dominican Republic and the United States shall implement the proposed modifications on a date the Parties stall determine.

I have the honor to propose that this letter and your letter of confirmation in reply shall constitute an agreement between our two Governments.

Sincerely,
[Signature]
Vilma I. Arbaje
Directora do Comercio Exterior
Secretaria de Estado de Industria y Comercio

cc:

The Honorable Amparo Pacheco, Vice Minster of Foreign Trade of Costa Rica
The Honorable Eduardo Ayala, Vice Minster of Foreign Trade of El Salvador
The Honorable Enrique Lacs, Vice Minster of Economy of Guatemala
The Honorable Jorge Rosa, Vice Minster of Industry and Foreign Trade of Honduras
The Honorable Julio Teran, Vice Minister of Trade of Nicaragua

STATE DEPARTMENT DOCUMENT NUMBER: 06-301

AGREEMENT BETWEEN THE UNITED STATES OF AMERICA AND THE REPUBLIC OF PERU ON BEEF SPS ISSUES FOR UNITED STATES–PERU TRADE PROMOTION, WITH ANNEX

EFFECTED BY EXCHANGE OF LETTERS AT LIMA AND WASHINGTON D.C., OCTOBER 6 AND 25, 2006
ENTERED INTO FORCE OCTOBER 25, 2006

CTIA DOCUMENT NUMBER: 13122.000

LETTER EXCHANGE ON BEEF SPS ISSUES FOR UNITED STATES–PERU TRADE PROMOTION AGREEMENT

October 6, 2006

Ambassador Susan C.
Schwab United States Trade Representative
Washington, DC 20508

Dear Ambassador Schwab:

We have the honor to confirm the following understanding reached between the Governments of Peru and the United States of America with respect to trade in beef and beef products of the United States, further to the exchanges of letters between our Governments of January 5, 2006 and April 10, 2006.

The Government of Peru recognizes the measures that the United States has taken with regard to Bovine Spongiform Encephalopathy (BSE), and confirms that, consistent with the World Organization for Animal Health (OIE) Terrestrial Animal Health Code, it shall permit, by no later than October 25, 2006, the importation of all beef and beef products of the United States, other than those listed in paragraphs 3 and 4 of the Annex to this letter, that are accompanied by a United States Department of Agriculture (USDA) Food Safety and Inspection Service (FSIS) Export Certificate of Wholesomeness with the additional certification statements set out in the Annex to this letter. Such USDA FSIS Export Certificate of Wholesomeness with the additional certification statements set out in the Annex shall meet all the Government of Peru's sanitary and health requirements.

The Governments of Peru and the United States recall that the World Trade Organization Agreement on the Application of Sanitary and Phytosanitary Measures allows Members to adopt measures necessary to protect human, animal or plant life or health, subject to the requirement that these measures are not applied in a manner that would constitute a means of arbitrary or unjustifiable discrimination or a disguised restriction on international trade.

We have the honor to propose that this letter, including the Annex thereto, and your letter in reply, confirming that your Government shares this understanding, shall constitute an agreement between our two Governments to enter into force on October 25, 2006.

Sincerely,

[Signature]
Macedes Araoz
Minister of Foreign Trade and Tourism

[Signature]
Juan Jose Salazar
Minister of Agriculture

[Signature]
CariosVallejos Sologuren
Minister of Health

ANNEX

Additional Certification Statements on *USDA FSIS Export Certificate of Wholesomeness* to Accompany U.S. Exports of Beef and Beef Products to Peru

1. The United States has an active BSE surveillance program which meets or exceeds international standards established by the World Organization for Animal Health (OIE).

2. The meat or meat products were derived from animals that were officially given an ante and post mortem inspection by Food Safety and Inspection Service (FSIS) inspection officials.

3. The meat or meat products were produced and handled in a manner which ensures that such products do not contain and are not contaminated with the following specified risk materials: for cattle 30 months of age and older, the brain, skull, eyes, trigeminal ganglia, spinal cord, vertebral column, and dorsal root ganglia; and for any cattle regardless of age, the tonsils and distal ileum of the small intestine.

4. The meat or meat products were produced and handled in a manner which ensures that such products do not contain and are not contaminated with mechanically separated meat from the skull and vertebral column from cattle over 30 months of age.

5. The meat or meat products were derived from federally certified slaughter or processing facilities, operating under the supervision of the FSIS.

6. The slaughter or processing plant where the meat was processed has a HACCP system in place.

7. The meat or meat products are fit for human consumption.

8. The meat or meat products were packed in authorized containers bearing the mark of inspection that includes the number of the facility, and labeled to include the name of the product, lot number, net weight, and date of packing.

9. The meat or meat products are transported in containers or thermo refrigerated vehicles that are monitored to assure that they maintain appropriate refrigerated or frozen temperatures.

10. Trucks and containers have been properly washed and disinfected.

11. The feeding of ruminants with ruminant origin meat-and-bone meal and greaves is prohibited in the United States, and this prohibition has been effectively enforced.

12. The meat or meat products were obtained from cattle that were not subjected to a stunning process, prior to slaughter, with a device injecting compressed air or gas into the cranial cavity, or to a pithing process.

13. The meat or meat products were not derived from animals imported from Canada for immediate slaughter.

LETTERHEAD OF EXECUTIVE OFFICE OF THE PRESIDENT
THE UNITED STATES TRADE REPRESENTATIVE
WASHINGTON, D.C. 20508

LETTER EXCHANGE ON BEEF SPS ISSUES
FOR UNITED STATES–PERU TRADE PROMOTION AGREEMENT

October 25, 2006

The Honorable Mercedes Araoz
Minister of Foreign Trade and Tourism
Calle Uno Oeste No 50, Urb Corpac
San Isidro, Lima 27

The Honorable Juan José Salazar
Minister of Agriculture
Pasaje Francisco de Zela s/n, Piso 6
Jesús María, Lima 11

The Honorable Carlos Vallejos Sologuren
Minister of Health
Avenida Salaverry cuadra 8 s/n
Jesus Maria, Lima 11

Dear Ministers Araoz, Salazar, and Vallejos:

I am pleased to acknowledge your letter of October 6, 2006, which reads as follows:

> "We have the honor to confirm the following understanding reached between the Governments of Peru and the United States of America with respect to trade in beef and beef products of the United States, further to the exchanges of letters between our Governments of January 5, 2006 and April 10, 2006.
>
> The Government of Peru recognizes the measures that the United States has taken with regard to Bovine Spongiform Encephalopathy (BSE), and confirms that, consistent with the World Organization for Animal Health (OIE) Terrestrial Animal Health Code, it shall permit, by no later than October 25, 2006, the importation of all beef and beef products of the United States, other than those listed in paragraphs 3 and 4 of the Annex to this letter, that are accompanied by a United States Department of Agriculture (USDA) Food Safety and Inspection Service (FSIS) Export Certificate of Wholesomeness with the additional certification statements set out in the Annex to this letter. Such USDA FSIS Export Certificate of Wholesomeness with the additional certification statements set out in the Annex shall meet all the Government of Peru's sanitary and health requirements.
>
> The Governments of Peru and the United States recall that the World Trade Organization Agreement on the Application of Sanitary and Phytosanitary Measures allows Members to adopt measures necessary to protect human, animal or plant life or health, subject to the requirement that these measures are not applied in a manner that would constitute a means of arbitrary or unjustifiable discrimination or a disguised restriction on international trade.

> We have the honor to propose that this letter, including the Annex thereto, and your letter in reply, confirming that your Government shares this understanding, shall constitute an agreement between our two Governments to enter into force on October 25, 2006."

I have the honor to confirm that my Government shares this understanding and that your letter, including the Annex thereto, and this reply shall constitute an agreement between our two Governments to enter into force on October 25, 2006.

Sincerely,
[Signature]
Susan C. Schwab

STATE DEPARTMENT DOCUMENT NUMBER: 06-302

MEMORANDUM OF UNDERSTANDING BETWEEN THE DEPARTMENT OF DEFENSE OF THE UNITED STATES OF AMERICA AND THE SECRETARY OF STATE FOR DEFENCE OF THE UNITED KINGDOM OF GREAT BRITAIN AND NORTHERN IRELAND FOR TEST AND EVALUATION PROGRAM (TEP COOPERATION), WITH ANNEXES

SIGNED AT WASHINGTON D.C. AND LONDON,
OCTOBER 18 AND NOVEMBER 7, 2006
ENTERED INTO FORCE NOVEMBER 7, 2006

CTIA DOCUMENT NUMBER: 13123.000

DATE: October 16, 2006
THIS DOCUMENT IS CERTIFIED TO BE A TRUE COPY
CERTIFIED BY: THOMAS BLANN, SES
[Signature]

INTRODUCTION

The Department of Defense of the United States of America (U.S. DoD) and the Secretary of State for Defence of the United Kingdom of Great Britain and Northern Ireland (UK MoD), hereinafter referred to as the "Participants":

Recognizing that the Agreement Concerning Defence Cooperation Arrangements of May 27, 1993 between the Government of the United States of America and the Government of the United Kingdom of Great Britain and Northern Ireland (Chapeau Agreement) will apply to this MOU;

Recognizing the NATO Agreement for the Mutual Safeguarding of Secrecy of Inventions Relating to Defense and for Which Applications for Patents Have Been Made, done in Paris on September 21, 1960, and its implementing procedures (NATO Agreement on Secrecy of Inventions and its Implementing Procedures);

Recognizing the General Security Agreement between the Government of the United Kingdom of Great Britain and Northern Ireland and the Government of the United States of America, dated April 14, 1961, as amended, including the Security Implementing Arrangement thereto, of January 27, 2003 (Security Agreement);

Having a common interest in defense;

Recognizing the benefits to be obtained from standardization, rationalization, and interoperability of military equipments;

Desiring to improve their mutual conventional defense capabilities through the application of emerging technology;

Having a mutual need to engage in a broad range of cooperative or reciprocal Test and Evaluation (T&E) Activities to satisfy common operational requirements; and

Having independently conducted testing of the applications of various technologies, and having recognized the benefits of cooperation in the T&E arena;

Have reached the following understandings:

SECTION I

DEFINITIONS

The Participants have jointly decided upon the following definitions for terms used in this MOU:

Approval in Principle (AIP)	The Performing Participant Managing Agent's preliminary acceptance of a proposed RUTF PA, which will enable both Participants to enter into technical discussions to formulate implementation plans, negotiate costs, and develop a RUTF PA for final approval.
Classified Information	Official information that requires protection in the interests of national security and is so designated by the application of a security classification marking. This Information may be in oral, visual, magnetic, or documentary form or in the form of equipment or technology.
Computer Data Base	A collection of data recorded in a form capable of being processed by a computer. This definition does not include Computer Software.
Computer Program	A set of instructions, rules, or routines recorded in a form that is capable of causing a computer to perform a specific operation or series of operations.
Computer Software	Computer Programs, source code, source code listings, design details, algorithms, processes, flow charts, formulae, and related materials that would enable the software to be reproduced, recreated, or recompiled. Computer Software does not include Computer Data Bases or Computer Software Documentation.
Computer Software Documentation	Owner's manuals, user's manuals, installation instructions, operating instructions, and other similar items, regardless of storage medium, that explain the capabilities of the Computer Software or provide instructions for using the Computer Software.
Contract	Any mutually binding legal relationship under national laws that obligates a Contractor to furnish supplies or services, and obligates one or both of the Participants to pay for them.

Contracting Agency	The entity within the government organization of a Participant, which has authority to enter into, administer, or terminate Contracts.
Contracting Officer	A person representing a Contracting Agency of a Participant who has the authority to enter into, administer, or terminate Contracts.
Contractor	Any entity awarded a Contract by a Participant's Contracting Agency.
Contractor Support Personnel	Persons specifically identified as providing administrative, managerial, scientific, or technical support services to a Participant under a support Contract that prohibits those persons from using Information received under the Contract for any purpose other than those authorized under this MOU.
Controlled Unclassified Information	Unclassified Information to which access or distribution limitations have been applied in accordance with applicable national laws or regulations. It could include Information that has been declassified but remains controlled.
Cooperative Project Personnel (CPP)	Military members or civilian employees of a Participant assigned under a specific Project Arrangement (PA) who perform managerial, engineering, technical, administrative, contracting, logistics, financial, planning, or other functions in furtherance of a Cooperative Test and Evaluation Project Arrangement.
Cooperative Test & Evaluation (CTE) Project Arrangement (PA)	An implementing arrangement under this MOU that specifies the provisions for cooperation on a specific TEP Activity.
Customer Participant	The Participant on whose behalf a test effort is conducted at a Test Facility of the Performing Participant.
Defense Purposes	Manufacture or other use in any part of the world by or for the armed forces of either Participant.
Designated Security Authority (DSA)	The security office approved by national authorities to be responsible for the security aspects of this MOU.
Direct Cost (Applies only to U.S. DoD, but correlates to UK MoD Variable Costs.)	Any item of cost that is easily and readily identified to a.specific unit of work or output within the Test Facility where the use occurred that would not have been incurred if such use had not occurred; it may include costs of labor, materials, facilities, utilities, equipment, supplies, and any other resources of the Test Facility that are consumed or damaged in connection with the use or the maintenance of the Test Facility for the purposes of the use.
Financial Costs	Any costs that, due to their nature, will be paid using monetary contributions from the Participants.
Fixed Costs (Applies only to UK MoD, but correlates to U.S. DoD Indirect Costs.)	Any item of cost that is not easily and readily identified to a specific unit of work or output within a Test Facility where the use occurred. These costs may include salary, insurance, cost of capital, administration costs, general overheads, and any other resources of the Test Facility that are related to the operation or the maintenance of the Test Facility.
Host Participant	The Participant to which Cooperative Project Personnel are assigned for duty pursuant to a CTE PA.

Indirect Cost (Applies only to U.S. DoD, but correlates to UK MoD Fixed Costs.)	Any item of cost that is not easily and readily identified to a specific unit of work or output within the Test Facility where the use occurred; may include general and administrative expenses for such activities as supporting base operations, manufacturing, supervision, procurement of office supplies, and utilities that are accumulated costs allocated among several users.
Information	Any information provided to, generated in, or used in a TEP Activity under this MOU regardless of form or type, including, but not limited to, that of a scientific, technical, business, or financial nature, and also including photographs, reports, manuals, threat data, experimental data, test data, Computer Software, designs, specifications, processes, techniques, inventions, drawings, technical writings, sound recordings, pictorial representations, and other graphical presentations, whether in magnetic tape, computer memory, or any other form and whether or not subject to copyright, Patent, or other legal protections.
Non-financial Costs	Any costs that, due to their nature, will be met using non-monetary contributions from the Participants.
Parent Participant	The Participant to which Cooperative Project Personnel belong.
Participant	A signatory to this MOU represented by its military and civilian personnel. Contractors and Contractor Support Personnel will not be representatives of a Participant under this MOU.
Patent	Grant by the Government of the right to exclude others from making, using, or selling an invention. The term refers to any and all Patents including, but not limited to, Patents of implementation, improvement or addition, petty Patents, utility models, appearance design Patents, registered designs, and inventor certificates or like statutory protection as well as divisions, reissues, continuations, renewals, and extensions of any of these.
Performing Participant	The Participant conducting a test effort at its Test Facilities on behalf of the Customer Participant.
Preferred Rate (Applies only to UK MoD)	The special rate some non-governmental T&E facilities in the United Kingdom charge the UK MoD for T&E services, which is less than the rate charged to commercial customers.
Project Background Information	Information not generated in the performance of a TEP Activity.
Project Equipment	Any test articles, material, equipment, end item, subsystem, component, special tooling or test equipment jointly acquired or provided for use in a TEP PA or a Project Equipment Transfer (PET).
Project Foreground Information	Information generated in the performance of a TEP Activity.
Project Invention	Any invention or discovery formulated or made (conceived or "first actually reduced to practice") in the course of work performed under a PA. The term "first actually reduced to practice" means the first demonstration, sufficient to establish to one skilled in the art to which the invention pertains, of the operability of an invention for its intended purpose and in its intended environment.

Prospective Contractor	Any entity that seeks to enter into a Contract awarded by a Participant's Contracting Agency and that, in the case of a solicitation involving the release of export-controlled Information, is eligible to receive such information.
Reciprocal Use of Test Facilities (RUTF) PA	An implementing arrangement under this MOU that specifies the cost, schedule and performance aspects of a test effort conducted by the Performing Participant's test facility for the Customer Participant.
TEP	The U.S. DoD - UK MoD Test & Evaluation Program.
TEP Activity	Any activity in support of Information exchange, Working Groups, Project Arrangements and PETs, as specified in Section HI (Scope of Work) of this MOU.
TEP Project Arrangement	An implementing arrangement under this MOU that can be either a Reciprocal Use of Test Facilities (RUTF) PA or a Cooperative Test & Evaluation (CTE) PA.
Test and Evaluation (T&E)	The overall process of data taking, data reduction, and the analysis of that data for a specific purpose or application.
Test Facility	Range, facility, or other capability where testing of defense equipment may be performed.
Third Party	A government other than the government of a Participant and any person or other entity whose government is not the government of a Participant.
Variable Costs (Applies only to UK MoD, but correlates to U.S. DoD Direct Costs.)	Any item of cost that is easily and readily identified to a specific unit of work or output within the Test Facility where the use took place, which would not have been incurred if that use had not occurred. This may include: travel and subsistence allowances for personnel involved in support of activities; accommodation and messing; running costs of military equipment/assets; repairs; raw materials, consumable stores and utilities; and services and facilities obtained under existing MoD Contracts.
Working Group	Any group authorized to conduct TEP-related T&E activities by the Management Agents (MAs), in accordance with Section III (Scope of Work) and Section IV (Management).

SECTION II

OBJECTIVES

2.1 This MOU establishes a comprehensive framework for implementing a program of cooperation on mutually determined topics related to defense Test & Evaluation (T&E). Specific objectives of this MOU are:

2.1.1 to share test resources through reciprocal and cooperative use of Test Facilities, ranges, and other test capabilities and testing tools;

2.1.2 to provide for the conduct of cooperative test and evaluation of systems of shared interest;

2.1.3 to conduct joint T&E-related tests and experiments to advance test technologies and procedures;

2.1.4 to conduct cooperative development of test capabilities, test procedures and methods, and test standards and criteria;

2.1.5 to exchange testing-related Information such as test capability specifications, test criteria, standards, procedures, lessons learned, and certain test data;

2.1.6 to provide for the transfer of test technologies and procedures; and

2.1.7 to maximize the effective utilization of each Participant's Test Facilities.

2.2 The Participants intend to use their best efforts to accommodate testing requirements of the other Participant. Each Participant may, however, refuse to conduct a proposed TEP Activity in its country on a case-by-case basis.

SECTION III

SCOPE OF WORK

3.1 The scope of work for this MOU will include the following TEP Activities:

3.1.1 accommodation of testing requirements on a customer-reimbursable basis under the provisions of a Reciprocal Use of Test Facilities Project Arrangement (RUTF PA). This may include access to, or transfer of, test instrumentation and other testing tools;

3.1.2 conduct of Cooperative T&E (CTE PA) on systems of shared interest;

3.1.3 conduct of joint tests and experiments to advance the state of the art of test technology;

3.1.4 cooperative development of new or existing test instrumentation, equipment, other testing tools and Test Facilities;

3.1.5 cooperative development of testing criteria, standards, and procedures;

3.1.6 exchange of information on T&E policy, testing criteria, standards and procedures, and other test-related or test-derived information including, but not limited to, doctrine, tactics and operational requirements related to TEP;

3.1.7 transfer of test technologies and procedures;

3.1.8 familiarization with each other's facilities and identification of potential cooperative T&E opportunities; and

3.1.9 assignment of personnel between the Participants to facilitate development of test capabilities and to assist with the conduct of T&E efforts.

3.2 The following mechanisms will be used to undertake the TEP Activities described in paragraph 3.1:

3.2.1 Information Exchange:

3.2.1.1 Information exchange will take place on an equitable basis in all areas concerning TEP. Computer Data Bases, Computer Software and Computer Software Documentation may be exchanged as Information under this MOU. Information may be exchanged for any purpose concerning TEPs, including harmonizing the Participants' respective TEP requirements and for formulating, developing, and negotiating any TEP Activity. Information exchange need not necessarily coincide in time, technical field, or in the form of Information.

3.2.1.2 Computer Data Bases, Computer Software or Computer Software Documentation associated with TEP Activities may be transferred under this MOU in accordance with national procedures.

3.2.2 Working Groups (WGs):

3.2.2.1 WGs may be established to explore, study, and report on specific T&E issues. A WG normally will be limited in scope to a well-defined area and will endeavor to assess the T&E

issue based on information provided by both Participants in such a way as to arrive at a jointly determined position within a set time limit. Each WG will have its own written terms of reference (TOR).

3.2.3 TEP Project Arrangements (PAs):

3.2.3.1 Reciprocal Use of Test Facilities (RUTF) PA: This type of PA will include specific provisions, consistent with this MOU, that specify the Performing and Customer Participants' responsibilities concerning the objectives, scope of work, estimated test schedule, management structure, financial provisions, contracting provisions, Project Equipment Transfers (PETs) (if required), additional disclosure and use-of-information provisions, security classification for the PA, and other special provisions as required. An Approval in Principle (ALP) will be required prior to negotiating a RUTF PA.

3.2.3.2 Cooperative T&E (CTE) PA: This type of PA will include specific provisions, consistent with this MOU, concerning the objectives, scope of work, sharing of work, management structure, financial provisions (if required), contracting provisions, PETs (if required), additional disclosure and use of information provisions, security classification for the applicable PA and other special provisions as required.

3.2.3.3 The Participants recognize that there may be instances where a project contains elements including cooperative effort as well as the reciprocal use of Test Facilities. Such projects will be treated as cooperative projects. Equitability will be required in all such projects.

3.2.4 Project Equipment Transfer:

3.2.4.1 The Participants recognize that it may be necessary to transfer Project Equipment for the purpose of implementing this MOU but not for the purposes of a specific TEP PA. In such cases, the Participants may conclude PETs consistent with the model at Annex C.

3.2.5 Familiarization Visits:

3.2.5.1 Familiarization visits may occur, in accordance with Section X (Visits to Establishments), to promote awareness of each other's facilities and to identify potential cooperative T&E opportunities.

3.3 Acquisition or production programs that may evolve from cooperation under one or more PAs under this MOU are outside the scope of this MOU and require conclusion of separate arrangements.

SECTION IV

MANAGEMENT (ORGANIZATION AND RESPONSIBILITY)

4.1 The Director, Operational Test & Evaluation (DOT&E), Office of the Secretary of Defense (or his/her successor in the event of reorganization) is designated U.S. MOU Director (U.S. MD). The Director General (Research & Technology) (or his/her successor in the event of reorganization) is designated UK MOU Director (UK MD). The MDs will consult or meet as mutually determined. The chairperson for each meeting will be the host Participant's MD or his/her designee. During such meetings, all decisions will be made unanimously. In the event that the Participants' representatives are unable to reach a timely decision on an issue, they will refer the issue to their respective higher authority for resolution. In the meantime, approved TEP Activities will continue to be implemented without interruption until the issue is resolved by higher authority. The MDs will be responsible for:

4.1.1 monitoring implementation of this MOU and exercising executive-level oversight;

4.1.2 monitoring the overall use and effectiveness of the MOU;

4.1.3 recommending amendments to this MOU to the Participants;

4.1.4 resolving issues brought forth by the Management Agents; and

4.1.5 approving PAs pursuant to paragraph 3.2.3 and the Participants' respective national procedures.

4.2 The Principal Deputy Director, Operational Test & Evaluation (PD, OT&E) (or his/her successor in the event of reorganization or his/her designee), is designated U.S. Management Agent (U.S. MA) for the MOU. The Director of Analysis, Experimentation and Simulation (DAES) (or his/her successor in the event of reorganization or his/her designee) is designated UK Management Agent (UK MA). The MAs will be responsible for:

4.2.1 monitoring and evaluating the work conducted under each TEP Activity and providing guidance and direction as necessary;

4.2.2 designating points of contact (POCs) and exercising overall supervision for Information exchanges pursuant to paragraph 3.2.1;

4.2.3 approving the formation of WGs and their TORs pursuant to paragraph 3.2.2;

4.2.4 granting AIP for RUTF PAs, as specified in paragraph 4.7 below;

4.2.5 developing PAs pursuant to paragraph 3.2.3 and recommending approval of such PAs to the MDs;

4.2.6 establishing a Steering Committee (SC), when considered necessary, to monitor conduct of a CTE PA and exercising overall supervision of the SC members, if established, a Joint Project Office (JPO), if established, or Project Officers (POs) (if no SC or JPO is established);

4.2.7 obtaining Designated Security Authority (DSA) approval for Project Security Instructions and Classification Guides for CTE PAs that contain provisions for the generation or exchange of Classified Information;

4.2.8 developing and entering into PETs pursuant to paragraph 3.2.4;

4.2.9 approving familiarization visits pursuant to paragraph 3.2.5;

4.2.10 monitoring Third Party Sales and Transfers authorized in accordance with Section XII (Third Party Sales and Transfers);

4.2.11 Discussing and employing their best efforts to resolve, with one or both Participants' export control authorities, any export control issues raised by the POs;

4.2.12 approving a Financial Management Procedures Document (FMPD) pursuant to paragraph 5.5, in the absence of an SC; and

4.2.13 forwarding, when necessary, issues to the MDs for resolution.

4.3 Each WG established by the MAs under this MOU will be responsible for:

4.3.1 submitting a proposed TOR to the MAs for approval;

4.3.2 conducting its assigned tasks and providing periodic progress reports to the MAs, including requesting further guidance as necessary; and

4.3.3 submitting final reports to the MAs for submission to the MDs.

4.4 If an SC is established under a particular PA, it will be responsible for:

4.4.1 providing policy and management direction to the POs during PA execution;

4.4.2 monitoring overall implementation, including technical, cost, and schedule performance against requirements;

4.4.3 approving plans for transfers of Project Equipment or disposal of jointly acquired Project Equipment, in accordance with Section VII;

4.4.4 monitoring export control arrangements required to implement this MOU and, if applicable, discussing and resolving export control issues with one or both Participants' export control authorities;

4.4.5 maintaining oversight of the security aspects of a project, including preparing a Project Security Instruction and a Classification Guide in the event that a CTE PA contains provisions for the generation or exchange of Classified Information;

4.4.6 approving assignment of personnel working on a project at the other Participant's facilities in accordance with the provisions set out in Appendix 1 to Annex B;

4.4.7 establishing and approving the detailed financial procedures of a CTE PA through an FMPD in the event that one Participant contracts on behalf of the other Participant or on behalf of both Participants;

4.4.8 resolving issues brought forward by the POs; and

4.4.9 reporting status and activity of assigned PAs on an annual basis to the MAs and MDs.

4.5 In accordance with the terms of any TEP PA, the POs will have primary responsibility for effective implementation, efficient management, and direction of their assigned PA including technical, cost, and schedule performance against requirements. Additionally, the POs will have the responsibilities under paragraph 4.4 if no SC is established for their CTE PA, except that the MAs will be responsible for approving the FMPD and resolving issues brought forth by the POs. The POs will also maintain a list of all PETs by either of the Participants under a TEP PA.

4.6 In accordance with the terms of an approved CTE PA and with the provisions set out in Appendix 1 to Annex B of this MOU attached to the approved CTE PA, a Participant may assign Cooperative Project Personnel (CPP) to the JPO, or to the other Participant's facilities to assist in the implementation of an approved PA.

4.7 Special Procedures for RUTF PAs. The following special procedures will apply only to RUTF PAs:

4.7.1 The Customer Participant's MA will submit a project proposal to the Performing Participant's MA. The project proposal will briefly describe the test effort requested.

4.7.2 The Performing Participant's Test Facility will review the project proposal to determine if it is able and willing to provide the requested test effort.

4.7.3 If the Performing Participant's MA determines that performing the requested test effort is feasible, he or she will notify the Customer Participant's MA of an AIP. AIP does not constitute a commitment to perform the test effort, but provides authority for the Participants to proceed with development and approval of the RUTF PA. If AIP will not be granted, the Performing Participant's MA will notify the Customer Participant's MA as soon as possible.

4.7.4 Each Participant's MA will submit a 12-month forecast of proposed tests to the other Participant's MA for AIP in accordance with a mutually determined schedule. Out-of-cycle project proposals may also be submitted for AIP to the Performing Participant's MA.

4.8 The MAs, SCs, and/or POs will consult or meet as required, but at least annually. The chairperson for each meeting will be the senior representative of the host Participant. During such meetings, all decisions will be made unanimously. In the event that the Participants' representatives are unable to reach a timely decision on an issue, they will refer the issue to their respective higher authority for resolution. In the meantime, approved PAs will continue to be implemented without interruption under the direction of the SC and/or POs while the issue is being resolved by higher authority.

SECTION V

FINANCIAL PROVISIONS

5.1 This MOU creates no financial commitments regarding individual TEP Activities. Detailed descriptions of the financial provisions for a specific project, including the total cost of the project and each Participant's cost share, will be contained in the specific RUTF or CTE PA.

5.2 For RUTF PAs, charges between Participants will be mutually determined on a case-by-case basis and specified in the PA.

5.2.1 For the U.S. DoD, charges will consist of Direct Costs and applicable Indirect Costs. Direct Costs, except for the cost of military personnel chargeable to the Customer Participant, will not be greater than what one component of the Performing Participant would charge to another component of the Performing Participant for the type and scope of the services provided. If required, Indirect Costs may also be charged depending on the nature and specifics of the effort. Indirect Costs charged to the Customer Participant will be only those required by the Performing Participant's laws and regulations.

5.2.2 For the UK MoD, T&E charges for services provided by government facilities will consist of Variable Costs and applicable Fixed Costs. Variable Costs, with the exception of the costs for military personnel chargeable to the Customer Participant, will not exceed those which one component of the Performing Participant would charge to another component of the Performing Participant for the type and scope of the services provided. If necessary, and depending on the nature and specifics of the T&E effort, Fixed Costs may also be charged. Fixed Costs charged to the Customer Participant will only be those required by the Performing Participant's laws and regulations. T&E services provided by nongovernmental facilities will be provided by the UK MoD only when the UK MoD has established a Preferred Rate.

5.2.3 The methods used for determining charges for T&E services by the U.S. DoD and UK MoD are deemed to be substantially equivalent.

5.3 For CTE PAs, each Participant will contribute its equitable share of the full Financial and Non-Financial Costs, including overhead costs, administrative costs and cost of claims, and will receive an equitable share of the results of each CTE PA as mutually determined.

5.4 The financial and non-financial provisions for a CTE PA, including the total cost of the CTE PA and each Participant's share of the total cost, will be included in the CTE PA.

5.5 For each CTE PA, the POs will be responsible for establishing the detailed financial management procedures under which the project will operate. Where necessary, these procedures will be detailed in an FMPD proposed by the POs, and subject to the approval of the MAs or SC, if one is established.

5.6 Each Participant will perform, or have performed, its tasks and will use its best efforts to perform the tasks within the cost estimates specified in each PA. Each Participant will bear the full costs it incurs for performing, managing, and administering its own activities under this MOU and participation in each PA, including its share of the costs of any Contracts awarded pursuant to paragraph 5.13.

5.7 The following costs will be borne entirely by the Participant incurring the costs or on whose behalf the costs are incurred:

5.7.1 costs associated with any unique national requirements identified by a Participant; and

5.7.2 any other costs not expressly stated as shared costs or any other costs outside the scope of this MOU and its PAs.

5.8 For CTE PAs with shared costs that involve the establishment of a JPO with CPP assignments to the other Participant's facilities or the JPO, the CTE PA will address the financial and non-financial contributions required for JPO administration and associated support services including, but not limited to, JPO costs of travel incurred in support of project efforts, JPO training costs, Contract award, Contract administration, office space, security services, information technology services, communications services, and supplies.

5.9 In addition to the shared costs of JPO administration and associated support services costs described in paragraph 5.8, the costs of CPP in the JPO or assigned to the other Participant's facilities will be borne as follows:

5.9.1 The Host Participant will bear the costs of all pay and allowances of Host Participant personnel in the JPO;

5.9.2 The Parent Participant will bear the following CPP-related costs:

5.9.2.1 all pay and allowances;

5.9.2.2 transportation of the CPP, the CPP's dependents, and their personal property to the place of assignment in the Host Participant's nation prior to the CPP's commencement of a tour of duty in the JPO or field activity, and return transportation of the foregoing from the place of assignment in the Host Participant's nation upon completion or termination of the tour of duty;

5.9.2.3 compensation for loss of, or damage to, the personal property of CPP or the CPP's dependents, subject to the Parent Participant's laws and regulations;

5.9.2.4 preparation and shipment of remains and funeral expenses in the event of the death of the CPP or the CPP's dependents; and

5.9.2.5 all temporary duty costs, including travel costs, when such duty is carried out pursuant to a unique requirement of the Parent Participant.

5.10 For CTE PAs that do not involve the establishment of a JPO, but do involve the assignment of one Participant's CPP to the facilities of the other Participant, the Participants will bear the costs as set forth in 5.9. The Host Participant will also be responsible for the following:

5.10.1 all temporary duty costs, including travel costs in connection with the performance of any duty carried out in support of a CTE PA or pursuant to a requirement of the Host Participant;

5.10.2 costs incurred as a result of a change in location of work ordered by the Host Participant during the period of exchange; and

5.10.3 administrative and support costs such as CPP-related training, office space, security services, information technology services, communication services, supplies, and use of facilities and equipment necessary for the performance of tasks assigned to CPP.

5.11 For PETs concluded pursuant to Annex C in which operator personnel from the providing Participant are required, the responsibility for bearing all costs associated with such personnel, including but not limited to salaries and overhead, transportation, and subsistence, will be specified in the PET Form.

5.12 A Participant will promptly notify the other Participant if available funds will not be adequate to fulfill its obligations as mutually determined under any TEP PA, or if it appears that the cost estimates in a PA will be exceeded. The Participants will immediately consult with a view toward continuation on a modified basis.

5.13 For CTE PAs where a Participant contracts on behalf of the other Participant or on behalf of both Participants, the POs or SC as appropriate will be responsible for establishing the detailed financial management procedures under which the PA will operate prior to the transfer of funds between the Participants. The procedures, which will accord with the national accounting and audit requirements of the Participants, will be detailed in an FMPD. Each Participant will provide funds in the amounts and at the times set forth in the estimated schedule for monetary contributions, as specified in the FMPD.

5.14 For CTE PAs, the Participants recognize that it may become necessary for one . Participant, with the written authority of the other Participant, to incur contractual or other responsibilities for the benefit of the other Participant prior to the receipt of the other Participant's funds. In the event that one Participant incurs such responsibilities, the other Participant will make such funds available in such amounts and at such times as may be required by the Contract or other responsibility, and where such performance or cancellation is done following prior consultation by the MAs, will pay its equitable share as mutually determined of any damages and costs that may accrue from the performance or cancellation of the Contract or other responsibility, in advance of the time such payments, damages, or costs are due. Such consultation will be appropriately documented.

5.15 Each Participant will be responsible for the audit of its activities or its Contractors' activities pursuant to a TEP PA. A Participant's audits will be in accordance with its own national practices. For CTE PA efforts where funds are transferred between the Participants, the receiving Participant will be responsible for the internal audit regarding administration of the other Participant's funds in accordance with the receiving Participant's national practices. Audit reports of such funds will be promptly made available by the receiving Participant to the other Participant.

SECTION VI

CONTRACTING PROVISIONS

6.1 If either Participant determines that Contracting is necessary to fulfill its obligations under the scope of work of any TEP PA, that Participant will contract in accordance with its respective national laws, regulations, and procedures.

6.2 When one Participant contracts on its own behalf to perform a task under a PA, it will be solely responsible for its own Contracting, and the other Participant will not be subject to any liability arising from such Contracts without its prior written consent.

6.3 If the Participants determine that it is appropriate under a CTE PA that one Participant contracts on behalf of the other Participant or for both Participants for tasks under that PA, the relevant Contracting Agency will contract in accordance with its national laws, regulations, and procedures. In such cases, appropriate implementing provisions will be specified in the particular PA. If necessary to meet the requirements of a PA, the U.S. DoD or the UK MoD Contracting Agency, as appropriate, will seek deviations from national regulations and procedures wherever possible. Sources from both Participants' industries will be allowed to compete on an equal basis for such

Contracts. The Contracting Agency will be the exclusive source for providing contractual direction and instructions to Contractors and prospective Contractors.

6.4 For all Contracting activities performed by either Participant, the POs will, upon request, be provided a copy of all statements of work prior to the development of invitations to tender/negotiate or solicitations to ensure that they are consistent with the provisions of this MOU and the applicable PA.

6.5 Each Participant's Contracting Agency will insert into its prospective Contracts (and require its Contractors to insert in subcontracts) suitable provisions to satisfy the requirements of this MOU, including Section VIII (Disclosure and Use of Information), Section IX (Controlled Unclassified Information), Section XI (Security), and Section XII (Third Party Sales and Transfers), and Section XVI (General Provisions), including suitable provisions to ensure compliance with the Participants' respective export control laws and regulations, and any corresponding provisions in the PAs. During the Contracting process, each Participant's Contracting Officer will advise prospective Contractors of their obligation to notify the Contracting Agency immediately if they are subject to any license or agreement that will restrict that Participant's freedom to disclose Project Information or permit its use. The Contracting Officer will also advise prospective Contractors to employ their best efforts not to enter into any new agreement or arrangement that will result in such restrictions.

6.6 Each Participant will establish legal arrangements with its Contractors to ensure that its Contractors do not retransfer or otherwise use export-controlled Information furnished by the other Participant for any purpose other than the purposes authorized under this MOU. Such legal arrangements will also provide that the Contractor will not retransfer the export-controlled Information to another Contractor or subcontractor unless that Contractor or subcontractor has been legally bound to limit use of the Information to the purposes authorized under this MOU. Export-controlled Information furnished by one Participant under this MOU may be retransferred by the other Participant to its Contractors only if the legal arrangements required by this paragraph have been established.

6.7 Each Participant will establish legal arrangements with its Prospective Contractors to ensure that its Prospective Contractors do not retransfer or otherwise use export-controlled Information furnished by the other Participant for any purpose other than responding to a solicitation issued in furtherance of the purposes authorized under this MOU. Prospective Contractors will not be authorized any other end use if they are not awarded a Contract. Such legal arrangements will also provide that the Prospective Contractors will not retransfer the export-controlled Information to a prospective subcontractor unless that prospective subcontractor has been legally bound to limit use of the export-controlled Information for the purpose of responding to the solicitation. Export-controlled Information furnished by one Participant under this MOU may be retransferred by the other Participant to its Prospective Contractors only if the legal arrangements required by this paragraph have been established. Upon request, either Participant will provide visibility into the identity of Prospective Contractors and prospective subcontractors receiving export-controlled Information.

6.8 In the event a Participant's Contracting Agency is unable to secure adequate rights to use and disclose Information as required by Section VIII (Disclosure and Use of Information), or is notified by Contractors or prospective Contractors of any restrictions on the disclosure and use of Project Information, that Participant's PO will notify the other Participant's PO of the restriction(s). The Participants will immediately consult, at the appropriate level, to assess the consequences and determine the way ahead.

6.9 Each Participant's PO will promptly advise the other Participant's PO of any cost growth, schedule delay, or performance problems of any Contractor for which its Contracting Agency is responsible. If a Contract has been awarded on behalf of the other Participant or for both Participants, the Participant whose Contracting Agency is responsible for the Contract will consult with the other Participant before terminating the Contract.

6.10 No requirement will be imposed by either Participant for work sharing or other industrial or commercial compensation in connection with this MOU that is not in accordance with this MOU.

SECTION VII

PROJECT EQUIPMENT

7.1 For the purpose of carrying out a TEP PA, each Participant may transfer, without charge to the other Participant, such Project Equipment identified as being necessary for implementing a TEP PA. The TEP PA will provide specific details of any transfer of Project Equipment. Project Equipment identified at the time of TEP PA signature will be detailed in the RUTF PA as set out in Annex A (Model RUTF PA) or the CTE PA as set out in Annex B (Model CTE PA). Project Equipment which cannot be identified at the time of PA signature will be documented, when identified, in a list to be developed and maintained by the POs in the format at Annexes A and B, Appendix 2, Inventory of Project Equipment Transfers (PETs). Approval for all PETs will be in accordance with national procedures.

7.2 For PETs concluded pursuant to Annex C, each Participant may transfer, without charge to the other Participant, Project Equipment, in accordance with the model at Annex C (PET Form). Approval for all PETs will be in accordance with national procedures.

7.3 Project Equipment transferred will be used by the receiving Participant for the purposes specified in the PA or PET Form only. Project Equipment will remain the property of the providing Participant. In addition, the receiving Participant will maintain the Project Equipment in good order, repair, and operable condition. Unless the providing Participant has consented that the transferred Project Equipment may be expended or otherwise consumed without reimbursement to the providing Participant, the receiving Participant will return the Project Equipment to the providing Participant in as good condition as received, reasonable wear and tear excepted, or return the Project Equipment and pay the cost to restore the Project Equipment to such condition. If the Project Equipment is damaged beyond economical repair, the receiving Participant will return the Project Equipment to the providing Participant (unless otherwise specified in writing by the providing Participant) and pay the replacement value as computed pursuant to the providing Participant's national laws, regulations, and procedures. If the Project Equipment is lost or stolen while in the custody of the receiving Participant, the receiving Participant will issue a certificate of loss to the providing Participant and pay the replacement value as computed pursuant to the providing Participant's national laws, regulations, and procedures. The providing and receiving Participants will specify that in no case will any payment respecting damage or loss exceed the amount indicated in the applicable TEP PA or PET Form.

7.4 The providing Participant will make every effort to ensure that the Project Equipment is furnished in a serviceable and usable condition according to its intended purpose. However, the providing Participant makes no warranty or guarantee of fitness of the Project Equipment for a particular purpose or use, and makes no commitment to alter, improve, or adapt the Project Equipment, or any part thereof.

7.5 The providing Participant will transfer the Project Equipment for the approved period, unless extended by written amendment or terminated by either Participant. The duration of the transfer period will not exceed the effective period of the TEP PA or PET Form.

7.6 The providing Participant, at its expense, will deliver the Project Equipment to the receiving Participant at the location mutually approved. Responsibility for Project Equipment will pass from the providing Participant to the receiving Participant at time of receipt. Any further transportation will be mutually determined by the Participants and specified in the TEP PA or PET Form.

7.7 The providing Participant will furnish the receiving Participant such information as is necessary to enable the Project Equipment to be used.

7.8 The receiving Participant will inspect and inventory the Project Equipment upon receipt. The receiving Participant will also inspect and inventory the Project Equipment prior to its return (unless the Project Equipment is to be expended or consumed).

7.9 Upon expiration or termination of the transfer period specified in the TEP PA or the PET Form (taking into account any extension), the receiving Participant will return the Project Equipment and related Information, at its expense, to the providing Participant at the location mutually approved. Responsibility for the Project Equipment will pass from the receiving Participant to the providing Participant at the time of its receipt. Any further transportation is the responsibility of the providing Participant.

7.10 The receiving Participant will provide written notice of consumption or expenditure of Project Equipment approved for such consumption or expenditure. In the event the intended consumption or expenditure does not occur, the receiving Participant will, unless otherwise determined by the providing Participant, return the Project Equipment, at its expense, to the providing Participant to the location mutually approved. Any further transportation is the responsibility of the providing Participant.

7.11 The Participants will ensure, by all reasonable means, the protection of intellectual property rights in Project Equipment.

7.12 Each Participant waives all claims against the other Participant for damage to or loss of jointly acquired Project Equipment arising from the performance of official duties. However, if the Participants mutually decide to repair damaged jointly acquired Project Equipment in order to complete PA efforts, the cost of such repair will be shared in a manner that results in sharing the total costs of the PA in the proportions established for the Participants' contributions under the PA. In any case, if the damage or loss is caused by reckless acts, reckless omission, willful misconduct or gross negligence, the costs of any liability, including the cost of repairs, will be borne by the responsible Participant.

7.13 Any Project Equipment that is jointly acquired on behalf of the Participants for use under any TEP PA will be disposed of as mutually approved by the SC, or the MAs, if an SC is not established.

7.14 Disposal of jointly acquired Project Equipment may include a transfer of the interest of one of the Participants in such Project Equipment to the other Participant, the sale or transfer of such Project Equipment to a Third Party in accordance with Section XII (Third Party Sales and Transfers), or sale or transfer to other entities. The Participants will share the consideration from jointly acquired Project Equipment transferred or sold to a Third Party or other entity in the same ratio as costs are shared in the CTE PA.

SECTION VIII

DISCLOSURE AND USE OF INFORMATION

8.1 General

Both Participants recognize that successful cooperation depends on full and prompt exchange of Information necessary for carrying out each TEP Activity. The Participants intend to acquire sufficient Information, and rights to use such Information to promote the objectives of this MOU.

The nature and amount of Information to be acquired will be consistent with Section II (Objectives), Section III (Scope of Work), Section VI (Contracting Provisions), and the PAs and PET Forms under this MOU. Subject to the rights both Participants are accorded under this MOU, title to Project Foreground Information generated by a Participant or its Contractor will reside in that Participant and/or its Contractors, in accordance with that Participant's national laws, regulations, and policies. Nothing in this MOU will affect title to Project Background Information of the Participants or their Contractors.

8.2 Transfer of Project Information will be consistent with furnishing Participant's applicable export control laws and regulations. Unless otherwise restricted by duly authorized officials of the furnishing Participant at the time of transfer to the other Participant, all export-controlled Information furnished by one Participant to the other Participant may be retransferred to the other Participant's Contractors, subcontractors, Prospective Contractors, and prospective subcontractors, subject to the requirements of paragraphs 6.6 and 6.7 of Section VI (Contracting Provisions). Export-controlled Information may be furnished by U.S. Contractors and their subcontractors or U.S. Prospective Contractors and their prospective subcontractors to the other Participant's Contractors, subcontractors, Prospective Contractors, and prospective subcontractors pursuant to this MOU subject to the conditions established in licenses or other approvals issued by the U.S. Government under the requirements of the Arms Export Control Act and the International Traffic in Arms Regulations, and the Export Administration Act and the Export Administration Regulations, and any amendments thereto. Export-controlled Information may be furnished by UK Contractors and their subcontractors or UK Prospective Contractors and their prospective subcontractors to the other Participant's Contractors, subcontractors, Prospective Contractors, and prospective subcontractors pursuant to this MOU subject to the conditions established in licenses or other approvals issued by the UK Government under the requirements of the Export Control Act and its relevant UK regulations, and the Council of the European Union Regulation Setting up a Community Regime for the Control of Exports of Dual-use Items and Technology, and any amendments thereto. The furnishing of all export-controlled Information by the Contractors and subcontractors of one Participant's nation to those of the other pursuant to this MOU will be subject to the conditions established in export licenses or other approvals issued by the government of the exporting Contractor or subcontractor in accordance with that exporting nation's applicable export control laws and regulations.

8.3 Information Exchange and Working Groups. The disclosure and use provisions that govern exchange of Information and WGs authorized in Section III (Scope of Work), paragraphs 3.2.1 and 3.2.2 are as follows:

8.3.1 Disclosure: At its discretion, the furnishing Participant may disclose Information to the other Participant. Prior written permission from the furnishing Participant will be required for further disclosure of the Information by the receiving Participant to any other entity, for example, a Contractor. Such permission will not be required in the case of further disclosure to the receiving Participant's Contractor support personnel, who are under a legally binding non-disclosure agreement.

8.3.2 Use: Use of Information will be for information and evaluation purposes only. Written permission from the furnishing Participant will be required for any other use.

8.4 RUTF PAs. Unless the Participants mutually determine otherwise in writing, the following provisions will apply to RUTF PAs:

8.4.1 Unless mutually determined otherwise, test results and/or analyses will be transferred via government-to-government channels only.

8.4.2 The Customer Participant's use of test results and/or analyses will be for Defense Purposes only. Written permission from the Performing Participant will be required for any other use.

8.4.3 The Performing Participant and its contractors will use test results and/or analyses for information and evaluation purposes only. Written permission from the Customer Participant will be required for any other use.

8.5 Other TEP Activities. Unless the Participants mutually determine otherwise in writing, and except as noted above in paragraph 8.4 regarding RUTF PAs, the following disclosure and use provisions which govern other TEP Activities authorized in Section III (Scope of Work), paragraphs 3.2.3 and 3.2.4, will apply.

8.6 Government Project Foreground Information:

8.6.1 Disclosure: Project Foreground Information generated by a Participant's military or civilian employees will be disclosed without charge to the other Participant.

8.6.2 Use: Each Participant may use or have used on its behalf government Project Foreground Information without charge for its Defense Purposes only. The furnishing Participant will retain all its rights with respect to such government Project Foreground Information. The sale or other transfer of government Project Foreground Information will be subject to the provisions of Section XII (Third Party Sales and Transfers) of this MOU.

8.7 Contractor Project Foreground Information:

8.7.1 Disclosure: Contractor Project Foreground Information generated and delivered by Contractors will be disclosed without charge to the other Participant.

8.7.2 Use: Each Participant may use or have used on its behalf all Contractor Project Foreground Information without charge for its Defense Purposes only. The Participant whose Contractors generate and deliver Contractor Project Foreground Information will also retain rights of use therein in accordance with the applicable Contract(s). The sale or other transfer of Contractor Project Foreground Information will be subject to the provisions of Section XII (Third Party Sales and Transfers) of this MOU.

8.8 Government Project Background Information:

8.8.1 Disclosure: Each Participant, upon request, will disclose to the other Participant any relevant government Project Background Information generated by its military or civilian employees, provided that:

8.8.1.1 such government Project Background Information is necessary to or useful in the TEP Activity, with the furnishing Participant determining whether it is necessary to or useful in the TEP Activity;

8.8.1.2 such government Project Background Information may be made available without incurring liability to holders of proprietary rights;

8.8.1.3 disclosure of such government Project Background Information is consistent with national disclosure policies and regulations of the disclosing Participant; and

8.8.1.4 any disclosure or transfer of such government Project Background Information to Contractors is consistent with the furnishing Participant's export control laws and regulations.

8.8.2 Use: A Participant may use or have used on its behalf all government Project Background Information disclosed by the other Participant without charge for conducting the TEP Activity for which it was provided only. However, subject to proprietary rights held by other than the Participants, government Project Background Information may be used for Defense Purposes by the receiving Participant without charge when the use of such government Project Background Information is necessary for the use of Project Foreground Information. The furnishing Participant (after consultation with the receiving Participant) will determine whether such use of government Project Background Information is necessary. The furnishing Participant will retain all its rights with respect to such government Project Background Information.

8.9 Contractor Project Background Information:

8.9.1 Disclosure: Any relevant Contractor Project Background Information (including information subject to proprietary rights), which is or has been generated outside of the TEP Activity and delivered by Contractors of one of the Participants, will be disclosed to the other Participant provided the following provisions are met:

8.9.1.1 such Contractor Project Background Information is necessary to or useful in the TEP Activity, with the furnishing Participant determining whether it is necessary to or useful in the TEP Activity;

8.9.1.2 such Contractor Project Background Information may be made available without incurring liability to holders of proprietary rights;

8.9.1.3 disclosure of such Contractor Project Background Information is consistent with national disclosure policies and regulations of the furnishing Participant; and

8.9.1.4 any disclosure or transfer of such Contractor Project Background Information to Contractors is consistent with the furnishing Participant's export control laws and regulations.

8.9.2 Use: Project Background Information delivered by Contractors under Contracts awarded in accordance with a PA may be used by or for the receiving Participant without charge for project purposes, and for other Defense Purposes in accordance with such fair and reasonable terms as are arranged with the Contractor. Any other Contractor Project Background Information furnished by one Participant's Contractors may be used by the other Participant without charge for project purposes only and for other Defense Purposes in accordance with such fair and reasonable terms as arranged with the Contractor, and may be subject to further restrictions by holders of proprietary rights. The furnishing Participant will retain all its rights with respect to Contractor Background Information.

8.10 Alternative Uses of Project Information:

8.10.1 The prior written consent of each Participant's government will be required for the use of Project Foreground Information for any purposes other than those provided for in this MOU or any of its PAs.

8.10.2 Any Project Background Information provided by one Participant will be used by the other Participant for the purposes set forth in this MOU only, unless otherwise consented to in writing by the furnishing Participant's government.

8.11 Project Information Subject to Proprietary Rights:

8.11.1 All unclassified project Information subject to proprietary rights will be identified, marked, and handled as Controlled Unclassified Information in accordance with Section IX (Controlled Unclassified Information). All classified project Information subject to proprietary rights will be identified, marked, and handled in accordance with Section IX (Controlled Unclassified Information) and Section XI (Security).

8.12 Patents

8.12.1 Each Participant will include in its Contracts a provision governing the disposition of rights in regard to Project Inventions and Patent rights relating thereto, which either:

8.12.1.1 Provides that the Participant will hold title to all Project Inventions together with the right to make Patent applications for the same, free of encumbrance from the Contractor; or

8.12.1.2 Provides that the Contractor will hold title (or may elect to retain title) for Project Inventions together with the right to make Patent applications for the same, while securing for the Participant a license for the Project Inventions, and any Patents therefore, on terms in compliance with the provisions of paragraph 8.12.2 below.

8.12.2 In the event that a Contractor holds title (or elects to retain title) for a Project Invention, the contracting Participant will secure for both Participants nonexclusive, irrevocable, royalty-free licenses under all Patents secured for that invention, to practice or have practiced the patented Project Invention for Defense Purposes throughout the world.

8.12.3 The provisions of paragraphs 8.12.4 through 8.12.8 below will apply in regard to Patent rights for all Project Inventions made by any Participant's military or civilian employees, including those within Government-owned facilities, and for all Project Inventions made by Contractors for which the contracting Participant holds title or is entitled to acquire title.

8.12.4 Where a Participant owns title to a Project Invention, or has the right to receive title to a Project Invention, that Participant will consult with the other Participant regarding the filing of a Patent application for such Project Invention. The Participant which has or receives title to such Project Invention will, in other countries, file, cause to be filed, or provide the other Participant with the opportunity to file on behalf of the Participant holding title, or its Contractors, as appropriate, Patent applications covering that Project Invention. If a Participant having filed or caused to be filed a Patent application decides to stop prosecution of the application or maintenance of the Patent granted thereon, that Participant will notify the other Participant of that decision and permit the other Participant to continue the prosecution or the maintenance.

8.12.5 The Participants will provide to each other copies of Patent applications filed and Patents granted with regard to Project Inventions.

8.12.6 Each Participant will grant to the other Participant a non-exclusive, irrevocable, royalty-free license under its Patents for Project Inventions, to practice or have practiced, by or on behalf of the Participant, the patented Project Invention for Defense Purposes throughout the world.

8.12.7 Patent applications that contain Classified Information to be filed under this MOU or any of its PAs will be protected and safeguarded in accordance with the requirements contained in Section XI (Security) of this MOU.

8.12.8 Each Participant will notify the other Participant of any Patent infringement claims made in its territory arising in the course of work performed under any PA of this MOU. Insofar as possible, the other Participant will provide Information available to it that may assist in defending the claim. Each Participant will be responsible for handling all Patent infringement claims made in its territory, and will consult with the other Participant during the handling, and prior to any settlement, of such claims. The Participants will share the costs of resolving Patent infringement claims in a manner they determine to be fair at the time the Patent infringement claim is resolved. The Participants will, in accordance with their national laws and practices, give their authorization and consent for all use and manufacture in the course of work performed under the project of any invention covered by a Patent issued by their respective countries.

SECTION IX

CONTROLLED UNCLASSIFIED INFORMATION

9.1 Except as otherwise provided in this MOU or as authorized in writing by the originating Participant, Controlled Unclassified Information provided or generated pursuant to this MOU and any of its PAs will be controlled as follows:

9.1.1 such Information will be used only for the purposes authorized for use of Project Information as specified in Section VIII (Disclosure and Use of Project Information);

9.1.2 access to such Information will be limited to personnel whose access is necessary for the permitted use under subparagraph 9.1.1, and will be subject to the provisions of Section XII (Third Party Sales and Transfers);

9.1.3 each Participant will take all lawful steps, which may include national classification, available to it to keep such Information free from further disclosure (including requests under any legislative provisions), except as provided in subparagraph 9.1.2, unless the originating Participant consents to such disclosure. In the event of unauthorized disclosure, or if it becomes probable that the Information may have to be further disclosed under any legislative provision, immediate notification will be given to the originating Participant.

9.2 To assist in providing the appropriate controls, the originating Participant will ensure that Controlled Unclassified Information is appropriately marked. All U.S. export-controlled Information will be marked as either –International Traffic in Arms Regulations (ITAR)-Controlled" or –Export Administration Regulations (EAR) Controlled", or other U.S. export controlled markings, as appropriate. All UK export-controlled Information will be marked as –UK Export Controlled" or other UK export control markings, as appropriate. The Participants will decide, in advance and in writing, on the markings to be placed on any other type of Controlled Unclassified Information. Where necessary appropriate markings will be specified:

9.2.1 for Working Groups in the TOR;

9.2.2 for RUTF PAs or PETs, through an exchange of correspondence between the POs; or

9.2.3 for CTE PAs in the Project Security Instruction.

9.3 Controlled Unclassified Information provided or generated pursuant to this MOU will be handled in a manner that ensures control as provided for in paragraph 9.1.

9.4 Prior to authorizing the release of Controlled Unclassified Information to Contractors, the Participants will ensure the Contractors are legally bound to control such Information in accordance with the provisions of this Section.

SECTION X

VISITS TO ESTABLISHMENTS

10.1 Each Participant will permit visits to its government establishments, agencies, and laboratories, and Contractor industrial facilities by employees of the other Participant or by employees of the other Participant's Contractor(s), provided that the visit is authorized by both Participants and the employees have any necessary and appropriate security clearances and a need-to-know.

10.2 All visiting personnel will be required to comply with security regulations of the host Participant. Any Information disclosed or made available to visitors will be treated as if supplied to the Participant sponsoring the visiting personnel, and will be subject to the provisions of this MOU.

10.3 Requests for visits by personnel of one Participant to a facility of the other Participant will be coordinated through official channels, and will conform to the established visit procedures of the host Participant. Requests for visits will bear the name of this MOU and the appropriate PA.

10.4 Lists of personnel of each Participant required to visit, on a continuing basis, facilities of the other Participant will be submitted through official channels in accordance with recurring international visit procedures.

SECTION XI

SECURITY

11.1 All Classified Information provided or generated pursuant to this MOU and any of its PAs will be stored, handled, transmitted, and safeguarded in accordance with the Security Agreement between the United Kingdom of Great Britain and Northern Ireland and the United States of America, dated April 14, 1961, amended July 5 and December 19, 1983, and its Implementing Arrangement of January 27, 2003.

11.2 Classified Information will be transferred only through official government-to-government channels or through channels approved by the Designated Security Authorities (DSAs) of the Participants. Such Classified Information will bear the level of classification, denote the country of origin, the conditions of release, and the fact that the information relates to this MOU and the applicable PA.

11.3 Each Participant will take all lawful steps available to it to ensure that Classified Information provided or generated pursuant to this MOU and any of its PAs is protected from further disclosure, except as permitted by paragraph 11.8, unless the other Participant consents to such disclosure. Accordingly, each Participant will ensure that:

11.3.1 the recipient will not release the Classified Information to any government, national, organization, or other entity of a Third Party without the prior written consent of the originating Participant in accordance with the procedures set forth in Section XII (Third Party Sales and Transfers);

11.3.2 the recipient will not use the Classified Information for other than the purposes provided for in this MOU; and

11.3.3 the recipient will comply with any distribution and access restrictions on Classified Information that is provided under this MOU.

11.4 The Participants will investigate all cases in which it is known or where there are grounds for suspecting that Classified Information provided or generated pursuant to this MOU has been lost or disclosed to unauthorized persons or other entities. Each Participant also will promptly and fully inform the other Participant of the details of any such occurrences, and of the final results of the investigation and of the corrective action taken to preclude recurrences.

11.5 When a CTE PA contains provisions for the exchange of Classified Information, the POs will prepare a Project Security Instruction (PSI) and a Classification Guide (CG) for the CTE PA. The PSI and the CG will describe the methods by which Project Information will be classified, marked, used, transmitted, and safeguarded. The PSI and CG will require that markings for all export-controlled Classified Information also include the applicable export-controlled markings as specified in paragraph 9.2 of Section DC (Controlled Unclassified Information). The PSI and CG will be developed by the PO within three months after the CTE PA enters into effect. They will be reviewed and forwarded to the Participants' DSAs for approval and will be applicable to all government and Contractor personnel participating in the project. The CG will be subject to regular review and revision with the aim of downgrading the classification whenever this is appropriate. The PSI and the CG will be approved by the appropriate DSA prior to the transfer of any Classified Information or Controlled Unclassified Information.

11.6 The DSA of the Participant in which a classified Contract is awarded pursuant to this MOU will assume responsibility for administering within its territory security measures for the protection of the Classified Information, in accordance with its laws and regulations. Prior to the release to a Contractor, prospective Contractor, subcontractor, or prospective subcontractor of any Classified Information provided or generated under this MOU, the DSAs will:

> 11.6.1 ensure that such Contractor, prospective Contractor, subcontractor or prospective subcontractor and their facility (ies) have the capability to protect the Classified Information adequately under the Participant's national security laws, regulations, and policies;
>
> 11.6.2 grant a security clearance to the facility (ies);
>
> 11.6.3 grant a security clearance for all personnel whose duties require access to Classified Information;
>
> 11.6.4 ensure that all persons having access to the Classified Information are informed of their responsibilities to protect the Classified Information in accordance with national security laws and regulations, and provisions of this MOU;
>
> 11.6.5 carry out periodic security inspections of cleared facilities to ensure that the Classified Information is properly protected; and
>
> 11.6.6 ensure that access to the Classified Information is limited to those persons who have a need-to-know for purposes of the MOU and any of its PAs.

11.7 Contractors, prospective Contractors, subcontractors or prospective subcontractors that are determined by the DSAs to be under financial, administrative, policy or management control of nationals or entities of a Third Party, may participate in a Contract or subcontract requiring access to Classified Information provided or generated pursuant to this MOU or any of its PAs only when enforceable measures are in effect to ensure that nationals or other entities of a Third Party will not have access to Classified Information. If enforceable measures are not in effect to preclude access by nationals or other entities of a Third Party, the other Participant will be consulted for approval prior to permitting such access.

11.8 For any facility wherein Classified Information is to be used, the responsible Participant or Contractor will approve the appointment of a person or persons to exercise effectively the responsibilities for safeguarding at such facility the Classified Information pertaining to this MOU and any of its PAs. These officials will be responsible for limiting access to Classified Information involved in this MOU and any of its PAs to those persons who have been properly approved for access and have a need-to-know.

11.9 Each Participant will ensure that access to the Classified Information is limited to those persons who possess requisite security clearances and have a specific need for access to the Classified Information in order to participate under this MOU or any of its PAs.

11.10 Information provided or generated pursuant to this MOU may be classified as high as SECRET. The existence of this MOU is UNCLASSIFIED and the contents are UNCLASSIFIED. The classification of the existence of any PA and its contents will be stated in that PA.

SECTION XII

THIRD PARTY SALES AND TRANSFERS

12.1 Except to the extent permitted in paragraph 12.2, the Participants will not sell, transfer title to, disclose, or transfer possession of Project Foreground Information (or any item produced either wholly or in part from the Project Foreground Information) or jointly acquired or produced Project Equipment to any Third Party without the prior written consent of the government of the other Participant. Furthermore, neither Participant will permit any such sale, disclosure, or transfer, including by the owner of the item, without the prior written consent of the government of the other Participant. Such consent will not be given unless the government of the intended recipient consents in writing with the Participants that it will:

12.1.1 not retransfer, or permit the further retransfer of, any equipment or Information provided; and

12.1.2 use, or permit the use of, the equipment or Information provided only for the purposes specified by the Participants.

12.2 Each Participant will retain the right to sell, transfer title to, disclose, or transfer possession of Project Foreground Information that:

12.2.1 is generated solely by either that Participant or that Participant's Contractors in the performance of that Participant's work allocation under Section III (Scope of Work);

12.2.2 does not include any Project Foreground Information or Project Background Information of the other Participant, and whose generation, test, or evaluation has not relied on the use of Project Equipment of the other Participant.

12.3 In the event questions arise as to whether the Project Foreground Information (or any item produced either wholly or in part from the Project Foreground Information) that a Participant intends to sell, transfer title to, disclose, or transfer possession of to a Third Party is within the scope of paragraph 12.2, the matter will be brought to the immediate attention of the other Participant's MA. The Participants will resolve the matter prior to any sale or other transfer of such Project Foreground Information (or any item produced either wholly or in part from the Project Foreground Information) to a Third Party.

12.4 A Participant will not sell, transfer title to, disclose, or transfer possession of Project Equipment or Project Background Information provided by the other Participant to any Third Party without the prior written consent of the government of the Participant that provided such equipment or Information. The providing Participant's government will be solely responsible for authorizing such transfers and, as applicable, specifying the method and provisions for implementing such transfers.

12.5 Consent for Third Party sales and transfers of Project Foreground Information, jointly acquired Project Equipment, or any item produced either wholly or in part from Project Foreground Information, will be subject to foreign policy, national security considerations, and national laws, regulations, and policies.

SECTION XIII

LIABILITY AND CLAIMS

13.1 With the exception of claims for loss of or damage to Project Equipment transferred from one Participant to the other Participant, which is addressed in Section VII (Project Equipment), claims arising under this MOU, including RUTF PAs, will be dealt with in accordance with paragraph 1 of the Chapeau Agreement.

13.2 CTE PAs. The Participants will share any costs of third party claims required to be shared under subparagraph 1(b) (ii) of the Chapeau Agreement in the same proportions as costs are shared in the PA.

13.3 The Participants will share any costs required to be shared under subparagraph 1(b) (iv) of the Chapeau Agreement as follows:

13.3.1 For Contracts where one Participant contracts solely on its own behalf, the Participant awarding the Contract will pay the cost of claims arising under that Contract.

13.3.2 For Contracts where one Participant contracts on behalf of the other Participant, the Participant on whose behalf the Contract was awarded will pay the cost of claims arising under the Contract. The contracting Participant will not indemnify Contractors against third party liability claims, unless otherwise mutually determined in the PA.

13.3.3 For Contracts awarded on behalf of both Participants, the costs of claims arising under such Contracts will be shared in a manner that results in sharing the total costs of the PA in the proportions established for the Participants' contributions under the PA. The contracting Participant will not indemnify Contractors against third party liability claims, unless otherwise mutually determined in a PA.

13.4 RUTF PAs. Unless mutually determined in a PA, the Performing Participant will pay all costs of third party claims under subparagraph 1(b) (ii) of the Chapeau Agreement.

13.5 Under subparagraph 1(b) (iv) of the Chapeau Agreement, where one Participant contracts to fulfil its commitments under a PA, the Participant awarding the Contract will pay the cost of claims arising under that Contract.

SECTION XIV

CUSTOMS DUTIES, TAXES, AND SIMILAR CHARGES

14.1 Customs duties, import and export taxes, and similar charges will be administered in accordance with each Participant's respective laws and regulations. Insofar as existing national laws and regulations permit, the Participants will endeavor to ensure that such readily identifiable duties, taxes, and similar charges, as well as quantitative or other restrictions on imports and exports, are not imposed in connection with work carried out under a TEP Activity.

14.2 Each Participant will use its best efforts to ensure that customs duties, import and export taxes, and similar charges are administered in a manner favorable to the efficient and economical conduct of the work. If any such duties, taxes, or similar charges are levied, the Participant in whose country they are levied will bear such costs. Any such costs will not be considered to fall under either Participant's shared costs.

14.3 If, in order to apply European Union (EU) regulations, it is necessary to levy duties, then these will be met by the EU member end recipient. To this end, parts of the components of the equipment coming from outside the EU will proceed to their final destination accompanied by the relevant customs document enabling settlement of duties to take place. The duties will be levied as a cost over and above that Participant's shared cost of the project.

SECTION XV

SETTLEMENT OF DISPUTES

15.1 Disputes between the Participants arising under or relating to this MOU or any of its PAs will be resolved by consultation between the Participants only and will not be referred to a national court, an international tribunal, or to any other person or entity for settlement.

SECTION XVI

GENERAL PROVISIONS

16.1 All activities of the Participants under this MOU and its PAs will be carried out in accordance with their national laws and regulations, including their export control laws and regulations. The commitments of the Participants will be subject to the availability of funds for such purposes.

16.2 In the event of a conflict between the provisions of this MOU and any TEP PA or PET Form, this MOU will take precedence.

16.3 The Participants will not communicate with representatives of the press, television, radio, internet or other communication media on any matter concerning a TEP Activity conducted under this MOU without prior consultation between the Participants. Such approval shall not be unreasonably withheld or delayed.

SECTION XVII

AMENDMENT, TERMINATION, ENTRY INTO EFFECT, AND DURATION

17.1 This MOU, or PAs to this MOU, may be amended by the mutual written consent of the Participants.

17.2 This MOU, or PAs to this MOU, may be terminated at any time by the mutual written consent of the Participants. In the event the Participants consent to terminate this MOU, or PAs to this MOU, the Participants will consult prior to the date of termination to ensure termination on the most economical and equitable terms. Termination of this MOU will result in the termination of all PAs to this MOU.

17.3 Either Participant may terminate this MOU, or PAs to this MOU, upon 180 days written notice of its intent to terminate to the other Participant. Such notice will be the subject of immediate consultation to decide upon the appropriate course of action to conclude the activities under this MOU or PA. In the event of such termination, the following rules apply:

17.3.1 The Participants will continue participation, financial or otherwise, in all PAs subject to the notice of termination, up to the effective date of termination;

17.3.2 Except as to Contracts awarded on behalf of both Participants, each Participant will be responsible for its own project-related costs associated with termination of the Project. For Contracts awarded on behalf of both Participants, the terminating Participant will pay all Contract modification and termination costs that would not otherwise have been incurred but for the decision to terminate. However, in no event will a terminating Participant's total financial contribution, including Contract termination costs, exceed that Participant's total financial contribution for the PA being terminated;

17.3.3 All Project Information and rights therein received under the provisions of this MOU or PAs prior to termination of the MOU or its PAs will be retained by the Participants, subject to the provisions of this MOU and its PAs;

17.3.4 If requested by the other Participant, the terminating Participant may continue to administer the project Contract(s) which it awarded on behalf of the other Participant on a reimbursable basis; and

17.3.5 Additional PA termination provisions consistent with this Section may be established in the PA.

17.4 The respective benefits and commitments of the Participants regarding Section VII (Project Equipment), Section VIII (Disclosure and Use of Project Information), Section IX (Controlled Unclassified Information), Section XI (Security), Section XII (Third Party Sales and Transfers), Section XIII (Liability and Claims), and Section XV (Settlement of Disputes) will continue notwithstanding termination or expiration of this MOU or any of its PAs.

17.5 This MOU, which consists of seventeen (17) Sections and three (3) Annexes, will come into effect on the date of last signature, and will remain in effect for fifteen (15) years unless terminated by either Participant. This MOU will be automatically extended for successive five-year periods unless one Participant notifies the other in writing that it does not desire this MOU to be extended.

The foregoing represents the understandings reached between the Department of Defense of the United States of America and the Secretary of State for Defence of The United Kingdom of Great Britain and Northern Ireland, upon the matters referred to herein.

SIGNED, in duplicate, in the English language.

FOR THE DEPARTMENT OF DEFENSE OF THE UNITED STATES OF AMERICA	FOR THE SECRETARY OF STATE FOR DEFENCE OF THE UNITED KINGDOM OF GREAT BRITAIN AND NORTHERN IRELAND
[Signature]	[Signature]
Dr. Charles E. McQueary Name	*P. Sotton* Name
Director. Operational Test and Evaluation Title	*Director General Research and Technology* Title
18 October 2006 Date	*7 November 2006* Date
Pentagon, Washington DC Location	*London* Location

ANNEX A
MODEL RECIPROCAL USE OF TEST FACILITIES (RUTF) PROJECT ARRANGEMENT
(PA)
RUTF PA NUMBER*
UNDER THE U.S. DoD-UK MoD
TEST AND EVALUATION PROGRAM (TEP) COOPERATION MEMORANDUM OF UNDERSTANDING (MOU)

DATED

CONCERNING
(FULL DESIGNATION OF THE PROJECT AND LOCATION)

(DATE)

INTRODUCTION

This Reciprocal Use of Test Facilities (RUTF) Project Arrangement (PA) is entered into pursuant to the MOU between the Department of Defense of the United States of America (U.S. DoD) and the Secretary of State for Defence of The United Kingdom of Great Britain and Northern Ireland (UK MoD) for Test and Evaluation Program (TEP) Cooperation of (*date*).

The Participants have determined that conducting ______________at ______________ is mutually beneficial.

(RUTF PAs may involve performance of multiple test events at multiple Test Facilities over multiple years.)

SECTION I

DEFINITION OF TERMS AND ABBREVIATIONS

(Define only those terms used in this PA that have not been defined in the MOU.)

SECTION II

T&E OBJECTIVES

The T&E objectives of this _________ PA are:

a. To determine the _____________

b. To evaluate the ______________

c. To accomplish/improve _______

SECTION III

SCOPE OF WORK

Test Description

a.______is designed to ______

b.______is comprised of _____

* The US. DoD will assign the Project Arrangement number.

(Include any Customer Participant-provided test personnel, equipment (other than Project Equipment), or other assistance in this Section, and provide the applicable details in the PA.)

Test Facility Services

(Outline the tasks and services to be performed by the Test Facility.)

The following T&E Activities will be performed by ________during a period of up to _______ days/weeks during _____.

a.

b.

c.

The following support will be provided by the Test Facility:

(For example: Technical and analytical assistance, consultation for preparation of the test plan, qualified personnel to conduct the T&E, any other specified support to customer.)

SECTION IV

ESTIMATED TEST SCHEDULE

Day/Week/Month 1: ***(List of activities to occur each day)***
Dates

Day/Week/Month 2: ***(List of activities to occur each day)***
Dates

Day/Week/Month 3: ***(List of activities to occur each day)***
Dates

The dates and duration of the test are subject to change by either Participant. The U.S. DoD and UK MoD POs will keep each other informed of progress and apprise each other of potential schedule change, delay, or cancellation.

The final report will be transmitted to the MAs six months before the termination date of this PA.

SECTION V

MANAGEMENT

This PA will be directed and administered on behalf of the Participants by one PO from each Participant. POs are responsible for the implementation of the provisions of the MOU and PA. Direct liaison between the Participants' POs is authorized. Alternate POs may also be designated. The POs are:

U.S. DoD PO: Name:________________________

Title/Position ____________________

Organization ____________________

Mail Address ____________________

Phone & Fax ____________________

E-mail ________________________

UK MoD PO: Name: ________________________

Title/Position ____________________

Organization ____________________

Mail Address ____________________

Phone & Fax ____________________

E-mail ________________________

(The POs, as appropriate, may develop and agree to a test plan.)

Command, Control, Safety, and Security Considerations

The performing Participant will retain command and control over all facilities, personnel, equipment, and support units. Both Participants will adhere to standing operating procedures regarding command, control, safety, and security, except where mutually determined otherwise in writing. In accordance with Section XI (Security) of the MOU:

a. The Participants are responsible for the security of all publications and reference material.

b. The performing Participant is responsible for the security of test site materials and . publications.

c. POs will coordinate security requirements prior to all classified testing.

SECTION VI

FINANCIAL PROVISIONS

The cost estimate for performance of the tasks under this PA is $ (USD)________ and/or £ (GBP) _______. In no event will the Performing Participant exceed this cost estimate without the prior written consent of the Customer Participant. If the Performing Participant has reason to believe that this cost estimate will be exceeded, the Performing Participant will immediately notify the Customer Participant and will set forth a new cost estimate together with supporting documentation. The Participants will consult as soon as possible regarding the action to be taken in view of the revised cost estimate.

The Performing Participant will submit a request for payment to the Customer Participant at least 45 days in advance of the test requiring payment of the estimated cost. The Customer Participant will review the request for payment and respond with payment no later than five (5) days prior to the scheduled commencement of the test. The test effort will not commence until the funds are received.

(The Participants may adjust the time periods as necessary for each test)

Upon completion of the test (including submission of the final report), the Performing Participant will provide a final statement of account to the Customer Participant, which details the actual costs incurred and payments received from the Customer Participant. After completing review of the final statement of account, the Participants will reconcile the account and make any final payments.

Requests for payment will contain the following information:

Date
PA Number
Invoice ID
Financial Manager's Contact Information
Financial Coding
Invoice Total

SECTION VII

CONTRACTING PROVISIONS

(Insert any contracting provisions required for the PA. If none, so state.)

SECTION VIII

ADDITIONAL DISCLOSURE AND USE OF INFORMATION PROVISIONS

(Insert any additional disclosure and use of information provisions needed to implement the PA. If none, so state.)

SECTION IX

CLASSIFICATION

(Only one of the three following possibilities must be selected:)

a. No Classified Information will be exchanged under this PA; or

b. The highest level of Classified Information exchanged under this PA is: CONFIDENTIAL; or

c. The highest level of Classified Information exchanged under this PA is: SECRET.

The existence of this PA is ***[Insert classification]*** and its contents are ***[Insert classification]***.

SECTION X

PRINCIPAL ORGANIZATIONS INVOLVED

(List Test Facilities and other organizations of the Participants.)

SECTION XI

PROJECT EQUIPMENT TRANSFERS

NOTES:

Providing Participant	Receiving Participant	QTY	Description	Part/ Stock #	Consumables/ Non-Consumables	Return Date	Replacement Value

1. Specifically identify the test article. In the event that the cooperative efforts under the PA require the provision of other Project Equipment to either Participant, a list of such Project Equipment must be developed in general accordance with the preceding table. (Project Equipment that cannot be identified at the time of PA signature will be documented, when identified, in a list to be developed and maintained by the POs, and in the format at Appendix 2 to this Annex.)

2 If jointly acquired Project Equipment is an aspect of the cooperative efforts under the PA, then terms and conditions for the disposal of such jointly acquired Project Equipment must be included in the PA.

SECTION XII

SPECIAL PROVISIONS

All activities of the Participants under this RUTF PA will be carried out in accordance with their national laws and regulations, including their export control laws and regulations.

(Insert any other special provisions needed to implement the PA.)

SECTION XIII

ENTRY INTO EFFECT, DURATION, AND TERMINATION

This ______ RUTF PA, a TEP Activity under the MOU between the Department of Defense of the United States of America and the Secretary of State for Defence of The United Kingdom of Great Britain and Northern Ireland, will come into effect upon signature by the Participants, and will remain in effect for ____ years unless terminated by either Participant. It may be extended by the written mutual determination of the Participants.

FOR THE DEPARTMENT OF DEFENSE OF THE UNITED STATES OF AMERICA

____

[Signature]

____

Name

Director. Operational Test and Evaluation

Title

____

Date

____

Location

FOR THE SECRETARY OF STATE FOR DEFENCE OF THE UNITED KINGDOM OF GREAT BRITAIN AND NORTHERN IRELAND

____

[Signature]

____

Name

Director General Research and Technology

Title

____

Date

____

Location

APPENDIX 1 – COST ESTIMATE MODEL

COST ESTIMATE FOR THE *(Name of Test)*
Test Period *(Insert Date)*

DIRECT COSTS

Item	Task Description/Service	Labor	Facility Use	Materials	Travel	Total
1	Test Planning					
2	Test Article Safety Inspection					
3	Test Preparation & Setup					
4	Flight Time & Flt Support					
5	Range Firings					
6	Ground Support (Telemetry & Communications)					
7	Toxic Fumes Test					
8	Human Factors Evaluation					
9	Technical / Review Meetings					
10	Secure Storage					
11	Supplies & Materials					
12	Contingencies (Retest, etc...)					
13	Data Analysis					
n	Report Preparation					

INDIRECT COSTS

(Indirect Costs charged to the Customer Participant will be only those required by the Performing Participant's laws and regulations.

These costs may be itemized in a format similar to the table above.)

RUTF PA ID # XXXX

Note: The above table is a notional example. Cost estimate tables should be tailored to align with the requirements of particular tests.

APPENDIX 2 – INVENTORY OF PROJECT EQUIPMENT TRANSFERS

Providing Participant	Receiving Participant	QTY	Description	Part/ Stock #	Consumables/ Non-Consumables	Return Date	Replacement Value

ANNEX B
MODEL COOPERATIVE TEST & EVALUATION (CTE)
PROJECT ARRANGEMENT (PA)
CTE PA NUMBER*
UNDER THE U.S. DoD – UK MoD
TEST AND EVALUATION PROGRAM (TEP)
COOPERATION MEMORANDUM OF
UNDERSTANDING (MOU) DATED

CONCERNING
(FULL DESIGNATION OF THE PROJECT)

INTRODUCTION

This Cooperative Test & Evaluation (CTE) Project Arrangement (PA) is entered into pursuant to the MOU between the Department of Defense of the United States of America (U.S. DoD) and the Secretary of State for Defence of The United Kingdom of Great Britain and Northern Ireland (UK MoD) for Test and Evaluation Program (TEP) Cooperation ***(date).***

SECTION I

DEFINITION OF TERMS AND ABBREVIATIONS

(Define only those terms used in this PA that have not been defined in the MOU.)

SECTION II

OBJECTIVES

The objectives of this __________ PA are:

a. The development of ______________________________
____.

b. The improvement of ______________________________.
____.

SECTION III

SCOPE OF WORK

The following work will be performed under this PA.

a. Develop __________________________
____.

b. Evaluate __________________________
____.

c. Design, fabricate, and test ____________________________
____.

* The U.S. DoD will assign the Project Arrangement number.

SECTION IV

SHARING OF TASKS

The sharing of tasks will be as follows:

a. The U.S. DoD will ________________________________
____.

b. The UK MoD will ________________________________
____.

c. U.S. DoD and UK MoD will jointly ___________________
____.

SECTION V

BREAKDOWN AND SCHEDULE OF TASKS (OPTIONAL)

(Use this format when the tasks covered under this project may be performed using multiple phases, requiring milestones, or decision points.)

The Project will proceed according to the following phases and schedule. Note that national priorities may pre-empt agreed-upon schedules in PAs.

Phase 1 Description of Phase 1	*Start* MM/DD/YYYY	*End* MM/DD/YYYY

(Milestone 1) (e.g., Transmittal of Feasibility Report)

Phase 2 Description of Phase 2	*Start* MM/DD/YYYY	*End* MM/DD/YYYY

(Milestone 2) (e.g., Decision to proceed to Phase 3)

Phase 3 Description of Phase 3	*Start* MM/DD/YYYY	*End* MM/DD/YYYY

(Milestone 3) (e.g., Evaluation, analysis of results)

(Add as many phases as necessary.)

The final report must be transmitted to the MAs six months before the termination date for this PA.

SECTION VI

MANAGEMENT

(If a PA does not require a Steering Committee, use the following format to set forth how the PA will be managed.)

Alternative 1

1. This PA will be directed and administered on behalf of the Participants by one Project Officer (PO) from each Participant. The POs are:

U.S. DoD PO Name: ___________________________

Title/Position ____________________

Organization ____________________

Address______________________

____

____

Email__________________________

UK MoD PO Name: ________________________

Title/Position ____________________

Organization _____________________

Address _______________________

____

____

Email __________________________

2. Project offices will be established in _________ ***(name of U.S. facility and location)*** and in _________ ***(name of UK facility and location)***. The POs are responsible for management of those tasks listed as national responsibilities in Section IV (Sharing of Tasks) in this PA.

3. Particular Management Procedures:

[Mention only those additional management responsibilities not covered under Section IV–Management (Organization and Responsibility) of the MOU.]

(If a Project requires the establishment of a Steering Committee, use the following format to set forth how the Project will be managed.)

Alternative 2

1. This PA will be directed and administered on behalf of the Participants by an

organization consisting of a Steering Committee (SC) and one Project Officer (PO) from each Participant. The SC members are:

U.S. DoD Co-Chairman Name _______________________

Title/Position _________________________

Organization _______________________

Address ________________________

____

____

Email ____________________________

UK MoD Co-Chairman Title/Position ______________________

Organization _______________________

Address ________________________

____

____

Email ___________________________

2. The POs are:

U.S. DoD PO________________________

Title/Position ________________________

Organization ________________________

Address ________________________

____

____

Email ________________________

U.S. DoD PO Title/Position________________________

Organization ________________________

Address ________________________

____

____

Email ________________________

3. Project offices will be established in ***(name of U.S. facility and location)*** and in ***(name of UK facility and location)***. The POs are responsible for management of those tasks listed as national responsibilities in Section IV (Sharing of Tasks) in this PA.

4. Particular Management Procedures:

(Mention only those additional management responsibilities not covered under Section IV of the MOU. For instance, if a PA will be administered by one joint program office (JPO) staffed by members from each Participant, add the following paragraph:

4.X Either Participant may assign personnel to the JPO to assist in administering a PA. The Host Participant will provide office space and administrative support to personnel of the other Participant in accordance with the Host Participant's normal practice. A Participant's assigned personnel will be subject to the normal procedures and regulations of the Host Participant. Provisions for the personnel provided are described in Appendix 1 to this PA.)

SECTION VII

FINANCIAL PROVISIONS

The Participants estimate that the cost of performance of the tasks under this PA will not exceed \$(USD) ___ and £(GBP) ___.

Cooperative efforts of the Participants over and above the mutually determined tasks set forth in the Scope of Work, Sharing of Tasks, and Financial Provisions Sections will be subject to amendment to this PA or signature of a new PA.

(If a PA will involve the assignment of CPP, the PA will include a provision that refers to paragraphs 5.8 - 5.10 of the MOU, identifies which Participant is sending or hosting CPP, and specifies the number of CPP to be assigned. In addition, the PA will include the amount of financial and non-financial contributions related to CPP in one of the two alternatives below in this Section.)

(If a PA will not involve one Participant contracting for the other or both Participants, and no funds will be exchanged between the Participants, use the following format for the financial arrangements. Both financial and non-financial contributions should be included in the total US DoD and UK MoD costs.)

Alternative 1

The U.S. DoD tasks will not cost more than: $(USD) ________.

The UK MoD tasks will not cost more than: £(GBP) ________.

Or:

(If a PA will involve one Participant contracting for the other Participant or both Participants, or the Participants will transfer or exchange funds between them, use the following format for the financial arrangements.)

Alternative 2

(Cost of performance includes Financial and Non-financial Costs.)

	Year 1	Year 2	Year 3	Year 4	Year 5	Total
U.S. DOD						
UK MOD						

(Using the above table and whatever description is necessary, explain and demonstrate how the PA will be funded Identify both financial (funds) and non-financial (range time, use of equipment, etc.) contributions and identify the amount of funds to be transferred between the Participants.)

(The Financial Management Procedures Document (FMPD) should be developed by the POs and submitted to the SC (if appropriate) for approval The FMPD should include, as a minimum, schedule, handling, funding levels by year, and auditing procedures for monetary contributions anticipated for this PA.)

SECTION VIII

CONTRACTING PROVISIONS

(Insert any contracting provisions required for the PA. If none, so state.)

SECTION IX

ADDITIONAL DISCLOSURE AND USE OF INFORMATION PROVISIONS

(Insert any additional disclosure and use of Information provisions unique to the PA. If none, so state.)

SECTION X

CLASSIFICATION

Only one of the three following possibilities must be selected:

a. No Classified Information will be exchanged under this PA;

b. The highest level of Classified Information exchanged under this PA is CONFIDENTIAL; or

c. The highest level of Classified Information exchanged under this PA is SECRET.

The existence of this PA is ***[Insert classification]*** and its contents are ***[Insert classification]***.

SECTION XI

PRINCIPAL ORGANIZATIONS INVOLVED

(List Test Facilities and other organizations of the Participants.)

SECTION XII

PROJECT EQUIPMENT TRANSFERS

NOTES:

Providing Participant	Receiving Participant	QTY	Description	Part/ Stock #	Consumables/ Non-Consumables	Return Date	Replacement Value

1. In the event that the cooperative efforts under the PA require the provision of Project Equipment to either Participant, a list of such Project Equipment must be developed in general accordance with the preceding table. (Project Equipment that cannot be identified at the time of PA signature will be documented, when identified, in a list to be developed and maintained by the POs in the format at Appendix 2 to this Annex.)

2. If jointly acquired Project Equipment is an aspect of the cooperative efforts under the PA, provisions for the disposal of such jointly acquired Project Equipment must be included in the PA.

SECTION XIII

SPECIAL PROVISIONS

All activities of the Participants under this CTE PA will be carried out in accordance with their national laws and regulations, including their export control laws and regulations.

(Insert any other special provisions needed to implement the PA.)

SECTION XIV

ENTRY INTO EFFECT, DURATION, AND TERMINATION

This ________________________ CTE PA, a Project under the MOU between the Department of Defense of the United States of America and the Secretary of State for Defence of The United Kingdom of Great Britain and Northern Ireland, will come into effect upon signature by the Participants, and will remain in effect for ______ years unless terminated by either Participant. It may be extended by the written mutual determination of the Participants.

FOR THE DEPARTMENT OF DEFENSE OF THE UNITED STATES OF AMERICA

[Signature]

Name
Director. Operational Test and Evaluation
Title

Date

Location

FOR THE SECRETARY OF STATE FOR DEFENCE OF THE UNITED KINGDOM OF GREAT BRITAIN AND NORTHERN IRELAND

[Signature]

Name
Director General Research and Technology
Title

Date

Location

APPENDIX 1 - COOPERATIVE PROJECT PERSONNEL (CPP)

ASSIGNMENT OF (*Insert name of Project*) COOPERATIVE PROJECT PERSONNEL

1.0 Purpose and Scope.

1.1 This Appendix to the Project Arrangement (PA) establishes the provisions that will govern the conduct of the U.S. DoD or UK MoD Cooperative Project Personnel (CPP). During the term of the PA, each Participant will be permitted to assign military members or civilian employees of its U.S. DOD/UK MoD to the Joint Project Office (JPO) if established, or to U.S. DoD or UK MoD field activities in accordance with this Appendix. CPP will be able to perform all the responsibilities for the positions assigned to them under this PA. Commencement of assignments will be subject to any requirements that may be imposed by the other Participant or its government regarding acceptance of PA CPP, such as, but not limited to, visas and visit request documentation. The U.S. DoD and UK MoD SC representatives, or in the event no SC is established the POs, will determine the length of tour for the positions at the time of initial assignment.

1.2 CPP will be assigned to the JPO or to U.S. DoD or UK MoD field activities for project work (including work at U.S. or UK Contractor facilities) and will report to their designated supervisor within those organizations regarding that work. The designated supervisor will be responsible for the creation of a document describing the duties of each CPP position, which will be subject to approval by the SC or, in the event no SC is established the POs. CPP will not act as liaison officers for their parent organizations or governments. Such personnel, however, may act from time to time on behalf of their SC representative (or PO as applicable), if the latter so authorizes in writing.

1.3 CPP will not be assigned to command or other positions that would require them to exercise responsibilities that are reserved by law or regulation to an officer or employee of the Host Participant's government.

2.0 Security.

2.1 The U.S. DoD and UK MoD SC representatives (or POs as applicable) will establish the maximum level of security clearance required, if any, to permit CPP to have access to Classified Information and facilities in which Classified Information is used in accordance with the Project Security Instruction (PSI) and Classification Guide (CG). Access to Classified Information and facilities in which Classified Information is used will be consistent with, and limited by, Section II (Objectives) and Section III (Scope of Work) of this PA and the corresponding provisions of this Appendix, and will be kept to the minimum required to accomplish the work assignments.

2.2 The Parent Participant will file visit requests for the CPP through prescribed channels in compliance with the Host Participant's procedures. The Participants will cause security assurances to be filed, through their respective embassies, specifying the security clearances for the CPP being assigned. The security assurances will be prepared and forwarded through prescribed channels in compliance with established procedures.

2.3 The Participants will use their best efforts to ensure that both the U.S. DoD and UK MoD personnel assigned to the JPO or field activities are made aware of, and required to comply with, applicable laws and regulations, as well as the requirements of Section VIII (Disclosure and Use of Project Information), Section IX (Controlled Unclassified Information), and Section XI (Security) of the MOU, and the corresponding provisions of this Appendix, and the PSI and CG. Prior to commencing assigned duties, CPP will, if required by the Host Participant's laws, regulations, policies, or procedures, sign a certification concerning the conditions and responsibilities of CPP.

2.4 CPP will at all times be required to comply with the security and export laws, regulations, and procedures of the Host Participant, as briefed in accordance with paragraph 3.2 of this Appendix.

Any violation of security or export procedures by CPP during their assignment will be reported to the Parent Participant for appropriate action. CPP committing willful violations of security or export laws, regulations, or procedures during their assignments will be withdrawn from the project with a view toward appropriate administrative or disciplinary action by the Parent Participant.

2.5 All Classified Information made available to CPP will be considered as Classified Information furnished to the U.S. DoD or UK MoD, and will be subject to all of the provisions and safeguards provided for in this PA, this Appendix, the MOU, the PSI, and the CG.

2.6 CPP will not have personal custody of Classified Information or Controlled Unclassified Information, unless approved by the JPO, if established and as authorized by the Parent Participant. They will be granted access to such Information in accordance with the provisions of the PSI during normal duty hours when access is necessary to perform project work. They may not have unsupervised access to classified libraries or operating centers, or to document catalogues, unless the Information therein is releasable to the public.

2.7 CPP will not serve as a conduit between the U.S. DoD and the UK MoD for requests for and/or transmission of Classified Information or Controlled Unclassified Information unless specifically authorized by the PSI.

3.0 Administrative Matters.

3.1 The tax treatment of income received by CPP from the Parent Participant will be determined by reference to the tax legislation of the government of the Host Participant and the government of the Parent Participant, subject to the terms of any double taxation agreement in force between the government of the host Participant and the government of the Parent Participant, or by the terms of the NATO Status of Forces Agreement.

3.2 Upon or shortly after arrival, CPP will be informed by the JPO or Host Participant duty station about applicable laws, orders, regulations, and customs and the need to comply with them. CPP will also be provided briefings arranged by the JPO or Host Participant duty station regarding applicable entitlements, privileges, and obligations such as:

3.2.1 Any medical or dental care that may be provided to CPP and their dependents at the Host Participant medical facilities, subject to applicable laws and regulations, including reimbursement when required by such laws and regulations, and any bilateral or multilateral agreements or arrangements;

3.2.2 Purchasing and patronage privileges at military commissaries, exchanges, theaters, and clubs for CPP and their dependents, subject to applicable laws and regulations, and any bilateral or multilateral agreements or arrangements; and

3.2.3 Responsibility of CPP and those dependents accompanying them to obtain motor vehicle liability insurance coverage in accordance with laws and regulations applicable in the area where they are residing. In case of claims involving the use of private motor vehicles by CPP and their dependents, the recourse will be against such insurance.

3.3 The POs, through the JPO and Host Participant field activities, will establish standard operating procedures for CPP in the following areas:

3.3.1 Working hours, including holiday schedules;

3.3.2 Leave authorization, consistent to the extent possible with the military or civilian personnel regulations and practices of both Participants;

3.3.3 Dress regulations, consistent to the extent possible with the military or civilian personnel regulations and practices of both Participants; and

3.3.4 Performance evaluations, recognizing that such evaluations must be rendered in accordance with the providing Participant's military or civilian personnel regulations and practices.

3.4 CPP committing an offense under the laws of the government of either Participant may be withdrawn from this project with a view toward further administrative or disciplinary action by the Parent Participant. Disciplinary action, however, will not be taken by the Host Participant against CPP from the Parent Participant, nor will CPP from the Parent Participant exercise disciplinary authority over Host Participant personnel. In accordance with the Host Participant's laws, regulations, and procedures, the Host Participant will assist the Parent Participant in carrying out investigations of offenses involving CPP.

APPENDIX 2 - INVENTORY OF PROJECT EQUIPMENT TRANSFERS

Providing Participant	Receiving Participant	QTY	Description	Part/ Stock #	Consumables/ Non-Consumables	Return Date	Replacement Value

ANNEX C
MODEL PROJECT EQUIPMENT TRANSFER (PET) FORM
PET NUMBER *(PET-XXXX*)*

UNDER THE U.S. DoD-UK MoD
TEST AND EVALUATION PROGRAM (TEP) COOPERATION
MEMORANDUM OF UNDERSTANDING (MOU)

DATED

BETWEEN

(Insert titles of the Organizations participating in the transfer)

INTRODUCTION

This Project Equipment Transfer (PET) is entered into pursuant to the Memorandum of Understanding (MOU) between the Department of Defense of the United States of America (U.S. DoD) and the Secretary of State for Defence of The United Kingdom of Great Britain and Northern Ireland (UK MoD) for Test and Evaluation Program (TEP) Cooperation dated ***(insert effective date of the TEP MOU)***. This TEP PET Form is being executed by authorized representatives of the providing and receiving Participants pursuant to Section VII (Project Equipment) of the TEP MOU.

SECTION I

DESCRIPTION AND QUANTITY

1.1 The following Project Equipment will be transferred by the providing Participant to the receiving Participant:

Providing Participant	Receiving Participant	QTY	Description	Part/ Stock #	Consumables/ Non-Consumables	Return Date	Replacement Value

(Fill in as appropriate)

1.2 ***(Choose one of the following alternatives, or use both if both situations apply.)***

Alternative A – Use when return of Project Equipment is planned.

None of the Project Equipment identified in paragraph 1.1 is intended to be consumed or expended during the course of the TEP Activity described in paragraph 2.1.1.

Alternative B – Use when return of Project Equipment is not planned due to its consumption during the activity.

The Project Equipment (specify as appropriate by highlighting in paragraph 1.1) described in paragraph 1.1 is intended to be consumed or expended during the course of the TEP Activity described in paragraph 2.1.1.

* The U.S. DoD will assign the PET number.

SECTION II

PURPOSE

2.1 The purpose of this PET is to support the following TEP Activity.

2.1.1 ***(Fill in as appropriate)***

SECTION III

MANAGEMENT AND RESPONSIBILITIES

3.1 Each Participant will establish a point of contact that will be responsible for implementing this PET.

3.1.1 For the providing Participant the point of contact is:

Name______________________________

Title/Position_______________________

Organization________________________

Address____________________________

____

____

Email______________________________

3.1.2 For the receiving Participant the point of contact is:

Name______________________________

Title/Position_______________________

Organization________________________

Address____________________________

____

____

Email______________________________

3.2 Responsibilities of the Providing Participant

3.2.1 Transfer of the Project Equipment - The providing Participant will transfer the Project Equipment listed above for the duration of the transfer period specified in paragraph 6.4 of this PET unless extended by mutual written consent.

3.2.2 Project Equipment Delivery - The providing Participant will deliver the Project Equipment ***(specify arrangements)***. Responsibility for the Project Equipment will pass from the providing Participant to the receiving Participant at the time of receipt of the Project Equipment. Any further transportation is the responsibility of the receiving Participant unless otherwise specified in this paragraph.

3.2.3 Information - The providing Participant will furnish the receiving Participant such Information as is necessary to enable the Project Equipment to be used in the TEP Activity described in paragraph 2.1.1 of this PET in accordance with Section VIII (Disclosure and Use of Information) of the TEP MOU.

3.3 Responsibilities of the Receiving Participant

3.3.1 Inspection and Inventory - The receiving Participant will inspect and inventory the Project Equipment upon receipt. The receiving Participant will also inspect and inventory the Project Equipment prior to its return to the providing Participant, unless the Project Equipment is consumed in accordance with paragraph 3.3.2.

3.3.2 ***(Choose one of the following alternatives, or use both if both situations apply.)***

Alternative A – Use when return of Project Equipment is planned.

Return of Project Equipment: Upon expiration or termination of the transfer period specified in paragraph 6.4 (taking into account any approved extension by the providing Participant), the receiving Participant will return the Project Equipment to the providing Participant ***(specify arrangements)***. If the Project Equipment is lost, unintentionally destroyed, or damaged beyond economical repair, while in the custody of the receiving Participant, the receiving Participant will issue a certificate of loss/destruction/irreparable damage to the providing Participant.

Alternative B – Use when return of Project Equipment is not planned due to its consumption during the Activity.

Consumption of Project Equipment: It is intended that the receiving Participant will consume the Project Equipment specified in paragraph 1.1 during the course of the TEP Activity described in paragraph 2.1.1. If this does occur, the receiving Participant will provide written notice of its consumption to the providing Participant. In the event consumption does not occur prior to the end of the transfer period specified in paragraph 6.4, the receiving Participant will return the Project Equipment to the providing Participant ***(specify arrangements)***. If the Project Equipment is lost, unintentionally destroyed, or damaged beyond repair prior to its intended consumption while in the custody of the receiving Participant, the receiving Participant will issue a certificate of loss/destruction/irreparable damage to the providing Participant.

3.4 This TEP PET Form provides only for transfer of Project Equipment associated with the TEP Activity described in paragraph 2.1.1. Signature of this TEP PET Form does not imply any commitment by a Participant to participate in any activities beyond the PET described herein.

SECTION IV

SPECIAL PROVISIONS

4.1 ***(Insert any special provisions as required. If none, so state.)***

SECTION V

CLASSIFICATION

5.1 ***(Insert only one of the two following paragraphs; note that one of these two options must be selected.)***

No classified Project Equipment will be transferred under this TEP PET Form.

or

The highest level of classified Project Equipment under this TEP PET Form is ***(insert level of classification)***.

SECTION VI

MODIFICATION, TERMINATION, AND TRANSFER PERIOD

6.1 The provisions of this PET Form may be modified or extended by written mutual consent of authorized representatives of the Participants in accordance with Section VII (Project Equipment) of the TEP MOU.

6.2 The PET described in this TEP PET Form may be terminated at any time in accordance with the following provisions:

6.2.1 Through the mutual written consent of the authorized representatives of the Participants;

6.2.2 Unilaterally by the receiving Participant on 60 days written notice to the providing Participant; and

6.2.3 Unilaterally by the providing Participant at any time.

6.3 Responsibilities regarding security and protection against unauthorized use, disclosure, or transfer that accrued prior to termination or expiration of the transfer period will continue to apply without limit of time in accordance with Section XVII (Amendment, Termination, Entry Into Effect, and Duration) of the TEP MOU.

6.4 The transfer period for the Project Equipment described herein begins on the date of the last signature below, and, unless terminated or extended, will continue until ***(enter date or amount of time)***.

FOR THE DEPARTMENT OF DEFENSE
OF THE UNITED STATES OF AMERICA

____
[Signature]

____
Name
Director. Operational Test and Evaluation
Title

____
Date

____
Location

FOR THE SECRETARY OF STATE FOR
DEFENCE OF THE UNITED KINGDOM OF
GREAT BRITAIN AND NORTHERN
IRELAND

____
[Signature]

____
Name
Director General Research and Technology
Title

____
Date

____
Location

STATE DEPARTMENT DOCUMENT NUMBER: 06-303

AGREEMENT BETWEEN THE UNITED STATES OF AMERICA AND THE REPUBLIC OF PANAMA REGARDING THE STATUS OF UNITED STATES PERSONNEL WHO MAY BE TEMPORARILY PRESENT IN PANAMA IN CONNECTION WITH A VISIT BY TWELVE OFFICIALS FROM THE U.S. NAVAL SPECIAL WARFARE DETACHMENT SOUTH

EFFECTED BY EXCHANGE OF NOTES AT PANAMA,
OCTOBER 27 AND NOVEMBER 8, 2006
ENTERED INTO FORCE NOVEMBER 8, 2006

CTIA DOCUMENT NUMBER: 13124.000

No. 2058

The Embassy of the United States of America presents its compliments to the Ministry of Foreign Relations of the Republic of Panama and has the honor to refer to recent discussions between representatives of the two Governments regarding the status of United States personnel, as defined in the Embassy's Note No. 834, dated July 3, 2001, and the Ministry's Note DM No. 0301/2001, dated July 10, 2001, who may be temporarily present in Panama in connection with a visit by twelve officials from the U.S. Naval Special Warfare Detachment South, who will be in uniform and who will carry their regulatory weapons, as authorized. The officials will stay in Panama from November 2, 2006 through September 30, 2007. The purpose of the visit is to conduct counter narcotics training (CNT-017) with the Panamanian Public Forces. The Panamanian counterparts are Vice Minister for Government and Justice Severino Mejia and Deputy Director General of the Panamanian National Police Emanuel Landau.

As a result of these discussions, the Embassy proposes that such personnel shall be accorded a status equivalent to that accorded to the administrative and technical staff of the Embassy of the United States of America under the Vienna Convention of Diplomatic Relations of April 18, 1961 (Vienna Convention). The understanding contained in the Embassy's Note. 835 dated July 3, 2001 and the Ministry's reply in Note No. D.M. 0300/2001 dated July 10, 2001, shall apply.

United States personnel shall be permitted to enter and exit Panama with United States identification and with collective movement or individual travel orders, in accordance with an agreement on non-immigrant visas between the United States and Panama, which has been in force since June 1, 1956, as amended, except that the Government of Panama will waive the requirement for tourist cards and related fees. Panamanian authorities shall accept as valid driving licenses or permits issued by the appropriate U.S. authorities to U.S. personnel for operation of vehicles; and such personnel shall be authorized to wear U.S. Government attire (uniforms) and to carry authorized equipment when required for their mission while performing official duties.

The Embassy of the United States further proposes that the Government of Panama accord duty-free importation and exportation, as well as exemption from inspection and taxation of products, services, property, materials, equipment, vehicles, vessels, and aircraft introduced and/or imported into, acquired in or exported from Panama by or on behalf of the U.S. Government or its personnel, in connection with their mission in Panama; except that United States personnel shall not be exempt from Panamanian taxes on items purchased in Panama for their personal use.

The two Governments shall cooperate in taking the necessary steps to ensure the security of United States personnel and property in Panama.

Vehicles, vessels, and aircraft owned or operated by or for United States Armed Forces shall not be subject to payment of landing or port fees, pilotage charges, navigation, overflight or parking charges or light or harbor dues while in Panama, except for the charges related to the normal transit of the Panama Canal, previously agreed to; however, United States Armed Forces shall pay reasonable charges for services requested and received.

It shall be the responsibility of United States personnel to respect the laws of Panama and to abstain from any activity inconsistent with the spirit of their mission. Authorities of the Government of the United States shall take the necessary steps to that end.

Appropriate Panamanian and U.S. military or civilian police authorities shall cooperate in the investigation of any crime believed to have been committed by or against United States personnel.

The Government of Panama shall accept full responsibility for, and shall hold the United States Government harmless from, any and all claims arising from the use of projects constructed, or in the process of being constructed in whole or in part, by United States personnel in connection with their mission in Panama.

Finally, both governments shall waive any and all claims (other than contractual claims) against each other for personal injury to or death of their military or civilian personnel, or for damage, loss, or destruction of the other's property arising out of activities covered by this agreement. The United States shall pay, in accordance with United States law, fair and reasonable compensation in settlement of meritorious claims by third parties arising out of acts or omissions of United States personnel, or which are otherwise incident to agreed activities by United States personnel in connection with their mission in Panama.

Additional arrangements as may be necessary may be entered into by the appropriate authorities of the two Governments.

The Embassy of the United States of America proposes that this note and the Ministry's reply thereto shall constitute an agreement between the two Governments on this subject and that its provisions shall be in effect as of the date of the Ministry's. reply.

Embassy of the United States of America
Panama, October 27, 2006.

[Seal]

Letter head of the U.S. Department of State
Office of Language Services
Translating Division

REPUBLIC OF PANAMA
MINISTRY OF FOREIGN RELATIONS
Panama City 4, Panama

No. DT/451

The Ministry of Foreign Relations presents its compliments to the Embassy of the United States of America and has the honor to acknowledge receipt of its note verbale No. 2058 of October 27, 2006, which reads as follows:

[See U.S. Text.]

In this regard, the Ministry of Foreign Relations has the honor to inform the Embassy of the United States of America that the above proposal is acceptable to the Government of the Republic of Panama and that the Embassy's note and this note in reply shall constitute an agreement between our two governments, which shall enter into force on the date of this note.

[Complimentary close]

Panama City, November 8, 2006

[Initialed]

[Ministry stamp]

Embassy of the United States of America,
Panama City.

STATE DEPARTMENT DOCUMENT NUMBER: 06-304

AGREEMENT CONCERNING CERTAIN ASPECTS OF TRADE IN AGRICULTURAL PRODUCTS, WITH ATTACHMENT AND ANNEXES

SIGNED AT WASHINGTON D.C.,
JULY 27, 2004
ENTERED INTO FORCE SEPTEMBER 10, 2004

CTIA DOCUMENT NUMBER: 13125.000

LETTERHEAD OF EXECUTIVE OFFICE OF THE PRESIDENT
THE UNITED STATES TRADE REPRESENTATIVE
WASHINGTON, D.C. 20508

His Excellency Ehud Olmeri
Vice Prime Minister and
Minister of Industry, Trade, Labor and Communications
State of Israel

Dear Mr. Minister:

I have the honor to confirm the following agreement reached between the delegation of the Government of the United States of America ("United States") and the delegation of the Government of Israel ("Israel") concerning certain aspects of trade in agricultural products. Israel and the United States acknowledge that the *Agreement on the Establishment of a Free Trade Area between the Government of Israel and the Government of the United States of America* ("FTAA"), dated April 22, 1985 (which corresponds to the first day of Iyar, 5745), applies in full to U.S. and Israeli agricultural products and to trade in these products between the two countries. However, both countries also acknowledge that they have differing interpretations as to the meaning of certain rights and obligations in Articles 2 and 6 of the FTAA as they relate to agricultural products. In the interest of achieving practical improvement in agricultural trade between the two countries, the United States and Israel have therefore agreed to set aside their differences and enter into this agreement through December 31, 2008, with regard to certain border measures of each party that relate to agricultural products of the other party (as defined in Annex 3 of the FTAA entitled "Rules of Origin").

This agreement is without prejudice to the parties' rights and obligations under Articles 2.1, 2.2, and 6 of the FTAA with respect to agricultural products and is without prejudice to the parties' other rights and obligations under the FTAA or the *Marrakesh Agreement Establishing the World Trade Organization*.

During the period January 1, 2004, through December 31, 2008, Israel shall accord agricultural products of the United States treatment no less favorable than that specified in the attachment to this agreement, and the United States shall accord agricultural products of Israel treatment no less favorable than that specified in the attachment to this agreement. The attachment and annexes to this agreement are an integral part of this agreement. During the period January 1, 2004, through December 31, 2008, both governments shall refrain from adopting, applying or otherwise maintaining any measures pursuant to Article 6 of the FTAA, unless such measures are otherwise specifically permitted by this agreement.

Beginning February 2004, the two governments agree to consult quarterly on the administration and utilization of quantities provided under the agreement by Israel for free import into Israel from the United States and by the United States for tree import into the United States from Israel. The lead offices for these discussions shall be the Office of the U.S. Trade Representative and the U.S. Department of Agriculture for the United States and the Ministry of Industry and Trade and the Ministry of Agriculture for Israel.

To facilitate a better understanding of each party's agricultural economy in the course of future discussions on improving agricultural market access, either party may present information on factors of importance to their respective agricultural sectors. Such factors may include, but are not limited to: annual overall trade in a product, the scope of U.S.–Israeli trade in that product and the interests which each party has in expanding access to the other's market; trends in domestic production, prices and profitability of a product and the capacity for further market access; economic circumstances of producers, such as changes in rural income; the benefits of liberalization ot agricultural trade, including benefits to consumers, trade and food processors: and additional agricultural policy considerations related to issues such as national and regional development priorities, government assistance, food security, special security conditions, and multilateral agricultural policy objectives. The aforementioned factors may be referenced by the parties and provide guidance in future discussions, including in the U.S.–Israel Joint Committee, on further improvements in agricultural market access

No later than June 1, 2007, our two governments shall initiate a review of the operation of this agreement and seek ways to make further improvements. In the event it appears that negotiations will not be concluded by December 31, 2008, the parties mutually agree to address the issue of maintaining the treatment that each provides to the agricultural products of the other party under this agreement until such time as a new agreement is in force.

I have the honor to propose that this letter, the attachment to this letter, and annexes, which are authentic in English, and your letter of confirmation in reply constitute an agreement between our two governments, to enter into effect on this date.

Sincerely,
[Signature]
Robert B. Zoellick
United States Trade Representative

Attachment

1. The Government of Israel shall, with respect to products of the United States:

(A) Listed in Annex A, permit the importation into Israel free of any customs duty, fee, or other import charge;

(B) Listed in Annex B:

i. permit the importation into Israel free of any customs duty, fee, or other import charge of not less than the quantity specified in that Annex for the applicable year, other than for items 08.02.1100 and 08.02.1200; and

ii. for items 08.02.1100 and 08.02.1200, permit the importation into Israel of not less than the quantity specified in Annex B at a rate not greater than that specified in that Annex; and

iii. permit the importation of any quantity in excess of the quantity specified in Annex B, at a rate not greater than the lesser of:

a. the most-favored-nation rate of customs duty applied by the Government of Israel as specified in Annex C or

b. the most-favored-nation rate of customs duty applied by the Government of Israel at the time of importation

each reduced by the percentage specified in Annex C.

(C) Listed in Annex C provide treatment at a rate not greater than the lesser of:

i. the most-favored-nation rate of customs duty applied by the Government of Israel as specified in Annex C for the applicable year or

ii. the most-favored-nation rate of customs duty applied by the Government of Israel at the time of importation

each reduced by the percentage specified in Annex C.

2. With respect to any good within chapters 1 through 24 of the Harmonized System that is not listed in Annex A, B, or C, the Government of Israel shall permit its importation into Israel at a rate no greater than ninety percent of the rate applied at the time of importation to imports of that good from other countries. With respect to any agricultural product listed in paragraph l (ii) of Annex 1 of the *Agreement on Agriculture* annexed to the *Marrakesh Agreement Establishing the World Trade Organization* that is not listed in Annex A, B, or C of this agreement, the Government of Israel shall permit its importation free of any customs duty, fee, or other import charge.

3. The Government of the United States shall, with respect to products of Israel imported into the customs territory of the United States listed in Annex D, permit the importation free of any customs duty, fee or other import charge of not less than the quantity specified in that Annex for the applicable year. For products in Annex D, the U.S. treatment of quantities above the quantity specified in that Annex for the applicable year shall be no less favorable that what is specified in the U.S. WTO Schedule. The U.S. treatment of over-quota quantities for products of Israel imported into the customs territory of the United States of the type listed in WTO notifications G/AG/N/USA/2 dated March 8, 1995, and G/AG/N/USA/2 Add. 1, dated April 21, 1995, ("WTO notifications") that are not listed in Annex D, shall be no less favorable than what is specified in the U.S. WTO Schedule, and, as specified in the U.S. WTO Schedule, the in-quota quantities for such products shall be imported free of any customs duty, fee, or other import charge. With respect to any agricultural product of Israel imported into the customs territory of the United States listed in paragraph 1 of Annex 1 of the *Agreement on Agriculture* annexed to the *Marrakesh Agreement Establishing the*

World Trade Organization that is not listed in either Annex D of this agreement or of the type listed in the WTO notifications, the Government of the United States shall permit its importation free of any customs duty, fee, or other import charge.

4. The item numbers in Annexes A, B, and C refer to the item numbers in the 2004 Israeli Customs Tariff in effect on January 1, 2004. The item numbers in Annex D refer to the Harmonized Tariff Schedule of the United States 2004 in effect on January 1, 2004.

5. Each successive annual quantity in Annex B or Annex D shall be made effective on January 1 of the applicable year.

6. The Annexes to this attachment are an integral part of this Attachment.

7. The term "customs duty, fee, or other import charge" shall not include any such charge:

(A) imposed pursuant to Article 4, 5, 7, 11, or 20 of the FTAA; or

(B) to the extent not inconsistent with the FTAA, permitted by the agreements listed in Annex 1 to the *Marrakesh Agreement Establishing the World Trade Organization*, other than Article 5 of the *Agreement on Agriculture*.

Annex A: Free Import into Israel from USA

Only items for which "A" appears in column 3 are in Annex A. Other items appear for purposes of information and definition only.		
ISRAEL TARIFF CODE	**SHORT DESCRIPTION OF PRODUCT**	**Annex A**
0101.0000	Horses, asses, mules or hinnies, live	A
0101.1000	Pure bred breeding Horses	A
0101.9000	Other	A
0102.0000	Bovine, live	
0102.1000	Pure bred breeding bovine	
0102.1010	- within Annex 5	
0102.1090	Pure bred breeding bovine-others	A
0102.9012	-calves for raising approved by the Ministry of Agriculture	A
0103.0000	Swine, live	A
0103.1000	Pure bred breeding swine	A

ISRAEL TARIFF CODE	SHORT DESCRIPTION OF PRODUCT	Annex A
0103.9000	Others	A
0103.9100	-weighing, < 50 kg	A
0103.9200	- weighing, => 50kg	A
0104.0000	Sheeps and goats, live'.	
0104.1000	Sheeps:	
0104.1010	Pure bred breeding sheep	A
0104.2000	Goats:	
0104.2010	Pure bred breeding goats	A
0105.0000	Fowls of the sp. gallus, ducks, geese and guinea fowls	
0105.1000	weighing <=185g	
0105.1100	- fowls of the species gallus	
0105 1110	-- <=4.5 NS/unit	
0105.1190	-- others	A
0105.1200	- fowls of turkey	
0105.1210	-- < 12 NS/unit	
0105.1290	-- others	A
0105.1900	- other fowls	
0105.1910	--< 12 NS/unit	
0105.1990	-- others	A
0106.0000	Other live animals	A
0106.3910	-- fancy/song/pet birds	A
0106.3911	--- for public zoos	A
0106.3990	---- others	A
0106.9000	---- others	A
0202.1090	Meat of bovine, frozen, - others	A
0202.2090	Other cuts with bone-in, - others	A

Continued

ISRAEL TARIFF CODE	SHORT DESCRIPTION OF PRODUCT	Annex A
0202.3090	Bovine, boneless- others	A
0206.2000	Edible offal of bovine animals, frozen	A
0206.2110	-- within Annex 5	
0206.2200	- livers	A
0206.2210	-- within Annex 5	
0206.2190	-tongues, others	A
0206.2290	-- others	A
0206.2900	- others	
0206.2910	-within Annex 5	
0206.2990	-- others	A
0206.9000	Others, frozen	A
0208.0000	Other meat and offal of other animals	A
0208.1000	Meat of rabbits or hares	A
0208.2000	Frogs legs	A
0208.9000	Other meat & edible offal	A
0301.0000	Live fish	A
0301.1010	---imported with the approval of the adminstration for...zoo	A
0301.1090	---others	A
0301.9110	---approved by the D.G. of Min. of Agr. For breeding	A
0301.9190	---others	A
0301.9210	---approved by the D.G. of Min. of Agr. For breeding	A
0301.9310	---approved by the D.G. of Min. of Agr. For breeding	A
0301.9390	---others	A
0301.9910	---approved by the D.G. of Min. of Agr. For breeding	A
0301.9990	---others	A

ISRAEL TARIFF CODE	SHORT DESCRIPTION OF PRODUCT	Annex A
ex 0302.0000	Fish, fresh or chilled, not fillet or other parts in 0304.-	
0302.1230	Salmonidae, other	A
0302.2230	Flat fish, plaice	A
0302.3230	Yellowfin Tunas, other	A
0302.3300	Skipjack or other striped-bellied bonito, other	A
0302.3930	Other fishes, other	A
0302.4030	Herrings, excl livers and roes, other	A
0302.5030	Cod, excl livers and roes, other	A
0302.6100	Sardines, sardinella, brisling or sprats, other	A
0302.6330	Coalfish, other	A
0302.6400	Mackerel	A
0302.6530	Dogfish and other sharks, other	A
0302.7020	Livers and roes, chilled	A
0303.3390	Sole, other	A
0303.4290	Yellowfin tunas, other	A
0303.4390	Skipjackor striped-bellied bonito, other	A
0303.4990	Other fishes, other	A
0303.7620	Eels, other	A
0304.0000	Fish, fillets and other fish meat, fresh, chilled or frozen	
0304.1020	---fillet of Pacific, Atlantic or Danube salmon	A
0304.1029	---fillet of Pacific, Atlantic or Danube salmon, other	A
ex 0304.1040	---flat fish, herring, cod, gadus	A
0304.1060	fillet of other fish approved by the D.G. of the Min. of Agr. Not being grown nor fished in Israel or in Mediterranean sea	A
0304.1099	-- other	A
ex.0304.2000	-- frozen, from salt water only	

Continued

ISRAEL TARIFF CODE	SHORT DESCRIPTION OF PRODUCT	Annex A
0304.2029	---other	A
0304.2049	---fillet of tunnus, skipjack, sardinas, sardinella	A
0304.2059	Frozen fillet, eels other	A
0305.0000	Fish , dried salted (exl Trout)	A
0306.1100	--rock lobster & other sea crawfish	A
0306.1200	-- lobsters	A
0306.1490	--crabs, other	A
0306.1990	--other, other	A
0306.2100	--rock lobster & other sea crawfish, not frozen	A
0306.2200	-- lobsters	A
0306.2490	--crabs, other	A
0306.2999	-- Others	A
0307.1090	Mollusks, other	A
0307.2190	Scallops, live, fresh or chilled, other	A
0307.2990	Scallops, live, fresh or chilled, other, other	A
0307.3190	Mussels, live, fresh or chilled, other	A
0307.3990	Mussels, other, other	A
0307.6099	Other, frozen, Snails	A
0307.9190	Other, live fresh, other	A
0307.9990	Others, other, frozen	A
0402.1020	Milk powder, granules, fat <= 1.5 % approved for industry	A
0402.2120	Milk powder, granules, 'fat > 1.5 % no sugar approved for industry	A
0404.1010	Whey, for industry	A
0407.0011	Hatching eggs of chickens, with value > NS 1.35/unit	A
0501.0000	Human hair, .., waste	A

ISRAEL TARIFF CODE	SHORT DESCRIPTION OF PRODUCT	Annex A
0502.0000	- Pigs, hogs or boars bristles ...,	A
0502.1000	- pigs, hogs or boars bristles and hair	A
0502.9000	- other	A
0503.0000	Horsehair and horsehair waste	A
0504.0000	Guts, bladders & stomachs of animals...	A
0504.0010	---sheep guts	A
0504.0020	---large intestines	A
0504.0030	--- rennet bags of calves	A
0504.0090	--- other	A
0505.0000	Skins & other parts of birds ..	
0505.1000	Feathers of a kind used for stuffing...	A
0506.0000	Bones & horn-cores, unworked...	A
0506.1000	-ossein and bones treated with acid	A
0506.9000	- other	A
0507.0000	Ivory, tortoise-shell, whalebone & ..	A
0507.1000	- ivory, ivory powder and waste	A
0507.9000	- other	A
0508.0000	Coral, shells of mollusks, crustacean	A
0509.0000	Natural sponges of animal origin	A
0510.0000	Ambergris, castreum, civet and musk....	A

Continued

ISRAEL TARIFF CODE	SHORT DESCRIPTION OF PRODUCT	Annex A
0511.0000	Animal products not else-where specified	A
0511.1000	Bovine semen	A
0511.9000	Other	A
0511.9100	- products of fish or crustaceans	A
0511.9130	---used for pet fish or birds food	A
0511.9140	---other	A
0511.9900	--other	A
0511.9920	--- used for pet food or birds' food	A
0511.9930	--- other	A
All Chapter 6	Live trees and plants, bulbs, root; cut flowers and ornamental foliage	A
0710.2920	Other frozen leguminous vegetables, " garden phaselous" , other	A
0710.8090	Other vegetables, other	A
0711.0000	Vegetables provisionally preserved	
0711.3000	Capers	A
0711.4000	Cucumbers and gherkins	A
0711.9042	Onions	A
0712.0000	Dried vegetables, whole, sliced, powder...	A
0712.2000	Onions	A
0712.3000	Mushrooms and truffles	A
0712.3100	---mushrooms	A
0712.3200	--- truffles	A
0712.9000	Other vegetables; mixtures of vegetables	A
0712.9010	---garlic	A
0712.9011	----sliced, flacks, powder	A
0712.9019	---- others	A

ISRAEL TARIFF CODE	SHORT DESCRIPTION OF PRODUCT	Annex A
0712.9020	---marjoram	A
0712.9030	--- asparagus, curly cabbage, powder	A
0712.9040	--- sweet corn	A
0712.9060	--- potatoes, ... with no prev. preparations	A
0712.9090	--- other	A
0713.0000	Dried leguminous vegetables..	
0713.1000	Peas (Pisum sativum)	A
0713.3000	Beans (Vigna...)	A
0713.3100	-- beans of species	A
0713.3200	-- small red (adzuki) beans	A
0713.3300	-- kidney beans, incl. White pea beans	A
0713.3900	-- others	A
0713.4000	Lentils	A
0713.5000	Broad beans	A
0713.9000	Others	A
0714.0000	Manioc, arrowroot, salep, .. sweet, potatoes...	
0714.1000	Manioc	A
0714.9000	Other	A
0801.0000	Coconuts, brazil nuts & cashew nuts...	A
0801.1000	Coconuts	A
0801.1100	- dried	A
0801.1900	-- other	A
0801.2000	Brazil nuts	A
0801.2100	--in shell	A
0801.2200	-- shelled	A

Continued

ISRAEL TARIFF CODE	SHORT DESCRIPTION OF PRODUCT	Annex A
0801.3000	Cashew nuts	A
0801.3100	-- in shell	A
0801.3200	-- shelled	A
0802.0000	Other nuts...	
0802.1000	Almonds	
0802.1100	- in shell	
0802.1110	-- for chocolate	A
0802.1200	- shelled	
0802.1210	-- for chocolate	A
0802.2000	Hazelnuts or filberts	A
0802.2100	-- in shell	A
0802.2200	-- shelled	A
0802.2210	--- for chocolate	A
0802.2290	--- not for chocolate	A
0802.3000	Walnuts	A
0802.3100	- in shell	A
0802.3110	-- within Annex 5	
0802.3190	--others	A
3802.3200	- shelled	A
0802.3210	-- within Annex 5	
0802.3290	-- others	A
0802.4000	Chestnuts	A
0802.5000	Pistachios	A
0802.9000	Others:	
0802.9020	- pecan & macadamia	A
0802.9022	-- within Annex 5	
0802.9029	-- others	A
0802.9090	- other nuts	A
0802.9092	-- within Annex 5	

ISRAEL TARIFF CODE	SHORT DESCRIPTION OF PRODUCT	Annex A
0802.9099	-- others	A
0804.0000	Dates, figs, pineapples, avocados, guavas, mangoes, mangosteens, fresh or dried	
0804.2000	Figs:	
0804.2010	- fresh	A
0804.2011	-- (May-Nov.)	A
0804.2019	--(Dec.-Apr.)	A
0804.2020	- dried	A
0804.2021	-within Annex 5	
0804.2029	-- others	A
0804.3000	Pineapples	A
0804.3010	--- fresh	A
0804.3020	--- dried	A
0804.5000	Guavas, mangoes, mangosteens	
0804.5090	- Dried	A
0810.0000	Other fruit, fresh	
0810.2000	Raspberries, blackberries...	A
0810.3000	Gooseberries & currants	A
0810.4000	Cranberries, bilberries...	A
0811.0000	Frozen fruits	
0811.1010	Strawberries, in packages over 10 kg	A
0811.2000	Raspberries, blackberries, ... loganberries	A
0811.2010	--- in pack. over 10 kg	A
0811.2090	--- others	A
0811.9010	Cherries, Blueberries	A

Continued

ISRAEL TARIFF CODE	SHORT DESCRIPTION OF PRODUCT	Annex A
0811.9091	Others, in packages over 10 kg	A
0811.9099	Others, others	A
0812.0000	Fruit and nuts preserved by sulfur dioxide, in salt water, not edible	A
0812.1000	- cherries	A
0812.9010	- strawberries	A
0812.9090	- others	A
0813.0000	Fruits, dried, except 0801.-: 0806.-, mixtures of nuts or dried fruits of this Chapter	
0813.1000	Apricots	A
0813.3000	Apples	A
0813.4000	Other fruit	A
0813.5000	- Mix. of nuts or dried fruits of this chapter	
0813.5010	-- mixed nuts	
0813.5012	---- containing 50% or more almonds	A
0813.5019	---- other	A
0813.5020	-- Mixed dried fruits	
0813.5022	---- containing 50% or more dried grapes	A
0813.5029	---- other	A
0814.0000	Fruit peels, fresh, frozen, dried, preservec	A
All Chapter 9	Coffee, tea, mate, spices	A
1001.0000	Wheat & meslin	
1001.1000	Durum wheat	A
1001 1010	-within Annex 5	

ISRAEL TARIFF CODE	SHORT DESCRIPTION OF PRODUCT	Annex A
1001.1090	- other	A
1001.9000	Other	
1001.9010	- within Annex 5	
1001.9090	- other	A
1002.0000	Rye	A
1002.0010	- within Annex 5	
1002.0090	- other	A
1003.0000	Barley	A
1003.0010	- within Annex 5	
1003.0090	- other	A
1004.0000	Oats	A
1005.0000	Maize (corn)	
1005.1000	Seed	A
1005.9000	Other, exclud. 9010	A
1005.9090	--- other	A
1006.0000	Rice	A
1006.1000	In the husk	A
1006.2000	Husked (brown) rice	A
1006.3000	Semi-milled or wholly milled rice	A
1006.3010	- within Annex 5	
1006.3090	- other	A
1006.4000	Broken rice	A

Continued

ISRAEL TARIFF CODE	SHORT DESCRIPTION OF PRODUCT	Annex A
1007.0000	Grain sorghum	A
1008.0000	Buckwheat, millet & canary seed; other	A
1008.1000	Buckwheat	A
1008.2000	Millet	A
1008.3000	Canary seeds	A
1008.9000	Other cereals	A
1101.0000	Wheat or meslin flour	A
1101.0010	--- up to 31.12.2004	A
1101.0090	--- others	A
1102.0000	Cereal flours other than of wheat or meslin	A
1102.1000	- rye flour	A
1102.1010	--- up to 31.12.2004	A
1102.1090	--- other	A
1102.2000	- maize (corn) flour	A
1102.3000	- rice flour	A
1102.9000	- other	A
1103.0000	Cereal groats, meal and pellets	A
1103.1000	- groats & meal	A
1103.1100	- of wheat	A
1103.1390	--- others	A
1103.1900	-- of other cereals	A
1103.2000	- pellets	A

ISRAEL TARIFF CODE	SHORT DESCRIPTION OF PRODUCT	Annex A
1104.0000	Cereals grains otherwise workea...	A
1104.1000	- rolled or flaked grains	A
1104.1210	-- in the form of flakes	A
1104.1900	-- of other cereals	A
1104.2000	- other worked grains	A
1104.2200	-- of oats	A
1104.2300	-- of maize (corn)	A
1104.2900	-- of other cereals	A
1104.2910	--- crushed or pounded wheat	A
1104.2920	--- other	A
1104.3000	Germ of cereals, whole, rolled, flaked...	A
1104.3010	--- of barely	A
1104.3090	--- other	A
1105.0000	Flour, meal & flakes of potatoes	A
1105.1000	- flour and mea	A
1105.2000	-flakes	A
1106.0000	Flour or meal of dried leguminous vegetables...	A
1106.1000	- of heading no. 0713.-	A
1106.2000	- of sago, roots or tubers of head. 0714-	A
1106.3000	- flour, meal & powder of the products of chapter 8	A
1107.0000	Malt, whether or not roasted	A
1107.1000	- not roasted	A
1107.2000	- roasted	A

Continued

ISRAEL TARIFF CODE	SHORT DESCRIPTION OF PRODUCT	Annex A
1108.0000	Starches, inulin	
1108.1000	- starches	
1108.1100	-- wheat starch	A
1108.1200	-- maize (corn) starch	
1108.1210	---waxy	A
1108.1300	-- potato starch	A
1108.1400	-- manioc (cassava) starch	A
1108.1900	-- other starches	A
1108.2000	- inulin	A
1109.0000	Wheat gluten, whether or not dried	A
1201.0000	Soya beans, whether or not broken	A
1203.0000	Copra	A
1204.0000	Linseec	A
1205.0000	Rape or colsa seeds	A
1206.0000	Sunflower seeds	
1206.0010	For oil	A
1206.0020	Sunfiower seeds-birds feed (Ministry of Agriculture approved)	A
1207.0000	Other oil seeds & oleaginous fruits	A
1207.1000	Palm nuts & kernels	A
1207.2000	Cotton seeds	A
1207.2010	--- with value <= NS 0.75/Kc	A
1207.2090	--- others	A
1207.3000	Castor oil seeds	A

ISRAEL TARIFF CODE	SHORT DESCRIPTION OF PRODUCT	Annex A
1207.4000	Sesamum seeds	A
1207.5000	Mustard seeds	A
1207.6000	Safflower seeds	A
1207.6010	-- with value <= NS 1.30/Kg	A
1207.6090	--- others	A
1207.9000	Other	A
1207.9100	-- poppy seeds	A
1207.9900	-- other	A
1208.0000	Flours & meals..., except of mustard	A
1208.1000	Of soya beans	A
1208.9000	Other	A
1208.9010	--- of poppy seeds	A
1208.9030	--- other, flours	A
1209.0000	Seeds, fruits & spores, for sowing	A
1209.1000	Beet seed	A
1209.2000	Seeds of forage plants, other than beet seed	A
1209.2100	--lucerne seed	A
1209.2200	-- clover seed	A
1209.2300	-- fescue seed	A
1209.2400	-- kentucky blue grass seed	A
1209.2500	-- rye grass seed	A
1209.2600	-- timothy grass seed	A
1209.2900	-- other, forage	A
1209.3000	Seeds of herbaceous plants	A
1209.9000	Other	A

Continued

ISRAEL TARIFF CODE	SHORT DESCRIPTION OF PRODUCT	Annex A
1209.9919	---- other	A
1209.9922	---- for sowing	A
1209.9929	---- other	A
1209.9930	---- other	A
1209.9990	--- other	A
1210.0000	Hop cones	A
1210.1000	- not ground...	A
1210.2000	- ground...	A
1211.0000	Plants for pharmacy, perfumery	A
1211.1000	Liquorice roots	A
1211.1010	--- herb tea bags	A
1211.1090	--- others	A
1211.2000	Ginseng roots	A
1211.2010	--- herb tea bags	A
1211.2090	--- others	A
1211.9000	Other plants for pharmacy, perfumery	A
1211.9010	--- of palaver seeds	A
1211.9020	--- tea of plants in personal bag	A
1211.9090	--- others	A
1212.0000	Locust beans, seaweed & algae...	A
1212.1000	Locust beans	A
1212.2000	Seaweed & algae	A
1212.2010	--- for perfum./pharm. or insecticid...	A
1212.2011	---- seaweeds for medicine (Health Min)	A
1212.2019	---- other seaweeds	A
1212.2090	--- others	A

ISRAEL TARIFF CODE	SHORT DESCRIPTION OF PRODUCT	Annex A
1212.3000	Apricot, peach, plum stones & kernels	A
1212.9000	Other	A
1212.9100	--sugar beet	A
1212.9920	--- chicory roots	A
1212.9990	---- other	A
1213.0000	Cereal straw & husks..	A
1214.0000	Swedes, mangolds, fodder roots, hey...	A
1214.1000	Lucerne (alfalfa)	A
1214.9000	Other	A
All Chapter 13	Lac.Gum. Resins, and other Vegetable Extracts	A
1401.1000	Bamboo	A
1401.2000	Rattans	A
1401.9000	Other weaving reeds	A
1402.0000	Veg. Stuffing material	A
1403.0000	Veg. Material for brooms	A
1404.1000	Raw vegetable materials for coloring:	A
1404.1010	Henna	A
1404.1020	Other	A
1404.2000	Cotton linters	A
1404.9000	Other	
1404.9090	Other	A

Continued

ISRAEL TARIFF CODE	SHORT DESCRIPTION OF PRODUCT	Annex A
1502.0000	Fatty greases of cow, sheep or goats:	A
1502.0010	Edible	A
1502.0090	Other	A
1503.0010	Sitarine lard, Tallow, oliostianne, edible	A
1503.0090	Other	A
1504.1000	Fish-liver oils and their fractions-	A
1504.1020	Edible	A
1504.1090	Other	A
1504.2000	Fats and oilsof fish, other than liver:	A
1504.3000	Fats and oils and their fractions, of marine mammals:-	A
1504.3020	Edible	A
1504.3030	Other edible oils, or with a high vitamin	
1504.3040	Sperm oil	A
1504.3090	Other	A
1505.0000	wool grease, and fractions	A
1506.0000	Oils and their fractions, animal:	A
1507.1000	Soya bean Crude oil, whether or not degummed -	
1507.1090	Other	A
1507.9000	Soya bean oil, Other:-	
1507.9090	Other	A
1508.1000	Groundnut oil, Crude	A
1508.9000	Groundnut oil, Other:-	A
1508.9010	Other, containing not less than 90%	
1508.9020	Edible	A
1508.9090	Other	A
1509.9000	Olive oil, Other-(not virgin):	

ISRAEL TARIFF CODE	SHORT DESCRIPTION OF PRODUCT	Annex A
1509.9030	Edible	A
1509.9090	Other	A
1510.0000	Other oils from olives, Hardened or solidified:	
1510.0030	Edible	A
1510.0090	Other	A
1511.0000	Palm Oil and fractions, distilled	A
1511.1000	Crude oil	A
1511.1010	Edible	A
1511.1020	Other	A
1511.9000	Other	A
1511.9020	Edible	A
1511.9090	Other	A
1512.1000	Sunflower seed oil, safflower oil and their fractions:-	
1512.1100	Crude oil:-	
1512.1190	Other	A
1512.1900	Other-	
1512.1920	Other -	
1512.1929	Other	A
1512.2100	Crude oil, whether or not Gossypol has been removed:-	A
1512.2190	Other	A
1512.2900	Other(not crude):-	
512.2910	Other, containing not less than 90%	
512.2920	Other, edible	A
512.2990	Other -	A
513.1000	Coconut (copra) oil and its fractions.	A
513.1100	Crude oil,	A
513.1110	Edible	A
513.1190	Other	A

Continued

ISRAEL TARIFF CODE	SHORT DESCRIPTION OF PRODUCT	Annex A
513.1900	Other	A
513.1920	Edible	A
513.1990	Other	A
1513.2000	Palm kernel oil or babassu oil and its fractions	A
1513.2100	Crude oil	A
1513.2110	Edible	A
1513.2120	Other	A
1513.2900	Other	A
1513.2920	Edible	A
1513.2990	Other	A
1514.0000	Rape seed oil, colza oil, and mustard seed oil and their fractions	
1514.1000	Crude oil:-	
1514.1020	Other	A
1514.9000	Other -	
1514.9020	Other-	
1514.9024	Oil, edible, other	A
1514.9029	Other	A
1514.9090	Other	A
1515.1000	Linseed oil and its fractions	A
1515.1100	Crude oil	A
1515.1110	Edible	A
1515.1190	Other	A
1515.1900	Other	A
1515.1910	Hardened or solidified	A
1515.1920	Other	A
1515.1921	Edible	A
1515.1929	Other	A
1515.1930	Edible	A
1515.1990	Other	A
1515.2000	Maize (corn) oil and its fractions-	

ISRAEL TARIFF CODE	SHORT DESCRIPTION OF PRODUCT	Annex A
1515.2100	Crude oil:-	
1515.2110	Crude oil, edible	A
1515.2120	Other	A
1515.2900	Other:-	
1515.2920	Other -	A
1515.2990	Other	A
1515.3000	Castor oil and its fractions:-	A
1515.3010	Hardened or solidified	A
1515.3020	Other	A
1515.4000	Tung oil and its fractions:-	A
1515.5000	Sesame oil and its fractions	A
1515.5020	Edible	A
1515.9000	Other Oils:-	A
1515.9020	Other, edible	A
1515.9021	Sweet almond oil	A
1515.9022	Other oils, of nuts or of kernel;	A
1515.9029	Other	A
1515.9030	Other	A
1516.1000	Hydrogenated Animal fats and oils and their fractions:-	A
1516.1010	Partly or wholly hydrogenated, hardened	A
1516.1011	Edible	A
1516.1019	Other	A
1516.1090	Other	A
1516.1091	Edible fish oil or with a high vitamin	A
1516.1092	Sperm oil	A
1516.1093	Other, from fish or sea mammals	A
1516.1099	Other	A
1516.2000	Vegetable fats and oils and their fractions:-	
1516.2010	Partly or whooly hydrogenated hardened	A

Continued

ISRAEL TARIFF CODE	SHORT DESCRIPTION OF PRODUCT	Annex A
1516.2011	Edible	A
1516.2019	Other	A
1516.2030	Other, edible -	
1516.2031	Sweet almond oil	A
1516.2032	Other oils of nuts or of kernels	A
1516.2039	Other	A
1516.2090	Other -	A
1516.2091	Castor oil	A
1516.2092	Linseed oil	A
1516.2099	Other	A
1517.1000	Margarine, excluding liquid margarine	A
1517.9000	Other-	
1517.9020	Mixtures of fixed vegetable oils, not volatile -	
1517.9029	Other	A
1517.9030	Oil preparations -	A
1518.0010	Animal or vegetable fats and oils and their fractions,	A
1518.0012	Oils containing in their compounds epoxy	A
1518.0013	Linseed oil	A
1518.0015	Other	A
1518.0020	Inedible mixtures or preparations of animal	A
1518.0021	Castor bean oil	A
1518.0022	Linseed oil	A
1518.0023	Animal fats and oil	A
1518.0029	Other	A
1519.1000	Industrial monocarboxylic fatty acids:	A
1519.1100	Steanc acid	A
1519.1200	Oleic acid	A
1519.1300	Tall oil fatty acids	A
1519.1900	Other	A
1519.2000	Industrial fatty alcohol	A

ISRAEL TARIFF CODE	SHORT DESCRIPTION OF PRODUCT	Annex A
1604.1500	Mackerel:-	
1604.1520	Fillets covered with batter	A
1604.1590	Mackerel, other	A
1604.1600	Anchovies:-	A
1604.1900	Other:-	A
1604.1910	Of the "lax" type	A
1604.1920	Fillets covered with batter	A
1604.1990	Other:-	A
1604.2000	Other prepared or preserved fish:-	
1604.2010	Of the "lax" kind and Salmon	A
1604.2020	Homogenised preparation	A
1604 2090	Other	A
1604.3000	Caviar and caviar substitutes	A
1605.0000	Crab, shrimps and prawns, lobsters, preparec	
1605.1000	Crab	A
1605.3000	Lobster	A
1605.4000	Other crustaceans	
1605 4900	Other	A
1605.9000	Other	A
1701.0000	Raw sugar pure or beet sugar	A
1701.1000	Raw sugar, not containing added flavoring or coloring	A
1701.1100	Cane sugar	A
1701.1200	Beet sugar	A
1701.9000	Other	A
1701.9100	Containing added flavouring orcolouring matter	A
1701.9910	Crystal cubes, piece and candy sugar	A
1701.9990	Other	A

Continued

ISRAEL TARIFF CODE	SHORT DESCRIPTION OF PRODUCT	Annex A
1702.0000	Other types of sugar	
1702.1000	Lactose and lactose syrup	A
1702.1100	containing 99% lactose, liquid	A
1702.1900	Other	A
1702.2000	Maple sugar and maple syrup	A
1702.3090	Others	A
1702.4000	Glucose and glucose syrup, containing in the dry state	A
1702.5000	Chemically pure fructose	A
1702.6000	Other fructose and fructose syrup, containing in the	A
1702.9000	Other, including invert sugar:-	A
1702.9010	Artificial honey	A
1702.9020	A mixture of caramel with mineral salts	A
1702.9030	In solid form, containing additional falvouring	A
1702.9040	Chemically pure maltose	A
1702.9090	Other	A
1703.0000	Cane molasses	A
1703.1000	Cane molasses	A
1703.9000	Other	A
1704.0000	Sugar candy, not containing cocor	A
1704.1000	Chewing gum whether or not sugar-coated -	A
1704.1010	Containing by weight, 10% or more of chewing gum	A
1704.1090	other-	A
1704.9000	othet-	
1704.9010	Halva	A
1704.9030	other-	A
1704.9031	Sugar-coated almonds or walnuts	A
1704.9032	White chocolate	A
1704.9033	Sugar-coated cereal flakes	A

ISRAEL TARIFF CODE	SHORT DESCRIPTION OF PRODUCT	Annex A
1704.9039	other -	A
All Chapter 18	Cocoa and preparations of cocoa	A
1901.0000	Malt, starch that do not contain cocoa, containing less than 40% cocoa unfatted from articles 0401, to 0404 not containing cocoa	A
1901.1000	Preparations for infant use, put up tor retail sale:-	A
1901.1010	Dietetic preparations of soya fiour, containing	A
1901.1020	Food preparation, of meal, of starch or malt extract	A
1901.1090	Pood preparations of other goods of heading 04.01-04.04	A
1901.2000	Mixes and dough for the preparation of bakers' wares	A
1901.2010	Food preparations of flour, of meal, of starch or malt extract	A
1901.2020	Other, containing cocoa	A
1901.2090	Other	A
1901.9000	Other-	A
1901.9010	Dietetic preparations of soya flour, containing	A
1901.9030	Food preparations fo flour, of meal, of starch or malt extract	A
1901.9090	Other	A
1903.0000	Tapioca and substitutes, flakes or grains...	A
1904.0000	Prepared foods obtained by the swelling of wheat flakes or obtained differently	A
1904.1000	Prepared foods obtained by the swelling or roasting	A
1904.1010	Containing cocoa	A
1904.1090	Other	A
1904.2000	Prepared oats from oat flakes not cooked	A
1904.2010	Containing cocoa	A
1904.2090	Other	A

Continued

ISRAEL TARIFF CODE	SHORT DESCRIPTION OF PRODUCT	Annex A
1904.9000	Other:-	A
1904.9010	Containing COCOa	A
1904.9090	Other:-	A
1905.0000	Bread, cakes, waffle, whether or not containing cocoa, communion wafers, sealing wafers, rice paper and similar product;	
1905.1000	Crispbread	A
1905.1010	with flour not from wheat	A
1905.1020	Food preparation, of meal, of starch or malt extract	A
1905.2000	Ginger bread and the like	
1905.2010	-especially for diabetics	A
1905.4000	Rusks, toasted bread and similar toasted products:-	
1905.4090	Other	A
1905.9000	Other:-	
1905.9020	Biscuits or cakes especially for diabetics(old Annex A says “Gelating capsules”; tariff schedule says biscuits...)	A
1905.9090	Other	A
2001.0000	Vegetables, fruit, nuts, preserved in vinegar	
2001.1000	Cucumbers and gherkins	A
2001.9000	Other:-	
2001.9010	Olives	A
2001.9040	Yams, sweet potatoes, other starchy vegetables	A
2001.9090	Others	A
2002.0000	Tomatoes, prepared or preserved other then in vinegar	
2002.1000	Tomatoes, whole or in pieces	
2002.9000	Other:- (not whole or in pieces)	

ISRAEL TARIFF CODE	SHORT DESCRIPTION OF PRODUCT	Annex A
2002.9020	Tomatoes in powder form	A
2003.0000	Preserved or prepared mushrooms	A
2003.1000	Mushrooms	A
2003.2000	Truffles	A
2004.0000	Other vegetables, prepared or preserved, frozen, other than those in 20.06:-	
2004.1000	Potatoes:	
2004.1010	Products of flour or meal	A
2004.1020	Homogenized food preparations	A
2004.9000	Other frozen veaetables and mixtures of veaetables:-	
2004.9020	Homogenized food preparations	A
2004.9090	Other:- (frozen vegetables)	
ex 2004.9093	Miniature corn-on-the-cob	A
2005.0000	Other vegetables, preserved otherwise than frozen other than in 20.06-	
2005.1000	Homogenized vegetables	A
2005.2000	Potatoes:-	
2005.2010	Products of flour or meal	A
2005.2020	Homogenized food preparations	A
2005.4000	Peas (Pisum sativum):-	
2005.4010	Products of flour or meal	A
2005 4020	Homogenized food preparations	A
2005.5000	Beans (Vigna spp., Phaseolus spp .) -	
2005.5100	Shelled	A
2005.5900	Other:-	

Continued

ISRAEL TARIFF CODE	SHORT DESCRIPTION OF PRODUCT	Annex A
2005.5910	Products of flour or meal	A
2005.5920	Homogenized food preparations	A
2005.6000	Asparagus	A
2005.7000	Olives	A
2005.8000	Sweet corn (Zee mays var. saccharata) -	
2005.8091	Miniature (Baby) corn-on-the-cob	A
2005.9000	Other vegetables and mixtures of vegetables	
2005.9010	Products of flour or meal	A
2005.9020	Homogenized food preparations	A
2005.9090	Other preserved or prepared vegetables	A
2006.0000	Fruit, nuts, fruit peels and other plant parts	A
2006.0010	Glaced or crystallised	A
2006.0090	Other	A
2007.0000	Jams or marmalade, whether or not naturally or artificially sweetened	
2007.1000	Homogenized food preparations	A
2007.9000	Other	
2007.9100	Citrus fruit	A
2007.9900	Other	
2007.9990	Other	A
2008.1000	Nuts, groundnuts and other seeds, whether or not mixed	
2008.1110	Food preparations (peanut butter)	A
2008.1900	Other, including mixtures:- (other nuts)	
2008.1910	Food preparations	A
2008.1920	Other, cooked or not, preserved by freezing	A
2008.1930	Other, roasted:-	
2008.1931	Approved by the Director General of the Ministry of Industry, for chocolate & sweets	A

ISRAEL TARIFF CODE	SHORT DESCRIPTION OF PRODUCT	Annex A
2008.1939	Other roasted nuts	A
2008.1940	Other, in spirits containing more than	A
2008.1990	Other:-	
2008.1999	Others	A
2008.2000	Pineapples	A
2008.2010	Cooked not by ... & freezed, without added sugar	A
2008.2020	In spirits containing more than 2% alcohol by volume	A
2008.2090	Other	A
2008.3000	Citrus fruit-	A
2008.3010	Cooked not by ... & freezed, without added sugar	A
2008.3020	In spirits containing more than 2% alcohol by volume	A
2008.3090	Other	A
2008.4000	Pears:-	A
2008.4010	Cooked not by ... & freezed, without added sugar	A
2008.4020	In spirits containing more than 2% alcohol by volume	A
2008.4090	Other	A
2008.5000	Apricots-	A
2008.5010	Cooked not by ... & freezed, without added sugar	A
2008.5020	In spirits containing more than 2% alcohol by volume	A
2008.5090	Other	A
2008.6000	Cherries-	A
2008.6020	In spirits containing more than 2% alcohol by volume	A
2008.6090	Other	A
2008.7000	Peaches:-	A
2008.7010	Cooked not by ... & freezed, without added sugar	A
2008.7020	In spirits containing more than 2% alcohol by volume	A
2008.7090	Other	A
2008.8000	Strawberries:-	A
2008.8010	Cooked not by ... & freezed, without added sugar	A

Continued

ISRAEL TARIFF CODE	SHORT DESCRIPTION OF PRODUCT	Annex A
2008.8020	In spirits containing more than 2% alcohol by volume	A
2008.8090	Other	A
2008.9000	Other including mixtures other than those of subheading	
2008 9100	Palm hearts	A
2008.9200	Mixtures:-	A
2008.9220	Cooked not by ... & freezed, without added sugar	A
2008.9230	In spirits containing more than 2% alcohol by volume	A
2008.9290	Other	A
2008 9900	Other:-	
2008.9910	Plums and prunes:-	
2008.9911	Cooked or not, preserved by freezing, without added sugar	A
2008 9912	Other, in spirits containing more than 2% alcohol by volume	A
2008.9920	Other, cooked or not, preserved by freezing	A
2008 9930	Other, in spirits containing more than	A
2008.9990	Other	A
2009.0000	Juices of Fruits and Vegetablei	
2009.4000	Pineapple juice:	A
2009.8090	Juice of any other single fruit or vegetable	A
2009.9000	Mixtures of juices	
2009.9090	Other juices	A
2101.1000	Extracts, essences and concentrates, of coffee, and tea:-	A
2101.1100	Extracts, essences and concentrates, of coffee	A
2101.1200	Other preparations based on coffee	A
2101.2000	Extracts. essences and concentrates of tea or mate -	A
2101.2010	Mixtures of tea with sugar, milk, fats	A
2101.2090	Other	A
2101.3000	Roasted chicory and other roasted coffee substitutes:-	A
2101.3010	Roasted chicory	A

ISRAEL TARIFF CODE	SHORT DESCRIPTION OF PRODUCT	Annex A
2101.3020	Instant coffee substitutes	A
2101.3090	Other	A
2102.0000	Yeast, other micro organisms, baking powder	A
2102.1000	Active yeast	A
2102.1010	- Dried, for backing	A
2102.1090	- other	A
2102.2000	Inactive yeast; other single-cell micro-organisms, dead:-	A
2102.2010	Inactive yeasts	A
2102.2090	Other	A
2102.3000	Prepared baking powder:	A
2103.1000	Soya sauce	A
2103.2000	Tomato ketchup and other tomato sauces	A
2103.3000	Mustard flour and meal and prepared mustard	A
2103.9000	Other:-	A
2103.9020	Products of flour, meal, of starch or malt extract	A
2103.9090	Other:-	A
2104.1000	Soups and broths and preparations therefor:-	A
2104.1010	Of flour, meal, starch or malt extract	A
2104.1090	Other	A
2104.2000	Homogenized composite food preparations	A
2106.0000	Other food preparations nes	
2106.1000	Protein concentrates and textured protein substances	A

Continued

ISRAEL TARIFF CODE	SHORT DESCRIPTION OF PRODUCT	Annex A
2106.9000	Other food preparations -	
2106.9010	Jelly powders ice-cream powders and other	A
2106.9040	Cream substitutes and mixtures of fats and sugar	A
2106.9050	Non-alcoholic concentrated extracts	A
2106.9060	Saccharine, including substances of similar properties	A
2106.9070	Candies	A
2106.9080	Preparations solely approved by the Director General of the Ministry of Health as necessary for health care	A
2106.9090	Other -	
2106.9091	Food preparations made of or containing potatoes	A
2106.9092	Alcoholic preparations for producing mixed drinks, whose price is more than $ 0.05 per centiliter	A
2106.9093	Alcoholic preparations for producing mixed drinks, whose price is not more than $ 0.05 per centiliter	A
2106.9095	F&;V juices conc., with min./vit. Of one F/V'	A
2106.9096	F&;V juices conc., with min./vit. Of mixt of F/V	A
2106.9097	F&;V juices conc., of prod. cont > 50% milk	A
2106.9098	Alcoholic preparations	A
2106.9099	Other	A
2201.0000	Water, not sweetened or spiced:-	A
2201.1000	Mineral waters and aerated waters	A
2201.9000	Other water, not sweetened or spicec	A
2202.0000	Waters, sweetened or spiced, or other non-alcoholic beverages, other than fruit and vegetable juices-	A
2202.1000	Waters	A
2202.9000	Other	A
2202.9010	F&;V juices with minerals & vitam	A
2202.9011	- of one F&;V	A
2202.9019	- mixture of F/V juices	
2202.9020	- containing mill	A

ISRAEL TARIFF CODE	SHORT DESCRIPTION OF PRODUCT	Annex A
2202.9090	- other	A
2203.0000	Beer made from malt:-	A
2203.0010	- containing not more than 2% alcohol	A
2203.0020	- containing not more than 3.8% alcohol in reusable bottles	A
2203.0090	- other beer containing malt	A
2207.0000	Ethyl alcohol or neutral spirits	
2207.1000	Undenatured ethyl alcohol of more than 80%; ethyl alcohol and other spirits, denatured:-	
2207.1010	Which the Dir-Gen of the Ministry of Health certifies for the use in medical practice	A
2207.1020	Which the Dir.-Gen. of the Ministry of Health certifies for use in the production of pharmaceuticals	A
2207.1030	Which the Director of Customs certifies for use in the production of vinegar	A
2207.1040	Which the Dir. -Gen of the Ministry of Defense certifies for the production of ethel	A
2207.1050	To be used in the production of an alcoholic beverage.-	
2207.1059	-Other	A
2207.1090	Other	
2207.1099	-Other	A
2207.2000	Ethyl alcohol and other spirits denatured-	A
2207.2010	Denatured alcohol, denatured under special Israeli conditions	A
2207.2090	Other	A
2208.0000	Undenatured ethyl alcohol less than 80%; spirits, liquors and other spiritous beverages	
2208.2000	Alcoholic beverages from grapes.-	
2208.2010	-less than 17% alcohol and less than $0.05/centiliter	A
2208.2020	-more than $0.05/centiliter	A
2208.3000	Whiskies	A

Continued

ISRAEL TARIFF CODE	SHORT DESCRIPTION OF PRODUCT	Annex A
2208.4000	Rum and Tafia:-	A
2208.4010	- less than 17% alcohol and less than $0.05/centiliter	A
2208.4020	- more than $0.05/centiliter	A
2208.4090	Other -	A
2208.5000	Gin and Geneva -	A
2208.5010	- less than 17% alcohol and less than $0.05/centiliter	A
2208.5020	- more than $0.05/centiliter	A
2208.5090	Other	A
2208.6000	Vodka	A
2208.6010	- more than $0.05/centiliter	A
2208.6090	Other -	A
2208.7000	Liqueurs	A
2208.7010	- less than 17% alcohol and less than $0.05/centiliter	A
2208.7020	- more than $0.05/centiliter	A
2208.7090	Other:-	A
2208.9000	Other:-	A
2208.9010	- less than 17% alcohol and less than $0.05/centiliter	A
2208.9020	- more than $0.05/centiliter	A
2208.9021	- like swed. Bitter	A
2208.9029	other	A
2208.9030	-undenatured ethyl alcohol, other	A
2208.9031	--which the Dir-Gen. Of the Ministry of Health certifies for use in Hospitals and Clinics	A
2208.9032	--which the Dir-Gen. Of the Ministry of Health certifies for use in pharmaceuticals	A
2208.9039	-other	A
2208.9090	-other	A
2209.0000	Vinegar and substitutes - acetic acic	A
2301.1000	Flours, meals and pellets of meat or meat offal; greaves	A

ISRAEL TARIFF CODE	SHORT DESCRIPTION OF PRODUCT	Annex A
2301.2000	Flours, meals and pellets, of fish or of crustaceans,	A
2302.0000	Sharps and bran	A
2302.1000	Of maize (corn)	A
2302.2000	Of rice	A
2302.3000	Of wheat	A
2302.4000	Of other cereals	A
2302.5000	Of leguminous plants	A
2303.000C	Residues of starch beet pulp, aregs waste	A
2303.1000	Residues of starch manufacture and similar residues	A
2303.2000	Beet-pulp, bagasse and other waste of sugar manufacture	A
2303.3000	Brewing or distilling dregs and waste	A
2307.0000	Wine lees; argol	A
2308.0000	Other vegetable material and waste for animal feed:-	A
2308.1000	Acorns and horse-chestnuts	A
2308.9000	Other	A
2309.0000	Animal food	
2309.1000	Dog or cat food put up for retail sale	A
2309.1020	- containing by weight, between 15% and 35% protein and not less than 4% fat	A
2309.1029	other	A

Continued

ISRAEL TARIFF CODE	SHORT DESCRIPTION OF PRODUCT	Annex A
2309.9000	Other:-	A
2309.9020	- containing by weight, between 15% and 35% protein and not less than 4% fat	A
2309.9030	Prepared foods for pet fish and birds	A
2309.9090	Other	A
All Chapter 24	Tobacco and prepared tobacco substitutes	
3505.1021	Starches, wheat or corn based (other than waxy corn starch)	A
3505.1029	- Other	A

Annex B: Quantities for Free Import into Israel from USA

ISRAEL TARIFF CODE	SHORT DESCRIPTION OF PRODUCT	**ANNUAL RATE OF GROWTH OF QUANTITY**	**2004 QUANTITY (Metric tons)**	**2005 QUANTITY (Metric tons)**	**2006 QUANTITY (Metric tons)**	**2007 QUANTITY (Metric tons)**	**2008 QUANTITY (Metric tons)**	Additional Notes
0102.9019	--Others	0%	2,000 head	2,000 head	2,000 head	2,000 head	2,000 head	
0201.0000	Meat of bovine, fresh/chilled	4%	1,217	1,266	1,316	1,369	1,424	
0201.1000	Carcass & half carcass							
0201.1010	-within Annex 5							
0201.1090	Others							
0201.2000	Other cuts with bone in							
0201.2010	- within Annex 5							
0201.2090	Others							
0201.3000	Bovine boneless							
0201.3010	- within Annex 5							
0201.3090	Others							

Continued

ISRAEL TARIFF CODE	SHORT DESCRIPTION OF PRODUCT	ANNUAL RATE OF GROWTH OF QUANTITY	2004 QUANTITY (Metric tons)	2005 QUANTITY (Metric tons)	2006 QUANTITY (Metric tons)	2007 QUANTITY (Metric tons)	2008 QUANTITY (Metric tons)	Additional Notes
0202.0000	Meat of bovine, frozen	8%	8,816	9,521	10,283	11,106	11,994	
0202.1000	Carcass & half carcass							
0202.1010	- within Annex 5							
0202.1090	Others							
0202.2000	Other cuts with bone in							
0202.2010	- within Annex 5							
0202.2090	Others							
0202.3000	Same, boneless							
0202.3010	-within Annex 5							
0202.3090	Others							
0204.0000	Meat of sheep or goats; fresh. chilled frozen	4%	608	632	658	684	711	

ISRAEL TARIFF CODE	SHORT DESCRIPTION OF PRODUCT	**ANNUAL RATE OF GROWTH OF QUANTITY**	**2004 QUANTITY (Metric tons)**	**2005 QUANTITY (Metric tons)**	**2006 QUANTITY (Metric tons)**	**2007 QUANTITY (Metric tons)**	**2008 QUANTITY (Metric tons)**	Additional Notes
0204.1000	Carcasses & half care, of lamb: fresh or chilled							
0204.1010	-fresh							
0204.1011	--within Annex 5							
0204.1019	Others							
0204.1090	- other							
0204.1091	- within Annex 5							
0204.1099	Others							
0204.2000	Other meat of sheep, fresh or chilled							
0204.2100	- carcass & half carcass							
0204.2110	- fresh							
0204.2111	-within Annex 5							
0204.2119	Others							
0204.2190	- other							
0204.2191	- within Annex 5							

Continued

ISRAEL TARIFF CODE	SHORT DESCRIPTION OF PRODUCT	**ANNUAL RATE OF GROWTH OF QUANTITY**	**2004 QUANTITY (Metric tons)**	**2005 QUANTITY (Metric tons)**	**2006 QUANTITY (Metric tons)**	**2007 QUANTITY (Metric tons)**	**2008 QUANTITY (Metric tons)**	Additional Notes
0204.2199	Others							
0204.2200	- Other cuts with bone in							
0204.2210	- fresh							
0204.2211	-within Annex 5							
0204.2219	Others							
0204.2290	- other							
0204.2291	-- within Annex 5							
0204.2299	Others							
0204.2300	Boneless							
0204.2310	-fresh							
0204.2311	--within Annex 5							
0204.2319	Others							
0204.2390	- other							
0204.2391	-- within Annex 5							
0204.2399	Others							

ISRAEL TARIFF CODE	SHORT DESCRIPTION OF PRODUCT	**ANNUAL RATE OF GROWTH OF QUANTITY**	**2004 QUANTITY (Metric tons)**	**2005 QUANTITY (Metric tons)**	**2006 QUANTITY (Metric tons)**	**2007 QUANTITY (Metric tons)**	**2008 QUANTITY (Metric tons)**	Additional Notes
0204.3000	Carc & half carc. of lamb, frozen							
0204.3010	-- within Annex 5							
0204.3090	Others							
0204.4000	Other meat of sheep, frozen							
0204.4100	-carcass & half carcass							
0204.4110	--within Annex 5							
0204.4190	Others							
0204.4200	Other cuts with bone in							
0204.4210	-- within Annex 5							
0204.4290	Others							
0204.4300	Boneless							
0204.4310	--within Annex 5							
0204.4390	Others							
0204.5000	Meat of goats							
0204.5010	- fresh							

Continued

ISRAEL TARIFF CODE	SHORT DESCRIPTION OF PRODUCT	**ANNUAL RATE OF GROWTH OF QUANTITY**	**2004 QUANTITY (Metric tons)**	**2005 QUANTITY (Metric tons)**	**2006 QUANTITY (Metric tons)**	**2007 QUANTITY (Metric tons)**	**2008 QUANTITY (Metric tons)**	Additional Notes
0204.5011	- within Annex 5							
0204.5019	Others							
0204.5090	- other							
0204.5091	-within Annex 5							
0204.5099	Others							
0207.0000	Meat and edible offal, of the poultry of the heading #0105; fresh, chilled or frozen	3%	290	299	308	317	326	
0207.1000	Of species gallus domesticus							
0207.1100	- not cut in pieces; fresh or chilled							
0207.1110	--kosher							
0207.1190	- others							
0207.1200	-not cuts in pieces, frozen							
0207.1210	-kosher							
0207.1290	-others							

ISRAEL TARIFF CODE	SHORT DESCRIPTION OF PRODUCT	**ANNUAL RATE OF GROWTH OF QUANTITY**	**2004 QUANTITY (Metric tons)**	**2005 QUANTITY (Metric tons)**	**2006 QUANTITY (Metric tons)**	**2007 QUANTITY (Metric tons)**	**2008 QUANTITY (Metric tons)**	Additional Notes
0207.1300	Cuts and offal, fresh or chilled							
0207.1400	Cuts and offal, frozen							
0207.1410	Liver							
0207.1490	Other cuts and offal							
0207.2000	Fowls of turkeys							
0207.2400	Not cut in pieces, fresh or chilled							
0207.2500	Not cut in pieces, frozen							
0207.2600	Cuts and offal, fresh or chilled							
0207.2710	Liver, frozen							
0207.2790	Other cuts and offal, frozen							
0207.3000	Fowls of ducks, geese or guinea							
0207.3200	Not cut in pieces, fresh or chilled							

Continued

ISRAEL TARIFF CODE	SHORT DESCRIPTION OF PRODUCT	**ANNUAL RATE OF GROWTH OF QUANTITY**	**2004 QUANTITY (Metric tons)**	**2005 QUANTITY (Metric tons)**	**2006 QUANTITY (Metric tons)**	**2007 QUANTITY (Metric tons)**	**2008 QUANTITY (Metric tons)**	Additional Notes
0207.3300	Not cut in pieces, frozen							
0207.3400	Fatty livers, fresh or chilled							
0207.3500	Others, fresh or chilled							
0207.3610	Liver, frozen							
0207.3690	Other cuts frozen							
0210.0000	salted in brine, dried, smoked: edible flours & meals of meat or meat offal	8%	735	794	857	926	1,000	
0210.2000	Meat of bovine							
0303.0000	Fish frozen, not fillet or other parts in 0304	7%	281	301	322	344	368	Tariff items in Chapter 3 remain subject to non-automatic licensing outside of quantities In
ex 0303 -	Fish, frozen, not fillet, from fresh water							

ISRAEL TARIFF CODE	SHORT DESCRIPTION OF PRODUCT	**ANNUAL RATE OF GROWTH OF QUANTITY**	**2004 QUANTITY (Metric tons)**	**2005 QUANTITY (Metric tons)**	**2006 QUANTITY (Metric tons)**	**2007 QUANTITY (Metric tons)**	**2008 QUANTITY (Metric tons)**	Additional Notes
ex 0303 -	Fish, frozen, not fillet, from salt water	7%	4,909	5,253	5,620	6,014	6,435	
0306.1300	Shrimps & prawns	0%	50	50	50	50	50	
0307.5000	Octopus and calamari	0%	40	40	40	40	40	TRQ joint quantity for 0307.5000 and 1605.4100
0402.0000	Milk & cream concentrated or containing added sugar	4%	1,317	1,370	1,424	1,481	1,541	TRQ joint quantity for 0402.1000 and 0402.2000
0402.1000	Milk powder, granules, fat <=1.5%							
0402.1010	- within Annex 5							

Continued

ISRAEL TARIFF CODE	SHORT DESCRIPTION OF PRODUCT	ANNUAL RATE OF GROWTH OF QUANTITY	2004 QUANTITY (Metric tons)	2005 QUANTITY (Metric tons)	2006 QUANTITY (Metric tons)	2007 QUANTITY (Metric tons)	2008 QUANTITY (Metric tons)	Additional Notes
0402.1090	Others							
0402.2000	Milk powder, granules, fat >1.5%							
0402.2100	- no sugar							
0402.2110	-within Annex 5							
0402.2190	Others							
0402.2900	-others							
0404.0000	Whey & products consisting of natural milk	7%	701	750	803	859	919	
0404.1010	- for industry							
0404.1020	-- within Annex 5							
0404.1090	Others							
0405.0000	Butter & other milk fats, dairy spreads	0%	365	365	365	365	365	

ISRAEL TARIFF CODE	SHORT DESCRIPTION OF PRODUCT	**ANNUAL RATE OF GROWTH OF QUANTITY**	**2004 QUANTITY (Metric tons)**	**2005 QUANTITY (Metric tons)**	**2006 QUANTITY (Metric tons)**	**2007 QUANTITY (Metric tons)**	**2008 QUANTITY (Metric tons)**	Additional Notes
0405.1000	Butter							
0405.1010	-within Annex 5							
0405.1030	- for industry							
0405 1099	Others							
0405.2000	Dairy spreads							
0405.2010	-within Annex 5							
0405.2090	Others							
0405.9000	Other							
0405.9010	- within Annex 5							
0405.9090	Others							
0406.0000	Cheese & Curd	2%	600	612	624	637	649	
0406.1000								
0406.1010	-within Annex 5							
0406.1090	Others							

Continued

ISRAEL TARIFF CODE	SHORT DESCRIPTION OF PRODUCT	ANNUAL RATE OF GROWTH OF QUANTITY	2004 QUANTITY (Metric tons)	2005 QUANTITY (Metric tons)	2006 QUANTITY (Metric tons)	2007 QUANTITY (Metric tons)	2008 QUANTITY (Metric tons)	Additional Notes
0406.2000	Grated or powdered cheese							
0406.2010	-within Annex 5							
0406.2090	Others							
0406.3000	Processed cheese, not grated							
0406.3010	- within Annex 5							
0406.3090	Others							
0406.4000	Blue-veined cheese							
0406.4010	- within Annex 5							
0406.4090	Others							
0406.9000	Other cheese							
0407.0011	--- Hatching eggs of chickens	3%	4,173,387	4,298,589	4,427,546	4,560,373	4,697,184	
0407.0019	---others							
0407.0020	--- hatching eggs of turkeys							
0407.0090	---eggs, other							

ISRAEL TARIFF CODE	SHORT DESCRIPTION OF PRODUCT	**ANNUAL RATE OF GROWTH OF QUANTITY**	**2004 QUANTITY (Metric tons)**	**2005 QUANTITY (Metric tons)**	**2006 QUANTITY (Metric tons)**	**2007 QUANTITY (Metric tons)**	**2008 QUANTITY (Metric tons)**	Additional Notes
0701.0000	Potatoes, fresh/ chilled	8%	2,939	3.174	3.428	3.702	3,998	
0701.1000	Seeds							
0701.1010	-(June -Sept)							
0701.1011	--within Annex 5							
0701.1019	Others							
0701.1090	-(Oct. -May)							
0701.1091	--within Annex 5							
0701.1099	Others							
0702.0000	Tomatoes; fresh or chilled	8%	147	159	171	185	200	
0702.0010	-(June-Oct)							
0703.0000	Onions, shallots, garlic, leeks	8%	147	159	171	185	200	
0703.1000	Onions & shallots							
0703.1010	(July-April)							
0703.1090	- others							

Continued

ISRAEL TARIFF CODE	SHORT DESCRIPTION OF PRODUCT	ANNUAL RATE OF GROWTH OF QUANTITY	2004 QUANTITY (Metric tons)	2005 QUANTITY (Metric tons)	2006 QUANTITY (Metric tons)	2007 QUANTITY (Metric tons)	2008 QUANTITY (Metric tons)	Additional Notes
0703.2000	Garlic	4%	122	127	132	137	143	
0703.2010	(July-April)							
0703.2090	- others							
0704.0000	Cabbages, cauliflower, kohlrabi & similar...	4%	1,217	1,266	1,316	1,369	1,424	
0704.1000	Cauliflower & headed broccoli							
0704.1010	Cauliflower (March-August)							
0704.1020	Cauliflower, other (Sept.-February)							
0704.1090	Broccoli, other							
0710.0000	Vegetables, frozen	3%	687	708	729	751	773	
0710.1000	Potatoes							
0710.2000	Leguminous vegetables shelled or unshelled							

ISRAEL TARIFF CODE	SHORT DESCRIPTION OF PRODUCT	**ANNUAL RATE OF GROWTH OF QUANTITY**	**2004 QUANTITY (Metric tons)**	**2005 QUANTITY (Metric tons)**	**2006 QUANTITY (Metric tons)**	**2007 QUANTITY (Metric tons)**	**2008 QUANTITY (Metric tons)**	Additional Notes
0710.2100	-peas							
0710.2110	-- within Annex 5							
0710.2190	Others							
0710.2200	-beans							
0710.2210	-- within Annex 5							
0710.2290	Others							
0710.2900	- others							
0710.2910	--within Annex 5							
0710.2920	---Broad beans(VICIA FABA VAR. MAJOR)							
0710.2990	Others							
0710.3000	spinach							
0710.3010	-- within Annex 5							
0710.3090	Others							
0710.4000	Sweet corn, frozen							

Continued

ISRAEL TARIFF CODE	SHORT DESCRIPTION OF PRODUCT	ANNUAL RATE OF GROWTH OF QUANTITY	2004 QUANTITY (Metric tons)	2005 QUANTITY (Metric tons)	2006 QUANTITY (Metric tons)	2007 QUANTITY (Metric tons)	2008 QUANTITY (Metric tons)	Additional Notes
0710.8000	Other vegetables							
0710.8080	-- within Annex 5							
0710.8090	Others							
0710.9000	Mixtures of vegetables							
0710.9090	Others							
0711.0000	Vegetables provisionally preserved	7%	491	525	562	601	644	
0711.2000	Olives							
0711.9000	Other vegeta-bles, mixtures of vegetables	4%	182	189	197	205	213	
0711.9020	-tomatoes, including juice and puree							
0711.9021	puree							
0711.9029	--other							

ISRAEL TARIFF CODE	SHORT DESCRIPTION OF PRODUCT	**ANNUAL RATE OF GROWTH OF QUANTITY**	**2004 QUANTITY (Metric tons)**	**2005 QUANTITY (Metric tons)**	**2006 QUANTITY (Metric tons)**	**2007 QUANTITY (Metric tons)**	**2008 QUANTITY (Metric tons)**	Additional Notes
0713.0000	Dried legumi-nous vegetables...	4%	180	187	195	202	211	
0713.2000	Chickpeas. dried							
0713.2010	Annex 5							
0713.2090	- other							
0802.1100	Almonds, in shell	0%	530	530	530	530	530	In-quota levy is $1.35/kilo
0802.1200	Almonds, shelled	0%	2,650	2,650	2,650	2,650	2,650	In-quota levy is $1.80/kilo
0805.0000	Citrus fruit, fresh/dried	6%	1,338	1,418	1,503	1,594	1,689	
0805.1000	Oranges							
0805.1010	-fresh							
0805.5000	Lemons and limes	6%	401	425	451	478	506	
0805.5010	-fresh							

Continued

ISRAEL TARIFF CODE	SHORT DESCRIPTION OF PRODUCT	**ANNUAL RATE OF GROWTH OF QUANTITY**	**2004 QUANTITY (Metric tons)**	**2005 QUANTITY (Metric tons)**	**2006 QUANTITY (Metric tons)**	**2007 QUANTITY (Metric tons)**	**2008 QUANTITY (Metric tons)**	Additional Notes
0805.4000	Grapefruit	6%	1,338	1,418	1,503	1,594	1,689	
0806.4010	-fresh.							
0805.9000	Others	6%	1,338	1,418	1,503	1,594	1,689	
0805.9010	-fresh							
0805.9011	-Etrog, kumquat or lime							
0805.9020	-- others							
0806.0000	Grapes, fresh or dried	5%	638	670	703	739	775	TRQ from 15 Oct. until 31 Jan
0806.1000	-fresh							
0806.2000	-dried	2%	1,180	1,204	1,228	1,252	1,277	
0806.2010	Annex 5							
0806.2090	-- others							
0808.0000	Apples, pears & quinces, fresh	3%	2,700	2,781	2,864	2,950	3,039	
0808.1000	Apples							
0808.1020	-- within Annex 5							
0808.1090	Others							

ISRAEL TARIFF CODE	SHORT DESCRIPTION OF PRODUCT	**ANNUAL RATE OF GROWTH OF QUANTITY**	**2004 QUANTITY (Metric tons)**	**2005 QUANTITY (Metric tons)**	**2006 QUANTITY (Metric tons)**	**2007 QUANTITY (Metric tons)**	**2008 QUANTITY (Metric tons)**	Additional Notes
0808.2000	Pears & quinces	5%	638	670	703	739	775	
0808.2010	Quinces							
0808.2012	--within Annex 5							
0808.2019	Others							
0808.2020	-Pears	3%	1,212	1,248	1,286	1,324	1,364	TRQ from 1 Nov. until 31 May
0809.0000	Apricots, cherries, peaches (incl. nectarines) plums & sloes, fresh	7%	561	600	642	687	735	
0809.3000	Peaches & nectarines							
0809.3010	(Apr.-Nov)							
0809.3090	(Dec - Mar.)							
0809.4000	Plums & sloes	8%	367	396	428	462	499	
0809.4010	(May-Nov.)							
0809.4090	(Dec-Apr.)							

Continued

ISRAEL TARIFF CODE	SHORT DESCRIPTION OF PRODUCT	ANNUAL RATE OF GROWTH OF QUANTITY	2004 QUANTITY (Metric tons)	2005 QUANTITY (Metric tons)	2006 QUANTITY (Metric tons)	2007 QUANTITY (Metric tons)	2008 QUANTITY (Metric tons)	Additional Notes
0813.0000	Fruits, dried, except 0801-0806- mixtures of nuts or dried fruits of this Chapter	3%	1,211	1,247	1,285	1,323	1,363	
0813.2000	prunes							
0813.2020	Annex 5							
0813.2090	--other							
1005.0000	Maize (corn)	8%	132	143	154	180	180	
1005.9010	- for pop corn							
1202.0000	Ground-nuts	4%	243	253	263	273	284	
1202.1000	In shell							
1202.1010	- wtih value <= NS 3.20/Kg							
1202.1090	- others							
1202.2000	Shelled							
1202.2010	- for oil							
1202.2040	- with value <= NS 5.30/Kg							
1202.2090	- others							

ISRAEL TARIFF CODE	SHORT DESCRIPTION OF PRODUCT	ANNUAL RATE OF GROWTH OF QUANTITY	2004 QUANTITY (Metric tons)	2005 QUANTITY (Metric tons)	2006 QUANTITY (Metric tons)	2007 QUANTITY (Metric tons)	2008 QUANTITY (Metric tons)	Additional Notes
1206.0000	Sunflower seeds	2%	2,519	2,569	2,621	2,673	2,727	
1206.0040	with value <= NS 3.70/Kg							
1206.0090	Other							
1601.0000	Sausages of meat, of meat	7%	701	750	803	859	919	TRQ joint quantity for 1602.2090, 1602.5090, 1602.9090
1601.0090	Other							
1602.0000	Other prepared meat							
1602.2000	Of liver of any animal							
1602.2090	Other							
1602.2099	Other							
1602.3000	Of poultry of heading No. 01.05	3%	290	299	308	317	326	
1602.3100	Of turkeys:							
1602.3190	Other							
1602.3200	Of chickens gallus domesticus:							
1602.3290	Other							
1602.3900	Other-							
1602.3990	Other							

Continued

ISRAEL TARIFF CODE	SHORT DESCRIPTION OF PRODUCT	ANNUAL RATE OF GROWTH OF QUANTITY	2004 QUANTITY (Metric tons)	2005 QUANTITY (Metric tons)	2006 QUANTITY (Metric tons)	2007 QUANTITY (Metric tons)	2008 QUANTITY (Metric tons)	Additional Notes
1602.5000	Of bovine anmals:-	7%	701	750	803	859	919	TRQ joint quantity for 1602.2090. 1602.5090, 1602.9090
1602.5090	Other							
1602.9090	Other							
1604.2000	Other prepared or preserved fish-	10%	24	26	29	32	35	
1604.2030	Stuffed fish or fish balls							
ex. 1604.2030	Gelfite fish made of whitefish and other fish not containing carp	10%	161	177	195	214	236	
1605.0000	Crab, shrimps and prawns,	10%	10	11	12	13	14	joint quantity for 0307.5000, 1605.4100
1605.4000	Other crusta-ceans							
1605.4100	-Calamari							

ISRAEL TARIFF CODE	SHORT DESCRIPTION OF PRODUCT	**ANNUAL RATE OF GROWTH OF QUANTITY**	**2004 QUANTITY (Metric tons)**	**2005 QUANTITY (Metric tons)**	**2006 QUANTITY (Metric tons)**	**2007 QUANTITY (Metric tons)**	**2008 QUANTITY (Metric tons)**	Additional Notes
2002.0000	Tomatoes, prepared or preserved, other than in vinegar	4%	182	189	197	205	213	
2002.1000	Tomatoes, whole or in pieces:-							
2002.1010	Cooked or uncoooked, preserved by freezing							
2002.1090	Other							
2002.9000	Other (not whole or in pieces)	4%	426	443	461	479	498	
2002.9010	Tomato paste:-							
2002.9011	In packages over 100 kg.							
2002.9019	Other							
2004.0000	Other vegetables prepared or preserved frozen, other than those in 20 06 -	3%	222	229	236	243	250	

Continued

ISRAEL TARIFF CODE	SHORT DESCRIPTION OF PRODUCT	ANNUAL RATE OF GROWTH OF QUANTITY	2004 QUANTITY (Metric tons)	2005 QUANTITY (Metric tons)	2006 QUANTITY (Metric tons)	2007 QUANTITY (Metric tons)	2008 QUANTITY (Metric tons)	Additional Notes
2004,1000	Potatoes:-							
2004.1090	Other							
2004.9000	Other frozen vegetables and mixtures of vegetables							
2004.9010	Products of flour or meal							
2004.9011	In Annex 5							
2004.9090	Other- (frozen vegetables)							
2004.9091	in Annex 5							
2004.9099	Other							
2008.1000	Nuts, ground-nuts and other seeds , whether or not mixed	4%	97	101	105	109	113	
2008.1100	Groundnuts:-							
2008.1120	Other roasted							
2008.1991	Other Almonds	3%	50	52	53	55	56	

ISRAEL TARIFF CODE	SHORT DESCRIPTION OF PRODUCT	ANNUAL RATE OF GROWTH OF QUANTITY	2004 QUANTITY (Metric tons)	2005 QUANTITY (Metric tons)	2006 QUANTITY (Metric tons)	2007 QUANTITY (Metric tons)	2008 QUANTITY (Metric tons)	Additional Notes
2009.0000	Juices of Fruits and vegetables	5%	3,829	4,020	4,221	4,433	4,654	
2009.1000	Orange juice:-							
2009.1100	-Frozen							
2009.1110	-Frozen Concentrated in packs of more than 100 Kg							
2009.1111	---IN PACKAGES CONTAINING 230KG OR MORE							
2009.1130	Frozen Orange juice, not concentrated, in packs of more than 100 kg							
2009.1900	- Other (Orange juice, not frozen) -							
2009.1910	-Concentrated , in packs of more than 100 kg							

Continued

ISRAEL TARIFF CODE	SHORT DESCRIPTION OF PRODUCT	ANNUAL RATE OF GROWTH OF QUANTITY	2004 QUANTITY (Metric tons)	2005 QUANTITY (Metric tons)	2006 QUANTITY (Metric tons)	2007 QUANTITY (Metric tons)	2008 QUANTITY (Metric tons)	Additional Notes
2009.1911	----IN PACKAGES CONTAINING 230KG OR MORE							
2009.1990	--Not concen-trated, in packs of more than 100 kg							
2009.2000	Grapefruit Juice	5%	1,000	1,050	1,103	1,158	1,216	
2009.2110	-Not concen-trated, in packs over 100 kg							
2009.2190	others							
2009.3000	Juice of any other single kind of Citrus fruit	5%	638	670	703	739	775	
2009.3110	in packs over 100 kg							
2009.3190	in other packs							
2009.5000	Tomato juice:-	5%	191	201	211	221	232	
2009.5010	In powder form							

ISRAEL TARIFF CODE	SHORT DESCRIPTION OF PRODUCT	**ANNUAL RATE OF GROWTH OF QUANTITY**	**2004 QUANTITY (Metric tons)**	**2005 QUANTITY (Metric tons)**	**2006 QUANTITY (Metric tons)**	**2007 QUANTITY (Metric tons)**	**2008 QUANTITY (Metric tons)**	Additional Notes
2009.5090	Other tomato juice:-							
2009.5091	-In packaging over 100 kg							
2009.5099	-in other packaging							
2009.7000	Apple juice:	3%	116	119	123	127	131	
2009.7100	Not concen-trated apple juce:-							
2009.7110	- in packages over 100 kg							
2009.7190	-in other packages							
2009.7900	Concentrated Apple juice :-							
2009.7910	in packages over 100 kg							
2009.7930	-other conc apple juice							
2105.000	Ice Cream	3%	100	103	106	109	113	

Continued

ISRAEL TARIFF CODE	SHORT DESCRIPTION OF PRODUCT	**ANNUAL RATE OF GROWTH OF QUANTITY**	**2004 QUANTITY (Metric tons)**	**2005 QUANTITY (Metric tons)**	**2006 QUANTITY (Metric tons)**	**2007 QUANTITY (Metric tons)**	**2008 QUANTITY (Metric tons)**	Additional Notes
2204.2000	Wine made from grapes	0%	200,000 ltr	200,000 ltr	200,000 ltr	200,000 ltr	200,000 ltr	

Annex C: Preferences on Imports to Israel from USA			
Israel Tariff Code	**Short Description of Product**	**Applied MFN Rate (2003)**	**Reduction percentage**
0102.0000	Bovine, live		
0102.9000	Other bovine		
0102.9010	within Annex 5		
0102.9019	-others	exempt	25%
0102.9090	other	NS1.20/kg	25%
0104.0000	Sheeps and goats, live		
0104.1000	Sheep		
0104.1090	Other sheep	NS6.22/kg, BNM 170%	15%
0104.2000	Goats		
0104.2090	Other goats	175%	25%
0105.0000	Fowls of the sp. gallus, ducks, geese and guinea fowls		
0105.1000	weighing <=185g		
0105.1100	-fowls of the species gallus		
0105.1110	- <= NS4.5/unit	NS1.50/unit, BNM 35%	15%
0105.1200	- fowls of turkey		
0105.1210	-<=NS 12/unit	NS6.60/unit, BNM 35%	15%
0105.1900	- other fowls		
0105.1910	-<=NS 12/unit	NS6.60/unit, BNM 35%	15%
0105.9000	Others		
0105.9200	- fowls of the sp. Gallus, <= 2 Kg	NS8.40/unit, BNM 185%	15%
0105.9300	- fowls of th sp. Gallus, >2Kg	NS8.40/unit, BNM 185%	15%
0105.9900	- others	NS67.5/unit, BNM 185%	15%

Continued

Israel Tariff Code	Short Description of Product	Applied MFN Rate (2003)	Reduction percentage
0201.0000	Meat of bovine, fresh/chilled		
0201.1000	Carcass & half carcass		
0201.1010	within Annex 5	100%	10%
0201.1090	- others	213%	10%
0201.2000	Other cuts with bone in		
0201.2010	within Annex 5	100%	10%
0201.2090	- others	213%	10%
0201.3000	Bovine, boneless		
0201.3010	within Annex 5	100%	10%
0201.3090	- others	213%	10%
0202.0000	Meat of bovine, frozen		
0202.1000	Carcass & half carcass		
0202.1010	within Annex 5	exempt	10%
0202.2000	Other cuts with bone in		
0202.2010	within Annex 5	exempt	10%
0202.3000	Bovine , boneless		
0202.3010	within Annex 5	exempt	10%
0203.0000	Meat of swine, fresh/chilled/frozen		15%
0203.1000	Fresh/chilled		
0203.1100	-carcass &;half carcass	30%	15%
0203.1200	- hams, shoulders and their cuts ..., with bone in	30%	15%
0203.1900	-others	30%	15%
0203.2000	Frozen		
0203.2100	carcass & half carcass	20%	15%

Israel Tariff Code	Short Description of Product	Applied MFN Rate (2003)	Reduction percentage
0203.2200	- hams, shoulders and their cuts ..., with bone in	20%	15%
0203.2900	others	20%	15%
0204.0000	Meat of sheep or goats, fresh, chjilled or frozen		
0204.1000	Carcasses & half carc. of lamb; fresh or chilled		
0204.1010	- fresh		
0204.1011	within Annex 5	50% + kosher certificate	10% and kosher certificate
0204.1019	-others	50% + kosher certificate	10% and kosher certificate
0204.1090	- other		
0204.1091	within Annex 5	50% + kosher certificate	10% and kosher certificate
0204.1099	- others	50% + kosher certificate	10% and kosher certificate
0204.2000	Other meat of sheep, fresh or chilled		
0204.2100	- carcass & half carcass		
0204.2110	- fresh		
0204.2111	within Annex 5	50% + kosher certificate	10% and kosher certificate
0204.2119	-- others	50% + kosher certificate	10% and kosher certificate
0204.2190	- other		
0204.2191	within Annex 5	50% + kosher certificate	10% and kosher certificate

Continued

Israel Tariff Code	Short Description of Product	Applied MFN Rate (2003)	Reduction percentage
0204.2199	-- others	50% + kosher certificate	10% and kosher certificate
0204.2200	Other cuts with bone in		
0204.2210	- fresh		
0204.2211	within Annex 5	50% + kosher certificate	10% and kosher certificate
0204.2219	-- others	50% + kosher certificate	10% and kosher certificate
0204.2290	- other		
0204.2291	within Annex 5	50% + kosher certificate	10% and kosher certificate
0204.2299	-others	50% + kosher certificate	10% and kosher certificate
0204.2300	Boneless		
0204.2310	- fresh		
0204.2311	within Annex 5	50% + kosher certificate	10% and kosher certificate
0204.2319	-- others	50% + kosher certificate	10% and kosher certificate
0204.2390	- other		
0204.2391	within Annex 5	50% + kosher certificate	10% and kosher certificate
0204.2399	-others	50% + kosher certificate	10% and kosher certificate
0204.3000	Carcasses & half carc. of lamb, frozen		
0204.3010	within Annex 5	50% + kosher certificate	10% and kosher certificate

Israel Tariff Code	Short Description of Product	Applied MFN Rate (2003)	Reduction percentage
0204.3090	- others	50% + kosher certificate	10% and kosher certificate
0204.4000	Other meat of sheep, frozen		
0204.4100	- carcass & half carcass		
0204.4110	within Annex 5	50% + kosher certificate	10% and kosher certificate
0204.4190	-- others	50% + kosher certificate	10% and kosher certificate
0204.4200	Other cuts with bone in		
0204.4210	within Annex 5	50% + kosher certificate	10% and kosher certificate
0204.4290	-others	50% + kosher certificate	10% and kosher certificate
0204.4300	Boneless		
0204.4310	within Annex 5	50% + kosher certificate	10% and kosher certificate
0204.4390	-others	50% + kosher certificate	10% and kosher certificate
0204.5000	Meat of goats		
0204.5010	- fresh		
0204.5011	within Annex 5	50% + kosher certificate	10% and kosher certificate
0204.5019	-others	50% + kosher certificate	10% and kosher certificate
0204.5090	- other		
0204.5091	within Annex 5	50% + kosher certificate	10% and kosher certificate

Continued

Israel Tariff Code	Short Description of Product	Applied MFN Rate (2003)	Reduction percentage
0204.5099	-- others	50% + kosher certificate	10% and kosher certificate
0205.0000	Meat of horses, asses, mules or hinnies, fresh/chilled/frozen		
0205.0010	- fresh	10%	15%
0205.0090	-other	10%	15%
0206.0000	Edible offal of bovine animals, swine, sheep, goats, horses, asses, mules, or hinnies, fresh, chilled or frozen		
0206.1000	Of bovine animals, fresh or chilled		
0206.1010	- fresh		
0206.1011	-- within Annex 5	50%	60%
0206.1019	-others	50%	60%
0206.1090	- other		
0206.1091	-within Annex 5	50%	60%
0206.1099	-- others	50%	60%
0206.3000	Of swine, fresh/chilled	30%	15%
0206.4000	Of swine, frozen	20%	15%
0206.8000	Others, fresh/chilled	60%	15%
0207.0000	Meat & edible offal, of the poultry of the heading #0105., fresh/chilled / frozen		
0207.1000	Of species gallus		
0207.1100	- not cut in pieces, fresh or chilled		
0207.1110	-- kosher	NS5.00/kg, BNM 170%	10%
0207.1190	-- others	NS5.00/kg,BNM 170%	10%
0207.1200	- not cut in pieces, frozen		

Israel Tariff Code	Short Description of Product	Applied MFN Rate (2003)	Reduction percentage
0207.1210	--kosher	NS5.00/kg,BNM 170%	10%
0207.1290	---others	NS5.00/kg, BNM 170%	10%
0207.1300	Cuts and offal, fresh or chilled	NS9.00/kg, BNM 111%	10%
0207.1400	Cuts and offal, frozen		
0207.1410	Liver	NS9.00/kg,BNM 115%	10%
0207.1490	Others cuts and offal	NS9.00/kg, BNM 191%	10%
0207.2000	Fowls of turkeys		
0207.2400	Not cut in pieces, fresh or chilled	NS5.00/kg, BNM 170%	10%
0207.2500	Not cut in pieces, frozen	NS5.00/kg, BNM 170%	10%
0207.2600	Cuts and offal, fresh or chilled	NS9.00/kg,BNM 111%	10%
0207.2700	Cuts and offal, frozen		
0207.2710	Liver	NS9.00/kg, BNM 102%	10%
0207.2790	Other cuts and offal	NS5.00/kg, BNM 170%	10%
0207.3000	Fowls of ducks, geese or guinea		
0207.3200	Not cut in pieces, fresh or chilled	NS9.00/kg, BNM 170%	10%
0207.3300	Not cut in pieces, frozen	NS9.00/kg, BNM 170%	10%
0207.3400	Fatty livers, fresh or chilled	NS12.0/kg, BNM 111%	10%
0207.3500	Others, fresh or chilled	NS9.00/kg,BNM 111%	10%
0207.3600	Others, frozen		
0207.3610	Liver	NS9.00/kg, BNM 102%	10%
0207.3690	Other cuts	NS9.00/kg, BNM 170%	10%
0209			15%
0210.0000	Meat & edible meat offal; salted, In brine, dried, smoked; edible flours & meals of meat or meat offal		
0210.1000	Meat of swine		
0210.1100	- hams, shoulders, cuts thereof, with bone in	NS417/ton, BNM 96%	15%
0210.1200	- bellies (streaky) and cuts thereof	NS417/ton, BNM 96%	15%
0210.1900	- other	NS417/ton, BNM 96%	15%
0210.2000	Meat of bovine	NS417/ton, BNM 191%	10%

Continued

Israel Tariff Code	Short Description of Product	Applied MFN Rate (2003)	Reduction percentage
0210.9000	Others, incl. edible flours and meals of meat or meat offal		
0210.9100	-Of upper mammals		
0210.9110	- meat and meat offal	NS417/ton, BNM 96%	15%
0210.9190	-other	16%+NS417/ton, BNM 96%	15%
0210.9200	Meat of whales, dolphines, cetasea, manatees, dugongs		
0210.9210	- meat and meat offal	NS417/ton, BNM 96%	15%
0210.9290	-other	16%+NS417/ton, BNM 96%	15%
0210.9300	Meat of reptiles (including snakes and turtles)		
0210.9310	- meat and meat offal	NS417/ton, BNM 96%	15%
0210.9390	-other	16%+NS417/ton, BNM 96%	15%
0210.9900	Others		
0210.9910	- poultry livers	exempt	15%
0210.9920	- meat and meat offal	NS417/ton, BNM 96%	15%
0210.9990	- other	16%+NS417/ton, BNM 96%	15%
0302.0000	Fish, fresh or chilled, not fillet or other parts in 0304.-		
0302.1100	Trout	15%+NS4005.13/ton	15%
0302.1210	mixture incldg items of 03.06 or 03.07 in any prctg	15%+NS4505.78/ton	15%
0302.1230	Others	10%+ns2503.21/ton	15%
0303.0000	Fish, frozen, not fillet or other parts in 0304.-	15%+NS4505.78/ton	10%
0304.0000	Fish, fillet or other parts, fresh, chilled or frozen		
0304.1000	- fresh or chilled		
0304.1020	Pacific Ocean Salmon, Atlantic and Danube		

Israel Tariff Code	Short Description of Product	Applied MFN Rate (2003)	Reduction percentage
0304.1021	Mixture of items from 03.06 and 03.07	15%+NS4505.78/ton	13%
0304.1029	-Others	NS313/ton	13%
0304.1030	Trout Fillet		
0304.1031	Mixture of items from 03.06 and 03.07	15%+NS4505.78/ton	13%
0304.1039	-Others	15%+NS6.51/kg	13%
0304.1040	Tuna	10%+NS4005.13/ton	13%
0304.1050	Fillet of Skipnack, Sardines, Mackerels		
0304.1051	Mixture of items from 03.06 and 03.07	15%+NS4505.78/ton	13%
0304.1059	-Others	15%+NS6.51/kg	13%
0304.1060	Fillet of other fish declared as not from the Mediteranean	10%+NS4005.13/ton	13%
0304.1070	Other Fillet		
0304.1071	Mixture of items from 03.06 and 03.07	15%+NS4505.78/ton	13%
0304.1079	-Others	15%+NS6.51/kg	13%
0304.1090	Other fish meat		
0304.1091	Mixture of items from 03.06 and 03.07	15%+NS4505.78/ton	13%
0304.9000	- other		
0304.9010	Mixture of items from 03.06 and 03.07	15%+NS4505.78/ton	13%
0305.0000	fish dried...	0 - 15% or 54.61 nis/t	13%
0306.0000	Crustaceans		
	Tariff Items In Chapter 3 remain subject to non-automatic licensing outside of quantities in List B		
0306.1000	frozen	15%+NS4505.78/ton	13%

Continued

Israel Tariff Code	Short Description of Product	Applied MFN Rate (2003)	Reduction percentage
0306.2000	not frozen	15%+NS4505.78/ton	13%
0307.0000	Mollusks	15%+NS4505.78/ton	13%
0401.0000	Milk & cream not conc., no sugar...		
0401.1000	Of a fat content, by weight, <=1%	172%	15%
0401.2000	Of a fat content, by weight, 1% - 6%	172%	15%
0401.3000	Of a fat content, by weight, >6%	172%	15%
0402.0000	Milk & cream conc./cont.added sugar...		
0402.1000	Milk powder, granules, fat <= 1.5%		
0402.1010	within Annex 5	85%	10%
0402.1090	- other	182%	10%
0402.2000	Milk powder, granules, fat >1.5%		
0402.2100	- no sugar		
0402.2110	within Annex 5	212%	10%
0402.2190	--others	212%	10%
0402.2900	--others	212%	10%
0402.9000	Others		
0402.9100	- no sugar		
0402.9110	-- Condensed milk	52%	15%
0402.9130	--other	153%	15%
0402.9900	- others		
0402.9910	-condensed milk	52%	15%
0402.9920	-other	153%	15%
0403.0000	Buttermilk. yogurt. cream, kephir,...		
0403.1000	Yogurt		

Israel Tariff Code	Short Description of Product	Applied MFN Rate (2003)	Reduction percentage
0403.1010	-with cocoa, with added flavor, with added fruit		spec. fee
0403.1011	powdered, granulated or other solid which contains, less than 1.5% milk fat, by weight	129%	spec. fee
0403.1012	powdered, granulated or other solid which contains, more than 1.5% milk fat, by weight	129%	spec. fee
0403.1013	others which contain more than 3% milk fat, by weight	129%	spec. fee
0403.1019	others	129%	spec. fee
0403.1020	with added fruit		
0403.1030	-drinks on yogurt basis	120%	15%
0403.1090	- other	134%	15%
0403.9000	other		
0403.9010	-with cocoa, with added flavor, with added fruit		
0403.9011	powdered or solid, contains milk fat less than 1.5% by weight	129%	15%
0403.9012	powdered or solid, contains milk fat less than 1.5% by weight	129%	15%
0403.9013	others, contain milk fat less than 3%	129%	15%
0403.9019	-other	129%	15%
0403.9090	- other	129%	15%
0404.0000	Whey & products consisting of natural milk		
0404.1000	Whey		
0404.1090	- others	40%	10%
0404.9000	Other		
0404.9090	- others	152%	15%
0405.0000	Butter & other milk fats, dairy spreads		

Continued

Israel Tariff Code	Short Description of Product	Applied MFN Rate (2003)	Reduction percentage
0405.1000	Butter		
0405.1090	- others	152%	10%
0405.2000	Dairy spreads		
0405.2010	within Annex 5	152%	10%
0405.2090	- others	152%	10%
0405.9000	Other		
0405.9010	within Annex 5	152%	10%
0405.9090	- others	152%	10%
0406.0000	Cheese & curd		
0406.1000	Fresh, cheese, uncured or unripend		
0406.1010	within Annex 5	148%	10%
0406.1090	- others	148%	10%
0406.2000	Grated or powdered cheese, all		
0406.2010	within Annex 5	150%	10%
0406.2090	- others	NS15.24/kg	10%
0406.3000	Processed cheese, not grated		
0406.3010	within Annex 5	50%	10%
0406.3090	- others	NS15.24/kg, BNM 214%	10% and license
0406.4000	Blue-veined cheese		
0406.4010	within Annex 5	120%	10%
0406.4090	- others	NS17.08/kg	10%
0406.9000	Other cheese		
0406.9010	within Annex 5	50%	10%
0406.9090	- others	NS17.08/kg, BNM 179%	10% and license

Israel Tariff Code	Short Description of Product	Applied MFN Rate (2003)	Reduction percentage
0407.0000	Fresh, preserved, cooked eggs in shell		
0407.0010	Hatching eggs of chickens		
0407.0019	- others	NS0.75/unit, BNM 50%	15%
0407.0020	Hatching eggs of turkey & other	NS3.60/unit, BNM 50%	15%
0407.0090	Eggs, other	NS0.30/unit, BNM 191%	10%
0408.0000	Bird's eggs, not in shell & egg yolks		
0408.1000	Egg yolks		
0408.1100	- dried	14%+NS8.0/kg, BNM 100%	20%
0408.1900	- others	14%+NS3.25/kg,BNM 100%	20%
0408.9000	Others		
0408.9100	- dried	14%+NS8.0/kg, BNM 100%	20%
0408.9900	- others	14%+NS3.25/kg,BNM 100%	20%
0409.0000	Natural honey		
0409.0010	within Annex 5, value <= NS14 Kg	NS7.00/kg	25%
0410.0000	Animal prod. n.e.s fit for hum. cons.		
0410.0010	Propolis	12%	15%
0410.0090	Others	32%	15%
0701.0000	Potatoes, fresh or chilled		
0701.1000	Seeds		
0701.1010	- (released June - Sept.)		
0701.1019	others	97%	10%
0701.1090	- (released Oct. - May)		
0701.1099	-- others	10%	10%
0701.9000	Others		
0701.9010	- (released July-Apr.), except 0701.9030	NS1.82/kg BNM 234%	15%

Continued

Israel Tariff Code	Short Description of Product	Applied MFN Rate (2003)	Reduction percentage
0701.9020	- (released May-June), except 0701.9030	NS1.53/kg BNM 234%	15%
0701.9030	- within Annex 5	250%	15%
0702.0000	Tomatoes, fresh or chilled		
0702.0010	- (released June-Oct.)	NS0.91/kg BNM 277.8%	25%
0702.0090	- (released Nov.-May)	NS1.22/kg BNM 277.8%	25%
0703.0000	Onion, shallots, garlic, leeks,..		
0703.1000	Onions & shallots		
0703.1010	-released July-April	NS1.11/kg, BNM 303.2%	10%
0703.1090	- others-	NS0.78/kg, BNM 303.2%	10%
0703.2000	Garlic	NS7.36/kg, BNM346%, BNL NS7.00/kg	25%
0703.9000	Leeks & other alliaceous vegetables	75%	25%
0704.0000	Cabbages, cauliflower, kohlrabi & similar..		
0704.1000	Cauliflower & headed broccoli		
0704.1010	Cauliflower released March -August	NS0.83/kg, BNM 130.2%	25%
0704.1020	Cauliflower, released September - February	NS1.11/kg, BNM 130.2%	25%
0704.1090	Broccoli	NS1.26/kg, BNM 130.2%	25%
0704.2000	Brussel sprouts	NS1.26/kg, BNM 130.2%	20%
0704.9000	Others		
0704.9010	Chinese leaves	NS0.64/kg, BNM 130.2%	20%
0704.9020	Kohlrabi	NS0.78/kg, BNM 130.2%	20%
0704.9030	Red and White Cabbage	NS0.74/kg	20%
0704.9090	Other	75%	20%

Israel Tariff Code	Short Description of Product	Applied MFN Rate (2003)	Reduction percentage
0705.0000	Lettuce (lactuca sativa) & chicory...		
0705.1000	Lettuce		
0705.1100	- head lettuce	NS0.73/kg, BNM90.6%	15%
0705.1900	- other lettuce	NS0.73/kg, BNM90.6%	15%
0705.2000	Chicory		
0705.2100	Witloof chicory	10%	25%
0705.2900	Other chicory	10%	25%
0706.0000	Carrots, turnips, salad beetroot,..		
0706.1000	Carrots and Turnips		
0706.1010	- (released Dec-May)	NS1.11/kg, BNM 216.7%	15%
0706.1090	(released June- Nov.)	NS1.44/kg, BNM 216.7%	15%
0706.9000	Others		
0706.9010	Celery roots	NS0.84/kg, BNM147.5%	25%
0706.9030	Radishes	NS0.51/kg, BNM147.5%	25%
0706.9050	Horseradish	NS3.93/kg, BNM147.5%	25%
0706.9090	Other edible roots	75%	25%
0707.0000	Cucumbers & gherkins fresh/chilled	NS0.99/kg BNM173%	25%
0708.0000	Leguminous vegetables		
0708.1000	Peas	NS1.04/kg, BNM 117.6%	30%
0708.2000	Beans	NS1.04/kg, BNM 117.6%	30%
0708.9000	Others leguminous vegetables		
0708.9010	- chickpeas	NS0.61/kg, BNM 117.6%	30%
0708.9020	Fava beans	NS0.87/kg, BNM 117.6%	30%
0708.9090	- other leguminous vegetables	75%	30%

Continued

Israel Tariff Code	Short Description of Product	Applied MFN Rate (2003)	Reduction percentage
0709.0000	Other vegetables, fresh/chilled		
0709.1000	Globe artichokes	NS1.49/kg, BNM 117.6%	25%
0709.2000	Asparagus	75	30%
0709.3000	Aubergines		
0709.3010	- (released May-Oct.)	NS0.47/kg, BNM 90.6%	30%
0709.3090	- (released Nov.-Apr.)	NS0.57/kg, BNM 90.6%	30%
0709.4000	Celery other than celeriac	NS0.79/kg, BNM 90.6%	30%
0709.5000	Mushrooms & truffles		
0709.5100	- mushrooms of the genus Agaricus		
0709.5110	(released June - September)	10%	25%
0709.5190	-- others	NS7.31/kg, BNM 350.1%	25%
0709.5200	- truffles	35%	25%
0709.5900	Others		
0709.5910	(released June - September)	105	25%
0709.5990	others	NS6.59/kg, BNM 350.15	25%
0709.6000	Fruits of the genus capsicum/pimenta		
0709.6010	- sweet peppers (capsicum grossum), not ground	NS1.88/kg, BNM 94.7%	25%
0709.6020	others	NS1.40/kg, BNM 94.7%	25%
0709.7000	Spinach	NS1.34/kg, BNM 107.9%	25%
0709.9000	Others		
0709.9010	- olives	NS1.83/kg, BNM 129.3%	35%
0709.9020	- sweet Corn, fresh	NS0.55/kg, BNM 130.0%	35%
0709.9030	Courgette		
0709.9031	-- (released May-Oct.)	NS0.55/kg, BNM 130.2%	35%

Israel Tariff Code	Short Description of Product	Applied MFN Rate (2003)	Reduction percentage
0709.9033	-- (Nov.-Apr.), with value <= NS 1.36/Kg	NS0.83/kg, BNM 130.2%	35%
0709.9090	Other	75%	35%
0710.0000	Vegetables, frozen		
0710.1000	Potatoes	17.1%+NS2.93/kg, BNM 64.3%	10%
0710.2000	Leguminous vegetables, shelled or unshelled		
0710.2100	- Peas		
0710.2110	within Annex 5	13.1%	10%
0710:2190	-others	18.8%+NS0.85/kg,BNM 69.1%	10%
0710.2200	- beans		
0710.2210	within Annex 5	13.1%	10%
0710.2290	--others	18.8%+NS0.80/kg,BNM 69.1%	10%
0710.2900	- others (excl 2920)		
0710.2910	within Annex 5	12.8%	10%
0710.2990	-- others	17.1%+NS1.14/kg, BNM64.3%	10%
0710.3000	- spinach		
0710.3010	within Annex 5	13.1%	10%
0710.3090	-- others	18.8%+NS0.51/kg,BNM 69.1%	10%
0710.4000	Sweet corn, frozen	18.8%+NS0.97/kg',BNM 69.1%	10%
0710.8000	Other veaetables		

Continued

Israel Tariff Code	Short Description of Product	Applied MFN Rate (2003)	Reduction percentage
0710.8010	Carrots, caulliflower, cabbage, broccoli, peppers, celery	18.8%+NS0.63/kg,BNM 69.1%	10%
0710.9000	Mixtures of vegetables	17.1%+NS0.98/kg, BNM64.3%	10%
0711.0000	Vegetables provisionally preserved		
0711.2000	Olives	30%+NS1.00/kg, BNM 100%	10%
0711.9000	Other vegetables, mixtures of vegetables		
0711.9010	-pepper (piper/pimenta/capsicum...)	25%	15%
0711.9020	- tomatoes, including juice and puree		
0711.9021	-- concentrated or puree	13.8%+NS1.63/kg, BNM100%	10%
0711.9029	-other	13.8%+NS0.50/kg, BNM100%	10%
0711.9030	- potato		
0711.9031	-sliced	30%+NS3.00/kg BNM 100%	15%
0711.9039	-others	30%+NS1.50/kg BNM 100%	15%
0711.9040	- other		
0711.9041	-sweet corn	30%+NS1.95/kg BNM 100%	15%
0711.9049	-others	30%+NS1.00/kg BNM 100%	15%
0713.0000	Dried leguminous vegetables...		
0713.2000	Chickpeas, dried		
0713.2010	-within Annex 5	NS0.4/kg	10%
0713.2090	- other	NS1.11/kg, BNM 152%	10%
0714.0000	Manioc, arrowroot, salep,.. sw. potatoes,..		
0714.2000	Sweet Potatoes	NS1.03/kg, BNM238%	20%

Israel Tariff Code	Short Description of Product	Applied MFN Rate (2003)	Reduction percentage
0802.0000	Other nuts, fresh, dried, shelled or unshelled		
0802.1000	Almonds		
0802.1100	- In shell		
0802.1190	- not for chocolate	NS9.72/kg, BNM 103.8%	10%
0802.1200	- shelled		
0802.1290	- not for chocolate	NS17.34/kg. BNM 103.8	10%
0803.0000	Bananas, including plantains, Fresh or dried		
0803.0010	Fresh	NS1.05/kg, BNM138.4%	15%
0803.0020	Dried	25%	15%
0804.0000	Dates, figs, pineapples, avocados, guavas, mangoes, mangosteens, fresh, dried		
0804.1000	Dates	NS5.46/kg, BNM 574%	15%
0804.4000	Avocados		
0804.4010	- fresh	NS1.92/kg, BNM86.5%	15%
0804.4020	- dried	25%	25%
0804.5000	Guavas, mangoes, mangosteens		
0804.5010	-- (released June-Dec),	NS2.08/kg, BNM86.5%	20%
0804.5020	- (released Jan.-May)	NS1.30/kg, BNM 87.5%	25%
0805.0000	Citrus fruit, fresh/dried		
0805.1000	Oranges		
0805.1010	- fresh	NS0.75/kg, BNM164.8%	10%
0805.1020	- dried	25%	20%

Continued

Israel Tariff Code	Short Description of Product	Applied MFN Rate (2003)	Reduction percentage
0805.2000	Mandarins		
0805.2010	- fresh	NS0.87/kg, BNM 224.9%	20%
0805.2020	- dried	25%	20%
0805.4000	Grapefruit		
0805.4010	-fresh	NS0.66/kg, BNM 164.8%	10%
0805.4020	-dried	25%	20%
0805.5000	Citrus limonum, Limon citrus, Latifolia citrus, Aurantifolia citrus		
0805.5010	- fresh	NS0.81/kg, BNM250.4%	10%
0805.5020	- dried	25%	25%
0805.9000	Others		
0805.9010	- fresh		
0805.9011	-- Etrog, kumquat, lime	NS2.67/kg, BNM 148.6%	10%
0805.9019	-- others	75%	10%
0805.9020	- dried	25%	20%
0806.0000	Grapes, fresh or dried		
0806.1000	-fresh	NS1.70/kg, BNM 355.1%	10%
0806.2000	- dried		
0806.2090	-- others	NS7.50/kg, BNM 346%	10%
0807.0000	Melons (incl. watermelons)/papaws, fresh		
0807.1000	Melons (incl. watermelons)		
0807.1100	Watermelons		
0807.1110	(released Oct.-May)	NS0.48/kg, BNM 103.8%	25%
0807.1190	-- (released June-Sept.)	NS0.46/kg, BNM 103.8%	25%
0807.1900	Others		

Israel Tariff Code	Short Description of Product	Applied MFN Rate (2003)	Reduction percentage
0807.1910	- (released Oct -May)	NS1.27/kg,BNM 103.8	20%
0807.1990	- (released June-Sept)	NS0.69/kg, BNM 103.8	20%
0807.2000	-Papaya	NS2.57/kg, BNM 86.5%	25%
0808.0000	Apples, Pears & Quinces		
0808.1000	Apples		
0808.1020	-within Annex 5	NS3.85/kg, BNM 569.5%	10%
0808.1090	- others	NS1.89/kg, BNM 562.9%	10%
0808.2000	Pears & quinces		
0808.2010	Quinces		
0808.2012	-within Annex 5	NS3.25/kg, BNM 324.2%	10%
0808.2019	-others	NS1.41/kg, BNM 320.5%	10%
0808.2020	- Pears	NS2.10/kg, BNM 445.7%	10%
0809.0000	Apricots, cherries, peaches (Incl. nectarines), plums & sloes, fresh		
0809.1000	Apricots		
0809.1010	-- (released Apr.-Aug.)	NS1.61/kg, BNM 90.6%	15%
0809.1090	- (released Sept.-Mar.)	NS1.02/kg, BNM 91.7%	20%
0809.2000	Cherries		
0809.2010	(released Apr.-July)	NS3.87kg, BNM 82.4%	15%
0809.2090	(released Aug.-Mar.)	NS1.82/kg, BNM 83.3%	20%
0809.3000	Peaches & nectarines		
0809.3010	(released Apr. - Nov.)	NS1.39/kg, BNM 90.6%	10%
0809.3090	(released Dec. - Mar)	NS0.88/kg,BNM 91.7%	10%
0809.4000	Plums & sloes		
0809.4010	(released May-Nov.)	NS1.18/kg, BNM 103.8%	25%

Continued

Israel Tariff Code	Short Description of Product	Applied MFN Rate (2003)	Reduction percentage
0809.4090	(released Dec.-Apr.)	NS0.74/kg,BNM 105%	25%
0810.0000	Other fruit, fresh		
0810.1000	Strawberries		
0810.1010	(released Oct.-May)	NS4.42/kg, BNM 95.6%	35%
0810.1090	(released June-Sept)	NS1.44/kg, BNM 97.2%	40%
0810.5000	Kiwifruit		
0810.5010	(released Sept-June)	NS3.59/kg, BNM 95.6%	15%
0810.5090	(released July-Aug)	NS1.70/kg, BNM 96.7%	15%
0810.9000	Others		
0810.9010	Persimmon		
0810.9011	(released Aug-Feb)	NS1.39/kg, BNM 95.6%	15%
0810.9019	(released Mar.-July)	NS0.97/kg, BNM 96.7%	20%
0810.9020	Lychee		
0810.9021	(released June-Sept.)	NS5.78/kg, BNM 95.6%	15%
0810.9029	(released Oct.- May)	NS3.65/kg, BNM 96.7%	20%
0810.9030	Loquat(Shesek)		
0810.9031	(released Mar.-July)	NS5.09/kg, BNM 95.6%	15%
0810.9039	(released Aug-Feb)	NS3.57/kg, BNM 96.7%	20%
0810.9090	Other fruit, fresh	100%	15%
0811.0000	Boiled, Steamed or Frozen fruits		
0811.1000	Strawberries		
0811.1090	- in packages <10kg	NS2.00/kg BNM 30%	20%
0811.9090	Other fruits		
0813.0000	Fruits. dried, except 0801-0806-, mixtures of nuts or dr. fruits of this Chapter		

Israel Tariff Code	Short Description of Product	Applied MFN Rate (2003)	Reduction percentage
0813.2000	-prunes		
0813.2020	-within Annex 5	NS2.00/kg	10%
0813.2090	--others		
0813.2091	-moisture less than 24% in packages>30kg	NS1.00/kg, BNM 30%	10%
0813.2099	--others	NS4.47/kg, BNM 103.8%	10%
0813.5000	- Mix of nuts or dried fruits of this chapter		
0813.5010	-- mixed nuts		
08135090	mixture of dry fruits		15%
1005.0000	Maize (corn)		
1005.9010	- for pop corn	NS2.30/kg, BNM 139%	10%
1108.0000	Starches, inulin		
1108.1000	-starches		
1108.1200	--maize (corn) starch		
1108.1290	-- - other (non waxy)	8%+NS0.40/kg, BNM 22.5%	62% BNM NS0.33/ kg
1202.0000	Ground-nuts		
1202.1000	In shell		
1202.1010	- with value <= NS 3.20/Kg	NS3.20/kg BNM 115%	10%
1202.1090	- others	20%+NS0.96/kg	10%
1202.2000	Shelled		
1202.2040	with value <=NS 5.30/kg	NS5.30/kg BNM 115%	10%
1202.2090	-others	20%+NS1.59/kg	10%
1206.0000	Sunflower seeds		
1206.0040	with value <= NS 3.70/Kg	NS3.70/kg,BNM 139%	10%
1206.0090	Other	20%+NS1.11/kg	10%

Continued

Israel Tariff Code	Short Description of Product	Applied MFN Rate (2003)	Reduction percentage
1404.9000	Other		
1404.9010	Polen, less than 15% moisture	NS19.50/kg	25%
1501.0000	Lard, other than pig or poultry fat	Exempted	15%
1507.1000	Soya bean Crude oil, whether or not degummed:-		
1507.1010	Edible	Exempted	40%
1507.9000	Soya bean oil, Other-		
1507.9010	Edible	Exempted	40%
1509.1000	Olive oil, Virgin-	12%+NS5.70/kg, BNM 50%	20%
1509.9000	Olive oil, Other-(not virgin):		
1509.9030	Edible	12%+NS4.07/kg, BNM65.5%	20%
1510.0000	Other oils from olives, Hardened or solidified:		
1510.0030	Edible	12%+NS5.70/kg, BNM 50%	20%
1510.0090	others	8%	Exempted
1512.1000	Sunflower seed oil, safflower oil and their fractions:-		
1512.1100	Crude oil-		
1512.1110	Edible	Exempted	40%
1512.1900	Other-		
1512.1920	Edible	Exempted	40%
1512.2000	Cotton seed oil and its fractions:-		
1512.2900	Others		
1512.2990	Other-	8%	Exempted
1514.0000	Rape seed oil, colza oil, and mustard seed oil and their fractions		

Israel Tariff Code	Short Description of Product	Applied MFN Rate (2003)	Reduction percentage
1514.1000	Rape seed oil, low Erucic Acid		
1514.1100	Crude oil-		
1514.1190	Others	8%	40%
1514.9000	Other:		
1514.9100	Crude oil-		
1514.9190	Other	8%	40%
1516.2030	Other, edible -		
1516.2032	Other nuts oils or fruit kernels as detailed in 08.02 and 12.12	8%	Exempted
1516.2033	Olive oil	12%+NS5.70/kg, BNM 50%	20%
1517.0000	Margarine, edible other than 15.16		
1517.9000	Other.-		
1517.9010	Liquid margarine	Exempted	40%
1517.9020	Mixtures of fixed vegetable oils, not volatile:-		
1517.9021	Containing olive oil	12%+NS5.70/kg, BNM 50%	20%
1517.9022	Containing soybean oil, sunflower oil, cottonseed oil, rapeseed oil, or corn oil,	Exempted	40%
1601.0000	Sausages of meat, of meat offal or blood		
1601.0010	Containing poultry meat	12%+NS2.90/kg,BNM 50%	15%
1601.0090	Other	12%	10%
1602.0000	Other prepared meat		
1602.2000	Of liver of any animal:-		
1602.2090	Other		
1602.2091	containing poultry liver	12%+NS9.75/kg,BNM 50%	15%
1602.2099	Other	12%	10%
1602.3000	Of poultry of heading No. 01.05:-		

Continued

Israel Tariff Code	Short Description of Product	Applied MFN Rate (2003)	Reduction percentage
1602.3100	Of turkeys:-		
1602.3190	Other	12%+NS4.90/kg,BNM 50%	10%
1602.3200	Of chickens gallus domesticus:-		
1602.3290	Other	12%+NS4.90/kg,BNM 50%	10%
1602.3900	Other-		
1602.3990	Other	12%+NS4.90/kg,BNM 50%	10%
1602.4000	Of swine:-		
1602.4100	Hams and cuts thereof	12%	15%
1602.4200	Shoulders and cuts thereof	12%	15%
1602.4900	Other, Including mixtures:-		
1602.4910	Mixed homogenized food preparations	12%	15%
1602.4990	Other	12%	15%
1602.5000	Of bovine animals:-		
1602.5090	Other		
1602.5091	Contains, by weight, more than 20% poultry meat	12%	10%
1602.5099	Other	12%	10%
1602.9000	Other, incl. preparations of blood of any animal:-		
1602.9090	Other	12%	10%
1604.0000	Fish, processed or preserved, Kaviar and Kaviar substitutes		
1604.1000	Fish, whole or in pieces, but not minced		
1604.1300	Sardines, sardinella and brisling or sprats:-		
1604.1310	within Annex 5	12%+NS4.50/kg, BNM 50%	10%
1604.1400	Tunas, skipjack and Atlantic bonito (Santa spp)		
1604.1410	within Annex 5	12%+NS3.25/kg, BNM 50%	10%

Israel Tariff Code	Short Description of Product	Applied MFN Rate (2003)	Reduction percentage
1604.1500	Mackerel:-		
1604.2000	Other prepared or preserved fish		
1604.2030	Stuffed fish or fish balls		
1604.2039	others	12%+NS4.90/kg, BNM 50%	10%
1605.0000	Crab, shrimps and prawns, lobsters, prepared		
1605.2000	Shrimps and prawns	12%	20%
1605.4000	Other crustaceans		
1605.4100	- Calamary	12%	10%
1702.3000	Glucose and glucose syrup, not containing fructose		
1702.3010	Liquid glucose	NS0.39/kg, BNM 18%	52% BNM 0.08/kg, from general
1902.0000	Uncooked Pasta, not stuffed with meat or		
1902.1000	Uncooked pasta, not stuffed or otherwise prepared:		
1902.1100	Containing eggs:-		
1902.1110	From durum wheat	Exempted	60% with max fee NS0.34/kg
1902.1190	Other	Exempted	60% with max fee NS0.34/kg
1902.1900	Other:		
1902.1910	From durum wheat	Exempted	60% with max fee NS0.34/kg
1902.1990	Other:	Exempted	60%with max fee NS0.34/kg

Continued

Israel Tariff Code	Short Description of Product	Applied MFN Rate (2003)	Reduction percentage
1902.2000	Stuffeded pasta, whether or not cooked or otherwise prepared:		
1902.2010	Stuffed with meat containing more than 20% of the weight	Exempted	35%
1902.2020	Stuffeded with fish, including caviar and substitutes, accounting for more than 20% of the weight	Exempted	35%
1902.2030	Stuffed with crabs and mollusks, including caviar and substitutes, accounting for more than 20% of the weight	Exempted	35%
1902.2090	Stuffed with other products	Exempted	60% with max fee NS0.34/kg
1902.3000	Other pasta	Exempted	60% with max fee NS0.34/kg
1902.4000	Couscous:-		
1902.4010	Prepared	Exempted	60% with max fee NS0.42/kg
1902.4090	Other	Exempted	60% with max fee NS0.42/kg
1905.0000	Bread, cakes, Waffel, whether or not containing cocoa, communion wafers, sealing wafers, rice paper and similar products.		
1905.3000	Sweet biscuits; waffles and wafers:		
1905.3110	Containing milk, eggs, or honey	12%+NS0.82/kg, BNM 112%	60% with max fee NS0.42/kg
1905.3190	Other	12%+NS0.32/kg, BNM 112%	60% with max fee NS0.34/kg

Israel Tariff Code	Short Description of Product	Applied MFN Rate (2003)	Reduction percentage
1905.4000	Rusks, toasted bread and similar toasted products:-		
1905.4030	Containing added sugar, honey, other sweetening		60% with max fee NS0.42/kg
19.05.4031	AINING FLOUR THAT IS NOT WHEAT FLOUR IN A QUANTITY NOT EXCEEDING 15%	12%+NS0.32/kg, BNM 112%	
19.05.4039	--other	12%+NS0.32/kg, BNM 112%	
1905.9000	Other.-		
1905.9091	Containing 10% or more eggs, nuts or dried fruits....	12%+NS0.82/kg, BNM 112%	60% with max fee NS0.42/kg
2001.0000	Vegetables, fruit, nuts, preserved in vinegar		
2001.9000	Other-		
2001.9030	Corn	12%+NS0.96/kg, BNM 50%	15%
2002.0000	Tomatoes, prepared or preserved other than in vinegar		
2002.1000	Tomatoes, whole or in pieces:-		
2002.1010	Cooked or uncooked, preserved by freezing	12%+NS0.49/kg, BNM 50%	10%
2002.1090	Other	12%+NS0.49/kg, BNM 50%	10%
2002.9000	Other:- (not whole or in pieces)		
2002.9010	Tomato paste:-		
2002.9011	In packages over 100 kg.	12%+NS1.63/kg, BNM 50%	10%
2002.9019	Other	12%+NS1.63/kg, BNM 50%	10%
2002.9090	Tomatoes, otherwise prepared or preserved	12%+NS0.49/kg, BNM 50%	15%
2004.0000	Other vegetables, prepared or preserved, frozen, other than those in 20.06:-		

Continued

Israel Tariff Code	Short Description of Product	Applied MFN Rate (2003)	Reduction percentage
2004.1000	Potatoes:-		
2004.1090	Other	12%+NS2.95/kg, BNM 50%, BNL NS2.25/kg	10%
2004.9000	Other frozen vegetables and mixtures of vegetables:-		
2004.9010	Products of flour or meal		
2004.9011	within Annex 5	12%+NS1.95/kg BNM 50%	10%
2004.9019	Other	12%+NS1.00/kg BNM 50%	10%
2004.9090	Other:- (frozen vegetables)		
2004.9091	within Annex 5	12%+NS1.95/kg, BNM 50%	10%
2004.9093	Other frozen corn	12%+NS0.96/kg, BNM 50%	10%
2004.9094	Frozen legumes	12%+NS0.71/kg, BNM 50%	10%
2004.9099	Other Frozen vegetables	12%+NS0.62/kg, BNM 50%	10%
2005.0000	Other vegetables, processed or preserved, not frozen, excl. 20.06		
2005.2000	Potatoes:-		
2005.2090	Other	12%	15%
2005.4000	Peas (Pisum sativum)		
2005.4090	Other peas	12%+NS0.76/kg, BNM 50%	15%
2005.5000	Beans (Vigna spp., Phaseolus spp .):-		
2005.5900	Other-		
2005.5990	Other beans	12%+NS1.10/kg, BNM 50%	15%
2005.8000	Sweet corn (Zea mays var. saccharata):-		
2005.8090	Others		
2005.8091	Baby corn	12.5%	15%
2005.8099	Others	12%+NS0.96/kg, BNM 50%	15%

Israel Tariff Code	Short Description of Product	Applied MFN Rate (2003)	Reduction percentage
2005.9000	Other vegetables and mixtures of vegetables:-		
2005.9030	Carrots, other than in 9020	12%+NS0.85/kg, BNM 50%	15%
2005.9040	Chickpeas:-	NS1.11/kg, BNM 50%	15%
2008.1000	Nuts, groundnuts and other seeds, whether or not mixed		
2008.1100	Groundnuts:-		
2008.1120	Other, roasted	12%+ns3.25/kg, BNM 50%	10%
2008.1190	Other	12%	15%
2008.1900	Other, Including mixtures:-(other nuts)		
2008.1930	Other, roasted:-		
2008.1932	Others	12%+NS8.34/kg, BNM 50%	15%
2008.1990	Others:-		
2008.1991	Almonds	12%+NS4.68/kg, BNM 50%	15%
2008.9000	Other, including mixtures other than those of subheading		
2008.9900	Other:-		
2008.9910	Plums and prunes:-		
2008.9919	Other plums or prunes	12%+NS4.90/kg, BNM 50%	25%
2009.0000	Juices of Fruits and Vegetables		
2009.1000	Orange juice:-		
2009.1110	-Frozen Concentrated, in packs of 100 kg or more		
2009.1111	-Frozen Concentrated in packs of 230 kg or more	12%	10%
2009.1119	-other	12%+NS1.63/kg, BNM 50%	10%
2009.1120	-Frozen Concentrated, In other packages	12%+NS1.63/kg, BNM 50%	15%
2009.1130	Frozen Orange juice, not concentrated In packs of 100 kg or more	12%+NS0.33/kg, BNM 50%	10%

Continued

Israel Tariff Code	Short Description of Product	Applied MFN Rate (2003)	Reduction percentage
2009.1190	Other Frozen orange juice, not concentrated	12%+NS0.33/kg, BNM 50%	15%
2009.1210	Not frozen, Brix<20, in package >100kg	12%+NS0.33/kg, BNM 50%	10%
2009.1290	Not frozen, Brix<20, in other package	12%+NS0.33/kg, BNM 50%	15%
2009.1900	- Other (Orange Juice, not frozen):-		
2009.1910	-Concentrated, in packs of 100 kg or more		
2009.1911	-Concentrated, in packagess of 230 kg or more	12%	10%
2009.1919	-other	12%+NS1.63/ka. BNM 50%	10%
2009.1990	---Other (not frozen, not concen-trated, not bulk)	12%+NS1.63/kg, BNM 50%	15%
2009.2000	Grapefruit juice		
2009.2100	Not concentrated, Brix value <20		
2009.2110	In packages > 100kg	12%+NS0.33/kg, BNM 50%	10%
2009.2190	Others	12%+NS0.33/kg, BNM 50%	15%
2009.2900	Brix value >20		
2009.2910	-Concentrated, in packs of 100 kg or more		
2009.2911	-Concentrated, in packagess of 230 kg or more	12%	15%
2009.2919	Other	12%+NS1.63/kg, BNM 50%	0.1
2009.2990	-Other	12%+NS5.30/kg, BNM 50%	15%
2009.3000	Juice of any other single kind of citrus fruit	12%	10%
2009.5000	Tomato Juice:-		
2009.5010	In powder form	8%	10%
2009.5090	Other tomato juice		

Israel Tariff Code	Short Description of Product	Applied MFN Rate (2003)	Reduction percentage
2009.5091	-In packaging over 100 kg	12%+ns0.22/kg, BNM 50%	10%
2009.5099	-in other packaging	12%+ns0.22/kg, BNM 50%	10%
2009.6000	Grape juice (including grape must)		
2009.6190	- that Brix value is <30	12.4%+NS1.80/kg,BNM 57.8%, BNL NS1.50	15%
2009.6990	-other grape juice	12%+NS5.50/kg, BNM 50%	15%
2009.7000	Apple juice		
2009.7100	with brix value <20		
2009.7110	-in packages over 100 kg	12%+NS0.65/kg, BNM 50%	10%
2009.7190	-other conc. apple juice	12%+NS0.65/kg, BNM 50%	10%
2009.7900	Other apple juice		
2009.7910	-in packages over 100 kg within Annex 5	12%+NS2.40/kg, BNM 50%	10%
2009.7930	-in packages over 100 kg, others	12%+NS2.40/kg, BNM 50%	10%
2009.7990	-in other packages	12%+NS2.40/kg, BNM 50%	10%
2009.9000	Mixture of juices:-		
2009.9010	-containing more than 50% grape juice:		
2009.9011	-concentrated	12%+NS3.90/kg, BNM 50%	15%
2009.9019	-other (not concentrated)	12%+NS1.25/kg, BNM 50%	15%
2009.9020	-containing more than 50% citrus juice, tomato juice, or apple juice:		
2009.9021	-Concentrated, in packages over 100 kg	12%+NS1.10/kg, BNM 50%	15%
2009.9022	--Concentrated, in other packages	12%+NS1.10/kg, BNM 50%	15%
2009.9023	-Not concentrated, packages aver 100 kg	12%+NS0.34/kg, BNM 50%	15%
2009.9024	--Not concentrated, in other packages	12%+NS0.34/kg, BNM 50%	15%
2105.0000	Ice Cream and other frozen food preparations		
2105.0010	Ice Cream:-		

Continued

Israel Tariff Code	Short Description of Product	Applied MFN Rate (2003)	Reduction percentage
2105.0011	- containing less than 3% milk fat	12%+NS0.70/kg	spec.Fee, max 0.55$/ kg
2105.0012	- containing 3% but less than 7% milk fat	12%+NS2.25/kg	spec.Fee, max 0.55$/ kg
2105.0013	-containing 7% or more milk fat	12%+NS3.40/kg	spec.Fee, max 0.55$/ kg
2105.0090	Other	12%	15%
2106.0000	Other food preparations nes		
2106.9000	Other food preparations:-		
2106.9020	Preparations based on hydrolyzed casein	25%	20%
2106.9094	Preparations containing pollen	12%+NS19.50/kg, BNM 50%	25% with Max 19.5 NS/KG
2204.0000	Wine made from grapes		
2204.1000	Sparkling wine:- .		
2204.1010	Chagne type wines	12%+NS0.68/lit, BNM 50%	25%
2204.1090	Other	12%+NS0.68/lit, BNM 50%	25%
2204.2000	Other wine or grape must with fermentation prevented by the addition of alcohol:-		
2204.2190	---Others	12%+NS1.35/lit, BNL NS5.00/lit	12%+1.35 nis/lit
2204.2990	---Others	12%+NS1.35/lit, BNL NS5.00/lit	12%+1.35 nis/lit
2204.3090	---Others	12%+NS1.15/lit, BNL NS2.50/lit	12%+1.15 nis/lit, BNM 50%
2205.0000	Vermouth and other spiced wines		
2205.1000	In containers holding 2 liters or less	12%+NS2.67/lit, BNM 50%	30%

Israel Tariff Code	Short Description of Product	Applied MFN Rate (2003)	Reduction percentage
2205.9000	Other	12%+NS2.67/lit, BNM 50%	30%
2206.0000	Other fermented beverages (ciders)	12%	25%
2207.0000	Ethyl alcohol or neutral spirits		
2207.1051	-Grape alcohol	8%+NS8.90/lit	15% with max fee NS8.90/lit
2207.1091	-Grape alcohol	8%+NS8.90/lit	15% with max fee NS8.90/lit
2208.0000	Undenatured ethyl alcohol less then 80%; spirits, liquors and other spirituous beverages		
2208.2000	Alcoholic beverages from grapes:		
2208.2090	-other	12%+NS9.90/lit	15% with max fee NS8.90/lit
2300.0000	Flour ,meals and pellets of meat Greaves		
2304.0000	Oil-cake and pellets resulting from soya-bean crush	Exempted	38%
2305.0000	Oil-cake and pellets resulting from ground nut oil crush	Exempted	30%
2306.0000	Oil-cake and pellets resulting from other oil crush:-		
2306.1000	Of cotton seeds	Exempted	30%
2306.2000	Of linseed	Exempted	30%
2306.3000	Of sunflower seeds	Exempted	30%
2306.4000	Of rape or colza seeds		
2306.4100	--Of low erucic acid rape or colza seeds	Exempted	30%

Continued

Israel Tariff Code	Short Description of Product	Applied MFN Rate (2003)	Reduction percentage
2306.4900	--Other	Exempted	30%
2306.5000	Of coconut or copra	Exempted	30%
2306.6000	Of palm nuts or kernels	Exempted	30%
2306.7000	Of corn sprouts	Exempted	30%
2306.9000	Other	Exempted	30%
3502.1000	Egg albumin		
3502.1100	Dried	10%+NS8.40/kg, BNM 50%	
3502.1900	- other	10%+NS3.25/kg, BNM 50%	20% with max fee NS8.00/kg
3505.1000	Dextrin and other modified starches:-		
3505.1020	Soluble starches		
3505.1021	-based on wheat or corn, excl. waxy corn	6%+NS0.39/kg, BNM 39%	38% with max fee NS0.39/kg
3505.1029	-others	6%	38%

Annex D: Additional Quantities for Free Import into the United States from Israel

U.S. TARIFF CODE	SHORT DESCRIPTION OF PRODUCT	ANNUAL RATE OF GROWTH	2004 QUANTITY MT	2005 QUANTITY MT	2006 QUANTITY MT	2007 QUANTITY MT	2008 QUANTITY MT
		3%	1,159	1194	1230	1266	1304
Ch.#4	Non-Fat Dried Milk						
	(Described in U.S. HTS Chapter 99, subchapter VIII, note 4)						
	Butter, and fresh or sour cream	5%	383	402	422	443	466
	(Described in U.S. HTS Chapter 99, subchapter VIII, note 3)						
	Certain cheeses	3%	2029	2090	2153	2217	2284
	(Described in U.S. HTS Chapter 99, subchapter VIII, note 5)						
Chs.#12&;20	Peanuts	3%	116	119	123	127	131
	(Described in U.S. HTS Chapter 99, subchapter VIII, note 6)						
Ch.#21	Ice cream	10%	483	531	584	643	707
	(Described in U.S. HTS Chapter 99, subchapter VIII, note 7)						

LETTERHEAD OF VICE PRIME MINISTER
MINISTER OF INDUSTRY, TRADE, LABOR
AND COMMUNICATIONS

Jerusalem, July 27, 2004
Tisha B'Av 5764

The Honorable Robert Zoellick
United States Trade Representative
Office of the U.S. Trade Representative
Washington, D.C.
United States of America

Dear Ambassador Zoellick,

I was pleased to receive your letter concerning certain aspects of trade in agricultural products, a copy of which is attached.

I have the honor to confirm that the understandings expressed in your letter (including its attachment and annexes) are shared by my government and that your letter and this reply shall constitute an agreement between our respective Governments, to come into force 45 days after the date of my letter.

With kind regards,

Sincerely,
[Signature]
Ehud Olmert

STATE DEPARTMENT DOCUMENT NUMBER: 06-305

AGREEMENT BETWEEN THE UNITED STATES OF AMERICA AND THE KINGDOM OF TONGA REGARDING GRANTS UNDER THE FOREIGN ASSISTANCE ACT OF 1961, AS AMENDED, OR SUCCESSOR LEGISLATION, AND THE FURNISHING OF DEFENSE ARTICLES, DEFENSE SERVICES AND RELATED TRAINING PURSUANT TO THE UNITED STATES INTERNATIONAL MILITARY AND EDUCATION TRAINING PROGRAM (IMET), FROM THE UNITED STATES OF AMERICA TO THE KINGDOM OF TONGA

EFFECTED BY EXCHANGE OF NOTES AT SUVA AND NUKU'ALOFA,
MARCH 16 AND AUGUST 24, 2006
ENTERED INTO FORCE AUGUST 24, 2006

CTIA DOCUMENT NUMBER: 13126.000

DIPLOMATIC NOTE

Note No. 10

Embassy of the United States of America presents its compliments to the Ministry of Foreign Affairs of the Kingdom of Tonga and has the honor to refer to earlier discussions between representatives of the two Governments regarding grants under the Foreign Assistance Act of 1961, as amended, or successor legislation, and the furnishing of defense articles, defense services, and related training, including pursuant to the United States International Military and Education Training Program, from the United States of America to the Kingdom of Tonga pursuant to the Foreign Assistance Act of 1961, or successor legislation.

In accordance with these discussions, it is proposed that the Kingdom of Tonga agree:

A. That unless the consent of the Government of the United States of America has been first obtained the Kingdom of Tonga shall not:

(I) Permit any use of much defence articles, related training, including training materials, or such defence services by anyone not an officer employee or agent of the Kingdom of Tonga;

(II) Transfer or permit any officer, employee or agent of the Kindom of Tonga to transfer such defense articles, related training, including training materials, or other defense services by gift, sale or otherwise, or

(III) Use or permit the use of such defence articles, related training, including training materials, or other defense services for pirposes other than those for which provided

B.That such defense articles or related training, including training materials, or defense services shall be returned to the Government of the United States of America when they are no longer needed for the purpose for which they were furnished, unless the Government of the United States of America consents toanother disposition.

C. That the net proceeds of the sale received by the Kingdom of Tonga in disposing of, with priority written consent of the Government of the United States of America, any defense article furnished by the Government of the United States of America on a grant basis, including scrap from such defense article, shall be paid to the Government of the United States of America;

D. That the Kingdom of Tonga shall maintain the security of such defense articles, related training, including training materials, and other defense services; that it shall provide substantially the same degree of security protection afforded to such defense articles, related training, including training materials, or other defense services by the Government of the United States of America; that it shall, as the United States of America may require, permit continuous observation and review by, and furnish necessary information to, representatives of the Government of the United States of America with regard to the use thereof by the Kingdom of Tonga, and

E. That the Government of the United States of America may also, from time to time, make the provision of articles, services, and related training furnished under other authority (except the United States Arms Export Act) subject to the terms and conditions of the agreement proposed herein, (Transfers under the United States Arms Export Control Act shall continue to be governed by the requirements of that Act shall continue to be governed by the requirements of that Act and United States regulations applicable to such transfers.)

The Ministry of Foreign Affairs note stating that the foregoing is acceptable to the Kingdom of Tonga shall, together with this note, constitute an agreement between the two Governments, which shall enter into force on the date of the Ministry's note.

The Embassy of the United States of America avails itself of this opportunity to renew to the Ministry of Foreign Affairs of the Government of the Kingdom of Tonga the assurances of its highest consideration.

[Seal]

Embassy of the United States of America,
Suva, 16 March, 2006

The Ministry of Foreign Affairs of the Kingdom of Tonga presents its complements to the Embassy of the United States of America and acknowledges receipt of the Embassy's Note No. 10, dated 16 March 2006, which reads as follows:

> "A. That unless the consent of the Government of the United States of America has been first obtained the Kingdom of Tonga shall not:
>
> (i) Permit any use of such defense articles, related training, including: Training materials, or other defense services by anyone not an officer employee or agent of the Kingdom of Tonga;
>
> (ii) Transfer or permit any officer, employee or agent of me Kingdom of Tonga to transfer such defense articles, related training, including training materials, or other defense services by gift, sale or otherwise; or
>
> (iii) Use or permit the use of such defense articles, related training, including training materials, or other defense services for purposes other than those for which provided;
>
> B. That such defense articles or related training, including training materials or defense services shall be returned to the Government of the United States of America when they are no longer needed for the purposes for which they were furnished, unless the Government of the United States of America consents to another disposition;
>
> C. That the net proceeds of the sale received by the Kingdom of Tonga in disposing of with priority written consent of the Government of the United States of America, any defense article furnished by the Government of the United States of America on a grant basis, including scrap from such defense article, shall be paid to the Government of the United States of America;
>
> D. That the Kingdom of Tonga shall maintain the security of such defense articles, related training, including training materials, and other defense services; that it shall provide substantially the same degree of security protection afforded to such defense articles, related training, including training materials, or other defense services by the Government of the United States of America; that it shall, as the Government of the United States of America may require, permit continuous observation and review by, and furnish necessary information to, representatives of the Government of the United States of America with regard to the use thereof by the Kingdom of Tonga, and
>
> E. That the Government of the United States of America may also, from time to time, make the provision articles, services, and related training furnished under authority (except the United States Arms Export Act) subject to the terms and conditions of the agreement proposed herein. (Transfers under the United States Arms Export Control Act shall continue to be governed by the requirements of that Act and United States regulations applicable to such transfers.)"

The Ministry of Foreign Affairs of the Government of the Kingdom of Tonga has the honor to confirm that the proposals set fort in the Embassy's note are acceptable to the Government of the Kingdom of Tonga and that the Embassy's note and this note in reply shall constitute an agreement between the two governments which shall enter into force on this date.

The Ministry of Foreign Affairs of the Kingdom of Tonga avails itself of this opportunity to renew to the Embassy of the United States of America the assurances of its highest consideration.

Nuku'alofa, 24 August 2006

[Seal]

Embassy of the United States of America
SUVA

STATE DEPARTMENT DOCUMENT NUMBER: 06-306

ACQUISITION AND CROSS-SERVICING AGREEMENT BETWEEN THE DEPARTMENT OF DEFENSE OF THE UNITED STATES OF AMERICA AND THE MINISTRY OF NATIONAL DEFENSE, DEMOBILIZATION, AND VETERANS OF THE DEMOCRATIC REPUBLIC OF THE CONGO, WITH ANNEXES

SIGNED AT STUTTGART AND KINSHASA,
JULY 14 AND SEPTEMBER 29, 2006
ENTERED INTO FORCE SEPTEMBER 29, 2006

CTIA DOCUMENT NUMBER: 13127.000

Effective Date: 29 SEP 2006

[Signature] USA

[Signature] COD

PREAMBLE

The Department of Defense of the United States of America and the Ministry of National Defense, Demobilization, and Veterans of the Democratic Republic of the Congo, hereinafter referred to as the Parties, desiring to further the interoperability, readiness, and effectiveness of their respective military forces through increased logistic cooperation, have resolved to conclude this Acquisition and Cross-Servicing Agreement (this Agreement).

ARTICLE I
PURPOSE

This Agreement is entered into for the purpose of establishing basic terms, conditions, and procedures to facilitate the reciprocal provision of Logistic Support, Supplies, and Services as that term is defined in Article II of this Agreement.

ARTICLE II
DEFINITIONS

1. As used in this Agreement and in any Implementing Arrangements which provide specific procedures, the following definitions apply:

a. *Equal Value Exchange.* Payment for a transfer conducted under this Agreement in which it is agreed that the Receiving Party shall replace Logistic Support, Supplies, or Services that it receives with Logistic Support, Supplies, or Services of an equal monetary value.

b. *Implementing Arrangement.* A written supplementary arrangement for Logistic Support, Supplies, and Services that specifies details, terms, and conditions to implement cross-servicing agreements effectively.

c. *Invoice.* A document from the Supplying Party that requests reimbursement or payment for specific Logistic Support, Supplies, or Services rendered pursuant to this Agreement and any applicable Implementing Arrangements.

d. *Logistic Support, Supplies, and Services.* Food, water, billeting, transportation (including airlift), petroleum, oils, lubricants, clothing, communication services, medical services, ammunition, base operations support (and construction incident to base operations support), storage services, use of facilities, training services, spare parts and components, repair and maintenance services, calibration services, and port services. This term also includes the temporary use of general purpose vehicles and other non-lethal items of military equipment, where such lease or loan is permitted under the national laws and regulations of the Parties.

e. *Order.* A written request, in an agreed upon format and signed by an authorized individual, for the provision of specific Logistic Support, Supplies, or Services pursuant to this Agreement and any applicable Implementing Arrangement.

f. *Receiving Party.* The Party ordering and receiving support.

g. *Replacement-In-Kind.* Payment for a transfer conducted under this Agreement in which it is agreed that the Receiving Party shall replace Logistic Support, Supplies, or Services that it receives with Logistic Support, Supplies, and Services of an identical, or substantially identical, nature which meet fit, form, and function criteria, under mutually agreed conditions.

h. *Supplying Party.* The Party providing support.

i. *Transfer.* Selling (whether for payment in currency, Replacement-In-Kind, or exchange of supplies or services of equal value), leasing, loaning, or otherwise temporarily providing Logistic Support, Supplies, and Services under the terms of this Agreement.

ARTICLE III
APPLICABILITY

1. This Agreement is designed to facilitate reciprocal logistic support between the Parties to be used primarily during combined exercises, training, deployments, operations, or other cooperative efforts, and for unforeseen circumstances or exigencies in which one of the Parties may have a need for Logistic Support, Supplies, and Services.

2. This Agreement applies to the provision of Logistic Support, Supplies, and Services from the military forces of one Party to the military forces of the other Party in return for either cash payment or the reciprocal provision of Logistic Support, Supplies, and Services to the military forces of the Supplying Party.

3. All activities of the Parties under this Agreement and any Implementing Arrangements shall be carried out in accordance with their respective national laws and regulations. All obligations of the Parties under this Agreement and any Implementing Arrangements shall be subject to the availability of funds for such purposes. Unless otherwise agreed in advance, a Party shall not place an Order and receive support under this Agreement and any Implementing Arrangement unless it has funds (or agreed-upon in-kind support) available to pay for such support. If a Party discovers that it does not have the funds to perform its obligations, it shall promptly notify the other Party, which shall have the right to discontinue its provision of any support that was to be paid with such funds. This shall not affect the obligation of a Party to pay for support already received.

4. The following items are *not* eligible for transfer under this Agreement and are specifically excluded from its coverage:

a. weapon systems;

b. major end items of equipment (except for the lease or loan of general purpose vehicles and other nonlethal items of military equipment where such lease or loan is permitted under the national laws and regulations of the Parties); and

c. initial quantities of replacement and spare parts associated with the initial order quantity of major items of organizational equipment; however, individual replacement and spare parts needed for immediate repair and maintenance services may be transferred.

5. Also excluded from transfer by either Party under this Agreement are any items the transfer of which is prohibited by its national laws or regulations. In accordance with U.S. law and regulation, the United States currently may not transfer the following items under this Agreement:

a. guided missiles;

b. naval mines and torpedoes;

c. nuclear ammunition (including items such as warheads, warhead sections, projectiles, demolition munitions, and training ammunition;

d. cartridge and propellant-actuated devices;

e. chaff and chaff dispensers;

f. guidance kits for bombs or other ammunition;

g. chemical munitions or ammunition (other than riot-control agents);

h. source, byproduct, or special nuclear materials, or any other material, article, data, or thing of value the transfer of which is subject to the Atomic Energy Act of 1954 (Title 42, United States Code, Section 2011, *et seq.*); and

i. items of military equipment designated as Significant Military Equipment on the United States Munitions List (Part 121 of Title 22 of the U.S. Code of Federal Regulations) not included in the definition of Logistic Support, Supplies and Services.

ARTICLE IV
TERMS AND CONDITIONS

1. Each Party shall make its best efforts, consistent with national priorities, to satisfy requests from the other Party under this Agreement for Logistic Support, Supplies, and Services. However, when an Implementing Arrangement contains a stricter standard for satisfying such requests, the standard in the Implementing Arrangement shall apply.

2. Orders may be placed or accepted only by the Points of Contact (POC), or designees, identified by the Parties in Annexes B through I of this Agreement. When military forces of the Democratic Republic of the Congo require Logistic Support, Supplies, or Services outside the United States European Command, hereafter referred to as USEUCOM, Area of Responsibility (AOR), they may place orders directly with the cognizant POC or may seek the assistance of USEUCOM or a USEUCOM Component Command, to place an order with a non-USEUCOM POC.

3. An Implementing Arrangement under this Agreement may be negotiated on behalf of the U.S. Department of Defense by Headquarters, USEUCOM, the Headquarters of other United States combatant commands, or their designees. Implementing Arrangements may be negotiated on behalf

of the Democratic Republic of the Congo, Ministry of National Defense, Demobilization, and Veterans by the Minister of National Defense, Demobilization, and Veterans or any delegated subcommand. Implementing Arrangements shall identify POCs and their specific authorizations or limitations.

4. Prior to submitting a written Order, the ordering Party should initially contact the Supplying Party's POC by personal contact, telephone, fax, or e-mail to ascertain capability, availability, price, and desired method of repayment for required materiel or services. Orders shall include all the data elements in Annex A/Tab A, as well as any other terms and details necessary to carry out the transfer. Minimum Essential Data Elements, a Standard ACSA Order Form – 2006, and completion instructions are attached at Annex A. The number of this Agreement, USA-COD-01, should be annotated on all Orders and related correspondence.

5. Both Parties shall maintain records of all transactions.

6. The Receiving Party is responsible for:

a. arranging pickup and transportation of supplies acquired under this Agreement. This does not preclude the Supplying Party from assisting with loading supplies acquired under this Agreement onto the transportation conveyance, if within its capability. The Supplying Party shall notify the Receiving Party when and where supplies are available to be picked up.

b. obtaining any applicable customs clearance and arranging other official actions required by national customs regulations.

7. The individual designated by the Receiving Party to receive the Logistic Support, Supplies, or Services on behalf of the Receiving Party shall sign the standard order form (Annex A) in the appropriate block as evidence of receipt. If the standard order form is not available at the Supplying Party's point of issue, the individual receiving the Logistic Support, Supplies, or Services shall sign the receipt document provided by the Supplying Party as a substitute. The number of this Agreement, USA-COD-01, shall be entered on the receipt document.

8. The Supplying Party shall be responsible for:

a. notifying the Receiving Party when and where Logistic Support, Supplies, or Services are available to be picked up; and

b. forwarding the signed receipt document to the POC authorized to accept Orders under this Agreement. The signed receipt document shall be attached to the original Order Form.

9. Logistic Support, Supplies, and Services received through this Agreement shall not be retransferred, either temporarily or permanently, to another country, international organization or entity (other than to officers, employees, or agents of the country whose military originally received the Logistics Support, Supplies, and Services) without the prior written consent of the Supplying Party, obtained through applicable channels.

ARTICLE V
REIMBURSEMENT

1. For transfers of Logistic Support, Supplies, and Services under this Agreement, the Parties shall agree for payment either by cash ("reimbursable transaction"), or by Replacement-In-Kind or an Equal Value Exchange (both of which are exchange transactions). The Receiving Party shall pay the Supplying Party as provided in either paragraph 1a. or paragraph 1b. of this Article.

a. *Reimbursable Transaction.* The Supplying Party shall submit Invoices to the Receiving Party after delivery or performance as applicable of the Logistic Support, Supplies, or Services. Both Parties shall provide for the payment of all transactions and each Party shall invoice the other

Party at least once every three (3) months for all transactions not previously invoiced. Invoices shall be accompanied by necessary support documentation and shall be paid within ninety (90) days of the date prepared. Payment shall be made in the currency of the Supplying Party or as otherwise agreed in the Order. In pricing a reimbursable transaction, the Parties agree to the following reciprocal pricing principles:

(1) In the case of specific acquisition by the Supplying Party from its contractors on behalf of a Receiving Party, the price shall be no less favorable than the price charged the military forces by the contractor of the Supplying Party for identical items or services, less any amounts excluded by Article VI of this Agreement. The price charged may take into account differentials due to delivery schedules, points of delivery, and other similar considerations.

(2) In the case of transfer from the Supplying Party's own resources, the Supplying Party shall charge the same price charged its own military forces for identical Logistic Support, Supplies, and Services, as of the date delivery or performance occurs, less amounts excluded by Article VI of this Agreement. In any case where a price has not been established or charges are not made for one's own military forces, the Parties shall agree on a price in advance, reflecting reciprocal pricing principles, excluding charges that are precluded under these same reciprocal pricing principles.

b. *Exchange Transaction.* Exchange transactions may be by Replacement-In-Kind or Equal Value Exchange. The Receiving Party shall pay by transferring to the Supplying Party Logistic Support, Supplies, or Services that are agreed between the Parties to be identical (or substantially identical) or to be of equal monetary value to the Logistic Support, Supplies, or Services delivered or performed by the Supplying Party. When Equal Value Exchange is the agreed method of payment, prior to the provision of the requested support, both Parties will agree, to the extent possible, on the goods and services that will be accepted for payment. The Receiving Party is responsible for arranging return transportation and delivery of the replacement Logistic Support, Supplies or Services to the location mutually agreed between the Parties at the time the order is signed. If the Receiving Party does not complete the exchange within the terms of a replacement schedule agreed to or in effect at the time of the original transaction, which may not exceed one year from the date of the original transaction, the transaction shall be deemed reimbursable and governed by paragraph 1a above, except that the price shall be established using actual or estimated prices in effect on the date replacement would otherwise have been due.

c. *Establishment of Price or Value.* The following pricing mechanisms are provided to clarify application of the reciprocal pricing principles. The price established for inventory stock materiel shall be the Supplying Party's stock list price. The price for new procurement shall be the same price paid to the contractor or vendor by the Supplying Party. The price for services rendered will be the Supplying Party's standard price, or, if not applicable, the costs directly associated with providing the services. Prices charged shall exclude all taxes and duties that the Receiving Party is exempted from paying under other agreements that the Governments of the Parties have concluded. Upon request, the Parties agree to provide information sufficient to verify that these reciprocal pricing principles have been followed and that prices do not include waived or excluded costs.

2. When a definitive price for the Order is not agreed to in advance, the Order, pending agreement on final price, shall set forth a maximum liability for the Party ordering the Logistic Support, Supplies, or Services. The Parties shall then promptly enter into negotiation to establish the final price.

3. POCs for payments and collections for each Party are identified in annexes B through I to this Agreement.

4. The price for Logistic Support, Supplies, and Services under this Agreement shall not be higher than the price for the same Logistic Support, Supplies, and Services available under any other agreement between the Parties or their Governments.

5. In all cases, prices and conditions are to be mutually agreed by both Parties.

ARTICLE VI
WAIVED OR EXCLUDED COSTS

Insofar as national laws and regulations permit, the Parties shall ensure that any readily identifiable duties, taxes, and similar charges are not imposed on activities conducted under this Agreement. The Parties shall cooperate to provide proper documentation to maximize tax and customs relief. The provisions of any applicable tax and customs relief agreements shall also apply under this Agreement. The Parties shall inform each other whether the price charged for Logistic Support, Supplies, or Services includes taxes or duties. In determining whether duties, taxes or similar charges should be levied, the pricing principles in Article V, and in particular Article V, paragraph 1., subparagraph c, will govern the value of the Logistic Support, Supplies, and Services provided by the Supplying Party.

ARTICLE VII
SECURITY OF INFORMATION

It is the intent of the Parties that activities under this Agreement and any Implementing Arrangements be carried out at the unclassified level. Unless specifically authorized by separate written agreement or arrangement, no classified information or material shall be provided or generated under this Agreement or any Implementing Arrangements.

ARTICLE VIII
INTERPRETATION AND, AMENDMENTS TO THE AGREEMENT, AND REVISION OF INFORMATION

1. Any disagreements regarding the interpretation or application of this Agreement, any Implementing Arrangements, or transactions executed hereunder shall be resolved through consultation between the Parties and shall not be referred to any international tribunal or third party for settlement.

2. Either Party may, at any time, request amendment of this Agreement by giving the other Party written notice. In the event such a request is made, the Parties shall promptly enter into negotiations. This Agreement may be amended only by written agreement between the Parties.

3. Replacement of Annexes B through I, which list POCs, may be done by a Party transmitting the replacement annex to the other Party through diplomatic channels, without formal amendment of this Agreement.

ARTICLE IX
ENTRY INTO FORCE AND TERMINATION

This Agreement, USA-COD-01, which consists of a Preamble, Articles I-IX, and Annexes A through I, shall enter into force upon the date of its signature. This Agreement shall remain in force unless terminated by the mutual consent of the Parties or by either Party giving not less than 180 days notice in writing to the other Party of its intent to terminate. Notwithstanding termination of this Agreement, all reimbursement obligations incurred pursuant to its terms shall remain binding on the responsible Party until satisfied.

IN WITNESS WHEREOF, the undersigned, being duly authorized by their respective governments, have signed this Agreement (USA-COD-01).

DONE, in duplicate in the English and French languages. In case of divergence between the two texts, the English text shall prevail.

FOR THE DEPARTMENT OF DEFENSE
OF THE UNITED STATES OF AMERICA

[Signature]
MICHAEL J. LYDEN
Rear Admiral, U.S. Navy
Director of Logistics and
Security Assistance
HQ, US European Command

at: Stuttgart, DEU
on: 14 JUL 2006

FOR THE MINISTRY
OF NATIONAL DEFENSE,
DEMOBILIZATION, AND VETERANS
OF THE DEMOCRATIC REPUBLIC OF THE
CONGO

[Signature]
S. E. ADOLPHE ONUSUMBA YEMBA
Minister of National Defense,
Demobilization, and Veterans

at: Kiashasa
on: 29 SEPTEMBER 2006

LIST OF ANNEXES

ANNEX A – ACSA Ordering Information

TAB A – Minimum Essential Data Elements

TAB B – Standard ACSA Order Form – 2006

TAB C – Instructions for Manual Completion of Standard ACSA Order Form – 2006

ANNEX B – The Democratic Republic of the Congo POC Annex

ANNEX C – USCENTCOM POCs

TAB A – USCENTCOM

TAB B – USARCENT (Army)

TAB C – USNAVCENT (Navy)

TAB D – USCENTAF (Air Force)

TAB E – USMARCENT (Marine Corps)

TAB F – SOCCENT (Special Operations)

ANNEX D – USPACOM/USFJ POCs

TABA–USPACOM

TAB B – PACFLT (Navy)

TAB C – USARPAC (Army)

TAB D – MARFORPAC (Marines)

TAB E – PACAF (Air Force)

TAB F – SOCPAC (Special Operations Command)

TAB G – USFJ (Japan)

TAB H – USARJ (Army)

TAB I – MARFORJ (Marines)

TAB J – USAFJ (Air Force)

TAB K–USFK (Korea)

ANNEX E – USEUCOM POCs

TAB A – USEUCOM

TAB B – USAFE (Air Force)

TAB C – USAREUR (Army)

TAB D – USNAVEUR (Navy)

TAB E – USMARFOREUR (Marine Corps)

TAB F – SOCEUR (Special Operations)

TAB G – US AREUR SFOR (Bosnia and Herzegovina)

TAB H – USAREUR KFOR (Kosovo)

ANNEX F – USJFCOM POCs

TAB A – USJFCOM

TAB B – ACC (Air Force)

TAB C – CDRLANTFLT (Navy)

TAB D – MARFORLANT (Marine Corps)

TAB E – FORSCOM (Army)

ANNEX G – USSOUTHCOM POCs

ANNEX H – USNORTHCOM POCs

ANNEX I – USTRANSCOM POCs

ANNEX A

ACSA ORDERING INFORMATION

TAB A – Minimum Essential Data Elements

TAB B – Standard ACSA Order Form – 2006

TAB C – Instructions for Manual Completion of Standard ACSA Order Form – 2006

ANNEX A / TAB A

MINIMUM ESSENTIAL DATA ELEMENTS

1) Implementing Arrangement or support Agreement

2) Date of Order

3) Designation and address of office to be billed

4) Numerical listing of stock numbers of items, if any

5) Quantity and description of material/services requested

6) Quantity furnished

7) Unit of Measurement

8) Unit price in currency of billing country or otherwise agreed to

9) Quantity furnished (6) multiplied by unit price (8)

10) Currency of billing country or other billing currency as agreed to

11) Total Order amount expressed in currency of billing country or otherwise agreed to

12) Name (typed or printed), signature, and title of authorized Ordering or requisitioning representative

13) Payee to be designated on remittance

14) Designation and address of office to receive remittance

15) Recipient's signature acknowledging service or supplies received on the Order or requisition or a separate supplementary document

16) Document number of Order or requisition

17) Receiving organization

18) Issuing organization

19) Transaction type

20) Fund citation or certification of availability of funds when applicable under Parties' procedures

21) Date and place of original transfer; in the case of an exchange transaction, a replacement schedule including time and place of replacement transfer

22) Name, signature and title of authorized acceptance official

23) Additional special requirement, if any, such as transportation, packaging, etc.

24) Limitation of government liability

25) Name, signature, date and title of Supplying Party official who actually issues supplies or services.

ANNEX A/ TAB B: STANDARD ACSA ORDER FORM – 2006

ACQUISITION AND CROSS-SERVICING AGREEMENT (ACSA) / MUTUAL LOGISTICS SUPPORT (MLS) ORDER FORM

1. Requisition No.	2. Support Agreement	3. Operation/Theater	4. Order Date
5. Requesting Unit	6. Requesting Nation	7. Providing Unit	8. Providing Nation
9. Deliver to Unit	10. Deliver to Country	11. Deliver Place	12. Deliver Time

13. REQUESTED LINE ITEM SUMMARY (SEE ATTACHED LINE ITEM DETAIL SHEET)

No.	Sub:	Attn:	Stock no. & Description	Unit of Mea	Quantity Request (Less Previously Received)	Quantity Received	Unit Price	Total

14. Method of Payment ☐ Cash ☐ Replacement-in-Kind (RIK) ☐ Equal-Value-Exchange (EVE)	15. Currency	16. Not to Exceed Amount	17. Line Item Cost
22. Authorized Requester	23. Authorized Supplier		18. Trans Costs
Signature	Signature		19. Other Costs
Name (Last, First MI, Rank/Title) / Date	Name (Last, First MI, Rank/Title) / Date		20. Total Claimed
Unit/Office / Nation/Organization	Unit/Office / Nation Organization		21. Agreed Return Date

24. Purchase Order No	25. Fund Citation	26. Bill To	30. Remarks
27. Invoice No.	28. Account No./Finance Tracking No.	29. Pay To	

31. Receipt	32. Invoice: I certify that the amount invoiced is exclusive of all taxes fro which excemption has been granted under provisions of existing agreements and that the invoice is correct.
Signature	Signature
Name (Last, First MI, Rank/Title) / Date	Name (Last, First MI, Rank/Title) / Date
Unit/Office / Nation/Organization	Unit/Office / Nation/Organization

ANNEX A/TAB C

INSTRUCTIONS FOR MANUAL COMPLETION OF STANDARD ACSA ORDER FORM (2006)

For manual Order, if the ACSA Global Automated Tracking and Recording Systems (AGATRS) is not available

1. REQUEST NUMBER: Enter an order identification number, with a unit / organization (Ex... USA, USAFE, etc .....) Specific prefix, Julian calendar date, and sequence number (001, 002, 003.....).

2. SUPPORT AGREEMENT: Enter the ACSA agreement number (such as USA-XXX-01), and the number of any associated Implementing Arrangement that the order will be done under.

3. OPERATION / THEATER: Enter the Operations / Theater where support is being provided (such as Bosnia, Kosovo, etc.....)

4. ORDER DATE: Self explanatory.

5. REQUESTING UNIT / DEMANDER: Enter the unit / organization actually receiving the LSSS.

6. REQUESTING NATION / ORGANIZATION: Enter the nation or organization (such as SHAPE, etc.....) of the Requesting Party.

7. PROVIDING UNIT / SUPPLIER: Enter the unit / organization actually providing the LSSS.

8. PROVIDING NATION / ORGANIZATION: Enter the nation or organization (such as US, SHAPE, etc.....).

9. DELIVER TO UNIT / DESTINATION: Enter Location of Unit to receive delivery.

10. DELIVERY TO COUNTRY: Enter the name of nation receiving delivery.

11. DELIVER PLACE: Enter Bldg Number / Location of delivery.

12. DELIVER TIME: Enter Date-Time (ZULU) Group (DDTTTTZ MMM YY) of desired delivery date and time (example: 061400Z AUG 04).

13. REQUESTED LINE ITEM SUMMARY:

a. Enter National Stock Number if applicable.

b. Enter a general description of each item requested.

c. Enter the appropriate or the agreed to unit of measure for specified type of LSSS.

d. Enter quantity of the specified item based on entered Unit of Measure.

e. Enter Unit Price of the specified item.

f. Enter Total Amount on the specified item(s) based on the entered Unit of Measure and Unit Price.

14. METHOD OF PAYMENT: Mark the appropriate block for "Cash", Replacement-In-Kind", or "Equal Value Exchange".

15. CURRENCY: Enter currency to be paid in.

16. NOT TO EXCEED AMOUNT: Maximum liability if applicable.

17. LINE ITEM COST: Enter the total amount of the order.

18. TRANSPORTATION COST: Enter the costs of transportation if any.

19. OTHER COSTS: Enter all additional costs (for example: customs, packing fees, etc.....)

20. TOTAL CLAIMED: Enter the total amount of the order

21. AGREED RETURN DATE: Enter return date for Replacement-In-Kind (RIK), or Equal Value Exchange (EVE) transactions, or for Temporary Transfers (Loans or Leases). Note: Dates RIK and EVE may not exceed one year from date of initial delivery.

22. AUTHORIZED REQUESTOR: Information for authorized (must hold office of listed POC organization in the POC Annex of applicable ACSA or IA) approving official for the requesting party. Enter Name, Title and Unit/Office of Requesting Official.

23. AUTHORIZED SUPPLIER/APPROVING OFFICIAL FOR SUPPLYING PARTY:

Approving official (must hold office of listed POC organization in POC Annex of applicable ACSA or IA) for Supplying Party. Enter Name, Title and Unit/Office of Approving Official.

24 – 29: TO BE FILLED IN BY INVOICING AUTHORITY

30. REMARKS: Enter date range for support or services that are continuous in nature (Example: Billeting Services that are scheduled from 1 January to 31 March).

31 – 32: TO BE FILLED IN BY INVOICING AUTHORITY

ANNEX B

THE DEMOCRATIC REPUBLIC OF THE CONGO, POINTS OF CONTACT (POC)

1. The Democratic Republic of the Congo POC responsible for **approving, placing and accepting orders**:

a. Unit: Minister of National Defense, Demobilization and Veterans

b. Commercial Telephone:

- 243 81 5199624

- 243 81 500 9854

- 243 9999 22734

c. 24 hours / after duty hours contact: same as above

d. Commercial fax: N/A

e. Mailing address: mindefac@yahoo.fr

2. The Democratic Republic of the Congo POC responsible for **collecting and making payments** for support, supplies and services:

a. Unit: Minister of National Defense, Demobilization and Veterans

b. Commercial Telephone:

- 243 81 5199624

- 243 81500 9854

- 243 9999 22734

c. 24 hours / after duty hours contact: same as above

d. Commercial fax: N/A

e. Mailing address : mindefac@yahoo.fr

ANNEX C

USCENTCOM
POINTS OF CONTACT, ORDERING AND FINANCIAL RESPONSIBILITIES

TAB A – HQ USCENTCOM
TAB B – USARCENT (Army)
TAB C – USNAVCENT (Navy)
TAB D – USCENTAF (Air Force)
TAB E – USMARCENT (Marine Corps)
TAB F – SOCCENT (Special Operations)

ANNEX C / TAB A

U.S. CENTRAL COMMAND (USCENTCOM)

1. The USCENTCOM POC for coordinated **placement and acceptance of orders** under this agreement is the USCENTCOM J4-Operations Directorate, Multinational Logistics and Contracting Branch (CCJ4-O/MLC)

a. Unit:	CCJ4-O/MLC
b. Telephone:	Com'l: 813-827-6420/5822 DSN: 651-6420/5822
c. Fax:	Com'l: 813-827-5828 DSN: 651-5828
d. Message Address:	USCENTCOM//J4/O/MLC//
e. Mailing Address:	USCENTCOM ATTN: CCJ4-O/MLC 7115 South Boundary Boulevard MacDill AFB, FL 33621-5101

2. The USCENTCOM agency responsible for **payments and collections** in support of this agreement is the USCENTCOM COMPTROLLER OFFICE.

a. Unit:	CCCO
b. Telephone:	Com'l: 813-827-5884 DSN: 651-5884
c. Fax:	Com'l: 813-827-4218/4648 DSN: 651-4218/4648
d. Message Address:	USCENTCOM//CCCO//

ANNEX C / TAB B

THIRD U.S. ARMY / U.S. ARMY FORCES CENTRAL COMMAND (USARCENT)

1. The USARCENT POC responsible for **approving, placing, and accepting orders** is the G-4, Logistics Sustainment Division.

a. Unit:	Third U.S. Army, G-4
b. Telephone:	Com'l: 404-464-2927 DSN: 367-2927
c. Fax:	Com'l: 404-464-4030 DSN: 367-4030 Com'l: 404-464-4579 (Classified) DSN: 367-4579 (Classified)
d. Message Address:	COMUSARCENT FT MCPHERSON GA//G4//
e. Mailing Address:	Third U.S. Army, ATTN: G-4, AFRD-GD-LS 18881 Hardee Ave SW Ft McPherson, GA 30330

2. The USARCENT agency responsible for **payments and collections** in support of this agreement is the USARCENT Comptroller.

a. Unit:	Third U.S. Army, Comptroller
b. Telephone:	Com'l: 404-464-4885/4049 DSN: 367-4885/4049
c. Fax:	Com'l: 404-464-4823 DSN: 367-4823
d. Message Address:	COMUSARCENT FT MCPHERSON GA// COMPTROLLER//
e. Mailing Address:	Third U.S. Army, ATTN: Comptroller, AFRD-CM 18881 Hardee Ave SW Ft McPherson, GA 30330

ANNEX C / TAB C

U.S. NAVAL FORCES CENTRAL COMMAND (USNAVCENT)

1. The USNAVCENT POC for coordinated **placement and acceptance of orders** under agreement is the USNAVCENT N4.

a. Unit:	COMUSNAVCENT-BAHRAIN Code: N4/Coalition Logistics Officer
b. Telephone:	Com'l: (CC) 973-1785-3721/3722 DSN: 318-439-3721/3722
c. Fax:	Com'l: 973-1785-9936 DSN: 318-439-9936 Com'l: 973-1785-4579 (Classified) DSN: 318-439-4579 (Classified)
d. Message Address:	COMUSNAVCENT//N4//COALITION LOGISTICS OFFICER//
e. Mailing Address:	COMUSNAVCENT Code: N4/LRC/Coalition Logistics Officer/ FPO AE 09501-6008

2. The USNAVCENT agency responsible for **payments and collections** in support of this agreement is the COMUSNAVCENT COMPTROLLER.

a. Unit:	COMUSNAVCENT Comptroller, CODE NOOCF
b. Telephone:	Com'l: 973-1785-3029/4254 DSN: 318-439-3029/4254
c. Fax:	Com'l: 973-1785-9936 DSN: 318-439-9936
d. Message Address:	COMUSNAVCENT//N00CF//
e. Mailing Address:	COMUSNAVCENT Code: NOOCF FPOAE 09501-6503

ANNEX C / TAB D

U.S. AIR FORCES CENTRAL COMMAND (USCENTAF)

1. The USCENTAF POC for coordinated **placement and acceptance of orders** under this agreement is the A4, Logistics Plans Office.

a. Unit:	US CENTAF/ A4-LGXP
b. Telephone:	Com'l: 803-895-4460/4455 DSN: 965-4460
c. Fax:	Com'l: 803-895-2947 DSN: 965-2947
d. Message Address:	COMUSCENTAF SHAW AFB SC//A4//
e. Mailing Address:	US CENTAF/ A4-LGXP 524 Shaw Drive, Suite 135 Shaw AFB, SC 29152

2. The USCENTAF agency responsible for **payments and collections** in support of this agreement is the 9th Air Force Financial Management Analysis Branch.

a. Unit:	9 AF/FMA
b. Telephone:	Com'l: 803-895-2806 DSN: 965-2806
c. UNCLASSIFIED Fax:	Com'l: 803-895-2809 DSN: 965-2809
d. Message Address:	USCENTAF SHAW AFB SC//FMA//
e. Mailing Address:	US CENTAF/9th AF-FMA 524 Shaw Drive, Suite 237 Shaw AFB, SC 29152

ANNEX C / TAB E

U.S. MARINE FORCES CENTRALCOMMAND (USMARCENT)

1. The USMARCENT POC for coordinated **placement and acceptance of orders** under this agreement is the MARFORPAC G-4-CENTCOM BRANCH.

a. Unit:	MARFORPAC, G4-RESOURCE BRANCH
b. Telephone:	Com'l: 808-477-8341 DSN: 477-8341
c. Fax:	Com'l: 808-477-8709 DSN: 477-8709 Com'l: 808-477-0077 (Classified) DSN: 477-0077 (Classified)
d. Message Address:	COMUSMARCENT//G4//
e. Mailing Address:	USMARCENT, G-4 ATTN: Resource Branch (Multinational Logistics) Box 64118 Camp H. M. Smith, HI 96861-4118

2. The USMARCENT agency responsible for **payments and collections** in support of this agreement is the USMARCENT G-8.

a. Unit:	USMARCENT G-8
b. Telephone:	Com'l: 808-477-8557 DSN: 477-8557
c. Fax:	Com'l: 808-477-8702 DSN: 477-8702 Com'l: 808-477-0077 (Classified) DSN: 477-0077 (Classified)
d. Message Address:	COMUSMARCENT//G8//
e. Mailing Address:	USMARCENT, G-8 Box 64112 Camp H. M. Smith, HI 96861-4112

ANNEX C / TAB F

SPECIAL OPERATIONS COMMAND CENTRAL (SOCCENT)

1. The Special Operations Command Central (SOCCENT) POC for **coordinated placement and acceptance of orders** under this agreement is the SOCCENT, J4.

a. Unit:	SOCCCENT, J4
b. elephone:	Com'l: 813-828-0297 DSN: 968-0297
c. Fax:	Com'l: 813-828-4826 DSN: 968-4826 Com'l: 813-828-8372 (Classified) DSN: 968-8372 (Classified)
d. Message Address:	COMSOCCENT MACDILL AFB FL//J4//
e. Mailing Address:	HQ, SOCCENT ATTN: SOCCENT, J4 7115 South Boundary Boulevard MacDill AFB, FL 33621-5101

2. The Special Operations Command Central (SOCCENT) agency responsible for **payments and collections** in support of this agreement is the SOCCENT Comptroller.

a. Unit:	SOCCENT, Comptroller
b. Telephone:	Com'l: (813)828-4614//DSN: 968-4614
c. Fax:	Com'l: 813-828-8747 DSN: 968-8747 Com'l: 813-828-1894 (Classified) DSN: 968-1894 (Classified)
d. Message Address:	COMSOCCENT MACDILL AFB FL//SOCCO//
e. Mailing Address:	HQ SOCCENT ATTN:SOCCO 7115 South Boundary Boulevard MacDill AFB, FL 33621-5101

ANNEX D

USPACOM/USFJ/USFK
POINTS OF CONTACT, ORDERING AND FINANCIAL RESPONSIBILITIES

TAB A – USPACOM
TAB B – PACFLT (Navy)
TAB C – USARPAC (Army)
TAB D – MARFORPAC (Marines)
TAB E – PACAF (Air Force)
TAB F – SOCPAC (Special Operations Command)
TAB G – USFJ (Japan)
TAB H – USARJ (Army)
TAB I – MARFORJ (Marines)
TAB J – USAFJ (Air Force)
TAB K – USFK (Korea)

ANNEX D TAB A

COMMANDER, U.S. PACIFIC COMMAND (CDRUSPACOM)

1. The USPACOM POC for coordinated **placement and acceptance of orders** under this agreement is the J45, Security Assistance and International Logistics Division:

a. Unit:	CDRUSPACOM J4
b. Telephone:	Com'l (808) 477-0387
c. Fax:	Com'l (808) 477-6669 Com'l (808) 477-0844 (Classified)
d. Message Address:	CDRUSPACOM HONOLULU HI//J4//
e. Mailing Address:	HQ CDRUSPACOM J4 Bldg 400, Box 64020 Camp H. M. Smith, HI 96861-4020

2. The USPACOM POC responsible for **payments and collections** in support of this agreement is the Comptroller:

a. Unit:	CDRUSPACOM J05
b. Telephone:	Com'l (808) 477-6680
c. Fax:	Com'l (808) 477-0535
d. Message Address:	CDRUSPACOM HONOLULU HI//J05//
e. Mailing Address:	HQ CDRUSPACOM J05 Box 64037 Camp H. M. Smith, HI 96861-4037

ANNEX D / TAB B

COMMANDER, U.S. PACIFIC FLEET (PACFLT)

1. The CDRPACFLT POC responsible for **approving, placing, and accepting orders** is:

a. Unit:	COMPACFLT (N401)
b. Telephone:	Com'l (808) 474-6445
c. Fax:	Com'l (808) 474-6448
d. Message Address:	COMPACFLT PEARL HARBOR HI//N401H//
e. Mailing Address:	Commander, U.S. Pacific Fleet Code N401 251 Makalapa Drive Pearl Harbor, HI 96860-3131

2. The CDRPACFLT POC for **collecting and making payments** for support, supplies, and services is:

a. Unit:	COMPACFLT (N00F)
b. Telephone:	Com'l (808) 474-6950
c. Fax:	Com'l (808) 474-6937
d. Message Address:	COMPACFLT PEARLHARBOR HI//N00F//
e. Mailing Address:	Commander, U.S. Pacific Fleet Code N00F 250 Makalapa Drive Pearl Harbor, HI 96860-3131

ANNEX D / TAB C

U.S. ARMY PACIFIC (USARPAC)

1. The USARPAC POC responsible for **approving, placing, and accepting orders** under this agreement is Headquarters USARPAC Logistics Plans and International Programs:

a. Unit:	USARPAC/APLG-PIL
b. Telephone:	Com'l (808) 438-8615
c. Fax:	Com'l (808) 438-3460
d. Message Address:	CDRUSARPAC FT SHAFTER HP//APLG-PIL//
e. Mailing Address:	Commander, U.S. Army, Pacific Attn: APLG-PIL, Logistics Plans and International Programs Ft. Shatter, HI 96858

2. The USARPAC POC responsible for **payments and collections** for this agreement is the Defense Finance and Accounting Service, Honolulu Operating Location:

a. Unit:	DFAS
b. Telephone:	Com'l (808) 472-3760
c. Fax:	Com'l (808) 472-8250
d. Message Address:	DFAS HONOLULU HI//
e. Mailing Address:	DFAS Box 77, Building 1392 Pearl Harbor, HI 96860-7552

ANNEX D / TAB D

MARINE FORCES PACIFIC (MARFORPAC)

1. The MARFORPAC POC responsible for **approving, placing, and accepting orders** under this agreement is:

a. Unit:	HQ MARFORPAC/G4
b. Telephone:	Com'l (808) 477-2066/2067
c. Fax:	Com'l (808) 477-0260
d. Message Address:	COMMARFORPAC//G4//
e. Mailing Address:	Commander MARFORPAC (GA Ops) Box 64118 Camp H. M. Smith, HI 96861-4118

2. The MARFORPAC POC responsible for **payments and collections** in support of this agreement is:

a. Unit:	MARFORPAC/G8
b. Telephone:	Com'l (808) 477-5051
c. Fax:	Com'l (808) 477-7100
d. Message Address:	COMMARFORPAC//G8//
e. Mailing Address:	Commander USMARFORPAC (G-8) Box 64112 Camp H. M. Smith, HI 96861-4112

ANNEX D / TAB E

PACIFIC AIR FORCES (PACAF)

1. The PACAF POC responsible for **approving, placing, and accepting orders** under this agreement is Headquarters PACAF Logistics Plans and Programs, Plans Branch:

a. Unit:	PACAF/LGR
b. Telephone:	Com'l (808) 449-3778
c. Fax:	Com'l (808) 449-3690
d. Message Address:	HQ PACAF HICKAM AFB HI//LGR//
e. Mailing Address:	HQ PACAF/LGR 25 E. Street, Suite H-302 Hickam AFB, HI 96853-5427

2. The PACAF POC responsible for **payments and collections** for this agreement is Headquarters PACAF Logistics Plans and Programs, Plans Branch:

a. Unit:	DFAS Pacific-AIF
b. Telephone:	Com'l (808) 472-7908
c. Fax:	Com'l (808) 472-5816
d. Message Address:	DFAS Honolulu// HI//LGXW//
e. Mailing Address:	DFAS Pacific-AIF 477 Essex Street Pearl Harbor, HI 96860-5806

ANNEX D / TAB F

SPECIAL OPERATIONS COMMAND PACIFIC (SOCPAC)

1. The SOCPAC POC responsible for **approving, placing, and accepting orders** under this agreement is:

a. Unit:	SOCPAC/SOJ4
b. Telephone:	Com'l (808) 477-0615
c. Fax:	Com'l (808) 477-2908
d. Message Address:	COMSOCPAC HONOLULU HI//SOJ4//
e. Mailing Address:	HQ SOCPAC/SOJ4 Box 64046 Camp H. M. Smith, HI 96861-4046

2. The SOCPAC POC responsible for **payments and collections** in support of this agreement is:

a. Unit:	SOCPAC/SOJ08
b. Telephone:	Com'l (808) 477-2603
c. Fax:	Com'l (808) 477-3880
d. Message Address:	COMSOCPAC HONOLULU HI//SOJO8//
e. Mailing Address:	HQ SOCPAC/SOJO8 Box 64046 Camp H. M. Smith, HI 96861-4046

ANNEX D / TAB G

US FORCES JAPAN (HQ USFJ)

1. The USFJ POC responsible for **approving, placing, and accepting orders** under this agreement is:

a. Unit:	USFJ/J43
b. Telephone:	Com'l: 0425-52-2511 ext. 5-2445 DSN: 225-2445
c. Fax:	Com'l: 0425-52-2511 ext. 5-4709 DSN: 225-4709
d. Message Address:	COMUSJAPAN YOKOTA AB JA//J4//
e. Mailing Address:	Headquarters, United States Forces, Japan Logistics Directorate/J4, Yokota Air Base Fussa-Shi, Tokyo 197

2. The USFJ agency responsible for **payments and collections** under this agreement is:

a. Unit:	DFAS-J
b. Telephone:	Com'l: 0425-52-2511, ext. 5-9838 DSN: 225-9838
c. Fax:	Com'l 0425-52-2511, ext. 5-9841 DSN: 225-3213
d. Message Address:	DFAS JAPAN YOKOTA JA//
e. Mailing Address:	DFAS-J, Unit 5220, Bldg 206 Yokota Air Base Fussa-Shi, Tokyo 197

ANNEX D/TAB H

US ARMY JAPAN (USARJ)

1. The USARJ POC responsible for **approving, placing, and accepting orders** under this agreement is:

a. Unit:	USARJ, DCS, G4
b. Telephone:	Com'l: 0462-51-1788 ext. 263-7204 DSN: 263-5471
c. Fax:	Com'l: 0462-51-1788 ext. 263-8372 DSN: 263-8372
d. Message Address:	CDRUSARJ 9th TSC CP ZAMA JA//DSCLOG//
e. Mailing Address:	HQ, USARJ/DCS, G4 ATTN: APAJ-GD-LOG, (ACSA POC) Camp Zama, Zama-Shi Kanagawa-Ken, 288-0000

2. The USARJ POC responsible for **approving, placing, and accepting orders** for the 836th U.S. Army Transportation Battalion under this agreement is:

a. Unit:	836th U.S. Army Transportation Bn
b. Telephone:	Com'l: 0454-53-4840 ext. 269-6630 DSN: 269-6330
c. Fax:	Com'l: 0454-53-4840 ext. 269-6246 DSN: 269-6739
d. Message Address:	CDR 836TH TRANS BN YOKOHAMA JA//SDPC-YO-XO//
e. Mailing Address:	836th U.S. Army Transportation Bn ATTN: SDPC-YO-XO Mizuho Sanbashi Kanagawa-Ku Yokohama-Shi, 221-0034

3. The USARJ POC responsible for approving, placing, and accepting orders for the 835th U.S. Army Transportation Bn under this agreement is:

a. Unit:	835th U.S. Army Transportation Bn
b. Telephone	Com'l: 098-857-3844 DSN: 648-7729
c. Fax:	Com'l: 098-892-5111 ext. 648-7731 DSN: 648-7731
d. Message Address:	CDR 835TH TRANS BN OKINAWA JA//MTPC-OK-XO//
e. Mailing Address:	835th U.S. Army Transportation Bn ATTN: MTPC-OK-XO Shisetsu, Bldg, 305 Nahagunko-Nai, Kakinohana-Cho Naha-Shi, Okinawa 900

4. The USARJ agency responsible for **payments and collections** under this agreement is:

a. Unit:	DFAS-J (Army Accounting)
b. Telephone:	Com'l: 042-552-2511 ext. 5-5340 DSN: 225-5340
c. Fax:	Com'l: 042-552-2511 ext. 5-3523 DSN: 225-3523
d. Message Address:	DFAS JAPAN YOKOTA JA//
e. Mailing Address:	DFAS-J (Army Accounting) Unit 5220 ATTN: AAOA Yokota Air Base Fussa-Shi, Tokyo 197

ANNEX D / TAB I

MARINE FORCES JAPAN (MARFORJ)

1. The MARFORJ POC responsible for **approving, placing, and accepting orders** for the III MEF under this agreement is:

a. Unit:	III Marine Expeditionary Force (G-4/Supply)
b. Telephone:	Com'l: 0988-92-5111 ext. 622-7137 DSN: 622-7137
c. Fax:	Com'l: 0988-92-5111 ext. 622-9019 DSN: 622-9019
d. Message Address:	CG III MEF//G4//
e. Mailing Address:	Commanding General ATTN: AC/S G4/MRB/SUP Unit 35601 FPO AP 96606-5061

2. The MARFORJ POC responsible for **approving, placing, and accepting orders** for Marine Forces Japan, Camp Butler under this agreement is:

a. Unit:	Marine Corps Base, Camp S.D. Butler (G-4/)
b. Telephone:	Com'l: 0988-92-5111 ext. 645-7223 DSN: 645-7223
c. Fax:	Com'l: 098-892-5111 ext. 645-7231 DSN: 6457231
d. Message Address:	CG MCB CP BUTLER JA//G4//SUPPLY//
e. Mailing Address:	Commanding General, Marine Corps Base, Camp
S.D. Butler (G4)	ATTN: ACSA POC Unit 35001 FPO AP 96373-5001, Central Post Office, Naha-shi, Okinawa-ken 900

3. The MARFORJ agency responsible for **payments and collections** under this agreement is:

a. Unit:	Marine Forces Japan, Camp Butler (Comptroller)
b. Telephone:	Com'l: 098-892-5111 ext. 645-7310 DSN: 645-7310
c. Fax:	Com'l: 098-892-5111 ext. 645-7351 DSN: 645-7759
d. Message Address:	DMS CG MCBUTLER COMPT JA//COMPT//
e. Mailing Address:	Commanding General Marine Forces Japan (Comptroller) Unit 35001 ATTN: ACSA POC FPO AP 96373-5001 Central Post Office, Naha-shi, Okinawa-ken 900

ANNEX D / TAB J

US AIR FORCES JAPAN (USAFJ)

1. The USAFJ POC responsible for **approving, placing, and accepting orders** under this agreement is:

a. Unit:	HQ 5AF 605 ASUS/LGX (Logistics Plans and Programs)
b. Telephone:	Com'l: 0425-52-2511, ext. 5-4173 DSN: 225-4173
c. Fax:	Com'l: 0425-52-2511, ext. 5-8831 DSN: 225-8831
d. Message Address:	5AF YOKOTA AB JA/LGX//
e. Mailing Address:	HQ 5 AF 605 Air Support Squadron/LGX Logistics Division, Plans and Programs Branch ATTN: ACSA POC, Yokota Air Base, Fussa-Shi, Tokyo 197

2. The USAFJ agency responsible for **payments and collections** under this agreement is:

a. Unit:	DFAS-J
b. Telephone:	Com'l: 0425-52-2511, ext. 5-9838 DSN: 225-9838
c. Fax:	Com'l: 0425-52-2511, ext. 5-9841 DSN: 225-3213
d. Message Address:	DFAS JAPAN YOKOTA JA//
e. Mailing Address:	DFAS-J, Unit 5220, Bldg 206 Yokota Air Base, Fussa-Shi, Tokyo 197

ANNEX D / TAB K

US FORCES KOREA (HQ USFK)

1. The HQ USFK POC for coordinated **placement and acceptance of orders** under this agreement is the J45, Security Assistance and International Logistics Division:

a. Unit:	CDRUSPACOM J4
b. Telephone:	Com'l (808) 477-0387
c. Fax:	Com'l (808) 477-6669 Com'l (808) 477-0844 (Classified)
d. Message Address:	CDRUSPACOM HONOLULU HI//J4//
e. Mailing Address:	HQ CDRUSPACOM J4 Bldg 400, Box 64020 Camp H. M. Smith, HI 96861-4020

2. The HQ USFK POC responsible for **payments and collections** in support of this agreement is the Comptroller:

a. Unit:	CDRUSPACOM J05
b. Telephone:	Com'l (808) 477-6680
c. Fax:	Com'l (808) 477-0535
d. Message Address:	CDRUSPACOM HONOLULU HI//J05//
e. Mailing Address:	HQ CDRUSPACOM J05 Box 64037 Camp H. M. Smith, HI 96861-4037

ANNEX E

UNITED STATES EUROPEAN COMMAND (USEUCOM)
POINTS OF CONTACT, ORDERING AND FINANCIAL RESPONSIBILITIES

TAB A – USEUCOM
TAB B – USAFE (Air Force)
TAB C – USAREUR (Army)
TAB D – USNAVEUR (Navy)
TAB E – USMARFOREUR (Marine Corps)
TAB F – SOCEUR (Special Operations)
TAB G – USAREUR SFOR (Bosnia and Herzegovina)
TAB H – USAREUR KFOR (Kosovo)

ANNEX E / TAB A

HQ U.S. EUROPEAN COMMAND (USEUCOM) POINTS OF CONTACT
POINTS OF CONTACT, POLICY, LEGAL, ORDERING, AND FINANCIAL RESPONSIBILITIES

1. The USEUCOM POC for **policy issues** under this agreement is the ECJ4 Logistics Sustainment Division, Multinational Logistics Branch, ACSA Program:

a. Unit:	HQ USEUCOM ECJ4-LS-ML-ACSA
b. Telephone:	Commercial 49-711-680-7474 /1490 DSN 430-7474 / 1490
c. Fax: CLASSIFIED Fax:	Commercial 49-711-680-7476 DSN 430-7476 Commercial 49-711-680-7402 DSN 430-7402
d. Message Address:	CDRUSEUCOM VAIHINGEN GE//ECJ4-LS//
e. Mailing Address:	HQ USEUCOM, ECJ4-LS ATTN: ML-ACSA Unit 30400, Box 1000 APO AE 09131

2. The EUCOM agency responsible for policy issues regarding **international law and legal matters** in support of this agreement is the Staff Judge Advocate:

a. Unit:	HQ USEUCOM-ECJA
b. Telephone:	Commercial 49-711-680-8001 DSN 430-8001
c. Fax:	Commercial 49-711-680-5370 DSN 430-5370
d. Message Address:	CDRUSEUCOM VAIHINGEN GE//ECJA//
e. Mailing Address:	HQ USEUCOM-ECJA Unit 30400 APOAE 09131

3. The USEUCOM POC's for coordination and authorized for **approving, placing, and acceptance of orders** under this agreement is:
3.1. The ECJ4 Logistics Sustainment Division, Multinational Logistics Branch, ACSA Program:

a. Unit:	HQ USEUCOM ECJ4-LS-ML-ACSA
b. Telephone:	Commercial 49-711-680-7474 /1490 DSN 430-7474/1490
c. Fax:	Commercial 49-711-680-7476 DSN 430-7476
CLASSIFIED Fax:	Commercial 49-711-680-7402 DSN 430-7402
d. Message Address:	CDRUSEUCOM VAIHINGEN GE//ECJ4-LS//
e. E-mail Address:	acsa@eucom.mil
f. Mailing Address:	HQ USEUCOM, ECJ4-LS ATTN: ML-ACSA Unit 30400, Box 1000 APO AE 09131

3.2. The ECJ4 EUCOM Deployment and Distribution Operation Center (EDDOC), to include the Logistics Readiness Center (LRC):

a. Unit:	HQ USEUCOM ECJ4-EDDOC
b. Telephone:	Commercial 49-711-680-8766 (24 hour) DSN 430-8766 (24 hour)
c. Fax:	Commercial 49-711-680-6104 (24 hour) DSN 430-7476 (24 hour)
CLASSIFIED Fax:	Commercial 49-711-680-7402 (24 hour) DSN 430-7402 (24 hour)
d. Message Address:	CDRUSEUCOM VAIHINGEN GE//ECJ4-EDDOC//
e. Mailing Address:	HQ USEUCOM, ECJ4-EDDOC Unit 30400, Box 1000 APO AE 09131

4. The EUCOM agency responsible for policy issues regarding **payments and collections** in support of this agreement is the Comptroller:

a. Unit:	HQ USEUCOM-ECCM
b. Telephone:	Commercial 49-711 -680-5119 or 7105 DSN 430-5119 or 7105
c. Fax:	Commercial 49-711-680-5370 DSN 430-5370
d. Message Address:	CDRUSEUCOM VAIHINGEN GE//ECCM//
e. Mailing Address:	HQ USEUCOM-ECCM Unit 30400 APO AE 09131

ANNEX E / TAB B

HQ U.S. AIR FORCES EUROPE (HQ USAFE) POINTS OF CONTACT ORDERING AND FINANCIAL RESPONSIBILITIES

1. The HQ USAFE agency responsible for approving, placing and accepting orders under this agreement is Headquarters USAFE Logistics Readiness Division, International Logistics Branch:

a. Unit:	HQ USAFE/A4RI
b. Telephone:	Commercial 49-6371-47-6788 DSN 480-6788
c. Fax:	Commercial 49-6371-47-9255 DSN 480-9255
d. Message	HQ USAFE RAMSTEIN AB GE//A4RI//
e. Mailing Address:	

(Military) HQ USAFE/A4RI Unit 3050, Box 105 APO AE 09094-0105	(Commercial) HQ USAFE/A4RI Gebaude 528, Zim. 102; Flugplatz 66877 Ramstein-Miesenbach, GE

2. The HQ USAFE agency responsible for payments and collections for this agreement is the Defense Finance and Accounting Service, Ramstein AB:

a. Unit:	DFAS-ADCJ
b. Telephone:	Com'l 49-6371-47-2068 DSN 480-2068
c. Fax:	Com'l 49-6371-47-7582 DSN 480-7582
d. Message Address:	USAFE DFAS-CCE/MSA Office
e. Mailing Address:	

(Military) HQ USAFE/DFAS CCE/ MSA Unit 3050, Box 5 APO AE 09094-0505	(Commercial) HQ USAFE/DFAS CCE/MSA Gebäude 413, Zim. 210, Flugplatz 66877 Ramstein-Miesenbach, GE

ANNEX E / TAB C

U.S. ARMY EUROPE (USAREUR)

The HQ USAREUR agencies responsible for **approving, placing, and accepting orders** under this agreement are:

1. For logistics support, supplies, and services **in connection with training**:

a. Unit/Address:	Commander 7th Army Training Command ATTN: AETT-RM-MGT Unit 28130, APO AE 09114-8130 Grafenwoehr Lager D-92655 Grafenwoehr, Germany
b Telephone:	Commercial 49-9641-83-7159 DSN 475-7159
c. Fax:	Commercial 49-9641-83-8416 DSN 475-8416
d. Message Address:	CDR7ATC GRAFENWOEHR GE//AETT-RM-MGT//

2. **For all other logistics support, supplies, and services:**

a. Unit/Address:	HQ USAREUR/7A ATTN: AEAGF-PB-TCS Unit 29351, APO AE 09014-9351 Roemerstr. 168 69128 Heidelberg, Germany
b. Telephone:	Commercial 49-6221-57-6375 DSN 370-6375
c. Fax:	Commercial 49-6221-57-6194 DSN 370-6194
d. Message Address:	CGUSAREUR HEIDELBERG GE//AEAGF-PM-TCS//

3. Paying Office for HQ USAREUR/7A:

a. Unit/Address:	DFAS Europe Army Vendor Pay Unit 23122 APO AE 09227 Mannheimer Strasse 218/219 D-67657 Kaiserslautern, Germany
b. Telephone:	Commercial 49-631-413-4278/4183/4109/4111 DSN 484-4278/4183/4109/4111
c. Fax:	Commercial 49-631-413-4290/4293 DSN 484-4290/4293

4. Paying Office for Balkans Area of Operations:

a. Unit/Address:	Commercial Vendor Service (CVS) Finance Detachment, Bldg 1330-C Camp Bondsteel Kosovo APO AE 09340
b. Telephone:	Commerical 49-621-730-781-5467 DSN 781-5467
c. Fax:	Commerical 49-621-730-781-5465 DSN 781-5465

ANNEX E / TAB D

U.S. NAVY EUROPE (USNAVEUR)

1. The USNAVEUR agency responsible for **approving, placing, and accepting orders** is:

a. Unit:	COMUSNAVEUR (NEPO LOG PLANS)
b. Telephone:	Com'l 39-081-568-5083 DSN 626-5083
c. Fax:	Com'l 39-081-568-8202 DSN 626-8202
d. Message Address:	COMSNAVEUR NAPLES IT//NEPO LOG PLANS//
e. Mailing Address:	

(Military)	(Commercial)
COMUSNAVEUR (NEPO LOG PLANS)	COMUSNAVEUR(NEPO LOG
PSC 817, Box 111	PLANS)
FPO AE 09622	Marina Militarie Americana Viale Fulco Ruffo Di Calabria Aereoporto Capodichino Napoli Italie 80144

2. The USNAVEUR agency for **collecting and making payments** for support, supplies, and services is:

a. Unit:	COMUSNAVEUR (COMPTROLLER)
b. Telephone:	Com'l 39-081-568-5295 DSN 626-5295
d. Message Address:	COMUSNAVEUR NAPLES IT//COMPT//
e. Mailing Address:	

(Military)	(Commercial)
COMUSNAVEUR (COMPROLLER)	COMUSNAVEUR
PSC 817, Box 111	(COMPTROLLER)
FPO AE 09622	Marina Militare Americana Viale Fulco Ruffo Di Calabria Aereoporto Capodichino Napoli Italie 80144

ANNEX E / TAB E

MARINE FORCES EUROPE (MARFOREUR)

1. The HQ MARFOREUR agency responsible for **approving, placing, and accepting orders** under this agreement is:

a. Unit:	HQ MARFOREUR/G4
b. Telephone:	Commercial 49-7031-15-438 DSN 431-2438
c. Fax:	Commercial 49-7031-15-519 DSN 431-2519
d. Message Address:	HQ MARFOREUR BOEBLINGEN GE//G4//
e. Mailing Address:	Commanding Officer Headquarters Marine Forces Europe Panzer Kaserne APO AE 09046

2. The HQ MARFOREUR agency responsible for **payments and collections** in support of this agreement is:

a. Unit:	HQ MARFOREUR/G4
b. Telephone:	Commercial 49-7031-15-438 DSN 431-5438
c. Fax:	Commercial 49-7031-15-519 DSN 431-5519
d. Message Address:	HQ MARFOREUR BOEBLNGEN GE//G4//
e. Mailing Address:	Commanding Officer Headquarters Marine Forces Europe Panzer Kaserne APO AE 09046

ANNEX E / TAB F

SPECIAL OPERATIONS COMMAND EUROPE (SOCEUR)

1. The HQ SOCEUR agency responsible for **approving, placing, and accepting orders** under this agreement is:

a. Unit:	SOCEUR/J4
b. Telephone:	Commercial 49-711-680-5250 DSN 430-5250
c. Fax:	Commercial 49-711-680-577 DSN 430-0577
d. Message Address:	COMSOCEUR VAIHINGEN GE//J4//
e. Mailing Address:	HQ USEUCOM SOCEUR/SOJ4 Unit 30400 APO AE 09131

2. The SOCEUR agency responsible for **payments and collections** in support of this agreement is:

a. Unit:	SOCEUR/J8
b. Telephone:	Commercial 49-711-680-7249 DSN 430-7249
c. Fax:	Commercial 49-711-5771 DSN 430-5771
d. Message Address:	COMSOCEUR VAIHINGEN GE//SOJ1//
e. Mailing Address:	HQ USEUCOM SOCEUR/SOJ8 Unit 30400 APOAE 09131

ANNEX E / TAB G

U.S. ARMY EUROPE (USAREUR) Stabilization Forces (SFOR)

The USAREUR SFOR agency responsible for **approving, placing, and accepting orders** under this agreement are:

1. For logistics support, supplies, and services:

a. Unit/Address:	Multinational Support Cell ATTN: G4, MNSC Eagle Base, Tuzla APO AE 09789
b. Telephone: Commercial	DSN 762-8856
c. Fax: Commercial	DSN 762-2287
d. Message Address:	EAGLE CAMP//S-4//

2. **Paying Office** for SFOR:

Bosnia:

a. Unit/Address:	Finance Office Eagle Base, Tuzla Operation Joint Forge APO AE 09789
b. Telephone:	DSN 762-2116
c. Fax:	Commercial 49-631-413-4300 DSN 370-4300

ANNEX E / TAB H

U.S. ARMY EUROPE (USAREUR) Kosovo Forces (KFOR)

The USAREUR KFOR agency responsible for **approving, placing, and accepting orders** under this agreement are:

1. For logistics support, supplies, and services:

a. Unit/Address:	Multinational Support Cell ATTN: G4, MNSC Camp Bondsteel, Kosovo APO AE 09340
b. Telephone: Commercial	DSN 781-4272
c. Fax:Commercial	DSN 781-3891
d. Message Address:	CAMP BONDSTEEL//S-4//
2. The USAREUR KFOR **Paying Office:**	
a. Unit/Address: Finance Office	Camp Bondsteel, Kosovo Task Force Falcon/ OJG APO AE 09340
b. Telephone:	DSN 781-3720
c. Fax:	Commercial 49-631-413-4300 DSN 370-4300

ANNEX F

USJFCOM
POINTS OF CONTACT, ORDERING AND FINANCIAL RESPONSIBILITIES

TAB A – USJFCOM
TAB B – ACC (Air Force)
TAB C – CINCLANTFLT (Navy)
TAB D – MARFORLANT (Marine Corps)
TAB E – FORSCOM (Army)

ANNEX F / TAB A

U.S. JOINT FORCES COMMAND (USJFCOM)

1. The USJFCOM POC for coordinated **placement and acceptance of orders** under this agreement is the J4 Plans, Programs, and Policy Division:

a. Unit:	USJFCOM J45
b. Telephone:	Com'l: (757) 836-8344 or 5924 DSN: 836-8344 or 5924
c. Fax:	Com'l: (757) 836-5937 DSN: 836-5937
d. Message Address:	COMUSJFCOM NORFOLK VA//J45//
e. Mailing Address:	Commander HQ, U.S. Joint Forces Command (J45) 1562 Mitscher Avenue, Suite 200 Norfolk, VA 23551-2488

2. The USJFCOM agency responsible for **payments and collections** in support of this agreement is the Comptroller:

a. Unit:	USJFCOM J02F3
b. Telephone	Com'l: (757) 836-5901 DSN: 836-5901
c. Fax:	Com'l: (757) 836-5901 DSN: 836-6648
d. Message Address:	COMUSJFCOM NORFOLK VA//J02F//
e. Mailing Address:	Commander HQ, U.S. Joint Forces Command (J02) 1562 Mitscher Avenue, Suite 200 Norfolk, VA 23551-2488

3. The USJFCOM agency for **legal matters** is J02L:

a. Unit:	USJFCOM J02L
b. Telephone:	Com'l: (757) 836-6416 or 6414 DSN: 836-6416 or 6414
c. Fax:	Com'l: (757) 836-5959 DSN: 836-5959
d. Message Address:	COMUSJFCOM NORFOLK VA//J02L//
e. Mailing Address:	Commander, U.S. Joint Forces Command (J02L) 1562 Mitscher Avenue Suite 200 Norfolk, VA 23551-2488

ANNEX F/ TAB B

AIR COMBAT COMMAND (ACC)

1. The ACC POC for coordinated **placement and acceptance of orders** and for **payment and collections** under this agreement is:

a. Unit:	Command Staff
b. Telephone:	Com'l: (757) 764-5462 DSN: 574-5462
c. Fax:	Com'l: (757) 764-3909 DSN: 574-3909
d. Message Address:	HQ ACC LANGLEY AFB VA//CS//
e. Mailing Address:	Headquarters Air Combat Command Langley AFB, VA 23665-5000

ANNEX F / TAB C

COMMANDER, ATLANTIC FLEET (CDRLANTFLT)

1. The CDRLANTFLT POC for coordinated **payment and collections** under this agreement is:

a. Unit:	N413
b. Telephone:	Com'l: (757) 836-3789 DSN: 836-3789
c. Fax:	Com'l: (757) 836-3772 DSN: 836-3772
d. Message Address:	CDRLANTFLT NORFOLK VA//N41
e. Mailing Address:	Commander, U.S Atlantic Fleet Code N413 1562 Mitscher Avenue, Suite 250 Norfolk, VA 23551-2487

2. The CDRLANTFLT POC for coordinated **placement and acceptance of orders** under this agreement is:

a. Unit:	N02F
b. Telephone:	Com'l: (757) 836-6929 DSN: 836-6929
c. Fax:	Com'l: (757) 836-6987 DSN: 836-6987
d. Message Address:	CDRLANTFLT NORFOLK VA//N02F
e. Mailing Address:	Commander, U.S Atlantic Fleet Code N02F 1562 Mitscher Avenue, Suite 250 Norfolk, VA 23551-2487

ANNEX F / TAB D

MARINE FORCES ATLANTIC (MARFORLANT)

1. The MARFORLANT POC for coordinated **payment and collections** under this agreement is:

a. Unit:	G4A
b. Telephone:	Com'l: (757) 836-1647 DSN: 836-1647
c. Fax:	Com'l: (757) 836-1678 DSN: 836-1678
d. Message Address:	COMMARFORLANT//G4
e. Mailing Address:	U.S. Marine Corps Forces Atlantic Code G4A 1468 Ingram Street Norfolk, VA 13551

2. The MARFORLANT POC for coordinated **placement and acceptance of orders** under this agreement is:

a. Unit:	G8
b. Telephone:	Com'l: (757) 836-1582 or 1583 DSN: 836-1582 or 1583
c. Fax:	Com'l: (757) 836-1753 DSN: 836-1753
d. Message Address:	COMMARFORLANT//G8
e. Mailing Address:	U.S. Marine Corps Forces Atlantic Code G8 1468 Ingram Street Norfolk, VA 13551

ANNEX F/TAB E

ARMY FORCES COMMAND (FORSCOM)

1. The FORSCOM POC for coordinated **payment and collections** under this agreement is:

a. Unit:	AFLG-POFP
b. Telephone:	Com'l: (404) 464-5636 DSN: 367-5636
c. Fax:	Com'l: (404) 464-5685 DSN: 367-5685
d. Message Address:	CDRFORSCOM FT MCPHERSONGA//AFLG-POT
e. Mailing Address:	Headquarters Forces Command Code AFLG-POT 1777 Hardee Avenue Ft. McPherson, GA 30330-1062

2. The FORSCOM POC for coordinated **placement and acceptance of orders** under this agreement is:

a. Unit:	AFRM-RI-O
b. Telephone:	Com'l: (404) 464-5460 or 6213 DSN: 367-5460 or 6213
c. Fax:	Com'l: (404) 464-6564 DSN: 367-6564
d. Message Address:	CDRFORSCOM FT MCPHERSONGA// AFRM-RI-O//
e. Mailing Address:	Headquarters Forces Command Code AFRM-RI-O 1777 Hardee Avenue Ft. McPherson, GA 30330-1062

ANNEX G

USSOUTHCOM
POINTS OF CONTACT, ORDERING AND FINANCIAL RESPONSIBILITIES

U.S. SOUTHERN COMMAND (USSOUTHCOM)

1. The USSOUTHCOM POC for coordinated **placement and acceptance of orders** under this agreement is the SCJ4 Joint Logistics Operations Center:

a. Unit:	SOUTHCOM-SCJ4
b. Telephone:	Com'l: (305) 437-1412 or 1400 DSN: 567-1412 or 1400
c. Fax:	Com'l: (305) 437-1443 DSN: 567-1443 Com'l: (305) 437-1444 (Classified) DSN: 567-1444 (Classified)
d. Message Address:	CDR USSOUTHCOM MIAMI FL//SCJ4//(CM)
e. Mailing Address:	COMMANDER HQ USOUTHCOM-SCJ4 3511 NW 91st Ave Miami, FL 33172-1217

2. The USSOUTHCOM agency responsible for coordinating **payments and collections** in support of this agreement is the Comptroller:

a. Unit:	USSOUTHCOM-SCJ8
b. Telephone:	Com'l: (305) 437-1814 or 1811 DSN: 567-1814 or 1811
c. Fax:	Com'l: (305)437-1840 DSN: 567-1840
d. Message Address:	CDR USSOUTHCOM MIAMI FL//SCJ8//(CM)
e. Mailing Address:	COMMANDER HQ USSOUTHCOM (Attn: SCJ8) 3511 NW 91st Ave Miami, FL 33172-1217

ANNEX H

USNORTHCOM POINTS OF CONTACT, ORDERING AND FINANCIAL RESPONSIBILITIES

U.S. NORTHERN COMMAND (USNORTHCOM)

1. The USNORTHCOM POC for coordinated **placement and acceptance of orders** under this agreement is:

a. Unit:	NORAD-USNORTHCOM/J4P
b. Telephone:	Com'l: (719) 554-2651 or 3205 DSN: 692-2651 or 3205
c. Fax:	Com'l: (719) 554-3062 or 0813 DSN: 692-3062 or 0813
d. Message Address:	NORAD-NORTHCOM PETERSON AFB CO//J4//
e. Mailing Address:	250 Vandenberg St. Ste. B016 Peterson AFB CO 80914-3816

2. The USNORTHCOM agency responsible for **payments and collections** in support of this agreement is:

a. Unit:	NORAD-USNORTHCOM/J8
b. Telephone:	Com'l: (719)554-6327 DSN: 692-6327
c. Fax:	Com'l: (719) 556-0335 DSN: 834-0335
d. Message Address:	NORAD-NORTHCOM PETERSON AFB CO//J8//
e. Mailing Address:	250 Vandenberg St. Rm 1031 Peterson AFB CO 80914-3816

ANNEX I

USTRANSCOM POINTS OF CONTACT, ORDERING AND FINANCIAL RESPONSIBILITIES

U.S. TRANSPORTATION COMMAND (USTRANSCOM)

1. The USTRANSCOM POC for coordinated **placement and acceptance of orders** under this agreement is the TCJ3 Deployment and Distribution Operations Center (DDOC):

a. Unit:	USTRANSCOM-TCJ3-R
b. Telephone:	Com'l: (618) 229-4172 or 1045 DSN: 779-4172 or 1045
c. Fax:	Com'l: (618)256-1363 DSN: 576-1363 Com'l: (618) 256-6859 (Classified) DSN: 576-6859 (Classified)
d. Message Address:	USTRANSCOM SCOTT AFB IL//TCJ3-R//
e. Mailing Address:	HQ USTRANSCOM TCJ3-R (DDOC) 508 Scott Drive Bldg. 1900 Scott AFB IL, 62225-5357

2. The USTRANSCOM agency responsible for **payments and collections** in support of this agreement is the TCJ8 Program Analysis and Financial Management Directorate:

a. Unit:	USTRANSCOM-TCJ8
b. Telephone:	Com'l: (618)229-1099 DSN: 779-1099
c. Fax:	Com'l: (618)256-8097 DSN: 576-8097
d. Message Address:	USTRANSCOM SCOTT AFB IL//TCJ8//
e. Mailing Address:	HQ USTRANSCOM - TCJ8 508 Scott Drive Bldg. 1900 Scott AFB IL 62225-5357

STATE DEPARTMENT DOCUMENT NUMBER: 06-307

MEMORANDUM OF UNDERSTANDING BETWEEN THE DEPARTMENT OF DEFENSE OF THE UNITED STATES OF AMERICA AND THE MINISTRY OF DEFENSE OF ITALY CONCERNING THE MUTUAL EXCHANGE OF MILITARY SATELLITE COMMUNICATIONS SERVICES AND SUPPORT, WITH ANNEX

SIGNED AT OFFUTT AFB AND ROME,
JULY 20 AND NOVEMBER 6, 2006
ENTERED INTO FORCE NOVEMBER 6, 2006

CTIA DOCUMENT NUMBER: 13128.000

INTRODUCTION

The Department of Defense of the United States of America (DoD U.S.) and the Ministry of Defense of Italy (MoD ITA), hereinafter referred to as the "Participants:"

Recognizing the Agreement Between the Member States of the North Atlantic Treaty on the Status of Forces, signed 19 June 1951 (NATO SOFA);

Recognizing the Agreement between the Government of Italy and the Government of the United States of America concerning the exchange of classified information that was concluded by an exchange of diplomatic notes on 4 August 1964 and amended by an exchange of diplomatic notes on 2 September 1982;

Recognizing the Bilateral Infrastructure Agreement (BIA) Between the United States of America and Italy, signed at Rome on 20 October 1954;

Having a common interest in defense;

Recognizing the benefits to be obtained from standardization, rationalization, and interoperability of communication systems;

Recognizing the need for the orderly use of space for communications purposes;

Recognizing that the satisfaction of the foregoing requirements may be sought through:

a. Shared use of each other's operational satellite communications (SATCOM);

b. Use of each other's spare SATCOM;

c. Use of each other's SATCOM systems by means of terrestrial interconnection;

d. Exchange of managerial and/or operational information to facilitate interoperability with each other's SATCOM systems;

Recognizing the Participants each have a desire to achieve interoperable SATCOM links over U.S. operational SATCOM between certain of each other's specified earth terminals and associated satellite communications facilities;

Recognizing the Participants each have a desire to achieve interoperable SATCOM links over Italian operational SATCOM between certain of each other's specified earth terminals and associated satellite communications facilities;

Recognizing the Participants have a need for a contingency and interoperability capability to use each other's satellites, satellite capacity, satellite ground terminals and interconnection facilities in support of joint and combined operations;

Recognizing the benefits that can be obtained from an exchange of communications services and capacity including SATCOM and other communications services;

Recognizing the benefits that can be achieved in achieving interoperable SATCOM broadcast services.

Have reached the following understandings:

SECTION I
DEFINITIONS

The Participants have jointly decided upon the following definitions for terms used in this Memorandum of Understanding (MOU) :

Classified Information

Information that requires protection in the interests of national security and is so designated by the application of a security classification. This information may be in oral, visual, electronic or documentary form, or in the form of material including equipment or technology.

Communications Interoperability and Interconnections Programs (CIIP)

Programs to meet both Participants' critical military operational requirements for communications interoperability and interconnections, as mutually determined through requirements harmonization discussions between the Participants. Programs will be identified under each CIIP, which will be set out in Communications Arrangements.

Communications Arrangement (CA)

A separate, mutually determined implementing arrangement, concluded after this MOU has come into effect, which details the provisions of collaboration between the Participants for particular Programs.

Contractor

Any individual or entity acting on behalf of a Participant in connection with this MOU or any of its CAs pursuant to a contract between that individual or entity and a Participant. Contractors can be involved in all aspects of this MOU, but cannot make binding decision on behalf of respective Participants.

Controlled Unclassified Information

Unclassified information to which access or distribution limitations have been applied in accordance with applicable national laws or regulations. Whether the information is provided or generated under this MOU and its CAs, the information will be designated so as to identify its "in confidence" nature. It could include information, which has been declassified, but remains controlled.

U.S. export-controlled information will be marked as "International Traffic in Arms Regulation (ITAR)-Controlled." Italy export controlled information will be marked as "US-ITA eyes only" with the proper classification.

Defense Purposes

Any purpose that is in furtherance of the mission of national defense of either Participant.

Designated Security Authority (DSA)/National Security Authority

The security office approved by the Participants' national authorities to be responsible for the security aspects of this MOU. For Italy, the DSA is the National Security Authority.

Financial Authority

The office(s) or organizations(s) responsible for determining and certifying the cost of services provided under this MOU.

Financial Costs

Program costs met with monetary contributions from the Participants.

Host Participant

The Participant whose facilities host, on behalf of the Providing Participant activities pursuant to this MOU and any of its CAs, including the hosting of the other Participant's personnel, property, equipment, material, or information. Such personnel, property, equipment, material, or information is hosted generally for the benefit of the Providing Participant and not for use by the Hosting Participant, absent express written authorization by the Providing Participant.

Participant

A signatory to the Agreement represented by its military and civilian personnel.

Program

An area of communications collaboration under this MOU to be carried out in a Communications Arrangement (CA) or an activity under this MOU. It can include a specific satellite communications system as a whole, which includes the space segment, ground segment, and control segment, delineated in a CA. It can also refer to a supporting area of SATCOM, such as a training exchange program, as described in a CA.

Providing Participant

Participant that provides personnel, property, equipment, material, or information in connection with this MOU or any if its CAs to the other Participant, regardless of whether the other Participant is acting as a Host Participant of a Receiving Participant.

Receiving Participant

The Participant that receives personnel, property, equipment, material, or information in connection with this MOU or any of its CAs from the Providing Participant for its own use.

Satellite Communications (SATCOM)

Military satellite communications including gateways, network connectivity and satellite terminal-to-terminal communications that are owned/operated by the U.S. Department of Defense or Italian Ministry of Defense.

Sub-Contractor

Any individual or entity acting on behalf of a Contractor pursuant to a contract.

Third Party

Any person or other entity whose governing authority is not a Participant to this MOU. It does not include a Contractor who is acting on behalf of either Participant in undertaking work for Defense Purposes.

SECTION II
OBJECTIVES

2.1 The objectives of this MOU are to:

2.1.1 Provide Participants access to bandwidth and SATCOM services from each other's satellites to enhance operational command of the Participants joint and combined forces, on an equitable exchange basis subject to reimbursement.

2.1.2 Promote mutual identification of Communications Interoperability and Interconnections Programs (CUP) to meet both Participants' critical military operational requirements. The specific level of cooperation and interconnection between U.S. DoD and Italian MoD systems will be mutually determined through requirements harmonization discussions conducted by the Participants under this MOU, consistent with their national interests.

2.1.3 Define and set forth details to establish the general principles that will apply to the initiation, conduct and management of separate Communications Arrangements (CAs) between authorized representatives in accordance with national procedures of the Participants.

2.1.4 CAs will be entered into pursuant to this MOU and will incorporate by reference the provisions of this MOU. Each CA will include specific provisions consistent with this MOU, concerning (but not limited to) the CAs' Objectives, Allocation of Tasks, Management, Implementation Procedures, Financial Arrangements, Communications Arrangements, Special Disclosure and Use Provisions, Entry in Effect, Duration, and Termination. Should any provision of a CA conflict with the provisions of this MOU; the provisions of this MOU will apply.

2.1.5 The exchange of military satellite communications services or support between the Participants under the provisions set out in this MOU or its CAs will only be used for Defense purposes. SATCOM and information exchanged consistent with the purposes of this MOU will not be made available to a Third Party without the express written consent of Participant that originally provided that information to the other (hereafter "Providing Participant").

2.1.6 Activities under this MOU are provided on an as available basis. Either Participant may deny a request by the other Participant for SATCOM access under this MOU, based upon its own operational commitments and requirements. To the extent possible, an explanation, at the appropriate classification level, will be provided to the Participant whose request was denied.

2.1.7 This MOU in no way limits the right of Participants to enter into any other arrangements in the satellite communications interoperability and interconnection area with other nations.

SECTION III
SCOPE OF MOU

3.0 The scope of this MOU includes the exchange of communications services and capacity between the Participants as well as information exchange for the purposes of facilitating activities under this MOU, including the development and implementation of CAs.

SECTION IV
MANAGEMENT (ORGANIZATION AND RESPONSIBILITY)

4.1 The Participants will designate appropriate "Principals" to oversee the full, smooth implementation of this MOU. The U.S. Strategic Command Director, Combat and Information Operations (or equivalent in the event of reorganization) is designated the U.S. Principal to this MOU. The Italian General Staff Chief of C4I and Transformation Department is designated the Italian Principal to this MOU.

4.2 This MOU establishes an Executive Committee (EC) to act on behalf of the Participants under the oversight of the Principal to facilitate the implementation of this MOU and its CAs. The U.S. Strategic Command Chief, SATCOM Operations Division, or his/her designated representative, will act as the US EC representative. The Italian General Staff C4I Department Chief of International Affairs Coordination Office, or his/her designated representative will act as the IT EC representative. The EC will normally meet on an annual basis with additional meetings held at the request of either representative. The representative of the Participant hosting the meeting will chair each meeting of the EC.

4.3 The EC will be responsible for:

4.3.1 Identifying and reviewing proposals regarding CAs.

4.3.2 Overseeing the Participants' day-to-day implementation of this MOU, including in the area of communications requirements activities under this MOU, the exchange of information conducted to support implementation of the MOU and the development of related CAs.

4.3.3 Establishing appropriate CAs in accordance with national procedures of the Participants.

4.3.4 Establishing broad executive-level oversight of CAs under this MOU.

4.3.5 Maintaining oversight of the security aspects associated with implementation of this MOU and its CAs.

4.3.6 Promptly appraising and consulting on matters that affect this MOU and resolving any issues brought forward by appropriate officials as provided in CAs.

4.3.7 Recommending amendments to this MOU to the Principals for the Principals' mutual approval. After mutually concurring in proposed amendments, the Participants will process such proposals for adoption through their respective national procedures.

4.3.8 Reviewing the annual financial balance of the communications services and systems exchanged under this MOU.

4.3.9 All decisions of the EC will be made unanimously. Any decisions that cannot be resolved will be referred to the Principals for resolution.

4.4 CAs will be managed in accordance with their respective provisions. Each CA will normally contain a management structure that consists of a Coordinating Team (CT) and Program Officers (POs) as described below:

4.4.1 The CT will consist of a senior representative designated by each Participant, both of whom will co-chair the CT. Each CT will appoint a Program Officer. Each Participant, as appropriate, will designate other team members.

4.4.2 The CT will meet on a periodic basis, as required, to resolve specific issues raised by POs and receive progress reports from the POs.

4.4.3 The senior representative of the CT of the Participant hosting the EC meeting will be responsible for briefing the EC on the CT. The brief to the EC will be mutually determined by the whole CT prior to presentation to the EC.

4.4.4 The POs identified in each CA will be responsible for day-to-day implementation of that CA. The POs will be responsible for:

4.4.4.1 Developing a management plan in accordance with the provisions of the CA for approval by the CT.

4.4.4.2 Managing the cost, schedule, technical and financial aspects associated with implementation of the CA.

4.4.4.3 Referring issues to the CT that cannot be resolved by the POs.

4.4.4.4 Providing progress reports to the CT, as necessary.

4.4.5 All decisions of the CT will be made unanimously. Any issues that cannot be resolved will be referred to the EC.

SECTION V
CO-LOCATED EQUIPMENT

5.1 With mutual consent of the Participants, either Participant may co-locate communications and/or cryptographic equipment, and any other necessary equipment, including spares and documentation, in the other Participant's nominated communications facilities to implement effectively the interoperability and intercommunication arrangements, and other activities under this MOU. Such co-located equipment will remain the property of the Providing Participant. A list of all such co-located equipment provided by the one Participant will be developed and maintained by the CT, approved by the EC, and incorporated into the appropriate CA in accordance with Section IV (Management) of this MOU prior to co-location of such equipment.

5.2 The Providing Participant will furnish the co-located equipment in a condition appropriate for the intended purpose stated in the CA. However, the Providing Participant makes no warranty or guarantee of fitness of the co-located equipment for a particular purpose or use, and makes no commitment to alter, improve, or adapt the co-located equipment or any part thereof.

5.3 Co-located equipment will be removed at the termination of this MOU, at the conclusion of the equipment's useful life, or not later than six months from the date of a written request from the Host Participant to remove such equipment.

5.4 The Providing Participant will pay all costs associated with transporting, maintaining, servicing, and repairing co-located equipment, unless otherwise agreed between the Participants.

5.5 The Participants may enter into appropriate arrangements allowing the Receiving Participant access to and use of co-located equipment for the purposes of facilitating activities under this MOU, consistent with this MOU and relevant CAs.

SECTION VI
DISCLOSURE AND USE OF INFORMATION

6.1 The Participants recognize that successful implementation of this MOU depends on the full and prompt exchange of information between the Participants, as necessary for carrying out this MOU and associated CAs. The Participants intend to exchange sufficient information to fully implement this MOU and its associated CAs. The nature and amount of information to be exchanged under the CAs will be consistent with this MOU and associated CAs, subject to the national requirements of the respective Participants.

6.2 The Participants invoke the Agreement between the Government of Italy and the Government of the United States of America concerning the exchange of classified information, in connection with the exchange of information under this MOU and any of its CAs.

6.3 Each Participant further recognizes that all classified information made available by a Providing Participant to the Receiving Participant will be considered to be classified information furnished under, and shall be subject to all the provisions and safeguards provided for by the Agreement between the Government of Italy and the Government of the United States of America concerning the exchange of classified information, which entered into force on 4 August 1964 and was amended by an exchange of diplomatic notes on 2 September 1982.

6.4 The Receiving Participant may, upon request, make available to the Providing Participant, a location for onsite storage of classified and controlled unclassified, sensitive information, under the same terms and conditions as provided for co-located equipment in Section V above.

6.5 Receiving or Host Participants will not release or permit access to equipment, property, or information of the Providing Participant to a Third Party, except a Contractor or Subcontractor thereof, without the express written authorization of the Providing Participant. Transfer of such information to Contractors will be consistent with each Participant's applicable export control laws.

SECTION VII
SECURITY

7.1 All Classified Information or material provided or generated pursuant to this MOU and its CAs will be stored, handled, transmitted, and safeguarded in accordance with the Agreement between the Government of Italy and the Government of the United States concerning the exchange of classified information which entered into force on 4 August 1964 and was amended by and exchange of diplomatic notes on 2 September 1982.

7.2 Classified Information and material will be transferred only through official government-to-government channels or through channels approved by the Designated Security Authorities (DSAs) of the Participants. To assist in providing the desired protection, each Participant will indicate, on or with the furnished information, the country of origin, the security classification, the conditions of release, and the fact that the information is related to this MOU, and the applicable CA, and that it is furnished in confidence.

7.3 Each Participant will take all appropriate lawful steps available to ensure that Classified Information provided, generated or exchanged in confidence under this MOU or any of its CAs is protected from disclosure under any legislative provision, unless the other Participant consents to such disclosure. Accordingly, each Participant will ensure that:

7.3.1 The recipient will not release the Classified Information to any government, national organization, or other entity of a Third Party without the prior written consent of the originating Participant.

7.3.2 The recipient will not use the Classified Information for other than the purpose provided in this MOU.

7.3.3 The recipient will comply with any distribution and access restrictions on information that is provided under this MOU.

7.4 Classified Information provided by either Participant to the other, and Classified Information produced by either Participant pursuant to this MOU, will be safeguarded in a manner that ensures its proper protection from unauthorized disclosure. To ensure this end, Classified Information will either retain its original classification, or be assigned a classification that will ensure a degree of protection against disclosure equivalent to that required by the other Participant. For Italy, Classified Information will be labelled Restricted, Confidential, Secret and Top Secret. The U.S. Classified Information is Confidential, Secret and Top Secret. Both the Italian Restricted and Confidential will be treated as U.S. Confidential.

7.5 The Participants will investigate all cases that it is known or where there are grounds for suspecting the Classified Information or material provided or generated pursuant to this MOU has been lost or disclosed to unauthorized persons. Each Participant will promptly and fully inform the other Participant of the details of any such occurrences, the final results of the investigation, and other corrective action taken to preclude recurrences.

7.6 When a CA contains provisions for the exchange of Classified Information, the CT or POs, as appropriate, will prepare a Program Security Instruction (PSI) and a Classification Guide (CG) for the CA. The PSI and the CG will describe the methods by which information generated by or exchanged in connection with this MOU or any of its CAs will be classified, marked, used, transmitted, and safeguarded. The CT or POs will develop the PSI and CG, as appropriate, within three months after CA enters into effect. They will be reviewed and forwarded to the Participants' DSAs for approval and will be applicable to all government and Contractor personnel participating in the Program. The CG will be subject to regular review and revision with the aim of downgrading the classification whenever this is appropriate. The PSI and the CG will be approved by the appropriate DSA prior to the transfer of any Classified Information or Controlled Unclassified Information.

7.7 Contractors, prospective Contractors, Subcontractors or prospective Subcontractors which are determined by the DSAs to be under financial, administrative, policy or management control of nationals or entities of a Third Party, may participate in a contract or subcontract requiring access to Classified Information provided or generated pursuant to this MOU or any of its CAs only when enforceable measures are in effect to ensure that nationals or other entities of a Third Party will not have access to Classified Information. If enforceable measures are not in effect to preclude access by nationals or other entities of a Third Party, the other Participant will be consulted for written approval prior to permitting such access.

7.8 For any facility wherein Classified Information or material is to be used, the responsible Participant or Contractor will approve the appointment of a person or persons to exercise effectively the responsibilities for safeguarding at such a facility the information or material generated or exchanged in connection with this MOU or any of its CAs. These officials will be responsible for limiting access to Classified Information or material involved in this MOU to those persons who have been properly approved for access and have a need-to-know.

7.9 Each Participant will ensure that access to the Classified Information is limited to those persons who possess requisite security clearances and have a specific need for access to the information in order to implement this MOU.

7.10 Information or material provided or generated pursuant to this MOU or any of its CAs may be classified as high as Secret. The existence of this MOU is Unclassified, and the contents are Unclassified.

SECTION VIII
CONTROLLED UNCLASSIFIED INFORMATION

8.1 Except as otherwise provided in this MOU or as authorized in writing by the Providing Participant, Controlled Unclassified Information provided or generated pursuant to this MOU will be controlled as follows:

8.1.1 Each Participant will disclose or cause to be disclosed to the other Participant such information as may be necessary for the implementation of this MOU or any of its CAs.

8.1.2 Any information provided under this MOU will be used solely for the purpose of this MOU or any of its CAs, unless otherwise approved in writing by the Providing Participant.

8.1.3 Access to such information will be limited to personnel whose access is necessary for the proper implementation of this MOU or any of its CAs.

8.2 Prior to authorizing the release of Controlled Unclassified Information to Contractors, the Receiving Participant will ensure the Contractors are legally bound to control such information.

8.3 Each Participant will take all appropriate lawful steps, which may include national classification, available to it to keep such information free from further disclosure (including requests under any legislative provisions), unless the Providing Participant consents to such disclosure. In the event of unauthorized disclosure, or if it becomes probable that the information may have to be further disclosed under any legislative provision, immediate notification will be given to the Providing Participant.

SECTION IX
CUSTOM DUTIES, TAXES AND SIMILAR CHARGES

9.1 All equipment, goods, provisions and supplies involved with this MOU will be exchanged or provided on a temporary basis.

9.2 Customs duties, import and export taxes, and similar charges on equipment, goods, provisions and supplies imported and exported in connection with activities undertaken in connection with this MOU or any of its CAs will be waived in accordance with the NATO SOFA and the BIA as well as associated memoranda of understanding.

SECTION X
VISITS TO ESTABLISHMENTS

10.1 Each Participant will permit visits to its facilities for the purposes of this MOU by personnel of the other Participant or by employees of the other Participant's Contractor(s), provided that the visit is authorized by both Participants and the visitors have necessary and appropriate access clearances.

10.2 All visiting personnel will be required to comply with security regulations of the host Participant. Any information disclosed or made available to visitors will be treated as if supplied to the Participant sponsoring the visiting personnel, and will be subject to the provisions of this MOU.

10.3 Requests for visits by personnel of one Participant to a facility of the other Participant will be coordinated through POs, and will conform with the established visit procedures of the host country.

10.4 Lists of personnel of each Participant required to visit, on a continuing basis, facilities of the other Participant, will be submitted through POs in accordance with each Participant's recurring international visit procedures.

SECTION XI
IMPLEMENTATION

11.1 Arrangements for familiarization and general administration of any personnel required for implementation of this MOU will be mutually determined by the Participants. All activities of the Participants under this MOU and its CAs will be carried out in accordance with their national laws and regulations, including their export control laws and regulations.

11.2 The obligations of the Participants will be subject to the availability of funds appropriated for such purposes.

11.3 The Participants have entered into this MOU with the understanding that the overall exchange of communications support and related supplies and services to be undertaken pursuant to this MOU as reflected in appropriate CAs, will be an exchange of equivalent value and that there will consistently be no requirement for liquidation payments. If actual practice demonstrates that the value of the communications support and related supplies and services being exchanged is not equivalent, then the Participants will enter into negotiations to adjust the arrangements so that the values remain substantially equivalent. If such adjustment is not possible, then any accrued credits or debits resulting from an unequal exchange of communications support and related supplies and services during the term of this MOU will be liquidated by direct payment to the Participant having provided the greater amount of communications support and related supplies and services. Such payments will be made at the termination of this MOU, but in any event no later than 30 days after termination.

11.4 The Participants will review activities undertaken in connection with this MOU and any of its CAs and determine the status of overall exchange of logistics, services, supplies, or support for the preceding 12 months. At every annual meeting there will be a discussion of exchange balancing with the goal of agreeing that there has been an exchange of equal value or establishing a plan to achieve an equitable exchange of value by the next annual meeting.

11.5 Each Participant will bear its own administrative costs in implementing this MOU and its CAs.

SECTION XII
LIABILITY AND CLAIMS

12.1 Claims arising under this Arrangement will be dealt with in accordance with Article VIII of the NATO SOFA.

12.2 Claims arising under a contract will be resolved in accordance with the terms of the contract. Unless otherwise mutually determined by the Participants, the costs of claims arising as a consequence of a contract awarded pursuant to this MOU will be the sole responsibility of the Participant, which is the party to the contract.

SECTION XIII
SETTLEMENT OF DISPUTES

13.0 Disputes between the Participants arising under or relating to this MOU will be resolved only by consultation between the Participants, and will not be referred to a national court, an international tribunal, or any other persons or entity for settlement.

SECTION XIV
EFFECT, DURATION, TERMINATION AND AMENDMENT

14.1 In the event of a conflict between a Section of this MOU and any CA to this MOU, this MOU will prevail.

14.2 This MOU between the Department of Defense of the United States of America and the Ministry of Defense of Italy will come into effect upon signature of both the Participants, and will remain in effect for five years.

14.3 Either Participant may terminate this MOU upon 60 days written notification to the other Participant. The terminating Participant will continue participation, financial or otherwise, up to the effective date of termination. Each Participant will pay the costs it incurs as a result of termination. The provisions contained in Section XI (Implementation) and Section XII (Liability and Claims) will survive the termination of this MOU and remain in effect until all issues arising as a result of this MOU are settled.

14.4 The respective benefits and responsibilities of the Participants regarding Section V (Co-located Equipment), Section VI (Disclosure and Use of Information), Section VII (Security), Section VIII (Controlled Unclassified Information), and Section XII (Liability and Claims), and this Section XIV (Effective, Duration, Termination, and Amendment) will continue to apply notwithstanding termination or expiration of this MOU or any CA.

14.5 Except as otherwise provided, this MOU may be amended by the mutual written consent of the Participants.

14.6 The foregoing represents the understandings reached between the Department of Defense of the United States of America and the Ministry of Defense of Italy upon the matters referred to therein.

Signed by the Participants:

For the Department of Defense of the United States of America	For the Ministry of Defense of the Republic of Italy
[Signature]	[Signature]
GAMES E. CARTWRIGHT Name General, USMC Commander, USSTRATCOM Title	Gino Bizzari Name V. Admiral, ITN MOD IT–C4I Systems and Transfer. Dep. Title
20 July 06 Date	6 november 2006 Date
OFFUTT AFB, NEBRASKA, USA Location	Rome, Italy Location

ANNEX A

SAMPLE COMMUNICATIONS ARRANGEMENT

COMMUNICATIONS ARRANGEMENT NO []

TO THE

MEMORANDUM OF UNDERSTANDING BETWEEN THE DEPARTMENT OF DEFENSE OF THE UNITED STATES OF AMERICA AND THE MINISTRY OF DEFENSE OF ITALY CONCERNING THE MUTUAL EXCHANGE OF MILITARY SATELLITE COMMUNICATIONS SERVICES AND SUPPORT

DATED MM/DD/YY

CONCERNING (FULL TITLE OF THE COMMUNICATIONS ARRANGEMENT)

INTRODUCTION

This Communication Arrangement (CA) establishes the [insert name of CA] and is entered into pursuant to the Memorandum of Understanding between the Department of Defense of the United States of America and the Ministry of Defense of Italy concerning The Exchange of Military Satellite Communications Services and Support of MM/DD/YY, the provisions of which are hereby incorporated by reference.

DEFINITIONS OF TERMS AND ABBREVIATIONS

(Define only those terms used in this CA that have not been defined in this MOU.)

OBJECTIVES

The objectives of this ________CA are:

a. ______________________

b. ______________________

c. ______________________

ALLOCATION OF TASKS

The allocation of tasks to meet the objectives will be as follows:

a. The U. S. DoD will______________________

b. The Italian MoD will______________________

c. U.S. DoD and Italian MoD will jointly__________

MANAGEMENT

The following CA management structure will operate under the authority of this MOU management authorities set out in Section IV of this MOU.

Coordination Team:
Members Title/Position
Organization
Contact Details

(This section will describe the frequency of meetings, arrangements for hosting and chairing management meetings, and arrangements for reporting to the Principals of this MOU.)

PROCEDURES

(This section will describe the arrangements for the day-to-day operations of the services provided under the CA. It may also call out specific standard operating procedures (SOPs) for the use of the services or for their implementation at short notice. It will also describe the technical and engineering aspects and constraints of any CA.)

FINANCIAL ARRANGEMENTS

(This section sets out the terms for establishing values for the services provided under this CA, and any arrangements for modifying these terms. It also sets out the information required in Section XII (Implementation) of this MOU.

COMMUNICATIONS ARRANGEMENTS AND CO-LOCATED EQUIPMENT

(This section will describe the provisions for any co-located equipment used to implement this CA. This may include the support arrangements for any co-located equipment of one Participant in the other Participant's facilities, or for the support arrangements of any co-located equipment to implement this CA. It also sets out the information required in Section XII (Implementation), of this MOU.)

If the collaborative efforts under the CA require the provision of equipment to a Participant, then a list of such equipment must be developed and included as an Annex to the CA.

The co-location of the following equipment is necessary for executing this CA;

Providing Participant	Receiving Participant	QTY	Description	Part/ Stock #	Consumables\ Non-Consumables	Approx Value	Loan Period

SPECIAL DISCLOSURE AND USE PROVISIONS

(Special provisions relating to disclosure and use of information under this CA may be included here.)

ENTRY INTO EFFECT, DURATION, AND TERMINATION

This CA is effective on the date signed by the Participants and will expire by mutual determination on thirty days notice in writing to the other Participant.

For the Department of Defense of the United States of America	For the Ministry of Defense of the Republic of Italy
Signature	Signature
Name	Name
Title	Title
Date	Date

STATE DEPARTMENT DOCUMENT NUMBER: 06-308

PROTOCOL BETWEEN THE DEPARTMENT OF STATE OF THE UNITED STATES OF AMERICA AND THE SECRETARIAT OF COMMUNICATIONS AND TRANSPORTATION OF THE UNITED MEXICAN STATES CONCERNING THE ALLOTMENT AND USE OF THE 698–806 MHZ BAND FOR TERRESTRIAL NON-BROADCASTING RADIOCOMMUNICATION SERVICES ALONG THE COMMON BORDER, WITH APPENDICES

SIGNED AT MEXICO CITY AND ANTALYA,
NOVEMBER 1 AND 8, 2006
ENTERED INTO FORCE NOVEMBER 8, 2006

CTIA DOCUMENT NUMBER: 7840.002

This Protocol is being concluded pursuant to the Agreement between the Government of the United States of America and the Government of the United Mexican States Concerning the Allocation and Use of Frequency Bands by Terrestrial Non-Broadcasting Radiocommunication Services along the Common Border, signed at Williamsburg, Virginia, June 16, 1994 (herein referred to as the "Agreement").

ARTICLE I
Purposes

The purposes of this Protocol are:

1. To establish and adopt a plan for the equitable allotment and use of frequency sub-bands in the 698–806 MHz band within the Sharing Zone defined in this Protocol;

2. To establish technical criteria that will permit each Administration to regulate the use of the frequency sub-bands referred to in paragraph 1 of this Article;

3. To establish conditions of use so that each Administration may use the frequency sub-bands allotted to the other country, provided this causes no harmful interference to stations operating within the other country; and

4. To continue interference protection for broadcasting services in both countries in a manner consistent with the terms set forth in the "Agreement Relating to Assignments and Usage of Television Broadcasting Channels in the Frequency Range 470–806 MHz (Channels 14–69) along the United States–Mexico border," signed by the United States and Mexico at Mexico City

June 18,1982, as amended (hereinafter the "1982 Agreement"), and the "Memorandum of Understanding between the Federal Communications Commission of the United States of America and the Secretaria de Comunicaciones y Transportes of the United Mexican States related to the use of the 54–72 MHz, 76–88 MHz, 174–216 MHz and 470–806 MHz bands for digital television broadcasting service along the common border," signed at Mexico City July 22,1998 (hereinafter the "1998 Memorandum") until these instruments are replaced by new instruments, or are modified or terminated.

ARTICLE II
Definitions

1. For the purpose of this Protocol and as provided for in Article IV of the Agreement, the term "Administration" or "Administrations" shall refer with equal effect to the Federal Communications Commission of the United States of America (hereinafter "FCC") and the Secretaria de Comunicaciones y Transportes of the United Mexican States (hereinafter "SCT").

2. For the purpose of this Protocol, the term "Sharing Zone" is defined to include the border areas within the United States and Mexico and their respective territorial waters as set forth in Appendix I.

3. For the purpose of this Protocol, the term "television station" is defined to include an assignment or allotment in the television broadcasting service, analog or digital.

4. For the purpose of this Protocol, the term "counterpart operators" is defined to include operators of communications networks operating in certain frequency sub-bands in the 698–806 MHz band with geographic coverage areas situated contiguous to each other and authorized by the Administrations to use the same sub-bands or portions of the same sub-bands.

ARTICLE III
Conditions of Use for Radiocommunication Services

1. For the frequency sub-bands 764–776 MHz and 794–806 MHz (TV Channels 63–64 and 68–69):

a. In the Sharing Zone, the frequencies in these sub-bands shall be allotted for the primary use of each Administration in accordance with Appendix II. Each Administration shall ensure that stations in its national territory are assigned and operated in such a way that the transmission bandwidth on radio channels shall not exceed the primary frequency allotments for that country in Appendix II.

b. Each Administration shall ensure that radiocommunication stations in these sub-bands that are assigned to primary frequency allotments within the Sharing Zone shall be operated in accordance with the effective radiated power (ERP) and antenna height limitations specified in the following table (Table I):

Table I

Average of the Antenna Height Above Average Terrain on Standard Radials in the Direction of the Common Border[1] **Meters**	**Maximum ERP in Any Direction Toward the Common Border** **Watts (Maximum)**
Up to 503	500
Above 503 to 609	350
Above 609 to 762	200
Above 762 to 914	140
Above 914 to 1066	100
Above 1066 to 1219	75
Above 1219 to 1371	70
Above 1371 to 1523	65
Above 1523	5

[1] Standard radials are 000°, 045°, 090°, 135°, 180°, 225°, 270° and 315°, relative to True North.

c. Frequencies in these sub-bands that are allotted for the primary use of one Administration may be assigned by the other Administration to stations located within the latter Administration's territorial segment of the Sharing Zone under the following conditions:

(i) The maximum power flux density (PFD) at any point at or beyond the common border shall not exceed −120 dBW/m^2 per 1 kHz;

(ii) Counterpart operators of communications networks in these frequency sub-bands (764–776 MHz and 794–806 MHz) may exceed the maximum PFD in subparagraph 1.c.i above if all potentially affected counterpart operators in the other country agree to a different PFD and approval is obtained from the appropriate Administration;

(iii) Each Administration shall take appropriate measures to eliminate any harmful interference caused by stations operating within its own territory to stations operating on frequency sub-bands allotted on a primary basis to the other country pursuant to this Protocol; and

(iv) Stations operating under this provision (subparagraph 1.c of Article III) shall be considered as secondary and shall not be granted protection against harmful interference from stations whose Administration has primary use of the frequency allotment as long as the stations on the primary frequency allotment operate in accordance with the technical limitations in subparagraphs 1.a and 1.b of this Article.

d. Beyond the Sharing Zone, the Administrations' use of the 764–776 MHz and 794–806 MHz frequency sub-bands shall in no way be restricted under this Protocol.

2. For the frequency sub-bands 698–764 MHz and 776–794 MHz (TV Channels 52–62 and 65–67):

a. All frequencies in these sub-bands are available to both Administrations on an equal basis for the provision of radiocommunication services within their respective national territories within the Sharing Zone in accordance with the following conditions:

(i) The maximum power flux density (PFD) at any point at or beyond the common border of all emissions shall not exceed −106 dBW/m^2 within the authorized bandwidth;

(ii) Both Administrations shall take appropriate measures to eliminate harmful interference to stations operating in the frequency sub-bands allotted under this paragraph (Article III, paragraph 2);

(iii) Measurements of transmitter power output shall be made in accordance with Appendix III;

(iv) The Administrations shall authorize counterpart operators in these frequency sub-bands (698–764 MHz and 776–794 MHz) to take the following actions:

1. Coordinate appropriate technical and operational network parameters when necessary to provide for cross-border roaming or other collaborative operations;

2. Exceed the PFD provided in subparagraph 2.a.i of this Article based upon a mutual understanding among the counterpart operators and based upon prior notification of the terms of the mutual understanding to the two Administrations;

3. Continue operations with a PFD greater than −106 dBW/m^2 within the authorized bandwidth either until the operator notifies its counterpart operator(s) that the mutual understanding referred to in the prior subparagraph (sub-paragraph 2.a.iv.*2* of this Article) is cancelled or until the operator is notified by the appropriate Administration to return to the PFD required in subparagraph 2.a.i; and

(v) The maximum out-of-band emission in the sub-bands 764–776 MHz and 794–806 MHz shall not exceed −120 dBW/m^2 per 1 kHz at any point at or beyond the common border.

b. Beyond the Sharing Zone, the Administrations' use of the 698–764 MHz and 776–794 MHz frequency sub-bands shall in no way be restricted under this Protocol.

ARTICLE IV
Transition and Protection of the Television Broadcasting Service

1. The protection to which this Article refers is intended to be provided consistent with the terms set forth in the 1982 Agreement, as amended, as well as the 1998 Memorandum until these instruments are replaced by new instruments, or are modified or terminated.

2. Assignments in the radiocommunication services in the band 698–806 MHz shall protect analog and digital television stations in accordance with the following desired-to-undesired (D/U) signal ratios:

a. For analog television stations. The minimum D/U ratio is 40 decibels (dB) for the co-channel case and 0 dB for the adjacent channel case. The minimum D/U ratio must be satisfied within the 64 dBμV/m coverage contour of the analog television station; if this contour extends beyond the common border, the minimum D/U ratio will be calculated at the common border. The interference criteria to be used for this provision (subparagraph 2.a of Article IV), is based on 50% of all locations no more than 10% of the time; and

b. For digital television stations. The minimum D/U ratio is 17 dB for the co-channel case and −23 dB for the adjacent channel case. The minimum D/U ratio must be satisfied within the 41 dBμV/m contour of the digital television station; if this contour extends beyond the common border, the minimum D/U ratio will be calculated at the common border. The interference criteria to be used for this provision (subparagraph 2.b of Article IV), is based on 50% of all locations no more than 10% of the time.

3. In order to promote spectrum efficiency under the terms of this Protocol, both Administrations will make their best efforts to support transitioning digital television stations to the 54–72 MHz, 76–88 MHz, 174–216 MHz and 470–698 MHz bands (TV Channels 2–51).

ARTICLE V
Appendices

Appendices I, II, and III are integral parts of this Protocol.

ARTICLE VI
Entry into Force and Termination

This Protocol shall enter into force on the last date of signature affixed below. It shall remain in force until it is replaced by a new or amended protocol, or until it is terminated in accordance with Article VII of the Agreement.

IN WITNESS WHEREOF, the respective representatives sign the present Protocol.

Signed at Mexico City on this first day of November, 2006 and at Antalya, Turkey, on this eighth day of November, 2006, in duplicate in the English and Spanish languages, both texts being equally authentic.

FOR THE DEPARTMENT OF STATE OF THE UNITED STATES OF AMERICA
[Signature]
Ambassador David A. Gross
U.S. Coordinator for International Communications and Information Policy

FOR THE SECRETARIAT OF COMMUNICATIONS AND TRANSPORTATION OF THE UNITED MEXICAN STATES
[Signature]
Mr. Jorge Alvarez Hoth
Under Secretary of Communications
[Signature]
Mr. Hector G. Osuna Jaime
Chairman, Federal Telecommunications Commission

APPENDIX I

Areas Within Which the Frequencies Are to Be Protected

U.S.–MEXICO SHARING ZONE

The Sharing Zone is defined as the areas covered by a distance of 110 kilometers (68.35 Miles) from the U.S.–Mexico common border into the national territory of each country and includes areas of the Pacific Ocean and the Gulf of Mexico.

These areas are enclosed by the boundaries shown on the map below and are further defined in Table II.

Table II

The following geographic coordinates (corresponding to NAD83) define the U.S.–Mexico Sharing Zone in the national territory of each country. Point 1 is located in the Pacific Ocean due west from the U.S.–Mexico common border and defines the starting point of the Sharing Zone. The boundary of the Sharing Zone is then defined by plotting each geographic point in advancing numerical order in a clockwise direction.

ID	longitude decimal degrees	latitude decimal degrees	longitude deg/min/sec	latitude deg/min/sec
1	−122.1324	31.5235	122/07/56 W	31/31/24 N
2	−119.2616	32.0537	119/15/41 W	32/03/13 N
3	−118.5985	33.3415	118/35/54 W	33/20/29 N
4	−118.1657	33.5837	118/09/56 W	33/35/01 N
5	−117.7038	33.6483	117/42/13 W	33/38/53 N
6	−117.0916	33.5693	117/05/29 W	33/34/09 N
7	−114.4342	33.7229	114/26/03 W	33/43/22 N
8	−113.5516	33.1732	113/33/05 W	33/10/23 N
9	−110.902	32.3491	110/54/07 W	32/20/56 N
10	−109.0659	32.3519	109/03/57 W	32/21/06 N
11	−108.6352	32.7974	108/38/06 W	32/47/50 N
12	−106.1107	32.8123	106/06/38 W	32/48/44 N
13	−103.8529	31.0554	103/51/10 W	31/03/19 N
14	−103.556	30.2756	103/33/21 W	30/16/32 N
15	−103.113	30.7142	103/06/46 W	30/42/51 N
16	−102.1958	30.9402	102/11/45 W	30/56/24 N
17	−100.4516	30.666	100/27/05 W	30/39/57 N
18	−97.9163	27.0978	97/54/58 W	27/05/52 N
19	−97.1379	26.9756	97/08/16 W	26/58/32 N
20	−96.5071	27.0384	96/30/25 W	27/02/18 N
21	−93.4156	27.0181	93/24/56 W	27/01/05 N
22	−91.0891	26.7119	91/05/20 W	26/42/42 N
23	−90.5847	26.7851	90/35/04 W	26/47/06 N
24	−88.1724	26.6918	88/10/20 W	26/41/30 N
25	−88.2459	24.698	88/14/45 W	24/41/52 N
26	−90.4566	24.7738	90/27/23 W	24/46/25 N
27	−90.9949	24.6998	90/59/41 W	24/41/59 N
28	−93.4595	24.9541	93/27/34 W	24/57/14 N
29	−96.6737	24.9901	96/40/25 W	24/59/24 N
30	−97.3714	24.7983	97/22/17 W	24/47/53 N
31	−98.0746	24.9511	98/04/28 W	24/57/03 N
32	−99.7404	25.5613	99/44/25 W	25/33/40 N
33	−101.9323	28.7236	101/55/56 W	28/43/24 N
34	−102.6689	28.0418	102/40/08 W	28/02/30 N
35	−103.354	27.8941	103/21/14 W	27/53/38 N
36	−105.1973	28.7692	105/11/50 W	28/46/09 N
37	−105.8133	29.9143	105/48/47 W	29/54/51 N
38	−106.9438	30.7571	106/56/37 W	30/45/25 N
39	−1073627	30.7571	107/21/45 W	30/45/25 N
40	−107.7697	30.3269	107/46/11 W	30/19/36 N
41	−111.2398	30.316	111/14/23 W	30/18/57 N
42	−115.4915	31.642	115/29/29 W	31/38/31 N
43	−117.2764	31.4945	117/16/34 W	31/29/40 N
44	−117.8588	30.4207	117/51/31 W	30/25/14 N
45	−118.2297	30.1897	118/13/47 W	30/11/22 N
46	−121.8613	29.5104	121/51/40 W	29/30/37 N

APPENDIX II

Allotment of Frequency Sub-bands in the 764–776 MHz and 794–806 MHz bands (TV Channels 63–64 and 68–69)

U.S. Primary	Mexico Primary
764.0 – 765.5 MHz	765.5 – 768.5 MHz
768.5 – 771.5 MHz	771.5 – 774.5 MHz
774.5 – 776.0 MHz	
794.0 – 795.5 MHz	795.5 – 798.5 MHz
798.5 – 801.5 MHz	801.5 – 804.5 MHz
804.5 – 806.0 MHz	

APPENDIX III

Measurement of Transmitter Power Output

Maximum (peak) composite transmitter power output shall be measured over any interval of continuous transmission using instrumentation calibrated in terms of root mean square (RMS) equivalent voltage. The measurement results shall be adjusted appropriately for any instrument limitations such as variations in detector times, limited resolution bandwidth capability when compared to the emission bandwidth, or other related characteristics, in order to obtain a true maximum composite measurement for the emission in question over the full bandwidth of the channel.

STATE DEPARTMENT DOCUMENT NUMBER: 06-309

PROTOCOL BETWEEN THE DEPARTMENT OF STATE OF THE UNITED STATES OF AMERICA AND THE MINISTRY OF DEFENSE OF THE REPUBLIC OF UZBEKISTAN PERTAINING TO FLIGHTS BY U.S. AIRCRAFT OVER THE TERRITORY OF THE REPUBLIC OF UZBEKISTAN

SIGNED AT TASHKENT,
NOVEMBER 14, 2006
ENTERED INTO FORCE NOVEMBER 14, 2006

CTIA DOCUMENT NUMBER: 13129.000

On January 23, 2006, talks were held in Tashkent between the Department of Defense of the United States of America and the Ministry of Defense of the Republic of Uzbekistan on matters pertaining to flights by U.S. aircraft over the territory of the Republic of Uzbekistan.

During the talks, the Parties discussed the matters set forth in the diplomatic note No. 03/412 of January 9, 2006, from the Ministry of Foreign Affairs of the Republic of Uzbekistan, and in the reply notes No. 0071/06 dated January 25, 2006, and No. 0094/06 dated February 1, 2006, from the U.S. Embassy in Uzbekistan.

In accordance with international practice and its domestic legislation, the Ministry of Defense of the Republic of Uzbekistan expressed its desire to resolve issues connected to flights by civil aircraft chartered by the Department of Defense of the United States of America over the territory of Uzbekistan as part of the operations to combat terrorism in Afghanistan.

Accordingly, the Ministry of Defense of the Republic of Uzbekistan and the Department of Defense of the United States of America have agreed as follows:

1.The Government of the Republic of Uzbekistan recognizes that the Department of Defense of the United States of America may carry out flights through the airspace of the Republic of Uzbekistan using civil aircraft chartered by the Department of Defense of the United States of America, and such flights will be subject to applicable fees to the extent consistent with the Convention on International Civil Aviation. The Department of Defense of the United States of America will not conduct flights through the airspace of the Republic of Uzbekistan with USAF aircraft except as specialty agreed.

2.The Department of Defense of the United States of America will ensure that operators of civil aircraft chartered by the Department of Defense of the United States of America will, when transporting munitions of war, implements of war, or other dangerous cargoes, inform the Government of the Republic of Uzbekistan about the flights at least six days in advance; the

Department of Defense of the United States of America will ensure that such aircraft have insurance sufficient to cover losses that may result from its operation.

This Protocol shall enter into force upon signature and remain in force for one year. The Parties may consult regarding the renewal of the Protocol for additional one-year periods. This Protocol may be amended by written agreement of the Ministry of Defense of the Republic of Uzbekistan and the Department of Defense of the United States of America, and may be terminated by either Party providing thirty days written notice to the other Party.

IN WITNESS THEREOF, the undersigned, being duly authorized by their respective Governments, have signed this Protocol.

DONE at Tashkent, this day of November 14, 2006, in the English and Russian languages, both texts being equally authentic.

For the Department of Defense of the United States of America
[Signature]

For the Ministry of Defense of the Republic of Uzbekistan
[Signature]

STATE DEPARTMENT DOCUMENT NUMBER: 06-310

MEMORANDUM OF UNDERSTANDING BETWEEN THE UNITED STATES OF AMERICA AND THE REPUBLIC OF INDONESIA REGARDING MUTUAL ASSISTANCE BETWEEN THEIR CUSTOMS ADMINISTRATIONS

SIGNED AT JAKARTA,
NOVEMBER 17, 2006
ENTERED INTO FORCE NOVEMBER 17, 2006

CTIA DOCUMENT NUMBER: 13130.000

The Government of the United States of America and the Government of the Republic of Indonesia, hereinafter referred to as "the Parties",

Considering that offenses against customs laws are prejudicial to the economic, fiscal and commercial interests of their respective countries;

Considering the importance of assuring the accurate assessment of customs duties and other taxes;

Recognizing the need for international cooperation is matters related to the administration and enforcement of the customs laws of their .respective countries;

Having regard to the international conventions containing prohibitions, restrictions and special measures of control in respect of specific goods;

Convinced that action against customs offenses can be made more effective by cooperation between their Customs Administrations; and

Having regard to the Recommendation of the Customs Cooperation Council regarding Mutual Administrative Assistance of December 5, 1953;

Have agreed as follows:

ARTICLE I
DEFINITIONS

For the purposes of the present Memorandum of Understanding:

1. the term "Customs Administration" means, in the United States of America, United States Customs and Border Protection and United States Immigration and Customs Enforcement, Department of Homeland Security, and in the Republic of Indonesia, the Directorate General of Customs and Excise, Ministry of Finance;

2. the term “customs laws” means the laws and regulations enforced by the Customs Administrations concerning the importation, exportation, and transit or circulation of goods as they relate to customs duties, charges, and other taxes or to prohibitions, restrictions, and other similar controls respecting the movement of controlled items across national boundaries;

3. the term “information” means data in any form, documents, records, and reports or certified copies thereof;

4. the term “offense” means any violation or attempted violation of the customs laws;

5. the term “person” means any natural or legal person;

6. the term “property” means assets of every kind, whether corporeal or incorporeal, movable or immovable, tangible or intangible, and legal documents or instruments evidencing title to or an interest in such assets;

7. the term “provisional measures” includes “seizure” or “freezing,” which means;

a. temporarily prohibiting the conversion, disposition, movement, or transfer of property, or

b. temporarily assuming custody or control of property on the basis of an order issued by a court or competent authority, or other means;

8. the term “forfeiture” means the deprivation of property by order of a court or competent authority and includes confiscation where applicable;

9. the term “requesting Administration” means the Customs Administration that requests assistance;

10. the term “requested Administration” means the Customs Administration from which assistance is requested.

ARTICLE II
SCOPE OF MEMORANDUM OF UNDERSTANDING

1. The Parties, through their Customs Administrations, shall assist each other, in accordance with the provisions of this Memorandum of Understanding, in preventing, investigating, and repressing any offense.

2. Each Customs Administration shall execute requests for assistance made pursuant to this Memorandum of Understanding in accordance with and subject to the limitations of its domestic laws and regulations, and within the limits of its competence and available resources.

3. This Memorandum of Understanding is intended solely for mutual legal assistance between the Parties; the provisions of this Memorandum of Understanding shall not give rise to a right on the part of any private person to obtain, suppress, or exclude any evidence, or to impede the execution of a request

4. This Memorandum of Understanding is intended to enhance and supplement mutual assistance practices in effect between the Parties. No provision in this Memorandum of Understanding may be interpreted in a manner that would restrict agreements and practices relating to mutual assistance and cooperation in effect between the Parties.

ARTICLE III
SCOPE OF GENERAL ASSISTANCE

1. Upon request a Customs Administration shall provide assistance in the form of information in bitter to ensure the enforcement of the customs laws and the accurate assessment of customs duties and other taxes by the Customs Administrations.

2. Upon request or upon its own initiative, a Customs Administration may provide assistance in the form of information including but not limited to, information concerning:

a. methods and techniques of processing passengers and cargo;

b. the successful application of enforcement aids and techniques;

c. enforcement actions that might be useful to suppress offenses and, in particular, special means of combating offenses; and

d. new methods used in committing offenses.

3. The Customs Administrations shall cooperate in:

a. establishing and maintaining channels of communication to facilitate the secure and rapid exchange of information;

b. facilitating effective co-ordination;

c. the consideration and testing of new equipment or procedures; and

d. any other general administrative matters that may from time to time require their joint action.

ARTICLE IV
SCOPE OF SPECIFIC ASSISTANCE

1. Upon request, the Customs Administrations shall inform each other whether goods exported from the territory of one Party have been lawfully imported into the territory of the other Party. If requested, the information shall contain the customs procedure used for clearing the goods.

2. Upon request, a Customs Administration shall exercise special surveillance of:

a. persons known to the requesting Party to have committed a customs offense or suspected of doing so, particularly those moving into and out of its territory;

b. goods either in transport or in storage identified by the requesting Party as giving rise to suspected illicit traffic toward its territory; and

c. means of transport suspected of being used in offenses within the territory of the requesting Party.

3. Upon request, the Customs Administrations shall furnish to each other information regarding the activities that may result in offenses within the territory of the other Party. In situations that could involve substantial damage to the economy, public health, public security, or similar vital interest of the other Party, the Customs Administrations, wherever possible, shall supply such information without being requested to do so. Nothing in this Memorandum of Understanding otherwise precludes the Customs Administrations from providing on their own initiative information regarding activities that may result to offenses within the territory of the other Party.

4. The Parties may provide assistance through the use of provisional measures and forfeiture, and in proceedings involving property subject to provisional measures or forfeiture.

5. The Parties may, consistent with any other agreement or Memorandum of Understanding between them pertaining to the sharing and disposition of forfeited assets:

a. dispose of property, proceeds, and instrumentalities forfeited as a result of assistance provided under this Memorandum of Understanding in accordance with the domestic law of the Party in control of the property, proceeds, and instrumentalities; and

b. to the extent permitted by their respective domestic laws, and without regard to the requirement of reciprocity, transfer forfeited property, proceeds, or instrumentalities, or the proceeds of their sale, to the other Party upon such terms as may be agreed.

ARTICLE V
FILES AND DOCUMENTS

1. Upon request, the Customs Administrations shall provide information relating to transportation and shipment of goods showing value, destination, and disposition of those goods.

2. A requesting Administration may request originals of files, documents, and other materials only where copies would be insufficient Upon request, the requested Administration shall provide properly certified copies of such files, documents, and other materials.

3. Unless the requesting Administration specifically requests originals or copies, the requested Administration may transmit computer-based information in any form. The requested Administration shall supply all information relevant for interpreting or utilizing computer-based information at the same time.

4. If the requested Administration agrees, officials designated by the requesting Administration may examine, in the offices of the requested Administration, information relevant to an offense and make copies thereof or extract information therefrom.

5. Originals of files, documents, and other materials that have been transmitted shall be returned at the earliest opportunity; any rights of the requested Party or of third parties relating thereto shall remain unaffected.

ARTICLE VI
WITNESSES

1. The requested Administration may authorize its employees to appear as witnesses in judicial or administrative proceedings in the territory of the other Party and to produce files, documents, or other materials or certified copies thereof.

2. Where a Customs official requested to appear as a witness is entitled to diplomatic or consular immunity, the requested Party may agree to a waiver of immunity under such conditions as it determines to be appropriate.

ARTICLE VII
COMMUNICATION OF REQUESTS

1. Requests pursuant to this Memorandum of Understanding shall be made in writing directly between officials designated by the Heads of the respective Customs Administrations. Information deemed useful for the execution of requests shall accompany the request, In urgent situations, oral requests may be made and accepted, but shall be promptly confirmed in writing, as expeditiously as possible.

2. Requests shall include:

a. the name of the authority making the request;

b. the nature of the matter or proceedings;

e. a brief statement of the facts and offenses involved;

d. the reason for the request; and

e. the names and addresses of the parties concerned in the matter or proceeding, if known.

ARTICLE VIII
EXECUTION OF REQUESTS

1. The requested Administration shall take all reasonable measures to execute a request and shall endeavor to secure any official measure necessary for that purpose.

2. If the requested Administration is not the appropriate agency to execute a request, it shall promptly transmit it to the appropriate agency and so advise the requesting Administration.

3. The requested Administration shall conduct to the fullest extent possible, or permit the requesting Administration to conduct, such inspections, verifications, fact-finding inquiries, or other investigative steps, including the questioning of experts, witnesses, and persons suspected of having committed an offense, as are necessary to execute a request.

4. Upon request, the requesting Administration shall be advised of the time and place of action to be taken in execution of a request.

5. Upon request, the requested Party shall authorize, to the fullest extent possible, officials of the requesting Party to be present in the territory of the requested Party to assist in execution of a request.

6. The requested Administration shall comply with a request that a certain procedure be followed to the extent that such procedure is not prohibited by the domestic law of the requested Party.

ARTICLE IX
LIMITATIONS OF USE

1. Information obtained under this Memorandum of Understanding shall be afforded the same degree of confidentiality by the receiving Party that it applies to similar information, in its custody.

2. Information obtained under this Memorandum of Understanding may only be used or disclosed for the purposes specified in this Memorandum of Understanding including use by the receiving Party in any proceedings. Such information may be used or disclosed for other purposes or by other authorities of the receiving Party if the supplying Customs Administration has expressly approved such use or disclosure in writing.

3. Information received by either Party shall upon request of the supplying Party, be treated as confidential. The reasons for such a request shall be stated.

4. This Article shall not preclude the use or disclosure of information to the extent that there is an obligation to do so under the Constitution of the receiving Party in connection with a criminal prosecution. The receiving Party shall give advance notice of any such proposed disclosure to the supplying Party.

5. Information made public in the territory of the receiving Party under paragraphs 2 and 4 of this Article may be used for any purpose.

ARTICLE X
EXEMPTIONS

1. Where a requested Party determines that granting assistance would infringe upon its sovereignty, security, public policy or other substantive national interest, or would be inconsistent with. its domestic law and regulations, including any legal requirement relating to non-compliance with assurances regarding limitations on use or confidentiality, it may refuse or withhold assistance, or may pant it subject to the satisfaction of certain conditions or requirements.

2. If the requesting Administration would be unable to comply if a similar request were made by the requested Administration, it shall draw attention to that fact in its request Compliance with such are request shall be at the discretion of the requested Administration.

3. The requested Administration may postpone assistance on the ground that it will interfere with an ongoing investigation, prosecution, or proceeding. In such instance, the requested Administration shall consult with the requesting Administration to determine if assistance can be given subject to such terms or conditions as the requested Administration may require.

4. In the event that a request cannot be complied with, the requesting Administration shall be promptly notified and provided with a statement of the reasons for postponement or denial of the request. Circumstances that might be of importance for the further pursuit of the matter shall also be provided to the requesting Administration.

ARTICLE XI
COSTS

1. The Requested Party shall normally pay all costs relating to the execution of the request, with the exception of expenses for experts and witnesses and the costs of translation, interpretation and transcription.

2. If during the execution of a request it becomes apparent that completion of the execution of the request will entail expenses of an extraordinary nature, the Customs Administrations shall consult to determine the terms and conditions under which execution may continue.

ARTICLE XII
IMPLEMENTATION OF THE MEMORANDUM OF UNDERSTANDING

1. The Customs Administrations of the Parties shall:

   a. communicate directly for the purpose of dealing with matters arising out of this Memorandum of Understanding;

   b. after consultation, issue any administrative directives necessary for the implementation of this Memorandum of Understanding; and

   c. endeavor by mutual accord to resolve problems or questions arising from the interpretation or application of the Memorandum of Understanding.

2. Conflicts for which no solutions can be found will be settled by diplomatic means.

3. The Customs Administrations of the Parties agree to meet periodically as necessary at the request of either Party in order to review the implementation of this Memorandum of Understanding.

ARTICLE XIII
APPLICATION

This Memorandum of Understanding shall be applicable to the Customs territories of both Parties as defined in their domestic legal and administrative provisions.

ARTICLE XIV
ENTRY INTO FORCE AND TERMINATION

1. This Memorandum of Understanding shall enter into force upon signature.

2. Either Party may terminate this Memorandum of Understanding at any time by notification through diplomatic channels. The termination shall take effect three months from the date of notification to the other Party. Ongoing proceedings at the time of termination shall nonetheless be completed in accordance with the provisions of this Memorandum of Understanding.

3. This Memorandum of Understanding may be amended at any time by mutual written consent.

IN WITNESS WHEREOF, the undersigned, being duly authorized by their respective Governments, have signed this Memorandum of Understanding.

DONE at Jakarta, on this 17th day of November 2006, in duplicate in English.

FOR THE GOVERNMENT OF THE
UNITED STATES OF AMERICA:

[Signature]

B. Lynn Pascoe

Ambassador of the United States of America
to the Republic of Indonesia

FOR THE GOVERNMENT OF THE
REPUBLIC OF INDONESIA:

[Signature]

Anwar Suprijadi

Director General of Customs and Excise
Ministry of Finance

STATE DEPARTMENT DOCUMENT NUMBER: 06-311

AGREEMENT BETWEEN THE UNITED STATES OF AMERICA AND THE REPUBLIC OF BOTSWANA CONCERNING THE ESTABLISHMENT OF A TROPICAL FOREST CONSERVATION FUND AND A TROPICAL FOREST CONSERVATION BOARD, WITH ATTACHMENTS

SIGNED AT GABORONE,
OCTOBER 5, 2006
ENTERED INTO FORCE NOVEMBER 19, 2006

CTIA DOCUMENT NUMBER: 13131.000

The Government of the United States of America (U.S. Government) and the Government of the Republic of Botswana (Government of Botswana), hereinafter known as the Parties,

Seeking to facilitate the conservation, protection, restoration, and sustainable management of tropical forests, which provide a wide range of benefits to humankind,

Acknowledging the work and contributions of the Government of the Botswana toward forest conservation under its national Forest Act and approved National Forest Policy;

Desiring to enhance the friendship and spirit of cooperation between the Parties,

Recognizing that tropical deforestation and forest degradation continue to be serious problems in many regions of the world,

Also recognizing that the alleviation of external debt can reduce economic pressures on countries and result in increased conservation of tropical forests,

Further recognizing that economic benefits to local communities of sustainable uses of tropical forests are critical to the protection and sustainable management of tropical forests,

Wishing to ensure that resources freed from debt are targeted to the conservation of tropical forests,

Also wishing to further the Agreement between the Government of the United States of America and the Government of the Republic of Botswana Regarding the Reduction of Certain Debts Owed to the Government of the United States and its Agencies, hereinafter known as the "Debt Reduction Agreement," which reduces certain debts owed the U.S. Government through the exchange of old obligations for new obligations, known as the New Tropical Forest Conservation Act (New TFCA) Obligations,

Have agreed as follows:

Article I
PURPOSE

The purpose of this Agreement is to provide for the establishment of a Tropical Forest Conservation Fund and an administering Tropical Forest Conservation Board to promote activities designed to conserve, maintain and restore the forests of Botswana. The agreement will be implemented in Botswana in accordance with the Forest Act and the National Forest Policy of Botswana.

Article II
TROPICAL FOREST CONSERVATION FUND

1. Within eight months of the signing of this Agreement, the Government of Botswana shall establish a Tropical Forest Conservation Fund, hereinafter known as the "Fund," in accordance with the laws of Botswana. The Fund shall be administered by the Board established pursuant to Article III of this Agreement. Any monies deposited in the Fund, or grants made from the Fund, will be free from any taxation, levies, fees or other charges imposed by the Parties to the extent permissible by the laws of the Parties.

2. The Fund shall consist of monies, in the form of local currencies or other currencies, as follows:

2.1 Monies appropriated by the Parliament of the Government of Botswana for this purpose;

2.2 Deposits made pursuant to Article II, paragraph 3 of the Debt Reduction Agreement; and

2.3 Grants and contributions from other sources.

3. The amounts deposited in the Fund shall be subject to the provisions of this Agreement. Deposits in the Fund made pursuant to Article II, paragraph 3 of the Debt Reduction Agreement shall be the property of the Government of Botswana until they are disbursed pursuant to the procedures set forth in Article VI of this Agreement. The Board and the Fiscal Agent shall develop a provision to be included in each Grant Agreement approved pursuant to Article IV, paragraph 2 of this Agreement to address the recovery of funds misspent or misused by, and the return of any unused grant funds held by a grantee.

4. Within eight months of the signing of this Agreement, the Government of Botswana shall appoint an accounting officer who shall act as Fiscal Agent for the Fund charged with monitoring payments into the Fund and disbursement and investment of the monies in the Fund. The Botswana Government Instructions appointing the accounting officer shall be reviewed by the U.S. Government prior to finalization. The Instructions shall be concluded within eight months of the signing of this Agreement and shall specify the subordinate relationship of the accounting officer to the Board established under Article III of this Agreement and shall also specify that the accounting officer shall take direction only from the Board. The Fiscal Agent is responsible for promptly notifying the Board in writing when monies are deposited in the Fund pursuant to paragraph 2 of this Article, or if a deposit is overdue.

5. Monies in the Fund shall be invested until disbursed, with every effort made to ensure that such investments yield a positive real rate within acceptable limits of risk in accord with sound investment practices. To accomplish this goal, the Parties may jointly request the conversion of all or part of the monies in the Fund into U.S. dollars or other hard currencies for investment purposes. Returns on investment shall be deposited by the Fiscal Agent in the Fund until disbursed, pursuant to the procedures set forth in Article VI of this Agreement.

Article III
ESTABLISHMENT AND COMPOSITION OF THE TROPICAL FOREST CONSERVATION BOARD

1. Within eight months of the signing of this Agreement, the Government of Botswana shall establish, in accordance with the Companies Act, in consultation with the U.S. Government and domestic Botswana nongovernmental entities with an interest in forests, a Tropical Forest Conservation Board, hereinafter known as the "Board," to administer the Fund. The Board shall have the authorities and functions conferred on it by this Agreement and implemented through the requisite documents of incorporation under Botswana law, which shall be reviewed by the US Government prior to finalization. The Board shall be discrete and separate from any existing Board, Commission, Foundation, or other entity in Botswana

2. The Board shall consist of nine members. It shall be composed of:

2.1 Two officials of the U.S. government appointed by the U.S. Government;

2.2 Two officials of the Government of Botswana appointed by the Minister of Environment, Wildlife and Tourism; and

2.3 Five representatives of a broad range of:

2.3.1 environmental nongovernmental organizations of, or active in, Botswana;

2.3.2 local community development nongovernmental organizations of Botswana; and

2.3.3 scientific, academic or forestry organizations of Botswana.

3. The representatives under paragraph 2.3 of this Article shall constitute a majority of the members of the Board. They shall be appointed to the Board by the Minister of Environment, Wildlife and Tourism of the Government of Botswana in consultation with a range of domestic nongovernmental entities in Botswana and the U.S. Government.

4. Board members named pursuant to paragraphs 2.1 and 2.2 above shall serve *ad honorem* and at the discretion of the naming Party. Board members described in paragraph 2.3 above shall serve *ad honorem*, except that the administrative expenses of such Board members may be paid as provided in Article IV, paragraph 9 of this Agreement. Board members described in paragraph 2.3 above shall serve in their expert capacity for a three year term, and may be removed prior to the end of their term only for malfeasance. Any such member of the Board may serve for a consecutive term if so recommended by the Board and agreed by the Parties.

5. A Board member may not participate in the approval of any proposed grant which if approved, would result in a financial benefit for the member or any person in his family, for an organization which employs the member or any person in his family, or for an organization in which the member or any person in his family has an affiliation or a direct financial interest.

Article IV
FUNCTIONS OF THE BOARD

1. The Board shall be responsible for administration and management of the Fund, for disbursements of grants from the Fund to support eligible activities, and for oversight of activities financed from the Fund, pursuant to this Agreement. The Board shall have full legal competence to carry out the functions assigned to it in this Agreement.

2. With respect to the management of the Fund, the Board shall:

2.1 Issue and widely disseminate a public announcement on the call for grant applications, which announcement shall state the purpose of the Fund, eligible activities and eligible entities in accordance with Article V of this Agreement, the criteria for the selection of grant recipients, the schedule of the grants process, and any other requirements established by the Board for the award of grants from the Fund;

2.2 Receive applications for grants from entities described in Article V, paragraph 3 of this Agreement and award grants consistent with Article V of this Agreement on the basis of an evaluation of applications on their merits;

2.3 Publicly announce grants awarded by the Board;

2.4 Develop with each grant recipient a Grant Agreement which shall include provisions on, *inter alia*, receipt and use of funds, audit and reporting requirements, improper use of funds and subsequent remedies, representations and warranties, and intellectual property.

2.5 Within six months of the Board's establishment, develop and submit to the Parties for their approval a long-term strategic plan for the operation of the Fund, including an annual budget showing prospective activities and expected administrative and program costs;

2.6 Take steps to meet the relevant "performance criteria" set forth in the "TFCA Performance Evaluation", the current form of which is contained in the Annex to this Agreement, recognizing the document may be amended from time to time;

2.7 Within 18 months after the signing of this Agreement, and on an annual basis thereafter, submit to the Parties a completed "TFCA Performance Evaluation" document, which shall include as annexes:

2.7.1 A report on grant activities for the previous year, including multi-year activities funded by the Board, which shall include information regarding the grants awarded, grant recipients, grant amounts, activities funded, and status of grant implementation, as well as information on the status of audits of randomly selected grants; and

2.7.2 A financial audit conducted in accordance with generally accepted international accounting standards by an independent auditor, covering the previous year.

2.8 Hire an Executive Director to coordinate and implement, with the guidance of the Board, all necessary actions required for the adequate functioning of the Board, including the hiring of necessary support staff with the approval of the Board.

3. A proposed grant which would over the project life require in excess of $100,000 to be disbursed from the Fund shall be submitted to the members of the Board appointed under Article III.2.1 and III.2.2 for approval. If the two members of the Board appointed under Article III.2.1 or the two members of the Board appointed under Article III.2.2 disapprove such a grant, those members must notify the rest of the Board of their disapproval, in which case the Board shall not award the proposed grant.

4. The Board shall adopt, by majority vote, guidelines, internal policies and procedures for its operation, which shall be subject to the approval of the Parties. No disbursements pursuant to Article VI may be made prior to the adoption of these procedures.

5. The Board shall approve procedures and schedules for the grant process, including procedures and schedules relating to public announcements, grant applications and review, monitoring, and auditing.

6. The Board shall establish and make public selection criteria for awarding grants, which should include criteria for evaluating the merits of application(s) and the prospects of success of proposed activities.

7. The Board shall monitor performance under Grant Agreements to determine whether time schedules and other performance goals are being achieved. Grant Agreements shall require periodic progress reports from the grantee to the Board. Such reports shall review all components essential to the successful achievement of the goals of the activity.

8. The Board shall meet at least once every three months.

9. The Board may draw sums from the Fund necessary to pay for reasonable administrative expenses of the Board, including the audit required pursuant to paragraph 2.7.2 of this Article. Board members appointed under Article III, paragraph 2.3 of this Agreement may be compensated from the Fund only for travel expenses and reasonable per diem. Such expenses incurred by Board members appointed under Article III, paragraphs 2.1 and 2.2 of this Agreement shall be borne by the Party which that member represents. Administrative expenses shall not exceed a ceiling established by the Parties' representatives on the Board, taking into account anticipated administrative expenses and funds available in the Fund. The Parties' representatives on the Board shall review and adjust, as appropriate, the ceiling for administrative expenses on an annual basis.

10. The Board's written policies, procedures, summaries of proceedings, books, records, reports, and any organizing statutes shall be retained in the files of the Board. A permanent record shall also be maintained of the decision to award each grant, including an explanation of the basis of the award decision. The Board shall make available for easy public inspection, such as by the Internet where appropriate, its written policies, operating procedures, summaries of proceedings, and explanations of award decisions. Upon request, authorities of either Party shall be granted access to all Board documents, including minutes of meetings, books, records, and reports.

Article V
ELIGIBLE ACTIVITIES AND GRANT RECIPIENTS

1. Amounts deposited in the Fund shall be used to provide grants to conserve, maintain, or restore tropical forest areas through one or more of the following activities and in a manner consistent with the Government of Botswana's Forest Act and approved National Forest Policy:

1.1 Establishment, restoration, protection and maintenance of parks, protected areas, and reserves. Such activities could include, for example, establishment of new or expanded protected forests and buffer zones, identification of unique or representative forest areas, or inventory and protection of areas featuring species richness and high levels of endemism.

1.2 Development and implementation of scientifically sound systems of natural resource management including land and ecosystem management practices. Such activities could include, for example, development and implementation of scientifically sound systems of forest land and forest resources management; forest resources assessment and inventory; land and resource use monitoring and evaluation; implementation of criteria and indicators for sustainable forest management; development and implementation of forest management information systems; development and implementation of watershed ecosystem management and community based forest management strategies; adoption of research-based forest technologies; plantation establishment on degraded lands; natural forest regeneration, rehabilitation and management; or testing and application of silvicultural techniques.

1.3 Training programs to increase scientific, technical and managerial capacities of individuals and organizations involved in forest conservation efforts. Such activities could include, for example, short-term training courses, internships and study tours; development of community extension services; environmental education and public awareness programs; enhancement of university curricula in forest management or conservation biology; or education and training to develop capacity of local nongovernmental organizations.

1.4 Restoration, protection, or sustainable use of diverse animal and plant species. Such activities could include, for example, rehabilitation of degraded forests; sustainable fishing and animal fanning; improvement of forest health and vitality and relevant research and development; efforts to assess and address problems of forest law enforcement and associated illegal practices.

1.5 Research and identification of medicinal uses of tropical forest plant life to treat human diseases, illnesses and health related concerns. Such activities could include, for example, ethnobotany studies; sample collection and analysis; or technical document preparation, publication and dissemination.

1.6 Development and support of the livelihoods of individuals living in or near a tropical forest in a manner consistent with protecting such a tropical forest. Such activities could include, for example, development of environmentally friendly community-based and women's enterprises involving wood or non-wood products; application of low impact logging practices; establishment of agroforestry systems; or development of multiple-use tree species outside natural forests.

2. The Board may establish priorities for financing among the eligible activities as it deems appropriate;

3. Entities in Botswana which shall be eligible to receive grants from the Fund are:

3.1 Nongovernmental environmental, forestry, conservation, and indigenous people organizations of, or active in, Botswana, including those organizations involved in development, education, science research, or forest management;

3.2 Other appropriate local or regional entities of, or active in, Botswana; and

3.3 In exceptional circumstances, the Government of Botswana.

4. In providing grants, priority shall be given to projects that are run by local nongovernmental organizations and other private entities and that involve local communities in their planning and execution.

5. Grants shall be awarded within the financial capacity of the Board and strictly on the merits of proposals presented to the Board.

Article VI
DISBURSEMENT OF FUNDS

1. The Board shall instruct the Fiscal Agent to disburse grant monies from the Fund to entities selected to receive grants pursuant to Article V of this Agreement. All disbursements shall be made pursuant to a Grant Agreement, as specified in Article IV, paragraph 2.4 of this Agreement.

2. The Fiscal Agent shall make disbursements promptly to designated recipients in accordance with directions received from the Board. In no case shall more than 10 Business Days elapse between the Fiscal Agent's receipt of a direction for disbursement from the Board and the actual disbursement of funds to a grant recipient.

Article VII
RESOLUTION AND REVIEW OF DISPUTES

1. Upon the written request of either Party, the Parties shall consult each other concerning the implementation or interpretation of this Agreement. These consultations shall be completed within 60 Business Days after a request for consultations is received from the other Party.

2. Consultations between the Parties concerning the interpretation or implementation of this Agreement may be conducted through written submissions between the Department of State of the U.S. Government and the Ministry of Environment, Wildlife and Tourism of the Government of Botswana. Unless the U.S. Government otherwise notifies the Government of Botswana, the Assistant Secretary of State for Oceans and International Environmental and Scientific Affairs shall be the contact point in the Department of State. Unless the Government of Botswana otherwise notifies the U.S. Government, the Director of the Department of Forestry and Range Resources shall be the contact point in the Ministry of Environment, Wildlife and Tourism.

3. Either Party may request consultations with the Board and with the other Party after reviewing the Boards reports and audits presented pursuant to Article IV of this Agreement. Such request shall be made in writing. These consultations shall be completed within 60 Business Days after a request for consultations is received from the other Party, unless the period of consultation is extended by mutual agreement of the Parties.

4. The Parties shall meet to review the operation of this Agreement one year from the date of its entry into force, and periodically thereafter as the Parties so agree.

Article VIII
SUSPENSION OF DISBURSEMENTS

1. If at any time either of the Parties determines that any issue requiring consultation under Article VII of this Agreement has not been satisfactorily resolved, such Party may notify the other Party in writing.

2. Notwithstanding any other provision of this Agreement, the US Government reserves the right to direct the Board in writing to direct the Fiscal Agent to suspend disbursements from the Fund under Article VI of monies in the fund resulting from payments on the New TFCA Obligations under the Debt Reduction Agreement, 30 days after consultations with Government of Botswana if the Government of Botswana fails to take action to rectify the situation to the satisfaction of both Parties in the event that:

2.1 The Board is operating under circumstances of undue influence and interference from the Government of Botswana; or

2.2 The Board lacks the appropriate authority to effectively implement the terms of this Agreement; or

2.3 Botswana ceases to meet the U.S. Government program eligibility requirements found at 22 U.S.C. Sec. 2431c.

3. Suspension of disbursements pursuant to paragraph 2 of this Article shall mean that no further approval of grants shall be undertaken until the Parties have jointly agreed to resume such activity. However, disbursements pursuant to previously-approved Grant Agreements shall proceed unless the specific Grant Agreement is suspended pursuant to the terms of that Grant Agreement.

4. Should the Parties jointly certify in writing to the Board that the manner in which a Grant Agreement was awarded was inconsistent with Articles III, IV or V of this Agreement or the

operating procedures of the Board, the Parties may require the Board to suspend disbursements under that Grant Agreement. Should disbursements be so suspended, no further approval of any grants shall be undertaken until both Parties agree to resume the receipt, review and award of grants

5. If disbursements have not been suspended within seven (7) Business Days of the written notification referred to paragraph 2 above, ("the Notification Period"), the Government of Botswana agrees that it will take any and all actions necessary to freeze the Fund until both Parties confirm in writing that the issues that led to freezing of those amounts have been resolved.

Article IX
TERMINATION

1. The Agreement shall automatically terminate in the event that the Debt Reduction Agreement automatically terminates under Article VII, paragraph 2(a) of the Debt Reduction Agreement.

2. The Agreement may be terminated by either Party upon six months' written notice if: (i) the Debt Reduction Agreement is terminated under Article VII, paragraph 2(b) of the Debt Reduction Agreement, and (ii) all funds resulting from the Payments in accordance with the Debt Reduction Agreement have been expended.

3. The Agreement may also be terminated by either Party pursuant to the process set forth in Article VII, paragraph 3 of the Debt Reduction Agreement. In such event, no disbursements from the Fund shall occur after a Party has given written notice to terminate the Agreement, unless the Parties expressly agree in writing to permit disbursements pursuant to specific Grant Agreements concluded before the notice to terminate has been given. The termination of the Agreement shall not prevent grantees' expenditure of funds that were disbursed before the notice to terminate was given.

4. Upon termination under either paragraphs 2 or 3 of this Article IX, the provisions of this Agreement shall continue to apply for the purpose of completion of any previously-authorized grants.

Article X
ENTRY INTO FORCE, AMENDMENT AND OTHER ARRANGEMENTS

1. This Agreement shall enter into force 45 calendar days after signature and shall remain in force unless terminated by the Parties in accordance with Article IX of this Agreement.

2. This Agreement may be amended by written agreement of the Parties.

3. Nothing in this Agreement shall prejudice other arrangements between the Parties concerning debt reduction or cooperation and assistance for tropical forest conservation purposes.

IN WITNESS WHEREOF the undersigned, being duly authorized by their respective Governments, have signed this Agreement.

Done at Gaborone, Botswana, this 5th day of October 2006, in duplicate, in the English language.

[Signature]
FOR THE GOVERNMENT OF THE
UNITED STATES OF AMERICA

[Signature]
FOR THE GOVERNMENT OF
THE REPUBLIC OF BOTSWANA

TFCA Evaluation Sheet

	Category	Function	Criteria	Fund Comments (w/ supporting material citation as appropriate)	Rating
			definition: "OC/B and its implementor" = The Oversight Committee/ Board and its Fund Administrator or Office of Exectutive Director.		Excellent (4); Acceptable (3); Needs Improvement (2); Unacceptable (1); NA
A.	**Implementation of Agreements**		A. 1.1 The OC/B and its implementor become operational within one year from the signing of the agreements.		
			A. 1.2 The Fund, or other implementor of the TFCA agreement, is in compliance with all articles of the agreements, including the legal registry of the appropriate implementing bodies.		
			A. 1.3 The Fund, or other implementor of the TFCA agreement, completes, and makes accessible, annual audits, plans and reports as may be required in the agreements.		

Continued

	Category	Function	Criteria	Fund Comments (w/ supporting material citation as appropriate)	Rating
B.	**Governance**	**Planning**	B. 1.1 Within one year of January 1, 2005 or within one year of becoming operational, the OC/B has established a written strategic plan that includes (a) specific, key objectives, (b) a list, in order of importance, of conservation and funding priorities in order to meet those objectives, and (c) target dates for completion of objectives.		
			B.1.2 The established goals & objectives complement plans/programs of others (eg. national environmental plans, donors, swap partners).		
			B.1.3 The OC/B, or its implementors, have establised all internal operational policies and procedures in accordance with normal business standards.		

	Category	Function	Criteria	Fund Comments (w/ supporting material citation as appropriate)	Rating
		Implementation	B.2.1 The OC/B meets in accordance with the bilateral agreement with achieves a quorum at these meetings.	(info should include no. of meetings, no. of meetings at which quorum was achieved)	
		Monitoring	B.3.1 The OC/B evaluates, on an annual basis, progress toward the key objectives specified in the strategic plan, and implements any changes judged necessary to remedy deficiencies in meeting the key objectives.		
			B.3.2 Within one year of January 1, 2005 or within one year of becoming operational, the OC/B has established and implemented a monitoring and evaluation plan for determining the conservation impact of funded projects. OC/B monitors assessment of impact of projects.	(please provide details of monitoring and evaluation methodology, percentage of projects undergoing M&E; number of visits per project; results of monitoring, administrator/OC/B corrective actions as applicable)	

Continued

	Category	Function	Criteria	Fund Comments (w/ supporting material citation as appropriate)	Rating
			B.3.3 The OC/B conducts an annual performance review of institutional management (itself, the implementors, and, if applicable, the Trustee or Investment Manager).		
C.	**Grant Management**	**Planning**	C. 1.1 The percentage of total funds paid into the Foundation or Fund (or other vehicle established to receive payments resulting from the Forest Conservation Agreement) disbursed as grants annually, is at a reasonable level.		
		Implementation	C.2.1 Request for Applications (RFAs), or other grant soliciation mechanisms used, are undertaken on a schedule consistent with an OC/B approved expenditure plan, if applicable, and widely publicized (if		

	Category	Function	Criteria	**Fund Comments** (w/ supporting material citation as appropriate)	Rating
			C.2.2 Grant processing, including fund disbursement periods, is maintained within reasonable targeted time-frames.		
		Monitoring	C.3.1 Grant agreements require reporting on the conservation impact of project.		
			C.3.2 The OC/B has a policy on the need for, and the frequency of, financial audits of grant recipients.		
			C.3.3 Implementor ensures that all necessary grant recipient financial audits and/or impact reports are submitted as required by agreements.		
			C.3.4 The OC/B, through its implementors, ensures periodic on-site reviews of grant projects.	(e.g. number of active projects, number of active projects receiving site inspections, and number of site inspections per project).	

Continued

	Category	Function	Criteria	Fund Comments (w/ supporting material citation as appropriate)	Rating
D.	**Financial Management**	**Planning**	D.1.1 The OC/B has established a financial plan (complete with budgets, forecasts of income and expenditures).		
			D. 1.2 As appropriate, the OC/B has established a written investment policy (guidance for the implementor or fund manager).		
		Implementation	D.2.1 The administrative costs were kept within the limits established by the bilateral agreement or its amendments during the last fiscal year.		
			D.2.2 The OC/B has established, as appropriate, in-house or out-sourced investment monitoring capabilities (separate from the Investment Manager).		
			D.2.3 Assuming fund sustainability beyond the life of the TFCA agreement is an objective, the fund has diversified its sources of revenue (fund raising).		

STATE DEPARTMENT DOCUMENT NUMBER: 06-312

AGREEMENT BETWEEN THE UNITED STATES OF AMERICA AND THE REPUBLIC OF BOTSWANA REGARDING THE REDUCTION OF CERTAIN DEBTS OWED TO THE GOVERNMENT OF THE UNITED STATES AND ITS AGENCIES, WITH ATTACHMENT

SIGNED AT GABORONE,
OCTOBER 5, 2006
ENTERED INTO FORCE NOVEMBER 19, 2006

CTIA DOCUMENT NUMBER: 13132.000

The Government of the United States of America (the "USG") and the Government of the Republic of Botswana (the "GOB"),

Seeking to facilitate the conservation, protection, restoration, and sustainable use and management of tropical forests in Botswana, which provide a wide range of benefits to the people of Botswana,

Noting that tropical deforestation and forest degradation continue to be serious problems in many regions of the world,

Recognizing that the alleviation of external debt in the context of broader economic reforms can reduce economic pressures on countries and result in increased protection for tropical forests,

Also recognizing that economic benefits to local communities of sustainable uses of tropical forests are critical to their protection and sustainable management,

Considering Botswana's positive record in implementing market-based economic reforms including sustained efforts to liberalize its investment regime, and

In furtherance of the goals of the U.S. Tropical Forest Conservation Act of 1998, as amended, and the Foreign Operations, Export Financing, and Related Programs Appropriations Acts for U.S. fiscal year 2005,

Have agreed as follows:

Article I
DEFINITIONS

1. "633H001 November 2006 Payment" means, if the Closing Date is after November 23, 2006, the amount due on November 23, 2006 from, and paid by or on behalf of, the GOB to USAID with respect to Loan 633H001 that shall be transferred by USAID according to the provisions of Article III, paragraph 2 or 3 of this Agreement.

2. "Agreement" means this debt reduction agreement, as it may be amended from time to time.

3. "Board" has the meaning ascribed to it in Article III of the Tropical Forest Agreement.

4. "Business Day" means any day on which the Central Bank of Botswana is open for business, or, with respect to the provisions of Article II, paragraphs 1 and 2, and, if applicable, with respect to Articles III, paragraphs 2 and 3, Article V, paragraph 4(b)(iii), and Article VII, paragraph 2, of this Agreement, any day on which both the Bank of Botswana and the Federal Reserve Bank of New York are open for business.

5. "Closing" has the meaning set forth in Article II of this Agreement.

6. "Closing Date" has the meaning set forth in Article II of this Agreement.

7. "Effective Date" has the meaning set forth in Article VII, paragraph 1 of this Agreement.

8. "Exchange Rate" means the daily reference exchange rate for Local Currency expressed in U.S. Dollars as certified by the Bank of Botswana for the Business Day preceding the Business Day on which the Payment is due.

9. "Executive Director" has the meaning ascribed to it in the Tropical Forest Agreement.

10. "Fiscal Agent" has the meaning ascribed to it in Article II, paragraph 4, of the Tropical Forest Agreement.

11. "Fund" means the new Tropical Forest Conservation Fund established in accordance with the laws of Botswana pursuant to the Tropical Forest Agreement.

12. "GOB" means the Government of the Republic of Botswana, its agencies or instrumentalities, acting primarily through the Ministry of Finance.

13. "Local Currency" means the lawful currency of the Republic of Botswana.

14. "New TFCA Obligations" means the GOB's new obligations concluded pursuant to this Agreement, which shall replace the Old Obligations and obligate the GOB to make the Payments to the Fund in accordance with the Tropical Forest Agreement and the terms and conditions set forth herein.

15. "Notification Date" has the meaning set forth in Article V, paragraph 4 of this Agreement.

16. "Old Obligations" means Loans 633H001, 633H002, and 633H002A, under the agreements entitled "Loan and Grant Agreement between the Government of Botswana and the Government of the United States of America Acting through the Agency for International Development," dated June 30, 1971, August 31, 1972, and June 13, 1973, respectively, that obligate the GOB to repay principal and interest on debt whose outstanding principal sums at the Effective Date amount to U.S. $7,438,975.24.

17. "Overdue Interest" means interest that accrues at a rate of three (3) percent per annum on any overdue and unpaid Payment. Overdue Interest shall be paid in Local Currency, unless Article V, paragraph 4(b) (iii) of this Agreement applies.

18. "Party" means either the USG or the GOB, and "Parties" means both the USG and the GOB.

19. "Payment(s)" means the payment(s) to be made by the GOB under the New TFCA Obligations as shown in Schedule A. A Payment shall be made in Local Currency calculated by the Government of Botswana using the Exchange Rate unless the Agreement specifically requires a U.S. Dollar Payment.

20. "Payment Due Date" has the meaning set forth in Article V of this Agreement.

21. "Schedule A" means the attached repayment schedule for the New TFCA Obligations. Schedule A lists the dates and amounts due for Payments under the New TFCA Obligations. Payments under the New TFCA Obligations are listed on Schedule A as U.S. Dollar Interest Payments, but, as provided in this Agreement, are to be paid in Local Currency using the Exchange Rate unless Article III or Article IV, paragraph 4(b) of this Agreement apply.

22. "Signature Date" has the meaning set forth in Article VII of this Agreement.

23. "Termination" has the meaning set forth in Article VII of this Agreement.

24. "Tropical Forest Agreement" means the "Agreement Between the Government of the United States of America and the Government of Botswana Concerning the Establishment of a Tropical Forest Conservation Fund and a Tropical Forest Conservation Board", dated as of the same date as this Agreement, to provide for the establishment and operation of a fund and the operation of an administering board in order to promote activities designed to conserve, maintain, restore or promote sustainable use the tropical forests of Botswana.

25. "USAID" means the United States Agency for International Development.

26. "USG" means the Government of the United States of America, acting primarily through the U. S. Department of the Treasury.

27. "U.S. Treasury Escrow Account" has the meanings set forth in Article III, and Article V, paragraph 4(b) (iii) of this Agreement.

Article II
CLOSING AND REDUCTION OF OUTSTANDING DEBT

1. Pursuant to the terms and subject to the conditions hereof, at the Closing, the USG and the GOB shall cancel the Old Obligations, and in its place substitute the New TFCA Obligations.

2. The consummation of the transactions set forth in paragraph 1 of this Article (the "Closing") shall occur on the Business Day (the "Closing Date") which is either: (a) December 4, 2006; or (b) such other Business Day on or before January 20, 2007, as may be agreed by the Parties in writing on or before the date set forth in subsection (a) of this paragraph.

3. The GOB agrees to make Payments to the Fund in Local Currency in accordance with the New TFCA Obligations as specified in Schedule A and in accordance with the terms and conditions set forth herein and in the Tropical Forest Agreement. If the respective Payment Due Date for the payment to the Fund is not a Business Day, then the Payment Due Date for that payment shall be the next succeeding day which is a Business Day.

4. The GOB agrees not to assign the New TFCA Obligations to any third party.

Article III
PAYMENTS ON THE NEW TFCA OBLIGATIONS TO THE U.S. TREASURY ESCROW ACCOUNT AND OTHER PAYMENT ADJUSTMENTS

1. In the event that Closing has occurred, but the Fund has not been fully constituted under Botswanan law, the Board appointed, and a Fiscal Agent or Executive Director selected, the GOB shall make any Payment when due under Schedule A in U.S. dollars in the amount set forth in Schedule A into a USG account, as directed by Treasury through information provided to the GOB before the Closing Date (the "U.S. Treasury Escrow Account.") Amounts deposited in the U.S. Treasury Escrow Account shall not bear interest. Once the Fund is constituted, the Board appointed, and a Fiscal Agent or Executive Director selected, Treasury shall transfer promptly to an account, as designated by the GOB, all U.S. dollar funds in the U.S. Treasury Escrow Account. Within three (3) Business Days

thereafter, the GOB shall then make a payment to the Fund in Local Currency, calculated by using the Exchange Rate, of an amount equivalent to the U.S. dollar funds transferred by the U.S. Treasury.

2. If the Closing occurs after November 23, 2006, and the following three events have all occurred: (a) the Fund has been fully constituted under Botswanan law, (b) the Board has been appointed, and (c) a Fiscal Agent has been selected, the GOB instructs USAID, to transfer the 633H001 November 2006 Payment to an account designated by the GOB. Such transfer shall occur no later than fourteen (14) Business Days after the Closing Date. Within three (3) Business Days after its receipt of the transferred funds, the GOB shall then make a payment to the Fund in Local Currency, calculated by using the Exchange Rate, of an amount equivalent to the U.S. dollar funds transferred by USAID.

3. If the Closing occurs after November 23, 2006, the GOB instructs USAID to transfer the 633H001 November 2006 Payment to the U.S. Treasury Escrow Account referred to in paragraph 1 above if, by the Closing Date, (a) the Fund has not been fully constituted under Botswanan law, (b) the Board has not been appointed, and (c) a Fiscal Agent has not yet been selected. Such transfer shall occur no later than 14 Business Days after the Closing Date.

Article IV
CONDITIONS TO CLOSING

The obligation of USG hereunder to cancel the Old Obligations and substitute the New TFCA Obligations shall be subject to the fulfillment or waiver on or prior to the Closing Date of the following conditions, each of which shall be performed to the satisfaction of the USG:

(a) The GOB shall have paid in full to USAID any amounts due under the Old Obligations up to, but not including, the Closing Date. For the avoidance of doubt, GOB shall continue to make payments to USAID under the terms and conditions, and according to the payment schedules, of the Old Obligations on any amounts due to USAID under the Old Obligations for the period between the Signature Date and the Closing Date. After the Closing Date, the 633H001 November 2006 Payment, if applicable, shall be transferred by USAID to the U.S. Treasury Escrow Account, or an account designated by GOB, in accordance with the procedures set forth in Article III., paragraphs 2 or 3.

(b) The GOB shall have signed this Agreement and the Tropical Forest Agreement and both agreements shall have entered into force.

(c) If applicable, the Parliament of the Republic of Botswana shall have approved this Agreement and the Tropical Forest Agreement.

(d) The USG shall have received from the GOB such further documents, opinions, and certificates as the USG shall reasonably request.

Article V
FAILURE TO MAKE A PAYMENT OF PRINCIPAL OR INTEREST ON THE NEW TFCA OBLIGATION WHEN DUE

1. In the event the GOB does not make full payment of any installment under the New TFCA Obligations when due under this Agreement (each such due date hereinafter referred to as a "Payment Due Date"), the GOB shall within 7 Business Days commence discussions with USG to resolve such payment default. The GOB and the USG agree to use their best efforts to find a mutually acceptable solution.

2. Overdue Interest shall accrue on any overdue and unpaid installment of the New TFCA Obligations. The GOB shall make an Overdue Interest payment as soon as possible, without waiting for the due date of the next scheduled payment under the New TFCA Obligations.

3. Except as otherwise provided below, the GOB shall pay any Overdue Interest accruing on a due and unpaid Payment under a New TFCA Obligation directly to the Fund.

4. (a) Notwithstanding any other provision of this Agreement or the Tropical Forest Agreement, if the USG determines that any other condition under this Agreement or the Tropical Forest Agreement is not being substantially fulfilled and so notifies the GOB (the date of receipt of the notification being the "Notification Date"), the GOB shall commence discussions with the USG within seven (7) Business Days after the Notification Date to seek to resolve such matter. The GOB and the USG agree to use their best efforts to find a mutually acceptable solution. The GOB shall continue to make any Payment when due to the Fund after the Notification Date, unless otherwise instructed.

(b) If the GOB and the USG are unable to find a mutually acceptable solution within sixty (60) Business Days following either a Notification Date or GOB's failure to make a full Payment on the Payment Due Date, including any accrued Overdue Interest, if applicable, the following procedures shall apply:

(i) the USG may require the GOB to pay immediately in U.S. Dollars any unpaid Payment under the New TFCA Obligations, including any accrued Overdue Interest, to the Fund;

(ii) the USG may, in its sole discretion, declare all, or any part of, future Payments under the New TFCA Obligations due and payable immediately in U.S. Dollars ("Accelerated Payments"), in which case, such amounts shall be paid to the Fund for distribution in accordance with the Tropical Forest Agreement unless Article IV, paragraph 4(b)(iii) below applies; or

(iii) the USG may, in its sole discretion, require that the GOB make unpaid and future Payments, including any accrued Overdue Interest, or Accelerated Payments, in U.S. Dollars to the U.S. Treasury Escrow Account until the USG, in its sole discretion, is satisfied that the conditions under this Agreement and the Tropical Forest Agreement are being fulfilled. If satisfied, the USG shall transfer funds to the Fund from the U.S. Treasury Escrow Account within 14 Business Days of such determination.

Article VI
AMENDMENT AND NOTIFICATION

1. This Agreement may be amended with the written consent of both Parties.

2. All notices, consents, requests, instructions, approvals, and other communications provided for in this Agreement shall be in writing and shall be deemed validly given (a) on the date of delivery when delivered by hand, (b) on the date of transmission when sent by facsimile transmission during normal business hours with telephone confirmation of receipt, or (c) on the date of receipt in accordance with the records of receipt by a reputable overnight courier that maintains records of receipt, all addressed as set forth below (or to such other address as any Party shall have designated by notice in accordance with this Article VI to the other Party).

FOR THE USG:	Deputy Assistant Secretary International Development Finance and Debt Department of the Treasury 1500 Pennsylvania Avenue Washington DC 20220 Tel. (202) 622 0070 Fax (202) 622 0658
FOR THE GOB:	Secretary for Economic Affairs Ministry of Finance and Development Planning P/Bag 008 Gaborone, Botswana Tel. (267)3950372

Article VII
ENTRY INTO FORCE AND TERMINATION

1. This Agreement shall enter into force on the date (the "Effective Date") that is forty-five calendar days after the date of the last signature hereto (the "Signature Date"), unless a party gives notice to the other party, prior to the expiration of that forty-five-day period, that it is unable to bring the Agreement into force.

2. This Agreement shall automatically terminate: (a) in the event that the Closing has not taken place on or before (i) December 4, 2006 or (ii) such later Business Day on or before January 20, 2007, as may be agreed by the Parties in writing on or before the date in subparagraph (i) of this paragraph; or (b) if the Closing has occurred, upon the payment by the Government of Botswana of all amounts due under the New TFCA Obligations.

3. Either Party may terminate this Agreement upon six months' written notice to the other Party. The Parties agree to use best efforts to avoid the provision of such notice, including use of the resolution and review of disputes procedures provided under Article VII of the Tropical Forest Agreement and the amendment procedures provided under Article VI, paragraph 1 of this Agreement and Article X, paragraph 2 of the Tropical Forest Agreement. Upon termination of this Agreement, amounts generated by the Debt Reduction Agreement remaining in the Fund (including accrued interest traceable to Payments into the Fund) and any unpaid and remaining Payments under the New TFCA Obligations shall be made in U.S. Dollars into the U.S. Treasury Escrow Account, on the dates and in the U.S. Dollar amounts set forth in Schedule A, until both Parties reach a mutually-acceptable arrangement as to the future use of such funds.

IN WITNESS WHEREOF the under signed, being duly authorized by their respective Governments, have signed this Agreement.

DONE at Gaborone, Botswana, this 5th day of October, 2006, in duplicate in the English language.

FOR THE GOVERNMENT OF THE UNITED STATES OF AMERICA	FOR THE GOVERNMENT OF THE REPUBLIC OF BOTSWANA
[Signature]	[Signature]

Schedule A
Schedule of Payments under New TFCA Obligations

Obligation 1				Obligation 2				Obligation 3
	Scheduled Principal	Scheduled Interest		Scheduled Principal	Scheduled Interest		Scheduled Principal	Scheduled Interest
**11/23/2006	139,155.38	27,221.32	2/28/2007	257,124.11	59,589.98	1/21/2007	75,770.82	24,773.33
5/23/2007	141,242.71	25,133.99	8/28/2007	260,980.97	55,733.12	7/21/2007	76,907.38	23,636.77
11/23/2007	143,361.35	23,015.35	2/28/2008	264,895.69	51,818.40	1/21/2008	78,060.99	22,483.16
5/23/2008	145,511.78	20,864.92	8/28/2008	268,869.12	47,844.97	7/21/2008	79,231.91	21,312.24
11/23/2008	147,694.45	18,682.25	2/28/2009	272,902.16	43,811.93	1/21/2009	80,420.38	20,123.77
5/23/2009	149,909.87	16,466.83	8/28/2009	276,995.69	39,718.40	7/21/2009	81,626.69	18,917.46
11/23/2009	152,158.52	14,218.18	2/28/2010	281,150.63	35,563.46	1/21/2010	82,851.09	17,693.06
5/23/2010	154,440.89	11,935.81	8/28/2010	285,367.89	31,346.20	7/21/2010	84,093.86	16,450.29
11/23/2010	156,757.51	9,619.19	2/28/2011	289,648.40	27,065.69	1/21/2011	85,355.26	15,188.89
5/23/2011	159,108.87	7,267.83	8/28/2011	293,993.13	22,720.96	7/21/2011	86,635.59	13,908.56
11/23/2011	161,495.50	4,881.20	2/28/2012	298,403.03	18,311.06	1/21/2012	87,935.13	12,609.02
5/23/2012	163,917.60	2,458.76	8/28/2012	302,879.07	13,835.02	7/21/2012	89,254.15	11,290.00
			2/28/2013	307,422.26	9,291.83	1/21/2013	90,592.97	9,951.18
			8/28/2013	312,033.16	4,680.50	7/21/2013	91,951.86	8,592.29
						1/21/2014	93,331.14	7,213.01
						7/21/2014	94,731.11	5,813.04
						1/21/2015	96,152.07	4,392.08
						7/21/2015	97,594.35	2,949.80
						1/21/2016	99,058.75	1,485.88
Total	1,814,754.43	181,765.62	Total	3,972,665.31	461,331.52	Total	1,651,555.50	258,783.83

**See definition of 633H001 November 2006 Payment and related provisions

State Department Document Number: 06-313

Memorandum of Understanding Between the Republic of Indonesia and the United States of America on General Cooperation in Science and Technology for Natural Hazard Assessment, Analysis, Warning, Preparedness, and Mitigation, with Annexes

Signed at Jakarta,
November 20, 2006
Entered into force November 20, 2006

CTIA DOCUMENT NUMBER: 13133.000

Preamble

The Government of the Republic of Indonesia (Indonesia), and the Government of the United States of America (United States) hereinafter referred to as the "Parties":

Recognize the importance of scientific and technical cooperation to understand, observe, monitor climate, oceanography, meteorology, hydrology, seismology, volcanology, coastal zone changes, and the natural hazards associated with these disciplines;

Recognize the importance of promoting a closer working relationship to address environmental and social issues of common concern that are associated with climate, oceanography, meteorology, hydrology, seismology, volcanology, and coastal zone changes;

Recognize that to reduse loss of life, economic disruption, destruction of communities, and damage to the environment from natural hazards and disasters, end-to-end multi-hazard warning and mitigation systems must address the technology, structure, and the culture of assessment, warning, communication, preparedness, mitigation, and community resilience;

Understand that such cooperation has mutual benefits for both countries in the conduct of scientific and technical investigation and development and discharge of operational responsibilities, and can benefit the international community;

Note that both Parties are members of the intergovernmental Oceanographic Commission (IOC), the World Meteorological Organization (WMO), and the United Nations EconomicEducation, ScienceScientific, and Cultural Organization (UNESCO) with common interests in climate, oceanography, meteorology, hydrology, seismology, volcanology, and coastal zone management and the natural hazards associated with these disciplines; and

Note that the Parties have made mutual commitments to support development of the Indian Ocean Tsunami Warning and Mitigation System (IOTWS) and the activities of the Global Earth Observation System of Systems (GEOSS) in a manner that builds on and strengthens the existing global observational and multi-hazard warning systems, especially the Indian Ocean Tsunami Warning and Mitigation System.

Therefore, pursuant to the prevailing laws and regulations in their respective countries, the Parties have reached an understanding as follows:

I. Purpose of Memorandum

1) The purpose of this Memorandum of Understanding (MOU) is to facilitate the Parties' coordination of activities in climate, oceanography, meteorology, hydrology, geology, including seismology and volcanology, coastal zone changes, and the natural hazards associated with these disciplines; and end-to-end multi-hazard warning systems. This MOU will facilitate exchange of scientific resources, personal, and technical knowledge for mutual benefit that will support the purposes of this MOU for the Parties.

2) The Parties specifically acknowledge that this MOU does not constitute an obligation of funds. Nothing in this MOU shall be construed as superseding or interfering in any way with other agreements or contracts entered into between the Parties, or any component thereof, either prior to or subsequent to the signing of this MOU.

3) This MOU and its Implementing Arrangements (see Section IV) will support the Parties' efforts to: understand, observe, monitor, analyze, and predict multi-hazards processes and multi-hazard events; improve multi-hazard early warning systems; promote preparedness, mitigation, and community resilience to red the impact of multi-hazard events on lives, economies, communities, and the environment; support regional efforts to detect, analyze, and warn of multi-hazard events, including tsunamis; arid enhance the GEOSS. Other cooperation cooperative efforts of mutual interest to the Parties related to climate, oceanography, meteorology, hydrology, geology, including seismology and, volcanology, coastal zone changes, and the natural hazards associated with these disciplines may be undertaken pursuant to the MOU.

II. Scope of Cooperative Activities

Cooperative activities are specific projects undertaken by the Parties. Activities may include the following:

1) Scientific investigation and research that improves the understanding and analysis of climate, oceanography, meteorology, hydrology, geology, including seismology, and volcanology, coastal zone changes, and hazards associated with these disciplines, including observations and monitoring and support for observational and monitoring networks;

2) Activities that promote climate analysis and forecasts;

3) Activities that support meteorological analysis and forecasts;

4) Activities that advance and sustain multi-hazard detection, analysis, warning, preparedness, and mitigation systems that save lives and reduce impacts from multi-hazards events, including tsunamis, on societies and natural systems;

5) Activities that support the improvement of hydrological forecasts and services such as flood forecasting and warning systems development;

6) Activities to advance seismic event analysis;

7) Activities to advance monitoring, analysis and understanding of crustal deformation and volcanic eruptions and hazards;

8) Activities to promote community resilience to natural hazards, minimize impacts from natural disasters, and accelerate post-disaster recovery;

9) Studies and activities that support operational data collection, data sharing, compilation, and processing;

10) Activities that allow the collaborative and mutual exchange of scientific and technical expertise for the enhancement of mutual project objectives;

11) Activities that support one or more international objectives as identified in international fora in which the Parties participate that a consistent with the purposes of this MOU; and,

12) Other activities that support and advance the purposes of this MOU as agreed by the Parties.

III. Responsibilities of the Parties

1) The Parties are responsible for coordinating and engaging with specific organizational entities in their own countries, as appropriate and necessary, for the completion of the tasks designated pursuant to this MOU.

2) Each Party is to provide staff, facilities, and other support necessary for implementation of projects as mutually determined by the Parties. Such support will be subject to the availability of personnel and appropriated funds and will be in accordance with the laws and regulations of the contributing Party's country.

3) Each Party shall facilitate, in accordance with its laws and regulations, entry into and exit from its territory of appropriate personnel, scientific specimens and equipment of the other Party, including field survey parties, engaged in or used in projects and programs, including maritime research cruises, under this MOU.

4) Exemption and relief from taxes, including value-added taxes and customs duties, in relation to the implementation of a project pursuant to this MOU will be provided in terms set forth in relevant implementing arrangements, consistent with the laws and regulations of both countries.

5) Funding and other assistance from the United States to Indonesia under this MOU may be provided to Indonesia's government agencies directly, or to third parties in the form of contracts, grants, cooperative agreements, and other mechanisms. Such third parties may include, but are not limited to, universities, commercial entities, international and national non-governmental organizations, and international private voluntary organizations, as appropriate. The Parties will coordinate regarding the selection of any such third parties.

6) The Government of the Republic of Indonesia will co-finance cooperative activities under this MOU in accordance with its laws and regulations and as described in Implementing Arrangements.

7) Each Party, in conjunction with appropriate ministries and offices of the respective governament, shall facilitate, as appropriate and in accordance with its laws, regulations and policies, prompt and efficient approval of access of persons of the other Party, participating in cooperative activities under this MOU, to its relevant geographic areas, institutions, data, materials, and individual scientists, specialists and researchers as needed to carry out those activities. Any activities conducted by persons of one Party in another Party's geographical areas shall be accompanied by the relevant officials of the latter at the option of the Party in whose geographical areas the activities will take place.

IV. Implementing Arrangements

1) The Parties shall encourage and facilitate, where appropriate, the development of direct contacts and cooperation between government agencies, universities, research centers, institutions, private sector companies and other entities of the two countries.

2) The Government agencies and designated entities of the Parties may conclude under this MOU Implementing Arrangements as annexes under this MOU, as appropriate, in areas of climate, oceanography, meteorology, hydrology, geology, including seismology and volcanology, coastal zone changes, and the natural hazards associated with these disciplines. These Implementing Arrangements shall cover, as appropriate, topics of cooperation, procedures for transfer and use of materials, equipment and funds, and other relevant issues.

3) Periodic reports will be submitted to the Executive Agents (see Section V) of the Parties or their designees as specified in Implementing Arrangements. Such reports should outline future activity areas, represent proceedings of working groups, seminars or meetings, and document the progress and results of a particular project or program.

4) Responsibilities for the payment of costs of the cooperative activities authorized by this MOU shall be decided by mutual agreement on a case-by-case basis, consistent with the responsibilities of the Parties set forth in Section III, above, and with each Party's rules on reimbursement. Reimbursable financial arrangements, when deemed appropriate to carry out specific projects; will be described in the Implementing arrangements agreed to under this MOU.

V. Coordination of Cooperative Activities

1) Each Party hereby designates an Executive Agent responsible for the coordination and facilitation of cooperative activities under this MOU:

- For the Government of the Republic of Indonesia: The State Ministry of Research and Technology of the Republic of Indonesia Office of Assistant to the Deputy Minister for Science and Technology Needs.
- For the Government of the United States of America: The U.S. Department of State Office of Science and Technology Cooperation.

2) The Executive Agents of the Parties shall discuss and review, on a regular basis, the implementation of this MOU, including matters of importance in the field of natural hazards assessment, warning, and mitigation and policy matters related to the overall science and technology relationship of the Parties.

VI. Scientific and Technical Information and Dissemination of Data

1) Distribution of information will be through customary channels and in accordance with the normal procedures of the Parties.

2) The suppliesr of scientific and technical information will make take appropriate measures to ensure that the best scientific information will be transferred and/or exchanged. The application or use of any information exchanged or transferred under this MOU will be the responsibility of the recipient. The supplier does not guarantee the suitability of such information for any particular application.

3) All operational observational data collected as a result of activities under the MOU that are part of the IOTWS, Indonesian Tsunami Early Warning System, or other natural hazard event detection, analysis, warning, and warning dissemination system will be available openly and freely in real time through the WMO Global telecommunications System (GTS), the Global Seismic Network (GSN),

or other dissemination systems as agreed to by the Parties. Distribution and dissemination of such data will be made in accordance with standards and protocols adopted by the IOC's Intergovernmental Coordination Group for the IOTWS, as appropriate.

VII. Third Parties' Participation

1) The Parties may, by mutual consent, request the participation of third parties in implementing and financing programs and projects carried out under this MOU.

2) The Parties shall support the participation of scientific and research organizations, enterprises and other entities concerned from the two countries in international scientific and technological activities.

3) Scientists, experts, and institutions from third party countries may be invited to participate in the activities conducted under this MOU upon the mutual consent of the Parties.

VIII. Intellectual Property

1) The treatment of intellectual property created or furnished in the course of cooperative activities under this MOU is provided for in Annex I.

2) The treatment of security arrangements for sensitive information or equipment transferred under this MOU is provided for in Annex II, which shall apply to all activities conducted under the auspices of the MOU unless agreed otherwise by the Parties in writing.

3) These Annexes I and II shall be an integral part of this MOU.

IX. Non-Exclusivity

Nothing in this MOU shall restrict the Parties from engaging in similar or related agreements and activities with entities not part of this MOU.

X. Temporarily Suspension

Each Party reserves the right for reasons of national security, public order or public health to suspend temporarily either in whole or in part the implementation of this MOU. Such suspension shall take effect immediately after notification has been given to the other Party through diplomatic channels.

XI. Limitation of Personnel

1) Without any prejudices to any applicable privileges and immunities, all persons engaged in activities related to this MOU shall respect political independence, sovereignty, and territorial integrity of the host country, shaft have a duty not to interfere in the internal affairs of the host country, and will avoid any activities inconsistent with the purposes and objectives of this MOU;

2) Persons who enjoy privileges and immunities provided by international agreement or by the relevant laws and regulations of the host country have the duty to respect the laws and regulations of the host country.

XII. Settlement of Disputes

Any disputes regarding interpretation or implementation of this MOU or its associated Implementing Arrangements will be resolved through consultations and negotiations by the Parties amicably and in a spirit of cooperation.

XIII. Entry into Force, Duration, Amendment and Termination

1) This MOU shall enter into force on the date on upon signature by both Parties and shall remain in force for a period of five (5) years. It may be amended, or This MOU many be extended for further five-year periods by written agreement of the Parties.

2) This MOU may be amended by mutual written agreement of the Parties.

3) This MOU may be terminated at any time by either Party upon three (3) months' written notice to the other Party.

4) Termination of this MOU shall not affect the implementation of any cooperative activity carried out under the MOU and not completed upon termination of the AgreementMOU, unless otherwise agreed to by the Parties.

In witness whereof, the undersigned, being duly authorized by their respective governments, have signed this MOU.

DONE in duplicate in the English language at Jakarta on this twentieth day of November, two thousand and six.

FOR THE GOVERNMENT OF THE
REPUBLIC OF INDONESIA:
[Signature]
KUSMAYANTO KADIMAN
State Minister for Research and Technology

FOR THE GOVERNMENT OF THE
UNITED STATES OF AMERICA:
[Signature]
B. LYNN PASCOE
U.S. Ambassador to the Republic of Indonesia

ANNEX I
Intellectual Property Rights

I. General Obligation

The Parties shall ensure adequate and effective protection of intellectual property created or furnished under this MOU and relevant Implementing Arrangements. Rights to such intellectual property shall be allocated as provided in this Annex.

II. Scope

A. This Annex is applicable to all cooperative activities undertaken pursuant to this MOU, except as otherwise specifically agreed by the Parties or their designees.

B. For purposes of this MOU, "Intellectual property" shall mean the subject matter listed in Article 2 of the Convention Establishing the World Intellectual Property Organization, done at Stockholm, July 14, 1967, and may include other subject matter as agreed by the Parties.

C. Each Party shall ensure, through contracts or other legal means with its own participants, if necessary, that the other Party can obtain the rights to intellectual property allocated in accordance with this Annex. This Annex does not otherwise after or prejudice the allocation between a Party and its nationals, which shall be determined by that Party's laws and practices.

D. Except as otherwise provided in this MOU, disputes concerning intellectual property arising under this MOU shall be resolved through discussions between the concerned participating institutions, or, if necessary, the Parties or their designees. Upon mutual agreement of the Parties, a dispute shall be submitted to an arbitral tribunal for binding arbitration in accordance with the applicable rules of international law. Unless the Parties or their designees agree otherwise in writing, the arbitration rules of United Nations Commission on International Trade Law (UNCITRAL) shall govern.

E. Termination or expiration of this MOU shall not affect rights or obligations under this Annex.

III. Allocation of Rights

A. Each Party shall be entitled to a non-exclusive, irrevocable, royalty-free licence in all countries to translate, reproduce, and publicly distribute scientific and technical journal articles, reports, and books directly arising from cooperation under this MOU. All publicly distributed copies of a copyrighted work prepared under this provision shall indicate the names of the authors of the work unless an author explicitly declines to be named.

B. Rights to all forms of intellectual property, other than those rights described in paragraph III.A above, shall be allocated as follows:

1. Visiting researchers shall receive rights, awards, bonuses and royalties in accordance with the policies of the host institution.

2.

(a) Any intellectual property created by persons employed or sponsored by one Party under cooperative activities other than those covered by paragraph III.B(1) shall be owned by that Party. Intellectual property created by persons employed or sponsored by both Parties shall be jointly owned by the Parties. In addition, each creator shall be entitled to awards, bonuses and royalties in accordance with the policies of the institution employing or sponsoring that person.

(b) Unless otherwise agreed in an implementing or other arrangement, each Party shaft have within its territory all rights to exploit or license intellectual property created in the course of the cooperative activities.

(c) The rights of a Party outside its territory shall be determined by mutual agreement considering the relative contributions of the Parties and their participants to the cooperative activities, the degree of commitment in obtaining legal protection and licensing of the intellectual property and such other factors deemed appropriate.

(d) Notwithstanding paragraphs III.B(2)(a) and (b) above, if a particular project has led to the creation of intellectual property protected by the laws of one Patty but not the other, the Party whose laws provide for this type of protection shall be entitled to all rights to exploit or license intellectual property worldwide although creators of intellectual property shall nonetheless be entitled to awards, bonuses and royalties as provided in paragraph III.13(2)(a).

(e) For each invention made under any cooperative activity, the Party employing or sponsoring the inventor(s) shall disclose the invention promptly to the other Party together with any documentation and information necessary to enable the other Party to establish any rights to which it may be entitled. Either Party may ask the other Party in writing to delay publication or public disclosure of such documentation or information for the purpose of protecting its rights in the invention. Unless otherwise agreed in writing, the delay shall not exceed a period of six months from the date of disclosure by the inventing Party to the other Party.

IV. Business Confidential Information

In the event that information identified in a timely fashion as business-confidential is furnished or created under this MOU, each Party and its participants shall protect such information in accordance with applicable laws, regulations, and administrative practices. Information may be identified as "business-confidential" if a person having the information may derive an economic benefit from it or may obtain a competitive advantage over those who do not have it, and the information is not generally known or publicly available from other sources, and the owner has not previously made the information available without imposing in a timely manner an obligation to keep it confidential.

ANNEX II
Security Obligations

I. Protection of Sensitive Technology

Both Parties agree that no information or equipment requiring protection in the interest of national defense or foreign relations classified in accordance with its applicable national laws and regulations shall be provided under this MOU. In the event that information or equipment which is known or behind to require such protection is identified in the course of cooperative activities pursuant to this MOU, it shall be brought immediately to the attention of the appropriate officials and the Parties shall consult to identify appropriate security measures to be agreed upon by the Parties in writing and applied to this information and equipment and shall, if appropriate, amend this MOU to incorporate such measures.

II. Technology Transfer

The transfer of unclassified export-controlled information or equipment between the Parties shall be in accordance with the relevant laws and regulations of each Party. If either Party deems it necessary, detailed provisions for the prevention of unauthorized transfer or retransfer of such information or equipment shall be incorporated into the contracts or Implementing Arrangements. Export controlled information shall be marked to Identify it as export controlled and identify any restrictions on further use or transfer.

Senate Treaty Document Number: 109-20

Protocol Amending the Convention Between the United States of America and the Federal Republic of Germany for the Avoidance of Double Taxation and the Prevention of Fiscal Evasion with Respect to Taxes on Income and on Capital and to Certain Other Taxes, with a Joint Declaration

Signed at Berlin,
June 1, 2006

CTIA Document Number: 15621.001

LETTER OF TRANSMITTAL

The White House, *September 29, 2006.*

To the Senate of the United States:

I transmit herewith, for Senate advice and consent to ratification, a Protocol Amending the Convention Between the United States of America and the Federal Republic of Germany for the Avoidance of Double Taxation and the Prevention of Fiscal Evasion with Respect to Taxes on Income and Capital and to Certain Other Taxes, Signed on August 29, 1989, signed at Berlin June 1, 2006 (the "Protocol"), along with a related Joint Declaration. Also transmitted for the information of the Senate is the report of the Department of State with respect to the Protocol.

The Protocol eliminates the withholding tax on certain cross-border dividend payments. Like a number of recent U.S. tax agreements, the proposed Protocol provides for the elimination of the withholding tax on dividends arising from certain direct investments and cross-border dividend payments to pension funds. The Protocol also provides for mandatory arbitration of certain cases before the competent authorities. This provision is the first of its kind in a U.S. tax treaty. In addition, the Protocol also modernizes the Convention to bring it into closer conformity with current U.S. tax-treaty policy, including strengthening the treaty's provisons preventing so-called treaty shopping.

I recommend that the Senate give early and favorable consideration to the Protocol, along with the Joint Declaration and give it advice and consent to ratification.

George W. Bush.

LETTER OF SUBMITTAL

DEPARTMENT OF STATE,
Washington, August 2, 2006.

The PRESIDENT,
The White House.

THE PRESIDENT: I have the honor to submit to you, with a view to its transmission to the Senate for advice and consent to ratification, a Protocol Amending the Convention Between the United States of America and the Federal Republic of Germany for the avoidance of Double Taxation and the Prevention of Fiscal Evasion with Respect to Taxes on Income and Capital and to Certain Other Taxes, Signed on 29th August 1989, signed at Berlin June 1, 2006 (the "Protocol"), along with a related Joint Declaration.

The Protocol eliminates the withholding tax on certain cross-border dividend payments. Like a number of recent U.S. tax agreements, the Protocol provides for the elimination of the withholding tax on dividends arising from certain direct investments and cross-border dividend payments to tension funds.

The Protocol also provides for mandatory arbitration of certain cases before the competent authorities. This provision is the first of its kind in a U.S. tax treaty. In addition, the Protocol modernizes the Convention to bring into closer conformity with current U.S. tax-treaty policy, including strengthening the treaty's provisions preventing so-called treaty shopping.

The Protocol was concluded in recognition of the importance of the United States' economic relations with Germany. The Department of the Treasury and the Department of State cooperated in the negotiation of the Protocol. It has the full approval of both Departments.

Respectfully submitted.

CONDOLEEZZA RICE.

Enclosures.

KEY PROVISIONS OF THE U.S.-GERMANY INCOME TAX PROTOCOL

The Protocol to the income tax Convention with Germany was negotiated to bring the current Convention, concluded in 1989, into closer conformity with current U.S. tax treaty policy. There are, as with all bilateral tax conventions, some variations from these norms. In the Protocol, these differences reflect particular aspects of German law and treaty policy, the interaction of U.S. and German law, and U.S.-German economic relations.

The most important aspect of the Protocol relates to the taxation of cross-border dividend payments. Under the Protocol, most dividends paid by a subsidiary in one country to its parent in the other country will be exempt from withholding tax in the subsidiary's home country, rather than being subject to the current treaty's maximum withholding tax rate for direct dividends of five percent. The proposed Protocol also provides for a withholding rate of zero on cross-border dividend payments to pension funds. Eliminating withholding taxes on cross-border direct dividends and cross-border dividend payments to pension funds is consistent with an overall view that investment income should be taxed by the country of residence, not the country of source.

The Protocol also provides for mandatory arbitration of certain cases before the competent authorities. The arbitration provided for in the Protocol is at the taxpayer's election with respect to competent authority cases that cannot be resolved within a specified period, generally two years from the commencement of the case. The determination of an arbitration board constitutes a resolution by mutual agreement under the Convention and is binding on both countries, unless the taxpayer does not accept the determination. This provision is the first of its kind in a U.S. tax treaty and will be well received by the business community.

In addition, the Protocol also updates the current treaty's treatment of pensions. It removes barriers to the flow of personal services between the United States and Germany that could otherwise result from discontinuities in the laws of the two countries regarding the deductibility of pension contributions.

The Protocol also strengthens the treaty's provisions preventing so-called treaty shopping, which is the inappropriate use of a tax treaty by third-country residents.

Moreover, the Protocol updates the current treaty to reflect U.S. and German legislative changes since 1989. For example, the Protocol updates the "saving clause" to provide that former citizens or long-term residents of the United States may, for the period of ten years following the loss of such status, be taxed in accordance with the laws of the United States.

The Protocol also modernizes our treaty relationship and brings it into closer conformity with current U.S. tax treaty policy by making technical changes to the article dealing with the elimination of double taxation and by eliminating the article dealing with the taxation of independent personal services.

The proposed Protocol will enter into force upon the exchange of instruments of ratification. It will have effect, with respect to taxes withheld at source, for amounts paid or credited on or after the first day of January of the year upon which the Protocol enters into force and, with respect to other taxes, for taxable years beginning on or after the first day of January next following the date upon which the Protocol enters into force. However, where any person would be entitled to greater benefits under the Convention as unmodified by the Protocol, the Convention as unmodified, at the election of the person, continues to have effect in its entirety with respect to such person for a period of twelve-months from the date the provisions of the Protocol are effective.

PROTOCOL AMENDING THE CONVENTION BETWEEN THE UNITED STATES OF AMERICA AND THE FEDERAL REPUBLIC OF GERMANY FOR THE AVOIDANCE OF DOUBLE TAXATION AND THE PREVENTION OF FISCAL EVASION WITH RESPECT TO TAXES ON INCOME AND CAPITAL AND TO CERTAIN OTHER TAXES, SIGNED ON 29th AUGUST 1989

The United States of America and the Federal Republic of Germany, desiring to amend the Convention Between the United States of America and the Federal Republic of Germany for the Avoidance of Double Taxation and the Prevention of Fiscal Evasion with Respect to Taxes on Income and Capital and to Certain Other Taxes, and the related Protocol signed at Bonn on August 29, 1989 (hereinafter referred to as "the Convention" and "Protocol to the Convention", respectively).

Have agreed as follows:

ARTICLE I

Article 1 (Personal Scope) of the Convention is deleted and the following Article substituted:

"Article 1
General Scope

1. This Convention shall apply to persons who are residents of one or both of the Contracting States, except as otherwise provided in this Convention.

2. This Convention shall not restrict in any manner any exclusion, exemption, deduction, credit, or other allowance now or hereafter accorded:

a) by the laws of either Contracting State; or

b) by any other agreement to which the Contracting States are party.

3.

a) Notwithstanding the provisions of subparagraph b) of paragraph 2:

aa) the Contracting States agree that any question arising as to the interpretation or application of the Convention and, in particular, whether a taxation measure is within the scope of the Convention, shall be determined exclusively in accordance with the provisions of Article 25 (Mutual Agreement Procedure) of the Convention; and

bb) the provisions of any other agreement shall not apply to a taxation measure unless the competent authorities agree that the measure is not within the scope of Article 24 (Nondiscrimination) of this Convention.

b) For the purposes of this paragraph, a "measure" is a law, regulation, rule, procedure, decision, administrative action, or any similar provision or action.

4.

a) Except to the extent provided in paragraph 5, this Convention shall not affect the taxation by the United States of its residents (as determined under Article 4 (Residence)) and its citizens.

b) Notwithstanding the other provisions of this Convention, a former citizen or long-term resident of the United States may, for the period of ten years following the loss of such status, be taxed in accordance with the laws of the United States.

5. The provisions of paragraph 4 shall not affect the benefits conferred by the United States:

a) under paragraph 2 of Article 9 (Associated Enterprises), paragraph 6 of Article 13 (Gains), paragraphs 3, 4 and 5 of Article 18 (Pensions, Annuities, Alimony, Child Support, and Social Security), paragraph 1 and 5 of Article 18A (Pension Plans), paragraph 3 of Article 19 (Government Service), and under Articles 23 (Relief from Double Taxation), 24 (Nondiscrimination), and 25 (Mutual Agreement Procedure); and

b) under paragraph 2 of Article 18A (Pension Plans), subparagraph b) of paragraph 1 of Article 19 (Government Service), and under Articles 20 (Visiting Professors and Teachers; Students and Trainees) and 30 (Members of Diplomatic Missions and Consular Posts), upon individuals who are neither citizens of, nor have immigrant status in, the United States.

6. Nothing in the Convention shall be construed to prevent the Federal Republic of Germany from imposing its taxes on amounts included in the income of a resident of the Federal Republic of Germany according to part 4, 5, and 7 of the German "Außensteuergesetz". Where such imposition of tax gives rise to double taxation, the competent authorities shall consult for the elimination of such double taxation according to paragraph 3 of Article 25 (Mutual Agreement Procedure).

7. In the case of an item of income, profit or gain derived by or through a person that is fiscally transparent under the laws of either Contracting State, such item shall be considered to be derived by a resident of a State to the extent that the item is treated for the purposes of the taxation law of such State as the income, profit or gain of a resident."

ARTICLE II

Article 4 (Residence) of the Convention is amended by deleting paragraph 1 and substituting the following paragraph:

"1. For the purposes of this Convention, the term "resident of a Contracting State" means any person who, under the laws of that State, is liable to tax therein by reason of his domicile, residence, place of management, place of incorporation, or any other criterion of a similar nature, and also includes that State and any political subdivision or local authority thereof. The term, however, does not include any person who is liable to tax in that State in respect only of income from sources in that State or of profits attributable to a permanent establishment in that State or capital situated therein."

ARTICLE III

Article 7 (Business Profits) of the Convention is modified by:

a) deleting paragraph 3 and substituting the following paragraph:

"3. In determining the business profits of a permanent establishment, there shall be allowed as deductions expenses that are incurred for the purposes of the permanent establishment, including executive and general administrative expenses so incurred, whether in the State in which the permanent establishment is situated or elsewhere."; and

b) in paragraph 7, adding the words "and income from the performance of professional services and of other activities of an independent character".

ARTICLE IV

Article 10 (Dividends) of the Convention is deleted and the following Article substituted:

"Article 10
Dividends

1. Dividends paid by a company that is a resident of a Contracting State to a resident of the other Contracting State may be taxed in that other State.

2. However, such dividends may also be taxed in the Contracting State of which the company paying the dividends is a resident and according to the laws of that State, but if the dividends are derived and beneficially owned by a resident of the other Contracting State, the tax so charged shall not exceed:

a) 5 percent of the gross amount of the dividends if the beneficial owner is a company that owns directly at least 10 percent of the voting stock of the company paying the dividends;

b) 15 percent of the gross amount of the dividends in all other cases.

This paragraph shall not affect the taxation of the company in respect of the profits out of which the dividends are paid.

3. Notwithstanding the provisions of paragraph 2, such dividends shall not be taxed in the Contracting State of which the company paying the dividends is a resident if the beneficial owner is:

a) a company that is a resident of the other Contracting State that has owned directly shares representing 80 percent or more of the voting power in the company paying the dividends for a 12-month period ending on the date entitlement to the dividend is determined and;

aa) satisfies the conditions of clause aa) or bb) of subparagraph c) of paragraph 2 of Article 28 (Limitation on Benefits);

bb) satisfies the conditions of clauses aa) and bb) of subparagraph f) of paragraph 2 of Article 28, provided that the company satisfies the conditions described in paragraph 4 of Article 28 with respect to the dividends;

cc) is entitled to benefits with respect to the dividends under paragraph 3 of Article 28; or

dd) has received a determination pursuant to paragraph 7 of Article 28 with respect to this paragraph; or

b) a pension fund that is a resident of the other Contracting State, provided that such dividends are not derived from the carrying on of a business, directly or indirectly, by such pension fund.

4. Subparagraph a) of paragraph 2 and subparagraph a) of paragraph 3 shall not apply in the case of dividends paid by a United States person that is a U.S. Regulated Investment Company (RIC), a United States person that is a U.S. Real Estate Investment Trust (REIT) or a German Investment Fund or a German *Investmentaktiengesellschaft* (collectively referred to as *Investmentvermögen).* In the case of dividends paid by a RIC or an Investmentvermögen, subparagraph b) of paragraph 2 and subparagraph b) of paragraph 3 shall apply. In the case of dividends paid by a REIT subparagraph b) of paragraph 2 shall apply only if:

a) the beneficial owner of the dividends is an individual holding an interest of not more than 10 percent in the REIT;

b) the dividends are paid with respect to a class of stock that is publicly traded and the beneficial owner of the dividends is a person holding an interest of not more than 5 percent of any class of the REIT's stock; or

c) the beneficial owner of the dividends is a person holding an interest of not more than 10 percent in the REIT and the REIT is diversified.

For purposes of this paragraph a REIT shall be diversified if no single interest in real property exceeds 10 percent of its total interests in real property. For the purposes of this paragraph foreclosure property shall not be an interest in real property. Where a REIT holds an interest in a partnership, it shall be treated as owning directly a proportion of the partnership's interests in real property corresponding to its interest in the partnership.

5. The term "dividends" as used in this Article means income from shares, "jouissance" shares or "jouissance" rights, founders' shares, or other rights (not being debt-claims) participating in profits, as well as other income from other rights that is subjected to the same taxation treatment as income from shares by the laws of the Contracting State of which the company making the distribution is a resident. The term "dividends" also includes in the Federal Republic of Germany income under a sleeping partnership (Stille Gesellschaft), a participating loan (partiarisches Darlehen), or "Gewinnobligation", as well as distributions on certificates of a German *Investmentvermögen*.

6. Notwithstanding the first sentence of paragraph 2 of this Article, paragraph 3 of this Article and paragraph 1 of Article 11 (Interest), income from arrangements carrying the right to participate in profits (including in the Federal Republic of Germany income under a sleeping partnership (Stille Gesellschaft), a participating loan (partiarisches Darlehen), or "Gewinnobligation", or "jouissance" shares or "jouissance" rights and in the United States contingent interest of a type that would not qualify as portfolio interest) that is deductible in determining the profits of the payor may be taxed in the Contracting State in which it arises according to the laws of that State.

7. The provisions of paragraphs 2 and 3 shall not apply if the beneficial owner of the dividends, being a resident of a Contracting State, carries on business in the other Contracting State, of which the company paying the dividends is a resident, through a permanent establishment situated therein, and the holding in respect of which the dividends are paid forms part of the business property of such permanent establishment. In such case, the provisions of Article 7 (Business Profits) shall apply.

8. A Contracting State may not impose any tax on dividends paid by a company which is a resident of the other Contracting State, except insofar as such dividends are paid to a resident of the first-mentioned State or insofar as the holding in respect of which the dividends are paid forms part of the business property of a permanent establishment situated in that State, nor may it impose tax on a company's undistributed profits except as provided in paragraph 9 of this Article, even if the dividends paid or the undistributed profits consist wholly or partly of profits or income arising in that State.

9. A company that is a resident of a Contracting State and that has a permanent establishment in the other Contracting State, or that is subject to tax on a net basis in that other Contracting State on items of income that may be taxed in that other State under Article 6 (Income from Immovable (Real) Property) or under paragraph 1 of Article 13 (Gains), may be subject in that other Contracting State to a tax in addition to the tax allowable under the other provisions of this Convention. Such tax, however, may be imposed only on:

a) the portion of the business profits of the company attributable to the permanent establishment, and

b) the portion of the income referred to in the preceding sentence that is subject to tax under Article 6 or paragraph 1 of Article 13, that represents the "dividend equivalent amount" of those profits and income; the term "dividend equivalent amount" shall, for the purposes of this subparagraph,

aa) in the case of the United States, have the meaning that it has under the law of the United States as it may be amended from time to time without changing the general principle thereof; and

bb) in the case of the Federal Republic of Germany, be that portion of the income described in subparagraph a) that is comparable to the amount that would be distributed as a dividend by a locally incorporated subsidiary.

10. The tax referred to in subparagraphs a) and b) of paragraph 9 of this Article shall not be imposed at a rate exceeding the rate specified in subparagraph a) of paragraph 2. In any case, it shall not be imposed on a company that:

a) satisfies the conditions of clause aa) or bb) of subparagraph c) of paragraph 2 of Article 28 (Limitation on Benefits);

b) satisfies the conditions of clauses aa) and bb) of subparagraph f) of paragraph 2 of Article 28, provided that the company satisfies the conditions described in paragraph 4 of that Article with respect to an item of income, profit or gain described in paragraph 9 of this Article;

c) is entitled under paragraph 3 of Article 28 to benefits with respect to an item of income, profit or gain described in paragraph 9 of this Article; or

d) has received a determination pursuant to paragraph 7 of Article 28 with respect to this paragraph.

11. The term "pension fund" as used in this Article means any person that:

a) is established under the laws of a Contracting State;

b) is established and maintained in that Contracting State primarily to administer or provide pensions or other similar remuneration, including social security payments, disability pensions and widow's pensions or to earn income for the benefit of one or more of such persons; and

c) is either,

aa) in the case of the United States, exempt from tax in the United States with respect to the activities described in subparagraph b) of this paragraph, or

bb) in the case of the Federal Republic of Germany, a plan the contributions to which are eligible for preferential treatment under the *Income Tax Act*."

ARTICLE V

Article 11 (Interest) of the Convention is modified by:

a) inserting the following new paragraph 6:

"6. Notwithstanding the provisions of paragraph 1, interest that is an excess inclusion with respect to a residual interest in a U.S. real estate mortgage investment conduit may be taxed by the United States in accordance with its domestic law."; and

b) in paragraph 5, deleting the words "paragraph 8(a)(bb)" where they appear and substituting the words "subparagraph b) of paragraph 9".

ARTICLE VI

Article 13 (Gains) of the Convention is modified by deleting paragraph 6 and substituting the following new paragraph:

"6. Where an individual who, upon ceasing to be a resident of one of the Contracting States, is treated under the taxation law of that State as having alienated property and is taxed in that State by reason thereof, the individual may elect to be treated for purposes of taxation in the other Contracting State as if the individual had, immediately before ceasing to be a resident of the first-mentioned State, alienated and reacquired the property for an amount equal to its fair market value at that time."

ARTICLE VII

1. Article 14 (Independent Personal Services) of the Convention shall be deleted and the Articles following Article 14 shall not be re-numbered.

2. Paragraph 3 of Article 11 (Interest) of the Convention shall be modified by deleting the words ", or performs in that other State independent personal services from a fixed base situated therein,", "or fixed base", and "or Article 14 (Independent Personal Services), as the case may be," where they appear.

3. Paragraph 5 of Article 11 of the Convention shall be modified by deleting the words "or a fixed base" where they appear.

4. Paragraph 3 of Article 12 (Royalties) of the Convention shall be modified by deleting the words ", or performs in that other State independent personal services from a fixed base situated therein," and "or Article 14 (Independent Personal Services), as the case may be," where they appear.

5. Paragraph 3 of Article 13 (Gains) of the Convention shall be modified by deleting the words "or of movable property pertaining to a fixed base available to a resident of a Contracting State in the other Contracting State for the purpose of performing independent personal services" and "or of such fixed base" where they appear.

6. Subparagraph c) of paragraph 2 of Article 15 (Dependent Personal Services) of the Convention shall be modified by deleting the words "or a fixed base" where they appear.

7. Paragraph 1 of Article 17 (Artistes and Athletes) of the Convention shall be modified by deleting the words ", 14 (Independent Personal Services)" where they appear.

8. Paragraph 2 of Article 17 of the Convention shall be modified by deleting the words "and 14 (Independent Personal Services)," where they appear.

9. Paragraph 2 of Article 21 (Other Income) of the Convention shall be modified by deleting the words "; or the recipient performs in that other State independent personal services from a fixed base situated therein, and the income is attributable to the fixed base" where they appear.

10. Paragraph 2 of Article 22 (Capital) of the Convention shall be modified by deleting the words ", or by movable property pertaining to a fixed base available to a resident of a Contracting State in the other Contracting State for the purpose of performing independent personal services," where they appear.

ARTICLE VIII

Article 18 (Pensions, Annuities, Alimony, and Child Support) of the Convention is modified by:

a) deleting the title "Article 18 (Pensions, Annuities, Alimony, and Child Support)" and replacing it with the title "Article 18 (Pensions, Annuities, Alimony, Child Support, and Social Security)";

b) by adding a new paragraph 5 as follows:

> "5. Social security benefits paid under the social security legislation of a Contracting State and other public pensions (not dealt with in Article 19 (Government Service)) paid by a Contracting State to a resident of the other Contracting State shall be taxable only in that other Contracting State. In applying the preceding sentence, that other Contracting State shall treat such benefit or pension as though it were a social security benefit paid under the social security legislation of that other Contracting State."

ARTICLE IX

The following new Article 18A (Pension Plans) shall be added to the Convention:

"Article 18A
Pension Plans

1. Where an individual who is a resident of a Contracting State is a member or beneficiary of, or participant in, a pension plan established in the other Contracting State, income earned by the pension plan may be taxed as income of that individual only when, and, to the extent that, it is paid to, or for the benefit of, that individual from the pension plan (and not transferred to another pension plan in that other Contracting State).

2. Where an individual who is a beneficiary of, or participant in, a pension plan established in a Contracting State exercises an employment or self-employment in the other Contracting State:

a) contributions paid by or on behalf of that individual to the pension plan during the period or attributable to the period that he exercises an employment or self-employment in the other State shall be deductible (or excludable) in computing his taxable income in that other State; and

b) any benefits accrued under the pension plan, or contributions made to the pension plan by or on behalf of the individual's employer, during that period shall not be treated as part of the employee's taxable income; any such contributions shall be allowed as a deduction in computing the business profits of his employer in that other State.

The relief available under this paragraph shall not exceed the relief that would be allowed by the other State to residents of that State for contributions to, or benefits accrued under, a pension plan or plans established in that State. The competent authorities of the Contracting States shall determine the relief available under this paragraph pursuant to the preceding sentence.

3. The provisions of paragraph 2 shall not apply unless:

a) contributions by or on behalf of the individual, or by or on behalf of the individual's employer were made before the individual began to exercise an employment or self-employment in the other State; and

b) the pension plan is accepted by the competent authority of that State as generally corresponding to a pension plan recognized as such for tax purposes by that State.

4. The term "pension plan" means an arrangement established in a Contracting State which is operated principally to administer or provide pension or retirement benefits or to earn income for the benefit of one or more such arrangements.

5. a) Where a citizen of the United States who is a resident of the Federal Republic of Germany exercises an employment in the Federal Republic of Germany the income from which is taxable in the Federal Republic of Germany and is borne by an employer who is a resident of the Federal Republic of Germany or by a permanent establishment situated in the Federal Republic of Germany, and the individual is a beneficiary of, or participant in, a pension plan established in the Federal Republic of Germany,

aa) contributions paid by or on behalf of that individual to the pension plan during the period or attributable to the period that he exercises the employment in the Federal Republic of Germany, and that are attributable to the employment, shall be deductible (or excludable) in computing his taxable income in the United States; and

bb) any benefits accrued under the pension plan, or contributions made to the pension plan by or on behalf of the individual's employer, during that period or attributable to that period, and that are attributable to the employment, shall not be treated as part of the employee's taxable income in computing his taxable income in the United States.

This paragraph shall apply only to the extent that the contributions or benefits qualify for tax relief in the Federal Republic of Germany.

b) The relief available under this paragraph shall not exceed the relief that would be allowed by the United States to its residents for contributions to, or benefits accrued under, a generally corresponding pension plan established in the United States.

c) For purposes of determining an individual's eligibility to participate in and receive tax benefits with respect to a pension plan established in the United States, contributions made to, or benefits accrued under, a pension plan established in the Federal Republic of Germany shall be treated as contributions or benefits under a generally corresponding pension plan established in the United States to the extent relief is available to the individual under this paragraph.

d) This paragraph shall not apply unless the competent authority of the United States has agreed that the pension plan generally corresponds to a pension plan established in the United States."

ARTICLE X

Article 19 (Government Service; Social Security) of the Convention is deleted and the following Article substituted:

"Article 19
Government Service

1. Notwithstanding the provisions of Articles 15 (Dependent Personal Services), 16 (Directors' Fees), and 17 (Artistes and Athletes):

a) salaries, wages and other similar remuneration, other than a pension, paid by a Contracting State or a political subdivision, local authority or an instrumentality thereof to an individual in respect of services rendered to that Contracting State or a political subdivision, local authority or an instrumentality thereof shall, subject to the provisions of subparagraph b), be taxable only in that State;

b) such remuneration, however, shall be taxable only in the other Contracting State if the services are rendered in that State and the individual is a resident of that State who:

aa) is a national of that State; or

bb) did not become a resident of that State solely for the purpose of rendering the services.

2. a) Notwithstanding the provisions of paragraph 1, pensions and other similar remuneration paid by, or out of funds created by, a Contracting State or a political subdivision, local authority or an instrumentality thereof to an individual in respect of services rendered to that State or subdivision, authority or instrumentality shall be taxable only in that State.

b) However, such pensions and other remuneration shall be taxable only in the other Contracting State if the individual is a

aa) resident of, and a national of, that State; or

bb) the pension is not subject to tax in the Contracting State for which the services were performed because the services were performed entirely in the other Contracting State.

3. Pensions, annuities, and other amounts paid by one of the Contracting States or by a juridical person organized under the public laws of that State as compensation for an injury or damage sustained as a result of hostilities or political persecution shall be exempt from tax by the other State.

4. The provisions of Articles 15 (Dependent Personal Services), 16 (Directors' Fees), 17 (Artistes and Athletes), and 18 (Pensions, Annuities, Alimony, Child Support, and Social Security) shall apply to salaries, wages and other similar remuneration, and to pensions, in respect of services rendered in connection with a business carried on by a Contracting State or by a political subdivision, local authority or an instrumentality thereof.

5. In this Article, the term "instrumentality" means any agent or entity created or organized by a Contracting State, one of its states or a political subdivision or local authority thereof in order to carry out functions of a governmental nature which is specified and agreed to in letters exchanged between the competent authorities of the Contracting States."

ARTICLE XI

Article 20 (Visiting Professors and Teachers; Students and Trainees) of the Convention is modified by:

a) deleting paragraph 1 and substituting the following paragraph:

"1. Remuneration that a professor or teacher who is a resident of a Contracting State and who is temporarily present in the other Contracting State for the primary purpose of carrying out advanced study or research or for teaching at an accredited university or other recognized educational institution, or an institution engaged in research for the public benefit, receives for such work shall be taxable only in the first-mentioned Contracting State for a period not exceeding two years from the date of his arrival. This Article shall not apply to income from research if such research is undertaken not in the public interest but primarily for the private benefit of a specific person or persons. The benefits provided in this paragraph shall not be granted to an individual who, during the immediately preceding period, enjoyed the benefits of paragraph 2, 3, or 4."; and

b) in paragraph 4, deleting the words "$5,000 (five thousand United States dollars)" and substituting the words "$9,000 (nine thousand United States dollars)".

ARTICLE XII

Article 23 (Relief from Double Taxation) of the Convention is deleted and the following Article substituted:

"Article 23
Relief from Double Taxation

1. In accordance with the provisions and subject to the limitations of the law of the United States (as it may be amended from time to time without changing the general principle hereof), the United States shall allow to a resident or citizen of the United States as a credit against the United States tax on income:

a) the income tax paid or accrued to the Federal Republic of Germany by or on behalf of such resident or citizen; and

b) in the case of a United States company owning at least 10 percent of the voting stock of a company that is a resident of the Federal Republic of Germany and from which the United States company receives dividends, the income tax paid or accrued to the Federal Republic of Germany by or on behalf of the payer with respect to the profits out of which the dividends are paid.

For the purposes of this paragraph, the taxes referred to in subparagraph b) of paragraph 1 of Article 2 (Taxes Covered) and paragraph 2 of Article 2, other than the capital tax *(Vermögensteuer)*, shall be considered income taxes.

2. For the purposes of applying paragraph 1 of this Article, an item of gross income, as determined under the laws of the United States, derived by a resident of the United States that, under this Convention, may be taxed in the Federal Republic of Germany shall be deemed to be income from sources in the Federal Republic of Germany.

3. Where a resident of the Federal Republic of Germany derives income or owns capital which, in accordance with the provisions of this Convention, may be taxed in the United States or is exempt from United States tax under paragraph 3 of Article 10 (Dividends), tax shall be determined as follows:

a) Except as provided in subparagraph b), the income or capital shall be excluded from the basis upon which German tax is imposed. The Federal Republic of Germany, however, retains the right to take into account in the determination of its rate of tax items of income and capital excluded under the provisions of this Convention. In the case of income from dividends the foregoing provisions shall apply only to such income from distributions of profits on corporate rights subject to corporate income tax under United States law as are paid to a company (not including partnerships) being a resident of the Federal Republic of Germany by a company being a resident of the United States at least 10 percent of the voting shares of which is owned directly by the German company. The exclusion provided by the first sentence of this subparagraph shall not apply to dividends paid by a U.S. Regulated Investment Company (RIC) or a U.S. Real Estate Investment Trust (REIT) and distributions that are deductible for United States tax purposes by the company distributing them. For the purposes of taxes on capital there shall also be excluded from the basis upon which German tax is imposed any shareholding the dividends of which, if paid, would be excluded, according to the two immediately foregoing sentences, from the basis upon which German tax is imposed.

b) There shall be allowed as a credit against German tax on income, subject to the provisions of German tax law regarding credit for foreign tax, the United States tax paid in accordance with the law of the United States and with the provisions of this Convention on the following items of income:

aa) income from dividends within the meaning of Article 10 (Dividends) to which subparagraph a) does not apply;

bb) gains to which Article 13 (Gains) applies provided such gains are taxable in the United States by reason only of subparagraph b) of paragraph 2 of Article 13;

cc) income to which Article 16 (Directors' Fees) applies;

dd) income to which Article 17 (Artistes and Athletes) applies;

ee) income which would, but for Article 28 (Limitation on Benefits), remain exempt from United States tax under this Convention.

For the purposes of this paragraph, income, profit or gain derived by a resident of the Federal Republic of Germany that, under this Convention, may be taxed in the United States shall be deemed to be income from sources within the United States.

4. a) Notwithstanding subparagraph a) of paragraph 3, double taxation shall be avoided by a credit as provided for in subparagraph b) of paragraph 3, if income or capital would be subject to double taxation due to the placement of such income or capital under different provisions of the Convention and this conflict cannot be settled by a procedure pursuant to Article 25 (Mutual Agreement Procedure).

b) The provisions of subparagraph a) of paragraph 3 shall not apply to income or capital where the United States applies the provisions of the Convention to exempt such income or capital from tax, or applies paragraphs 2 or 3 of Article 10 (Dividends) to such income, or may under the provisions of the Convention tax such income or capital but is prevented from doing so under its laws.

c) The provisions of subparagraph b) and not the provisions of subparagraph a) of paragraph 3 shall apply to items of income or capital of which the Federal Republic of Germany has, after due consultation, notified the United States through diplomatic channels. In such a case, the provisions of subparagraph b) shall apply for any taxable year following the year of such notification.

5. Where a United States citizen is a resident of the Federal Republic of Germany:

a) With respect to items of income not excluded from the basis of German tax under paragraph 3 that are exempt from United States tax or that are subject to a reduced rate of United States tax when derived by a resident of the Federal Republic of Germany who is not a United States citizen, the Federal Republic of Germany shall allow as a credit against German tax, subject to the provisions of German tax law regarding credit for foreign tax, only the tax paid, if any, that the United States may impose under the provisions of this Convention, other than taxes that may be imposed solely by reason of citizenship under paragraph 4 of Article 1 (General Scope);

b) For purposes of computing United States tax, the United States shall allow as a credit against United States tax the income tax paid to the Federal Republic of Germany after the credit referred to in subparagraph a); the credit so allowed shall not reduce that portion of the United States tax that is creditable against the German tax in accordance with subparagraph a); and

c) For the exclusive purpose of relieving double taxation in the United States under subparagraph b), items of income referred to in subparagraph a) shall be deemed to arise in the Federal Republic of Germany to the extent necessary to avoid double taxation of such income under subparagraph b)."

ARTICLE XIII

Paragraph 5 of Article 25 (Mutual Agreement Procedure) of the Convention shall be deleted and replaced with the following paragraph:

"5. Where, pursuant to a mutual agreement procedure under this Article, the competent authorities have endeavored but are unable to reach a complete agreement in a case, the case shall be resolved through arbitration conducted in the manner prescribed by, and subject to, the requirements of paragraph 6 and any rules or procedures agreed upon by the Contracting States, if:

a) tax returns have been filed with at least one of the Contracting States with respect to the taxable years at issue in the case;

b) the case

aa) is a case that

A) involves the application of one or more Articles that the Contracting States have agreed shall be the subject of arbitration, and

B) is not a particular case that the competent authorities agree, before the date on which arbitration proceedings would otherwise have begun, is not suitable for determination by arbitration, or

bb) is a particular case that the competent authorities agree is suitable for determination by arbitration; and

c) all concerned persons agree according to the provisions of subparagraph d) of paragraph 6.

6. For the purposes of paragraph 5 and this paragraph, the following rules and definitions shall apply:

a) The term "concerned person" means the presenter of a case to a competent authority for consideration under this Article and all other persons, if any, whose tax liability to either Contracting State may be directly affected by a mutual agreement arising from that consideration;

b) The "commencement date" for a case is the earliest date on which the information necessary to undertake substantive consideration for a mutual agreement has been received by both competent authorities;

c) Arbitration proceedings in a case shall begin on the later of:

aa) Two years after the commencement date of that case, unless both competent authorities have previously agreed to a different date, and

bb) The earliest date upon which the agreement required by subparagraph d) has been received by both competent authorities;

d) The concerned person(s), and their authorized representatives or agents, must agree prior to the beginning of arbitration proceedings not to disclose to any other person any information received during the course of the arbitration proceeding from either Contracting State or the arbitration board, other than the determination of such board;

e) Unless any concerned person does not accept the determination of an arbitration board, the determination shall constitute a resolution by mutual agreement under this Article and shall be binding on both Contracting States with respect to that case; and

f) For purposes of an arbitration proceeding under paragraph 5 and this paragraph, the members of the arbitration board and their staffs shall be considered "persons or authorities" to whom information may be disclosed under Article 26 (Exchange of Information and Administrative Assistance) of the Convention."

ARTICLE XIV

Article 28 (Limitation on Benefits) of the Convention is deleted and the following Article substituted:

"Article 28
Limitation on Benefits

1. Except as otherwise provided in this Article, a resident of one of the Contracting States that derives income from the other Contracting State shall be entitled, in that other Contracting State, to all the benefits of this Convention otherwise accorded to residents of a Contracting State only if such resident is a "qualified person" as defined in paragraph 2 of this Article and satisfies any other conditions specified in the Convention for the obtaining of such benefits.

2. A resident of one of the Contracting States is a qualified person for a taxable year only if such resident is either:

a) an individual;

b) a Contracting State, political subdivision or local authority thereof;

c) a company, if

aa) its principal class of shares (and any disproportionate class of shares) is regularly traded on one or more recognized stock exchanges, and either

A) its principal class of shares is primarily traded on a recognized stock exchange located in the Contracting State of which the company is a resident; or

B) the company's primary place of management and control is in the Contracting State of which it is a resident; or

bb) shares representing at least 50 percent of the aggregate voting power and value (and at least 50 percent of any disproportionate class of shares) of the company are owned directly or indirectly by five or fewer companies entitled to benefits under clause aa) of this subparagraph, provided that, in the case of indirect ownership, each intermediate owner is a resident of either Contracting State;

d) an entity organized under the laws of one of the Contracting States and established and maintained in that Contracting State exclusively for a religious, charitable, educational, scientific, or other similar purpose;

e) an entity organized under the laws of one of the Contracting States and established and maintained in that Contracting State to provide, pursuant to a plan, pensions or other similar benefits to employed and self-employed persons, provided that:

aa) more than 50 percent of the entity's beneficiaries, members or participants are individuals resident in either Contracting State; or

bb) the organization sponsoring such person is entitled to the benefits of the Convention pursuant to this paragraph;

f) a person other than an individual, if:

aa) on at least half the days of the taxable year at least 50 percent of each class of shares or other beneficial interests in the person is owned, directly or indirectly, by residents of that Contracting State that are entitled to the benefits of this Convention under subparagraph a), subparagraph b), clause aa) of subparagraph c), subparagraph d) or subparagraph e) of this paragraph, provided that, in the case of indirect ownership, each intermediate owner is a resident of that Contracting State; and

bb) less than 50 percent of the person's gross income for the taxable year is paid or accrued, directly or indirectly, to persons who are not residents of either Contracting State entitled to the benefits of this Convention under subparagraph a), subparagraph b), clause aa) of subparagraph c), subparagraph d) or subparagraph e) of this paragraph in the form of payments that are deductible for purposes of the taxes covered by this Convention in the person's State of residence.

3. Notwithstanding that a company that is a resident of a Contracting State may not be a qualified person, it shall be entitled to all the benefits of this Convention otherwise accorded to residents of a Contracting State with respect to an item of income if it satisfies any other specified conditions for the obtaining of such benefits and:

a) shares representing at least 95 percent of the aggregate voting power and value (and at least 50 percent of any disproportionate class of shares) of the company are owned, directly or indirectly, by seven or fewer persons who are equivalent beneficiaries; and

b) less than 50 percent of the company's gross income for the taxable year in which the item of income arises is paid or accrued, directly or indirectly, to persons who are not equivalent beneficiaries, in the form of payments that are deductible for the purposes of the taxes covered by this Convention in the Contracting State of which the company is a resident.

4.

a) Notwithstanding that a resident of a Contracting State may not be a qualified person, it shall be entitled to all the benefits of this Convention otherwise accorded to residents of a Contracting State with respect to an item of income derived from the other Contracting State, if the resident is engaged in the active conduct of a trade or business in the first-mentioned Contracting State (other than the activities of making or managing investments for the resident's own account, unless these activities are banking, insurance or securities dealing carried on by a bank, insurance company or registered securities dealer), the income derived from the other Contracting State is derived in connection with, or is incidental to, that trade or business and that resident satisfies any other specified conditions for the obtaining of such benefits.

b) If a resident of one of the Contracting States or any of its associated enterprises carries on a trade or business activity in the other Contracting State which gives rise to an item of income, subparagraph a) of this paragraph shall apply to such item only if the trade or business activity in the first-mentioned Contracting State is substantial in relation to the trade or business activity in the other Contracting State.

c) In determining whether a person is engaged in the active conduct of a trade or business in a Contracting State under subparagraph a) of this paragraph, activities conducted by persons connected to such person shall be deemed to be conducted by such person. A person shall be connected to another if one possesses at least 50 percent of the beneficial interest in the other (or, in the case of a company, shares representing at least 50 percent of the aggregate voting power and value of the company or of the beneficial equity interest in the company) or another person possesses, directly or indirectly, at least 50 percent of the beneficial interest (or, in the case of a company, shares representing at least 50 percent of the aggregate voting power and value of the company or of the beneficial equity interest in the company) in each person. In any case, a person shall be considered to be connected to another if, on the basis of all the facts and circumstances, one has control of the other or both are under the control of the same person or persons.

5. Notwithstanding the preceding provisions of this Article, where an enterprise of a Contracting State derives income from the other Contracting State, and that income is attributable to a permanent establishment which that enterprise has in a third jurisdiction, the tax benefits that would otherwise apply under the other provisions of the Convention will not apply to that income if the combined tax that is actually paid with respect to such income in the first-mentioned Contracting State and in the third jurisdiction is less than 60 percent of the tax that would have been payable in the first-mentioned State if the income were earned in that Contracting State by the enterprise and were not attributable to the permanent establishment in the third jurisdiction. Any dividends, interest or royalties to which the provisions of this paragraph apply shall be subject to tax at a rate that shall not exceed 15 percent of the gross

amount thereof. Any other income to which the provisions of this paragraph apply will be subject to tax under the provisions of the domestic law of the other Contracting State, notwithstanding any other provision of the Convention. The provisions of this paragraph shall not apply if:

a) in the case of royalties, the royalties are received as compensation for the use of, or the right to use, intangible property produced or developed by the permanent establishment itself; or

b) in the case of any other income, the income derived from the other Contracting State is derived in connection with, or is incidental to, the active conduct of a trade or business carried on by the permanent establishment in the third jurisdiction (other than the business of making, managing or simply holding investments for the person's own account, unless these activities are banking or securities activities carried on by a bank or registered securities dealer).

6. Notwithstanding the preceding provisions of this Article, a German Investment Fund or German *Investmentaktiengesellschaft* (collectively referred to as *Investmentvermögen*) may only be granted the benefits of this Convention if at least 90 percent of the shares or other beneficial interests in the German *Investmentvermögen* are owned, directly or indirectly, by residents of the Federal Republic of Germany that are entitled to the benefits of this Convention under subparagraph a), subparagraph b), clause aa) of subparagraph c), subparagraph d) or subparagraph e) of paragraph 2 of this Article or by persons that are equivalent beneficiaries with respect to the income derived by the German *Investmentvermögen* for which benefits are being claimed. For the purposes of this paragraph, beneficiaries of entities that are subject to numbers 3 and 5 of paragraph 1 of section 1 of the German Corporate Tax Act shall be treated as indirectly owning shares of a German Investmentvermögen. Foundations referred to in number 5 of paragraph 1 of section 1 of the German Corporate Tax Act, other than those referred to in subparagraph d) of paragraph 2 of this Article, shall not be taken into account in determining whether a German Investmentvermögen meets the 90 percent minimum ownership threshold.

7. A person resident of one of the Contracting States, who is not entitled to some or all of the benefits of this Convention because of the foregoing paragraphs, may, nevertheless, be granted benefits of this Convention if the competent authority of the Contracting State in which the income in question arises so determines. In making such determination, the competent authority shall take into account as its guidelines whether the establishment, acquisition or maintenance of such person or the conduct of its operations has or had as one of its principal purposes the obtaining of benefits under this Convention. The competent authority of the Contracting State in which the income arises will consult with the competent authority of the other Contracting State before denying the benefits of the Convention under this paragraph.

8. For the purposes of this Article the following rules and definitions shall apply:

a) the term "recognized stock exchange" means:

aa) the NASDAQ System and any stock exchange registered with the U.S. Securities and Exchange Commission as a national securities exchange under the *U.S. Securities Exchange Act of 1934*;

bb) any German stock exchange on which registered dealings in shares take place;

cc) any other stock exchange which the competent authorities agree to recognize for the purposes of this Article;

b)

aa) the term "principal class of shares" means the ordinary or common shares of the company, provided that such class of shares represents the majority of the voting power and value of the company. If no single class of ordinary or common shares represents the majority of the aggregate voting power and value of the company, the "principal class of shares" is that class or those classes that in the aggregate represent a majority of the aggregate voting power and value of the company;

bb) the term "shares" shall include depository receipts thereof or trust certificates thereof;

c) the term "disproportionate class of shares" means any class of shares of a company resident in one of the Contracting States that entitles the shareholder to disproportionately higher participation, through dividends, redemption payments or otherwise, in the earnings generated in the other Contracting State by particular assets or activities of the company;

d) the company's primary place of management and control will be in the Contracting State of which it is a resident only if executive officers and senior management employees exercise day-to-day responsibility for more of the strategic, financial and operational policy decision making for the company (including its direct and indirect subsidiaries) in that Contracting State than in any other state and the staffs conduct more of the day-to-day activities necessary for preparing and making those decisions in that Contracting State than in any other state.

e) an equivalent beneficiary is a resident of a member state of the European Union or of a European Economic Area state or of a party to the North American Free Trade Agreement but only if that resident:

aa)

A) would be entitled to all the benefits of a comprehensive convention for the avoidance of double taxation between any member state of the European Union or a European Economic Area state or any party to the North American Free Trade Agreement and the State from which the benefits of this Convention are claimed under provisions analogous to subparagraph a), subparagraph b), clause aa) of subparagraph c), subparagraph d) or subparagraph e) of paragraph 2 of this Article provided that if such convention does not contain a comprehensive limitation on benefits article, the person would be a qualified person under subparagraph a), subparagraph b), clause aa) of subparagraph c), subparagraph d) or subparagraph e) of paragraph 2 of this Article if such person were a resident of one of the States under Article 4 (Resident) of this Convention; and

B) with respect to insurance premiums and to income referred to in Article 10 (Dividends), 11 (Interest) or 12 (Royalties) of this Convention, would be entitled under such convention to a rate of tax with respect to the particular class of income for which benefits are being claimed under this Convention that is at least as low as the rate applicable under this Convention; or

bb) is a resident of a Contracting State that is a qualified person by reason of subparagraph a), subparagraph b), clause aa) of subparagraph c), subparagraph d) or subparagraph e) of paragraph 2 of this Article.

For the purposes of applying paragraph 3 of Article 10 (Dividends) in order to determine whether a person, owning shares, directly or indirectly, in the company claiming the benefits of this Convention, is an equivalent beneficiary, such person shall be deemed to hold the same voting power in the company paying the dividend as the company claiming the benefits holds in such company;

f) with respect to dividends, interest or royalties arising in the Federal Republic of Germany and beneficially owned by a company that is a resident of the United States, a company that is a resident of a member state of the European Union will be treated as satisfying the requirements of clause aa) B) of subparagraph e) for purposes of determining whether such United States resident is entitled to benefits under this paragraph if a payment of dividends, interest or royalties arising in the Federal Republic of Germany and paid directly to such resident of a member state of the European Union would have been exempt from tax pursuant to any directive of the European Union, notwithstanding that the income tax convention between the Federal Republic of Germany and that other member state of the European Union would provide for a higher rate of tax with respect to such payment than the rate of tax applicable to such United States company under Article 10 (Dividends), 11 (Interest), or 12 (Royalties) of this Convention."

ARTICLE XV

Paragraph 1 of Article 17 (Artistes and Athletes) of the Convention and paragraph 4 and 5 of Article 20 (Visiting Professors and Teachers; Students and Trainees) of the Convention are modified by deleting the words "Deutsche Mark" where they appear and replacing them with the word "Euro".

ARTICLE XVI

The Protocol to the Convention is amended by deleting paragraphs 1 through 28 and replacing them with the following paragraphs:

"1. *WITH REFERENCE TO SUBPARAGRAPH b) OF PARAGRAPH 4 OF ARTICLE 1 (GENERAL SCOPE)*

The term "long-term resident" shall mean any individual who is a lawful permanent resident of the United States in eight or more taxable years during the preceding 15 taxable years. In determining whether the threshold in the preceding sentence is met, an individual shall not be treated as a lawful permanent resident of the United States for any taxable year in which such individual is treated as a resident of a country other than the United States under the provisions of a tax treaty of the United States and the individual does not waive the benefits of such treaty provided by the United States to a resident of the other country. Consequently, if during each of the 15 taxable years preceding the loss of his status as a lawful permanent resident an individual was a resident of the Federal Republic of Germany (as determined under Article 4 (Residence)) and claimed the benefits provided by the United States to a resident of the Federal Republic of Germany, the individual shall not be considered a long-term resident.

2. *WITH REFERENCE TO PARAGRAPH 1 OF ARTICLE 4 (RESIDENCE)*

a) The Federal Republic of Germany shall treat a United States citizen or an alien lawfully admitted for permanent residence (a "green card" holder) as a resident of the United States only if such person has a substantial presence, permanent home, or habitual abode in the United States.

b) It is understood that a German Investment Fund and a German *Investmentaktiengesellschaft* (collectively referred to as *Investmentvermögen*) to which the provisions of the Investment Act (*Investmentgesetz*) apply are residents of the Federal Republic of Germany and that a U.S. Regulated Investment Company (RIC) and a U.S. Real Estate Investment Trust (REIT) are residents of the United States.

3. *WITH REFERENCE TO ARTICLE 5 (PERMANENT ESTABLISHMENT)*

A resident of a Contracting State that performs in the other Contracting State concerts, theatrical or artistic performances, or similar shows and revues and that may not be taxed in that other State under the provisions of Article 17 (Artistes and Athletes) shall not be deemed to have a permanent establishment in that State if its presence does not exceed in the aggregate 183 days in the calendar year concerned.

4. *WITH REFERENCE TO ARTICLE 7 (BUSINESS PROFITS)*

It is understood that the business profits to be attributed to a permanent establishment shall include only the profits derived from the assets used, risks assumed, and activities performed by the permanent establishment. The principles of the OECD Transfer Pricing Guidelines will apply for purposes of determining the profits attributable to a permanent establishment, taking into account the different economic and legal circumstances of a single entity. Accordingly, any of the methods described therein as acceptable methods for determining an arm's-length result may be used to determine the income of a permanent establishment so long as those methods are applied in accordance with the Guidelines. In particular, in determining the amount of attributable profits, the permanent establishment shall be treated as having the same amount of capital that it would need to support its activities if it were a distinct and separate enterprise engaged in the same or similar activities. With respect to financial institutions other than insurance companies, a Contracting State may determine the amount of capital to be attributed to a permanent establishment by allocating the institution's total equity between its various offices on the basis of the proportion of the financial institution's risk-weighted assets attributable to each of them. A financial institution may determine the amount of the capital attributed to its permanent establishment using its risk weighted assets only if it risk weights its assets in the ordinary course of its business.

5. *WITH REFERENCE TO PARAGRAPHS 1 AND 2 OF ARTICLE 7 (BUSINESS PROFITS) AND PARAGRAPH 3 OF ARTICLE 13 (GAINS)*

For the implementation of paragraphs 1 and 2 of Article 7 and paragraph 3 of Article 13 any income, gain, or expense attributable to a permanent establishment is taxable or deductible in the Contracting State where such permanent establishment is situated even if the payments are deferred until such permanent establishment ceases to exist. Nothing in the preceding sentence shall prevent the application to such deferred payments of rules regarding the accrual of income and expenses according to the domestic law of a Contracting State.

6. *WITH REFERENCE TO ARTICLE 7 (BUSINESS PROFITS) AND ARTICLE 13 (GAINS)*

Gains from the alienation of movable property that at any time formed part of the business property of a permanent establishment that a resident of one Contracting State has or had in the other Contracting State may be taxed by that other State only to the extent of the gain that accrued during that time. Notwithstanding any provision of Article 7 or Article 13, such tax may be imposed on such gains at the time when realized and recognized under the laws of that other State, if it is within ten years of the date on which the property ceases to be part of the business property of the permanent establishment (or such shorter period provided by the laws of either Contracting State).

7. *WITH REFERENCE TO ARTICLE 9 (ASSOCIATED ENTERPRISES)*

Either State may apply the rules of its national law that permit the distribution, apportionment, or allocation of income, deductions, credits, or allowances between related persons with a view to apportioning or allocating such deductions, credits, or allowances in accordance with the general principles of paragraph 1 of Article 9. Article 9 shall not be construed to limit either Contracting State in allocating income between persons that are related other than by direct or indirect participation within the meaning of paragraph 1, such as by commercial or contractual relationships resulting in controlling influence, so long as such allocation is otherwise in accordance with the general principles of paragraph 1 of Article 9.

8. *WITH REFERENCE TO PARAGRAPH 3 OF ARTICLE 10 (DIVIDENDS)*

a) If the Federal Republic of Germany introduces a taxation regime that exempts from taxation Real Estate Investment Companies, subparagraph b) of paragraph 3 of Article 10 shall not apply.

b) It is understood that in the case of the Federal Republic of Germany, subparagraph b of paragraph 3 of Article 10 applies to the person treated as the owner of the assets of the pension fund under section 39 of the Fiscal Code, provided the dividends may only be used for providing retirement benefits through such fund.

9. *WITH REFERENCE TO PARAGRAPH 9 OF ARTICLE 10 (DIVIDENDS)*

The general principle of the "dividend equivalent amount", as used in the United States law, is to approximate that portion of the income mentioned in paragraph 9 that is comparable to the amount that would be distributed as a dividend if such income were earned by a locally incorporated subsidiary.

10. *WITH REFERENCE TO ARTICLE 11 (INTEREST)*

The excess of the amount of interest deductible by a United States permanent establishment of a German company over the interest actually paid by such permanent establishment shall be treated as interest derived and beneficially owned by a resident of the Federal Republic of Germany.

11. *WITH REFERENCE TO ARTICLE 12 (ROYALTIES)*

Where an artiste resident in one Contracting State records a performance in the other Contracting State, has a copyrightable interest in the recording, and receives consideration for the right to use the recording based on the sale or public playing of such recording, then such consideration shall be governed by this Article.

12. *WITH REFERENCE TO PARAGRAPH 2 OF ARTICLE 13 (GAINS)*

The term "immovable property situated in the other Contracting State", as described in this paragraph, when the United States is that other Contracting State includes a United States real property interest.

13. *WITH REFERENCE TO PARAGRAPH 3 OF ARTICLE 13 (GAINS)*

Nothing in this Article shall prevent gains from the alienation by a resident of a Contracting State of an interest in a partnership, trust, or estate that has a permanent establishment situated in the other Contracting State from being treated as gain under paragraph 3.

14. *WITH REFERENCE TO PARAGRAPH 1 OF ARTICLE 17 (ARTISTES AND ATHLETES)*

If an artiste or athlete is not subject to tax in the Federal Republic of Germany under the provisions of paragraph 1 of Article 17, tax may be withheld at source in the Federal Republic of Germany, and shall be refunded to the taxpayer only upon application at the end of the calendar year concerned. Paragraph 6 of Article 29 (Refund of Withholding Tax) shall remain unaffected.

15. *WITH REFERENCE TO PARAGRAPH 3 OF ARTICLE 18 (PENSIONS, ANNUITIES, ALIMONY, CHILD SUPPORT, AND SOCIAL SECURITY)*

In determining the taxable income of an individual who is a resident of the Federal Republic of Germany there shall be allowed as a deduction in respect of alimony or similar allowances paid to an individual who is a resident of the United States the amount that would be allowed as a deduction if that last-mentioned individual were subject to unlimited tax liability in the Federal Republic of Germany.

16. *WITH REFERENCE TO PARAGRAPH 4 OF ARTICLE 18A (PENSION PLANS)*

a) For purposes of paragraph 4 of Article 18A, the term "pension plan" shall include the following and any identical or substantially similar plans established pursuant to legislation enacted after the date of signature of this Protocol:

> aa) In the case of the United States, qualified plans under section 401(a) of the Internal Revenue Code, individual retirement plans (including individual retirement plans that are part of a simplified employee pension plan that satisfies section 408(k), individual retirement accounts, individual retirement annuities, and section 408(p) accounts, and Roth IRAs under Section 408A), section 403(a) qualified annuity plans, section 403(b) plans, and section 457(b) governmental plans.
>
> bb) In the case of the Federal Republic of Germany, arrangements under section 1 of the German law on employment-related pensions (*Betriebsrentengesetz*).

b) For purposes of subparagraph b) of paragraph 3 and subparagraph d) of paragraph 5 of Article 18A, it is understood that:

> aa) The Federal Republic of Germany recognizes qualified plans specifically listed in clause aa) of subparagraph a), other than Roth IRAs, as arrangements that correspond to pension plans referred to under section 1 of the German law on employment-related pensions (*Betriebsrentengesetz*). The Federal Republic of Germany shall provide the corresponding relief under section 3 No. 63 of the *Income Tax Act*; and
>
> bb) The United States recognizes arrangements under section 1 of the German law on employment-related pensions (*Betriebsrentengesetz*) as arrangements that correspond to pension plans referred to in clause aa) of subparagraph a) above.

17. *WITH REFERENCE TO PARAGRAPH 2 OF ARTICLE 20 (VISITING PROFESSORS AND TEACHERS; STUDENTS AND TRAINEES).*

Payments that are made out of public funds of a Contracting State or by a scholarship organization endowed with such funds shall be considered to arise in full from sources outside the other Contracting State. The preceding sentence shall also apply when such payments are made under programs funded jointly by organizations of both Contracting States if more than 50 percent of these funds are provided out of public funds of the first-mentioned State or by a scholarship organization endowed with such funds. The competent authorities shall consult with each other to identify those scholarship programs whose payments shall be treated as arising from sources outside a Contracting State under the foregoing rules.

18. *WITH REFERENCE TO PARAGRAPH 2 OF ARTICLE 21 (OTHER INCOME)*

Where the recipient and the payor of a dividend are both residents of the Federal Republic of Germany and the dividend is attributed to a permanent establishment that the recipient of the dividend has in the United States, the Federal Republic of Germany may tax such a dividend at the rates provided for in paragraphs 2 and 3 of Article 10 (Dividends). The United States shall give a credit for such tax according to the provisions of Article 23 (Relief from Double Taxation).

19. *WITH REFERENCE TO PARAGRAPH 1 OF ARTICLE 23 (RELIEF FROM DOUBLE TAXATION)*

For purposes of paragraph 1 of Article 23, the "general principle hereof" means the avoidance of double taxation by allowing a credit for taxes imposed on items of income arising in the Federal Republic of Germany, as determined under the applicable United States source rules, as modified by the Convention. While the details and limitations of the credit pursuant to this paragraph may change as provisions of United States law change, any such changes must preserve a credit for German taxes imposed with respect to items of income that the Federal Republic of Germany may tax pursuant to the Convention.

20. *WITH REFERENCE TO PARAGRAPH 1 OF ARTICLE 24 (NON-DISCRIMINATION)*

Paragraph 1 of Article 24 does not obligate the United States to subject an individual who is a German national not resident in the United States to the same taxing regime as that applied to a citizen of the United States not resident in the United States.

21. *WITH REFERENCE TO PARAGRAPH 4 OF ARTICLE 24 (NON-DISCRIMINATION)*

It is understood that paragraph 4 of Article 24 shall not be construed as obligating a Contracting State to permit cross-border consolidation of income or similar benefits between enterprises.

22. *WITH REFERENCE TO PARAGRAPHS 5 AND 6 OF ARTICLE 25 (MUTUAL AGREEMENT PROCEDURE)*

In respect of any case where the competent authorities have endeavored but are unable to reach an agreement under Article 25 regarding the application of one or more of the following Articles of the Convention: 4 (Residence) (but only insofar as it relates to the residence of a natural person), 5 (Permanent Establishment), 7 (Business Profits), 9 (Associated Enterprises), 12 (Royalties), binding arbitration shall be used to determine such application, unless the competent authorities agree that the particular case is not suitable for determination by arbitration. In addition, the competent authorities may, on an ad hoc basis, agree that binding arbitration shall be used in respect of any other matter to which Article 25 applies. If an arbitration proceeding (the Proceeding) under paragraph 5 of Article 25 commences, the following rules and procedures will apply:

a) The Proceeding will be conducted in the manner prescribed by, and subject to the requirements of, paragraphs 5 and 6 of Article 25 and these rules and procedures, as modified or supplemented by any other rules and procedures agreed upon by the competent authorities pursuant to subparagraph q) below.

b) The determination reached by an arbitration board in the Proceeding shall be limited to a determination regarding the amount of income, expense or tax reportable to the Contracting States.

c) Notwithstanding the initiation of the Proceeding, the competent authorities may reach a mutual agreement to resolve a case and terminate the Proceeding. Correspondingly, a concerned person may withdraw a request for the competent authorities to engage in the Mutual Agreement Procedure (and thereby terminate the Proceeding) at any time.

d) The requirements of subparagraph d) of paragraph 6 of Article 25 will be met when the competent authorities have each received from each concerned person a statement agreeing that the concerned person and each person acting on the concerned person's behalf will not disclose to any other person any information received during the course of the Proceeding from either Contracting State or the Arbitration Board, other than the determination of the Proceeding. A concerned person that has the legal authority to bind any other concerned person(s) on this matter may do so in a comprehensive statement.

e) Each Contracting State will have 60 days from the date on which the Proceeding begins to send a written communication to the other Contracting State appointing one member of the arbitration board. Within 60 days of the date on which the second such communication is sent, the two members appointed by the Contracting States will appoint a third member, who will serve as Chair of the board. If either Contracting State fails to appoint a member, or if the members appointed by the Contracting States fail to agree upon the third member in the manner prescribed by this paragraph, the remaining member(s) will be appointed by the highest-ranking member of the Secretariat at the Centre for Tax Policy and Administration of the Organisation for Economic Co-operation and Development (OECD) who is not a citizen of either Contracting State, by written notice to both Contracting States within 60 days of the date of such failure. The competent authorities will develop a non-exclusive list of individuals with familiarity in international tax matters who may potentially serve as the Chair of the board. In any case, the Chair shall not be a citizen of either Contracting State.

f) The arbitration board may adopt any procedures necessary for the conduct of its business, provided that the procedures are not inconsistent with any provision of Article 25 or the Protocol to the Convention.

g) Each of the Contracting States will be permitted to submit, within 90 days of the appointment of the Chair of the arbitration board, a Proposed Resolution describing the proposed disposition of the specific monetary amounts of income, expense or taxation at issue in the case, and a supporting Position Paper, for consideration by the arbitration board. Copies of the Proposed Resolution and supporting Position Paper shall be provided by the board to the other Contracting State on the date on which the later of the submissions is submitted to the board. In the event that only one Contracting State submits a Proposed Resolution within the allotted time, then that Proposed Resolution shall be deemed to be the determination of the board in that case and the Proceeding shall be terminated. Each of the Contracting States may, if it so desires, submit a Reply Submission to the board within 180 days of the appointment of its Chair, to address any points raised by the Proposed Resolution or Position Paper submitted by the other Contracting State. Additional information may be submitted to the arbitration board only at its request, and copies of the board's request and the Contracting State's response shall be provided to the other Contracting State on the date on which the request or the response is submitted. Except for logistical matters such as those identified in subparagraphs 1), n) and o) below, all communications from the Contracting States to the arbitration board, and vice versa, shall take place only through written communications between the designated competent authorities and the Chair of the board.

h) The arbitration board will deliver a determination in writing to the Contracting States within six months of the appointment of its Chair. The board will adopt as its determination one of the Proposed Resolutions submitted by the Contracting States.

i) In making its determination, the arbitration board will apply, as necessary and in descending order of priority:

aa) the provisions of the Convention;

bb) any agreed commentaries or explanations of the Contracting States concerning the Convention;

cc) the laws of the Contracting States to the extent they are not inconsistent with each other; and

dd) any OECD Commentary, Guidelines or Reports regarding relevant analogous portions of the OECD Model Tax Convention.

j) The determination of the arbitration board in a particular case shall be binding on the Contracting States. The determination of the board will not state a rationale. It will have no precedential value.

k) As provided in subparagraph e) of paragraph 6 of Article 25, the determination of an arbitration board shall constitute a resolution by mutual agreement under Article 25. Each concerned person must, within 30 days of receiving the determination of the board from the competent authority to which the case was first presented, advise that competent authority whether that concerned person accepts the determination of the board. If any concerned person fails to so advise the relevant competent authority within this time frame, the determination of the board will be considered not to have been accepted in that case. Where the determination of the board is not accepted, the case may not subsequently be the subject of a Proceeding.

l) Any meeting(s) of the arbitration board shall be in facilities provided by the Contracting State whose competent authority initiated the mutual agreement proceedings in the case.

m) The treatment of any associated interest or penalties will be determined by applicable domestic law of the Contracting State(s) concerned.

n) No information relating to the Proceeding (including the board's determination) may be disclosed by the members of the arbitration board or their staffs or by either competent authority, except as permitted by the Convention and the domestic laws of the Contracting States. In addition, all material prepared in the course of, or relating to, the Proceeding shall be considered to be information exchanged between the Contracting States. All members of the arbitration board and their staffs must agree in statements sent to each of the Contracting States in confirmation of their appointment to the arbitration board to abide by and be subject to the confidentiality and nondisclosure provisions of Article 26 (Exchange of Information and Administrative Assistance) of the Convention and the applicable domestic laws of the Contracting States. In the event those provisions conflict, the most restrictive condition shall apply.

o) The fees and expenses will be borne equally by the Contracting States. In general, the fees of members of the arbitration board will be set at the fixed amount of $2,000 (two thousand United States dollars) per day or the equivalent amount in euro, subject to modification by the competent authorities. In general, the expenses of members of the arbitration board will be set in accordance with the International Centre for Settlement of Investment Disputes (ICSID) Schedule of Fees for arbitrators (as in effect on the date on which the arbitration proceedings begin), subject to modification by the competent authorities. Any fees for language translation will also be borne equally by the Contracting States. Meeting facilities, related resources, financial management, other logistical support, and general administrative coordination of the Proceeding will be provided, at its own cost, by the Contracting State whose competent authority initiated the mutual agreement proceedings in the case. Any other costs shall be borne by the Contracting State that incurs them.

p) For purposes of paragraphs 5 and 6 of Article 25 and this paragraph, each competent authority will confirm in writing to the other competent authority and to the concerned person(s) the date of its receipt of the information necessary to undertake substantive consideration for a mutual agreement. Such information will be:

aa) in the United States, the information required to be submitted to the United States competent authority under Revenue Procedure 2002–52, section 4.05 (or any applicable successor provisions) and, for cases initially submitted as a request for an Advance Pricing Agreement, the information required to be submitted to the Internal Revenue Service under Revenue Procedure 2006–9, section 4 (or any applicable successor provisions), and

bb) in the Federal Republic of Germany, the information required to be submitted to the competent authority in the Federal Republic of Germany under the circular of July 1, 1997,—IV C 5–S 1300–89/96—, published by the Ministry of Finance (or any applicable successor circular).

However, this information shall not be considered received until both competent authorities have received copies of all materials submitted to either Contracting State by the concerned person(s) in connection with the mutual agreement procedure.

q) The competent authorities of the Contracting States may modify or supplement the above rules and procedures as necessary to more effectively implement the intent of paragraph 5 of Article 25 to eliminate double taxation.

23. *WITH REFERENCE TO ARTICLE 26 (EXCHANGE OF INFORMATION AND ADMINISTRATIVE ASSISTANCE)*

a) It is understood that the powers of each Contracting State's competent authorities to obtain information include powers to obtain information held by financial institutions, nominees, or persons acting in an agency or fiduciary capacity, and information relating to the ownership of legal persons, and that each Contracting State's competent authority is able to exchange such information in accordance with Article 26.

b) The Federal Republic of Germany shall under this Article exchange information with or without request to the extent provided for in the law of 19 December 1985 (*EG-Amtshilfe-Gesetz*) as amended from time to time without changing the general principles thereof.

24. *WITH REFERENCE TO PARAGRAPH 6 OF ARTICLE 28 (LIMITATION ON BENEFITS)*

The competent authorities of the Contracting States shall establish procedures for determining indirect ownership for purposes of determining whether the 90 percent ownership threshold contained in paragraph 6 of Article 28 is satisfied. It is anticipated that these procedures may include the use of statistically valid sampling techniques."

ARTICLE XVII

1. This Protocol shall be subject to ratification and the instruments of ratification shall be exchanged as soon as possible.

2. This Protocol shall enter into force on the date on which the instruments of ratification are exchanged and shall have effect in both Contracting States:

a) in respect of taxes withheld at source, for amounts paid or credited on or after the first day of January of the year in which this Protocol enters into force;

b) in respect of other taxes on income for any taxable year beginning on or after the first day of January next following the date this Protocol enters into force; and

c) in respect of taxes on capital for the taxes levied on items of capital owned on or after the first day of January next following the date this Protocol enters into force.

3. Notwithstanding the provisions of paragraph 2,

a) the provisions of paragraphs 2 and 3 of Article 1 (General Scope) shall have effect after the entry into force of this Protocol and shall apply in respect of any tax claim irrespective of whether such tax claim pre-dates the entry into force of this Protocol or the effective date of any of its provisions; and

b) the amendments made by Article X of this Protocol shall not have effect with respect to individuals who, at the time of the signing of the Convention, were employed by the United States, a political subdivision or local authority thereof.

4. Article XIII of this Protocol shall have effect with respect to

a) cases that are under consideration by the competent authorities as of the date on which this Protocol enters into force, and

b) cases that come under such consideration after that time, and the commencement date for a case described in subparagraph a) of this paragraph shall be the date on which this Protocol enters into force.

5. Notwithstanding paragraph 2, where any person entitled to benefits under the Convention as unmodified by this Protocol would have been entitled to greater benefits thereunder than under the Convention as modified by this Protocol, the Convention as unmodified shall, at the election of such person, continue to have effect in its entirety with respect to such person for a twelve-month period from the date on which the provisions of this Protocol would have effect under paragraph 2 of this Article.

6. The Notes exchanged on 29 August 1989 and referring to paragraph 5 of Article 25 (Mutual Agreement Procedure) and Article 28 (Limitation on Benefits) as well as the German Note of 3 November 1989 referring to paragraph 21 of the Protocol to the Convention shall cease to have effect when the provisions of this Protocol take effect in accordance with this Article.

Done in duplicate at Berlin on the first day of June, 2006, in the English and German languages, both texts being equally authentic

FOR THE
UNITED STATES OF AMERICA:
[Signature]

FOR THE
FEDERAL REPUBLIC OF GERMANY:
[Signature]
[Signature]

Joint Declaration
by the United States of America and the Federal Republic of Germany
on the Occasion
of the Signing on 1 June 2006
of the Protocol Amending the Convention
Between the United States of America and the Federal Republic of Germany
for the Avoidance of Double Taxation and the Prevention of Fiscal Evasion
with Respect to Taxes on Income and Capital and to Certain Other Taxes
Signed on 29th August 1989

The United States of America and the Federal Republic of Germany on the occasion of the signing on 1 June 2006 of the Protocol Amending the Convention Between the United States of America and the Federal Republic of Germany for the Avoidance of Double Taxation and the Prevention of Fiscal Evasion with Respect to Taxes on Income and Capital and to Certain Other Taxes signed on 29th August 1989 (hereafter "Protocol of 1 June 2006"), and with regard to Article 18 (Pensions, Annuities, Alimony, Child Support, and Social Security) of the Convention as amended by the Protocol of 1 June 2006, in which it is agreed that pensions and other similar remuneration paid in consideration of past employment as well as benefits paid under the social security legislation of a Contracting State shall be taxable only in the Contracting State of which the recipient of that pension or benefits on the basis of the social security legislation is a resident,

Have reached the following understanding:

I

1. The Federal Republic of Germany draws attention to the fact

a) that, effective as of 1 January 2005, legislation introduced on 5 July 2004 (Federal Law Gazette part I page 1427) has fundamentally changed in the Federal Republic of Germany the taxation of retirement income,

b) that these changes combine full taxation of retirement income with extended tax exemption of contributions to pension plans.

2. The Federal Republic of Germany therefore expresses its conviction

a) that, as a result of these legislative changes, Article 18 of the Convention as amended by the Protocol of 1 June 2006 should be further amended to such effect as to also provide for the taxation of retirement income in the Contracting State in which the income arises or in which the contributions to the pension plan were exempt from taxation;

b) that taking into account the successive implementation in the Federal Republic of Germany of the taxation of retirement income, as amended by legislation of 5 July 2004, any further amendment to Article 18 of the Convention of 29 August 1989 as amended by the Protocol of 1 June 2006 should not enter into force before 1 January 2015.

II

The Federal Republic of Germany and the United States of America therefore reaffirm their intentions declared during negotiations on the Protocol of 1 June 2006 to enter into consultations at the appropriate time, but not before 1 January 2013, with a view to further amending Article 18 of the Convention as amended by the Protocol of 1 June 2006 to allow for the taxation of retirement income in the Contracting State in which the income arises based on the following principles:

1. Benefits paid under the social security legislation of a Contracting State may also be taxed by that Contracting State; the tax may not however exceed 15 percent of the gross amount of such payments;

2. Pensions and other similar remuneration paid in consideration of past employment may also be taxed in the Contracting State in which the employment had been exercised for a substantial period of time; the tax may not however exceed 15 percent of the gross amount of such payments.

This Joint Declaration is signed in duplicate, in the English and German languages.

Berlin, 1 June 2006

FOR THE
UNITED STATES OF AMERICA:
[Signature]

FOR THE
FEDERAL REPUBLIC OF GERMANY:
[Signature]
[Signature]

SENATE TREATY DOCUMENT NUMBER: 109-21

GENEVA ACT OF THE HAGUE AGREEMENT CONCERNING THE INTERNATIONAL REGISTRATION OF INDUSTRIAL DESIGNS

ADOPTED AT GENEVA,
JULY 2, 1999
SIGNED BY THE UNITED STATES OF AMERICA,
JULY 6, 1999

CTIA DOCUMENT NUMBER: 10291.004

LETTER OF TRANSMITTAL

The White House, *November 13, 2006.*

To the Senate of the United States:

With a view to receiving the advice and consent of the Senate to ratification, I transmit herewith the Geneva Act of the Hague Agreement Concerning the International Registration of Industrial Designs (the "Agreement"), adopted in Geneva on July 2, 1999, and signed by the United States on July 6, 1999. I also transmit, for the information of the Senate, a report of the Department of State with respect to the Agreement.

This Agreement promotes the ability of U.S. design owners to protect their industrial designs by allowing them to obtain multinational design protection through a single deposit procedure. Under the Agreement, U.S. design owners would be able to file for design registration in any number of the Contracting Parties with a single standardized application in English at either the U.S. Patent and Trademark Office or at the International Bureau of the World Intellectual Property Organization (WIPO). Similarly, renewal of a design registration in each Contracting Party may be made by filing a single request along with payment of the appropriate fees at the International Bureau of WIPO. This Agreement should make access to international protection of industrial designs more readily available to U.S. businesses.

In the event that the Senate provides its consent to ratify the Agreement, the United States would not deposit its instrument of ratification until the necessary implementing legal structure has been established domestically.

I recommend that the Senate give early and favorable consideration to this Agreement and give its advice and consent to its ratification, subject to the declarations described in the accompanying report of the Department of State.

George W. Bush.

LETTER OF SUBMITTAL

Department of State,
Washington, April 14, 2006.

The President,
The White House.

The President: I have the honor hereby to submit to you, with a view to its transmittal to the Senate for advice and consent to ratification, the Geneva Act of the Hague Agreement Concerning the International Registration of Industrial Designs (hereinafter the "Agreement"), adopted at Geneva, July 2, 1999. This treaty was adopted under the auspices of the World Intellectual Property Organization ("WIPO") with the objective of simplifying the process of seeking protection for designs in multiple countries.

The Agreement traces its roots to the Hague Agreement Concerning the International Deposit of Industrial Designs done at The Hague, Netherlands, on November 6, 1925, which entered into force in 1928, and was revised numerous times. For the 42 current member states of the Hague Union, these existing agreements facilitate the obtainment of intellectual property protection for industrial designs by allowing multinational patent protection in a number of countries through a single "international deposit" procedure. However, these Acts did not meet the needs of nations, such as the United States, that review each application individually. This Agreement allows the United States to partake in the benefits of facilitating multinational design protection for applicants while continuing its system of individual review.

The Department of Commerce and the Office of the United States Trade Representative join the Department of State in re-questing that the Geneva Act of the Hague Agreement Concerning the International Registration of Industrial Designs be transmitted to the Senate for its advice and consent to ratification as soon as possible, subject to the declarations described in the enclosed document.

Respectfully submitted.

CONDOLEEZZA RICE.

Enclosure: Key Provisions of the Geneva Act of the Hague Agreement Concerning the International Registration of Industrial Designs.

KEY PROVISIONS OF THE GENEVA ACT OF THE HAGUE AGREEMENT CONCERNING THE INTERNATIONAL REGISTRATION OF INDUSTRIAL DESIGNS

The Operation of the Treaty

The Agreement will permit a U.S. design applicant to file for protection in any of the Contracting Parties, including the United States, by filing a single standardized application in English. Pursuant to Articles 3 and 4(1) of the Agreement, any person who is a national of or is domiciled in the United States may file an international design application with the United States Patent and Trademark Office (USPTO) or directly with the International Bureau (IB) of the World Intellectual Property Organization (WIPO). The filing date of the international design application is the date that the application is received by either the IB or the USPTO (Article 9(1) and Rule 13(3)).

The USPTO must transmit any application to the IB within one month from the date on which the USPTO receives it. If, however, a security clearance is required by law, then the USPTO can notify the Director General of WIPO (Director General) as to this fact, and the USPTO has six months to transmit the application to the IB.

Article 5(1) sets forth the mandatory requirements as to the contents of an international design application. Article 5(2) provides additional mandatory contents as to Contracting Parties that have an intellectual property office that is an Examining Office, such as the USPTO.

The Agreement also provides a basis for rights of priority with regard to international design applications filed under the Agreement. Article 6(1) states that the application may contain a declaration under Article 4 of the Paris Convention for the Protection of Industrial Property (1967) claiming the priority of one or more earlier applications filed in or for any country party to the Paris Convention or any member of the World Trade Organization. Article 6(2) provides that an international design application is deemed, as from its filing date and regardless of its subsequent fate, equivalent to a regular filing within the meaning of Article 4 of the Paris Convention. Thereby, international design applications under the Agreement may serve as a basis for claiming priority in a national or regional application.

Article 7 states that the fees shall include a designation fee for each designated Contracting Party. However, any Contracting Party, such as the United States, whose Office is an Examining Office, may declare that the prescribed designation fees be replaced by an individual designation fee, which may be payable in two parts.

According to Article 10(1) and Rule 15 of the Agreement, the IB will register each design that is the subject of an international design application immediately upon receipt by the IB of the application. The general rule under Article 10(2) is that the date of the international registration will be the filing date of the application, provided it is complete and complies with the mandatory requirements of the Agreement. Pursuant to Article 9(3) and Rule 14, if the application contains any of the following missing parts or irregularities, the date of the international registration is the date on which the correction is received by the IB: (1) the application is not in a prescribed language (English or French); (2) the application lacks any indication that registration under the Agreement is sought; (3) the application is missing indications allowing the identity of the applicant to be established; (4) the application lacks a reproduction, or a specimen, as required; or (5) the application does not contain the designation of at least one Contracting Party. If an irregularity is discovered other than the five listed above, the international registration date is the filing date, provided that the irregularity is corrected within the prescribed time limit of three months. If not corrected within the time limit, the application is considered abandoned. However, pursuant to Article 8(2)(b), if the irregularity relates to additional elements that may be required by an Examining Office, or to a special requirement notified to the Director General by a Contracting Party, and the applicant has not complied within the prescribed time limit of three months, the application is merely deemed not to contain the designation of the concerned Contracting Party.

In accordance with Article 10(3) and Rule 17, the IB will normally publish the international registration within six months of the registration date, unless the applicant requests that the publication be made immediately after the registration. Article 11 (1) and Rule 16(1) provide that applicants may also request deferment of publication, which shall be granted for a period of less than 30 months from the filing date if such deferment is allowed by the laws of all the Contracting Parties designated in an application. Article 11 (1)(b) provides that where a Contracting Party does not provide for the deferment of the publication of an industrial design, as is the case in the United States, the Contracting Party shall notify the Director General of that fact in a declaration.

Pursuant to Article 12(1), the USPTO may refuse registration, in whole or in part, of the international registration, when the conditions for the grant of protection under the laws of the United States are not met. Under Article 12(2), the refusal shall be communicated by the USPTO to the IB within the prescribed period of six months from the date on which the IB sends to the USPTO a copy of the publication of the international registration, as set forth in Rule 18(1)(a). However, the USPTO, as an Examining Office, may notify the Director General that the period for refusal for the United States shall be 12 months.

According to Article 14(2) and Rule 18(1), if the USPTO does not communicate a notification of refusal, the international registration will have the same effect as a grant of protection for the industrial design under the laws of the United States at the latest on the last day of the period in which USPTO could have transmitted a notice of refusal to the IB. However, if the USPTO unintentionally does not communicate a notice of refusal within that time period, the USPTO may notify the IB and communicate the decision to the holder of the international registration promptly thereafter (Rule 8(1)(c)(ii))

Article 14(1) provides that the international registration has the same effect in the USPTO as a regularly-filed application for the grant of protection of the design under U.S. law. The applicant has the same remedies as if the design had been the subject of a U.S. national application. Under Article 12(4), the USPTO may with-draw a notification of refusal, in whole or in part, at any time. However, in that case, a grant of protection will ensue from the latest date on which the refusal was withdrawn (see Article 14(2)(b)).

Article 15 provides that invalidation by the competent authorities in a designated Contracting Party may not be pronounced without the right holder having, in good time, the opportunity to defend his rights. Additionally, in the United States, the USPTO must, where it is aware of the invalidation, notify the IB. Article 16 provides that the IB must record changes of ownership and other matters regarding international registrations and that such changes are to have the same effect as if the recording had been made in the Office of the concerned Contracting Party.

Pursuant to Article 17, an international registration shall be effected for a term of five years from the date of international registration. Registrations may be renewed for additional terms of five years. As long as they are renewed according to Article 17(2), Article 17(3) provides that protection shall not terminate before 15 years from the date of international registration. Renewal requires the payment of fees as specified in Rule 24.

Article 19 sets forth provisions regarding a common patent office being substituted for national offices when a group of member states agrees to unify domestic legislation on designs.

Article 20 of the Agreement provides that the Contracting Parties shall be members of the "same Union as the States party to the 1934 Act or the 1960 Act," and Article 21(1) of the Act provides that the Contracting Parties shall be members "of the same Assembly as the States bound by Article 2 of the Complementary Act of 1967."

Article 21(2) sets forth the tasks to be performed by the Assembly. These tasks include: dealing with all matters concerning maintenance and development of the Union and the implementation of the Agreement; exercising rights and performing such tasks as are specifically conferred upon it or assigned to it under this Agreement or the Complementary Act of 1967; giving directions to the Director General concerning preparations for conferences of revision and deciding on the convocation of any such conference; amending the Regulations; giving the Director General all necessary instructions concerning matters within the competence of the Union; adopting the biennial budget and financial regulations of the Union; establishing committees and working groups as appropriate; and determining which States and organizations shall be admitted to its meetings as observers.

Article 21(4) sets forth the general voting procedures in the Assembly. Each Contracting Party that is a state shall have one vote and shall vote only in its own name. Any Contracting Party that is an intergovernmental organization may vote in place of its member states, with a number of votes equal to the number of its member states that are party to the Agreement, but no such organization may participate in the vote if anyone of its member states exercises its right to vote, and vice versa.

Article 21(5) provides that subject to Articles 24(2) and 26(2), the decisions of the Assembly require two-thirds of the votes cast (abstentions do not count as votes). However, as is common practice in multilateral intellectual property treaties that include provisions for an assembly to facilitate treaty implementation, certain provisions of the Agreement may be amended by a super-majority of the Assembly, without the need for a revision conference. In particular, proposals for the adoption of any amendment to Articles 21, 22, 23, and 26 may be submitted by any Contracting Party or the Director General. Adoption of amendments to those Articles requires a three-fourths majority, except that amendments to Articles 21 and 26(2) shall require a four-fifths majority. Pursuant to Article 26(3), any such amendment enters into force one month after the Director General receives written notifications of acceptance from three-fourths of those Contracting Parties, which, at the time the amendment was adopted, were members of the Assembly and had the right to vote on the amendment. Pursuant to Article 26(3)(c), any such amendment that enters into force will bind all the States and intergovernmental organizations that are Contracting Parties to the Agreement.

Article 22 details the duties of the International Bureau of WIPO as they relate to the Agreement. Pursuant to Article 22(5)(c), the Director General and persons designated by the Director General shall take part, without the right to vote, in discussions at any revision conference.

Pursuant to Article 23 of the Agreement, the budget of the Union will include income and expenses proper to the Union and its contribution to the budget of expenses to the Unions administered by WIPO. Its budget will be established with due regard to the requirements of coordination with the budgets of the other WIPO Unions. The finances of the Union include a working capital fund, established pursuant to Article 23(5), which will be constituted by the excess receipts and, if such excess does not suffice, by a single payment made by each member of the Union.

The USPTO is expected to incur some initial costs for items such as new forms and other updates of procedures in order to allow for appropriate processing of international design applications under the Agreement. However, the Agreement authorizes the United States to set an individual designation fee payable in two parts that will be equivalent to the filing and issue fees currently charged with respect to a regular United States design application. The substantive requirements of chapter 16 of title 35 of the United States Code, which currently defines the substantive requirements for the patenting of designs, will also apply to international design applications. Therefore, these fees should cover the cost of processing applications filed under the Agreement. Much of the examination of an international design application will be the same as that of a regular national application for design patent.

Implementing Legislation

In the event that the Senate provides its advice and consent to ratify this Agreement, the United States would not deposit its instrument of ratification until the necessary implementing legal structure had been established domestically, so as to ensure that the United States was capable of complying with the provisions of this Agreement. Such implementation requirements include the enactment of legislation, and the promulgation of new regulations by the USPTO.

Declarations to Accompany United States Ratification

The Agreement contemplates that Contracting Parties may make declarations with respect to certain articles. The Department of State recommends that the United States ratification to the Agreement be accompanied by nine declarations, pursuant to Agreement Articles 5(2)(a), 7(2), 11(1)(b), 13(1), 16(2), and 17(3)(c), and Agreement Rules 8(1), 13(4) and 18(1)(b).

The first listed declaration, authorized under Article 5(2)(a), permits the USPTO, as an Examining Office under the Agreement, to declare those additional elements listed in Article 5(2)(b), which it requires be included in an application for grant of protection of the design. Current United States statutes and regulations governing the protection of design patents require: indications concerning the identity of the creator of the industrial design that is the subject of the application (35 U.S.C. 114, 37 CFR 1.63(a)(3)); a brief description of the reproduction or of the characteristic features of the industrial design (35 U.S.C. 112, 1st paragraph; 37 CFR 1.154(b)(5)); and a claim (35 USC 111). In addition, Rule 11(3) of the Agreement requires that a Party making a declaration under Article 5(2)(a) to the effect that a claim is required must specify in its declaration the exact wording of the required claim (as found in 37 CFR 1.153(a)).

The USPTO has ascertained that a declaration is necessary to ensure that its substantive examination of industrial designs is maintained. Accordingly, the Department of State recommends that the following declaration be included in the U.S. instrument of ratification:

> Pursuant to Article 5(2)(a) and Rule 11(3) of the Agreement, the United States declares that it is an Examining Office under the Agreement whose law requires that an application for the grant of protection to an industrial design contain: (i) indications concerning the identity of the creator of the industrial design that is the subject of the application; (ii) a brief description of the reproduction or of the characteristic features of the industrial design that is the subject of the application; and (iii) a claim. The specific wording of the claim shall be in formal terms to the ornamental design for the article (specifying name of article) as shown, or as shown and described.

The second declaration, authorized under Article 7(2), authorizes a Party whose office is an Examining Office (such as USPTO) to declare that its individual designation fee, whose amount is to be indicated in the declaration and can be changed in future declarations, shall replace the designation fee prescribed in the Regulations of the Agreement. In addition, Rule 12(3) provides that a declaration made pursuant to Article 7(2) may also specify that the individual designation fee be payable in two parts. The first part would be paid at the time of filing and the second part would be paid at a later date determined by the law of the Contracting Party.

The USPTO has determined that such a declaration is necessary in order to keep its fees for processing international design applications filed under the Agreement the same as those for regularly filed national design applications. Further, it is necessary to have the fee payable in two parts in order to maintain USPTO's current fee practice that comprises a filing fee, due at the time of filing of the application, and an issue fee, due before the patent is to be granted. Accordingly, the Department of State recommends that the following declaration be included in the U.S. instrument of ratification:

> Pursuant to Article 7(2) and Rule 12(3) of the Agreement, the United States declares that, as an Examining Office under the Agreement, the prescribed designation fee referred to in Article 7(1) of the

> Agreement shall be re-placed by an individual designation fee, that is payable in a first part at filing and a second part payable upon allowance of the application. The current amount of the designation fee is US$790, payable in a first part of US$330 at filing and a second part of US$460 upon allowance of the application. However, for those entities that qualify for "small entity" status within the meaning of section 41(h) of title 35 of the United States Code and section 3 of the Small Business Act, the amount of the individual designation fee is US$395, payable in a first part of US$165 and a second part of US$230. In addition, these amounts are subject to future changes upon which notification to the Director General will be made in future declarations as authorized in Article 7(2) of the Agreement.

The third declaration, authorized by Article 11(1)(b) of the Agreement, allows the USPTO to notify the Director General that its law does not provide for deferment of publications under the Agreement. The USPTO has ascertained that such a declaration is necessary in order to prohibit deferments of publication of international design registrations designating the United States under the Agreement. Accordingly, the Department of State recommends that the U.S. instrument of ratification be accompanied by the following declaration:

> Pursuant to Article 11(1)(b) of the Agreement, the United States declares that the law of the United States does not provide for the deferment of the publication of an industrial design.

The fourth declaration, authorized under Article 13(1) of the Agreement, authorizes the USPTO to maintain its restriction of al-lowing only one independent and distinct design to be claimed in a single application. The USPTO has ascertained that such a declaration is necessary so that the USPTO may maintain its practice of issuing one patent for one design, which is defined by a single claim. Accordingly, the Department of State recommends that the following declaration be included in the U.S. instrument of ratification:

> Pursuant to Article 13(1) of the Agreement, the United States declares that its laws require that only one independent and distinct design may be claimed in a single application.

The fifth declaration, authorized by Article 16(2) of the Agreement, allows the USPTO to refuse the effect of recordings regarding change of ownership in the international registration until the USPTO receives assignment statements or documents. This would allow the USPTO to maintain its current practice of requiring that a statement to the effect that a conveyance has been made be submitted to the USPTO and be made available to the public. Under U.S. patent law, if such an assignment is not recorded within three months, the transfer is void against subsequent bona fide purchasers or mortgagees. This protects subsequent purchasers by al-lowing them to view the contents of any agreement that purports to transfer ownership.

The USPTO has ascertained that such a declaration is necessary in order to maintain its current practice of requiring that assignment documents be provided to the USPTO before they are given effect. Accordingly, the Department of State recommends that the United States instrument of ratification be accompanied by the following declaration:

> Pursuant to Article 16(2) of the Agreement, the United States declares that a recording by the International Bureau under Article 16(1)(i) of the Agreement shall not have effect in the United States until the USPTO has received the statements or documents recorded thereby.

The sixth declaration is mandated by Article 17(3)(c) of the Agreement. That Article requires that each Contracting Party notify the Director General as to the maximum duration of protection provided for by its law. Accordingly, the Department of State recommends that the U.S. instrument of ratification be accompanied by the following declaration:

> Pursuant to Article 17(3)(c) of the Agreement, the United States declares that the maximum duration of protection for designs provided for by its law is 15 years from grant.

The seventh declaration, authorized by Rule 8(1)(a) of the Agreement, allows the USPTO to continue its practice of requiring that an application for the protection of an industrial design be filed in the name of the creator of the design. In addition, Rule 8(1)(b) states that any declaration pursuant to Rule 8(1)(a) specify the form and mandatory contents of any statement or document required for the purposes of that rule.

The USPTO has determined that such a declaration is necessary in order to maintain its current examination practice of requiring that the applicant for protection of an industrial design be the creator of that design. Accordingly, the Department of State recommends that the United States instrument of ratification be accompanied by the following declaration:

> Pursuant to Rule 8(1) of the Agreement, the United States declares that the law of the United States requires that an application for protection of an industrial design be filed in the name of the creator of the industrial design. The specific form and mandatory contents of a statement required for the purposes of Rule 8(2) of the Agreement are contained in section 1.63 of title 37 of the Code of Federal Regulations of the United States.

The eighth declaration, authorized by Rule 13(4) of the Agreement, allows the USPTO to notify the Director General that the law of the United States requires a security clearance and that the period of one month identified in Rule 13(3) for the Office of a Contracting Party to forward an application to the IB, shall be replaced by a period of six months. This will allow for time to complete the security review of the applications currently required by 35 U.S.C. 181, *et seq.*

The USPTO has ascertained that a declaration is necessary in order to ensure that international design applications can be re-viewed for secrecy and security purposes. Accordingly, the Department of State recommends that the following declaration be included in the U.S. instrument of ratification:

> Pursuant to Rule 13(4) of the Agreement, the United States declares that the period of one month referred to in Rule 13(3) of the Agreement shall be replaced by a period of six months as to the United States in light of the security clearance required by United States law.

The ninth declaration, authorized by Rule 18(1)(b), allows the USPTO, as an Examining Office, to notify the Director General that the period of six months for notification of refusal referred to in Rule 18(1)(a) shall be replaced by a period of 12 months as to the United States. The USPTO has ascertained that such a declaration is necessary in order to maintain the integrity of its substantive examination procedures for applications filed under the Agreement. Accordingly, the Department of State recommends that the following declaration be included in the U.S. instrument of ratification:

> Pursuant to Rule 18(1)(b), the United States declares that the period of six months referred to in Rule 18(1)(a) of the Agreement shall be replaced by a period of twelve months with respect to the United States, as the Office of the United States is an Examining Office under the Agreement."

Geneva Act of The Hague Agreement Concerning The International Registration Of Industrial Designs

INTRODUCTORY PROVISIONS

Article 1
Abbreviated Expressions

For the purposes of this Act:

(i) "the Hague Agreement" means the Hague Agreement Concerning the International Deposit of Industrial Designs, henceforth renamed the Hague Agreement Concerning the International Registration of Industrial Designs;

(ii) "this Act" means the Hague Agreement as established by the present Act;

(iii) "Regulations" means the Regulations under this Act;

(iv) "prescribed" means prescribed in the Regulations;

(v) "Paris Convention" means the Paris Convention for the Protection of Industrial Property, signed at Paris on March 20, 1883, as revised and amended;

(vi) "international registration" means the international registration of an industrial design effected according to this Act;

(vii) "international application" means an application for international registration;

(viii) "International Register" means the official collection of data concerning international registrations maintained by the International Bureau, which data this Act or the Regulations require or permit to be recorded, regardless of the medium in which such data are stored;

(ix) "person" means a natural person or a legal entity;

(x) "applicant" means the person in whose name an international application is filed;

(xi) "holder" means the person in whose name an international registration is recorded in the International Register;

(xii) "intergovernmental organization" means an intergovernmental organization eligible to become party to this Act in accordance with Article 27(1)(ii);

(xiii) "Contracting Party" means any State or intergovernmental organization party to this Act;

(xiv) "applicant's Contracting Party" means the Contracting Party or one of the Contracting Parties from which the applicant derives its entitlement to file an international application by virtue of satisfying, in relation to that Contracting Party, at least one of the conditions specified in Article 3; where there are two or more Contracting Parties from which the applicant may, under Article 3, derive its entitlement to file an international application, "applicant's Contracting Party" means the one which, among those Contracting Parties, is indicated as such in the international application;

(xv) "territory of a Contracting Party" means, where the Contracting Party is a State, the territory of that State and, where the Contracting Party is an intergovernmental organization, the territory in which the constituent treaty of that intergovernmental organization applies;

(xvi) "Office" means the agency entrusted by a Contracting Party with the grant of protection for industrial designs with effect in the territory of that Contracting Party;

(xvii) "Examining Office" means an Office which *ex officio* examines applications filed with it for the protection of industrial designs at least to determine whether the industrial designs satisfy the condition of novelty;

(xviii) "designation" means a request that an international registration have effect in a Contracting Party; it also means the recording, in the International Register, of that request;

(xix) "designated Contracting Party" and "designated Office" means the Contracting Party and the Office of the Contracting Party, respectively, to which a designation applies;

(xx) "1934 Act" means the Act signed at London on June 2, 1934, of the Hague Agreement;

(xxi) "1960 Act" means the Act signed at The Hague on November 28, 1960, of the Hague Agreement;

(xxii) "1961 Additional Act" means the Act signed at Monaco on November 18, 1961, additional to the 1934 Act;

(xxiii) "Complementary Act of 1967" means the Complementary Act signed at Stockholm on July 14, 1967, as amended, of the Hague Agreement;

(xxiv) "Union" means the Hague Union established by the Hague Agreement of November 6, 1925, and maintained by the 1934 and 1960 Acts, the 1961 Additional Act, the Complementary Act of 1967 and this Act;

(xxv) "Assembly" means the Assembly referred to in Article 21(1)(a) or any body replacing that Assembly;

(xxvi) "Organization" means the World Intellectual Property Organization;

(xxvii) "Director General" means the Director General of the Organization;

(xxviii) "International Bureau" means the International Bureau of the Organization;

(xxix) "instrument of ratification" shall be construed as including instruments of acceptance or approval.

Article 2
Applicability of Other Protection Accorded by Laws of Contracting Parties and by Certain International Treaties

(1) [*Laws of Contracting Parties and Certain International Treaties*] The provisions of this Act shall not affect the application of any greater protection which may be accorded by the law of a Contracting Party, nor shall they affect in any way the protection accorded to works of art and works of applied art by international copyright treaties and conventions, or the protection accorded to industrial designs under the Agreement on Trade-Related Aspects of Intellectual Property Rights annexed to the Agreement Establishing the World Trade Organization.

(2) [*Obligation to Comply with the Paris Convention*] Each Contracting Party shall comply with the provisions of the Paris Convention which concern industrial designs.

CHAPTER I
INTERNATIONAL APPLICATION AND INTERNATIONAL REGISTRATION

Article 3
Entitlement to File an International Application

Any person that is a national of a State that is a Contracting Party or of a State member of an intergovernmental organization that is a Contracting Party, or that has a domicile, a habitual residence or a real and effective industrial or commercial establishment in the territory of a Contracting Party, shall be entitled to file an international application.

Article 4
Procedure for Filing the International Application

(1) [*Direct or Indirect Filing*] (a) The international application may be filed, at the option of the applicant, either directly with the International Bureau or through the Office of the applicant's Contracting Party.

(b) Notwithstanding subparagraph (a), any Contracting Party may, in a declaration, notify the Director General that international applications may not be filed through its Office.

(2) [*Transmittal Fee in Case of Indirect Filing*] The Office of any Contracting Party may require that the applicant pay a transmittal fee to it, for its own benefit, in respect of any international application filed through it.

Article 5
Contents of the International Application

(1) [*Mandatory Contents of the International Application*] The international application shall be in the prescribed language or one of the prescribed languages and shall contain or be accompanied by

(i) a request for international registration under this Act;

(ii) the prescribed data concerning the applicant;

(iii) the prescribed number of copies of a reproduction or, at the choice of the applicant, of several different reproductions of the industrial design that is the subject of the international application, presented in the prescribed manner; however, where the industrial design is two-dimensional and a request for deferment of publication is made in accordance with paragraph (5), the international application may, instead of containing reproductions, be accompanied by the prescribed number of specimens of the industrial design;

(iv) an indication of the product or products which constitute the industrial design or in relation to which the industrial design is to be used, as prescribed;

(v) an indication of the designated Contracting Parties;

(vi) the prescribed fees;

(vii) any other prescribed particulars.

(2) [*Additional Mandatory Contents of the International Application*] (a) Any Contracting Party whose Office is an Examining Office and whose law, at the time it becomes party to this Act, requires that an application for the grant of protection to an industrial design contain any of the elements specified in subparagraph (b) in order for that application to be accorded a filing date under that law may, in a declaration, notify the Director General of those elements.

(b) The elements that may be notified pursuant to subparagraph (a) are the following:

(i) indications concerning the identity of the creator of the industrial design that is the subject of that application;

(ii) a brief description of the reproduction or of the characteristic features of the industrial design that is the subject of that application;

(iii) a claim.

(c) Where the international application contains the designation of a Contracting Party that has made a notification under subparagraph (a), it shall also contain, in the prescribed manner, any element that was the subject of that notification.

(3) [*Other Possible Contents of the International Application*] The international application may contain or be accompanied by such other elements as are specified in the Regulations.

(4) [*Several Industrial Designs in the Same International Application*] Subject to such conditions as may be prescribed, an international application may include two or more industrial designs.

(5) [*Request for Deferred Publication*] The international application may contain a request for deferment of publication.

Article 6
Priority

(1) [*Claiming of Priority*] (a) The international application may contain a declaration claiming, under Article 4 of the Paris Convention, the priority of one or more earlier applications filed in or for any country party to that Convention or any Member of the World Trade Organization.

(b) The Regulations may provide that the declaration referred to in subparagraph (a) may be made after the filing of the international application. In such case, the Regulations shall prescribe the latest time by which such declaration may be made.

(2) [*International Application Serving as a Basis for Claiming Priority*] The international application shall, as from its filing date and whatever may be its subsequent fate, be equivalent to a regular filing within the meaning of Article 4 of the Paris Convention.

Article 7
Designation Fees

(1) [*Prescribed Designation Fee*] The prescribed fees shall include, subject to paragraph (2), a designation fee for each designated Contracting Party.

(2) [*Individual Designation Fee*] Any Contracting Party whose Office is an Examining Office and any Contracting Party that is an intergovernmental organization may, in a declaration, notify the Director General that, in connection with any international application in which it is designated, and in connection with the renewal of any international registration resulting from such an international application, the prescribed designation fee referred to in paragraph (1) shall be replaced by an individual designation fee, whose amount shall be indicated in the declaration and can be changed in further declarations. The said amount may be fixed by the said Contracting Party for the initial term of protection and for each term of renewal or for the maximum period of protection allowed by the Contracting Party concerned. However, it may not be higher than the equivalent of the amount which the Office of that Contracting Party would be entitled to receive from an applicant for a grant of protection for an equivalent period to the same number of industrial designs, that amount being diminished by the savings resulting from the international procedure.

(3) [*Transfer of Designation Fees*] The designation fees referred to in paragraphs (1) and (2) shall be transferred by the International Bureau to the Contracting Parties in respect of which those fees were paid.

Article 8
Correction of Irregularities

(1) [*Examination of the International Application*] If the International Bureau finds that the international application does not, at the time of its receipt by the International Bureau, fulfill the requirements of this Act and the Regulations, it shall invite the applicant to make the required corrections within the prescribed time limit.

(2) [*Irregularities Not Corrected*] (a) If the applicant does not comply with the invitation within the prescribed time limit, the international application shall, subject to subparagraph (b), be considered abandoned.

(b) In the case of an irregularity which relates to Article 5(2) or to a special requirement notified to the Director General by a Contracting Party in accordance with the Regulations, if the applicant does not comply with the invitation within the prescribed time limit, the international application shall be deemed not to contain the designation of that Contracting Party.

Article 9
Filing Date of the International Application

(1) [*International Application Filed Directly*] Where the international application is filed directly with the International Bureau, the filing date shall, subject to paragraph (3), be the date on which the International Bureau receives the international application.

(2) [*International Application Filed Indirectly*] Where the international application is filed through the Office of the applicant's Contracting Party, the filing date shall be determined as prescribed.

(3) [*International Application with Certain Irregularities*] Where the international application has, on the date on which it is received by the International Bureau, an irregularity which is prescribed as an irregularity entailing a postponement of the filing date of the international application, the filing date shall be the date on which the correction of such irregularity is received by the International Bureau.

Article 10
International Registration, Date of the International Registration, Publication and Confidential Copies of the International Registration

(1) [*International Registration*] The International Bureau shall register each industrial design that is the subject of an international application immediately upon receipt by it of the international application or, where corrections are invited under Article 8, immediately upon receipt of the required corrections. The registration shall be effected whether or not publication is deferred under Article 11.

(2) [*Date of the International Registration*] (a) Subject to subparagraph (b), the date of the international registration shall be the filing date of the international application.

(b) Where the international application has, on the date on which it is received by the International Bureau, an irregularity which relates to Article 5(2) , the date of the international registration shall be the date on which the correction of such irregularity is received by the International Bureau or the filing date of the international application, whichever is the later.

(3) [*Publication*] (a) The international registration shall be published by the International Bureau. Such publication shall be deemed in all Contracting Parties to be sufficient publicity, and no other publicity may be required of the holder.

(b) The International Bureau shall send a copy of the publication of the international registration to each designated Office.

(4) [*Maintenance of Confidentiality Before Publication*] Subject to paragraph (5) and Article 11(4)(b), the International Bureau shall keep in confidence each international application and each international registration until publication.

(5) [*Confidential Copies*] (a) The International Bureau shall, immediately after registration has been effected, send a copy of the international registration, along with any relevant statement, document or specimen accompanying the international application, to each Office that has notified the

International Bureau that it wishes to receive such a copy and has been designated in the international application.

(b) The Office shall, until publication of the international registration by the International Bureau, keep in confidence each international registration of which a copy has been sent to it by the International Bureau and may use the said copy only for the purpose of the examination of the international registration and of applications for the protection of industrial designs filed in or for the Contracting Party for which the Office is competent. In particular, it may not divulge the contents of any such international registration to any person outside the Office other than the holder of that international registration, except for the purposes of an administrative or legal proceeding involving a conflict over entitlement to file the international application on which the international registration is based. In the case of such an administrative or legal proceeding, the contents of the international registration may only be disclosed in confidence to the parties involved in the proceeding who shall be bound to respect the confidentiality of the disclosure.

Article 11
Deferment of Publication

(1) [*Provisions of Laws of Contracting Parties Concerning Deferment of Publication*] (a) Where the law of a Contracting Party provides for the deferment of the publication of an industrial design for a period which is less than the prescribed period, that Contracting Party shall, in a declaration, notify the Director General of the allowable period of deferment.

(b) Where the law of a Contracting Party does not provide for the deferment of the publication of an industrial design, the Contracting Party shall, in a declaration, notify the Director General of that fact.

(2) [*Deferment of Publication*] Where the international application contains a request for deferment of publication, the publication shall take place,

(i) where none of the Contracting Parties designated in the international application has made a declaration under paragraph (1), at the expiry of the prescribed period or,

(ii) where any of the Contracting Parties designated in the international application has made a declaration under paragraph (1)(a), at the expiry of the period notified in such declaration or, where there is more than one such designated Contracting Party, at the expiry of the shortest period notified in their declarations.

(3) [*Treatment of Requests for Deferment Where Deferment Is Not Possible Under Applicable Law*] Where deferment of publication has been requested and any of the Contracting Parties designated in the international application has made a declaration under paragraph (1)(b) that deferment of publication is not possible under its law,

(i) subject to item (ii), the International Bureau shall notify the applicant accordingly; if, within the prescribed period, the applicant does not, by notice in writing to the International Bureau, withdraw the designation of the said Contracting Party, the International Bureau shall disregard the request for deferment of publication;

(ii) where, instead of containing reproductions of the industrial design, the international application was accompanied by specimens of the industrial design, the International Bureau shall disregard the designation of the said Contracting Party and shall notify the applicant accordingly.

(4) [*Request for Earlier Publication or for Special Access to the International Registration*] (a) At any time during the period of deferment applicable under paragraph (2), the holder may request publication of any or all of the industrial designs that are the subject of the international registration,

in which case the period of deferment in respect of such industrial design or designs shall be considered to have expired on the date of receipt of such request by the International Bureau.

(b) The holder may also, at any time during the period of deferment applicable under paragraph (2), request the International Bureau to provide a third party specified by the holder with an extract from, or to allow such a party access to, any or all of the industrial designs that are the subject of the international registration.

(5) [*Renunciation and Limitation*] (a) If, at any time during the period of deferment applicable under paragraph (2), the holder renounces the international registration in respect of all the designated Contracting Parties, the industrial design or designs that are the subject of the international registration shall not be published.

(b) If, at any time during the period of deferment applicable under paragraph (2), the holder limits the international registration, in respect of all of the designated Contracting Parties, to one or some of the industrial designs that are the subject of the international registration, the other industrial design or designs that are the subject of the international registration shall not be published.

(6) [*Publication and Furnishing of Reproductions*] (a) At the expiration of any period of deferment applicable under the provisions of this Article, the International Bureau shall, subject to the payment of the prescribed fees, publish the international registration. If such fees are not paid as prescribed, the international registration shall be canceled and publication shall not take place.

(b) Where the international application was accompanied by one or more specimens of the industrial design in accordance with Article 5(1)(iii), the holder shall submit the prescribed number of copies of a reproduction of each industrial design that is the subject of that application to the International Bureau within the prescribed time limit. To the extent that the holder does not do so, the international registration shall be canceled and publication shall not take place.

Article 12
Refusal

(1) [*Right to Refuse*] The Office of any designated Contracting Party may, where the conditions for the grant of protection under the law of that Contracting Party are not met in respect of any or all of the industrial designs that are the subject of an international registration, refuse the effects, in part or in whole, of the international registration in the territory of the said Contracting Party, provided that no Office may refuse the effects, in part or in whole, of any international registration on the ground that requirements relating to the form or contents of the international application that are provided for in this Act or the Regulations or are additional to, or different from, those requirements have not been satisfied under the law of the Contracting Party concerned.

(2) [*Notification of Refusal*] (a) The refusal of the effects of an international registration shall be communicated by the Office to the International Bureau in a notification of refusal within the prescribed period.

(b) Any notification of refusal shall state all the grounds on which the refusal is based.

(3) [*Transmission of Notification of Refusal; Remedies*] (a) The International Bureau shall, without delay, transmit a copy of the notification of refusal to the holder.

(b) The holder shall enjoy the same remedies as if any industrial design that is the subject of the international registration had been the subject of an application for the grant of protection under the law applicable to the Office that communicated the refusal. Such remedies shall at least consist of the possibility of a re-examination or a review of the refusal or an appeal against the refusal.

(4) [*Withdrawal of Refusal*] Any refusal may be withdrawn, in part or in whole, at any time by the Office that communicated it.

Article 13
Special Requirements Concerning Unity of Design

(1) [*Notification of Special Requirements*] Any Contracting Party whose law, at the time it becomes party to this Act, requires that designs that are the subject of the same application conform to a requirement of unity of design, unity of production or unity of use, or belong to the same set or composition of items, or that only one independent and distinct design may be claimed in a single application, may, in a declaration, notify the Director General accordingly. However, no such declaration shall affect the right of an applicant to include two or more industrial designs in an international application in accordance with Article 5(4), even if the application designates the Contracting Party that has made the declaration.

(2) [*Effect of Declaration*] Any such declaration shall enable the Office of the Contracting Party that has made it to refuse the effects of the international registration pursuant to Article 12(1) pending compliance with the requirement notified by that Contracting Party.

(3) [*Further Fees Payable on Division of Registration*] Where, following a notification of refusal in accordance with paragraph (2), an international registration is divided before the Office concerned in order to overcome a ground of refusal stated in the notification, that Office shall be entitled to charge a fee in respect of each additional international application that would have been necessary in order to avoid that ground of refusal.

Article 14
Effects of the International Registration

(1) [*Effect as Application Under Applicable Law*] The international registration shall, from the date of the international registration, have at least the same effect in each designated Contracting Party as a regularly-filed application for the grant of protection of the industrial design under the law of that Contracting Party.

(2) [*Effect as Grant of Protection Under Applicable Law*] (a) In each designated Contracting Party the Office of which has not communicated a refusal in accordance with Article 12, the international registration shall have the same effect as a grant of protection for the industrial design under the law of that Contracting Party at the latest from the date of expiration of the period allowed for it to communicate a refusal or, where a Contracting Party has made a corresponding declaration under the Regulations, at the latest at the time specified in that declaration.

(b) Where the Office of a designated Contracting Party has communicated a refusal and has subsequently withdrawn, in part or in whole, that refusal, the international registration shall, to the extent that the refusal is withdrawn, have the same effect in that Contracting Party as a grant of protection for the industrial design under the law of the said Contracting Party at the latest from the date on which the refusal was withdrawn.

(c) The effect given to the international registration under this paragraph shall apply to the industrial design or designs that are the subject of that registration as received from the International Bureau by the designated Office or, where applicable, as amended in the procedure before that Office.

(3) [*Declaration Concerning Effect of Designation of Applicant's Contracting Party*] (a) Any Contracting Party whose Office is an Examining Office may, in a declaration, notify the Director General that, where it is the applicant's Contracting Party, the designation of that Contracting Party in an international registration shall have no effect.

(b) Where a Contracting Party having made the declaration referred to in subparagraph (a) is indicated in an international application both as the applicant's Contracting Party and as a designated Contracting Party, the International Bureau shall disregard the designation of that Contracting Party.

Article 15
Invalidation

(1) [*Requirement of Opportunity of Defense*] Invalidation, by the competent authorities of a designated Contracting Party, of the effects, in part or in whole, in the territory of that Contracting Party, of the international registration may not be pronounced without the holder having, in good time, been afforded the opportunity of defending his rights.

(2) [*Notification of Invalidation*] The Office of the Contracting Party in whose territory the effects of the international registration have been invalidated shall, where it is aware of the invalidation, notify it to the International Bureau.

Article 16
Recording of Changes and Other Matters Concerning International Registrations

(1) [*Recording of Changes and Other Matters*] The International Bureau shall, as prescribed, record in the International Register

(i) any change in ownership of the international registration, in respect of any or all of the designated Contracting Parties and in respect of any or all of the industrial designs that are the subject of the international registration, provided that the new owner is entitled to file an international application under Article 3,

(ii) any change in the name or address of the holder,

(iii) the appointment of a representative of the applicant or holder and any other relevant fact concerning such representative,

(iv) any renunciation, by the holder, of the international registration, in respect of any or all of the designated Contracting Parties,

(v) any limitation, by the holder, of the international registration, in respect of any or all of the designated Contracting Parties, to one or some of the industrial designs that are the subject of the international registration,

(vi) any invalidation, by the competent authorities of a designated Contracting Party, of the effects, in the territory of that Contracting Party, of the international registration in respect of any or all of the industrial designs that are the subject of the international registration,

(vii) any other relevant fact, identified in the Regulations, concerning the rights in any or all of the industrial designs that are the subject of the international registration.

(2) [*Effect of Recording in International Register*] Any recording referred to in items (i), (ii), (iv), (v), (vi) and (vii) of paragraph (1) shall have the same effect as if it had been made in the Register of the Office of each of the Contracting Parties concerned, except that a Contracting Party may, in a declaration, notify the Director General that a recording referred to in item (i) of paragraph (1) shall not have that effect in that Contracting Party until the Office of that Contracting Party has received the statements or documents specified in that declaration.

(3) [*Fees*] Any recording made under paragraph (1) may be subject to the payment of a fee.

(4) [*Publication*] The International Bureau shall publish a notice concerning any recording made under paragraph (1). It shall send a copy of the publication of the notice to the Office of each of the Contracting Parties concerned.

Article 17
Initial Term and Renewal of the International Registration and Duration of Protection

(1) [*Initial Term of the International Registration*] The international registration shall be effected for an initial term of five years counted from the date of the international registration.

(2) [*Renewal of the International Registration*] The international registration may be renewed for additional terms of five years, in accordance with the prescribed procedure and subject to the payment of the prescribed fees.

(3) [*Duration of Protection in Designated Contracting Parties*] (a) Provided that the international registration is renewed, and subject to subparagraph (b), the duration of protection shall, in each of the designated Contracting Parties, be 15 years counted from the date of the international registration.

(b) Where the law of a designated Contracting Party provides for a duration of protection of more than 15 years for an industrial design for which protection has been granted under that law, the duration of protection shall, provided that the international registration is renewed, be the same as that provided for by the law of that Contracting Party.

(c) Each Contracting Party shall, in a declaration, notify the Director General of the maximum duration of protection provided for by its law.

(4) [*Possibility of Limited Renewal*] The renewal of the international registration may be effected for any or all of the designated Contracting Parties and for any or all of the industrial designs that are the subject of the international registration.

(5) [*Recording and Publication of Renewal*] The International Bureau shall record renewals in the International Register and publish a notice to that effect. It shall send a copy of the publication of the notice to the Office of each of the Contracting Parties concerned.

Article 18
Information Concerning Published International Registrations

(1) [*Access to Information*] The International Bureau shall supply to any person applying therefor, upon the payment of the prescribed fee, extracts from the International Register, or information concerning the contents of the International Register, in respect of any published international registration.

(2) [*Exemption from Legalization*] Extracts from the International Register supplied by the International Bureau shall be exempt from any requirement of legalization in each Contracting Party.

CHAPTER II
ADMINISTRATIVE PROVISIONS

Article 19
Common Office of Several States

(1) [*Notification of Common Office*] If several States intending to become party to this Act have effected, or if several States party to this Act agree to effect, the unification of their domestic legislation on industrial designs, they may notify the Director General

(i) that a common Office shall be substituted for the national Office of each of them, and

(ii) that the whole of their respective territories to which the unified legislation applies shall be deemed to be a single Contracting Party for the purposes of the application of Articles 1, 3 to 18 and 31 of this Act.

(2) [*Time at Which Notification Is to Be Made*] The notification referred to in paragraph (1) shall be made,

(i) in the case of States intending to become party to this Act, at the time of the deposit of the instruments referred to in Article 27(2);

(ii) in the case of States party to this Act, at any time after the unification of their domestic legislation has been effected.

(3) [*Date of Entry into Effect of the Notification*] The notification referred to in paragraphs (1) and (2) shall take effect,

(i) in the case of States intending to become party to this Act, at the time such States become bound by this Act;

(ii) in the case of States party to this Act, three months after the date of the communication thereof by the Director General to the other Contracting Parties or at any later date indicated in the notification.

Article 20
Membership of the Hague Union

The Contracting Parties shall be members of the same Union as the States party to the 1934 Act or the 1960 Act.

Article 21
Assembly

(1) [*Composition*] (a) The Contracting Parties shall be members of the same Assembly as the States bound by Article 2 of the Complementary Act of 1967.

(b) Each member of the Assembly shall be represented in the Assembly by one delegate, who may be assisted by alternate delegates, advisors and experts, and each delegate may represent only one Contracting Party.

(c) Members of the Union that are not members of the Assembly shall be admitted to the meetings of the Assembly as observers.

(2) [*Tasks*] (a) The Assembly shall

(i) deal with all matters concerning the maintenance and development of the Union and the implementation of this Act;

(ii) exercise such rights and perform such tasks as are specifically conferred upon it or assigned to it under this Act or the Complementary Act of 1967;

(iii) give directions to the Director General concerning the preparations for conferences of revision and decide the convocation of any such conference;

(iv) amend the Regulations;

(v) review and approve the reports and activities of the Director General concerning the Union, and give the Director General all necessary instructions concerning matters within the competence of the Union;

(vi) determine the program and adopt the biennial budget of the Union, and approve its final accounts;

(vii) adopt the financial regulations of the Union;

(viii) establish such committees and working groups as it deems appropriate to achieve the objectives of the Union;

(ix) subject to paragraph (1)(c), determine which States, intergovernmental organizations and non-governmental organizations shall be admitted to its meetings as observers;

(x) take any other appropriate action to further the objectives of the Union and perform any other functions as are appropriate under this Act.

(b) With respect to matters which are also of interest to other Unions administered by the Organization, the Assembly shall make its decisions after having heard the advice of the Coordination Committee of the Organization.

(3) [*Quorum*] (a) One-half of the members of the Assembly which are States and have the right to vote on a given matter shall constitute a quorum for the purposes of the vote on that matter.

(b) Notwithstanding the provisions of subparagraph (a), if, in any session, the number of the members of the Assembly which are States, have the right to vote on a given matter and are represented is less than one-half but equal to or more than one-third of the members of the Assembly which are States and have the right to vote on that matter, the Assembly may make decisions but, with the exception of decisions concerning its own procedure, all such decisions shall take effect only if the conditions set forth hereinafter are fulfilled. The International Bureau shall communicate the said decisions to the members of the Assembly which are States, have the right to vote on the said matter and were not represented and shall invite them to express in writing their vote or abstention within a period of three months from the date of the communication. If, at the expiration of this period, the number of such members having thus expressed their vote or abstention attains the number of the members which was lacking for attaining the quorum in the session itself, such decisions shall take effect provided that at the same time the required majority still obtains.

(4) [*Taking Decisions in the Assembly*] (a) The Assembly shall endeavor to take its decisions by consensus.

(b) Where a decision cannot be arrived at by consensus, the matter at issue shall be decided by voting. In such a case,

(i) each Contracting Party that is a State shall have one vote and shall vote only in its own name, and

(ii) any Contracting Party that is an intergovernmental organization may vote, in place of its Member States, with a number of votes equal to the number of its Member States which are party to this Act, and no such intergovernmental organization shall participate in the vote if any one of its Member States exercises its right to vote, and *vice versa*.

(c) On matters concerning only States that are bound by Article 2 of the Complementary Act of 1967, Contracting Parties that are not bound by the said Article shall not have the right to vote, whereas, on matters concerning only Contracting Parties, only the latter shall have the right to vote.

(5) [*Majorities*] (a) Subject to Articles 24(2) and 26(2), the decisions of the Assembly shall require two-thirds of the votes cast.

(b) Abstentions shall not be considered as votes.

(6) [*Sessions*] (a) The Assembly shall meet once in every second calendar year in ordinary session upon convocation by the Director General and, in the absence of exceptional circumstances, during the same period and at the same place as the General Assembly of the Organization.

(b) The Assembly shall meet in extraordinary session upon convocation by the Director General, either at the request of one-fourth of the members of the Assembly or on the Director General's own initiative.

(c) The agenda of each session shall be prepared by the Director General.

(7) [*Rules of Procedure*] The Assembly shall adopt its own rules of procedure.

Article 22
International Bureau

(1) [*Administrative Tasks*] (a) International registration and related duties, as well as all other administrative tasks concerning the Union, shall be performed by the International Bureau.

(b) In particular, the International Bureau shall prepare the meetings and provide the secretariat of the Assembly and of such committees of experts and working groups as may be established by the Assembly.

(2) [*Director General*] The Director General shall be the chief executive of the Union and shall represent the Union.

(3) [*Meetings Other than Sessions of the Assembly*] The Director General shall convene any committee and working group established by the Assembly and all other meetings dealing with matters of concern to the Union.

(4) [*Role of the International Bureau in the Assembly and Other Meetings*] (a) The Director General and persons designated by the Director General shall participate, without the right to vote, in all meetings of the Assembly, the committees and working groups established by the Assembly, and any other meetings convened by the Director General under the aegis of the Union.

(b) The Director General or a staff member designated by the Director General shall be *ex officio* secretary of the Assembly, and of the committees, working groups and other meetings referred to in subparagraph (a).

(5) [*Conferences*] (a) The International Bureau shall, in accordance with the directions of the Assembly, make the preparations for any revision conferences.

(b) The International Bureau may consult with intergovernmental organizations and international and national non-governmental organizations concerning the said preparations.

(c) The Director General and persons designated by the Director General shall take part, without the right to vote, in the discussions at revision conferences.

(6) [*Other Tasks*] The International Bureau shall carry out any other tasks assigned to it in relation to this Act.

Article 23
Finances

(1) [*Budget*] (a) The Union shall have a budget.

(b) The budget of the Union shall include the income and expenses proper to the Union and its contribution to the budget of expenses common to the Unions administered by the Organization.

(c) Expenses not attributable exclusively to the Union but also to one or more other Unions administered by the Organization shall be considered to be expenses common to the Unions. The share of the Union in such common expenses shall be in proportion to the interest the Union has in them.

(2) [*Coordination with Budgets of Other Unions*] The budget of the Union shall be established with due regard to the requirements of coordination with the budgets of the other Unions administered by the Organization.

(3) [*Sources of Financing of the Budget*] The budget of the Union shall be financed from the following sources:

(i) fees relating to international registrations;

(ii) charges due for other services rendered by the International Bureau in relation to the Union;

(iii) sale of, or royalties on, the publications of the International Bureau concerning the Union;

(iv) gifts, bequests and subventions;

(v) rents, interests and other miscellaneous income.

(4) [*Fixing of Fees and Charges; Level of the Budget*] (a) The amounts of the fees referred to in paragraph (3)(i) shall be fixed by the Assembly on the proposal of the Director General. Charges referred to in paragraph 3(ii) shall be established by the Director General and shall be provisionally applied subject to approval by the Assembly at its next session.

(b) The amounts of the fees referred to in paragraph (3)(i) shall be so fixed that the revenues of the Union from fees and other sources shall be at least sufficient to cover all the expenses of the International Bureau concerning the Union.

(c) If the budget is not adopted before the beginning of a new financial period, it shall be at the same level as the budget of the previous year, as provided in the financial regulations.

(5) [*Working Capital Fund*] The Union shall have a working capital fund which shall be constituted by the excess receipts and, if such excess does not suffice, by a single payment made by each member of the Union. If the fund becomes insufficient, the Assembly shall decide to increase it. The proportion and the terms of payment shall be fixed by the Assembly on the proposal of the Director General.

(6) [*Advances by Host State*] (a) In the headquarters agreement concluded with the State on the territory of which the Organization has its headquarters, it shall be provided that, whenever the working capital fund is insufficient, such State shall grant advances. The amount of those advances and the conditions on which they are granted shall be the subject of separate agreements, in each case, between such State and the Organization.

(b) The State referred to in subparagraph (a) and the Organization shall each have the right to denounce the obligation to grant advances, by written notification. Denunciation shall take effect three years after the end of the year in which it has been notified.

(7) [*Auditing of Accounts*] The auditing of the accounts shall be effected by one or more of the States members of the Union or by external auditors, as provided in the financial regulations. They shall be designated, with their agreement, by the Assembly.

Article 24
Regulations

(1) [*Subject Matter*] The Regulations shall govern the details of the implementation of this Act. They shall, in particular, include provisions concerning

(i) matters which this Act expressly provides are to be prescribed;

(ii) further details concerning, or any details useful in the implementation of, the provisions of this Act;

(iii) any administrative requirements, matters or procedures.

(2) [*Amendment of Certain Provisions of the Regulations*] (a) The Regulations may specify that certain provisions of the Regulations may be amended only by unanimity or only by a four-fifths majority.

(b) In order for the requirement of unanimity or a four-fifths majority no longer to apply in the future to the amendment of a provision of the Regulations, unanimity shall be required.

(c) In order for the requirement of unanimity or a four-fifths majority to apply in the future to the amendment of a provision of the Regulations, a four-fifths majority shall be required.

(3) [*Conflict Between This Act and the Regulations*] In the case of conflict between the provisions of this Act and those of the Regulations, the former shall prevail

CHAPTER III
REVISION AND AMENDMENT

Article 25
Revision of This Act

(1) [*Revision Conferences*] This Act may be revised by a conference of the Contracting Parties.

(2) [*Revision or Amendment of Certain Articles*] Articles 21, 22, 23 and 26 may be amended either by a revision conference or by the Assembly according to the provisions of Article 26.

Article 26
Amendment of Certain Articles by the Assembly

(1) [*Proposals for Amendment*] (a) Proposals for the amendment by the Assembly of Articles 21, 22, 23 and this Article may be initiated by any Contracting Party or by the Director General.

(b) Such proposals shall be communicated by the Director General to the Contracting Parties at least six months in advance of their consideration by the Assembly.

(2) [*Majorities*] Adoption of any amendment to the Articles referred to in paragraph (1) shall require a three-fourths majority, except that adoption of any amendment to Article 21 or to the present paragraph shall require a four-fifths majority.

(3) [*Entry into Force*] (a) Except where subparagraph (b) applies, any amendment to the Articles referred to in paragraph (1) shall enter into force one month after written notifications of acceptance, effected in accordance with their respective constitutional processes, have been received by the Director General from three-fourths of those Contracting Parties which, at the time the amendment was adopted, were members of the Assembly and had the right to vote on that amendment.

(b) Any amendment to Article 21(3) or (4) or to this subparagraph shall not enter into force if, within six months of its adoption by the Assembly, any Contracting Party notifies the Director General that it does not accept such amendment.

(c) Any amendment which enters into force in accordance with the provisions of this paragraph shall bind all the States and intergovernmental organizations which are Contracting Parties at the time the amendment enters into force, or which become Contracting Parties at a subsequent date.

CHAPTER IV
FINAL PROVISIONS

Article 27
Becoming Party to This Act

(1) [*Eligibility*] Subject to paragraphs (2) and (3) and Article 28,

(i) any State member of the Organization may sign and become party to this Act;

(ii) any intergovernmental organization which maintains an Office in which protection of industrial designs may be obtained with effect in the territory in which the constituting treaty of the intergovernmental organization applies may sign and become party to this Act, provided that at least one of the member States of the intergovernmental organization is a member of the Organization and provided that such Office is not the subject of a notification under Article 19.

(2) [*Ratification or Accession*] Any State or intergovernmental organization referred to in paragraph (1) may deposit

(i) an instrument of ratification if it has signed this Act, or

(ii) an instrument of accession if it has not signed this Act.

(3) [*Effective Date of Deposit*] (a) Subject to subparagraphs (b) to (d), the effective date of the deposit of an instrument of ratification or accession shall be the date on which that instrument is deposited.

(b) The effective date of the deposit of the instrument of ratification or accession of any State in respect of which protection of industrial designs may be obtained only through the Office maintained by an intergovernmental organization of which that State is a member shall be the date on which the instrument of that intergovernmental organization is deposited if that date is later than the date on which the instrument of the said State has been deposited.

(c) The effective date of the deposit of any instrument of ratification or accession containing or accompanied by the notification referred to in Article 19 shall be the date on which the last of the instruments of the States members of the group of States having made the said notification is deposited.

(d) Any instrument of ratification or accession of a State may contain or be accompanied by a declaration making it a condition to its being considered as deposited that the instrument of one other State or one intergovernmental organization, or the instruments of two other States, or the instruments of one other State and one intergovernmental organization, specified by name and eligible to become party to this Act, is or are also deposited. The instrument containing or accompanied by such a declaration shall be considered to have been deposited on the day on which the condition indicated in the declaration is fulfilled. However, when an instrument specified in the declaration itself contains, or is itself accompanied by, a declaration of the said kind, that instrument shall be considered as deposited on the day on which the condition specified in the latter declaration is fulfilled.

(e) Any declaration made under paragraph (d) may be withdrawn, in its entirety or in part, at any time. Any such withdrawal shall become effective on the date on which the notification of withdrawal is received by the Director General.

Article 28
Effective Date of Ratifications and Accessions

(1) [*Instruments to Be Taken into Consideration*] For the purposes of this Article, only instruments of ratification or accession that are deposited by States or intergovernmental organizations referred to in Article 27(1) and that have an effective date according to Article 27(3) shall be taken into consideration.

(2) [*Entry into Force of This Act*] This Act shall enter into force three months after six States have deposited their instruments of ratification or accession, provided that, according to the most recent annual statistics collected by the International Bureau, at least three of those States fulfill at least one of the following conditions:

(i) at least 3,000 applications for the protection of industrial designs have been filed in or for the State concerned, or

(ii) at least 1,000 applications for the protection of industrial designs have been filed in or for the State concerned by residents of States other than that State.

(3) [*Entry into Force of Ratifications and Accessions*] (a) Any State or intergovernmental organization that has deposited its instrument of ratification or accession three months or more before the date of entry into force of this Act shall become bound by this Act on the date of entry into force of this Act.

(b) Any other State or intergovernmental organization shall become bound by this Act three months after the date on which it has deposited its instrument of ratification or accession or at any later date indicated in that instrument.

Article 29
Prohibition of Reservations

No reservations to this Act are permitted.

Article 30
Declarations Made by Contracting Parties

(1) [*Time at Which Declarations May Be Made*] Any declaration under Articles 4(1)(b), 5(2)(a), 7(2), 11(1), 13(1), 14(3), 16(2) or 17(3)(c) may be made

(i) at the time of the deposit of an instrument referred to in Article 27(2), in which case it shall become effective on the date on which the State or intergovernmental organization having made the declaration becomes bound by this Act, or

(ii) after the deposit of an instrument referred to in Article 27(2), in which case it shall become effective three months after the date of its receipt by the Director General or at any later date indicated in the declaration but shall apply only in respect of any international registration whose date of international registration is the same as, or is later than, the effective date of the declaration.

(2) [*Declarations by States Having a Common Office*] Notwithstanding paragraph (1), any declaration referred to in that paragraph that has been made by a State which has, with another State or other States, notified the Director General under Article 19(1) of the substitution of a common Office for their national Offices shall become effective only if that other State or those other States makes or make a corresponding declaration or corresponding declarations.

(3) [*Withdrawal of Declarations*] Any declaration referred to in paragraph (1) may be withdrawn at any time by notification addressed to the Director General. Such withdrawal shall take effect three months after the date on which the Director General has received the notification or at any later date indicated in the notification. In the case of a declaration made under Article 7(2), the withdrawal shall not affect international applications filed prior to the coming into effect of the said withdrawal.

Article 31
Applicability of the 1934 and 1960 Acts

(1) [*Relations Between States Party to Both This Act and the 1934 or 1960 Acts*] This Act alone shall be applicable as regards the mutual relations of States party to both this Act and the 1934 Act or the 1960 Act. However, such States shall, in their mutual relations, apply the 1934 Act or the 1960 Act, as the case may be, to industrial designs deposited at the International Bureau prior to the date on which this Act becomes applicable as regards their mutual relations.

(2) [*Relations Between States Party to Both This Act and the 1934 or 1960 Acts and States Party to the 1934 or 1960 Acts Without Being Party to This Act*] (a) Any State that is party to both this Act and

the 1934 Act shall continue to apply the 1934 Act in its relations with States that are party to the 1934 Act without being party to the 1960 Act or this Act.

(b) Any State that is party to both this Act and the 1960 Act shall continue to apply the 1960 Act in its relations with States that are party to the 1960 Act without being party to this Act.

Article 32
Denunciation of This Act

(1) [*Notification*] Any Contracting Party may denounce this Act by notification addressed to the Director General.

(2) [*Effective Date*] Denunciation shall take effect one year after the date on which the Director General has received the notification or at any later date indicated in the notification. It shall not affect the application of this Act to any international application pending and any international registration in force in respect of the denouncing Contracting Party at the time of the coming into effect of the denunciation.

Article 33
Languages of This Act; Signature

(1) [*Original Texts; Official Texts*] (a) This Act shall be signed in a single original in the English, Arabic, Chinese, French, Russian and Spanish languages, all texts being equally authentic.

(b) Official texts shall be established by the Director General, after consultation with the interested Governments, in such other languages as the Assembly may designate.

(2) [*Time Limit for Signature*] This Act shall remain open for signature at the headquarters of the Organization for one year after its adoption.

Article 34
Depositary

The Director General shall be the depositary of this Act.

HAGUE AGREEMENT CONCERNING THE INTERNATIONAL REGISTRATION OF INDUSTRIAL DESIGNS

of November 6, 1925

I. *London Act 1934*

II. *Hague Act 1960*

III. *Additional Act of Monaco 1961*

IV. *Complementary Act of Stockholm 1967*, as amended on September 28, 1979

V. *Geneva Act 1999*

Common Regulations
(as in force on April 1, 2004)
and
Administrative Instructions
(as in force on April 1, 2004)

World Intellectual Property Organization
Geneva 2004

PREFACE

The present publication contains the texts of the *London Act (1934)*, the *Hague Act (1960)* and the *Geneva Act (1999)* of the Hague Agreement Concerning the International Registration of Industrial Designs, as well as the texts of the *Additional Act of Monaco (1961)* and the *Complementary Act of Stockholm (1967)*.

It also contains the Common Regulations under the 1999 Act, the 1960 Act and the 1934 Act of the Hague Agreement and the corresponding Administrative Instructions.

I. London Act of June 2, 1934

Article 1

Nationals of any of the contracting countries, as well as persons who, upon the territory of the restricted Union, have satisfied the conditions of Article 3 of the General Convention, may, in all the other contracting countries, secure protection for their industrial designs by means of an international deposit made at the International Bureau of Industrial Property at Berne.

Article 2

(1) The international deposit shall include designs, either in the form of the industrial product for which they are intended, or in the form of a drawing, a photograph, or any other adequate graphic representation of the said design.

(2) The articles submitted shall be accompanied by an application for international deposit, in duplicate, containing, in French, the particulars specified in the Regulations.

Article 3

(1) As soon as the International Bureau receives an application for international deposit it shall record the application in a special Register and shall publish it, sending free of charge to each Office the desired number of copies of the periodical journal in which it publishes such records.

(2) Deposits shall be kept in the archives of the International Bureau.

Article 4

(1) Any person making an international deposit of an industrial design shall, in the absence of proof to the contrary, be deemed to be the owner of the work.

(2) International deposit is purely declaratory. The deposit, as such, shall have in the contracting countries the same effect as if the designs had been deposited there direct on the date of the international deposit, subject however to the special rules established by this Agreement.

(3) The publicity mentioned in the foregoing Article shall be deemed in all the contracting countries to be sufficient, and no other publicity may be required of the depositor, apart from any formalities to be complied with for the exercise of rights in accordance with the domestic law.

(4) The right of priority established by Article 4 of the General Convention shall be guaranteed to every design which has been the subject of an international deposit, without requiring compliance with any of the formalities prescribed in the said Article.

Article 5

The contracting countries agree not to require designs which have been the subject of an international deposit to bear any compulsory marking. They shall not cause the designs to lapse either by reason of non-exploitation or as a result of the introduction of articles similar to those protected.

Article 6

(1) The international deposit may consist of either a single design or several, the number thereof being stated in the application.

(2) Such deposit may be made under open cover or under sealed cover. In particular, there shall be accepted as a means of deposit under sealed cover double envelopes having a perforated control number (Soleau system) or any other system for ensuring identification.

(3) The maximum dimensions of covers or packets eligible for deposit shall be fixed by the Regulations.

Article 7

The duration of international protection is fixed at fifteen years from the date of deposit at the International Bureau at Berne; this term is divided into two periods, namely, one period of five years and one period of ten years.

Article 8

During the first period of protection, deposits shall be accepted either under open cover or under sealed cover; during the second period of protection, they shall be accepted only under open cover.

Article 9

During the first period, deposits under sealed cover may be opened at the request of the depositor or of a competent court; upon expiration of the first period, they shall, with a view to transition to the second period, be opened upon application for prolongation.

Article 10

In the course of the first six months of the fifth year of the first period, the International Bureau shall give unofficial notice of expiration to the depositor of the design.

Article 11

(1) When the depositor desires to secure extension of the protection by transition to the second period he shall, before the expiration of the first period, file with the International Bureau an application for prolongation.

(2) The International Bureau shall open the package, if sealed, shall publish in its journal notice of the prolongation granted, and shall notify all Offices thereof by sending to each the desired number of copies of the said journal.

Article 12

Designs forming the subject of deposits which have not been prolonged, as well as those in respect of which protection has expired, shall, upon the request of the proprietors and at their expense, be returned to them as they stand. If unclaimed, they shall be destroyed at the end of two years.

Article 13

(1) Depositors may, at any time, renounce their deposit, either wholly or in part, by means of a declaration addressed to the International Bureau; the Bureau shall give such declaration the publicity referred to in Article 3.

(2) Renunciation shall entail the return of the deposit to the depositor, at his expense.

Article 14

If a court or any other competent authority orders the communication to it of a secret design, the International Bureau, when duly required, shall open the deposited package, shall extract therefrom the requested design, and shall remit it to the authority so requiring. Similar communication shall take place on request in the case of an unsealed design. The article thus communicated shall be returned in the shortest possible time and reincorporated in the sealed package or in the envelope, as the case may be. Such transactions may be subject to a fee, which shall be fixed by the Regulations.

Article 15

The fees for an international deposit and for the prolongation thereof, which shall be paid before registration of the deposit or of the prolongation can be proceeded with, shall be as follows:

1. for a single design, and in respect of the first period of five years: 5 francs;
2. for a single design, upon expiration of the first period and in respect of the duration of the second period of ten years: 10 francs;
3. for a multiple deposit, and in respect of the first period of five years: 10 francs;

4. for a multiple deposit, upon expiration of the first period and in respect of the duration of the second period of ten years: 50 francs.

Article 16

The net annual proceeds from fees shall be divided, as provided in Article 8 of the Regulations, among the contracting countries by the International Bureau, after deduction of the common expenses necessitated by the implementation of this Agreement.

Article 17

(1) The International Bureau shall record in its Registers all changes affecting the proprietorship of designs which are notified to it by the parties concerned; it shall publish them in its journal and shall announce them to all Offices by sending to each the desired number of copies of the said journal.

(2) These transactions may be subject to a fee, which shall be fixed by the Regulations.

(3) The proprietor of an international deposit may assign the rights in respect of part only of the designs included in a multiple deposit or in respect of one or several of the contracting countries only; but, in such cases, if the deposit has been made under sealed cover, the International Bureau shall open the package before recording the transfer in its Registers.

Article 18

(1) The International Bureau shall deliver to any person, upon application, and on payment of a fee fixed by the Regulations, an abstract of the entries in the Register in connection with any given design.

(2) Such abstract may, if the design lends itself thereto, be accompanied by a copy or a reproduction of the design, which has been supplied to the International Bureau and which the latter shall certify as being in conformity with the article deposited under open cover. If the Bureau is not in possession of such copies or reproductions, it shall have them made, on the request of interested parties and at their expense.

Article 19

The archives of the International Bureau, in so far as they contain unsealed deposits, shall be accessible to the public. Any person may inspect them, in the presence of an official, or may obtain from the Bureau written information on the contents of the Register, subject to payment of fees to be fixed by the Regulations.

Article 20

The details of the application of this Agreement shall be determined by Regulations the provisions of which may, at any time, be amended with the common consent of the Offices of the contracting countries.

Article 21

The provisions of this Agreement offer only a minimum of protection; they shall not preclude the claiming of the application of wider provisions that may be enacted by the domestic legislation of a contracting country, nor shall they prejudice the application of the provisions of the Berne Convention, as revised in 1928, relating to the protection of artistic works and works of art applied to industry.

Article 22

(1) Countries members of the Union which are not party to this Agreement may accede thereto at their request and in the manner prescribed by Articles 16 and 16*bis* of the General Convention.

(2) Notification of accession shall, of itself, ensure, upon the territory of the acceding country, the benefits of the foregoing provisions to industrial designs which, at the time of accession, are the subject of international deposit.

(3) However, any country may, in acceding to this Agreement, declare that application of this Act shall be limited to designs deposited from the date on which its accession becomes effective.

(4) In the case of denunciation of this Agreement, Article 17*bis* of the General Convention shall apply. International designs deposited up to the date on which denunciation becomes effective shall continue, throughout the period of international protection, to enjoy in the denouncing country, as well as in all other countries of the restricted Union, the same protection as if they had been deposited direct in such Countries.

Article 23

(1) This Agreement shall be ratified and ratifications shall be deposited at London not later than July 1, 1938.

(2) It shall enter into force, between the countries which have ratified it, one month after that date, and shall have the same force and duration as the General Convention.

(3) This Act shall, as regards the relations between the countries which have ratified it, replace the Hague Agreement of 1925. However, the latter shall remain in force as regards the relations with countries which have not ratified this Act.

II. The Hague Act of November 28, 1960

Article 1

(1) The contracting States constitute a Special Union for the international deposit of industrial designs.

(2) Only States members of the International Union for the Protection of Industrial Property may become party to this Agreement.

Article 2

For the purposes of this Agreement:

"1925 Agreement" shall mean the Hague Agreement concerning the International Deposit of Industrial Designs of November 6, 1925;

"1934 Agreement" shall mean the Hague Agreement concerning the International Deposit of Industrial Designs of November 6, 1925, as revised at London on June 2, 1934;

"this Agreement" or "the present Agreement" shall mean the Hague Agreement concerning the International Deposit of Industrial Designs as established by the present Act;

"Regulations" shall mean the Regulations for carrying out this Agreement;

"International Bureau" shall mean the International Bureau of Intellectual Property;

"international deposit" shall mean a deposit made at the International Bureau;

"national deposit" shall mean a deposit made at the national Office of a contracting State;

"multiple deposit" shall mean a deposit including several designs;

"State of origin of an international deposit" shall mean the contracting State in which the applicant has a real and effective industrial or commercial establishment or, if the applicant has such establishments in several contracting States, the contracting State which he has indicated in his application; if the applicant has no such establishment in any contracting State, the contracting State in which he has his domicile; if he has no domicile in a contracting State, the contracting State of which he is a national;

"State having a novelty examination" shall mean a contracting State the domestic law of which provides for a system which involves a preliminary *ex officio* search and examination by its national Office as to the novelty of each deposited design.

Article 3

Nationals of contracting States and persons who, without being nationals of any contracting State, are domiciled or have a real and effective industrial or commercial establishment in the territory of a contracting State may deposit designs at the International Bureau.

Article 4

(1) International deposit may be made at the International Bureau:

1. direct, or

2. through the intermediary of the national Office of a contracting State if the law of that State so permits.

(2) The domestic law of any contracting State may require that international deposits of which it is deemed to be the State of origin shall be made through its national Office. Non-compliance with this

requirement shall not prejudice the effects of the international deposit in the other contracting States.

Article 5

(1) The international deposit shall consist of an application and one or more photographs or other graphic representations of the design, and shall involve payment of the fees prescribed by the Regulations.

(2) The application shall contain:

1. a list of the contracting States in which the applicant requests that the international deposit shall have effect;

2. the designation of the article or articles in which it is intended to incorporate the design;

3. if the applicant wishes to claim the priority provided for in Article 9, an indication of the date, the State, and the number of the deposit giving rise to the right of priority;

4. such other particulars as the Regulations may prescribe.

(3) *(a)* In addition, the application may contain:

1. a short description of characteristic features of the design;

2. a declaration as to who is the true creator of the design;

3. a request for deferment of publication as provided in Article 6(4).

(b) The application may be accompanied also by samples or models of the article or articles incorporating the design.

(4) A multiple deposit may include several designs intended to be incorporated in articles included in the same class of the International Design Classification referred to in Article 21(2), item 4.

Article 6

(1) The International Bureau shall maintain the International Design Register and shall register international deposits therein.

(2) The international deposit shall be deemed to have been made on the date on which the International Bureau received the application in due form, the fees payable with the application, and the photograph or photographs or other graphic representations of the design, or, if the International Bureau received them on different dates, on the last of these dates. The registration shall bear the same date.

(3) *(a)* For each international deposit, the International Bureau shall publish in a periodical bulletin:

1. reproductions in black and white or, at the request of the applicant, in color of the deposited photographs or other graphic representations;

2. the date of the international deposit;

3. the particulars prescribed by the Regulations.

(b) The International Bureau shall send the periodical bulletin to the national Offices as soon as possible.

(4) *(a)* The publication referred to in paragraph (3)*(a)* shall, at the request of the applicant, be deferred for such period as he may request. The said period may not exceed twelve months from the date of the international deposit. However, if priority is claimed, the starting date of such period shall be the priority date.

(b) At any time during the period referred to in subparagraph *(a)*, the applicant may request immediate publication or may withdraw his deposit. Withdrawal of the deposit may be limited to one or a few only of the contracting States and, in the case of a multiple deposit, to some only of the designs included therein.

(c) If the applicant fails to pay within the proper time the fees payable before the expiration of the period referred to in subparagraph *(a)*, the International Bureau shall cancel the deposit and shall not effect the publication referred to in paragraph (3)*(a)*.

(d) Until the expiration of the period referred to in subparagraph *(a)*, the International Bureau shall keep in confidence the registration of deposits made subject to deferred publication, and the public shall have no access to any documents or articles concerning such deposits. These provisions shall apply without limitation as to time if the applicant has withdrawn his deposit before the expiration of the said period.

(5) Except as provided in paragraph (4), the Register and all documents and articles filed with the International Bureau shall be open to inspection by the public.

Article 7

(1) *(a)* A deposit registered at the International Bureau shall have the same effect in each of the contracting States designated by the applicant in his application as if all the formalities required by the domestic law for the grant of protection had been complied with by the applicant and as if all administrative acts required to that end had been accomplished by the Office of such State.

(b) Subject to the provisions of Article 11, the protection of designs the deposit of which has been registered at the International Bureau is governed in each contracting State by those provisions of the domestic law which are applicable in that State to designs for which protection has been claimed on the basis of a national deposit and in respect of which all formalities and administrative acts have been complied with and accomplished.

(2) An international deposit shall have no effect in the State of origin if the laws of that State so provide.

Article 8

(1) Notwithstanding the provisions of Article 7, the national Office of a contracting State whose domestic law provides that the national Office may, on the basis of an administrative *ex officio* examination or pursuant to an opposition by a third party, refuse protection shall, in case of refusal, notify the International Bureau within six months that the design does not meet the requirements of its domestic law other than the formalities and administrative acts referred to in Article 7(1). If no such refusal is notified within a period of six months the international deposit shall become effective in that State as from the date of that deposit. However, in a contracting State having a novelty examination, the international deposit, while retaining its priority, shall, if no refusal is notified within a period of six months, become effective from the expiration of the said period unless the domestic law provides for an earlier date for deposits made with its national Office.

(2) The period of six months referred to in paragraph (1) shall be computed from the date on which the national Office receives the issue of the periodical bulletin in which the registration of the international deposit has been published. The national Office shall communicate that date to any person so requesting.

(3) The applicant shall have the same remedies against the refusal of the national Office referred to in paragraph (1) as if he had deposited his design in that Office; in any case, the refusal shall be subject to a request for re-examination or appeal. Notification of such refusal shall indicate:

1. the reasons for which it has been found that the design does not meet the requirements of the domestic law;

2. the date referred to in paragraph (2);

3. the time allowed for a request for re-examination or appeal;

4. the authority to which such request or appeal may be addressed.

(4) *(a)* The national Office of a contracting State whose domestic law contains provisions of the kind referred to in paragraph (1) requiring a declaration as to who is the true creator of the design or a description of the design may provide that, upon request and within a period of not less than sixty days from the dispatch of such a request by the said Office, the applicant shall file in the language of the application filed with the International Bureau:

1. a declaration as to who is the true creator of the design;

2. a short description emphasizing the essential characteristic features of the design as shown by the photographs or other graphic representations.

(b) No fees shall be charged by a national Office in connection with the filing of such declarations or descriptions, or for their possible publication by that national Office.

(5) *(a)* Any contracting State whose domestic law contains provisions of the kind referred to in paragraph (1) shall notify the International Bureau accordingly.

(b) If, under its legislation, a contracting State has several systems for the protection of designs one of which provides for novelty examination, the provisions of this Agreement concerning States having a novelty examination shall apply only to the said system.

Article 9

If the international deposit of a design is made within six months of the first deposit of the same design in a State member of the International Union for the Protection of Industrial Property, and if priority is claimed for the international deposit, the priority date shall be that of the first deposit.

Article 10

(1) An international deposit may be renewed every five years by payment only, during the last year of each period of five years, of the renewal fees prescribed by the Regulations.

(2) Subject to the payment of a surcharge fixed by the Regulations, a period of grace of six months shall be granted for renewal of the international deposit.

(3) At the time of paying the renewal fees, the international deposit number must be indicated and also, if renewal is not to be effected for all the contracting States for which the deposit is about to expire, those of the contracting States for which the renewal is to be effected.

(4) Renewal may be limited to some only of the designs included in a multiple deposit.

(5) The International Bureau shall record and publish renewals.

Article 11

(1) *(a)* The term of protection granted by a contracting State to designs which have been the subject of an international deposit shall not be less than:

1. ten years from the date of the international deposit if the deposit has been renewed;
2. five years from the date of the international deposit in the absence of renewal.

(b) However, if, under the provisions of the domestic law of a contracting State having a novelty examination, protection commences at a date later than that of the international deposit, the minimum terms provided for in subparagraph *(a)* shall be computed from the date at which protection commences in that State. The fact that the international deposit is not renewed or is renewed only once shall in no way affect the minimum terms of protection thus defined.

(2) If the domestic law of a contracting State provides, in respect of designs which have been the subject of a national deposit, for protection whose duration, with or without renewal, is longer than ten years, protection of the same duration shall, on the basis of the international deposit and its renewals, be granted in that State to designs which have been the subject of an international deposit.

(3) A contracting State may, under its domestic law, limit the term of protection of designs which have been the subject of an international deposit to the terms provided for in paragraph (1).

(4) Subject to the provisions of paragraph (1)*(b)*, protection in a contracting State shall terminate at the date of expiration of the international deposit, unless the domestic law of that State provides that protection shall continue after the date of expiration of the international deposit.

Article 12

(1) The International Bureau shall record and publish changes affecting ownership of a design which is the subject of an international deposit in force. It is understood that transfer of ownership may be limited to the rights arising from the international deposit in one or a few only of the contracting States and, in the case of a multiple deposit, to some only of the designs included therein.

(2) The recording referred to in paragraph (1) shall have the same effect as if it had been made in the national Offices of the contracting States.

Article 13

(1) The owner of an international deposit may, by means of a declaration addressed to the International Bureau, renounce his rights in respect of all or some only of the contracting States and, in the case of a multiple deposit, in respect of some only of the designs included therein.

(2) The International Bureau shall record and publish such declaration.

Article 14

(1) No contracting State may, as a condition of recognition of the right to protection, require that the article incorporating the design bear a sign or notice concerning the deposit of the design.

(2) If the domestic law of a contracting State provides for a notice on the article for any other purpose, such State shall regard such requirement as satisfied if all the articles offered to the public with the authorization of the owner of the rights in the design, or the tags attached to such articles, bear the international design notice.

(3) The international design notice shall consist of the symbol [(D)] (a capital D in a circle) accompanied by:

1. the year of the international deposit and the name, or the usual abbreviation of the name, of the depositor, or

2. the number of the international deposit.

(4) The mere appearance of the international design notice on the article or the tags shall in no case be interpreted as implying a waiver of protection by virtue of copyright or on any other grounds, whenever, in the absence of such notice, such protection may be claimed.

Article 15

(1) The fees prescribed by the Regulations shall consist of:

1. fees for the International Bureau;

2. fees for the contracting States designated by the applicant, namely:

(a) a fee for each contracting State;

(b) a fee for each contracting State having a novelty examination and requiring the payment of a fee for such examination.

(2) Any fees paid in respect of one and the same deposit for a contracting State under paragraph (1), item 2(*a*), shall be deducted from the amount of the fee referred to in paragraph (1), item 2*(b)*, if the latter fee becomes payable for the same State.

Article 16

(1) The fees for contracting States referred to in Article 15(1), item 2, shall be collected by the International Bureau and paid over annually to the contracting States designated by the applicant.

(2) *(a)* Any contracting State may notify the International Bureau that it waives its right to the supplementary fees referred to in Article 15(1), item 2*(a)*, in respect of international deposits of which any other contracting State making a similar waiver is deemed to be the State of origin.

(b) Such State may make a similar waiver in respect of international deposits of which it is itself deemed to be the State of origin.

Article 17

The Regulations shall govern the details concerning the implementation of this Agreement and in particular:

1. the languages and the number of copies in which the application for deposit must be filed, and the data to be supplied in the application;

2. the amounts and the dates and method of payment of the fees for the International Bureau and for the States, including the limits imposed on the fee for contracting States having a novelty examination;

3. the number, size, and other characteristics, of the photographs or other graphic representations of each design deposited;

4. the length of the description of characteristic features of the design;

5. the limits within which and conditions under which samples or models of the articles incorporating the design may accompany the application;

6. the number of designs that may be included in a multiple deposit and other conditions governing multiple deposits;

7. all matters relating to the publication and distribution of the periodical bulletin referred to in Article 6(3)*(a)*, including the number of copies of the bulletin which shall be given free of charge to the national Offices and the number of copies which may be sold at a reduced price to such Offices;

8. the procedure for notification by contracting States of any refusal provided for under Article 8(1), and the procedure for communication and publication of such refusals by the International Bureau;

9. the conditions for recording and publication by the International Bureau of the changes affecting the ownership of a design referred to in Article 12(1), and for the renunciations referred to in Article 13;

10. the disposal of documents and articles concerning deposits for which the possibility of renewal has ceased to exist.

Article 18

The provisions of this Agreement shall not preclude the making of a claim to the benefit of any greater protection which may be granted by domestic legislation in a contracting State, nor shall they affect in any way the protection accorded to works of art and works of applied art by international copyright treaties and conventions.

Articles 19 to 22

[Repealed by Article 7(2) of the *Complementary Act of Stockholm (1967)*]

Article 23

(1) This Agreement shall remain open for signature until December 31, 1961.

(2) It shall be ratified and the instruments of ratification shall be deposited with the Government of the Netherlands.

Article 24

(1) States members of the International Union for the Protection of Industrial Property which have not signed this Agreement may accede thereto.

(2) Such accessions shall be notified through diplomatic channels to the Director General, and by the latter to the Governments of all contracting States.

Article 25

(1) Each contracting State undertakes to provide for the protection of industrial designs and to adopt, in accordance with its constitution, the measures necessary to ensure the application of this Agreement.

(2) At the time a contracting State deposits its instrument of ratification or accession, it must be in a position under its domestic law to give effect to the provisions of this Agreement.

Article 26

(1) This Agreement shall enter into force one month after the date on which the Director General has dispatched a notification to the contracting States of the deposit of ten instruments of ratification or accession, at least four of which are those of States which, at the date of the present Agreement, are not party either to the 1925 Agreement or to the 1934 Agreement.

(2) Thereafter, the deposit of instruments of ratification and accession shall be notified to the contracting States by the Director General. Such ratifications and accessions shall become effective one month after the date of the dispatch of such notification unless, in the case of accession, a later date is indicated in the instrument of accession.

Article 27

Any contracting State may at any time notify the Director General that this Agreement shall also apply to all or part of those territories for the external relations of which it is responsible. Thereupon, the Director General shall communicate such notification to the contracting States and the Agreement shall apply also to the said territories one month after the dispatch of the communication by the Director General to the contracting States unless a later date is indicated in the notification.

Article 28

(1) Any contracting State may, by notification addressed to the Director General, denounce this Agreement in its own name and on behalf of all or part of the territories designated in the notification under Article 27. Such notification shall take effect one year after its receipt by the Director General.

(2) Denunciation shall not relieve any contracting State of its obligations under this Agreement in respect of designs deposited at the International Bureau prior to the date on which the denunciation takes effect.

Article 29

(1) This Agreement shall be submitted to revision with a view to the introduction of amendments designed to improve the protection resulting from the international deposit of designs.

(2) Revision conferences shall be called at the request of not less than one-half of the contracting States.

Article 30

(1) Two or more contracting States may at any time notify the Director General that, subject to the conditions indicated in the notification:

1. a common Office shall be substituted for the national Office of each of them;
2. they shall be deemed to be a single State for the purposes of the application of Articles 2 to 17 of this Agreement.

(2) Such notification shall not take effect until six months after the date of dispatch of the communication thereof by the Director General to the other contracting States.

Article 31

(1) This Agreement alone shall be applicable as regards the mutual relations of States party to both the present Agreement and the 1925 Agreement or the 1934 Agreement. However, such States shall,

in their mutual relations, apply the 1925 Agreement or the 1934 Agreement, as the case may be, to designs deposited at the International Bureau prior to the date on which the present Agreement becomes applicable as regards their mutual relations.

(2) *(a)* Any State party to both the present Agreement and the 1925 Agreement shall continue to apply the 1925 Agreement in its relations with States party only to the 1925 Agreement, unless the said State has denounced the 1925 Agreement.

(b) Any State party to both the present Agreement and the 1934 Agreement shall continue to apply the 1934 Agreement in its relations with States party only to the 1934 Agreement, unless the said State has denounced the 1934 Agreement.

(3) States party to the present Agreement only shall not be bound to States which, without being party to the present Agreement, are party to the 1925 Agreement or the 1934 Agreement.

Article 32

(1) Signature and ratification of, or accession to, the present Agreement by a State party, at the date of this Agreement, to the 1925 Agreement or the 1934 Agreement shall be deemed to include signature and ratification of, or accession to, the Protocol annexed to the present Agreement, unless such State makes an express declaration to the contrary at the time of signing or depositing its instrument of accession.

(2) Any contracting State having made the declaration referred to in paragraph (1), or any other contracting State not party to the 1925 Agreement or the 1934 Agreement, may sign or accede to the Protocol annexed to this Agreement. At the time of signing or depositing its instrument of accession, it may declare that it does not consider itself bound by the provisions of paragraphs (2)*(a)* or (2)*(b)* of the Protocol; in such case, the other States party to the Protocol shall be under no obligation to apply, in their relations with that State, the provisions mentioned in such declaration. The provisions of Articles 23 to 28 inclusive shall apply by analogy.

Article 33

This Act shall be signed in a single copy which shall be deposited in the archives of the Government of the Netherlands. A certified copy shall be transmitted by the latter to the Government of each State which has signed or acceded to this Agreement.

PROTOCOL[1]

States party to this Protocol have agreed as follows:

(1) The provisions of this Protocol shall apply to designs which have been the subject of an international deposit and of which one of the States party to this Protocol is deemed to be the State of origin.

(2) In respect of designs referred to in paragraph (1), above:

(a) the term of protection granted by States party to this Protocol to the designs referred to in paragraph (1) shall not be less than fifteen years from the date provided for in paragraphs (1)*(a)* or (1)*(b)*, as the case may be, of Article 11;

(b) the appearance of a notice on the articles incorporating the designs or on the tags attached thereto shall in no case be required by the States party to this Protocol, either for the exercise in their territories of rights arising from the international deposit, or for any other purpose.

[1] This Protocol is not yet in force.

III. Additional Act of Monaco of November 18, 1961

Article 1

(1) Over and above the fees established in Article 15 of the Hague Agreement as revised at London, the following additional fees shall be payable in respect of the transactions hereinafter specified, that is to say:

1. for the deposit of a single design and in respect of the first period of five years: 20 Swiss francs;
2. for the deposit of a single design, upon expiration of the first period and in respect of the duration of the second period of ten years: 40 Swiss francs;
3. for a multiple deposit and in respect of the first period of five years: 50 Swiss francs;
4. for a multiple deposit, upon expiration of the first period and in respect of the duration of the second period of ten years: 200 Swiss francs.

(2) If the fees prescribed in Article 15.2 and Article 15.4 of the Hague Agreement as revised at London have been paid after the date of this Act but before its entry into force—the latter being determined for each State in accordance with the provisions of paragraphs 7(2) and 7(3) where the first period of protection expires after such entry into force, the person making the deposit must pay the additional prolongation fee specified in items (1)2 and (1)4 of this Article. Upon entry into force of this Act, the International Bureau shall advise the depositors concerned that they must pay the additional fee within a period of six months from the receipt of such notice. If payment is not effected within such period the prolongation shall be deemed to be null and the reference thereto shall be deleted from the Register. In such case, the fee for prolongation already paid shall be refunded.

Article 2

Additional fees of 20 Swiss francs or 10 Swiss francs shall likewise be payable in respect of every other transaction provided for by the Hague Agreement as revised at London and for which the Regulations of the said Agreement prescribe a fee of 5 Swiss francs or 2.50 Swiss francs.

Article 3

(1) The fees prescribed in Articles 1 and 2 of this Act may be modified on the proposal of the International Bureau or of the Swiss Government, in accordance with the procedure hereinafter defined.

(2) Such proposals shall be communicated to the Offices of States party to this Act, which shall communicate their views to the International Bureau within a period of six months. If, after that period, a modification of a fee is adopted by a majority of the said Offices without giving rise to any opposition, such modification shall enter into force on the first day of the month following the date of dispatch of the notification thereof by the International Bureau to the aforesaid Offices.

Article 4

(1) There shall be established from the excess receipts derived from the application of the additional fees a reserve fund not exceeding 50,000 Swiss francs.

(2) When the reserve fund has reached this amount, any further excess receipts shall be distributed among the States party to this Act in proportion to the number of designs deposited by their nationals, or by the other persons referred to in Article 1 of the Hague Agreement as revised at London.

Article 5

For such time as all countries members of the Union created by the Hague Agreement as revised at London are not party to this Act or to the Hague Agreement of November 28, 1960, the International Bureau shall draw up separate accounts for countries which are party to this Act and for those which are party only to the Hague Agreement as revised at London.

Article 6

(1) This Act shall remain open for signature until March 31, 1962.

(2) States party to the Hague Agreement as revised at London which have not signed this Act may accede thereto. In such cases, the provisions of Articles 16 and 16*bis* of the Paris Convention for the Protection of Industrial Property shall be applicable.

Article 7

(1) This Act shall be ratified and the instruments of ratification shall be deposited with the Government of the Principality of Monaco. Such deposits shall be notified by the latter Government to the Government of the Swiss Confederation, which shall notify them to the contracting States.

(2) This Act shall come into force at the expiration of a period of one month from the date of dispatch by the Government of the Swiss Confederation to the contracting States of the notification of the deposit of the second instrument of ratification.

(3) As regards States which deposit their instruments of ratification subsequently to the deposit of the second such instrument of ratification as is mentioned in the preceding paragraph, this Act shall enter into force upon expiration of a period of one month from the date of dispatch by the Government of the Swiss Confederation to the contracting States of the notification of the deposit of the instrument of ratification concerned.

Article 8

This Act shall be signed in a single copy and shall be deposited in the archives of the Government of the Principality of Monaco. A certified copy thereof shall be sent by the latter to each of the Governments of the countries of the Hague Union.

IV. Complementary Act of Stockholm of July 14, 1967 as amended on September 28, 1979

Article 1 *[Definitions]*

For the purposes of this Complementary Act:

"1934 Act" shall mean the Act signed at London on June 2, 1934, of the Hague Agreement concerning the International Deposit of Industrial Designs;

"1960 Act" shall mean the Act signed at The Hague on November 28, 1960, of the Hague Agreement concerning the International Deposit of Industrial Designs;

"1961 Additional Act" shall mean the Act signed at Monaco on November 18, 1961, additional to the 1934 Act;

"Organization" shall mean the World Intellectual Property Organization;

"International Bureau" shall mean the International Bureau of Intellectual Property;

"Director General" shall mean the Director General of the Organization;

"Special Union" shall mean the Hague Union established by the Hague Agreement of November 6, 1925, concerning the International Deposit of Industrial Designs, and maintained by the 1934 and 1960 Acts, by the 1961 Additional Act, and by this Complementary Act,

Article 2 *[Assembly]*

(1)(a) The Special Union shall have an Assembly consisting of those countries which have ratified or acceded to this Complementary Act.

(b) The Government of each country shall be represented by one delegate, who may be assisted by alternate delegates, advisors, and experts.

(c) The expenses of each delegation shall be borne by the Government which has appointed it.

(2)(a) The Assembly shall:

(i) deal with all matters concerning the maintenance and development of the Special Union and the implementation of this Agreement;

(ii) give directions to the International Bureau concerning the preparation for conferences of revision, due account being taken of any comments made by those countries of the Special Union which have not ratified or acceded to this Complementary Act;

(iii) modify the Regulations, including the fixation of the amounts of the fees relating to the international deposit of industrial designs;

(iv) review and approve the reports and activities of the Director General concerning the Special Union, and give him all necessary instructions concerning matters within the competence of the Special Union;

(v) determine the program and adopt the biennial budget of the Special Union, and approve its final accounts;

(vi) adopt the financial regulations of the Special Union;

(vii) establish such committees of experts and working groups as it may deem necessary to achieve the objectives of the Special Union;

(viii) determine which countries not members of the Special Union and which intergovernmental and international non-governmental organizations shall be admitted to its meetings as observers;

(ix) adopt amendments to Articles 2 to 5;

(x) take any other appropriate action designed to further the objectives of the Special Union;

(xi) perform such other functions as are appropriate under this Complementary Act.

(b) With respect to matters which are of interest also to other Unions administered by the Organization, the Assembly shall make its decisions after having heard the advice of the Coordination Committee of the Organization.

(3) (a) Each country member of the Assembly shall have one vote.

(b) One-half of the countries members of the Assembly shall constitute a quorum.

(c) Notwithstanding the provisions of subparagraph (b), if, in any session, the number of countries represented is less than one-half but equal to or more than one-third of the countries members of the Assembly, the Assembly may make decisions but, with the exception of decisions concerning its own procedure, all such decisions shall take effect only if the conditions set forth hereinafter are fulfilled. The International Bureau shall communicate the said decisions to the countries members of the Assembly which were not represented and shall invite them to express in writing their vote or abstention within a period of three months from the date of the communication. If, at the expiration of this period, the number of countries having thus expressed their vote or abstention attains the number of countries which was lacking for attaining the quorum in the session itself, such decisions shall take effect provided that at the same time the required majority still obtains.

(d) Subject to the provisions of Article 5(2), the decisions of the Assembly shall require two-thirds of the votes cast.

(e) Abstentions shall not be considered as votes.

(f) A delegate may represent, and vote in the name of, one country only.

(g) Countries of the Special Union not members of the Assembly shall be admitted to the meetings of the latter as observers.

(4) (a) The Assembly shall meet once in every second calendar year in ordinary session upon convocation by the Director General and, in the absence of exceptionnal circumstances, during the same period and at the same place as the General Assembly of the Organization.

(b) The Assembly shall meet in extraordinary session upon convocation by the Director General, at the request of one-fourth of the countries members of the Assembly.

(c) The agenda of each session shall be prepared by the Director General.

(5) The Assembly shall adopt its own rules of procedure.

Article 3
[International Bureau]

(1) (a) International deposit of industrial designs and related duties, as well as all other administrative tasks concerning the Special Union, shall be performed by the International Bureau.

(b) In particular, the International Bureau shall prepare the meetings and provide the secretariat of the Assembly and of such committees of experts and working groups as may have been established by the Assembly.

(c) The Director General shall be the chief executive of the Special Union and shall represent the Special Union.

(2) The Director General and any staff member designated by him shall participate, without the right to vote, in all meetings of the Assembly and of such committees of experts or working groups as may have been established by the Assembly. The Director General, or a staff member designated by him, shall be ex officio secretary of those bodies.

(3) (a) The International Bureau shall, in accordance with the directions of the Assembly, make the preparations for the conferences of revision of the provisions of the Agreement.

(b) The International Bureau may consult with intergovernmental and international non-governmental organizations concerning preparations for conferences of revision.

(c) The Director General and persons designated by him shall take part, without the right to vote, in the discussions at those conferences.

(4) The International Bureau shall carry out any other tasks assigned to it.

Article 4
[Finances]

(1) (a) The Special Union shall have a budget.

(b) The budget of the Special Union shall include the income and expenses proper to the Special Union, its contribution to the budget of expenses common to the Unions, and, where applicable, the sum made available to the budget of the Conference of the Organization.

(c) Expenses not attributable exclusively to the Special Union but also to one or more other Unions administered by the Organization shall be deemed to be expenses common to the Unions. The share of the Special Union in such common expenses shall be in proportion to the interest the Special Union has in them.

(2) The budget of the Special Union shall be established with due regard to the requirements of coordination with the budgets of the other Unions administered by the Organization.

(3) The budget of the Special Union shall be financed from the following sources:

(i) international deposit fees and other fees and charges due for other services rendered by the International Bureau in relation to the Special Union;

(ii) sale of, or royalties on, the publications of the International Bureau concerning the Special Union;

(iii) gifts, bequests, and subventions;

(iv) rents, interests, and other miscellaneous income.

(4) (a) The amounts of the fees referred to in paragraph (3)(i) shall be fixed by the Assembly on the proposal of the Director General.

(b) The amounts of such fees shall be so fixed that the revenues of the Special Union from fees and other sources shall be at least sufficient to cover the expenses of the International Bureau concerning the Special Union.

(c) If the budget is not adopted before the beginning of a new financial period, it shall be at the same level as the budget of the previous year, as provided in the financial regulations.

(5) Subject to the provisions of paragraph (4)(a), the amount of the fees and charges due for other services rendered by the International Bureau in relation to the Special Union shall be established, and shall be reported to the Assembly, by the Director General.

(6) (a) The Special Union shall have a working capital fund which shall be constituted by the excess receipts and, if such excess does not suffice, by a single payment made by each country of the Special Union. If the fund becomes insufficient, the Assembly shall decide to increase it.

(b) The amount of the initial payment of each country to the said fund or of its participation in the increase thereof shall be a proportion of the contribution of that country as a member of the Paris Union for the Protection of Industrial Property to the budget of the said Union for the year in which the fund is established or the decision to increase it is made.

(c) The proportion and the terms of payment shall be fixed by the Assembly on the proposal of the Director General and after it has heard the advice of the Coordination Committee of the Organization.

(7) (a) In the headquarters agreement concluded with the country on the territory of which the Organization has its headquarters, it shall be provided that, whenever the working capital fund is insufficient, such country shall grant advances. The amount of those advances and the conditions on which they are granted shall be the subject of separate agreements, in each case, between such country and the Organization.

(b) The country referred to in subparagraph (a) and the Organization shall each have the right to denounce the obligation to grant advances, by written notification. Denunciation shall take effect three years after the end of the year in which it has been notified.

(8) The auditing of the accounts shall be effected by one or more of the countries of the Special Union or by external auditors, as provided in the financial regulations. They shall be designated, with their agreement, by the Assembly.

Article 5
[Amendment of Articles 2 to 5]

(1) Proposals for the amendment of this Complementary Act may be initiated by any country member of the Assembly, or by the Director General. Such proposals shall be communicated by the Director General to the member countries of the Assembly at least six months in advance of their consideration by the Assembly.

(2) Amendments referred to in paragraph (1) shall be adopted by the Assembly. Adoption shall require three-fourths of the votes cast, provided that any amendment to Article 2 and to the present paragraph, shall require four-fifths of the votes cast.

(3) Any amendment referred to in paragraph (1) shall enter into force one month after written notifications of acceptance, effected in accordance with their respective constitutional processes, have been received by the Director General from three-fourths of the countries members of the Assembly at the time it adopted the amendment. Any amendment thus accepted shall bind all the countries which are members of the Assembly at the time the amendment enters into force, or which become members thereof at a subsequent date.

Article 6
[Amendment of the 1934 Act and the 1961 Additional Act]

(1) (a) References in the 1934 Act to "the International Bureau of Industrial Property at Berne," to "the Berne International Bureau," or to "the International Bureau," shall be construed as references to the International Bureau as defined in Article 1 of this Complementary Act.

(b) Article 15 of the 1934 Act is repealed.

(c) Any amendment of the Regulations referred to in Article 20 of the 1934 Act shall be effected in accordance with the procedure prescribed under Article 2(2)(a)(iii) and Article 2(3)(d).

(d) In Articles 21 of the 1934 Act, for the words "revised in 1928" there shall be substituted the words "for the Protection of Literary and Artistic Works."

(e) References in Article 22 of the 1934 Act to Articles 16, 16*bis*, and 17*bis*, of the "General Convention" shall be construed as references to those provisions of the Stockholm Act of the Paris Convention for the Protection of Industrial Property which, in the said *Stockholm Act*, correspond to Articles 16, 16*bis*, and 17*bis*, of the earlier Acts of the Paris Convention.

(2) (a) Any modification of the fees referred to in Article 3 of the *1961 Additional Act* shall be effected in accordance with the procedure prescribed under Article 2(2)(a)(iii) and 2(3)(d).

(b) Article 4(1) of the *1961 Additional Act*, and the words "When the reserve fund has reached this amount" in Article 4(2) are repealed.

(c) References in Article 6(2) of the *1961 Additional Act* to Articles 16 and 16*bis* of the Paris Convention for the Protection of Industrial Property shall be construed as references to those provisions of the Stockholm Act of the said Convention which, in the Stockholm Act, correspond to Article 16 and 16*bis* of the earlier Acts of the Paris Convention.

(d) References in paragraph 7(1) and paragraph 7(3) of the *1961 Additional Act* to the Government of the Swiss Confederation shall be construed as references to the Director General.

Article 7
[Amendment of the 1960 Act]

(1) References in the 1960 Act to "the Bureau of the International Union for the Protection of Industrial Property" or to "the International Bureau" shall be construed as references to the International Bureau as defined in Article 1 of this Complementary Act.

(2) Articles 19, 20, 21, and 22, of the 1960 Act are repealed.

(3) References in the 1960 Act to the Government of the Swiss Confederation shall be construed as references to the Director General.

(4) In Article 29 of the 1960 Act, the words "periodical" (paragraph 29(1)) and "of the International Design Committee or" (paragraph 29(2)) are deleted.

Article 8
[Ratification of, and Accession to,
the Complementary Act]

(1) (a) Countries which, before January 13, 1968, have ratified the 1934 Act or the 1960 Act, and countries which have acceded to at least one of those Acts, may sign this Complementary Act and ratify it, or may accede to it.

(b) Ratification of, or accession to, this Complementary Act by a country which is bound by the 1934 Act without being bound also by the *1961 Additional Act* shall automatically entail ratification of, or accession to, the *1961 Additional Act*.

(2) Instruments of ratification and accession shall be deposited with the Director General.

Article 9
[Entry Into Force of the Complementary Act]

(1) With respect to the first five countries which have deposited their instruments of ratification or accession, this Complementary Act shall enter into force three months after the deposit of the fifth such instrument of ratification or accession.

(2) With respect to any other country, this Complementary Act shall enter into force three months after the date on which its ratification or accession has been notified by the Director General, unless a subsequent date has been indicated in the instrument of ratification or accession. In the latter case, this Complementary Act shall enter into force with respect to that country on the date thus indicated.

Article 10
[Automatic Acceptance of Certain Provisions by Certain Countries]

(1) Subject to the provisions of Article 8 and the following paragraph, any country which has not ratified or acceded to the 1934 Act shall become bound by the *1961 Additional Act* and by Articles 1 to 6 of this Complementary Act from the date on which its accession to the 1934 Act enters into force, provided that, if on the said date this Complementary Act has not yet entered into force pursuant to Article 9(1), then, such country shall become bound by the said Articles of this Complementary Act only from the date of entry into force of the Complementary Act pursuant to Article 9(1).

(2) Subject to the provisions of Article 8 and the foregoing paragraph, any country which has not ratified or acceded to the 1960 Act shall become bound by Articles 1 to 7 of this Complementary Act from the date on which its ratification of, or accession to, the 1960 Act enters into force, provided that, if on the said date this Complementary Act has not yet entered into force pursuant to Article 9(1), then, such country shall become bound by the said Articles of this Complementary Act only from the date of entry into force of the Complementary Act pursuant to Article 9(1).

Article 11
[Signature, etc., of the Complementary Act]

(1) (a) This Complementary Act shall be signed in a single copy in the French language and shall be deposited with the Government of Sweden.

(b) Official texts shall be established by the Director General, after consultation with the interested Governments, in such other languages as the Assembly may designate.

(2) This Complementary Act shall remain open for signature at Stockholm until January 13, 1968.

(3) The Director General shall transmit two copies, certified by the Government of Sweden, of the signed text of this Complementary Act to the Governments of all countries of the Special Union and, on request, to the Government of any other country.

(4) The Director General shall register this Complementary Act with the Secretariat of the United Nations.

(5) The Director General shall notify the Governments of all countries of the Special Union of signatures, deposits of instruments of ratification or accession, entry into force, and all other relevant notifications.

Article 12
[Transitional Provision]

Until the first Director General assumes office, references in this Complementary Act to the International Bureau of the Organization or to the Director General shall be construed as references to the Bureau of the Union established by the Paris Convention for the Protection of Industrial Property or its Director, respectively.

Common Regulations Under the 1999 Act, the 1960 Act and the 1934 Act of the Hague Agreement

(as in force on April 1, 2004)

CHAPTER 1
GENERAL PROVISIONS

Rule 1
Definitions

(1) [*Abbreviated Expressions*] For the purposes of these Regulations,

(i) "1999 Act" means the Act signed at Geneva on July 2, 1999, of the Hague Agreement;

(ii) "1960 Act" means the Act signed at The Hague on November 28, 1960, of the Hague Agreement;

(iii) "1934 Act" means the Act signed at London on June 2, 1934, of the Hague Agreement;

(iv) an expression which is used in these Regulations and is referred to in Article 1 of the 1999 Act has the same meaning as in that Act;

(v) "Administrative Instructions" means the Administrative Instructions referred to in Rule 34;

(vi) "communication" means any international application or any request, declaration, invitation, notification or information relating to or accompanying an international application or an international registration that is addressed to the Office of a Contracting Party, the International Bureau, the applicant or the holder by means permitted by these Regulations or the Administrative Instructions;

(vii) "official form" means a form established by the International Bureau or any form having the same contents and format;

(viii) "International Classification" means the Classification established under the Locarno Agreement Establishing an International Classification for Industrial Designs;

(ix) "prescribed fee" means the applicable fee set out in the Schedule of Fees;

(x) "Bulletin" means the periodical bulletin in which the International Bureau effects the publications provided for in the 1999 Act, the 1960 Act, the 1934 Act or these Regulations, whatever the medium used;

(xi) "Contracting Party designated under the 1999 Act" means a designated Contracting Party in respect of which the 1999 Act is applicable, either as the only common Act to which that designated Contracting Party and the applicant's Contracting Party are bound, or by virtue of Article 31(1), first sentence, of the 1999 Act;

(xii) "Contracting Party designated under the 1960 Act" means a designated Contracting Party in respect of which the 1960 Act is applicable, either as the only common Act to which that designated Contracting Party and the State of origin referred to in Article 2 of the 1960 Act are bound, or by virtue of Article 31(1), first sentence, of the 1960 Act;

(xiii) "Contracting Party designated under the 1934 Act" means a designated Contracting Party in respect of which the 1934 Act is applicable, as the only common Act to which that designated Contracting Party and the contracting country referred to in Article 1 of the 1934 Act are bound;

(xiv) "international application governed exclusively by the 1999 Act" means an international application in respect of which all designated Contracting Parties are Contracting Parties designated under the 1999 Act;

(xv) "international application governed exclusively by the 1960 Act" means an international application in respect of which all designated Contracting Parties are Contracting Parties designated under the 1960 Act;

(xvi) "international application governed exclusively by the 1934 Act" means an international application in respect of which all designated Contracting Parties are Contracting Parties designated under the 1934 Act;

(xvii) "international application governed by both the 1999 Act and the 1960 Act" means an international application in respect of which

—at least one Contracting Party has been designated under the 1999 Act,

—at least one Contracting Party has been designated under the 1960 Act, and

—no Contracting Party has been designated under the 1934 Act;

(xviii) "international application governed by both the 1999 Act and the 1934 Act" means an international application in respect of which

—at least one Contracting Party has been designated under the 1999 Act,

—at least one Contracting Party has been designated under the 1934 Act, and

—no Contracting Party has been designated under the 1960 Act;

(xix) "international application governed by both the 1960 Act and the 1934 Act" means an international application in respect of which

—at least one Contracting Party has been designated under the 1960 Act,

—at least one Contracting Party has been designated under the 1934 Act, and

—no Contracting Party has been designated under the 1999 Act;

(xx) "international application governed by the 1999 Act, the 1960 Act and the 1934 Act" means an international application in respect of which

—at least one Contracting Party has been designated under the 1999 Act,

—at least one Contracting Party has been designated under the 1960 Act, and

—at least one Contracting Party has been designated under the 1934 Act.

(2) [*Correspondence Between Some Expressions Used in the 1999 Act, the 1960 Act and the 1934 Act*] For the purposes of these Regulations,

(i) reference to "international application" or "international registration" shall be deemed, where appropriate, to include a reference to "international deposit" as referred to in the 1960 Act and the 1934 Act;

(ii) reference to "applicant" or "holder" shall be deemed, where appropriate, to include a reference to, respectively, "depositor" or "owner" as referred to in the 1960 Act and the 1934 Act;

(iii) reference to "Contracting Party" shall be deemed, where appropriate, to include a reference to a State party to the 1960 Act or to a country party to the 1934 Act;

(iv) reference to "Contracting Party whose Office is an examining Office" shall be deemed, where appropriate, to include a reference to "State having a novelty examination" as defined in Article 2 of the 1960 Act;

(v) reference to "individual designation fee" shall be deemed, where appropriate, to include a reference to the fee mentioned in Article 15(1)2(b) of the 1960 Act;

(vi) reference to "renewal" shall be deemed, where appropriate, to include a reference to "prolongation" referred to in the 1934 Act.

Rule 2
Communication with the International Bureau

Communications addressed to the International Bureau shall be effected as specified in the Administrative Instructions.

Rule 3
Representation Before the International Bureau

(1) [*Representative; Number Representatives*] (a) The applicant or the holder may have a representative before the International Bureau.

(b) Only one representative may be appointed in respect of a given international application or international registration. Where the appointment indicates several representatives, only the one indicated first shall be considered to be a representative and be recorded as such.

(c) Where a partnership or firm composed of attorneys or patent or trademark agents has been indicated as representative to the International Bureau, it shall be regarded as one representative.

(2) [*Appointment of the Representative*] (a) The appointment of a representative may be made in the international application, provided that the application is signed by the applicant.

(b) The appointment of a representative may also be made in a separate communication which may relate to one or more specified international applications or international registrations of the same applicant or holder. The said communication shall be signed by the applicant or the holder.

(c) Where the International Bureau considers that the appointment of a representative is irregular, it shall notify accordingly the applicant or holder and the purported representative.

(3) [*Recording and Notification of Appointment of a Representative; Effective Date of Appointment*] (a) Where the International Bureau finds that the appointment of a representative complies with the applicable requirements, it shall record the fact that the applicant or holder has a representative, as well as the name and address of the representative, in the International Register. In such a case, the effective date of the appointment shall be the date on which the International Bureau received the international application or separate communication in which the representative is appointed.

(b) The International Bureau shall notify the recording referred to in subparagraph (a) to both the applicant or holder and the representative.

(4) [*Effect of Appointment of a Representative*] (a) Except where these Regulations expressly provide otherwise, the signature of a representative recorded under paragraph (3)(a) shall replace the signature of the applicant or holder.

(b) Except where these Regulations expressly require that a communication be addressed to both the applicant or holder and the representative, the International Bureau shall address to the representative recorded under paragraph (3)(a) any communication which, in the absence of a representative, would have to be sent to the applicant or holder; any communication so addressed to the said representative shall have the same effect as if it had been addressed to the applicant or holder.

(c) Any communication addressed to the International Bureau by the representative recorded under paragraph (3)(a) shall have the same effect as if it had been addressed to the said Bureau by the applicant or holder.

(5) [*Cancellation of Recording; Effective Date of Cancellation*] (a) Any recording under paragraph (3)(a) shall be canceled where cancellation is requested in a communication signed by the applicant, holder or representative. The recording shall be canceled *ex officio* by the International Bureau where a new representative is appointed or where a change in ownership is recorded and no representative is appointed by the new holder of the international registration.

(b) The cancellation shall be effective from the date on which the International Bureau receives the corresponding communication.

(c) The International Bureau shall notify the cancellation and its effective date to the representative whose recording has been canceled and to the applicant or holder.

Rule 4
Calculation of Time Limits

(1) [*Periods Expressed in Years*] Any period expressed in years shall expire, in the relevant subsequent year, in the month having the same name and on the day having the same number as the month and the day of the event from which the period starts to run, except that, where the event occurred on February 29 and in the relevant subsequent year February ends on the 28th, the period shall expire on February 28.

(2) [*Periods Expressed in Months*] Any period expressed in months shall expire, in the relevant subsequent month, on the day which has the same number as the day of the event from which the period starts to run, except that, where the relevant subsequent month has no day with the same number, the period shall expire on the last day of that month.

(3) [*Periods Expressed in Days*] The calculation of any period expressed in days shall start with the day following the day on which the relevant event occurred and shall expire accordingly.

(4) [*Expiry on a Day on Which the International Bureau or an Office Is Not Open to the Public*] If a period expires on a day on which the International Bureau or the Office concerned is not open to the public, the period shall, notwithstanding paragraphs (1) to (3), expire on the first subsequent day on which the International Bureau or the Office concerned is open to the public.

Rule 5
Irregularities in Postal and Delivery Services

(1) [*Communications Sent Through a Postal Service*] Failure by an interested party to meet a time limit for a communication addressed to the International Bureau and mailed through a postal service shall be excused if the interested party submits evidence showing, to the satisfaction of the International Bureau,

(i) that the communication was mailed at least five days prior to the expiry of the time limit, or, where the postal service was, on any of the ten days preceding the day of expiry of the time limit, interrupted on account of war, revolution, civil disorder, strike, natural calamity, or other like reason, that the communication was mailed not later than five days after postal service was resumed,

(ii) that the mailing of the communication was registered, or details of the mailing were recorded, by the postal service at the time of mailing, and

(iii) in cases where not all classes of mail normally reach the International Bureau within two days of mailing, that the communication was mailed by a class of mail which normally reaches the International Bureau within two days of mailing or by airmail.

(2) [*Communications Sent Through a Delivery Service*] Failure by an interested party to meet a time limit for a communication addressed to the International Bureau and sent through a delivery service shall be excused if the interested party submits evidence showing, to the satisfaction of the International Bureau,

(i) that the communication was sent at least five days prior to the expiry of the time limit, or, where the delivery service was, on any of the ten days preceding the day of expiry of the time limit, interrupted on account of war, revolution, civil disorder, natural calamity, or other like reason, that the communication was sent not later than five days after the delivery service was resumed, and

(ii) that details of the sending of the communication were recorded by the delivery service at the time of sending.

(3) [*Limitation on Excuse*] Failure to meet a time limit shall be excused under this Rule only if the evidence referred to in paragraph (1) or (2) and the communication or a duplicate thereof are received by the International Bureau not later than six months after the expiry of the time limit.

Rule 6
Languages

(1) [*International Application*] The international application shall be in English or French.

(2) [*Recording and Publication*] The recording in the International Register and the publication in the Bulletin of the international registration and of any data to be both recorded and published under these Regulations in respect of that international registration shall be in English and French. The recording and publication of the international registration shall indicate the language in which the international application was received by the International Bureau.

(3) [*Communications*] Any communication concerning an international application or the international registration resulting therefrom shall be

(i) in English or French where such communication is addressed to the International Bureau by the applicant or holder or by an Office;

(ii) in the language of the international application where the communication is addressed by the International Bureau to an Office, unless that Office has notified the International Bureau that all such communications are to be in English or that all such communications are to be in French;

(iii) in the language of the international application where the communication is addressed by the International Bureau to the applicant or holder unless the applicant or holder expresses the wish to receive all such communications in English although the international application was in French, or *vice versa*.

(4) [*Translation*] The translations needed for the recordings and publications under paragraph (2) shall be made by the International Bureau. The applicant may annex to the international application a proposed translation of any text matter contained in the international application. If the proposed translation is not considered by the International Bureau to be correct, it shall be corrected by the International Bureau after having invited the applicant to make, within one month from the invitation, observations on the proposed corrections.

CHAPTER 2
INTERNATIONAL APPLICATIONS AND INTERNATIONAL REGISTRATIONS

Rule 7
Requirements Concerning the International Application

(1) [*Form and Signature*] The international application shall be presented on the official form. The international application shall be signed by the applicant.

(2) [*Fees*] The prescribed fees applicable to the international application shall be paid as provided for in Rules 27 and 28.

(3) [*Mandatory Contents of the International Application*] The international application shall contain or indicate

(i) the name of the applicant, given in accordance with the Administrative Instructions;

(ii) the address of the applicant, given in accordance with the Administrative Instructions;

(iii) the Contracting Party or Parties in respect of which the applicant fulfills the conditions to be the holder of an international registration;

(iv) the product or products which constitute the industrial design or in relation to which the industrial design is to be used, with an indication whether the product or products constitute the industrial design or are products in relation to which the industrial design is to be used; the product or products shall preferably be identified by using terms appearing in the list of goods of the International Classification;

(v) the number of industrial designs included in the international application, which may not exceed 100, and the number of reproductions or specimens of the industrial designs accompanying the international application in accordance with Rule 9 or 10;

(vi) the designated Contracting Parties;

(vii) the amount of the fees being paid and the method of payment, or instructions to debit the required amount of fees to an account opened with the International Bureau, and the identification of the party effecting the payment or giving the instructions.

(4) [*Additional Mandatory Contents of an International Application*] (a) With respect to Contracting Parties designated under the 1999 Act in an international application, that application shall contain, in addition to the indications referred to in paragraph (3)(iii), the indication of the applicant's Contracting Party.

(b) Where a Contracting Party designated under the 1999 Act has notified the Director General, in accordance with Article 5(2)(a) of the 1999 Act, that its law requires one or more of the elements referred to in Article 5(2)(b) of the 1999 Act, the international application shall contain such element or elements, as prescribed in Rule 11.

(c) Where Rule 8 applies, the international application shall contain the indications referred to in Rule 8(2) and, where applicable, be accompanied by the statement or document referred to in that Rule.

(5) [*Optional Contents of an International Application*] (a) An element referred to in item (i) or (ii) of Article 5(2)(b) of the 1999 Act or in Article 8(4)(a) of the 1960 Act may, at the option of the applicant, be included in the international application even where that element is not required in consequence of a notification in accordance with Article 5(2)(a) of the 1999 Act or in consequence of a requirement under Article 8(4)(a) of the 1960 Act.

(b) Where the applicant has a representative, the international application shall state the name and address of the representative, given in accordance with the Administrative Instructions.

(c) Where the applicant wishes, under Article 4 of the Paris Convention, to take advantage of the priority of an earlier filing, the international application shall contain a declaration claiming the priority of that earlier filing, together with an indication of the name of the Office where such filing was made and of the date and, where available, the number of that filing and, where the priority claim relates to less than all the industrial designs contained in the international application, the indication of those industrial designs to which the priority claim relates or does not relate.

(d) Where the applicant wishes to take advantage of Article 11 of the Paris Convention, the international application shall contain a declaration that the product or products which constitute the industrial design or in which the industrial design is incorporated have been shown at an official or officially recognized international exhibition, together with the place where the exhibition was held and the date on which the product or products were first exhibited there and, where less than all the industrial designs contained in the international application are concerned, the indication of those industrial designs to which the declaration relates or does not relate.

(e) Where the applicant wishes that publication of the industrial design be deferred, the international application shall contain a request for deferment of publication.

(f) The international application may also contain any declaration, statement or other relevant indication as may be specified in the Administrative Instructions.

(g) The international application may be accompanied by a statement that identifies information known by the applicant to be material to the eligibility for protection of the industrial design concerned.

(6) [*No Additional Matter*] If the international application contains any matter other than that required or permitted by the 1999 Act, the 1960 Act, the 1934 Act, these Regulations or the Administrative Instructions, the International Bureau shall delete it *ex officio*. If the international application is accompanied by any document other than those required or permitted, the International Bureau may dispose of the said document.

(7) [*All Products to Be in Same Class*] All the products which constitute the industrial designs to which an international application relates, or in relation to which the industrial designs are to be used, shall belong to the same class of the International Classification.

Rule 8
Special Requirements Concerning the Applicant

(1) [*Notification of Special Requirements*] (a) Where the law of a Contracting Party bound by the 1999 Act requires that an application for the protection of an industrial design be filed in the name of the creator of the industrial design, that Contracting Party may, in a declaration, notify the Director General of that fact.

(b) The declaration referred to in subparagraph (a) shall specify the form and mandatory contents of any statement or document required for the purposes of paragraph (2).

(2) [*Identity of the Creator and Assignment of International Application*] Where an international application contains the designation of a Contracting Party that has made the declaration referred to in paragraph (1),

(i) it shall also contain indications concerning the identity of the creator of the industrial design, together with a statement, complying with the requirements specified in accordance with paragraph (1)(b), that the latter believes himself to be the creator of the industrial design; the person so identified as the creator shall be deemed to be the applicant for the purposes of the designation of that Contracting Party, irrespective of the person named as the applicant in accordance with Rule 7(3)(i);

(ii) where the person identified as the creator is a person other than the person named as the applicant in accordance with Rule 7(3)(i), the international application shall be accompanied by a statement or document, complying with the requirements specified in accordance with paragraph (1)(b), to the effect that it has been assigned by the person identified as the creator to the person named as the applicant. The latter person shall be recorded as the holder of the international registration.

Rule 9
Reproductions of the Industrial Design

(1) [*Form and Number of Reproductions of the Industrial Design*] (a) Reproductions of the industrial design shall, at the option of the applicant, be in the form of photographs or other graphic representations of the industrial design itself or of the product or products which constitute the industrial design. The same product may be shown from different angles; views from different angles shall be included in different photographs or other graphic representations.

(b) Any reproduction shall be submitted in the number of copies specified in the Administrative Instructions.

(2) [*Requirements Concerning Reproductions*] (a) Reproductions shall be of a quality permitting all the details of the industrial design to be clearly distinguished and permitting publication.

(b) Matter which is shown in a reproduction but for which protection is not sought may be indicated as provided for in the Administrative Instructions.

(3) [*Views Required*] (a) Subject to subparagraph (b), any Contracting Party bound by the 1999 Act which requires certain specified views of the product or products which constitute the industrial design or in relation to which the industrial design is to be used shall, in a declaration, so notify the Director General, specifying the views that are required and the circumstances in which they are required.

(b) No Contracting Party may require more than one view where the industrial design or product is two-dimensional, or more than six views where the product is three-dimensional.

(4) [*Refusal on Grounds Relating to the Reproductions of the Industrial Design*] A Contracting Party may not refuse the effects of the international registration on the ground that requirements relating to the form of the reproductions of the industrial design that are additional to, or different from, those notified by that Contracting Party in accordance with paragraph (3)(a) have not been satisfied under its law. A Contracting Party may however refuse the effects of the international registration on the ground that the reproductions contained in the international registration are not sufficient to disclose fully the industrial design.

Rule 10
Specimens of the Industrial Design Where Deferment of Publication Is Requested

(1) [*Number of Specimens*] Where an international application governed exclusively by the 1999 Act contains a request for deferment of publication in respect of a two-dimensional industrial design and, instead of being accompanied by the reproductions referred to in Rule 9, is accompanied by specimens of the industrial design, the following number of specimens shall accompany the international application:

(i) one specimen for the International Bureau, and

(ii) one specimen for each designated Office that has notified the International Bureau under Article 10(5) of the 1999 Act that it wishes to receive copies of international registrations.

(2) [*Specimens*] All the specimens shall be contained in a single package. The specimens may be folded. The maximum dimensions and weight of the package shall be specified in the Administrative Instructions.

Rule 11
Identity of Creator; Description; Claim

(1) [*Identity of Creator*] Where the international application contains indications concerning the identity of the creator of the industrial design, his name and address shall be given in accordance with the Administrative Instructions.

(2) [*Description*] Where the international application contains a description, the latter shall concern those features that appear in the reproductions of the industrial design and may not concern technical features of the operation of the industrial design or its possible utilization. If the description exceeds 100 words, an additional fee, as set out in the Schedule of Fees, shall be payable.

(3) [*Claim*] A declaration under Article 5(2)(a) of the 1999 Act that the law of a Contracting Party requires a claim in order for an application for the grant of protection to an industrial design to be accorded a filing date under that law shall specify the exact wording of the required claim. Where the international application contains a claim, the wording of that claim shall be as specified in the said declaration.

Rule 12
Fees Concerning the International Application

(1) [*Prescribed Fees*] (a) The international application shall be subject to the payment of the following fees:

(i) a basic fee;

(ii) a standard designation fee in respect of each designated Contracting Party that has not made a declaration under Article 7(2) of the 1999 Act or under Rule 36(1);

(iii) an individual designation fee in respect of each designated Contracting Party that has made a declaration under Article 7(2) of the 1999 Act or under Rule 36(1);

(iv) a publication fee.

(b) The amounts of the fees referred to in items (i), (ii) and (iv) are set out in the Schedule of Fees.

(2) [*When Fees to Be Paid*] The fees referred to in paragraph (1) are, subject to paragraph (3), payable at the time of filing the international application, except that, where the international application contains a request for deferment of publication, the publication fee may be paid later, in accordance with Rule 16(3)(a).

(3) [*Individual Designation Fee Payable in Two Parts*] (a) A declaration under Article 7(2) of the 1999 Act or under Rule 36(1) may also specify that the individual designation fee to be paid in respect of the Contracting Party concerned comprises two parts, the first part to be paid at the time of filing the international application and the second part to be paid at a later date which is determined in accordance with the law of the Contracting Party concerned.

(b) Where subparagraph (a) applies, the reference in paragraph (1)(iii) to an individual designation fee shall be construed as a reference to the first part of the individual designation fee.

(c) The second part of the individual designation fee may be paid either directly to the Office concerned or through the International Bureau, at the option of the holder. Where it is paid directly to the Office concerned, the Office shall notify the International Bureau accordingly and the International Bureau shall record any such notification in the International Register. Where it is paid through the International Bureau, the International Bureau shall record the payment in the International Register and notify the Office concerned accordingly.

(d) Where the second part of the individual designation fee is not paid within the applicable period, the Office concerned shall notify the International Bureau and request the International Bureau to cancel the international registration in the International Register with respect to the Contracting Party concerned. The International Bureau shall proceed accordingly and so notify the holder.

Rule 13
International Application Filed Through an Office

(1) [*Date of Receipt by Office and Transmittal to the International Bureau*] Where an international application governed exclusively by the 1999 Act is filed through the Office of the applicant's Contracting Party, that Office shall notify the applicant of the date on which it received the application. At the same time as it transmits the international application to the International Bureau, the Office shall notify the International Bureau of the date on which it received the application. The Office shall notify the applicant of the fact that it has transmitted the international application to the International Bureau.

(2) [*Transmittal Fee*] An Office that requires a transmittal fee, as provided for in Article 4(2) of the 1999 Act, shall notify the International Bureau of the amount of such fee, which should not exceed the administrative costs of receiving and transmitting the international application, and its due date.

(3) [*Filing Date of International Application Filed Indirectly*] Subject to Rule 14(2), the filing date of an international application filed through an Office shall be

(i) where the international application is governed exclusively by the 1999 Act, the date on which the international application was received by that Office, provided that it is received by the International Bureau within one month of that date;

(ii) in any other case, the date on which the International Bureau receives the international application.

(4) [*Filing Date Where Applicant's Contracting Party Requires a Security Clearance*] Notwithstanding paragraph (3), a Contracting Party whose law, at the time that it becomes party to the 1999 Act, requires security clearance may, in a declaration, notify the Director General that the period of one month referred to in that paragraph shall be replaced by a period of six months.

Rule 14
Examination by the International Bureau

(1) [*Time Limit for Correcting Irregularities*] If the International Bureau finds that the international application does not, at the time of its receipt by the International Bureau, fulfill the applicable requirements, it shall invite the applicant to make the required corrections within three months from the date of the invitation sent by the International Bureau.

(2) [*Irregularities Entailing a Postponement of the Filing Date of the International Application*] Where the international application has, on the date on which it is received by the International Bureau, an irregularity which is prescribed as an irregularity entailing a postponement of the filing date of the international application, the filing date shall be the date on which the correction of such

irregularity is received by the International Bureau. The irregularities which are prescribed as entailing a postponement of the filing date of the international application are the following:

(a) the international application is not in the prescribed language or one of the prescribed languages;

(b) any of the following elements is missing from the international application:

(i) an express or implicit indication that international registration under the 1999 Act, the 1960 Act or the 1934 Act is sought;

(ii) indications allowing the identity of the applicant to be established;

(iii) indications sufficient to enable the applicant or its representative, if any, to be contacted;

(iv) a reproduction, or, in accordance with Article 5(1)(iii) of the 1999 Act, a specimen, of each industrial design that is the subject of the international application;

(v) the designation of at least one Contracting Party.

(3) [*International Application Considered Abandoned; Reimbursement of Fees*] Where an irregularity, other than an irregularity referred to in Article 8(2)(b) of the 1999 Act, is not remedied within the time limit referred to in paragraph (1), the international application shall be considered abandoned and the International Bureau shall refund any fees paid in respect of that application, after deduction of an amount corresponding to the basic fee.

Rule 15
Registration of the Industrial Design in the International Register

(1) [*Registration of the Industrial Design in the International Register*] Where the International Bureau finds that the international application conforms to the applicable requirements, it shall register the industrial design in the International Register and send a certificate to the holder.

(2) [*Contents of the Registration*] The international registration shall contain

(i) all the data contained in the international application, except any priority claim under Rule 7(5)(c) where the date of the earlier filing is more than six months before the filing date of the international application;

(ii) any reproduction of the industrial design;

(iii) the date of the international registration;

(iv) the number of the international registration;

(v) the relevant class of the International Classification, as determined by the International Bureau.

Rule 16
Deferment of Publication

(1) [*Maximum Period of Deferment*] (a) The prescribed period for deferment of publication in respect of an international application governed exclusively by the 1999 Act shall be 30 months from the filing date or, where priority is claimed, from the priority date of the application concerned.

(b) The maximum period for deferment of publication in respect of an international application governed exclusively by the 1960 Act or by both the 1999 Act and the 1960 Act shall be 12 months from the filing date or, where priority is claimed, from the priority date of the application concerned.

(2) [*Period for Withdrawal of Designation Where Deferment Is Not Possible Under Applicable Law*] The period referred to in Article 11(3)(i) of the 1999 Act for the applicant to withdraw the designation of a Contracting Party whose law does not allow the deferment of publication shall be one month from the date of the notification sent by the International Bureau.

(3) [*Period for Paying Publication Fee and Submitting Reproductions*] (a) The publication fee referred to in Rule 12(1)(a)(iv) shall be paid, and, where specimens have been submitted instead of reproductions in accordance with Rule 10, those reproductions shall be submitted, not later than three months before the period of deferment applicable under Article 11(2) of the 1999 Act or under Article 6(4)(a) of the 1960 Act expires or not later than three months before the period of deferment is considered to have expired in accordance with Article 11(4)(a) of the 1999 Act or with Article 6(4)(b) of the 1960 Act.

(b) Six months before the expiry of the period of deferment of publication referred to in subparagraph (a), the International Bureau shall, by sending an unofficial notice, remind the holder of the international registration, where applicable, of the date by which the publication fee referred to in paragraph (3) shall be paid and the reproductions referred to in paragraph (3) shall be submitted.

(4) [*Registration of Reproductions*] The International Bureau shall record in the International Register any reproduction submitted under paragraph (3).

(5) [*Requirements Not Complied With*] If the requirements of paragraph (3) are not complied with, the international registration shall be canceled and shall not be published.

Rule 17
Publication of the International Registration

(1) [*Timing of Publication*] The international registration shall be published

(i) where the applicant so requests, immediately after the registration,

(ii) where deferment of publication has been requested and the request has not been disregarded, immediately after the date on which the period of deferment expired or is considered to have expired,

(iii) in any other case, six months after the date of the international registration or as soon as possible thereafter.

(2) [*Contents of Publication*] The publication of the international registration in the Bulletin shall contain

(i) the data recorded in the International Register;

(ii) the reproduction or reproductions of the industrial design;

(iii) where publication has been deferred, an indication of the date on which the period of deferment expired or is considered to have expired.

CHAPTER 3
REFUSALS AND INVALIDATIONS

Rule 18
Notification of Refusal

(1) [*Period for Notification of Refusal*] (a) The prescribed period for the notification of refusal of the effects of an international registration in accordance with Article 12(2) of the 1999 Act or Article

8(1) of the 1960 Act shall be six months from the publication of the international registration as provided for by Rule 26(3).

(b) Notwithstanding subparagraph (a), any Contracting Party whose Office is an Examining Office, or whose law provides for the possibility of opposition to the grant of protection, may, in a declaration, notify the Director General that, where it is designated under the 1999 Act, the period of six months referred to in that subparagraph shall be replaced by a period of 12 months.

(c) The declaration referred to in subparagraph (b) may also state that the international registration shall produce the effect referred to in Article 14(2)(a) of the 1999 Act at the latest

(i) at a time specified in the declaration which may be later than the date referred to in that Article but which shall not be more than six months after the said date or

(ii) at a time at which protection is granted according to the law of the Contracting Party where a decision regarding the grant of protection was unintentionally not communicated within the period applicable under subparagraph (a) or (b); in such a case, the Office of the Contracting Party concerned shall notify the International Bureau accordingly and endeavor to communicate such decision to the holder of the international registration concerned promptly thereafter.

(2) [*Notification of Refusal*] (a) The notification of any refusal shall relate to one international registration, shall be dated and shall be signed by the Office making the notification.

(b) The notification shall contain or indicate

(i) the Office making the notification,

(ii) the number of the international registration,

(iii) all the grounds on which the refusal is based together with a reference to the corresponding essential provisions of the law,

(iv) where the grounds on which the refusal is based refer to similarity with an industrial design which has been the subject of an earlier national, regional or international application or registration, the filing date and number, the priority date (if any), the registration date and number (if available), a copy of a reproduction of the earlier industrial design (if that reproduction is accessible to the public) and the name and address of the owner of the said industrial design, as provided for in the Administrative Instructions,

(v) where the refusal does not relate to all the industrial designs that are the subject of the international registration, those to which it relates or does not relate,

(vi) whether the refusal may be subject to review or appeal and, if so, the time limit, reasonable under the circumstances, for any request for review of, or appeal against, the refusal and the authority to which such request for review or appeal shall lie, with the indication, where applicable, that the request for review or the appeal has to be filed through the intermediary of a representative whose address is within the territory of the Contracting Party whose Office has pronounced the refusal, and

(vii) the date on which the refusal was pronounced.

(3) [*Notification of Division of International Registration*] Where, following a notification of refusal in accordance with Article 13(2) of the 1999 Act, an international registration is divided before the Office of a designated Contracting Party in order to overcome a ground of refusal stated in that notification, that Office shall notify the International Bureau of such data concerning the division as shall be specified in the Administrative Instructions.

(4) [*Notification of Withdrawal of Refusal*] (a) The notification of any withdrawal of refusal shall relate to one international registration, shall be dated and shall be signed by the Office making the notification.

(b) The notification shall contain or indicate

(i) the Office making the notification,

(ii) the number of the international registration,

(iii) where the withdrawal does not relate to all the industrial designs to which the refusal applied, those to which it relates or does not relate, and

(iv) the date on which the refusal was withdrawn.

(5) [*Recording*] The International Bureau shall record any notification received under paragraph (1)(c)(ii), (2) or (4) in the International Register together with, in the case of a notification of refusal, an indication of the date on which the notification of refusal was sent to the International Bureau.

(6) [*Transmittal of Copies of Notifications*] The International Bureau shall transmit copies of notifications received under paragraph (1)(c)(ii), (2) or (4) to the holder.

Rule 19
Irregular Refusals

(1) [*Notification Not Regarded as Such*] (a) A notification of refusal shall not be regarded as such by the International Bureau and shall not be recorded in the International Register

(i) if it does not indicate the number of the international registration concerned, unless other indications contained in the notification permit the said registration to be identified,

(ii) if it does not indicate any grounds for refusal, or

(iii) if it is sent to the International Bureau after the expiry of the period applicable under Rule 18(1).

(b) Where subparagraph (a) applies, the International Bureau shall, unless it cannot identify the international registration concerned, transmit a copy of the notification to the holder, shall inform, at the same time, the holder and the Office that sent the notification that the notification of refusal is not regarded as such by the International Bureau and has not been recorded in the International Register, and shall indicate the reasons therefor.

(2) [*Irregular Notification*] If the notification of refusal

(i) is not signed on behalf of the Office which communicated the refusal, or does not comply with the requirements established under Rule 2,

(ii) does not comply, where applicable, with the requirements of Rule 18(2)(b)(iv),

(iii) does not indicate, where applicable, the authority to which a request for review or an appeal lies and the applicable time limit, reasonable under the circumstances, for lodging such a request or appeal (Rule 18(2)(b)(vi)),

(iv) does not indicate the date on which the refusal was pronounced (Rule 18(2)(b)(vii)),

the International Bureau shall nevertheless record the refusal in the International Register and transmit a copy of the notification to the holder. If so requested by the holder, the International Bureau shall invite the Office which communicated the refusal to rectify its notification without delay.

Rule 20
Invalidation in Designated Contracting Parties

(1) [*Contents of the Notification of Invalidation*] Where the effects of an international registration are invalidated in a designated Contracting Party and the invalidation is no longer subject to any review or appeal, the Office of the Contracting Party whose competent authority has pronounced the invalidation shall, where it is aware of the invalidation, notify the International Bureau accordingly. The notification shall indicate

(i) the authority which pronounced the invalidation,

(ii) the fact that the invalidation is no longer subject to appeal,

(iii) the number of the international registration,

(iv) where the invalidation does not relate to all the industrial designs that are the subject of the international registration, those to which it relates or does not relate,

(v) the date on which the invalidation was pronounced and its effective date.

(2) [*Recording of the Invalidation*] The International Bureau shall record the invalidation in the International Register, together with the data contained in the notification of invalidation.

CHAPTER 4
CHANGES AND CORRECTIONS

Rule 21
Recording of a Change

(1) [*Presentation of the Request*] (a) A request for the recording shall be presented to the International Bureau on the relevant official form where the request relates to any of the following:

(i) a change in the ownership of the international registration in respect of all or some of the industrial designs that are the subject of the international registration;

(ii) a change in the name or address of the holder;

(iii) a renunciation of the international registration in respect of any or all of the designated Contracting Parties;

(iv) a limitation, in respect of any or all of the designated Contracting Parties, to one or some of the industrial designs that are the subject of the international registration.

(b) The request shall be presented by the holder and signed by the holder; however, a request for the recording of a change in ownership may be presented by the new owner, provided that it is

(i) signed by the holder, or

(ii) signed by the new owner and accompanied by an attestation from the competent authority of the holder's Contracting Party that the new owner appears to be the successor in title of the holder.

(2) [*Contents of the Request*] The request for the recording of a change shall, in addition to the requested change, contain or indicate

(i) the number of the international registration concerned,

(ii) the name of the holder, unless the change relates to the name or address of the representative,

(iii) in case of a change in the ownership of the international registration, the name and address, given in accordance with the Administrative Instructions, of the new owner of the international registration,

(iv) in case of a change in the ownership of the international registration, the Contracting Party or Parties in respect of which the new owner fulfills the conditions to be the holder of an international registration,

(v) in case of a change in the ownership of the international registration that does not relate to all the industrial designs and to all the Contracting Parties, the numbers of the industrial designs and the designated Contracting Parties to which the change in ownership relates, and

(vi) the amount of the fees being paid and the method of payment, or instruction to debit the required amount of fees to an account opened with the International Bureau, and the identification of the party effecting the payment or giving the instructions.

(3) [*Request Not Admissible*] A change in the ownership of an international registration may not be recorded in respect of a designated Contracting Party if that Contracting Party is not bound by an Act to which the Contracting Party, or one of the Contracting Parties, indicated under paragraph (2)(iv) is bound.

(4) [*Irregular Request*] If the request does not comply with the applicable requirements, the International Bureau shall notify that fact to the holder and, if the request was made by a person claiming to be the new owner, to that person.

(5) [*Time Allowed to Remedy Irregularity*] The irregularity may be remedied within three months from the date of the notification of the irregularity by the International Bureau. If the irregularity is not remedied within the said three months, the request shall be considered abandoned and the International Bureau shall notify accordingly and at the same time the holder and, if the request was presented by a person claiming to be the new owner, that person, and shall refund any fees paid, after deduction of an amount corresponding to one-half of the relevant fees.

(6) [*Recording and Notification of a Change*] (a) The International Bureau shall, provided that the request is in order, promptly record the change in the International Register and shall inform the holder. In the case of a recording of a change in ownership, the International Bureau will inform both the new holder and the previous holder.

(b) The change shall be recorded as of the date of receipt by the International Bureau of the request complying with the applicable requirements. Where however the request indicates that the change should be recorded after another change, or after renewal of the international registration, the International Bureau shall proceed accordingly.

(7) [*Recording of Partial Change in Ownership*] Assignment or other transfer of the international registration in respect of some only of the industrial designs, or some only of the designated Contracting Parties shall be recorded in the International Register under the number of the international registration of which a part has been assigned or otherwise transferred; any assigned or otherwise transferred part shall be canceled under the number of the said international registration and recorded as a separate international registration. The separate international registration shall bear the number of the international registration of which a part has been assigned or otherwise transferred, together with a capital letter.

(8) [*Recording of Merger of International Registrations*] Where the same person becomes the holder of two or more international registrations resulting from a partial change in ownership, the registrations shall be merged at the request of the said person and paragraphs (1) to (6) shall apply *mutatis mutandis*. The international registration resulting from the merger shall bear the number of the international registration of which a part had been assigned or otherwise transferred, together, where applicable, with a capital letter.

Rule 22
Corrections in the International Register

(1) [*Correction*] Where the International Bureau, acting *ex officio* or at the request of the holder, considers that there is an error concerning an international registration in the International Register, it shall modify the Register and inform the holder accordingly.

(2) [*Refusal of Effects of Correction*] The Office of any designated Contracting Party shall have the right to declare in a notification to the International Bureau that it refuses to recognize the effects of the correction. Rules 18 and 19 shall apply *mutatis mutandis.*

CHAPTER 5
RENEWALS

Rule 23
Unofficial Notice of Expiry

Six months before the expiry of a five-year term, the International Bureau shall send to the holder and the representative, if any, a notice indicating the date of expiry of the international registration. The fact that the said notice is not received shall not constitute an excuse for failure to comply with any time limit under Rule 24.

Rule 24
Details Concerning Renewal

(1) [*Fees*] (a) The international registration shall be renewed upon payment of the following fees:

(i) a basic fee;

(ii) a standard designation fee in respect of each Contracting Party designated under the 1999 Act that has not made a declaration under Article 7(2) of the 1999 Act, and each Contracting Party designated under the 1960 Act, for which the international registration is to be renewed;

(iii) an individual designation fee for each Contracting Party designated under the 1999 Act that has made a declaration under Article 7(2) of the 1999 Act and for which the international registration is to be renewed.

(b) The amounts of the fees referred to in items (i) and (ii) of subparagraph (a) are set out in the Schedule of Fees.

(c) The payment of the fees referred to in subparagraph (a) shall be made at the latest on the date on which the renewal of the international registration is due. However, it may still be made within six months from the date on which the renewal of the international registration is due, provided that the surcharge specified in the Schedule of Fees is paid at the same time.

(d) If any payment made for the purposes of renewal is received by the International Bureau earlier than three months before the date on which the renewal of the international registration is due, it shall be considered as having been received three months before that date.

(2) [*Further Details*] (a) Where the holder does not wish to renew the international registration

(i) in respect of a designated Contracting Party, or

(ii) in respect of any of the industrial designs that are the subject of the international registration,

payment of the required fees shall be accompanied by a statement indicating the Contracting Party or the numbers of the industrial designs for which the international registration is not to be renewed.

(b) Where the holder wishes to renew the international registration in respect of a designated Contracting Party notwithstanding the fact that the maximum period of protection for industrial designs in that Contracting Party has expired, payment of the required fees, including the standard designation fee or the individual designation fee, as the case may be, for that Contracting Party, shall be accompanied by a statement that the renewal of the international registration is to be recorded in the International Register in respect of that Contracting Party.

(c) Where the holder wishes to renew the international registration in respect of a designated Contracting Party notwithstanding the fact that a refusal is recorded in the International Register for that Contracting Party in respect of all the industrial designs concerned, payment of the required fees, including the standard designation fee or the individual designation fee, as the case may be, for that Contracting Party, shall be accompanied by a statement specifying that the renewal of the international registration is to be recorded in the International Register in respect of that Contracting Party.

(d) The international registration may not be renewed in respect of any designated Contracting Party in respect of which an invalidation has been recorded for all the industrial designs under Rule 20 or in respect of which a renunciation has been recorded under Rule 21. The international registration may not be renewed in respect of any designated Contracting Party for those industrial designs in respect of which an invalidation in that Contracting Party has been recorded under Rule 20 or in respect of which a limitation has been recorded under Rule 21.

(3) [*Insufficient Fees*] (a) If the amount of the fees received is less than the amount required for renewal, the International Bureau shall promptly notify at the same time both the holder and the representative, if any, accordingly. The notification shall specify the missing amount.

(b) If the amount of the fees received is, on the expiry of the period of six months referred to in paragraph (1)(c), less than the amount required for renewal, the International Bureau shall not record the renewal, shall refund the amount received and shall notify accordingly the holder and the representative, if any.

Rule 25
Recording of the Renewal; Certificate

(1) [*Recording and Effective Date of the Renewal*] Renewal shall be recorded in the International Register with the date on which renewal was due, even if the fees required for renewal are paid within the period of grace referred to in Rule 24(1)(c).

(2) [*Certificate*] The International Bureau shall send a certificate of renewal to the holder.

CHAPTER 6
BULLETIN

Rule 26
Bulletin

(1) [*Information Concerning International Registrations*] The International Bureau shall publish in the Bulletin relevant data concerning

(i) international registrations, in accordance with Rule 17;

(ii) refusals recorded under Rule 18(5), with an indication as to whether there is a possibility of review or appeal, but without the grounds for refusal;

(iii) invalidations recorded under Rule 20(2);

(iv) changes in ownership, changes of name or address of the holder, renunciations and limitations recorded under Rule 21;

(v) corrections effected under Rule 22;

(vi) renewals recorded under Rule 25(1);

(vii) international registrations which have not been renewed.

(2) [*Information Concerning Declarations; Other Information*] The International Bureau shall publish in the Bulletin any declaration made by a Contracting Party under the 1999 Act, the 1960 Act or these Regulations, as well as a list of the days on which the International Bureau is not scheduled to open to the public during the current and the following calendar year.

(3) [*Mode of Publishing the Bulletin*] The Bulletin referred to in Rule 1(1)(x) shall be published on the website of the Organization. The date on which each issue of the Bulletin is published on that website shall be electronically communicated by the International Bureau to the Office of each Contracting Party. Such communication shall be deemed to replace the sending of the Bulletin referred to in Article 10(3)(b) of the 1999 Act and Article 6(3)(b) of the 1960 Act, and, for the purposes of Article 8(2) of the 1960 Act, the Bulletin shall be deemed to have been received by each Office concerned also on the date of the said communication.

CHAPTER 7
FEES

Rule 27
Amounts and Payment of Fees

(1) [*Amounts of Fees*] The amounts of fees due under the 1999 Act, the 1960 Act, the 1934 Act and these Regulations, other than individual designation fees referred to in Rule 12(1)(a)(iii), shall be specified in the Schedule of Fees which is annexed to these Regulations and forms an integral part thereof.

(2) [*Payment*] (a) Subject to subparagraph (b) and Rule 12(3)(c), the fees shall be paid directly to the International Bureau.

(b) Where the international application is filed through the Office of the applicant's Contracting Party, the fees payable in connection with that application may be paid through that Office if it accepts to collect and forward such fees and the applicant or the holder so wishes. Any Office which accepts to collect and forward such fees shall notify that fact to the Director General.

(3) [*Modes of Payment*] Fees shall be paid to the International Bureau in accordance with the Administrative Instructions.

(4) [*Indications Accompanying the Payment*] At the time of the payment of any fee to the International Bureau, an indication must be given,

(i) before international registration, of the name of the applicant, the industrial design concerned and the purpose of the payment;

(ii) after international registration, of the name of the holder, the number of the international registration concerned and the purpose of the payment.

(5) [*Date of Payment*] (a) Subject to Rule 24(1)(d) and subparagraph (b), any fee shall be considered to have been paid to the International Bureau on the day on which the International Bureau receives the required amount.

(b) Where the required amount is available in an account opened with the International Bureau and that Bureau has received instructions from the holder of the account to debit it, the fee shall be considered to have been paid to the International Bureau on the day on which the International

Bureau receives an international application, a request for the recording of a change, or an instruction to renew an international registration.

(6) [*Change in the Amount of the Fees*] (a) Where an international application is filed through the Office of the applicant's Contracting Party and the amount of the fees payable in respect of the filing of the international application is changed between, on the one hand, the date on which the international application was received by that Office and, on the other hand, the date of the receipt of the international application by the International Bureau, the fee that was valid on the first date shall be applicable.

(b) Where the amount of the fees payable in respect of the renewal of an international registration is changed between the date of payment and the due date of the renewal, the fee that was valid on the date of payment, or on the date considered to be the date of payment under Rule 24(1)(d), shall be applicable. Where the payment is made after the due date, the fee that was valid on the due date shall be applicable.

(c) Where the amount of any fee other than the fees referred to in subparagraphs (a) and (b) is changed, the amount valid on the date on which the fee was received by the International Bureau shall be applicable.

Rule 28
Currency of Payments

(1) [*Obligation to Use Swiss Currency*] All payments made under these Regulations to the International Bureau shall be in Swiss currency irrespective of the fact that, where the fees are paid through an Office, such Office may have collected those fees in another currency.

(2) [*Establishment of the Amount of Individual Designation Fees in Swiss Currency*] (a) Where a Contracting Party makes a declaration under Article 7(2) of the 1999 Act or under Rule 36(1) that it wants to receive an individual designation fee, the amount of the fee indicated to the International Bureau shall be expressed in the currency used by its Office.

(b) Where the fee is indicated in the declaration referred to in subparagraph (a) in a currency other than Swiss currency, the Director General shall, after consultation with the Office of the Contracting Party concerned, establish the amount of the fee in Swiss currency on the basis of the official exchange rate of the United Nations.

(c) Where, for more than three consecutive months, the official exchange rate of the United Nations between the Swiss currency and the currency in which the amount of an individual designation fee has been indicated by a Contracting Party is higher or lower by at least 5% than the last exchange rate applied to establish the amount of the fee in Swiss currency, the Office of that Contracting Party may ask the Director General to establish a new amount of the fee in Swiss currency according to the official exchange rate of the United Nations prevailing on the day preceding the day on which the request is made. The Director General shall proceed accordingly. The new amount shall be applicable as from a date which shall be fixed by the Director General, provided that such date is between one and two months after the date of the publication of the said amount in the Bulletin.

(d) Where, for more than three consecutive months, the official exchange rate of the United Nations between the Swiss currency and the currency in which the amount of an individual designation fee has been indicated by a Contracting Party is lower by at least 10% than the last exchange rate applied to establish the amount of the fee in Swiss currency, the Director General shall establish a new amount of the fee in Swiss currency according to the current official exchange rate of the United Nations. The new amount shall be applicable as from a date which shall be fixed by the Director General, provided that such date is between one and two months after the date of the publication of the said amount in the Bulletin.

Rule 29
Crediting of Fees to the Accounts of the Contracting Parties Concerned

Any standard designation fee or individual designation fee paid to the International Bureau in respect of a Contracting Party shall be credited to the account of that Contracting Party with the International Bureau within the month following the month in the course of which the recording of the international registration or renewal for which that fee has been paid was effected or, as regards the second part of the individual designation fee, immediately upon its receipt by the International Bureau.

CHAPTER 8
INTERNATIONAL APPLICATIONS GOVERNED EXCLUSIVELY OR PARTLY BY THE 1934 ACT AND INTERNATIONAL REGISTRATIONS RESULTING THEREFROM

Rule 30
Applicability of These Regulations to International Applications Governed Exclusively by the 1934 Act and International Registrations Resulting Therefrom

(1) [*General Principle*] Unless otherwise specified and subject to paragraph (2), these Regulations shall be applicable to international applications governed exclusively by the 1934 Act and to international registrations resulting therefrom.

(2) [*Exceptions*] (a) Notwithstanding Rule 6, any international application governed exclusively by the 1934 Act shall be in French. Any communication concerning that international application or the international registration resulting therefrom shall be in French.

(b) Notwithstanding Rule 7(5)(a), a description of the reproduction or of the characteristic features of the industrial designs and the identity of the creator of the industrial designs may not be included in an application governed exclusively by the 1934 Act.

(c) Notwithstanding Rule 7(5)(e), deferment of publication may not be requested with respect to an international application governed exclusively by the 1934 Act.

(d) Notwithstanding Rule 7(7), the industrial designs contained in an international application governed exclusively by the 1934 Act may belong to different classes of the International Classification.

(e) Notwithstanding Rule 9(1), an international application governed exclusively by the 1934 Act may, instead of containing reproductions, be accompanied by specimens.

(f) Notwithstanding Rule 12(1)(a), an international application governed exclusively by the 1934 Act shall be subject only to the payment of the basic fee referred to in Rule 12(1)(a)(i).

(g) Notwithstanding Rule 15(1), the reproductions of the industrial designs contained in an international application governed exclusively by the 1934 Act shall not be registered in the International Register.

(h) Notwithstanding Rule 17(1), an international registration resulting from an international application governed exclusively by the 1934 Act shall be published immediately after registration.

(i) Notwithstanding Rule 17(2)(ii), the reproductions of industrial designs contained in an international registration resulting from an international application governed exclusively by the 1934 Act shall not be published in the Bulletin.

(j) Notwithstanding Rule 18, the effects of an international registration resulting from an international application governed exclusively by the 1934 Act may not be the subject of a notification of refusal of protection.

(k) Notwithstanding Rule 21(3), a change in ownership may not be recorded in respect of a Contracting Party designated under the 1934 Act if, on the basis of the indications referred to in Rule 21(2)(iv), the 1934 Act would cease to be applicable in respect of that Contracting Party.

(l) Notwithstanding Rule 24(1)(a), an international registration resulting from an international application governed exclusively by the 1934 Act shall be renewed upon payment only of the basic fee referred to in Rule 24(1)(a)(i).

(m) Notwithstanding Rule 24(2)(b), an international registration resulting from an international application governed exclusively by the 1934 Act shall not be renewed where the duration of international protection of fifteen years referred to in Article 7 of the 1934 Act has expired.

(n) The renewal of an international registration resulting from an international application governed exclusively by the 1934 Act, for the second period of protection of ten years referred to in Article 7 of the 1934 Act, may be requested at the time of filing the international application concerned. In such case, the fee referred to in Rule 24(1)(a)(i) shall be payable at the time of filing of the said international application, failing which the request for renewal shall be disregarded by the International Bureau.

(3) [*International Applications Under Sealed Cover*] (a) An international application governed exclusively by the 1934 Act shall contain, in addition to the indications referred to in Rule 7(3), an indication as to whether such application is made under open or sealed cover.

(b) Upon expiry of the first period of five years of international protection referred to in Article 7 of the 1934 Act, any international registration which is under sealed cover shall be opened by the International Bureau upon renewal of the said registration.

Rule 31
Applicability of These Regulations to International Applications Governed Partly by the 1934 Act and International Registrations Resulting Therefrom

(1) [*General Principle*] These Regulations shall be applicable to international applications referred to in Rule 1(1)(xviii) to (xx), and to international registrations resulting therefrom, subject to paragraph (2).

(2) [*Exceptions*] (a) Notwithstanding Rule 7(5)(e), deferment of publication may not be requested with respect to an international application referred to in paragraph (1). Where deferment of publication has been requested and one of the designated Contracting Parties in the international application has been designated under the 1934 Act, the International Bureau shall notify the applicant accordingly; if, within the period of one month from the date of the notification sent by the International Bureau, the applicant does not, by notice in writing to the International Bureau, withdraw the designation of the said Contracting Party, the International Bureau shall disregard the request for deferment of publication.

(b) Notwithstanding Rule 21(3), a change in ownership may not be recorded in respect of a designated Contracting Party if, on the basis of the indications referred to in Rule 21(2)(iv), the 1934 Act would cease to be applicable, or would become applicable, in respect of that Contracting Party.

(c) With respect to Contracting Parties designated under the 1934 Act in an international application referred to in paragraph (1), or in an international registration resulting therefrom,

(i) the fees referred to in Rule 12(1)(a)(ii) to (iv) shall not be payable;

(ii) the effects of the international registration concerned may not be the subject of a notification of refusal of protection referred to in Rule 18;

(iii) the renewal fees referred to in Rule 24(1)(a)(ii) and (iii) shall not be payable;

(iv) the international registration concerned shall not be renewed where the duration of international protection of fifteen years referred to in Article 7 of the 1934 Act has expired, notwithstanding Rule 24(2)(b).

CHAPTER 9
MISCELLANEOUS

Rule 32
Extracts, Copies and Information Concerning Published International Registrations

(1) [*Modalities*] Against payment of a fee whose amount shall be fixed in the Schedule of Fees, any person may obtain from the International Bureau, in respect of any published international registration:

(i) extracts from the International Register;

(ii) certified copies of recordings made in the International Register or of items in the file of the international registration;

(iii) uncertified copies of recordings made in the International Register or of items in the file of the international registration;

(iv) written information on the contents of the International Register or of the file of the international registration;

(v) a photograph of a specimen.

(2) [*Exemption from Authentication, Legalization or any Other Certification*] In respect of a document referred to in paragraph (1)(i) and (ii), bearing the seal of the International Bureau and the signature of the Director General or a person acting on his behalf, no authority of any Contracting Party shall require authentication, legalization or any other certification of such document, seal or signature, by any other person or authority. The present paragraph applies *mutatis mutandis* to the international registration certificate referred to in Rule 15(1).

Rule 33
Amendment of Certain Rules

(1) [*Requirement of Unanimity*] Amendment of the following provisions of these Regulations shall require unanimity of the Contracting Parties bound by the 1999 Act:

(i) Rule 13(4);

(ii) Rule 18(1).

(2) [*Requirement of Four-Fifths Majority*] Amendment of the following provisions of the Regulations and of paragraph (3) of the present Rule shall require a four-fifths majority of the Contracting Parties bound by the 1999 Act:

(i) Rule 7(7);

(ii) Rule 9(3)(b);

(iii) Rule 16(1)(a);

(iv) Rule 17(1)(iii).

(3) [*Procedure*] Any proposal for amending a provision referred to in paragraph (1) or (2) shall be sent to all Contracting Parties at least two months prior to the opening of the session of the Assembly which is called upon to make a decision on the proposal.

Rule 34
Administrative Instructions

(1) [*Establishment of Administrative Instructions; Matters Governed by Them*] (a) The Director General shall establish Administrative Instructions. The Director General may modify them. The Director General shall consult the Offices of the Contracting Parties with respect to the proposed Administrative Instructions or their proposed modification.

(b) The Administrative Instructions shall deal with matters in respect of which these Regulations expressly refer to such Instructions and with details in respect of the application of these Regulations.

(2) [*Control by the Assembly*] The Assembly may invite the Director General to modify any provision of the Administrative Instructions, and the Director General shall proceed accordingly.

(3) [*Publication and Effective Date*] (a) The Administrative Instructions and any modification thereof shall be published in the Bulletin.

(b) Each publication shall specify the date on which the published provisions become effective. The dates may be different for different provisions, provided that no provision may be declared effective prior to its publication in the Bulletin.

(4) [*Conflict with the 1999 Act, the 1960 Act, the 1934 Act or These Regulations*] In the case of conflict between, on the one hand, any provision of the Administrative Instructions and, on the other hand, any provision of the 1999 Act, the 1960 Act, the 1934 Act or of these Regulations, the latter shall prevail.

Rule 35
Declarations Made by Contracting Parties to the 1999 Act

(1) [*Making and Coming into Effect of Declarations*] Article 30(1) and (2) of the 1999 Act shall apply *mutatis mutandis* to the making of any declaration under Rules 8(1), 9(3)(a), 13(4) or 18(1)(b) and to its coming into effect.

(2) [*Withdrawal of Declarations*] Any declaration referred to in paragraph (1) may be withdrawn at any time by notification addressed to the Director General. Such withdrawal shall take effect upon receipt by the Director General of the notification of withdrawal or at any later date indicated in the notification. In the case of a declaration made under Rule 18(1)(b), the withdrawal shall not affect an international registration whose date is earlier than the coming into effect of the said withdrawal.

Rule 36
Declarations Made by Contracting Parties to the 1960 Act

(1) [*Individual Designation Fee*] For the purpose of Article 15(1)2(b) of the 1960 Act, any Contracting Party to the 1960 Act whose Office is an Examining Office may, in a declaration, notify the Director General that, in connection with any international application in which it is designated under the 1960 Act, the standard designation fee referred to in Rule 12(1)(a)(ii) shall be replaced by an individual designation fee, whose amount shall be indicated in the declaration and can be changed in further declarations. The said amount may not be higher than the equivalent of the amount which the Office of that Contracting Party would be entitled to receive from an applicant for a grant of protection for an equivalent period to the same number of industrial designs, that amount being diminished by the savings resulting from the international procedure.

(2) [*Maximum Duration of Protection*] Each Contracting Party to the 1960 Act shall, in a declaration, notify the Director General of the maximum duration of protection provided for by its law.

(3) [*Time at Which Declarations May Be Made*] Any declaration under paragraphs (1) and (2) may be made

(i) at the time of the deposit of an instrument referred to in Article 26(2) of the 1960 Act, in which case it shall become effective on the date on which the State having made the declaration becomes bound by this Act, or

(ii) after the deposit of an instrument referred to in Article 26(2) of the 1960 Act, in which case it shall become effective one month after the date of its receipt by the Director General or at any later date indicated in the declaration but shall apply only in respect of any international registration whose date of international registration is the same as, or is later than, the effective date of the declaration.

SCHEDULE OF FEES
(as in force on April 1, 2004)

I. ***International Applications Governed Exclusively or Partly by the 1960 Act or by the 1999 Act***

	Swiss francs
1. Basic fee	
1.1 For one design	397
1.2 For each additional design included in the same international application	19
2. Publication fee	
2.1 For each reproduction to be published in black and white	12
2.2 For each reproduction to be published in color	75
2.3 For each page, in addition to the first, on which one or more reproductions are shown (where the reproductions are submitted on paper)	150
3. Additional fee where the description exceeds 100 words per word exceeding 100 words	2
4. Standard designation fee	
4.1 For one design	42
4.2 For each additional design included in the same international application	2
5. Individual designation fee (the amount of the individual designation fee is fixed by each Contracting Party concerned)	

II. ***International Applications Governed Exclusively by the 1934 Act***

	Swiss francs
6. Basic fee	
6.1 For one design	216
6.2 For two to 50 designs included in the same international application	432
6.3 For 51 to 100 designs included in the same international application	638

III. *Renewal of an International Registration Resulting From an International Application Governed Exclusively or Partly by the 1960 Act or by the 1999 Act*

7. Basic fee	
7.1 For one design	200
7.2 For each additional design included in the same international registration	17
8. Standard designation fee	
8.1 For one design	21
8.2 For each additional design included in the same international registration	1
9. Individual designation fee (the amount of the individual designation fee is fixed by each Contracting Party concerned)	
10. Surcharge (period of grace)	**

50% of the renewal basic fee.

IV. *Renewal of an International Registration Resulting From an International Application Governed Exclusively by the 1934 Act*

	Swiss francs
11. Basic fee	
11.1 For one design	422
11.2 For two to 50 designs included in the same international registration	844
11.3 For 51 to 100 designs included in the same international registration	1236
12. Surcharge (period of grace)	

50% of the renewal basic fee.

V. *Miscellaneous Recordings*

13. Change in ownership	144
14. Change of name and/or address of the holder	
14.1 For one international registration	144
14.2 For each additional international registration of the same holder included in the same request	72
15. Renunciation	144
16. Limitation	144

VI. *Information Concerning Published International Registrations*

17. Supply of an extract from the International Register relating to a published international registration	144
18. Supply of non-certified copies of the International Register or of items in the file of a published international registration	
18.1 For the first five pages	26
18.2 For each additional page after the fifth if the copies are requested at the same time and relate to the same international registration	2
19. Supply of certified copies from the International Register or of items in the file of a published international registration	
19.1 For the first five pages	46
19.2 For each additional page after the fifth if the copies are requested at the same time and relate to the same international registration	2

20. Supply of a photograph of a specimen	57
21. Supply of written information on the contents of the International Register or of the file of a published international registration	
21.1 Concerning one international registration	82
21.2 Concerning any additional international registration of the same holder if the same information is requested at the same time	10
22. Search in the list of owners of international registrations	
22.1 Per search by the name of a given person or entity	82
22.2 For each international registration found beyond the first one	10
23. Surcharge for the communication of extracts, copies, information or search reports by telefacsimile (per page)	4

Administrative Instructions for the Application of the Hague Agreement

(as in force on April 1, 2004)

Part One
Definitions

Section 101
Abbreviated Expressions

(a) For the purposes of these Administrative Instructions:

(i) "Regulations" means the Common Regulations under the Hague Agreement Concerning the International Registration of Industrial Designs;

(ii) "Rule" means a Rule of the Regulations.

(b) An expression which is used in these Administrative Instructions and is referred to in Rule 1 has the same meaning as in the Regulations.

Part Two
Communications with the International Bureau

Section 201
Communication in Writing; Several Documents in One Envelope

(a) Communications addressed to the International Bureau shall be effected in writing by typewriter or other machine and shall be signed.

(b) If several documents are mailed in one envelope, they should be accompanied by a list identifying each of them.

Section 202
Signature

A signature shall be hand written, printed or stamped; it may be replaced by the affixing of a seal or, as regards the electronic communication referred to in Section 204, by a mode of identification to be determined by the International Bureau.

Section 203
Communication by Telefacsimile

(a) Any communication, other than an international application containing a reproduction to be published in color, may be addressed to the International Bureau by telefacsimile, provided that where the communication must be presented on an official form, the official form is used for the purposes of the telefacsimile communication.

(b) An international application addressed to the International Bureau by telefacsimile shall not have effect unless, prior to the expiration of 20 days counted from the date of receipt of such communication, the original of the international application bearing the prescribed signature along with the reproductions and/or specimens concerned, have been received by the International Bureau. When so confirmed, the said international application shall have effect as of the date on which it was received by telefacsimile by the International Bureau.

(c) Where an international application has been transmitted to the International Bureau by telefacsimile, the Bureau shall promptly and by telefacsimile inform the sender of the receipt of that international application, and where such telefacsimile communication received by the International Bureau is incomplete or illegible, of that fact also, provided that the sender can be identified and can be reached by telefacsimile.

Section 204
Electronic Communications

(a) Communications with the International Bureau, including the presentation of the international application, may take place by electronic means at a time and in a manner and format to be ascertained by the International Bureau, the particulars of which shall be published in the Bulletin.

(b) The International Bureau shall promptly and by electronic transmission inform the originator of an electronic transmission of the receipt of that transmission and, where the electronic transmission received is incomplete or otherwise unusable, also of that fact, provided that the originator can be identified and can be reached.

(c) For the purpose of the communication by the International Bureau to Offices of Contracting Parties of the date on which each issue of the Bulletin is published, as provided for in Rule 26(3), each such Office shall indicate to the International Bureau the email address to which the said communication shall be sent.

Part Three
Requirements Concerning Names and Addresses

Section 301
Names and Addresses

(a) In the case of a natural person, the name to be indicated is the family or principal name and the given or secondary name(s) of the natural person.

(b) In the case of a legal entity, the name to be indicated is the full official designation of the legal entity.

(c) In the case of a name in characters other than Latin characters, the indication of that name shall consist of a transliteration into Latin characters which shall follow the phonetics of the language of the international application. In the case of a legal entity whose name is in characters other than Latin characters, the said transliteration may be replaced by a translation into the language of the international application.

(d) An address shall be given in such a way as to satisfy the customary requirements for prompt postal delivery and shall consist, at least, of all the relevant administrative units up to, and including, the house number, if any. In addition, telephone and telefacsimile numbers, an e-mail address as well as a different address for correspondence, may be indicated.

Section 302
Address for Correspondence

Where there are two or more applicants or new owners with different addresses and no representative is appointed, one address for correspondence shall be indicated. Where no such address has been indicated, the address of the person named first shall be treated as the address for correspondence.

Part Four
Reproduction of the Industrial Design; Disclaimer; Numbering; Description of Characteristic Features

Section 401
Presentation of Reproductions

(a) One and the same international application may comprise both photographs and other graphic representations, in black and white or in color.

(b) Each reproduction accompanying an international application shall be submitted in a single copy.

(c) The photographs or other graphic representations accompanying the international application shall be either pasted or printed directly onto a separate sheet of A4 paper which is white and opaque. The separate sheet of paper shall be used upright and shall not contain more than 25 reproductions.

(d) The reproductions must be arranged on the separate sheet referred to in subparagraph (c) in the orientation in which the applicant wishes them to be published. A margin of at least 5 millimeters should be left around the representation of each industrial design.

(e) Each reproduction must fall within a right-angled quadrilateral containing no other reproduction or part of another reproduction and no numbering. The photographs or other graphic representations shall not be folded, stapled or marked in any way.

Section 402
Representation of the Industrial Design

(a) The photographs and other graphic representations shall represent the industrial design alone, or the product in relation to which the industrial design is to be used, to the exclusion of any other object, accessory, person or animal.

(b) The dimensions of the representation of each industrial design appearing in a photograph or other graphic representation may not exceed 16 x 16 centimeters, and one of those dimensions must be at least 3 centimeters.

(c) The following shall not be accepted:

(i) technical drawings, particularly with axes and dimensions;

(ii) explanatory text or legends.

Section 403
Disclaimer

Matter which is shown in a reproduction but for which protection is not sought may be indicated

(i) in the description referred to in Rule 7(5)(a) and/or

(ii) by means of dotted or broken lines.

Section 404
Requirements for Photographs and
Other Graphic Representations

(a) The photographs supplied must be of professional standard and have all the edges cut at right angles. The industrial design must be shown against a neutral plain background. Photographs retouched with ink or correcting fluid shall not be allowed.

(b) Graphic representations must be of professional standard produced with drawing instruments or by electronic means on good quality white, opaque paper, all of whose edges are cut at right angles. The industrial design represented may comprise shading and hatching to provide relief. Graphic representations executed by electronic means may be shown against a background, provided that it is neutral and plain and has only edges cut at right angles.

Section 405
Numbering of Reproductions

(a) The numbering stipulated for multiple international applications shall appear in the margin of each photograph or other graphic representation. When the same industrial design is represented from different angles, the numbering shall consist of two separate figures separated by a dot (e.g., 1.1, 1.2, 1.3, etc. for the first design, 2.1, 2.2, 2.3, etc. for the second design, and so on).

(b) The reproductions shall be pasted or printed in ascending numerical order on the separate sheet referred to in Section 401(c).

Section 406
Requirements for Specimens

(a) A specimen in two dimensions which accompanies an international application shall not exceed 26.2 centimeters x 17 centimeters in size (unfolded), 50 grams in weight or 3 millimeters in thickness. Such specimens shall be pasted on sheets of A4 paper and numbered in accordance with Section 405(b). The same number shall be assigned to each reproduction corresponding to these specimens when submitted to the International Bureau.

(b) None of the dimensions of a package containing specimens shall exceed 30 centimeters and the weight of such package and its packing shall not exceed 4 kilograms.

(c) Perishable products or products which may be dangerous to store shall not be accepted.

Part Five
Refusals

Section 501
Date of Sending of Notification of Refusal

In the case of a notification of refusal sent through a postal service, the date of dispatch shall be determined by the postmark. If the postmark is illegible or missing, the International Bureau shall treat such notification as if it had been sent 20 days before the date of its receipt by the International Bureau. However, if the date of dispatch thus determined is earlier than any date of refusal or date of sending mentioned in the notification, the International Bureau shall treat such notification as if it had been sent on the latter date. In the case of a notification of refusal sent through a delivery service, the date of dispatch shall be determined by the indication given by such delivery service on the basis of the details of the mailing as recorded by it.

Section 502
Notification of Division of an International Registration

Where an international registration has been divided before the Office of a designated Contracting Party following a notification of refusal as provided for in Rule 18(3), that Office shall notify the International Bureau of that fact, together with the following additional particulars:

(i) the Office making the notification;

(ii) the number of the international registration concerned;

(iii) the numbers of the industrial designs which have been the subject of the division with the Office concerned, and

(iv) the resulting national or regional application numbers or registration numbers.

Part Six
Request for the Recording of a Limitation or Renunciation when Publication Deferred

Section 601
Latest Time to Request the Recording of a Limitation or Renunciation

Where the publication of an international registration is deferred, a request for the recording of a limitation or renunciation concerning that registration, complying with the applicable requirements, must be received by the International Bureau not later than three months prior to the expiry of the period of deferment. In default of this, the international registration is published at the expiration of the period of deferment without account being taken of the request for the recording of a limitation or renunciation. Provided that the request for limitation or renunciation complies with the applicable requirements, the limitation or renunciation is however recorded in the International Register.

Part Seven
Renewal

Section 701
Unofficial Notice of Expiry

When, pursuant to Rule 23, the International Bureau sends to the holder and the representative, if any, a notice indicating the date of expiration of an international registration, such notice shall contain also an indication of the Contracting Parties for which, at the date of the notice, and in accordance with the maximum duration of protection notified by each Contracting Party pursuant to Article 17(3)(c) of the 1999 Act and Rule 36(2), renewal of the international registration is possible.

Part Eight
Fees

Section 801
Mode of Payment

Fees may be paid to the International Bureau

(i) by debit to a current account with the International Bureau,

(ii) by payment into the Swiss postal check account or to any of the specified bank accounts of the International Bureau,

(iii) by a banker's check,

(iv) by payment in cash at the International Bureau.

I hereby certify that the foregoing text is a true copy of the original text in English of the Geneva Act of the Hague Agreement Concerning the International Registration of Industrial Designs and the Common Regulations under the 1999 Act, the 1960 Act and the 1934 Act of the Hague Agreement.

[Signature]
Kamil Idris
Director General
World Intellectual Property Organization

November 4, 2005

SENATE TREATY DOCUMENT NUMBER: 109-22

TREATY BETWEEN THE UNITED STATES OF AMERICA AND MALAYSIA ON MUTUAL LEGAL ASSISTANCE IN CRIMINAL MATTERS, WITH ANNEX

SIGNED AT KUALA LUMPUR,
JULY 28, 2006

CTIA DOCUMENT NUMBER: 13030.000

LETTER OF TRANSMITTAL

THE WHITE HOUSE, *November 14, 2006.*

To the Senate of the United States:

With a view to receiving the advice and consent of the Senate to ratification, I transmit herewith the Treaty between the United States of America and Malaysia on Mutual Legal Assistance in Criminal Matters, signed on July 28, 2006, at Kuala Lumpur. I transmit also, for the information of the Senate, the report of the Department of State with respect to the Treaty.

The Treaty is one of a series of modern mutual legal assistance treaties being negotiated by the United States in order to counter criminal activities more effectively. The Treaty should enhance our ability to investigate and prosecute a wide variety of crimes. The Treaty is self-executing.

The Treaty provides for a broad range of cooperation in criminal matters. Under the Treaty, the Parties agree to assist each other by, among other things: providing evidence (such as testimony, documents, items, or things) obtained voluntarily or, where necessary, by compulsion; arranging for persons, including persons in custody, to travel to the other country to provide evidence; serving documents; executing searches and seizures; locating and identifying persons, items, or places; examining objects and sites; freezing and forfeiting assets or property; and identifying or tracing proceeds of crime.

I recommend that the Senate give early and favorable consideration to the Treaty, and give its advice and consent to ratification.

GEORGE W. BUSH.

LETTER OF SUBMITTAL

DEPARTMENT OF STATE,
Washington, September 27, 2006.

The PRESIDENT,

The White House.

THE PRESIDENT: I have the honor to submit to you the Treaty on Mutual Legal Assistance in Criminal Matters between the United States and Malaysia signed on July 28, 2006. I recommend that the Treaty be transmitted to the Senate for its advice and consent to ratification.

The Treaty covers mutual legal assistance in criminal matters. In recent years, similar bilateral treaties have entered into force with a number of countries. This Treaty contains all of the essential provisions of such treaties sought by the United States. It will enhance our ability to investigate and prosecute a wide variety of offenses. The Treaty is self-executing and will not require implementing legislation.

A detailed, article-by-article analysis is enclosed with this report. The Department of Justice joins the Department of State in favoring approval of this Treaty by the Senate at the earliest possible date.

Respectfully submitted.

CONDOLEEZZA RICE.

Enclosures: As stated.

U.S.-MALAYSIA MUTUAL LEGAL ASSISTANCE TREATY

OVERVIEW

The Treaty on Mutual Legal Assistance in Criminal Matters between the United States and Malaysia creates for the first time a treaty-based relationship of mutual legal assistance between the United States and Malaysia.

The following is an article-by-article description of the provisions of the Treaty.

Article 1 sets out the scope of assistance available under the Treaty. Article 1(1) requires the Parties to provide each other the widest measure of mutual legal assistance in connection with investigations and proceedings pertaining to criminal matters. During the negotiations, both Parties expressed their understanding that this creates an international obligation on each Party to provide mutual legal assistance. The Parties further expressed their understanding that their international obligation would be carried out pursuant to the terms of the Treaty and in compliance with domestic laws.

Assistance is to be available for "investigations and proceedings pertaining to criminal matters." This terminology is meant to incorporate not only the full range of proceedings in a criminal case, including grand jury and other investigative and pre-charge proceedings, but also ancillary matters such as forfeiture proceedings that may be civil in nature but are nonetheless covered by the Treaty because they pertain to a criminal matter.

Article 1(2) contains a non-exhaustive list of the major types of assistance to be provided under the Treaty, including producing evidence (such as testimony, documents, or items or things) obtained voluntarily or, where necessary, by compulsion; arranging for persons, including persons in custody, to travel to the other country to provide evidence; serving documents; executing searches and seizures; locating and identifying persons, items, or places; examining objects and sites; freezing and forfeiting assets or property; and identifying or tracing proceeds of crime. Most of these types of assistance are described in detail in subsequent articles in the Treaty.

The Treaty also authorizes provision of any other form of assistance not prohibited by the laws of the state receiving the request (referred to in the Treaty, as in other such treaties, as the "requested state" or "requested Party," while the state making the request is the "requesting state" or "requesting Party"). As long as there is no specific legal restriction barring the type of assistance requested, it may be provided pursuant to the Treaty.

Article 1(3), a standard provision in U.S. mutual legal assistance treaties, provides that the Treaty is intended solely for government-to-government mutual legal assistance. The Treaty is not intended to provide to private persons a means of evidence gathering, nor is it intended to extend generally to civil matters. Private persons in the United States may continue to obtain evidence from Malaysia by letters rogatory, an avenue of international assistance that the Treaty leaves undisturbed. Similarly, the paragraph provides that the Treaty is not intended to create any right in a private person to suppress or exclude evidence provided pursuant to the Treaty, or to impede the execution of a request.

Article 2 requires that each Party designate a "Central Authority" to make and receive Treaty requests. The Central Authority of the United States would make all requests to Malaysia on behalf of federal and state agencies and local law enforcement authorities in the United States. The Central Authority of Malaysia would make all requests emanating from officials in Malaysia.

In each state, the Central Authority is to be the Attorney General or a person designated by the Attorney General. In the United States, the authority to handle the duties of the Central Authority under mutual legal assistance treaties has been delegated to the Office of International Affairs in the Criminal Division of the Department of Justice.

The Central Authority of the requesting state exercises discretion as to the form and content of requests, as well as the number and priority of requests. The Central Authority of the requested state is responsible for receiving and evaluating each incoming request; transmitting it to the proper agency, court, or other authority for execution; and effecting a timely response.

Article 2(1) provides that, in Malaysia, requests are to be transmitted through the Ministry of Foreign Affairs to or from the Central Authority. This pass-through is necessary because of a provision of Malaysian law that requires use of the diplomatic channel in Malaysia to transmit requests. There is no such requirement in United States law, and the Treaty specifically provides that requests need not pass through the diplomatic channel in the United States. This provision also does not affect transmission of evidence or other responses to requests or any other followup communications, all of which, pursuant to Article 2(5), are to be done directly between the Central Authorities.

Article 3 sets forth the circumstances under which a requested state's Central Authority may deny assistance under the Treaty. Refusal under this Article is discretionary with the Central Authority of the requested state. Several of the grounds for refusal are common to most U.S. mutual legal assistance treaties. So, for example, a request may be denied if it relates to a political or a military offense, if it does not conform to the requirements of the Treaty, or if its execution would prejudice the sovereignty, security, public order, or other essential interest of the requested state.

In addition, the Treaty provides that a request may be denied if it relates to an act or omission that, if it had occurred in the requested state, would not have constituted an offense under the laws of that state punishable by a deprivation of liberty for a period of one year or more, or by a more severe penalty (Article 3(1)(e)). The United States does not generally impose this requirement—known as "dual criminality"—on mutual legal assistance requests, but under Malaysian law Malaysia is not permitted to provide assistance in support of the investigation or prosecution of an offense that is not recognized in Malaysia. To ensure that the Treaty would be available for assistance in the types of cases in which law enforcement authorities in the United States generally require assistance, the negotiators undertook a review of the respective criminal codes of the United States and Malaysia. That review revealed broad areas of commonality between the United States and Malaysia criminal codes, establishing that a dual criminality refusal ground would not unduly restrict the ability of U.S. authorities to obtain assistance.

To further provide certainty to U.S. (and Malaysian) authorities seeking assistance, the Parties agreed to include in an annex to the Treaty a non-exclusive list of offenses for which they have already established that dual criminality exists. A similar approach was previously adopted in the Mutual Legal Assistance Treaty between the United States and the Republic of Korea. If a request relates to an offense that appears on this annexed list, pursuant to Article 3(2), the request may not be denied on the grounds of an absence of dual criminality. The list in the Annex is not all-encompassing—indeed, it does not include most common crimes for which dual criminality is obvious—but rather is designed to cover some of the types of offenses regarding which mutual legal assistance requests are most commonly made. The Parties further agreed that the Annex could be modified by an exchange of notes, without requiring amendment of the Treaty. The Annex is an integral part of the Treaty.

Other grounds for refusal included in Article 3(1) reflect requirements in Malaysian law that a Central Authority maintain the discretion to consider certain factors in evaluating requests. Assistance may be refused if the request (a) was made for the purpose of investigating a person on account of that person's race, religion, sex, ethnic origin, nationality, or political opinions; (b) relates to an offense for which a person has already been convicted or acquitted by a court in the requested state; or (c) relates to an offense of insufficient gravity or an item of insufficient importance. The negotiators expressed their views that these grounds for refusal would be employed infrequently, if ever.

In keeping with the overall intent of the Treaty to facilitate assistance, the Parties also included in Article 3 several provisions designed to limit the use of grounds for refusal. Article 3(2), referred to above, restricts the use of the ground of absence of dual criminality. Article 3(3) provides that assistance shall not be refused solely on the ground of bank secrecy or that the offense involves fiscal matters. And Article 3(4) requires a Central Authority, before refusing assistance under Article 3(1), to consult with its counterpart in the requesting Party to consider whether assistance can be given subject to such conditions as the Central Authority of the requested Party deems necessary. If the requesting Party accepts assistance subject to these conditions, it is required to comply with them. Finally, if a Central Authority refuses assistance, it is required under Article 3(5) to inform the Central Authority of the requesting Party of the reasons for the refusal.

Articles 4 and 5 prescribe the form and contents of requests under the Treaty, specifying in detail the information required in each request. If the information in the request is not sufficient to enable the request to be executed, the Central Authority of the requested state may ask for additional information. A request for assistance must be in writing, except that in urgent situations a request may be made in another form so long as the request is confirmed in writing as soon as possible thereafter. The requirement that requests be in writing can be satisfied with an electronic version, the authenticity of which can be verified. As both countries move towards use of electronic signatures, it is anticipated that this method might be used more frequently.

Article 6 concerns the execution of requests. Article 6(1) includes three important concepts: the obligation to execute requests, and to do so promptly; a requirement that competent authorities do "everything in their power" to execute requests; and the granting of authority to courts in the requested state to issue subpoenas, search warrants, or other orders necessary to execute requests. Taken together, the latter two provisions specifically authorize United States courts to use all of their powers to issue whatever process is necessary to satisfy a request under the Treaty. They also reflect an understanding that the Parties intend to provide each other with every available form of assistance from judicial and executive branches of government in the execution of mutual legal assistance requests.

Article 6(2) addresses the manner in which requests are to be executed. It creates a hierarchy for a requested state to follow in determining the appropriate procedures for executing a request. In the first instance, requests themselves may specify a particular procedure to be followed, and such specified procedures are to be followed unless prohibited by law in the requested state. This can be important to ensure that evidence collected in one state satisfies requirements for admissibility at trial in the other. If no particular procedure is specified in the request, the request is to be executed in accordance with any specific provisions of the Treaty. Finally, if neither the Treaty nor the request specifies procedures to be followed, the requested state is to execute the request in accordance with its domestic criminal procedure laws. The negotiators intended this provision, like similar provisions in other MLATs, to allow the requested state to use its established procedures for obtaining evidence where procedures are not otherwise specified, so long as those procedures do not undermine the obligation in the Treaty to provide assistance. *See, e.g, In re Commissioner's Subpoenas*, 325 F.3d 1287 (11th Cir. 2003).

Article 6(3) states that the Central Authority of the requested state shall represent the requesting state or make other arrangements for representing the requesting state in the execution of a request for assistance. Thus, it is understood that if execution of the request entails action by a judicial authority or administrative agency, the Central Authority of the requested state shall arrange for the presentation of the request to that court or agency at no cost to the requesting state.

Under Article 6(5), if the Central Authority of the requested state determines that execution of a request would interfere with an ongoing investigation or proceeding pertaining to a criminal matter in that state, it may postpone execution or make execution subject to conditions deemed necessary after consultations with the Central Authority of the requesting state. If the requesting Party accepts assistance subject to such conditions, it must comply with them.

Article 6(6) is meant to address the possible circumstance in which the Central Authority of the requested state believes that the provision of assistance is likely to create a significant safety risk, for example, to a prospective witness or his or her family members. In such a circumstance, which the negotiators concluded would be unusual, the Parties would consult on reasonable measures to address the safety concern.

Confidentiality and limitations on use of evidence obtained under the Treaty are addressed in Article 7. Although requests themselves are generally not confidential, the requesting Party may ask that the request, the supporting documents, action taken pursuant to the request, and even the fact that assistance is granted be kept confidential (Article 7(2)). The requested Party is to use its best efforts to comply with such a request, but if assistance cannot be granted without breaching the confidentiality requirements, the decision whether to proceed is left to the requesting Party.

Article 7(1) requires that information or evidence provided under the Treaty not be used for investigations or proceedings other than those stated in the request without the consent of the requested Party. The requested Party may also request that the information or evidence produced under the Treaty be kept confidential or be used subject to certain conditions (Article 7(3)). The default rule, however, is that such information or evidence is not confidential, and Article 7(5) also provides that once such information or evidence has been disclosed in a public judicial or administrative proceeding, it may be used for any purpose. Moreover, the Treaty is explicit that it does not preclude the disclosure of information to the extent that there is an obligation to disclose it under the Constitution of the requesting state in a criminal prosecution. This contingency, found in Article 7(4), was included to ensure that the United States would be able to satisfy any obligations to disclose information under its Constitution, such as set forth in *Brady v. Maryland*, 373 U.S. 83 (1963). Malaysia's delegation indicated that there is no corresponding obligation under its laws.

As with other provisions of the Treaty, the confidentiality protections and use limitation provisions of Article 7 are for the benefit of the two governments that are Parties to the Treaty, and invocation and enforcement of these provisions is entirely a matter for the Parties.

Article 8 is the first of a series of articles that spell out in detail the procedures to be employed in the case of specific types of requests for assistance outlined in Article 1(2). Article 8 addresses the obtaining of evidence, whether it is a statement or testimony, documents, records, or particular items or things. A person from whom evidence is sought under the Treaty may appear voluntarily to provide such evidence, or, if necessary, the Treaty authorizes the Parties to compel production of evidence. This compulsion may be accomplished by subpoena or any other means available under the laws of the requested state. Article 8(2) specifically provides that use of compulsory process is authorized regardless of whether the proceeding for which the evidence is sought takes place in a court in the requesting state. This provision was necessary to ensure that Malaysia would be empowered to compel witness testimony when requested for use in U.S. grand jury proceedings.

Article 8(3) requires the requested Party to permit persons specified in the request to be present during execution of the request and, where permitted by law, to question the person giving testimony or evidence. Even where direct questioning is not permitted, persons could be permitted under this provision to propose questions to be asked of a witness. Consistent with Article 1(3), this provision does not create a right for private persons to be present during the execution of the request.

Article 8(4) contains the first of several provisions in the Treaty addressing the authentication of evidence produced pursuant to the Treaty. Similar provisions are found at Article 9(3) and 14(3). In the case of requests by Malaysia, the request will specify any authentication requirements that might apply. In the case of requests by the United States, evidence produced under the Treaty is to be authenticated by use of one of the forms appended to the Treaty. The appended forms are an integral part of the Treaty. It is the intent of the Parties that evidence produced and authenticated according to the procedure set forth in the Treaty be admissible in evidence in the requesting state.

In the event that a person from whom the request seeks testimony, documents, records, or items of evidence asserts a right to decline to provide such evidence (such as a privilege or immunity), Article 8(5) establishes two different methods to proceed depending on which state's law is invoked. If the claim is based on the requested state's law, it is to be resolved by the authorities of the requested state. If, however, the claim is based on the laws of the requesting state, the evidence may nonetheless be taken and the claim resolved by the authorities of the requesting state, although the requested state may request a statement from the requesting state of its views as to the validity of the claim. This formulation allows each Party to resolve privilege claims made under its own laws.

Article 8(6) provides that the Parties may agree to the use of live video or television links or other appropriate communications facilities for the purpose of executing a request for the taking of testimony on a case-by-case basis. Such technologies are to be employed according to the laws and procedures of the requested state. The United States can use and has used video technology, for example, to provide testimony to other countries upon request pursuant to 28 U.S.C. Section 1782.

Article 9 addresses provision of documents or other records in the possession of government agencies. The Parties are obligated to provide to each other copies of publicly available records upon request. With respect to documents that are not publicly available, whether to provide such documents is left to the discretion of the requested Party.

Article 10 provides a mechanism for the requesting Party to ask for the voluntary attendance in its territory of a person located in the requested state as a witness or expert in proceedings or to assist in an investigation. The requesting Party must indicate the extent to which the person's expenses will be paid, as well as any arrangements for the person's safety and accommodation while in the requesting state.

Article 11 provides a similar mechanism for persons in custody in the requested state. A need sometimes arises for the testimony in one country of a person who is incarcerated in another country. For example, a witness incarcerated in one country may have to give testimony in the presence of an incarcerated defendant in the other country. Attendance of the person is still voluntary, but is also subject to the discretion of the Parties and agreement of the Central Authorities. In addition, the Treaty imposes certain conditions on such transfers: the person must be held in custody by the requesting Party, unless otherwise authorized by the requested Party; the requesting Party must return the person in custody to the requested Party at the conclusion of the matter, or as soon as circumstances permit or as otherwise agreed; the return of the person shall not require any extradition or other proceedings, such as immigration proceedings; and the period that the person is in custody in the requesting state shall be counted towards the person's period of imprisonment or detention in the requested state.

When persons agree to travel to a requesting state to give evidence, whether in custody or not, Article 12 authorizes the Central Authority of the requesting state, in its discretion, to give such persons a guarantee of "safe conduct." This would ensure that a person attending in the requesting state would not be subject to service of process or any restriction on personal liberty by reason of any acts or convictions that preceded that person's departure from the requested state. It is understood that this provision would not prevent action against a person for perjury or any other crime committed while in the requesting state—rather, it applies only to past offenses. Under Article 12(2), any safe conduct so provided would cease seven days after the Central Authority of the requested state is notified that the person's presence is no longer required, or if the person has left the requesting state and voluntarily returns to it. Of course, as the Treaty sets forth, this article does not preclude a state from holding a person in custody as required by Article 11(2).

While Article 11 addresses the transfer of persons in custody from one Party to the other, Article 13 addresses the situation in which one Party may need to bring persons in custody through the territory of the other on the way to or from third states in order to participate in an investigation or proceeding. Article 13(2) provides that the state through which the person transits has the authority and obligation to keep that person in custody during the transit unless otherwise agreed.

Article 14 obligates the requested Party to execute a request for the search, seizure, and delivery of any documents, records, or items or things if the request includes the information justifying such action under the laws of the requested state. For requests from Malaysia to the United States, this means that a request would have to be supported by a showing of probable cause for the search. The evidentiary standard required under Malaysia law for requests by the United States is similar.

Article 15 provides for determining the whereabouts in the requested state of persons (such as witnesses, potential defendants, or experts) or items or things when such information is requested. The Treaty requires only that the requested state use its "best efforts" to locate the persons or items or things sought. The extent of such efforts will vary, of course, depending on the quality and extent of the information provided by the requesting state concerning the suspected location and last known location. The obligation is limited to persons or items or things that are reasonably believed to be in the territory of the requested state. Thus, the United States would not be obliged to attempt to locate persons or items that may be in third countries.

Article 16 relates to service of documents. It creates an obligation on the Parties to use their best efforts, upon request, to serve documents relating to a criminal investigation or proceeding such as summonses, complaints, subpoenas, or notices. When the document pertains to a response or appearance in the requesting state, it must be transmitted a reasonable time before the scheduled response or appearance. The Parties chose not to set a fixed period of time for this obligation, as circumstances may vary.

Article 17 obligates the Parties, upon request and to the extent permitted by their domestic laws, to endeavor to locate, trace, restrain, freeze, seize, forfeit, or confiscate the proceeds and instrumentalities of crime or recover pecuniary penalties. The types of actions that could be undertaken in the United States under this Article include actions to seize and forfeit property under 18 U.S.C. Section 981, which can be and is employed to temporarily restrain or to seize assets or proceeds of offenses committed abroad. The language of this Article, however, does not require either state to take any action that would exceed its domestic legal authority. Thus it does not mandate, for example, institution of forfeiture proceedings against property located in the United States in the absence of statutory authority to institute such proceedings.

Once property is confiscated, Article 17(2) permits the Party in control of the property to share it with the other Party or otherwise dispose of it in accordance with its own laws. United States law permits the government to transfer a share of certain forfeited property to other countries that participate directly or indirectly in the seizure or forfeiture of the property where, among other requirements, such transfer is authorized by an international agreement. This Article provides such authorization for asset sharing with Malaysia.

Article 17(3) requires the rights of bona fide third parties to be respected in any action taken under this Article.

Article 18 states that this Treaty shall not prevent the Parties from providing assistance to each other through the provisions of other treaties, arrangements, or practices that may be applicable, or through the provisions of their national laws. Thus, for example, the Treaty would leave the provisions of U.S. and Malaysian law on letters rogatory completely undisturbed, and would not alter any practices or arrangements concerning investigative assistance or prohibit the Parties from developing other such practices or arrangements.

Article 19 addresses the costs associated with providing assistance. As is standard in U.S. mutual legal assistance treaties, Article 19 provides that the requested Party must pay all costs relating to the execution of a request, except for the following items to be paid by the requesting Party: fees of private counsel retained at the request of the requesting Party; fees and reasonable expenses of expert witnesses; costs of translation, interpretation and transcription; and allowances and expenses related to travel of persons pursuant to Articles 10 and 11. The article also provides that the requesting Party shall pay the travel expenses of custodial or escorting officers, and the costs of utilizing live video links or other similar facilities, subject to agreement between the Parties. Finally, Article 19(3) provides that, in the event that fulfilling a request would require extraordinary and substantial resources, including expenses, consultation between Central Authorities shall occur in order to determine the terms and conditions for execution.

Article 20 provides for consultations between the Central Authorities to promote the effective use of the Treaty. The Parties discussed the importance of regular consultations between Central Authorities. Such contacts generally result in development of practical measures to more effectively implement the Treaty.

Article 21 is a dispute settlement clause. In keeping with the intent of the Treaty to make the Central Authorities the primary points of contact between the two governments in implementation of the

Treaty, the Central Authorities are also expected to resolve any disputes that arise. The article provides, however, that if the Central Authorities are not able to reach accommodation after a reasonable period, disputes shall be resolved through the diplomatic channel. No external dispute resolution mechanism is contemplated or provided for.

The final clauses are contained in Article 22. The Treaty will enter into force upon exchange of instruments of ratification. It is expressly retroactive—that is, once in force, it shall apply to all requests presented between the Parties regardless of when the acts or omissions constituting the offense occurred. Article 22 also provides procedures for termination of the Treaty, but specifies that termination shall not prevent completion of any requests made prior to termination.

TREATY BETWEEN THE GOVERNMENT OF THE UNITED STATES OF AMERICA AND THE GOVERNMENT OF MALAYSIA ON MUTUAL LEGAL ASSISTANCE IN CRIMINAL MATTERS

The Government of the United States of America and the Government of Malaysia (hereinafter referred to singularly as the "Party" and collectively as the "Parties"):

DESIRING to improve the effectiveness of the law enforcement authorities of the Parties in the investigation of crime and in proceedings pertaining to criminal matters through cooperation and mutual legal assistance in criminal matters,

HAVE AGREED as follows:

ARTICLE 1
SCOPE OF ASSISTANCE

1. The Parties shall, in accordance with this Treaty, render to one another the widest measure of mutual legal assistance in connection with investigations and proceedings pertaining to criminal matters.

2. Mutual legal assistance to be rendered in accordance with this Treaty shall include:

(a) taking of evidence, including testimony, documents, records and items or things, by way of judicial process;

(b) taking of voluntary statements of persons;

(c) providing documents, records and items or things;

(d) making arrangements for persons to give evidence or to assist in criminal investigations, including the transfer of persons in custody;

(e) effecting service of judicial documents;

(f) executing searches and seizures;

(g) locating and identifying persons or items or things and examining objects and sites;

(h) freezing and forfeiting assets or property and collecting fines;

(i) identifying or tracing proceeds of crime and property and instrumentalities derived from or used in the commission of an offence; and

(j) any other form of assistance not prohibited by the laws of the requested state.

3. This Treaty applies solely to the provision of mutual legal assistance between the Parties. The provisions of this Treaty shall not create any right on the part of any private person to obtain, suppress or exclude any evidence or to impede the execution of any request for assistance.

ARTICLE 2
DESIGNATION OF CENTRAL AUTHORITIES

1. Each Party shall designate a Central Authority to make and receive requests pursuant to this Treaty. Requests from the United States shall be transmitted through the Ministry of Foreign Affairs of Malaysia to the Malaysia Central Authority. Requests from Malaysia shall be transmitted through the Ministry of Foreign Affairs of Malaysia directly to the United States Central Authority.

2. For Malaysia, the Central Authority shall be the Attorney General or a person designated by the Attorney General.

3. For the United States of America, the Central Authority shall be the Attorney General or a person designated by the Attorney General.

4. Each Party shall expeditiously notify the other of any change in the designation of its Central Authority.

5. Except as otherwise provided in paragraph 1, the Central Authorities shall communicate directly with one another for the purposes of this Treaty.

ARTICLE 3
LIMITATIONS ON ASSISTANCE

1. The Central Authority of the requested state may refuse assistance if, in the opinion of the Central Authority of the requested state—

(a) the request relates to a political offence;

(b) the request relates to an offence under military law that if it had occurred in the requested state would not be an offence under ordinary criminal law in the requested state;

(c) there are substantial grounds for believing that the request was made for the purpose of investigating, prosecuting, or punishing a person on account of the person's race, religion, sex, ethnic origin, nationality or political opinions;

(d) the request relates to the investigation or prosecution of a person for an offence in a case where the person has been convicted or acquitted by a court in the requested state in respect of the same offence;

(e) the request relates to an act or omission that, if it had occurred in the requested state, would not have constituted an offence against the laws of the requested state punishable under the laws of that state by deprivation of liberty for a period of one year or more, or by a more severe penalty;

(f) the execution of the request would prejudice the sovereignty, security, public order or other essential interest of the requested state;

(g) the Central Authority of the requesting state has, in respect of that request, failed to comply with any material terms of this Treaty or failed to agree to reasonable conditions imposed under paragraph 4 of this Article;

(h) the facts constituting the offence to which the request relates do not indicate an offence of sufficient gravity;

(i) the item or thing requested is of insufficient importance to the investigation or could reasonably be obtained by other means.

2. Without prejudice to any other offences which satisfy dual criminality, a request that relates to an offence identified in the Annex to this Treaty shall not be refused pursuant to subparagraph (1)(e) of this Article as the Parties have determined that dual criminality exists for such offences. The Annex to this Treaty may be modified by the Parties by an exchange of notes.

3. Assistance shall not be refused solely on the ground of secrecy of banks and similar financial institutions or that the offence is also considered to involve fiscal matters.

4. Before denying assistance pursuant to this Article, the Central Authority of the requested state shall consult with the Central Authority of the requesting state to consider whether assistance can be

given subject to such conditions as it deems necessary. If the requesting Party accepts assistance subject to these conditions, it shall comply with the conditions.

5. If the Central Authority of the requested state refuses assistance, it shall promptly inform the Central Authority of the requesting state of the grounds of refusal.

ARTICLE 4
FORM OF REQUESTS

Requests for assistance shall be made in writing, including, where possible, by electronic means that are capable of establishing authenticity. In urgent situations, requests may be made orally or by any other means, but in such cases the requests shall be confirmed in writing as soon as possible, but not later than ten days thereafter, unless the Central Authority of the requested state agrees otherwise.

ARTICLE 5
CONTENTS OF REQUESTS

1. A request shall contain the following:

(a) the name of the competent authority conducting the investigation or proceedings to which the request relates;

(b) the purpose of the request and the nature of the assistance sought;

(c) a description of the offence to which the request relates, including the applicable penalty, and a statement or text of the relevant laws;

(d) a description of the facts alleged to constitute the offence; and

(e) a description of the evidence, information or other assistance sought.

2. Requests for assistance shall also, to the extent necessary, contain the following information:

(a) the identity and location of any person from whom evidence is sought;

(b) a list of questions to be asked of a witness;

(c) the identity and location of a person to be served, that person's relationship to the criminal proceedings, and the manner in which service is to be made;

(d) a precise description of the place or person to be searched and of the items or things to be seized;

(e) information on the identity and suspected whereabouts of a person to be located;

(f) a description of the property, asset or items or things to which the request relates, including its identity and location;

(g) in the case of a request for the enforcement of a forfeiture order or any other court order, a certified copy of the court order relating to the assistance requested and a statement relating to the finality of that order;

(h) a description of any particular procedure to be followed;

(i) specification of any time limit within which compliance with the request is desired;

(j) any special requirement for confidentiality and the reasons for it; and

(k) such other information or requirement as is necessary for the proper execution of the request.

3. Requests, supporting documents and other communications made pursuant to this Treaty shall be in the English language.

4. If the Central Authority of the requested state considers that the information contained in the request is not sufficient to enable the request to be executed, the Central Authority may request additional information. The requesting Party shall supply such additional information as the requested Party considers necessary to enable the request to be fulfilled.

ARTICLE 6
EXECUTION OF REQUESTS

1. The Central Authority of the requested state shall promptly execute the request or, when appropriate, shall transmit it to the authority having jurisdiction to do so. The competent authorities of the requested state shall do everything in their power to execute the request. The courts of the requested state shall have authority to issue subpoenas, search warrants or other orders necessary to execute the request.

2. Requests shall be executed in accordance with the laws of the requested state except to the extent that this Treaty provides otherwise. Procedures specified in the request shall be followed except to the extent that those procedures cannot lawfully be followed in the requested state. Where neither the Treaty nor the request specifies a particular procedure, the request shall be executed in accordance with the appropriate procedure under the laws applicable for criminal investigations or proceedings in the requested state.

3. The Central Authority of the requested state shall represent the interests of the requesting Party or may, if requested to do so, make other arrangements for the representation of the requesting Party in the requested state in any proceedings arising out of a request for assistance.

4. The Central Authority of the requested state shall respond within a reasonable period to reasonable inquiries by the Central Authority of the requesting state concerning progress toward execution of the request.

5. If the Central Authority of the requested state determines that execution of a request would interfere with an ongoing investigation or proceeding pertaining to a criminal matter in that state, it may postpone execution, or make execution subject to conditions determined necessary after consultations with the Central Authority of the requesting state. If the requesting Party accepts the assistance subject to the conditions, it shall comply with the conditions.

6. Where, in the opinion of the requested Party, the provision of assistance pursuant to a request is likely to create a significant safety risk in the requested state, the Parties shall consult on reasonable measures to address the safety concern.

7. The Central Authority of the requested state shall promptly inform the Central Authority of the requesting state of the outcome of the execution of the request. If execution of the request is denied, delayed or postponed, the Central Authority of the requested state shall inform the Central Authority of the requesting state of the reasons for the denial, delay or postponement.

ARTICLE 7
LIMITATIONS ON USE OF EVIDENCE OBTAINED AND PROTECTION OF CONFIDENTIALITY

1. The requesting Party shall not, without the consent of the requested Party and subject to such terms and conditions as the requested Party considers necessary, use or transfer information or evidence provided by the requested Party for investigations or proceedings pertaining to a criminal matter other than those stated in the request.

2. The requested Party shall, upon request and to the extent permitted by its laws, use its best efforts to keep confidential the request for assistance, its contents and its supporting documents, the fact of granting of such assistance and any action taken pursuant to the request. If the request cannot be executed without breaching the confidentiality requirements stated in the request, the requested Party shall so inform the requesting Party, which shall then determine whether the request should nevertheless be executed.

3. The Central Authority of the requested state may request that information or evidence furnished under this Treaty be kept confidential or be used only subject to terms and conditions it may specify. If the requesting Party accepts the information or evidence subject to such conditions, the requesting Party shall use its best efforts to comply with the conditions.

4. Nothing in this Article shall preclude the use or disclosure of information to the extent that there is an obligation to do so under the Constitution of the requesting state in a criminal prosecution. The requesting Party shall notify the requested Party in advance of any such proposed disclosure.

5. Information or evidence, the contents of which have been disclosed in a public judicial or administrative proceeding, may thereafter be used for any purpose.

ARTICLE 8
OBTAINING OF EVIDENCE

1. A person in the requested state from whom evidence is requested pursuant to this Treaty shall appear and provide a statement, or sworn or affirmed testimony, or produce documents, records or items of evidence. The person may provide such evidence voluntarily or the requested Party may compel the testimony or production of such evidence, as may be necessary.

2. The requested Party shall, as necessary, authorize the use of compulsory process to execute a request for testimony or evidence for use in a proceeding pertaining to a criminal matter regardless of whether such a proceeding takes place in a court.

3. Upon request, the requested Party shall permit the presence of persons set forth in the request during the execution of the request and, to the extent permitted by its laws, shall allow specified persons to question the person giving the testimony or evidence.

4. Evidence that has been produced in the requested state pursuant to this Article or that has been the subject of testimony taken under this Article shall, upon request, be authenticated, in the case of requests by Malaysia, as required under Malaysian laws and specified in the request, and in the case of requests by the United States of America, by use of Form A or Form B, as the case may require, appended to this Treaty.

5. If a person who is required to give sworn or affirmed testimony or produce documents, records or items of evidence under this Article claims that there is a right to decline to do so under the laws of the requested state, the claim shall be resolved by the authorities of the requested state. If such a claim is made regarding a right under the laws of the requesting state, the requesting Party shall, if so requested, provide a statement to the requested Party of its views as to the validity of the claim and whether the evidence shall nonetheless be taken and forwarded and the claim resolved by the authorities of the requesting state.

6. For the purpose of executing a request for the taking of testimony, the Parties may agree on a case by case basis to the use of live video or television links or other appropriate communications facilities in accordance with the laws and procedures of the requested state if it is expedient and in the interests of justice to do so.

ARTICLE 9
PROVISION OF PUBLICLY AVAILABLE DOCUMENTS AND OTHER RECORDS

1. The requested Party shall provide the requesting Party with copies of publicly available records, including documents or information in any form, in the possession of government departments and agencies in the requested state.

2. The requested Party may, to the extent permitted by its laws, provide the requesting Party with copies of any records, including documents or information in any form, that are in the possession of a government department or agency in the requested state but that are not publicly available. The requested Party may in its discretion deny, entirely or in part, a request pursuant to this paragraph.

3. Records produced in the requested state pursuant to this Article shall, upon request, be authenticated, in the case of requests by Malaysia, as required under Malaysian laws and specified in the request, and in the case of requests by the United States of America, by use of Form C or Form D, as the case may require, appended to this Treaty.

ARTICLE 10
ATTENDANCE OF PERSON IN THE REQUESTING STATE

1. The requested Party shall, upon request, invite a person to attend in the requesting state as a witness or expert in proceedings pertaining to a criminal matter or to assist in an investigation and where the person consents, assist in arranging that person's attendance.

2. The requesting Party shall indicate the extent to which the person's expenses will be paid. A person who agrees to attend in the requesting state may ask that the requesting Party advance money to cover these expenses. This advance may be provided through the Embassy or a Consulate of the requesting Party.

3. Where a person is asked to attend in the requesting state, the request shall contain information on the following matters:

(a) the fees, allowances and expenses, if any, to which he will be entitled;

(b) the arrangements for his security, if any, while he is traveling to and from the requesting state and while he is in the requesting state; and

(c) the arrangements for his accommodation, if any, while he is in the requesting state.

ARTICLE 11
ATTENDANCE OF PERSON IN CUSTODY IN THE REQUESTING STATE

1. The requested Party may, upon request, agree to allow a person in custody in the requested state, subject to his consent and if the Central Authorities agree, to be temporarily transferred to the requesting state to give evidence or to assist in an investigation.

2. The requesting Party shall hold the person in custody, unless otherwise authorized by the requested Party, and shall return that person in custody to the requested Party at the conclusion of the matter, or as soon as circumstances permit or otherwise agreed by both Central Authorities.

3. The requesting Party shall not require the requested Party to initiate extradition or any other proceedings for the return of the person transferred.

4. The period during which such person was under the custody of the requesting Party shall count towards the period of his imprisonment or detention in the requested state.

ARTICLE 12
SAFE CONDUCT

1. The Central Authority of the requesting state may, in its discretion, determine that a person attending in the requesting state pursuant to Article 10 or 11 shall not be subject to service of process or be detained or subjected to any restriction of personal liberty by reason of any acts or convictions that preceded his departure from the requested state. Nothing in this Article shall preclude the requesting Party from holding a person in custody pursuant to Article 11(2).

2. The safe conduct provided for by this Article shall cease seven days after the Central Authority of the requesting state has notified the Central Authority of the requested state that the person's presence is no longer required, or when the person, having left the requesting state, voluntarily returns to that state. The Central Authority of the requesting state may, in its discretion, extend this period up to fifteen days if it determines that there is good cause to do so.

ARTICLE 13
TRANSIT OF PERSONS IN CUSTODY

1. The requested Party may, upon request, authorize the transit through its territory of a person held in custody by the requesting Party or a third state whose attendance has been requested by the requesting Party in an investigation or proceedings pertaining to a criminal matter.

2. The requested Party shall have the authority and the obligation to keep the person in custody during transit unless otherwise agreed between the Parties.

3. Where a person is being held in custody in the requested state on transit and the person's transportation is not continued within a reasonable time, the person may be returned to the state from which the person was first transported.

ARTICLE 14
SEARCH AND SEIZURE

1. The requested Party shall, upon request, execute a request for the search, seizure and delivery of any documents, records or items or things to the requesting Party if the request includes the information justifying such action under the laws of the requested state.

2. The Central Authority of the requested state may require that the requesting Party agree to terms and conditions related to any seized documents, records or items or things which may be delivered to the requesting Party that are considered necessary by the requested Party to protect the documents, records or items or things to be transferred.

3. Upon request, every official who has custody of a seized article shall certify the identity of the article, the continuity of custody, and any changes in condition, in the case of requests by Malaysia, as specified in the request, and in the case of requests by the United States of America, by use of Form E appended to this Treaty. No further certification shall be required. The form shall be admissible in evidence in the requesting state.

ARTICLE 15
LOCATION OR IDENTIFICATION OF PERSONS OR ITEMS OR THINGS

The requested Party shall, upon request, use its best efforts to ascertain the location or identity of a person or item or thing specified in the request and reasonably believed to be within its territory.

ARTICLE 16
SERVICE OF DOCUMENTS

1. The requested Party shall, upon request, use its best efforts to effect service of any document relevant to an investigation or proceeding pertaining to a criminal matter arising in the requesting state that is transmitted to it for this purpose by the requesting Party.

2. If the document pertains to a response or appearance in the requesting state, it shall be transmitted a reasonable time before the scheduled response or appearance.

3. The requested Party shall return a proof of service in the manner mutually agreed by the Parties.

ARTICLE 17
ASSISTANCE IN FORFEITURE PROCEEDINGS

1. The requested Party shall, upon request and to the extent permitted by its laws, endeavor to locate, trace, restrain, freeze, seize, forfeit or confiscate the proceeds of crime and the instrumentalities of crime or recover pecuniary penalties.

2. A Party in control of forfeited or confiscated property or assets or pecuniary penalties recovered shall dispose of them according to its laws. To the extent permitted by its laws, that Party may transfer all or any part of such property or the proceeds of its sale or the pecuniary penalties recovered to the other Party upon mutually acceptable terms.

3. In the application of this Article, the rights of *bona fide* third parties shall be respected.

ARTICLE 18
COMPATIBILITY WITH OTHER ARRANGEMENTS

Nothing in this Treaty shall prevent the Parties from providing assistance to each other pursuant to other treaties, arrangements, practices or the provisions of their national laws.

ARTICLE 19
COSTS

1. The requested Party shall assume all ordinary expenses of fulfilling the request for assistance, except that the requesting Party shall bear—

(a) the fees of other counsel retained at the request of the requesting Party;

(b) the fees and reasonable expenses of expert witnesses;

(c) the costs of translation, interpretation and transcription;

(d) the expenses associated with conveying any person to or from the territory of the requested state and any fees, allowances and expenses payable to the person concerned while that person is in the requesting state pursuant to a request made under Article 10 or 11 of this Treaty; and

(e) the travel expenses of custodial or escorting officers as agreed between the Parties.

2. The costs of utilizing live video or television links or other appropriate communications facilities shall be borne by the requesting Party, unless the Parties mutually agree otherwise.

3. If during the execution of the request it becomes apparent that resources, including expenses, of an extraordinary or substantial nature are required to fulfill the request, the Parties shall consult to determine the terms and conditions under which the execution of the request is to be effected or continued.

ARTICLE 20
CONSULTATION

1. The Central Authorities shall consult, at times mutually agreed upon by them, to promote the most effective use of this Treaty.

2. The Central Authorities may develop such practical measures as may be necessary to facilitate the implementation of this Treaty.

ARTICLE 21
SETTLEMENT OF DISPUTES

Any difference or dispute between the Parties arising from the interpretation or implementation of the provisions of this Treaty shall be resolved through the diplomatic channel if the Central Authorities are not able to reach accommodation after a reasonable period.

ARTICLE 22
RATIFICATION, ENTRY INTO FORCE AND TERMINATION

1. This Treaty shall be subject to ratification and the instruments of ratification shall be exchanged as soon as possible.

2. This Treaty shall enter into force upon the exchange of instruments of ratification.

3. This Treaty shall apply to requests presented after the date of its entry into force whether the relevant acts or omissions constituting the offence occurred before or after that date.

4. Either Party may terminate this Treaty by written notification to the other. Termination shall take effect six months following the date of notification.

5. Termination of this Treaty shall be without prejudice to the completion of any requests made pursuant to this Treaty before or up to the date of termination.

IN WITNESS WHEREOF the undersigned, being duly authorized by their respective Governments, have signed this Treaty.

Done at Kuala Lumpur on this 28th day of July 2006 in two original copies in the English language.

FOR THE GOVERNMENT OF THE UNITED STATES OF AMERICA

[Signature]

Condoleezza Rice
Secretary of State

FOR THE GOVERNMENT OF MALAYSIA

[Signature]

Dato' Seri Syed Hamid Albar
Minister of Foreign Affairs

ANNEX

1. Offences against the laws relating to possession, trafficking, cultivation, manufacture, import or export of dangerous drugs including narcotics, and psychotropic substances, precursors and essential chemicals used in the illegal manufacture of narcotics and psychotropic substances.

2. Racketeering activity, including—

(a) using income derived from a pattern of criminal activity to establish, operate, or acquire an interest in an enterprise engaged in or affecting interstate commerce;

(b) acquiring or maintaining control of or an interest in such an enterprise through a pattern of criminal activity or collection of illegal debt; or

(c) conducting or participating in the conduct of such an enterprise's affairs through a pattern of criminal activity or collection of illegal debt.

3. Offences against the laws relating to money laundering, including—

(a) failing to make or causing another to fail to make to the Government a report which is required by law to be made in respect of a transfer of currency or other financial transaction;

(b) converting, transferring or receiving property knowing that such property is derived from a criminal offence, for the purpose of concealing or disguising the illicit origin of such property or of assisting any person involved in the commission of such offence to evade the legal consequences of his actions;

(c) concealing or disguising the true nature, source, location, disposition or movement or ownership of property knowing that such property is derived from a crime; or

(d) possessing or laundering of proceeds obtained from the commission of any offence for which mutual legal assistance may be granted in accordance with this Treaty.

4. Cheating, fraud (against the Government or individuals), obtaining property or pecuniary advantage by deception, willful issuance of a cheque under a false name or without having made arrangements with a financial institution, or after transactions have been suspended by such an institution, or the willful failure to honor a cheque.

5. Offences against the laws relating to securities and futures trading, and fraudulent securities practices including the use by any person of any means, directly or indirectly, in connection with the offer, purchase or sale of any security—

(a) to employ any device, scheme or artifice to defraud;

(b) to willfully make any misleading statement or provide any misleading information to shareholders or securities authorities or others; or

(c) to willfully engage in any act, practice or course of business which operates or would operate as a fraud or deceit upon any person.

6. Offences against the laws relating to insider trading, including the offer, purchase or sale of securities by any person while in possession of material non-public information directly or indirectly relating to the securities offered, purchased or sold in breach of a legally binding duty or trust or confidence.

7. Offences against the laws relating to bribery and corruption, including acts involving foreign public officials.

8. Offences against the laws relating to fiscal matters, taxes or duties notwithstanding that the laws of the requested Party do not impose the same kind of tax or duty or do not contain a tax, duty or customs regulation of the same kind as the laws of the requesting Party, including—

(a) tax evasion or fiscal fraud by individuals or corporate bodies;

(b) failure to submit returns;

(c) making a false statement or submitting false or misleading information, whether written or oral, to the relevant authorities; or

(d) intentionally failing to make a report or declaration as required by law, to relevant authorities in matters concerning customs duties or taxes.

9. Offences against the laws relating to the environment, including conduct directed at the destruction, defacing, deterioration or harming of the earth's environment, the seas or endangered species of plant or animal life, including illegal possession and trafficking of endangered plant or animal species.

10. Offences against the laws relating to export control, including conduct tending to evade the laws controlling the export of goods or arms.

11. Criminal exploitation of children, whether for sexual or other purposes, including—

(a) forcing children into prostitution;

(b) commercial dealing in child pornography;

(c) possessing obscene materials for sale, circulation, distribution or hire; or

(d) publicly exhibiting obscene material or distributing obscene materials through the Internet.

12. Offences against bankruptcy laws.

13. Offences against the laws relating to corporations or companies, including offences committed by officers, directors or promoters.

14. Offences against the laws relating to firearms, weapons, ammunition or explosives of any type.

15. Offences against the laws relating to protection of intellectual property.

16. Offences against the laws relating to immigration and nationality, including—

(a) harboring illegal immigrants;

(b) fraudulent acquisition or illegal possession or use of a passport or visa or any other means to engage in any form of criminal activity; and

(c) arranging or facilitating the illegal entry or exit of persons into or out of a jurisdiction.

17. Smuggling.

18. Offences against the laws relating to the international transfer of funds.

19. Offences against the laws relating to the protection of computers or computer systems, computer data or computer security (including passwords or other related devices).

20. Piracy involving ships or aircraft.

21. Obstruction of justice, including perjury and attempting to pervert the course of justice.

22. Offences under multilateral international conventions binding on both Parties for which offenders must be prosecuted or extradited.

23. Any offence derived from conduct described in this Annex or subject to mutual legal assistance in accordance with this Treaty where federal jurisdiction is based upon interstate transport or use of the mails, telecommunications or other interstate facilities.

24. Offences of criminal conspiracy, attempt, participation or aiding and abetting and conspiracy offences committed with the common intention of two or more persons.

25. Any offence under the laws of the requesting State which is connected with the commission of one or more offences derived from the conduct described in this Annex or subject to mutual legal assistance in accordance with this Treaty.

FORM A
CERTIFICATE OF AUTHENTICITY OF BUSINESS RECORDS

I, ______________________________ (*name*), attest on penalty of criminal punishment for false statement or attestation that I am employed by ______________________________ (*name of business from which documents are sought*) and that my official title is ______________________________ (*official title*). I further state that each of the records attached hereto is the original or a duplicate of the original record in the custody of ______________________________ (*name of business from which documents are sought*).

I further state that:

A) such records were made, at or near the time of the occurrence of the matters set forth, by (or from information transmitted by) a person with knowledge of those matters;

B) such records were kept in the course of a regularly conducted business activity;

C) the business activity made such records as a regular practice; and

D) if any such record is not the original, it is a duplicate of the original.

______________________________ ______________________________

(*signature*) (*date*)

Sworn to or affirmed before me, ______________________________ (*name*), a judicial officer, this __________ day of __________ 20 _____

FORM B
CERTIFICATION OF ABSENCE OR NONEXISTENCE OF BUSINESS RECORDS

I, ______________________________ (*name*), attest on penalty of criminal punishment for false statement or attestation that I am employed by/ associated with ______________________________ (*name of business from which documents are sought*) in the position of ______________________________ ________ (*business position or title*) and by reason of my position am authorized and qualified to make this attestation.

As a result of my employment/ association with the above-named business, I am familiar with the business records it maintains. The business maintains records that are:

A) made, at or near the time of the occurrence of the matters set forth, by (or from information transmitted by) a person with knowledge of those matters;

B) kept in the course of a regularly conducted business activity; and

C) made by the business as a regular practice.

Among the records so maintained are records of individuals and entities that have accounts or otherwise transact business with the above-named business. I have made or caused to be made a diligent search of those records. No records have been found reflecting any business activity between the business and the following individuals and entities:

____

____

____

____

(*date of execution*)

____

(*place of execution*)

____

(*signature*)

FORM C

I, ______________________________ (*name*), attest on penalty of criminal punishment for false statement or attestation that my position with the Government of ____________________________ (*country*) is ____________________________ (*official title*) ____________________________ and that in that position I am authorized by the law of ____________________________ (*country*) to attest that the documents attached and described below are true and accurate copies of original official records which are recorded or filed in ____________________________ (*name of office or agency*), which is a government office or agency of ____________________________ (*country*).

Description of Documents:

____
(*signature*)

____
(*title*)

____
(*date*)

FORM D

I, ______________________________ (*name*), attest on penalty of criminal punishment for false statement or attestation that:

1. ______________________________ (*name of office or agency*) is a government office or agency of ______________________________ (*country*) and is authorized by law to maintain official records setting forth matters authorized by law to be reported and recorded or filed;

2. records of the type described below set forth matters that are authorized by law to be reported and recorded or filed, and such matters regularly are recorded or filed by the above-named public authority;

3. my position with the above-named public authority is ______________________________ (*official title*);

4. in my official capacity I have caused the production of true and accurate copies of records maintained by that public authority; and

5. no such records have been found to exist therein.

Description of Documents:

____

(*signature*)

____

(*date*)

Official Seal

FORM E

I, ______________________________ (*name*), attest on penalty of criminal punishment for false statement or attestation that my position with the Government of ____________________ (*country*) is ______________________________ (*official title*). I received custody of the articles listed below from ______________________________ (*name of person*) on __________ (*date*), at ______________________________ (*place*) in the same condition as when I received them (or, if different, as noted below).

Description of Articles:

Changes in condition while in my custody:

______________________________ (*signature*)

______________________________ (*title*)

Official Seal

______________________________ (*place*)

______________________________ (*date*)

APPENDIX I
INDEX BY COUNTRY

Afghanistan

Economic Cooperation

Strategic Objective Grant Agreement Amendment Number Five for the Strategic Objective of a Thriving Economy Led by the Private Sector. Signed at Kabul, September 18, 2006. Entered into force September 18, 2006. **06-05 CTIA 1, DOS 06-251.**

Strategic Objective Grant Agreement Amendment Number Five for the Strategic Objective of a Better Educated and Healthier Population. Signed at Kabul, September 18, 2006. Entered into force September 18, 2006. **06-05 CTIA 5, DOS 06-252.**

Strategic Objective Grant Agreement Amendment Number Six for the Strategic Objective of a Thriving Economy Led by the Private Sector. Signed at Kabul, September 30, 2006. Entered into force September 30, 2006. **06-05 CTIA 307, DOS 06-266.**

Armenia

Economic Cooperation

Millennium Challenge Compact, with Annexes. Signed at Washington D.C., March 27, 2006. Entered into force September 29, 2006. **06-05 CTIA 17, DOS 06-256.**

Labor and Employment

Agreement on Employment of Dependents of Members of Diplomatic Missions and Consular Posts. Effected by Exchange of Notes at Yerevan, September 20 and December 30, 2005. Entered into force October 16, 2006. **06-05 CTIA 355, DOS 06-278.**

Australia

Defense

Memorandum of Understanding Concerning Cooperation on Land Force Capability Modernization, with Annexes. Signed at Washington D.C., July 26, 2006. Entered into force July 26, 2006. **06-05 CTIA 463, DOS 06-290.**

Memorandum of Understanding Regarding Assignment of an Operational Logistics Liaison Officer to USTRANSCOM, with Annex. Signed at Canberra and Belleville, July 27 and August 25, 2006. Entered into force August 25, 2006. **06-05 CTIA 531, DOS 06-296.**

Benin

Economic Cooperation

Millennium Challenge Compact, with Annexes. Signed at Washington D.C., February 22, 2006. Entered into force October 6, 2006. **06-05 CTIA 81, DOS 06-257.**

Botswana

Conservation

Agreement Concerning the Establishment of a Tropical Forest Conservation Fund and a Tropical Forest Conservation Board, with Attachments. Signed at Gaborone, October 5, 2006. Entered into force November 19, 2006. **06-05 CTIA 823, DOS 06-311.**

Debts

Agreement Regarding the Reduction of Certain Debts Owed to the Government of the United States and Its Agencies, with Attachment. Signed at Gaborone. October 5, 2006. Entered into force November 19, 2006. **06-05 CTIA 837, DOS 06-312.**

Cambodia

Economic Cooperation

Amendment No. 4 to the Strategic Objective Grant Agreement for Improved Health Services in HIV/AIDS and Infectious Diseases. Signed at Phnom Penh, September 18, 2006. Entered into force September 18, 2006. **06-05 CTIA 543, DOS 06-298.**

Congo, Democratic Republic of the

Defense

Agreement Regarding Grants and the Furnishing of Defense Articles, Defense Services and Related Training, Including Pursuant to the United States IMET Program and the Peacekeeping Operation (PKO) Program. Effected By Exchange of Notes at Kinshasa, June 5 and October 11, 2006. Entered into force October 11, 2006. **06-05 CTIA 319, DOS 06-268.**

Acquisition and Cross-Servicing Agreement, with Annexes. Signed at Stuttgart and Kinshasa, July 14 and September 29, 2006. Entered into force September 29, 2006. **06-05 CTIA 745, DOS 06-306.**

Dominican Republic

Textiles

Agreement on Trade in Textile and Apparel Goods. Effected by Exchange of Letters at Santo Domingo and Washington D.C., October 19 and 24, 2006. Entered into force October 24, 2006. **06-05 CTIA 571, DOS 06-300.**

Egypt

Scientific Cooperation

Extension to the Agreement of January 29, 2001 on Science and Technology Cooperation. Effected by Exchange of Notes at Cairo, May 11 and August 27, 2006. Entered into force August 27, 2006, Effective September 1, 2005. **06-05 CTIA 337, DOS 06-274.**

European Bank for Reconstruction and Development - EBRD

Economic Cooperation

Amendment to the Grant Agreement of November 21,1997, as Amended, for the Chernobyl Unit 4 Shelter Implementation Plan. Effected by Exchange of Letters at Washington D.C. and London, September 21 and 29, 2006. Entered into force September 29, 2006, Effective September 21, 2006. **06-05 CTIA 13, DOS 06-255.**

European Space Agency - ESA

Space

Amendment to the Agreement of October 7, 1977, as Amended, Concerning Cooperation with Respect to the Hubble Space Telescope Program, Signed at Washington, D.C., April 20 and 24, 2006. Entered into force April 24, 2006. **06-05 CTIA 203, DOS 06-259.**

Amendment and Extension of the Memorandum of Understanding Concerning ESA Participation in the Hubble Space Telescope Program. Signed on October 19 and October 23, 2001. Entered into force October 23, 2001. **06-05 CTIA 375, DOS 06-281.**

Finland

Nuclear Materials and Safety

Arrangement for the Exchange of Technical Information and Cooperation in Nuclear Safety Matters, with Addenda. Signed at Vienna, September 20, 2006. Entered into force September 20, 2006. **06-05 CTIA 339, DOS 06-275.**

France

Nuclear Materials and Safety

Agreement Regarding the Technical Exchange and Cooperation Arrangement in the Field of Nuclear Safety Research. Signed at Rockville and Paris, July 26 and August 4, 2006. Entered into force August 4, 2006. **06-05 CTIA 501, DOS 06-291.**

Georgia

Biological Weapons

Amendment to the Agreement of December 30, 2002 Concerning Cooperation in the Area of Prevention of Proliferation of Technology, Pathogens and Expertise Related to the Development of Biological Weapons. Signed at Tbilisi and Washington D.C., March 19 and 23, 2004. Entered into force July 22, 2004. **06-05 CTIA 329, DOS 06-271.**

Amendment to the Agreement of December 30, 2002, as Amended, Concerning Cooperation in the Area of Prevention of Proliferation of Technology, Pathogens, and Expertise Related to the Development of Biological Weapons. Signed at Tbilisi and Washington D.C., June 21 and 23, 2006. Entered into force October 25, 2006. **06-05 CTIA 373, DOS 06-280.**

Germany

Income Taxation

Protocol Amending the Convention for the Avoidance of Double Taxation and the Prevention of Fiscal Evasion with Respect to Taxes on Income and on Capital and to Certain Other Taxes, with a Joint Declaration. Signed at Berlin, June 1, 2006. **06-05 CTIA 855, Senate Treaty Document 109-20.**

Hungary

Defense

Memorandum of Understanding Regarding Assignment of Liaison Officers, with Annex. Signed at Budapest and Norfolk, September 22 and October 23, 2006. Entered into force October 23, 2006. **06-05 CTIA 361, DOS 06-279.**

Iceland

Military Operations

Agreement Regarding the Withdrawal of United States Forces from and the Return to Iceland of Certain Agreed Areas and Facilities in Iceland, with Attachments. Signed at Washington D.C. and Reykjavik, September 27 and 29, 2006. Entered into force September 29, 2006. **06-05 CTIA 297, DOS 06-265.**

India

Space

Memorandum of Understanding on Cooperation Concerning NASA's Miniature Synthetic Aperture Radar Instrument on ISRO's Chandrayaan - 1 Mission. Signed at Bangalore, May 9, 2006. Entered into force May 9, 2006. **06-05 CTIA 429, DOS 06-287.**

Memorandum of Understanding on Cooperation Concerning NASA's Moon Mineralogy Mapper (M3) Instrument on ISRO's Chandrayaan - 1 Mission. Signed at Bangalore, May 9, 2006. Entered into force May 9, 2006. **06-05 CTIA 443, DOS 06-288.**

Indonesia

Customs

Memorandum of Understanding Regarding Mutual Assistance Between Their Customs Administrations. Signed at Jakarta. November 17, 2006. Entered into force November 17, 2006. **06-05 CTIA 815, DOS 06-310.**

Economic Cooperation

Strategic Objective Grant Agreement to Support Improved Quality of Decentralized Basic Education in Indonesia. Signed at Jakarta, August 30, 2004. Entered into force August 30, 2004. **06-05 CTIA 389, DOS 06-282.**

Amendment No.1 to the Strategic Objective Grant Agreement to Support Improved Quality of Decentralized Basic Education in Indonesia. Signed at Jakarta, July 8, 2005. Entered into force July 8, 2005. **06-05 CTIA 411, DOS 06-283.**

Amendment No.1 to the Strategic Objective Grant Agreement of July 11, 2005 to Support Effective Democratic and Decentralized Governance in Indonesia. Signed at Jakarta, November 16, 2005. Entered into force November 16, 2005. **06-05 CTIA 425, DOS 06-285.**

Emergency Preparedness

Memorandum of Understanding on General Cooperation in Science and Technology for Natural Hazard Assessment, Analysis, Warning, Preparedness, and Mitigation, with Annexes. Signed at Jakarta, November 20, 2006. Entered into force November 20, 2006. **06-05 CTIA 845, DOS 06-313.**

Israel

Trade

Agreement Concerning Certain Aspects of Trade in Agricultural Products, with Attachment and Annexes. Signed at Washington D.C., July 27, 2004. Entered into force September 10, 2004. **06-05 CTIA 635, DOS 06-304.**

Italy

Defense

Memorandum of Agreement for Research, Development, Test and Evaluation Projects, with Annex and Appendix. Signed at Washington D.C. and Rome, September 15 and 26, 2006. Entered into force September 26, 2006. **06-05 CTIA 267, DOS 06-264.**

Memorandum of Understanding Concerning the Mutual Exchange of Military Satellite Communications Services and Support, with Annex. Signed at Offutt AFB and Rome, July 20 and November 6, 2006. Entered into force November 6, 2006. **06-05 CTIA 789, DOS 06-307.**

Japan

Defense

Agreement Concerning a Cash Contribution by Japan for Administrative and Related Expenses Arising from Implementation of the Mutual Defense Assistance Agreement of March 8, 1954. Effected By Exchange of Notes at Tokyo, October 13, 2006. Entered into force October 13, 2006. **06-05 CTIA 323, DOS 06-269.**

Jordan

Defense

Agreement Concerning the Training of Iraqi Police in Jordan. Signed at Amman and Washington D.C., September 24, 2004. Entered into force September 6, 2005. **06-05 CTIA 415, DOS 06-284.**

Economic Cooperation

Amendment No. 4 to the Strategic Objective Grant Agreement of February 23, 2004, as Amended, for the Improved Economic Opportunities for Jordanians Strategic Objective, with Annex. Signed at Amman, August 10, 2006. Entered into force August 10, 2006. **06-05 CTIA 513, DOS 06-292.**

Amendment No. 2 to the Strategic Objective Grant Agreement of June 2, 2004, as Amended, for the Improved Social Sector Development and Governance Strategic Objective, with Annex. Signed at Amman, August 10, 2006. Entered into force August 10, 2006. **06-05 CTIA 517, DOS 06-293.**

Amendment No. 2 to the Strategic Objective Grant Agreement of June 2, 2004, as Amended, for the Enhanced Integrated Water Resources Strategic Objective, with Annex. Signed at Amman, August 10, 2006. Entered into force August 10, 2006. **06-05 CTIA 521, DOS 06-294.**

Amendment No. 3 to the Strategic Objective Grant Agreement of March 23, 2004, as Amended, for the Cash Transfer Special Objective, with Annex. Signed at Amman, August 10, 2006. Entered into force August 10, 2006. **06-05 CTIA 525, DOS 06-295.**

Lebanon

Defense

Acquisition and Cross-Servicing Agreement. Signed at Beirut, May 3 and 20, 2006. Entered into force September 30, 2006. **06-05 CTIA 311, DOS 06-267.**

Malaysia

Aviation

Amendment to the Air Transport Agreement of June 21, 1997. Effected by Exchange of Notes at Kuala Lumpur, August 7 and October 20, 2006. **06-05 CTIA 569, DOS 06-299.**

Judicial Assistance and Extradition

Treaty on Mutual Legal Assistance in Criminal Matters, with Annex. Signed at Kuala Lumpur, July 28, 2006. **06-05 CTIA 965, Senate Treaty Document 109-22.**

Mali

Defense

Acquisition and Cross-Servicing Agreement, with Annexes. Signed at Bamako, September 20, 2006. Entered into force September 20, 2006. **06-05 CTIA 215, DOS 06-262.**

Mexico

Conservation

Agreement on Cooperation in the Management and Protection of National Parks and Other Protected Natural Area. Signed at Washington D.C., March 23, 2006. Entered into force March 23, 2006. **06-05 CTIA 331, DOS 06-272.**

Telecommunications

Protocol Concerning the Allotment and Use of the 698–806 MHz Band for Terrestrial Non-Broadcasting Radiocommunication Services Along the Common Border, with Appendices. Signed at Mexico City and Antalya, November 1 and 8, 2006. Entered into force November 8, 2006. **06-05 CTIA 803, DOS 06-308.**

Norway

Space

Extension the Agreement of October 20, 2000 and November 14, 2001 for the Cooperation in the Civil Uses of Outer Space. Signed at Washington D.C., October 23, 2006. Entered into force October 23, 2006; Effective November 14, 2006. **06-05 CTIA 327, DOS 06-270.**

Panama

Aviation

Amendment to the Air Transport Agreement of May 8, 1997. Effected by Exchange of Notes at Panama, August 7 and September 27, 2006. Entered into force September 27, 2006. **06-05 CTIA 11, DOS 06-254.**

Military Operations

Agreement Regarding the Status of United States Personnel Who May Be Temporarily Present in Panama in Connection with a Visit by Twelve Officials from the U.S. Naval Special Warfare Detachment South. Effected by Exchange of Notes at Panama, October 27 and November 8, 2006. Entered into force November 8, 2006. **06-05 CTIA 631, DOS 06-303.**

Peru

Trade

Agreement on Beef SPS Issues for United States - Peru Trade Promotion, with Annex. Effected by Exchange of Letters at Lima and Washington D.C., October 6 and 25 2006. Entered into force October 25, 2006. **06-05 CTIA 577, DOS 06-301.**

Poland

Defense

Memorandum of Arrangement Regarding Assignment of Liaison Officers, with Annex. Signed on September 22, 2006. Entered into force September 22, 2006. **06-05 CTIA 255, DOS 06-263.**

Russian Federation

Space

Extension to the Agreement of April 6, 2001 on the Flight of the Russian High Energy Neutron Detector (HEND) Instrument on the United States 2001 Mars Odyssey Orbiter Mission. Signed at Washington D.C., September 12 and 18, 2006. Entered into force September 18, 2006. **06-05 CTIA 205, DOS 06-260.**

Weapons

Amendment to the Agreement of August 26, 1993, as Amended, Concerning Cooperation in the Elimination of Strategic Offensive Arms. Signed at Washington D.C. and Moscow, May 15 and 25, 2006. Entered into force May 25, 2006. **06-05 CTIA 335, DOS 06-273.**

Saudi Arabia

Meteorology

Amendment No. 1 to the Memorandum of Understanding of March 3, 2001 for Technical Cooperation in a Meteorological and Environmental Program. Signed at Jeddah and Washington D.C., March 15 and April 27, 2006. Entered into force April 27, 2006. **06-05 CTIA 427, DOS 06-286.**

Swaziland

Courts and Tribunals

Agreement Regarding the Surrender of Persons to the International Criminal Court. Signed at Mbabane, May 10, 2006. Entered into force September 20, 2006. **06-05 CTIA 9, DOS 06-253.**

Sweden

Nuclear Materials and Safety

Arrangement for the Exchange of Technical Information and Cooperation in the Regulation of Nuclear Safety, with Addenda. Signed at Vienna, September 19, 2006. Entered into force September 19, 2006. **06-05 CTIA 207, DOS 06-261.**

Scientific Cooperation

Agreement on Science and Technology Cooperation, with Annexes. Signed at Stockholm, June 29, 2006. Entered into force June 29, 2006. **06-05 CTIA 455, DOS 06-289.**

Tonga

Defense

Agreement Regarding Grants Under the Foreign Assistance Act of 1961 and the Furnishing of Defense Articles, Defense Services and Related Training from the United States of America to the Kingdom of Tonga. Effected by Exchange of Notes at Suva and Nuku'alofa, March 16 and August 24, 2006. Entered into force August 24, 2006. **06-05 CTIA 741, DOS 06-305.**

United Kingdom

Defense

Amendment No.1 to the Memorandum of Understanding Concerning the Exchange and Replacement or Reimbursement of Marine Aviation and Propulsion Fuels at Sea and at Military Installation Worldwide. Signed at Fort Belvoir, October 6, 2006. Entered into force October 6, 2006. **06-05 CTIA 349, DOS 06-276.**

Memorandum of Understanding for Test and Evaluation Program (TEP Cooperation), with Annexes. Signed at Washington D.C. and London, October 18 and November 7, 2006. Entered into force November 7, 2006. **06-05 CTIA 583, DOS 06-302.**

Uzbekistan

Biological Weapons

Amendment to the Agreement Concerning Cooperation in the Area of Demilitarization of Biological Weapons Associated Facilities and the Prevention of Proliferation of Biological Weapons Technology. Signed at Tashkent and Washington D.C., September 29 and October 11, 2006. Entered into force October 11, 2006. **06-05 CTIA 353, DOS 06-277.**

Defense

Protocol Pertaining to Flights by U.S. Aircraft over the Territory of the Republic of Uzbekistan. Signed at Tashkent, November 14, 2006. Entered into force November 14, 2006. **06-05 CTIA 813, DOS 06-309.**

APPENDIX II
INDEX TO MULTILATERAL AGREEMENTS

Industrial Property

Geneva Act of the Hague Agreement Concerning the International Registration of Industrial Designs. Adopted at Geneva, July 2, 1999. Signed by the United States of America, July 6, 1999. **06-05 CTIA 883, Senate Treaty Document 109-21.**

Meteorology

Memorandum of Understanding for Cooperation In the Ocean Surface Topography Mission. Signed at Washington D.C., Darmstadt and Paris, March 21, 24, and 30, and April 7, 2006. Entered into force April 7, 2006. **06-05 CTIA 185, DOS 06-258.**

APPENDIX III
TOPICAL INDEX

Documents are listed by topic and within each topic, by the country which is the other party to the agreement. References are to Department of State numbers as all documents are printed in sequence by this number in this Release. All references in this index are to documents included in this volume.

United Kingdom, **06-05 CTIA 349, DOS 06-276; 06-05 CTIA 583, DOS 06-302**
Uzbekistan, **06-05 CTIA 813, DOS 06-309**

Economic Cooperation
Afghanistan, **06-05 CTIA 1, DOS 06-251; 06-05 CTIA 5, DOS 06-252; 06-05 CTIA 307, DOS 06-266**
Armenia, **06-05 CTIA 17, DOS 06-256**
Benin, **06-05 CTIA 81, DOS 06-257**
Cambodia, **06-05 CTIA 543, DOS 06-298**
EBRD, **06-05 CTIA 13, DOS 06-255**
Indonesia, **06-05 CTIA 389, DOS 06-282; 06-05 CTIA 411, DOS 06-283; 06-05 CTIA 425, DOS 06-285**
Jordan, **06-05 CTIA 513, DOS 06-292; 06-05 CTIA 517, DOS 06-293; 06-05 CTIA 521, DOS 06-294; 06-05 CTIA 525, DOS 06-295**

Emergency Preparedness
Indonesia, **06-05 CTIA 845, DOS 06-313**

Income Taxation
Germany, **06-05 CTIA 855, Senate Treaty Document 109-20**

Industrial Property
Multilateral, **06-05 CTIA 883, Senate Treaty Document 109-21**

Judicial Assistance and Extradition
Malaysia, **06-05 CTIA 965, Senate Treaty Document 109-22**

Labor and Employment
Armenia, **06-05 CTIA 355, DOS 06-278**

Meteorology
Multilateral, **06-05 CTIA 185, DOS 06-258**
Saudi Arabia, **06-05 CTIA 427, DOS 06-286**

Military Operations
Iceland, **06-05 CTIA 297, DOS 06-265**
Panama, **06-05 CTIA 631, DOS 06-303**

Nuclear Materials and Safety
Finland, **06-05 CTIA 339, DOS 06-275**
France, **06-05 CTIA 501, DOS 06-291**
Sweden, **06-05 CTIA 207, DOS 06-261**

The manufacturer's authorised representative in the EU for product safety is Oxford University Press España S.A. of El Parque Empresarial San Fernando de Henares, Avenida de Castilla, 2 - 28830 Madrid (www.oup.es/en or product.safety@oup.com). OUP España S.A. also acts as importer into Spain of products made by the manufacturer.
Printed and bound by CPI Group (UK) Ltd, Croydon, CR0 4YY
14/09/2026
02216312-0001